PoliSim 2.0 Contents

Note: new titles listed in red.

The Map of Freedom

The Constitution: What if You Were a Founding Father?

Political Survey: What Do You Believe?

The Great American Divide

Lobbying America

The Political Horizon

Election in Action: 2004 Presidential Election

Presidential Greatness: How Do We Judge Them?

Who's Got the Power?

Travel the Civil Rights Timeline

Balancing the Nation's Checkbook: What Can You Get for $4 Trillion?

The Impact of Foreign Aid

Running for Congress

Civil Liberties: The Great Balancing Act

Bureaucracy: A Place Where Ideals Meet Reality

Public Opinion: Spin Detection

Governor of Texas and the Veto

Read this text. Experience the simulations on the free PoliSim 2.0 CD that accompanies this text. And become an informed decision maker who considers the impact of political decisions before they are made. **After all, isn't that what politics is all about?**

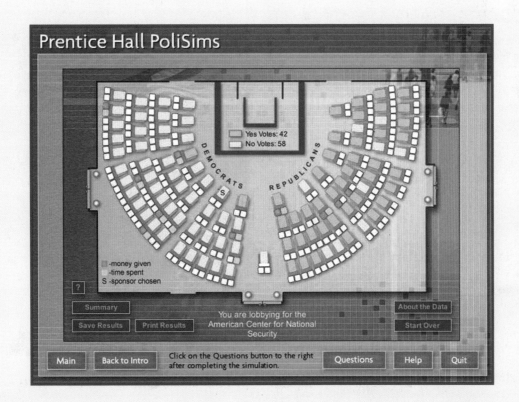

SINGLE PC LICENSE AGREEMENT AND LIMITED WARRANTY

READ THIS LICENSE CAREFULLY BEFORE OPENING THIS PACKAGE. BY OPENING THIS PACKAGE, YOU ARE AGREEING TO THE TERMS AND CONDITIONS OF THIS LICENSE. IF YOU DO NOT AGREE, DO NOT OPEN THE PACK-AGE. PROMPTLY RETURN THE UNOPENED PACKAGE AND ALL ACCOMPANYING ITEMS TO THE PLACE YOU OBTAINED THEM [[FOR A FULL REFUND OF ANY SUMS YOU HAVE PAID FOR THE SOFTWARE]]. *THESE TERMS APPLY TO ALL LICENSED SOFTWARE ON THE DISK EXCEPT THAT THE TERMS FOR USE OF ANY SHAREWARE OR FREEWARE ON THE DISKETTES ARE AS SET FORTH IN THE ELECTRONIC LICENSE LOCATED ON THE DISK:*

1. GRANT OF LICENSE and OWNERSHIP: The enclosed computer programs <<and data>> ("Software") are licensed, not sold, to you by Pearson Education, Inc. publishing as Prentice Hall ("We" or the "Company") and in consideration [[of your payment of the license fee, which is part of the price you paid]] [[of your purchase or adoption of the accompanying Company textbooks and/or other materials,]] and your agreement to these terms. We reserve any rights not granted to you. You own only the disk(s) but we and/or our licensors own the Software itself. This license allows you to use and display your copy of the Software on a single computer (i.e., with a sin-gle CPU) at a single location for academic use only, so long as you comply with the terms of this Agreement. You may make one copy for back up, or transfer your copy to another CPU, provided that the Software is usable on only one computer.

2. RESTRICTIONS: You may not transfer or distribute the Software or documentation to anyone else. Except for backup, you may not copy the documentation or the Software. You may not network the Software or otherwise use it on more than one computer or computer terminal at the same time. You may not reverse engineer, disassemble, decompile, modify, adapt, translate, or create derivative works based on the Software or the Documentation. You may be held legally responsible for any copying or copyright infringement that is caused by your failure to abide by the terms of these restrictions.

3. TERMINATION: This license is effective until terminated. This license will terminate automatically without notice from the Company if you fail to comply with any provisions or limitations of this license. Upon termination, you shall destroy the Documentation and all copies of the Software. All provisions of this Agreement as to limita-tion and disclaimer of warranties, limitation of liability, remedies or damages, and our ownership rights shall sur-vive termination.

4. LIMITED WARRANTY AND DISCLAIMER OF WARRANTY: Company warrants that for a period of 60 days from the date you purchase this SOFTWARE (or purchase or adopt the accompanying textbook), the Software, when properly installed and used in accordance with the Documentation, will operate in substantial conformity with the description of the Software set forth in the Documentation, and that for a period of 30 days the disk(s) on which the Software is delivered shall be free from defects in materials and workmanship under normal use. The Company does not warrant that the Software will meet your requirements or that the operation of the Software will be uninterrupted or error-free. Your only remedy and the Company's only obligation under these limited war-ranties is, at the Company's option, return of the disk for a refund of any amounts paid for it by you or replace-ment of the disk. THIS LIMITED WARRANTY IS THE ONLY WARRANTY PROVIDED BY THE COMPANY AND ITS LICENSORS, AND THE COMPANY AND ITS LICENSORS DISCLAIM ALL OTHER WARRANTIES, EXPRESS OR IMPLIED, INCLUDING WITHOUT LIMITATION, THE IMPLIED WARRANTIES OF MERCHANTABILITY AND FITNESS FOR A PAR-TICULAR PURPOSE. THE COMPANY DOES NOT WARRANT, GUARANTEE OR MAKE ANY REPRESENTATION REGARDING THE ACCURACY, RELIABILITY, CURRENTNESS, USE, OR RESULTS OF USE, OF THE SOFTWARE.

5. LIMITATION OF REMEDIES AND DAMAGES: IN NO EVENT, SHALL THE COMPANY OR ITS EMPLOYEES, AGENTS, LICENSORS, OR CONTRACTORS BE LIABLE FOR ANY INCIDENTAL, INDIRECT, SPECIAL, OR CONSEQUEN-TIAL DAMAGES ARISING OUT OF OR IN CONNECTION WITH THIS LICENSE OR THE SOFTWARE, INCLUDING FOR LOSS OF USE, LOSS OF DATA, LOSS OF INCOME OR PROFIT, OR OTHER LOSSES, SUSTAINED AS A RESULT OF INJURY TO ANY PERSON, OR LOSS OF OR DAMAGE TO PROPERTY, OR CLAIMS OF THIRD PARTIES, EVEN IF THE COMPANY OR AN AUTHORIZED REPRESENTATIVE OF THE COMPANY HAS BEEN ADVISED OF THE POSSIBILITY OF SUCH DAMAGES. IN NO EVENT SHALL THE LIABILITY OF THE COMPANY FOR DAMAGES WITH RESPECT TO THE SOFTWARE EXCEED THE AMOUNTS ACTUALLY PAID BY YOU, IF ANY, FOR THE SOFTWARE OR THE ACCOMPA-NYING TEXTBOOK. BECAUSE SOME JURISDICTIONS DO NOT ALLOW THE LIMITATION OF LIABILITY IN CERTAIN CIRCUMSTANCES, THE ABOVE LIMITATIONS MAY NOT ALWAYS APPLY TO YOU.

6. GENERAL: THIS AGREEMENT SHALL BE CONSTRUED IN ACCORDANCE WITH THE LAWS OF THE UNITED STATES OF AMERICA AND THE STATE OF NEW YORK, APPLICABLE TO CONTRACTS MADE IN NEW YORK, AND SHALL BENEFIT THE COMPANY, ITS AFFILIATES AND ASSIGNEES. THIS AGREEMENT IS THE COMPLETE AND EXCLUSIVE STATEMENT OF THE AGREEMENT BETWEEN YOU AND THE COMPANY AND SUPERSEDES ALL PRO-POSALS OR PRIOR AGREEMENTS, ORAL, OR WRITTEN, AND ANY OTHER COMMUNICATIONS BETWEEN YOU AND THE COMPANY OR ANY REPRESENTATIVE OF THE COMPANY RELATING TO THE SUBJECT MATTER OF THIS AGREEMENT. If you are a U.S. Government user, this Software is licensed with "restricted rights" as set forth in sub-paragraphs (a)-(d) of the Commercial Computer-Restricted Rights clause at FAR 52.227-19 or in subparagraphs (c)(1)(ii) of the Rights in Technical Data and Computer Software clause at DFARS 252.227-7013, and similar claus-es, as applicable.

Should you have any questions concerning this agreement or if you wish to contact the Company for any reason, please contact in writing: Social Sciences Media Editor, Prentice Hall, One Lake Street, Upper Saddle River, NJ 07458.

Government by the People

TWENTIETH EDITION

NATIONAL, STATE, AND LOCAL VERSION

James MacGregor Burns
University of Richmond

J. W. Peltason
University of California

Thomas E. Cronin
Whitman College

David B. Magleby
Brigham Young University

David M. O'Brien
University of Virginia

Paul C. Light
New York University
Brookings Institute

PEARSON

Prentice
Hall

Upper Saddle River, NJ 07458

Library of Congress Cataloging-in-Publication Data

Government by the people election update edition.—National, state, and
local version, 20th ed./James MacGregor Burns ... [et al.].

  p.   cm.

  Includes bibliographical references and index.

  ISBN 0-13-193886-X

  1. United States—Politics and government. 2. State
  governments—United States. 3. Local government—United States. I.
  Burns, James MacGregor.

JK276.B87 2004d

320.473—dc21   2002044557

VP, Editorial Director: *Charlyce Jones Owen*
Senior Acquisitions Editor: *Heather Shelstad*
Project Manager: *Rob DeGeorge*
Editor in Chief, Development: *Rochelle Diogenes*
Development Editor: *Betty Gatewood*
Editorial Assistant: *Jessica Drew*
Director of Marketing: *Beth Mejia*
Marketing Manager: *Claire Bitting*
Marketing Assistant: *Jennifer Bryant*
Copy Editor: *Bruce Emmer*
VP, Director of Production and Manufacturing: *Barbara Kittle*
Executive Managing Editor: *Ann Marie McCarthy*
Prepress and Manufacturing Manager: *Nick Sklitsis*
Prepress and Manufacturing Buyer: *Tricia Kenny*
Creative Design Director: *Leslie Osher*
Interior and Cover Designer: *Kathryn Foot*
Director, Image Resource Center: *Melinda Reo*
Interior Image Specialist: *Beth Brenzel*
Manager, Rights and Permissions: *Zina Arabia*
Image Permission Coordinator: *Michelina Viscusi*
Photo Researcher: *Yvonne Gerin*
Manager of Production Services: *Guy Ruggiero*
Electronic Page Layout: *Scott Garrison and Joh Lisa*
Illustrations: *Mirella Signoretto*
Photo Development Editor: *Melissa Whitcraft*
Cover Art: *©Corbis Digital Stock Royalty Free*

This book was set in 10/12.5 Minion
by Prentice Hall Production Services and was
printed and bound by RR Donnelley & Sons.
The cover was printed by Coral.

© 2005 by Pearson Education, Inc.
Upper Saddle River, New Jersey 07458

Printed in the United States of America
10 9 8 7 6 5 4 3 2 1

ISBN 0-13-193886-X

Pearson Education LTD., London
Pearson Education Australia PTY, Limited, Sydney
Pearson Education Singapore, Pte. Ltd
Pearson Education North Asia Ltd, Hong Kong
Pearson Education Canada, Ltd., Toronto
Pearson Educación de Mexico, S.A. de C.V.
Pearson Education—Japan, Tokyo
Pearson Education Malaysia, Pte. Ltd
Pearson Education, Upper Saddle River, New Jersey

BRIEF CONTENTS

CONTENTS

A MESSAGE FROM THE AUTHORS

Events of the past few years have underscored the importance of government and politics in people's lives. The terrorist attacks on the World Trade Center and Pentagon reminded all Americans that we live in a dangerous world. Citizens expect their national, state, and local governments to provide security, a theme President Bush repeatedly emphasized in his 2004 campaign appearances. The tragic events of September 11, 2001 also raised many questions about how our governments perform: How do we capture and punish those who planned and paid for these attacks? How could our intelligence services—the FBI, CIA, and others—have failed to detect an attack of this magnitude? How do we secure the homeland from future attacks? At the same time that we are asking these hard questions, we are affirming the enlarged role of governments at all levels in defending our country against those who encourage terrorism, in reorganizing our governments, especially our national government, to more effectively secure our homeland and to rebuild New York City and the Pentagon. We also ask a lot of our government. For example, what balance should we strike between protecting liberty and providing security?

The economic state of affairs is another topic that illustrates the importance of government at all levels. Many states have been forced to cut budgets and consider tax increases and at the national level, the Federal Reserve Board has been active in adjusting interest rates. How governments respond to these economic challenges provides another opportunity to learn about government and politics.

In terms of elected office and party preferences, our nation is evenly divided, with a slight edge to the Republicans at the national level. But as we were reminded in 2000, the Electoral College, and not the popular vote, decides who is president. And in the case of the 2000 presidential election, it was the Supreme Court's decision in Florida, one of many 5-to-4 decisions by the court in recent years, that effectively decided the election. Bush put talk of the disputed 2000 election aside with his successful bid for reelection in 2004.

Constitutional democracy—the kind we have in the United States—is exceedingly hard to achieve, equally hard to sustain, and often hard to understand without rigorous study. Our political history has been an evolution toward an enlarged role for citizens and voters. Citizens have more rights and political opportunities in 2003 and 2004 than they had in 1800 or 1900. The framers of our Constitution warned that we must be vigilant in safeguarding our rights, liberties, and political institutions. But to do this, we must first understand these institutions and the forces that have shaped them.

Many U.S. citizens take for granted civil liberties, civil rights, free and fair elections, the peaceful transfer of power, and economic freedom and prosperity. Yet many people live in places where these freedoms are nonexistent. This is a time of testing for new democracies as well as old ones. Contempt for government and politics is being expressed in the United States and abroad, yet politics and partisan competition are the lifeblood that enables free societies to achieve the ideal of government by the people.

The world we live in remains highly volatile. Although our defense policy changed with the collapse of communism and the emergence of a less powerful Russia, the world has not suddenly become a safer place in which to live. Terrorism, as evidenced by attacks not only in New York and Washington but around the world, has become the most pressing national security threat. How should we respond to terrorism? To what extent do we pursue those countries that may be producing weapons of mass destruction, such as Iraq? Should the war on terrorism be waged by the United States alone? Or should we work through the United Nations?

Although we constantly turn to government and to our elected officials with problems and requests, we are critical of their shortcomings. A recurrent theme of this book is the absolute need for politics and politicians, despite the widespread tendency to criticize nearly everything political. The reality is that our political system should not be taken for granted, even as we seek ways in which it can be improved.

We want you to come away from reading this book with a richer understanding of American politics, government, and the job of politicians, and we hope you will participate actively in making this constitutional democracy more vital and responsive to the urgent problems of the twenty-first century.

Reviewers

The writing of this book has profited from the informed, professional, and often sharp, critical suggestions of our colleagues around the country. This and previous editions have been considerably improved as a result of reviews by the following individuals, for which we thank them all.

James E. Anderson, Texas A&M University
Susan E. Baer, University of Wisconsin, Oshkosh
Alan Balboni, Community College of Southern Nevada
Thad Beyle, University of North Carolina
Robert R. Bland, University of North Texas
Wendell S. Broadwell, Georgia Perimeter College
Mark Cassel, Kent State University
Ray Christensen, Brigham Young University
Douglas Crane, Georgia Perimeter College
Veronica D. DiConti, American University
Cecile Durish, Austin Community College

Anthony Eksterowicz, James Madison University
Earl H. Fry, Brigham Young University
Bill Gangi, St. Johns University
G. David Garson, North Carolina State University
John Green, University of Akron
Conway Gregory, Chesapeake College
Yoram Haftel, Ohio State University
Kenneth G. Hartman, Longview Community College
Paul Herrnson, University of Maryland
Heidi Hobbs, North Carolina State University
Randal Hoyer, Madonna University

Terry Jack, Gulf Coast Community College
Ronald F. King, Tulane University
Ronald M. Labbe, University of Louisiana, Lafayette
Joseph Lamb, Macon State College
Christopher B. Mobley, De Paul University
Gary Moncrief, Boise State University
Grier Stephenson, Franklin & Marshall College
Regina Swopes, Northeastern Illinois University
Robert A. Taylor, Florida Institute of Technology
Lois Duke Whitaker, Georgia Southern University
Frank L. Wilson, Purdue University

Acknowledgments

Writing this book requires teamwork—first, among the authors, who read and rewrite each other's first drafts, then with our research assistants, who track down loose ends and give us the perspective of students, and with the editors and other professionals at Prentice Hall. Important to each revision are the detailed reviews by teachers and researchers, who provide concrete suggestions on how to improve the book. We are grateful to all who helped with this edition.

Research assistants for the current edition of *Government by the People* are: Elizabeth Esty, Andrew Jenson, Jeffrey R. Makin, Peter Stone, and Analisa Underdown at Brigham Young University; Elizabeth Schiller at the University of California, Irvine; and Joey Bristol at Whitman College. Donna Jones and JoAnn Collins at Whitman College provided secretarial assistance. Sherra Merchant at the Brookings Instituiton was also of assistance. We thank the Honorable David Sills, Presiding Justice of the California Court of Appeals, Fourth District, Division Three, for his most helpful comments.

Books for major college courses like this feature state of the art teaching tools and electronic ancillaries. We thank the professionals who produced the various supplements and media.

We gratefully acknowledge the enthusiasm and commitment of Political Science editor Heather Shelstad. Our production editor, Rob DeGeorge, kept us on schedule and orchestrated the production of this edition. Our thanks, too, to Brian Prybella and Jessica Drew, who assisted Heather Shelstad in the numerous tasks involved in publishing a book of this scope. Others at Prentice Hall we wish to thank for their continued support are Yolanda de Rooy, Charlyce Jones Owen, and Nancy Roberts.

Many skilled professionals were important to the publication of this book. They include Scott Garrison for page layout, Yvonne Gerin for photo research, Guy Ruggiero for line art coordination, Mirella Signoretto for line art creation, Kathryn Foot for interior and cover design, Leslie Osher for design supervision, Betty Gatewood for text development, and Melissa Whitcraft for photo editing.

We also want to thank you, the professors and students who use our book and who send us letters with suggestions for improving *Government by the People*. We welcome your notes, phone calls, and e-mail. Please write us in care of the Political Science Editor at Prentice Hall, 1 Lake Street, Upper Saddle River, New Jersey 07458, or contact us directly:

James MacGregor Burns Jenson School of Leadership Studies, University of Richmond, Richmond, VA 23173

J.W. Peltason School of Social Sciences, University of California, Irvine, CA 92717-5700 jwpeltas@uci.edu

Thomas E. Cronin Office of the President, Whitman College, Walla Walla, WA 99362 cronin@whitman.edu

David B. Magleby Dean of FHSS, Brigham Young University, Provo, UT 84602 david_magleby@byu.edu

David M. O'Brien Department of Government and Foreign Affairs, University of Virginia, Charlottesville, VA 22903 dmo2y@virginia.edu

Paul C. Light Paulette Goddard Professor of Public Service at New York University and Douglas Dillion Senior Fellow at the Brookings Institution. pclight@brookings.edu

A MESSAGE FROM THE PUBLISHER

Always one step ahead . . .

At Prentice Hall, we are extremely proud to continue to publish the book that always remains one step ahead by anticipating your needs as an educator and your students' needs as learners. In fact, *Government by the People* has set the standard that others strive to meet. And *Government by the People* continues to innovate in response to changes in our democratic environment and changes in how the government course is taught by introducing instructors and students to a cohesive presentation interwoven with interesting sidebars, political cartoons, and photos—all the while staying focused on the very document that serves as the foundation of our government: The Constitution. With this edition of *Government by the People*, we continue this proud legacy.

Esteemed authorship has always been a hallmark of this text. Our authorship is the reason *Government by the People* remains a bestseller. Every author on this text is among the most well known scholars in his respective field. As a result, *Government by the People* is considered the most authoritative text on the market. With this edition, we are extremely proud to continue this heritage by welcoming Paul C. Light as the newest member of our renowned author team.

New to this Edition:

- *New Co-Author* Paul C. Light is currently the Paulette Goddard Professor of Public Service at New York University's Wagner School of Public Service and Douglas Dillon Senior Fellow at the Brookings Institution. His diverse academic and professional experience, including having written fifteen books on government, public service, and public policy, make him the ideal new author for *Government by the People.* Paul contributed to the revision of several chapters in this edition, including chapters that deal with congress, the presidency, and the policy chapters.

- *Late-Breaking, Up-to-Date Content* Many chapters have undergone significant revision in this edition. The authors have paid particular attention to the material in Parts III and V (Policy-Making Institutions and The Politics of National Policy) as a result of dramatic events that have affected this mate-

rial over the course of the past two years. Chapters on Constitutional Democracy, Campaigns and Elections, Congress, The Presidency, Congress and the President, The Judiciary, Bureaucracy, Making Economic and Regulatory Policy, Making Social Policy, and Making Foreign and Defense Policy have been substantially rewritten. As a result, there is a very timely discussion of topics such as the passage of campaign finance reform and its effects, the Enron debacle and its fallout, the success of welfare reform, an analysis of why crime is increasing throughout the United States, and the war on terrorism as well as a possible war in Iraq. Every chapter's tone and coverage were assessed in view of the changing circumstances in our national life as a result of the events of September 11, 2001. Finally, owing to the unique connections these authors have to inside analyses, the new edition features extensive evaluation of the impact of the historic midterm elections of 2002.

Technology Initiatives

As in previous editions, *Government by the People* leads the industry in providing creative, innovative electronic solutions for your classroom. Whether in the form of tools that enable more effective communication or by providing dynamic presentation of content via the World Wide Web, Prentice Hall continues to anticipate your needs.

- *New PoliSim Version 2.0* PoliSim is a dynamic series of multi-level simulations developed by Prentice Hall exclusively for American government texts that require students to make politically-charged decisions based on the evaluation of data and information obtained from a variety of authentic sources. Students will use information such as real election results, real demographics, real maps, and real voting score cards from actual Senators to complete simulations in a highly interactive multimedia environment. Some of the simulations enable a Web browser so that students are encouraged to do additional research in order to make intelligent decisions. Simulations are current as of the midterm elections of 2002.

PoliSim 2.0 features several improvements over version 1.0. Most notably, there are six new simulations, for a total of 17, including a Running for Congress simulation and The Civil Rights Timeline. (For a complete list, these simulations are incorporated into the Table of Contents for your convenience.) A new user interface featuring a Results Reporter has been added to track progress and outcomes of each simulation for easy grading. For your added convenience, PoliSim is integrated into the end-of-chapter material in *Government by the People.*

PoliSim is included free with all new copies of the text and is CD-ROM based. A Web browser is required for the successful completion of some simulations.

- ### New and Improved Evaluating Online Resources for Political Science with Research Navigator™
  Our newest addition to the reliable Internet guide for political science, Prentice Hall's new Research Navigator™ keeps instructors and students abreast of the latest news and information and helps students create top quality research papers. From finding the right articles and journals to citing sources, drafting and writing effective papers, and completing research assignments, Research Navigator™ simplifies and streamlines the entire process. Complete with extensive help on the research process and three exclusive databases full of relevant and reliable source material, including EBSCO's *ContentSelect™* Academic Journal Database, *The New York Times* Search-by-Subject Archive, and *Best of the Web* Link Library.

  A unique access code for Research Navigator™ is provided on the inside front cover of the booklet. *Evaluating Online Resources for Political Science with Research Navigator™* is FREE when packaged with *Government by the People* and available for stand-alone sale. Take a tour on the Web at http://www.researchnavigator.com

- ### Improved Companion Website™
  (*www.prenhall.com/burns*)   Students can now take full advantage of the World Wide Web to enrich the study of American government through the *Government by the People* Website. Created by Jimmie McGee, South Plains College, the site features interactive practice tests, chapter objectives and overviews, additional graphs and charts, and over 150 primary source documents that are referenced in the text. Interactive Web exercises guide students to do research with a series of questions and links. Students can also tap into information regarding the midterm elections of 2002, writing in political science, career opportunities, and internship information. Students and instructors will benefit from material providing the latest news from highly regarded media outlets. Finally, a special feature allows instructors to create their syllabus customized to *Government by the People* and post it conveniently online.

- ### Course Management and Distance Learning Solutions
  For instructors interested in managing their courses online, whether locally on campus or in a distance-learning environment, Prentice Hall offers fully customizable, online courses in both WebCT and Blackboard platforms. Ask your local Prentice Hall representative for details or visit our special demonstration site at www.prenhall.com/cms for more information.

Enduring Features of the Text

Among the many attributes of *Government by the People* are the features that have come to support the balanced presentation of topics within the text. Each of these features has been appropriately revised to reflect those issues that are most significant within our political environment today.

- ### NEW: In Comparative Perspective.
  This new boxed feature uses data, maps, and figures to show students how the United States compares to other nations throughout the world with regard to a variety of topics, including: The British and American Systems: A Study in Contrasts, and Registration and Voting in the World's Democracies.

- ### NEW: People in Politics.
  This new boxed feature provides students with short profiles of influential political figures, some of historical importance as well as some contemporary figures. Many focus on the positive contributions of America's public servants, including: Justice Thurgood Marshall, Hillary Clinton, and James Lee Witt.

- ### NEW: PoliSim.
  Now featured within the end-of-chapter material, this feature introduces students to the PoliSim that correlates to that respective chapter, revealing how the chapter material relates to the simulation that the students are about to perform.

- ### People Debate.
  These box features have been completely revised to offer additional introductory material in which the authors provide a framework for the discussion. In addition, each debate now concludes with a set of critical thinking questions and a list of Websites where the students can do further research. People Debate boxes give students a chance to participate in a pro/con debate in the text, online, and through essays and links on the *Companion Website™* Topics include: Liberty Versus Security, Interpreting the Constitution, and Dissent in War.

- ### You Decide/Thinking It Through.
  Now streamlined, this feature has even greater presence in each chapter. It has been revised to include even broader discussion on current topics. This participatory question-and-answer feature is designed to strengthen students' critical

thinking skills as well as introduce interesting and challenging issues and ideas about American politics, including: Should Presidents Be Limited to Two Terms in Office? and How Should the United States Government Deal with Undocumented Aliens?

■ *We the People.*   This feature has been revised to address even more specifically the diverse nature of the American political system. These unique boxes are designed to reflect the concerns and experiences of ethnic and minority groups in American politics. Some of the topics include: Where We Learn the American Political Culture, Religion and Politics, Portrait of the Electorate, and Women Governors.

Supplements Available for the Instructor

■ *Instructor's Resource CD-ROM*   New from Prentice Hall, the Instructor's Resource CD-ROM allows you maximum flexibility as you prepare your lectures and manage your class. For presentation use, this CD contains a database featuring most of the line art from the text, more than thirty video and audio segments of classical and contemporary political science footage, and several simulations from PoliSim. An easy-to-use interface (organized logically by chapter) allows you to customize your lectures with your own original material and the assets we've provided. For your convenience, we've gotten you started with an entirely new pre-built PowerPoint presentation created especially for *Government by the People.* To allow for optimum organization, we have also included the Instructor's Resource Manual in MS Word format to allow you to customize resources depending on how you organize your course.

■ *Instructor's Manual with Test Item File*   For each chapter, a summary, review of concepts, lecture suggestions and topic outlines, and additional resource materials—including a guide to media resources—are provided. An electronic version is also included on the Instructor's Resource CD-ROM.

Thoroughly revised to ensure the highest level of quality and accuracy, the Test Item File offers over 2,000 questions in multiple choice, true/false, and essay format with page references to the text.

■ *Prentice Hall Test Manager*   A computerized test bank contains the items from the Test Item File. The program allows full editing of questions and the addition of instructor-generated items. Suitable for Windows and Macintosh operating systems.

■ *American Government Transparencies, Series VII*   This set of over 100 full-color transparency acetates reproduces illustrations, charts, and maps from the text as well as from additional sources. An instructor's guide is also available.

■ *New Prentice Hall American Government Video Series*   Corresponding to most parts within the text, this new video series portrays students debating today's most controversial political issues. Excellent for launching discussion in class or the beginning of a lecture, these 5–8-minute segments are created to engage students. Available free to adopters of *Government by the People.*

■ *Prentice Hall Custom Video: How a Bill Becomes a Law*   This 25-minute video chronicles an environmental law in Massachusetts—from its start as one citizen's concern to its passage in Washington, D.C. Students see the step-by-step process of how a bill becomes a law, complete through narrative and graphics.

■ *PowerPoint Gallery*   For each chapter, the PowerPoint Gallery provides electronic files for each figure and table in the text, along with ready-to-customize PowerPoint slides. With the use of this tool you may create a dynamic PowerPoint presentation or print your own customized four-color transparencies. The PowerPoint Gallery is included on the Instructor's Resource CD-ROM.

■ *Films for the Humanities and Social Sciences*   With a qualifying order of textbooks from Prentice Hall, you may select from a high quality library of political science videos from Films for the Humanities and Social Sciences. Please contact your local Prentice Hall representative for a complete listing.

■ *Choices: An American Government Custom Reader*   Exercise some real freedom of expression by creating an American Government reader that truly reflects your teaching style, your course goals, your perspective! *Choices: An American Government Custom Reader* delivers quality scholarship, pedagogy, and exceptional source materials. You choose the readings and the sequence. You can even add your own work or other favorite materials to create a reader that fits your course precisely. The price of your reader is determined by its length. Your students pay for what they need—no more. Over 250 articles, documents, book excerpts, and speeches—representing classic pieces as well as current articles and covering over 20 topical areas—are available. Visit the Choices Website: www.choicesreader.com and learn about updates.

Supplements Available for the Student

- *Study Guide*   Includes chapter outlines, study notes, a glossary, and practice tests designed to reinforce information in the text and help students develop a greater understanding of American government and politics.

- *Supplementary Books and Readings for American Government*   Each of the following books features specialized topical coverage allowing you to tailor your American government course to suit the needs of your region or your particular teaching style. Featuring contemporary issues or timely readings, any of the following books is available at a significant discount when bundled with *Government by the People*. Please visit our Online Catalog at www.prenhall.com/burns for additional details.

21 Debated: Issues in American Politics, 2nd Edition
Gregory M. Scott, University of Central Oklahoma
Randall J. Jones, Jr., University of Central Oklahoma
Louis S. Furmanski, University of Central Oklahoma
ISBN: 0130458295 © 2004

Government's Greatest Achievements: From Civil Rights to Homeland Security
Paul C. Light, New York University and the Brookings Institution
ISBN: 0131101927 © 2004

American Politics: Core Argument/Current Controversy, 2nd Edition
Peter Wooley, Fairleigh Dickenson University
Albert Papa, University of New Jersey
ISBN: 0130879193 © 2002

Contemporary Readings in American Government
Mark Rozell, The Catholic University of America
John White, The Catholic University of America
ISBN: 0130406457 © 2002

Issues in American Political Life: Money, Violence, and Biology, 4th Edition
Robert Thobaben, Wright State University
Donna Schlagheck, Wright State University
Charles Funderburk, Wright State University
ISBN: 0130336726 © 2002

Choices: An American Government Reader— Custom Publishing
Gregory M. Scott, University of Central Oklahoma
Katherine Tate, University of California–Irvine
Ronald Weber, University of Wisconsin–Milwaukee
ISBN: 013090399X © 2001

Prentice Hall's Real Politics in America Series
Series Editor: Paul Herrnson, University of Maryland. Another excellent resource for contemporary instructional material, the *Real Politics in America Series* attempts to bridge the gap between research and relevancy. These brief supplementary books are the ideal solution for bringing the latest political science research on the most contemporary topics to your classroom. Newest titles include the following (please contact your local Prentice Hall representative for a complete listing):

Congress and the Politics of Foreign Policy
Colton F. Campbell, Florida International University
Nicol C. Rae, Florida International University
John F. Stack, Jr., Florida International University
ISBN: 0130421545 © 2003

Congress and the Internet
James A. Thurber, American University
Colton C. Campbell, Florida International University
ISBN: 0130996173 © 2003

Celebrity Politics
Darrell West, Brown University
John Orman, Fairfield University
ISBN: 0130943258 © 2003

ABOUT THE AUTHORS

James MacGregor Burns

James MacGregor Burns is a Senior Scholar at the Jenson School of Leadership Studies, University of Richmond. He has written numerous books, including *The Power to Lead* (1984), *The Vineyard of Liberty* (1982), *Leadership* (1979), *Roosevelt: The Soldier of Freedom* (1970), *The Deadlock of Democracy: Four-Party Politics in America* (1963), and *Roosevelt: The Lion and the Fox* (1956). With his son, Stewart Burns, he wrote *A People's Charter: The Pursuit of Rights in America* (1991); with Georgia Sorenson, *Dead Center: Clinton, Gore, and the Perils of Moderation* (2000); and with Susan Dunn, *The Three Roosevelts* (2001). Burns is a past president of the American Political Science Association and winner of numerous prizes, including a Pulitzer Prize in History.

J.W. Peltason

J.W. Peltason is a leading scholar on the judicial process and public law. He is Professor Emeritus of Political Science at the University of California, Irvine. As past president of the American Council on Education, Peltason has represented higher education before Congress and state legislatures. His writings include *Federal Courts in the Political Process* (1955), *Fifty-Eight Lonely Men: Southern Federal Judges and School Desegration* (1961), and with Sue Davis, *Understanding the Constitution* (2000). Among his awards are the James Madison Medal from Princeton University, the Irvine Medal from the University of California, Irvine, and the American Political Science Association's Charles E. Merriam Award.

Thomas E. Cronin

Thomas E. Cronin is a leading student of the American presidency, leadership, and policy-making processes. He teaches at and serves as president of Whitman College. He was a White House Fellow and a White House aide and has served as president of the Western Political Science Association. His writings include *The State of the Presidency* (1980), *U.S. v. Crime in the Streets* (1981), *Direct Democracy: The Politics of Initiative, Referendum, and Recall* (1989), *Colorado Politics and Government* (1993), and *The Paradoxes of the American Presidency* (1998). Cronin is a past recipient of the American Political Science Association's Charles E. Merriam Award.

David B. Magleby

David B. Magleby is nationally recognized for his expertise on direct democracy, voting behavior, and campaign finance. He is dean as well as Professor of Political Science at Brigham Young University and has taught at the University of California, Santa Cruz, and the University of Virginia. His writings include *Direct Legislation* (1984), *The Money Chase: Congressional Campaign Finance Reform* (1990), *Myth of the Independent Voter* (1992), and is editor of *Outside Money: Soft Money and Issue Advocacy in the 1998 Congressional Elections* (2000). He was president of Pi Sigma Alpha, the national political science honor society, and has received numerous teaching awards. In 1996 he was a Fulbright Scholar at Nuffield College, Oxford University.

David M. O'Brien

David M. O'Brien is the Leone Reaves and George W. Spicer Professor at the University of Virginia. He was a Judicial Fellow and Research Associate at the Supreme Court of the United States, a Fulbright Lecturer at Oxford University, held the Fulbright Chair for Senior Scholars at the University of Bologna, and a Fulbright Researcher in Japan, as well as a Visiting Fellow at the Russell Sage Foundation. Among his publications are *Storm Center: The Supreme Court in American Politics, 5th ed.,* (2000); a two volume casebook, *Constitutional Law and Politics, 4th ed.,* (2000); an annual Supreme Court Watch; and *To Dream of Dreams: Religious Freedom in Postwar Japan* (1996). He received the American Bar Association's Silver Gavel Award for contributing to the public's understanding of the law.

Paul C. Light

Paul C. Light is currently the Paulette Goddard Professor of Public Service at New York University's Wagner School of Public Service and Douglas Dillon Senior Fellow at the Brookings Institution. Professor Light has a wide-ranging career in both academia and government. He has worked on Capitol Hill as a senior committee staffer in the U.S. Senate and as an American Political Science Association Congressional Fellow in the U.S. House. He has taught at the University of Virginia, University of Pennsylvania, and Harvard University's John F. Kennedy School of Government. He has also served as a senior adviser to several national commissions on federal, state, and local public service. He is the author of 15 books on government, public service, and public policy.

Government by the People

by

the People

NATIONAL, STATE, AND LOCAL VERSION

1
CHAPTER

CONSTITUTIONAL DEMOCRACY

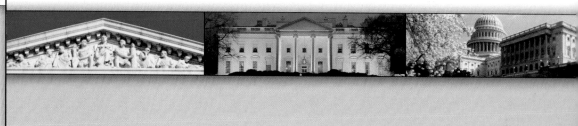

THE OLDEST CONSTITUTIONAL DEMOCRACY IN THE WORLD, THE UNITED STATES OF AMERICA, HAS SURVIVED FOR MORE THAN TWO centuries, yet it is still an experiment, still a work in progress. We think of it as an enduring, strong government, but in a real sense, our constitutional political system is built on a fragile foundation. The U.S. Constitution and Bill of Rights survive not because the parchment they were written on is still with us but because each generation of Americans respects, renews, and works at understanding the principles and values found in these precious documents. Different generations have faced different challenges in preserving, protecting, and defending our way of government. Some have faced depressions, others world wars; most recently, Americans have confronted foreign attacks on domestic soil.

The challenge to our government and our people posed by the events of September 11, 2001, will never be forgotten by this generation of Americans. Whether we learned of the terrorist attacks through television images or radio or Internet reports, we won't forget where we were when we first heard the news. Rarely in our history has the United States been directly attacked; most of our military actions have been on foreign soil. Yet on September 11, 2001, terrorists used hijacked commercial airliners as lethal missiles to destroy the World Trade Center in New York City and substantially damage the Pentagon in Washington, D.C. The impact of the attack was extraordinary. The death toll approached 3,000,[1] and the International Monetary Fund has estimated that the attacks could cost the U.S. economy more than $25 billion.[2] Repairing the Pentagon in Washington, D.C., and rebuilding the demolished areas of New York City will cost billions of dollars as well.[3]

In a fundamental way, the events of September 11, 2001, have forced people to rethink the meaning of citizenship, the successes and failures of government, the role of political leadership, and the need for strong defense and homeland security. Time will tell how enduring the impact of the terrorist attacks is on the American public, but in the

Some Key Terms

Let us define some of the basic terms we'll be using throughout this book. *Government* refers to the procedures and institutions (such as elections, courts, and legislatures) by which a people govern and rule themselves. *Politics* is the process by which people decide, at least in our system of government, who shall govern and what policies shall be adopted. Such processes invariably involve discussions, debates, and compromises over tactics and goals. *Politicians* are the people who fulfill the tasks of an operating government. Some politicians—legislators, mayors, and presidents—come to office through an election. Nonelected politicians may be political party officials or aides, advisers, or consultants to elected officials. *Political science* is the study of the principles, procedures, and structures of government and the analysis of political ideas, institutions, behavior, and practices.

The terrorist attacks on September 11, 2001 created a new cast of heroes in the American political arena. Former New York City Mayor Rudolph Giuliani (right) was transformed from being viewed as a rigid and insensitive bully to being viewed as a strong leader who was able to maintain order in the face of unprecedented chaos. Here New York Governor George Pataki (left) and former New York Mayor David Dinkins (center) are getting a tour of Ground Zero.

first weeks and months the impact was dramatic. One way to demonstrate that these issues have become more important is to contrast events after September 11 with things as they were before the attacks of that day.

Before September 11, many Americans believed that government was either irrelevant to solving problems, or worse, itself a problem. In 1981, Ronald Reagan summed up the latter perspective when he said in his inaugural address, "The problem is government."[4] The downsizing of government, which was a part of our politics in the 1980s and 1990s, reflected hostility toward government but was also a reaction to massive budget deficits and the presumed reduced threat to our national defenses. More fundamentally, skeptics of the influence of government contended that what really mattered was not who was elected president or which party controlled Congress but rather what Federal Reserve Board Chairman Alan Greenspan was doing to keep the economy humming.

Cynicism about government also carried over to politicians and was widespread. Neither presidential candidate generated much passion in 2000, and both were frequently criticized. Trust in the new president, George W. Bush, was further limited by the fact that opponent Al Gore won 500,000 more popular votes nationwide than Bush had and by a ballot-counting controversy in Florida that had to be resolved by the U.S. Supreme Court in a bitter 5-to-4 vote.[5] More than a few political pundits questioned whether Bush was up to the job, and his occasional grammatical errors and fractured syntax reinforced this impression. Trust in politicians and government generally had already been diminished by the prolonged attention given to Bush's predecessor, Bill Clinton, regarding his affair with Monica Lewinsky and subsequent grand jury testimony, impeachment, and Senate trial. Public trust in Congress was dealt another blow in 2001 when Representative Gary Condit (D.-Calif.) initially denied and later admitted having an affair with an intern, Chandra Levy, who mysteriously disappeared and was ultimately found to have been murdered.

Before September 11, our national politics were increasingly partisan and negative. Both parties could point to incidents along the way that reinforced this way of doing business. The close party division in both houses intensified the partisanship. The party switch from Republican to Independent in the summer of 2001 by Vermont Senator Jim Jeffords gave Democrats control of the U.S. Senate, leaving Republicans resentful. Although George W. Bush had advocated "bipartisan cooperation"[6] during his election campaign, strident partisanship continued during Bush's first eight months in office.

The attacks of September 11, 2001, and an outbreak of anthrax bioterrorism shortly thereafter, dramatically altered people's attitudes, at least for a time. The terrorist acts reminded people of the vital role of government in dealing with domestic and international crises. The scope of the attacks created a sense of vulnerability and heightened concerns about national defense. Airport security became a focus of attention for Congress and the president. Letters laced with anthrax sent to media outlets and politicians reminded citizens of the need for public health agencies and the role of government in defending homeland security and providing for the general welfare.

The terrorist attacks on the United States unified, at least initially, elected officials and the public. The contested presidential election of November 2000 faded into the background after the dramatic attacks. The widely perceived need for presidential leadership and President Bush's effectiveness in rallying the country earned him unprecedented job approval ratings of 90 percent.[7] Not surprisingly, public confidence in some institutions like Congress and the news media waned within months of the attack, but confidence in the presidency, military, police, and firefighters remained high.[8]

Skepticism about and even hostility toward politicians and strident partisanship were replaced, at least for a while, by genuine interparty cooperation. Following his speech to a joint session of Congress, President Bush openly embraced Senate Majority Leader Tom Daschle (D.-S.D.) and House Minority Leader Dick Gephardt (D.-Mo.). The fact that an anthrax-laced letter was sent to Daschle, the Democratic leader, only reinforced the sense that all institutions and parties were under attack. With strong bipartisan support, Congress authorized the use of military force in response to the terrorist attacks, enacted laws enhancing the tools law enforcement officials can use in combating domestic terrorism, strengthened airport security laws, provided bailout money to airlines, and expedited the payment of funds to public safety officers who were killed or injured in the attacks and rescue efforts.[9]

In response to September 11, there was widespread agreement that government should play a central role in rebuilding lower Manhattan, securing airports, and fighting terrorism abroad and at home. There was a renewed sense of patriotism, and displaying the American flag became commonplace. There was also an outpouring of philanthropy, large and small, toward the victims and their families in New York and Washington, D.C. In only seven weeks, Americans donated $564 million to the Red Cross and other organizations pledging to assist victims of the attack and their families.[10] Both parties and the president recognized that charity alone could not meet the challenge to the economy and people's lives following the attack.

Finally, after September 11, politicians were seen more favorably. President Bush has been especially effective in his speeches and public appearances, a dramatic reversal of earlier perceptions about him. Another politician who demonstrated the positive role elected officials can play was New York Mayor Rudolph Giuliani. Barred from seeking reelection by term limits and assumed to be leaving public life after withdrawing from the 2000 U.S. Senate race in New York, Giuliani soared in visibility and popularity as he praised police, firefighters, and rescue workers; encouraged contributions to disaster funds; and led the city in mourning its fallen citizens.

Bipartisanship, however, did not last long when it came to dealing with the economic recession that was worsened by the events of September 11. Democrats, following the lead of Senate Majority Leader Daschle, tried to focus the economic debate on the adverse consequences of the tax cut urged by President Bush and enacted in June 2001. Republicans countered that Democrats had obstructed President Bush's economic recovery proposals and that the terrorist attacks deserved most of the blame for the country's economic problems. Such a focus on the state of the economy is standard fare in midterm elections like 2002, and both parties worked hard to try to blame the other for rising unemployment, the return of budget deficits, and the depth and length of the recession.

The attacks on the World Trade Center and Pentagon building on September 11, 2001, and the subsequent outbreak of anthrax, dramatically altered people's attitude toward government intervention into the affairs of private citizens. Prior to these attacks, there was widespread cynicism in the United States about the ability of the government to address their needs.

President Bush, riding the crest of high popularity, campaigned aggressively for Republican candidates in the closing weeks of the 2002 midterm election and reaped a substantial reward—more GOP seats in the House and Senate. The economy and jobs were a major concern on the minds of voters, but so too was the looming war with Iraq and homeland security. A concerted strategy by the GOP was successful in making issues like prescription drug benefits for senior citizens and the solvency of social security less important in 2002. Republicans also made major inroads with the education issue, which had previously been an issue that helped Democrats. Democrats could take some solace in their party picking up more governorships. Individual candidates, with their strengths and shortcomings, remain very important to the outcome of competitive races. Going into the 2004 election, the country continued to have the two parties essentially tied in terms of state and federal offices but with the Republicans in charge of both houses of Congress and the White House. The 2002 elections clearly gave the GOP momentum and a sense of optimism.

American Government and Politicians in Context

The American Republic has endured and prospered for more than 225 years. During that time, we have held 108 presidential and midterm elections (including the recent 2002 election), and we have witnessed the peaceful transfer of power from one party to another on dozens of occasions.

Few democracies have survived this long. The United States has succeeded in large part because Americans love their country, revere the Constitution, and respect the free enterprise system. We also believe that our differences are best reconciled by debate, compromise, and free elections. From an early age, we practice democracy in elementary school class-

PEOPLE DEBATE

LIBERTY VERSUS SECURITY

As the nation responded to the terrorist attacks on New York City and the Pentagon, a debate ensued about how best to counter terrorism and how much liberty individuals should forgo.

Liberty

From the opening statement by Senator Russell Feingold (D.-Wis.) during the debate on the Senate floor over the Antiterrorism Bill, October 11, 2001.

At **feingold.senate.gov/releases/01/10/101101at.html**

❝ . . . There is no doubt that if we lived in a police state, it would be easier to catch terrorists. If we lived in a country where the police were allowed to search your home at any time for any reason; if we lived in a country where the government was entitled to open your mail, eavesdrop on your phone conversations, or intercept your e-mail communications; if we lived in a country where people could be held in jail indefinitely based on what they write or think, or based on mere suspicion that they were up to no good, the government would probably discover and arrest more terrorists, or would-be terrorists, just as it would find more lawbreakers generally. But that would not be a country in which we would want to live, and it would not be a country for which we could, in good conscience, ask our young people to fight and die. In short, that country would not be America.

I think it is important to remember that the Constitution was written in 1789 by men who had recently won the Revolutionary War. They did not live in comfortable and easy times of hypothetical enemies. They wrote the Constitution and the Bill of Rights to protect individual liberties in times of war as well as in times of peace.

There have been periods in our nation's history when civil liberties have taken a back seat to what appeared at the time to be the legitimate exigencies of war. Our national consciousness still bears the stain and the scars of those events: The Alien and Sedition Acts, the suspension of habeas corpus during the Civil War, the internment of Japanese-Americans during World War II and the injustices perpetrated against German-Americans and Italian-Americans, the blacklisting of supposed communist sympathizers during the McCarthy era, and the surveillance and harassment of antiwar protesters, including Dr. Martin Luther King Jr., during the Vietnam War. We must not allow this piece of our past to become prologue.

Preserving our freedom is the reason we are now engaged in this new war on terrorism. We will lose that war without a shot being fired if we sacrifice the liberties of the American people in the belief that by doing so we will stop the terrorists. ❞

rooms, and even though we may be critical of elected leaders, we recognize the need for political leadership. We also know that there are deep divisions and unsolved problems in the United States. Many people are concerned about the persistence of racism, about religious bigotry, about the gap in economic opportunities between rich and poor, and about the gun violence that disproportionately afflicts children and minorities. And we want our government, in addition to providing a defense against terrorism and foreign enemies, to provide basic health care and education as well as to address other domestic problems.

But what is this government of which we expect so much? The reality is that "government" is merely a shorthand term to refer to tens of thousands of our fellow Americans: the people we elect and the people they appoint to promote the general welfare, provide for domestic tranquillity, and secure the blessings of liberty for us.

More than any other form of government, the kind of democracy that has emerged under the U.S. Constitution requires active participation and a balance between faith and skepticism. Government by the people, however, does not require that *everyone* be involved in politics and policy making. Many citizens will always be too busy doing other things, and some people will always be apathetic toward government and politics. Government by the people does require a substantial segment of the public to be attentive, interested, involved, informed, and willing, when necessary, to criticize and change the direction of government.

Security

From the statement of Douglas W. Kmiec, Dean and St. Thomas More Professor, Columbus School of Law, Catholic University of America, Washington, D.C., before the Senate Judiciary Committee Hearing on the Constitutionality of Various Provisions of the Proposed Antiterrorism Act of 2001, October 3, 2001.

But as grievously wounded as we may be, American society and its principled understanding of freedom with responsibility does not fracture or panic that easily, but it does expect that justice will be done. It earnestly desires, along with our President, to see those who so mercilessly took sacred human life to be held to account—not in a local criminal court, but by the able men and women of the military and our law enforcement communities, working together, either to eliminate on a field of battle these "enemies of mankind," as Blackstone called them, or to apprehend and punish them—presumably before the bar of a properly convened military tribunal like those employed against Nazi saboteurs in World War II.

In considering this legislation it is useful to remember that our founders' conception of freedom was not a freedom to do anything or associate for any purpose, but to do those things which do not harm others and which, it was hoped, would advance the common good. Freedom separated from this truth is not freedom at all, but license. Congress can no longer afford, if it ever could, to confuse freedom and license—because doing so licenses terrorism, not freedom. Those opposing the Antiterrorism Act of 2001 submitted to you by the Attorney General seem to have both a more radical view of freedom and a less sober view of the threats we face.

The primary authority for dealing with terrorist threat resides both in the President as commander in chief, and this Congress, as the architect of various specific legal authorities, under the Constitution, to meet that threat. The President has courageously told the nations of the world that all are either for the United States in this, or with the terrorists. There is no middle ground. . . . The President has not been rash in the use of our military might, even as he has made unmistakably plain that the "hour is coming when America will act." However, for that hour to come, for the proportionate application of our military might to become successfully manifest, this Congress must equip our law enforcement and intelligence communities with adequate and constitutional legal authority to address a war crime on a scale that previously was not seen in this generation, or seen ever in peacetime.

1. What are the dangers in providing the same due process of law protections to those accused of terrorism as we would to others accused of breaking the law?

2. Does the history of limiting civil liberties in times of war give you pause in limiting them in the wake of the September 11, 2001 terrorist attacks? If so, why? If not, why not?

3. Which values are the foundation of the two perspectives in this debate? To what extent are they incompatible? What do you think of the idea that if we permit the government to limit fundamental liberties, we have permitted the terrorists to prevail in a fundamental way?

Thomas Jefferson, one of our best-known champions of constitutional democracy, believed in the common sense of the people and in the flowering possibilities of the human spirit. Jefferson warned that every government degenerates when it is left only in the hands of the rulers. The people themselves, Jefferson wrote, are the only safe repositories of government. His was a robust commitment to popular control, representative processes, and accountable leadership. But he was no believer in the simple participatory democracy of ancient Greece or revolutionary France. The power of the people, too, must be restrained from time to time.

Government by the people requires faith concerning our common human enterprise, a belief that if the people are informed and caring, they can be trusted with their own self-government and an optimism that when things begin to go wrong, the people can be relied on to set them right. But a healthy skepticism is needed as well. Democracy requires us to question our leaders and never trust a group or institution that holds too much power. And even though constitutional advocates prize majority rule, they must remain skeptical about whether the majority is always right.

Constitutional democracy requires constant attention to protecting the rights and opinions of others, to ensure that our democratic processes are effectively serving the principles of liberty, equality, and justice. Thus a peculiar blend of faith and skepticism is warranted when dealing with the will of the people.

Thomas Jefferson.

Constitutional democracy is necessarily government by representative politicians. A central feature of democracy is that those who hold power do so only by winning a free election. In our political system, the fragmentation of powers requires elected officials to mediate among factions, build coalitions, and work out compromises among and within the branches of our government to produce policy and action.

We expect a lot from our politicians. We expect them to operate within the rules of democracy and to be honest, humble, patriotic, compassionate, sensitive to the needs of others, well informed, competent, fair-minded, self-confident, and inspirational. They must be candidates of all the people, not just of the ones with money. They must not want power for itself but lead because of their concern for the public good. And finally, they must be willing to do the job and get out when finished.

Why does such a gap persist between our image of the ideal politician and our views about actual politicians? The gap exists in part because we have unrealistic expectations. We want politicians to be perfect, to have all the answers, and to have all the "correct" values (as we perceive them). We want politicians to solve our problems, yet we also want them to serve as scapegoats for the things we dislike about government: taxes, regulations, hard times, limits on our freedom. It is impossible for anyone to live up to these ideals. Like all individuals, politicians live in a world in which perfection may be the goal but compromise, ambition, fund raising, and self-promotion are necessary.

Americans will never be satisfied with their political candidates and politicians. The ideal politician is probably a fictional entity, for the perfect official would be able to please everyone, make conflict disappear, and not ask us to make any sacrifices. Politicians become "ideal" only when they are dead.

But the love of liberty invites disagreements of ideology and values. Politicians and candidates, as well as the people they represent, have different ideas about what is best for the nation. That's why we have politics, candidates, opposition parties, heated political debates, and elections.

Defining Democracy

The word "democracy" is nowhere to be found in the Declaration of Independence or in the U.S. Constitution, nor was it a term used by the founders of the Republic. It is both a very old term and a modern one. It was used at the time of the founding of this nation to refer to various undesirables: mobs, lack of standards, and a system that encourages leaders to gain power by appealing to the emotions and prejudices of the rabble.

The distinguishing feature of democracy is that government derives its authority from its citizens. In fact, the word comes from two Greek words: *demos* (the people) and *kratos* (authority or power). Thus **democracy** means *government by the people,* not government by one person (a monarch, dictator, or priest) or government by the few (an oligarchy or aristocracy).

Ancient Athens and a few other Greek city-states had a **direct democracy** in which citizens came together to discuss and pass laws and select their rulers. These Greek city-states did not last. Most degenerated into mob rule and then resorted to dictators. When the word "democracy" came into use in English in the seventeenth century, it denoted this kind of direct democracy. It was a term of derision, a negative word, a reference to power wielded by an unruly mob.

James Madison, writing in *The Federalist,* No. 10, reflected the view of many of the framers of the U.S. Constitution when he wrote, "Such democracies [as the Greek and Roman] . . . have ever been found incompatible with personal security, or the rights of property; and have in general been as short in their lives, as they have been violent in their deaths" (*The Federalist,* No. 10, is reprinted in the Appendix at the back of this book).

Today it is no longer possible, even if desirable, to assemble the citizens of any but the smallest towns to make their laws or to select their officials directly from among the citizenry. Rather, we have invented a system of representation. Democracy today means **representative democracy**, or, to use Plato's term, a *republic,* in which those

democracy
Government by the people, either directly or indirectly, with free and frequent elections.

direct democracy
Government in which citizens vote on laws and select officials more directly.

representative democracy
Government that derives its powers indirectly from the people, who elect those who will govern; also called a *republic.*

who have governmental authority get and retain authority directly or indirectly as a result of winning free elections in which all adult citizens are allowed to participate. The framers preferred to use the term "republic" to avoid any confusion between direct democracy, which they disliked, and representative democracy, which they liked and thought secured all the advantages of a direct democracy while curing its weaknesses. Today, as in this book, *democracy* and *republic* are used interchangeably.

In defining democracy, several other terms need to be clarified. **Constitutional democracy**, as used here, refers to a government in which the individuals who exercise substantial governmental powers do so as the result of winning free and relatively frequent elections. *It is a government in which there are recognized, enforced limits on the powers of all governmental officials.* It also generally involves a written set of governmental rules and procedures, a constitution.

Constitutionalism is a term we apply to arrangements—checks and balances, federalism, separation of powers, rule of law, due process, a bill of rights—that require our leaders to listen, think, bargain, and explain before they make laws. We then hold them politically and legally accountable for how they exercise their powers.

Like most political concepts, democracy encompasses many ideas and has many meanings. Democracy is a way of life, a form of government, a way of governing, a type of nation, a state of mind, and a variety of processes. We can divide these many meanings of democracy into three broad categories: a system of interacting values, a system of interrelated political processes, and a system of interdependent political structures.

Democracy as a System of Interacting Values

Belief in representative democracy may be as near a universal faith as the world has today. Respect for human dignity, freedom, liberty, individual rights, and other democratic values is wide spread. The ideas of personal liberty, respect for the individual, equality of opportunity, and popular consent are at the core of democratic values. As the Taliban government in Afghanistan demonstrated, there are governments that not only suppress democratic values but find them threatening enough to terrorize governments that embrace them.

PERSONAL LIBERTY   Liberty has been the single most important value in American history. It was for "life, liberty, and the pursuit of happiness" that independence was declared; it was to "secure the Blessings of Liberty" that the Constitution was drawn up and adopted. Even our patriotic songs extol the "sweet land of liberty." The essence of liberty is *self-determination*, meaning that all individuals must have the opportunity to realize their own goals. Liberty is not simply the absence of external restraint on a person (freedom *from*); it is the individual's freedom and capacity to act positively to reach his or her goals (freedom *to*). Moreover, both history and reason suggest that individual liberty is the key to social progress. The greater the people's freedom, the greater the chance of discovering better ways of life.

RESPECT FOR THE INDIVIDUAL   Popular rule in a democracy flows from a belief that every individual has the potential for common sense, rationality, and fairness. Individuals have important rights; collectively, those rights are the source of all legitimate governmental authority and power. These concepts pervade all democratic thought. They are woven into the writings of Thomas Jefferson, especially in the Declaration of Independence: "All men . . . are endowed by their Creator with certain unalienable rights" (the Declaration of Independence is reprinted in the Appendix). Constitutional democracies make the *person*—rich or poor, black or white, male or female—the central measure of value.

Not all political systems put the individual first. Some promote **statism**, a form of government based on centralized authority and control, especially over the economy. Examples of countries with this approach include China and Cuba. In a modern democracy, the nation, or even the community, is less important than the individuals who compose it.

"The Athenians are here, Sire, with an offer to back us with ships, money, arms, and men—and, of course, their usual lectures about democracy."

constitutional democracy
A government that enforces recognized limits on those who govern and allows the voice of the people to be heard through free, fair, and relatively frequent elections.

constitutionalism
The set of arrangements, including checks and balances, federalism, separation of powers, rule of law, due process, and a bill of rights, that requires leaders to listen, think, bargain, and explain before they act or make laws. We then hold them politically and legally accountable for how they exercise their powers.

statism
The idea that the rights of the nation are supreme over the rights of the individuals residing in that nation.

EQUALITY OF OPPORTUNITY   The importance of the individual is enhanced by the democratic value of *equality:* "All men are created equal and from that equal creation they derive rights inherent and unalienable, among which are the preservation of liberty and the pursuit of happiness." So reads Jefferson's first draft of the Declaration of Independence, and the words indicate the primacy of the concept. Alexis de Tocqueville and other international visitors who have studied American democracy were all struck by the strength of egalitarian thought and practice in our political and social lives.

But what does equality mean? Equality for whom? For blacks as well as whites? For women as well as men? For Native Americans, descendants of the Pilgrims, and recent immigrants? And what kind of equality? Economic, political, legal, social, or some other kind of equality? Equality of opportunity? Does equality of opportunity simply mean that everyone should have the same place at the starting line? Or does it mean an effort should be made to equalize the factors that determine how well a person fares economically or socially? These enduring issues arise often in our study of American politics.

POPULAR CONSENT   The animating principle of the American Revolution, the Declaration of Independence, and the resulting new nation was **popular consent**, the idea that a just government must derive its powers from the *consent of the people it governs.* A commitment to democracy thus entails a community's willingness to participate and make decisions in government. These principles sound unobjectionable intellectually, but in practice they mean that certain individuals or groups may not get their way. A commitment to popular consent must involve a willingness to lose when most people vote the other way.

DEMOCRATIC VALUES IN CONFLICT   The basic values of democracy do not always coexist happily. Individualism may conflict with the collective welfare or the public good. Self-determination may conflict with equal opportunity. For example, the right of a homeowner to add another floor to her home may conflict with the right of her neighbor to have an unobstructed view. Or the right of a person to smoke an after-dinner cigar in a restaurant may conflict with the right of others not to have to breathe tobacco smoke.

Much of our political combat revolves around how to strike a balance among democratic values, how to protect the Declaration of Independence's unalienable rights of life, liberty, and the pursuit of happiness while trying to "form," as the Constitution announces, "a more perfect Union, establish Justice, insure domestic Tranquility, provide for the common defence, promote the general Welfare, and secure the Blessings of Liberty to ourselves and our Posterity" (see the Preamble to the Constitution on page 47). Over the years, the American political system has moved, despite occasional setbacks, toward greater freedom and more democracy.

Expansion of democracy in the United States and elsewhere was in many ways a twentieth-century idea. Although on dozens of occasions in the past century, democracies collapsed and gave way to authoritarian regimes, even more democracies triumphed. Indeed, "the global range and influence of democratic ideas, institutions, and practices has made [the twentieth century] far and away the most flourishing period for democracy."[11]

Democracy as a System of Interrelated Political Processes

Far more people dream about democracy than ever experience it, and many new democracies fail. To be successful, democratic government requires a well-defined political process as well as a stable governmental structure. To become reality, democratic values must be incorporated into a political process, most importantly in the form of free and fair elections, majority rule, freedom of expression, and the right to assemble and protest.

popular consent
The idea that a just government must derive its powers from the consent of the people it governs.

FREE AND FAIR ELECTIONS   Democratic government is based on free and fair elections held at intervals frequent enough to make them relevant to policy choices. Elections are one of the most important devices for keeping officials and representatives accountable.

Free and fair elections are an important characteristic of democracies; however, participation requires time and patience, as is evident by these citizens standing in line to vote.

We previously described representative democracy as a government in which those who have the authority to make decisions with the force of law acquire and retain this authority either directly or indirectly as the result of winning free elections in which the great majority of adult citizens are allowed to participate. Crucial to modern-day definitions of democracy is the idea that opposition political parties can exist, can run candidates in elections, and can at least have a chance to replace those who are currently holding public office. Thus *political competition and choice* are crucial to the existence of democracy.

Although all citizens should have equal voting power, free and fair elections do not imply that everyone must or will have equal political influence. Some people, because of wealth, talent, or position, have more influence than others. How much extra influence key figures should be allowed to exercise in a democracy is frequently debated. But in an election, each citizen—president or plumber, corporate CEO or ditch digger—casts only one vote.

MAJORITY (PLURALITY) RULE   **Majority rule**—governance according to the expressed preferences of the majority—is a basic rule of democracy. The **majority** candidate or party is the one that receives *more than half* the votes and so wins the election and takes charge of the government until the next election. In practice, however, majority rule is often **plurality** rule, in which the candidate or party with the *most* votes wins the election, even though it may not constitute a true majority of more than half the votes. About a third of our presidents have won with pluralities in the popular vote rather than majorities.[12] Once elected, officials do not have a right to curtail the attempts of political minorities to use all peaceful means to become the new majority. Even as the winners take power, the losers are at work to try to get it back at the next election.[13]

Should the side with the most votes prevail in all cases? Americans answer this question in a variety of ways. Some insist that majority views should be enacted into laws and regulations. However, an effective representative democracy involves far more than simply ascertaining and applying the statistical will of most of the people. It is a more complicated and often untidy process in which the people and their agents debate, compromise, and arrive at a decision only after thoughtful deliberation.

The framers of the U.S. Constitution wanted to guard society against any one faction of the people acting unjustly toward any other faction of the people. The Constitution

majority rule
Governance according to the expressed preferences of the majority.

majority
The candidate or party that wins more than half the votes cast in an election.

plurality
Candidate or party with the most votes cast in an election, not necessarily more than half.

reflects their fear of tyranny by majorities, especially momentary majorities that spring from temporary passions. They insulated certain rights (such as freedom of speech) and institutions (such as the Supreme Court) from popular choice. Effective representation of the people, the framers insisted, should not be based solely on parochial interests or shifting breezes of opinion.

FREEDOM OF EXPRESSION   Free and fair elections depend on access to information relevant to voting choices. Voters must have access to facts, competing ideas, and the views of candidates. Free and fair elections require a climate in which competing, non-government-owned newspapers, radio stations, and television stations can flourish. If the government controls what is said and how it is said, there is no democracy. Without free speech, there are no free and fair elections.

THE RIGHT TO ASSEMBLE AND PROTEST   Citizens must be free to organize for political purposes. Obviously, individuals can be more effective if they join with others in a party, a pressure group, a protest movement, or a demonstration. The right to oppose the government, to form opposition parties, and to have a chance of defeating incumbents is more than vital; it is a defining characteristic of a democracy.

Democracy as a System of Interdependent Political Structures

Democracy is, of course, more than values and processes. It also entails political structures that safeguard these values and processes. The Constitution and its first ten amendments (the Bill of Rights) set up an ingenious structure—one that both grants and checks government power. This constitutional structure is reinforced by a system of political parties, interest groups, media, and other institutions that intercede between the electorate and those who govern and thus help maintain democratic stability.

The U.S. constitutional system has four distinctive elements: *federalism,* the division of powers between the national and state governments; *separation of powers* among the legislative, executive, and judicial branches; *checks and balances* in which each branch is given the constitutional means, the political independence, and the motives to check the powers of the other branches; and a judicially enforceable, written, explicit *Bill of Rights* that provides a guarantee of individual liberties and due process before the law.

Conditions Conducive to Constitutional Democracy

Although it is hard to specify the precise conditions that are essential for the establishment and maintenance of a democracy, here are a few things we have learned.

EDUCATIONAL CONDITIONS   The exercise of voting privileges takes some level of education on the part of the citizenry. But a high level of education does not guarantee democratic government, as the example of Nazi Germany readily illustrates. And there are some democracies, such as India, where large numbers of people are illiterate. Still, voting makes little sense unless a considerable number of the voters can read and write and express their interests and opinions. The poorly educated and illiterate often get left out in a democracy.

ECONOMIC CONDITIONS   A relatively prosperous nation, with an equitable distribution of wealth, provides the best context for democracy. Starving people are more interested in food than in voting. Where economic power is concentrated, political power is likely to be concentrated. Well-to-do nations have a greater chance of sustaining democratic governments than those with widespread poverty do. The reality is that extremes of wealth and poverty undermine the possibilities for a healthy constitutional democracy. Thus the prospects for an enduring democracy are greater in Canada or France than in Rwanda, Zimbabwe, or Mongolia.

Some measure of private ownership of property and a relatively favorable role for the market economy are also related to the creation and maintenance of democratic institutions. Democracies can range from heavily regulated economies with public ownership of many enterprises, such as Sweden, to those in which there is little government regulation of the marketplace. But there are no democracies with a highly centralized government-run economy and little private ownership of property, although there are many nations with a market economy and no democracy. There are no truly democratic communist states, nor have there ever been any.

SOCIAL CONDITIONS   Economic development generally makes democracy possible, yet proper social conditions are necessary to make it real.[14] In a society fragmented into warring groups that differ fiercely on fundamental issues, government by discussion and compromise is difficult, as we have seen in the Balkans. When ideologically separated groups consider the issues at stake to be vital, they may prefer to fight rather than accept the verdict of the ballot box.

In a society that consists of many overlapping associations and groupings, however, individuals are not as likely to identify completely with a single group and give their allegiance to it. For example, Joe Smith is a Baptist, an African American, a southerner, a Democrat, an electrician, and a member of the National Rifle Association, and he makes $50,000 a year. On some issues, Joe thinks as a Baptist, on others as a southerner, and on still others as an African American. Sue Jones is a Catholic, a white Republican, an auto dealer, and a member of the National Organization for Women (NOW); she comes from a Polish background, and she makes $150,000 a year. Sometimes she acts as a Republican, sometimes as an American of Polish descent, and sometimes as a member of NOW. Jones

STILL BOWLING ALONE
BUT MORE INTERESTED IN CURRENT EVENTS

You Decide... In his book *Bowling Alone*, Robert D. Putnam discussed a startling trend in American communities. At the end of the twentieth century, Americans "voted less, joined less, gave less, trusted less, . . . and engaged less with our friends, our neighbors, and even our families."* One of the primary manifestations of this phenomenon is the fact that though more Americans were bowling than ever before, the number of organized groups participating in bowling leagues was steadily decreasing.

Thinking It Through... Did the tragic events of September 11, 2001, change the increasingly detached behavior of Americans? Public opinion surveys found a surge in interest in public affairs, particularly among young Americans. Their interest in public affairs grew by 27 percent, whereas in older Americans the growth was only 8 percent. But Putnam also learned that behavior has not shifted as much as have attitudes. For example, while feelings of unity have increased, regular volunteering (at least twice a month) has not.

Putnam sees the growth in interest in current events as an opportunity to encourage greater participation in community life, including voting and volunteering. Putnam is not alone. In the aftermath of the terrorist attacks, Senators John McCain (R.-Ariz.) and Evan Bayh (D.-Ind.) proposed increased funding for AmeriCorps, the national youth service program.

Robert D. Putnam, "Bowling Together," American Prospect 13 (February 11, 2002), pp. 20–22.

and Smith differ on some issues and agree on others. In general, the differences between them are not likely to be greater than their common interest in maintaining a democracy.[15]

Democracy is more likely to survive in a nation where the people have acquired democratic habits and are inclined to participate in social, cultural, and civic groups. Political scientist Robert Putnam calls this interest in participation **social capital**.[16] Democratic social capital is generated when there are a rich variety of associations and social institutions that bind people together. Participation in voluntary organizations such as women's groups, bowling leagues, and environmental and conservation groups helps build and reinforce democratic habits of discussion, compromise, and respect for differences. It can "provide the social resources and the civic training that citizens need to make democracy tick."[17]

Civic and social engagement has been changing with the advent of the Internet. Today there are more advocacy and lobbying groups than ever, and environmental groups are on the rise. Beyond the traditional Boy Scouts, Girl Scouts, YMCA, YWCA, and Red Cross, there are myriad local volunteer and service groups and a vast network of youth as well as adult soccer, basketball, hockey, and snowboarding leagues. Women and minorities have been recognized and are active in many new ways. As Michael Schudson notes, if measures of civic health include "measures of political inclusion and protection for individual rights," then "Americans are unquestionably better off in the past quarter century than at any prior moment in our history."[18]

IDEOLOGICAL CONDITIONS   **Ideology** refers to basic beliefs about power, government, and political practices—beliefs that arise out of the educational, economic, and social conditions individuals experience. Out of these conditions must also develop a general acceptance of the ideals of democracy and a willingness of a substantial part of the people to agree to proceed democratically. This acceptance is sometimes called the *democratic consensus.*

The Constitutional Roots of the American Experiment

Americans often take democracy for granted. Most of us probably consider it inevitable. We take pride in our ability to make it work, yet we have essentially inherited a functioning system. Its establishment was the work of others, nine or ten generations ago. The challenge for us is not just to keep it going but to improve it and make it adapt to the challenges of our times. To do so, however, we must first understand it, and this requires systematic consideration of our democratic and constitutional roots.

The Colonial Beginnings

There were many reasons one might have expected our democratic experiment to fail. The 13 original states (formerly colonies) were independent and could have gone their separate ways. Sectional differences based on social and economic conditions, especially the southern states' dependence on slavery, were an obvious problem. Religious, ethnic, and racial diversity, which challenges so many governments around the world today, existed to a substantial degree in the United States during its formative years.

Given these potential problems, how did democracy survive? How did this nation establish democratic principles for its government? How did it limit potential abuses? These questions are of importance not only to Americans but also to all others who value freedom and democracy. The United States has been a world leader in promoting the use of democratic institutions, in effect universalizing its successful experiment.

The framers of the U.S. Constitution had experience to guide them. For almost two centuries, Europeans had been sailing to the New World in search of liberty—especially religious liberty—as well as land and work. While still aboard the *Mayflower*, the Pilgrims drew up a compact to protect their religious freedom and to make possible "just and equal

social capital
Participation in voluntary associations that reinforce democratic and civic habits of discussion, compromise, and respect for differences.

ideology
A consistent pattern of beliefs about political values and the role of government.

laws." In the American colonies, editors found they could speak freely in their newspapers, dissenters could distribute leaflets, and agitators could protest in taverns or in the streets.

But the picture of freedom in the colonies was mixed. The Puritans in Massachusetts soon established a **theocracy**, a system of government in which religious leaders claimed divine guidance and in which certain religious sects were denied religious liberty. Dissenters were occasionally chased out of town, and some printers were beaten and had their shops closed. In short, the colonists struggled with the balance between unity and diversity, stability and dissent, order and liberty. Puritans continued to worry "about what would maintain order in a society lacking an established church, an attachment to place, and the uncontested leadership of men of merit."[19] Nine of the 13 colonies eventually set up a state church. Throughout the 1700s, Puritans in Massachusetts barred certain men from voting on the basis of church membership. To the Anglican establishment in Virginia, campaigns for toleration were in themselves subversive. Women and slaves could not vote at all.

The Rise of Revolutionary Fervor

As resentment against British rule mounted during the 1770s and revolutionary fervor rose, Americans became determined to fight the British to win their rights and liberties. A year after the fighting broke out in Massachusetts, the Declaration of Independence proclaimed in ringing tones that all men are created equal, endowed by their Creator with certain unalienable rights; that among them are "life, liberty, and the pursuit of happiness"; that to secure those rights, governments are instituted among men; and that whenever a government becomes destructive of those ends, it is the right of the people to alter or abolish it. (Read the full text of the Declaration of Independence in the Appendix.)

We have all heard these great ideals so often that we take them for granted. Revolutionary leaders did not. They were deadly serious about these rights and willing to fight and pledge their lives, fortunes, and sacred honor for them. Indeed, by signing the Declaration of Independence they were effectively signing their own death warrants if the Revolution failed.[20] Bills of rights in the new state constitutions guaranteed free speech, freedom of religion, and the natural rights to life, liberty, and property. All their constitutions spelled out the rights of persons accused of crime, such as knowing the nature of the accusation, being confronted by their accusers, and receiving a timely and public trial by jury.[21] Moreover, these guarantees were set out *in writing*, in sharp contrast to the unwritten British constitution.

Toward Unity and Order

As the war against the British widened, the need arose for a stronger central government that could pull the colonies together and conduct a revolutionary war. For a time, the Continental Congress, which had led the way toward revolution, tried to direct hostilities against the British, but it took a man of George Washington's iron resolve to unify and direct the war effort. Sensing the need for more unity, Congress established a new national government under a written document called the **Articles of Confederation**. At first hardly worthy of the term "government," the Articles were not approved by all the state legislatures until 1781, after Washington's troops had been fighting for six years.

This new Confederation was a move toward a stronger central government, but a limited and inadequate one. Having fought a war against a strong central government in London, Americans were understandably reluctant to create another one, so the Articles established a fragile league of friendship rather than a national government. From 1777 to 1788, Americans made progress under the Confederation, but with the end of the war in 1783, the sense of urgency that had produced unity began to fade. Conflicts between creditors and debtors in the various states grew intense. Foreign threats continued; territories ruled by England and Spain surrounded the new nation, which, internally divided and lacking a strong central government, made a tempting prize.

theocracy
Government by religious leaders, who claim divine guidance.

Articles of Confederation
The first governing document of the confederated states, drafted in 1777, ratified in 1781, and replaced by the present Constitution in 1789.

Weaknesses of the Articles of Confederation

1. Congress had no direct authority over citizens but had to work through the states; it could not pass laws or levy taxes to carry out its responsibilities to defend the nation and promote its well-being.

2. Congress could not regulate trade between the states or with other nations. States taxed each other's goods and even negotiated their own trade agreements with other nations.

3. Congress could not forbid the states from issuing their own currencies, further complicating interstate trade and travel.

4. Congress had to handle all administrative duties because there was no executive branch.

5. The lack of a judicial system meant that the national government had to rely on state courts to enforce national laws and settle disputes between the states. In practice, state courts could overturn national laws.

Annapolis Convention
A convention held in September 1786 to consider problems of trade and navigation, attended by five states and important because it issued the call to Congress and the states for what became the Constitutional Convention.

Constitutional Convention
The convention in Philadelphia, May 25 to September 17, 1787, that framed the Constitution of the United States.

Shays' Rebellion
Rebellion by farmers in western Massachusetts in 1786–1787, protesting mortgage foreclosures; led by Daniel Shays and important because it highlighted the need for a strong national government just as the call for the Constitutional Convention went out.

As pressures on the Confederation mounted, many leaders became convinced it would not be enough merely to revise the Articles of Confederation. To create a union strong enough to deal with internal diversity and factionalism as well as to resist external threats, a stronger central government was needed.

In September 1786, under the leadership of Alexander Hamilton, supporters of a truly national government took advantage of the **Annapolis Convention**—a meeting in Annapolis, Maryland, on problems of trade and navigation attended by delegates from five states—to issue a call for a convention that would have full authority to consider basic amendments to the Articles of Confederation. The delegates in Annapolis asked the legislatures of all the states to appoint commissioners to meet in Philadelphia on the second Monday of May 1787, "to devise such further provisions as shall appear to them necessary to render the Constitution of the Federal Government adequate to the exigencies of the Union." The convention they called for became the **Constitutional Convention**.

For a short time, all was quiet. Then, late in 1786, messengers rode into George Washington's plantation at Mount Vernon with the kind of news he and other leaders had dreaded. Farmers in western Massachusetts, crushed by debts and taxes, were rebelling against foreclosures, forcing judges out of their courtrooms, and freeing debtors from jails. Washington was appalled. "What, gracious God, is man?" he exclaimed. Ten years before, he had been leading Americans in a patriotic war against the British, and now Americans were fighting Americans!

Not all Americans reacted as Washington did to what became known as **Shays' Rebellion** after Daniel Shays, its leader. When Abigail Adams, the politically knowledgeable wife of John Adams, sent news of the rebellion to Thomas Jefferson, the Virginian replied, "I like a little rebellion now and then," noting also that the "tree of liberty must be refreshed from time to time with the blood of patriots and tyrants. It is its natural manure."[22]

Shays' Rebellion petered out after the farmers attacked an arsenal and were cut down by cannon fire. Yet this "little rebellion" sent a stab of fear into the established leadership. It also acted as a catalyst. The message was now plain: Action must be taken to strengthen the machinery of government. Seven states appointed commissioners to attend the Philadelphia convention to strengthen the Articles of Confederation. Congress finally issued a cautiously worded call to all the state legislatures to appoint delegates for the "sole and express purpose of revising the Articles of Confederation." The suspicious congressional legislators specified that no recommendation would be effective unless approved by Congress and confirmed by all the state legislatures, as provided by the Articles.

The Constitutional Convention of 1787

The delegates who assembled in Philadelphia that May had to establish a national government powerful enough to prevent the young nation from dissolving but not so powerful that it would crush individual liberty. What these men did continues to have a major impact on how we are governed. It also provides an outstanding lesson in political science for the world.

The Delegates

Seventy-four delegates were appointed by the various states, but only 55 arrived in Philadelphia. Of these, approximately 40 actually took part in the work of the convention. It was a distinguished gathering. Many of the most important men of the nation were there: successful merchants, planters, bankers, lawyers, and former and present governors and congressional representatives (39 of the delegates had served in Congress). Most had read the classics of political thought. Most had participated vigorously in the practical task of constructing local and state governments. Many had also worked hard to create and direct the national Confederation of the states. And 8 of the 56 signers of the Declaration of Independence were present at the Constitutional Convention.

The convention was as representative as most political gatherings at the time: The participants were all white male landowners. These well-read, well-fed, well-bred, and often well-wed delegates were mainly state or national leaders, for in the 1780s, ordinary people were not likely to participate in politics. (Even today, farm laborers, factory workers, and truck drivers are seldom found in Congress, although a haberdasher, a peanut farmer, and a movie actor have made their way to the White House.)

Although active in the movement to revise the Articles of Confederation, George Washington had been reluctant to attend the convention. He accepted only when persuaded that his prestige was needed for its success. He was selected unanimously to preside over the meetings. According to the records, he spoke only twice during the deliberations, yet his influence was felt in the informal gatherings as well

The Framers: Hamilton and Madison

In the Constitution of the United States, the framers offered perhaps the most brilliant example of collective intellectual genius (combining theory and practice) in the history of the Western world. How could such a sparsely populated country by today's standards produce several dozen men of genius in Philadelphia and probably another hundred or so equally talented political thinkers who did not attend? The lives of two prominent delegates, Alexander Hamilton and James Madison, help explain the origins of this collective genius.

Alexander Hamilton had been the engineer of the Annapolis Convention, and as early as 1778, he had been urging that the national government be made stronger. Hamilton had come to the United States from the West Indies and while still a college student had won national attention for his brilliant pamphlets in defense of the Revolutionary cause. During the war, he served as General Washington's aide, and his experiences confirmed his distaste for a Congress so weak it could not even supply the Revolution's troops with enough food or arms.

James Madison was only 36 years old at the time of the convention, yet he was one of its most learned members. He had helped frame Virginia's first constitution and had served both in the Virginia Assembly and in the Continental Congress. Madison was also a leader of those who favored the establishment of a stronger national government.

Like most of the other framers, Hamilton and Madison were superbly educated. Both had extensive private tutoring—a one-to-one teacher-student ratio. Like scores of other thinkers of the day, both combined extensive practical experience with their schooling. Both were active in their political and religious groups; both took part in political contests and electoral struggles; both helped build political coalitions.

Both men were "moral philosophers" as well as political thinkers. They had strong views on the supreme value of liberty as well as on current issues. Instead of simply sermonizing about liberty, they analyzed it; they debated what kind of liberty, how to protect it, and how to expand it.

James Madison.

Alexander Hamilton.

as during the sessions. Everyone understood that Washington favored a more powerful central government led by a president. The general expectation that Washington would likely be the first president played a crucial role in the creation of the presidency. "No one feared that he would misuse power. . . . His genuine hesitancy, his reluctance to assume the position, only served to reinforce the almost universal desire that he do so."[23]

The proceedings of the convention were kept secret. To encourage everyone to speak freely, delegates were forbidden to discuss the debates with outsiders. It was feared that if a delegate publicly took a firm stand on an issue, it would be harder for him to change his mind after debate and discussion. The delegates also knew that if word of the inevitable disagreements got out, it would provide ammunition for the many enemies of the convention. There were critics of this secrecy rule, but without it, agreement might not have been possible.

Consensus

The Constitutional Convention is usually discussed in terms of its three famous compromises: the compromise between large and small states over representation in Congress, the compromise between North and South over the regulation and taxation of foreign commerce, and the compromise between North and South over the counting of slaves for the purpose of taxation and representation. There were many other important compromises; yet on many significant issues, most of the delegates were in agreement.

Although a few delegates might have privately favored a limited monarchy, all supported a republican form of government based on elected representatives of the people. This was the only form seriously considered and the only form acceptable to the nation. Equally important, all the delegates opposed arbitrary and unrestrained government.

The common philosophy accepted by most of the delegates was that of *balanced government.* They wanted to construct a national government in which no single interest would dominate. Because most of the delegates represented citizens who were alarmed by the tendencies of desperate farmers to interfere with the property rights of others,

Representing different constituencies and different ideologies, the Constitutional Convention devised a totally new form of government that provided for a central government strong enough to rule but still responsible to its citizens and to the member states.

they were primarily concerned with balancing the government in the direction of protection for property and business.

Benjamin Franklin, the 81-year-old delegate from Pennsylvania, favored extending the right to vote to all white males, but most of the delegates believed that owners of land were the best guardians of liberty. James Madison feared that those without property, if given the right to vote, might combine to deprive property owners of their rights. Delegates agreed in principle on limited voting rights but differed over the kind and amount of property one must own in order to vote. Because states were in the process of relaxing qualifications for the vote, the framers recognized that they would jeopardize approval of the constitution if they made the qualifications to vote in federal elections more restrictive than those of the states. As a result, each state was left to determine the qualifications for electing members of the House of Representatives, the only branch of the national government that was to be elected directly by the voters.

Within five days of its opening, the convention—with only the Connecticut delegates dissenting—voted that "a national government ought to be established consisting of a supreme legislative, executive, and judiciary." This decision to establish a supreme national government profoundly altered the nature of the union from a loose confederation of states to a true nation.

Few dissented from proposals to give the new Congress all the powers of the old Congress plus all other powers necessary to ensure that the integrity of the United States would not be challenged by state legislation. The framers agreed that a strong executive, which had been lacking under the Articles of Confederation, was necessary to provide energy and direction. An independent judiciary was also accepted without much debate. Other issues, however, sparked considerable conflict.

"Remember, gentlemen, we aren't here just to draft a constitution. We're here to draft the best damn constitution in the world."

Conflict and Compromise

There were serious differences among the various delegates, especially between those from the large and small states. One of the most contentious issues was how to distribute the land extending westward to the Mississippi, land that had been secured through the War for Independence. Several large states asserted claims to these western lands, but small states generally objected. The large states also favored a strong national government (which they expected they could dominate), while delegates from small states were anxious to avoid being dominated.

This tension surfaced in the first discussions of representation in Congress. Franklin favored a single-house national legislature, but most states had had two-chamber legislatures since colonial times, and the delegates were used to the system. **Bicameralism**—the principle of the two-house legislature—reflected delegates' belief in the need for balanced government. The Senate, the smaller chamber, would represent the states, and to some extent the aristocracy, and offset the larger, more democratic House of Representatives.

THE VIRGINIA PLAN   The Virginia delegation took the initiative. Its members had met before the convention, and as soon as it was convened, they presented 15 resolutions. These resolutions, known as the **Virginia Plan**, called for a strong central government with a legislature composed of two chambers. The members of the more representative chamber were to be elected by the voters; those of the smaller and more aristocratic chamber were to be chosen by the larger chamber from nominees submitted by the state legislatures. Representation in both houses would be based on either wealth or numbers, which would give the wealthier and more populous states—Massachusetts, Pennsylvania, and Virginia—a majority in the national legislature.

The Congress thus created was to be given all the legislative power of its predecessor under the Articles of Confederation, as well as the right "to legislate in all cases in which the separate States are incompetent." Further, it was to have the authority to veto state legislation

bicameralism
The principle of a two-house legislature.

Virginia Plan
Initial proposal at the Constitutional Convention made by the Virginia delegation for a strong central government with a bicameral legislature, the lower house to be elected by the voters and the upper chosen by the lower.

that conflicted with the proposed constitution. The Virginia Plan also called for a national executive with extensive jurisdiction who would be chosen by the legislature. A national Supreme Court, along with the executive, was to have a qualified veto over acts of Congress.

THE NEW JERSEY PLAN   The Virginia Plan dominated the discussion for the first few weeks. But by June 15, additional delegates from the small states arrived, and they began a counterattack. They rallied around William Paterson of New Jersey, who presented a series of resolutions known as the **New Jersey Plan**. Table 1-1 outlines the key features of both plans. Paterson did not question the need for a strengthened central government, but he was concerned about how this strength might be used. The New Jersey Plan would give Congress the right to tax and regulate commerce and to coerce states, and it would retain the single-house unicameral legislature (as under the Articles of Confederation) in which each state, regardless of size, would have the same vote.

The New Jersey Plan contained the germ of what eventually came to be a key provision of our Constitution: the *supremacy clause*. The national Supreme Court was to hear appeals from state judges, and the supremacy clause would require all judges—state and national—to treat laws of the national government and the treaties of the United States as superior to the constitutions and laws of each of the states.

To adopt the Virginia Plan—which would create a powerful national government dominated by Massachusetts, Pennsylvania, and Virginia and eliminate the states as important units of government—would guarantee that many of the other states would reject the new constitution. Still, the large states resisted, and for a time the convention was deadlocked. The small states believed that all states should be represented equally in Congress, especially in the smaller "upper house" if there were to be two chambers. The large states insisted that representation in both houses be based on population or wealth and that national legislators be elected by voters rather than by state legislatures. Finally, the so-called Committee of Eleven was elected to devise a compromise. On July 5, it presented its proposals.

THE CONNECTICUT COMPROMISE   Because of the prominent role of the Connecticut delegation in constructing this plan, it has since been known as the **Connecticut Compromise**. It called for one house in which each state would have an equal vote and a second house in which representation would be based on population and in which all bills for raising or appropriating money would originate. This proposal was a setback for the large states, which agreed to it only when the smaller states made it clear this was their price for union. After equality of state representation in the Senate was accepted, most objections to a strong national government dissolved.

New Jersey Plan
Proposal at the Constitutional Convention made by William Paterson of New Jersey for a central government with a single-house legislature in which each state would be represented equally.

Connecticut Compromise
Compromise agreement by states at the Constitutional Convention for a bicameral legislature with a lower house in which representation would be based on population and an upper house in which each state would have two senators.

TABLE 1–1   **The Virginia and New Jersey Plans**

Virginia Plan	New Jersey Plan
Legitimacy derived from citizens, based on popular representation	Derived from states, based on equal votes for each state
Bicameral legislature	Unicameral legislature
Executive size undetermined, elected and removable by Congress	More than one person, removable by state majority
Judicial life-tenure, able to veto state legislation	No power over states
Legislature can override state laws	Government can compel obedience to national laws
Ratification by citizens	Ratification by states

NORTH-SOUTH COMPROMISES   Other issues split the delegates from the North and South. Southerners were afraid a northern majority in Congress might discriminate against southern trade. They had some basis for this concern. John Jay, secretary of foreign affairs for the Confederation, had proposed a treaty with Great Britain that would have given advantages to northern merchants at the expense of southern exporters. To protect themselves, the southern delegates insisted that a two-thirds majority be required in the Senate before the president could ratify a treaty.

Differences between the North and South were also evident on the issue of representation in the House of Representatives. The question was whether to count slaves for the purpose of apportioning seats in the House. The South wanted to count slaves, thereby enlarging its number of representatives; the North resisted. After heated debate, the delegates agreed on the **three-fifths compromise**. Each slave would be counted as three-fifths of a free person for the purposes of apportionment in the House and of direct taxation; this fraction was chosen because it maintained a balance of power between North and South. The issue of balance would recur in the early history of our nation as territorial governments were established and territories applied for statehood.

OTHER ISSUES   Delegates found other issues to argue about. Should the national government have lower courts, or would one federal Supreme Court be enough? This issue was resolved by postponing the decision. The Constitution states that there shall be one Supreme Court and that Congress may establish lower courts.

How should the president be selected? For a long time, the convention accepted the idea that the president should be chosen by Congress, but the delegates feared that Congress would dominate the president, or vice versa. Election by the state legislatures was rejected because the delegates distrusted the state legislatures. Finally, the electoral college system was devised. This was perhaps the most novel and most contrived contribution of the delegates and has long been one of the most criticized provisions in the Constitution.[24] (See Article II, Section 1, of the Constitution, which is reprinted between Chapters 2 and 3.)

After three months, the delegates stopped debating. On September 17, 1787, they assembled for an impressive ceremony of signing the document they were recommending to the nation. All but three of those still present signed; others who opposed the general drift of the convention had already left. Their work well done, delegates adjourned to the nearby City Tavern to celebrate.

According to an old story, Benjamin Franklin was confronted by a woman as he left the last session of the convention.

"What kind of government have you given us, Dr. Franklin?" she asked. "A republic or a monarchy?"

"A republic, Madam," he answered, "if you can keep it."

To Adopt or Not to Adopt?

The delegates had gone far. Indeed, they had wholly disregarded Congress's instruction to do no more than revise the Articles. They had ignored Article XIII of the Articles of Confederation, which declared the Union to be perpetual and prohibited any alteration of the Articles unless agreed to by Congress and by *every one of the state legislatures*—a provision that had made it impossible to amend the Articles. The convention delegates, however, boldly declared that their newly proposed Constitution should go into effect when ratified by popularly elected conventions in nine states.

They turned to this method of ratification for practical considerations as well as for reasons of securing legitimacy for their newly proposed government. Not only were the delegates aware that there was little chance of winning approval of the new Constitution in all state legislatures; many also believed the Constitution should be ratified by an authority higher than a legislature. A constitution based on approval *by the people* would have

three-fifths compromise
Compromise agreement between northern and southern states at the Constitutional Convention that three-fifths of the slave population would be counted for determining direct taxation and representation in the House of Representatives.

higher legal and moral status. The Articles of Confederation had been a compact of state governments, but the Constitution was based on the people (recall its opening words: "We the People . . . "). Still, even this method of ratification would not be easy. The nation was not ready to adopt the Constitution without a thorough debate.

Federalists Versus Antifederalists

Supporters of the new government, by cleverly appropriating the name **Federalists**, took some of the sting out of charges they were trying to destroy the states and establish an all-powerful central government. By calling their opponents **Antifederalists**, they pointed up the negative character of the arguments of those who opposed ratification.

The split was in part geographic. Seaboard and city regions tended to be Federalist strongholds; backcountry regions from Maine (then a part of Massachusetts) through Georgia, inhabited by farmers and other relatively poor people, were generally Antifederalist. But as in most political contests, no single factor completely accounted for the division between Federalists and Antifederalists. Thus in Virginia, the leaders of both sides came from the same general social and economic class. New York City and Philadelphia strongly supported the Constitution, yet so did predominantly rural New Jersey.

The great debate was conducted through pamphlets, papers, letters to the editor, and speeches. The issues were important, but with few exceptions, the argument about the merits of the Constitution was carried on in a quiet and calm manner. Out of the debate came a series of essays known as ***The Federalist***, written (using the pseudonym Publius) by Alexander Hamilton, James Madison, and John Jay to persuade the voters of New York to ratify the Constitution. *The Federalist* is still "widely regarded as the most profound single treatise on the Constitution ever written and as among the few masterly works in political science produced in all the centuries of history."[25] (Three of the most important

Federalists
Supporters of ratification of the Constitution whose position promoting a strong central government was later voiced in the Federalist party.

Antifederalists
Opponents of ratification of the Constitution and of a strong central government generally.

The Federalist
Series of essays promoting ratification of the Constitution, published anonymously by Alexander Hamilton, John Jay, and James Madison in 1787 and 1788.

Creating the Republic

April 1775   American Revolution begins at Lexington and Concord, Massachusetts
June 1775   George Washington assumes command of Continental forces
July 1776   Declaration of Independence approved
November 1777   Articles of Confederation adopted by Continental Congress
March 1781   Articles of Confederation ratified by all 13 states
October 1781   British defeated at Yorktown
April 1783   Congress ratifies peace treaty with Britain
August 1786 to February 1787   Shays' Rebellion in western Massachusetts
May 1787   Constitutional Convention opens in Philadelphia
September 1787   Constitution of the United States adopted by Constitutional Convention
June 1788   Constitution ratified by nine states
January and February 1789   First national elections
March 1789   United States Congress meets for the first time in New York
April 1789   George Washington inaugurated as first president
September 1789   John Jay becomes first chief justice of the United States
September 1789   Congress proposes Bill of Rights
December 1791   Bill of Rights (first ten amendments) ratified as part of the U.S. Constitution

Note: It took about 15 years to win independence, form an interim government that tried to govern, fashion a "more perfect union," and actually set up a national government with functioning legislative, executive, and judicial branches.

Federalist essays, Nos. 10, 51, and 78, are reprinted in the Appendix of this book. We urge you to read them.) The great debate stands even today as an outstanding example of free people using public discussion to determine the nature of their fundamental laws.

The Antifederalists' most telling criticism of the proposed Constitution was its failure to include a bill of rights.[26] The Federalists believed a bill of rights was unnecessary because the proposed national government had *only* the specific powers delegated to it by the states and the people. Thus there was no need to specify that Congress could not, for example, abridge freedom of the press because the states and the people had not given it power to regulate the press. Moreover, the Federalists argued, to guarantee some rights might be dangerous, because it would then be thought that rights not listed could be denied. The Constitution already protected some important rights—trial by jury in federal criminal cases, for example. Hamilton and others also insisted that paper guarantees were weak supports on which to depend for protection against governmental tyranny.

The Antifederalists were unconvinced. If some rights were protected, what could be the objection to providing constitutional protection for others? Without a bill of rights, what was to prevent Congress from using one of its delegated powers to abridge free speech? If bills of rights were needed in state constitutions to limit state governments, why was a bill of rights not needed in the national constitution to limit the national government? This was a government farther from the people, they contended, with a greater tendency to subvert natural rights.

The Politics of Ratification

The absence of a bill of rights in the proposed constitution dominated the struggle over its adoption. In taverns and church gatherings and newspaper offices up and down the eastern seaboard, people were muttering, "No bill of rights—no constitution!" This feeling was

Challenges for Our Constitutional Democracy

1. *"All men are created equal":* What kinds of equality are—and should be—protected by the Constitution, and by what means?

2. *"Government by the people":* Does the evolving constitutional system, including political parties and interest groups, strengthen fair and effective representation of the people?

3. *Federalism:* Does the Constitution provide an efficient and realistic balance between national and state power?

4. *Checks and balances:* Does the constitutional separation of powers between the president and Congress lead too often to gridlock and stalemate?

5. *Minority rights:* Does the Constitution adequately protect the rights of women, African Americans, Native Americans, Hispanic Americans, other ethnic groups, and recent immigrants?

6. *Suspects' rights:* Can representative government uphold the rights of the criminally accused and yet protect its citizens?

7. *Individual liberties:* Are individual liberties adequately protected in the Constitution? Do big government and big business diminish the freedom of the individual?

8. *The judicial branch:* Is it too powerful? Are the federal courts exceeding their proper powers as interpreters of the Constitution?

9. *War and peace:* What are the responsibilities of the United States as the only superpower?

10. *Constitutional responsibilities:* Are Americans participating adequately in our democratic system? Do citizens have the social capital and understanding of our governmental processes to be heard and to make a difference?

TABLE 1–2 Ratification of the U.S. Constitution

State	Date
Delaware	December 7, 1787
Pennsylvania	December 12, 1787
New Jersey	December 18, 1787
Georgia	January 2, 1788
Connecticut	January 9, 1788
Massachusetts	February 6, 1788
Maryland	April 28, 1788
South Carolina	May 23, 1788
New Hampshire	June 21, 1788
Virginia	June 25, 1788
New York	July 26, 1788
North Carolina	November 21, 1789
Rhode Island	May 29, 1790

so strong that some Antifederalists, who were far more concerned with states' rights than individual rights, joined forces with bill of rights advocates in an effort to defeat the proposed Constitution.

The Federalists were first to begin the debate over the Constitution that opened as soon as the delegates left Philadelphia in mid-September 1787. The Federalists' tactic was to secure ratification in as many states as possible before the opposition had time to organize. The Antifederalists were handicapped. Most newspapers were owned by supporters of ratification. Moreover, Antifederalist strength was concentrated in rural areas, which were underrepresented in some state legislatures and difficult to arouse to political action. The Antifederalists needed time to perfect their organization and collect their strength, while the Federalists, composed of a more closely knit group of leaders throughout the colonies, moved in a hurry.

In most of the small states, now satisfied by equal Senate representation, ratification was gained without difficulty. Delaware was the first state to ratify, and by early 1788, Pennsylvania, New Jersey, Georgia, and Connecticut had also ratified (see Table 1-2). Reports were coming in from Massachusetts, however, that opposition was broadening. The position of such key leaders as John Hancock and Samuel Adams was in doubt. The debate in the ratifying convention in Boston pitched some of the most polished Federalist speakers against an array of eloquent but plainspoken Antifederalists. The debate raged for most of January 1788 into February. At times it looked as though the Constitution would lose, as Antifederalists raised the cry of "Why no bill of rights?" and other objections. But in the end, the Constitution was narrowly ratified in Massachusetts, 187 to 168.

The struggle over ratification continued through the spring of 1788. By June 21, Maryland, South Carolina, and New Hampshire had ratified, putting the Constitution over the top in the number (nine) required for ratification. But two big hurdles remained: Virginia and New York. It would be impossible to begin the new government without the consent of these two major states. Virginia was crucial. As the most populous state, the home of Washington, Jefferson, and Madison, it was a link between North and South. The Virginia ratifying convention rivaled the Constitutional Convention in the caliber of

Patrick Henry's famous cry of "Give Me Liberty or Give Me Death!" symbolizes the underlying spirit of optimism in the United States. This spirit has endured throughout this country's history, despite the many problems the country has experienced.

its delegates. Madison, who had only recently switched to favoring a bill of rights after saying earlier it was unnecessary, captained the Federalist forces. The fiery Patrick Henry led the opposition. In an epic debate, Henry cried that liberty was the issue: "Liberty, the greatest of earthly possessions . . . that precious jewel!" But Madison quietly rebutted him and then played his trump card, a promise that a bill of rights embracing the freedoms of religion and speech and assembly would be added to the Constitution as the first order of business once the new government was established. At a critical moment, Washington himself tipped the balance with a letter urging ratification. News of the Virginia vote, 89 for the Constitution and 79 opposed, was rushed to New York.[27]

The great landowners along New York's Hudson River, unlike their southern planter friends, were opposed to the Constitution. They feared federal taxation of their holdings, and they did not want to abolish the profitable tax New York had been levying on trade and commerce with other states. When the convention assembled, the Federalists were greatly outnumbered, but they were aided by Alexander Hamilton's strategy and skill and by word of Virginia's ratification. New York approved by a margin of three votes. Although North Carolina and Rhode Island still remained outside the Union (the former ratified in November 1789, the latter six months later), the new nation was created. In New York, a few members of the old Congress assembled to issue the call for elections under the new Constitution. Then they adjourned without setting a date for reconvening.

THE MAP OF FREEDOM

New democracies often fail. It is one thing to espouse democratic values and quite another to put them into practice. Some people say they believe in democracy until they lose power in an election. Or the citizens grow weary of the political wrangling that comes with democracy and long for a strong, charismatic leader with simple solutions for complex problems. The struggle to convert to a market economy in Russia has produced this kind of turmoil. Leaders like Napoleon or Adolf Hitler promise to make a country work more smoothly, often by disbanding democratic institutions. Citizens may turn to such leaders when they face economic difficulties or are under threat from a foreign power. Sectional differences can also pull apart the fabric of democracy. Parts of a country that have a distinctive racial, religious, or ethnic composition often distrust the national majority and seek guarantees or special concessions—as French-speaking residents in Quebec and ethnic Albanians in Kosovo have done. Muslim Kashmiris living in predominantly Hindu India have long sought independence from the country—a conflict that has spurred hostilities between India and Pakistan for decades.

Because democracies are so difficult to sustain, comparatively few have lasted long. More than half the world's constitutions have been written since 1960. On the entire continent of Asia, no democracy predates World War II, when a democratic constitution was imposed on Japan. In Africa,

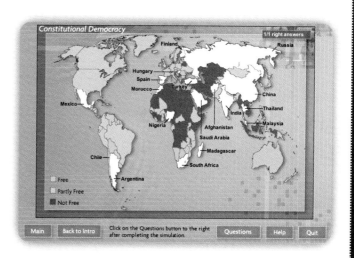

the oldest democracy is Botswana, which has had free elections and a multiparty system since 1966.

In this simulation, you are asked to categorize the nations of the world in terms of freedom (free, partly free, or not free), based on the extent to which they have such rights as universal suffrage, free and fair elections, and political participation by racial minorities. When you encounter a country that is more or less free than you thought, you might want to read more about that country and learn about its political history. Also, determine what factors seem to predict which countries will be free and which will be less free.

Go to PoliSim "The Map of Freedom."

Summary

1. The terrorist attacks of September 11, 2001, and the bioterrorism that followed transformed public attitudes about the importance of government, improved the image of President George W. Bush as a political leader, and fostered an outpouring of patriotism. The response of government at all levels to the attacks illustrate the ability of American government to respond to a crisis.

2. Americans have long been skeptical of politicians and politics. Yet politics is a necessary activity for a democracy. Indeed, politics and politicians are indispensable to making our system of separated institutions and checks and balances work.

3. "Democracy" is an often misused term, and it has many different meanings. We use it here to refer to a system of interacting values, interrelated political processes, and interdependent political structures. The vital principle of democracy is that a just government must derive its powers from the consent of the people and that this consent must be regularly renewed in free and fair elections.

4. The essential democratic values are a belief in personal liberty, respect for the individual, equality of opportunity, and popular consent. Essential elements of the democratic process are free and fair elections, majority rule, freedom of expression, and the right to assemble and protest.

5. Stable constitutional democracy is encouraged by various conditions, such as an educated citizenry, a healthy economy, and overlapping associations and groupings within a society in which major institutions interact to achieve a certain degree of consensus.

6. There has recently been some concern about a decline in *social capital*—the experiences people gain in working together in community groups. Lessons about compromise, accommodation, and participation are important building blocks for democracy. Some observers say we have experienced a decline in civic engagement, while others see a healthy level of voluntary and charitable engagement that is making our communities and our nation better.

7. Constitutionalism is a general label we apply to arrangements such as checks and balances, federalism, separation of powers, rule of law, due process, and the Bill of Rights that force our leaders and representatives to listen, think, bargain, and explain before they act and make laws. A constitutional government enforces recognized and regularly applied limits on the powers of those who govern.

8. Democracy developed gradually. A revolution had to be fought before a system of representative democracy in the United States could be tried and tested. It took several years before a national constitution could be written and almost another year to be ratified. It took still another two years before the Bill of Rights could be adopted and ratified. It has taken more than 200 years for democratic institutions to be refined and for systems of competition and choice to be hammered out. Democratic institutions such as free and fair elections and equal protection of the laws in the United States are still in the process of being refined and improved.

Key Terms

democracy
direct democracy
representative democracy
constitutional democracy
constitutionalism
statism
popular consent

majority rule
majority
plurality
social capital
ideology
theocracy
Articles of Confederation

Annapolis Convention
Constitutional Convention
Shays' Rebellion
bicameralism
Virginia Plan
New Jersey Plan
Connecticut Compromise

three-fifths compromise
Federalists
Antifederalists
The Federalist

Further Reading

BERNARD BAILYN, ED., *The Debate on the Constitution: Federalist and Antifederalist Speeches, Articles, and Letters During the Struggle over Ratification,* 2 vols. (Library of America, 1993).

LANCE BANNING, *The Sacred Fire of Liberty: James Madison and the Founding of the Federal Republic* (Cornell University Press, 1995).

WILLIAM J. CROTTY, ED., *The State of Democracy in America* (Georgetown University Press, 2001).

ROBERT A. DAHL, *On Democracy* (Yale University Press, 1998).

ALEXANDER HAMILTON, JAMES MADISON, AND JOHN JAY, *The Federalist Papers,* ed. Clinton Rossiter (New American Library, 1961). Also in several other editions.

SAMUEL P. HUNTINGTON, *The Third Wave: Democratization in the Late Twentieth Century* (University of Oklahoma Press, 1991).

DANIEL LESSARD LEVIN, *Representing Popular Sovereignty: The Constitution in American Political Culture* (State University of New York Press, 1999).

AREND LIJPHART, *Patterns of Democracy: Government Forms and Performance in Thirty-Six Countries* (Yale University Press, 1999).

DREW R. McCOY, *The Last of the Fathers: James Madison and the Republican Legacy* (Columbia University Press, 1989).

RICHARD B. MORRIS, *Witnesses at the Creation: Hamilton, Madison, and Jay and the Constitution* (Holt, Rinehart and Winston, 1985).

PIPPA NORRIS, ED., *Critical Citizens: Global Support for Democratic Institutions* (Oxford University Press, 1999).

JACK N. RAKOVE, *Original Meanings: Politics and Ideas in the Making of the Constitution* (Vintage Books, 1997).

MICHAEL J. SANDEL, *Democracy's Discontent: America in Search of a Public Philosophy* (Belknap Press, 1996).

MICHAEL SCHUDSON, *The Good Citizen: A History of American Civic Life* (Harvard University Press, 1998).

THEDA SKOCPOL AND MORRIS P. FIORINA, EDS., *Civic Engagement in American Democracy* (Brookings/Russell Sage, 1999).

CASS R. SUNSTEIN, *Designing Democracy: What Constitutions Do* (Oxford University Press, 2001).

ALEXIS DE TOCQUEVILLE, *Democracy in America,* 2 vols. (1835).

GARRY WILLS, *A Necessary Evil: A History of American Distrust of Government* (Simon & Schuster, 1999).

GORDON S. WOOD, *The Creation of the American Republic, 1776–1787* (University of North Carolina Press, 1969).

See also the *Journal of Democracy* (Johns Hopkins University Press).

THE LIVING CONSTITUTION

THE CONSTITUTION OF THE UNITED STATES, THE WORLD'S OLDEST WRITTEN CONSTITUTION, IS ALSO ONE OF THE SHORTEST. The original, unamended Constitution, which went into effect in 1789, contains just 4,543 words, yet it established the framers' experiment in free-government-in-the-making that each generation reinterprets and renews. The Constitution remains a document Americans revere. Optimists read it as expressing their hopes; pessimists put faith in its protections against tyranny and other abuses.

Why, after more than 215 years, have we not written another constitution—let alone two, three, or more, like other countries around the world? Part of the answer is the widespread acceptance of the Constitution by optimists and pessimists alike. But also part of the answer is the Constitution's brilliant structure for limited government and because the framers built into the document the capacity for adaptability and flexibility.

As the Constitution won the support of citizens of the early years of the Republic, it took on the aura of **natural law**—law that defines right from wrong, law that is higher than human law. "The [Founding] Fathers grew ever larger in stature as they receded from view; the era in which they lived and fought became a Golden Age; in that age there had been a fresh dawn for the world, and its men were giants against the sky."[1] This early Constitution worship helped bring unity to the diverse new nation. Like the crown in Great Britain, the Constitution became a symbol of national loyalty, evoking both emotional and intellectual support from Americans, regardless of their differences. The framers' work became part of the American creed and culture.[2] It stood for liberty, equality before the law, limited government—indeed, for just about whatever anyone wanted to read into it.

Even today, Americans generally revere the Constitution, yet many do not know what is in it. A poll by the National Constitution Center found that nine out of ten Americans are proud of the Constitution and feel it is important to them. However, a third think the Constitution establishes English as the country's official language. One in six believes the

"And there are three branches of government, so that each branch has the other two to blame everything on."

natural law
God's or nature's law that defines right from wrong and is higher than human law.

separation of powers
Constitutional division of powers among the legislative, executive, and judicial branches, with the legislative branch making law, the executive applying and enforcing the law, and the judiciary interpreting the law.

Constitution establishes America as a Christian nation. Only one out of four could name a single First Amendment right. Although two out of three knew that the Constitution creates three branches of the national government, only one in three could name all three branches.[3]

The Constitution, however, is more than a symbol. It is a supreme and binding law that both grants and limits powers. "In framing a government which is to be administered by men over men," wrote James Madison in *The Federalist*, No. 51, "the great difficulty lies in this: you must first enable the government to control the governed; and in the next place oblige it to control itself." (See *The Federalist*, No. 51, in the Appendix of this book, or go on the Web to www.law.ou.edu/hist/federalist/.) The Constitution is both a positive instrument of government, which enables the governors to control the governed, and a restraint on government, which enables the ruled to check the rulers. In what ways does the Constitution limit the power of the government? In what ways does it create governmental power? How has it managed to serve as a great symbol of national unity and at the same time as an adaptable instrument of government? The secret is an ingenious separation of powers and a system of checks and balances that check power with power.

Checking Power with Power

It may seem strange to begin by stressing the ways in which the Constitution *limits* governmental power, but keep in mind the dilemma the framers faced. They wanted a stronger and more effective national government than they had under the Articles of Confederation; at the same time, they were keenly aware that the people would not accept too much central control. Efficiency and order were important concerns, but they were not as important as liberty. The framers wanted to ensure domestic tranquillity and prevent future rebellions, but they also wanted to forestall the emergence of a homegrown King George III. Accordingly, they allotted certain powers to the national government and reserved the rest for the states, thus establishing a system of *federalism* (whose nature and problems we take up in Chapter 3). Even this was not enough. They believed they needed additional means to limit the national government.

The most important way they devised to make public officials observe the constitutional limits on their powers was through *free and fair elections;* voters would be able to throw out of office those who abuse power. Yet the framers were not willing to depend solely on political controls, because they did not fully trust the people's judgment. "Free government is founded on jealousy, and not in confidence," said Thomas Jefferson. "In questions of power, then, let no more be heard of confidence in man, but bind him down from mischief by the chains of the Constitution."[4]

No less important, the framers feared that a majority might deprive minorities of their rights. "A dependence on the people is, no doubt, the primary control on the government," Madison admitted in *The Federalist*, No. 51, "but experience has taught mankind the necessity of auxiliary precautions." What were these "auxiliary precautions" against popular tyranny?

Separation of Powers

The first step was the **separation of powers**, the distribution of constitutional authority among the three branches of the national government. In *The Federalist*, No. 47, Madison wrote, "No political truth is certainly of greater intrinsic value, or is stamped with the authority of more enlightened patrons of liberty, than that . . . the accumulation of all powers, legislative, executive, and judiciary, in the same hands . . . may justly be pronounced the very definition of tyranny."[5] Chief among the "enlightened patrons of liberty" to whose authority Madison was appealing were John Locke and Montesquieu, whose works were well known to most educated Americans.

The intrinsic value of the principle of dispersion of power does not by itself account for its inclusion in our Constitution. Dispersion of power had been the general practice in the colonies for more than 100 years. Only during the Revolutionary period did some of the states concentrate authority in the hands of the legislature, and that unhappy experience confirmed the framers' belief in the merits of the separation of powers. Many attributed the evils of state government and the lack of energy in the central government to the fact that there was no strong executive both to check legislative abuses and to give energy and direction to administration.

Still, separating power was not enough. There was always the danger—in the framers' view—that different officials with different powers might pool their authority and act together. Separation of powers by itself might not prevent governmental branches and officials from responding to the same pressures—from the demand of an overwhelming majority of the voters to suppress an offensive book, for example, or to impose confiscatory taxes on rich people. If separating power was not enough, what else could be done?

Checks and Balances: Ambition to Counteract Ambition

The framers' answer was a system of **checks and balances**. "The great security against a gradual concentration of the several powers in the same department," wrote Madison in *The Federalist,* No. 51, "consists in giving to those who administer each department the necessary constitutional means and personal motives to resist encroachments of the others: . . . Ambition must be made to counteract ambition." Each branch therefore has a role in the actions of the others (see Figure 2-1). Congress enacts laws, but the president can veto them.

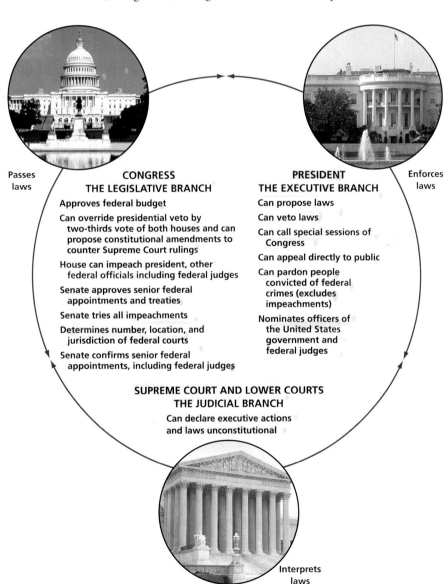

Passes
laws

**CONGRESS
THE LEGISLATIVE BRANCH**

Approves federal budget

Can override presidential veto by two-thirds vote of both houses and can propose constitutional amendments to counter Supreme Court rulings

House can impeach president, other federal officials including federal judges

Senate approves senior federal appointments and treaties

Senate tries all impeachments

Determines number, location, and jurisdiction of federal courts

Senate confirms senior federal appointments, including federal judges

**PRESIDENT
THE EXECUTIVE BRANCH**

Can propose laws

Can veto laws

Can call special sessions of Congress

Can appeal directly to public

Can pardon people convicted of federal crimes (excludes impeachments)

Nominates officers of the United States government and federal judges

Enforces
laws

**SUPREME COURT AND LOWER COURTS
THE JUDICIAL BRANCH**

Can declare executive actions and laws unconstitutional

Interprets
laws

FIGURE 2–1 **The Separation of Powers and Checks and Balances.**

checks and balances
Constitutional grant of powers that enables each of the three branches of government to check some acts of the others and therefore ensure that no branch can dominate.

The Exercise of Checks and Balances, 1789–2002

vetoes   The president has vetoed more than 2,500 acts of Congress. Congress has overridden presidential vetoes more than 100 times.

judicial review   The Supreme Court has ruled some 164 congressional acts or parts thereof unconstitutional. Its 1983 decision on legislative vetoes (*INS v. Chadha*) affects another 200 provisions.

impeachment   The House of Representatives has impeached two presidents and 15 federal judges; of these, the Senate has convicted seven judges but neither president.

confirmation   The Senate has refused to confirm nine cabinet nominations, and many other cabinet and subcabinet appointments were withdrawn because of likely Senate rejection.

For additional resources on the Constitution, go to www.prenhall.com/burns

The Supreme Court can declare laws passed by Congress and signed by the president unconstitutional, but the president appoints the justices and all the other federal judges, with the Senate's approval. The president administers the laws, but Congress provides the money. Moreover, the Senate and the House of Representatives have an absolute veto over each other in the enactment of laws, because both houses must approve bills.

Not only does each branch have some authority over the others, but each is politically independent of the others. Voters in each local district choose members of the House; voters in each state choose senators; the president is elected by the voters in all the states. With the consent of the Senate, the president appoints federal judges, who remain in office until they retire or are impeached.

The framers also ensured that a majority of the voters could win control over only part of the government at one time. Although in an off-year (nonpresidential) election a new majority might take control of the House of Representatives, the president would still have at least two more years, and senators hold office for six years. Finally, independent federal courts, which have developed their own powerful checks, were also provided.

Modifications of Checks and Balances

Distrustful of both the elites and the masses, the framers deliberately built inefficiency into our political system. They designed the decision-making process so that the national government can act decisively only when there is a consensus among most groups and after all sides have had a chance to have their say. "The doctrine of separation of powers was adopted by the convention of 1787," in the words of Justice Louis D. Brandeis, "not to promote efficiency but to preclude the exercise of arbitrary power. The purpose was not to avoid friction, but, by means of the inevitable friction incident to the distribution of the governmental powers among three departments, to save the people from autocracy."[6] Still, even though the fragmentation of political power written into the Constitution remains, several developments have modified the way the system of checks and balances works.

THE RISE OF NATIONAL POLITICAL PARTIES   Political parties can serve as unifying factors, at times drawing together the president, senators, representatives, and sometimes even judges behind common programs. When parties do this, they help bridge the separation of powers. Yet parties can be splintered and weakened by having to work through a system of fragmented governmental power, so they never become strong or cohesive. Moreover, when one party controls Congress or one of its chambers and the other controls the White House (**divided government**), as has generally been the case since the end of World War II, the parties may intensify checks and balances rather than moderate them, to the point that action on some important issues may be difficult.[7]

divided government
Governance divided between the parties, especially when one holds the presidency and the other controls one or both houses of Congress.

Divided government may lead to so much competition between the legislative and executive branches that we find "each institution protecting and promoting itself through a broad interpretation of its constitutional and political status, even usurping the other's power when the opportunity presents itself."[8] Thus we have had battles over presidential impoundment of funds appropriated by Congress, budget gridlock, and unseemly and angry confirmation hearings for the appointment of justices of the Supreme Court and even members of the executive branch. Divided government also makes it difficult for the voters to hold anybody or any party accountable. "Presidents blame Congress . . . while members of Congress attack the president. . . . Citizens genuinely cannot tell who is to blame."[9]

Yet when all the shouting dies down, political scientist David Mayhew concludes, there have been just as many congressional investigations and just as much important legislation passed when one party controls Congress and another controls the presidency as when the same party controls both branches.[10] And Charles Jones, a noted authority on Congress and the presidency, adds that not only is divided government not that important in determining how our government responds to crises, but divided government is precisely what the voters appear to have wanted through much of our history.[11]

EXPANSION OF THE ELECTORATE AND THE MOVE TOWARD MORE DIRECT DEMOCRACY   The framers wanted the president to be chosen by the electoral college—wise, independent citizens free from popular passions and hero worship—rather than by ordinary citizens. Almost from the beginning, however, that is not the way the electoral college worked.[12] Rather, voters actually do select the president, because presidential electors chosen by the voters are pledged in advance to cast their electoral votes for their party's candidates for president and vice president. Nevertheless, presidential candidates may very occasionally win the national popular vote but lose the vote in the electoral college, as demonstrated most recently in Al Gore's winning the popular vote in the 2000 presidential election but losing the electoral college with 266 votes to George W. Bush's 271.

The kind of people allowed to vote has expanded from white property-owning males to all citizens over 18 years of age. In addition, during the past century, American states have expanded the role of the electorate by adopting **direct primaries**, in which the voters elect party nominees for the House and Senate and even for president; by permitting the voters

direct primary
Election in which voters choose party nominees.

IN COMPARATIVE PERSPECTIVE

The Japanese Constitution

The Japanese Constitution of 1947 created a parliamentary democracy and established the power of American-style judicial review. Although drafted in part by the United States and the Allied Occupation Forces after World War II, the Japanese Constitution was made easier to amend than ours. A proposed amendment needs only to be passed by a two-thirds majority of both houses of Japan's parliament and then be ratified by a majority vote of the people in a national referendum. Yet it has never been amended. What explains the reluctance of the Japanese to amend their constitution? Part of the explanation may be that the Japanese Constitution goes well beyond our Bill of Rights to include a broad range of economic and social rights, so that progressive Japanese vigorously oppose changing it. Opposition also comes from older Japanese who remember World War II and revere their "Peace Constitution,"

while younger generations tend to be indifferent and more concerned with economic matters. Another explanation is that the Japanese have learned to reinterpret controversial provisions of their constitution, as Americans have, in ways that make formal amendments unnecessary. For example, although Article 9 of the Japanese Constitution forbids the maintenance of "land, sea, and air forces" and includes a renunciation of war, the Japanese have interpreted Article 9 to permit them to maintain "self-defense forces," thus making it less urgent to change the constitution. Japan now ranks among the top five countries in terms of military spending and looks toward a larger role in international peacekeeping missions, including participation in the global war against terrorism.

For more information on the Japanese Constitution, go to www.home.ntt.com/jap/constitution/english-constitution.html.

IN COMPARATIVE PERSPECTIVE

The European Union

The European Union grew out of a succession of alliances formed after World War II to promote economic integration and cooperation. Through a series of treaties, the union has grown to include 15 countries in Western Europe. One of the most important institutions created by the union is the European Court of Justice (ECJ). The ECJ has the power to declare national laws invalid when they conflict with treaty obligations and has created a uniform system of law that takes precedence over national laws and constitutions.

The member states of the European Union have also signed the European Convention on Human Rights, which establishes a long list of civil liberties. They are subject to the jurisdiction of the European Court of Human Rights, which resolves allegations of human rights abuses and enforces the Convention on Human Rights. This court has interpreted its powers broadly and has asserted its right to invalidate national laws that contravene obligations that the nations accepted in signing the convention.

For the most part, the issues coming before the ECJ have been economic and commercial in nature, but it has struck down laws based on gender discrimination and advanced the right to equal pay for equal work. Critics of the ECJ complain that it has become too activist and compare it to the U.S. Supreme Court in the early nineteenth century under Chief Justice John Marshall, whose rulings striking down state trade barriers promoted the growth of our unified economy. Even with these trends toward more active judicial review in the European Union, courts in the United States continue to exercise the power of judicial review more frequently and more broadly than the newer constitutional and supranational courts do.

In response in part to the growing economic integration promoted by the ECJ, additional treaties, and the introduction of the euro as the common currency of 12 of the 15 member states, a commission is deciding on the agenda and procedures for a constitutional convention to adopt a federal constitution for the European Union; it will make its recommendations in late 2003.

For more information on the European Union, go to www.userpage.chemie.fu-berlin.de/adressen/eu.html and www.lib.berkeley.edu/gssi/eugde.html. The ECJ maintains a site at www.europa.eu.int/cj/en containing recent decisions and other information.

in about half the states to propose and vote on laws (**initiatives**); and by allowing voters to reconsider actions of the legislature (**referendums**) and even to remove elected state and local officials from office (**recall**). And with the passage of the Seventeenth Amendment, senators are no longer elected by state legislatures but are chosen directly by the people.

ESTABLISHMENT OF AGENCIES DELIBERATELY DESIGNED TO EXERCISE LEGISLATIVE, EXECUTIVE, AND JUDICIAL FUNCTIONS   When the national government began to regulate the economy, it issued detailed rules on such complex matters as railroad safety, bank and stock exchange practices, employment conditions, union negotiations, and automobile emissions. It was impossible to assign these regulatory responsibilities without providing the power to make and apply rules and to decide disputes. Beginning in 1887, Congress created *independent regulatory commissions* such as the Interstate Commerce Commission (which went out of business in 1995, although many of its functions were transferred to the Surface Transportation Board within the Department of Transportation) and the Federal Communications Commission. More recently, it has established *independent executive agencies* such as the Environmental Protection Agency.

CHANGES IN TECHNOLOGY   The system of checks and balances operates differently today from the way it did in 1789. Back then, there were no televised congressional committee hearings; no electronic communications; no *Larry King Live* talk shows; no *New York Times, Wall Street Journal, USA Today,* CNN, or C-SPAN; no nightly news programs with national audiences; no presidential press conferences; and no live coverage of wars and of Americans fighting in foreign lands. Nuclear bombs, television, computers, cellular telephones, fax machines, the World Wide Web—these and other innovations create conditions today that are very different from those of two centuries ago. We also live in a time of instant polls that tell us what people are thinking about public issues.

initiative
Procedure whereby a certain number of voters may, by petition, propose a law or constitutional amendment and have it submitted to the voters.

referendum
Procedure for submitting to popular vote measures passed by the legislature or proposed amendments to a state constitution.

recall
Procedure for submitting to popular vote the removal of officials from office before the end of their term.

In some ways, these new technologies have added to the powers of presidents by permitting them to appeal directly to millions of people and giving them immediate access to public opinion. And these new technologies have also added leverage to organized interests by making it easier to target thousands of letters and calls at members of Congress, to organize the writing of letters to the editor, and to stage media events. New technologies have also given greater independence and influence to nongovernmental institutions such as the press. They have made it possible for rich people like Ross Perot and Steve Forbes and religious leaders like Pat Robertson, who have access to ample financial resources, to bypass political parties and carry their message directly to the electorate.

THE GROWTH OF PRESIDENTIAL POWER   Today problems elsewhere in the world—Afghanistan, Israel, Pakistan, North Korea, Iraq—often create crises for the United States. The need to deal with perpetual emergencies has concentrated power in the hands of the chief executive and the presidential staff. The president of the United States has emerged as the most significant player on the world stage, and media coverage of summit conferences with foreign leaders enhance his status. Headline-generating events give the president a visibility no congressional leader can achieve. The office of the president has on occasion served to modify the system of checks and balances and provide some measure of national unity. Drawing on constitutional, political, and emergency powers, the president is sometimes able to overcome the restraints imposed by the Constitution on the exercise of governmental power—to the applause of some Americans and the alarm of others.

Judicial Review and the "Guardians of the Constitution"

Judges have become so important in our system of checks and balances that they deserve special attention. Judges did not claim the power of **judicial review**—the power of a court to strike down a law or a government regulation that in the opinion of the judges conflicts with the Constitution—until some years after the Constitution was adopted. From the beginning, however, judges were expected to restrain legislative majorities. "The independence of judges," wrote Alexander Hamilton in *The Federalist,* No. 78 (which appears in the Appendix), "may be an essential safeguard against the effects of occasional ill humors in the society."

Judicial review is a major contribution of the United States to the art of government, a contribution that has been adopted at an increasing pace by other nations. In Japan, Germany, France, Italy, and Spain, constitutional courts are responsible for reviewing laws referred to them to ensure constitutional compliance, including compliance with the charter of rights that is now part of their constitutions.[13] (Also see the box on the growth of judicial power in the European Union.)

Origins of Judicial Review

The Constitution says nothing about who should have the final word in disputes that might arise over its meaning. Whether the delegates to the Constitutional Convention of 1787 intended to give the courts the power of judicial review is a question long debated. The framers clearly intended that the Supreme Court have the power to declare state legislation unconstitutional, but whether they intended to give it the same power over *congressional* legislation and the president is not clear. Why then didn't the framers specifically provide for judicial review? Probably because they believed the power could be inferred from certain general provisions and the necessity of interpreting and applying a written constitution.

The Federalists—who urged ratification of the Constitution and controlled the national government until 1801—generally supported a strong role for federal courts and favored judicial review. Their opponents, the Jeffersonian Republicans (called Democrats after 1832), were less enthusiastic. In the Kentucky and Virginia Resolutions of 1798 and 1799, respectively, Jefferson and Madison (who by this time had left the Federalist camp)

judicial review
The power of a court to refuse to enforce a law or a government regulation that in the opinion of the judges conflicts with the U.S. Constitution or, in a state court, the state constitution.

PEOPLE IN POLITICS
JUSTICE THURGOOD MARSHALL

Thurgood Marshall was a crusading lawyer for the NAACP's Legal Defense Fund and the civil rights movement in the 1940s and 1950s. He argued before the Supreme Court and won the landmark case of *Brown* v. *Board of Education of Topeka* (1954), which held that segregated public schools were unconstitutional. President John Kennedy appointed him to the federal appellate bench in 1961. President Lyndon Johnson then persuaded Marshall to become solicitor general of the United States, and he was appointed to the Supreme Court in 1967. As the first African American on the Supreme Court, Justice Marshall served until 1991 and continued to champion the cause of civil rights throughout his career.

In 1987, he spoke out in dissent from the celebration of the Bicentennial of the Constitution and defended his view of our "living Constitution":

I do not believe that the meaning of the Constitution was forever "fixed" at the Philadelphia Convention. Nor do I find the wisdom, foresight, and sense of justice exhibited by the framers particularly profound. To the contrary, the government they devised was defective from the start, requiring several amendments, a civil war,

and momentous social transformation to attain the system of constitutional government, and its respect for the individual freedoms and human rights, that we hold as fundamental today. When contemporary Americans cite "The Constitution," they invoke a concept that is vastly different from what the framers barely began to construct two centuries ago.

For a sense of the evolving nature of the Constitution we need look no further than the first three words of the document's preamble: "We the People." When the Founding Fathers used this phrase in 1787, they did not have in mind the majority of America's citizens. "We the People" included, in the words of the framers, "the whole Number of free Persons." On a matter so basic as the right to vote, for example, Negro slaves were excluded, although they were counted for representational purposes—at three-fifths each. Women did not gain the right to vote for over a hundred and thirty years.

These omissions were intentional. The record of the framers' debates on the slave question is

especially clear: the Southern states acceded to the demands of the New England states for giving Congress broad power to regulate commerce, in exchange for the right to continue the slave trade. . . .

And so we must be careful, when focusing on the events which took place in Philadelphia two centuries ago, that we not overlook the momentous events which followed, and thereby lose our proper sense of perspective. . . . If we seek, instead, a sensitive understanding of the Constitution's inherent defects, and its promising evolution through 200 years of history, the celebration of the "Miracle at Philadelphia" will, in my view, be a far more meaningful and humbling experience. We will see that the true miracle was not the birth of the Constitution, but its life, a life nurtured through two turbulent centuries of our own making, and a life embodying much good fortune that was not.*

*Remarks at the annual seminar of the San Francisco Patent and Trademark Law Association, Maui, Hawaii, May 16, 1987. In David M. O'Brien, ed., *Judges on Judging* (Chatham House, 1997), pp. 195–200.

came close to the position that state legislatures—and not the Supreme Court—had the ultimate power to interpret the Constitution. These resolutions seemed to question whether the Supreme Court even had final authority to review state legislation, something about which there had been little doubt.

When the Jeffersonians defeated the Federalists in the election of 1800, it was still undecided whether the Supreme Court would actually exercise the power of judicial review. Logical reasons to support such a doctrine were at hand, and some precedents could even be cited; nevertheless, judicial review was not an established power. Then in 1803 came *Marbury* v. *Madison*, the most pathbreaking Supreme Court decision of all time.[14]

Marbury Versus Madison

The election of 1800 marked the rise to power of the Jeffersonian Republicans. President John Adams and fellow Federalists did not take their defeat easily. Indeed, they were greatly alarmed at what they considered to be the "enthronement of the rabble." Yet there was nothing much they could do about it before leaving office—or was there? The Constitution gives the president, with the consent of the Senate, the power to appoint federal judges to hold office during "good Behaviour"—basically, lifetime tenure, subject to removal only by impeachment. With the judiciary in the hands of Federalists, thought Adams and his associates, they could stave off the worst consequences of Jefferson's victory.

The outgoing Federalist Congress consequently created dozens of new federal judgeships. By March 3, 1801, Adams had appointed and the Senate had confirmed loyal Federalists to all these new positions. Adams signed the commissions and turned them over to John Marshall, his secretary of state, to be sealed and delivered. Marshall had just received his own commission as chief justice of the United States, but he continued to serve as secretary of state until Adams's term as president expired. Working right up until nine o'clock on the evening of March 3, Marshall sealed, but was unable to deliver, all the commissions. The only ones left were for the justices of the peace for the District of Columbia. The newly appointed chief justice left these commissions for his successor to deliver.

This "packing" of the judiciary angered Jefferson, now inaugurated as president. When he discovered that some of the commissions were still lying on a table in the Department of State, he instructed a clerk not to deliver them. Jefferson could see no reason why the District needed so many justices of the peace, especially Federalist justices.[15]

Among the commissions not delivered was one for William Marbury. After waiting in vain, Marbury decided to seek action from the courts. Searching through the statute books, he came across Section 13 of the Judiciary Act of 1789, which authorized the Supreme Court "to issue writs of mandamus." A **writ of mandamus** is a court order directing an official, such as the secretary of state, to perform a duty about which the official has no discretion, such as delivering a commission. So, thought Marbury, why not ask the Supreme Court to issue a writ of mandamus to force James Madison, the new secretary of state, to deliver the commission? Marbury and his companions went directly to the Supreme Court and, citing Section 13, they made the request.

What could Marshall do? On the one hand, if the Court issued the writ, Madison and Jefferson would probably ignore it. The Court would be powerless, and its prestige, already low, might suffer a fatal blow. On the other hand, by refusing to issue the writ, the judges would appear to support the Jeffersonian Republicans' claim that the Court had no authority to interfere with the executive. Would Marshall issue the writ? Most people thought so; angry Republicans even threatened impeachment if he did so.

On February 24, 1803, the Supreme Court delivered its opinion. The first part was as expected. Marbury was entitled to his commission, said Marshall, and Madison should have delivered it to him. Moreover, the proper court could issue a writ of mandamus, even against so high an officer as the secretary of state.

Then came the surprise. Section 13 of the Judiciary Act appears to give the Supreme Court original jurisdiction in cases such as this one in question. But Section 13, said Marshall, is contrary to Article III of the Constitution, which gives the Supreme Court original jurisdiction only when an ambassador or other foreign minister is affected or when a state is a party. Even though this is a case of original jurisdiction, Marbury is neither a state nor a foreign minister. If we follow Section 13, wrote Marshall, we have jurisdiction; if we follow the Constitution, we have no jurisdiction.

Marshall then posed the question in a more pointed way: Should the Supreme Court enforce an unconstitutional law? Of course not, he concluded. *The Constitution is the supreme and binding law,* and the courts cannot enforce any action of Congress that conflicts with it. Thus by limiting the Court's power to what is granted in the Constitution, Marshall gained the much more important power to declare laws passed by Congress unconstitutional. It was a brilliant move.

Chief Justice John Marshall (1755–1835), our most influential Supreme Court justice. Appointed in 1801, Marshall served until 1835. Earlier he had been a staunch defender of the U.S. Constitution at the Virginia ratifying convention, a member of Congress, and a secretary of state. He was one of those rare people who served in all three branches of government.

writ of mandamus
Court order directing an official to perform an official duty.

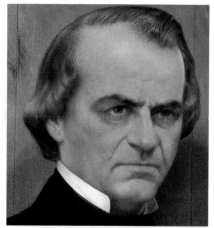

Two U.S. presidents, Andrew Johnson and Bill Clinton, have been impeached by the U.S. House of Representatives. In both cases the U.S. Senate did not muster a two-thirds majority vote, which would have been needed to convict these two presidents. President Richard Nixon almost surely would also have been impeached by the House of Representatives in 1974 but he resigned and left the presidency, and this decision preempted the House's action.

impeachment
Formal accusation against a public official, the first step in removal from office.

Marbury v. *Madison* might have been interpreted by subsequent generations in a very limited way. It could have been interpreted to mean that the Supreme Court had the right to determine the scope of its own powers under Article III, but Congress and the president had the authority to interpret their own powers under Articles I and II. Yet over the decades, building on Marshall's precedent, the Court has taken the commanding position as the authoritative interpreter of the Constitution.

Several important consequences follow from the acceptance of Marshall's argument that judges are the official interpreters of the Constitution. The most important is that people can challenge laws enacted by Congress and approved by the president. Simply by bringing a lawsuit, those who lack the clout to get a bill through Congress can often secure a judicial hearing. And organized interest groups often find that goals unattainable by legislation can be achieved by litigation. Litigation thus supplements, and at times even takes precedence over, legislation as a way to make public policy.[16]

The Constitution as an Instrument of Government

As careful as the Constitution's framers were to limit the powers they gave the national government, the main reason they had assembled in Philadelphia was to create a stronger national government. Having learned that a weak central government was a danger to liberty, they wished to establish a national government within the framework of a federal system with enough authority to meet the needs of all time. They made general grants of power, leaving it to succeeding generations to fill in the details and organize the structure of government in accordance with experience.

Hence our formal, written Constitution is only the skeleton of our system. It is filled out in numerous ways that must be considered part of our constitutional system in a larger sense. In fact, it is primarily through changes in the informal, unwritten Constitution that our system is kept up to date. These changes are found in certain basic statutes and historical practices of Congress, presidential practices, and decisions of the Supreme Court.

The Unwritten Constitution

CONGRESSIONAL ELABORATION   Because the framers gave Congress authority over many of the structural details of the national government, it is not necessary to amend the Constitution every time a change is needed. Rather, Congress can create legislation to meet the need. Examples of congressional elaboration appear in such legislation as the Judiciary Act of 1789, which laid the foundations of our national judicial system; in the laws establishing the organization and functions of all federal executive officials subordinate to the president; and in the rules of procedure, internal organization, and practices of Congress.

A dramatic example of congressional elaboration of our constitutional system is the use of the impeachment and removal power. An **impeachment** is a formal accusation against a public official and the first step in removal from office. Constitutional language defining the grounds for impeachment is sparse. Look at the Constitution (reprinted between this chapter and the next) and note that Article II (the Executive Article) calls for removal of the president, vice president, and all civil officers of the United States on impeachment for, and conviction of, "Treason, Bribery, or other High Crimes and Misdemeanors." It is up to Congress to give meaning to that language.

Article I (the Legislative Article) gives the House of Representatives the sole power to initiate impeachments and the Senate the sole power to try impeachments. In the event the president is tried, the chief justice of the United States presides, as Chief Justice William H. Rehnquist did in the impeachment of President Bill Clinton. Article I also requires conviction on impeachment charges to have the agreement of two-thirds of the senators present. Judgments shall extend no further than removal from office and disqualification from holding any office under the United States, but a person convicted may also be liable to indictment, trial, judgment, and punishment according to the law. Article I also exempts cases of impeachment from the president's pardoning power. Article III (the

IN COMPARATIVE PERSPECTIVE

The British and American Systems: A Study in Contrasts

Our political system is based on the Constitution; Britain has no such single document. Yet both systems are "constitutional" in the sense that the rulers are subject to well-defined restraints. Parliament is the guardian of the British constitution. In the United States, it is the courts—ultimately, the Supreme Court—that are the keepers of the constitutional conscience, not Congress or the president. The limitations in our written Constitution and the practices in the unwritten British constitution rest on underlying national values and attitudes toward government.

In the British system, voters elect members of the House of Commons from districts, much as we elect members of our House of Representatives. Like us, the party with the most votes in a district wins the seat, so that even with three or more parties, a plurality of the popular vote usually results in a majority of the parliamentary seats. So long as the parliamentary majority stays together, it can enact into law the ruling party's program.

Leaders of the majority party in the House of Commons serve as executive ministers who collectively form the cabinet, with the prime minister at its head. The majority selects the prime minister. If the ruling party loses the support of the majority in the Commons on a major issue, it must resign or call for new elections. Formerly, the House of Lords could check the Commons, but it is now almost powerless.

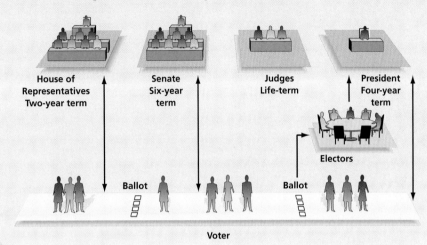

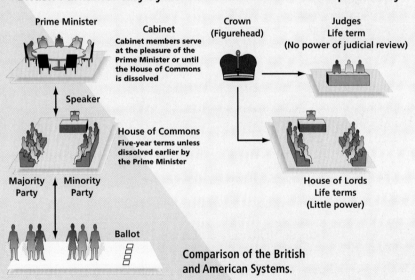

British Parliamentary System of Concentration of Responsibility

Comparison of the British and American Systems.

The House of Commons, when it chooses to act, has almost complete constitutional power. There is no high court with the power to declare acts of Parliament unconstitutional, and the prime minister cannot veto them, although he or she may ask the crown to dissolve Parliament and call new elections.

In British politics, parties are cohesive and disciplined; party members vote together and support their parliamentary leaders. In Britain, the party that wins an election has a very good chance of seeing its policies enacted. By contrast, our system depends on the agreement of many elements of society. The party that wins a presidential or congressional election or even one that controls both these branches may still have a tough time carrying out its campaign promises.

In recent years, the British system has been substantially modified. In addition to introducing elements of federalism by providing for regional parliaments in Scotland and Wales, the House of Lords has been stripped of its hereditary peers, peers who served as a result of hereditary titles. The House of Lords can still delay implementation of acts of the House of Commons, but it now consists only of people appointed by the prime minister for their accomplishments in the arts, business, and public service.

In October 2000, England made the European Convention on Human Rights part of domestic law, giving ordinary citizens their first American-style bill of rights. Civil libertarians praised the move as the most important change to the British constitutional system in more than 300 years.

PEOPLE DEBATE

INTERPRETING THE CONSTITUTION

Although we have the oldest written constitution in the world, we do not have an agreed-on theory of how it should be interpreted, nor does the document itself say how it should be read. Justices, no less than politicians and citizens, differ over how to interpret it. Here, Justice Antonin Scalia makes the case for adhering to the "original intent" of the Constitution, whereas Justice William J. Brennan Jr. advocates the view that the Constitution is a "living document" that requires contemporary ratification.

The Case for Adhering to the "Original Intent" of the Constitution

Supreme Court Justice Antonin Scalia.

Justice Scalia, a staunch conservative, contends that departing from the original intent of the Constitution undermines the legitimacy of the Court and leads to judicial legislation.

The principal theoretical defect of nonoriginalism, in my view, is its incompatibility with the very principle that legitimizes judicial review of constitutionality. Nothing in the text of the Constitution confers upon the courts the power to inquire into, rather than passively assume, the constitutionality of federal statutes.*

Justice Scalia maintains that originalism—holding to the original intent of the framers of the Constitution—is more compatible with the purpose of a constitution in a democracy:

A democratic society does not, by and large, need constitutional guarantees to insure that its laws will reflect "current values." Elections take care of that quite well. The purpose of constitutional guarantees—and in particular those constitutional guarantees of individual rights that are at the center of this controversy—is precisely to prevent the law from reflecting certain changes in original values that the society adopting the Constitution thinks fundamentally undesirable. Or, more precisely, to require the society to devote to the subject the long and hard consideration required for a constitutional amendment before those particular values can be cast aside.

Originalism, according to Justice Scalia,

establishes a historical criterion that is conceptually quite separate from the preferences of the judge himself. And the principal defect of that approach—that historical research is always difficult and sometimes inconclusive—will, unlike nonoriginalism, lead to a more moderate rather than a more extreme result. The inevitable tendency of judges to think that the law is what they would like it to be will, I have no doubt, cause most errors in judicial historiography to be made in the direction of projecting upon the age of 1789 current, modern values—so that as applied, even as applied in the best of faith, originalism will (as the historical record shows) end up as something of a compromise.

Judicial Article) exempts cases of impeachment from the jury trial requirement. That is all the relevant constitutional language about impeachment. We must look to history to answer most questions about the proper exercise of these and other powers.[17]

Fortunately, past experience has triggered few acute constitutional disputes about the interpretation of impeachment procedures, so there is little history to go on. The House of Representatives has investigated 67 individuals for possible impeachment and has impeached 17 (two presidents—Andrew Johnson and Bill Clinton—and 15 federal judges). The Senate has convicted only seven, all federal judges.

Presidential Practices

Although the formal constitutional powers of the president have not changed, the office is dramatically more important and more central today than it was in 1789. Vigorous presidents—George Washington, Thomas Jefferson, Andrew Jackson, Abraham Lincoln, Theodore Roosevelt, Woodrow Wilson, Franklin Roosevelt, Harry Truman, Lyndon Johnson, Bill Clinton, and George W. Bush—have boldly exercised their political and constitutional powers, especially

The Case for a Contemporary Ratification

Supreme Court Justice William J. Brennan, Jr.

Justice William J. Brennan Jr., a leading liberal on the Court from 1956 to 1990, points out the problems with appealing to original intent:

It is arrogant to pretend that from our vantage [point] we can gauge accurately the intent of the framers on application of principle to specific, contemporary questions. All too often, sources of potential enlightenment, such as records of the ratification debates, provide sparse or ambiguous evidence of the original intention. Typically, all that can be gleaned is that the framers themselves did not agree about the application or meaning of particular constitutional provisions and hid their differences in cloaks of generality. Indeed, it is far from clear whose intention is relevant—that of the drafters, the congressional disputants, or the ratifiers in the states?—or even whether the idea of original intention is a coherent way of thinking about a jointly drafted document drawing its authority from a general assent of the states. And apart from the problematic nature of the sources, our distance of two centuries cannot but work as a prism refracting all we perceive.†

Justice Brennan maintains that constitutional interpretation is compatible with democratic governance:

The view that all matters of substantive policy should be resolved through the majoritarian process has appeal under some circumstances, but I think it ultimately will not do. . . . Faith in democracy is one thing; blind faith, quite another. Those who drafted the Constitution understood the difference. One cannot read the text without admitting that it embodies substantive value choices; it places certain values beyond the power of any legislature.

We current justices read the Constitution in the only way that we can: as [contemporary] Americans. We look to the history of the time of framing and to the intervening history of interpretation. But the ultimate question must be: What do the words of the text mean in our time? For the genius of the Constitution rests not in any static meaning it might have had in a world that is dead and gone, but in the adaptability of its great principles to cope with current problems and current needs.

1. How persuasive do you find the arguments for adhering to the "original intent" of the Constitution, and how feasible is such an approach to constitutional interpretation?

2. If justices go beyond the historical context of specific constitutional provisions, what constrains their interpretation of the Constitution?

3. How and on what basis would you interpret guarantees for "free speech," "due process of law," and "equal protection of the law"?

---

*All Scalia quotes from Antonin Scalia, "Originalism: The Lesser Evil," *University of Cincinnati Law Review* 55 (1989), p. 894.

†Both quotes from William J. Brennan Jr., "The Constitution of the United States: Contemporary Ratification," lecture delivered at Georgetown University, October 12, 1985.

---

during times of national crisis like the current war against terrorism. Their presidential practices have established important precedents, building the power and influence of the office.

A major practice involves **executive orders**, which carry the full force of law. They may make major policy changes, such as withholding federal contracts from businesses engaging in racial discrimination, or they may simply be formalities, such as the presidential proclamation of Earth Day.

Other practices include **executive privilege** (the right to confidentiality of executive communications, especially those that relate to national security), **impoundment** by a president of funds previously appropriated by Congress, the power to send our armed forces into hostilities, and most important, the authority to propose legislation and work actively to secure its passage by Congress.

Foreign and economic crises as well as nuclear age realities have expanded the president's role: "When it comes to action risking nuclear war, technology has modified the Constitution: the President, perforce, becomes the only such man in the system capable of exercising judgment under the extraordinary limits now imposed by secrecy, com-

executive order
Directive issued by a president or governor that has the force of law.

executive privilege
The power to keep executive communications confidential, especially if they relate to national security.

impoundment
Presidential refusal to allow an agency to spend funds authorized and appropriated by Congress.

plexity, and time."[18] The presidency has also become the pivotal office for regulating the economy and promoting the general welfare. Plainly, the president has become a leader in sponsoring legislation as well as the nation's chief executive.

Custom and Usage

Custom and usage round out our governmental system. The development of structures outside the formal Constitution—such as national political parties and the expansion of suffrage in the states—has democratized our Constitution. Other examples of custom and usage are in televised press conferences and presidential and vice presidential debates. Through such developments, the president has become responsive to the people and has a political base different from that of Congress. Consequently, the constitutional relationship between the branches today is considerably different from that envisioned by the framers.

Judicial Interpretation

As discussed earlier, judicial interpretation of the Constitution, especially by the Supreme Court, plays an important role in keeping the constitutional system up to date. As social and economic conditions have changed and new national demands developed, the Supreme Court has changed its interpretation of the Constitution accordingly. Because the Constitution adapts to changing times, it does not require frequent formal amendment. The advantages of this flexibility may be appreciated by comparing the national Constitution with the rigid and often overly specific state constitutions. Many state constitutions are so detailed that they tie the hands of public officials and must be amended or replaced frequently.

Changing the Letter of the Constitution

The idea of a constantly changing system disturbs many people. How, they contend, can you have a constitutional government when the Constitution is constantly being twisted by interpretation and changed by informal methods? This view fails to distinguish between two aspects of the Constitution. As an expression of *basic and timeless personal liberties*, the Constitution does not, and should not, change. For example, a government cannot destroy free speech and still remain a constitutional government. In this sense, the Constitution is unchanging. But when we consider the Constitution as an *instrument of government* and a positive grant of power, we realize that if it does not grow with the nation it serves, it would soon be irrelevant and ignored.

The framers could never have conceived of the problems facing the government of a large, powerful, and wealthy nation of over 285 million people at the beginning of the twenty-first century. Although the general purposes of government remain the same—to establish liberty, promote justice, ensure domestic tranquillity, and provide for the common defense—the powers of government that were adequate to accomplish these purposes in 1787 are simply insufficient more than 215 years later. Through its remarkable adaptability, our Constitution has survived democratic and industrial revolutions, the turmoil of civil war, the tensions of major depressions, and the dislocations of world wars.

The framers knew that future experiences would call for changes in the text of the Constitution and that some means for formal amendment was necessary. In Article V, they gave responsibility for amending the Constitution to Congress and to the states. The president has no formal authority over constitutional amendments; presidential veto power does not extend to them, although presidential political influence is often crucial in getting amendments proposed and ratified.

Proposing Amendments

The first method for proposing amendments—and the only one used so far—is by *a two-thirds vote of both houses of Congress.* Dozens of resolutions proposing amendments are introduced in every session. Thousands have been introduced since 1789, but few make any headway. Throughout our history, Congress has proposed only 31 amendments, of

The Amending Power and How It Has Been Used

Leaving aside the first ten amendments (the Bill of Rights), the power of constitutional amendment has served a number of purposes:

To Add or Subtract National Government Power

The Eleventh took some jurisdiction away from the national courts.

The Thirteenth abolished slavery and authorized Congress to legislate against it.

The Sixteenth enabled Congress to levy an income tax.

The Eighteenth authorized Congress to prohibit the manufacture, sale, or transportation of liquor.

The Twenty-First repealed the Eighteenth and gave states the authority to regulate liquor sales.

The Twenty-Seventh limited the power of Congress to set members' salaries.

To Expand the Electorate and Its Power

The Fifteenth extended suffrage to all male African Americans over the age of 21.

The Seventeenth took the right to elect their United States senators away from state legislatures and gave it to the voters in each state.

The Nineteenth extended suffrage to women over the age of 21.

The Twenty-Third gave voters of the District of Columbia the right to vote for president and vice president.

The Twenty-Fourth outlawed the poll tax, thereby prohibiting states from taxing the right to vote.

The Twenty-Sixth extended suffrage to otherwise qualified persons 18 years of age or older.

To Reduce the Electorate's Power

The Twenty-Second took away from the electorate the right to elect a person to the office of president for more than two full terms.

To Limit State Government Power

The Thirteenth abolished slavery.

The Fourteenth granted national citizenship and prohibited states from abridging privileges of national citizenship; from denying persons life, liberty, and property without due process; and from denying persons equal protection of the laws. This amendment has come to be interpreted as imposing restraints on state powers in every area of public life.

To Make Structural Changes in Government

The Twelfth corrected deficiencies in the operation of the electoral college that were revealed by the development of a two-party national system.

The Twentieth altered the calendar for congressional sessions and shortened the time between the election of presidents and their assumption of office.

The Twenty-Fifth provided procedures for filling vacancies in the vice presidency and for determining whether presidents are unable to perform their duties.

which 27 have been ratified—including the Twenty-Seventh, which was originally part of the Bill of Rights but took more than 200 years to be ratified (see Figure 2-2).

Recent decades have seen a flurry of congressional attempts at constitutional amendments.[19] None has been formally proposed by both chambers; many remain under consideration. One given serious consideration is the Balanced Budget Amendment. Such an amendment has several times secured the two-thirds vote needed in the House but failed to do so in the Senate. Republicans tend to favor it; most Democrats oppose it. As a result of good economic times and some fiscal restraint, the budget generated a surplus in 1999, reducing pressure to pass the amendment. The return of deficit spending may renew debate over the Balanced Budget Amendment.

Why is proposing amendments to the Constitution so popular? In part because interest groups unhappy with Supreme Court decisions seek to overturn them. In part because groups frustrated by their inability to get things done in Congress hope to bypass Congress. And in part because scholars or interest groups (not necessarily mutually exclusive categories) seek to change the procedures and processes of government to make the system more responsive.[20]

The second method for proposing amendments—*a convention called by Congress* at the request of the legislatures in two-thirds of the states—has never been used. Under Article V of the Constitution, Congress could call for such a convention without the concurrence of the president. This method presents some difficult questions.[21] First, can state legislatures apply for a convention to propose specific amendments on one topic, or must they request a convention with full powers to revise the entire Constitution? How long do state petitions remain alive? How should delegates be chosen? How should such a convention be run? Congress has considered bills to answer some of these questions but has not passed any, in part because most members do not wish to encourage a constitutional convention for fear that once in session it might propose amendments on any and all topics.

The Equal Rights Amendment

Proposed March 22, 1972. Died June 30, 1982, three state legislatures short of the 38 needed for ratification.

Section 1. Equality of rights under the law shall not be denied or abridged by the United States or by any State on account of sex.

Section 2. The Congress shall have power to enforce, by appropriate legislation, the provisions of this article.

Section 3. This amendment shall take effect two years after the date of ratification.

Under most proposals, each state would have as many delegates to the convention as it has representatives and senators in Congress. Finally—a crucial point—the convention would be limited to considering only the subject specified in the state legislative petitions and described in the congressional call for the convention. Scholars are divided, however, on whether Congress has the authority to limit what a constitutional convention might propose.[22]

Ratifying Amendments

After an amendment has been proposed, it must be ratified by the states. Again, two methods are provided by the Constitution: approval by the legislatures in three-fourths of the states or approval by specially called ratifying conventions in three-fourths of the states. Congress determines which method is used. All amendments except one—the Twenty-First (to repeal the Eighteenth, the Prohibition Amendment)—have been submitted to the state legislatures for ratification.

Seven state constitutions specify that their state legislatures must ratify a proposed amendment to the U.S. Constitution by majorities of three-fifths or two-thirds of each chamber. Although a state legislature may change its mind and ratify an amendment after it has voted against ratification, the weight of opinion is that once a state has ratified an amendment, it cannot "unratify" it.[23]

The Supreme Court has said that ratification must take place within a "reasonable time." When Congress proclaims an amendment to be part of the Constitution, it must decide whether the amendment has been ratified within a reasonable time so that it is "sufficiently contemporaneous to reflect the will of the people."[24] However, Congress approved ratification of the Twenty-Seventh Amendment, which had been before the nation for almost 203 years, so there seems to be no limit on what it considers a "reasonable time." Because of the experience with the Twenty-Seventh Amendment, Congress will probably continue the current practice of stipulating in the text of a proposed amendment that the necessary number of states must ratify it within seven years from the date of submission by Congress. In fact, ratification ordinarily takes place rather quickly (see Figure 2-3).[25]

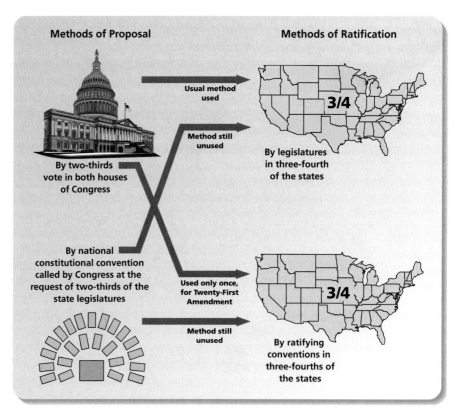

FIGURE 2–2 Four Methods of Amending the Constitution.

Gregory Watson and the Twenty-Seventh Amendment

In March 1982, Gregory Watson, a student at the University of Texas writing a paper on the Equal Rights Amendment, came across an amendment proposed in 1789 as part of the Bill of Rights that would prohibit a pay raise for members of Congress until the intervention of an election for members of the House. He found that only six of the original 13 states had ratified it and that during the intervening years only three more states had done so.

Gregory Watson.

Watson decided to start a ratification movement. He got some publicity for his efforts and, with the help of Texas Republican State Representative Don Mielke, persuaded six more state legislatures to ratify this long-forgotten proposed amendment. (By the way, Watson got only a C on his paper, although he is credited with influencing 26 state legislatures to ratify the Twenty-Seventh Amendment.)*

After members of Congress tried unsuccessfully in 1989 to avoid public anger by delegating their decision to increase their own salaries to an independent commission, anti-Congress sentiment began to grow, and the ratification movement picked up steam. On May 7, 1992, the Michigan legislature became the thirty-eighth state to ratify the amendment.

The first reaction of some congressional leaders was to question this action because the Supreme Court had made it clear that amendments must be ratified within a "reasonable time." However, when members of Congress realized that the issue could be used against them in the next election, they declared the Twenty-Seventh Amendment to be "valid as part of the Constitution of the United States." The vote was 99 to 0 in the Senate, 414 to 3 in the House.

*Ruth Ann Strickland, "The Twenty-Seventh Amendment and Constitutional Change by Stealth," *P.S.: Political Science and Politics* (December 1993), p. 720.

Ratification Politics

The failure of the Equal Rights Amendment to be ratified provides a vivid example of the pitfalls of ratification. First introduced in 1923 and frequently thereafter, the Equal Rights Amendment (ERA) did not get much support until the 1960s. An influential book by Betty Friedan, *The Feminine Mystique* (1963), challenged stereotypes about the role of women. The National Organization for Women (NOW), formed in 1966, made passage of the ERA its central mission. By the 1970s, the ERA had overwhelming support in both houses of Congress and in both national party platforms; not until 1980 did one party (the Republicans) adopt a stance of neutrality. Every president from Harry Truman to Ronald Reagan, and many of their wives, endorsed the amendment. More than 450 organizations with a total membership of more than 50 million were on record in support of the ERA.[26]

Soon after passage of the amendment by Congress in 1972 and submission to the states, many legislatures ratified it quickly—sometimes without hearings—and by overwhelming majorities. By the end of that year, 22 states had ratified the amendment, and it appeared that the ERA would soon become part of the Constitution.[27] Then the opposition organized under the articulate leadership of Phyllis Schlafly, a prominent spokesperson for conservative causes, and the ERA became controversial.

Opponents argued that "women would not only be subject to the military draft but also assigned to combat duty. Full-time housewives and mothers would be forced to join the labor force. Further, women would no longer enjoy existing advantages under state domestic relations codes and under labor law."[28] The ERA also became embroiled in the controversy over abortion. Many opponents contended that its ratification would jeopardize the power of states and Congress to regulate abortion and would compel public funding of abortions.[29]

People came from every state in the union to march in support of the passage of the Equal Rights Amendment.

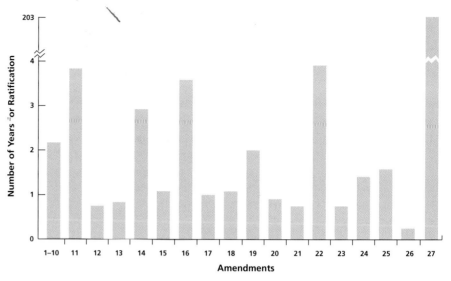

FIGURE 2–3 The Time for Ratification of the 27 Amendments to the Constitution.

After the ERA became controversial, state legislatures held lengthy hearings, and floor debates became heated. Legislators hid behind parliamentary procedures and avoided making a decision for as long as possible. Opposition to ratification arose chiefly in the same cluster of southern states that had opposed ratification of the Nineteenth Amendment, which gave women the vote. As the opposition grew more active, proponents redoubled their efforts.

In the autumn of 1978, it appeared that the ERA would fall three short of the necessary number of ratifying states before the expiration of the seven-year limit on March 22, 1979. After an extended debate, and after voting down provisions that would have authorized state legislatures to change their minds and rescind prior ratification, Congress, by a simple majority vote, extended the time limit until June 30, 1982. Nonetheless, by the final deadline, the amendment was still three states short.

The framers intended that amending the Constitution should be difficult, and the ERA ratification battle demonstrated how well they had planned. Still, through interpretation, practices, usages, and judicial decisions, the Constitution has proved an enduring and adaptable governing document.

PoliSim

THIS CONSTITUTION: WHAT IF YOU WERE A FOUNDING FATHER?

You have seen in this chapter that constitutions require trade-offs among competing principles and entail some form of checks and balances. The PoliSim for this chapter allows to you to see how constitutional principles and changes that you favor would conflict with and require modifications of the Constitution.

Go to PoliSim "The Constitution: What If You Were a Founding Father?"

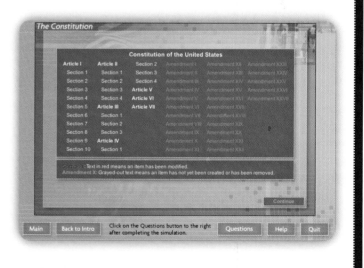

Summary

1. The U.S. Constitution, adopted in 1789, is the world's oldest. It has lasted because it is adaptable and flexible. It both grants and limits governmental power. The Constitution's separation of powers distributes authority among three branches of government: the legislative, executive, and judicial. Checks and balances limit the power of each branch.

2. Political parties may sometimes overcome the separation of powers, especially if the same party controls both houses of Congress and the presidency. Often, however, this is not the case, and a divided government intensifies checks and balances. Presidential power, which has increased over time, has sometimes been able to overcome the restraints imposed by the Constitution.

3. Judicial review is the power of the courts to strike down acts of Congress, the executive branch, and the states as unconstitutional. It is one of the unique features of the U.S. constitutional system. The Supreme Court's power of judicial review was established in the 1803 case of *Marbury* v. *Madison.*

4. The Constitution is the framework of our governmental system. The constitutional system has been modified over time, adapting to new conditions through congressional elaboration, presidential practices, custom and usage, and judicial interpretation.

5. Although adaptable, the Constitution itself needs to be altered from time to time, and the framers provided a procedure for its amendment. An amendment must be both proposed and ratified: proposed by either a two-thirds vote in each chamber of Congress or by a national convention called by Congress on petition of the legislatures in two-thirds of the states; ratified either by the legislatures in three-fourths of the states or by specially called ratifying conventions in three-fourths of the states.

6. The Constitution has been formally amended 27 times. The usual method has been proposal by a two-thirds vote in both houses of Congress and ratification by the legislatures in three-fourths of the states.

Key Terms

natural law
separation of powers
checks and balances
divided government

direct primary
initiative
referendum
recall

judicial review
writ of mandamus
impeachment
executive order

executive privilege
impoundment

Further Reading

Bruce A. Ackerman, *We the People* (Belknap Press, 1993).

Lance Banning, *The Sacred Fire of Liberty: James Madison and the Founding of the Federal Republic* (Cornell University Press, 1995).

Richard B. Bernstein, *Amending America: If We Love the Constitution So Much, Why Do We Keep Trying to Change It?* (Time, 1993).

James Bryce, *The American Commonwealth,* 2 vols. (Macmillan, 1889).

James MacGregor Burns, *The Vineyard of Liberty* (Knopf, 1982).

Gerhard Casper, *Separation of Powers: Essays on the Founding Period* (Harvard University Press, 1997).

Neil H. Cogan, *The Complete Bill of Rights: The Drafts, Debates, Sources, and Origins* (Oxford University Press, 1997).

Christopher L. Eisgruber, *Constitutional Self-Government* (Harvard University Press, 2001).

Michael Kammen, *A Machine That Would Go of Itself: The Constitution in American Culture* (Knopf, 1986).

Philip B. Kurland and Ralph Lerner, *The Founders' Constitution,* 5 vols. (University of Chicago Press, 1987).

David E. Kyvig, *Explicit and Authentic Acts: Amending the U.S. Constitution, 1776–1995* (University Press of Kansas, 1996).

Library of Congress, Congressional Research Service, *The Constitution of the United States of America: Analysis and Interpretation,* Senate Document 100-9 (U.S. Government Printing Office, 1991). Updated at www.findlaw.com/case_code.

William Nelson, Marbury v. Madison: *The Origins and Legacy of Judicial Review* (University Press of Kansas, 2000).

J. W. Peltason and Sue Davis, *Understanding the Constitution,* 15th ed. (Harcourt, 2000).

Charles H. Sheldon, *Essentials of the American Constitution: The Supreme Court and Fundamental Law,* ed. Stephen L. Wasby (Westview Press, 2002).

Cass Sunstein, *Designing Democracy: What Constitutions Do* (Oxford University Press, 2001).

John R. Vile, *Encyclopedia of Constitutional Amendments, Proposed Amendments, and Amending Issues, 1789–1995* (ABC-CLIO, 1996).

On Reading the Constitution

More than 215 years after its ratification, our Constitution remains the operating charter of our republic. It is neither self-explanatory nor a comprehensive description of our constitutional rules. Still, it remains the starting point. Many Americans who swear by the Constitution have never read it seriously, although copies can be found in most American government and American history textbooks.

Justice Hugo Black, who served on the Supreme Court for 34 years, kept a copy of the Constitution with him at all times. He read it often. Reading the Constitution would be a good way for you to begin (and then reread again to end) your study of the government of the United States. We have therefore included a copy of it at this point in the book. Please read it carefully.

The Constitution
of the
United States

THE PREAMBLE

We the People of the United States, in Order to form a more perfect Union, establish Justice, insure domestic Tranquility, provide for the common defense, promote the general Welfare, and secure the Blessings of Liberty to ourselves and our Posterity, do ordain and establish this Constitution for the United States of America.

"We the people"—three simple words of profound importance and contentious origin. The founders rejected monarchy as a form of government and proposed instead a republic, which would draw its sovereignty from the people.

The Articles of Confederation, under which the nation was governed from 1776 until 1789, started with "We the undersigned Delegates of the States." Early drafts of the new constitution started with "We the states." But the founders were interested not in another union of states but in the creation of a new national government. Therefore, "We the states" was changed to "We the people." The remainder of the preamble describes the generic functions of government.

ARTICLE I—THE LEGISLATIVE ARTICLE

Legislative Power

The first Article in the Constitution establishes the legislative branch. The framers believed it was the most important component of the new government.

Section 1   All legislative Powers herein granted shall be vested in a Congress of the United States, which shall consist of a Senate and House of Representatives.

Section I establishes a bicameral (two-chamber) legislature, with an upper chamber (Senate) and a lower chamber (House of Representatives), to serve as the legislative branch.

House of Representatives: Composition; Qualifications; Apportionment; Impeachment Power

Section 2

Clause 1.   The House of Representatives shall be composed of Members chosen every second Year by the People of the several States, and the Electors in each State shall have the Qualifications requisite for Electors of the most numerous Branch of the State Legislature.

This clause sets the term of office for House members (two years) and indicates that persons voting for members of Congress will have the same qualifications as those voting for the state legislatures.

Clause 2.   No Person shall be a Representative who shall not have attained to the Age of twenty five Years, and been seven Years a Citizen of the United States, and who shall not, when elected, be an Inhabitant of that State in which he shall be chosen.

This clause sets forth the basic qualifications for a representative: One must be at least 25 years of age, a U.S. citizen for at least seven years, and the resident of a state. Note that the Constitution does not require that one be a resident of the district one represents.

Clause 3.   Representatives and direct Taxes[1] shall be apportioned among the several States which may be included within this Union, according to their respective Numbers, which shall be determined by adding to the whole Number of free Persons, including those bound to Service for a Term of Years, and excluding Indians not taxed, three fifths of all other Persons.[2] The actual Enumeration shall be made within three Years after the first Meeting of the Congress of the United States, and within every subsequent Term of ten Years, in such Manner as they shall by Law direct. The Number of Representatives shall not exceed one for every thirty Thousand, but each State shall have at least one Representative; and until each enumeration shall be made, the State of New Hampshire shall be entitled to chuse three, Massachusetts eight, Rhode-Island and Providence Plantations one, Connecticut five, New-York six, New Jersey four, Pennsylvania eight, Delaware one, Maryland six, Virginia ten, North Carolina five, South Carolina five, and Georgia three.

This clause contains the three-fifths compromise, stipulating that slaves be counted as three-fifths of a person for the purpose of congressional representation. This clause also addresses the question of congressional reapportionment every ten years, which requires a census. Since the 1911 Reapportionment Act, the size of the House of Representatives has been set at 435. This is the designated size that is reapportioned every ten years. Based on changes of population, some states gain and some states lose representatives. This clause also provides that every state, regardless of population, will have at least one representative. Currently, there are seven states that have only one representative.

Clause 4.   When vacancies happen in the Representation from any State, the Executive Authority thereof shall issue Writs of Election to fill such Vacancies.

---

[1]Modified by the 16th Amendment

[2]Replaced by Section 2, 14th Amendment

48

This clause provides a procedure for replacing a U.S. representative in the case of death, resignation, or expulsion from the House. Generally, if less than half a term is left, the governor will appoint a successor. If more than half a term is remaining, most states will require a special election to fill the vacancy.

Clause 5. The House of Representatives shall chuse their Speaker and other Officers; and shall have the sole Power of Impeachment.

Only one officer of the House is specified—the Speaker. All other officers are created by the House. This clause also gives the House authority for bringing impeachments (accusations) against officials of the executive and judicial branches.

Senate Composition: Qualifications, Impeachment Trials

Section 3

Clause 1. The Senate of the United States shall be composed of two Senators from each State, chosen by the Legislature thereof,[3] for six Years; and each Senator shall have one Vote.

This clause treats each state equally—all have two senators each. Originally, senators were chosen by state legislatures, but since passage and ratification of the Seventeenth Amendment, they have been elected by popular vote. This clause also establishes the term of a senator: six years, three times that of a House member.

Clause 2. Immediately after they shall be assembled in Consequence of the first Election, they shall be divided as equally as may be into three Classes. The Seats of the Senators of the first Class shall be vacated at the Expiration of the second Year, of the second Class at the Expiration of the fourth Year, and of the third Class at the Expiration of the sixth Year, so that one third may be chosen every second Year; and if Vacancies happen by Resignation, or otherwise, during the Recess of the Legislature of any State, the Executive thereof may make temporary Appointments until the next Meeting of the Legislature, which shall then fill such Vacancies.[4]

To prevent a complete turnover of senators every six years, this clause provides that one-third of the Senate will be elected every two years. Senate vacancies are as in the House—either through appointment by the governor or a special election.

Clause 3. No person shall be a Senator who shall not have attained to the Age of thirty Years, and been nine Years a Citizen of the United States, and who shall not, when elected, be an inhabitant of that State for which he shall be chosen.

This clause sets forth the qualifications for a senator: One must be at least 30 years old, a U.S. citizen for at least nine years, and a resident of the state.

Clause 4. The Vice President of the United States shall be President of the Senate, but shall have no Vote, unless they be equally divided.

The only constitutional duty of the vice president is specified in this clause—president of the Senate. This official may vote only if there is a tie vote in the Senate; the vice president's vote thus breaks the tie.

Clause 5. The Senate shall chuse their other Officers, and also a President pro tempore, in the Absence of the Vice President, or when he shall exercise the Office of President of the United States.

One official office in the U.S. Senate is specified—the temporary president, who fills in when the vice president is absent (which is normally the case). All other Senate officers are designated and selected by the Senate.

Clause 6. The Senate shall have the sole Power to try all Impeachments. When sitting for that Purpose, they shall be on Oath or Affirmation. When the President of the United States is tried, the Chief Justice shall preside: And no Person shall be convicted without the Concurrence of two thirds of the Members present.

Judgment in Cases of Impeachment shall not extend further than to removal from Office, and disqualification to hold and enjoy any Office of honor, Trust or Profit under the United States; but the Party convicted shall nevertheless be liable and subject to Indictment, Trial, Judgment and Punishment, according to law.

The Senate acts as a trial court for impeached federal officials. If the accused is the president, the chief justice of the United States presides. Otherwise, the vice president presides.

Conviction of the charges requires a two-thirds majority vote of the senators present at the time of the vote. Conviction results in the federal official's removal from office and, if the Senate so decides, disqualification from holding any other federal office. Removal from office does not bar further prosecution under applicable criminal or civil laws, nor, apparently, does it bar one from running for elected office at the state or local level.

Congressional Elections: Times, Places, Manner

Section 4 The Times, Places and Manner of holding Elections for Senators and Representatives, shall be prescribed in each State by the Legislature thereof; but the Congress may at any time by Law make or alter such Regulations, except as to the Places of chusing Senators.

The Congress shall assemble at least once in every Year, and such Meeting shall be on the first Monday in December, unless they shall by Law appoint a different Day.[5]

The states determine the place and manner of electing representatives and senators, but Congress has the right to make or change these laws or regulations, except for the election sites. Congress is required to meet annually, and now, by law, sessions begin in January.

Powers and Duties of the Houses

Section 5

Clause 1. Each House shall be the Judge of the Elections, Returns and Qualifications of its own Members, and a Majority of each shall constitute a Quorum to do Business; but a smaller Number may adjourn from day to day, and may be authorized to compel the Attendance of absent Members, in such Manner, and under the Penalties as each House may provide.

This clause enables each legislative branch to make its own rules. Normally, to take a final vote, a quorum is necessary. But if no final votes are scheduled, fewer than a quorum can convene a session.

---

[3]Repealed by the 17th Amendment
[4]Modified by the 17th Amendment

[5]Changed by the 20th Amendment

Clause 2. Each House may determine the Rules of its Proceedings, punish its Members for disorderly Behaviour, and, with the Concurrence of two thirds, expel a Member.

Each branch promulgates its own rules and punishes its own members. The ultimate punishment is expulsion of the member, which requires a two-thirds vote. Expulsion does not prevent the member from running again.

Clause 3. Each House shall keep a Journal of its Proceedings, and from time to time publish the same, excepting such Parts as may in their Judgment require Secrecy; and the Yeas and Nays of the Members of either House on any question shall, at the Desire of one fifth of those Present, be entered on the Journal.

The Journal of Proceedings should not be confused with the *Congressional Record,* a daily account of House and Senate floor debates, votes, and members' remarks. However, a record is not printed if a proceeding is closed to the public for security reasons. Many votes are by voice vote, and if at least one-fifth of the members so request, a recorded vote of yeas and nays will be conducted and recorded. This procedure permits analysis of congressional roll call votes.

Clause 4. Neither House, during the Session of Congress, shall, without the Consent of the other, adjourn for more than three days, nor to any other place than that in which the two Houses shall be sitting.

This clause prevents one branch from adjourning for a long period of time or to some other location without the consent of the other branch.

Rights of Members

Section 6

Clause 1. The Senators and Representatives shall receive a Compensation for their Services, to be ascertained by Law, and paid out of the Treasury of the United States. They shall in all Cases, except Treason, Felony and Breach of the Peace, be privileged from Arrest during their Attendance at the Session of their respective Houses, and in going to and returning from the same; and for any Speech or Debate in either House, they shall not be questioned in any other Place.

This clause ensures that senators and representatives will be paid a salary from the U.S. Treasury. In addition, members of Congress receive many other benefits, including free health care, a fully funded retirement pension, free gyms, and 26 free round trips to their home state or district each year. This section also provides immunity from arrest or prosecution for congressional actions on the floor or in travel to and from Congress. See also the Twenty-Seventh Amendment.

Clause 2. No Senator or Representative, shall, during the time for which he was elected, be appointed to any civil Office under the Authority of the United States, which shall have been created, or the Emoluments whereof shall have been encreased during such time; and no Person holding any Office under the United States, shall be a Member of either House during his Continuance in Office.

This clause prevents the United States from becoming a parliamentary democracy, since congressional members cannot hold executive offices and members of the executive branch cannot be members of Congress.

Legislative Powers: Bills and Resolutions

Section 7

Clause 1. All Bills for raising Revenue shall originate in the House of Representatives; but the Senate may propose or concur with Amendments as on other Bills.

This clause specifies one of the few powers specific to the U.S. House: passing revenue bills.

Clause 2. Every Bill which shall have passed the House of Representatives and the Senate, shall, before it becomes a Law, be presented to the President of the United States; if he approve he shall sign it, but if not he shall return it, with his Objections to that House in which it shall have originated, who shall enter the Objections at large on their Journal, and proceed to reconsider it. If after such Reconsideration two thirds of that House shall agree to pass the Bill, it shall be sent, together with the Objections, to the other House, by which it shall likewise be reconsidered, and if approved by two thirds of that House, it shall become a Law. But in all such Cases the Votes of both Houses shall be determined by yeas and Nays, and the Names of the Persons voting for and against the Bill shall be entered on the Journal of each House respectively. If any Bill shall not be returned by the President within ten Days (Sundays excepted) after it shall have been presented to him, the Same shall be a Law, in like Manner as if he had signed it, unless the Congress by their Adjournment prevent its Return, in which Case it shall not be a Law.

The heart of the system of checks and balances is contained in this clause. Both the House and the Senate must pass a bill and present it to the president. If the president fails to act on the bill within ten days (not including Sundays), the bill will automatically become law unless Congress has adjourned. If the president signs the bill, it becomes law. If the president vetoes the bill and sends it back to Congress, this body may override the veto by a two-thirds majority in each branch. This must be a recorded vote.

Clause 3. Every Order, Resolution, or Vote to which the Concurrence of the Senate and House of Representatives may be necessary (except on a question of Adjournment) shall be presented to the President of the United States; and before the Same shall take Effect, shall be approved by him, or being disapproved by him, shall be repassed by two thirds of the Senate and House of Representatives, according to the Rules and Limitations prescribed in the Case of a Bill.

This clause covers all legislative actions with a few exceptions. For example, a joint resolution proposing a new constitutional amendment is not subject to presidential veto.

Powers of Congress

Section 8

Clause 1. The Congress shall have Power To lay and collect Taxes, Duties, Imposts and Excises, to pay the Debts and provide for the common Defence and general Welfare of the United States; but all Duties, Imposts and Excises shall be uniform throughout the United States.

To borrow Money on the Credit of the United States;

To regulate Commerce with foreign Nations, and among the several States, and with the Indian Tribes;

To establish an uniform Rule of Naturalization, and uniform Laws on the subject of Bankruptcies throughout the United States;

To coin Money, regulate the Value thereof, and of foreign Coin, and fix the Standard of Weights and Measures;

To provide for the Punishment of counterfeiting the Securities and current Coin of the United States;

To establish Post Offices and post Roads;

To promote the Progress of Science and useful Arts, by securing for limited Times to Authors and Inventors the exclusive Right to their respective Writings and Discoveries;

To constitute Tribunals inferior to the supreme Court;

To define and punish Piracies and Felonies committed on the high Seas, and Offences against the Law of Nations;

To declare War, grant Letters of Marque and Reprisal, and make Rules concerning Captures on Land and Water;

To raise and support Armies, but no Appropriation of Money to that Use shall be for a longer Term than two Years;

To provide and maintain a Navy;

To make Rules for the Government and Regulation of the land and naval Forces;

To provide for calling for the Militia to execute the Laws of the Union, suppress Insurrections and repel Invasions;

To provide for organizing, arming, and disciplining, the Militia, and for governing such Part of them as may be employed in the Service of the United States, reserving to the States respectively, the Appointment of the Officers, and the Authority of training the Militia according to the discipline prescribed by Congress;

This clause establishes the "express" or "specified" powers of Congress.

Clause 2. To exercise exclusive Legislation in all Cases whatsoever, over such District (not exceeding ten Miles square) as may, by Cession of particular States, and the Acceptance of Congress, become the Seat of the Government of the United States, and to exercise like Authority over all Places purchased by the Consent of the Legislature of the State in which the Same shall be, for the Erection of Forts, Magazines, Arsenals, dock-Yards, and other needful Buildings;—And

This clause establishes the seat of the federal government, which started out in New York but eventually moved to Washington, D.C., when both Maryland and Virginia ceded land to the new national government, which then established the District of Colombia.

Clause 3. To make all Laws which shall be necessary and proper for carrying into Execution the foregoing Powers, and all other Powers vested by this Constitution in the Government of the United States, or in any Department or Officer thereof.

This clause, known as the "elastic clause," provides the basis for the doctrine of "implied" congressional powers, which was first introduced in the U.S. Supreme Court case of *McCulloch* v. *Maryland* in 1819.

Powers Denied to Congress

Section 9

Clause 1. The Migration of Importation of such Persons as any of the States now existing shall think proper to admit, shall not be prohibited by the Congress prior to the Year one thousand eight hundred and eight, but a Tax or Duty may be imposed on such Importation, not exceeding ten dollars for each Person.

This clause was part of the three-fifths compromise. Essentially, the new Congress was prohibited from stopping the importation of slaves until 1808.

Clause 2. The privilege of the Writ of Habeas Corpus shall not be suspended, unless when in Cases of Rebellion or Invasion the public Safety may require it.

Neither Congress nor the president may suspend the writ of habeas corpus except in cases of rebellion or invasion. The writ of habeas corpus permits a judge to inquire about the legality of detention or deprivation of liberty of any citizen.

Clause 3. No Bill of Attainder or ex post facto Laws shall be passed.

This provision prohibits Congress from passing either a bill of attainder (legislative imposition of a punishment) or ex post facto laws (retroactive criminal laws). Similar restrictions were enshrined in many state constitutions.

Clause 4. No Capitation, or other direct, Tax shall be laid, unless in Proportion to the Census or Enumeration herein before directed to be taken.[6]

This clause prevents Congress from passing an income tax. Only with passage of the Sixteenth Amendment in 1913 did Congress gain this power.

Clause 5. No Tax or Duty shall be laid on Articles exported from any State.

The federal government cannot tax state exports.

Clause 6. No Preference shall be given by any Regulation of Commerce or Revenue to the Ports of one State over those of another; nor shall Vessels bound to, or from, one State, be obliged to enter, clear, or pay Duties in another.

This clause also applies to free trade within the United States. The national government cannot show any preference to any state or to maritime movements among the states.

Clause 7. No Money shall be drawn from the Treasury, but in Consequence of Appropriations made by Law; and a regular Statement and Account of the Receipts and Expenditures of all public Money shall be published from time to time.

This provision of the Constitution prevents any expenditure unless it has been funded in an appropriations bill. At the beginning of most fiscal years, Congress has not completed its work on the budget. Technically, the government could not spend any money according to this provision and would have to shut down. So Congress normally passes a continuing resolution authority providing temporary authority to continue to spend money until the final budget is approved and signed into law.

Clause 8. No Title of Nobility shall be granted by the United States; And no Person holding any Office of Profit or Trust under them, shall, without the Consent of Congress, accept of any present, Emolument, Office, or Title, of any kind whatever, from any King, Prince, or foreign State.

This clause prohibits the government from granting titles of nobility and prohibits federal officials from accepting such titles without congressional approval.

---

[6]Modified by the 16th Amendment

Powers Denied to the States

Section 10

Clause 1. No State shall enter into any Treaty, Alliance, or Confederation; grant Letters of Marque and Reprisal; coin Money; emit Bills of Credit; make any Thing but gold and silver Coin a Tender in Payment of Debts; pass any Bill of Attainder, ex post facto Law, or Law impairing the Obligation of Contracts, or grant any Title of Nobility.

This clause is a laundry list of powers denied to the states. Note that these restrictions cannot be waived by Congress. States are not to engage in foreign relations or acts of war. A letter of marque and reprisal was used to provide legal cover for privateers. The clause establishes the federal government's currency monopoly. The sanctity of contracts is specified. And prohibitions are placed on state legislatures for various legal actions.

Clause 2. No State shall, without the Consent of the Congress, lay any Imposts or Duties on Imports or Exports, except what may be absolutely necessary for executing its inspection Laws: and the net Produce of all Duties and Imposts, laid by any State on Imports or Exports, shall be for the Use of the Treasury of the United States; and all such Laws shall be subject to the Revision and Controul of the Congress.

This clause established the monopoly control of the national government in matters of international trade. The only concession to states is health and safety inspections.

Clause 3. No State shall, without the Consent of Congress, lay any Duty of Tonnage, keep Troops, or Ships of War in time of Peace, enter into any Agreement or Compact with another State, or with a foreign Power, or engage in War, unless actually invaded, or in such imminent Danger as will not admit of Delay.

This final clause of the legislative article establishes the war power of the national government. The only exception to state action is actual invasion or threat of imminent danger.

ARTICLE II—THE EXECUTIVE ARTICLE

Nature and Scope of Presidential Power

Section 1

Clause 1. The executive Power shall be vested in a President of the United States of America. He shall hold his Office during the Term of four Years and, together with the Vice President, chosen for the same Term, be elected as follows:

This clause vests the executive power in the office of the president of the United States of America. It also establishes a second office, vice president. A four-year term was established, with no limit on the number of terms. (A limit was later established by the Twenty-Second Amendment.)

Clause 2. Each State shall appoint, in such Manner as the Legislature thereof may direct, a Number of Electors, equal to the whole Number of Senators and Representatives to which the State may be entitled in the Congress: but no Senator or Representative, or Person holding an Office of Trust or Profit under the United States, shall be appointed an Elector.

This clause essentially creates the electoral college to choose the president and vice president.

Clause 3. The Electors shall meet in their respective States, and vote by Ballot for two Persons, of whom one at least shall not be an Inhabitant of the same State with themselves. And they shall make a List of all the Persons voted for, and of the Number of Votes for each; which List they shall sign and certify, and transmit sealed to the Seat of the Government of the United States, directed to the President of the Senate. The President of the Senate shall, in the Presence of the Senate and House of Representatives, open all the Certificates, and the Votes shall then be counted. The Person having the greatest Number of Votes shall be the President, if such Number be a Majority of the whole Number of Electors appointed; and if there be more than one who have such Majority, and have an equal Number of Votes, then the House of Representatives shall immediately chuse by Ballot one of them for President; and if no person have a Majority, then from the five highest on the List the said House shall in like Manner chuse the President. But in chusing the President, the Votes shall be taken by States, the Representation from each State having one Vote; A quorum for this Purpose shall consist of a Member or Members from two thirds of the States, and a Majority of all the States shall be necessary to a Choice. In every Case, after the Choice of the President, the person having the greatest Number of Votes of the Electors shall be the Vice President. But if there should remain two or more who have equal Vote, the Senate shall chuse from them by Ballot the Vice President.[7]

This clause has been superseded by the Twelfth Amendment. The original language did not require a separate vote for president and vice president. This resulted in a tied vote in the electoral college in 1800 when both Thomas Jefferson and Aaron Burr received 73 electoral votes. The Twelfth Amendment requires a separate vote for each. Only one of the two can be from the state of the elector. This makes it highly unlikely that the candidates for president and vice president would be from the same state.

The original language provided for a House election in the case of no majority vote or a tie vote among the top five candidates. The Twelfth Amendment reduced the candidates to the top three. The Senate is to select the vice president if a candidate does not have an electoral majority or is locked in a tie vote, in which case the Senate considers only the top two candidates. The amendment also clarifies that the qualifications for the vice president are the same as those for the president.

Clause 4. The Congress may determine the Time of chusing the Electors, and the Day on which they shall give their Votes; which Day shall be the same throughout the United States.

This clause lets Congress set the date on which the electoral college meets.

Clause 5. No Person except a natural born Citizen, or a Citizen of the United States, at the time of the Adoption of this Constitution, shall be eligible to the Office of President; neither shall any Person be eligible to that Office who shall not have attained to the Age of thirty five Years, and been fourteen Years a Resident within the United States.

The qualifications for the office of president and vice president are specified in this clause: Candidates must be at least 35 years old, 14 years resident in the United States, and a citizen from birth.

Clause 6. In Case of the Removal of the President from Office, or of his Death, Resignation, or Inability to discharge the Powers and Duties of the said

---

[7]Changed by the 12th and 20th Amendments

Office, the same shall devolve on the Vice President, and the Congress may by Law provide for the Case of Removal, Death, Resignation, or Inability, both of the President and Vice President, declaring what Officer shall then act as President, and such Officer shall act accordingly, until the Disability be removed, or a President shall be elected.[8]

This clause has been modified by the Twenty-Fifth Amendment. Upon the death, resignation, or impeachment conviction of the president, the vice president becomes president. The new president nominates a new vice president, who assumes the office, if approved by a majority vote in both houses of Congress.

Clause 7. The President shall, at stated Times, receive for his Services, a Compensation, which shall neither be encreased nor diminished during the Period of which he shall have been elected, and he shall not receive within that Period any other Emolument from the United States, or any of them.

This clause covers the compensation of the president, which cannot be increased or decreased during his term of office.

Clause 8. Before he enter on the Execution of his Office, he shall take the following Oath or Affirmation:—"I do solemnly swear (or affirm) that I will faithfully execute the Office of President of the United States, and will to the best of my Ability, preserve, protect and defend the Constitution of the United States."

This clause sets forth the presidential oath of office.

Powers and Duties of the President

Section 2

Clause 1. The President shall be the Commander in Chief of the Army and Navy of the United States, and of the Militia of the several States, when called into the actual Service of the United States, he may require the Opinion, in writing, of the principal Officer in each of the executive Departments, upon any Subject relating to the Duties of their respective Offices, and he shall have the Power to grant Reprieves and Pardons for Offences against the United States, except in Cases of Impeachment.

The president is commander in chief of the U.S. armed forces. The only U.S. president to actually lead U.S. armed forces was George Washington during the Whiskey Rebellion.

Clause 2. He shall have Power, by and with the Advice and Consent of the Senate to make Treaties, provided two thirds of the Senators present concur; and he shall nominate, and by and with the Advice and Consent of the Senate, shall appoint Ambassadors, other public Ministers and Consuls, Judges of the supreme Court, and all other Officers of the United States, whose Appointments are not herein otherwise provided for, and which shall be established by Law: but the Congress may by Law vest the Appointment of such inferior Officers, as they think proper, in the President alone, in the Courts of Law, or in the Heads of Departments.

This clause covers two important presidential powers: treaty making and appointments. The president (via the State Department) can negotiate treaties with other nations, but these do not become official until the Senate concurs by a two-thirds vote. The president is empowered to appoint federal judges, ambassadors, and other U.S. officials (cabinet officers, military officers, federal agency heads) subject to Senate approval by

a majority vote. Congress can and does delegate this approval to the president in the case of inferior officers. For example, junior military officer promotions are not submitted to the Senate, but senior officer promotions are.

Clause 3. The President shall have Power to fill up all Vacancies that may happen during the Recess of the Senate, by granting Commissions which shall expire at the End of their next Session.

This provision allows recess appointments of the officials listed in clause 2. These appointments automatically expire by the end of the next session of Congress, unless the Senate approves a formal nomination to fill the appointment. Sometimes presidents use this provision to fill positions when a nomination is being held up in the Senate.

Section 3 He shall from time to time give to the Congress Information of the State of the Union, and recommend to their Consideration such Measures as he shall judge necessary and expedient; he may, on extraordinary Occasions, convene both Houses, or either of them, and in Case of Disagreement between them, with Respect to the Time of Adjournment, he may adjourn them to such Time as he shall think proper; he shall receive Ambassadors and other public Ministers; he shall take Care that the Laws be faithfully executed, and shall Commission all the Officers of the United States.

This section provides the basis for, but does not require, the annual State of the Union Address to a joint session of Congress and the American people. The president is also authorized to call special meetings of either the House or the Senate. If there is disagreement between the House and the Senate regarding adjournment, the president is empowered to adjourn them. This has been extremely rare. The president formally receives other nations' ambassadors. The next-to-last provision, to faithfully execute laws, provides the basis for the whole administrative apparatus of the presidency. All officers of the United States receive a formal commission from the president (most of these are signed by machine).

Section 4 The President, Vice President and all civil Officers of the United States, shall be removed from Office on Impeachment for, and Conviction of, Treason, Bribery, or other High Crimes and Misdemeanors.

This section provides the constitutional authority for the impeachment and trial of the president, vice president, and all civil officers for treason, bribery, or other "high crimes and misdemeanors" (the exact meaning of this phrase is a matter of debate).

ARTICLE III—THE JUDICIAL ARTICLE

Judicial Power, Courts, Judges

Section 1 The judicial Power of the United States, shall be vested in one supreme Court, and in such inferior Courts as the Congress may from time to time ordain and establish. The Judges, both the supreme and inferior Courts, shall hold their Offices during good Behaviour, and shall, at stated Times, receive for their Services, a Compensation, which shall not be diminished during their Continuance in Office.

This section establishes the judicial branch in very general terms. It specifically provides only for the Supreme Court. Congress is given the responsibility to flesh out the court system.

---

[8]Modified by the 25th Amendment

It initially did so in the Judiciary Act of 1789, which established 13 district courts (one for each state) and appellate courts. All federal judges hold their offices for life and can be removed only by impeachment and conviction.

The salary of federal judges is set by Congress but cannot be reduced.

Jurisdiction

Section 2 The judicial Power shall extend to all Cases, in Law and Equity, arising under this Constitution, the Laws of the United States, and Treaties made, or which shall be made, under their Authority;—to all Cases affecting Ambassadors, other public Ministers and Consuls;—to all Cases of admiralty and maritime Jurisdiction;—to Controversies to which the United States shall be a Party;—to Controversies between two or more States; between a State and Citizens of another State;[9]—between Citizens of different States;—between Citizens of the same State claiming Lands under Grants of different States, and between a State, or the Citizens thereof, and foreign States, Citizens, or Subjects.

In all Cases affecting Ambassadors, other public Ministers and Consuls, and those in which a State shall be Party, the supreme Court shall have original Jurisdiction. In all the other Cases before mentioned, the supreme Court shall have appellate Jurisdiction, both as to Law and Fact, with such Exceptions, and under such Regulations as Congress shall make.

The Trial of all Crimes, except in Cases of Impeachment, shall be by Jury; and such Trial shall be held in the State where the said Crimes shall have been committed; but when not committed within any State, the Trial shall be at such Place or Places as the Congress may by Law have directed.

This section establishes the original and appellate jurisdiction of the U.S. Supreme Court. Since the Congress of Vienna's 1815 implementation of "diplomatic immunity," the U.S. Supreme Court no longer hears cases involving ambassadors. The Supreme Court no longer hears every case on appeal but has discretionary jurisdiction to select which cases it will accept. This section also establishes the right of trial by jury for federal crimes.

Treason

Section 3 Treason against the United States, shall consist only in levying War against them, or in adhering to their Enemies, giving them Aid and Comfort. No Persons shall be convicted of Treason unless on the Testimony of two Witnesses to the same overt Act, or on Confession in open Court.

The Congress shall have Power to declare the Punishment of Treason, but no Attainder of Treason shall work Corruption of Blood, or Forfeiture except during the Life of the Person attainted.

Treason is the only crime defined in the U.S. Constitution. Congress established the penalty of death for treason convictions. Two witnesses are required to convict a person of treason.

ARTICLE IV—INTERSTATE RELATIONS

Full Faith and Credit Clause

Section 1 Full Faith and Credit shall be given in each State to the public Acts, Records, and judicial Proceedings of every other State. And the Congress may by general Laws prescribe the Manner in which such Acts, Records and Proceedings shall be proved, and the Effect thereof.

This section provides that the official acts and records of one state (marriages, divorces, and so on) will be recognized and given credence by other states.

Privileges and Immunities; Interstate Extradition

Section 2

Clause 1. The Citizens of each State shall be entitled to all Privileges and Immunities of Citizens in the several States.

This clause requires states to treat citizens of other states equally. For example, if you have a driver's license from one state, you may drive in all states.

Clause 2. A person charged in any State with Treason, Felony or other Crime, who shall flee from Justice, and be found in another State, shall on Demand of the executive Authority of the State from which he fled, be delivered up, to be removed to the State having jurisdiction of the Crime.

A criminal fleeing to another state, if captured, can be returned to the state where the crime was committed. But extradition is not absolute. A state's governor can refuse, for good reason, to extradite someone to another state.

Clause 3. No person held to Service or Labour in one State, under the Laws thereof, escaping into another, shall, in Consequence of any Law or Regulation therein, be discharged from such Service or Labour, but shall be delivered up on Claim of the Party to whom such Service or Labour may be due.[10]

This clause was included to cover runaway slaves. It has been made inoperable by the Thirteenth Amendment, which abolished slavery.

Admission of States

Section 3 New States may be admitted by the Congress into this Union; but no new State shall be formed or erected within the Jurisdiction of any other State; nor any State to be formed by the Junction of two or more States, or Parts of States, without the Consent of the Legislatures of the States concerned as well as of the Congress.

The Congress shall have Power to dispose of and make all needful Rules and Regulations respecting the Territory or other Property belonging to the United States; and nothing in this Constitution shall be so construed as to Prejudice any Claims of the United States, or of any particular State.

This section concerns the admission of new states to the Union. In theory, no state can be created from part of another state without permission of the state legislature. But West Virginia was formed from Virginia during the Civil War without the permission of Virginia, which was part of the Confederacy.

Republican Form of Government

Section 4 The United States shall guarantee to every State in this Union a Republican Form of Government, and shall protect each of them against Invasion; and on Application of the Legislature, or of the Executive (when the Legislature cannot be convened) against domestic Violence.

This section commits the federal government to guarantee a republican form of government to each state and to protect all states against foreign invasion or domestic insurrection.

---

[9]Modified by the 11th Amendment

[10]Repealed by the 13th Amendment

54

ARTICLE V—THE AMENDING POWER

The Congress, whenever two thirds of both Houses shall deem it necessary, shall propose Amendments to this Constitution, or, on the Application of the Legislatures of two thirds of several States, shall call a Convention for proposing Amendments, which, in either Case, shall be valid to all Intents and Purposes, as Part of this Constitution, when ratified by the Legislatures of three fourths of the several States, or by Conventions in three fourths thereof, as the one or the other Mode of Ratification may be proposed by the Congress; Provided that no Amendment which may be made prior to the Year One thousand eight hundred and eight shall in any Manner affect the first and fourth Clauses in the Ninth Section of the first Article; and that no State, without its Consent, shall be deprived of its equal Suffrage in the Senate.

Amendments to the Constitution may be proposed by a two-thirds vote in both the House and the Senate or by a convention called by Congress at the request of the legislatures in two-thirds of the states. Proposed amendments by either route must be ratified by either the state legislatures in three-quarters of the states or by conventions in three-quarters of the states. Congress chooses which method of ratification should be used. Only one amendment has been ratified by the convention method—the Twenty-first. There have been only 27 amendments to the U.S. Constitution.

ARTICLE VI—THE SUPREMACY ACT

Clause 1. All Debts contracted and Engagements entered into, before the Adoption of this Constitution, shall be as valid against the United States under the Constitution, as under the Confederation.

This clause made the new national government responsible for all debts incurred during the Revolutionary War. This was very important to banking and commercial interests.

Clause 2. This Constitution, and the Laws of the United States which shall be made in Pursuance thereof; and all Treaties made, or which shall be made, under the Authority of the United States, shall be the supreme Law of the Land; and the Judges in every State shall be bound thereby, any Thing in the Constitution or Laws of any State to the Contrary notwithstanding.

This "supremacy clause" makes the U.S. Constitution, national laws, and U.S. treaties binding no matter what a state constitution, state law, or city ordinance might provide.

Clause 3. The Senators and Representatives before mentioned, and the Members of the several State Legislatures, and all executive and judicial Officers, both of the United States and of the several States, shall be bound by Oath or Affirmation, to support this Constitution; but no religious Test shall ever be required as a Qualification to any Office or public Trust under the United States.

All federal and state officials must swear or affirm their allegiance and support of the U.S. Constitution. Note that a religious test is prohibited for federal office.

ARTICLE VII—RATIFICATION

The Ratification of the Conventions of nine States, shall be sufficient for the Establishment of this Constitution between the States so ratifying the Same.

Realizing that unanimous approval of the new Constitution by all 13 states might not be attainable, the framers specified that only *nine* states would be needed for ratification.

Done in Convention by the Unanimous Consent of the States present the Seventeenth Day of September in the Year of our Lord one thousand seven hundred and Eighty seven and of the Independence of the United States of America the Twelfth In Witness whereof We have hereunto subscribed our Names.

AMENDMENTS

The Bill of Rights

[The first ten amendments were ratified on December 15, 1791, and form what is known as the "Bill of Rights."]

The Bill of Rights applied initially only to the federal government and not to state or local governments. The U.S. Supreme Court selectively incorporated the Bill of Rights, making its provisions applicable to state and local governments. There are only three exceptions, discussed at the appropriate amendment.

Amendment 1—Religion, Speech, Assembly, and Politics

Congress shall make no law respecting an establishment of religion, or prohibiting the free exercise thereof; or abridging the freedom of speech, or of the press; or the right of the people peaceably to assemble, and to petition the government for a redress of grievances.

This amendment protects five fundamental freedoms: religion, speech, press, assembly, and petition.

Amendment 2—Militia and the Right to Bear Arms

A well-regulated Militia, being necessary to the security of a free State, the right of the people to keep and bear Arms, shall not be infringed.

This amendment has not been incorporated for state and local governments; in other words, state and local governments are free to regulate arms within their jurisdiction.

Amendment 3—Quartering of Soldiers

No Soldier shall, in time of peace be quartered in any house, without the consent of the Owner, nor in time of war, but in manner to be prescribed by law.

It was the practice of the British government to insist that colonists provide room or board to British troops. This amendment prohibits that practice.

Amendment 4—Searches and Seizures

The right of the people to be secure in their persons, houses, papers, and effects, against unreasonable searches and seizures, shall not be violated, and no Warrants shall issue, but upon probable cause, supported by Oath or affirmation, and particularly describing the place to be searched, and the persons or things to be seized.

This amendment prevents the abuse of police powers. Essentially, unreasonable searches or seizures of homes, persons, or property cannot be undertaken without probable cause or a warrant that specifically describes the place to be searched and the person and/or things to be seized.

Amendment 5—Grand Juries, Self-Incrimination, Double Jeopardy, Due Process, and Eminent Domain

No person shall be held to answer for a capital, or otherwise infamous crime, unless on a presentment or indictment of a Grand jury, except in cases arising in the land or naval forces, or in the Militia, when in actual service in time of War or public danger; nor shall any person be subject for the same offence to be twice put in jeopardy of life or limb; nor shall be compelled in any criminal case to be a witness against himself, nor be deprived of life, liberty, or property, without due process of law; nor shall private property be taken for public use, without just compensation.

The provision for a grand jury indictment of a person accused of a crime does not apply to state and local governments. This amendment also covers double jeopardy, or being tried twice for the same crime in the same jurisdiction. Note that since the federal government and state governments are different jurisdictions, one can be tried in each jurisdiction for essentially the same crime. Further, this amendment also covers the prohibition of self-incrimination. The deprivation of life, liberty, or property by any level of government is prohibited unless due process of law is applied. Finally, private property may not be taken under the doctrine of "eminent domain" unless the government provides just compensation.

Amendment 6—Criminal Court Procedures

In all criminal prosecutions, the accused shall enjoy the right to a speedy and public trial, by an impartial jury of the State and district wherein the crime shall have been committed, which district shall have been previously ascertained by law, and to be informed of the nature and cause of the accusation; to be confronted with the witnesses against him; to have compulsory process for obtaining Witnesses in his favor, and to have the Assistance of Counsel for his defense.

Persons accused of a crime are entitled to be prosecuted before an impartial jury in a public trial. They are guaranteed the right to be informed of the charges, to confront witnesses, to subpoena witnesses for their defense, and to have a lawyer for their defense.

Amendment 7—Trial by Jury in Common Law Cases

In Suits at common law, where the value in controversy shall exceed twenty dollars, the right of trial by jury shall be preserved, and no fact tried by a jury shall be otherwise re-examined in any Court of the United States, than according to the rules of the common law.

This amendment does not apply to state and local governments. Statutory law has largely superseded common law. Federal civil lawsuits with a guaranteed jury are now restricted to cases that exceed $50,000.

Amendment 8—Bail, Cruel and Unusual Punishment

Excessive bail shall not be required, nor excessive fines imposed, nor cruel and unusual punishments inflicted.

This amendment prohibits excessive bail, fines, and cruel and unusual punishments.

Amendment 9—Rights Retained by the People

The enumeration in the Constitution, of certain rights, shall not be construed to deny or disparage others retained by the people.

This amendment implies that there are other rights of the people not specified by the previous amendments, such as the right of privacy.

Amendment 10—Reserved Powers of the States

The powers not delegated to the United States by the Constitution, nor prohibited by it to the States, are reserved to the States respectively, or to the people.

This amendment reaffirms the principles of limited government and federalism in recognizing that the states retain all powers not delegated to the national government.

Amendment 11—Suits Against the States
[Ratified February 7, 1795]

The Judicial power of the United States shall not be construed to extend to any suit in law or equity, commenced or prosecuted against one of the United States by Citizens of another State, or by Citizens or Subjects of any Foreign State.

Article III of the U.S. Constitution originally allowed federal jurisdiction in cases of one state citizen against another state citizen or state. This amendment removes federal jurisdiction in this area. In essence, states may not be sued in federal court by citizens of another state or country without their consent.

Amendment 12—Election of the President
[Ratified June 15, 1804]

The Electors shall meet in their respective states, and vote by ballot for President and Vice-President, one of whom, at least, shall not be an inhabitant of the same state with themselves; they shall name in their ballots the person voted for as President, and in distinct ballots the person voted for as Vice-President, and they shall make distinct lists of all persons voted for as President, and of all persons voted for as Vice-President, and of the number of votes for each, which lists they shall sign and certify, and transmit sealed to the seat of the government of the United States, directed to the President of the Senate;—The President of the Senate shall, in presence of the Senate and House of Representatives, open all the certificates and the votes shall then be counted;—The person having the greatest number of votes for President, shall be the President, if such number be a majority of the whole number of Electors appointed; and if no person have such majority, then from the persons having the highest numbers not exceeding three on the list of those voted for as President, the House of Representatives shall choose immediately, by ballot, the President. But in choosing the President, the votes shall be taken by states, the representation from each state having one vote; a quorum for this purpose shall consist of a member or members from two-thirds of the states, and a majority of all states shall be necessary to a choice. And if the House of Representatives shall not choose a President whenever the right of choice shall devolve upon them, before the fourth day of March next following, then the Vice-President shall act as President, as in the case of the death or other constitutional disability of the President.[11] The person having the greatest number of votes as Vice-President, shall be the Vice-President, if such a number be a majority of the whole numbers of Electors appointed, and if no person have a majority, then from the two highest numbers on the list, the Senate shall choose the Vice-President; a quorum for the purpose shall consist of two-thirds of the whole number of Senators, and a majority of the whole number shall be necessary to a choice. But no person constitutionally ineligible to the office of President shall be eligible to that of Vice-President of the United States.

This was a necessary amendment to correct a flaw in the Constitution covering the operation of the electoral college. Article II originally specified that each elector would cast two ballots for president; the candidate with the second-highest number of electoral votes would become vice president. In the election of 1800, both Thomas Jefferson and Aaron Burr received the same number of electoral votes, 73. The tie was broken as provided in Article II, with Jefferson becoming president and Burr vice president. Luckily, they were both from the same political party. But Article II made no accommodation for parties. This amendment therefore stipulates that the electors' votes must be specific for president and vice president. Article II originally provided that if no candidate received a majority of electoral votes, the House would decide from the candidates with the top five vote totals. This amendment reduces the candidate field to the top three vote totals for each position. If the House delays its selection of the president past the fourth day of March, the elected vice president will act as president until the House selects the president. If no vice presidential candidate receives an electoral vote majority, selection passes to the Senate.

Amendment 13—Prohibition of Slavery
[Ratified December 6, 1865]

Section 1   Neither slavery nor involuntary servitude, except as a punishment for crime whereof the party shall have been duly convicted, shall exist within the United States, or any place subject to their jurisdiction.

Section 2   Congress shall have power to enforce this article by appropriate legislation.

This is the first of the three Civil War amendments. It abolishes slavery and prohibits involuntary servitude except as punishment for a convicted crime.

Amendment 14—Citizenship, Due Process, and Equal Protection of the Laws
[Ratified July 9, 1868]

Section 1   All persons born or naturalized in the United States, and subject to the jurisdiction thereof, are citizens of the United States and of the State wherein they reside. No State shall make or enforce any law which shall abridge the privileges or immunities of citizens of the United States; nor shall any State deprive any person of life, liberty, or property, without due process of law; nor deny to any person within its jurisdiction the equal protection of the laws.

This section defines the meaning of U.S. citizenship and the protection of citizenship rights. It extends the provisions of the

Fifth Amendment's due process clause and makes them applicable to the states. It also establishes that each state must guarantee equal protection to its citizens.

Section 2   Representatives shall be apportioned among the several States according to their respective numbers, counting the whole number of persons in each State, excluding Indians not taxed. But when the right to vote at any election for the choice of electors for President and Vice President of the United States, Representatives in Congress, the Executive and Judicial officers of a State, or the members of the Legislature thereof, is denied to any of the male inhabitants of such State, being twenty-one[12] years of age, and citizens of the United States, or in any way abridged, except for participation in rebellion, or other crime, the basis of representation therein shall be reduced in the proportion which the number of such male citizens shall bear to the whole number of male citizens twenty-one years of age in such State.

This section changes the three-fifths clause of Article I, Section 2, Clause 3. All male citizens, age 21 or older, are counted to calculate representation in the House of Representatives. If a state denies the right to vote to any male 21 or older, the number of denied citizens will be deducted from the overall state total to determine representation.

Section 3   No person shall be a Senator or Representative in Congress, or elector of President and Vice President, or hold any office, civil or military, under the United States, or under any State, who, having previously taken an oath, as a member of Congress, or as an officer of the United States, or as a member of any State legislature, or as an executive or judicial officer of any State, to support the Constitution of the United States, shall have engaged in insurrection or rebellion against the same, or given aid or comfort to the enemies thereof. But Congress may by a vote of two-thirds of each House, remove such disability.

This section disqualifies from federal office or elector for president or vice president anyone who has rebeled or participated in an insurrection against the Constitution. This was specifically directed against citizens of southern states. Congress could override this provision by a two-thirds vote.

Section 4   The validity of the public debt of the United States, authorized by law, including debts incurred for payment of pensions and bounties for services in suppressing insurrection or rebellion, shall not be questioned. But neither the United States nor any State shall assume or pay any debt or obligation incurred in aid of insurrection or rebellion against the United States, or any claim for the loss or emancipation of any slave; but all such debts, obligations and claims shall be held illegal and void.

Section 5   The Congress shall have power to enforce, by appropriate legislation, the provisions of this article.

These sections cover the Civil War debts.

Amendment 15—The Right to Vote
[Ratified February 3, 1870]

Section 1   The right of citizens of the United States to vote shall not be denied or abridged by the United States or by any State on account of race, color, or previous condition of servitude.

Section 2   The Congress shall have power to enforce this article by appropriate legislation.

---

[11]Changed by the 20th Amendment

[12]Changed by the 26th Amendment

This final Civil War amendment states that voting rights cannot be denied by any state on account of race, color, or previous servitude.

Amendment 16—Income Taxes
[Ratified February 3, 1913]

The Congress shall have power to lay and collect taxes on incomes, from whatever source derived, without apportionment among the several States, and without regard to any census or enumeration.

Article I, Section 9 prohibited Congress from enacting a direct tax (head tax) unless in proportion to a census. Congress in 1894 passed an income tax law, levying a 2 percent tax on incomes over $4,000. In 1895, the U.S. Supreme Court, in a split decision (5-4), found that the income tax was a direct tax not apportioned among the states and was thus unconstitutional. This amendment authorizes a federal income tax.

Amendment 17—Direct Election of Senators
[Ratified April 8, 1913]

The Senate of the United States shall be composed of two Senators from each State, elected by the people thereof, for six years; and each Senator shall have one vote. The electors in each State shall have the qualifications requisite for electors of the most numerous branch of the State legislatures.

When vacancies happen in the representation of any State in the Senate, the executive authority of such State shall issue writs of election to fill such vacancies: Provided, That the Legislature of any State may empower the executive thereof to make temporary appointment until the people fill the vacancies by election as the legislature may direct.

This amendment shall not be so construed as to affect the election or term of any Senator chosen before it becomes valid as part of the Constitution.

Prior to this amendment, U.S. senators were selected by state legislatures. They are now selected by popular vote in each state. Further, the governor of each state may fill vacancies, subject to state laws.

Amendment 18—Prohibition
[Ratified January 16, 1919. Repealed December 5, 1933 by Amendment 21]

Section 1 After one year from the ratification of this article the manufacture, sale, or transportation of intoxicating liquors within, the importation thereof into, or the exportation thereof from the United States and all territory subject to the jurisdiction thereof for beverage purposes is hereby prohibited.

Section 2 The Congress and the several states shall have concurrent power to enforce this article by appropriate legislation.

Section 3 This article shall be inoperative unless it shall have been ratified as an amendment to the Constitution by the legislatures of the several states, as provided in the Constitution, within seven years from the date of the submission hereof to the States by the Congress.[13]

This amendment was largely the work of the Women's Christian Temperance Union and essentially banned the manufacture, sale, or transportation of alcoholic beverages. It was repealed by the Twenty-First Amendment.

Amendment 19—For Women's Suffrage
[Ratified August 18, 1920]

The right of the citizens of the United States to vote shall not be denied or abridged by the United States or by any State on account of sex.

Congress shall have power, by appropriate legislation, to enforce the provision of this article.

This amendment grants women the right to vote.

Amendment 20—The Lame Duck Amendment
[Ratified January 23, 1933]

Section 1 The terms of the President and Vice President shall end at noon on the 20th day of January, and the terms of the Senators and Representatives at noon on the 3rd day of January, of the years in which such terms would have ended if this article had not been ratified; and the terms of their successors shall then begin.

Section 2 The Congress shall assemble at least once in every year, and such meeting shall begin at noon on the 3rd day of January, unless they shall by law appoint a different day.

Section 3 If, at the time fixed for the beginning of the term of the President, the President elect shall have died, the Vice President elect shall become President. If a President shall not have been chosen before the time fixed for the beginning of his term, or if the President elect shall have failed to qualify, then the Vice President elect shall act as President until a President shall have qualified; and the Congress may by law provide for the case wherein neither a President elect nor a Vice President elect shall have qualified, declaring who shall then act as President, or the manner in which one who is to act shall be selected, and such person shall act accordingly until a President or Vice President shall have qualified.

Section 4 The Congress may by law provide for the case of the death of any of the persons from whom the House of Representatives may choose a President whenever the right of choice shall have developed upon them, and for the case of the death of any of the persons from whom the Senate may choose a Vice President whenever the right of choice shall have devolved upon them.

Section 5 Sections 1 and 2 shall take effect on the 15th day of October following the ratification of this article.

Section 6 This article shall be inoperative unless it shall have been ratified as an amendment to the Constitution by the legislatures of three-fourths of the several States within seven years from the date of its submission.

This amendment fixes the dates for the end of presidential and legislative terms. A new president is elected in November, but the current president remains in office until January 20 of the following year, during which time his influence is diminished. Legislative terms begin earlier, on January 3.

Amendment 21—Repeal of Prohibition
[Ratified December 5, 1933]

Section 1 The eighteenth article of amendment to the Constitution of the United States is hereby repealed.

Section 2 The transportation or importation into any State, Territory, or Possession of the United States for delivery or use therein of intoxicating liquors, in violation of the laws thereof, is hereby prohibited.

Section 3 This article shall be inoperative unless it shall have been ratified as an amendment to the Constitution by conventions in the several States, as provided

---

[13]Repealed by the 21st Amendment

58

in the Constitution, within seven years from the date of the submission hereof to the States by the Congress.

This amendment nullifies the Eighteenth, ending the prohibition of alcohol under federal law.

Amendment 22—Number of Presidential Terms
[Ratified February 27, 1951]

Section 1   No person shall be elected to the office of the President more than twice, and no person who has held the office of President, or acted as President, for more than two years of a term to which some other person was elected President shall be elected to the Office of the President more than once. But this Article shall not apply to any person holding the office of President when this article was proposed by the Congress, and shall not prevent any person who may be holding the office of President, or acting as President, during the term within which this Article becomes operative from holding the office of President or acting as President during the remainder of such term.

Section 2   This Article shall be inoperative unless it shall have been ratified as an amendment to the Constitution by the legislatures of three-fourths of the several states within seven years from the date of its submission to the States by the Congress.

In the 1930s and 1940s, Franklin D. Roosevelt, a Democrat, won an unprecedented four terms as president. When the Republicans gained control of the Congress in 1948, they pushed through this amendment limiting the president to two full four-year terms of office.

Amendment 23—Presidential Electors for the District of Columbia
[Ratified March 29, 1961]

Section 1   The District constituting the seat of Government of the United States shall appoint in such manner as the Congress may direct:

A number of electors of President and Vice President equal to the whole number of Senators and Representatives in Congress to which the District would be entitled if it were a State, but in no event more than the least populous State; they shall be in addition to those appointed by the States, but they shall be considered, for the purposes of the election of President and Vice President, to be electors appointed by a State; and they shall meet in the District and perform such duties as provided by the twelfth article of amendment.

Section 2   The Congress shall have power to enforce this article by appropriate legislation.

This amendment gives electoral votes to the citizens of Washington, D.C., which is not a state. The District of Columbia has three electoral votes, bringing the total of presidential electoral votes to 538.

Amendment 24—The Anti-Poll Tax Amendment
[Ratified January 23, 1964]

Section 1   The right of citizens of the United States to vote in any primary or other election for President or Vice President, for electors for President or Vice President, or for Senator or Representative in Congress, shall not be denied or abridged by the United States or any State by reason of failure to pay any poll tax or other tax.

Section 2   The Congress shall have power to enforce this article by appropriate legislation.

Poll taxes were used mostly in southern states to discourage poor white and black voters from registering to vote. This amendment, part of an effort to prevent the disenfranchisement of potential voters, abolishes the poll tax. Literacy tests, another device once used to disqualify voters, were abolished by the Voting Rights Act of 1965.

Amendment 25—Presidential Disability, Vice Presidential Vacancies
[Ratified February 10, 1967]

Section 1   In case of the removal of the President from office or his death or resignation, the Vice President shall become President.

Section 2   Whenever there is a vacancy in the office of the Vice President, the President shall nominate a Vice President who shall take the office upon confirmation by a majority vote of both houses of Congress.

Section 3   Whenever the President transmits to the President pro tempore of the Senate and the Speaker of the House of Representatives his written declaration that he is unable to discharge the powers and duties of his office, and until he transmits to them a written declaration to the contrary, such powers and duties shall be discharged by the Vice President as Acting President.

Section 4   Whenever the Vice President and a majority of either the principal officers of the executive departments, or of such other body as Congress may by law provide, transmit to the President pro tempore of the Senate and the Speaker of the House of Representatives their written declaration that the President is unable to discharge the powers and duties of his office, the Vice President shall immediately assume the powers and duties of the office as Acting President.

Thereafter, when the President transmits to the President pro tempore of the Senate and the Speaker of the House of Representatives his written declaration that no inability exists, he shall resume the powers and duties of his office unless the Vice President and a majority of either the principal officers of the executive departments, or of such other body as Congress may by law provide, transmit within four days to the President pro tempore of the Senate and the Speaker of the House of Representatives their written declaration that the President is unable to discharge the powers and duties of his office. Thereupon Congress shall decide the issue, assembling within forty-eight hours for that purpose if not in session. If the Congress, within twenty-one days after receipt of the latter written declaration, or, if Congress is not in session, within twenty-one days after Congress is required to assemble, determines by two-thirds vote of both houses that the President is unable to discharge the powers and duties of his office, the Vice President shall continue to discharge the same as Acting President; otherwise, the President shall resume the powers and duties of his office.

President Woodrow Wilson's final year in office, 1920, was marked by serious illness. There was no constitutional provision to cover an incapacitated president. This amendment provides a procedure for this eventuality. The president can inform congressional leaders of his or her incapacitation, and the vice president takes over. When the president recovers, he or she can so inform congressional leaders and resume office.

The amendment also recognizes that the president may not be able or wish to indicate this debilitation, so the vice president and a majority of cabinet members can inform congressional leaders, and the vice president takes over. When the president informs congressional leadership that he or she is back in form, he or she resumes the presidency unless the vice president and majority of the cabinet disagree. Then Congress must decide.

Amendment 26—Eighteen-Year-Old Vote
[Ratified July 1, 1971]

Section 1 The right of citizens of the United States, who are eighteen years of age, or older, to vote shall not be denied or abridged by the United States or by any State on account of age.

Section 2 The Congress shall have power to enforce this article by appropriate legislation.

During the Vietnam War, 18-year-olds were drafted and sent to fight and possibly die in the service of their country, yet they did not have the right to vote. This incongruity led to the Twenty-Second amendment, which lowered the legal voting age from 21 to 18.

Amendment 27—Congressional Salaries
[Ratified May 7, 1992]

No law, varying the compensation for the services of the Senators and Representatives, shall take effect, until an election of Representatives shall be intervened.

This "sleeper" amendment was one of 12 amendments originally submitted by the first Congress to the states for ratification. The states ratified only 10 of the 12, which collectively became known as the Bill of Rights. But since Congress did not set a time limit for ratification, the other two amendments remained on the table. In 1992, three-fourths of the states ratified this original amendment, 203 years after it was proposed. The amendment delays any increase of compensation for at least one election cycle.

AMERICAN FEDERALISM

CHAPTER OUTLINE

- Defining Federalism

- The Constitutional Structure of American Federalism

- The Role of the Federal Courts: Umpires of Federalism

- Regulatory Federalism, Federal Grants, and Federal Mandates

- The Politics of Federalism

- The Future of Federalism

I N THE AFTERMATH OF THE TERRORIST ATTACKS ON THE WORLD TRADE CENTER AND THE PENTAGON, CONGRESS AND THE AMERICAN people rallied behind President George W. Bush's calls for a massive economic package to rebuild lower Manhattan and for passage of the USA Patriot Act, expanding executive powers to prevent future attacks; responsibility for airport security was also turned over to the national government. There is virtually unanimous agreement that the national government must take the lead in protecting homeland security and rooting out international terrorism. President Bush has also pushed for expanding the role of the federal government, particularly in education. Whereas in the early 1980s, President Ronald Reagan pressed for abolishing the Department of Education, Bush campaigned on becoming the "education president" and in 2002 signed into law his "No Child Left Behind" education bill, which among other things mandates the annual standardized testing of children in grades three through eight by 2005–2006 and provides funds for tutoring children in failing schools.

Since the founding of the Republic, Americans have debated the relationship of the national government to the states.[1] In 1787, the Federalists defended the creation of a strong national government, whereas the Antifederalists warned that a strong national government would overshadow the states. More recently, Republicans have led the charge against big government, urging the return of many functions to the states—a **devolution revolution**.[2] They had some success, for example, when President Bill Clinton agreed to turn over more responsibilities for welfare to the states.

Federalism has recently emerged as a hot topic in other countries as well. Western European countries have formed the European Union (EU), with member nations giving up considerable authority over the regulation of businesses and labor, adopting a common monetary policy and currency (the euro), and now debating whether to call a convention to recommend a federal constitution for the EU.[3]

This independence celebration in Quebec, Canada illustrates how the debate over federalism is still a vital issue throughout the world today. The citizens of this French-speaking province are demanding the right to determine their own destiny rather than leaving it in the hands of the Canadian government, which they believe does not always act in their interest.

Heightened interest in federalism also comes from demands for greater autonomy for ethnic nationalities. The Canadian federal system strains under the demands of the French-speaking province of Quebec for special status and even independence. In the United Kingdom, devolution has occurred with Scotland and Wales gaining their own parliaments with considerable authority and, in the case of Scotland, limited power to tax. Belgium, Italy, and Spain are devolving powers from their central governments to regional governments. Central European nations have divided and subdivided over ethnic tensions.

In contrast to some countries, the United States has had a relatively peaceful experience with the shifting balances of power under federalism. Since the New Deal in the 1930s, power and responsibility have drifted from the states to the national government. Although presidents from Richard Nixon to Bill Clinton slowed the growth of the national government, it was not until the late 1990s that the Republican-controlled Congress sought major reforms that heated the debate over federalism. As with welfare reform in 1996, Congress promoted decentralization in education with the Educational Flexibility Partnership Demonstration Act of 1999, authorizing the secretary of education to grant states waivers from federal rules setting educational goals. Still, in spite of such moves toward decentralization, Congress continues to expand federal law by making such offenses as carjacking and the burning of churches federal crimes, even though they are already state and local crimes.

After more than half a century, the Supreme Court has placed some constraints on congressional powers in the name of federalism.[4] Like Congress, however, the Court's recent record on federalism is mixed. In spite of rulings in the 1990s holding that Congress exceeded its powers and may not authorize individuals to sue states to enforce federal laws,[5] the Court nevertheless ruled that state welfare programs may not restrict benefits to new residents to what they would have received in the states from which they moved[6] and that Congress may restrict states from selling drivers' personal information.[7]

Debates over federalism resemble those over whether "the glass is half-empty or half-full."[8] People who think they can get more of what they want from the national government usually advocate national action. Those who view states as more responsive and accountable argue for decentralization. Although Republicans generally favor action at the state level and Democrats tend to support action by the national government, neither party is consistent in its positions on the balance of power between the national government and the states. It depends on the issue at stake.

In this chapter, we first define federalism and its advantages. We look next at the constitutional basis for our federal system. Then we see how court decisions and political developments have shaped, and continue to shape, federalism in the United States.

Defining Federalism

Scholars argue and wars (including our own Civil War) have been fought over what federalism means. One scholar counted 267 definitions.[9]

Federalism, as we define it here, is a form of government in which a constitution distributes powers between a central government and subdivisional governments—usually called states, provinces, or republics—giving to both the national government and the regional governments substantial responsibilities and powers, including the power to collect taxes and to pass and enforce laws regulating the conduct of individuals.

The mere existence of both national and state governments does not make a system federal. What is important is that a *constitution divides governmental powers between the national government and the subdivisional governments,* giving clearly defined functions to each. Neither the central nor the subdivisional government receives its powers from the other; both derive them from a common source—the Constitution. No ordinary act of legislation at either the national or the state level can change this constitutional distribution of powers. Both levels of government operate through their own agents and exercise power directly over individuals.

devolution revolution
The effort to slow the growth of the federal government by returning many functions to the states.

federalism
Constitutional arrangement whereby power is distributed between a central government and subdivisional governments, called states in the United States. The national and the subdivisional governments both exercise direct authority over individuals.

At the official opening of Scotland's parliament on July 1, 1999, Queen Elizabeth was presented with the Scottish crown. The 129-member assembly is Scotland's first parliament in nearly 300 years.

Our definition of federalism is broad enough to include competing visions of it and the range of federal systems around the world. The following are some of the leading visions of federalism.

- *Dual federalism* views the Constitution as giving a limited list of powers—primarily foreign policy and national defense—to the national government, leaving the rest to sovereign states. Each level of government is dominant within its own sphere. The Supreme Court serves as the umpire between the national government and the states in disputes over which level of government has responsibility for a particular activity. During our first hundred years, dual federalism was the favored interpretation given by the Supreme Court.

- *Cooperative federalism* stresses federalism as a system of intergovernmental relations in delivering governmental goods and services to the people and calls for cooperation among various levels of government.

- *Marble cake federalism,* a term coined by political scientist Morton Grodzins, conceives of federalism as a marble cake in which all levels of government are involved in a variety of issues and programs, rather than a layer cake, or dual federalism, with fixed divisions between layers or levels of government.[10]

- *Competitive federalism,* a term first used by political scientist Thomas R. Dye, views the national government, 50 states, and thousands of other units as competing with each other over ways to put together packages of services and taxes. Applying the analogy of the marketplace, Dye emphasizes that at the state and local levels, we have some choice about which state and city we want to "use," just as we have choices about what kind of automobile we drive.[11]

- *Permissive federalism* implies that although federalism provides "a sharing of power and authority between the national and state government, the states' share rests upon the permission and permissiveness of the national government."[12]

- *"Our federalism,"* championed by Ronald Reagan, Justice Sandra Day O'Connor, and Chief Justice William Rehnquist, presumes that the power of the federal government is limited in favor of the broad powers reserved to the states.

TABLE 3–1   Number of Governments in the United States

National	1
States	50
Counties	3,043
Municipalities	19,279
Townships or towns	16,656
School districts	14,422
Special districts	31,555
Total	85,006

SOURCE: U.S. Bureau of the Census, *Statistical Abstract of the United States, 1998* (Government Printing Office, 1998).

Federal nations are diverse and include Australia, Canada, Germany, Russia, and Switzerland. Although their number is not large, they "cover more than half of the land surface of the globe and include almost half of the world's population."[13] Federalism thus appears well suited for large countries with large populations, even though only 21 of the world's approximately 185 nation-states claim to be federal.

Constitutionally, the federal system of the United States consists of only the national government and the 50 states. "Cities are not," the Supreme Court reminded us, "sovereign entities." But in a practical sense, we are a nation of about 85,000 governmental units, from the national government to the school board district (see Table 3-1). This does not make for a tidy, efficient, easy-to-understand system; yet, as we shall see, it has its virtues.

Alternatives to Federalism

Among the alternatives to federalism are **unitary systems** of government, in which a constitution vests all governmental power in the central government. The central government, if it so chooses, may delegate authority to constituent units, but what it delegates it may take away. England, France, Israel, and the Philippines have unitary governments. In the United States, state constitutions usually create this kind of relationship between the state and its local governments.

At the other extreme from unitary governments are **confederations**, in which sovereign nations, through a constitutional compact, create a central government but carefully limit the power of the central government and do not give it the power to regulate the conduct of individuals directly. The central government makes regulations for the constituent governments, but it exists and operates only at their direction. The 13 states under the Articles of Confederation operated in this manner (see Figure 3-1), and so did the southern Confederacy during the Civil War. The European Union is another example, though it is moving toward greater integration and perhaps even the eventual adoption of a federal constitution.[14]

Why Federalism?

In 1787, federalism was an obvious choice. Confederation had been tried but proved unsuccessful. A unitary system was out of the question because most people were too deeply attached to their state governments to permit subordination to central rule. Federalism was, and still is, thought to be ideally suited to the needs of a heterogeneous people spread over a large continent, suspicious of concentrated power, and desiring unity but not uniformity. Federalism offered, and still offers, many advantages for such a people.

FEDERALISM CHECKS THE GROWTH OF TYRANNY   Although in the rest of the world, federal forms have not always been notably successful in preventing tyranny, and many unitary governments are democratic, Americans tend to associate freedom with federalism.[15] As James Madison pointed out in *The Federalist*, No. 10: If "factious leaders . . . kindle a flame within their particular states," national leaders can check the spread of the "conflagration through the other states" (*The Federalist*, No. 10, appears in the Appendix of this book). Moreover, when one political party loses control of the national government, it is still likely to hold office in a number of states. It can then regroup, develop new policies and new leaders, and continue to challenge the party in power at the national level.

Such diffusion of power creates its own problems. It makes it difficult for a national majority to carry out a program of action, and it permits those who control state governments to frustrate the policies enacted by Congress and administered by federal agencies. To the framers, these obstacles were an advantage. They feared that a single-interest group might capture the national government and attempt to suppress the interests of others. Of course, the size of the nation and the many interests within it are the greatest obstacles to the formation of a single-interest majority—a point often overlooked today but emphasized by Madison in *The Federalist*, No. 10. If such a majority were to occur, having to work through a federal system would check its power.

unitary system
Constitutional arrangement in which power is concentrated in a central government.

confederation
Constitutional arrangement in which sovereign nations or states, by compact, create a central government but carefully limit its power and do not give it direct authority over individuals.

Government Under the Articles of Confederation, 1781–1788

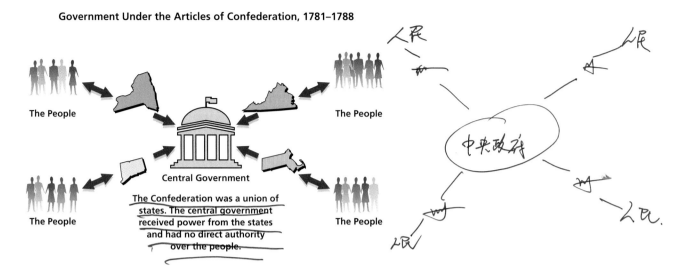

Government Under the U.S. Constitution (Federation) Since 1789

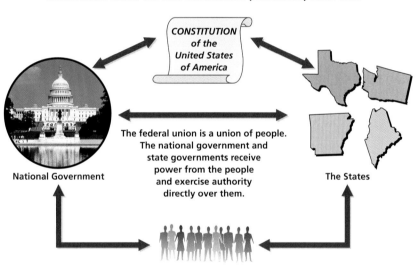

FIGURE 3–1 A Comparison of Federalism and Confederation.

FEDERALISM ALLOWS UNITY WITHOUT UNIFORMITY   National politicians and parties do not have to iron out every difference on every issue that divides us, whether it be abortion, same-sex marriage, gun control, capital punishment, welfare financing, or assisted suicide. Instead, these issues are debated in state legislatures, county court-houses, and city halls. But this advantage of federalism is becoming less significant as many local issues become national and as events in one state immediately affect policy debates at the national level.

FEDERALISM ENCOURAGES EXPERIMENTATION   Supreme Court Justice Louis Brandeis pointed out that state governments provide great "laboratories" for public policy experimentation, with states serving as proving grounds. If they adopt pro-grams that fail, the negative effects are limited; if programs succeed, they can be adopted by other states and by the national government. Georgia, for example, was the first state to permit 18-year-olds to vote; Wisconsin experimented with putting welfare recipients to work; California pioneered air pollution control programs; Ore-gon and Hawaii are creating new systems for the delivery of health care; Nevada is the only state, so far, to legalize statewide gambling, but aspects of legalized casino gambling are now found in more than half the states. Not all innovations, even those considered successful, become widely adopted. Nebraska is the only state to have a unicameral legislature, although in recent years both Minnesota and California considered adopting one.

FEDERALISM KEEPS GOVERNMENT CLOSER TO THE PEOPLE   By providing numerous arenas for decision making, federalism involves many people and helps keep government closer to the people. Every day, thousands of Americans are busy serving on city councils, school boards, neighborhood associations, and planning commissions. Since they are close to the issues and have firsthand knowledge of what needs to be done, they may be more responsive to problems than the experts in Washington.

We should be cautious, however, about generalizing that state and local governments are necessarily closer to the people than the national government. True, more people are involved in local and state politics than in national affairs, and confidence in state governments has increased while respect for national agencies has diminished. A majority of the public often appears dissatisfied with the federal government. Yet national and international affairs are on people's minds more often than state or local politics. And fewer voters participate in state and local elections than in congressional and presidential elections.

The Constitutional Structure of American Federalism

Dividing powers and responsibilities between the national and state governments has resulted in thousands of court decisions, hundreds of books, and endless speeches to explain them—and even then the division lacks precise definition. Nonetheless, a basic understanding of how the Constitution divides these powers and responsibilities and of what obligations are imposed on each level of government is helpful (see Table 3-2).

The formal constitutional framework of our federal system may be stated relatively simply:

1. The national government has only those powers delegated to it by the Constitution (with the important exception of the inherent power over foreign affairs).
2. Within the scope of its operations, the national government is supreme.
3. The state governments have the powers not delegated to the central government, except those denied to them by the Constitution and their state constitutions.
4. Some powers are specifically denied to both the national and state governments; others are specifically denied only to the states; still others are denied to the national government but not the states.

TABLE 3–2 The Federal Division of Powers		
Powers Delegated to the National Government	**Some Powers Reserved for the States**	**Some Concurrent Powers Shared by the National and State Governments**
▪ Express powers stated in the Constitution ▪ Implied powers that may be inferred from the express powers ▪ Inherent powers that allow the nation to present a united front to foreign powers	▪ To create a republican form of government ▪ To charter local governments ▪ To conduct elections ▪ To exercise all powers not delegated to the national government or denied to the states by the Constitution	▪ To tax citizens and businesses ▪ To borrow and spend money ▪ To establish courts ▪ To pass and enforce laws ▪ To protect civil rights

Powers of the National Government

The Constitution, chiefly in the first three articles, delegates legislative, executive, and judicial powers to the national government. In addition to these **express powers**, such as the power to regulate interstate commerce and to appropriate funds, Congress has assumed constitutionally **implied powers**, such as the power to create banks, which are inferred from the express powers. The constitutional basis for the implied powers of Congress is the **necessary and proper clause** (Article I, Section 8, Clause 18). This clause gives Congress the right "to make all Laws which shall be necessary and proper for carrying into Execution the foregoing Powers, and all other Powers vested . . . in the Government of the United States."

In the field of foreign affairs, the Constitution gives the national government **inherent powers.** The national government has the same authority to deal with other nations as if it were the central government in a unitary system. Such inherent powers do not depend on specific constitutional provisions. For example, the government of the United States may acquire territory by purchase or by discovery and occupation, though no specific clause in the Constitution allows such acquisition. Even if the Constitution were silent about foreign affairs—which it is not—the national government would still have the power to declare war, make treaties, and appoint and receive ambassadors.

Together, these express, implied, and inherent powers create a flexible system that allows the Supreme Court, Congress, the president, and the people to expand the central government's powers to meet the needs of a modern nation in a global economy. This expansion of central government functions rests on four constitutional pillars.

These four constitutional pillars—the *national supremacy article,* the *war power,* the *commerce clause,* and most especially, the *power to tax and spend* for the general welfare—have permitted a tremendous expansion of the functions of the national government, so much so that despite the Supreme Court's recent declaration that some national laws exceed Congress's constitutional powers, the national government has, in effect, almost full power to enact any legislation that Congress deems necessary, so long as it does not conflict with the provisions of the Constitution designed to protect individual rights and the powers of the states.

THE NATIONAL SUPREMACY ARTICLE   One of the most important pillars is found in Article VI of the Constitution: "This Constitution, and the Laws of the United States which shall be made in Pursuance thereof; and all Treaties made . . . under the Authority of the United States, shall be the supreme Law of the Land; and the Judges in every State shall be bound thereby; any Thing in the Constitution or Laws of any State to the Contrary notwithstanding." All officials, state as well as national, swear an oath to support the Constitution of the United States. States may not override national policies; this restriction also applies to local units of government, since they are agents of the states. National laws and regulations of federal agencies *preempt* the field so that conflicting state and local regulations are unenforceable.

THE WAR POWER   The national government is responsible for protecting the nation from external aggression, whether from other nations or international terrorism. The government's power to protect national security includes the power to wage war. In today's world, military strength depends not only on troops in the field but also on the ability to mobilize the nation's industrial might as well as to apply scientific and technological knowledge to the tasks of defense. The national government has the power to do whatever is necessary and proper to wage war successfully. Thus the national government has the power to do almost anything not in direct conflict with constitutional guarantees.

THE POWER TO REGULATE INTERSTATE AND FOREIGN COMMERCE   Congressional authority extends to all commerce that affects more than one state. Commerce includes the production, buying, selling, renting, and transporting of goods, services, and properties.

express powers
Powers specifically granted to one of the branches of the national government by the Constitution.

implied powers
Powers inferred from the express powers that allow Congress to carry out its functions.

necessary and proper clause
Clause of the Constitution (Article I, Section 8, Clause 18) setting forth the implied powers of Congress. It states that Congress, in addition to its express powers, has the right to make all laws necessary and proper for carrying out all powers vested by the Constitution in the national government.

inherent powers
The powers of the national government in the field of foreign affairs that the Supreme Court has declared do not depend on constitutional grants but rather grow out of the very existence of the national government.

An Expanding Nation

A great advantage of federalism—and part of the genius and flexibility of our constitutional system—has been the way in which we acquired territory and extended rights and guarantees by means of statehood, commonwealth, or territorial status, and thus grew from 13 to 50 states, plus territories.

Louisiana Purchase	1803
Florida	1819
Texas	1845
Oregon	1846
Mexican Cession	1848
Gadsden Purchase	1853
Alaska	1867
Hawaii	1898
Philippines	1898–1946
Puerto Rico	1899
Guam	1899
American Samoa	1900
Canal Zone	1904–2000
U.S. Virgin Islands	1917
Pacific Islands Trust Territory	1947

commerce clause
The clause in the Constitution (Article I, Section 8, Clause 3) that gives Congress the power to regulate all business activities that cross state lines or affect more than one state or other nations.

The **commerce clause** (Article I, Section 8, Clause 3) packs a tremendous constitutional punch; it gives Congress the power "to regulate Commerce with foreign Nations, and among the several States, and with the Indian Tribes." In these few words, the national government has been able to find constitutional justification for regulating a wide range of human activity, since very few aspects of our economy today affect commerce in only one state and are thus outside the scope of the national government's constitutional authority.[16]

The broad authority of Congress over interstate commerce was affirmed in the landmark ruling of *Gibbons* v. *Ogden* in 1824. There, in interpreting the commerce clause, Chief Justice John Marshall asserted national interests over those of the states and laid the basis for the subsequent growth in congressional power over commerce.

Gibbons v. *Ogden* arose from a dispute over a monopoly to operate steamboats in New York waters that was granted to Robert Livingston and Robert Fulton. They in turn licensed Aaron Ogden to exclusively operate steamboats between New York and ports in New Jersey. Ogden sued to stop Thomas Gibbons from running a competing ferry. Gibbons countered that his boats were licensed under a 1793 act of Congress governing vessels "in the coasting trade and fisheries." But New York courts sided with Ogden in holding that both Congress and the states may regulate commerce, just as each has the power to tax. Congress, therefore, had not preempted New York from granting the monopoly. Gibbons appealed to the Supreme Court.

The stakes were high in *Gibbons* v. *Ogden,* for at issue was the very concept of "interstate commerce." May both Congress and the states regulate interstate commerce? And when conflicts arise between national and state regulations, which prevails?

Chief Justice Marshall asserted that national interests prevail and astutely defined "interstate commerce" as "intercourse that affects more states than one." Unlike the power of taxation, Congress's power over interstate commerce is complete and overrides conflicting state laws.[17]

Gibbons v. *Ogden* was immediately heralded for promoting a national economic common market in holding that states may not discriminate against interstate transportation and out-of-state commerce. Chief Justice Marshall's brilliant definition of "commerce" as *intercourse among the states* provided the basis clause for national regulation of an expanding range of economic activities, from the sale of lottery tickets[18] to prostitution[19] to radio and television broadcasts,[20] and telecommunications and the Internet.

The commerce clause has also been used to sustain legislation that goes beyond commercial matters. When the Supreme Court upheld the Civil Rights Act of 1964, forbidding discrimination because of race, religion, gender, or national origin in places of public accommodation, it said: "Congress's action in removing the disruptive effect which it found racial discrimination has on interstate travel is not invalidated because Congress was also legislating against what it considers to be moral wrongs."[21] Discrimination restricts the flow of interstate commerce; therefore, Congress could legislate against discrimination. Moreover, the law applies even to local places of public accommodation because local incidents of discrimination have a substantial and harmful impact on interstate commerce. The Court, however, has recently limited congressional power to address some other similar harms because it did not find a substantial connection with interstate commerce.[22]

THE POWER TO TAX AND SPEND   Congress lacks constitutional authority to pass laws solely on the grounds that they will promote the general welfare, but it may raise taxes and spend money for this purpose. For example, Congress lacks the power to regulate education or agriculture directly, yet it does have the power to appropriate money to support education or to pay farm subsidies. By attaching conditions to its grants of money, Congress may thus regulate what it cannot directly control by law.

When Congress puts up the money, it determines how the money will be spent. By withholding or threatening to withhold funds, the national government can influence or control state operations and regulate individual conduct. For example, Congress has stipulated that federal funds should be withdrawn from any program in which any person is denied benefits because of race, color, national origin, sex, or physical handicap. Congress has also used its power of the purse to force states to raise the drinking age to 21 by tying such a condition to federal dollars for highways.

Congress frequently requires states to do certain things—for example, provide services to indigent mothers and clean up the air and water. These requirements are called **federal mandates**. Often Congress does not supply the funds required to carry out these mandates—called "unfunded mandates"—and its failure to do so has become an important issue as states face growing expenditures with limited resources. The Supreme Court has also ruled that Congress may not compel states to enact particular laws or require state officials to enforce federal laws, for example, requiring checks on the backgrounds of handgun purchasers.[23]

Powers of the States

The Constitution *reserves for the states all powers not granted to the national government*, subject only to the limitations of the Constitution. Powers not given exclusively to the national government by provisions of the Constitution or by judicial interpretation may be exercised concurrently by the states, as long as there is no conflict with national law. Such **concurrent powers** with the national government include the power to levy taxes and regulate commerce internal to each state.

In general, a state may levy a tax on the same item as the national government does, but a state cannot, by a tax, "unduly burden" commerce among the states, interfere with a function of the national government, complicate the operation of a national law, or abridge the terms of a treaty of the United States. Where Congress has not preempted the field, states may regulate interstate businesses, provided that these regulations do not cover matters requiring uniform national treatment or unduly burden interstate commerce.

Who decides what matters require "uniform national treatment" or what actions might place an "undue burden" on interstate commerce? Congress does, subject to final review by the Supreme Court. When Congress is silent or does not clearly state its intent, the courts—ultimately, the Supreme Court—decide if there is a conflict with the national Constitution or if there has been federal preemption by law or regulation.

Constitutional Limits and Obligations

To make federalism work, the Constitution imposes certain restraints on both the national and the state governments. States are prohibited from:

1. Making treaties with foreign governments
2. Authorizing private persons to prey on the shipping and commerce of other nations
3. Coining money, issuing bills of credit, or making anything but gold and silver coin legal tender in payment of debts
4. Taxing imports or exports
5. Taxing foreign ships
6. Keeping troops or ships in time of peace (except the state militia, now called the National Guard)
7. Engaging in war, unless invaded or in such imminent danger as will not admit of delay

The national government, in turn, is required by the Constitution to refrain from exercising its powers, especially its powers to tax and to regulate interstate commerce, in such a way as to interfere substantially with the states' abilities to perform their responsibilities. Today, the protection states have from intrusions by the national government comes primarily from the political process because senators and

federal mandate
A requirement imposed by the federal government as a condition for the receipt of federal funds.

concurrent powers
Powers that the Constitution gives to both the national and state governments, such as the power to levy taxes.

Same-Sex Marriages and the Full Faith and Credit Clause

The full faith and credit clause has become part of a national debate because one state now recognizes same-sex unions. In April 2000, Vermont enacted a law recognizing "civil unions," granting same-sex couples the same rights and protections as married couples. It was the first state to do so. As a result, same-sex couples were entitled to 300 state benefits, ranging from health care and inheritance rights to property transfers. However, in March 2001, the Vermont House of Representatives reversed course and passed a bill outlawing same-sex marriages.

Same-sex partnerships are legally recognized in several European countries, including Belgium, Denmark, France, Hungary, Luxembourg, Norway, and Sweden. However, such unions are banned in 32 states. Congress passed and President Bill Clinton signed the Defense of Marriage Act of 1996, which relieves states of any obligation to recognize same-sex marriages even if they are recognized in other states and stipulates that the national government recognizes only heterosexual marriages for federal benefits such as Social Security.

The Defense of Marriage Act may well be challenged in the courts for going beyond the power of Congress to provide states with an exemption from their constitutional obligation under the full faith and credit clause. Supporters of the act point to the Constitution, which gives Congress the responsibility for prescribing the manner in which states are to comply with the clause.

The Supreme Court has not addressed the issue squarely, and precedents provide no clear answer. It is the view of one authority that in light of recent Court rulings showing the present Court's tilt toward states' rights and "the fact that marriage has traditionally been an almost exclusive sphere of state authority, the Court would

Gay couples renew their vows to each other in this ceremony in San Francisco's Metropolitan Community church.

likely maintain the noncentralized and dual nature of American domestic relations that exist today, and allow the states to decide whether to recognize same-sex marriages."*

*John P. Feldmeier, "Federalism and Full Faith and Credit: Must States Recognize Out-of-State Same-Sex Marriages?" *Publius* 25 (Fall 1995), p. 126. See also Jeremy D. Mayer and Louis-Philippe Rochon, "Gay Rights in the USA: The States Lead the Way," *Federations* 2 (November 2001).

representatives elected from the states participate in the decisions of Congress. However, the Court has held that Congress may not command states to enact laws to comply with or order state employees to enforce unfunded federal mandates; for example, as noted earlier, Congress may not require local law enforcement officials to make background checks prior to handgun sales.[24] It has also ruled that the Eleventh Amendment's guarantee of states' sovereign immunity from lawsuits forbids state employees from suing states in federal and state courts in order to force state compliance with federal employment laws.[25] Although Congress may not use those sticks, it may offer the carrot of federal funding if states comply with national policies, such as establishing a minimum drinking age or setting 55-mile-an-hour speed limits.

The Constitution also requires the national government to guarantee to each state a "republican form of government." The framers used this term to distinguish a republic from a monarchy, on the one side, and from a pure, direct democracy, on the other. Congress, not the courts, enforces this guarantee and determines what is or is not a republican form of government. By permitting the congressional delegation of a state to be seated in Congress, Congress acknowledges that the state has the republican form of government guaranteed by the Constitution.

In addition, the national government is obliged by the Constitution to protect states against *domestic insurrection*. Congress has delegated to the president the authority to dispatch troops to put down such insurrections when so requested by the proper state authorities. If there are contesting state authorities, the president decides which is the proper one. The president does not have to wait, however, for a request from state authorities to send federal troops into a state to enforce federal laws.

IN COMPARATIVE PERSPECTIVE

Three Different Approaches to Federalism

There is no single model for dividing authority between national and state governments or for power sharing in intergovernmental relations. The federal systems in Canada, Germany, and Switzerland are illustrative.

Canada combines a federal system with a parliamentary form of government that has authority to legislate on all matters pertaining to "peace, order, and good government." The system was established in 1867, in part to prevent conflicts similar to those between the states that led to the American Civil War. In each of the ten provinces, the lieutenant governor is appointed on the advice of the prime minister and must approve any provincial law before it goes into effect. The legislative powers of the provinces are thus checked and limited. However, the provinces retain residual powers, and unlike the U.S. Supreme Court, the Canadian judiciary has generally encouraged decentralization in recognition of its multicultural society. Thus Canadian provinces exercise greater power and the national government is weaker than in the United States. In addition, the special status claimed by French-speaking Quebec has led to intergovernmental relations that alternate between periods of centralization and decentralization.

The Federal Republic of Germany, whose Basic Laws of 1949 became the constitution with the reunification of East and West Germany in 1990, is often referred to as an example of cooperative federalism. Its 16 states, or Länder, exercise a great deal of power, far more than states do in the United States. The central government has a president and a bicameral parliament composed of an upper house, the Federal Council, and a lower house, the National Assembly, as well as an independent judiciary. The central government has exclusive authority over foreign affairs, money, immigration, and telecommunications. But the Länder retain residual powers over all other matters and have concurrent powers over civil and criminal law, along with matters related to education, health, and the public welfare. Moreover, national legislation does not become law unless approved by a majority of the Federal Council, whose members are selected by legislatures in the Länder, not by popular elections.

Switzerland established a confederation on the basis of regional governments (cantons). The cantons reflect the ethnic and linguistic differences of their German-, French-, and Italian-speaking populations. All three languages are officially recognized by the central government. But of the 22 cantons, there are 18 that are unilingual, three that are bilingual, and one that is trilingual. They exercise most lawmaking powers and are represented in the National Council, a bicameral legislature, and the Council of States.

For more information on comparative federalism, go to the Web site of the International Political Science Association's Section on Comparative Federalism at www.iu.edu/~soeaweb/IPSA and to the site of the Forum on Federations at www.forumfed.org.

Interstate Relations

Three clauses in the Constitution, taken from the Articles of Confederation, require states to give full faith and credit to each other's public acts, records, and judicial proceedings; to extend to each other's citizens the privileges and immunities of their own citizens; and to return persons who are fleeing from justice.

FULL FAITH AND CREDIT   The **full faith and credit clause** (Article IV, Section 1), one of the more technical provisions of the Constitution, requires state courts to enforce the civil judgments of the courts of other states and accept their public records and acts as valid. It does not require states to enforce the criminal laws of other states; in most cases, for one state to enforce the criminal laws of another would raise constitutional issues. The clause applies especially to enforcement of judicial settlements and court awards.

INTERSTATE PRIVILEGES AND IMMUNITIES   Under Article IV, Section 2, states must extend to citizens of other states the privileges and immunities granted to their own citizens, including the protection of the laws, the right to engage in peaceful occupations, access to the courts, and freedom from discriminatory taxes. Because of this clause, states may not impose unreasonable residency requirements, that is, withhold rights to American citizens who have recently moved to the state and thereby have become citizens of that state. For example, a state may not set unreasonable time limits to withhold state-funded medical benefits from new citizens or to keep them

full faith and credit clause
Clause in the Constitution (Article IV, Section 1) requiring each state to recognize the civil judgments rendered by the courts of the other states and to accept their public records and acts as valid.

from voting. How long a residency requirement may a state impose? A day seems about as long as the Court will tolerate to withhold welfare payments or medical care, 50 days or so for voting privileges, and one year for eligibility for in-state tuition for state-supported colleges and universities.

Financially independent adults who move into a state just before enrolling in a state-supported university or college may be required to prove that they have become citizens of that state and intend to remain after finishing their schooling by supplying such evidence of citizenship as tax payments, a driver's license, car registration, voter registration, and a continuous, year-round off-campus residence. Students who are financially dependent on their parents remain citizens of the state of their parents.

EXTRADITION   In Article IV, Section 2, the Constitution asserts that when individuals charged with crimes have fled from one state to another, the state to which they have fled is to deliver them to the proper officials upon the demand of the executive authority of the state from which they fled. This process is called **extradition**. "The obvious objective of the Extradition Clause," the courts have claimed, "is that no State should become a safe haven for the fugitives from a sister State's criminal justice system."[26] Congress has supplemented this constitutional provision by making the governor of the state to which fugitives have fled responsible for returning them. Despite their constitutional obligation, governors of asylum states have on occasion refused to honor a request for extradition.

INTERSTATE COMPACTS   The Constitution also requires states to settle disputes with one another without the use of force. States may carry their legal disputes to the Supreme Court, or they may negotiate **interstate compacts**. Interstate compacts often establish interstate agencies to handle problems affecting an entire region. Before most interstate compacts become effective, congressional approval is required. After a compact has been signed and approved by Congress, it becomes binding on all signatory states, and its terms are enforceable by the federal judiciary. A typical state may belong to 20 compacts dealing with such subjects as environmental protection, crime control, water rights, and higher education exchanges.[27]

The Role of the Federal Courts: Umpires of Federalism

Although the political process ultimately decides how power will be divided between the national and the state governments, the federal courts—and especially the Supreme Court—have often been called on to umpire the ongoing debate about which level of government should do what, for whom, and to whom. This role for the courts was claimed in the celebrated case of *McCulloch* v. *Maryland*.

McCulloch Versus Maryland

In *McCulloch* v. *Maryland* (1819), the Supreme Court had the first of many chances to define the division of power between the national and state governments.[28] The state of Maryland had levied a tax against the Baltimore branch of the Bank of the United States, a semipublic agency established by Congress. James William McCulloch, the cashier of the bank, refused to pay on the grounds that a state could not tax an instrument of the national government.

Maryland was represented before the Court by some of the country's most distinguished lawyers, including Luther Martin, who had been a delegate to the Constitutional Convention. Martin said that the power to incorporate a bank was not expressly delegated to the national government in the Constitution. He maintained that the necessary and proper clause gives Congress only the power to choose those

extradition
Legal process whereby an alleged criminal offender is surrendered by the officials of one state to officials of the state in which the crime is alleged to have been committed.

interstate compact
An agreement among two or more states. The Constitution requires that most such agreements be approved by Congress.

You Decide / Thinking It Through

DO WE NEED A STRONGER OR A WEAKER GOVERNMENT IN WASHINGTON?

You Decide... Should responsibility for welfare, education, and health care be given back to the states? If the national government sets the standards, should it provide the funds but leave the details to the states? Do the facts, as you know them, support the need for federal standards? Or can state and local governments be trusted to handle most domestic problems in their own way?

Thinking It Through... The great debate about which level of government can best perform functions continues to rage. The Republican party started its history as the party of the National Union, while the Democrats were then the champion of states' rights, but over the past several decades, there has been a switch. After winning majority status in Congress in 1994, Republicans led the charge on Washington, demanding the return of functions to the states. Democrats tend to be reluctant about removing all federal standards, especially with respect to regulation of the environment and of the workplace, and they tend to be in favor of providing minimum standards for programs, especially welfare and health care.

Centralists' Arguments

1. State and local officials tend to be less competent than national officials.
2. State and local officials tend to be concerned only with the interests of their own areas.
3. State and local governments are unable or unwilling to raise taxes needed to carry out vital government functions.
4. State and local governments are more apt to reflect local racial and ethnic biases as well as the biases of dominant local industries.
5. State and local governments are afraid to regulate industries for fear the industries will move elsewhere.

Decentralists' Arguments

1. Increased urbanization has made states more responsive to the needs of city people.
2. In recent years, state and local governments have shown a greater willingness to raise taxes than the national government.
3. State and local governments have become as sensitive to the needs of the poor and minorities as the national government.
4. State and local governments have reformed and modernized and thus become more effective governments.

means and to pass those laws absolutely essential to the execution of its expressly granted powers. Because a bank is not absolutely necessary to the exercise of any of its delegated powers, Congress had no authority to establish it. As for Maryland's right to tax the bank, the power to tax is one of the powers reserved to the states; they may use it as they see fit.

The national government was represented as well by distinguished counsel, including Daniel Webster. Webster conceded that the power to create a bank is not one of the express powers of the national government. However, the power to pass laws necessary and proper to carry out Congress's express powers is specifically delegated to Congress. Therefore, Congress may incorporate a bank as an appropriate, convenient, and useful means of exercising the granted powers of collecting taxes, borrowing money, and caring for the property of the United States. Although the power to tax is reserved to the states, Webster argued that states cannot interfere with the operations of the national government. The Constitution leaves no room for doubt; in cases of conflict between the national and state governments, the national government is supreme.

Speaking for a unanimous Court, Chief Justice John Marshall rejected every one of Maryland's contentions. He summarized his views on the powers of the national government in these now-famous words: "Let the end be legitimate, let it be within the scope of the Constitution, and all means which are appropriate, which are plainly adapted to that end, which are not prohibited, but consist with the letter and spirit of the constitution, are constitutional." Having thus established the doctrine of *implied national powers,* Marshall set forth the doctrine of **national supremacy.** No state, he said, can use its taxing powers to tax a national instrument. "The power to tax involves the power to destroy. . . . If the right of the States to tax the means employed by the general government be conceded, the declaration that the Constitution, and the laws made in pursuance thereof, shall be the supreme law of the land, is empty and unmeaning declamation."

The long-range significance of *McCulloch* v. *Maryland* in providing support for the developing forces of nationalism and a unified economy cannot be overstated. The contrary arguments in favor of the states, if they had been accepted, would have strapped the national government in a constitutional straitjacket and denied it powers needed to handle the problems of an expanding nation.

Federal Courts and the Role of the States

The authority of federal judges to review the activities of state and local governments has expanded dramatically in recent decades because of modern judicial interpretations of the Fourteenth Amendment, which forbids states to deprive any person of life, liberty, or property without *due process of the law;* nor can states deny to any person the *equal protection of the laws* and congressional legislation enacted to implement this amendment. Almost every action by state and local officials is now subject to challenge before a federal judge as a violation of the Constitution or of federal law.

Preemption occurs when a federal law or regulation takes precedence over enforcement of a state or local law or regulation. State and local laws are preempted not only when they conflict directly with federal laws and regulations but also if they touch

national supremacy
Constitutional doctrine that whenever conflict occurs between the constitutionally authorized actions of the national government and those of a state or local government, the actions of the federal government prevail.

preemption
The right of a federal law or regulation to preclude enforcement of a state or local law or regulation.

There have been times throughout U.S. history when federal law has superseded state and local law. One example of this in recent history is the Voting Rights Act of 1965, which enforced the voting rights of African Americans in the South. In this photo, African American citizens in Montgomery, Alabama, are registering to vote for the very first time following a march that took place during one of the many voter registration drives of 1964 and 1965.

a field in which the "federal interest is so dominant that the federal system will be assumed to preclude enforcement of state laws on the same subject."[29] Examples of federal preemption include laws regulating hazardous substances, water quality, and clean air standards and many civil rights acts, especially the Civil Rights Act of 1964 and the Voting Rights Act of 1965.

Over the years, federal judges, under the leadership of the Supreme Court, have generally favored the powers of the federal government over the states. In spite of the Supreme Court's recent bias in favor of state over national authority, few would deny the Supreme Court the power to review and set aside state actions. As Justice Oliver Wendell Holmes of the Supreme Court once remarked: "I do not think the United States would come to an end if we lost our power to declare an Act of Congress void. I do think the Union would be imperiled if we could not make that declaration as to the laws of the several States."[30]

The Great Debate: Centralists Versus Decentralists

From the beginning of the Republic, there has been an ongoing debate about the "proper" distribution of powers, functions, and responsibilities between the national government and the states. Did the national government have the authority to outlaw slavery in the territories? Did the states have the authority to operate racially segregated schools? Could Congress regulate labor relations? Does Congress have the power to regulate the sale and use of firearms? Does Congress have the right to tell states how to clean up air and water pollution? Even today, as in the past, such debates are frequently phrased in constitutional language, with appeals to the great principles of federalism. But they are also arguments over who gets what, where, when, and how.

During the Great Depression of the 1930s, the nation debated whether Congress had the constitutional authority to enact legislation on agriculture, labor, education, housing, and welfare. Only 40 years ago, some legislators and public officials—as well as some scholars—questioned the constitutional authority of Congress to legislate against racial discrimination. The debate continues between **centralists**, who favor national action, and **decentralists**, who defend the powers of the states and favor action at the state and local levels.

THE DECENTRALIST POSITION   Among Americans favoring the decentralist or **states' rights** interpretation were the Antifederalists, Thomas Jefferson, John C. Calhoun, the Supreme Court from the 1920s to 1937, and more recently, Presidents Ronald Reagan and George Bush, the Republican leaders of Congress, Chief Justice William H. Rehnquist, and Justices Antonin Scalia, Clarence Thomas, and Sandra Day O'Connor.

Most decentralists contend that the Constitution is a treaty among sovereign states that created the central government and gave it very limited authority. As Justice Clarence Thomas, an ardent advocate of states' rights, wrote in a dissenting opinion supporting the argument that a state has the power to impose term limits on members of Congress, "The ultimate source of the Constitution's authority is the consent of the people of each individual State, not the consent of the undifferentiated people of the Nation as a whole."[31] Thus the national government is little more than an agent of the states, and every one of its powers should be narrowly defined. Any question about whether the states have given a particular function to the central government or have reserved it for themselves should be resolved in favor of the states.

Decentralists hold that the national government should not interfere with activities reserved for the states. The Tenth Amendment, they claim, makes this clear: "The powers not delegated to the United States by the Constitution, nor prohibited by it to the States, are reserved to the States respectively, or to the people." Decentralists insist that state governments are closer to the people and reflect the people's wishes more accurately than the national government does. The national government, they add, is inherently heavy-handed and bureaucratic; to preserve our federal system and our liberties, central authority must be kept under control.

centralists
People who favor national action over action at the state and local levels.

decentralists
People who favor state or local action rather than national action.

states' rights
Powers expressly or implicitly reserved to the states and emphasized by decentralists.

THE CENTRALIST POSITION   The centralist position has been supported by Chief Justice John Marshall, Presidents Abraham Lincoln, Theodore Roosevelt, and Franklin Roosevelt, and throughout most of our history, the Supreme Court.

Centralists reject the whole idea of the Constitution as an interstate compact. Rather, they view the Constitution as a supreme law established by the people. The national government is an agent of the people, not of the states, because it was the people who drew up the Constitution and created the national government. They intended that the central government's powers should be defined by the national political process and that it should be denied authority only when the Constitution clearly prohibits it from acting.

Centralists argue that the national government is a government of all the people, whereas each state speaks only for some of the people. Although the Tenth Amendment clearly reserves powers for the states, it does not deny the national government the authority to exercise, to the fullest extent, all of its powers. Moreover, the supremacy of the national government restricts the states, because governments representing part of the people cannot be allowed to interfere with a government representing all of them.

The Supreme Court and the Role of Congress

From 1937 until the 1990s, the Supreme Court essentially removed federal courts from what had been their traditional role of protecting states from acts of Congress. The Supreme Court broadly interpreted the commerce clause to allow Congress to do whatever Congress thought necessary and proper to promote the common good, even if the federal laws and regulations infringed on the activities of state and local governments. In 1985, the Court went so far as to tell the states that they should look to the political process to protect their interests, not to the federal courts.[32]

In the past decade, however, the Supreme Court signaled that federal courts should no longer remain passive in resolving federalism issues.[33] In 1995, the Court declared that a state could not impose term limits on its members of Congress, but it did so only by a 5 to 4 vote. Justice John Paul Stevens, writing for the majority, built his argument on the concept of the federal union as espoused by the great Chief Justice John Marshall, as a compact among the people, with the national government serving as the people's agent. By contrast, Justice Clarence Thomas, writing for the dissenters, espoused a view of federalism not heard from a justice of the Supreme Court since prior to the New Deal. He interpreted the Tenth Amendment as requiring the national government to justify its actions in terms of an enumerated power and granting to the states all other powers not given to the national government.[34]

The Court also declared that the clause in the Constitution empowering Congress to regulate commerce with the Indian tribes did not give Congress the power to authorize federal courts to hear suits against a state brought by Indian tribes.[35] The effect of this decision goes beyond Indian tribes. As a result, except to enforce rights stemming from the Fourteenth Amendment, which the Court explicitly acknowledged to be within Congress's power, Congress may no longer authorize individuals to bring legal actions against states in order to force their compliance with federal law in either federal or state courts.[36]

Building on those rulings, the Court continues to press ahead with its "constitutional counterrevolution"[37] in returning to an older vision of federalism not embraced since the constitutional crisis over the New Deal in the 1930s. Among other recent rulings,[38] the Court struck down the Violence Against Women Act, which had given women who are victims of violence the right to sue their attackers for damages.[39] Congress had found that violence against women annually costs the national economy $3 billion, but the Court held that Congress exceeded its powers in enacting the law and intruded on the powers of the states.

These Supreme Court decisions—most of which split the Court 5 to 4 along ideological lines, with the conservative justices favoring states' rights—may signal a major shift in the Court's interpretation of the constitutional nature of our federal system. Chief Justice Rehnquist, joined by Justices Scalia, Thomas, O'Connor, and frequently Justice Anthony M. Kennedy, veered the Court back to a decentralist position. President Clinton's two appointees, Justices Ruth Bader Ginsburg and Stephen Breyer, joined by Justices David Souter and John Paul Stevens, are resisting this movement back to a states' rights interpretation of our federal system. Consequently, federalism issues are likely to come up in future Supreme Court confirmation hearings, and the outcome of presidential elections—which greatly influence who gets appointed to the Supreme Court—could well determine how these and other federalism issues will be decided.

Regulatory Federalism, Federal Grants, and Federal Mandates

Congress authorizes programs, establishes general rules for how the programs will operate, and decides whether and how much room should be left for state or local discretion. Most important, Congress appropriates the funds for these programs and generally has deeper pockets than even the richest states. One of Congress's most potent tools for influencing policy at the state and local levels has been federal grants.

Federal grants serve four purposes, the most important of which is the fourth:

1. To supply state and local governments with revenue.

2. To establish minimum national standards for such things as highways and clean air.

3. To equalize resources among the states by taking money from people with high incomes through federal taxes and spending it, through grants, in states where the poor live.

4. To attack national problems yet minimize the growth of federal agencies.

Types of Federal Grants

Three types of federal grants are currently being administered: *categorical-formula grants, project grants,* and *block grants* (sometimes called *flexible grants*). From 1972 to 1987, there was also *revenue sharing*—federal grants to state and local governments to be used at their discretion and subject only to very general conditions. But when budget deficits soared in the second Reagan administration (1985–1989) and there was no revenue to share, revenue sharing was terminated—to the states in 1986 and to local governments in 1987.

CATEGORICAL-FORMULA GRANTS   Congress appropriates funds for specific purposes, such as school lunches or the building of airports and highways. These funds are allocated by formula and are subject to detailed federal conditions, often on a matching basis; that is, the local government receiving the federal funds must put up some of its own dollars. Categorical grants, in addition, provide federal supervision to ensure that the federal dollars are spent as Congress wants. There are hundreds of grant programs, but two dozen, including Medicaid, account for more than half of total spending for categoricals.

PROJECT GRANTS   Congress appropriates a certain sum, which is allocated to state and local units and sometimes to nongovernmental agencies, based on applications from those who wish to participate. Examples are grants by the National Science Foundation to universities and research institutes to support the work of scientists or grants to states and localities to support training and employment programs.

BLOCK GRANTS   These are broad grants to states for prescribed activities—welfare, child care, education, social services, preventive health care, and health services—with only a few strings attached. States have great flexibility in deciding how to spend block grant dollars, but when the federal funds for any fiscal year are gone, there are no more matching federal dollars.

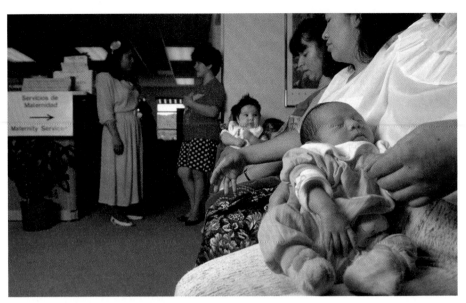

This maternity clinic is funded in part by federal block grants, which provide federal money to states for various services, such as health care, education, and welfare. States have great flexibility in deciding how to spend block grant dollars.

The Politics of Federal Grants

Republicans "have consistently favored fewer strings, less federal supervision, and the delegation of spending discretion to the state and local governments."[40] Democrats have generally been less supportive of broad discretionary block grants, favoring instead more detailed, federally supervised spending. The Republican-controlled Congress in the 1990s gave high priority to the creation of block grants, but it ran into trouble by trying to lump together welfare, school lunch and breakfast programs, prenatal nutrition programs, and child protection programs in one block grant.

With President Clinton's enthusiastic support, however, the Republicans succeeded in making a major change in federal-state relations—a devolution of responsibility for welfare from the national government to the states. The Personal Responsibility and Work Opportunity Reconciliation Act of 1996 put an end to the 61-year-old program of Aid to Families with Dependent Children (AFDC), a federal guarantee of welfare checks for all eligible mothers and children. The 1996 act substituted for AFDC a welfare block grant to each state, with caps on the amount of federal dollars that the state will receive. It also put another big federal child care program into another block grant—the Child Care and Development Block Grant (CCDBG).

Welfare block grants give states flexibility in how they provide for welfare, but no federal funds can be used to cover recipients who do not go to work within two years, and no one can receive federally supported benefits for more than five years. In order to slow down the "race to the bottom" in which states may try to make themselves "the least attractive state in which to be poor,"[41] Congress also stipulated that in order for states to receive their full share of federal dollars, they must continue to spend at least 75 percent of what they had been spending on welfare.

The battle over the appropriate level of government to control funding and to exercise principal responsibility for social programs tends to be cyclical. As one scholar of federalism explains, "Complaints about excessive federal control tend to be followed by proposals to shift more power to state and local governments. Then, when problems arise in state and local administration—and problems inevitably arise when any organization tries to administer anything—demands for closer federal supervision and tighter federal controls follow."[42]

Federal Mandates

Fewer federal dollars do not necessarily mean fewer federal controls. On the contrary, the federal government has imposed mandates on states and local governments, often without providing federal funds. State and local officials complained, and protests from state and local officials against unfunded federal mandates were effective. Congress, with President Clinton's support, passed the Unfunded Mandates Reform Act of 1995. The act requires the Congressional Budget Office (CBO) and federal agencies to issue reports about the impact of unfunded mandates. The act also imposed some mild constraints on Congress itself. A congressional committee that approves any legislation containing a federal mandate must draw attention to the mandate in its report and describe its cost to state and local governments. If the committee intends any mandate to be partially unfunded, it must explain why it is appropriate for the cost to be borne by state and local government.

Whether the Unfunded Mandates Reform Act significantly slows down federal mandates remains to be seen. So far, it has had little effect. The Americans with Disabilities Act (1990), for example, called on state and local governments to build ramps and alter curbs—renovations that are costing millions of dollars. Environmental Protection Agency regulations require states to build automobile pollution-testing stations and take other actions to reduce pollution, but without corresponding federal dollars. Still, state officials praise the law for increasing congressional awareness of unfunded mandates. It has forced members of Congress to take into account how a bill would affect state and local governments.[43]

The Politics of Federalism

The formal structures of our federal system have not changed much since 1787, but the political realities, especially during the past half-century, have greatly altered how federalism works. To understand these changes, we need to look at some of the trends that continue to fuel the debate about the meaning of federalism.

The Growth of Big Government

Over the past two centuries, power has accrued to the national government. "No one planned the growth, but everyone played a part in it."[44] How did this shift come about? For a variety of reasons. One is that many of our problems have become national in scope. Much that was local in 1789, in 1860, or in 1930 is now national, even global. State governments could supervise the relations between small merchants and their few employees, but only the national government can supervise relations between multinational corporations and their thousands of employees, many organized in national unions.

As industrialization proceeded, powerful interests made demands on the national government. Business groups called on the government for aid in the form of tariffs, a national banking system, subsidies to railroads and the merchant marine, and uniform rules relating to the environment. Farmers learned that the national government could give more aid than the states, and they too began to demand help. By the beginning of the twentieth century, urban groups in general and organized labor in particular pressed their claims. Big business, big agriculture, and big labor all added up to big government.

The growth of the national economy and the creation of national transportation and communications networks altered people's attitudes toward the national government. Before the Civil War, the national government was viewed as a distant, even foreign, government. Today, in part because of television and the Internet, most people identify as closely with Washington as with their state capitals. People are apt to know more about the president than about their governor and more about their national senators and representatives than about their state legislators or even about the local officials who run their cities and schools.

New Technologies of Federal Control

Direct Orders

In a few instances, federal regulation takes the form of direct orders that must be complied with under threat of criminal or civil sanction. An example is the Equal Employment Opportunity Act of 1972, barring job discrimination by state and local governments on the basis of race, color, religion, sex, and national origin.

Cross-Cutting Requirements

Certain conditions on one federal grant may be extended to all activities supported by federal funds, regardless of their source. The first and most famous of these is Title VI of the 1964 Civil Rights Act, which holds that in the use of federal funds, no person may be discriminated against on the basis of race, color, or national origin. Other laws extend these protections to persons because of gender or handicapped status. More than 60 cross-cutting requirements concern such matters as the environment, historic preservation, contract wage rates, access to governmental information, the care of experimental animals, and the treatment of human subjects in research projects.

Cross-Over Sanctions

These sanctions permit the use of federal dollars in one program to influence state and local policy in another. One example is a 1984 act that threatened to reduce federal highway aid by up to 15 percent for any state that failed to adopt a minimum drinking age of 21 by 1987.

Total Preemption

This kind of control rests not on the national government's power to spend but on its powers under the supremacy and commerce clauses to preempt conflicting state and local activities. Building on this constitutional authority, federal law in certain areas just preempts state and local governments from the field. "There are fourteen types of total preemption laws, ranging from ones removing all regulatory powers from the states to ones authorizing states to cooperate in enforcing a statute."*

Partial Preemption

Sometimes federal law establishes basic policies but requires states to administer them. Some programs give states an option not to participate, but if a state chooses not to do so, the national government then steps in and runs the programs. Even worse from the state's point of view is *mandatory partial preemption,* in which the national government requires the state to act on peril of losing other funds but provides no funds to support the state action. The Clean Air Act of 1990 is an example of mandatory partial preemption; the federal government set national air quality standards and required states to devise plans and pay for their implementation and enforcement.† Medicaid is another example of the national government providing some funds but mandating states to provide services that cost more than the federal funds cover.

*Joseph F. Zimmerman, "Congressional Regulation of Subnational Governments," *P.S.: Political Science and Politics* 26 (June 1993), p. 179.

†Mel Dubnick and Alan Gitelson, "Nationalizing State Policies," in Jerome J. Hanus, ed., *The Nationalization of State Government* (Heath, 1981), pp. 56–57.

The Great Depression of the 1930s stimulated extensive national action on welfare, unemployment, and farm surpluses. World War II brought federal regulation of wages, prices, and employment, as well as national efforts to allocate resources, train personnel, and support engineering and inventions. After the war, the national government helped veterans obtain college degrees and inaugurated a vast system of support for university research. The United States became the most powerful leader of the free world, maintaining substantial military forces even in times of peace. The Great Society programs of the 1960s poured out grants-in-aid to states and localities. City dwellers who had migrated from the rural South to northern cities began to seek federal funds for—at the very least—housing, education, and mass transportation.

Although economic and social conditions created many of the pressures for expansion of the national government, so did political claims. Until federal budget deficits became a hot issue in the 1980s and early 1990s, members of Congress, presidents, federal judges, and federal administrators actively promoted federal initiatives. With the return of more balanced federal budgets and even with deficit spending in 2002 and 2003, Congress appears willing to actively promote some federal programs, at least in the areas of education and homeland security. True, when there is widespread conflict about what to do—how to reduce the federal deficit, adopt a national energy policy, reform Social Security, provide health care for the indigent—Congress waits for a national consensus. But when an organized constituency wants something and there is no counterpressure, Congress "responds often to everyone, and with great vigor."[45] Once established, federal programs generate groups with vested interests in promoting, defending, and expanding them. Associations are formed and alliances are made. "In a word, the growth of government has created a constituency of, by, and for government."[46]

The politics of federalism are changing, however, and Congress is being pressured to reduce the size and scope of national programs. At the same time, the cost of entitlement programs such as Social Security and Medicare are going up because there are more older people and they are living longer. These programs have widespread public support, and to cut them is politically risky. "With all other options disappearing, it is politically tempting to finance tax cuts by turning over to the states many of the social programs . . . that have become the responsibility of the national government."[47]

The Devolution Revolution: Rhetoric Versus Reality

The Republican sweep of Congress in the 1994 elections carried with it a pledge to return many functions, especially welfare, back to the states. President Clinton appeared to agree with the general tone of the Republicans. In his 1996 State of the Union Address, he proclaimed, "The era of big government is over." However, he tempered his comments by saying, "But we cannot go back to the time when our citizens were left to fend for themselves." Congress and the president came together for a major overhaul of welfare and, to a lesser degree, education. Congress also freed the states to set their own highway speed limits, changed the Safe Drinking Water Act to allow states to operate certain programs, and gave states a greater role over how federal rural development funds can be used.

Yet despite these shifts, recent Congresses, like their predecessors, have increased the authority of the national government in many areas. Congress established national criteria for state-issued drivers' licenses, ended state registration of mutual funds, created national food safety standards, nullified state laws restricting telecommunications competition, and made a host of offenses federal crimes, including carjacking and stalking. Appropriation bills pressured states to keep criminals behind bars by threatening to take grants away from states that failed to meet federal standards. The only two major achievements of the devolution revolution remain the 1996 reform of welfare and the repeal of a national speed limit.[48] As one reporter concluded, "The 'devolution' promised by Congressional Republicans . . . has mostly fizzled. Instead of handing over authority to state and local governments, they're taking it away."[49] In the aftermath of the attacks on the World Trade Center and the Pentagon and in confronting the continuing threats of terrorism, the role of the federal government in defending homeland security is certain to continue to expand.

The Future of Federalism

In 1933, during the Great Depression, with state governments helpless, one writer stated, "I do not predict that the states will go, but affirm that they have gone."[50] Such prophets of doom were wrong; the states are stronger than ever. During recent decades, state governments have undergone a major transformation. Most have improved their governmental structures, taken on greater roles in funding education and welfare, launched programs to help distressed cities, and—despite new constitutional limitations—expanded their tax bases. Able men and women have been attracted to the governorship. "Today, states, in formal representational, policy making, and implementation terms at least, are more representative, more responsive, more activist, and more professional in their operations than they ever have been. They face their expanded roles better equipped to assume and fulfill them."[51]

Until the civil rights revolution of the 1960s, segregationists had feared that national officials would work for racial integration. Thus they praised local government, emphasized the dangers of centralization, and argued that the protection of civil rights was not a proper function of the national government. As one political scientist observed, "Federalism has a dark history to overcome. For nearly two hundred years, states' rights have been asserted to protect slavery, segregation, and discrimination."[52]

Today the politics of federalism, even with respect to civil rights, is more complicated than in the past. The national government is not necessarily more favorable to the claims of minorities than state or city governments are. When the Supreme Court did

Although each state has its own Division of Motor Vehicles, which issues drivers' licenses, the federal government now has considerable say in determining the criteria necessary to qualify for a license to operate a motor vehicle.

not extend marital privacy rights to gays and lesbians, Vermont and some other state courts interpreted their state constitutions to provide more protection for these rights than the U.S. Constitution does. However, other states are passing legislation that would eliminate such protections.

As states more actively regulate the economy and as state attorneys general prosecute anticompetitive business practices, as they did in joining the suit against Microsoft in 2000, business interests have been arguing that conflicting state regulations are unduly burdening interstate commerce. They are asking for preemptive federal regulation, barring state taxes on e-commerce, for instance, in order to save them not only from stringent state regulations but also from having to adjust to 50 different state laws. "One national dumb rule is better than 50 inconsistent rules of any kind," says a lawyer who represents trade groups in the food and medical devices industries.[53]

The national government is not likely to retreat to a pre-1930 posture or even a pre-1960 one. Indeed, the underlying economic and social conditions that generated the demand for federal action have been altered substantially by international terrorism. In addition to such traditional issues as helping people find jobs and preventing inflation and depressions—which still require national action—countless new issues have been added to the national agenda by the growth of a global economy based on the information explosion and e-commerce, advancing technologies, and combating international terrorism.

Most Americans have strong attachments to our federal system—in the abstract. They remain loyal to their states and show a growing skepticism about the national government. Some evidence suggests, however, that the anti-Washington sentiment "is 3,000 miles wide but only a few miles deep."[54] The fact is that Americans are pragmatists: We appear to prefer federal-state-local power sharing[55] and are prepared to use whatever level of government necessary to meet our needs and new challenges.

Summary

1. A federal system is one in which the constitution divides powers between the central government and subdivisional governments—states or provinces. Alternatives to federalism are unitary systems, in which all constitutional power is vested in the central government, and confederations, which are loose compacts among sovereign states.

2. Federal systems check the growth of tyranny, allow unity without uniformity, encourage state experimentation, permit power sharing between the national government and the states, and keep government closer to the people.

3. The national government has the constitutional authority, stemming primarily from the national supremacy clause, the war powers, and its powers to regulate commerce among the states to tax and spend, to do what Congress thinks is necessary and proper to promote the general welfare and to provide for the common defense. These constitutional pillars have permitted tremendous expansion of the functions of the federal government.

4. States must give full faith and credit to each other's public acts, records, and judicial proceedings; extend to each others' citizens the privileges and immunities it gives its own; and return fugitives from justice.

5. The federal courts umpire the division of power between the national and state governments. The Marshall Court, in decisions such as *Gibbons* v. *Ogden* and *McCulloch* v. *Maryland,* asserted the power of the national government over the states and promoted a national economic common market. These decisions also reinforced the supremacy of the national government over the states.

6. Today debates about federalism are less often about its constitutional structure than about whether action should come from the national or state and local levels. Recent Supreme Court decisions favor a decentralist position and may presage shifts in the Court's interpretation of the constitutional nature of our federal system.

7. The major instruments of federal intervention in state programs have been various kinds of financial grants-in-aid, of which the most prominent are categorical-formula grants, project grants, and block grants. The national government also imposes federal mandates and controls some activities of state and local governments by other means.

8. Over the past 215 years, power has accrued to the national government, but recently Congress has been pressured to reduce the size and scope of national programs and to shift some existing programs back to the states. Although responsibility for welfare has been turned over to the states, the authority of the national government has increased in many other areas.

Key Terms

devolution revolution	implied powers	concurrent powers	preemption
federalism	necessary and proper clause	full faith and credit clause	centralists
unitary system	inherent powers	extradition	decentralists
confederation	commerce clause	interstate compact	states' rights
express powers	federal mandate	national supremacy	

Further Reading

SAMUEL H. BEER, *To Make a Nation: The Rediscovery of American Federalism* (Harvard University Press, 1993).

CENTER FOR THE STUDY OF FEDERALISM, *The Federalism Report* (published quarterly by Temple University; this publication notes research, books and articles, and scholarly conferences).

CENTER FOR THE STUDY OF FEDERALISM, *Publius: The Journal of Federalism* (published quarterly by Temple University; one issue each year is an "Annual Review of the State of American Federalism"; and has a Web site at www.lafayette.edu/~publius).

TIMOTHY J. CONLAN, *From New Federalism to Devolution: Twenty-Five Years of Intergovernmental Reforms* (Brookings Institution, 1998).

DANIEL J. ELAZER AND JOHN KINCAID, *The Covenant Connection: From Federal Theology to Modern Federalism* (Lexington Books, 2000).

JOHN FEREJOHN AND BARRY WEINGAST, *The New Federalism: Can the States Be Trusted?* (Hoover Institute Press, 1998).

FRANK GOODMAN, ED., *The Supreme Court's Federalism: Real or Imagined?* (Sage, 2001).

ELLIS KATZ AND G. ALAN TARR, EDS., *Federalism and Rights* (Rowman & Littlefield, 1996).

NEIL C. McCABE, ED., *Comparative Federalism in the Devolution Era* (Rowman & Littlefield, 2002).

FORREST McDONALD, *States' Rights and the Union: Imperim in Imperio, 1776–1876* (Univeristy Press of Kansas, 2000).

KALYPSO NICOLAIDIS AND ROBERT HOWSE, EDS., *The Federal Vision: Legitimacy and Levels of Governance in the United States and the European Union* (Oxford University Press, 2001).

DAVID M. O'BRIEN, *Constitutional Law and Politics: Struggles for Power and Governmental Accountability,* 5th ed. (Norton, 2002).

LAURENCE J. O'TOOLE Jr., *American Intergovernmental Relations,* 3d ed. (CQ Press, 2000).

PAUL E. PETERSON, *The Price of Federalism* (Brookings Institution, 1995).

PAUL J. POSNER, *The Politics of Unfunded Mandates: Whither Federalism?* (Georgetown University Press, 1998).

WILLIAM H. RIKER, *The Development of American Federalism* (Academic, 1987).

4

CHAPTER

POLITICAL CULTURE AND IDEOLOGY

OR MANY AMERICANS, THE FIRST EXPERIENCE WITH DEMOCRACY IS A SCHOOL ELECTION, OFTEN IN AN ELEMENTARY SCHOOL. WHAT ARE the expectations of these young voters, and what do these expectations teach us about our political culture? Were we to observe such an election, we would see recurrent patterns. For example, it would be considered unfair if someone suggested that some students' votes count more than others' or that some not be allowed to vote at all. It is likely that the candidates will be asked to speak, and they may even make a few campaign promises. When the votes are counted, the young participants expect the person with the most votes to be elected. These and other elements of our political culture are a central focus of this chapter.

The specifics of a nation's political culture can be discovered not only by what people believe and say but also by how they behave. Political culture is the underlying beliefs, assumptions, attitudes, and patterns of behavior people have toward government and politics. Political culture relates to such fundamental issues as who may participate in political decisions, what rights and liberties citizens have, how decisions are made, and how people view politicians and government generally. Some elements of our political culture—like our fear of concentrated power and our concern with individual liberty—have remained constant over time. In other respects, our political culture has changed from believing that only property-owning men should be allowed to vote to a conviction that all adults should have the right to vote and that participation should include a wider range of political activities. For example, citizens now vote in party primaries to select nominees for office, whereas previously, party leaders determined who would run for office.

The idea of people coming together, listening to each other, exchanging ideas, learning to appreciate each other's differences, and defending their opinions is sometimes called deliberation. Such interaction is thought to build community and relationships in ways that do not happen when citizens only cast ballots. Because of a decline in public participation in town council meetings, community groups, the PTA, labor unions, business associations, and other civic groups, some social scientists, including Harvard professor Robert Putnam, believe that we as a people are losing the skills and learned behaviors people develop in such settings, which help build social capital. Putnam has defined **social capital** as "features of social organization such as networks, norms, and social trust that facilitate coordination and cooperation for mutual benefit."[1] But as we noted in Chapter 1, not all political scientists agree with Putnam's assessment that social capital is in decline.[2] More recently, Putnam found evidence of expanded civic engagement in the weeks after the terrorist attacks of September 11, 2001.[3]

The social capital debate has rekindled an interest in the nature and viability of the American political culture and an examination of how it is changing. Americans have conflicting ideas and beliefs about the proper role of government and where and how political power should be exercised. These attitudes and beliefs, when coherent and consistent, are what political scientists call *ideology*. In this chapter, we look at our political culture and ideology.

The American Political Culture

Political scientists use the term **political culture** to refer to the widely shared beliefs, values, and norms concerning the relationship of citizens to government and to one another.

American political culture centers on democratic values like liberty, equality, individualism, democracy, justice, the rule of law, nationalism, optimism, and idealism. There is no "official" list of American political values, however, and as we noted in Chapter 1, these widely shared democratic values overlap and sometimes conflict.

Shared Values

Before the American and French Revolutions of the late eighteenth century, discussions about individual liberty, freedom, equality, private property, limited government, and popular consent were rare. Europe had been dominated by aristocracies, had experienced centuries of political and social inequality, and had been ruled by governments that were often arbitrary in their exercise of power. Liberal political philosophers rebelled against these traditions and proclaimed the principles of classical liberalism. They claimed individuals have certain **natural rights**—the rights of all people to dignity and worth—and that government, as a primary threat to those rights, must be limited and controlled. During this same period, the economic system was changing from a mercantile to a free market system. People began to think they could improve their lot in life and own property. Radical new ideas like these influenced the thinking of the founders of our nation.

LIBERTY   No value in the American political culture is more revered than liberty. "We have always been a nation obsessed with liberty. Liberty over authority, freedom over responsibility, rights over duties—these are our historic preferences," wrote the late Clinton Rossiter, a noted political scientist. "Not the good man but the free man has been the measure of all things in this sweet 'land of liberty'; not national glory but individual liberty has been the object of political authority and the test of its worth."[4] The predominance of freedom and individualism over virtue and the public good is not universally accepted by students of American thought, and in reality both perspectives are built on some mix of the two views.[5]

EQUALITY   Jefferson's famous words in the Declaration of Independence express the primacy of our views of equality: "We hold these truths to be self-evident, that all men are created equal, that they are endowed by their Creator with certain unalienable rights, that among these are life, liberty, and the pursuit of happiness." Americans

social capital
Democratic and civic habits of discussion, compromise, and respect for differences, which grow out of participation in voluntary organizations.

political culture
The widely shared beliefs, values, and norms concerning the relationship of citizens to government and to one another.

natural rights
The rights of all people to dignity and worth; also called *human rights*.

Values We Share

Americans distrust government: 57 percent think government regulation of business usually does more harm than good, and 64 percent think that when something is run by the government, it is usually inefficient and wasteful.

Americans are more distrustful of the federal government than of local government: 75 percent think the federal government should run only those things that cannot be run at the local level.

Americans are patriotic and share a sense of civic responsibility: 90 percent say they are "very patriotic," 89 percent feel it is their "duty to always vote," and 67 percent think that voting gives them some say in how the government runs things.

Most Americans believe in providing equal opportunity: 91 percent of Americans believe that "our society should do what is necessary to make sure that everyone has an equal opportunity to succeed."

Americans believe that government should help those in need: 61 percent of Americans believe that "it is the responsibility of government to take care of people who can't take care of

themselves," and 62 percent think "the government should guarantee every citizen enough to eat and a place to sleep."

Americans are religious: 88 percent of Americans believe in the existence of God, and 78 percent see prayer as an important part of their daily life.

Americans see family and marriage as important: 85 percent of Americans say they have "old-fashioned values about family and marriage," and 74 percent think "too many children are being raised in day-care centers these days."

Americans distrust large corporations: 73 percent of Americans think "too much power is concentrated in the hands of a few big companies," and 58 percent think "business corporations make too much profit."

Americans are optimistic: 71 percent think that the United States can always find a way to solve our problems and get what we want.

SOURCE: The Pew Research Center for the People and the Press, *Pew Values Update: American Social Beliefs, 1997–98,* April 1998.

have always believed in social equality. In contrast to Europeans, our nation shunned aristocracy, and our Constitution explicitly prohibits governments from granting titles of nobility.

In addition to social equality, Americans belive in *political equality,* the idea that every individual has a right to equal protection under the law and equal voting power. Although political equality has always been a goal, it has not always been a reality. In the past, African Americans, Native Americans, and women were denied the right to vote and otherwise participate in the nation's political life.

Equality encompasses the idea of *equal opportunity,* especially with regard to improving our economic status. Americans believe that social background should not limit our opportunity to achieve to the best of our ability, nor should race, gender, or religion. The nation's commitment to public education programs like Head Start for underprivileged preschool children, state support for public colleges and universities, and federal financial aid for higher education reflect this belief in equal opportunity.

INDIVIDUALISM The United States is characterized by a persistent commitment to the individual. Under our system of government, individuals have both rights and responsibilities. Concern for preserving individual freedom of choice and what limits, if any, to place on individual choice generate intense political conflict. The debate over legalized abortion is often framed in these terms. Although Americans agree with individual rights and freedoms, they also understand that their rights can conflict with another person's rights or with the government's need to maintain order.

RESPECT FOR THE COMMMON PERSON Americans have faith in the common sense and collective wisdom of ordinary people. We prefer action to reflection. We are often anti-expert and sometimes anti-intellectual. The emphasis on practicality and common sense has become part of our national image. Poets like Walt Whitman and Carl Sandburg and storytellers like Mark Twain, Will Rogers, Eudora Welty, and Garrison Keillor have helped shape this tradition. This reverence for the common people helps explain our ambivalence toward power, politics, and government authority. In the United States, government is often viewed as a necessary evil.

DEMOCRATIC CONSENSUS   The most important feature that binds us together is **democratic consensus**, a fairly widespread agreement on fundamental principles of governance and the values that undergird them. We are a people from many different cultural and ethnic backgrounds, histories, and religions. Despite these differences, our political culture includes widely shared attitudes and beliefs about principles of government, procedures, documents, and institutions. Americans have strong opinions about who has power to do what, how people acquire power, and how they are removed from power. These are fundamental "rules of the game" in which widespread consensus is important.

Elements of the democratic consensus are majority rule and popular sovereignty. We believe in **majority rule**—governance according to the expressed preferences of the majority at regular elections. Yet we also believe that people in the minority should be free to try to win majority support for their opinions. Despite the fact that large numbers of Americans lack strong party attachments, we favor a two-party system. Our institutions are based on the principle of representation and consent of the governed. We believe in **popular sovereignty**—that ultimate power resides in the people. Government, from this perspective, exists to serve the people rather than the other way around. The means by which the government learns the will of the people is through *elections*, perhaps the most important expression of popular consent. But there are instances when popular sovereignty and majority rule must be limited by other fundamental rights, as in the case of referendums limiting civil rights.[6] Examples include California's 1964 vote, subsequently overturned, to permit people to discriminate in the sale of residential housing and the same state's 1996 vote to prohibit affirmative action in state governmental bodies, including universities and colleges.

Many of the limits on governments are specified in the Constitution, especially in the first ten amendments (the Bill of Rights) and the Thirteenth, Fourteenth, Fifteenth, and Nineteenth. The Constitution is revered as a national symbol, yet we often differ over the framers' original intentions. We honor many of these rights more in the abstract than in the particular. More than half of us, for instance, think that books with dangerous ideas should be banned from public school libraries (see Table 4-1). Intolerance of dissenting or offensive views is amply demonstrated in many public opinion polls and is observed on college and university campuses. Still, Americans can ordinarily be characterized as affirming support for democratic and constitutional values.

democratic consensus
Widespread agreement on fundamental principles of democratic governance and the values that undergird them.

majority rule
Governance according to the expressed preferences of the majority.

popular sovereignty
A belief that ultimate power resides in the people.

TABLE 4–1 **What Do You Mean by Rights and Freedoms? It Depends . . .**			
	Agree	Disagree	Don't Know*
Freedom of speech should apply to groups such as communists and the Ku Klux Klan.	57%	39%	4%
There has been real improvement in the position of African Americans.	53	38	9
Books that contain dangerous ideas should be banned from public school libraries.	55	43	2
Affirmative action programs to help African American women get better jobs and education should be continued.	65	31	4
The police should be allowed to search the houses of known drug dealers without a court order.	45	53	2
School boards ought to have the right to fire teachers who are known homosexuals.	33	62	4

SOURCE: The Pew Research Center for the People and the Press, *Retro-Politics: The Political Typology*, November 14, 1999.

Includes those who said "neither."

WE THE PEOPLE

Where We Learn the American Political Culture

The Family

One of the important sources of political culture in the United States, as in other nations, is the family. Children are taught from an early age what it means to be an American. They are curious about why people vote, what the president does, and whether Grandpa fought in Vietnam. The questions may vary somewhat from family to family, but the themes of authority, freedom, equality, liberty, and partisanship are common. Families are the most important reference groups, and compared to families in other cultures, American families are much more egalitarian.

The Schools

Public schools are another source of the American political culture. Children and teachers often begin the school day by saluting the flag, reciting the Pledge of Allegiance, or singing the national anthem. Teaching American political and economic values is part of the curriculum. Not only are values taught in American history classes, but they are put into practice in school elections and newspapers and in encouraging students to participate in small-scale economic ventures.

Colleges and universities also play a role in fostering the American political culture. Students who attend college are often more confident than other persons in dealing with bureaucracy and politics generally, more likely to participate in politics and to vote, and more knowledgeable about government. Many states require students at state colleges and universities to take courses in American government or state government, in part to instill a sense of civic duty while imparting knowledge about state and national governance.

Religious and Civic Organizations

Religious freedom and diversity have played a part in the formation and maintenance of the American political culture. American churches, synagogues, and mosques have long fostered a common understanding of right and wrong.

Freedom, including freedom of religion, individualism, pluralism, and civic duty, have all been fostered by churches. As churches do not all take the same positions on political issues, their impact is sometimes mitigated, but they have been important to such major social and political movements as the abolition of slavery, the expansion of civil rights, and opposition to war. Civic organizations like the Boy Scouts, 4-H, League of Women Voters, Rotary Club, and Chamber of Commerce encourage citizen participation and pride in community and nation.

The Mass Media

In modern times, the mass media have taken over some functions previously performed by the family. By the time children leave high school, they will have spent more time watching television than in conversation with their parents. They may have had more political instruction from MTV than from their parents or their schools.

Political Activities

Finally, Americans educate each other about political values in the workplace, at the PTA meeting, or in more expressly political activities.

TABLE 4–2 Satisfaction with the Way Democracy Works

	Satisfied	Dissatisfied
United States	64%	27%
Canada	62	24
Germany	55	27
Iceland	54	23
Thailand	54	27
Costa Rica	52	25
Chile	43	31
France	43	32
Dominican Republic	40	38
United Kingdom	40	43
Japan	35	32
India	32	43
Spain	31	30
Venezuela	28	59
Taiwan	25	18
Hungary	17	50
Mexico	17	67

SOURCE: "People Throughout the World Largely Satisfied with Personal Lives," *Gallup Poll,* June 1995, p. 6.

American dream
The widespread belief that the United States is a land of opportunity and that individual initiative and hard work can bring economic success.

capitalism
An economic system characterized by private property, competitive markets, economic incentives, and limited government involvement in the production and pricing of goods and services.

JUSTICE AND THE RULE OF LAW   Inscribed over the entrance to the U.S. Supreme Court are the words "Equal Justice Under Law." The rule of law means that government is based on a body of law applied equally and by just procedures, as opposed to rule by an elite whose whims decide policy or resolve disputes. Chief Justice John Marshall succinctly summarized this principle: "The government of the United States has been emphatically termed a government of laws, not of men."[7] Americans believe strongly in the principle of fairness: All individuals are entitled to the same legal rights and protections.

For government to adhere to the rule of law, its policies and laws should follow these five rules:

- *Generality:* Laws should be stated generally, not singling out any group or individual.
- *Prospectivity:* Laws should apply to the future, not punish something someone did in the past.
- *Publicity:* Laws cannot be kept secret and then enforced.
- *Authority:* Valid laws are made by those with legitimate power, and the people legitimate that power through some form of popular consent.
- *Due process:* Laws must be enforced impartially with fair processes.

NATIONALISM, OPTIMISM, AND IDEALISM   Americans are highly nationalistic, sharing a sense of values and identity. This nationalism was reinforced by the terrorist attacks of 2001, which illustrated that unity under threat is a widely shared value. As President George W. Bush said, "We are a different country than we were on September 10th: sadder and less innocent; stronger and more united; and in the face of ongoing threats, determined and courageous."[8] We are proud of our past and our role in the world today. We are optimistic, though more about people than about government.

We believe in opportunity, choice, individualism, and most of all, the freedom to improve ourselves and to achieve success with as little interference as possible from others or from government. As Table 4-2 indicates, U.S. citizens are more satisfied with their democratic government than the citizens of other countries.

We know that our system is not perfect, yet we have an abiding faith in government by the people. We often grumble that elected officials have lost touch with us, we are disgusted by scandals, and we are impatient with the slowness of the system to solve problems like health care, crime, drug abuse, and terrorism. Despite the dissatisfactions, a remarkable belief persists that this nation is better, stronger, and more virtuous than other nations. Like every country, the United States has interests and motives that are selfish as well as generous, cynical as well as idealistic. Still, our support of human needs and rights throughout the world is evidence of an enduring idealism.

The American Dream

Many of our political values come together in the **American dream**, a complex set of ideas holding that the United States is a land of opportunity and that individual initiative and hard work can bring economic success. Whether realized or not, this American dream speaks to our most deeply held hopes and goals. The essence of the American dream can be found in our enthusiasm for **capitalism**, an economic system characterized by private property, competitive markets, economic incentives, and limited government involvement in the production and pricing of goods and services.

The concept of *private property* enjoys extraordinary popularity. In many European democracies, the state owns and operates transportation systems and other businesses that are privately owned and operated in the United States, although there has been some privatization of communications systems like telephone companies and broadcast media. Americans cherish the dream of acquiring property. Moreover, most Americans believe that the owners of property have the right to decide how to use it.

Oprah Winfrey: Achieving the American Dream

Is the American Dream a reality? If you don't think so, ask Oprah Winfrey. Born in Kosciusko, Mississippi, in 1954 to parents who never married, Oprah had a less than ideal childhood. At age 6, she moved from her grandmother's farm in Mississippi to live with her mother in Wisconsin. At age 12, a family member sexually molested her. Later she attempted to run away from home. To avoid being put in a detention center, she was sent to live with her father in Nashville.

Under her father's direction, Oprah began to straighten out her life. She enrolled in Tennessee State University but dropped out during her sophomore year to become the first African American anchor for Nashville's WTVF-TV. She moved to Baltimore to anchor a TV news broadcast and was later fired. But she found her niche as host of a Baltimore morning talk show. Building on this success, she moved to Chicago and hosted *A.M. Chicago,* which was later syndicated as *The Oprah Winfrey Show.*

Today Oprah Winfrey is a household name and for many Americans a household personality. She has amassed a net worth of over a half a billion dollars, owns her own production company, and has her own women's magazine. She has starred in several films and was nominated for an Academy Award for her role in *The Color Purple.* She has even been active in the political arena. In 1994, Bill Clinton signed into law the "Oprah Bill," federal legislation to protect children from abuse.

Coming from humble beginnings, Oprah Winfrey—television host, movie actress, and one of the highest-paid people in the country—epitomizes the American dream.

SOURCE: Deborah Tannen, "The T.V. Host Oprah Winfrey," www.time.com/time/time100/artists/profile/winfrey.html; "Oprah Winfrey: The Real Story," *Bibliobytes, 2000,* www.bb.com/looptestlive.cfm?BOOKID=1581&StartRow=1.

The right to private property is just one of the economic incentives that cement our support for capitalism and fuel the American dream. This is the land of opportunity for the enterprising. Here the competitive, practical go-getter can make a fortune, build a dream home, and retire early. We assume that people who have more ability or who work extremely hard will get ahead, earn more, and enjoy economic rewards. We also believe that people should be able to pass most of what they have accumulated along to their children and relatives. Even the poorest Americans generally oppose high inheritance taxes or limits on how much someone can earn. Americans believe that the free market system gives almost everyone a fair chance, that capitalism is necessary, and that freedom depends on it. We reject communism and socialism—a rejection fortified in recent years as most communist nations shifted toward capitalism. In the United States, individuals and corporations have acquired wealth and, at the same time, exercised political clout. Their power has in turn bred some resentment. The Enron Corporation, for example, made over $2 million in political contributions in the 2000 election cycle, and between January 1, 1995, and June 30, 2001, Enron ranked among the top 15 political soft-money donors.[9] Enron later filed for bankruptcy and became a widely criticized example of corporate mismanagement and accounting problems.[10]

The conflict in values between a *competitive economy,* in which individuals reap large rewards for their initiative and hard work, and an *egalitarian society,* in which everyone earns a decent living, carries over into politics. How the public resolves this tension changes over time and from issue to issue.

As important as the American dream is to the national consciousness, Americans know it remains unfulfilled. An underclass persists in the form of impoverished families, ill-nourished and poorly educated children, and people living on the streets.[11] Many cities are actually two cities, where some residents live in luxury while others live in squalor. The gap between rich and poor has grown in recent years, and a sharp difference between white and black income persists tenaciously.[12] For more people than we want to admit, chances for success still depend on the family you were born in, the neighborhood you grew up in, or the college you attended.

Political and Economic Change

Political values are clearly affected by historical developments and by economic and technological growth. The Declaration of Independence and the Constitution identified such important political values as individual liberty, property rights, and limited government.[13] Early in our history, we emphasized separation of powers, checks and balances, states' rights, and the Bill of Rights. It took an additional generation or two before we also began to take seriously the expansion of suffrage and competitive nominations and elections. Notions of political equality and effective participation emerged during the presidency of Andrew Jackson and matured in the course of the nineteenth century. By the end of the nineteenth century, populists and suffragists turned ideals into action and formed large-scale movements to achieve more democratic forms of participation and more responsive forms of governance.

THE INDUSTRIAL TRANSFORMATION   By 1900, the agrarian society the framers knew had largely been replaced by industrial capitalism and the growth of giant corporations. With these changes, ideology was irreversibly transformed. Large privately owned corporations changed the economic order, including changes in the role of government and how people viewed each other. No one captures the implications of this shift better than political scientist Robert A. Dahl:

> One of the consequences of the new order has been a high degree of inequality in the distribution of wealth and income, and far greater inequality than had ever been thought likely or desirable under an agrarian order by Democratic Republicans like Jefferson and Madison, or had ever been thought consistent with democratic or republican government in the historic writings on the subject from Aristotle to Locke, Montesquieu, and Rousseau. Previous theorists and advocates had, like many of the framers of our own Constitution, insisted that a republic could exist only if the citizen body continued neither rich nor poor. Citizens, it was argued, must enjoy a rough equality of conditions.[14]

The success of the American economy led to the accumulation of great wealth in the hands of a few—the "robber barons" or tycoons. Many had taken great risks or earned their fortunes through inventions and efficient production practices. But as disparities of income grew, so did disparities in political resources. Economic resources can be converted into political resources, as when time is spent on political campaigns and money is contributed to parties and candidates.[15] At the turn of the twentieth century, the rise of the corporations and the concentration of individual wealth in the United States created divisions and resentment. Muckraking journalists charged that the huge corporations had become **monopolies**, using their dominance of their industry to exploit workers and limit competition. Unsafe work conditions led to some regulation of the workplace by the states, but only the national government, it seemed, had the power to ensure fair treatment in the marketplace. This sentiment not only gave rise to the nation's first **antitrust legislation**— federal laws that try to prevent monopolies from dominating an industry and restraining

monopoly
Domination of an industry by a single company by fixing prices and discouraging competition; also, the company that dominates the industry by these means.

antitrust legislation
Federal laws (starting with the Sherman Act of 1890) that try to prevent a monopoly from dominating an industry and restraining trade.

trade—but also sowed the idea that the national government could—and should—as the Constitution asserts, "promote the general Welfare" by regulating working conditions, product safety, and labor-management disputes.

THE GREAT DEPRESSION AND THE NEW DEAL   Much of our thinking about the role of government in a capitalistic system was shaped by the Great Depression of the 1930s and the near collapse of the capitalistic system. Unrestrained capitalism and an unregulated market were faulted as causes of the Depression. The collapse of the stock market, massive unemployment, and a failed banking system caused widespread suffering among the nation's citizens. Americans had no unemployment compensation, no guarantee on bank savings, no federal regulation of the securities exchanges, and no Social Security. People turned to the government to improve the lot of millions of jobless and homeless citizens. Beginning with President Franklin D. Roosevelt's New Deal, the idea gradually gained widespread acceptance that governments, at both the national and state levels, should use their powers and resources to ensure some measure of equal opportunity and social justice.

Roosevelt's State of the Union Address in 1944 outlined a "Second Bill of Rights" for all citizens in which he declared that this nation must make a firm commitment to "economic security and independence." Included in his Second Bill of Rights were the following:

- The right to a useful and remunerative job in the industries, shops, farms, or mines of the nation
- The right to earn enough to provide adequate food and clothing and recreation
- The right of every farmer to raise and sell his products at a return that would give him and his family a decent living
- The right of every businessman, large and small, to trade in an atmosphere of freedom from unfair competition and domination by monopolies at home or abroad
- The right of every family to a decent home
- The right to adequate medical care and the opportunity to achieve and enjoy good health
- The right to adequate protection from the economic fears of old age, sickness, accident, and unemployment
- The right to a good education[16]

Breadlines like this provided handouts of food to thousands of unemployed and destitute people during the Great Depression.

Senator Ted Kennedy (D.-Mass) has been a champion of liberal programs and legislation for many years. He is shown here at a press conference on Capitol Hill urging Secretary of Labor Elaine Chao to fulfill her stated commitment to worker safety and health by developing an ergonomics standard.

Roosevelt's policies and later efforts by Presidents John F. Kennedy and Lyndon B. Johnson in the 1960s to pass civil rights and voting rights legislation and launch a "war on poverty" defined the ideological and political fights of the second half of the twentieth century. Modern-day liberalism and conservatism turn, in large measure, on how much one believes in Roosevelt's Second Bill of Rights and how much government assistance one thinks is owed to minorities, women, and others who have suffered discrimination or have been left behind by the industrial or technological revolutions of the twentieth century.

Today, free enterprise is no longer unbridled. Government regulations, antitrust laws, job safety regulations, environmental standards, and minimum wage laws all balance freedom of enterprise against the rights of individuals. Most people today support a semi-regulated or mixed free enterprise system that checks the worst tendencies of capitalism, but they reject excessive government intervention (see Table 4-3). Much of American politics centers on how to achieve this balance. Currently, liberals and conservatives agree that some governmental intervention is necessary to assist Americans who fall short in the competition for education and economic prosperity.

Political Ideology and Attitudes Toward Government

Political ideology refers to a consistent pattern of ideas or beliefs about political values and the role of government. It includes the views people have about how government should work and how it actually works. Ideology links our basic values to the day-to-day operations or policies of government.

Two major schools of political ideology dominate American politics: *liberalism* and *conservatism*. Three lesser schools of thought, *socialism, environmentalism,* and *libertarianism,* also help define the spectrum of ideology in the United States. Table 4-4 provides a general distribution of political ideology in the United States.

Liberalism

In the seventeenth and eighteenth centuries, classical liberals fought to minimize the role of government. They stressed individual rights and perceived government as the primary threat to rights and liberties. Classical liberals favored *limited government* and sought ample protections from governmental harassment. Over time, the emphasis on individualism remained constant, but the perception of the need for government changed.

political ideology
A consistent pattern of beliefs about political values and the role of government.

TABLE 4–3 **Attitudes on Business and Welfare**			
	Agree	Disagree	Don't Know*
There is too much power concentrated in the hands of a few big companies.	74%	25%	1%
Business corporations make too much profit.	56	38	6
Regulation of business does more harm than good.	55	37	8
It is the responsibility of the government to take care of people who can't take care of themselves.	62	35	3
The government should help more needy people even if it means going deeper into debt.	49	47	4
The government should guarantee every citizen enough to eat and a place to sleep.	64	33	2

SOURCE: The Pew Research Center for the People and the Press, *Retro-Politics: The Political Typology,* November 14, 1999.

Includes those who said "neither."

TABLE 4–4 Differences in Political Ideology

	Conservative	Moderate	Liberal
Sex			
Male	39%	45%	16%
Female	25	55	20
Race			
White	34	46	20
Black	10	78	12
Age			
18–34	19	58	24
35–45	37	44	18
46–55	35	44	21
56–64	36	55	10
65+	32	52	16
Religion			
Protestant	37	51	12
Catholic	25	55	20
Jewish	18	64	18
Education			
Less than high school	11	80	9
High school diploma	23	66	11
Some college	32	43	25
Bachelor's degree	44	34	21
Advanced degree	41	39	20
Party			
Democrat	15	54	31
Independent	26	58	16
Republican	71	24	6

SOURCE: Center for Political Studies, University of Michigan, *American National Election Study,* 2000.

Note: We have combined with the moderates persons who do not know their ideology or had not thought much about it. For party identification, we have combined Independent leaners with their respective parties. Rows may not add up to 100 percent due to rounding.

CONTEMPORARY LIBERALS   In its current American usage, **liberalism** refers to a belief in the positive uses of government to bring about justice and equality of opportunity. Modern-day liberals wish to preserve the rights of the individual and the right to own private property, yet they are willing to have the government intervene in the economy to remedy the defects of capitalism. Liberals advocate equal access to health care, housing, and education for all citizens. They generally believe in affirmative action programs, workers' health and safety protections, tax rates that rise with income, and unions' rights to organize and strike.

On a more philosophical level, liberals generally believe in the probability of progress. They believe that the future will be better, that obstacles can be overcome. This positive set of beliefs may explain their willingness to trust government programs. Modern liberals contend that modern technology and industrialization cry out for government programs to offset the loss of liberties suffered by the poor and the weak. Liberals such as Edward Kennedy, Hillary Rodham Clinton, Paul Wellstone, and Jesse Jackson frequently stress the need for an involved and affirmative government.

Liberals charge that conservatives usually act out of self-interest and follow the maxim "Let the government take care of the rich, and the rich will in turn take care of the

liberalism
A belief in the positive uses of government to bring about justice and equality of opportunity.

Enron: Will Business Failure Result in Reregulation?

How could the seventh-largest corporation in the United States, known for high profits and solid political connections, fall into bankruptcy in a matter of months, see its stock fall from $90 in August 2000 to 28 cents 15 months later? How could its corporate leaders transform from icons of entrepreneurial success to witnesses before congressional committees claiming Fifth Amendment protection against self-incrimination? All of this happened to the Enron Corporation, a Texas-based energy company. Enron's growth and early success was enhanced by the government's policy of energy deregulation. At its peak, the company was seen as a leader in corporate governance and was successful enough to help fund the new Houston baseball stadium, Enron Field.

The Demise of Enron

What went wrong at Enron? One problem was that Enron, in an effort to appear more profitable to investors, set up sham partnerships that allowed it to remove debt-ridden portions of the company from Enron's bottom line. Another problem was that many employees invested most or all of their retirement savings in Enron stock, a practice encouraged by the company's policy and leadership. When Enron's stock value plummeted, so did the retirement savings of many employees, and some lost virtually all their financial assets. The fact that corporate leaders at Enron were issuing misleadingly positive reports of the company's performance at the same time that they were cashing in their own stock only added to the controversy surrounding the company.

Where Were the Accountants?

The image of accountants shredding documents is also part of the Enron story. Arthur Andersen, one of the so-called Big Five accounting firms in the United States, was presumably auditing the Enron books and reporting the company's financial status objectively to investors and the public. Yet Andersen overlooked or failed to catch the financial shenanigans that were taking place. As the story of the collapse of Enron broke Andersen employees reportedly shredded documents, in an apparent effort to destroy incriminating evidence. These mistakes damaged Andersen's reputation and prompted Congress to impose sweeping reforms of the way accounting firms do business.

Deregulation and Reform

The Enron and Andersen failures have revived a long-standing debate about the role of government in regulating corporations. Some, like former Treasury Secretary Paul O'Neil, see the Enron collapse as part of free market economics: "Companies come and go. It's part of the genius of capitalism."* This view implies that it is the investors' responsibility to beware of possible failures. Others see in the Enron case a need for more meaningful regulation of accounting firms and corporations, especially in conflict of interest situations like those faced by Andersen and in prohibiting the use of partnerships to hide from investors the real profitability of publicly traded corporations. Finally, the Enron collapse may lead to reform of pension systems.

*Dana Milbank, "Bush Aide Was Told of Enron's Plea," *Washington Post*, January 14, 2002, p. A4.

poor." Liberals prefer that government take care of the weak, for the strong can always take care of themselves. "We have rejected the discredited theory that the fortunes of the nation should be in the hands of a privileged few," said President Harry Truman. "Instead, we believe that our economic system should rest on a democratic foundation and that wealth should be created for the benefit of all. . . . Every segment of our population and every individual has a right to expect from his government a fair deal."[17]

Equality of opportunity is viewed by liberals as essential, and to achieve that end, liberals believe that discriminatory practices must be eliminated. Some liberals favor the reduction of great inequalities of wealth that make equality of opportunity impossible. Most favor a certain minimum level of income. Rather than placing a cap on wealth, they want a floor placed beneath the poor. In short, liberals seek to lessen the impact of great inequalities of wealth and work to extend opportunities to all, regardless of their economic standing. If you are interested in learning more about the liberal ideology you may find www.prospect.org or www.turnleft.com/liberal.html helpful.

CRITICISMS OF LIBERALISM   Critics of liberalism say that liberals place too much reliance on governmental solutions, higher taxes, and bureaucracy. These opponents argue that somewhere along the line, liberals forgot that government, to serve our best interests, has to be limited. Power tends to corrupt, and too much dependence on government can corrupt the spirit, undermine self-reliance, and make people forget those cherished personal freedoms and property rights our Republic was founded to secure and protect. Too many governmental regulations and too much taxation tend to undermine the self-help ethic that "made America great." In short, critics of liberalism contend that the welfare and regulatory state pushed by liberals will ultimately destroy individual initiative, the entrepreneurial spirit, and the very engine of economic growth that might lead to true equality of economic opportunity.

In recent elections, Republicans have made liberalism a villain while at the same time have attempted to position their presidential candidates more in the mainstream. George Bush, in 1988, consistently referred to Michael Dukakis as from the "liberal Democratic party." Bill Clinton was careful not to label his program as liberal, focusing on the need for economic growth, jobs, and a lower budget deficit. He insisted he was a "New Democrat." Al Gore positioned himself in the tradition of Clinton as a centrist, not a liberal, but George W. Bush charged that Gore was an advocate of big government. The same charge was leveled against congressional Democratic candidates in 2002 by their Republican opponents and their allied interest groups.

The movement to the center by some Democrats and the conventional wisdom that liberal or progressive approaches are in decline is disputed by political commentator E. J. Dionne Jr., whose book on how progressives can regain power is aptly titled *They Only Look Dead.* Dionne contends that the current political upheaval should be defined less as a revolt against *big* government than as a rebellion against *bad* government—government that has proved ineffectual in grappling with the political, economic, and moral crises that have shaken the country. Dionne challenges the claims that big government is bad or even over. Pointing to past progressive or liberal successes, Dionne contends Americans want a government that eases economic transitions, helps "preserve a broad middle class," and "expands the choices available to individuals."[18]

The popularity of liberalism and conservatism and the importance of particular issues change with world events. For a time, we were preoccupied with budget deficits. With the end of the cold war, we became more concerned about domestic policy than about foreign policy. Policy concerns changed with the terrorist attacks of September 11, 2001, and the war on terrorism that followed. Budget deficits replaced projected surpluses, and Americans became focused on places like Afghanistan, North Korea, Iraq, and Iran, or what President George W. Bush called the "Axis of Evil."[19]

The 2002 midterm election was a referendum on President George W. Bush's popularity. Because of his high approval, the President, along with the First Lady, Vice President Cheney, and former New York Mayor Rudy Giuliani, campaigned aggressively for Republican candidates. Congressional consideration of a possible war with Iraq and sniper shootings in the Washington, D. C. area in October 2002 diverted attention from the economy, education, and other issues important to voters in the 2002 campaign.

Grover Norquist, head of Americans for Tax Reform, is a major proponent of lowering federal, state, and local taxes. Conservatives believe that by lowering taxes, people will have more money to invest in the economy and to donate to charitable organizations.

Conservatism

Private property rights and belief in free enterprise are cardinal attributes of contemporary **conservatism**. In contrast to liberals, conservatives want to enhance individual liberty by keeping government small, especially the national government, except in the area of national defense. Conservatives take a more pessimistic view of human nature than liberals do. They maintain that people need strong leadership institutions, firm laws, and strict moral codes to keep their appetites under control. Government, they think, needs to ensure order. Conservatives also believe that people who fail in life are in some way the architects of their own misfortune and must bear the main responsibility for solving their own problems. Conservatives prefer a reversal of laws on judicial rulings permitting abortion, affirmative action programs, and various worker protection laws.

TRADITIONAL CONSERVATIVES   Traditional conservatives are emphatically pro-business. They oppose higher taxes and resist all but the most necessary antitrust, trade, and environmental regulations on corporations. They believe that the functions of government should be to protect the nation from foreign enemies, preserve law and order, enforce private contracts, foster competitive markets, encourage free and fair trade, and promote family values. Traditional conservatives favor dispersing power broadly throughout the political and social systems to avoid concentration of power at the national level. They favor having the market, rather than the government, provide services.

Until recent decades, conservatives opposed the New Deal programs of the 1930s, the War on Poverty in the 1960s, and many civil rights and affirmative action programs.

conservatism
A belief that limited government ensures order, competitive markets, and personal opportunity.

Event hosts Courtney Cox Arquette, Lisa Kudrow, and Jennifer Aniston arrive at the 10th Annual Fire & Ice Ball, an event that raises funds for the Revlon–UCLA Women's Cancer Research Program. Conservatives believe that social problems, poverty, and health issues should be addressed by private individuals and private institutions and not by the government.

Human needs, they say, can and should be taken care of by families and charities. Conservatives are more inclined to put their faith in the private sector and dislike the tendency to turn to government, especially the national government, for solutions to societal problems. Government social activism, they say, has been expensive and counterproductive. They prefer private giving and individual voluntary efforts targeted at social and economic problems rather than government programs. As noted, conservatives have come to see some social problems as needing a government response. They differ from liberals in the extent to which they see problems this way and in a preference for state and local government over national government activity when a government response is needed.

Conservatives, especially when in office, selectively advocate government activism, often while continuing to criticize government generally. Early in the 2000 presidential campaign, for example, George W. Bush said, "Too often, my party has confused the need for a limited government with a disdain for government itself." Love of country, he said, "is undermined by sprawling, arrogant, aimless government. It is restored by focused and effective and energetic government."[20] To learn more about conservative beliefs, go to www.conservativedigest.net and www.aei.org.

SOCIAL CONSERVATIVES   Some conservatives focus less on economics and more on morality and lifestyle. Social conservatives favor strong governmental action to protect children from pornography and drugs. They want stringent limits on abortions. This brand of conservatism—sometimes called the New Right, ultraconservatism, or even the Radical Right—emerged in the 1980s. The New Right shares the traditional conservative's love of freedom and backs an aggressive effort to defend America's interests abroad. It favors the return of organized prayer in public schools and opposes policies like job quotas, busing, and tolerance of homosexuality. In sum, a defining characteristic of the New Right is a strong desire to impose various *social controls.*

A New Right or Religious Right group that supports social conservatism includes among others, Pat Robertson, a minister who sponsors a nightly cable television program. Robertson's Christian Coalition was a major political force in the 1980s and early 1990s but has weakened in recent years.[21] Although ostensibly working in a bipartisan fashion, it is more at home in the Republican party. The Coalition endorses candidates who are profamily, antiabortion, and antigay. It favors a constitutional amendment that would guarantee the rights to organized prayer in public schools and religious symbols in public places.

Some conservatives are uncomfortable with the close association between the Republican party and the Christain Right. Former U.S. Senator Warren Rudman of New Hampshire has observed, "Politically speaking, the Republican Party is making a terrible mistake if it appears to ally itself with the Christian right. There are some fine, sincere people in its ranks, but there are also enough anti-abortion zealots, would-be censors, homophobes, bigots, and latter-day Elmer Gantrys to discredit any party that is unwise enough to embrace such a group."[22] Rudman's statement was later used to justify phone calls by Robertson to Christian Coalition members urging them to vote for George W. Bush in the 2000 South Carolina and Michigan primaries instead of for John McCain, whose campaign Rudman co-chaired.[23]

CRITICISMS OF CONSERVATISM   Not everyone agreed with Ronald Reagan's statement that "government is the problem." Indeed, critics of conservatism point out that conservatives themselves urge more government when it serves their needs—regulating pornography and abortion, for example—but are opposed to it when it serves somebody else's. Hence conservative opposition to government is selective and inconsistent.

Conservatives place great faith in the market economy—critics would say too much faith. This posture often puts conservatives at odds with labor unions and consumer activists and in close alliance with businesspeople, particularly large corporations. Hostility to regulation and a belief in competition leads them to push for deregulation. This approach has not always had the intended positive effects, as the collapse of many savings and loan companies in the 1980s, the energy crisis in California in the early 2000s, and the business and accounting failures at Enron and other major corporations in 2002 revealed.[24] Conservatives counter that relying on market solutions and encouraging the free market are still the best course of action in most policy areas.

The Reagan administration policy of lowering taxes was consistent with the conservative hostility to big government. Many conservatives embraced the idea that if taxes are lowered on the rich, their increased economic activity will "trickle down" to the poor. This view was criticized by many Democrats, who pointed out that the growth in income and wealth in the 1980s was largely concentrated among the well-to-do.[25] They also pointed out that reduced taxes and increased government spending, especially for defense, tripled the deficit during the 1980s, when conservatives were in control.

Liberals charge that some conservatives repeatedly fail to acknowledge and endorse policies that deal with racism and sexism. Their opposition to civil rights laws in the 1960s and to affirmative action more recently is cited. Not only did some conservatives oppose new laws in these areas, liberals charge, they hampered the executive branch and sought to limit the courts implementation of civil rights laws.

The selective application of government by liberals and social conservatives demonstrates the lack of consistency by some in both groups. Liberals favor vigorous governmental programs to help the poor but oppose governmental intrusion into people's private lives to protect our national security, while some social conservatives preach less government except when they consider it necessary to counter drugs, pornography, and other social evils.

Bernard Sanders, a self-described Socialist, represents Vermont in the U.S. House of Representatives as an Independent.

Socialism

Socialism is an economic and governmental system based on public ownership of the means of production and exchange. Karl Marx once described socialism as a transitional stage of society between capitalism and communism. In a capitalist system, the means of production and most property are privately owned; in a communist system, property is controlled by the state in common for all the people, and the government is in charge of a single political party representing the working classes, with no opposition allowed. Communist countries like Cuba are ruled by one party, the Communist party. Some countries, like Sweden, have combined some aspects of government ownership and operation of businesss with democracy. Others have experimented with socializing medicine and telecommunications while keeping other economic sectors private.

In one of the most dramatic transformations in recent times, Russia, its sister republics, and its former eastern European satellites abandoned communism in the early 1990s and have been attempting to establish free markets. These countries had previously had a system of state ownership and centralized government planning of the economy. But political and economic failure in the Soviet Union resulted in the disintegration of its communist leadership and its empire. Once central power was loosened over the Soviet republics and satellites, a tide of political and economic reform left communism intact in only a few countries, such as Cuba and China.

American socialists—of whom there are only a few prominent examples—favor a greatly expanded role for the government but argue that such a system is compatible with democracy. They would nationalize certain industries, institute a public jobs program so that all who want work would be put to work, place a much steeper tax burden on the wealthy, and drastically cut defense spending.[26] Most of the democracies of western Europe are more influenced by socialist ideas than we are in the United States, but they remain, like the United States, largely market economies. Many countries appear to be turning to market solutions for problems once assumed to be the responsibility of government. Debate will continue about the proper role of government and what the market can do better than government can.[27]

socialism
An economic and governmental system based on public ownership of the means of production and exchange.

PEOPLE DEBATE

IDEOLOGY

The ideological left and right have very different views about government's role in citizens' lives. Pete DuPont, a "contemporary conservative" and Mitchell Cohen, a proponent of "social democracy," discuss their political values and beliefs about government's preferred role.

Conservative Manifesto

Pete DuPont

Former governor of Delaware and Republican presidential candidate Pete DuPont is a strong advocate for what he calls "contemporary conservatism." According to DuPont, conservatives are troubled by the inability of many individuals to accept the responsibility that living independently and morally in a free society entails.

Pointing to the Declaration of Independence, which states that "that all men are created equal, that they are endowed by their creator with certain unalienable rights," DuPont asserts that people receive their rights from God rather than from government. The problem is that today's government has unnecessarily restricted rights and freedoms by regulating the economy and replacing private initiative with publicly financed social programs. These actions have encouraged many individuals to abandon responsibility for their own welfare in favor of dependence on government programs. DuPont asserts that "even in America, amid the greatest success of political and economic freedom in the history of the world, generations of central social and economic planning have finally fostered a new culture—a culture of dependency, rampant crime, single parenthood, broken families, tribal-like group competition, and a turn away from personal responsibility." Human beings, in the conservative view, are competitive and individualistic. Like many conservatives, DuPont applauds the open marketplace in which people can establish their own businesses and compete freely to build enterprises that contribute to the general welfare of society. Conservatives enjoy the exhilaration of risk and competition. They find personal dignity in facing adversity with courage and overcoming obstacles with determination. They find personal irresponsibility and immorality to be the two most negative features of human nature. Irresponsible people rely on government or private handouts or resort to crime to meet their needs; immoral people have extramarital affairs and desert their families in their pursuit of pleasure.

What, then, is the conservative vision of the good society? DuPont repeatedly emphasizes strength as he identifies explicit principles for creating a prosperous and just society. Conservatives would (1) strengthen our national defense by increasing the military forces and improving technology; (2) strengthen law enforcement by building more prisons, reinvigorating drug enforcement programs, and reaffirming the public's right to own firearms; (3) strengthen our economy by reducing taxes, minimizing government regulation of business, abolishing affirmative action programs, and paring down social programs such as health and welfare subsidies; and (4) strengthen families by making divorce and abortion more difficult and allowing families to select the schools their children will attend.

SOURCE: "Conservative Manifesto," *National Review,* March 21, 1994, pp. 32–38.

environmentalism
An ideology that is dominated by concern for the environment but also promotes grassroots democracy, social justice, equal opportunity, nonviolence, respect for diversity, and feminism.

Environmentalism

An intense concern with the environment and related matters is **environmentalism**, an ideology that has taken root in several democracies in recent decades. The so-called Green movement has elected members of parliament in Finland, Germany, Switzerland, Sweden, Luxembourg, Austria, and the Netherlands and is part of the liberal-left coalition governing Germany today. In the United States, the Green party emphasizes such values as grassroots democracy, social justice, equal opportunity, nonviolence, respect for diversity, and feminism. In these areas, environmentalism is little different from liberalism, but it is in the emphasis on ecology and the environment that Greens are distinct.

Why I'm Still Left

Mitchell Cohen

Mitchell Cohen, an editor of *Dissent* magazine, offers a different vision: one of American liberalism (or "social democracy," as he calls it). He explains that he uses the word "left" in order to identify with three "entwined" ideas: "liberty, equality, and solidarity." Conservatives, he says, have distorted what it means to be "liberal" or "left" and have tried to give these words negative connotations. Cohen maintains that at the heart of leftist values are democracy and social justice. This does not mean creating a utopia in which all people are forced to be equal. It does, however, include "siding with working people and the dispossessed, especially against private economic power." He hopes to convince people that "democracy ought to pervade socioeconomic in addition to political domains of life so that . . . the conditions for the freedom of one would be the conditions for the freedom of all."

Cohen insists that when conservatives claim that all people are equally free to pursue opportunity in our society, this is a myth. Citizens don't begin life at the same starting place. Our "free market" economy is in fact highly undemocratic because of the power of corporations and the advantages enjoyed by the upper social strata. People are not actually born with equal resources. We are born into a world in which some possess considerable advantages and many others are at a disadvantage. Cohen writes (following philosopher John Rawls) that "our parents are a matter of chance, not choice. Unless you can be said to have rated your progenitors, why should advantages or disabilities that attend accidents of birth be translated into social privileges?" He points to national income data that indicate that the top 20 percent of the population has nine times as much wealth as the bottom 20 percent. This imbalance, he believes, is inherently unjust. Cohen also thinks that conservatives are too one-sided when they say that people are competitive, "rugged individualists" by nature. Cohen argues that we are "social individuals" who want freedom but who also feel solidarity with other human beings. So while Cohen believes that markets are an important part of economic life, he also contends that they need to be regulated on behalf of broader human values. Cohen advocates an "equality-friendly society" and "social citizenship." He wants to ensure equal access to education and health care and to restrain the power of large corporations. According to Cohen, a healthy political democracy requires economic democracy.

SOURCE: Mitchell Cohen, "Why I'm Still Left," *Dissent* 44 (Spring 1997), pp. 43–50.

1. Which specific value is most important to DuPont and Cohen, and why do you think that is so?
2. What are the underlying assumptions that each author makes in his argument?
3. What is the most important omission or flaw in DuPont's and Cohen's thinking?

The Web site of the U.S. Green party says, "We must practice agriculture which replenishes the soil; move to an energy-efficient economy; and live in ways that respect the integrity of natural systems."[28] In 2004, Green party candidate David Cobb, lacking the visibility or stature of Ralph Nader, received less than one-tenth of one percent of the vote. Many environmental groups supported John Kerry in the 2004 election.

Libertarianism

Libertarianism is a political ideology that cherishes individual liberty and insists on sharply limited government. It carries some overtones of anarchism, of the classical English liberalism of the past, and of a 1930s-style conservatism. The Libertarian party has

libertarianism
An ideology that cherishes individual liberty and insists on a sharply limited government, promoting a free market economy, a noninterventionist foreign policy, and an absence of regulation in the moral and social spheres.

Harry Browne, Libertarian candidate for president in 1996 and 2000, was on the ballot in all 50 states but received less than 1 percent of the total vote.

gained a small following among people who believe that both liberals and conservatives lack consistency in their attitude toward the power of the national government.

Libertarians preach opposition to almost all government programs. They favor massive cuts in government spending and an end to the Federal Bureau of Investigation, the Central Intelligence Agency, and most regulatory commissions. They oppose participation in the United Nations and favor a defense establishment that would defend the United States only if directly attacked. They oppose *all* government regulation, including, for example, mandatory seat-belt and helmet laws. Unlike conservatives, libertarians would repeal laws that regulate personal morality, including abortion, pornography, prostitution, and illicit drugs.

A Libertarian party candidate for president has been on the ballot in all 50 states in recent presidential elections, although never obtaining more than 1 percent of the vote. The Libertarian party's 2004 candidate, Michael Badnarik, received 380,000 votes, just 20,000 behind Nader. Badnarik received the most votes of the offical candidates for the minor parties.[29] In 2004, the Libertarian party endorsed same-sex marriage, legalizing drugs, repealing the Patriot Act, withdrawing from Iraq, eliminating all gun control laws, retracting business regulations, and eliminating the FDA. To learn more about libertarianism, go to www.lp.org.

A Word of Caution

Political labels have different meanings across national boundaries as well as over time. To be a liberal in certain European nations is to be on the right; to be a liberal in the United States is to be on the left. In recent elections, the term "liberal"—which back in Franklin Roosevelt's day had been popular—became "the L-word," a label most politicians sought to avoid. But liberalism is more than a label. On big questions—such as the role of government in the economy, in promoting equality of opportunity, and in regulating the behavior of individuals or businesses—real differences separate conservative and liberal groups. This does not mean, however, that people who are conservative in one area are necessarily conservative in another or that liberals always hold similar views.

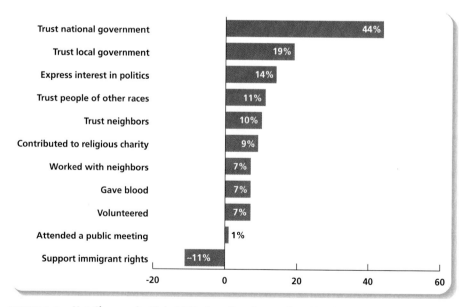

FIGURE 4–1   Net Changes in Civic Attitudes after September 11, 2001.

SOURCE: Robert D. Putnam, "Bowling Together," *American Prospect* 13 (February 11, 2002):20–22.

It is important to appreciate that ideology both causes events and is affected by them. Just as the Great Depression resulted in a tidal wave of ideological change, so did our involvement in World War II. The attacks on the World Trade Center and the Pentagon on September 11, 2001, may also have a lasting impact. For example, World War II, with its positive example of how government can work to defend freedom, strengthened positive views about the role of the national government. The Vietnam War probably had the opposite effect, producing disillusionment with government. The antigovernment sentiment in recent presidential elections is undoubtedly related to Vietnam, the Watergate scandal, and allegations of sexual misconduct by political leaders in recent years. The surge in patriotism and sense of national unity in the war against terrorism after September 11 stands in sharp contrast to the national mood during the final years of the Vietnam War. It also reflects at least in the short term a view that government has an important role to play in responding to a crisis (see Figure 4-1).

Political Ideology and the American People

For some people, ideological controversy today centers on the role of the government in improving schools, encouraging a stronger work ethic, and stopping the flow of drugs into the country. For others, ideology is centered on whether to permit openly gay people into the military or sanction same-sex marriages and on the best ways to instill moral values, build character, and encourage cohesive and lasting families.

Despite the twists and turns of American politics, the distribution of ideology in the nation has been remarkably consistent (see Figure 4-2). Conservatives outnumber liberals, but the proportion of conservatives did not increase substantially with the decisive Republican presidential victories of the 1980s or congressional victories of the 1990s.

Another important fact about ideology in the United States is that few people see themselves as extremists. In 2000, only 2 percent of the population saw themselves as extreme conservatives, and the same percentage saw themselves as extreme liberals (see Figure 4-3). These percentages have changed very little over time. The tendency toward muted ideology is also demonstrated by the fact that more people consider themselves *slightly* liberal or *slightly* conservative than liberal or conservative. Despite claims by ideological factions in both parties to move to the right or to the left, there are simply more votes in the middle.[30]

Both major parties targeted moderate or centrist voters in the 2000 presidential election, as reflected in the stands of the candidates on key issues, including their efforts to minimize ideological battles at the conventions. Governor Tommy Thompson of Wisconsin, who chaired the Republican Platform Committee, stated that their more conservative partisans

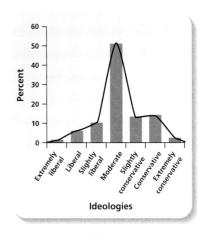

FIGURE 4–3 Ideology Curve.

Source: Center for Political Studies, University of Michigan, *2000 National Election Study.*

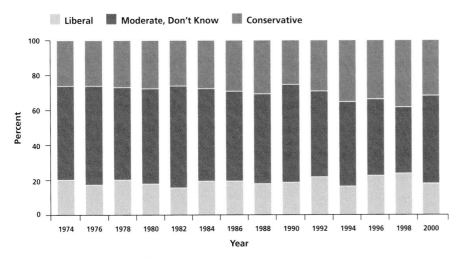

FIGURE 4–2 Ideology over Time.

Source: Center for Political Studies, University of Michigan, National Election Study Cumulative Data File, 1952–1992; *1994, 1996, 1998, and 2000 National Election Study.*

did not push their issues because "they want to win."[31] Democrats adopted a similar strategy. For example, they stressed the need to limit violence and sexuality in video games sold to children. This move to the center by both parties at the presidential level does not mean that there are not liberal and conservative wings in both parties, especially in the House of Representatives, with the liberal wing more powerful in the Democratic party and the conservative wing more powerful in the Republican party. In 2002, candidates typically sought to portray themselves as moderates while hoping their party and interest groups would succeed in labeling their opponent as out of the mainstream. (We analyze party identification in greater detail in Chapter 7.)

For those who have a liberal or conservative preference, ideology provides a lens through which to view candidates and public policies. It helps simplify the complexities of politics, policies, personalities, and programs. However, most Americans do not organize their political views systematically. A voter may want increased spending for defense but vote for the party that is for reducing defense spending because he or she has always voted for that party or prefers its stand on the environment. Or a person may favor tax cuts and balancing the budget while at the same time being unwilling to see government programs cut back substantially.

The degree to which people have ideologically consistent attitudes and opinions varies but is often relatively low. Much of the time, people view political issues as isolated matters and do not apply an overall standard of performance in evaluating parties or candidates. Indeed, many citizens find it difficult to relate what happens in one policy situation to what happens in another. This problem becomes more complex as government gets into more and more policy areas. Hence many people, not surprisingly, have difficulty finding candidates who reflect their ideological preferences across a wide range of issues.

The absence of widespread and solidified liberal and conservative positions in the United States makes for politics and policy-making processes that are markedly different from those in many European and other nations. Policy making in this country is characterized more by coalitions of the moment than by fixed alignments that pit one set of ideologies against another. Our politics is marked more by moderation, pragmatism, and accommodation than by a prolonged battle among two, three, or more competing philosophies of government. Elsewhere, especially in countries where a strong Socialist or Christian Democratic party exists, like Germany or Sweden, things are different.

This does not, however, mean that policies or ideas are not important elements in American politics. There has been, for instance, a shift to strongly partisan and ideological voting in the House of Representatives. Part of the explanation for the increasing importance of ideology in Congress is Republican gains in the South, with remaining southern Democrats becoming more liberal;[32] in other parts of the country where moderate Republicans were once successful, liberal Democrats now hold many seats. Perhaps even more important, congressional districts are now being drawn in such a way as to make more of them safe for one or the other party, so Republican members of Congress tend to appeal to the more conservative wing of their party, while the more liberal Democratic members of Congress tend to appeal to the more liberal wing of their party.

Ideology and Tolerance

Is there a connection between the ideologies of liberalism and conservatism and support for civil liberties and tolerance for racial minorities? Some political scientists assert that conservatives are generally less tolerant than liberals.[33] This view is stoutly contested by conservatives, who have charged liberals with trying to impose a "politically correct" position on faculty and students in universities, colleges, and the media. Liberals are usually more tolerant of dissent from some quarters and the expression of some unorthodox opinions. However, liberals, too, can be intolerant—of abortion foes, for example, or the National Rifle Association or the views of Pat Robertson. On the other side, some conservatives have worked to seek dismissal of faculty members and ministers who have been critical of the war against terrorists.

Most liberals are strongly opposed to crime and lawbreaking, yet they are as concerned about the roots or causes of crime as they are about the punishment of criminals. Perhaps for this reason, liberals exhibit somewhat greater concern than conservatives for the rights of the accused and are more willing to expand the rights of due process. Conservatives usually take a harder line and, in recent years, have won widespread popular support for their greater concern for the victims of crime than for the rights of the accused.

Such differences are most evident in the responses of liberals and conservatives to questions of civil rights and civil liberties. In the area of free speech, conservatives are usually seen as less willing to permit speech that is out of the political or cultural mainstream. Perhaps conservatives are less tolerant because those who claim to be exercising the right of free speech often attack established values. Liberals favor limiting speech in areas like cigarette advertising or campaign spending but favor fewer restrictions than conservatives do on countercultural individuals or groups.[34]

Conservatives believe that the United States has become morally too permissive. Many conservatives, especially in the New or Religious Right, are highly critical of homosexuals, drug users, prostitutes, unwed mothers, and pornographers. They worry about what they claim has been a decline in moral standards and, interestingly, call on government to help reverse these trends. Most liberals, by contrast, generally accept nonconformity in conduct and opinion as an inescapable byproduct of freedom.[35] In this regard, liberals are like libertarians.

Ideologies have consequences. It is these sharp cleavages in political thinking that stir opposing interest groups into action. A wide variety of groups promote their views of what is politically desirable. It is also these differences in ideological perspectives that reinforce party loyalties and divide us at election time. Policy fights in Congress, between Congress and the White House, and during judicial confirmation hearings also have their roots in our uneasily coexisting ideological values.

Our hard-earned rights and liberties are never entirely safeguarded; they are fragile and are shaped by the political, economic, and social climate of the day. In later chapters, we examine the interest groups and political parties that are battling to advance their values and compete in the American political culture. But before turning to those topics, we examine the social and economic diversity of the American political landscape in Chapter 5 and see why agreement on shared democratic values is all the more remarkable.

"It's been hell! The breakfast bagels aren't toasted, I can't sleep with a nightlight, there's no "dry hair" formula shampoo in the showers, and the guard won't get close enough for me to stab him with a spoon!."

By Steve Sack, *Minneapolis Star-Tribune.* Reprinted with permission of the Star Tribune.

POLITICAL SURVEY: WHAT DO YOU BELIEVE?

Political scientists measure ideology by asking people about their beliefs and values and then placing those individual responses in a context of a broader public. The PoliSim for this chapter provides a sample of these polling questions, allowing you to see how you would be categorized. You can also compare your views with those of the general public.

Go to PoliSim "Political Survey: What Do You Believe?"

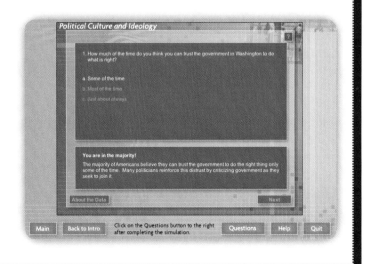

Summary

1. The United States, like every other nation or society, has a distinctive political culture. It consists of a widely held set of fundamental political values and accepted processes and institutions that help us manage conflict and resolve problems. In the United States, at least in the abstract, people respect the Constitution, the Bill of Rights, the two-party system, and the right to elect officials on the basis of majority rule. Our belief in social equality has fostered acceptance of the notion that government should guarantee equality of opportunity through programs like education and job training.

2. Americans share a widespread commitment to classical liberalism, which embraces the importance of individual liberty, equality, individualism, power to the people, private property, limited government, nationalism, optimism, idealism, the democratic consensus, and justice and the rule of law. They also believe that the American dream should be something we can all pursue.

3. American political values have been and continue to be affected by historical and economic developments. Among these have been the industrial transformation, the development of large corporations and other large institutions, the Great Depression, and a global economy.

4. The sources of the American political culture include the family, schools, religious and civic organizations, the mass media, and political activities.

5. Two broad schools of thought are important in American politics today: liberalism, a belief in the positive uses of government to bring about justice and equality of opportunity; and conservatism, a belief that limited government ensures order, competitive markets, and personal opportunity. Socialism, environmentalism, and libertarianism also attract a modest following in America.

6. Most Americans are nonideological and are guided primarily by moderate pragmatism. Few Americans are extremists.

7. Ideological orientation has a bearing on how tolerant we are of the views and conduct of others. Liberals tend to be more tolerant, whereas conservatives generally favor tradition, stability, and greater levels of "law and order." These differences have consequences for electoral contests and policy development in our political system.

Key Terms

social capital
political culture
natural rights
democratic consensus

majority rule
popular sovereignty
American dream
capitalism

monopoly
antitrust legislation
political ideology
liberalism

conservatism
socialism
environmentalism
libertarianism

Further Reading

H. W. BRANDS, *The Strange Death of American Liberalism* (Yale University Press, 2001).

JAMES W. CEASER, *Reconstructing America: The Symbol of America in Modern Thought* (Yale University Press, 1997).

E. J. DIONNE JR., *They Only Look Dead: Why Progressives Will Dominate the Next Political Era* (Simon & Schuster, 1996).

JEAN BETHKE ELSHTAIN, *Democracy on Trial* (Basic Books, 1995).

AMY GUTMANN AND DENNIS THOMPSON, *Democracy and Disagreement: Why Moral Conflict Cannot Be Avoided in Politics, and What Should Be Done About It* (Harvard University Press, 1996).

LAWRENCE E. HARRISON AND SAMUEL P. HARRINGTON, EDS., *Culture Matters: How Values Shape Human Progress* (Basic Books, 2000).

LOUIS HARTZ, *The Liberal Tradition in America* (Harcourt, 1955).

GEORGE KLOSKO, *Democratic Procedures and Liberal Consensus* (Oxford University Press, 2000).

IRVING KRISTOL, *Neoconservatism: The Autobiography of an Idea* (Free Press, 1995).

HERBERT MCCLOSKY AND JOHN ZALLER, *The American Ethos: Public Attitudes Toward Capitalism and Democracy* (Harvard University Press, 1984).

LISA MCGIRR, *Suburban Warriors: The Origins of the New American Right* (Princeton University Press, 2001).

CHARLES MURRAY, *What It Means to Be a Libertarian: A Personal Interpretation* (Broadway Books, 1997).

JOHN RENSENBRINK, *Against All Odds: The Green Transformation of American Politics* (Leopold Press, 1999).

JONATHON M. SCHOENWALD, *A Time for Choosing: The Rise of American Conservatism* (Oxford University Press, 2001).

ROGER SCRUTON, *The Meaning of Conservatism* (St. Augustine Press, 2001).

ALEXIS DE TOCQUEVILLE, *Democracy in America,* 2 vols. (1835).

JOHN TOMASI, *Liberalism Beyond Justice: Citizens, Society, and the Boundaries of Political Theory* (Princeton University Press, 2001).

GARRY WILLS, *A Necessary Evil: A History of American Distrust of Government* (Simon & Schuster, 1999).

DANIEL YERGIN AND JOSEPH STAINSLAW, *The Commanding Heights: The Battle Between Government and the Marketplace That Is Remaking the Modern World* (Simon & Schuster, 1998).

5
CHAPTER

THE AMERICAN POLITICAL LANDSCAPE

THE UNITED STATES IS A NATION OF IMMIGRANTS, A FACT THAT IS A SOURCE OF PRIDE. FRANKLIN D. ROOSEVELT ONCE BEGAN A speech to the Daughters of the American Revolution by saying, "You and I, especially, are descended from immigrants and revolutionists."[1] Immigrants have long been drawn to America by the hope for prosperity and freedom. However, the American dream is rarely achieved in the first generation. There are notable exceptions. Take, for example, George Soros, an international financier who is among the most successful businesspeople in the United States. Soros was born in Hungary, educated in England, and then moved to the United States. Madeleine Albright, secretary of state in the Clinton administration, is another example. Albright and her family fled Czechoslovakia at the outbreak of World War II. Largely educated in the United States, she became a policy adviser and professor at Georgetown University. Both George Soros and Madeline Albright illustrate the potential for fortunate and hardworking individuals to succeed in our political and economic system.

We have conflicting ideas about immigration. We celebrate our immigrant past and proudly recite the words of Emma Lazarus inscribed at the base of the Statue of Liberty: "Give me your tired, your poor, your huddled masses yearning to breathe free." And yet our borders are not open to all who wish to come here, and immigration is limited, with specific numbers of immigrants allowed to enter from each country each year. Hundreds of thousands avoid these limitations by crossing our borders illegally, seeking employment, refuge, and freedom.

After the terrorist attacks on the World Trade Center and the Pentagon in 2001, there was some anti-Arab and anti-Muslim sentiment, including some efforts in Congress to restrict student visas.[2] President Bush urged Americans to "treat each other with respect."[3] Disagreements about the admission of aliens into this country and about their rights and privileges have been featured in political campaigns for more than two centuries. In 1994, Californians passed a controversial ballot initiative, Proposition 187, restricting public services to illegal immigrants. Even though a federal judge found portions of the proposition un-constitutional, the furor about Proposition 187 demonstrated the intense feelings on both sides of the issue, especially in a border state like California.

Albert Einstein once said that most people are incapable of expressing opinions that differ much from the prejudices of their social upbringing.[4] This **ethnocentrism**—selective perception based on one's background, attitudes, and biases—is not uncommon, even among college students, who often assume that others share their economic opportunities, social attitudes, sense of civic responsibility, and self-confidence. In this chapter, we consider how our social environment explains, or at least shapes, our opinions and prejudices. We also look at our diversity as Americans and the implications of geographic, social, and economic divisions for politics and government. Specifically, this chapter explores the effects of regional or state identity on political perspectives; the implications of differences in race, ethnicity, gender, family structure, religion, wealth and income, occupation, and social class for opinions and voting choices; and the relationship between age and education and political participation.

A Land of Diversity

Most nations consist of groups of people who have lived together for hundreds of years and who speak the same language, embrace the same religious beliefs, and share a common history. Most Japanese citizens are Japanese in the fullest sense of the word, and this sense of identity and oneness is generally the same in Germany, Sweden, Saudi Arabia, China, and France. The United States is different. We have attracted the poor and oppressed, the adventurous, and the talented from all over the world, and we have been more open to accepting these people than other nations have.

One reason so many people want to come to the United States is that it holds a promise of religious, political, and economic freedom. It is also a place of opportunity for the enterprising. Our economic system has provided widespread (but not universal) opportunity for individuals to improve their economic standing. The American dream—that anyone can find success in the United States—is widely shared.

Some elements of our diversity have political significance. Many Americans retain an identity with the native land of their ancestors, even after three or four generations. Holding on to such differences reflects socialization in families, churches, and other close-knit groups. **Political socialization** is the process by which parents and others teach children about political values, beliefs, and attitudes. This teaching occurs in the home, in school, on the playground, and in the neighborhood. In addition to fostering group identities, political socialization strongly influences how individuals see politics and which political party they prefer. Where we live and who we are in terms of age, education, religion, and occupation affect how we vote. Such characteristics of populations are called **demographics**. Persons in certain demographic categories tend to vote alike and to have certain **political predispositions** in common, and these characteristics sometimes predict political behavior. Although demographics can be important in both explaining and predicting political behavior, there are sometimes large individual differences within socioeconomic and demographic categories.

When social and economic differences coincide, they reinforce each other and make the differences between groups more important. Social scientists call these differences **reinforcing cleavages**; where these differences are reinforcing, political conflict becomes more intense and there is greater polarization in society. In Italy, for example, the regional divide between north and south is reinforced by the tendency of the north to lean toward the Socialist or Communist party and the south to be Christian Democratic and Catholic in orientation.

Nations can also have **cross-cutting cleavages**, instances where differences among people do not reinforce each other but rather create counterpulls. To illustrate, if all the rich individuals in a nation are of one religion and the poor of another, the nation would have

ethnocentrism
Belief in the superiority of one's nation or ethnic group.

political socialization
The process by which we develop our political attitudes, values, and beliefs.

demographics
The study of the characteristics of populations.

political predisposition
A characteristic of individuals that is predictive of political behavior.

reinforcing cleavages
Divisions within society that reinforce one another, making groups more homogeneous or similar.

cross-cutting cleavages
Divisions within society that cut across demographic categories to produce groups that are more heterogeneous or different.

You Decide — Thinking It Through

HOW SHOULD PEOPLE BE COUNTED?

You Decide... The Census Bureau, which conducts the once-a-decade count of all persons in the United States, proposed using random sampling rather than attempting to count all households in the 2000 census. Republicans opposed sampling because they considered it unreliable. The proposed sample approach would contact 90 percent of the households in a census tract consisting of roughly 1,700 individuals. The bureau would then check the accuracy of the sample by surveying 750,000 households throughout the nation and adjusting the final total accordingly.

The sample approach responds to complaints about the flawed 1990 census, which cost $2.6 billion (a 400 percent increase over the cost of the 1980 census) and failed to account for 10 million people and double-counted 6 million others, according to a study by the National Academy of Sciences. Do you think that sampling is a fair and effective solution?

Thinking It Through... The battle over sampling was not so much about *how* to count as *whom* to count. The proposed sampling would have produced a more accurate count of inner-city Hispanics and African Americans—the most difficult to count. This approach would likely have resulted in a greater representation for Hispanics and African Americans in state legislatures and the U.S. House of Representatives. A more complete count of minorities could also mean that the Republican party could lose a few seats in the House to Democrats, which is why Republicans generally opposed the sampling approach while Democrats favored it. The constitutionality of sampling was also disputed, as the Constitution calls for an "actual enumeration" of the people. Democrats are quick to point out that under three presidents— Jimmy Carter, George Bush, and Bill Clinton—the Justice Department concluded that sampling is legal.

In 1998, in order to get a ruling on the constitutionality of sampling, then Speaker Newt Gingrich filed suit on behalf of the House of Representatives in the District Court of the Eastern District of Virginia and District Court of the District of Columbia. Both courts declared that sampling violated the Census Act 13 as amended in 1976. In January 1999, the Supreme Court upheld that decision and ordered an actual count.* The Census Bureau supplemented its actual count with sampling in 2000, which was upheld in *Utah* v. *Evans*, 122 S.Ct. 2191 (2002).

SOURCE: Steven A. Holmes, "Political Interests Arouse Raging Debate on Census," *New York Times*, April 12, 1998, p. 1; Holmes, "Gingrich Files Suit to Prevent Use of Sampling in 2000 Census," *New York Times*, February 22, 1998, p. 21.

*Department of Commerce et al. v. United States House of Representatives et al., 119 S.Ct. 765 (1999).

---

reinforcing cleavages, and political conflict between the groups would be intensified. But if there are both rich and poor in all religions and if people sometimes vote on the basis of their religion and sometimes on the basis of their wealth, the divisions would be cross-cutting. American diversity has generally been more of the cross-cutting type than the reinforcing type, lessening political conflict because individuals have multiple allegiances.

In some societies, politics centers largely on passions over economic and religious differences. Although socioeconomic differences are important to understanding American government and politics, they are not as central to our politics as religion is in Bosnia or tribal identity in Rwanda. In Northern Ireland, the religious differences between Catholics and Protestants have produced centuries of violent strife that is yet to be resolved.

Despite the fact that America has been more hospitable to people from different religions, classes, and races than almost any other nation in the world, we Americans often prefer to associate only with people "like us" and are suspicious of people "like them."

From hostility toward different religions in the early colonies to the anti-immigration movements of the late 1800s and early 1900s to the various anti-immigration and anti–civil rights ballot initiatives of the 1990s, Americans have exhibited ethnocentrism, and for much of our history, minorities have been excluded from full participation in American political and economic life.

Geography and National Identity

The United States is a geographically large and historically isolated country. In the 1830s, French commentator Alexis de Tocqueville studied the early development of the United States and observed that the country had no major political or economic powers on its borders "and consequently no great wars, financial crises, invasions, or conquests to fear."[5] Geographic isolation from the major powers of the world during our government's formative period helps explain American politics. The Atlantic Ocean served as a barrier to foreign meddling, giving us time to establish our political tradition and develop our economy. The western frontier provided room to grow and avoid some of the social and political tensions that Europe experienced. Two great oceans also reinforced our sense of isolation from Europe and foreign alliances. American reluctance to become involved in foreign wars and controversies still emerges in debates over foreign policy.

Before the terrorist attacks of September 2001, only one foreign enemy had struck the United States on our own soil—England in the War of 1812. (The war against Mexico of 1846–1848 was fought almost entirely on Mexican land, some of which later became American land as a result of the war. The only other war fought on our soil was, of course, the Civil War.) By contrast, Poland has been invaded repeatedly and was partitioned by Austria, Prussia, and Russia in the eighteenth century and by Nazi Germany and the Soviet Union in the twentieth century. The difference is explained largely by location: Poland was surrounded by Europe's great powers. Had the United States been closer to Europe and not isolated by two oceans, it might have been overrun like Poland and our Constitution and institutions repeatedly changed or eliminated to suit the victorious invaders. The presence of powerful and aggressive neighbors impedes the development of democracy in relatively weak nations.

Part of our national identity is bound up with the physical isolation and hardship many families endured as pioneers.

September 11, 2001, showed us that the ability of terrorists to promulgate war, especially if willing to die along with their enemies, and access to the modern tools of war mean that isolation and national security have to be rethought. No longer does the United States have the luxury of developing our democracy behind the protection of two oceans; our newly recognized vulnerability to attacks on our own soil has changed the context in which we debate the balance between liberty and security. New York, San Francisco, and Chicago are now on the front line.

Size also confers an advantage. The landmass of the United States exceeds that of all but three nations in the world. In contrast, India has a population more than three times that of the United States on a landmass one-third the size. Geographic space gave the expanding population of the United States room to spread out. This possibility meant that some of the political conflicts arising from religion, social class, and national origin were defused because groups could isolate themselves from one another. This was what Madison hoped for in his concept of a "large republic" (see *The Federalist*, No. 10, in the Appendix). Moreover, the large and accessible landmass helped foster the perspective that the United States had a **manifest destiny** to be a continental nation reaching from the Atlantic to the Pacific oceans. Early settlers used the notion that the United States was "destined" to expand across the continent to justify taking land occupied by Native Americans and Mexicans, especially the land acquired following victory in the Mexican-American War.

The United States is also a land of abundant natural resources. We have rich farmland, which not only feeds our population but also makes us the largest exporter of food in the world.[6] We are rich in such natural resources as coal, iron, uranium, and precious metals. All these resources enhance economic growth, provide jobs, and stabilize government. As de Tocqueville observed long ago, "Yet what takes place in the United States is much less attributable to the institutions of the country than to the country itself."[7]

Geography also helps explain our diversity. Parts of the United States are wonderfully suited to agriculture, others to mining or ranching, and still others to shipping. These differences produce different regional economic concerns, which in turn influence politics. For instance, a person from the agricultural heartland may have a perception of foreign trade that is different from that of an automobile worker in Detroit. But if that automobile worker is African American, this fact may be more important to her politics than what she does or where she lives. To understand American politics, we must appreciate these differences and their relative importance.

Sectional Differences

Unlike many other countries, geography in the United States does *not* define an ethnic or religious division. All the Serbs in the United States do not live in one place, all French-speaking Catholics in another, and all German immigrants in another. Sectional differences in the United States are primarily geographic, not ethnic or religious.

The most distinct section of the United States remains the South, although the South's differences are diminishing. From the beginning of the Republic, the agricultural South differed from the North, where commerce and manufacturing were more significant. But the most important difference between the regions was the institution of slavery. Northern opposition to slavery, which grew increasingly intense by the middle of the nineteenth century, reinforced sectional economic interests. The 11 Confederate states, by virtue of their decision to secede from the Union, reinforced a common political identity, and after the Civil War, sectional differences were strengthened by the policy of Reconstruction and the problems of race relations.

The South is becoming less distinct from the rest of the United States. In addition to undergoing tremendous economic change, a large in-migration has diminished the sense of regional identity, and the South has undergone tremendous economic change. The civil rights revolution eliminated roadblocks preventing African Americans from voting, opened up new educational opportunities, and helped integrate the South into the

Evidence of the persistent racial divide in this country was brought out by the dispute over the flag of the Confederacy (bottom flag) flying over the South Carolina capitol building. After bitter debate between descendents of slave-owning families and descendents of slaves, the flag was relocated near a small statue on the capitol grounds.

manifest destiny
A notion held by nineteenth-century Americans that the United States was destined to rule the continent, from the Atlantic to the Pacific.

TABLE 5–1 Voting Patterns in the 11 Former Confederate States

Republican for President

1980	50%
1984	62
1988	59
1992	43
1996	46
2000	54
2004	57

Republican Vote for U.S. Representatives

1980	40%
1982	39
1984	42
1986	41
1988	42
1990	43
1992	48
1994	58
1996	53*
1998	58
2000	53
2002	56
2004	55

Republican Share of State Legislators

	House	Senate
1980	18%	17%
1982	22	14
1984	23	17
1986	24	20
1988	27	24
1990	28	26
1992	31	31
1994	37	37
1996	44	44
1998	42	40
2000	44	42
2002	47	46
2004	50	49

SOURCE: U.S. Bureau of the Census, *Statistical Abstract of the United States*, 1993–2000. For 2004, CNN, at www.cnn.com/elections/2004/results, and *Congressional Quarterly Weekly Report*, November 11, 2000, pp. 2694–2703; and Todd Edwards, Council of State Governments, Southern Office, personal communication, December 22, 2000; and Doris Smith, Council of State Governments Southern Office, November 10, 2004.

*The 1996 Texas runoff elections are not included.

national economy. African Americans still lag behind whites in voter registration, but the gap is now no wider in the South than elsewhere and is explained more by differences in education than by race.[8] In economic terms, the South still falls below the rest of the country in per capita income and education, but much less so than 50 years ago. The religious and moral conservatism of the South remains notable.

Until the 1970s, political observers spoke of the "solid South"—a region that voted for Democrats at all levels. "The Civil War made the Democratic party the party of the South, and the Republican party, the party of the North."[9] The Democratic "solid South" remained a fixture of American politics for more than a century. Since 1968 that has changed dramatically, first at the presidential level and increasingly at the state and local levels. As two respected observers of the region comment, "The fall of the South as an assured stronghold of the Democratic Party in presidential elections is one of the most significant developments in modern American politics."[10] The political alignment has shifted as African Americans have been enfranchised and become overwhelmingly Democrats and many whites have become Republicans. In 1992 and 1996, even with two southerners (Bill Clinton and Al Gore) on the ticket, Democrats won only 4 of the 11 former Confederate states. In 2000, George W. Bush carried all 11 southern states, including Al Gore's home state of Tennessee. George W. Bush won all 11 former Confederate states in the 2004 election.

What explains this dramatic reversal? Part of the explanation is that the Democrats' advocacy of aggressive action on civil rights in the 1960s alienated some southern whites. In addition, the debate within the Democratic party over Vietnam policy in the late 1960s and 1970s was "perceived by many southern voters as unpatriotic."[11] Republican presidential candidates have more recently emphasized family values, opposition to taxes, and law-and-order issues that appeal to conservative southern voters.

Republican success at the presidential level was slow to affect contests for Congress and state legislatures. Yet in recent years, Republicans had more than half of southern votes for the U.S. House of Representatives (see Table 5-1), and by 2000, they had 7 of the 11 governorships in the former Confederate states (this was still the case in 2004). In the state legislatures of several southern states, remnants of the old "solid South" remain, but Republicans have made major inroads, and politics in the region is now predictably Republican, at least at the presidential level.

Both parties could point to successes in the South in 2002. The Democrats picked up the Governorship in Tennessee and the Republicans did the same in Georgia and Alabama. In Georgia, this was the first GOP elected governor since 1966 and in Alabama, the last Republican was elected in 1995. Overall, Republicans controlled more governorships than Democrats in the South after 2002. In 2004, the GOP gained a larger advantage in the Confederate States holding 18 of the 22 Senate seats.

Another sectional division is the Sun Belt—the 11 former Confederate states plus New Mexico, Arizona, and the southern half of California. Sun Belt states are growing much more rapidly than the rest of the country. Arizona, California, Florida, Georgia, Nevada, North Carolina, and Texas gained 12 seats in the House of Representatives after the 2000 census.[12] Moreover, population growth in the South and West is occurring in different age groups. In the South, growth is largest among those over 65; in the West, younger persons provide the growth. Sun Belt states have also experienced greater economic growth as industries have headed south and southwest, where land and labor are cheaper and more abundant (see Figure 5-1).

State and Local Identity

Different states have rather distinctive political traditions. Mention Utah, Mississippi, Oregon, New York, or Kansas, and a certain type of politics comes to mind. The same is true for many other states. Like most stereotypes, these images are often misleading, yet they reflect the fact that there is a sense of identity to states as political units that goes

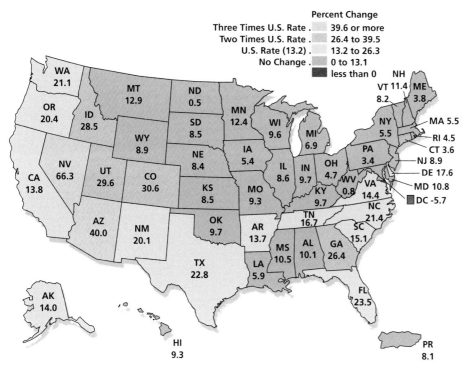

Percent Change

Three Times U.S. Rate . ▨ 39.6 or more
Two Times U.S. Rate . ▨ 26.4 to 39.5
U.S. Rate (13.2) . ▨ 13.2 to 26.3
No Change . ▨ 0 to 13.1
▨ less than 0

FIGURE 5–1   Percent Change in Resident Population, 1990–2000.

SOURCE: U.S. Bureau of the Census, at www.census.gov/population/cen2000/tab01.

beyond demographic characteristics and is supported by recent empirical evidence. States have distinctive political cultures that affect public opinion and policy outcomes.[13] Our electoral rules and other laws reinforce these state identities.

In American politics today, one state—California—stands out. More than one out of eight Americans is a Californian.[14] In terms of economic and political importance, California is in a league by itself; its 53 members of the House of Representatives exceed the total number of representatives from the smallest 20 states. California's 55 electoral votes are key for any presidential candidate.[15]

Where We Live

Four out of five Americans now live in central cities and their suburbs—what the Census Bureau calls *metropolitan areas*.[16] During the early twentieth century, the movement of population was from rural areas to central cities, but the movement since the 1950s has been from the central cities to their suburbs. Today the most urban state is California (93 percent of its population lives in cities or suburbs). Vermont is the least urban, with only 32 percent living in cities or suburbs.[17] Regionally, the West and Northeast are the most urban, the South and Midwest the most rural.

People move from cities to the suburbs for many reasons—better housing, new transportation systems that make it easier to get to work, the desire for cleaner air and safer streets. Another reason is white flight, the movement of whites away from the central cities so that children can avoid being bused for racial balance and attend generally better schools. White, middle-class migration to the suburbs has made American cities increasingly poor, African American, and Democratic. More than half of all African Americans now live in central cities, as opposed to only about one-fifth of whites, and the poverty level among blacks living in central cities is higher than among whites living in the same cities.[18] The proportions are very nearly reversed for the suburbs, where more than half of all white Americans reside. Almost one-third of African Americans

TABLE 5–2   Cities with Populations of 100,000 or More That Are at Least 50 Percent African American, 2000

City	Population	Percent African American
Atlanta, Ga.	416,474	61.4%
Baltimore, Md.	651,154	64.3
Birmingham, Ala.	242,820	73.5
Detroit, Mich.	951,270	81.6
Gary, Ind.	102,746	84
Jackson, Miss.	184,256	70.6
Memphis, Tenn.	650,100	61.4
Newark, N.J.	273,546	53.5
New Orleans, La.	484,674	67.3
Richmond, Va.	197,790	57.2
Savannah, Ga.	131,510	57.1
Washington, D.C.	572,059	60.0

SOURCE: U.S. Bureau of the Census, at www.census.gov/population/cen2000/phc-t6/tab05.pdf.

live in the suburbs, up from one-fifth in 1980.[19] In large cities such as Washington, D.C., Detroit, Baltimore, Atlanta, and New Orleans, the city population is now more than 50 percent African American (see Table 5-2). Hispanics constitute roughly two-thirds of the population of El Paso, Texas; Santa Ana, California; and Miami, Florida.[20]

As the better off have left the cities, the cities' problems have become more acute, and their tax base has not increased proportionate to their problems. Older suburban areas now face the same problems as the inner cities, as they too suffer from out-migration to newer cities and towns. High-tech and professional service companies frequently relocate to the suburbs to avoid traffic congestion and to be closer to the bedroom communities of their workers. Political boundaries, which define local governments and delineate responsibility for services, create understandable tensions among cities, suburbs, and rural areas. Tax revenues, legislative representation, zoning laws, and governmental priorities are hotly contested issues in most metropolitan areas.

Who We Are

Sectional distinctions are less prominent today than they were a century or even a half-century ago. Today Americans are more likely to define themselves by a number of characteristics, each of which may influence how they vote or think about various candidates, issues, or policies.

Race and Ethnicity

Racial and ethnic differences have always had political significance. **Race** can be defined as a grouping of human beings with distinctive physical characteristics determined by genetic inheritance. **Ethnicity** is a social division based on national origin, religion, and language, often within the same race, and includes a sense of attachment to that group. In the United States, race and ethnicity issues focus on African Americans, Asian Americans, Native Americans, and Hispanics.

There are more than 35 million African Americans in the United States, roughly 12.5 percent of the population. Asian Americans constitute about 4 percent of the population, and Native Americans, around 1.5 percent.[21] The Census Bureau classifies most American Hispanics as white, although Hispanics can be of any race. Hispanics are the

race
A grouping of human beings with distinctive characteristics determined by genetic inheritance.

ethnicity
A social division based on national origin, religion, language, and often race.

Percentage of the Population by Race and Origin

	1990	2000	2025	2050
White	83.9%	82.2%	78.5%	74.9%
African American	12.2	12.8	13.9	14.7
American Indian, Inuit, Aleut	0.8	0.9	1.0	1.1
Asian and Pacific Islander	3.0	4.1	6.5	9.3
Hispanic	8.9	11.8	18.2	24.3

SOURCE: U.S. Bureau of the Census, *Statistical Abstract of the United States, 2001* (Government Printing Office, 2001), pp. 16–17.

Note: Percentages do not equal 100 because Hispanics can be of any race. Figures for 2025 and 2050 are projections.

fastest-growing ethnic group; the Census Bureau estimates that there are 32 million American Hispanics, constituting over 11 percent of the population.[22] Because of differences in immigration and birthrates, whites in America will have declined to fewer than three-quarters of the population by the year 2050.[23]

AFRICAN AMERICANS   Most immigrants came to this country of their free will in search of freedom and opportunity. In contrast, African Americans came against their will as slaves. Although they were freed as a result of the Civil War, racial divisions continue as one of the enduring issues of American politics. Until 1900, more than 90 percent of all African Americans lived in the South; by the end of the twentieth century, the figure was 55 percent.[24] Many African Americans left the South hoping to improve their lives by settling in the large cities of the Northeast, Midwest, and West. The reality for many was urban poverty. More recently, some African Americans have been returning to the South, especially to its urban areas.

Most African Americans are economically worse off than most whites in the United States. African American median family income is close to $32,000, compared to more than $51,000 for whites.[25] About one-quarter of African American incomes are below the poverty level, compared to less than 10 percent of the incomes of whites.[26] Poverty among Native Americans and Alaskan Natives has averaged 26 percent in recent years, a proportion quite similar to that found among African Americans and Hispanics.[27] However, some African Americans have been doing better in recent years; 27 percent of African American households have earnings of over $50,000 (compared to 62 percent of white households).[28] Some African Americans, like Kobe Bryant, a basketball player with the Los Angeles Lakers, and Oprah Winfrey, a syndicated talk show host, have risen to top earnings in their professions.

Another way to measure economic well-being is in terms of assets or wealth. *Wealth* is the economic value of the things you own (savings, stocks, property), compared to *income,* which is how much money you make from your job or investments. As a group, African Americans' net wealth is only one-tenth that of whites, and Hispanics have only slightly more wealth than African Americans (see Figure 5-2).[29] As a result, most African Americans and Hispanics have fewer resources to fall back on in hard times, and they are less likely to have the savings to help a child pay for college.[30]

Middle-class African Americans, of whom there are a growing number, are role models for the young of all races, yet their still comparatively small number serves as a reminder that most African Americans remain behind whites in an economy that relies more and more on education and job skills. About 28 percent of whites graduate from

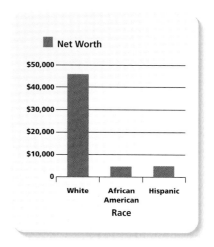

FIGURE 5–2 Wealth Distribution in the United States by Race.

SOURCE: U.S. Bureau of the Census, at www.census.gov/hhes/www/wealth.

The 2002 Texas Democratic gubernatorial candidate Tony Sanchez is the first Hispanic American nominated by a major party to run for governor of Texas.

The 2002 Democratic candidate for U.S. Senate from Texas state senate, Ron Kirk, mayor of Dallas, was the first African American to be elected mayor in a major city in Texas.

The 2002 New York Democratic gubernatorial candidate Carl McCall is the first African American nominated by a major party to run for governor of New York.

college, whereas only about 17 percent of African Americans do.[31] Among recent high school graduates, 61 percent of whites go on to college, but only 50 percent of African Americans do.[32]

Finally, the African American population is much younger than the white population; the median age for whites in 2000 was 37.7, compared to 30.2 for African Americans.[33] The combination of a younger African American population, a lower level of education, and their concentration in economically depressed urban areas has resulted in a much higher unemployment rate for young African Americans. Unemployment can in turn lead to social problems like crime, drug and alcohol abuse, and family dissolution.

African Americans had little political power until after World War II. Owing their freedom from slavery to the "party of Lincoln," most African Americans initially identified with the Republicans, but this loyalty started to change with Franklin Roosevelt, who insisted on equal treatment for African Americans in his New Deal programs.[34] After World War II, African Americans came to see the Democrats as the party of civil rights. The 1964 Republican platform position on civil rights espoused *states' rights*—at the time, the creed of southern segregationists—in what appeared to be an effort to win the support of southern white voters. Virtually all African Americans voted for Lyndon Johnson in 1964, and in presidential elections between 1984 and 2000, their Democratic vote averaged 86 percent.[35]

Recently, African Americans have become much more important politically because of their increased voter participation and their concentrated population. African Americans constitute only 0.3 percent of the population in Montana and 0.6 percent in South Dakota, but 36 percent in Mississippi, 33 percent in Louisiana, and 30 percent in South Carolina.[36] Southern senators and representatives cannot afford to ignore the African American vote.[37] Evidence of growing African American political power is the dramatic increase in the number of African American state legislators, which rose from 168 in 1970 to 583 in 1999.[38] Mississippi has 45 African American state legislators, the most of any state. Alabama, Georgia, South Carolina, Maryland, and Louisiana all have over 30.[39]

Underrepresentation of Hispanics

In the 1990s, America's Hispanic population grew by 58 percent. This surge in growth has not, however, been accompanied by a similar surge in political participation or representation. Researchers cite many reasons for this, including redistricting, low rates of citizenship and voting, and a lack of common party commitment.

Hispanics have fared worse in redistricting than other groups. The large number of noncitizens and younger population among Hispanics diminishes their political power. For example, 9.5 million foreign-born Hispanics are not citizens, and more than half—5.4 million—are in this country illegally. This group of Hispanics cannot vote, nor can those under 18, which is a greater percentage of the Hispanic population than for others. Language problems also reduce Hispanic citizens' voter registration and turnout. Despite their huge increase in population, Hispanic groups were disappointed by the redrawing of legislative district boundaries after the 2000 census.* This has spurred some lawsuits as Hispanic activists seek to eliminate gerrymandering, the drawing of district boundaries to benefit a group or party.

Neither party has yet to develop an effective strategy to mobilize the Hispanic vote. The Democrats, which have historically been the party of new immigrant groups, have done somewhat better among Hispanics than the Republicans have. But President George W. Bush and the Republican party have mounted efforts to win Hispanic support.

The diversity of political perspective in the Hispanic population limits the impact of the group as a whole. Hispanics are not politically homogeneous. For example, Cuban Americans tend to be Republican, and Dominicans and other Caribbean islanders tend to be Democrats. This prevents them from uniting as a voting block.

*Robert Pear, "Race Takes Back Seat as States Prepare to Redistrict," *New York Times*, February 4, 2001, p. 17.

HISPANICS (LATINOS) Hispanic Americans, who generally prefer to be called Latinos, are not a monolithic group, and while they share a common linguistic heritage, they often differ, depending on which country they or their forebears emigrated from. Cuban Americans, for instance, tend to be Republicans, while Mexican Americans and Puerto Ricans are disproportionately Democrats.[40] Latinos are politically important in a growing number of states. Nearly two-thirds of Cuban immigrants live in Florida, especially in greater Miami; Puerto Rican immigrants are concentrated in and around New York City; and many Mexican American immigrants live in the Southwest and California. Almost 11 million Hispanics live in California.[41]

Cuban Americans are more in the upper-middle income levels, while Puerto Rican Americans and Mexican Americans are generally in lower and lower-middle income categories.[42] A recent study found differences among Latinos of Mexican, Puerto Rican, and Cuban descent in partisanship, ideology, and rates of participation, but widespread support for a liberal domestic agenda, including increased spending on health care, crime and drug control, education, the environment, child services, and bilingual education.[43]

Given the overall growth of the Latino population, it is not surprising that both major parties are aggressively cultivating Latino candidates. Three Latinos, all from New Mexico, have won election to the U.S. Senate, although none is currently serving. Several Hispanics have been cabinet members; in the George W. Bush administration, Mel Martinez is secretary of Housing and Urban Development (HUD). Alberto R. Gonzales left the Texas Supreme Court to join the Bush administration as White House counsel.

A prominent advisor to President George W. Bush is Alberto Gonzales, White House General Counsel. Mr. Gonzales previously served on the Texas Supreme Court.

ASIAN AMERICANS Asian Americans are classified together by the Census Bureau for statistical purposes, but there are significant differences among them in culture, language, and political experience in the United States. Asian Americans include, among others, persons of Chinese, Japanese, Indian, Korean, Vietnamese, Filipino, and Thai origin, as well as persons from the Pacific Islands.

The United States is home to more than 11 million Asian Americans and Pacific Islanders, residing primarily in the western states, especially Hawaii, California, and Washington.[44] The numbers of Asian Americans grew during the 1970s and 1980s, largely as a result of immigration from Southeast Asia. Immigrants from China, India, Korea, the Philippines, and Vietnam account for five of the top ten leading countries of foreign-born persons living in this country.[45]

Many Asian Americans have done well both economically and educationally. More than two out of every five Asian Americans have graduated from college, compared to one out of every four white Americans and one in six African Americans.[46] Asian Americans are becoming more politically important and more visible in politics. In 1996, Washington elected the first Chinese American governor of a state in the continental United States—Gary Locke. He was reelected in 2000.

THE TIES OF ETHNICITY Except for Native Americans and the descendants of slaves, all Americans have immigrant ancestors. Early settlers were generally English-speaking Protestants; even today, people of English, Scottish, and Welsh background are the largest "ethnic" group in the United States. Irish immigrants, largely Catholics, started coming before the potato famine in the 1840s and came in larger numbers after it. Upon their arrival, they experienced economic exploitation and religious bigotry. Irish Americans responded by retreating among themselves, forming a strong ethnic consciousness. Other ethnic groups that followed—Italians, Greeks, Chinese—each experienced a similar cycle: flight from their homeland and happy arrival here, then discrimination, exploitation, residential clustering, and the formation of a strong group identity.

The largest number of immigrants came between 1900 and 1924, when 17.3 million people relocated to the United States—by far the largest immigration to one country in any quarter-century in human history. From 1991 to 1998, the United States welcomed more than 7.6 million immigrants,[47] primarily from the Caribbean and Mexico and from Asian countries

Transportation Secretary Norman Mineta is an Asian American, former Congressman, and the only Democrat in President George W. Bush's cabinet.

EMILY's List and Wish List

One of the groups that has most aggressively promoted female candidates is EMILY's List, a group that funds pro-choice Democrats. EMILY is an acronym for "Early Money Is Like Yeast," meaning that campaign contributions given to candidates early in their campaigns can help raise more money, just as yeast helps dough rise. EMILY's List supporters are proud of the fact that there are more women in the U.S. House than ever before. EMILY's List has also helped fund racial and ethnic female candidates, with roughly one-third of the candidates supported being African American or Latina. Republicans have duplicated EMILY's List with their own political action committee, Wish List, which gives to Republican female candidates who are pro-choice.

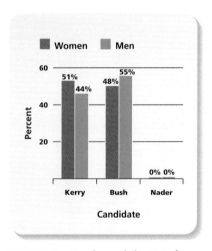

FIGURE 5–3   Gender and the Vote for President, 2004

SOURCE: 2004 Exit Polls from Edison Media Research and Mitofsky International at www.cnn.com/ELECTION/2004/pages/results/states/US/P/00/epolls.0.html

gender gap
The difference between the political opinions or political behavior of men and of women.

such as the Philippines, Vietnam, and China. The foreign-born proportion of the U.S. population has increased in recent years, rising from 14 million in 1980 to nearly 28 million in 2000, the largest number of foreign-born in U.S. history.[48] Recently, the proportion of Asian and Mexican immigrants has pulled even with or surpassed the number of Europeans.

Having large numbers of immigrants can pose challenges to any political and social system. Immigrants are often a source of social conflict as they compete with more established groups for jobs, rights, political power, and influence.

Gender

For most of U.S. history, politics and government were men's business. Women first gained the right to vote primarily in the western territories, beginning with Wyoming in 1869 and Utah in 1870, and then in Colorado and Idaho before the turn of the twentieth century.[49] The right was not extended nationally until 1920 with passage of the Nineteenth Amendment. The fears of some opponents and some proponents of *women's suffrage* (the right to vote)— that women would form their own party and vote largely for women or fundamentally alter our political system—have not been realized. During Susan B. Anthony's suffrage campaign, Jonas H. Upton, editor of the *Democratic Salem Monitor* in Salem, Oregon, contended that women, if given the right to vote, would combine to vote for war because they were exempt from the draft.[50] Others feared that women would unite to vote for prohibition.[51]

For a half-century after gaining the right to vote, American women voted at a lower rate than women in other Western democracies.[52] But in the past 20 years, slightly more women than men have voted in presidential elections, and there is no significant difference between the genders in rates of voting in midterm elections.[53] Because women outnumber men, there are more female than male voters.[54] Women have chosen to work within the existing political parties and do not overwhelmingly support female candidates, especially if they must cross party lines to do so.[55]

The women's movement in American politics encompasses a comprehensive agenda, including voting and political rights as well as extending the basic liberties of the Bill of Rights and the Fourteenth Amendment. In addition to rights and liberties, women seek equal opportunity, education, jobs, skills, and respect in what has been a male-dominated system.[56]

Since 1917, less than 6 percent of representatives in the U.S. House have been women. A common way women entered Congress was through appointment after their husband's death. The number of women in the House of Representatives and U.S. Senate reached new highs in the 1990s. Following the 2000 elections, there were three female governors, 13 women serving in the Senate, and 58 in the U.S. House of Representatives. There were ten female major-party gubernatorial candidates in 2002, and on election day, four of them were elected. Three of the four successful candidates were Democrats. After the 2002 elections, thirteen women will serve in the Senate during the 108th Congress. The proportion of women serving in the House of Representatives is about the same as in the Senate: below 15 percent. In contrast, some state legislative chambers are nearly 40 percent female. The number of female officeholders is rising in part because women are increasingly running in contests in which there is no incumbent.[57]

Is there a **gender gap**? Do women vote differently from men? Women have typically divided their vote between the two major political parties. However, in recent elections, women have been more likely than men to vote for Democratic presidential candidates (see Figure 5-3). In the 2004 presidential election, John Kerry's share of the vote among women was 7 percent higher than among men.[58]

Women are more likely than men to oppose violence in any form—the death penalty, new weapon systems, or the possession of handguns. Women, as a group, are more compassionate than men in that they are more likely to favor government that provides health insurance and family services. Women are generally more concerned than men about women's rights—enforcement of child support, punishment for sexual abuse and rape, and equal treatment in the legal system. They also identify work and family issues such as day care, maternity leave, and equal treatment in the workplace as important.[59]

Other gender issues, some of them focal points in recent elections, include reproductive rights, restrictions on pornography, gun control, and sexual harassment.[60]

There are serious income inequalities between men and women. Nearly twice as many women than men have an annual income of $15,000 or less.[61] Because an increasing number of women today are the sole breadwinners for their families, the implications of this low income level are significant. Women earn on average less than men for the same work. Even among college graduates aged 25 to 34, women earn an average of 80 cents for every dollar earned by men of the same age and education. After controlling for characteristics such as job experience, education, occupation, and other measures of productivity, studies show that wage discrimination is somewhere between 89 and 98 cents on every dollar.[62] As age increases, the earnings gap widens.

Sexual Orientation

Differences in sexual orientation have become important politically in recent years. The modern movement for expanded rights for gays and lesbians traces its roots to 1969, when New York City police raided the Stonewall Inn in Greenwich Village and a riot ensued.[63] Precise data on the number of homosexuals in the United States are in dispute. The gay and lesbian communities talk in terms of 10 percent; other estimates come in much lower.[64] One source estimates that 2.8 percent of men and 1.4 percent of women identify themselves as homosexual or bisexual.[65] Regardless of its overall size, the homosexual community has become important politically in several cities, most notably San Francisco. Both parties have openly professed gay members of Congress.

In 2000, Vermont became the first state to enact legislation granting gay and lesbian couples "civil union" status, which confers many of the benefits of marriage. Before this law took effect, the Vermont Supreme Court had ruled that denying gay couples the same rights and benefits as heterosexual couples is unconstitutional. The legislation prompted some voter backlash in the Vermont 2000 elections, and court challenges are also likely to continue.[66]

The political agenda for gay and lesbian advocacy groups includes fighting discrimination, including the military's "Don't ask, don't tell" policy. On some fronts, the groups have been successful. In several cities and among some employers, gays and lesbians have been able to secure health care and other benefits for domestic partners. Antidiscrimination statutes protecting people from discrimination in housing and employment on the basis of sexual orientation have been passed in several cities and states. Groups like the Human Rights Campaign are visible advocates of eliminating restrictions based on sexual orientation. Hate crimes against gays and lesbians have led the Senate to include sexual orientation in federal hate crimes legislation.[67]

Conservative groups have, however, largely been successful in banning same-sex marriage in a series of statewide ballot initiatives. Among the groups who have been active in the protest movement have been some conservative Protestants, Catholics, and Mormons. The courts have also been drawn into the battle over sexual orientation. In a 5-to-4 decision, the Supreme Court upheld the right of the Boy Scouts of America to bar homosexuals from leadership positions, as well as general membership, in its organization.[68] As the Boy Scouts controversy illustrates, policies relating to sexual orientation are among the most contentious in our society.

Family Structure

Over the past half-century, the typical American family has been transformed from a "traditional family" (mother and father married with children in the home) to a variety of living arrangements and varying family structures. Americans are much more likely to approve of premarital sex than in the early 1970s. And at some point in their lives, over half of Americans will *cohabit* (live with someone of the opposite sex to whom they are not married). Cohabitation raises public policy questions such as whether the live-in partner is eligible for employment benefits and welfare payments. Contraception is widely used and accepted, and yet one-third of all births are now illegitimate. These children will often be in need of social services and financial assistance.

Rosie O'Donnell, a gay parent, is a vocal advocate for gays who want to adopt children.

The risk of having children later in life has recently been the subject of cover stories in news magazines.

People now marry later in life, with men marrying at average age 26 and women at 24.[69] Yet marrying later has not improved the chances of avoiding divorce. The average marriage today lasts only about 7.2 years. Before World War II, only 9 out of every 1,000 marriages ended in divorce; between 1950 and 1996, the divorce rate nearly doubled. Today it is estimated that about half of all marriages will end in divorce.[70]

Since the 1960s, birthrates have steadily declined in the United States. In the early 1960s, a woman statistically averaged about 3.5 children. By 1999, that number dropped to 2 children, below the 2.1 needed to replace the population. In other words, if the current trend continues, the American native-born population will actually decrease over time.[71]

Divorce is one reason why some women go to work and why the number of households headed by women has risen. Attitudes about the role of women in marriage and the family have also changed. In 1972, one-third of Americans thought that a woman belonged in the home and should not work outside the home, but in 1998, only one-sixth of all Americans felt this way.[72]

Religion

In many parts of the world, religious differences, especially when combined with disputes over territory or sovereignty, are a source of violent conflict. The conflict in Israel between Israelis and Palestinians escalated with homicide bombers willing to kill themselves while killing Israeli civilians and with Israeli troops and tanks rolling into Palestinian areas. In Iraq and Turkey, the Kurdish people have been subjected to expulsion and even genocide. The war between India and Pakistan over Kashmir is a religious and ethnic battle among Muslims and Hindus, as is the conflict between Muslims and Christians in Indonesia. Other countries like Afghanistan, Lebanon, Sri Lanka, and Sudan have also experienced intense religious conflicts in recent years.

Jews have often been the target of religious discrimination and persecution (anti-Semitism), which reached its greatest intensity in the Holocaust of the 1930s and 1940s, during which an estimated 6 million Jews were murdered.[73] The United States has not been immune from such hatred, despite its principle of religious freedom. In 1838, Governor Lilburn W. Boggs of Missouri issued an extermination order against the Mormons.[74]

Our government is founded on the premise that religious liberty is more likely when there is not one predominant or official faith, which is why the framers of our Constitution did not sanction a national church. In fact, James Madison wrote in *The Federalist,* No. 51, "In a free government the security for civil rights must be the same as that for religious rights. It consists in the one case in the multiplicity of interests, and in the other in the multiplicity of sects" (see the Appendix).

The absence of an official American church does not mean that religion is unimportant in American politics; indeed, there were established state churches in this country until the 1830s. Some observers contend that "the root of American political and social values . . . is the distinctive Puritanism of the early New England settlers."[75] Politicians frequently refer to God in their speeches or demonstrate their piety in other ways. Democratic vice presidential candidate Joseph Lieberman, an observant Jew, made frequent references to God and religion in the 2000 campaign. President George W. Bush, addressing Congress in response to the events of September 11, 2001, said, "May God grant us wisdom and may He watch over the United States of America."[76]

Many Americans take their religious beliefs seriously, more so than people of other industrial democracies.[77] Nearly three-quarters of Americans attend houses of worship at least several times a year, 59 percent at least once a month, and 42 percent nearly every week.[78] Religion, like ethnicity, is a *shared identity.* People identify themselves as Baptist, Catholic, or Buddhist. To find out more information about religion in the United States, go to www.ipl.org/ref/RR/static/hum80.10.00.html. Sometimes church attendance or nonattendance is more important than differences

WE THE PEOPLE

Religion and Politics

At one time, it was thought that a Catholic could not be elected president. With the election of 1960, that issue was resolved. John F. Kennedy directly confronted the question of whether a Catholic would put aside religious teachings if they conflicted with constitutional obligations. He said, "I am not the Catholic candidate for President. I am the Democratic party's candidate for President who happens also to be Catholic. I do not speak for my church on public matters, and the church does not speak for me." Nevertheless, today it is still the case that a candidate's religion may become an issue if religious convictions on sensitive issues such as abortion threaten to conflict with public obligations.

Religion can be an important catalyst for social change, as the Catholic church was in the overthrow of communism in central Europe and the leadership of the black church was instrumental in the American civil rights movement. As writer Taylor Branch explains, the black church "served not only as a place of worship but also as a bulletin board to a people who owned no organs of communication, a credit union to those without banks, and even a kind of people's court."* African American ministers, like the Reverend Martin Luther King Jr., became leaders of the civil rights movement; others, like the Reverend Jesse Jackson, have run for national office. Hence religion can be important not only as a source of personal values and attitudes but also as a means of political activity and organization.

More recently, there has been an increase in political activity among fundamentalist Christians. Led by ministers like Jerry Falwell and Pat Robertson, they have supported political organizations such as the Moral Majority and the Christian Coalition. For two decades, they have sought to influence the national agenda, and Robertson taped telephone endorsements for George W. Bush in 2000. They also focus their attention at the local level—school boards, city councils, mayorships, and local GOP leadership.† Their agenda includes the return of school prayer, the outlawing of abortion, restrictions on homosexuals, and opposition to gun control. To learn more about the Christian Coalition, go to www.cc.org.

In the 2000 presidential election, both sets of major party nominees emphasized their religious faith.‡ Al Gore's running mate, Senator Joseph Lieberman, often spoke about God and religion during campaign stops. One of President Bush's first actions was to propose government use of churches to deliver social services, his "faith-based" initiative.

*Taylor Branch, *Parting the Waters: America in the King Years, 1954–63* (Simon & Schuster, 1988), p. 3.

†Kevin Lange, "An Energized Religious Right? Strategies for the Clinton Era," *Christian Century* 110 (February 17, 1993), pp. 177–79.

‡Janine Zacharia, "The Role of God in U.S. Elections," *Jerusalem Post,* September 7, 2000, p. 6.

John F. Kennedy.

Pat Robertson.

Joseph Lieberman.

---

between religions in explaining attitudes. "Among both Catholics and Protestants, opposition to abortion increases with frequency of church attendance, but the percentages expressing pro-choice and pro-life sentiments are almost identical for the Catholic and Protestant groups."[79]

One defining characteristic of religion in the United States is the tremendous variety of denominations. About half the people in the United States describe themselves

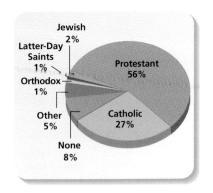

FIGURE 5–4   Religious Groups in America.

Source: "Largest Religious Groups in the United States of America," at www.adherents.com/relUSA.htm.

as Protestant (see Figure 5-4). The largest Protestant denomination is Baptist, followed by Methodists, Lutherans, Presbyterians, Pentecostals, and Episcopalians. Because Protestants are divided among so many different churches, Catholics have the largest single membership in the United States, constituting more than one-quarter of the population. Jews constitute 2 percent of the population. Followers of Islam number more than 500,000.[80] Protestants came to the United States first; most Catholics and Jews immigrated after the 1840s. It was not until 1960, however, that Americans elected a Catholic president.

Religion is important in American politics in part because of the concentrations of people of particular religions in a few states. Catholics, as noted, make up about one-quarter of the U.S. population, yet they make up more than 50 percent of the population of Rhode Island, Massachusetts, and Connecticut. Baptists represent 19 percent of the U.S. population, yet they account for more than 50 percent of the population of Mississippi, Alabama, and Georgia. Mormons represent only 2 percent of the U.S. population but more than 70 percent of the population of Utah. The South is the most Protestant—61 percent. The state of New York has the highest percentage of Jews, 7 percent; New York City is 14 percent Jewish.

In recent presidential elections, a majority of Protestants voted Republican, while majorities of Catholics and Jews voted Democratic.[81] The perception among many Catholics and Jews that the Democratic party is more open to them helps explain the strength of their Democratic identification. Democrats won the loyalty of many Catholics by their willingness to nominate Al Smith for the presidency in 1928 and John Kennedy in 1960. Jewish voters' long-standing identification with the Democratic party may have been reinforced by Al Gore's selection of Joseph Lieberman to be his running mate in 2000. Southern Protestants have been Democrats for different reasons, having largely to do with the sectional issues discussed earlier. Religious groups vary in their rates of participation. Jews have the highest rate of reported voter turnout, 93 percent in 2000, while those who claim no religious affiliation have the lowest, 47 percent.[82] Catholics (62 percent) voted at a slightly higher rate than Protestants (59 percent).[83] Religion can be related to other politically important characteristics. For instance, Jews are the most prosperous and best educated of any ethnic or religious group. More than 46 percent of Jewish adults are college graduates, compared to 22 percent of Protestants and 20 percent of Catholics.[84] In this example, as in others, religion is a cross-cutting cleavage in American politics; the differences do not reinforce one another. On the basis of income and education, we might expect Jews to be Republicans, but 79 percent of American Jews voted for Al Gore in 2000.[85] Similarly, we might predict that southern Protestants would be heavily Republican, but many are Democrats.

Wealth and Income

The United States is a wealthy nation. Compared to other nations, our purchasing power is higher than that of any other advanced democracy.[86] Indeed, to some knowledgeable observers, "the most striking thing about the United States has been its phenomenal wealth."[87] Most Americans lead comfortable lives. They eat and live well and have first-class medical care. But the unequal distribution of wealth and income still results in important political divisions and conflicts.

Wealth (total value of possessions) is more concentrated than income (annual earnings). The wealthiest families hold most of the property and other forms of wealth like stocks and savings. Traditionally, one of the problems with concentrated wealth has been that it fosters an aristocracy. Thomas Jefferson sought to break up the "aristocracy of wealth" by changing from laws based on *primogeniture* (the eldest son's exclusive right to inherit his father's estate) to laws that encouraged people to divide their estates equally among all their children, resulting in smaller landholdings. Jefferson sought to encourage an "aristocracy of virtue and talent" through a public school system open to all for the primary grades and for the best students through the university level.[88]

The Impact of Rising College Costs on Low-Income Students

College tuition and other costs have climbed substantially in recent years. Tuition, for example, climbed 185 percent, on average, at public colleges and universities and 173 percent at private institutions during the 1990s.

The impact of rising costs affects low-income students more than others. These students come from families that are less likely to be able to help with the rising costs. "Last year, the cost of college as a percentage of real family income was 62 percent for low-income families, 16 percent for middle-class families and 7 percent for the wealthier."*

Low-income students have also been hurt by a shift in some colleges away from a need-based system of scholarships. Part of the problem for low-income students is also a success story. There are now more of them qualifying for admission, making the competition for support more intense.

Finally, in recent years, the agenda for college aid has been more focused on the middle class, with tax breaks for tuition and college savings accounts, rather than on aid to low-income students. All of these factors combine to make obtaining a college education more of a hurdle for low-income students.

SOURCE: "Rising Costs Burden Poor College Students," *New York Times,* February 22, 2001, p. A18; U.S. Bureau of the Census, *Statistical Abstract of the United States, 2001* (Government Printing Office, 2001), p. 173.

*Kristin Davis, "College by the Numbers," *Kiplinger's Personal Finance Magazine* 55 (November 2001), p. 86.

Most college students come from the top quarter of American families in income—those earning $50,000 a year or more. Education is in turn one of the most important means to achieve upward economic and social mobility. People who go to college earn more than those who have not, and those from wealthier families are more inclined to get an education at nearly twice the rate as those positioned elsewhere on the socioeconomic ladder.[89]

"The most common and durable source of factions has been the various and unequal distribution of property," wrote James Madison in *The Federalist,* No. 10 (reprinted in the Appendix). "Those who hold, and those who are without property, have ever formed distinct interests in society." Madison was right. Economic differences often lead to conflict, and Americans remain divided politically along economic lines. Aside from race, income may be the single most important factor in explaining views on issues, partisanship, and ideology. Most rich people are Republicans, and most poor people are Democrats, and this has been true since at least the Great Depression of the 1930s. In terms of income, the Northeast is the most prosperous region and the South the least prosperous.

For most Americans, income has been rising. After adjusting for inflation, income doubled in the period between the 1950s and the 1970s. Since then, inflation-adjusted income has gone up and down, but the steady rise seen earlier has not occurred (see Figure 5-5).[90] Economists debate the causes for this change; some cite higher energy costs, low levels of personal savings, and the worldwide slowdown in productivity growth.[91]

Despite the general rise in income, the bottom 10 percent of the population in terms of income has actually seen a decline in wages. At the same time, the top 10 percent has experienced substantial growth in income. Economists refer to this as *dispersion,* or the difference in growth patterns among income levels.

The bottom 10 percent in income is also the segment of the population that falls below the poverty line.[92] In 2001, the official poverty level for a family of four was an income below $17,960.[93] Families headed by a female are three times more likely to fall below the poverty line than families headed by a man, and 36.2 percent of all households headed by females fall below the poverty line.[94] Close to 35 percent of the

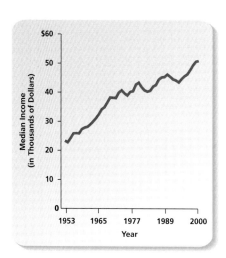

FIGURE 5–5   Median Family Income, 1953–2000.

SOURCE: U.S. Bureau of the Census, at www.census.gov/hhes/income/histinc/f06.html.

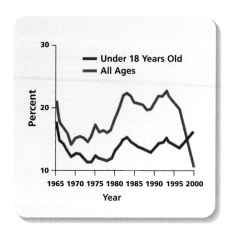

FIGURE 5–6   Percentage of Americans Living in Poverty, by Age, 1959–2000.

SOURCE: U.S. Bureau of the Census, at www.census.gov/prod/3/97pubs/p60–198.pdf.

"It's like this. If the rich have money, they invest. If the poor have money, they eat."

gross domestic product (GDP)
The total output of all economic activity in the nation, including goods and services.

poor are children under 18 years of age, and many appear to be trapped in a cycle of poverty (see Figure 5-6).[95] African American and Hispanic children are nearly three times as likely to be poor than white children.[96]

The definition of poverty is itself political, and a change in the definition of poverty can make it appear that there are more or fewer poor people than before. The poverty classification is intended to identify persons who cannot meet a minimum standard in such basics as housing, food, and medical care. Regardless of how one defines poverty, however, the poor are a minority who lack political power. The poor vote less than wealthier groups and are less confident and organized in dealing with politics and government. Over the past two decades, inequality between rich and poor has been increasing, a trend quite different from the 1960s, when the gap between rich and poor narrowed.[97] Although the gap began to decrease under the first Bush administration (1989–1993), inequality between rich and poor has again been on the rise since then.[98]

The distribution of income in a society can have important consequences for democratic stability. If there is a perception that only the few at the top of the economic ladder can hope to earn enough for an adequate standard of living, domestic unrest and revolution may follow. Income is related to participation in politics. People who need the most help from government are the least likely to participate. They are also the most likely to favor social welfare programs.

Occupation

Americans at the time of Jefferson and for several generations thereafter worked primarily on farms, but by the end of World War I, the United States had become the world's leading industrial nation. This dramatic transformation also resulted in the expansion of American cities as workers moved to find jobs. Labor conditions, including child labor practices, became important political issues. Inventions and the application of technology, combined with abundant natural and human resources, meant that the U.S. **gross domestic product (GDP)** rose, after adjusting for inflation, by more than 392 percent over the period from 1960 to 2000.[99]

The United States several years ago entered what Daniel Bell, a noted sociologist, labeled the "postindustrial" phase of our development. "A post-industrial society, being primarily a technical society, awards less on the basis of inheritance or property . . . than on education and skill."[100] *Knowledge* is the organizing device of the postindustrial era. Postindustrial societies have greater affluence and a class structure less defined along traditional labor-versus-management lines.

The changing dynamics of the American labor force can be seen in Figure 5-7, which shows the percentage of the U.S. labor force in various occupations. There has been tremendous growth in the white-collar sector of our economy. This sector includes managers, accountants, and lawyers, as well as professionals and technicians in such rapid-growth areas as computers, communications, finance, insurance, and research. This shift has been accompanied by a dramatic decline in the number of people engaged in agriculture and a more modest decline in the number of people in manufacturing (the blue-collar sector). Today only 11.6 percent of working Americans produce goods, and only 2 percent work on farms.[101] Governments are among the biggest employers in this country. Federal, state, and local governments produce more than one-sixth of our gross domestic product.[102]

Women and racial minorities have distinct occupational patterns. The majority of blue-collar jobs are held by men, while women hold over 62 percent of jobs in the service sector—especially in education, social services, and health care.[103] As noted earlier, women generally earn less than men of the same age and education. Occupations in which women predominate, like teaching and clerical work, are generally lower-paying than industrial or management jobs. And as women advance in their careers, especially in management, they encounter a barrier to advancement that has been referred to as the "glass ceiling."

Social Class

Why do Americans not divide themselves into social classes as Europeans do? American workers have not formed their own political party, nor does class seem to dominate our political life. Marxist categories of *proletariat* (those who sell their labor) and *bourgeoisie* (those who own or control the means of production) are far less important here than they are in Europe. Still, we do have social classes and what social scientists call **socioeconomic status (SES)**—a division of the population based on occupation, income, and education.

Most Americans, when asked what class they belong to, say "middle class." Very few see themselves as lower class or upper class. In many other industrial democracies, large proportions of the population think of themselves as "working class" rather than middle class.[104] In England, nearly three out of five persons identify themselves as working class.[105] But Americans rarely use that designation.

What constitutes the "middle class" in the United States is highly subjective. For instance, some individuals perform working class tasks (such as plumbing), but their income places them in the middle class or even the upper-middle class. A schoolteacher's income is below that of many working class jobs, but in terms of status, the job ranks among middle-class fields.

One explanation for Americans' responses may be the elements of the American dream that involve upward mobility. Or their responses may reflect the hostility many feel toward organized labor. In any case, compared to many countries, class divisions in the United States are less defined and less important to politics. As political scientist Seymour Martin Lipset has written, "The American social structure and values foster an emphasis on competitive individualism, an orientation that is not congruent with class consciousness, support for socialist or social democratic parties, or a strong union movement."[106]

Age

Americans are living longer, a phenomenon that has been dubbed the "graying of America" (Figure 5-8). This demographic change is having important consequences; it has increased the demand for medical care, retirement benefits, and a host of other age-related services. Persons over the age of 65 constitute less than 13 percent of the population yet account for 31 percent of the total medical expenditures.[107] With the decreasing birthrate discussed earlier, there is some concern about maintaining an adequate work force in the future.

Older Americans are politically aware, and they vote. Past legislative victories have changed the lives of older citizens. For instance, the poverty rate among this group dropped from 15.7 percent in 1980 to 9.7 percent in 1999, a change partly due to improved medical benefits passed during the 1960s.[108] As a group, older Americans fight to

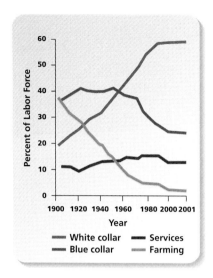

FIGURE 5–7 Occupational Groups, 1900–1999.

SOURCE: U.S. Department of Labor, *Employment and Earnings,* vol. 43, no. 1 (Government Printing Office, 1996), p. 30; vol. 44, no. 1 (1997), p. 31; and vol. 47, no. 1 (2000), p. 31. See also www.bls.gov/cps/home.htm#charemp.

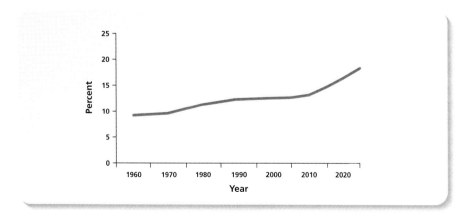

FIGURE 5–8 Percent of Population over Age 65, 1960–2050.

SOURCE: U.S. Bureau of the Census, at www.census.gov/population/www/projections/natsum-T3.html.

socioeconomic status (SES)
A division of population based on occupation, income, and education.

ensure that Social Security is protected; they value Medicare and favor prescription drug coverage. Despite their desire for services that benefit themselves, they also favor tax cuts.

In recent presidential elections, 28 percent of all 18- to 20-year-olds voted; in contrast, 67.6 percent of Americans 65 and older turned out to vote.[109] Their vote is especially important in western states and in Florida, the state with the largest proportion of people over 65. The "gray lobby" not only votes in large numbers but also has four other political assets not found in other age groups that make it politically powerful: disposable income, discretionary time, a clear focus on issues, and effective organization. When older Americans compete for their share of the budget pie, the young, minorities, and the poor often lose out.[110] In his 2000 presidential campaign, Al Gore proposed a prescription drug benefit through Medicare while Bush promoted Social Security privatization, which seemed to threaten seniors. These campaign dynamics helped Democrats gain support from seniors.

Age is important to politics in two additional ways: life cycle and generational. *Life-cycle effects* have shown that as people become middle-aged, they become more politically conservative, less mobile, and more likely to participate in politics. As they age further and rely more on the government for services, they tend to grow more liberal.[111] Young people, in contrast, are more mobile and less concerned about the delivery of government services.

There are also *generational effects* in politics that arise when a particular generation has had experiences that make it politically distinct. An example is the experience of those who lived through the Great Depression of the 1930s, which shaped their lifelong views of parties, issues, and political leaders. Some members of this generation saw Franklin Roosevelt as the leader who saved the country by pulling it out of the Depression; others felt he sold the country down the river by launching too many government programs. More recently and to a lesser extent, the baby boomers shared a common and distinctive political experience. These Americans came of age politically in the 1960s and 1970s during the civil rights movement and the Vietnam War.

Education

Differences in education affect not only economic well-being but political participation and involvement as well. Thomas Jefferson wrote of education, "Enlighten the people gener-

TABLE 5–3 Distribution of Education in the United States

	Population (1,000)	Not a High School Graduate	High School Graduate	Bachelor's Degree	Advanced Degree
Age					
18 to 24 years old	26,532	10.8%	30.4%	7.0%	0.6%
25 to 34 years old	37,786	11.8	30.6	22.7	6.6
35 to 44 years old	44,805	11.4	33.7	18.4	8.6
45 to 54 years old	36,630	11.1	31.0	18.7	11.5
55 to 64 years old	23,387	17.7	35.7	13.7	10.9
65 to 74 years old	17,796	26.4	37.4	10.4	7.1
75 years old or over	14,825	35.4	34.1	8.7	4.7
Sex					
Male	96,901	17.2	31.8	16.2	8.7
Female	104,861	16.6	33.7	15.3	6.5
Race					
White	148,091	12.3	3.6	17.4	8.4
Black	23,308	21.5	35.2	10.2	4.3
Hispanic	21,109	43.0	28.3	6.3	2.7
Asian/Pacific Islander	7,859	14.7	21.8	26.4	13.3

SOURCE: U.S. Bureau of the Census, *Current Population Reports,* P217 (Government Printing Office, 2001); U.S. Bureau of the Census, *Statistical Abstract of the United States, 2001* (Government Printing Office, 2001), p. 140.

ally, and tyranny and oppressions of body and mind will vanish like evil spirits at the dawn of day."[112] The vast majority of people in the United States are educated in public schools. Nine out of every ten students in kindergarten through high school attend public schools, and more than three out of four students in college are in public institutions.[113]

Only recently has the number of college graduates in America surpassed the number of persons who did not graduate from high school.[114] Just over half of all Americans have not gone to college, though many college students assume that the college experience is widely shared. The proportion of whites who are college graduates is nearly double that for African Americans and more than double that for Hispanics; roughly 24 percent of African Americans and nearly half of all Hispanics stopped their schooling before completing high school (see Table 5-3).[115]

Education is one of the most important variables in predicting political participation, confidence in dealing with government, and awareness of issues. Education is also related to the acquisition of democratic values. People who have failed to learn the prevailing norms of American society are far more likely to express opposition to democratic and capitalist ideals than those who are well educated and politically knowledgeable.[116]

Unity in a Land of Diversity

As remarkable as American diversity is, the existence of a strong and widely shared sense of national unity and identity may be even more remarkable. Writing about the United States some years ago, a famous reporter, John Gunther, summarized his insights from extensive travels:

> Whoever invented the motto *E Pluribus Unum* [out of many, one] has given the best three-word description of the United States ever written. The triumph of America is the triumph of a coalescing federal system. Complex as the nation is almost to the point of insufferability, it interlocks. Homogeneity and diversity—these are the stupendous rival magnets. . . . Think of the United States as an immense blanket or patchwork quilt solid with different designs and highlights. But, no matter what colors burn and flash in what corners, the warp and woof, the basic texture and fabric, is the same from corner to corner, from end to end.[117]

Social scientists sometimes speak of the "melting pot," meaning that as various ethnic groups associate with other groups, they are assimilated into American society and come to share democratic values like majority rule, individualism, and the notion that America is the land of opportunity. The melting pot idea has been criticized as assuming

IN COMPARATIVE PERSPECTIVE

Politics and Urbanization in Mexico

The migration from rural to urban areas, important to American politics during the nineteenth century, has more recently had an impact on the politics of Mexico. In Mexico's 2000 presidential election, Vicente Fox surprised many when his party defeated the candidate of the Institutional Revolution Party (PRI). The PRI had not lost a presidential election in more than 70 years. One factor in Fox's defeat of the PRI appears to have been the migration to Mexico City and other population centers of voters who opposed the PRI.

Why is urbanization important? One reason is that it is easier to organize and mobilize voters living in closer proximity to one another. Another reason is that educational opportunities are more available in the urban sections of Mexico. The success of Fox and his party in organizing and mobilizing these new urban voters is another example of the importance of place in politics. It often makes a difference where one lives, at least if one or more parties are willing and able to appeal to issues of concern to voters from these places.

SOURCE: Julia Preston, "The Defiant Ones: 4 Mexicans Exult in Party's Fall," *New York Times*, July 12, 2000, p. A3.

that differences between groups are to be discouraged. In its place, critics propose the notion of the "salad bowl," in which "though the salad is an entity, the lettuce can still be distinguished from the chicory, the tomatoes from the cabbage."[118]

As we have seen, important differences persist among groups, and in that sense the salad bowl analogy is accurate. Divisive issues like immigration, affirmative action, and programs for the poor have reinforced our differences. But in another way, our society has achieved a unity of commitment to democratic values and processes—a political culture that is, at least in part, a consequence of such elements of the melting pot theory as public schools, a common language, and hope for a better life for one's children. Ethnic divisions in the United States pose challenges to the institutions and processes of government, yet the public has generally accepted diversity in political appointments, government jobs and contracts, and other aspects of policy. This acceptance is in sharp contrast to the violent ethnic conflicts in other parts of the world. But we are still seeking the appropriate balance among recognition, preservation, and representation of ethnic groups and the needs for assimilation, common commitments, and a shared identity.

THE GREAT AMERICAN DIVIDE

This PoliSim examines the demographic makeup of the two major parties. The cross-cutting nature of American politics is more evident among some groups, while others are strongly inclined toward one party. Based on your reading of this chapter and your political experience, test your knowledge about which types of people identify with the Republican or Democratic party.

Go to PoliSim "The Great American Divide."

Summary

1. The character of a political society and its social environment are important to understanding our politics and government.

2. As a nation of immigrants, Americans are more diverse than the citizens of most other nations. Diversity in race and ethnicity are reflected in different family structures and religions. The nation's citizens also differ in wealth and income, occupation, social class, age, and education. Divisions by gender and sexual orientation have recently become more important. This diversity is often significant in our politics, though most divisions cut across demographic categories rather than reinforce them.

3. Geography, room to grow, abundant natural resources, wealth, and relative isolation from foreign entanglements help explain American politics and traditions, including the notions of manifest destiny, ethnocentrism, and isolationism.

4. Until recently, the South was a very distinct region in the United States, in large part because of its agricultural base and its history of slavery and troubled race relations. With in-migration and the impact of the civil rights movement, it is no longer solidly Democratic. Recently, the most significant migration has been from cities to suburbs. Today large cities are increasingly poor, African American, and Democratic,

surrounded by suburbs that are primarily middle class, white, and Republican.

5. Race has been among the most important of the differences in our political landscape. Although we fought a civil war over freedom for African Americans, racial equality was largely postponed until the latter half of the twentieth century. Race remains an important issue in our politics and government. Ethnicity, including the rising numbers of Hispanics, continues to be a factor in politics.

6. Gender is important in American politics. Women have gradually acquired political rights. They now play important roles in our government, and they differ from men in their attitudes on some issues. Sexual orien-

tation policies are among the most contentious in our society.

7. Since World War II, attitudes toward sexuality, marriage, and family have changed in important ways. People cohabit at much higher rates, and those who marry are older. Divorce has also become much more commonplace. Changing family structures and attitudes affect our tax policies, child care, parental leave, and gender equality. They are also important political issues.

8. The United States has a large variety of religious denominations, and these differences help explain public opinion and political behavior. Important differences also exist between Americans who are religious and those who are not.

9. Although the United States is a land of wealth with a large middle class, not everyone has an adequate share in the American economic success. Poverty has grown over the past two decades, and it is most concentrated among African Americans, Native Americans, Hispanics, and single-parent households. Women as a group continue to earn less than men, even in the same occupations. Differences in income and wealth remain important.

10. The United States has shifted from an agricultural to an industrial and now to a postindustrial society, with consequences for occupations and politics. Governments are a major source of employment. Social class is less important in America than in other industrialized democracies.

11. Age and education are important to understanding American politics. Older citizens participate much more than young voters and are a potent political force. Education not only opens up economic opportunities in America but also explains many important aspects of political participation.

12. Despite our diversity, Americans share an important unity. We are united by our shared commitment to democratic values, economic opportunity, the work ethic, and the American dream.

Key Terms

ethnocentrism
political socialization
demographics

political predisposition
reinforcing cleavages
cross-cutting cleavages

manifest destiny
race
ethnicity

gender gap
gross domestic product (GDP)
socioeconomic status (SES)

Further Reading

Douglas L. Anderson, Richard Bartnett, and Donald Bogue, *The Population of the United States*, 3d ed. (Free Press, 1996).

David H. Bennett, *The Party of Fear* (University of North Carolina Press, 1990).

Earl Black and Merle Black, *The Vital South: How Presidents Are Elected* (Harvard University Press, 1992).

Urie Bronfenbrenner et al., *The State of Americans: The Disturbing Facts and Figures on Changing Values, Crime, the Economy, Poverty, Family, Education, the Aging Population, and What They Mean for Our Future* (Free Press, 1996).

David T. Canon, *Race, Redistricting, and Representation: The Unintended Consequences of Black Majority Districts* (University of Chicago Press, 1999).

Rodolfo O. de la Garza, Louis De Sipio, F. Chris Garcia, John Garcia, and Angelo Falcon, *Latino Voices: Mexican, Puerto Rican, and Cuban Perspectives on American Politics* (Westview Press, 1992).

Lois Lovelace Duke, ed., *Women in Politics: Outsiders or Insiders?* 2d ed. (Prentice Hall, 1995).

Sarah H. Evans, *Born for Liberty: A History of Women in America* (Free Press, 1989).

Geoffrey Fox, *Hispanic Nation: Culture, Politics and the Constructing of Identity* (Birch Lane Press, 1996).

Donald R. Kinder and Lynn M. Sanders, *Divided by Color: Racial Politics and Democratic Ideals* (University of Chicago Press, 1996).

Jan E. Leighley, *Strength in Numbers? The Political Mobilization of Racial and Ethnic Minorities* (Princeton University Press, 2001).

Seymour Martin Lipset, *Continental Divide: The Values and Institutions of the United States and Canada* (Routledge, 1990).

Nancy E. McGlen and Karen O'Connor, *Women, Politics, and American Society,* 2d ed. (Prentice Hall, 1998).

Peter Nabokov, ed., *Native American Testimony: A Chronicle of Indian-White Relations from Prophecy to the Present, 1492–1992* (Viking, 1991).

Kevin Phillips, *The Politics of Rich and Poor: Wealth and the American Electorate in the Reagan Aftermath* (Random House, 1990).

Stanley A. Renshon, ed., *One America? Political Leadership, National Identity, and the Dilemmas of Diversity* (Georgetown University Press, 2001).

Steven J. Rose, *Social Stratification in the United States: The American Profile Poster Revised and Expanded* (New Press, 1992).

Ruben G. Rumbaut and Alejandro Portes, *Ethnicities: Children of Immigrants in America* (University of California Press, 2001).

Arthur M. Schlesinger Jr., *The Disuniting of America* (Norton, 1992).

Jeffrey M. Stonecash, *Class and Party in American Politics* (Westview Press, 2000).

Studs Terkel, *Race: How Blacks and Whites Think and Feel About the American Obsession* (Norton, 1992).

Alexis de Tocqueville, *Democracy in America,* ed. J. P. Mayer, trans. George Lawrence (Doubleday, 1969). Originally published 1835.

Kenneth D. Wald, *Religion and Politics in the United States*, 3d ed. (CQ Press, 1996).

6
CHAPTER

INTEREST GROUPS
The Politics of Influence

DURING THE FINAL TWO WEEKS OF THE 2000 PRESIDENTIAL ELECTION CAMPAIGN, A GROUP CALLING ITSELF AMERICANS FOR Equality, a project of the National Association for the Advancement of Colored People's National Voter Fund, ran a commercial criticizing Texas governor and presidential candidate George W. Bush. The ad begins with harsh black-and-white images and eerie, metallic sounds of a truck dragging a chain along a gravel road. Then a female voice says, "On June 7, 1998, in Texas, my father was killed. He was beaten, chained, and then dragged three miles to his death, all because he was black." The woman speaking is the eldest daughter of James Byrd Jr., and she continues by saying that when Governor Bush "refused to support hate crime legislation, it was like my father was killed all over again." According to Mike Lux, an NAACP National Voter Fund consultant, it was designed to stimulate turnout among new and infrequent African American voters in hope of electing candidates with a strong record on civil rights issues. Research with focus groups found that the ad would need to convey passion and force to have the desired effect.[1] The NAACP National Voter Fund ran the ad along with a voter registration and get-out-the-vote effort in states where the African American vote was crucial, and it seemed to make a difference in Florida, Missouri, Arkansas, and New York, where black voter turnout went up dramatically.[2]

Group-sponsored campaign activity in recent elections has included many groups whose names you will likely recognize: Christian Coalition, American Federation of Labor–Congress of Industrial Organizations (AFL-CIO), National Education Association, National Abortion and Reproductive Rights Action League (NARAL), National Right to Life, U.S. Chamber of Commerce, Sierra Club. All these *interest groups*, dedicated to advancing specific interests through the political process, have run ads on television and radio and mounted telephone or mail campaign efforts in recent election cycles. The U.S. Supreme Court has ruled that as long as such communications avoid words like "vote for" or "vote against," they are **issue advocacy** ads, and as such, they are not subject to the same disclosure requirements and contribution limitations as candidate campaign advertising.

Groups can engage in issue advocacy in addition to contributing money to candidates and parties through their political action committees (PACs)[3] and to political parties. Much of this election activity is done late in the campaign, when there is little time for a reply, and communicated in ways designed to avoid media scrutiny. Groups can also spend unlimited amounts using words like "vote for" and "vote against" candidates if those expenditures are completely independent. Such campaign communications are called independent expenditures and differ from issue ads only in the language used. The campaign finance reforms enacted in 2002 change some aspects of the laws relating to issue advocacy, but interest groups may well become even more important in competitive elections as a result of these reforms, as we will explain later.

How interest groups compete for influence, the role they play in elections, and efforts to rein them in are the subjects of this chapter. We begin by discussing the types of interest groups and the roles they play. Then we turn to one of their most important activities, lobbying. Finally, we examine the problems interest groups pose and ways to regulate them.

Interest Groups Past and Present: The "Mischiefs of Faction"

What we call interest groups today, the founders of the Republic called **factions**. (They also thought of political parties as factions.) For the framers of the Constitution, the daunting problem was how to establish a stable and orderly constitutional system that would also respect the liberty of free citizens and prevent the tyranny of the majority or of a single dominant interest. As a good practical politician and a brilliant theorist, James

issue advocacy
Unlimited and undisclosed spending by an individual or group on communications that do not use words like "vote for" or "vote against," although much of this activity is actually about electing or defeating candidates.

faction
A term used by the founders of this country to refer to political parties and special interests or interest groups.

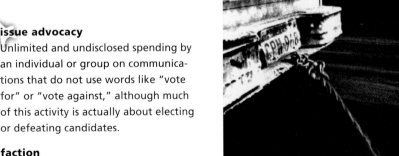

Interest groups often use advertising to promote issues that they consider important. This advertisement created by the NAACP was designed to attract new and infrequent African American voters to vote for candidates with a strong record on civil rights issues.

Madison offered both a diagnosis and a solution in *The Federalist,* No. 10 (reprinted in the appendix). He began with a basic proposition: "The latent causes of faction are thus sown in the nature of man." Acknowledging that Americans live in a maze of group interests, Madison went on to argue that the "most common and durable source of factions has been the various and unequal distribution of property."

A Nation of Interests

As we noted in Chapter 5, some Americans identify with groups distinguished by race, gender, ethnic background, age, occupation, or sexual orientation. Others form groups based on issues like gun control or tax reduction. When such associations seek to influence government in some way, they are **interest groups**.

Interest groups are sometimes called "special interests." Politicians and the media often use this term in a pejorative way. What makes an interest group a "special" one? The answer is highly subjective. One person's special interest is another's public interest. Some interest groups claim to speak for the "public interest," yet so-called public interest groups like Common Cause or the Center for Responsive Politics support policies that not everyone agrees with. Politics is best seen as a clash among interests with differing concepts of what is in the public interest rather than a battle between the special interests on one side and "the people" or the public intent on the other.

When political scientists call something an "interest group" or a "special interest," they are not calling it names. These are analytic terms to describe a group that speaks for some but not all of us. Much of our politics focuses on arguments about what is in the national interest. In a democracy, there are many interests and many organized interest groups. The democratic process exists to decide among those competing interests. Part of the politics of interest groups is to persuade the general public that your group's interest is better, broader, more beneficial, and more general than other groups' and at the same time label groups that oppose yours as "special interests." The term "special interest" conveys a selfish or narrow view, one that may lack credibility. For this reason, we use the neutral term "interest groups."

Social Movements

Interest groups sometimes begin as movements. A **movement** consists of a large body of people who are interested in a common issue, idea, or concern that is of continuing significance and who are willing to take action. Examples include the abolitionist, temperance, civil rights, environmental, antitax, animal rights, and women's rights movements. Each movement represents groups who have felt unrepresented by government. Such groups often arise at the grassroots level and evolve into national groups. Movements tend to see their causes as morally right and the positions of the opposition as morally wrong.

To a marked degree, our Constitution protects the liberties and independence of movements. The Bill of Rights guarantees movements, whether popular or unpopular, by supporting free assembly, free speech, and due process. Consequently, militants do not have to engage in violence or other extreme activities in the United States, as they do in some countries, and they need not fear persecution for demonstrating peacefully. In a democratic system that restricts the power of the people in positions of authority, movements have considerable room to operate *within* the constitutional system.

Types of Interest Groups

Interest groups vary widely. Some are formal associations or organizations like the National Rifle Association; others have no formal organization like Bubba's List, a group from Austin, Texas (Bubba stands for Brothers United for Building a Better America). Some are organized primarily to lobby for limited goals such as restrictions on gun ownership, conducting research, or broadly influencing public opinion by publishing reports and mass mailings.

interest group
A collection of people who share some common interest or attitude and seek to influence government for specific ends. Interest groups usually work within the framework of government and employ tactics such as lobbying to achieve their goals.

movement
A large body of people interested in a common issue, idea, or concern that is of continuing significance and who are willing to take action. Movements seek to change attitudes or institutions, not just policies.

Interest groups can be categorized into several broad types: (1) economic, including both business and labor; (2) ideological or single-issue; (3) public interest; (4) foreign policy; and (5) government itself. Obviously, these categories are not mutually exclusive. The varied and overlapping nature of interest groups in the United States has been described as *interest group pluralism,* meaning that competition among open, responsive, and diverse groups helps preserve democratic values and limits the concentration of power in any single group.

Most Americans are represented by a number of interest groups, some of which they are aware of and others of which they may not be and often with which they differ. For instance, citizens over 50 may not be aware that the AARP (which began as the American Association of Retired Persons) claims to represent their interests, and now is open to anyone over fifty years of age. Others may not know that when they join the American Automobile Association (AAA), they are not only purchasing travel assistance and automobile towing when needed but also joining a group that lobbies Congress and the Federal Highway Administration on behalf of motorists.

Economic Interest Groups

There are thousands of economic interests: agriculture, consumers, plumbers, northern businesses, southern businesses, labor unions, the airplane industry, landlords, truckers, bondholders, property owners, and on and on.

BUSINESS   The most familiar business institution is probably the large corporation. Corporations range from one-person enterprises to vast multinational entities. Large corporations—General Motors, AT&T, Microsoft, Coca-Cola, McDonald's, and other large companies—exercise considerable political influence, as do hundreds of smaller corporations. Corporate power and the implications of a changing domestic and global economy make business practices important political issues.

TRADE AND OTHER ASSOCIATIONS   Businesses with similar interests in government regulations and other issues join together as *trade associations,* which are as diverse as the products and services they provide. In addition, businesses of all types are organized into large, nationwide associations such as the Conference Board, the National Association for the Self-Employed, the National Association of Realtors, and the Chamber of Commerce.

The broadest business trade association is the Chamber of Commerce of the United States. Organized in 1912, the Chamber is a federation of several thousand local Chambers of Commerce representing tens of thousands of firms. Loosely allied with the Chamber on most issues is the National Association of Manufacturers, which, since its founding in the wake of the depression of 1893, has tended to speak for the more conservative elements of American business.

LABOR   Workers' associations have a range of interests, from professional standards to wages and working conditions. Labor unions are one of the most important groups representing workers. The American work force is the least unionized of almost any industrial democracy (see Figure 6-1).

Probably the oldest unions in the United States were farm organizations. The largest farm group now is the American Farm Bureau Federation, which is especially strong in the Corn Belt. Originally organized around government agents who helped farmers in rural counties, the federation today is almost a semigovernmental agency, but it retains full freedom to fight for such goals as price supports and expanded credit. As farming has grown in scale and workers are less and less likely to be members of the farmer's family, there have been efforts to organize farm workers into unions. Noteworthy here have been the efforts of the late César Chávez and others to organize migrant farm workers.

Throughout the nineteenth century, workers organized political parties and local unions. Their most ambitious effort at national organization, the Knights of Labor, claimed 700,000 members. By the beginning of the twentieth century, the American Federation of

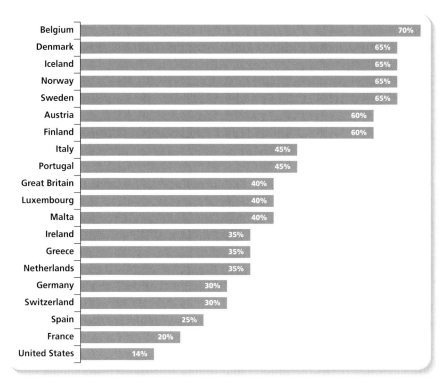

FIGURE 6–1 Union Membership in the United States Compared to Other Countries (Estimated Percentage of the Work Force).

Source: *The World Almanac and Book of Facts, 2000;* based on data from Henri J. Wamenhoven, *Western Europe,* 5th ed. (Dushkin/McGraw-Hill, 1997), p. 46.

Labor (AFL), a confederation of strong and independent-minded national unions mainly representing craft workers, was the dominant organization. During the ferment of the 1930s, unions more responsive to industrial workers broke away from the AFL and formed a rival national organization organized by industry, the Congress of Industrial Organizations (CIO). In 1955, the AFL and CIO reunited in the organization that exists today.

Union membership is optional in states whose laws permit the **open shop**, in which union membership cannot be required as a condition of employment. In states with the **closed shop**, union membership may be required as a condition of employment if most employees so vote. In both cases, the unions conduct negotiations with management, and the benefits the unions gain will be shared with all workers. In open-shop states, many workers choose not to affiliate with a union, as they can secure the same benefits without incurring the costs associated with union membership. When a person benefits from the work or service of an organization like a union or even a public radio station without joining or contributing, this condition is referred to as the **free rider** problem.

The AFL-CIO speaks for about 80 percent of unionized labor, but unions represent only about 14 percent of the nation's work force (see Figure 6-2).[4] The drop in the proportion of the work force belonging to unions is explained in part by the shift from an industrial to a service economy. Dwindling membership limits organized labor's political and lobbying muscle, and its prospects for increasing influence in the future are dim. Recently there has been growth in public sector unions, however, and even some doctors have unionized.

For some years, the Committee on Political Education (COPE) of the AFL-CIO was one of the most respected—and most feared—political organizations in the country. In the Kennedy and Johnson years, it won a reputation for political effectiveness. It encouraged and supervised grassroots political activity, and at the national level, it prepared and adopted a detailed platform that spelled out labor's position on issues. Labor

open shop

A company with a labor agreement under which union membership cannot be required as a condition of employment.

closed shop

A company with a labor agreement under which union membership can be a condition of employment.

free rider

An individual who does not join a group representing his or her interests yet receives the benefit of the influence the group achieves.

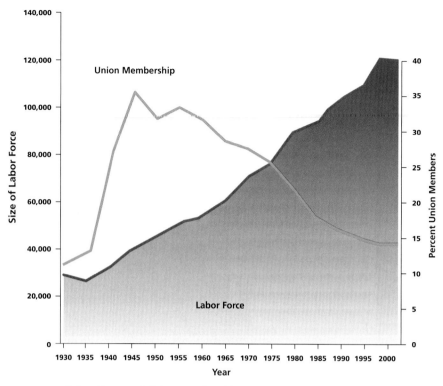

FIGURE 6-2 **Labor Force and Union Membership, 1930–1999.**

Source: *The World Almanac and Book of Facts, 2000.* Copyright © 1999 Primedia Reference, Inc. Reprinted with permission; all rights reserved. U.S. Bureau of Labor Statistics, at www.stats.bls.gov/news.release/union2.toc.htm. and www.bls.gov/cps/cpsaat40.pdf.

contributed money to candidates, ran registration and get-out-the-vote campaigns, and otherwise supported its favorites. In recent elections, COPE has had a fairly successful record of wins for its endorsed House and Senate candidates.[5] Labor unions invested heavily in the fight against the North American Free Trade Agreement (NAFTA), claiming it would cost jobs. Labor's defeat in this battle was compounded by the 1994 election, which put Republicans in charge of Congress, and the 2000 election, which put the GOP in charge of the White House and briefly also of Congress until Vermont Senator James Jeffords left the Republican party in 2001, giving Democrats control of the Senate. Despite labor's efforts to help Domocrats, Republicans regained control of the Senate in 2002.

In recent elections, the AFL-CIO has mounted vigorous campaigns to elect a Democratic majority in Congress and to keep the White House Democratic. Some foes of labor have proposed legislation and ballot initiatives called "paycheck protection," which would require annual authorization by union members for portions of their dues to be used for political purposes. Labor unions have successfully defeated these measures.

Unions have been effective in communicating with their members and organizing them for political purposes. In the 1998 elections and again in 2000 and 2002, unions sent mailings to their members, organized get-out-the-vote drives, and paid for television advertising. The voter identification and mobilization done by the AFL-CIO for Al Gore in the Iowa caucuses and New Hampshire primary were important to his victories in those states. The strong labor backing of Gore continued through the general election and was also aimed at key congressional contests.

Traditionally identified with the Democratic party, unions have not enjoyed a close relationship with Republican administrations. Given labor's limited resources, one option for unions is to form temporary coalitions with consumer, public interest, liberal, and sometimes even with industry groups, especially on issues related to foreign imports. Few of labor's recent legislative initiatives have been successful, and turning to the courts has yielded mixed results.[6]

PROFESSIONAL ASSOCIATIONS   Professional people have organized some of the strongest unions in the nation. Some are well known, such as the American Medical Association and the American Bar Association. Others are divided into many subgroups. Teachers, for example, are organized into large groups such as the National Education Association, the American Federation of Teachers, and the American Association of University Professors and also into subgroups based on specialties, such as the Modern Language Association and the American Political Science Association.

Government, especially on the state level, regulates many professions. Lawyers, for example, are licensed by states, which, often as a result of pressure from lawyers themselves, have set up certain standards of admission to the state bar. Professional associations also use the courts to pursue their agenda. In the area of medical malpractice, for example, doctors lobby hard for limited liability laws, while the trial lawyers resist such efforts. Teachers, hair stylists, and marriage therapists work for legislation or regulations of concern to them. It is not surprising, then, that among the largest donors to political campaigns through political action committees are those representing professional associations such as the American Medical Association and the American Realtors Association (see Table 6-1). Professional associations, in addition to lobbying legislative bodies, use the courts to pursue their agendas.

Ideological or Single-Issue Interest Groups

Ideological groups behave very much like economic interest groups, although they may not be driven by a desire to make money. Some of these groups are *single-issue groups,* often highly motivated and seeing politics primarily as a means to pursue their one issue. Such groups are often adamant about their position and unwilling to negotiate compromises. Right-to-life and pro-choice groups on abortion fit this description, as does the National Rifle Association.

Countless groups have organized around other specific issues, such as civil liberties, environmental protection, nuclear energy, and nuclear disarmament.[7] Such associations are not new. The Anti-Saloon League of the 1890s was single-mindedly

---

TABLE 6–1   PACs That Gave the Most to Federal Candidates, 1998–2002 (millions of dollars)

	2002	2000	1998
Realtors Political Action Committee	5.44	3.42	2.47
Association of Trial Lawyers of America Political Action Committee	6.72	2.66	2.43
American Federation of State, County, and Municipal Employees	8.48	2.59	2.37
Dealers Election Action Committee of the National Automobile Dealers	3.47	2.50	2.10
Democrat Republican Independent Voter Education Committee	9.62	2.50	2.18
International Brotherhood of Electrical Workers Committee on Political Action	9.18	2.46	1.88
Machinists Non-Partisan Political League	4.98	2.18	1.64
United Auto Workers Voluntary Community Action Program	6.54	2.16	1.92
Service Employees International Union Political Action Committee	7.10	1.89	1.30
American Medical Association Political Action Committee	5.17	1.94	2.34

SOURCE: Federal Election Commission, "PAC Activity Increases in 1995–96 Election Cycle," press release, April 22, 1997, p. 19; FEC/Info: Political Action Committee and Party Committee home page: www.fecinfo/_pac.htm. Also: Harold E. Stanley and Richard G. Niemi, eds., *Vital Statistics on American Politics 2001–2002* (CQ Press, 2001). Political Money Line, "Total PAC Disbursements," March 11, 2003, http://www.fecinfo.com/cgi-win/x_ps.exe?DoFn=, March 11, 2003.

devoted to barring the sale and manufacture of alcoholic beverages, and it did not care whether legislators were drunk or sober, as long as they voted dry. One of the best-known ideological groups today is the American Civil Liberties Union (ACLU), with roughly 250,000 members committed to the protection of civil liberties.[8] Religious groups are thriving in the otherwise pragmatic, pluralistic politics of today; an example is the Christian Coalition, which distributes voter guides before elections, although it has had less of a presence in recent years than it had earlier in the 1990s.[9] African American churches have long been important politically and continue to encourage voter participation.

Public Interest Groups

Out of the political ferment of the 1960s came groups that make a specific claim to promote "the public interest." For example, Common Cause, founded in 1970 by independent Republican John W. Gardner and later led by noted Watergate prosecutor Archibald Cox, campaigns for electoral reform and for making the political process more open. Its Washington staff raises money through direct-mail campaigns, oversees state chapters, issues research reports and press releases on current issues, and lobbies on Capitol Hill and in major government departments.

Ralph Nader started a conglomerate of consumer organizations that investigates and reports on governmental and corporate action—or inaction—relating to consumer interests. Public Interest Research Groups (PIRGs) founded by Nader are among the largest interest groups in the country. PIRGs have become important players on Capitol Hill and

A New Movement: Opposition to International Trade and Globalization

Movements arise around particular issues but often lack widespread support. To generate interest and support for their cause, movements often use protest demonstrations. A recent example of a movement that sought to use protest demonstrations to achieve its aims is the diverse set of interest groups that assembled an estimated 10,000 protesters in Seattle, Washington, December 11–13, 1999, to oppose the labor, environmental, and trade practices fostered by the World Trade Organization (WTO). Some of the same groups who protested in Seattle took part in later demonstrations in Washington, D.C., aimed at the World Bank and again in 2002 in Seattle to protest the WTO and globalization.

What started out in 1999 as a peaceful protest turned into a riot. Peaceful groups like Public Citizen and the AFL-CIO were brushed aside by more violent protesters, such as the Ruckus Society and the Direct Action Network. Vandals abandoned any pretense of peaceful protest by smashing store windows and spray-painting the anarchist symbol of an "A" in a circle on buildings. The Seattle police, unable to contain the situation and fearful they would be unable to protect delegates from 135 countries, resorted to riot control tactics, including tear gas, rubber bullets, and pepper spray. They also arrested more than 400 protesters. Newspapers and television broadcasts around the world showed the confrontations, arrests, and destruction.

In the days and weeks that followed, the tactics of the protesters and the police were debated. By most accounts, the protests led to an abrupt end to the meeting, and despite high hopes of important progress on international trade issues before the meeting, no new agreements were reached. More broadly, the protesters succeeded in forcing the topic of globalization and the negative consequences of increased international trade onto the political agenda. Before the protests in Seattle, few Americans knew much about the WTO

or the concept of globalization. The antiglobalization movement has been successful in getting media attention but has had a limited impact on policy.

SOURCES: Kim Murphy, "Anarchists Deployed New Tactics in Violent Seattle Demonstrations," *Los Angeles Times,* December 16, 1999, p. A3; Marc Cooper, "Street Fight in Seattle," *Nation,* December 20, 1999, pp. 3–4; Kenneth Klee, "The Siege of Seattle," *Newsweek,* December 13, 1999, p. 30.

Thousands of protesters from a variety of interest groups took over the streets of Seattle during the World Trade Organization meeting in December 1999.

The Women's Christian Temperance Union, a movement dedicated to the Prohibition of drinking liquor, succeeded in passing the Eighteenth Amendment, which outlawed the manufacture and sale of alcoholic beverages. It was later repealed by the Twenty-first Amendment.

in several state legislatures, promoting environmental issues, safe energy, consumer protection, and good government. Nader ran for president in 2000 as the nominee of the Green party. Despite his reputation as an advocate for consumers, he received only 3 percent of the popular vote.

A specific type of public interest group is the tax-exempt public charity. Examples include the American Heart Association, the Girl Scouts of the U.S.A., and the American Cancer Society. These organizations must meet certain conditions, such as educational or philanthropic objectives, to qualify for this preferred status. Not only are public charities tax-exempt, but donations to these organizations are tax-deductible, and the organizations are not required to disclose information about their donors publicly. These organizations cannot participate in elections or support candidates, nor can they benefit an individual or small group. Despite these limitations, tax-exempt charitable organizations have been very active in voter registration efforts and in advertising campaigns designed to influence public opinion.

Foreign Policy Interest Groups

Domestic policy is not the only matter of concern to interest groups. Groups also organize to promote or oppose certain foreign policies. Among the most prestigious foreign affairs groups is the Council on Foreign Relations in New York City. Other groups, devoted to narrower areas of American foreign policy, exert pressure on members of Congress and the president to enact specific policies. For example, interest group pressure influenced U.S. policy toward South Africa and played a role in South Africa's decision to abandon apartheid. Groups ranging from student organizations to national lobbies like the American Committee on Africa urged divestment, sanctions, or other policy measures that ultimately promoted change in South Africa.

The American-Israel Political Action Committee (AIPAC) has more than 50,000 members and has been very successful. Because AIPAC's primary focus is lobbying and not distributing campaign funds, it is not required to disclose where its money comes from or goes. Included in the long list of AIPAC lobbying successes are enactment of aid packages to Israel, passage of the 1985 United States–Israel Free Trade Agreement, and emergency assistance to Israel in the wake of the 1992 Gulf War. Its counterpart,

Interest groups such as Greenpeace stage demonstrations and call attention to environmental issues.

A group of Hassidic Jews joined advocates for Palestine on April 20, 2002 in Washington, D.C. to protest, among other issues, the U.S. government's support for Israel.

the National Association of Arab Americans, lobbies for action in support of Arab causes and hosted events at both major parties' 2000 national conventions. Efforts to secure a negotiated settlement between the Palestinians and Israel have meant that American interest groups on both sides of the dispute remain visible and important.

An example of the efforts of interest groups to influence U.S. foreign policy were demonstrations in 2002 in Washington, D.C., after multiple suicide bombs had been used against civilians by Palestinians in Israel and after Israel had sent troops into Palestinian areas in the West Bank. As is often the case with such demonstrations, news coverage is sought in hopes of reaching a much wider audience. Those who report on such demonstrations often assess the stature of congressional or administration leaders speaking to the group, the size of the group, and any controversy surrounding the event.

Government and Government Employee Interest Groups

Governments are themselves important interest groups. Many cities and most states retain Washington lobbyists, and cities also hire lobbyists to represent them at the state legislature. Governors are organized through the National Governors Association, cities through the National League of Cities, and counties through the National Association of Counties.

Government employees form a large and well-organized group. The National Education Association (NEA), for example, claims 2.7 million members.[10] Public employees are also important to organized labor, and they are the fastest-growing unions.

Other Interest Groups

Americans are often emotionally and financially involved in a variety of groups: veterans' groups such as American Legion or Veterans of Foreign Wars; nationality groups such as the multitude of German, Irish, Hispanic, Palestinian, and Korean organizations; or religious organizations such as the Knights of Columbus or B'nai B'rith. More than 150 nationwide organizations are based on national origin alone. In recent years, there has been a virtual explosion in the number and variety of interests and associations. This is especially true for environmental groups (see Table 6-2).

TABLE 6–2   Some Environmental Groups and How They Do Business

Group	Membership	Issues	Activities
Greenpeace USA	250,000	Oceans, global warming, genetically engineered foods	Media events; mass mailings; grassroots activity; does not lobby government
Natural Resources Defense Council	500,000	Resources, energy, pollution	Lobbying; litigation; watchdog; its scientists compete with experts from agencies and industry
Sierra Club	700,000	Wilderness, pollution, endangered species	Grassroots action; media; hierarchy of 67 chapters
Wilderness Society	200,000	Strictly public lands	Headquarters in Washington, D.C., with eight regional offices; mostly an analysis and advocacy group

SOURCE: Greenpeace USA, at www.greenpeaceusa.com; Natural Resources Defense Council, at www.nrdc.org; Sierra Club, at www.sierraclub.org; Wilderness Society, at www.wilderness.org.

Characteristics and Power of Interest Groups

Groups vary in their goals, methods, and power. Among the most important group characteristics are size, resources, cohesiveness, leadership, and techniques.

Size and Resources

Obviously, size is important to political power; an organization representing 5 million voters has more influence than one speaking for 5,000. Perhaps even more important than size is the extent to which members are actively involved and fight for policy objectives. Often people join an organization for reasons that have little to do with its political objectives. They may want to secure group insurance, take advantage of travel benefits, participate in professional meetings, or get a job.

How do associations motivate potential members to join them? Organizations must provide incentives, material or otherwise, that are compelling enough to attract the potential free rider.[11] Unions are organized not just for lobbying but also to perform other important services for their members. They derive much of their strength from their negotiating position with corporations, which they use to obtain wage increases or improved safety standards. Similarly, the AARP, in addition to lobbying against Social Security cuts and speaking out on other issues of concern to older citizens, offers incentives such as a free subscription to one of its magazines and member discounts at certain hotels. This combination of size and strength sets these groups apart from other large organizations in their effectiveness, as members derive numerous benefits from joining.

While the size of an interest group is often important, so, too, is its *spread*—the extent to which membership is concentrated or dispersed. Automobile manufacturing is concentrated in Michigan and a few other states, and as a result, the auto industry's influence does not have the same spread as that of the American Medical Association, which has an active chapter in virtually every congressional district. An association consisting of 3 million supporters concentrated in a few states will usually have less influence than another group consisting of 3 million supporters spread out in a large number of states.

Interest groups also differ in the extent to which they preempt a policy area or share it with other groups. Doctors and the AMA have effectively preempted the health care policy area because they play such an important role in the delivery of health care. But in the transportation policy area, railroads must compete with interstate trucking and even air freight companies.

Groups also differ in their *resources,* which include money, volunteers, expertise, and reputation. Some groups can influence many centers of power—both houses of Congress, the White House, federal agencies, the courts, and state and local governments—while others cannot.

Cohesiveness

Usually, a mass membership organization is made up of three types of members: (1) a relatively small number of formal leaders who may hold full-time, paid positions or devote much time, effort, and money to the group's activities; (2) people intensely involved in the group who identify with the group's aims, attend meetings, faithfully pay dues, and do a lot of the legwork; and (3) people who are members in name only, do not participate actively, and cannot be depended on to vote in elections or otherwise act as the leadership wants.[12] In a typical large organization, for every top leader, there might be a few hundred hard-core activists and thousands of essentially inactive members.

Another factor in group cohesiveness is its *organizational structure.* Some associations have a strong formal organization; others are local organizations that have joined together in a loose state or national federation in which they retain a measure of separate power and independence. Separation of powers may be found as well: The national assembly of an organization establishes, or at least ratifies, policy; an executive committee meets more frequently; a president or director is elected to head and speak for the group; and permanent paid officials form the organization's bureaucracy. Power may be further divided between the organization's main headquarters and its Washington office. An organization of this sort tends to be far less cohesive than a centralized, disciplined group such as the army or some trade unions.

Militia groups have sprung up in many parts of the United States. They generally object to gun control laws and tend to be suspicious of the federal government.

Leadership

Closely related to cohesion is the nature of the leadership. In a group that embraces many attitudes and interests, leaders may either weld the various elements together or sharpen their disunity. The leader of a national business association, for example, must tread cautiously between big business and small business, between exporters and importers, between chain stores and corner grocery stores, and between the producers and the sellers of competing products. The group leader is in the same position as a president or a member of Congress; he or she must know when to lead followers and when to follow them.

Techniques

Interest groups seeking to wield influence choose from a variety of political weapons and targets. They present their case to both houses of Congress, the White House staff, state and local governments, and federal agencies and departments. They also become involved in litigation. Other techniques include election activities, establishing political parties, and lobbying.

PUBLICITY AND MASS MEDIA APPEALS   Interest groups exploit the communications media—television, radio, newspapers, leaflets, signs, direct mail, and word of mouth—to influence voters during elections and to motivate constituents to contact their representatives between elections. Business enjoys a special advantage in this arena, and businesspeople have the money and staff to use propaganda machinery. As large-scale advertisers, they know how to deliver their message effectively or can find an advertising agency to do it for them. But organized labor is also effective in communicating with its membership through shop stewards, mail, and phone calls.

As people communicate more and more via e-mail, this technology will become an important means of political mobilization. John McCain effectively used e-mail in the 2000 primary campaign to turn out crowds in New Hampshire; after his big win in that state, he was able to raise campaign funds nationally. Candidates at all levels used e-mail for fund raising and to motivate supporters. E-mail will likely become part of political communication at the workplace, as management communicates information to its workers about the candidates and ballot issues.

MASS MAILING   One means of communication that has increased the reach and effectiveness of interest groups is computerized and targeted mass mailing.[13] Before computers, interest groups had to cull from telephone directories and other sources lists of people to contact, and managing these lists was time-consuming. As a result, some groups sent out mailings indiscriminately. Today the computer permits easy data storage and efficient management of mailing lists. Mass mailing is now used by all kinds of interest groups. Today's technology can produce personalized letters targeted to specific groups. Such targeted direct mail can also appeal to people who share a common concern, such as environmental groups.

INFLUENCE ON RULE MAKING   Organized groups have ready access to the executive and regulatory agencies that write the rules implementing laws passed by Congress. Government agencies publish proposed regulations in the ***Federal Register*** and invite responses from all interested persons before the rules are finalized. The *Federal Register* is published every weekday. You can find it at school, at the library, or on the Internet at www.access.gpo.gov. Well-staffed associations and corporations peruse the *Register,* ever alert for actions that will affect their interests. Lobbyists prepare written responses to the proposed rules, draft alternative rules, and appear at the hearings to make their case. These lobbyists seek to be on good terms with the staff of the agencies so that they can learn what rules are being considered long before they are released publicly and thus have input in the early stages. Administrative rules are defined over time through legal cases and agency modifications, so even if an interest group fails to get what it wants, it can fight the rules in court or press for a reinterpretation when the agency leadership changes hands.

Federal Register
Official document, published every weekday, that lists the new and proposed regulations of executive departments and regulatory agencies.

Finally, an interest group can seek to modify rules it does not like by pressuring Congress to change the legal mandate for the agency or have the agency's budget reduced, making enforcement of existing rules difficult. In short, interest groups and lobbyists never really quit fighting for their point of view.

LITIGATION   When groups find the political channels closed to them, they may turn to the courts.[14] The Legal Defense and Education Fund of the National Association for the Advancement of Colored People (NAACP), for example, initiated and won numerous court cases in its efforts to end racial segregation and to protect the right to vote for African Americans. Urban interests and environmental groups, feeling underrepresented in state and national legislatures, turned to the courts to influence the political agenda.[15] Women's groups, such as the National Organization for Women and the American Civil Liberties Union's Women's Rights Project, also used the courts to pursue their objectives.[16] Conservative religious groups like the Washington Legal Foundation or groups identified with the Religious Right have also actively used litigation as a strategy to pursue their objectives.[17]

In addition to initiating lawsuits, associations can gain a forum for their views in the courts by filing **amicus curiae** briefs (literally, "friend of the court" briefs) in cases in which they are not direct parties. Despite the general impression that associations achieve great success in the courts, groups are no more likely than individuals to win their cases at the district court level.[18]

ELECTION ACTIVITIES   Although nearly all large organizations say they are nonpolitical, almost all are politically involved in some way. What they usually mean when they say they are nonpolitical is that they are *nonpartisan*. A distinguishing feature of organized interest groups is that they often try to work through *both* parties. Another regularity is that they want to be friendly with the winners, which often means that they contribute to incumbents. But as competition for control of both chambers of Congress has intensified and with presidential contests also up for grabs, interest groups have generally invested more in one party or the other.

Labor usually favors Democrats. The AFL-CIO has supported every Democratic candidate for president since the New Deal, although the Teamsters Union has often endorsed Republicans. In 2000, the Teamsters joined most other unions in backing Al Gore. Business groups occasionally endorse Democratic incumbents but generally favor Republicans.

Some organizations are prevented from taking a firm position because of the differing views of their members. A local retailers' group, for example, might be composed equally of Republicans and Democrats, and many of its members might refuse to openly support a candidate for fear of losing business.

Ideological groups target certain candidates, seeking to change a candidate's positions or, failing that, to influence voters to vote against that candidate. Americans for Democratic Action and the American Conservative Union publish ratings of members of Congress's voting records on liberal and conservative issues; so do the U.S. Chamber of Commerce, the AFL-CIO, and other groups.

How effective is electioneering by interest groups? In general, the mass membership organizations' power to mobilize their full strength in elections has been exaggerated in the press. Although when a group's interests are directly attacked, as was the case with the anti-union "paycheck protection" ballot initiatives in 1998 and 2000, these groups can effectively mobilize their membership.[19] More typically, there are too many cross-pressures operating in the pluralistic politics of the United States for any one group to assume a commanding role. Some groups reach their maximum influence only by allying themselves closely with one of the two major parties. They may place their members on local, state, and national party committees and help send them to party conventions as delegates, but such alliances mean losing some independence.

FORMING A POLITICAL PARTY   Another interest group strategy is to form a political party. These parties are organized less with the intent to win elections than to publicize a

amicus curiae brief
Literally, a "friend of the court" brief, filed by an individual or organization to present arguments in addition to those presented by the immediate parties to a case.

cause. The Free Soil party was formed in the mid-1840s to work against the spread of slavery into the territories, and the Prohibition party was organized two decades later to ban the sale of liquor. Farmers have formed a variety of such parties. More often, however, interest groups prefer to work through existing parties. Today, environmental groups and voters for whom the environment is a central issue must choose between supporting the Green party, which has yet to elect a person to federal office, and one of the two major parties. In a New Mexico congressional special election in 1997, the Green party candidate won 17 percent of the vote, taking some votes from the Democrat and thereby helping elect a Republican to the seat. In the 1998 election, environmental groups campaigned aggressively for the Democrat, who obtained 53 percent of the vote, while all minor parties combined only got 4 percent.[20] In the 2000 presidential election, most environmental groups supported Al Gore over Green party nominee Ralph Nader. In the 2002 midterm congressional elections, minor parties rarely got more than one or two percent of the vote. Yet this is enough for them to be accused of being "spoilers" for the major party candidate closer to their position on issues. A minor party candidate got more votes than the difference between the front-runners in some races. In South Dakota's race between Tim Johnson (D) and John Thune (R), the Libertarian candidate got more than three thousand votes. Johnson defeated Thune by just over 500 votes.

COOPERATIVE LOBBYING   Like-minded groups often join together as cooperative groups. In 1987, the Leadership Conference on Civil Rights and People for the American Way brought together many groups in the battle to defeat the nomination of outspoken federal judge Robert Bork to the U.S. Supreme Court.[21] Different types of environmentalists work together, as do consumer and ideological groups on the right and on the left. Women continue to be represented by a large variety of groups that reflect diverse interests, but the larger the coalition, the greater the chance that members may divide over such issues as abortion. Another example of a cooperative group is the Business Roundtable (BRT), an association of chief executive officers of the 200 largest U.S. corporations. The BRT, which has been in existence for more than 30 years, promotes policies that help large businesses, such as free trade and less government regulation of business.

The Influence of Lobbyists

The terms "lobbying" and "lobbyist" were not generally used until around the middle of the nineteenth century in the United States. The root in these words refers to the lobby or hallway outside House and Senate chambers in the U.S. Capitol. It also refers to those who hung around the lobby of the old Willard Hotel when presidents dined. The noun "lobby" has been turned into a verb in this political context. Thus "to lobby" is to seek to influence legislators and government officials, and we call this **lobbying** even if there is no lobby in sight.

Despite their negative public image, lobbyists perform useful functions for government. They provide information for the decision makers of all three branches of government, they help educate and mobilize public opinion, they help prepare legislation and testify before legislative hearings, and they contribute a large share of the costs of campaigns. Yet many people are concerned that lobbyists have too much influence on government and add to legislative gridlock by being able to stop action on pressing problems.

Who Are the Lobbyists?

The typical image is of powerful, hard-nosed lobbyists who skillfully employ a combination of knowledge, persuasiveness, personal influence, charm, and money to influence legislators and bureaucrats. **Lobbyists** are the employees of associations who try to influence policy decisions and positions in the executive and especially in the legislative branches of our government. They are experienced in the ways of government, often having been public servants before going to work for an organized interest group, association, or corporation. They might start as staff in Congress, perhaps on a congressional committee. Later, when

lobbying
Engaging in activities aimed at influencing public officials, especially legislators, and the policies they enact.

lobbyist
A person who is employed by and acts for an organized interest group or corporation to try to influence policy decisions and positions in the executive and legislative branches.

Personal contact and access to decision makers continue to be key elements of lobbying today, as they were at the time of President Grant's administration.

their party wins the White House, they gain an administration post, often in the same policy area as their congressional committee work. After a few years in the administration, they are ready to make the move to lobbying, either by going to work for one of the interests they dealt with while in the government or by obtaining a position with a lobbying firm.

Moving from a government job to one with an interest group is quite common, a practice called the **revolving door**. Despite the fact that it is illegal for former national government employees to directly lobby the agency from which they came, their contacts made during government service are helpful to interest groups. Many former members of Congress make use of their congressional experience as full-time lobbyists.

The revolving-door tendency between government and interest groups produces networks of people who care about certain issues. These networks have been called **iron triangles**, consisting of mutually dependent relationships among interest groups, congressional committees and subcommittees, and the government agencies that share a common policy concern. Sometimes these relationships become so strong and mutually beneficial that the iron triangle becomes very powerful and a sort of subgovernment forms. A former senior staff person from a House or Senate agriculture committee now working for an agricultural corporation as a lobbyist who has ongoing friendships with his former staff colleagues including some who now work at the Department of Agriculture is an example of how personal relationships work within iron triangles. Powerful iron triangles may serve to enhance the policy preferences of narrow interests and not those of the broader public interest.

Legal and political skills, along with specialized knowledge, have become so crucial in executive and legislative policy making as to become a form of power in themselves. Elected representatives increasingly depend on their staffs for guidance, and these issue specialists know more about "Section 504" or "Title IX" or "the amendment of 1972"—and who wrote it and why—than most political and administrative leaders, who are usually generalists. It is in this gray area of policy making that many interest groups and lobbyists play a vital role, as people move freely from congressional or agency staff to association staff and perhaps back again. These groups of experts are sometimes called *issue networks*. Like iron triangles, issue networks are made up of people with similar policy concerns; however, they differ in two important ways. First, issue networks can include more players, such as the media, than iron triangles. Second, because members of issue networks are less dependent on one another than members of iron triangles are, organization is more amorphous and less structured.[22]

What Do Lobbyists Do?

Thousands of lobbyists are active in Washington, but few are as glamorous or as unscrupulous as the media suggest, nor are they necessarily influential. One limit on their power is the competition among interest groups. Rarely does any one group have a policy area all to itself. For example, transportation policy involves airplanes, trucks, cars, railroads, consumers, suppliers, state and local governments—the list goes on and on.

To members of Congress, the single most important thing lobbyists provide is money for their next reelection campaign. "Reelection underlies everything else," writes political scientist David Mayhew.[23] Money from interest groups has become instrumental in this driving need among incumbents. Interest groups also provide volunteers for campaign activity. In addition, their failure to support the opposition can enhance an incumbent's chances of being reelected.

Some people defend lobbyists as a kind of "third house" of Congress. Whereas the Senate and House are set up on a geographical basis, lobbyists represent people on the basis of interests and money. Small but important groups can sometimes get representation in the "third house" when they cannot get it in the other two. In a nation of vast and important interests, this kind of functional representation, if it is not abused, can be a useful supplement to geographical representation.

revolving door
Employment cycle in which individuals who work for governmental agencies regulating interests eventually end up working for interest groups or businesses with the same policy concern.

iron triangle
A mutually supporting relationship among interest groups, congressional committees and subcommittees, and government agencies that share a common policy concern.

Beyond their central role in campaigns and elections, interest groups provide another essential commodity to legislators: information of two important types, political and substantive. The *political information* provided by lobbyists includes such matters as who supports or opposes legislation and how strongly they feel.[24] *Substantive information,* such as the impact of proposed laws, might not be available from any other source. Lobbyists often provide technical assistance on the drafting of bills and amendments, identify persons to testify at legislative hearings, and formulate questions to ask of administration officials at oversight hearings.

Money and Politics

A **political action committee** (**PAC**) is the political arm of an interest group that is legally entitled to raise funds on a voluntary basis from members, stockholders, or employees in order to contribute funds to favored candidates or political parties. PACs link two vital techniques of influence—giving money and other political aid to politicians and persuading officeholders to act or vote "the right way" on issues. Thus PACs are the means by which interest groups seek to influence which legislators are elected and what they do once they take office.[25] PACs can be categorized according to the type of interest they represent: corporations, trade and health organizations, labor unions, ideological organizations, and so on.

The Growth of PACs

Surprisingly, considering the explosion of PACs that has occurred mainly in the business world, it was organized labor that invented this device. In the 1930s, John L. Lewis, president of the United Mine Workers, set up the Non-Partisan Political League as the political arm of the newly formed Congress of Industrial Organizations. When the CIO merged with the American Federation of Labor, the new labor group established the Committee

SHOULD PACS BE ABOLISHED?

You Decide... As a new member of Congress who almost lost to a candidate supported by PACs in the last election, you are urged by your local newspaper and some constituents to take a bold step and introduce legislation to abolish all PACs. If such legislation were introduced, how would you defend it?

Thinking It Through... As an incumbent, your self-interest would dictate that you oppose a ban on PACs because you stand to benefit from them and your challengers do not. PAC contributions provide a major advantage to you and a huge obstacle to most challengers. This is why many incumbents who ran against PACs in their first race suddenly discover, once elected, that PACs are not all bad. Defenders of PACs label PAC contributions an important form of participation. They argue that such contributions are constitutionally protected. Or they point to a PAC from their district that has supported them and claim that PACs are merely groups of constituents.

If you want to stand by your original opposition to PACs and win others to your point of view, you will need to find a way to substitute "untainted" money like public financing of elections for what you see as "tainted" PAC money. You will have to overcome an intense lobbying effort by PACs to defend what they have been doing. Your best argument against them is that they give so heavily to incumbents (especially incumbents on committees that deal with their concerns) that they make competitive elections unlikely.

political action committee (PAC) The political arm of an interest group that is legally entitled to raise funds on a voluntary basis from members, stockholders, or employees in order to contribute funds to favored candidates or political parties.

on Political Education (COPE), whose activities we have already described. This unit came to be the model for most political action committees: "From the outset, national, state, and local units of COPE have not only raised and distributed funds, but have also served as the mechanism for organized and widespread union activity in the electoral process, for example, in voter registration, political education, and get-out-the-vote drives."[26] Some years later, manufacturers formed the Business-Industry Political Action Committee, but the most active business PAC is the one affiliated with the U.S. Chamber of Commerce.[27]

The 1970s brought a near revolution in the role and influence of PACs—ironically, as the result of reforms intended to reduce the influence of money in elections. The number of PACs increased dramatically, from about 150 to nearly 4,000 today.[28] Corporations and trade associations contributed most to this growth; today their PACs constitute the majority of all PACs. Labor PACs, by contrast, increased only slightly in number, representing less than 10 percent of all PACs.[29] But the increase in the number of PACs is less important than the intensity of recent PAC participation in elections and in lobbying.

How PACs Invest Their Money

PACs take part in the entire election process, but their main influence lies in their capacity to contribute money to candidates. Candidates today need a lot of money to wage their campaigns. It is no longer uncommon for House candidates to spend more than $1 million and for many senators and would-be senators to spend several times that amount.[30] And as PACs contribute more, their influence grows. What counts is not only the amounts they give but also to whom they give. PACs give to the most influential incumbents, to committee chairs, to party leaders and whips, and to the Speaker. PACs give not only to the majority party but also to key incumbents in the minority party as well, because they understand that today's minority could be tomorrow's majority.

PACs, like individuals, are limited by law in the amount of money they can contribute to any single candidate in an election cycle. The Federal Election Campaign Act of 1971 as amended in 2002 limits PACs to $5,000 per election or $10,000 per election cycle (primary and

Labor PACs tend to favor Democratic candidates, as did these fire fighters.

general elections). Individuals have a limit of $4,000 per candidate per election cycle. PACs have found some creative ways around this limit. They can host fund-raisers attended by other PACs to boost their reputation with the candidate, or they can collect money from several persons and give it to the candidate as a bundle. Through **bundling**, PACs and interested individuals can increase their clout with elected officials. Until the 2003–2004 election cycle, PACs were not limited in how much they could give the political parties for "party-building" purposes, so called **soft money** contributions. Some of the largest PAC soft money contributors in the 1999–2000 election cycle came from labor unions, AT&T, Philip Morris, and Microsoft.[31] For data on soft money through the 2002 election cycle, go to www.crp.org.

The Effectiveness of PACs

The strong tendency of PACs to give more money to incumbents has meant that challengers face real difficulties in getting their campaigns funded. Challengers have to rely more on individual contributors, and until 2003, PACs could give five times as much to a candidate as individuals could. The campaign finance reform law enacted in 2002 doubled the individual contribution limit and thus reduced the difference in PAC contributions over individual contributions from 2½ to 1. Moreover, as noted, PACs for years helped friendly incumbents with soft money contributions until these were banned by the campaign finance reforms of 2002. (We discuss this legislation in greater detail later in this chapter and in Chapters 7 and 9.)

In highly competitive races, interest groups mount issue advocacy campaigns to help elect or defeat candidates. These campaigns are highly professional, are often negative, and can be substantial in scope. Moreover, interest group electioneering includes all modes of communication with voters—phone calls, mail, personal contact, e-mail, and radio and television commercials. Groups—and even individuals—sometimes run their campaigns hiding behind phony names like Citizens for Good Sense or the Foundation for Responsible Government or Republicans for Clean Air. Mailings and ads by groups with names like these

bundling
A tactic of political action committees whereby they collect contributions from like-minded individuals (each limited to $2,000) and present them to a candidate or political party as a "bundle," thus increasing their influence.

soft money
Money raised in unlimited amounts by political parties for party-building purposes. Now largely illegal except for limited contributions to state and local parties for voter registration and get-out-the-vote efforts.

Campaigning via Telephone: Candidate Communication Masquerading as Issue Advocacy

During the 2000 presidential primaries, interest groups ran phone banks communicating with voters about candidates. In South Carolina, for example, some groups attacked John McCain on the telephone. In partial response, McCain's campaign ran its own phone message operation in the Michigan presidential primary, seeking to mobilize Catholic voters. The complete text of McCain's February 2000 Michigan "Catholic Voter Alert" follows:

> "This is a Catholic Voter Alert. Governor George Bush has campaigned against Senator John McCain by seeking the support of Southern fundamentalists who have expressed anti-Catholic views. Several weeks ago, Governor Bush spoke at Bob Jones University in South Carolina. Bob Jones has made strong anti-Catholic statements, including calling the Pope the anti-Christ [and] the Catholic Church a satanic cult! John McCain, a pro-life senator, has strongly criticized this anti-Catholic bigotry, while Governor Bush has stayed silent while seeking the support of Bob Jones University. Because of this, one Catholic pro-life Congressman has switched his support from Bush to McCain, and many Michigan Catholics support John McCain for president."

When confronted with the misrepresentation of his campaign communicating as "Catholic Voter Alert," McCain stated that he had not authorized the message and asked that it be stopped. The misrepresentation of who was really behind the Catholic Voter Alert put McCain on the defensive and robbed him of some of his claim to be the advocate of campaign reform.

As with other candidates today, Al Gore's campaign staffers got the word out by using phone banks.

Campaign fund-raisers such as this one often charge donors $1,000 a plate for the privilege of meeting the candidates and mingling with influential policy makers.

make it difficult for voters to evaluate the source of the communications. Voters assume that candidates are responsible for the tone and content of campaigns, but the growth in issue advocacy campaigns raises doubts about the validity of that assumption.

The 2002 campaign finance reform legislation bans unions and corporations from using treasury funds to pay for election ads in the month before a primary and two months before a general election. The law also expands the definition of an election ad to include ads that mention the candidate by name, show the image or likeness of the candidate, or mention the election. The law also requires greater disclosure of groups involved in this activity. For example, the NAACP ad mentioned at the beginning of this chapter would now be considered illegal unless paid for through a PAC using disclosed and limited contributions of hard money.

How much does PAC money influence election outcomes, legislation, and representation? One critic has written, "When politicians start to see a dollar sign behind every vote, every phone call, every solicitation, those other factors sometimes weighed during governance, like the public good and equal access to government, become less and less important."[32] In this area, as in others, money obviously talks. But it is easy to exaggerate that influence. Although a candidate may receive a great amount of PAC money, only a fraction of that total comes from any single interest. In addition, it is debatable how much campaign contributions affect election outcomes and uncertain that winning candidates will be willing and able to "remember" their financial angels or that the money in the end produces a real payoff in legislation.

One likely result of the campaign finance reforms of 2002 will be a surge in issue advocacy, especially via the mail and on the telephone, in 2004. By closing down party soft money and limiting issue advocacy on television and radio in the weeks leading up to an election, the most recent reform makes issue advocacy via mail and telephone more attractive to individuals and groups. Examples of groups with substantially enlarged issue advocacy efforts in 2000 and 2002 included the NAACP Voter Fund, the pharmaceutical industry (Citizens for Better Medicare), the Sierra Club, National Abortion and Reproductive Rights Action League, and other groups. EMILY's List did issue advocacy in over a dozen 2002 primaries and ended up losing in at least five. In some of these races, both candidates were strong proponents of the pro-choice position on abortion. In selected Republican primaries, the NRA did issue advocacy with a higher success rate. In the 2002 general election, the most active new group was United Seniors. This group, with admitted connections to the pharmaceutical drug industry, invested heavily in the prescription drug and social security issues. Planned Parenthood, however, spent several million dollars less because one donor, Jane Fonda, did not make as much of a contribution to the group in 2002 as she had in 2000.

Much depends, however, on the context in which money is given and received. Many campaigns—especially state and local campaigns—are small-scale undertakings in which a big contribution makes a difference. Amid all the murk of campaigning, a candidate may feel grateful for so tangible and convertible a contribution as money. Studies demonstrate a significant relationship between the frequency of lobbying contacts and favorable treatment in the Ways and Means and House Agriculture committees. Campaign contributions were found to predict lobbying patterns.[33]

Curing the Mischiefs of Faction—Two Centuries Later

If James Madison were to return today, he would not be surprised by the existence of interest groups, nor would he be surprised by their variety. He might be surprised, however, by the varied weapons of group influence, the deep involvement of interest groups in the electoral process, and the vast number of lobbyists in Washington and the state capitals. And doubtless Madison, were he alive today, would still be concerned about the power of faction, especially its tendency toward instability and injustice.

One of the main arguments against factions is that people are not represented equally. For example, fewer interest groups represent young or low-income people than represent corporations. Further, some groups are better organized and better financed, allowing them a decided advantage over more general groups. Another problem with factions is that the existence of a multiplicity of interests often leads to incoherent policies, inefficiency, and delay as lawmakers try to appease conflicting interests. In addition, the propensity of interest groups to support incumbents in elections increases their advantage, which is often seen as undesirable. Finally, the ability of interest groups to supply needed and accurate information to government officials increases their power. Providing inaccurate information spells trouble for interest groups.

Concern about the evils of interest groups has been a recurrent theme throughout U.S. history. President Ronald Reagan in his Farewell Address warned of the power of "special interests,"[34] and President Dwight Eisenhower used his Farewell Address to warn against the "military-industrial complex."

Single-interest groups organized for or against particular policies—abortion, handgun control, tobacco subsidies, animal rights—have aroused much concern in recent years. "It is said that citizen groups organizing in ever greater numbers to push single issues ruin the careers of otherwise fine politicians who disagree with them on one emotional issue, paralyze the traditional process of governmental compromise, and ignore the common good in their selfish insistence on getting their own way."[35] But which single issues reflect narrow interests? Women's rights—even a specific issue such as sexual harassment—are hardly "narrow," women's rights leaders contend, because they would help over half the population. Peace groups, too, claim that they represent the whole population, as do those who support prayer in schools. These issues may seem quite different from those related to subsidies to dairy farmers, for example.

What—if anything—should be done about factions? For decades, Americans have tried to find ways to keep interest groups in check. They have agreed with James Madison that the "remedy" of outlawing factions would be worse than the disease. It would be absurd to abolish liberty simply because it nourished faction. And the existence and activity of interest groups and lobbies are solidly protected by the Constitution. But by safeguarding the value of liberty, have Americans allowed interest groups to threaten equality, the second great value in our national heritage? The question remains: How can interest groups be regulated in a way that does not threaten their constitutional liberties?

Federal and State Regulation

Americans have generally responded to this question by seeking to regulate lobbying in general and political money in particular. Concern over the use of money—especially corporate funds—to influence politicians goes back well over a century, to the Crédit Mobilier scandals during the administration of Ulysses S. Grant, when members of Congress promoted the Crédit Mobilier construction company in exchange for the right to buy shares of the company's stock below market value, on which they made huge profits. In the "progressive" era during the first two decades of the twentieth century, Congress legislated against corporate contributions in federal elections and required disclosure of the use of the money.

In 1925, Warren G. Harding's administration allowed private companies to secretly lease naval oil reserve lands. In response to this event, known as the Teapot Dome scandal, Congress passed the Federal Corrupt Practices Act. It required disclosure reports, both before and after elections, of receipts and expenditures by Senate and House candidates and by political committees that sought to influence federal elections in more than one state. Note that these were *federal* laws applying to *federal* elections; regulation of state lobbying and elections was left to the states.

Federal legislation, including the 1925 Federal Corrupt Practices Act and the 1946 Federal Regulation of Lobbying Act, was not very effective. It was, in fact, largely unenforced. Many candidates filed incomplete reports or none at all. The reform mood of the 1960s brought basic changes. The upshot was the Federal Election Campaign Act (FECA) of 1971, which supplanted the earlier legislation.

FECA, which was amended three times, established reporting or disclosure requirements for all candidates for the U.S. House of Representatives, the Senate, and the presidency, as well as their political parties and campaign committees. It also required disclosure of the amounts spent to influence federal elections by others, including individuals and political action committees. The act established partial public financing for presidential candidates, financed by a voluntary checkoff on federal income tax forms. Spending by candidates was not limited, but contributions to these candidates and to presidential candidates were limited. Two candidates for president in 2000, Steve Forbes and George W. Bush, turned down the federal matching funds to avoid state-by-state limits in the primaries, a move likely to be copied by wealthy or well-funded candidates in the future.

FECA has had its critics, and Congress has frequently debated reforming campaign financing and did in fact enact legislation in 2002. There have also been significant attempts to regulate interest group activity in elections at the state level. Some states, including Maine, Wisconsin, Minnesota, and Hawaii, provide for public financing of state offices and state legislative races; others, including Michigan, New Jersey, and Massachusetts, provide partial public financing of gubernatorial elections; a dozen more help underwrite parties with public funds.[36]

During President Bill Clinton's first term, Congress passed the first major overhaul of lobbying laws since 1946. Under the Lobbying Disclosure Act of 1995, the definition of a lobbyist was significantly expanded to include part-time lobbyists, those who deal with congressional staff or executive branch agencies, and those who represent foreign-owned companies and foreign entities. This act was expected to increase the number of registered lobbyists to as much as ten times its then current level.[37] In fact the number of registered "clients" is basically unchanged seven years after enactment of the act.[38] The act also included specific disclosure and information requirements.

Just six months before leaving office, President Clinton signed into law legislation expanding disclosure requirements by interest groups running issue ads. Some groups had previously been able to avoid disclosure because they fell outside the disclosure requirements of either the Federal Election Commission or the Internal Revenue Service. One group with an innocuous name, Republicans for Clean Air, attacked Senator McCain's environmental record in the 2000 primaries. The new law will have only a minor impact, however, as interest groups desiring to engage in issue advocacy can continue to do so, hiding behind vague names like the Foundation for Responsible Government or the Coalition to Make Our Voices Heard—two groups that have run ads in recent election cycles. These advertisements generally attack one candidate or praise another, and they are difficult to distinguish from candidate or party ads. But to limit them, as some reformers propose, means some wider limitation on freedom of speech.

Interest group issue advocacy ads permit the interest group to circumvent the contribution limits and some of the disclosure requirements imposed on candidates. This strategic advantage has made issue advocacy increasingly important in competitive election contests. Interest groups have also been a major source of soft money to the parties and also the primary donor to incumbents.

The 2002 Campaign Finance Reforms

For more than 15 years, campaign finance reform had been under consideration in one or both houses of Congress; in 1992, it passed in both houses only to be vetoed by President George H. W. Bush. The issue gained momentum after the 2000 elections, in large part due to the attention Republican presidential candidate and Arizona senator John McCain brought to the issue. The 2000 elections changed the dynamics of the issue even more fundamentally when the Democrats had a net gain of four seats in the Senate, all four replacing senators who had previously voted for unlimited debate, effectively killing campaign finance reform in the Senate.[39]

The collapse in 2002 of the Enron Corporation, the seventh-largest corporation in the United States and a major contributor to candidates and parties, made it hard for opponents of reform to defend a system in which individuals and corporations could give unlimited amounts of money to the parties. Enron had given more than $3.7 million in unregulated, unlimited soft money to political parties since 1995—$1.7 million of that to the national parties in 2000 alone.[40]

Vice President Cheney's Ties to the Energy Industry

That both Republican nominees, George W. Bush and Dick Cheney, had worked in the energy industry and had benefited from energy companies' donations to their party and campaign was no secret during the 2000 presidential election campaign. Early in his business career, Bush had been an owner of an energy company, and Cheney had been the top executive of Halliburton, the world's largest oilfield services and construction company. Indeed, Cheney's reentry into government is an example of the revolving door phenomenon, in which public officials leave public life for lucrative business careers and occasionally return to government. Cheney's retirement package from Halliburton was generous, valued at more than $20 million.

Once in office, the vice president turned to corporate leaders in the energy industry to advise the new administration on energy policy. The Bush administration insists that exactly who participated in these discussions does not need to be disclosed. The controversy over who did and did not participate in the activity of this issue network was heightened by the collapse of the Enron Corporation, another giant energy company. The Bush administration position was that government needs to be able to seek the candid advice of experts and that some will shy away from providing advice if their role is disclosed. Advocates of disclosure in Congress and elsewhere argued that the public has a right to know who is providing policy advice to top government officials. Access to policy makers is helpful in influencing public policy. The Cheney task force consulted leaders in the energy business but not others with concerns about energy policy, like environmentalists. The implication is that Cheney may have acted to shape energy policy that would suit narrow business interests.

Vice President Dick Cheney speaks at the Nuclear Energy Institute's annual conference. Many say that Cheney's close ties with the energy industry prevent him from being objective on energy-related issues and have a great influence on the Bush administration's energy policies.

Opponents of the bill hoped that President George W. Bush, like his father, would veto the bill. Early in the legislative consideration, Bush indicated he would not veto the bill. Ultimately, he signed the bill without any fanfare, denying his former presidential rival, John McCain, the celebratory moment of participating in a White House bill signing. The courts will eventually have the last say on the 2002 round of campaign finance reform, just as they did with the reforms of a quarter-century earlier.

The Bipartisan Campaign Reform Act of 2002 banned most forms of soft money, leaving individuals and PACs free to contribute $10,000 to state or local party committees for voter registration or mobilization. The law raised the individual contribution limits while leaving PAC contribution limits where they were. The law also redefined issue advocacy electioneering to include much of what had been exempt from regulation, and it restricted broadcast issue advocacy in the periods before primary and general elections. The law did not include public financing of congressional candidates or parties or free television time, as had been proposed in the past.

Advocates of campaign finance reform have seen large amounts of money flowing into candidate and party campaign accounts for more than a century. Many see these donations as money with strings attached, linked to organized interests that stand to benefit from government action or inaction. This kind of influence, in which a group seeks to get something in return for something given, is known as a **quid pro quo**. In 1976, the U.S. Supreme Court, in *Buckley* v. *Valeo,* cited this potential for undue influence as a valid reason to limit direct contributions.[41] But the remaining ability to give unlimited amounts of money to party committees effectively removed all contribution limits. The party committees have even gone so

quid pro quo
Something given with the expectation of receiving something in return.

far as to create "victory committees" that allow a candidate to host a fund-raiser and raise not only the limited contributions to his or her campaign but also, at the same time and in the same check, unlimited amounts for the party. The donor implicitly understands that the entire contribution will go to help elect that candidate.[42] A prominent example of the use of victory funds was Hillary Rodham Clinton in her 2000 Senate campaign in New York.[43]

Reformers for more than a century have sought disclosure of money in politics. This is consistent with efforts to have more complete disclosure of conflicts of interest in potential executive branch appointees and among legislators and judges. In campaigns and elections, disclosure was often incomplete, and groups quickly found ways to avoid it. However, the disclosure provisions of the 1971 Federal Election Campaign Act, as amended in 1974, were quite effective. Until the mid-1990s, citizens, journalists, and scholars had a quite complete picture of who was giving what to whom, and who was spending money and in what ways, to influence elections. That changed with the discovery of issue advocacy as an electioneering tool in the 1996 election cycle. Disclosure of a possible quid pro quo between an interest group and a politician was also diminished by soft money. A large donor could give millions to a party with the expectation that it was going to a particular U.S. senate campaign, but such a connection is not traceable because the soft money is passed through the party before going to candidates.

The 2002 reforms seek to enhance disclosure first by banning soft money and then by broadening the definition of electioneering to capture much more of the issue advocacy of recent election cycles. The former test for whether a communication was or was not about an election was a language test, the so called "magic words" test, included in the *Buckley* v. *Valeo* decision in a footnote. If the communication used words such as "vote for," "elect," "support," "cast your ballot for," "Smith for Congress," "vote against," "defeat," or "reject," it was presumed to be election advocacy. If the communication did not use words like those, it was presumed to be *issue* advocacy and was not subject to disclosure or limitation. The hate crimes ad described at the beginning of this chapter is an example of an issue ad. Because the ad does not use any of the "magic words," the sponsors avoid all disclosure. The new legislation defines election communication to include mentioning a candidate by name, mentioning an election, or showing the image or likeness of a candidate within 60 days of a general election and 30 days of a primary election and makes such communications subject to disclosure.

The Supreme Court in 1976 declared that limits on independent expenditures were unconstitutional but upheld disclosure by individuals and groups spending independently to influence the outcome of an election. The new legislation seeks to apply the same disclosure requirements to broadcast issue advocacy messages that meet the broader definition. Interest groups would continue to be able to skirt disclosure should they communicate with voters through the mail, in newspaper ads, on billboards, on the phone, and by e-mail even in the period leading up to the election.

One other dimension of campaign finance regulation has been limitations on candidate spending when those candidates accept partial public financing. The 2002 legislation does not add a system of public financing to congressional elections. The public financing of the presidential elections (see Chapter 9) had worked rather well until 2000, when George W. Bush declined public funds in the primary phase of his campaign. Because of his extraordinary fund raising, he wished to avoid the constraints of spending limits that accompany public financing. It remains unclear whether spending limits will be viable in the future.

Can groups and individuals still seek to influence the electoral process through financial contributions? The new legislation permits them to make contributions to a federal candidate for a primary election and for a general election, with additional contributions allowed if runoffs become necessary. For each of these types of elections, individuals can contribute $2,000. Individuals have an aggregate two-year federal election cycle limit of $95,000 in contributions to parties or candidates. Individuals can make unlimited contributions to interest groups and other types of political actors.

TABLE 6–3 The Big Givers, 2001–2002

Donor (Industry)	Republicans	Democrats	Total
Saban Capital Group	$0	$12,280,000	$12,280,000
Newsweb Corp	0	7,390,000	7,390,000
American Federation of State, County, and Municipal Employees	500	6,586,000	6,586,500
Shangri-La Entertainment	0	6,525,000	6,525,000
Service Employees International Union	41,622	4,571,117	4,612,739
Freddie Mac	2,335,615	1,687,500	4,023,115

SOURCE: The Center for Responsive Politics, "Soft Money to National Parties," March 11, 2003 at www.opensecrets.org/softmoney/softtop.asp?txtCycle-2002&txtSort=amt, March 11, 2003.

Interest groups under the new legislation will continue to participate through PACs. Many members of Congress thrive on the present arrangements, and the leaders and members of both parties actually compete for PAC dollars (see Table 6-3). Although Republicans have generally received larger amounts, Democrats in recent election cycles put pressure on the pharmaceutical and insurance industries to give more to Democratic candidates.[44] More pragmatic PACs contribute to both parties to be in a favored position with whichever party wins the majority. One reason members of Congress become entrenched in their seats is that PACs fund them. The PAC contribution limits were not changed in 2002, remaining at $5,000 per candidate for each of up to three elections (primary, general, and runoff). In most cases, the maximum a PAC can give a candidate is $10,000, since most states do not have runoff elections. PACs are also limited to $30,000 in contributions to a national party committee in a two-year election cycle. Beyond these hard money contribution limits, PACs were previously able to give unlimited amounts of soft money to the parties. With the soft money ban in the 2002 legislation, these contributions will probably dry up.

One likely consequence of the 2002 reforms will be interest groups spending more in issue advocacy. Many interest groups have already been diversifying their investment strategy. An example of diversification before the current reforms is the pharmaceutical industry, whose PACs donated an estimated $5.2 million to federal candidates in 2000 and then also gave another $15.2 million in soft money to the political parties.[45] The pharmaceutical industry exemplifies another recent development—the willingness of groups to spend money on issue advocacy. Beginning in 1999, the pharmaceutical industry contributed heavily to a group named Citizens for Better Medicare, which reported it would spend $40 million in issue advertising in 2000.[46] It ran ads in states with competitive Senate races.[47] The industry was also active in 2002.

The Effects of Regulation

What have been the effects of past reforms on interest groups? Ironically, one has been to increase the number and importance of such groups. The strategy of the 1971 law was to authorize direct and open participation by both labor and corporate organizations in elections and lobbying in the hope that a visible role for interest group activity, backed by effective enforcement, would be constitutional under the First Amendment. The 1971 act allowed unions and corporations to communicate on political matters to members or stockholders, to conduct registration and get-out-the-vote drives, and to spend union and company funds to set up "separate segregated funds" (PACs) to use for political purposes.

Corporations, trade associations, and unions made PACs a central part of their government relations strategy. But what changed the rules of the game for corporate interests was passage in 1974 of limits on individual contributions, something not part of the 1971 act. An explosion of corporate PACs followed this 1974 amendment.[48] In 1978, there was little difference in the level of campaign activity of PACs representing corporations, labor unions, or trade associations.[49] But that has changed, with corporate PACs spending more than the others and ideological PACs at roughly half the level of spending of trade and labor PACs.

Even with the surge in issue advocacy and party soft money contributions by interest groups, all three major types of PACs also substantially expanded their contributions to candidates in 1999–2000. Labor PACs saw the greatest increase in spending, climbing to $126 million, or a 28 percent increase over 1997–1998. Trade association PACs exceeded their past cycle contributions by $23 million, for a total of $114 million. Corporate PACs again led all PACs in contributions in 1999–2000, giving nearly $162 million, a 17 percent increase over 1997–1998.[50]

With each successive election cycle, PACs spend more money. Most of this money goes to incumbents, especially committee chairs and party leaders. The result, labor leaders contend, has been a greater imbalance than ever between the political action and power of a relatively small number of corporate executives and stockholders, on the one hand, and the labor unions, on the other.

A centerpiece of past efforts to regulate interest group activity was disclosure of how politicians fund their campaigns. Until the 1996 election cycle, with the important exception of soft money, we had a much better idea of how much money candidates raised and how they spent it. Without disclosure, much of what we have written here about PACs, for instance, would not be public knowledge. Disclosure permits the press and public to assess the implications of how candidates finance their campaigns. The growth of soft money and the advent of issue advocacy by interest groups now means that we know less and less about how campaigns are financed. Groups and individuals can avoid disclosure, and the public remains uninformed about who is trying to influence its vote. The campaign finance reforms enacted in 2002 require that the sponsors of all election-related advertising be identified in the communication, with enhanced visibility of this disclosure. Furthermore, the 2002 reform requires that everything filed with the Federal Election Commission be made available to the public within 48 hours.

Candidates and some appointed officials must also disclose their personal finances, permitting voters and the press to see what investments and resources candidates have that may affect their ability to be impartial. Such public disclosure of personal assets, the value of property owned, and outstanding debts no doubt discourages some persons from entering public life, but it also makes officeholders accountable for certain obligations and actions once they enter office.

POLISIM

LOBBYING AMERICA

In this PoliSim, you will lobby on behalf of a fictional interest group. Your goal is to get legislation passed for your interest group. To accomplish this goal, you will research different members of Congress and finally disburse your limited resources of time and money (campaign contributions). Only if you use your resources efficiently will the legislation be passed.

Go to PoliSim "Lobbying America."

Summary

1. Interest groups exist to make demands on government. The dominant interest groups in the United States are economic or occupational, but a variety of other groups—ideological, public interest, foreign policy, government itself, as well as ethnic, religious, and racial—have memberships that cut across the big economic groupings; thus their influence is both reduced and stabilized.

2. Movements of large numbers of people who are frustrated with government policies have always been with us in the United States. Blacks, women, and the economic underdogs have at various times organized themselves into movements.

3. Elements in interest group power include size, resources, cohesiveness, leadership, and techniques, especially the ability to contribute to candidates and political parties as well as the ability to fund lobbyists. But the actual power of an interest group stems from the manner in which these elements relate to the political and governmental environment in which the interest group operates.

4. For many decades, interest groups have engaged in lobbying, but these efforts have become far more significant as groups become more deeply involved in the electoral process, especially through the expanded use of political action committees (PACs). Interest groups also take their messages directly to the public through mass mailings and advertising campaigns. Other interest group techniques include influencing rule making, litigation, election activities, and cooperative lobbying.

5. Concern about PACs centers on their ability to raise money and spend it on elections on behalf of endorsed candidates, typically incumbents. This concern has led to proposals to ban PACs or more strictly limit their activities. Yet their existence and rights are protected by the First Amendment.

6. Reforms of interest group excesses often include regulations that seek fairness, disclosure, and balance. All reform efforts must operate so as not to infringe on the basic constitutional rights of individuals. The key issue today in "controlling factions" is whether to allow groups to proliferate and so balance each other, to try to regulate groups, or to seek reforms outside the groups by fostering balanced power in political parties or elsewhere.

Key Terms

issue advocacy
faction
interest group
movement
open shop

closed shop
free rider
Federal Register
amicus curiae brief
lobbying

lobbyist
revolving door
iron triangle
political action committee (PAC)
bundling

soft money
guid pro quo

Further Reading

Jeffrey M. Berry, *New Liberalism: The Rising Power of Citizen Groups* (Brookings Institution, 1999).

Robert Biersack et al., eds., *After the Revolution: PACs, Lobbies, and the Republican Congress* (Addison-Wesley, 1999).

Jeffrey H. Birnbaum, *The Money Men: The Real Story of Fund-Raising's Influence on Political Power in America* (Crown, 2000).

William P. Browne, *Groups, Interests, and Public Policy* (Georgetown University Press, 1998).

Allan J. Cigler and Burdett A. Loomis, eds., *Interest Group Politics,* 6th ed. (CQ Press, 2002).

Martha A. Derthick, *Up in Smoke* (CQ Press, 2002).

Kenneth M. Goldstein, *Interest Groups, Lobbying, and Participation in America* (Cambridge University Press, 1999).

Gene Grossman and Elhanan Helpman, *Special Interest Politics* (MIT Press, 2001).

Paul S. Herrnson, Ronald G. Shaiko, and Clyde Wilcox, *The Interest Group Connection: Electioneering, Lobbying, and Policymaking in Washington* (Chatham House, 1998).

Allen D. Hertzke, *Representing God in Washington: The Role of Religious Lobbies in the American Polity* (University of Tennessee Press, 1988).

Kevin W. Hula, *Lobbying Together: Interest Group Coalitions in Legislative Politics* (Georgetown University Press, 1999).

David B. Magleby, ed., *The Other Campaign: Soft Money and Issue Advocacy in the 2000 Congressional Elections* (Rowman & Littlefield, 2003).

Mancur Olson, *The Logic of Collective Action* (Harvard University Press, 1965).

David Vogel, *Kindred Strangers: The Uneasy Relationship Between Politics and Business in America* (Princeton University Press, 1996).

Jack L. Walker, Jr., *Mobilizing Interest Groups in America: Patrons, Professions, and Social Movements* (University of Michigan Press, 1991).

Darrell M. West and Burdett A. Loomis, *The Sound of Money: How Political Interests Get What They Want* (Norton, 1999).

7
CHAPTER

POLITICAL PARTIES
Essential
to Democracy

SOME YEARS AGO, A COMMUNITY COLLEGE DISTRICT IN LOS ANGELES HELD A NONPARTISAN ELECTION FOR ITS TRUSTEES IN WHICH ANY registered voter could run if he or she paid the $50 filing fee and gathered 500 valid signatures on a petition. A total of 133 candidates ran, and each voter could cast up to seven votes in the election. Political parties were not allowed to nominate candidates, and party labels did not appear on the ballot to help orient voters to the candidates.[1]

How did people vote in an election without parties? Candidates were listed alphabetically, and those whose names began with the letters A to F did better than those later in the alphabet. Being well known helped. Endorsements by the *Los Angeles Times* also influenced the outcome, as did campaigning by a conservative group. A Mexican American surname also helped. In this election, an important voting cue was absent: incumbency. Because the board of trustees was newly created, none of the candidates were incumbents.

Rarely do American voters face such unorganized and plentiful choices, because parties give structure to national and state elections. E. E. Schattschneider, a noted political scientist, once said, "The political parties created democracy, and modern democracy is unthinkable save in terms of the parties."[2] This provocative statement is true, but such a favorable evaluation of political parties runs counter to a long-standing and deep-seated American fear and distrust of them. Experience has taught us that free people create political parties to promote their own goals. Even though our founders hoped to discourage them, political parties quickly became an integral part of our political system.

Parties serve many functions, including the important one of narrowing the choices for voters.[3] They are both a consequence of democracy and an instrument of it. Parties need not be strong and cohesive like those in Britain and most European democracies, but without some kind of party system, democracies are not likely to survive. Elections serve the vital task of deciding who can legitimately exercise political power, and parties are an integral part of making national and state elections work. We Americans take for granted the peaceful transfer of power from one elected official to another and from one party to another, yet in new democracies, the transfer of power following an election is often problematic. In such democracies, the holding of power may be more important than the principle of democratic competition. Well-established parties help stabilize democracy.

This chapter begins by examining the purposes parties serve that make them so vital to the functioning of democracy. We then examine the evolution of American political parties. Although American political parties have changed over time, they remain important in three different settings: as institutions, in government, and in the electorate. It is important to understand how parties facilitate democracy in all three settings. Finally, we turn to a discussion of the strength of parties today and the prospects for party reform and renewal.

What Parties Do for Democracy

Party Functions

Political parties are organizations that seek political power by electing people to office so that their positions and philosophy become public policy. American political parties serve a variety of political and social functions, some obvious and some not so obvious. They perform some functions well and others not so well, and how they perform them differs from place to place and time to time.

ORGANIZE THE COMPETITION   One of the most important functions of parties is to organize the competition by designating candidates to run under their label. For some races, parties recruit and nominate candidates for office; they register and activate voters; and they help candidates by training them, raising money for them, providing them with research and voter lists, and enlisting volunteers to work for them.[4] For more visible contests, especially ones where there is a real chance of winning, multiple candidates often compete with each other for the nomination, often without party efforts to recruit them. Recently, campaign consultants rather than party officials have taken over some of these responsibilities; we explore this topic at some length in Chapter 10.[5]

The ability of parties to influence the selection of candidates varies by the type of nominating system used in the state. A few states use a *caucus* or *convention system,* which permits party leaders to play a role in the selection of nominees. Other states hold *primary elections.* As more and more states turn to primary elections, the ability of party leaders to influence who runs under their party label is reduced. Candidates with little party experience but with well-known names or ample personal funds can often win in a primary over a person with a known track record of prior party service or success in a less visible office. New Jersey Senator Jon Corzine had never run for office and was not well known in the state before spending $60 million in his successful 2000 campaign. Not all little-known, self-financed candidates win; in fact, they are often defeated. For example, Michael Huffington spent nearly $30 million in an unsuccessful bid for the Senate in California in 1994, and Steve Forbes spent a combined $129 million in unsuccessful bids for the Republican presidential nomination in 1996 and 2000.

A party's ability to organize the competition is also influenced by how states organize their ballots. In many states, candidates are listed in party columns—on a **party column ballot**—which makes it easier for voters to vote a *straight ticket* for all the party candidates. Straight-ticket voting is also more likely in voting systems that permit flipping one switch or punching one spot on the computer card to vote for all candidates from one party. Other states organize the ballot by office—the **office block ballot**—which makes straight-ticket voting harder. Even though many voters cast votes for candidates in more than one party, the party label of a candidate means something to most voters and is important in their voting decision.

Local and judicial elections in most states are **nonpartisan elections**, which means no party affiliation is indicated. Such systems make it more difficult for political parties to operate—precisely why many jurisdictions have adopted this reform. Proponents of

political party

An organization that seeks political power by electing people to office so that its positions and philosophy become public policy.

party column ballot

Type of ballot that encourages party-line voting by listing all of a party's candidates in a column under the party name.

office block ballot

Ballot on which all candidates are listed under the office for which they are running making split-ticket voting easier.

nonpartisan election

A local or judicial election in which candidates are not selected or endorsed by political parties and party affiliation is not listed on ballots.

nonpartisan local and judicial elections contend that party affiliation is not important to being a good judge or school board member.

UNIFY THE ELECTORATE   Parties are often accused of creating conflict, but they actually help unify the electorate and moderate conflict. There is a strong incentive in both parties to fight out their differences inside the party but then come together to take on the opposition. Moreover, in order to win elections, parties need to reach out to voters outside their party and gain their support. This action also helps unify the electorate, at least into the two large national political parties in our system.

Parties have great difficulty building coalitions on controversial issues like abortion or gun control. Not surprisingly, candidates and parties generally try to avoid defining themselves or the election in single-issue terms. Rather, they hope that if voters disagree with the party's stand on one issue, they will still support the party because they agree with it on other issues. Deemphasizing single issues in this way helps defuse conflict and unify the electorate.

HELP ORGANIZE GOVERNMENT   Although political parties in the United States are not as cohesive as in some other democracies, parties are important when it comes to organizing our state and national governments. Congress is organized along party lines. The political party with the most votes in each chamber elects the officers of that chamber, selects the chair of each committee, and has a majority on all the committees. State legislatures, with the notable exception of Nebraska, are also organized along party lines.

Following the 2000 election, the U.S. Senate was evenly split between Republicans and Democrats, and the Republicans could have relied on Vice President Cheney to cast a tie-breaking vote on which party would chair all committees. Instead, leaders of both parties negotiated a power-sharing arrangement in which Republicans chaired all committees, but membership on committees was evenly split, with both parties having the same allocation of staff on all committees.[6] This unusual arrangement soon came to an end with the decision by Vermont Senator James Jeffords to leave the Republican party, becoming an Independent but voting with the Democrats on which party controlled the chamber and all committees and subcommittees. The 2004 election enlarged the Republican majorities in the U. S. Senate and the U. S. House of Representatives. In the Senate, the GOP rose from 51 to 55 members, but this number remained below the number needed to override a filibuster. Republicans continued to control all committee chairs but due to party rules there was some rotation among Republicans. The Senate Judiciary Committee chairmanship, for example, switched from Orrin Hatch (R.-Utah) to Arlen Specter (R.-Penn.).

The party that controls the White House, the governor's mansion, or city hall gets **patronage**, which means it can select party members as public officials or judges. Such appointments are limited only by civil service regulations that restrict patronage typically to the top posts, but these posts, which number about 4,000 in the federal government, are also numerous at the state and local levels. Patronage provides an incentive for people to become involved in politics and gives the party leaders and elected politicians loyal partisans in key positions to help them achieve their policy objectives.

TRANSLATE PREFERENCES INTO POLICY   One of the great strengths of our democracy is that even the party that wins an election usually has to moderate what it does in order to win reelection. For that reason, public policy does not change dramatically with each election. Nonetheless, the party that wins the election has a chance to enact its policies and implement its campaign promises.

American parties have had only limited success in setting the course of national policy, especially when compared with countries with strong parties. The European model of party government, which has been called a *responsible party system,* assumes that parties discipline their members through their control over nominations and campaigns. Officeholders in such

patronage
The dispensing of government jobs to persons who belong to the winning political party.

party-centered systems are expected to act according to party wishes or they will not be allowed to run again under the party label. Moreover, candidates run on fairly specific party platforms and are expected to implement those policies if they win control in the election.

Although we lack a European-type party system, most, but not all Democrats in Congress vote together, as do most, but not all, Republicans. And then there are times, rather unusual but not unprecedented, when a president of one party receives more congressional votes from the opposing party than from his own, as President Bill Clinton did in 2000 on legislation granting China permanent normal trade relations status with the United States.[7] And when the House passed the Enhanced Border Security and Visa Entry Reform Act of 2002, which President Bush wanted, nearly twice as many Democrats voted yes—182, compared to 92 yes votes from the Republicans.[8]

Because American parties do not control nominations, they are unable to discipline members who express views contrary to those of the party. The American system is largely *candidate-centered;* politicians are nominated largely on the basis of their qualifications and personal appeal, not party loyalty. In fact, it is more correct to say that in most contests, we have *candidate* politics rather than *party* politics. As a consequence, party leaders cannot guarantee passage of their program, even if they are in the majority.

Even though parties cannot exert tight control over candidates, their ability to spend money has had a significant influence. In recent years, parties played an important role in competitive federal elections through their **soft money** expenditures. Soft money consisted of contributions given to the political parties by individuals, corporations, labor unions, and political action committees (PACs) for "party-building" purposes that came to be used for candidate promotion. Because such contributions were unlimited, parties put a premium on raising them. The ads soft money paid for were often candidate-centered and focused on the broad policy agenda of the election.[9] The 2002 campaign finance reform abolished soft money at the federal level.

PROVIDE LOYAL OPPOSITION   Accountability in a democracy comes from the party out of power closely monitoring and commenting on the actions of the party in power. When national security issues are involved or the country is under attack, parties restrain their criticism, as the Democrats in Congress did after September 11, 2001. There is usually a polite interval following an election—known as the **honeymoon**—after which the opposition party begins to criticize the party that controls the White House, especially when the opposition party controls one or both houses of Congress.[10] The length of the honeymoon depends in part on how contentious the agenda of the new administration is and on the leadership skills of the new president. Early success in enacting policy can prolong the honeymoon; mistakes or controversies can shorten it.

The Nomination of Candidates

From the beginning, parties have been the mechanism by which candidates for public office are chosen. The **caucus** played an important part in pre-Revolutionary politics. Elected officials organized themselves into groups or parties and together selected candidates to run for higher office, including the presidency. This method of nomination operated for several decades after the United States was established.

As early as the 1820s, however, charges of "secret deals" in "smoke-filled rooms" were made against this method. Moreover, it was not representative of people from areas where a party was in a minority or nonexistent, as only officeholders took part in the caucus. Efforts were made to make the caucus more representative of rank-and-file party members. The *mixed caucus* brought in delegates from districts in which the party had no elected legislators.

Then, during the 1830s and 1840s, a system of **party conventions** was instituted. Delegates, usually chosen directly by party members in towns and cities, selected the party candidates, debated and adopted a platform, and built party spirit by celebrating noisily. But the convention method soon came under criticism that it was subject to control by the party bosses and their machines.

soft money
Money raised in unlimited amounts by political parties for party building purposes. Now largely illegal except for limited contributions to state or local parties for voter registration and get-out-the-vote efforts.

honeymoon
Period at the beginning of a new president's term during which the president enjoys generally positive relations with the press and Congress, usually lasting about six months.

caucus
A meeting of local party members to choose party officials or candidates for public office and to decide the platform.

party convention
A meeting of party delegates to vote on matters of policy and in some cases to select party candidates for public office.

A precinct caucus in West Des Moines, Iowa, counts U.S. presidential preference votes by placing slips in piles sorted by each candidate's name.

To involve more voters and reduce the power of the bosses to pick party nominees, states adopted the **direct primary**, in which people could vote for the party's nominees for office. Primaries spread rapidly after Wisconsin adopted them in 1905—in the North as a Progressive era reform and in the South as a way to bring democracy to a region that had seen no meaningful general elections since the end of Reconstruction due to one-party rule by the Democrats. By 1920, direct primaries were the norm for some offices in almost all states.

Today the direct primary is the typical method of picking party candidates. Primaries vary significantly from state to state. They differ in terms of (1) who may run in a primary and how one qualifies for the ballot; (2) whether the party organization can or does endorse candidates before the primary; (3) who may vote in a party's primary—that is, whether a voter must register with a party in order to vote; and (4) how many votes are needed for nomination—a plurality, a majority, or some other number determined by party rule or state law. The differences among primaries are not trivial; they have an important impact on the role played by party organization and on the strategy used by candidates.

In states with **open primaries**, any voter, regardless of party, can participate in whichever primary he or she chooses. This kind of primary permits **crossover voting**—Republicans and Independents helping determine who the Democratic nominee will be, and vice versa. Other states use **closed primaries**, in which only persons already registered in that party may participate. Some states, like Washington and California, experimented with *blanket primaries* in which all voters could vote for any candidate, regardless of party. In 2000, the Supreme Court held that California's blanket primary violated the free association rights of political parties, in part because blanket primaries permit people who have "expressly affiliated with a rival" party to have a vote in the selection of a nominee from a different party.[11] In a detailed study of California's blanket primary, political scientists found that fewer than 5 percent of voters associated with one party actually voted for nominees from another party. More broadly, they concluded that the rules of a primary are important in determining the winner.[12]

direct primary
Election in which voters choose party nominees.

open primary
Primary election in which any voter, regardless of party, may vote.

crossover voting
Voting by a member of one party for a candidate of another party.

closed primary
Primary election in which only persons registered in the party holding the primary may vote.

Along with modern communications and fund-raising techniques, direct primaries have diminished the influence of leaders of political parties. Many critics believe that this change has had more undesirable than desirable consequences. Party leaders now have less influence over who gets to be the party's candidate, and candidates are less accountable to the party both during the election and after it.

Direct primaries are used to nominate most party candidates for most offices. Yet in some states, local caucuses choose delegates to attend regional meetings, which in turn select delegates to state and national conventions, where they nominate party candidates for offices. The Iowa presidential caucuses, in which roughly 100,000 Iowans in each major party participate, are highly publicized as the first important test of potential presidential nominees.[13]

In a few states, conventions still play a role in the nominating process for state and federal candidates. In Connecticut, for example, convention choices become the party nominees unless they are challenged. Candidates who attain at least 15 percent of the vote in the convention have an automatic right to challenge the winner at the convention, but they do not always exercise this right.[14] In Utah, if a candidate gets 60 percent of the delegate vote at the convention, there is no primary election vote for that office. Should no candidate reach 60 percent, only the top two candidates are listed on the primary ballot. In other states, convention nominees are designated as such on the primary ballot; they may or may not receive help from the party organization. Conventions are also used to invigorate the party faithful by enabling them to meet with their leaders.

In most states, candidates can get their names on the ballot as an Independent or minor party candidate by securing the required number of signatures on a nomination petition. This is hard to do, but it can be done, as Ross Perot demonstrated in 1992. He spent his own money to build an organization of volunteers who put his name on the ballot in all 50 states. Minor party gubernatorial candidates like the Minnesota Reform party's Jesse Ventura in 1998 or the Green party's presidential candidate Ralph Nader in 2000 secured their nominations as candidates of existing minor parties.[15]

Party Systems

Ours is a two-party system; most other democracies have a multiparty system. Although we have many minor parties, only the two major parties have much of a chance to win elections. Multiparty systems are almost always found in countries that have a parliamentary government, in contrast to our presidential system. This is, however, not always true. For example, England has a parliamentary system but also a strong two-party system.

Parliamentary systems usually have a *head of the nation,* often called the president, but they also have a *head of the government,* often called the prime minister or chancellor, who is the leader of one of the large parties in the legislature. In democracies with multiparty systems, such as Israel and Italy, because no one party has a majority of the votes, *coalition* governments are necessary. Minor parties can gain concessions—positions in a cabinet or support of policies they want implemented—in return for their participation in a coalition. Major parties need the minor parties and are therefore willing to bargain. Thus the multiparty system favors the existence of minor parties by giving them incentives to persevere.

proportional representation
An election system in which each party running receives the proportion of legislative seats corresponding to its proportion of the vote.

winner-take-all system
An election system in which the candidate with the most votes wins.

In some multiparty parliamentary systems, parties run slates of candidates for legislative positions, and winners are determined by **proportional representation**, in which the parties receive a proportion of the legislators corresponding to their proportion of the vote. In our **winner-take-all system**, only the candidate with the most votes in a district or state takes office. Because a party does not gain anything by finishing second, minor parties in a two-party system can rarely overcome the assumption that a vote for them is a wasted vote.[16] Even if a third-party candidate can keep either major party candidate from receiving more than 50 percent (a *majority*) of the vote, the candidate with the most votes (a *plurality*) wins.

IN COMPARATIVE PERSPECTIVE

Israel's Coalition Government

Israel has a multiparty system. Though Israelis vote for prime minister and parliament separately, the prime minister must still have the support of the majority of the members of parliament. If he doesn't, he is in danger of facing a parliamentary vote of no confidence. A vote of no confidence leads to new elections for prime minister and parliament. Because there are many parties, it is difficult—if not impossible—for any one party to gain a majority of the seats in the Knesset, the Israeli parliament. Usually one party can only get a plurality of the seats. A party with only a plurality of seats must form a coalition with other parties in order to rule. Certain concessions must be made to those parties to convince them to join. If the ruling party loses the support of its coalition partners, the prime minister and his party must form a new coalition, or else their government will be toppled by a parliamentary vote of no confidence.

In July 2000, three religious or rightist parties withdrew from Prime Minister Ehud Barak's coalition government in protest over peace talks with the Palestinians. This left Barak without a parliamentary majority. Though he survived the subsequent vote of no confidence, he was forced into forming a new coalition government. This effort even led to talks of forming a unity party with the Likud party. The Likud party leader, Ariel Sharon, was one of Barak's most outspoken critics. Sharon demanded that if his party were to join a unity government with Barak, it must have a veto over any future concessions in

peace talks. These negotiations were ultimately unfruitful, and in a surprise move in November, Barak exercised his authority to call an early election for prime minister. On February 6, 2001, Ariel Sharon soundly defeated Ehud Barak.

The conflict between Israel and Palestine escalated in 2002 with Palestinian suicide bombers killing Israeli civilians and Israeli troops taking military action against Palestinian refugee settlements. These problems led to stresses and strains on the coalition government in Israel. The strong Likud party central committee voted never to support the creation of a Palestinian state, a condition of the Palestinian Authority for any type of concessions or peace talks. Binyamin Netanyahu, the prime minister who held power before Barak, brought the motion before the party committee for the vote. Netanyahu is considered a likely candidate for the elections in 2003 against Sharon. Members of the Labour party and other minor parties that are part of Sharon's coalition would likely support the establishment of a Palestinian state in efforts to bring peace to the area. The Israeli coalition government may therefore be hard to hold together.

SOURCE: John Kifner, "Barak Seems in Position to Survive Vote in Parliament," *New York Times,* July 31, 2000, p. A8; Joel Greenberg, "Barak and Sharon Open Talks on Forming a Coalition," *New York Times,* October 24, 2000, p. A18; Deborah Sontag, "Barak Declares Early Elections, in Surprise Move," *New York Times,* November 29, 2000, p. A1; Michael Voss, "Likud Embarrasses Sharon," *BBC News,* May 12, 2002, at news.bbc.co.uk/2/hi.html.

In multiparty systems, parties at the extremes are apt to have more influence than in our two-party system, and in nations with a multiparty system, their legislatures more accurately reflect the full range of the views of the electorate. Political parties in multiparty systems can be more doctrinaire than ours because they do not have to appeal to masses of people. Even though parties that do not become part of the governing coalition may have little to say in setting government policy, they survive because they appeal to some voters. Under such a system, an incentive exists for third, fourth, or additional parties to run because they may win some seats. In contrast, our two-party system tends to create *centrist* parties that appeal to moderate elements and suppress the views of extremists in the electorate. Moreover, once elected, our parties do not form as cohesive a voting bloc as ideological parties do in multiparty systems.

Multiparty parliamentary systems make governments unstable as coalitions form and collapse. In addition, swings in policy when party control changes can be quite dramatic. In contrast, two-party systems produce governments that tend to be stable and centrist, and as a result, policy changes occur incrementally.

Minor Parties: Persistence and Frustration

Although we have a primarily two-party system in the United States, we also have **minor parties**, sometimes called *third parties*. Those that arise around a candidate usually disappear when the charismatic personality does. Examples of such parties are

minor party
A small political party that rises and falls with a charismatic candidate or, if composed of ideologies on the right or left, usually persists over time; also called a *third party.*

Theodore Roosevelt's Bull Moose party and George Wallace's American Independent party. Wallace's party polled more than 13 million votes and won 46 electoral votes in 1968. Ross Perot won 19 million votes, 19 percent of the total vote in 1992. He did only about half as well in 1996, despite the fact that he had organized a political party. Without Ross Perot to lead it, the Reform party was badly divided in 2000, and its presidential candidate, Pat Buchanan, failed to reach 1 percent of the national popular vote. More visible than the Reform party was the Green party, which although not on the ballot in seven states mounted a major effort to reach 5 percent of the popular vote for presidential candidate Ralph Nader and thereby qualify the party for federal funding in the 2004 elections. The effort failed. The Green party mustered only 3 percent of the popular vote. In 2004, Nader, running as an independent, but endorsed by the Reform party, received 1 percent of the vote.

Minor parties that are organized around an *ideology* usually persist over a longer time than those built around a particular leader. Communist, Prohibition, Libertarian, Right to Life, and Green parties are of the ideological type. Minor parties of both types come and go, and there are usually several minor parties running in any given election.[17] Some parties arise around a single issue, like the Right to Life party active in states like New York.

Minor parties have had an indirect influence in our country by drawing attention to controversial issues and by organizing such groups as the antislavery and the civil rights movements.[18] Ross Perot, for example, elevated the importance of balanced budgets in 1992 and made it more difficult for George Bush to attack Bill Clinton on character issues.[19] However, they have never won the presidency or more than a handful of congressional seats (see Table 7-1).[20] They have never shaped national policy from *inside* the government, and their influence on national policy and on the platforms of the two major parties has been limited.[21]

Minor parties have been criticized by major parties as "spoilers," diverting votes away from the major party candidate and costing that candidate the election. Green party candidate Ralph Nader was accused of doing this to Al Gore in 2000. Interest groups identified with environmental issues ran ads urging voters not to waste their vote on

Minor Parties

- The **Natural Law party** was started at the Maharishi International University in Fairfield, Iowa, with the stated purpose to "bring the light of science into politics." The party's platform includes preventive health care and sustainable agriculture without pesticides; it favors using renewable energy to reduce pollution and create national energy self-sufficiency and advocates transcendental meditation as a solution to major health and crime problems, as well as a foreign policy tool. The Natural Law party also wanted a 10 percent flat tax by 2002. The party had more than 213 candidates running for office in 2000. [www.natural-law.org]

- The **Libertarian party** places heavy emphasis on individual liberties, personal responsibility, and freedom from government. Its agenda calls for an end to the federal government's role in education and crime control. Libertarians believe the income tax is the "biggest intrusion into the lives of the American people," and they perceive Social Security as a "fraudulent scheme." They think the United States should wash its hands of foreign involvement—bring all U.S. troops home and only maintain sufficient military for our own defense. In 2000, a total of 1,431 Libertarians ran for office. [www.lp.org]

- The **Green party** takes its name from other pro-environment parties throughout Europe. In the United States, the Greens not only embrace pro-environment positions but are also committed to social justice, decentralization, respect for diversity, community-based economics, nonviolence, feminism, ecological wisdom, grassroots democracy, and personal and global responsibility. The party's 1996 and 2000 presidential candidate, Ralph Nader, called for public campaign financing, greater environmental protection, and affordable housing. His main themes included facilitating social justice, eliminating discrimination, and promoting self-reliance. [www.greenpartyus.org]

- The **Reform party** was organized on September 25, 1995, by Ross Perot. It focuses on national government reform, fiscal responsibility, and political accountability. In 1996, Perot won 9 percent of the popular vote in the presidential election and qualified the party for official party status. In 2000, Pat Buchanan ran as the Reform party's presidential nominee and managed to win only 1 percent of the vote. Recently, the Reform party has been characterized by internal strife; a number of states withdrew from the party, and many of the top party leaders resigned in 2002. [www.reformparty.org]

TABLE 7–1   Minor Parties in the United States

Year	Party	Presidential Candidate	Percent of Popular Vote Received	Electoral Votes Received
1832	Anti-Masonic	William Wirt	8%	7
1856	American (Know-Nothing)	Millard Fillmore	22	8
1860	Democratic (Secessionist)	John C. Breckinridge	18	72
1860	Constitutional Union	John Bell	13	39
1892	People's (Populist)	James B. Weaver	9	22
1912	Bull Moose	Theodore Roosevelt	27	88
1912	Socialist	Eugene V. Debs	6	0
1924	Progressive	Robert M. La Follette	17	13
1948	States' Rights (Dixiecrat)	Strom Thurmond	2	39
1948	Progressive	Henry A. Wallace	2	0
1968	American Independent	George C. Wallace	14	46
1980	National Unity	John Anderson	7	0
1992	Reform	Ross Perot	19	0
1996	Reform	Ross Perot	8	0
2000	Reform	Pat Buchanan	0	0
2000	Green	Ralph Nader	3	0
2004	Reform	Ralph Nader	1	0

Nader, who could not win the election. In the end, it is debatable whether Nader affected the outcome of the contest. However, some research indicates that if no minor party candidate had been on the ballot in 2000, the popular vote would have been split evenly between Bush and Gore.[22]

A Brief History of American Political Parties

Our First Parties

To the founders of the young Republic, parties meant bigger, better-organized, and fiercer factions, and they did not want that. Benjamin Franklin worried about the "infinite mutual abuse of parties, tearing to pieces the best of characters." In his Farewell Address, George Washington warned against the "baneful effects of the Spirit of Party." And Thomas Jefferson said, "If I could not go to heaven but with a party, I would not go there at all."[23]

How, then, did parties get started? Largely out of practical necessity. The same early leaders who so frequently stated their opposition to political parties also recognized the need to organize officeholders who shared their views so that government could act. To get its measures passed by Congress, the Washington administration had to fashion a coalition among factions. This job fell to Treasury Secretary Alexander Hamilton, who built an informal Federalist party, while Washington stayed "above politics."

Secretary of State Jefferson and other officials, many of whom despised Hamilton and his aristocratic ways as much as they opposed the policies he favored, were uncertain about how to deal with these political differences. Their overriding concern was the success of the new government; personal loyalty to Washington was a close second. Thus Jefferson stayed in the cabinet, despite his opposition to administration policies, during most of Washington's first term. When he left the cabinet at the end of 1793, many who joined him in opposition to the administration's economic policies remained in Congress, forming a group of legislators opposed to Federalist fiscal policies and eventually to Federalist foreign policy, which appeared "soft on Britain." This party was later known as Republicans, then as Democratic-Republicans, and finally as Democrats.[24]

Ross Perot, organizer of the Reform party and its presidential candidate in 1992 and 1996.

Some Realities About American Political Parties

- Parties began in this country as soon as people started taking sides in the debate over ratifying the U.S. Constitution, although it took a few years for them to organize into formal bodies.

- Political parties, and especially our two-party system, have persisted over the course of our history.

- Ours has almost always been a two-party system, differentiating us from most nations, which have a one-party or multiparty system.

- Since 1830, we have witnessed reasonably effective competition in our national party system.

- Our parties have historically been decentralized and fragmented. Parties are organized around states, congressional districts, counties, and cities, with state parties the most important units.

- Winning office and power has been more important to party leaders than specific issues or platforms; political parties in the United States are primarily organized to win and hold political power.

- Our parties can be characterized as moderate, centrist, and pragmatic, with only modest ideological cohesion and voting discipline, especially when compared to European political parties.

realigning election

An election during periods of expanded suffrage and change in the economy and society that proves to be a turning point, redefining the agenda of politics and the alignment of voters within parties.

Realigning Elections

American political parties have evolved and changed over time, but some underlying characteristics have been constant. Historically, we have had a two-party system with minor parties. Our parties are moderate and accommodative, meaning that they are open to people with diverse outlooks. Political scientist V. O. Key and others have argued that our party system has been shaped in large part by **realigning elections**, turning points that define the agenda of politics and the alignment of voters within parties during periods of historic change in the economy and society. Realigning elections are characterized by intense electoral involvement by the voters, disruptions of traditional voting patterns, changes in the relations of power within the community, and the formation of new and durable electoral groupings. They have occurred cyclically, not randomly. These elections tend to coincide with expansions of the suffrage or changes in the rate of voting.[25] We focus here on four realigning elections: 1824, 1860, 1896, and 1932.

1824: ANDREW JACKSON AND THE DEMOCRATS Party politics was invigorated following the election of 1824, in which the leader in the popular vote—the hero of the battle of New Orleans, Democrat Andrew Jackson—failed to achieve the necessary majority of the electoral college and was defeated by John Quincy Adams in the runoff election in the House of Representatives. Jackson, brilliantly aided by Martin Van Buren, a veteran party builder in New York State, later knitted together a winning combination of regions, interest groups, and political doctrines to win the presidency in 1828. The Whigs succeeded the Federalists as the opposition party. By the time Van Buren followed Jackson in the White House in 1837, the Democrats had become a large, nationwide movement with national and state leadership, a clear party doctrine, and grassroots organization. The Whigs were almost as strong; in 1840, they put their own man, General William Henry Harrison ("Old Tippecanoe") into the White House. A two-party system had been born, and we have had that two-party system ever since—one of few such systems worldwide.

1860: THE CIVIL WAR AND THE RISE OF THE REPUBLICANS Out of the crisis over slavery evolved a new party: the second Republican party—ultimately dubbed the "Grand Old Party" (GOP).[26] Abraham Lincoln was elected in 1860 with the support not only of financiers, industrialists, and merchants but also of large numbers of workers and farmers. For 50 years after 1860, the Republican coalition won every presidential race except for Grover Cleveland's victories in 1884 and 1892. The Democratic party survived with its durable white male base in the South.

1896: A PARTY IN TRANSITION The Republican party's response to industrialization and hard times for farmers changed it in the late 1800s. A combination of western and southern farmers and western mining interests sought an alliance with workers in the East and Midwest to "recapture America from the foreign moneyed interests responsible for industrialization. The crisis of industrialization squarely placed an agrarian-fundamentalist view of life against an industrial-progress view."[27] The two parties also differed over whether U.S. currency should be tied to a silver or gold standard, with Republicans favoring gold and Democrats silver. William Jennings Bryan, the Democratic candidate for president in 1896, was a talented orator but lost the race to William McKinley.[28] The 1896 realignment differs from the others, however, in that the party in power did not change hands. In that sense it was a *converting realignment* because it reinforced the Republican majority status that had been in place since 1860.[29]

The Progressive era, the first two decades of the twentieth century, was a period of political reform led by the Progressive wing of the Republican party. Much of the agenda of the Progressives focused on the corrupt political parties. Civil service reforms shifted some of the patronage out of the hands of party officials. The direct primary election took control of nominations from party leaders and gave it to the rank-and-file. And in a number of cities, nonpartisan governments were instituted, totally eliminating the role of a party. With the ratification of the Seventeenth Amendment to the Constitution in 1913, U.S. senators came to be popularly elected. Women obtained the right to vote when the Nineteenth

Amendment was ratified in 1920. Thus within a short time, the electorate changed, the rules changed, and even the stakes of the game changed. Democrats were unable to build a durable winning coalition during this time and remained the minority party until the early 1930s, when the Hoover administration was overwhelmed by the Great Depression.

1932: FRANKLIN ROOSEVELT AND THE NEW DEAL ALIGNMENT   The 1932 election was a turning point in American politics. In the 1930s, the United States faced a devastating economic collapse. Between 1929 and 1932, the gross national product fell over 10 percent per year, and unemployment rose from 1.5 million to more than 15 million, with millions more working only part time. Herbert Hoover and the Republican majority in Congress had responded to the Depression by arguing that the problems with the economy were largely self-correcting and that their long-standing policy of following **laissez-faire economics**, a hands-off approach, was appropriate.

Green party presidential candidate in 2000, Ralph Nader.

Voters wanted more. Franklin D. Roosevelt and the Democrats were swept into office in 1932 by a tide of anti-Hoover and anti-Republican sentiment. Roosevelt rode this wave and promised that his response to the Depression would be a "New Deal for America." He rejected laissez-faire economics and instead relied on **Keynesian economics**, which asserted that government could influence the direction of the economy through fiscal and monetary policy. After a century of sporadic government action, the New Dealers stepped in and fundamentally altered the relationship between government and society.

The central issue on which the Republicans and Democrats disagreed in the New Deal period was the role of government with respect to the economy. Roosevelt Democrats argued that the government had to take action to pull the country out of the Depression, but Republicans objected to enlarging the scope of government activity and intruding it into the economy. This basic disagreement about whether the national government should play an active role in regulating and promoting our economy remains one of the most important divisions between the Democratic and Republican parties today, although, with time, the country and both parties accepted many of the New Deal programs.

For the two decades following the 1932 election, the Republican party was relegated to watching the majority Democrats—a new coalition of union households, immigrant workers, and people hurt by the Great Depression—implement their domestic policies. During World War II, both parties cooperated in embracing a bipartisan foreign policy.

We have gone a long time since the last critical or realigning election. You will note that each realignment lasted roughly 36 years, or a couple of generations. Some political scientists anticipated that we were ripe for realignment in 1968 or 1972, but it did not happen. A shift in party allegiances among many southern whites, from the Democratic to the Republican party, coincided with the enfranchisement of southern blacks, who largely identify with the Democratic party. But this was more important regionally and did not constitute a national realignment. Now, as memories of the New Deal fade and the agenda of American politics shifts, the alignments of the 1930s and 1940s hold less and less relevance. Yet, to a surprising degree, the parties are stable and closely competitive, as the 2000 and 2002 elections demonstrated. Whether one party can seize the agenda of politics and fashion itself as the new majority party is one of the interesting political questions for the future.

Divided Government

Major shifts in the demographics of the parties have occurred in recent decades. The once "Solid South" that the Democrats could count on to bolster their legislative majorities and help win the White House has now become the "Solid Republican South" in presidential and, increasingly, in congressional elections as well. Republican congressional leaders—House Majority Leader Tom DeLay of Texas and Senate Majority Leader Bill Frist of Tennessee— came from states that once rarely elected Republicans. Further evidence of partisan change in the South is the sweep of U.S. Senate victories Republicans had in 2004 in Florida, North Carolina, South Carolina, and Georgia, picking up seats that had been held by Democrats going into the 2004 elections. This shift is explained by the movement of whites from the Democratic party, largely because of the party's position on civil rights. The rise of the Re-

laissez-faire economics
Theory that opposes governmental interference in economic affairs beyond what is necessary to protect life and property.

Keynesian economics
Theory based on the principles of John Maynard Keynes, stating that government spending should increase during business slumps and be curbed during booms.

Religion is sometimes linked to partisanship. In reality, devoutly religious people are found in both major parties.

publican South reinforced the shift to conservatism in the Grand Old Party. This shift, combined with the diminished ranks of conservative southern Democrats, made the Democratic party, especially the congressional Democrats, more unified and more liberal than in the days when more of its congressional members had "safe" southern seats.

Since 1953, **divided government**, with one party controlling Congress and the other the White House, has been in effect twice as long as one-party control of both legislative and executive branches. Until the 1992 and 1994 elections, the Republicans' strength had been in presidential elections, where they often won with landslide margins. Part of the explanation was their ability to attract popular candidates like Dwight Eisenhower and Ronald Reagan, but Republicans also reaped the rewards of Democratic party divisiveness and generally weaker Democratic presidential candidates. Evidence that voters are inclined to favor divided government came when voters elected a Republican congressional majority in 1994 and then retained it in 1996 and 1998. In 2004, the GOP expanded its congressional majorities. This was especially the case in 2005, when the Republican majority in the U.S. Senate climbed to 55 Republicans and 45 Democrats.

The 2000 and 2002 Elections: Into the New Century

Neither party could claim a mandate after the tightly contested 2000 elections, which resulted in a 50–50 partisan tie in the Senate, a slim Republican majority in the House, and a presidential contest whose outcome was unresolved for weeks as ballots were recounted in Florida. Although the outcome was essentially a tie, the breakdown of the vote was anything but random. The 2000 presidential results and exit polls revealed a divided nation. Al Gore carried the Northeast and Pacific states and a few urban states in the nation's midsection. George W. Bush carried the South and interior of the country, minus a few states like New Mexico. Demographically, the Democrats received large majorities of votes from African Americans, Hispanics, union households, Jews, and gays. Republicans did well among white males, religious conservatives, and higher-income voters.[30] People's positions on most issues in the 2000 election were not as strongly held as on issues in the past, like Vietnam, civil rights, or Lyndon Johnson's Great Society programs, but there were clear differences between Democratic and Republican voters on tax cuts, school vouchers, and privatization of Social Security.

The 2002 election departed from historic patterns in several respects. First, the longstanding pattern had been for the party of the president to lose seats in the House of Representatives. Since 1934, in only two elections—1998 and 2002—has the president's party gained seats. In 2002, the Republicans picked up seats in both the House and Senate, returning to the majority in the Senate and expanding their majority in the House. In 2004, George W. Bush not only secured reelection but his party picked up seats in the Senate and House. Most of the open and competitive seats in 2004 were in predictably Republican states in terms of presidential voting, such as Alaska, Oklahoma, and South Dakota. Bush carried all of these states by wide margins. The Senate Republican candidate won in all of these states, including South Dakota, where the Senate Democratic Leader, Tom Daschle, was defeated by John Thune. Republicans also swept the open Senate seats in Florida, South Carolina, Georgia, and North Carolina. All of these seats were held by Democrats going into 2004. Democrats picked up a Republican Senate seat in 2004 with the election of Ken Salazar. Democrats also picked up a net gain of three state legislative majorities in 2004.

American Parties Today

divided government
Governance divided between the parties, as when one holds the presidency and the other controls one or both houses of Congress.

Americans are largely indifferent about political parties.[31] If anything, most people are critical or even fearful of the major parties. Parties are, in a word, distrusted. Some see parties as corrupt institutions, interested only in the spoils of politics. Critics charge that the parties evade the issues; they fail to deliver on their promises; they have no new ideas; they follow public opinion rather than lead it; or they are just one more special interest.

Still, Americans understand that parties are necessary. They want party labels kept on the ballot, at least for congressional and presidential elections as well as for statewide offices. Most voters think of themselves as Democrats or Republicans and typically vote for candidates from their party. They even contribute millions of dollars to the two major parties. Far more individual contributions go to the Republicans than to the Democrats.[32] Thus Americans appreciate, at least vaguely, that you cannot run a big democracy without parties.

Both the Democratic and Republican national parties and most state parties are moderate in their policies and leadership.[33] Successful party leaders must be diplomatic; to win presidential elections and congressional majorities, they must find a middle ground among more or less hostile groups. Members of the House of Representatives, in order to be elected and reelected, have to appeal to a majority of the voters from their own district. As more House districts have become "safe" for incumbents, the House of Representatives has become less moderate and the home of partisan ideological clashes to a greater extent than the Senate or the White House.

Although each party usually takes its extremist supporters more or less for granted and seeks out the voters in the middle, both parties retain some ideological diversity. The Democratic umbrella encompasses the conservative Coalition for a Democratic Majority, the moderate Democratic Leadership Council (dominated by an array of southern governors and senators), and the liberal Americans for Democratic Action. The Democratic coalition embraces activists in the civil rights and other liberal-left movements. Republicans, while more homogeneous, have their contentious factions as well. On the more conservative side are the Religious Right, staunch supporters of the right to bear arms, and antitax activists. As noted in Chapter 5, a gender gap exists in voting in presidential and congressional elections, with women voting Democratic more than men. As political scientist Virginia Sapiro has written, "Women and men may still be socialized to think about politics somewhat differently, or at least some groups of women and men are. The two sexes play different kinds of roles in society and family life and thus have different kinds of experiences."[34] Some interest groups also seek to reinforce the gender gap, emphasizing issues like reproductive rights, gun control, or the environment with women and often urging them to vote Democratic. Some individual Republican candidates have been successful in narrowing the gender gap.

Among Republican elected officials, the split has been between more liberal northeastern Republicans like Governors John G. Rowland of Connecticut and George Pataki of New York and the dominant conservative wing. Democratic officeholders also have substantial policy differences. Georgia Senator Zell Miller and conservative House Democrats are often at odds with the more liberal and dominant wing of their party. Democratic Senator Joseph Lieberman from Connecticut, known for his willingness to consider school vouchers and his concerns about affirmative action, had to modify his positions in order to reconcile with more liberal Democratic party activists after being selected as Al Gore's running mate in 2000.

Marc Racicot, Former Montana governor and Republican National Committee chair.

Parties as Institutions

Like other institutions of American government—Congress, the presidency, and the courts—political parties have rules, procedures, and organizational structure. What are the institutional characteristics of political parties?

NATIONAL PARTY LEADERSHIP   The supreme authority in both major parties is the **national party convention**, which meets every four years for four days to nominate candidates for president and vice president, to ratify the party platform, and to adopt rules.

In charge of the national party when it is not assembled in convention is the *national committee*. In recent years, both parties have strengthened the role of the national committee and enhanced the influence of individual committee members. The committees are now more representative of the party rank-and-file. This enhanced role and more representative membership will not end with the ban on soft money to federal candidates. But in neither party is the national committee the center of party leadership.

national party convention
A national meeting of delegates elected in primaries, caucuses, or state conventions who assemble once every four years to nominate candidates for president and vice president, ratify the party platform, elect officers, and adopt rules.

Party Platforms

The typical party platform—the official statement of party policy—is often a vague and ponderous document that hardly anyone reads. Platforms are ambiguous by design, giving voters few obvious reasons to vote against the party. This generalization about party platforms does not mean that political parties do not stand for anything. Most business and professional people believe the Republican party best serves their interests, while working people tend to look to the Democrats to speak for them. The proportion of voters discerning important differences between the parties increased sharply, as the parties became more polarized.*

Many politicians contend that platforms rarely help elect anybody, but platform positions can hurt a presidential candidate. Because the platform-writing process is not always controlled by the nominee, it is possible for presidential candidates to disagree with their own party platform. But the platform-drafting process gives partisans, especially those motivated by particular issues, an opportunity to express their views, and it serves to identify the most important values and principles on which the parties are based. Once elected, politicians are rarely reminded of what their platform position was on a given issue. One major exception to this was former President George Bush's promise not to raise taxes if elected in 1988 with his memorable quote, "Read my lips—no new taxes." He was forced to eat those words when taxes were raised.

Party platforms in 2000 were carefully controlled by the Gore and Bush campaigns. The Republican platform reflected Bush's "compassionate conservative" themes, but Bush was criticized for not softening the party position on abortion.† The Bush campaign decided not to risk a convention fight by removing the plank, preferring to present an image of a unified party, and pro-choice Republicans at the convention did not challenge the platform language. The platform language did not become an issue in the general election campaign. Vice President Gore tried to reinforce centrist themes in his party's platform. For example, the Democratic platform included the death penalty as a means of fighting crime.

Differences between 2000 Democratic and Republican platforms are highlighted in the following chart. The platforms in their entirety are available at www.democrats.org/about/platform.html and www.rnc.org/gopinfo/platform.

Key Party Differences: Excerpts from the Democratic and Republican Party Platforms, 2000

Democrats	Republicans
Abortion	
Support the right of every woman to choose, consistent with *Roe* v. *Wade,* and regardless of ability to pay. Individual—not government—can best take responsibility for making the most difficult and intensely personal decisions regarding reproduction.	Support a human life amendment to the Constitution and endorse legislation to make clear that the Fourteenth Amendment's protections apply to unborn children. Oppose using public revenues for abortion and will not fund organizations that advocate it.
Campaign Finance Reform	
Propose tough new lobbying reform, publicly guaranteed TV time for debates and advocacy by candidates, a crackdown on special-interest issue ads, and a public-private, nonpartisan Democracy Endowment that will raise money from Americans and finance congressional elections—with no other contributions allowed to candidates who accept the funding.	Enact "paycheck protection," ensuring that no union member is forced to contribute to anybody's campaign. Preserve the right of every individual and all groups to express their opinions and advocate their issues.

Each major party has a *national chair* as its top official. The national committee formally elects the chair, but in reality it is the choice of the presidential nominee. For the party that controls the White House, the chair actually serves at the pleasure of the president and does the president's bidding. Following the 2000 election, the Republican national party chair, James Gilmore, was replaced by former Montana Governor Marc Racicot, a move initiated by the Bush White House.[35] The chair of the party without an incumbent president has considerable independence yet works closely with the party's congressional leadership. The national committee often elects a new head after an electoral defeat. Although chairs are the heads of their national party apparatus, they remain largely unknown to the voters. The chair may play a major role in running the national campaign; after the election, the power of the national chair of the victorious party tends to dwindle.

National party organizations are often agents of an incumbent president in securing his renomination. When there is no incumbent president seeking reelection, the national party committee is generally neutral until the nominee is selected. Although heated primary contests often preclude having a united party in the general election, national parties are helpless to prevent them.[36]

Foreign Policy and Military Deployment

"We cannot be the world's policemen, and we must be discriminating in our approach. But where the stakes are high, when nothing short of military engagement can secure our national interest, when we have the military forces available and have made our best efforts to join with allies, and cost is proportionate to the objective, we must be ready to act."

"The military is not a civilian police force or a political referee. . . . A Republican president will identify and pursue vital American national interests, and build and secure the peace. Republicans know what it takes to accomplish this: robust military forces, strong alliances, expanding trade, and resolute diplomacy."

Missile Defense

Support the development of the technology for a limited national missile defense system. Any such system is compatible with the Anti-Ballistic Missile Treaty.

Favor "deploying an effective missile defense . . . at the earliest possible date, and designed to protect all 50 states. America's deployed forces overseas, and our friends and allies . . . will seek a negotiated change in the Anti-Ballistic Missile Treaty."

School Choice

Favor public schools that compete with one another and are held accountable for results. Oppose private school vouchers.

Expand parental choice and encourage competition by providing parents with information on their child's school, increasing the number of charter schools, and expanding education savings accounts.

Gun Control

Favor mandatory child safety locks, a photo license ID, a full background check, and a gun safety test to buy a new handgun.

Support background checks. Oppose federal licensing of law-abiding gun owners and national gun registration.

Status of Gays

Support continued efforts to end workplace discrimination against gay men and lesbians.

Support the traditional definition of "marriage" as the legal union of one man and one woman.

*Bruce E. Keith et al., *The Myth of the Independent Voter* (University of California Press, 1992), p. 148.

†Richard Benedetto, "Bush's Influence on Platform Results in 'More Upbeat' Tone," *USA Today,* July 31, 2000, p. A6.

In addition to the national party committees, there are also congressional and senatorial *campaign committees.* In recent years, congressional and senatorial campaign committees have become much more active—recruiting candidates, training them, and assisting with campaign finance.[37] Senatorial campaign committees are composed of senators chosen for two-year terms by their fellow party members in the Senate; congressional campaign committees are chosen in the same manner by the House. Chairs of campaign committees are nominated by their party leadership and typically ratified by their party caucus. For information on the party committees and their leadership, go to www.nrcc.org, www.nrsc.org, www.dccc.org, and www.dscc.org. They have a lot of say about which candidates get party campaign funds. This will likely diminish with the abolition of party soft money.

The surge in soft money in recent years has enhanced the power of the congressional and senatorial party committee leaders who allocated unlimited amounts of soft money to particular races. Table 7-2 shows the party soft money allocations to key 2000 U.S. Senate races. An example of a powerful congressional campaign committee leader was Mitch McConnel of Kentucky, who headed the National Republican

TABLE 7–2   Soft Money Transfers to State Parties in Five Competitive 2000 Senate Races

| | Democratic Senatorial Campaign Committee | | | National Republican Senatorial Committee | | |
State	Hard Money	Soft Money	Percent Soft Money	Hard Money	Soft Money	Percent Soft Money
Delaware	$ 1,402,032	$ 2,954,313	68%	$ 0	$ 250,000	100%
Michigan	2,391,714	4,280,606	64	1,668,200	2,821,560	63
Missouri	1,649,107	4,110,334	71	1,270,800	2,691,900	68
Montana	824,089	1,886,558	70	516,700	778,900	60
Virginia	4,132,687	4,968,600	55	2,303,800	3,052,100	57
Total	10,399,629	18,200,911	64	5,759,500	9,594,460	62

SOURCE: Federal Election Commission, "National Party Financial Activity Through the End of the Election Cycle," press release, May 15, 2001, at www.fec.gov/press/05150partyfund/tables/cong2state2000.html; David B. Magleby, ed., *Election Advocacy: Soft Money and Issue Advocacy in the 2000 Congressional Elections* (Brigham Young University, Center for the Study of Elections and Democracy, 2001); David B. Magleby, *The Other Campaign: Soft Money and Issue Advocacy in the 2000 Congressional Elections* (Rowman & Littlefield, 2003).

Senatorial Committee between 1997 and 2000. McConnell, an outspoken opponent of campaign finance reform, generated controversy when he sent soft money to Wisconsin in 1998 rather than to the Senate race in Washington. Some believed that McConnell wanted to defeat Russell Feingold, the Wisconsin Democrat and a major sponsor of campaign finance reform. Linda Smith, the Republican candidate in Washington, supported campaign finance reform. McConnell's work for the party helped him win election to Majority Whip after the 2002 election.[38]

PARTIES AT THE GRASS ROOTS   The two major parties are decentralized, organized around elections in states, cities, or congressional districts. They have organizations for each level of government, national, state, and local. Party organization at the state and local levels is structured much like the national level. Each state has a *state committee* headed by a *state chair*. State law determines the composition of the state committees and sets rules regulating them. Members of state committees are usually elected from local areas. Party auxiliaries such as the Young Democrats or the Federation of Republican Women are sometimes represented as well. In many states, these committees are dominated by governors, senators, or coalitions of locally elected business and ethnic leaders. State chairs are normally elected by the state committees, although in approximately one-quarter of the states they are chosen at state conventions. When the party controls the governorship, chairs are often agents of the governor.[39]

Some powerful state parties have developed in recent years. Despite much state-to-state variation, the trend is toward stronger state organizations, with Republicans typically being much better funded.[40] In some states, third and fourth parties play a role in local elections. New York, for instance, has both a Liberal party and a Conservative party in addition to the Democratic and Republican parties. The role minor parties play in statewide elections can be important, even though they rarely win office themselves.

Below the state committees are *county committees,* which vary widely in function and power. The key role of these committees is recruiting candidates for such offices as county commissioner, sheriff, and treasurer. The recruiting job often involves finding a candidate for the office, not deciding among competing contenders. For a party that rarely wins an election, the county committee has to struggle to find someone willing to run. When the chance of winning is greater, primaries, not the party leaders, usually decide the winner.[41] Many county organizations maintain a significant level of activity, distributing campaign literature, organizing telephone campaigns, putting up posters and lawn signs, and canvassing door-to-door. Other county committees do not function at all, and many party leaders are just figureheads.

In recent elections, state party organizations have been the means by which millions of dollars in soft money have been spent. Rulings of the Federal Election Commission made it advantageous for national parties to spend their soft money through the state parties. The focus of their soft money expenditures was candidate promotion. In many instances, broadcast ads paid for with soft money did not even mention the party.[42]

It is not clear that soft money helped build stronger parties at the state and local levels. Some soft money spending may have enhanced such party activities as building a list of active partisans in the state or district or improving the computer technology of the party offices or may have had secondary benefits when party supporters were mobilized for a U.S. Senate or House race. But for most soft money spending, state parties simply became local bank accounts for national party committee candidate-centered campaign communications. Even after the scores of millions of dollars of soft money spent by party committees, strong local party organization is rare at the city, town, ward, and precinct levels. Most local party committees are poorly financed and inactive except during the few weeks before election day.[43] In a few places, local ward and precinct leaders still do favors for constituents, from getting more police patrols in a neighborhood to organizing clambakes or obtaining horse-racing passes in a state like Arkansas.

Parties in Government

Political parties are central to the operation of our governments. They help bridge the separation of powers and facilitate coordination between levels of government in a federal system.

IN THE LEGISLATIVE BRANCH   Members of Congress take their partisanship seriously, at least while they are in Washington. Their power and influence are determined by whether their party is in control of the House or Senate; they also have a stake in which party controls the White House. The chairs of all standing committees in Congress come from the majority party, as do the presiding officials of both chambers. Members of both houses sit together with fellow partisans on the floor and in committee.

Members of congressional staffs are also partisan. From the volunteer intern to the senior staffer, members of Congress expect their staff to be loyal first to them and then to their party. Should you decide to go to work for a representative or senator, you would be expected to identify yourself with that person's party, and you would have some difficulty working for the other party later. Employees of the House and Senate—from elevator operators to the Capitol Hill police and even including the chaplain—hold patronage jobs. With few exceptions, such jobs go to persons from the party that has a majority in the House or the Senate.

IN THE EXECUTIVE BRANCH   Presidents select almost all senior White House staff and cabinet members from their own party. Presidents, however, typically surround themselves with advisers who have campaigned with them and have proved their party loyalty.

Partisanship is also important in presidential appointments to the highest levels of the federal bureaucracy. The party that wins the White House has around 5,000 noncareer positions to fill.[44] Included in these positions are cabinet-level appointments and ambassadorships around the world. Party commitment, including making campaign contributions, is expected of those who seek these positions.

IN THE JUDICIAL BRANCH   The judicial branch of the national government, with its lifetime tenure and political independence, is designed to operate in an expressly nonpartisan manner. Judges, unlike Congress, do not sit together by political party. But the appointment process for judges has been partisan from the beginning. The landmark case

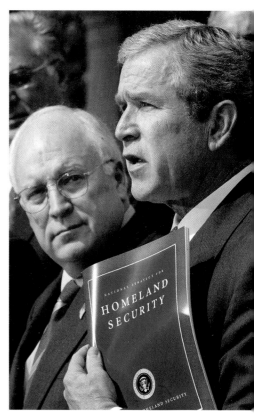

Presidents have many advisers. One of George W. Bush's most influential advisers is Vice President Dick Cheney, who played a major role in Bush's presidential campaign and who continues to shape the president's agenda.

178   PART II   THE POLITICAL PROCESS

establishing the principle of judicial review, *Marbury* v. *Madison* (1803), concerned the efforts of one party to stack the judiciary with fellow partisans before leaving office.[45] Today party identification remains an important consideration in the naming of federal judges. Although the party affiliation of a judicial nominee is not called for on any form, the individuals responsible for screening and evaluating candidates do take party and ideology into account. Appointees must be acceptable to certain power centers in the party. For example, Republicans in the Ronald Reagan and George Bush administrations insisted on conservative judges; Bill Clinton, although nominating Democrats, placed more importance on gender and race than on ideology in selecting judges. The confirmation process can also be partisan. Republicans claimed that Democrats were delaying hearings for George W. Bush's judicial nominees, and Democrats countered that they were responding in kind to what Republicans had done to Clinton nominees when the GOP controlled the Senate.

AT THE STATE AND LOCAL LEVELS   The importance of party in the operation of local government varies among states and localities. In some states, such as New York and Illinois, local parties play an even stronger role than they do at the national level. In others, such as Nebraska, parties play almost no role. In Nebraska, the state legislature is expressly nonpartisan, though factions perform like parties and still play a role. Parties are likewise unimportant in the government of most city councils. But in most states and many cities, parties are important to the operation of the legislature, governorship, or mayoralty. Judicial selection in most states is also a partisan matter. Much was made by the Bush campaign of the fact that six of the seven Florida Supreme Court justices deciding the 2000 ballot-counting case in favor of Gore are Democrats. Democrats made much of the fact that the five U.S. Supreme Court justices who decided in favor of Bush are Republicans.

Parties in the Electorate

Political parties would be of little significance if they did not have meaning to the electorate. Adherents of the two parties are drawn to them by a combination of factors, including their stand on the issues; personal or party history; religious, racial, or social peer grouping; and the appeal of their candidates. The emphases among these factors change over time, but they are remarkably consistent with those identified by political scientists more than 40 years ago.[46]

PARTY REGISTRATION   For citizens in most states, "party" has a particular legal meaning—**party registration**. At the time voters register to vote in these states, they are asked to state their party preference. They then become registered Democrats, Republicans, Libertarians, or whatever. Voters can subsequently change their party registration. The purpose of party registration is to limit the participants in primary elections to members of that party and to make it easier for parties to contact people who might vote for their party.

PARTY ACTIVISTS   Activists tend to fall into three broad categories: party regulars, candidate activists, and issue activists. *Party regulars* place the party first. They value winning elections and understand that compromise and moderation may be necessary to reach that objective. They also realize that it is important to keep the party together as much as possible, because a fractured party only helps the opposition.

Candidate activists are followers of a particular candidate who see the party as the means to place their candidate in power. Candidate activists are often not concerned with the other operations of the party—with nominees for other offices or with raising money for the party. For example, people who supported Pat Buchanan in his unsuccessful run for the presidency as a Reform party candidate in 2000 would be classified as candidate activists. Buchanan, a television commentator and unsuccessful Republican candidate for the Republican nomination in 1996, built a personal following. Reform party members who traced their roots in the party to Ross Perot found Buchanan so repellent that they split from him and nominated their own candidate for president. Buchanan fared poorly in the 2000

party registration
The act of declaring party affiliation; required by some states when one registers to vote.

Portrait of the Electorate

	Republican	Democrat	Independent	Other
Sex				
Male	32%	32%	32%	4%
Female	31	35	26	7
Race				
White	36	29	30	6
Black	7	70	20	3
Hispanic	23	38	35	4
Age				
18–34	30	32	32	6
35–45	37	30	25	7
46–55	28	36	30	6
56–64	29	36	31	4
65+	32	37	27	5
Income				
$0–$14,999	20	47	27	10
$15,000–$34,999	25	41	30	17
$35,000–$49,999	29	31	33	17
$50,000–$64,999	35	31	28	12
$65,000–$84,999	36	30	26	25
$84,999+	40	27	29	16
Religion				
Protestant	46	29	22	3
Catholic	30	37	31	2
None/Atheist/Agnostic	13	38	38	13
Other/Jewish	19	40	28	13
Ideology				
Liberal	9	55	30	5
Moderate	20	35	20	5
Conservative	48	20	28	4
Region				
Northeast	30	34	33	3
North-Central	33	33	27	7
South	32	35	28	5
West	32	32	29	8
Total	31	33	28	7

Source: *2002 National Election Study* (Center for Political Studies, University of Michigan, 2002).

Note: Numbers may not add up to 100 due to rounding.

election, getting less than 1 percent of the vote and as a result losing millions of dollars in federal subsidies for the 2004 elections. The federal subsidy from Perot's 8 percent vote total in 1996 on the Reform party ticket largely funded the Buchanan 2000 campaign.[47]

Issue activists wish to push the parties in a particular direction on a single issue or a narrow range of issues: abortion, taxes, school prayer, the environment, or civil rights. To issue activists, the party platform is an important battleground because they seek party endorsement for their position. Issue activists are also often candidate activists if they can find a candidate willing to embrace their position.

Both issue activists and candidate activists insist on making their "statement" regardless of the electoral consequences. They would rather lose the election than compromise. Party activists thus include a diverse group of people who come to the political party with different objectives. It is not surprising, then, that some of the most interesting politics are over candidate selection and issue positions within the political parties. Fights over strategy and party position are conducted in open meetings and under democratic procedures. Political parties foster democracy not only by competition *between* the parties but *within* the parties as well.

Party Identification

Most Americans are mere spectators of party activity. They lack the partisan commitment and interest needed for active party involvement. This is not to say that parties are irrelevant or unimportant to them. For them, partisanship is what political scientists call **party identification**—an informal and subjective affiliation with a political party that most people acquire in childhood, a standing preference for one party over another.[48] This type of voter may sometimes vote for a candidate from the other party, but in the absence of a compelling reason to do otherwise, most will vote according to their party identification. Peers and early political experiences reinforce party identification, generally acquired from parents. It is part of the political socialization process described in Chapter 4.

Party identification is the single best predictor of how people will vote. Unlike candidates and issues, which come and go, party identification is a long-term element in voting choice. The strength of party identification is also important in predicting participation and political interest. Strong Republicans and strong Democrats participate more actively in politics than any other groups and are generally more knowledgeable and informed. Pure Independents are just the opposite; they vote at the lowest rates and have the lowest levels of interest and awareness of any of the categories of party identification. This evidence runs counter to the notion that persons who are strong partisans are unthinking party adherents.[49]

Partisan Realignment and Dealignment

With the exception of the shift of southern whites to the Republican party and the enfranchisement of blacks who remain Democrats, the current system of party identification is built on a foundation of the New Deal and the critical election of 1932, events that took place nearly three-quarters of a century ago. How can events so removed from the present still be important in shaping our party system? When will there be another realignment—an election that dramatically changes the voters' partisan identification? Or has such a realignment already occurred? The question is frequently debated in the literature of political science. Most scholars believe that we have not experienced a major re-

party identification
An informal and subjective affiliation with a political party that most people acquire in childhood.

TABLE 7–3   Party Identification, 1950s–2002

Decade	Strong Democrat	Weak Democrat	Independent-Leaning Democrat	Independent	Independent-Leaning Republican	Weak Republican	Strong Republican	Apolitical
1950s*	23%	23%	8%	7%	7%	15%	13%	4%
1960s	22	25	8	10	7	15	12	2
1970s	17	24	12	14	10	14	9	2
1980s	18	26	11	12	11	14	11	2
1990s	18	19	13	10	12	15	13	1
2000s	18	16	14	9	13	14	15	1

SOURCE: *2000 and 2002 National Election Study* (Center for Political Studies, University of Michigan).

Note: Data may not sum to 100 percent due to averaging.

1950s percentages based on years 1952, 1956, and 1958.

alignment since 1932.[50] Partisan identification has been stable for more than four decades, and even though new voters have been added to the electorate—minorities and 18- to 21-year-olds—the basic nature of the party system has not changed dramatically. Table 7-3 presents the party identification breakdown for the period from the 1950s to 2000.

Evidence of a possible voting realignment came in the early 1980s, when Republicans won several close Senate elections and gained a majority in that body.[51] Democrats, however, won back the Senate in 1986, and until 1994 they appeared to have a permanent majority in the House. All that changed with the 1994 election, as Republicans were swept into office on a tidal wave of victories. Republicans made major inroads in the South and strengthened their share of the vote among white males.

The 1998 election gave the Democrats renewed hope that they could regain control of Congress, or at least the House of Representatives, in the 2000 elections. Overcoming their worst fears that the Bill Clinton–Monica Lewinsky scandal would enlarge Republican majorities in the Senate and House, the Democrats effectively mobilized their core voters and actually picked up five seats in the House of Representatives. Allies of the Democratic party, such as organized labor, were also encouraged by gains they saw in 1998. Republicans were disheartened by the congressional election outcome but pointed to their strength in several key governorships as cause for optimism.

The 2000 presidential and congressional elections were exceedingly close. The Republicans narrowly held on to their majority in the House in 2000, but the Democrats picked up a net gain of four seats in the Senate, resulting in an evenly divided Senate after the election.

Following September 11, 2001, the President had high approval ratings, which declined somewhat in the ensuing months but which were still strong during the 2002 election. In an election that lacked a national theme and during which the public seemed distracted by talk of war with Iraq and by a series of sniper murders in Washington, D.C., the Democrats had difficulty communicating a theme and a message. Into this void stepped President Bush, who gave focus and energy to Republican candidates and volunteers. The result was a net gain in seats in the Senate and House. Republicans did not do as well in contests for governor, however. While the President's popularity helped Republicans, it did not alter long-standing partisan identification and falls short of a realignment.

"Very Republican. I love it."

Party Identification

Party identification is measured by the answers to the following questions:

- *Generally speaking, in politics do you usually think of yourself as a Republican, a Democrat, an Independent, or what?*

Persons who answer Republican or Democrat to this question are then asked:

- *Would you call yourself a strong or a not very strong Republican/Democrat?*

Persons who answered Independent to the first question are asked this follow-up question:

- *Do you think of yourself as closer to the Republican or the Democratic party?*

Persons who do not indicate Democrat, Republican, or Independent to the first question rarely exceed 2 percent of the electorate and include those who are apolitical or who identify with one of the minor political parties. Because of their consistently small numbers, they are typically not important to election outcomes. In a close race, like the 2000 presidential contest, Green party supporters became an important target for both Al Gore and Ralph Nader.

The party identification questions produce seven categories of persons: strong Democrats, weak Democrats, Independent-leaning Democrats, Pure Independents, Independent-leaning Republicans, weak Republicans, and strong Republicans. Over the nearly 50-year period during which political scientists have been conducting such surveys, the partisan preferences of the American public have remained remarkably stable.

TABLE 7–4 **Voting Behavior of Partisans and Independents, 1992–2002**

	Percent Voting Democratic							
	President			U.S. House				
	1992	1996	2000	1994	1996	1998	2000	2002
Strong Democrats	93%	96%	97%	88%	87%	77%	90%	89%
Weak Democrats	60	82	80	73	70	57	73	71
Independent-leaning Democrats	70	76	72	68	69	63	73	67
Pure Independents	41	35	44	55	41	41	50	35
Independent-leaning Republicans	11	20	13	25	21	24	26	27
Weak Republicans	14	20	14	21	21	25	18	25
Strong Republicans	3	5	2	7	3	7	12	8

SOURCE: *2000 American National Election Study* (Center for Political Studies, University of Michigan, 2000). Update by authors.

In presidential voting, Republicans have done well, winning six of the last nine presidential elections, although they lost the popular vote in 2000. Bill Clinton's victories in 1992 and 1996 demonstrated, however, that Democrats could still assemble a winning coalition. But as discussed previously, the 2000 presidential vote showed an evenly divided nation. Whether one party can expand its support to make it dominant remains an open question.

We may therefore conclude from recent national elections that American voters overall have no consistent preference for one party over the other. In a time of such electoral volatility and low turnout, the winners and losers are determined by the basics of politics: who attracts positive voter attention, who strikes themes that motivate voters to participate, who does a better job in communicating with voters. Party identification remains important for those voters who come out to vote, and strength of partisanship remains positively correlated with turnout.

Thus there are few signs of voter realignment but stronger signs of voter disengagement. Some observers feel that we are experiencing a rejection of partisanship in favor of becoming Independents, and there has indeed been an increase in the number of persons who characterize themselves as Independents. Journalist Hedrick Smith expresses a widespread view: "The most important phenomenon of American politics in the past quarter century has been the rise of independent voters, who have at times outnumbered Republicans."[52]

The **dealignment** argument—that people have abandoned both parties to become Independents—would be more persuasive were it not that two-thirds of all self-identified Independents are really partisans in their voting behavior and attitudes. One-third of those who claim to be Independents lean toward the Democratic party and vote Democratic in election after election. Another third of Independents lean toward Republicans and just as predictably vote Republican. The remaining third, who appear to be genuine Independents and who do not vote predictably for one party, turn out to be people with little interest in politics. Despite the reported growth in Independents, there are proportionately about the same number of Pure Independents now as there were in 1956.[53] There are, in short, at least three types of Independents, and most of them are predictably partisan. Table 7-4 summarizes voting behavior in recent contests for president and the House of Representatives.

Why has realignment moved so slowly? Why aren't all conservatives now happily ensconced in the Republican party and all liberals gladly lodged in the Democratic party? Americans do not casually cross party lines. If you grew up in a conservative New Hampshire family whose forebears voted Republican for a century, you are pretty much conditioned to stay with the GOP. Even if that party took a direction you disliked, you might continue to register as a Republican but quietly vote Democratic to avoid friction in the family. Or if you come from a "yellow dog" Democratic family in Texas (meaning your

dealignment
Weakening of partisan preferences that points to a rejection of both major parties and a rise in the number of Independents.

family would vote for a "yellow dog" before it would vote for a Republican), you might continue to vote for Democrats locally even though you disliked various Democratic candidates for president or senator. This pattern was once common throughout the South.[54]

Another reason for slow realignment is the local nature of the parties. For decades, conservative Democrats in the South have been voting for Republican candidates for president—not just George W. Bush and Ronald Reagan but also Richard Nixon and even Dwight Eisenhower—without changing their identification from the Democratic party to the Republican.[55] Why? Partly because they still see themselves as Democrats, but also because the Democratic party remains stronger at the state and local levels in many southern states. So if candidates and voters want to have an impact on local politics, in which the only meaningful elections may be in the Democratic primaries, they retain their Democratic affiliation.

Are the Political Parties Dying?

Critics of the American party system make three allegations against it: (1) parties do not take meaningful and contrasting positions on most issues, (2) party membership is essentially meaningless, and (3) parties are so concerned with accommodating the middle

The Progressives

From the late 1800s until around 1920, a group of Americans calling themselves "Progressives" pushed for economic, social, and political reforms. On the economic front, they sought more regulation of business, hostility to monopolies, and tax reforms including income taxes. Socially, the Progressives pressed for improved living and working conditions for the poor. Politically, they sought to substitute direct democracy for what they saw as corrupt legislatures, governors, and local governments. Examples of Progressive era reforms include the direct election of senators (taking this power away from state legislatures), the direct primary (putting voters, not party leaders, in charge of nominations), and the initiative, referendum, and recall, whereby voters could enact laws or veto actions of legislatures. These reforms have had a lasting impact on American politics.

The political reform agenda of the Progressives became important again in the 1970s as the number of states using primaries in presidential elections rose substantially and as states experienced much greater use of the initiative process. During the 1970s and again in the late 1990s, advocates of a national initiative became more vocal.

President Theodore Roosevelt.

of the ideological spectrum that they are incapable of serving as an avenue for social progress. Are these statements accurate? And if they are accurate, are they important?

Some analysts fear that parties are in a severe decline or even mortally ill. They point first to the long-run adverse impact on political parties of the Progressive movement reforms early in this century, reforms that robbed party organizations of their control of the nomination process by allowing masses of independent and "uninformed" voters to enter the primaries and nominate candidates who might not be acceptable to party leaders. They also point to the spread of nonpartisan elections in cities and towns and the staggering of national, state, and local elections that made it harder for parties to influence the election process.

Legislation limiting the viability and functions of parties was bad enough, say the party pessimists, but parties suffer from additional ills. The rise of television and electronic technology and the parallel increase in the number of campaign, media, and direct-mail consultants have made parties less relevant in educating, mobilizing, and organizing the electorate. Television, radio, the Internet, and telephones have strengthened the role of candidates and lessened the importance of parties. (See Chapter 10 for more on the media in this role.)

Advocates of strong parties concede that parts of this diagnosis may be correct: the demise of political machines at the local level, the decline in strong partisan affiliations, the weakness of grassroots party membership. Yet they also see signs of party revival, or at least the persistence of party. The national party organizations—the national committees and the congressional and senatorial campaign committees—are significantly better funded than they were in earlier days; they even own permanent, modern headquarters buildings in Washington, D.C., located a few blocks from the U.S. Capitol. Moreover, the parties through 2002 were capable of providing assistance to candidates in competitive races and to state and local party organizations because of their financial base, especially from soft money contributions. However, the new campaign finance reforms will likely lessen party activity. Advocates hope that strong national parties will exercise some leverage over the positions that candidates and officeholders take on party issues.[56]

Since the first years of the Reagan administration, both the Republican and Democratic parties have demonstrated a remarkable cohesiveness in Congress. This trend can be measured by the *party unity score,* defined as the percentage of members of a party who vote together on roll call votes in Congress on which a majority of the members of one party vote against a majority of the members of the other party. During the 107th Congress (2001), House and Senate Republicans voted together 90 percent of the time. Democrats were only slightly less united at 85 percent, tying their previous unity record.[57] These numbers demonstrate the growing partisanship within the two chambers. Thus while rank-and-file voters do not display strong partisan ties, party organizations and the party in government do show significant signs of strength.[58]

Reform Among the Democrats

In Chicago in 1968, the Democratic National Convention saw disputes inside the hall and riots outside, largely because of protests against the country's policy in Vietnam. Responding to the disarray and to disputes about the fairness of delegate selection procedures, members of the party agreed to a number of reforms. They established a process that led to greater use of direct primaries for the selection of delegates to the national convention and greater representation of younger voters, women, and minorities as elected delegates. Another reform was the abolition of the rule that a winner of a state's convention or primaries got all the state's delegates (the *unit rule*). This rule was replaced by a system of *proportionality* in which candidates won delegates in rough proportion to the votes they received in the primary election or convention in each state.

Chicago's former mayor Richard J. Daley, father of the current mayor of Chicago, and many other party stalwarts argued that these reforms would make the party reflective of the views of minorities within the party, such as college professors and intellectuals who would have time and resources to invest in the political process, and not working-class people, unionists, the elderly, and elected officials who depend more on group leaders to make their case. The new process also meant that elected officials who wanted a voice in determining presidential candidates had to run for delegate to the national convention. Responding to this criticism, the party created "superdelegate" positions for elected officials and party leaders who were not required to run for election as delegates.

Reform Among the Republicans

Republicans have not been immune to criticism that their party conventions and party procedures were keeping out the rank-and-file. They did not make changes as drastic as those made by the Democrats, but they did give the national committee more control over presidential campaigns, and state parties were urged to encourage broader participation by all groups, including women, minorities, youth, and the poor.

The Republican party has long had a party organization superior to that of the Democrats. In the 1970s, the GOP emphasized grassroots organization and membership recruitment. Seminars were held to teach Republican candidates how to make speeches and hold press conferences, and weekend conferences were organized for training young party professionals. The Democrats have become better organized and more professional. Both parties now conduct training sessions for candidates on campaign planning, advertising, fund raising, using phone banks, recruiting volunteers, and campaign scheduling.[59] But Republicans have cultivated a larger donor base and have been less reliant on the large-donor soft money contributions that became so controversial in recent elections.

Campaign Finance Reform and Political Parties

Following the 1976 election, both parties pressed for amendments to the Federal Election Campaign Act, claiming that campaign finance reforms resulted in insufficient money for generic party activities like billboard advertising and get-out-the-vote drives. The 1979 amendments to the act and the interpretations of this legislation by the Federal Election Commission permitted unlimited contributions to the parties by individuals and PACs for these party building purposes. Corporations and unions could also give the parties soft money from their general funds, something they could not do in support of candidates or other party activities. Over time, both parties found ways to spend this soft money in unlimited amounts to promote the election or defeat of specific candidates, effectively circumventing the campaign finance reform rules.[60]

Competitive federal elections since the 1990s were not only contests between candidates but included substantial campaigns mounted by the political parties through soft money. Soft money was intended to be for generic party activity like get-out-the-vote drives or ads that urged a Democratic or Republican vote. But in the 1996 campaign, parties shifted to using soft money for candidate-specific messages—often attacking the opposing party's candidates. Soft money was controversial because of its sources—generally interest groups or wealthy individuals—and the fact that it was unlimited and often came in large amounts.

In the 1998, 2000, and 2002 elections, congressional campaign committees, following the lead of the national party committees in previous presidential elections, raised unprecedented amounts of soft money. Soft money was spent in the most competitive races where it could help determine which party controlled Congress or the most competitive states in the 1996 and 2000 contests for the White House. This is why banning soft money became

TABLE 7–5 Effects of the 2002 Campaign Finance Reforms

	Before 2002 Reform	After 2002 Reform
Party contributions to candidates	$5,000 per election or $10,000 per election cycle	Unchanged
Party-coordinated expenditures with candidates	*Senate:* State voting age population times 2 cents, multiplied by the cost-of-living adjustment (COLA), or $20,000 multiplied by the COLA, whichever is greater. *House:* $10,000 multiplied by the COLA; if only one representative in the state, same as the Senate limit.	Unchanged (but the Federal Election Commission is considering new rules on this). Parties may choose either independent expenditures or coordinated but not both
Party soft money contributions to the national party committee	Unlimited	Banned
Soft money to national or state and local parties for voter registration and get-out-the-vote drives	Unlimited	Limit of $10,000 per group to each state or local party committee (Levin Amendment)
Contributions to parties for buildings	Unlimited	Banned
Party-independent expenditures	Unlimited	Unlimited, except if ad falls under "electioneering communications definition." Then source of funding is subject to FECA regulations and limits, and the ad may not be broadcast within 30 days of a primary or 60 days of a general election. Parties may choose either independent expenditures or coordinated but not both.
Individual contributions to candidates per two-year election cycle	$2,000	$4,000
Aggregate individual contribution limit to candidate or parties per two-year election cycle	$50,000	$95,000

such a dedicated cause for Arizona Senator John McCain, a cosponsor of the McCain-Feingold campaign finance reform legislation. Despite repeated defeats in one or both houses of Congress over 15 years, Congress passed the Bipartisan Campaign Reform Act in 2002, much of it drawn from the McCain-Feingold bill. This campaign finance reform legislation, which takes effect in the 2003–2004 election cycle, bans soft money to the national and congressional party committees. Table 7-5 shows the effects on the parties.

What were the implications of this surge in soft money in presidential and congressional elections? First, because soft money contributions were unlimited, the priority given to raising soft money elevated the importance of large contributors. Parties came to rely heavily on these large donors. Among the largest soft money donors to the Democrats were the Affiliated Federal State County and Municipal Employees (AFSCME), the Service Employees International Union, and the Communications Workers of America. The largest Republican soft money donors were Phillip Morris and AT&T.

Central to the arguments for passage of the 2002 reforms was the perception that the ability of individuals and groups to give unlimited amounts of money to the parties gives these donors extraordinary access and influence over elected officials. As McCain said during floor debate on the 2002 reform, "Why can't we all agree to this very simple, very obvious truth that campaign contributions from a single source that run to the hundreds of thousands or millions of dollars are not healthy to a democracy?"[61] An unexpected event in 2002 helped highlight the role well-funded interest groups play and gave renewed momentum to supporters of campaign finance reform. The collapse of the Enron Corporation and the loss of retirement savings of many of its employees stood in stark contrast to the revelations of Enron's having made nearly $2.8 million in soft money contributions over a period of 5½ years.[62]

One uncertainty following the 2002 campaign finance reform is whether soft money donors will attempt to find another way to spend money on electing or defeating candidates. Some soft money donors may abandon large donations altogether, instead making the limited and disclosed PAC or individual contributions. A more likely scenario will be soft money donors contributing to issue advocacy organizations, either existing interest groups or new ones that may be created for this purpose. One possible new interest group would be linked to party leaders through former senior staff who would have access to former soft money donor lists and the expertise to spend such issue advocacy money on key races. As noted in Chapter 6, such issue advocacy groups may not use radio or television ads in the 60 days before a general election and 30 days before a primary unless the ads are paid for by PACs.

As discussed earlier, it is unclear whether soft money had a positive effect on the parties. In competitive contests, parties have become major players, mounting their own campaigns, often against the other party's candidate. Most party spending has been on ads placed on television and radio, sent through the mail, or delivered over the telephone. To a lesser extent, parties have worked to register voters and mobilize them on election day. This latter type of activity is the only one to have an enduring effect on state and local parties. The 2002 campaign finance legislation provides for limited contributions to state and local party committees; individuals and groups may donate up to $10,000 per party committee. This provision has the potential to encourage parties to continue to invest in mobilizing voters. Individuals or groups who want to make unlimited contributions to parties to influence federal races will now have to give their money to nonparty entities such as interest groups, which are less regulated than the parties (see Chapter 6).

While the particular role parties play in financing elections may be changing, the broader roles of organizing electoral competition, simplifying voter choices, and providing an enduring psychological identification for voters have not changed. Parties are also remarkably permeable organizations that provide citizens who want to influence the course of their government an accessible and often consequential way to get involved. Finally, parties continue to reinforce federalism through the distinctive nature of many state parties.

THE POLITICAL HORIZON

This PoliSim examines party ideologies and the changes that have occurred in America's political parties. People affiliate with a party in part because of their stands on particular issues. Based on your beliefs and opinions, find out with which political party you agree most.

Go to PoliSim "The Politcal Horizon."

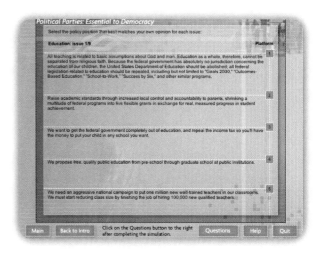

Summary

1. Political parties are essential to democracy—they simplify voting choices, organize the competition, unify the electorate, help organize government by bridging the separation of powers and fostering cooperation among branches of government, translate public preferences into policy, and provide loyal opposition.

2. Political parties help structure voting choice by nominating candidates to run for office. Before the advent of direct primaries, in which voters determine the party nominees, the parties had more control over who ran under their label. States determine the nomination rules. While most states employ the direct primary, some use a caucus or mixed caucus system where more committed partisans have a larger role in the decision of who gets nominated. Recently, some states adopted a blanket primary in which voters could vote for a candidate from any party. These primaries were declared unconstitutional.

3. American parties are moderate. Bringing factions and interests together, they are broad enough to win the presidency and other elections. Third parties have been notably less successful. One reason for this is our single-member-district, winner-take-all election rules. In systems with proportional representation or multimember districts, there is a greater tendency for more parties to form and consequently a need to assemble governing coalitions of several parties.

4. American parties have experienced critical elections and realignments. Most political scientists agree that the last realignment occurred in 1932. In recent years, there has been divided government and an increase in the number of persons who call themselves Independents. This trend is sometimes called dealignment, but most Independents are closet partisans who vote fairly consistently for the party toward which they lean.

5. For half a century, it has been routine to have divided government, with one party in control of the presidency and the other in control of one or both houses of Congress. Successful presidents have found ways to cope with divided government and enact important parts of their agenda. The 2002 election gave Republicans unified government with control of both houses of Congress and the White House.

6. Parties are governed by their national and state committees, and the focal points of party organization are the national and state party chairs. When the party controls the executive branch of government, the executive (governor or president) usually has a determining say in selecting the party chair. With the rise of soft money in recent elections, parties had more resources to spend on politics. In 2002, Congress banned soft money except for some narrowly defined and limited activities.

7. Party platforms are vague and general by design, giving the other party and voters little to oppose.

8. Parties are vital in the operation of government. They are organized around elected offices at the state and local levels. Congress is also organized around parties, and judicial and many executive branch appointments are based in large part on partisanship.

9. Parties are also active in the electorate, seeking to organize elections, simplify voting choices, and strengthen party identification.

10. Frequent efforts have been made to reform our parties. The Progressive movement saw parties, as then organized, as an impediment to democracy and pushed direct primaries as a means to reform them. Following the 1968 election, the Democratic party took the lead in pushing primaries and stressing greater diversity among the individuals elected as delegates. Republicans have also encouraged broader participation, and they have improved their party structure and finances. One likely consequence of the campaign finance reforms enacted in 2002 will be a renewed emphasis on building a large individual donor base.

11. Compared to some European parties, ours remain organizationally weak. There has been some party renewal in recent years as party competition has grown in the South and the parties themselves have initiated reforms.

Key Terms

political party	**honeymoon**	**closed primary**	**Keynesian economics**
party column ballot	**caucus**	**proportional representation**	**divided government**
office block ballot	**party convention**	**winner-take-all system**	**national party convention**
nonpartisan election	**direct primary**	**minor party**	**party registration**
patronage	**open primary**	**realigning election**	**party identification**
soft money	**crossover voting**	**laissez-faire economics**	**dealignment**

Further Reading

JOHN H. ALDRICH, *Why Parties? The Origin and Transformation of Party Politics in America* (University of Chicago Press, 1995).

PAUL ALLEN BECK AND MARJORIE RANDON HERSHEY, *Party Politics in America*, 9th ed. (Longman, 2001).

JOHN F. BIBBY, *Politics, Parties, and Elections in America*, 4th ed. (Thomson Learning, 1999).

DAVID BOAZ, *Libertarianism: A Primer* (Free Press, 1998).

MARY C. BRENNAN, *Turning Right in the Sixties: The Conservative Capture of the GOP* (University of North Carolina Press, 1995).

BRUCE E. CAIN AND ELISABETH R. GERBER, EDS., *Voting at the Political Fault Line: California's Experiment with the Blanket Primary* (University of California Press, 2002).

LEON EPSTEIN, *Political Parties in the American Mold* (University of Wisconsin Press, 1986).

JOHN C. GREEN AND DANIEL M. SHEA, EDS., *The State of the Parties: The Changing Role of Contemporary American Parties,* 3d ed. (Rowman & Littlefield, 1999).

PAUL S. HERRNSON, *Party Campaigning in the 1980s: Have the National Parties Made a Comeback as Key Players in Congressional Elections?* (Harvard University Press, 1988).

PAUL S. HERRNSON AND JOHN C. GREEN, EDS., *Multiparty Politics in America: Prospects and Performance,* 2d ed. (Rowman & Littlefield, 2002).

WILLIAM J. KEEFE, *Parties, Politics, and Public Policy in America,* 8th ed. (Congressional Quarterly Press, 1998).

BRUCE E. KEITH, DAVID B. MAGLEBY, CANDICE J. NELSON, ELIZABETH ORR, MARK C. WESTLYE, AND RAYMOND E. WOLFINGER, *The Myth of the Independent Voter* (University of California Press, 1992).

THEODORE J. LOWI AND JOSEPH ROMANCE, *A Republic of Parties? Debating the Two-Party System* (Rowman & Littlefield, 1998).

G. CALVIN MACKENZIE, *The Irony of Reform: Roots of American Political Disenchantment* (Westview Press, 1996).

DAVID B. MAGLEBY, ED., *Financing the 2000 Election* (Brookings Institution, 2002).

L. SANDY MAISEL, *The Electoral Process,* 3d ed. (Rowman & Littlefield, 2002).

WILLIAM G. MAYER, *The Divided Democrats: Ideological Unity, Party Reform, and Presidential Elections* (Westview Press, 1996).

SIDNEY M. MILKIS, *The President and the Parties: The Transformation of the American Party System Since the New Deal* (Oxford University Press, 1993).

WARREN E. MILLER AND J. MERRILL SHANKS, *The New American Voter* (Harvard University Press, 1996).

KELLY D. PATTERSON, *Political Parties and the Maintenance of Liberal Democracy* (Columbia University Press, 1996).

STEVEN J. ROSENSTONE, ROY L. BEHR, AND EDWARD H. LAZARUS, *Third Parties in America: Citizen Response to Major Party Failure,* 2d ed. (Princeton University Press, 1996).

JOSEPH A. SCHLESINGER, *Political Parties and the Winning of Office* (University of Michigan Press, 1998).

JAMES SUNDQUIST, *Dynamics of the Party System: Alignment and Realignment of Political Parties in the United States,* rev. ed. (Brookings Institution, 1983).

MARTIN P. WATTENBERG, *The Decline of American Political Parties, 1952–1992* (Harvard University Press, 1994).

JOHN K. WHITE AND DANIEL M. SHEA, *New Party Politics: From Jefferson and Hamilton to the Information Age* (Bedford/St. Martin's, 2000).

PUBLIC OPINION, PARTICIPATION, AND VOTING

UNDECIDED OR "SWING VOTERS" GOT A LOT OF ATTENTION IN 2002 IN STATES OR DISTRICTS WITH COMPETITIVE CONTESTS FOR governor, the U.S. Senate, or the U.S. House, just as they did in battleground states in 2000. Because so much was at stake in the 2002 elections—Democrats holding a one-vote majority in the U.S. Senate and Republicans holding a narrow majority in the House of Representatives, and five open-seat gubernatorial races—the candidates, parties, and interest groups made voter registration and turnout high priorities. Voters who had already made up their minds and indicated they were likely to vote were bombarded with postcards reminding them to vote and phone calls reminding them it was election day and that their vote was needed. For example, in 2000 the National Abortion and Reproductive Rights Action League (NARAL) made phone calls to pro-choice women under 40 years of age with a recorded message from Sarah Jessica Parker of HBO's *Sex and the City*, reminding them of the importance of electing pro-choice candidates.[1]

Candidate preferences and issue positions of potential voters are discovered by a telephone or personal interview, a process called a *canvas*. If these persons are undecided and probable voters, they receive lots of mail and many telephone calls aimed at persuading them to support one candidate over another. Mailings emphasize the stand of the candidate on such issues as Social Security, education, and prescription drug benefits. Interest groups and political parties send out similar persuasion pieces to undecided voters, often reinforcing the same themes as the candidates use. In 2002, both major political parties and their allied interest groups sought to activate friendly voters through personal contact, mail, and telephone. House Republicans added a new program called STOMP (Strategic Taskforce to Organize and Mobilize People), which placed volunteers and paid staff in battleground districts for the final 72 hours of the campaign. Volunteers made personal contact with selected voters and worked to get them to the polls. President Bush's blitz through fifteen states in the closing days of the campaign energized these efforts.

In addition to polls conducted by Gallup, Pew, and other such organizations, newspapers and TV networks conduct polls on election preferences and numerous other subjects.

Some voters received conflicting messages. For instance, in the newly-created seventh Congressional district in Colorado, voters in the last week of the campaign reported on an average day seeing between twelve and thirteen television ads, hearing six radio ads, receiving two telephone calls, receiving four pieces of political mail, and having one person talk to them face-to-face about the congressional race. All of this political communication was about the House race, not all contests combined.

We learned from the 2000 and 2002 elections that a few hundred votes can determine an election outcome. Candidates cannot take any votes for granted, so in close contests, voter mobilization is critical. In this chapter, we look at the nature of public opinion, how to measure it, the factors that affect the formation of opinions, the nature and level of political participation in the United States, and why people vote as they do.

Public Opinion

All governments in all nations must be concerned with public opinion. In nondemocratic nations, unrest and protest can topple those in power. And in a constitutional democracy, citizens can express opinions in a variety of ways, including demonstrations, letters to newspaper editors, and voting in free and regularly scheduled elections. There are clear and direct connections between what voters want and what our governments do. In short, democracy and public opinion go hand in hand.

What Is Public Opinion?

Everybody talks about "public opinion." Everybody claims to speak for "the public." But social scientists use the term more precisely: We define **public opinion** as the distribution of individual preferences for, or evaluations of, a given issue, candidate, or institution

How You Ask It Shapes How You Answer It

How you ask a polling question makes a lot of difference in the responses people give, as demonstrated by the way three different polls asked about special interests and campaign finance. The first question was written by Ross Perot's organization, not by a survey researcher. It was published in *TV Guide* and asked individuals to send in their answers. Perot's survey was criticized widely by survey organizations for its skewed sample and biased questions. The second and third questions were part of national surveys conducted by professional polling firms using random samples.

1. Should laws be passed to eliminate all possibilities of special interests giving huge sums of money to candidates?

   Yes   99%

2. Should laws be passed to prohibit interest groups from contributing to campaigns? Or do groups have a right to contribute to the candidate they support?

   Prohibit contribution   40%

   Groups have right   55%

3. Please tell me whether you favor or oppose this proposal: New laws should eliminate all possibility of special interests giving large sums of money to candidates.

   Favor   70%

   Oppose   28%

SOURCE: Daniel Goleman, "Pollsters Enlist Psychologists in Quest for Unbiased Results," *New York Times,* September 7, 1993, pp. C1, C11.

public opinion
The distribution of individual preferences for or evaluations of a given issue, candidate, or institution within a specific population.

within a specific population. *Distribution* means the proportion of the population that holds a particular opinion, compared to people with opposing opinions or those with no opinion at all. For instance, final preelection polls in 2004 by the Gallup Organization found that among potential voters, 49 percent reported they would vote for George W. Bush, 49 percent for John Kerry, and 1 percent for Ralph Nader.[2] The actual vote was Bush 51 percent, Kerry 48 percent, and Nader 1 percent.[3]

TAKING THE PULSE OF THE PEOPLE   Proper *sampling* is based on randomly selecting people to survey. In a *random sample,* every individual has an equal chance of being selected. The sample of randomly selected respondents should be appropriate for the questions being asked. For instance, a survey of 18- to 24-year-olds should not be done solely among college students, since roughly three-quarters of the members of this age group do not attend college. Even with proper sampling, surveys have a *margin of error,* meaning that the sample accurately reflects the population within a certain margin—usually plus or minus 3 percent for a sample of at least 1,500 individuals. The final preelection survey results in 2004 were indeed within this margin of error for the actual vote.

The *art of asking questions* is also important to scientific polling. The wording of questions can influence the answers. Question order can also alter the responses. Good questions have to be pretested to be sure that the way a question is asked does not bias how it is answered. Questions should be delivered by trained and professional interviewers, who read them exactly as written and without any intonation in their voices. Questions can be worded in different ways to measure factual knowledge, opinions, the intensity of opinion, or views on hypothetical situations. Sometimes *open-ended questions* are asked to permit respondents to answer in their own words rather than in set categories. Open-ended questions are harder to record and compare but allow respondents to express their views more clearly and may provide insight into their thinking.

In addition to random sampling and clearly worded questions, thorough *analysis and reporting of the results* are required of scientific polls. Scientific polls inform the public of the sample size, the margin of error, and when and where the poll was conducted. It is also important to realize that public opinion can change from day to day and hour to hour. Polls are really snapshots of opinion at a point in time rather than moving pictures of opinions over time.

Individual preference emphasizes that when we measure public opinion, we are asking *individuals*—not groups, elected officials, or journalists—about their opinions. The *universe* or *population* is the relevant group of people for the question. When a substantial percentage of a sample agrees on an issue—for example, that we should honor the American flag—there is a *consensus.* But on most issues, opinions are divided. When a large portion of opposing sides feels intensely about an issue, voters are said to be *polarized.* The Vietnam War in the 1960s and abortion in the present decade are polarizing issues (see Table 8-1).

INTENSITY   The factor called *intensity* produces the brightest and deepest hues in the fabric of public opinion. The fervor of people's beliefs varies greatly. For example, some individuals mildly favor gun control legislation and others mildly oppose it, some people are emphatically for or against it, and some have no interest in the matter at all; still others may not have even heard of it. People who lost their jobs or retirement savings because of corporate scandals likely feel more intensely about enhanced regulation of corporations and accounting firms than people who have not been directly affected by the scandals. Intensity is typically measured by asking people how strongly they feel about an issue or about a politician. Such a question is often called a *scale.*

LATENCY   *Latency* refers to political opinions that exist merely as a potential; they may not have crystallized, yet they are still important, for they can be aroused by leaders and converted into political action. Latent opinions set rough boundaries for leaders who know that if they take certain actions, they will trigger either opposition or support from millions of people. If leaders have some understanding of latent opinions—people's unexpressed wants, needs,

TABLE 8–1 Differing Opinions on Abortion: Percentage of Individuals Who Say That Abortion Should Be Legal in Few or No Cases

Total	55%
Age	
18–29	55
30–49	54
50–64	54
65+	62
Sex	
Men	57
Women	54
Education	
High school or less	62
Some college	57
College graduate	47
Postgraduate	40
Race	
White	55
Black	62
Hispanic	63
Religion	
Very important	68
Fairly important	48
Not important	26
Political philosophy	
Liberal	33
Moderate	50
Conservative	70
Party identification	
Republican	68
Democrat	49
Independent	52
Income	
Less than $20,000	65
$20,000–$29,900	60
$30,000–$49,900	53
$50,000–$74,900	57
More than $75,000	46

SOURCE: Gallup Organization, *Public Opinion About Abortion: An In-Depth Review,* May 2001, at www.gallup.com.

THE WALL STREET JOURNAL

"It should be 'yes' or 'no' or 'undecided' – we don't accept a 'don't give a damn answer!'"

Cartoon Features Syndicate.

and hopes—they will know how to mobilize people and draw them to the polls on election day. Many who lived in communist Poland, East Germany, Czechoslovakia, or Yugoslavia must have had latent opinions favorable to democracy—opinions supporting majority rule, freedom, and meaningful elections. The speed with which these countries embraced democratic reforms was possible when leaders encouraged widespread expression of such ideas. A more recent example of a latent opinion is the desire for security from foreign enemies, which had not been a concern before the terrorist attacks of September 11, 2001. Wanting homeland security became a manifest opinion thereafter.

SALIENCE   By *salience* we mean the extent to which people believe issues are relevant to them. Most people are more concerned about personal issues like paying their bills and keeping their jobs than about national issues, but if national issues somehow threaten their security or safety, salience of national issues rises sharply.

The salience of issues may change over time. During the Great Depression of the 1930s, Americans were concerned mainly about jobs, wages, and economic security. By the 1940s, foreign affairs came to the forefront. In the 1960s, problems of race and poverty aroused intense feelings. In the 1970s, Vietnam and then Watergate riveted people's attention. By the early 2000s, concern about Social Security, health care, education, terrorism, and national security had become salient issues. The war on terrorism mounted by the United States after September 11, 2001, made more salient to Americans how Israel dealt with suicide bombings. Support for Israel's actions to deal with terrorists rose, with 59 percent saying Israeli action against Palestinians is no different than U.S. action against al-Qaeda.[4]

How Do We Get Our Political Opinions and Values?

No one is born with political views. We learn them from many mentors and teachers. The process by which we develop our political attitudes, values, and beliefs is called **political socialization**. This process starts in childhood, and the family and the schools are probably the two most important political teachers. Children learn the content of our culture in childhood and adolescence but reshape it as they mature.[5] Socialization lays the foundation for political beliefs, values, ideology, and partisanship.

A common element of political socialization in all cultures is *nationalism,* a consciousness of the nation-state and of belonging to that entity. Robert Coles describes it this way:

> As soon as we are born, in most places on this earth, we acquire a nationality, a membership in a community. . . . A royal doll, a flag to wave in a parade, coins with their engraved messages—these are sources of instruction and connect a young person to a country. The attachment can be strong, indeed, even among children yet to attend school, wherever the flag is saluted, the national anthem sung. The attachment is as parental as the words imply—homeland, motherland, fatherland. . . . Nationalism works its way into just about every corner of the mind's life.[6]

The sources of our views are immensely varied in the pluralistic political culture of the United States. Political attitudes may stem from religious, racial, gender, ethnic, or economic beliefs and values. But we can make at least one generalization safely: We form our attitudes in *groups,* and not only in groups such as schools, social organizations, and some more political ones like the National Rifle Association or Planned Parenthood but especially in close-knit groups like the family. When we identify closely with the attitudes and interests of a particular group, we tend to see politics through the "eyes" of that group.[7]

Group affiliation does not necessarily mean that individual members do not think for themselves. Each member brings his or her own emotions, feelings, memories, and resistance to groups. The extent to which people are captive to groups is indeed a running argument among scholars from different disciplines. Sociologists tend to emphasize the pervasive influence of groups over their members. Psychologists focus more on the developmental stages within individuals that prompt them to be joiners or loners. Political scientists have traditionally tended to agree more with the sociological approach.[8] Political psychologists seek to combine both approaches.

political socialization

The process most notably in families and schools by which we develop our political attitudes, values, and beliefs.

Children in the United States tend at an early age to adopt common values that provide continuity with the past and legitimate the American political system. Young children know what country they live in, and their loyalty to the nation develops early. Although the details of our political system may still elude them, most young Americans acquire a respect for the Constitution and for the concept of participatory democracy, as well as an initially positive view of the most visible figure in our democracy, the president.[9]

FAMILY   Most social psychologists agree that family is the most powerful socializing agent.[10] American children typically show political interest by the age of ten, and by the early teens their interest may be fairly high. Consider your own political learning process. You probably formed your picture of the world by listening to a parent at dinner or by absorbing the tales your older brothers and sisters brought home from school. Perhaps you heard about politics from grandparents, aunts, and uncles. You, in turn, influenced your family, if only by bringing some of your own hopes and concerns home from school. What we first learn in the family is not so much specific political opinions as basic *attitudes* that shape our opinions—attitudes toward our neighbors, political parties, other classes or types of people, particular leaders (especially presidents), and society in general.

Studies of high school students indicate a high correlation between the political party of the parents and the partisan choice of their children. This relatively high degree of correspondence continues throughout life. Such a finding raises some interesting questions: Does the direct influence of parents create the correspondence? Or does living in the same social environment—neighborhood, church, socioeconomic group—influence parents and children? The answer is *both,* and one influence often strengthens the other. For example, a daughter of Democratic parents growing up in a small southern town with strong Democratic leanings will be affected by friends, by other adults, and perhaps by youngsters in a church group, all of whom may reinforce the attitudes of her parents.[11] What happens when a young person's parents and friends disagree? Young people tend to go along with parents rather than friends on party affiliation, with friends rather than parents on issues like the death penalty or gun control, and somewhere in between in their actual votes in presidential elections.[12]

SCHOOLS   Schools also mold young citizens' political attitudes. American schools see part of their purpose as preparing students to be citizens and active participants in governing their communities and nation. At an early age, schoolchildren begin to pick up specific political values and acquire basic attitudes toward our system of government. Education, like the family, prepares Americans to live in society.

From kindergarten through college, students generally develop political values consistent with the democratic process and supportive of the American political system. In their study of American history, they are introduced to our nation's heroes and heroines, the important events in our history, and the ideals of our society. Other aspects of their experience, such as the daily Pledge of Allegiance and occasional programs or assemblies, seek to reinforce respect of country. Children also gain practical experience in the workings of democracy through elections for class or school officers and student government. In some high schools and colleges, the state legislature or college trustees require students to take courses in U.S. history or American government to graduate.

Do school courses and activities give young people the skills needed to participate in elections and democratic institutions? A study of 18- to 24-year-olds commissioned by the National Association of Secretaries of State found that young people "lack any real understanding of citizenship . . . , information and understanding about the democratic process . . . , and information about candidates and political parties."[13] "Furthermore, the Secretaries of State report noted that most young people do not seek out political information and that they are not very likely to do so in the future."[14] You and your classmates are not a representative sample in part because you are taking this course and therefore have more interest and knowledge than most people.

American children learn early the importance of participatory democracy.

The Chicago Herald Tribune was so sure of its polling data in the 1948 election, they predicted a win for Republican Thomas Dewey before the results were final. A victorious Harry Truman displays the mistaken headline.

The debate about whether there is peer pressure on college campuses to conform to certain acceptable ideas or to use particular language highlights the role higher education can play in shaping attitudes and values. How does college influence political opinions? One study suggests that college students are more likely than people of the same age who are not attending college to be knowledgeable about politics, more in favor of free speech, and more likely to talk and read about politics.[15] Is this the influence of the professors, the curriculum, the students, or the party leadership in the White House? It is difficult to generalize. Parents sometimes fear that professors have too much influence on their college-age children; however, most professors doubt that they have a significant influence on the political views of their students.

MASS MEDIA   Like everybody else, young people are exposed to a wide range of media—school newspapers, national newspapers, the Internet, movies, radio, television—all of which influence what they think. They, like adults, pick and choose the media with which they agree, so their exposure is *selective.* The mass media also serve as agents of socialization by providing a link between individuals and the values and behavior of others. The popular media help shape the attitudes and opinions of the people who watch, listen to, or read them. News broadcasts present information about our society; events that get intensive media coverage often focus our attention on certain issues. For example, the hours of TV coverage of the presidential vote count in Florida in 2000 directed widespread attention to voting systems and the electoral college. Similarly, many Americans turned their attention to Islamic fundamentalism and the recent history of Afghanistan in the aftermath of the terrorist attacks of September 11, 2001.

OTHER INFLUENCES   Religious, ethnic, and racial attitudes also shape opinions, both within and outside the family. Generalizations about how people vote are useful, but we have to be careful about stereotyping people. For example, many Catholics agree with their church's position against abortion, but some do not. It is dangerous to assume that because we know a person's religious affiliation or ethnic background, we know his or her political opinions.

Stability and Change in Public Opinion

Adults are not simply the sum of all their early experiences, but few change their opinions very often. Even if the world around us changes rapidly, we are slow to shift our loyalties or to change our minds about things that matter to us. In general, people who remain in the same place, in the same occupation, and in the same income group throughout their lives tend to have stable opinions. People often carry their attitudes with them, and families who move from cities to suburbs often retain their big-city attitudes long after they have moved. Political analysts are becoming more interested in the ways in which adults modify their views. A major factor may be a harsh experience—a war, economic depression, or loss of a job—that shocks people out of their existing attitudes.

The terrorist attacks on the World Trade Center in New York and the Pentagon in Washington, D.C. had at least a short-term impact on public trust and confidence in government. Political Scientist Robert D. Putnam has for several years been studying how the public views political institutions and community interaction. Putnam had done a national survey in the summer of 2000. Following the terrorist attacks, he reinterviewed the same respondents to see how their views had changed. Table 8-2 shows the changes in selected dimensions. Putnam found that more than half of his sample expressed greater confidence in government after the attacks. Interest in public affairs grew by 27 percent among younger people (age 35 and under) and 8 percent among older respondents. Putnam concludes, "Americans don't only trust political institutions more: We also trust one another more, from neighbors and co-workers to shop clerks and perfect strangers. More Americans now express confidence that people in their community would cooperate, for example, with voluntary conservation measures in an energy or water shortage." The events of September 11 also appear to have led people to be "somewhat more generous."[16] How enduring these changes are is not yet clear and may be more consequential in peoples' private lives than in their public activities like voting, volunteering, or becoming more involved in politics.

Some of our political opinions change very little because they are part of our core values. Thus our views on abortion, the death penalty, and doctor-assisted suicide remain relatively stable over time. On issues that are less central to our values, such as our view of how a president is performing his job, opinions can show substantial change over time. On many issues, public opinion can change once the public learns more about the issue or perceives that there is another side to the question. It is on these issues that politicians can help shape attitudes. The decisions by Dwight Eisenhower, John Kennedy, and Lyndon Johnson to enforce school desegregation are examples of leadership of public opinion, as were the positions of Jimmy Carter on the Panama Canal Treaty and George Bush and Bill Clinton on the North American Free Trade Agreement (NAFTA).

Public Opinion and Public Policy

For much of human history, it has been difficult to measure public opinion. "What I want," Abraham Lincoln once said, "is to get done what the people desire to be done, and the question for me is how to find that out exactly."[17] Politicians in our day do not face

TABLE 8–2 Change in Selected Civic Attitudes and Behavior, 2000–2001

	Increased	Decreased	Net Change
Trust national government	51%	7%	44%
Trust local government	32	13	19
Watch TV	40	24	16
Express interest in politics	29	15	14
Trust local police	26	12	14
Trust people of other races	31	20	11
Trust shop clerks	28	17	11
Support keeping unpopular books in the library	28	18	10
Trust neighbors	23	13	10
Contributed to religious charity	29	20	9
Expect crisis support from friends	22	14	8
Trust the "people running my community"	32	24	8
Worked with neighbors	15	8	7
Trust local news media	30	23	7
Gave blood	11	4	7
Volunteered	36	29	7
Expect local cooperation in crisis	23	17	6
Worked on a community project	17	11	6
Attended a political meeting	11	6	5
Read a newspaper	27	24	3
Visited relatives	43	40	3
Attended a club meeting	29	26	3
Attended a public meeting	27	26	1
Contributed to a secular charity	28	27	1
Attend church	20	19	1
Belong to organizations	39	39	0
Had friends visit your home	39	45	–6

SOURCE: Robert D. Putnam, "Bowling Together," *American Prospect* 13 (February 11, 2002), p. 22.

such uncertainty about public opinion; far from it. Polling informs them of public opinion on all major policy issues. In addition to polls politicians commission themselves, they can turn to public or media polls. More than 80 percent of newspapers and half of all television stations conduct or commission their own polls.[18]

Here are some examples of how public opinion can shape policy and in turn how policies shape opinion. During the Vietnam War, antiwar demonstrations on college campuses spread to cities all over the country. "Public opinion had a substantial impact on the rate of troop withdrawals."[19] In the Persian Gulf War, opposition to the use of U.S. forces was greatly reduced after a few days of success in the air and ground war. When American forces were dispatched to Somalia in Operation Restore Hope in January 1993, fully 79 percent of the public approved of the use of troops to ensure the delivery of humanitarian aid, food, and medical provisions. But when U.S. soldiers were killed and dragged through the streets of Mogadishu, support fell to only 17 percent in October of the same year.[20] The terrorist attacks of September 11, 2001, had at least a short-term impact on public opinion and behavior. A CNN/*USA Today*/Gallup poll in June 2002 found that 64 percent of Americans "check more often on the whereabouts of their loved ones," 23 percent "report they avoid public events or crowded areas," and 42 percent "say they are 'personally more afraid to fly.'"[21]

Typically, elected officials seek to follow public opinion. Winning reelection is a strong motive for members of Congress.[22] "Legislators show greater attention to public opinion as election day looms," and the closeness of the fit between constituent opinion and roll call voting reflects that connection.[23] Candidates use polls to determine where to campaign, how to campaign, and even whether to campaign. Early on, political candidates and political activists were monitoring polling figures for presidential hopefuls thinking about a challenge to President Bush in 2004.[24]

Surely polls are no substitute for elections. With a ballot before them, voters must translate their opinions into concrete decisions. They must decide what is important and what is not. Democracy is more than the expression of views, more than a simple mirror of opinion. It also involves choosing among leaders, taking sides on certain issues, and selecting the governmental actions that may follow. Democracy is the thoughtful participation of people in the political process. Elections, despite their failings, still establish the link between the many opinions "We the People" hold and the selection of our leaders.

Renewed Patriotism

The terrorist attacks of September 11, 2001, changed many Americans' perspectives on life and patriotism. Before these attacks, displays of patriotism were more reserved and isolated. Afterward, however, flags began to sell at extraordinary rates, hearing patriotic songs became more common, and a renewed respect for U.S. war veterans was more apparent. Many Americans had, in a sense, revived their love for the country. Their patriotism had been a kind of latent opinion, activated in response to a diabolical attack on the nation.

Because of this renewed patriotism, July 4, 2002, was different from previous Independence Days. There were frequent references to the heroism of firefighters, and more people participated in parties, barbecues, sightseeing, and other activities than had done so in previous years. Houston Police Department spokesman Robert Hurst said, "After the events of September 11, many citizens across the country are being more aware of their patriotism."

Citizens have also become more aware of other things, such as family, friends, and the importance of life. Almost everyone can describe the personal effects of September 11; it was a life-changing experience for many people, not just those directly affected by the attacks. The events of September 11 changed the perspectives of Americans. Will the resurgence in patriotism translate into political actions like voting in elections, running for office, or contributing time or money to a candidate or party? Only time will tell.

SOURCE: Pam Belluck, "With Patriotism Renewed, July 4 Hits a Deeper Chord," *New York Times,* July 4, 2002, p. A1.

Awareness and Interest

For most people, politics is of secondary importance to earning a living, raising a family, and having a good time; some Americans are more concerned about which team wins the World Series or the Super Bowl than they are about who wins the school board elections, who gets to be mayor, or even who gets to be president of the United States. Most people find politics complicated and difficult to understand. And they should, for democracy *is* complicated and difficult to understand. But it helps to understand the mechanics and structures of our government such as how the government operates, how the electoral college works, how Congress is set up, and the length of terms for the president and for members of the Senate and House of Representatives.

Details about how the government works are typically best known by younger adults, who remember learning them in school. The general adult public, however, fares poorly when quizzed about their elected officials. Just over 15 percent of Americans are able to recall the name of the congressional candidates from their district.[25] With so many voters not knowing who represents them in Congress, it is not surprising that "on even hotly debated congressional issues, few people know where their Congress member stands."[26]

Although the public's knowledge of institutional and candidate issues is poor, its knowledge of important public policy issues is worse. In 1982, after approximately 59 years of debate over ratification of the Equal Rights Amendment, nearly one-third of the adults in the United States indicated they had never heard of it. The same is true for many issues.[27] Fortunately, not all Americans are uninformed or uninterested. About 25 percent of the public is interested in politics most of the time. This is the **attentive public**, people who know and understand how the government works. They vote in most elections, read a daily newspaper, and "talk politics" with their families and friends. They tend to be better educated and more committed to democratic values than other Americans.

At the opposite end of the spectrum are *nonvoters,* people who are rarely interested in politics or public affairs and who rarely vote. About 57 percent of Americans have indicated that they are only somewhat interested, not very interested, or not at all interested in politics.[28] A subset of this group might be called *political know-nothings.* These individuals not only avoid political activity but also have little interest in government and limited knowledge about it.

These college students feel responsible to vote and line up on campus to fill out absentee ballots.

attentive public
Those citizens who follow public affairs carefully.

What If They Held an Election and No One Voted?

Such an election actually happened in Centreville, Mississippi, in 1993. Candidate Danny Jones appeared to be a sure winner for a seat on the board of aldermen (city council), in part because he was the only candidate. But no one actually voted, including Jones, who had to work late on election day. State law requires winners to get at least one vote, so a special election had to be held, in which Jones received 45 votes.

SOURCE: *Parade,* January 2, 1994, p. 4.

Between the attentive public and the political know-nothings are the *part-time citizens,* roughly 40 percent of the American public. These individuals participate selectively in elections, voting in presidential elections but usually not in others. Politics and government do not greatly interest them; they pay only minimal attention to the news, and they rarely discuss candidates or elections with others.

Democracy can survive even when a large number of citizens are passive and uninformed, as long as a substantial number of people serve as opinion leaders and are interested and informed about public affairs. Obviously, these activists will have much greater influence than their less active fellow citizens.

Participation: Translating Opinions into Action

Americans influence their government's actions in several ways, many of which are protected by the Constitution. They vote in elections, join interest groups, go to political party meetings, ring doorbells, call friends urging them to vote for issues or candidates, sign petitions, write letters to the editors of newspapers, and make calls to radio talk shows.

Protest is also a form of political participation. Our political system is remarkably tolerant of protest that is not destructive or violent. Boycotts, picketing, sit-ins, and marches are all legally protected. Rosa Parks and Martin Luther King Jr. used nonviolent protest to call attention to what they saw as unfair laws (see Chapter 18). The number of Americans who participate in protests is small, but the impact of their actions in shaping public opinion can be substantial.

A distinguishing characteristic of a democracy is that citizens can influence government decisions by participating in politics. When the citizens of Belgrade turned out night after night to protest the nullification of their election, they forced Slobodan Milosevic to permit the victorious candidate, Vojislav Kostunica, to take power. But protests and demonstrations are not always peaceful or successful. In totalitarian societies, participation is very limited, forcing people who want to influence government to resort to violence or revolution. The protest of Chinese students in Tiananmen Square in 1989 failed to stop the onslaught of tanks and the repression that followed. Americans sometimes forget that our democracy was born of revolution but that maintaining a constitutional democracy after the revolution is difficult and demands public participation.

Even in an established democracy, people may feel so strongly about an issue that they would rather fight than accept the verdict of an election. The classic example is the Amer-

When the student pro-democracy protest was stopped by Chinese government tanks in Tiananman Square on June 5, 1989, one man stood up in defiance until he was pulled to safety by bystanders.

ican Civil War. Following the election of 1860, in which Lincoln, an antislavery candidate who did not receive a single electoral vote from a slave state, won the presidency, the South took up arms. The ensuing war marked the breakdown of democracy. Examples in our own time include antiabortion groups that use violence to press their political agenda and militia groups that arm themselves for battle against government regulations.

Participation can also include less intense activity and even engaging in patriotic rituals. For example, large numbers of Americans routinely sing the national anthem or recite the Pledge of Allegiance. They communicate their views about government and politics to their representatives in Washington and the state capitol. They serve as jurors in courtrooms and enlist in the military. They express concern about the involvement of American military forces in foreign hostilities. They complain about taxes and government regulations. And many families feel it important that their children visit Washington, D.C., and other historic sights.

For most people, politics is a private activity. Some books on manners still consider it impolite to discuss politics at dinner parties. To say that politics is private does not mean people do not have opinions or will not discuss them when asked by others, including pollsters. But often politics is avoided in discussions with neighbors, work associates, even friends and family, as too divisive or upsetting. Typically, less than one person in four attempts to influence how another person votes in an election. An even smaller number actually work for a candidate or party. Only one in 20 people make a contribution to a candidate, and only one in six designates $3 of their taxes to the fund that pays for presidential general elections (see Table 8-3).[29]

Few individuals attempt to influence others by writing letters to elected officials or to editors of newspapers for publication. Even smaller numbers participate in protest groups or activities. Despite the small number of persons who engage in these activities, it would be a mistake to assume that small numbers of individuals cannot make a difference to politics and government. An individual or small group can generate media interest in an issue and expand the impact. Peaceful protests for civil rights, about environmental issues, and both for and against abortion have generated public attention and even changed opinions.

Voting

Americans' most typical political activity is voting. The United States is a constitutional democracy with more than 200 years of free and frequent elections and a tradition of the peaceful transfer of power between competing groups and parties.

Originally, the Constitution left it to the individual states to determine the crucial question of who could vote, and the qualifications for voting differed considerably from state to state. All states except New Jersey barred women from voting, many did not permit African Americans to vote, and until the 1830s, property ownership was often a requirement. By the time of the Civil War, the franchise had been extended to all white male citizens in every state. Since that time, eligibility standards for voting have been expanded seven times by legislation and constitutional amendments (see Table 8-4).

TABLE 8–3 Political Participation and Awareness in the United States

Watched Campaign on TV	62%
Vote in presidential elections	55
Vote in congressional elections	42
Try to persuade vote of others	29
Display campaign button, sticker, or sign	9
Gave money to help a campaign	11
Attend dinner, meeting, or rally for candidate	5

SOURCE: U.S. Bureau of the Census, *Statistical Abstract of the United States, 2003* (U.S. Government Printing Office, 2003), p. 269; The 2002 National Election Study, Center for Political Studies, University of Michigan. The NES Guide to Public Opinion and Electoral Behavior, at www.umich.edu/~nes/nesguide/gd-index.htm#6; See also www.census.gov.

TABLE 8–4 Changes in Voting Eligibility Standards Since 1870

Year	Change
1870	Fifteenth Amendment forbade states from denying the right to vote because of "race, color, or previous condition of servitude."
1920	Nineteenth Amendment gave women the right to vote.
1924	Congress granted Native Americans citizenship and voting rights.
1961	Twenty-Third Amendment permitted District of Columbia residents to vote in federal elections.
1964	Twenty-Fourth Amendment prohibited the use of poll taxes in federal elections.
1965	Voting Rights Act removed restrictions that kept African Americans from voting.
1971	Twenty-Sixth Amendment extended the vote to citizens age 18 and older.

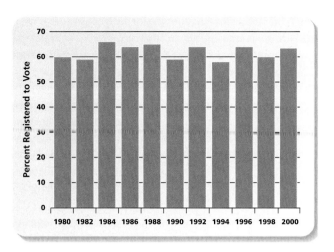

FIGURE 8–1 **Percentage of African Americans Registered to Vote, 1980–2000.**

SOURCE: U.S. Bureau of the Census, *Statistical Abstract of the United States,* 2001 (U.S. Government Printing Office, 2001), p. 251.

The civil rights movement in the 1960s, which made voting rights a central issue, secured adoption of the Twenty-Fourth Amendment and passage of the 1965 Voting Rights Act. The Voting Rights Act banned literacy tests, eased registration requirements, and provided for the replacement of local election officials with federal registrars in areas where the denial of the right to vote had been most blatant. Its passage resulted in a dramatic expansion of black registration and voting. Once African Americans were permitted to register to vote, "the focus of voting discrimination shifted . . . to preventing them from winning elections."[30] In southern legislative districts where blacks are in the majority, however, there has been a "dramatic increase in the proportion of African American legislators elected" (see Figure 8-1).[31]

Registration

One peculiarly American legal requirement—**voter registration**—arose in response to concerns about voting abuses, but it also discourages voting. Most other democracies have automatic voter registration. Average turnout in the United States is more than 30 percentage points lower than in countries like Australia, Austria, Belgium, Denmark, Germany, and Italy.[32] This was not always the case. In fact, in the 1800s, turnout in the United States was much like that of Europe today. Turnout began to drop significantly around the turn of the twentieth century, in part as a result of election reform (see Figure 8-2).

American elections in the 1800s were different from those of today. Ballots were prepared by the parties, often using different colors of paper that allowed party officials to monitor how people had voted. In some areas, charges of multiple voting generated a re-

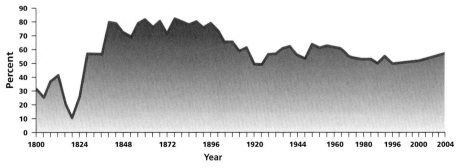

FIGURE 8–2 **Voter Turnout in Presidential Elections, 1800–2004.**

SOURCE: Howard W. Stanley and Richard G. Niemi, *Vital Statistics on American Politics, 1999–2000* (CQ Press, 2000). See also "National Voter Turnout in Federal Elections, 1996–2000," at www.infoplease.com/ipa/A0781453.html. Updated by authors.

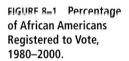

voter registration
System designed to reduce voter fraud by limiting voting to those who have established eligibility by submitting the proper form.

ican Civil War. Following the election of 1860, in which Lincoln, an antislavery candidate who did not receive a single electoral vote from a slave state, won the presidency, the South took up arms. The ensuing war marked the breakdown of democracy. Examples in our own time include antiabortion groups that use violence to press their political agenda and militia groups that arm themselves for battle against government regulations.

Participation can also include less intense activity and even engaging in patriotic rituals. For example, large numbers of Americans routinely sing the national anthem or recite the Pledge of Allegiance. They communicate their views about government and politics to their representatives in Washington and the state capitol. They serve as jurors in courtrooms and enlist in the military. They express concern about the involvement of American military forces in foreign hostilities. They complain about taxes and government regulations. And many families feel it important that their children visit Washington, D.C., and other historic sights.

For most people, politics is a private activity. Some books on manners still consider it impolite to discuss politics at dinner parties. To say that politics is private does not mean people do not have opinions or will not discuss them when asked by others, including pollsters. But often politics is avoided in discussions with neighbors, work associates, even friends and family, as too divisive or upsetting. Typically, less than one person in four attempts to influence how another person votes in an election. An even smaller number actually work for a candidate or party. Only one in 20 people make a contribution to a candidate, and only one in six designates $3 of their taxes to the fund that pays for presidential general elections (see Table 8-3).[29]

Few individuals attempt to influence others by writing letters to elected officials or to editors of newspapers for publication. Even smaller numbers participate in protest groups or activities. Despite the small number of persons who engage in these activities, it would be a mistake to assume that small numbers of individuals cannot make a difference to politics and government. An individual or small group can generate media interest in an issue and expand the impact. Peaceful protests for civil rights, about environmental issues, and both for and against abortion have generated public attention and even changed opinions.

Voting

Americans' most typical political activity is voting. The United States is a constitutional democracy with more than 200 years of free and frequent elections and a tradition of the peaceful transfer of power between competing groups and parties.

Originally, the Constitution left it to the individual states to determine the crucial question of who could vote, and the qualifications for voting differed considerably from state to state. All states except New Jersey barred women from voting, many did not permit African Americans to vote, and until the 1830s, property ownership was often a requirement. By the time of the Civil War, the franchise had been extended to all white male citizens in every state. Since that time, eligibility standards for voting have been expanded seven times by legislation and constitutional amendments (see Table 8-4).

TABLE 8–3 **Political Participation and Awareness in the United States**	
Watched Campaign on TV	62%
Vote in presidential elections	55
Vote in congressional elections	42
Try to persuade vote of others	29
Display campaign button, sticker, or sign	9
Gave money to help a campaign	11
Attend dinner, meeting, or rally for candidate	5

SOURCE: U.S. Bureau of the Census, *Statistical Abstract of the United States, 2003* (U.S. Government Printing Office, 2003), p. 269; The 2002 National Election Study, Center for Political Studies, University of Michigan. The NES Guide to Public Opinion and Electoral Behavior, at www.umich.edu/~nes/nesguide/gd-index.htm#6; See also www.census.gov.

TABLE 8–4 **Changes in Voting Eligibility Standards Since 1870**	
Year	**Change**
1870	Fifteenth Amendment forbade states from denying the right to vote because of "race, color, or previous condition of servitude."
1920	Nineteenth Amendment gave women the right to vote.
1924	Congress granted Native Americans citizenship and voting rights.
1961	Twenty-Third Amendment permitted District of Columbia residents to vote in federal elections.
1964	Twenty-Fourth Amendment prohibited the use of poll taxes in federal elections.
1965	Voting Rights Act removed restrictions that kept African Americans from voting.
1971	Twenty-Sixth Amendment extended the vote to citizens age 18 and older.

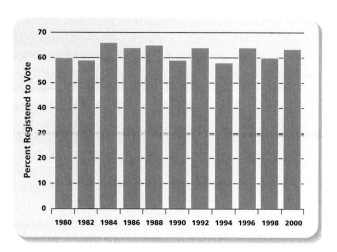

FIGURE 8–1   Percentage of African Americans Registered to Vote, 1980–2000.

SOURCE: U.S. Bureau of the Census, *Statistical Abstract of the United States,* 2001 (U.S. Government Printing Office, 2001), p. 251.

The civil rights movement in the 1960s, which made voting rights a central issue, secured adoption of the Twenty-Fourth Amendment and passage of the 1965 Voting Rights Act. The Voting Rights Act banned literacy tests, eased registration requirements, and provided for the replacement of local election officials with federal registrars in areas where the denial of the right to vote had been most blatant. Its passage resulted in a dramatic expansion of black registration and voting. Once African Americans were permitted to register to vote, "the focus of voting discrimination shifted . . . to preventing them from winning elections."[30] In southern legislative districts where blacks are in the majority, however, there has been a "dramatic increase in the proportion of African American legislators elected" (see Figure 8-1).[31]

Registration

One peculiarly American legal requirement—**voter registration**—arose in response to concerns about voting abuses, but it also discourages voting. Most other democracies have automatic voter registration. Average turnout in the United States is more than 30 percentage points lower than in countries like Australia, Austria, Belgium, Denmark, Germany, and Italy.[32] This was not always the case. In fact, in the 1800s, turnout in the United States was much like that of Europe today. Turnout began to drop significantly around the turn of the twentieth century, in part as a result of election reform (see Figure 8-2).

American elections in the 1800s were different from those of today. Ballots were prepared by the parties, often using different colors of paper that allowed party officials to monitor how people had voted. In some areas, charges of multiple voting generated a re-

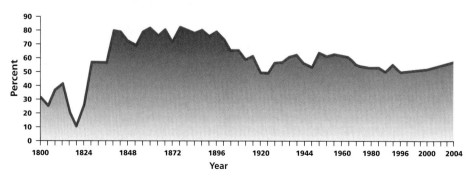

FIGURE 8–2   Voter Turnout in Presidential Elections, 1800–2004.

SOURCE: Howard W. Stanley and Richard G. Niemi, *Vital Statistics on American Politics, 1999–2000* (CQ Press, 2000). See also "National Voter Turnout in Federal Elections, 1996–2000," at www.infoplease.com/ipa/A0781453.html. Updated by authors.

voter registration
System designed to reduce voter fraud by limiting voting to those who have established eligibility by submitting the proper form.

IN COMPARATIVE PERSPECTIVE

Registration and Voting in the World's Democracies

	Turnout as a Percentage of the Eligible Vote	Compulsion Penalties*	Automatic Registration†		Turnout as a Percentage of the Eligible Vote	Compulsion Penalties*	Automatic Registration†
Australia	84%	Yes	No	New Zealand	86	No	No
Austria	85	No	Yes	Norway	80	No	Yes
Belgium	85	Yes	Yes	Spain	77	No	Yes
Canada	68	No	Yes	Sweden	83	No	Yes
Denmark	84	No	Yes	Switzerland	49	No	Yes
Finland	79	No	Yes	United Kingdom	75	No	Yes
France	67	No	No	United States	48	No	No
Germany	81	No	Yes				
Greece	80	Yes	Yes				
Ireland	75	No	Yes				
Israel	80	No	Yes				
Italy	93	Yes	Yes				
Japan	69	No	Yes				
Netherlands	85	No	Yes				

SOURCE: Thomas T. Mackie and Richard Rose, *The International Almanac of Electoral History*, 3d ed. (CQ Press, 1991); International Institute for Democracy and Electoral Assistance, "Voter Turnout from 1945 to Date: A Global Report on Political Participation," at www.idea.int/voter_turnout/index.html.

*Compulsion penalties are fines or other state actions against nonvoters.

†Automatic registration uses another form of citizen identification, such as an identity card or a driver's license.

form movement that substituted the **Australian ballot**, a secret ballot printed by the state, and initiated voter registration to reduce multiple voting and limit voting to those who had previously established their eligibility.

Registration laws vary by state, but in every state except North Dakota, registration is required in order to vote. Six states permit election day voter registration: Idaho, Maine, Minnesota, New Hampshire, Wisconsin, and Wyoming. The most important provision regarding voter registration may be the closing date. A few years ago, it was not uncommon for closing dates to be six months before the election; now, by federal law, no state can stop registration more than 30 days before a federal election.[33] Voter registration places a responsibility on voters to take an extra step—usually filling out a form at the county courthouse, when renewing a driver's license, or with a roving registrar—some days or weeks before the election and every time they move to a new address. Other important provisions include places and hours of registration.[34] The problem Florida encountered in counting ballots in the 2000 presidential election helped propel reform of election administration onto the national political agenda. However, modernizing how we vote involves complex legislation and even constitutional amendments because U.S. elections are largely governed by state law and administered at the county level. In 2002, Congress passed legislation creating minimum federal standards for all U.S. elections, including keeping computerized statewide lists of voters to combat election fraud. The legislation also provides states with $3.9 billion to improve voting equipment, assist with voter education, and train poll workers. The law also requires some form of identification at the time of registration.

Motor Voter

The burdens of voter registration were eased a bit when, on May 20, 1993, President Bill Clinton signed the National Voter Registration Act—called the "Motor Voter" bill because it allows people to register to vote while applying for or renewing a driver's license. Offices that provide welfare and disabled assistance can also facilitate voter registration. States have the option to include public schools, libraries, and city and county clerks' offices as registration sites. The law also requires states to allow registration by mail using a standardized form. Motor Voter requires a questionnaire be mailed to registered voters

Australian ballot
A secret ballot printed by the state.

every four years to purge for death and change of residence but forbids purging for any other reasons, such as nonvoting.

The law has been successful, at least in terms of numbers of new voters registered.[35] Early data on the impact of Motor Voter suggest that neither Democrats nor Republicans are the primary beneficiaries because most who have registered claim to be Independent.[36] Yet even with the increase in registration, Motor Voter does not appear to have increased turnout.[37]

Turnout

Americans hold more elections for more offices than the citizens of any other democracy. In part because there are so many elections, American voters tend to pick and choose which elections to vote in. Americans elect officeholders in *general elections,* determine party nominees in *primary elections,* and replace senators who have died or left office in *special elections.*

Elections held in years when the president is on the ballot are called *presidential elections,* elections held midway between presidential elections are called *midterm elections,* and elections held in odd-numbered calendar years are called *off-year elections.* Midterm elections (like the one in 2002) elect about one-third of the U.S. Senate, all members of the House of Representatives, and most governors and other statewide officeholders as well as large numbers of state legislators. Many local elections to elect city councils and mayors are held in the spring of odd-numbered years.

Turnout—the proportion of the voting-age public that votes—is highest in presidential general elections (see Figure 8-3). Turnout is higher in general elections than in primary elections and higher in primary elections than in special elections. Turnout is higher in presidential general elections than in midterm general elections, and higher in presidential primary elections than in midterm primary elections.[38] Turnout is higher in elections in which candidates for federal office are on the ballot (U.S. senator, member of the House of Representatives, president) than in state elections in years when there are no federal contests. Some states elect their governor and other state officials in odd-numbered years to separate state from national politics. The result is generally lower turnout. Finally, local or municipal elections have lower turnout than state elections, and municipal primaries generally have the lowest rates of participation.

WE THE PEOPLE

Voter Turnout by Demographic Factors

	1992	1994	1996	1998	2000	2002
Sex						
Men	60.2%	44.4%	52.8%	41.4%	53.1%	41.4%
Women	62.3	44.9	55.5	42.4	56.2	43.0
Race						
White	63.6	46.9	56.0	43.3	56.4	44.1
Black	54.0	37.0	50.6	39.6	53.5	39.7
Hispanic	28.9	19.1	26.7	20.0	27.5	18.9
Education						
Some high school	41.2	27.0	33.8	25.0	33.6	23.3
High school graduate	57.5	40.5	49.1	37.1	49.4	37.1
Some college	68.7	49.1	60.5	46.2	60.3	45.8
College graduate	81.0	63.1	73.0	57.2	72.0	58.5
Age						
18 to 24	42.8	20.1	32.4	16.6	32.3	17.2
25 to 34	53.2	32.2	43.1	28.0	43.7	27.1
35 to 44	63.6	46.0	54.9	40.7	55.0	40.2
45 to 64	70.0	56.0	64.4	53.6	64.1	53.1
65 and over	70.1	60.7	67.0	59.5	67.6	61.0

SOURCE: U.S. Census Bureau, *Statistical Abstract of the United States, 2003* (U.S. Government Printing Office, 2003), p. 269; U.S. Census Bureau, "Voting and Registration in the Election of November 2002: Detailed Tables for Current population Report," at www.census.gov/prod/2004pubs/p20-552.pdf.

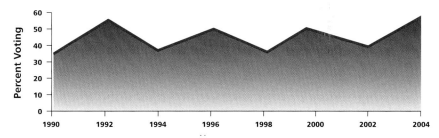

FIGURE 8–3   Voter Turnout in Presidential and Midterm Elections, 1990–2004.

SOURCE: U.S. Bureau of the Census, *Statistical Abstract of the United States,* 1998 (U.S. Government Printing Office, 1998), p. 97; Louis V. Gerstner, "Next Time, Let Us Boldly Vote as No Democracy Has Before," *USA Today,* November 16, 1998, p. A15; www.infoplease.com/ipa/A0781453.html; National Voter Turnout in Federal Elections: 1960–2000. Update by authors.

Turnout peaked in 1960 at more than 65 percent of persons eligible to vote, but it has since declined to 36 percent in 1998 and 51 percent in 2000.[39] Turnout was 39 percent nationally in 2002, up 3 percent from 1998. In states with more competitive contests, like Minnesota and South Dakota, it was even higher. The number of potential voters has increased since the 1960s because the Voting Rights Act of 1965 added large numbers of African Americans to the pool of registered voters. Younger voters were also given the right to vote with the Twenty-Sixth Amendment in 1971. Our electorate has also grown richer and more educated since the 1960s. Since wealth and education are related to voting, we should have seen an increase instead of a decrease in voting. However, 97 million eligible Americans failed to vote in the 2000 presidential election; the nonvoting figures are even higher for congressional, state, county, and local elections.[40]

Who Votes?

The extent of voting varies widely among different groups. Level of education especially helps predict whether people will vote; as education increases, so does the propensity to vote. "Education increases one's capacity for understanding complex and intangible subjects such as politics," according to one study, "as well as encouraging the ethic of civic responsibility. Moreover, schools provide experience dealing with a variety of bureaucratic problems, such as coping with requirements, filling out forms, and meeting deadlines."[41] Race and ethnic background are linked with different levels of voting, in large part because

In an effort to make registration easier, states have made registration forms available at motor vehicle stations, schools, public buildings, and even highway tollbooths.

turnout
The proportion of the voting-age public that votes, sometimes defined as the number of registered voters that vote.

This poster, published by the League of Women Voters, urged women to use the vote the Nineteenth Amendment had given them.

they correlate with education. Blacks in general turn out at lower rates than whites, although this is beginning to change. Women, another historically underrepresented group, have increased their voting levels to the point that since 1984, more women than men vote.[42] In 2002, with an eye to the 2004 elections, both parties mounted major efforts to register and mobilize Hispanic voters, a group likely to be of growing importance.

Income and age are also important factors. Those with higher family incomes are more likely to vote than those with lower incomes. Income, of course, corresponds to occupation, and those with higher-status careers are more likely to vote than those with lower-status jobs. Poor people are less likely to feel politically involved and confident, and their social norms tend to deemphasize politics.[43] Older people, unless they are very old and infirm, are more likely to vote than younger people. The greater propensity of older persons to vote will only amplify the importance of this group as baby boomers age and retire. In recent elections, pollsters have spoken of the key "swing" or undecided voters as "soccer moms," evidence of the growing relevance of female voters. Women's recent higher turnout is generally attributed to increasing levels of education and employment.

How Serious Is Nonvoting?

Although Americans can hardly avoid reading or hearing about political campaigns, half of all Americans fail to vote in presidential elections. Who are they? Why don't they vote? Is the fact that so many Americans choose not to vote a cause for alarm? If so, what can we do about it?

The simplest explanation for low turnout is that people are lazy, but there is more to it than that. Of course, some people are apathetic, but the vast majority of Americans are not. Paradoxically, we compare favorably with other nations in political interest and awareness, but for a variety of institutional and political reasons, we fail to convert these qualities into votes (see Table 8-5).

The difficulty of voting in the United States, the cost in time and effort, is higher than in other democracies. In our system, individuals are required to register to vote, and they must decide how to vote for a large number of offices, and in many states decide how to vote on ballot questions relating to public policy or constitutional amendments. Elections in the United States are held on weekdays rather than holidays or weekends as they often are elsewhere. Another factor in the decline of voter turnout since the 1960s is the Twenty-Sixth Amendment, which lowered the voting age to 18. It increased the number of eligible voters, but that group is the least likely to vote. With ratification of the amendment in 1971, turnout fell from 62 percent in 1968 to 57 percent in 1972.[44] The effect of adding this low-turnout group to the electorate has been to lower the overall turnout rate.

Mobilizing African American Turnout in 2000

Turnout among black voters surged in many states in 2000. Although nationwide, African Americans accounted for 10 percent of the total vote, the same percentage as in 1996, some states experienced exceptional increases. For example, in Florida, African American turnout increased by 68 percent, from 530,000 in 1996 to 893,000 in 2000. Missouri and Illinois also experienced exceptional turnout among black Americans. One of the major reasons was an unprecedented voter mobilization effort mounted by the National Association for the Advancement of Colored People. The NAACP's National Voter Fund spent $10 million on a get-out-the-vote campaign. Mobilization efforts can affect an election outcome in a race as close as that of 2000.

SOURCE: Michael A. Fletcher, "In Targeted States, a Striking Turnout of Black Voters," *Washington Post,* November 17, 2000, p. A29.

Some political scientists argue that nonvoting is not a critical problem. "Nonvoting is not a social disease," contends Austin Ranney, a noted scholar of politics. He points out that legal and extralegal denial of the vote to African Americans, women, Hispanics, persons over 18, and other groups has now been outlawed, so nonvoting is voluntary. He quotes the late Senator Sam Ervin of North Carolina: "I don't believe in making it easy for apathetic, lazy people to vote."[45] The late Dick Scammon used to say nonvoting was a sign of satisfaction.

Those who argue that nonvoting is a critical problem cite the "class bias" of those who do vote. The social makeup and attitudes of nonvoters are significantly different from those of voters and hence greatly distort the representative system. "The very poor . . . have about two-thirds the representation among voters than their numbers would suggest." Thus the people who need help the most from the government lack their fair share of electoral power to obtain it. And, it is argued, this situation is growing worse.[46]

Low voting, according to those who see a class bias in voting, reflects "the underdevelopment of political attitudes resulting from the historic exclusion of low-income groups from active electoral participation."[47] In short, part of the problem of nonvoting among low-income, less educated people is their failure to be conscious of their interests. Dynamic leadership or strong party organization, or both, would not only attract the poor to the polls but also make clear their "class grievances and aspirations."[48]

Others reject this class bias argument. They admit that nonvoters are demographically different but cite polls showing that nonvoters' attitudes are not much different from voters' attitudes. One study, comparing the party identification of voters with that of all Americans, found that the proportion of Democrats was nearly identical (51.4 percent of all citizens and 51.3 percent of voters), while Republicans as voters were slightly overrepresented (36 percent of citizens and 39.7 percent of voters). All other political differences are considered to be much smaller than this 3.7 percent gap. Further, voters are not "disproportionately hostile" to social welfare policies.[49]

What effect might increased voter turnout have in national elections? It might make a difference, since there are partisan differences between different demographic groups, and candidates would have to adjust to the demands of an expanded electorate. A noted political scientist, while acknowledging that no political system could achieve 100 percent participation, pointed out that the entire balance of power in the political system could be overturned if the large nonvoter population decided to vote.[50] However, others contend more persuasively that the difference may not be as pronounced. Nonvoters are not more in favor of government ownership or control of industry, and they are not more egalitarian. Nonvoters are, however, more inclined to favor additional spending on welfare programs.[51]

Another way to think of low voter turnout is to see it as a sign of approval of things as they are, whereas high voter turnout would signify disapproval and widespread desire for change. Even on the subject of how to interpret low turnout there is disagreement.

Voting Choices

Why do people vote as they do? Political scientists have identified three main elements of the voting choice: party identification, candidate appeal, and issues. These elements often overlap.

Voting on the Basis of Party

Party identification is the subjective sense of identification or affiliation that a person has with a political party (see Chapter 7). Party identification often predicts a person's stand on issues. It is part of our national mythology that Americans vote for the person and not the party, but as you will see, the person we vote for is most often from the party we prefer.

As discussed, partisanship is typically acquired in childhood or adolescence as a result of the socialization process in the family and then reinforced by peer groups in adolescence. In the absence of reasons to vote otherwise, people depend on party identification

TABLE 8–5 Why People Don't Vote	
Too busy, conflicting schedule	20.9%
Illness or disability (own or family's)	14.8
Not interested, felt vote would not make a difference	12.2
Out of town or away from home	10.2
Other reason, not specified	10.2
Did not like candidates or campaign issues	7.7
Refused or don't know	7.5
Registration problems	6.9
Forgot to vote (or send in absentee ballot)	4.0
Inconvenient polling place or hours or lines too long	2.6
Transportation problems	2.4
Bad weather conditions	0.6

SOURCE: U.S. Bureau of the Census, "Reasons for Not Voting, by Sex, Age, Race and Hispanic Origin, November 2000," at www.census.gov.

party identification
An informal and subjective affiliation with a political party that most people acquire in childhood.

You Decide   Thinking It Through

SHOULD WE ALLOW VOTING BY MAIL AND ON THE INTERNET?

You Decide... During the past two centuries of constitutional government, this nation has gradually adopted a more expansive view of popular participation. Not only has the right to vote been extended to more people, but the decisions made in the voting booth have been expanded as well to include primary elections to nominate party candidates and ballot referendums in which state constitutional amendments and state laws are adopted.

It seems logical that the next step in our democratic progress is permitting voters to cast ballots through the mail or via the Internet. Not only would such a reform make voting easier, but it would permit us to have more elections. For example, when a city council wants voters to decide whether to build a new football stadium or when there is need for a special election to fill the term of a member of Congress who has died or resigned, election officials could mail out the ballots and then in two or three weeks count up those that have been returned. The state of Oregon has already conducted several general elections by mail, and other states are considering adopting the Oregon system.

What do you think? Should we move toward a system in which we replace the ballot box with the mailbox or the computer? What arguments would you make for and against such an idea?

Thinking It Through... One of the problems with making elections more frequent is that voters will get fed up. Americans already vote more frequently and for more offices than citizens of any other democracy. Asking them to make voting choices even more frequently could result in lower turnout and less rational consideration. Many voters may be unaware that an election is going on. Yet the advantage of the vote-by-mail system employed by Oregon and some cities and counties is that it increases turnout, at least initially. What political scientists dispute is whether such increases in participation will continue when the novelty wears off.

Some critics of voting by mail or electronic democracy worry about fraud. Even when voters are required to sign their mailed-in ballots, the possibility of forgery still exists. Also, voting by mail or computer has the possibility of allowing people to pressure or harass voters. Another concern is late returns, as occurred in 2000.

Another criticism is that mail and electronic voting could be skewed toward participation by better-educated and higher-income voters, who routinely pay their bills by mail, make purchases on their computer, and own a personal computer with Internet access. Advocates of these new voting procedures contend that voters who do not own computers can drop off their ballots in some public building and that eventually computers will be available widely enough that access will not be a problem.

However, if voting can be made easier and more convenient, why not do it? If the integrity of the vote can be protected and the new ways of voting become widely accessible, such changes are probably inevitable.

SOURCE: David B. Magleby, "Participation in Mail Ballot Elections," *Western Political Quarterly* 40 (March 1987), pp. 79–91; Michael W. Traugott, "An Evaluation of Voting by Mail in Oregon," paper presented at a workshop cosponsored by the University of Michigan and the League of Women Voters, Washington, D.C., August 27, 1997. See also Adam J. Berinsky, Nancy Burns, and Michael W. Traugott, "Who Votes by Mail? A Dynamic Model of the Individual-Level Consequences of Voting-by-Mail Systems," *Public Opinion Quarterly* 65 (Summer 2001), pp. 178–197.

to simplify their voting choices. Party identification is not the same as party registration; it is not party membership in the sense of being a dues-paying, card-carrying member, as in some European parties. Rather, it is a psychological sense of attachment to one party or another.

There has been a dramatic increase in the number of self-declared Independents since the mid-1970s. Nominally, there are more Independents in the electorate today than Republicans. But two-thirds of all Independents are, in fact, partisans in their voting be-

Problems Counting Ballots and Administering Elections

The chaos in the counting of ballots in Florida in the 2000 election surprised many Americans, who assumed that vote counting is simple and precise. They were wrong. The problems were not isolated to Florida's clogged voting machines, defective punch cards, and inconsistent standards for dealing with problems. Ballots were misplaced in New Mexico, voting machines broke down in several states, people's names were incorrectly purged from voting lists, and long lines of people waiting to vote led to court challenges in many states. In the weeks and months following the election, at least half the states launched efforts to study the problems and propose solutions; in addition, national commissions, advisory groups, and experts undertook extensive analyses of our voting procedures.

Most people agree that many communities need new voting equipment and that the antiquated and flawed punch card technology used by "roughly 30 percent of the nation's voters" must be abandoned.* Whether jurisdictions adopt the less expensive optically scannable ballots or more expensive high-tech computer systems will depend in part on how much money Congress is willing to provide. Estimates vary, but the cost could be as high as $6.5 billion.

The National Association of Secretaries of State—the state officials charged with election administration—issued recommendations that included better pay for poll workers; aggressive voter education on matters like how to ask for a second ballot if the first is spoiled; equal access to balloting for minorities, the poor, and elderly voters; maintaining up-to-date voter lists; ensuring the integrity of absentee ballots; and providing federal money to local communities to upgrade their voting systems.†

The debate over electoral reform growing out of the 2000 election is not limited to machines and ballots but includes standards for recounts, ways to ensure that the process is open to all citizens, and concerns about the news media projecting winners before the polls close.

As a result of voting rights violations including discriminatory treatment and failure to provide ample resources for disabled persons and persons with limited English proficiency, the Bush administration's Justice Department filed five lawsuits in the summer of 2002. Three lawsuits targeted Florida counties, and the other two targeted Missouri and Tennessee. The cases were filed to "ensure that minority voters are not disenfranchised in the 2002 elections."‡

Angry voters in Palm Beach County protested that the "butterfly ballot" caused them to vote incorrectly and demanded an opportunity to vote over again, but were not allowed to do so.

Florida again experienced problems with voting in the 2002 primary election. Florida abandoned punch-card ballots, replacing them with touch-screen computer systems. Among the problems in the 2002 primary were precincts opening late, officials who were not able to explain the new technology or properly use it, and some election officials who failed to retrieve voting data from some equipment.

*Robert Tanner, "Ballot Reforms Are Slow in Coming, Despite Hundreds of Ideas, Studies," *Deseret News*, March 4, 2001, p. A3.

†Katharine Q. Seelye, "Panel Suggests Election Changes That Let States Keep Control," *New York Times*, February 5, 2001, p. A16.

‡Lynette Clemetson, "Justice Dept. to File 5 Suits on Voting Problems in 2000," *New York Times*, May 22, 2002, p. A25.

havior. Independent-leaning Democrats are predictably Democratic in their voting behavior, and Independent-leaning Republicans vote heavily Republican. Independent leaners are thus very different from each other and from the Pure Independents. Pure Independents have the lowest rate of turnout but generally do side with the eventual winner in presidential elections. These data on Independents only reinforce the importance of partisanship as an explanation of voting choice, because when we consider Independent-leaning Democrats and Independent-leaning Republicans as Democrats and Republicans, respectively, there were only 11 percent Pure Independents or others without a party in 2000, and the average for the period 1952–2000 was just that, 11 percent.[52]

Although party identification has fluctuated somewhat in the past 40 years, it remains more stable than attitudes about issues or political ideology. Fluctuations in party identification appear to come in response to economic conditions and political performance, especially of the president. The more information voters have about their choices, the more likely they are to defect from their party and vote for a candidate from the other party.

Permission of Harley Schwadron.

Voting on the Basis of Candidates

While long-term party identification is important, it is clearly not the only factor in voting choices; otherwise the Democrats would have won every presidential election since the last realignment in 1932. In fact, since 1952, Republicans have been more successful in winning the White House than Democrats. The answer to this puzzle is largely found in a second major explanation of voting choice—**candidate appeal**.

The elections of the 1980s marked a critical threshold in the emergence of the candidate-centered era in American electoral politics. This change in focus from parties to candidates is an important historical trend that has been gradually taking place over the past several decades.[53]

Candidate appeal often involves an assessment of a candidate's character. Is the candidate honest? Is the candidate consistent? Is the candidate dedicated to "family values"? Does the candidate have religious or spiritual commitments? The press in recent elections has sometimes played the role of "character cop," asking questions about private lives and lifestyles. The press asks these questions because voters are interested in a political leader's background—perhaps even more interested in personal character than in a political position on hard-to-understand health care or regulatory policy issues.

Ronald Reagan's effort to generate positive candidate appeal was successful. Carter had hoped that Reagan would behave more like Barry Goldwater, who in his speech accepting the nomination in 1964 had said, "Extremism in the defense of liberty is no vice. . . . Moderation in the pursuit of justice is no virtue."[54] Lyndon Johnson, Goldwater's opponent, benefited from public perception that Goldwater and those who nominated him were out of the mainstream of American politics, an idea reinforced by Goldwater's acceptance speech.

Like Barry Goldwater in 1964, George McGovern, who ran as the Democratic candidate for president in 1972, had negative appeal. Many of his supporters, by their dress and manner, appeared out of the mainstream of American politics. McGovern raised doubts about his judgment and leadership by how he handled his choice of a vice president. McGovern named Missouri Senator Tom Eagleton as his running mate, only to discover that Eagleton had once been hospitalized for emotional exhaustion and depression and received electric shock therapy. McGovern initially stood behind Eagleton, but as press coverage and criticism of McGovern's lack of investigation into Eagleton's past grew, McGovern dropped Eagleton and named a new running mate, Sargent Shriver. In the end, "only about one-third of the public thought McGovern could be trusted as president."[55]

Candidate appeal or the lack of it—in terms of leadership, experience, good judgment, integrity, competence, strength, and energy—is often more important than party or issues. Dwight Eisenhower had great candidate appeal. He was a five-star general, a legendary hero of the Allied effort in World War II. His unmilitary manner, his moderation, his personal charm, and his lack of a strong party position made him appealing across the ideological spectrum. Ronald Reagan generated positive candidate appeal, in part by asserting characteristics the public found lacking in Jimmy Carter—leadership and strength. Neither George W. Bush nor Al Gore was able to convey a vision that led to decisive victory in 2000. Bush was seen as more "likable" and Gore as more "competent." But both candidates had liabilities. Bush fought the image of not being up to the job, and Gore tried to make himself more likable.

Increasingly, campaigns today focus on the negative elements of candidates' history and personality. Opponents and the media are quick to point out the limitations or problems of any given candidate. The political parties and interest groups did most of the attacking in 2000. Bush was attacked for his stand on abortion, his lack of support for hate crime legislation, his environmental record, and his dubious competence.[56] Gore was attacked for the 1996 fund-raising scandals, his misstatement about his having invented the Internet, and his position on gun control.[57] Voters indicated that the

candidate appeal
How voters feel about a candidate's background, personality, leadership ability, and other personal qualities.

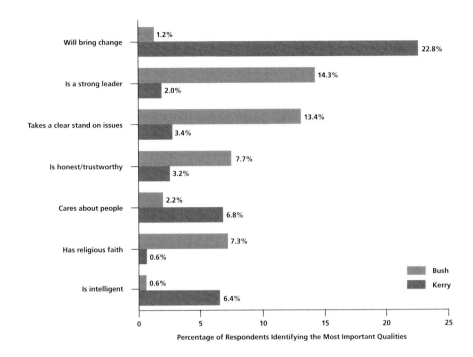

FIGURE 8–4 Which Quality Mattered Most in the 2004 Vote for President?

SOURCE: 2004 Exit Polls from Edison Media Research and Mitofsky International at www.cnn.com/ELECTION/2004/pages/results/states/US/P/00/epolls.0.html.

candidate quality that mattered most was being "honest or trustworthy," which one in four voters mentioned. For these voters, Bush was preferred by 80 percent over Gore, Ralph Nader (the Green party candidate), and Patrick Buchanan (the Reform party candidate). All other candidate attributes—"understands issues," "cares about people," "has experience," is a "strong leader," and exhibits "good judgment"—were mentioned by 12 to 15 percent of voters as the quality that mattered most. Bush also was preferred by respondents who said strong leadership mattered most. For voters who saw understanding issues as most important, Gore got 75 percent of the vote. Gore also was the preferred candidate for voters who valued "cares about people" and "has experience," where he got 63 and 82 percent, respectively, of the vote. Among the 2 percent who said likability was the candidate quality that mattered most, Bush got 82 percent of the vote (see Figure 8-4).[58]

Voting on the Basis of Issues

Most political scientists agree that issues, while important, are not as central to the decision process as party identification and candidate appeal.[59] Part of the reason is that candidates often intentionally obscure their positions on issues—an understandable strategy.[60] Richard Nixon said he had a plan to end the Vietnam War in 1968, clearly the most important issue in that year, but he would not reveal the specifics. By not detailing his plan, he stood to gain votes from those who wanted a more aggressive war effort as well as those who wanted a cease-fire.

For issue voting to become of major significance, the issue must be important to a substantial number of voters, opposing candidates must take opposing stands on the issues, and voters must know these positions and vote accordingly. Rarely do candidates focus on only one issue. Voters often will agree with one candidate on one issue and with the opposing candidate on another. In such an instance, issues will likely not be the determining factor. But lack of interest by voters in issues does not mean candidates can take any issue position they wish.[61]

More likely than *prospective issue voting* (voting based on what a candidate pledges to do in the future about an issue if elected) is *retrospective issue voting* (holding incumbents, usually the president's party, responsible for past performance on issues such as the economy or foreign policy).[62] In times of peace and prosperity, voters will reward the incumbent; if the nation falls short on either, voters will elect the opposition.

But good economic times do not always lead to the retention of an administration, as Al Gore learned in 2000. Part of Gore's problem in 2000 was that only half the public saw their family's financial situation as having gotten better. Of these voters, Gore received 61 percent of the vote.[63] But his inability to effectively claim credit for the good economic times hurt him, especially when Republicans contended that it was the American people, not the government, that produced the strong economy. A similar debate arose in 2004 over the state of the economy and the extent to which President Bush's policies or the terrorist attacks of September 11, 2001 had resulted in job loss and other economic problems. Democrats argued that the tax cuts had been irresponsible, especially when the country was at war. The Republicans countered that the tax cuts had helped stimulate the economy. The state of the economy is often the central issue in midterm elections as well as presidential ones. Several studies have found a positive relationship between the state of the economy and "out" party gains and "in" party losses in congressional seats.[64] Political scientists have been able to locate the sources of this effect in individual voters' decision making. Voters tend to vote against the party in power if they perceive a decline or standstill in their personal financial situations.[65]

Voters see responsibility for the economy resting with the president and Congress more than with governors or local officials.[66] In 2004, the electorate was divided over the economy, jobs, and Bush's tax cut. More voters felt the economy was "not good or poor" than felt it was "excellent or good." The view of the economy appeared to be influenced by which candidate one preferred, with Bush voters more positive and Kerry voters more negative.

PUBLIC OPINION: SPIN DETECTION

Public opinion is important in a democracy because the government depends on the consent of the governed. This simulation describes survey techniques and identifies possible problems with surveys. Test your knowledge about survey research and attempt to identify problems with which surveyors deal.

Go to the PoliSim "Public Opinion: Spin Detection."

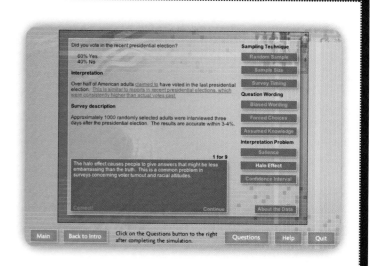

Summary

1. Public opinion is a complex combination of views and attitudes individuals acquire through various influences from childhood on. Public opinion takes on qualities of intensity, latency, consensus, and polarization—each of which is affected by people's feelings about the salience of issues.

2. The American public has a generally low level of interest in politics, and most people do not follow politics and government closely. The public's knowledge of political issues is poor.

3. Americans who are interested in public affairs can participate by voting, joining interest groups and political parties, working on campaigns, writing letters to newspaper editors or elected officials, attempting to influence how another person will vote, or even protesting.

4. Better-educated, older, and party- and group-involved people tend to vote more; the young tend to vote the least. Voter turnout tends to be higher in national than in state and local elections, higher in presidential than in midterm elections, and higher in general than in primary elections.

5. Party identification remains the most important element in the voting choice of most Americans. It represents a long-term attachment and is a "lens" through which voters view candidates and issues as they make their voting choices. Candidate appeal, including character and record, is another key factor in voter choice. Voters decide their vote less frequently on the basis of issues.

Key Terms

public opinion	**attentive public**	**Australian ballot**	**party identification**
political socialization	**voter registration**	**turnout**	**candidate appeal**

Further Reading

JOSEPH A. AISTRUP, *The Southern Strategy Revisited: Republican Top-Down Advancement in the South* (University Press of Kentucky, 1996).

HERBERT ASHER, *Polling and the Public: What Every Citizen Should Know,* 5th ed. (CQ Press, 2001).

EARL BLACK AND MERLE BLACK, *The Vital South: How Presidents Are Elected* (Harvard University Press, 1992).

M. MARGARET CONWAY, *Political Participation in the United States,* 4th ed. (CQ Press, 2000).

ROBERT S. ERIKSON AND KENT L. TEDIN, *American Public Opinion: Its Origins, Content and Impact,* 6th ed. (Allyn & Bacon, 2000).

WILLIAM H. FLANIGAN AND NANCY H. ZINGALE, *Political Behavior of the American Electorate,* 10th ed. (CQ Press, 2002).

ROBERT HUCKFELDT AND JOHN SPRAGUE, *Citizens, Politics, and Social Communication: Information and Influence in an Election Campaign* (Cambridge University Press, 1995).

LAWRENCE R. JACOBS AND ROBERT Y. SHAPIRO, *Politicians Don't Pander: Political Manipulation and the Loss of Democratic Responsiveness* (University of Chicago Press, 2000).

KATHLEEN HALL JAMIESON, *Everything You Think You Know About Politics and Why You're Wrong* (Basic Books, 2000).

BRYAN D. JONES, *Reconceiving Decision Making in Democratic Politics: Attention, Choice and Public Policy* (University of Chicago Press, 1994).

BRUCE E. KEITH, DAVID B. MAGLEBY, CANDICE J. NELSON, ELIZABETH ORR, MARK C. WESTLYE, AND RAYMOND E. WOLFINGER, *The Myth of the Independent Voter* (University of California Press, 1992).

V. O. KEY JR., *Public Opinion and American Democracy* (Knopf, 1961).

PAUL J. LAVRAKAS AND MICHAEL W. TRAUGOTT, EDS. *Election Polls, the News Media, and Democracy* (Seven Bridges Press, 2000).

WARREN E. MILLER AND J. MERRILL SHANKS, *The New American Voter* (Harvard University Press, 1996).

MICHAEL NELSON, ED., *The Elections of 2000* (CQ Press, 2001).

RICHARD G. NIEMI AND HERBERT F. WEISBERG, *Classics in Voting Behavior* (CQ Press, 1993).

RICHARD G. NIEMI AND HERBERT F. WEISBERG, *Controversies in Voting Behavior,* 4th ed. (CQ Press, 2001).

BENJAMIN I. PAGE AND ROBERT Y. SHAPIRO, *The Rational Public: Fifty Years of Trends in Americans' Policy Preferences* (University of Chicago Press, 1992).

FRANK R. PARKER, *Black Votes Count: Political Empowerment in Mississippi After 1965* (University of North Carolina Press, 1990).

GERALD M. POMPER, ED., *The Election of 2000: Reports and Interpretations* (Seven Bridges Press, 2001).

JACOB SHAMIR AND MICHAL SHAMIR, *The Anatomy of Public Opinion* (University of Michigan Press, 2000).

JOHN ZALLER, *The Nature and Origins of Public Opinion* (Cambridge University Press, 1992).

See also *Public Opinion Quarterly, the American Journal of Political Science,* and *American Political Science Review.*

9
CHAPTER

CAMPAIGNS AND ELECTIONS
Democracy in Action

S OME CYNICS CONTEND THAT ELECTIONS DO NOT MATTER AND THERE IS LITTLE POINT IN VOTING. STRONG EVIDENCE TO THE CONTRARY comes from the 2000 elections, in which Al Gore won the popular vote by 539,947 votes, or only slightly more than 180 votes per county! The contest was especially close in Florida and New Mexico, where the statewide margins were 537 and 366 votes, respectively. The contest for the presidency was not the only one that required recounts. In Michigan, Mike Rogers won election to the House by 88 votes. In the 2000 election, you could truthfully say that every vote counted. In 2004, there were again some very close elections. Senate Minority Leader Tom Daschle, a Democrat, lost by 4,535 votes in South Dakota. In the Presidential race, Bush carried New Mexico by only 8,000 votes. At the state and local level, there are often races decided by only a few votes.

In the United States, citizens vote more often and for more offices than citizens of any other democracy. We hold thousands of elections for everything from community college directors to county sheriffs. About half a million persons hold elected state and local offices.[1] In 2002, we elected 34 U.S. senators, all 435 members of the U.S. House of Representatives, 36 governors, and dozens of treasurers, secretaries of state, and, in most states, judges.

In addition to electing people, voters in 27 states vote on laws or constitutional amendments proposed by initiative petitions or on popular referendums put on the ballot by petition. In all states except Delaware, voters must approve all changes in the state constitution.

In this chapter, we explore our election rules. We note four important problems: the lack of competition for some offices, the complexities of nominating presidential candidates, the distortions of the electoral college, and the influence of money in our elections. We also discuss proposed reforms in each of these areas.

Important Factors in Winning an Election

Uncontrollable Factors

- Incumbent running
- Strength of party organization
- National tides or landslide possibility
- Socioeconomic makeup of district

Organizational Factors

- Registration drives
- Fund-raising machinery
- Campaign organization
- Volunteers
- Media campaign
- Direct-mail campaign efforts
- Get-out-the-vote efforts

Candidate's Personal Leadership Factors

- Personal appeal
- Knowledge of issues
- Speaking and debating ability
- Commitment and determination
- Ability to earn free, positive media coverage

Elections: The Rules of the Game

The rules of the game—the electoral game—make a difference. Although the Constitution sets certain conditions and requirements, most electoral rules remain matters of state law.

Regularly Scheduled Elections

In our system, elections are held at fixed intervals that cannot be changed by the party in power. It does not make any difference if the nation is at war, as we were during the Civil War, or in the midst of a crisis, as in the Great Depression; when the calendar calls for an election, the election is held. Elections for members of Congress occur on the first Tuesday after the first Monday in November of even-numbered years. Although there are some exceptions (for special elections or peculiar state provisions), participants know *in advance* just when the next election will be. In many parliamentary democracies, such as Great Britain and Canada, the party in power calls elections at a time of its choosing.

Fixed, Staggered, and Sometimes Limited Terms

Our electoral system is based on *fixed terms*, meaning that the length of a term in office is specified, not indefinite. The Constitution has set the term of office for the U.S. House of Representatives at two years, the Senate at six years, and the presidency at four years.

Our system also has *staggered terms* for some offices; not all offices are up for election at the same time. All House members are up for election every two years, but only one-third of the senators are up for election at the same time. Since presidential elections occur two or four years into a senator's six-year term, senators can run for the presidency with-out fear of losing their seat. But if their Senate term expires the same year as the presi-dential election, the laws of many states require them to give up their Senate seat to run for president or vice president or any other position. An example of a state that permits a candidate to run for election to two offices is Connecticut, where Joseph Lieberman was reelected to the U.S. Senate in 2000 while being narrowly defeated in his race for vice pres-ident. Had he been victorious in both campaigns, he would have resigned his Senate seat.

Term Limits

The Twenty-Second Amendment to the Constitution, adopted in 1951, limits presidents to two terms. Knowing that a president cannot run again changes the way members of Congress, the voters, and the press regard the president. A politician who cannot, or has announced he or she will not, run again is called a *lame duck.* Efforts to limit the terms of other politicians have become a major issue in several American states. The most frequent targets have been state legislators. One consequence of term limits is more lame ducks.

Term limits are popular. Voters in 15 states have enacted them for their state legisla-ture, and in two states, the legislature imposed term limits on themselves. Even more states limit the term of governors.[2] Three-fourths of all voters favor term limits (9 out of 10 strong Republicans and 7 out of 10 strong Democrats).[3] Still, despite their popularity, proposals for term limits have repeatedly been defeated when they have come to a vote in Congress.

The Supreme Court, by a vote of 5 to 4, declared that a state does not have the consti-tutional power to impose limits on the number of terms for which its members of the U.S. Congress are eligible, either by amending its own constitution or by state law.[4] Congress has refused to propose a constitutional amendment to impose a limit on congressional terms.

Winner Take All

An important feature of our electoral system is the **winner-take-all system**.[5] In most American electoral settings, the candidate with the most votes wins. The winner does not need to have a *majority* (more than half the votes cast); in a multicandidate race, the win-ner may have only a *plurality* (the largest number of votes). In 2000, three senators and seven House members were elected by pluralities. In 2002, again there were seven House races and three Senate races decided by a plurality.

Most American electoral districts are **single-member districts**, meaning that in any district for any given election—senator, governor, U.S. House, state legislative seat— the voters choose *one* representative or official.[6] When the single-member-district and winner-take-all systems are combined, minor parties find it hard to win. For example, even if a third party gets 25 percent of the vote in several districts, it still gets no seats.

The combination of single-member districts and winner-take-all is different from a **proportional representation** system, in which political parties secure legislative seats and power in proportion to the number of votes they receive in the election. Let's assume that a state has three representatives up for election. In each of the three contests, the Re-publican defeats the Democrat, but in one district by only a narrow margin. If you add up the statewide vote, the Republicans get 67 percent and the Democrats 33 percent. Under our single-member-district and winner-take-all system, the Republicans get all three seats. But under a system of proportional representation, in which the three seats represent the whole state, the Democrats would receive one seat because they got rough-ly one-third of the vote in the entire state. Proportional representation thus rewards minor parties and permits them to participate in government. Countries that practice some form of proportional representation include Germany, Israel, and Japan.

The Electoral College

We elect our president and vice president not by a national vote but by an indirect device known as the **electoral college**. The framers of the U.S. Constitution devised this system because they did not trust the choice of president to a direct vote of the people. Under this

winner-take-all system
An election system in which the candi-date with the most votes wins.

single-member district
An electoral district in which voters choose one representative or official.

proportional representation
An election system in which each party running receives the proportion of leg-islative seats corresponding to its pro-portion of the vote.

electoral college
The electoral system used in electing the president and vice president, in which vot-ers vote for electors pledged to cast their ballots for a particular party's candidates.

Advantages and Disadvantages of Proportional Representation

The winner-take-all rule of most American elections has some advantages but also means that substantial minorities go unrepresented. In cases where there are multiple candidates and the winner only has a plurality, it means that a majority goes unrepresented.

A system of proportional representation could be applied to the allocation of electoral votes by state, or in states with more than one member of the House of Representatives, it could be applied to the allocation of seats as it is in many democracies.

Proportional representation has some advantages. It more accurately reveals the preferences of voters and gives those who do not vote for the winning candidate a sense that they have some influence as a result of their vote. In this sense, proportional representation may encourage greater turnout for people who identify with parties that rarely win elections, like Democrats in Utah or Wyoming. Proportional representation may also encourage issue-oriented campaigns and enhance the representation of women and minorities.

But there are some problems with proportional representation. It may make it harder to have a clear winner. This problem is even greater if minor parties are likely to receive representation as well. In this sense, it may encourage minor parties. Opponents of proportional representation worry that it can contribute to political instability.

system, each state has as many electors as it has representatives and senators. California will therefore have 55 electoral votes (53 House seats and two Senate seats) and Vermont three electoral votes for the election of 2004.

Each state legislature is free to determine how its electors are selected. Each party nominates a slate of electors, usually longtime party workers. Electors are expected to cast their electoral votes for the party's candidates for president and vice president. In our entire history, no "faithless elector"—an elector who does not vote for his or her state's popular vote winner—has ever cast the deciding vote. There were no faithless electors in 2000, but one elector from the District of Columbia abstained.

The Twelfth Amendment requires electors to vote separately for president and vice president. To demonstrate how this works, if you voted for the Republican candidate in 2000, you actually voted for the Republican slate of electors pledged to vote for George W. Bush for president and Dick Cheney for vice president in the electoral college.

Candidates who win a plurality of the popular vote in a state secure all that state's electoral votes, except in Nebraska and Maine, which allocate electoral votes to the winner in each congressional district plus two electoral votes for the winner of the state as a whole. Winning electors go to their state capital on the first Monday after the second Wednesday in December to cast their ballots. These ballots are then sent to Congress, and early in January, Congress formally counts the ballots and declares who won the election for president and vice president.

It takes a majority of the electoral votes to win. If no candidate gets a majority of the electoral votes for president, the House chooses among the top three candidates, with each state delegation having one vote. If no candidate gets a majority of the electoral votes for vice president, the Senate chooses among the top two candidates, with each senator casting one vote.

When there are only two major candidates for the presidency, the chances of an election being thrown into the House are remote. But twice in our history the House has had to act: In 1800, before the Twelfth Amendment was written, the House had to choose in a tie vote between Thomas Jefferson and Aaron Burr; and in 1824, the House picked John Quincy Adams over Andrew Jackson and William Crawford. Henry Clay, who was forced out of the race when he came in fourth in the electoral college, threw his support behind Adams. When Adams was elected, he made Clay his secretary of state. The 1824 vote in the House was especially contentious. Jackson, winner of the popular vote, was not elected when the decision passed to the House. This outcome infuriated Jackson, who won the electoral college vote by a wide margin four years later.

The Electoral Commission of 1877 met in secret session to decide the controversial presidential election between Rutherford B. Hayes and Samuel Tilden. After many contested votes the presidency was eventually awarded to Hayes.

As we were reminded in 2000, our electoral college system makes it possible for a presidential candidate to receive the most popular votes, as Al Gore did, and yet not get enough electoral votes to be elected president. Al Gore won the popular vote by over 500,000 votes but lost the electoral college 271 to 266.[7] This also happened in 1824, when Andrew Jackson won 12 percent more of the vote than John Quincy Adams; in 1876, when Samuel Tilden received more popular votes than Rutherford B. Hayes; and in 1888, when Benjamin Harrison won in the electoral college despite Grover Cleveland's receiving more popular votes. It almost happened in 1960 and 1976, when the shift of a few votes in a few key states could have resulted in the election of a president without a popular majority. In a year with a serious minor party candidate, the result could be the election of a president without a plurality of the vote, as happened in 2000, when the Green party took enough votes away from Gore to have made the difference in Florida and New Hampshire.

In two of the four elections in which winners of the popular vote did not become president, the electoral college did not decide the winner. The 1824 election was decided by the U.S. House of Representatives. In 1876, the electoral vote in three southern states and Oregon was disputed, resulting in the appointment of an electoral commission to decide how those votes should be counted. In 1888 and 2000, the electoral college awarded the presidency to the candidate with fewer popular votes.

Concern about the electoral college is renewed every time there is a serious third-party candidate for the presidency. Even a candidate like Green party candidate Ralph Nader, who got less than 3 percent of the vote in 2000, prompted preelection discussions about his impact on the electoral college vote. People began to ask, which Congress casts the vote, the one serving during the election or the newly elected one? The answer is the new one, the one elected in November and taking office the first week in January. Since each state has one vote in the House, what happens if a state's delegation is tied in its vote, 2 to 2 or 3 to 3? Then its vote does not count. Would it be possible to have a president of one party and a vice president of another? Yes, if the election were thrown into the House and Senate and each chamber were controlled by a different party.

The electoral college sharply influences presidential politics. To win a presidential election, a candidate must appeal successfully to several big states like California, Texas, Ohio, and Illinois, and when the contest is close, as it was in 2000, a candidate must also win in the competitive states.[8] California's electoral vote of 54 in

2000 exceeded the combined electoral votes of the 14 least populous states plus the District of Columbia. The map inside the front cover of this book provides a visual comparison of state size based on electoral votes.

Presidential candidates do not ordinarily waste time campaigning in a state unless they have at least a fighting chance of carrying that state; nor do they waste time in a state in which their party is a sure winner. Richard Nixon in 1960 was the last candidate to campaign in all 50 states, but he lost valuable time traveling to and from Alaska, while John Kennedy focused on the more populous states in which he had a chance to win. The contest usually narrows down to the medium-sized and big states, where the balance between the parties tends to be fairly even.

Running for Congress

How candidates run for Congress differs, depending on the nature of their district or state, on whether candidates are incumbents or challengers, on the strength of their personal organization, on how well known they are, and on how much money they have to spend on their campaign. We can also note several similarities in House and Senate elections.

First, most congressional elections are not close. In districts where most people belong to one party or where incumbents are popular and enjoy fund-raising and other campaign advantages, there is often little competition.[9] Those who believe competition

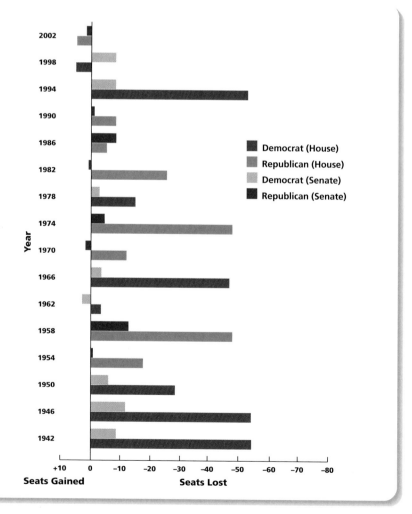

FIGURE 9–1   Seats Lost by the President's Party in Midterm Elections for the House of Representatives and the Senate, 1938–2002.

is essential to constitutional democracy are concerned that so many officeholders have **safe seats**. When officeholders do not have to fight to retain their seat, elections are not performing their proper role.[10]

Competition is more likely when funding is adequate for both candidates, which is not often the case in U.S. House elections. Elections for governor and for the U.S. Senate are more seriously contested and more adequately financed than those for the U.S. House of Representatives.

Presidential popularity affects both House and Senate elections during presidential election years as well as midterm elections. The impact of presidential candidate popularity in a presidential election is the **coattail effect**, the boost candidates from the president's party get from a popular presidential candidate running in the same election. But winning presidential candidates do not always provide such a boost. The Republicans suffered a net loss of six House seats in 1988, even though George H. W. Bush won the presidency, and the Democrats suffered a net loss of ten house seats in 1992 when Bill Clinton won the presidential election. Democrats fared better in 1996, registering a net gain of nine house seats. There were no discernible coattails in the 2000 elections. Overall, "measurable coattail effects continue to appear," according to congressional elections scholar Gary Jacobson, but they are "erratic and usually modest" in their impact.[11]

In midterm elections, presidential popularity and economic conditions have long been associated with the number of House seats a president's party loses.[12] These same factors are associated with how well the president's party does in Senate races, but the association is not as strong.[13] Figure 9-1 shows the number of seats in the House of Representatives and U.S. Senate gained or lost by the party controlling the White House in midterm elections since 1938. Republicans did better in 1994 than in any midterm election since 1946, picking up 53 seats. The Republican tide was not limited to the House but included a net gain of nine Senate seats.[14] In all of the midterm elections between 1934 and 1998, the party controlling the White House lost seats in the House. The range of losses, however, is quite wide, from a low of four seats for the Democrats in 1962 to a high of 71 seats for the Democrats in 1938. But in 2002, as in 1998, the longstanding pattern of the president's party losing seats did not hold. Republicans picked up a net gain of 2 seats in the Senate and 6 seats in the House. As noted, there were comparatively few competitive races in 2002, especially for a year following redistricting.

When presidential landslides occur, as they did with Lyndon Johnson in 1964, the victorious party is especially vulnerable and likely to lose seats in the next midterm election, as the Democrats did in 1966. Given the historic pattern of the president's party's losing seats and the close party balance resulting from the 2000 elections, Democrats believed they were well positioned in 2002 to recapture control of both houses of Congress. The Democrats' hopes were dashed by a set of strong Republican candidates for the House and Senate, recruited in part with the assistance of the White House. President Bush invested a great deal of time and effort into helping Republican candidates in competitive races with early visits to their states and districts to help with fundraising and an intense series of campaign stops in the last five days that more resembled the close to a presidential election than the close to a midterm election. Despite the heavy investment by President Bush, many 2002 contests revolved around more local issues. Arkansas voters rejected Republican Tim Hutchinson for another term in the Senate in part because of his private life and South Dakota returned Democrat Tim Johnson despite five visits to the state by Bush. Johnson closely linked himself to fellow South Dakota Democrat Tom Daschle, whose power as Senate Majority Leader was at stake in 2002.

The House of Representatives

Every two years, as many as 1,000 candidates—including approximately 400 incumbents—campaign for Congress. After deciding to take the plunge, candidates must first plan a primary race, unless they face no opponents for their party nomination. Incumbents are rarely challenged for renomination from within their own party, and when they are, the challenges are seldom serious. In the 1990s, for example, on average only two House incumbents were denied renomination each election cycle. Challengers from other parties running against entrenched incumbents rarely encounter opposition in their own party.[15]

safe seat
An elected office that is predictably won by one party or the other, so the success of that party's candidate is almost taken for granted.

coattail effect
The boost that candidates may get in an election because of the popularity of candidates above them on the ballot, especially the president.

Democrat Mark Pryor, Arkansas Attorney General, debated the incumbent U.S. Senator Tim Hutchinson, Republican, when he successfully challenged Hutchinson for the Senate seat from Arkansas in 2002.

MOUNTING A PRIMARY CAMPAIGN   The first step for would-be challengers is to raise hundreds of thousands of dollars and sometimes more to mount a serious campaign. This requires asking friends and acquaintances as well as interest groups for money. Candidates need money to hire campaign managers and technicians, buy television and other advertising, conduct polls, and pay for a variety of activities. Parties can sometimes help, but they shy away from giving money in primary contests. The party organization usually stays neutral until the nomination is decided.

Another early step is to build a *personal organization.* A candidate can build an organization while holding another office, such as a seat in the state legislature, by serving in civic causes, helping other candidates, and being conspicuous without being controversial.

A candidate's main hurdle is gaining visibility. Candidates work hard to be mentioned by the media. In large cities with many simultaneous campaigns, congressional candidates are frequently overlooked, and in all areas, television is devoting less time to political news.[16] Candidates rely on personal contacts, on hand shaking and door-to-door campaigning, and on identifying likely supporters and courting their favor—the same techniques used in campaigns for lesser offices. Despite these efforts, the turnout in primaries tends to be low, except in campaigns in which large sums of money are expended on advertising.

CAMPAIGNING FOR THE GENERAL ELECTION   As we have mentioned, most incumbent members of Congress win reelection.[17] Since 1970, over 95 percent of incumbent House members seeking reelection have won, and in 2000, 98 percent of incumbent House members running for reelection were successful (see Figure 9-2).[18] In 2002, again 98 percent of incumbents running in the general election won. Incumbents outspent their challengers roughly 3 to 1; in the Senate the difference was closer to 1.75 to 1.[19] Most challengers spend little money, run campaigns that are not significantly more visible than primary campaigns, contact few voters, and lose badly.

Serious challengers in House races are hard to find. Many are scared away by the prospect of having to raise more than $1 million in campaign funds, others realize that the district has been drawn with fewer persons from their party than the incumbent's, and some do not want to face the media scrutiny that comes with a serious race for Congress. Nonetheless, in each election, a few challengers mount serious campaigns because of a desire to serve and to influence public policy or because of the incumbent's perceived vulnerability, the challengers' own wealth, party or political action committee efforts, or other factors.

Why is keeping a House seat so much easier than gaining it? Incumbents have a host of advantages that help them win reelection. These perquisites, or "perks," include free mailings to constituents (the *franking privilege*), the free use of broadcast studios to record radio and television tapes to be sent to local media outlets, and, perhaps most important of all, a large staff to perform countless favors for constituents and send a stream

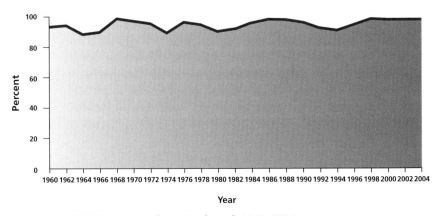

FIGURE 9–2   U.S. House Incumbents Reelected, 1946–2004.

SOURCE: Harold W. Stanley and Richard G. Niemi, eds., *Vital Statistics on American Politics 2001– 2002* (CQ Press, 2001), pp. 53–55. Updated by authors.

of press reports and mail back to the district.[20] Representatives also try to win committee posts, even on minor committees, that relate to the needs of their districts and build connections with constituents.[21]

If incumbents win so often, how do we get any significant turnover in the House of Representatives? Turnover comes when incumbents die, decide to retire, or seek some other office. *Redistricting,* which happens once each decade, often promotes some turnover, as it did in 2002, when eight incumbents were forced to run against other incumbents, either in primaries or general elections.[22] More than one-third of the U.S. House retired between 1992 and 1996. This amount of turnover was unusual and included some members who were disillusioned by partisan bickering.

The 2002 redistricting process largely protected incumbents in both parties. Few incumbents were seriously challenged. Retirements and redistricting create *open seats,* which can result in more competitive elections. Potential candidates, as well as political action committees and political party committees, all watch open-seat races closely. But as noted, most races have incumbents and most incumbents win, lending credibility to the charge that we have a "permanent Congress." Occasionally, one party has a big victory, as the Republicans did in 1994, with a 57-seat gain in the House, securing the majority for the first time in 40 years. Large shifts like 1994 are rare in part because state legislatures through redistricting have created fewer competitive districts.

The Senate

Running for the Senate is big-time politics. The six-year term and the national exposure make a Senate seat a glittering prize, so competition is usually intense. Senate campaigns generally feature state-of-the-art campaign techniques; a race normally costs millions of dollars (see Figure 9-3).[23] The essential tactics are to raise lots of money, get good people involved, make as many personal contacts as possible (especially in the states with smaller populations), avoid giving the opposition any positive publicity, and have a clear and consistent campaign theme. Incumbency is an advantage for senators, although not as much as for representatives.[24] Incumbent senators are widely known, but so are their opponents, who often raise and spend significant amounts of money.[25]

When one party controls the Senate by only a few seats, as has been the case in recent years, more good candidates run, and the number of competitive elections increases. The cost of Senate campaigns can vary greatly. California has nearly 70 times the

"My former opponent is supporting me in the general election. Please disregard all the things I said about him in the primary."

Dunagin's People. Tribune Media Services.

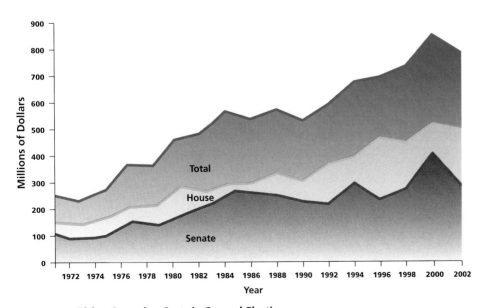

FIGURE 9–3 **Rising Campaign Costs in General Elections.**

SOURCE: Federal Election Commission, at ftp.fcc.gov/fec.

The Iowa caucuses are an important first step in terms of media exposure for candidates running for president. Here, Republican presidential candidate Alan Keyes speaks at a caucus site in Des Moines, Iowa on January 24, 2000.

number of potential voters as Wyoming; not surprisingly, running for a seat from Wyoming is much cheaper than running for a seat from California. As a result, interest groups and parties direct more money to competitive races in small states when the stakes for control of the Senate are high.[26] Going into the 2002 elections, the Senate had 50 Democrats, 49 Republicans, and one Independent. Jim Jeffords was reelected as a Republican in 2000 but switched parties in 2001, putting the Democrats in control of Senate leadership and all standing committees. The narrow margin of Democratic control meant that a net loss of one seat would put the Republicans back in the majority. The GOP mounted a major effort to reclaim the Senate in 2002. Part of the strategy was candidate recruitment. In South Dakota, President Bush persuaded Representative John Thune to run for Senate instead of for governor. In Minnesota, Vice President Cheney urged former Democrat and St. Paul mayor, Norm Coleman, to run for Senate and also pressed Tim Pawlenty to run for governor rather than Senator, clearing the way for Coleman. Democrats also made candidate recruitment a priority, finding strong candidates in Arkansas and New Hampshire. Because 2002 was the last election allowing party soft money at the federal level, both parties raised and spent record amounts of soft money. The 2002 election was unusual in that there were two late candidate replacements. In New Jersey, Senator Robert Torricelli dropped out and was replaced by former Senator Frank Lautenberg, who ended up winning. In Minnesota, Democratic incumbent Paul Wellstone died in a plane accident only eleven days before the election, and former Vice President Walter Mondale ran in Wellstone's place. Mondale lost narrowly to Norm Coleman.

Running for President

Presidential elections are major media events, with candidates seeking as much positive television coverage as possible and trying at the same time to avoid negative coverage. The formal campaign has three stages: winning the nomination, campaigning at the convention, and mobilizing support in the general election.

Stage 1: The Nomination

Presidential hopefuls must make a series of critical tactical decisions. The first is when to start campaigning. For the presidential election of 2000, some candidates, like Al Gore, Steve Forbes, and Lamar Alexander, began almost as soon as the 1996 presidential election was over. Early decisions are increasingly necessary for candidates to raise the money and assemble an organization. Campaigning begins well before any actual declaration of candidacy as candidates try to line up supporters to win caucuses or primaries in key states and to raise money for their nomination effort.

One of the hardest jobs for candidates and their strategists is calculating how to deal with the complex maze of presidential primaries and caucuses that constitutes the delegate selection system. The system for electing delegates to the national party convention varies from state to state and often from one party to the other in the same state. In some parties in some states, for example, candidates must provide lists of delegates supporting them months in advance of the primary. The presidential campaign finance system provides funds to match small individual contributions for candidates who agree to remain within spending limitations. George W. Bush declined the federal funds in 2000 in part to have greater flexibility in when and where he spent his campaign money.

PRESIDENTIAL PRIMARIES   State presidential primaries, unknown before 1900, have become the main method of choosing delegates to the national convention. Today, more than three-fourths of the states use presidential primaries. In 2000, some 84 percent of the Democratic delegates and 89 percent of the Republican delegates were chosen in the primaries.[27] The rest of the delegates were chosen by party caucuses or conventions.

Presidential primaries often have two features: a *beauty contest,* or popularity vote in which voters indicate which candidate they prefer but do not actually elect delegates to the convention, and *actual voting* for delegates pledged to a candidate. Candidates may win the beauty contest and find their opponents doing better in actual delegates elected because they failed to put a full slate of delegates on the ballot or because local notables were listed on the ballot as delegates pledged to another candidate. Different combinations of these two features have produced the following systems[28]:

- *Proportional representation:* Delegates to the national convention are allocated on the basis of the votes candidates win in the beauty contest. This system has been used in most of the states, including several of the largest ones. The Democrats mandate proportional representation for all their primaries.[29] In some states, Republicans use this same system, but Republicans are much more varied in their delegate selection processes.[30]

- *Winner take all:* Whoever gets the most votes wins all that state's delegates, as George W. Bush did in the California Republican primary in 2000. To win all the delegates of a state like California is an enormous bonus to a candidate. Republicans still use the winner-take-all system at the state level, and in 2000, about half of all states used this rule at either the state or congressional district levels.

- *Delegate selection:* In several states, large and small, voters choose delegates who may or may not have pledged how they will vote in the national party convention. The names of the presidential hopefuls do not appear separately on the ballot, and there is no declared presidential preference. Under this arrangement, delegates are free to exercise their independent judgment at the convention. Only Republicans use this system; in 2000, it was used most prominently in New York and Illinois.

- *Delegate selection and separate presidential poll:* In several states, voters decide twice: once to indicate their choice for president and again to choose delegates pledged, or at least favorable, to a presidential candidate.

Voters in states like Iowa and New Hampshire, which are the first states to pick delegates, bask in media attention for weeks and even months before they cast the first ballots in the presidential sweepstakes. Because these early contests have had the effect of limiting the choices of voters in states that come later in the process, there has been a tendency for states to move their primaries up. This process is called "front loading." California, which traditionally held its primary in June, moved it to March in 2000 so that its voters would play a more important role in selecting the nominee. Other states did the same thing. This had the effect of compressing the nomination battle into several weeks of intense activity in the spring followed by months of much less activity before the fall general election campaign. For 2004, as in the past, states that felt overlooked in 2000 pushed for revision to the schedule, including possibly having four regional groupings (East, South, Midwest, and West).[31] States that gain visibility and importance through early primaries continue to want to maintain that advantage.

CAUCUSES AND CONVENTIONS   A **caucus** is a meeting of party members and supporters of various candidates. About a dozen states use a caucus or convention system (or both) for choosing delegates.[32] Each state's parties and legislature regulate the methods used. The caucus or convention is the oldest method of choosing delegates and differs from the primary system in that it centers on party organization.

Delegates who will attend the national party conventions are chosen by delegates to state or district conventions, who themselves are chosen earlier in county, precinct, or town caucuses. The process starts at local meetings open to all party members, who discuss and take positions on candidates and issues and elect delegates to represent their views at the next level. This process is repeated until national nominating convention delegates are chosen by conventions of delegates throughout a district or state.

The best-known example of a caucus is in Iowa, because Iowa has held the earliest caucuses in the most recent presidential nominating contests. Every January or February in a presidential election year, Iowans have the opportunity to attend Republican and Democratic precinct meetings. Large numbers of voters attend these small town meetings and have a chance to meet and exchange views on issues and candidates, rather than merely pulling a lever in a voting booth or placing an *X* on a ballot.[33]

caucus
A meeting of local party members to choose party officials or candidates for public office and to decide the platform.

Presidential hopefuls face a dilemma: To get the Republican nomination, you have to appeal to the more intensely conservative Republican partisans, those who vote in primaries and support campaigns. Democratic hopefuls have to appeal to the liberal wing of their party as well as minorities, union members, and environmental activists. But to win the general election, candidates have to win support from moderates and pragmatic voters, many of whom do not vote in the primaries. If candidates get out too far from the moderates in their nomination campaign, they risk being labeled extreme in the general election.

STRATEGIES   Strategies for securing the nomination have changed over the years. Some candidates think it wise to skip some of the earlier contests and enter first in states where their strength lies. John McCain pursued such a strategy in 2000, ignoring Iowa and concentrating on New Hampshire. Most candidates choose to run hard in Iowa and New Hampshire, hoping that early showings in these states, which receive a great deal of media attention, will move them into the spotlight for later efforts.

During this early phase, especially important is the ability of candidates to manage the media's expectations of their performance. Lyndon Johnson actually won the New Hampshire primary in 1968, but because his challenger, Eugene McCarthy, did better than the press had predicted, McCarthy was interpreted as the "winner."

Winning in the primaries thus becomes a game of expectations, and candidates may intentionally downplay their expectations so that "doing better than expected" might generate momentum for their campaign. John McCain's surprise victory in New Hampshire in 2000 generated a lot of free publicity and garnered more than $1 million in campaign contributions via the Internet in just three days.[34] As the race moved to more friendly turf for George W. Bush in South Carolina, Bush won. Al Gore's early victories in Iowa and New Hampshire knocked Bill Bradley out of the race and effectively gave Gore the Democratic nomination.

Stage 2: The Convention

The delegates elected in primaries, caucuses, or state conventions assemble at their **national party convention** in the summer before the election to pick the party's presidential and vice presidential candidates. In the past, delegates arrived at national nominating conventions with differing degrees of commitment to presidential candidates; some delegates were pledged to no candidate at all, others to a specific candidate for one or two ballots, and others firmly to one candidate only. Recent conventions have merely ratified decisions already made in the primaries and caucuses, in part because delegates are required to pledge themselves to a specific presidential hopeful (in the Democratic party) or because one candidate has been able to amass a majority of delegates. And because of reforms encouraging delegates to stick with the person to whom they are pledged, there has been no room to maneuver at conventions. National party conventions used to be events of high excitement because they determined who would be the party nominee, but in every election since the Republican convention of 1948 and the Democratic convention of 1952, the party primaries have decided who would be the nominee.

As recently as 1988, Democratic and Republican national conventions were given gavel-to-gavel coverage by the major networks, meaning that from the beginning of the first night to the end of the fourth night, television covered the conventions. Now the major networks leave comprehensive coverage to C-SPAN and CNN. National nominating conventions have ceased to dominate the national news, for the very good reason that they are no longer the place where candidates are selected.[35] The long-term trend of declining viewership and reduced hours of coverage has altered the parties' strategies. In 2004, the parties featured their most important speakers and highlighted their most important messages in the limited time given them by the networks. There were modest increases in viewership of the conventions in 2004.

Conventions follow standard rules, routines, and rituals. Usually, the first day is devoted to a keynote address and other speeches touting the party and denouncing the opposition; the second day, to committee reports, including party and convention rules and the party platform; the third day, to presidential and vice presidential balloting; and the

national party convention
A national meeting of delegates elected in primaries, caucuses, or state conventions who assemble once every four years to nominate candidates for president and vice president, ratify the party platform, elect officers, and adopt rules.

The Role of Conventions

Every four years since 1856, both major parties have held conventions to nominate candidates for president and vice president. Conventions bring together delegates from the state parties to represent the wishes of their voters. Successful conventions build party unity, mobilize support for the party nominees, and capture the interest and attention of the nation. Conventions also decide on rules and regulations governing the party, settling controversies surrounding delegate selection (credentials) and party platforms.

The 1968 Democratic National Convention will long be remembered for the more than 10,000 protesters who came to Chicago to oppose the war in Vietnam. Security concerns were high because Martin Luther King Jr. and Robert Kennedy had been assassinated earlier that year. Televised images of Chicago police using tear gas and night sticks to disperse the crowd not only hurt the Democrats in 1968 but also meant that neither party held a convention in Chicago for the next 28 years. The intense battle in the streets of Chicago carried over onto the convention floor as delegates debated the Vietnam plank of the party platform into the early hours of the morning. Civil rights issues nearly tore the Democratic party apart as some southern states still had all-white delegations to the convention. African American delegates sought recognition, and the convention voted to seat some of them over the protest of the white delegates. The party remained badly divided after the Chicago convention and later changed its rules to encourage greater diversity in delegations and more extensive use of direct primaries.

Who attends conventions? Delegates come from all walks of life, yet many are former party leaders or public officials. Republican delegates are more likely to be male than their Democratic counterparts. Aside from the candidates and delegates, the most important people at the conventions are journalists and TV reporters. Thousands from all over the world view these festivities. The parties have an interest in getting a positive "spin" out of the convention, so they work hard to manage the news coverage. Reporters, by contrast, have an interest in stirring up controversy.

Because the choice of the party nominees has been decided well before the convention, there has been relatively little controversy on the floor of the conventions in recent years. The parties have turned to theatrics and celebrities in an effort to boost the audience watching the televised conventions. They have also shortened the proceedings on network television to only a few hours in the evening.

fourth day, to the presidential candidate's acceptance speech.[36] For sample coverage of the 2000 Republican convention go to www.pbs.org/newshour/election2000/gopconvention/, and for the Democrats see www.pbs.org/newshour/election2000/demconvention/.

THE PARTY PLATFORM   Delegates to the national party conventions decide on the *platform,* a statement of party perspectives on public policy. Why does anyone care what is in the party platform? Critics have long pointed out that the party platform is binding on no one and is more likely to hurt than to help a candidate. But presidential candidates as well as delegates take the platform seriously because it defines the direction a party wants to take. Also, despite the charge that the platform is ignored, most presidents make an effort to implement it.[37] For example, when President George W. Bush signed an education bill into law, he pointed to his party's commitment to "leave no child behind."[38] Neither party had a platform fight in 2000.

THE VICE PRESIDENTIAL NOMINEE   The choice of the vice presidential nominee garners widespread attention. Rarely does a person actually "run" for the vice presidential nomination because only the president's vote counts. But there is a good deal of maneuvering to capture that one vote. Sometimes the choice of a running mate is made at the convention—not a time conducive to careful and deliberate thought. More often the choice is made before the convention, and the announcement is timed to enhance media coverage and momentum going into the convention. The last time a presidential candidate left the choice of vice president to the delegates was for the Democrats in 1956.

The hoopla and excitement of the national convention reach a nationwide audience on TV.

Traditionally, the presidential nominee chooses a running mate who will "balance the ticket." Democratic presidential nominee Walter Mondale raised this tradition to a dramatic new height in 1984 by selecting a woman, New York Representative Geraldine A. Ferraro, to run with him. Mondale's bold decision was an effort to strengthen his appeal to women voters. But presidential candidates can also ignore the idea of a balanced ticket, as George W. Bush did when he chose another Texan from the oil industry to be his running mate. Dick Cheney moved his official residence to Wyoming and registered to vote there so that if the Bush-Cheney ticket won the popular vote in Texas, Republican Texas electors could vote for him, since the Constitution (Article II, Section 1) prohibits electors from voting for more than one person for president and vice president from their own state.

THE VALUE OF CONVENTIONS   Why do the parties continue to have conventions if the nominee is known in advance and the vice presidential nominee is the choice of one person? What role do conventions play in our system? For the parties, they are a time of "coming together" to endorse a party program and to build unity and enthusiasm for the fall campaign. For candidates as well as other party leaders, conventions are a chance to capture the national spotlight and further their political ambitions. For nominees, they are an opportunity to define themselves in positive ways. The potential is there to heal wounds festering from the primary campaign and move into the general election united, but the potential is not always achieved. Conventions can be potentially divisive, as the Republicans learned in 1964 when conservative Goldwater delegates loudly booed New York Governor Nelson Rockefeller and as the Democrats learned in 1968 when the convention spotlighted divisions within the party over Vietnam as well as ugly battles between police and protesters near the convention hotels.

NOMINATION BY PETITION   There is a way to run for president of the United States that avoids the grueling process of primary elections and conventions—if you are rich enough or well known enough. John Anderson in 1980 and H. Ross Perot in 1992 met the various state requirements and made it onto the ballot in all 50 states. In 2000, the petition process was as simple as submitting the signatures of 200 registered voters in Washington State or as difficult as getting the signatures of 2 percent of voters who voted in the last election in North Carolina (52,000 signatures).[39] Patrick Buchanan, candidate of the Reform party, was able to get his name on the ballot in all but one state and the District of Columbia, and Ralph Nader, candidate of the Green party, in all but seven states.[40]

Stage 3: The General Election

The national party convention adjourns immediately after the presidential and vice presidential candidates deliver their acceptance speeches to the delegates and the national television audience. Traditionally, the time between the conventions and Labor Day was a time for resting, binding up wounds from the fight for nomination, gearing up for action, and planning campaign strategy. In recent elections, however, the candidates have not paused after the convention but launched directly into all-out campaigning.

PRESIDENTIAL DEBATES   Televised presidential debates are a major feature of presidential elections. The 1960 debate between John Kennedy and Richard Nixon boosted Kennedy's campaign and elevated the role of television in national politics.[41] In 1976, President Gerald Ford debated Jimmy Carter and mistakenly said that each country in eastern Europe "is independent, autonomous, it has its own territorial integrity, and the United States does not conceive that those countries are under the domination of the Soviet Union."[42] That mistake damaged his credibility. Ronald Reagan's performance in the 1980 and 1984 debates confirmed the public view of him as decent, warm, and dignified. Bill Clinton's skirmishes with George Bush in 1992 and Bob Dole in 1996 showed him to be a skilled performer.

The 2004 presidential debates were widely watched and largely reinforced the candidate preferences of the viewers.[43] Neither candidate made a major mistake and both candidates were able to state their positions and draw contrasts with their opponent. Challengers generally benefit more from debates and in 2004, Kerry was seen as the "winner" in public opinion surveys following all three debates."[44] The vice presidential debate followed the same pattern as the presidential debates, with no major mistakes and few surprises. During both the presidential and vice presidential debates, the Democrats brought up the fact that Vice President Cheney's daughter is a lesbian. The Republicans, and especially Mrs. Cheney, criticized the Democrats after the debate for drawing her daughter's sexual orientation into the campaign.

The Commission on Presidential Debates once again ran the 2004 debates. The candidates again negotiated such things as whether they would be standing or sitting. An important departure from the presumed format was the use by the networks of split screens where one candidate was seen reacting while the other was speaking. President Bush, especially during the first debate, reacted with what was widely described as a "scowl" to some of the criticisms leveled by Senator Kerry. In a later debate, Bush made mention of his "scowl." The president seemed more comfortable in the format where questions came from the audience.

Presidential debates give candidates an opportunity to show how quickly and accurately they can respond to questions and outline their goals. In the debates of the 2004 elections, there were no major mistakes made by any of the candidates but many felt that John Kerry outperformed George W. Bush in the three presidential debates.

Charles Keating, Jr. answers questions during a Senate hearing on the Lincoln Federal Savings and Loan scandal. Keating attempted to win favors from senators by giving them substantial campaign contributions.

Ralph Nader, the Green party candidate in 2000, charged that the commission had a bias in favor of the two major parties when he and Reform party candidate Pat Buchanan were excluded from the debates. But Nader and Buchanan failed to meet the commission's criteria for inclusion of minor parties; neither had an average of 15 percent or higher in the five major polls used by the commission for this purpose. The other criteria for inclusion of a minor party candidate in the presidential debates are that the candidate be legally eligible and be on the ballot in enough states to be able to win at least 270 electoral votes.[45] In 1992, Ross Perot and his running mate, James Stockdale, had been included in the presidential and vice presidential debates, which generated large viewing audiences, averaging more than 80 million for each debate. The issue of excluding minor party candidates remains contentious. Including them takes time away from the major party candidates, especially if two or more minor party candidates are invited. Including them may also reduce the likelihood of both major parties' candidates' participating. But excluding them raises issues of fairness and free speech.

Although some critics are quick to express their dissatisfaction with presidential candidates for being so concerned with makeup and rehearsed answers, and although the debates have not significantly affected the election outcomes, they have provided important opportunities for candidates to distinguish themselves and for the public to weigh their qualifications. Candidates who do well in these debates are at a great advantage. They have to be quick on their feet, seem knowledgeable but not overly rehearsed, and project a positive image. Most candidates are adept at all of these skills.

Although each election is unique, politicians, pollsters, and political scientists have collected enough information to agree broadly on a number of basic factors that they believe affect election outcomes. Whether the nation is prospering probably has the most to do with who wins a presidential election, but as we have noted, most voters vote on the basis of party and candidate appeal.[46] Who wins depends on voter turnout. The Democrats' advantage in the number of people who identify themselves as Democrats is mitigated by higher voter turnout among Republicans. Republicans also usually have better access to money, which means they can run more television ads in more places and more often. In 2000, the Democrats as a party achieved financial parity with the Republicans and more effectively targeted resources to key Senate races.

Money in U.S. Elections

Election campaigns cost money, and the methods of obtaining the money have long been controversial. Campaign money can come from a candidate's own wealth, political parties, interested individuals, or interest groups. Money is contributed to candidates for a variety of reasons, ranging from altruism to self-interest. Individuals or groups, in hopes of influencing the outcome of an election and subsequently influencing policy, give **interested money**. Concern about campaign finance stems from the possibility that candidates or parties, in their pursuit of campaign funds, will decide that it is more important to represent their contributors than their conscience or the voters. The potential corruption that results from politicians' dependence on interested money concerns many observers of American politics.

Scandals involving money's influence on policy are not new. In 1925, responding to the Teapot Dome scandal, in which a cabinet member was convicted of accepting bribes, Congress passed the Corrupt Practices Act, which required disclosure of campaign funds but was "written in such a way as to exempt virtually all [members of Congress] from its provisions."[47]

The 1972 Watergate scandal—an illegal break-in at Democratic party headquarters by persons associated with the Nixon campaign to steal campaign documents and plant listening devices—led to discoveries by news reporters and congressional investigators that large amounts of money from corporations and individuals were "laundered" in secret bank accounts outside the country for political and campaign purposes. Nixon's 1972 campaign spent more than $60 million, more than twice what it had expended in 1968. Investigators discovered that wealthy individuals and corporations made large contributions to influence the outcome of the election or secure ambassadorships and administrative appointments.

interested money
Financial contributions by individuals or groups in the hope of influencing the outcome of an election and subsequently influencing policy.

In the early 1990s, Charles Keating and his failed Lincoln Savings and Loan spotlighted the possibility that undue influence comes with large contributions. Keating had asked five U.S. senators, all of whom had received substantial campaign contributions or other perks from him, to intervene on his behalf with federal bank regulators looking into his savings and loan business. These senators came to be called the Keating Five. One of the senators was John McCain, who later became a strong advocate of campaign finance reform. The Bipartisan Campaign Finance Reform Act, most closely identified with McCain, became law in 2002.

Efforts at Reform

Reformers have tried three basic strategies to prevent abuse in political contributions: (1) imposing limitations on giving, receiving, and spending political money; (2) requiring public disclosure of the sources and uses of political money; and (3) giving governmental subsidies to presidential candidates, campaigns, and parties. Recent campaign finance laws have tended to use all three strategies.

THE FEDERAL ELECTION CAMPAIGN ACT   In 1971, Congress passed two significant laws dealing with campaign funding. The Federal Election Campaign Act (FECA) limited amounts that candidates for federal office could spend on advertising, required the disclosure of the sources of campaign funds as well as how they are spent, and required political action committees to register with the government and report all major contributions and expenditures. This law also provided a checkoff that allowed taxpayers to contribute $1 to a fund to subsidize presidential campaigns by checking a box on their income tax form. The checkoff option is now $3.

In 1974, Congress passed and President Gerald Ford signed the most sweeping campaign reform measure in U.S. history. These amendments to the Federal Election Campaign Act established somewhat more realistic limits on contributions and spending, tightened disclosure, and provided for public financing of presidential campaigns.

IN COMPARATIVE PERSPECTIVE

The Soft Money Loophole in Japan

The Japanese strategy to combat corruption and money politics has been to create some of the most stringent campaign regulations in the world:

- Door-to-door campaigning is banned.
- Candidates may not run campaign advertisements in the media, although parties may.
- Each campaign may produce only two versions of its campaign brochure, and only a limited number may be distributed; the number varies according to the number of registered voters in a district.
- Campaign posters are allowed only on government-provided poster boards that are set up in several locations across a district during the campaign.
- Direct mailing of campaign literature is not allowed except for a specified number of government-provided campaign postcards.
- The number of campaign offices, employees, and vehicles is restricted by law.

These regulations should make it impossible for candidates to raise and spend large sums of money in a campaign, but Japanese candidates have found a giant loophole in these restrictions by avoiding "official" campaign activities. A candidate will go door to door or mail out literature to voters or put up posters *before* the official campaign period. In these precampaign activities, the candidates will be very careful never to mention the upcoming election, so their efforts are not covered by law.

Attempts to limit these activities have run into constitutional concerns. If a campaign has not begun and a person has not declared his or her candidacy, how can the Japanese government restrict the right of a citizen to hold meetings, discuss issues with people, mail information to people, or put up posters? In a similar manner, concern for free speech led to the soft money loophole in U.S. campaign restrictions.

The 1974 law was again extensively amended after the Supreme Court's 1976 *Buckley v. Valeo* decision, which overturned several of its provisions on grounds that they violated the First Amendment.[48] The *Buckley* decision emphasized limitations on contributions and full and open disclosure of all fund-raising activities by candidates for federal office, as well as the system of public financing for presidential elections.[49] The Supreme Court made a distinction between campaign spending and campaign contributions, holding that the First Amendment protects spending; therefore, legislatures may not limit how much of their own money people spend on elections, but Congress may limit how much people contribute to somebody else's campaign. Later modifications of the law and interpretations by the Federal Election Commission sought to encourage volunteer activities and party building by permitting national political parties, corporations, labor unions, and individuals to give unlimited amounts, called **soft money**, to state parties, provided that the funds are used for party-building purposes.

The public subsidy of presidential candidates has broken down. Until 2000, presidential candidates (except wealthy self-financed candidates) accepted the voluntary limitations that come with partial public financing of presidential campaigns. George W. Bush, who raised more than $125 million for his campaign, declined federal matching funds in the 2000 primaries but accepted the federal subsidy of $67.5 million for the general election and with it the limits on how much his campaign could spend.[50] Whether future candidates will also pass up some federal funds depends on how well funded their opponents are and their own ability to raise money. Beyond the problem of candidates' passing up federal funds, the number of taxpayers checking the campaign subsidy on their income tax forms has been declining, although enough did so to cover all the costs of the 2000 elections.[51]

THE 2002 CAMPAIGN FINANCE REFORMS   The most serious problem with the presidential campaign finance system was soft money—funds given to state and local parties by political parties, individuals, or political action committees ostensibly for party-building registration drives, mailings, and advertising, which do not specify a candidate by name. No limits were set on the amount of such contributions. The money was called "soft" because federal law did not limit how much individuals or groups could contribute or how much parties could spend. Although soft money was supposed to benefit only parties, it was used by the parties to influence the election of federal candidates. Both parties made raising soft money a high priority, and soft money spending rose dramatically. All national party committees

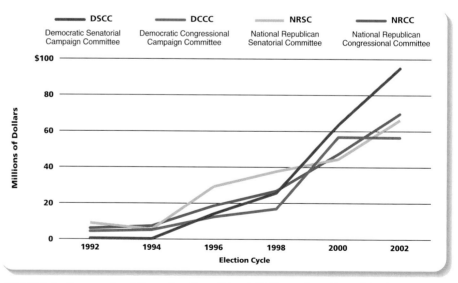

FIGURE 9–4   Congressional Campaign Committee Soft Money Spending, 1994–2002.

SOURCE: Federal Election Commission, "Party Committees Raise more than $1 Billion in 2002–2003," press release, March 20, 2002. At www.fec.gov/press/20030320party/20030320party.html, April 29, 2003. Adjusted by CPI. At bls.gov/pub/special.requests/cpi/cpiai.txt, January 15, 2003.

Note: The totals for each party do not equal the sum of the party committee receipts because the numbers provided by the FEC have been adjusted to account for transfers between party committees so as not to double count money in the total receipts.

soft money
Contributions to a state or local party for party-building purposes.

combined raised over $487 million of soft money in the 1999–2000 election cycle, up from $78 million in 1991–1992[52] (see Figure 9-4). In 2001–2002, all party committees combined raised over $420 million in soft money.

Soft money brought back the large donors as major players in campaign finance. It also strengthened the power of the national party committees, which allocate the money to state parties and indirectly to candidates. In the past, soft money had been more important in presidential than in congressional contests, but that changed in a dramatic way with the 1998 and 2000 congressional elections. The most dramatic growth in 2000 came among Senate Democrats, who raised only $372,000 in soft money in 1993–1994 but $63 million in 1999–2000—a surge in spending that helped Senate Democrats pick up a net gain of four Senate seats. Figure 9-4 plots the surge in soft money funds for the four congressional campaign committees. The 2002 election cycle also saw extraordinary soft money activity by all party committees. Overall, the parties raised nearly as much soft money in 2001–2002 as they raised in 1999–2000, which was a presidential election year. When we compare 2002 with the last midterm year, 1998, we see soft money more than doubling in four years. With President Bush leading the way, the Republican National Committee raised nearly $114 million, up from $74 million in 1998. Again in 2002, the Democratic Senatorial Campaign Committee outpaced all other committees, raising more than $95 million.

The 2002 campaign finance reforms banned most forms of soft money. All soft money contributions to national party committees were banned, as was soft money spending by state parties for or against federal candidates. However, the 2002 reforms permit

The 2002 Campaign Finance Reforms: Continuity and Change

Federal campaign finance legislation passed in 2002 does all of the following:

- Keeps the Federal Election Commission, appointed by the president with the advice and consent of the Senate, to regulate the campaign financing of candidates for president, senator, and representative

- Retains for public financing of presidential general election campaigns with funds from the income tax checkoff

- Retains partial public financing on a matching basis of presidential nominating campaigns

- Retains subsidies to the two national parties for their convention expenses and to any minor party that polled 5 percent of the total vote in the previous presidential election

- Keeps limits on spending by candidates for presidential nominations (on a state-by-state basis and in total) and in the presidential general elections for those candidates who accept public funding

- Keeps limits on the amounts that national parties may spend on presidential campaigns and on individual congressional and senatorial campaigns

- Sets a limit of $2,000 on the amount that any individual can give to a candidate for the U.S. Senate or for the U.S. House of Representatives in the primary election; a limit of $2,000 per candidate in the general election; and a limit of $5,000 per candidate in the primary and $5,000 in the general election for political action committees

- Sets an overall limitation of $37,500 for individuals over a two-year cycle election

- Sets no limit on the amount of their own money candidates can spend on their campaign

- Sets no limit on the amount that individuals or groups can spend independently

- Bans soft money except for $10,000 per state and local party committee for voter registration and activation

- Bans the use of corporate and union treasury funds for all electioneering, including issue advocacy

- Redefines such "issue advocacy" as electioneering and makes more consistent with independent expenditure disclosure.

You Decide   Thinking It Through

WHEN IS AN ISSUE AD AN ELECTION AD?

You Decide... Political ads have many different purposes. Some are about issues, attempting to persuade the audience to a point of view; others are about a candidate's qualifications; and still others are about both issues and candidates. But does the content of an advertisement indicate the ad's purpose?

Assume it is a few weeks before an election, and you are watching an ad on TV or listening to one on the radio. Ask yourself if what you are seeing or hearing is only about issues, or if it is about electing or defeating a candidate.

- Does it feature the image or likeness of a candidate?
- Does it mention a candidate by name?
- Does it mention an election?
- Does it use words like "vote for," "vote against," or "support"?
- Is it shown in the weeks before an election?

The answers to questions like these can determine whether this is a campaign communication and therefore subject to the disclosure and other requirements of federal law.

Thinking It Through... Based on a distinction in the *Buckley* v. *Valeo* Supreme Court decision, communications that do not use words such as "vote for" or "vote against" are considered issue ads, which are not subject to the same disclosure rules as ads that are about electing or defeating a candidate. But in the context of an election, it is possible to convey a positive or negative election message without using these words. Some of these ads end by telling viewers to "call" or "write" the candidate to express support or opposition. But the real intent of the message is to get the audience to vote for or against a candidate.

Research on the types of ads run in recent election cycles has found that less than 10 percent were only about issues and not about candidates. Research also shows that people do not think it necessary to use words like "vote for" in order to convey an election message but that even showing the candidate's image is enough to convey that the ad is about electing or defeating a candidate.

Opponents to limiting or prohibiting issue ads point out that Congress is often in session until a few days before an election, and interest groups need to be able to inform the public about important issues that are being considered. To limit issue ads during this period may stifle the free speech of groups with a more legislative than electoral agenda.

---

state and local party committees to raise and spend limited amounts of soft money for voter registration and get-out-the-vote efforts. Such activities may be funded with soft money contributions of no more than $10,000 per individual or group as permitted by state law.

ISSUE ADVOCACY ADVERTISING   The 1996 election saw a surge in **issue advocacy**. Money spent on issue advocacy ads is unlimited and undisclosed because it presumably deals with issues, not candidates. Issue ad spending in some U.S. House races exceeded $1 million in recent elections; for example, in 2000, one group, the Alliance for Quality Nursing Home Care, spent more than $1 million on issue ads in the Delaware U.S. Senate race.[53] In the 1998, 2000, and 2002 elections, businesses, labor unions, health maintenance organizations, the Sierra Club, the League of Conservation Voters, the Business Roundtable, pro- and antigun groups, pro- and antiabortion groups, and the pharmaceutical industry ran issue ads (see Table 9-1). The 2002 election saw an expansion of seniors groups doing issue advocacy. Among those involved were 60 Plus, Seniors Coalition, United Seniors, and the American Association for Retired People (AARP). The AARP, by far the largest and best known of seniors groups, urged voters to study the issues. The seniors group that spent the most money was United

issue advocacy
Promoting a particular position or an issue paid for by interest groups or individuals but not candidates. Much issue advocacy is often electioneering for or against a candidate, and until 2004 had not been subject to any regulation.

TABLE 9–1   Some Frequent Issue Advertisers

Advertiser	Expenditures (in millions)*
Citizens for Better Medicare	$64
AFL-CIO	45
Coalition to Protect America's Health Care	30
National Rifle Association	25
U.S. Chamber of Commerce	15
Planned Parenthood Action Fund	14
Business Roundtable	13
Federation for American Immigration Reform	12
NAACP National Voter Fund	11
Americans for Job Security	10

SOURCE: Data from David B. Magleby, ed., *Election Advocacy: Soft Money and Issue Advocacy in the 2000 Congressional Elections* (Center for the Study of Elections and Democracy, Brigham Young University, 2001); Erika Falk, "Issue Advocacy Advertising Through the Presidential Primary, 1999–2000 Election Cycle," Annenberg Public Policy Center, press release, September 20, 2000.

The numbers estimate total spending on issue advocacy and express advocacy; however, a large proportion went to issue advocacy.

Seniors, a group largely funded by the pharmaceutical industry. United Seniors ran ads in several competitive races. By masking its identity, the pharmaceutical industry could present its message without a stigma. Voters have an unfavorable impression of the pharmaceutical industry but know very little about United Seniors. Other groups that engaged in substantial issue advocacy in 2002 included the Sierra Club, Planned Parenthood, and Club for Growth. These ads not only help the candidate that interest groups prefer or punish the candidate they oppose but also force candidates to discuss the interest group's agenda. Although these ads do not specifically say to vote for or against a candidate, they may contain candidates' images and names, and for voters they are indistinguishable from candidate or party ads.[54] The Bipartisan Campaign Finance Reform Act of 2002 bans broadcast ads that show the image or likeness of a candidate, mention a candidate's name, and occur in the 60 days before a general election or 30 days before a primary election not paid for with disclosed money. This act also bans unions and corporations from using treasury funds for issue ads.

The use of issue ads and the growth in soft money meant that competitive congressional elections shifted from candidate-centered elections to party-centered and interest group–centered campaigns.[55] Soft money spending combined with interest group issue advocacy spending exceeded the candidate campaigns in radio and television advertising by a margin of 2 to 1 in 17 of the most competitive congressional races of 2000.[56] Parties and interest groups also spend large sums of money on mailings and telephone calls. For example, in some congressional races in 2000, targeted voters received as many as 12 pieces of political mail per day as election day approached. The intensity of issue advocacy and soft money-funded communications in competitive races in 2002 was again extraordinary. In contests like the South Dakota Senate race, hour-long programs could have had only political commericals. Because television time was sold out, some groups purchased radio time. Others turned to mail. Many groups with membership lists used these for personal contact and get-out-the-vote efforts.[57]

One of the problems with issue ads is accountability. Since interest groups using this form of electioneering are not required to disclose how much they spend or how they raise their money, voters have a hard time knowing the source of the funds. Ads by these groups also tend to be more negative.[58] Often candidates get blamed for the attacks made by these groups because voters assume that the ads are run by the candidates.

One predictable consequence of the 2002 campaign finance reform ban on soft money was increased interest group electioneering via issue advocacy in 2004. The most visible of these new electioneering groups is America Coming Together (ACT),

Issue ads, such as this one used by the U.S. Chamber of Commerce to promote pro-business candidates, try to influence voters in their favor.

which raised and spent a little under an estimated $61.9 million in presidential bat-tleground states in 2004. The advent of groups like ACT, while benefitting John Kerry and the Democrats, constitutes a shift in power toward groups and away from candi-dates and parties.

The group that may have had the greatest impact on the campaign were the Swift Boat Veterans for Truth, who attacked Senator Kerry's war record. Their modest initial ad budget generated considerable news coverage. The message of the ads cut to the core of the persona that Kerry had presented at the Democratic National Convention.

Defenders of issue ads point to recent ad campaigns that focused on legislation, like those mounted by tobacco companies in 1998 to defeat a tobacco tax in the Senate or ads run by insurance companies attacking the Clinton health care plan in 1994. Pro-ponents of unlimited issue advocacy claim that it should be protected as free speech. Drawing a distinction between genuine issue advocacy and election issue advocacy is not easy, but voters clearly see a difference.[59]

The 2002 reforms did not address the fund-raising advantages enjoyed by incum-bents. Hence it is not only the source of campaign money that is a problem but the pat-tern of unequal distribution as well. The high costs of television advertising diminish the ability of challengers to mount visible campaigns, resulting in declining competition. Only months after passage of the 2002 reforms, John McCain announced his support and sponsorship of legislation creating a "broadcast bank" where political parties would be given vouchers for free advertising time, with one-third of the time to go to challengers. Television stations, under McCain's proposal, are required to devote at least two hours per week to political coverage in which the candidates are on camera during the last month of the general election campaign.[60]

CANDIDATES' PERSONAL WEALTH   Campaign finance legislation cannot constitutionally restrict rich candidates—the Rockefellers, the Kennedys, the Perots—from giving heavily to their own campaigns. Big money can make a big difference, and wealthy candidates can afford to spend big money. In presidential politics, this advantage can be most meaningful in the period before the primaries begin. There may be no constitutional way to limit how much money people can spend on their own campaigns. The 2000 New Jersey U.S. Senate race set new records for a candidate's spending personal wealth in an election. Wall Street investment banker Jon Corzine, a newcomer to elections, spent a total of $60 million, $35 million of it on the primary alone.[61] Corzine was elected. The 2002 reforms do not alter the millionaire's loophole.

INDEPENDENT EXPENDITURES   Current finance laws, including the 2002 campaign finance reforms, do not constrain **independent expenditures** by groups or individuals who are separate from political candidates. This exemption was permitted by the Supreme Court on free speech grounds. Groups sympathetic to but independent of candidates are allowed to raise and spend unlimited funds to help elect candidates or to defeat their opponents. In the 1999–2000 election cycle, interest groups spent a total of $22 million on independent expenditures. The National Rifle Association (NRA) led all other interest groups

independent expenditures
Money spent by individuals or groups not associated with candidates to elect or defeat candidates for office.

IN COMPARATIVE PERSPECTIVE

Campaign Financing in Britain and Canada

United States election campaigns go on for months or even years and are very expensive. In contrast, Canadian general election campaigns are limited by law to about five weeks. Public opinion polls cannot be published during the last three days of a campaign, and the media are prohibited by law from reporting results from earlier time zones on the evening of the election in any district where voting is still taking place.

Expenditures are strictly limited for Canadian political parties and individual candidates. During the 1997 general election campaign to fill the 301 seats in the House of Commons, political parties that fielded candidates in all districts were limited by law to spending no more than approximately $8 million each for the entire election, and individual candidates could spend about $35,000 to $45,000, depending on the number of voters per district. In return, media outlets were required to sell a certain amount of airtime to the parties, and national and regional television and radio networks had to donate some free airtime to these parties. If individual candidates received more than 15 percent of the vote in their districts, the government reimbursed 50 percent of their election-related expenses. Political parties receiving at least 2 percent of the national vote or at least 5 percent of the votes cast in electoral districts where they ran candidates were reimbursed 22.5 percent of their expenses.

In the June 1997 Canadian elections, 1,672 candidates ran for office, and ten political parties received registered status. Total spending by the parliamentary candidates and political parties was approximately $70 million—less than half the $157 million spent by candidates in the United States during the 1996 election campaign ($29 million on seats in the House of Representatives and $128 million on seats in the Senate).

British general elections also offer an interesting contrast to elections in the United States. The election campaign lasts only three weeks. Candidates for the House of Commons, the most critical election in Britain, are allowed to raise and spend only $15,000. If they spend more, they are disqualified. Each candidate gets the same amount of free airtime, and each candidate is allowed one free election leaflet mailed to each voter in the constituency. About 75 percent of voters turn out, and about 95 percent of eligible voters are registered to vote. At the voting booth, the voter is handed a slip of paper with the names of three or four candidates for the House of Commons. No other offices or ballot questions are presented at the same time.

SOURCE: Adapted from Dudley Fishburn, "British Campaigning—How Civilized!" *New York Times*, April 14, 1992, p. 25.

Candidates willing to spend personal wealth on their campaign enjoy important advantages. They are not subject to the contribution limitations imposed on other individuals. New Jersey Senator Jon Corzine spent $60 million of his own money on his 2000 race. Corzine was selected by the Democratic leadership to head the Democratic Senatorial Campaign Committee for 2003–2004.

with $4.2 million mostly for Republicans, but the League of Conservation Voters ($3.2 million), the National Education Association (NEA) ($2.4 million), and the National Abortion and Reproductive Rights Action League ($2.2 million) all combined to spend $7.8 million, mostly on behalf of Democrats. Individuals can also engage in independent expenditures. In the 2000 presidential election, Stephen Adams, owner of an outdoor advertising firm, spent $2 million in support of Governor George W. Bush.[62] As long as there is no collusion or coordination between the independent spender and the candidate, an individual or PAC can spend an unlimited amount of money for or against a candidate.

Issue ads have largely replaced independent expenditures in recent election cycles because interest groups can spend the same amount of money without having to disclose the activity. Some groups like the NRA and the NEA continue to use independent expenditures, however, perhaps because they want to urge voters to "vote for" or "vote against" specific candidates, words that cannot appear in an issue ad. But most groups, including several who have never engaged in independent expenditures, have adopted issue advocacy; they want to try to help elect or defeat a candidate. Should the Supreme Court uphold the 2002 campaign finance reform law's provisions about issue ads, some of this activity is likely to shift to independent expenditures. If the court upholds the soft money ban but strikes the issue advocacy provision of the law, there will likely be a surge in issue advocacy.

Continuing Problems with Campaign Finance

The continuing problems with federal election fund raising are easy to identify: dramatically escalating costs, a growing dependence on PAC money, decreasing visibility and competitiveness of challengers (especially in the House), and the ability of wealthy individuals to fund their own campaigns. The danger of large contributions altering election outcomes was reduced through the recently enacted soft money ban and limitations placed on issue advocacy.

TABLE 9–2 Average Campaign Expenditures of Candidates for the House of Representatives, 1988–2002 General Election (in thousands of 2002 dollars)

	Incumbent	Challenger	Open Seat
Republican			
1988	$603.1	$148.0	$1,201.8
1990	531.1	147.8	1,109.1
1992	660.7	234.6	778.2
1994	541.7	281.4	1,189.3
1996	820.3	234.9	699.0
1998	715.5	262.2	758.6
2000	944.5	331.7	1,283.6
2002	860.9	188.3	1,080.0
Democrat			
1988	$528.0	$211.9	$658.9
1990	536.2	147.4	714.3
1992	751.6	199.8	599.2
1994	711.3	186.3	684.2
1996	635.1	329.4	698.0
1998	577.1	249.1	759.3
2000	787.0	485.6	1,176.7
2002	785.1	313.4	1,020.6

SOURCE: Federal Election Commission, "Congressional Fundraising and Spending Up Again in 1996," press release, April 14, 1997, p. 13; Federal Election Commission, "1998 Congressional Financial Activity Declines," press release, December 29, 1998, p. 5; Federal Election Commission, at ftp.fec.gov/fec.

RISING COSTS OF CAMPAIGNS   The American ideal that anyone—even a person of modest wealth—can run for public office has become more a myth than a reality. And rising costs also mean that incumbents spend more time raising funds and therefore less time legislating and representing their districts. Since the Federal Election Campaign Act became law in 1972, total expenditures by candidates for the House of Representatives have more than doubled after controlling for inflation, and they have risen even more in Senate elections (see Table 9-2). One reason for escalating costs is television. Organizing and running a campaign is expensive, limiting the field of challengers to those who have resources of their own or are willing to spend more than a year raising money from interest groups and individuals.

DECLINING COMPETITION   Unless something is done to help finance challengers, incumbents will continue to have the advantage in seeking reelection. Nothing in the 2002 legislation addresses this problem. Challengers in both parties are typically underfunded. House Democratic challengers averaged $168,650 in spending in 2000.[63] House Democratic challengers raised on average $384,081 in 2002. In today's expensive campaigns, candidates are invisible if they can spend only $200,000 or $300,000.

The high cost of campaigns dampens competition by discouraging individuals from running for office. Potential challengers look at the fund-raising advantages enjoyed by incumbents—at incumbents' campaign war chests carried over from previous campaigns, which can reach $1 million or more, and at the time it will take for them to raise enough money to launch a minimal campaign—and they decide to direct their energies elsewhere. Moreover, unlike incumbents, who are being paid while campaigning and raising money, most challengers have to support themselves and their families throughout the campaign, which for a seat in Congress lasts roughly two years.

INCREASING DEPENDENCE ON PACS AND WEALTHY DONORS   Where does the money come from to finance these expensive election campaigns? For most House incumbents, it comes from political action committees (PACs), which we discussed in Chapter 6. In 2000, for instance, 191 of the 408 incumbents seeking reelection raised more money from PACs than from individuals (see Figure 9-5).[64] In 2002, 186 of the 408 incumbents seeking reelection raised more money from PACs than from individuals. Senators get a smaller percentage of their campaign funds from PACs, but because they spend so much more, they need to raise even more money from PACs than House incumbents do. PACs are pragmatic, giving largely to incumbents. Challengers receive little from PACs because PACs do not want to offend politicians in power. The 2002 legislation raised the individual contribution limit to a candidate in the two-year campaign cycle to $4,000, still well below the PAC contribution limit for an election cycle of $10,000. Some individuals who formerly gave $2,000 will now double their contribution to particular candidates, but politicians will continue to rely on PACs because relatively few individuals have the means to give this much money. It also often takes less time to raise money from PACs than from individuals.

To be sure, PACs and individuals give money to campaigns, including issue advocacy, for many reasons. Most of them want certain laws to be passed or repealed, certain funds to be appropriated, or certain administrative decisions to be rendered. At a minimum, they want access to officeholders, a chance to talk with members before key votes.

Defenders of PACs point out that there is no demonstrable relationship between contributions and legislators' votes. But influence in the legislative process depends on access to staff and members of Congress, and most analysts agree that campaign contributions give donors extraordinary access. PACs influence the legislative process in other ways as well. Their access helps them structure the legislative agenda with friendly legislators and influence the drafting of legislation or amendments to existing bills. These are all advantages that others do not have.

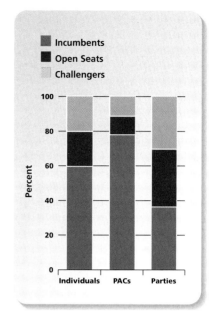

FIGURE 9–5   PAC Money Favors Incumbents.

Source: Federal Election Commission, at ftp.fec.gov/fec.

Improving Elections

A combination of party rules and state laws determines how we choose nominees for president. Reformers agree that the current process is flawed but disagree over which aspects require change. Concern over how we choose presidents now centers on four issues[65]: (1) the number, timing, and representativeness of presidential primaries; (2) the role of the electoral college, including the possibility that a presidential election might be thrown into the House of Representatives; (3) how we vote; and (4) how we fund presidential elections.

Reforming Presidential Primaries

Presidential primaries open the nominating process to more voters than caucus or convention methods for selecting presidential candidates do. Today, the media play up the primary in every important state, and voters follow the races in other states as well as their own. In so doing, they can judge the candidates' political qualities: their abilities to organize campaigns, communicate through the media, stand up under pressure, avoid making mistakes (or recover if they do make them), adjust their appeals to shifting events and to different regions of the country, control their staffs as well as make good use of them, and be decisive, articulate, resilient, humorous, informed, and ultimately successful in winning votes. In short, supporters claim, primaries test candidates on the very qualities they must exhibit in the presidency.[66]

Critics of primaries grant that more voters take part in primaries than in the caucus and convention methods of choosing delegates, but they question the quality of the participation. For one thing, supporters of the different candidates have no opportunity to deliberate together in public. Voters in caucuses can argue and persuade one another in small meetings; voters in primaries must depend largely on the news media and advertising for their information and basis for judgment. Voters in primaries tend to be more influenced by candidates' personalities and media skills than their positions on vital issues.[67] Participation in primaries has been low in recent years (see Figure 9-6). In the 2000 primaries, turnout was generally under 18 percent of the voting-age population, and it declined as the primary season progressed and the field of candidates narrowed.[68] Low levels

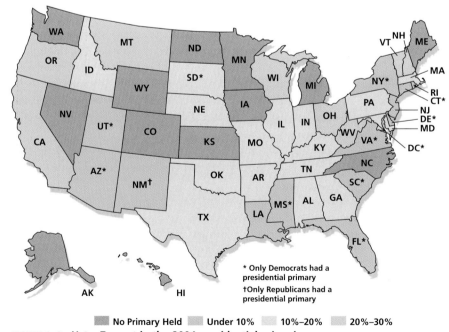

* Only Democrats had a presidential primary

†Only Republicans had a presidential primary

No Primary Held   Under 10%   10%–20%   20%–30%

FIGURE 9–6   Voter Turnout in the 2004 presidential primaries.

SOURCE: Data is based on the voting age population of each state and has been collected from the following sources: Dr. Michael McDonald, Department of Public and International Affairs, George Mason University; Curtis B. Gans, Director, Committee for the Study of the American Electorate, in a facsimile to the author on September 22, 2004; the secretary of state Web sites for each state; the Federal Election Commission.

of turnout in primaries open the possibility that extreme groups will have a dispropor-tionate say; the "selectorate" replaces the electorate. In addition, candidates are forced to appeal to highly motivated voters, usually from the conservative wing of the Republican party and the liberal wing of the Democratic party.

For many years, the primary season was criticized for being too long.[69] Some states, by virtue of coming early in the process, had a disproportionate say in determining the nominee and therefore were more influential with presidents. Several states moved up their primary dates in 2000 so that 48 percent of the Republican and 37 percent of the De-mocratic delegates were selected by March 7.[70] Not surprisingly, Al Gore and George W. Bush had their nominations locked up by this date. States that came later in the process found that the nominee had already been selected.

Finally, some critics question whether primaries test the qualities needed to be pres-ident. To win the "media game," candidates must be witty, resourceful, attractive, and ar-ticulate—not necessarily the most important qualities to be a good president. Thomas Jefferson, Abraham Lincoln, and Harry Truman were able presidents, but how much "media appeal" would they have in the age of television? Critics are disturbed by the gap between the qualities required to carry primary contests and the qualities needed to gov-ern: to organize an administration, get support on issues, make hard decisions, and deal with congressional leaders, governors, and mayors.

Reforming the Nominating Process

What would the critics substitute for state presidential primaries? Some argue in favor of a *national presidential primary* that would take the form of a single nationwide election, probably held in May or September, or separate state primaries held in all the states on the same day.[71] Supporters contend that a one-shot national presidential primary (though a runoff might be necessary) would be simple, direct, and representative. It would cut down the wear-and-tear on candidates, and it would attract a large turnout because of media cov-erage. Opponents argue that such a reform would make the present system even worse. It would enhance the role of showmanship and gamesmanship, and being enormously ex-pensive, it would hurt the chances of candidates who lack strong financial backing.

A more modest proposal is to hold *regional primaries,* possibly at two- or three-week intervals across the country. Regional primaries might bring more coherence to the process and encourage more emphasis on issues of regional concern. But such primaries would retain most of the disadvantages of the present system—especially the emphasis on money and media. Clearly, they would give an advantage to candidates from whatever region held the first primary, and this advantage would encourage regional candidates and might increase polarization among sections of the country.

A different proposal is to drastically reduce the number of presidential primaries and make more use of the caucus system. The turnout of voters in the Iowa caucuses in recent elections shows that participation can be high, and the time participants spent discussing candidates and issues shows that such participation can be thoughtful and in-formed. In caucus states, candidates are less dependent on the media and more depend-ent on convincing political activists. By centering delegate selection in party meetings, the caucus system would also, some say, enhance the role of the party.[72]

Still another idea—used by Colorado for nominations to state offices and by Utah for nominations to federal and state offices—would turn the process around. Beginning in May, local caucuses and then state conventions would be held in every state. They would then send delegates—a certain percentage of whom would be unpledged to any presiden-tial candidate—to the national party conventions, which would be held in the summer. The national conventions would select two or three candidates to compete in a national pri-mary to be held in September. In this plan, voters registered by party would be allowed to vote for their party nominee in the September primaries.[73] Such a plan would likely add voter engagement in the party process but also be more expensive as candidates would mount two national campaigns, one in September and another in November.

Reforming the Electoral College

The Florida ballot counting and recounting at the close of the 2000 election and the fact that the popular vote winner did not become president prompted a national debate on the electoral college. The most frequently proposed reform of the electoral college system is *direct popular election* of the president. Presidents would be elected directly by the voters, just as governors are, and the electoral college and individual electors would be abolished. Such proposals usually provide that if no candidate receives at least 40 percent of the total popular vote, a *runoff election* would be held between the two contenders with the most votes. Supporters argue that direct election would give every voter the same weight in the presidential balloting in accordance with the one-person, one-vote doctrine. Winners would take on more legitimacy because their victories would reflect the will of the voters.

Opponents contend that the plan would further undermine federalism, encourage unrestrained majority rule and hence political extremism, and hurt the smaller states, which would lose some of their present influence. Others fear that the plan would make presidential campaigns more remote from the voters; candidates might stress television and give up their forays into shopping centers and city malls.[74]

From time to time, Congress considers proposals for a constitutional amendment to elect presidents directly. Such proposals, however, seldom get far because of the strong opposition of various interests that believe they may be disadvantaged by such a change, especially small states and minority groups whose role is enlarged by the electoral college. Groups such as African Americans and farmers, for example, fear they might lose their swing vote power—their ability to make a difference in key states that may tip the electoral college balance.

Another alternative to the electoral college is sometimes called the National Bonus Plan. This plan adds to the current 538 electoral college members another 102 electoral votes, to be awarded on a winner-take-all basis to the candidate with the most votes, so long as that candidate received more than 40 percent of the popular vote. This system would avoid elections' being thrown into the House of Representatives and would help the popular vote winner take over the White House. The most serious liabilities of the plan are that it is complicated and that it requires a runoff election if there is no winner.

Finally, two states, Maine and Nebraska, have already modified the electoral college, adopting a district system in which the candidate who carries each congressional district gets that electoral vote and the candidate who carries the state gets the state's two additional electoral votes. This quasi-proportional representation system has the advantage of not shutting out a candidate who is strong in some areas of a state but not others, but otherwise it does not address the larger concerns with the electoral college.

The failure of attempts to change the system of elections points to an important conclusion about procedural reform: Americans normally do not focus on procedures. Only after an electoral college crisis like the one we experienced in 2000 is any significant change likely. As the crucial importance of ballot counts dragged on, citizens focused on actual problems with the electoral system, not on hypothetical problems discussed by political scientists and democratic theorists.

Reforming How We Vote

The 2000 presidential election ended with a monthlong controversy over ballots and how to count them. While Florida became the focal point of national and international attention with its problems with punch-card ballots, dangling chads, voter confusion over ballot formats, and when to count or not count absentee ballots, such problems are common to all 50 states. As we noted earlier, election administration is a state and local matter, and election law is constitutionally assigned to the individual states.

Following the 2000 election, the state of Florida enacted legislation modernizing its election process and establishing minimum standards for polling places and voting machines. These standards include certification of electronic voting machines and requirements for the use and storage of these machines. Despite this legislation and spending more than $30 million on the new electronic machines, their first use in the 2002 primary reminded many of the problems with punch card ballots in 2000. Some new machines failed to record votes, others had too many votes, and precint workers were not adequately prepared to help voters with the new technology. At the national level, both houses of Congress passed legislation providing $3.9 billion in federal funds to modernize how Americans vote, mandating that states maintain accurate statewide voter registration lists.

The changes considered by Congress in election administration are just the start of a broader effort to modernize democracy. It is likely that state legislatures and Congress will debate permitting people to vote via the Internet. The argument will be that if people can make purchases over the Internet, why not let them vote electronically as well. Some states experimented with "e-voting" on a small scale in presidential primaries in 2000. A shift to e-voting is in some respects an extension of the Oregon vote-by-mail experience since 1996. Yet critics worry that important elements of community and democracy are lost when people do not vote collectively at the local schoolhouse or fire station. Another concern with e-voting is that it may encourage a proliferation of elections and direct democracy. If we can vote from home, why not vote on more things and more often? E-voting could also foster a political culture of more and more ballot referendums.

The touch-screen voting machine is an example of a new way for voters to register their choice. This computerized machine prevents voters from choosing more than one candidate, as many did erroneously during the 2000 election in Florida.

Reforming Campaign Finance

The campaign finance reforms of 2002 and subsequent court decisions about them will set the ground rules for only a short time before campaign finance reform is again an issue. This is because those who want to influence the outcome of elections and the consultants who spend their money are creative in getting around the rules. It is also because the federal agency charged with administering these rules is often deadlocked. Finally, those who wanted more fundamental reforms—such as public financing—will continue to press for their more comprehensive solutions. At the same time, those who favor deregulation of campaign finance will seek to overturn the 2002 reforms in favor of a system of disclosure without limits. The 2002 reforms ignored the major problems with the presidential campaign finance system, including the declining level of participation in the tax checkoff, the unreasonably low state-by-state spending limits for presidential nominations in the early contests, and the probability that candidates will choose to bypass the system in the nomination phase altogether, as George W. Bush did in 2000. These and other problems that will arise with the implementation of the 2002 act are likely to keep campaign finance reform an important topic for the next few years at least.

ELECTION IN ACTION: 2004 PRESIDENTIAL ELECTION

Try your hand as the campaign manager for either major party candidate in the 2004 presidential campaign. You will make the strategic decisions that guide your candidate to victory. As you travel through the virtual process of coordinating campaign advertisements, budgeting the available funds through election day, and deciding which states to travel to, you will better understand the impact of the electoral college and the work that goes into electing a president of the United States.

Go to PoliSim "Election in Action: 2004 Presidential Election."

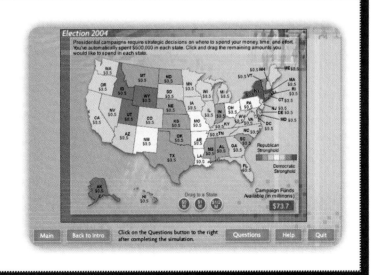

Summary

1. American elections, even presidential elections, are largely governed by state law and administered by local election officials. Following the 2000 elections, governments at all levels began to look for ways to improve the system.

2. Our electoral system is based on winner-take-all rules, with typically single-member-district or single-officeholder arrangements. These rules encourage a moderate, two-party system. That we have fixed and staggered terms of office adds predictability to our electoral system.

3. The electoral college is the means by which presidents are actually elected. To win a state's electoral votes, a candidate must have a plurality of votes in that state. Except in two states, the winner takes all. Thus candidates cannot afford to lose the popular vote in the most populous states. The electoral college also gives disproportionate power to the largest states and has the potential to defeat the popular vote winner.

4. Many congressional, state, and local races are not seriously contested. The extent to which a campaign is likely to be hotly contested varies with the importance of the office and the chance a challenger has of winning. Senate races are more likely to be contested, though most incumbents win.

5. The race for the presidency actually takes place in three stages: winning enough delegate support in presidential primaries and caucuses to secure the nomination, campaigning at the national party convention, and mobilizing voters for a win in the electoral college.

6. Even though presidential nominations today are usually decided weeks or months before the national party conventions, these conventions still have an important role in setting the parties' direction, unifying their ranks, and firing up enthusiasm.

7. Because large campaign contributors are suspected of improperly influencing public officials, Congress has long sought to regulate political contributions. The main approaches to reform have been (1) imposing limitations on giving, receiving, and spending political money; (2) requiring public disclosure of the sources and uses of political money; and (3) giving governmental subsidies to presidential candidates, campaigns, and parties, including incentive arrangements. Present regulation includes all three approaches.

8. Loopholes in federal law—including soft money, issue advocacy, and independent expenditures—and rising costs of campaigns have led to declining competition for congressional seats and increasing dependence on PACs and wealthy donors.

9. The present presidential selection system is under criticism because of its length and expense, because of uncertainties and biases in the electoral college, and because it seems to test candidates for media skills less needed in the White House than the ability to govern, including the capacity to form coalitions and make hard decisions.

10. Reform efforts center on presidential primaries and the electoral college as well as on voting methods and campaign finance.

Key Terms

winner-take-all system
single-member district
proportional representation

electoral college
safe seat
coattail effect

caucus
national party convention
interested money

soft money
issue advocacy
independent expenditures

Further Reading

R. MICHAEL ALVAREZ, *Information and Elections* (University of Michigan Press, 1998).

LARRY M. BARTELS, *Presidential Primaries and the Dynamics of Public Choice* (Princeton University Press, 1988).

LARRY M. BARTELS AND LYNN VAVRECK, EDS., *Campaign Reform: Insights and Evidence* (University of Michigan Press, 2000).

JUDITH A. BEST, *The Choice of the People? Debating the Electoral College* (Rowman & Littlefield, 1996).

EARL BLACK AND MERLE BLACK, *The Vital South: How Presidents Are Elected* (Harvard University Press, 1992).

DAVID W. BRADY, JOHN F. COGAN, AND MORRIS P. FIORINA, EDS., *Continuity and Change in House Elections* (Stanford University Press, 2000).

ANDREW E. BUSH, *Horses in Midstream: U.S. Midterm Elections and Their Consequences, 1894–1998* (University of Pittsburgh Press, 2000).

LINDA L. FOWLER AND ROBERT D. MCCLURE, *Political Ambition: Who Decides to Run for Congress* (Yale University Press, 1993).

RONALD KEITH GADDIE AND CHARLES S. BULLOCK III, EDS., *Elections to Open Seats in the U.S. House: Where the Action Is* (Rowman & Littlefield, 2000).

THOMAS GAIS, *Improper Influence: Campaign Finance Law, Political Interest Groups, and the Problem of Equality* (University of Michigan Press, 1996).

PAUL GRONKE, *The Electorate, the Campaign, and the Office: A Unified Approach to Senate and House Elections* (University of Michigan Press, 2000).

RODERICK P. HART, *Campaign Talk* (Princeton University Press, 2000).

RODERICK P. HART AND DARON SHAW, EDS., *Communication in U.S. Elections* (Rowman & Littlefield, 2001).

PAUL S. HERRNSON, *Playing Hardball: Campaigning for the U.S. Congress* (Prentice Hall, 2000).

PAUL S. HERRNSON, *Congressional Elections: Campaigning at Home and in Washington,* 3d ed. (CQ Press, 2000).

GARY C. JACOBSON, *The Politics of Congressional Elections,* 5th ed. (Longman, 2000).

KATHLEEN HALL JAMIESON, *Everything You Think You Know About Politics . . . and Why You're Wrong* (Basic Books, 2000).

KATHLEEN HALL JAMIESON AND PAUL WALDMAN, EDS., *Electing the President, 2000: The Insiders' View—Election Strategy from Those Who Made It* (University of Pennsylvania Press, 2001).

KIM F. KAHN AND PATRICK J. KENNEDY, *The Spectacle of U.S. Senate Campaigns* (Princeton University Press, 1999).

DAVID LUBLIN, *The Paradox of Representation: Racial Gerrymandering and Minority Interests in Congress* (Princeton University Press, 1997).

LOUIS SANDY MAISEL, *Parties and Elections in America: The Electoral Process* (Altamira Press, 2001).

DAVID B. MAGLEBY, ED., *Financing the 2000 Election* (Brookings Institution, 2002).

DAVID B. MAGLEBY, ED., *The Other Campaign: Soft Money and Issue Advocacy in the 2000 Congressional Elections* (Rowman & Littlefield, 2003).

STEPHEN K. MEDVIC, *Political Consultants in U.S. Congressional Elections* (Ohio State University Press, 2001).

JOHN J. PITNEY JR., *The Art of Political Warfare* (University of Oklahoma Press, 2000).

POLITICAL STAFF OF THE *WASHINGTON POST, Deadlock: The Inside Story of America's Closest Election* (Public Affairs, 2001).

NELSON W. POLSBY AND AARON B. WILDAVSKY, *Presidential Elections: Contemporary Strategies of American Politics,* 10th ed. (Chatham House, 2000).

SAMUEL L. POPKIN, *The Reasoning Voter: Communication and Persuasion in Presidential Campaigns,* 2nd ed. (University of Chicago Press, 1994).

JACK N. RAKOVE, ED., *The Unfinished Election of 2000* (Basic Books, 2001).

PAUL D. SCHUMAKER AND BURDETT A. LOOMIS, EDS., *Choosing a President: The Electoral College and Beyond* (Seven Bridges Press, 2002).

JAMES A. THURBER, ED., *The Battle for Congress: Consultants, Candidates, and Voters* (Brookings Institution Press, 2001).

JAMES A. THURBER AND CANDICE J. NELSON, EDS., *Campaign Warriors: Political Consultants in Elections* (Brookings Institution, 2000).

JAMES A. THURBER, CANDICE J. NELSON, AND DAVID A. DULIO, EDS., *Crowded Airwaves: Campaign Advertising in Elections* (Brookings Institution, 2000).

STEPHEN J. WAYNE, *The Road to the White House, 2000: The Politics of Presidential Elections* (St. Martin's Press, 2000).

STEPHEN J. WAYNE AND CLYDE WILCOX, EDS., *The Election of the Century and What It Tells Us About the Future of American Politics* (Sharpe, 2002).

See also *Public Opinion Quarterly, the American Journal of Politics,* and *American Political Science Review.*

10
CHAPTER

THE MEDIA
AND AMERICAN
POLITICS

AT 7:50 P.M. (EST) ON ELECTION NIGHT, NOVEMBER 7, 2000, TELEVISION NETWORKS PROJECTED AL GORE AS THE WINNER OF FLORIDA; they soon had second thoughts and revoked their announcement. At 2:16 A.M. (EST), Fox News projected George W. Bush as winning Florida and, based on electoral votes, the presidency. Within minutes, the other networks followed. The truth was that the vote in Florida was by every measure too close to call, and no network should have called the race. In the days and weeks after the election, the Voter News Service, which conducts exit polls for the television networks and some newspapers, admitted that its Florida sample was flawed, that it underestimated the Florida absentee vote, and that it relied on incomplete actual vote totals.[1] The mistaken projections by the networks were embarrassing. Tom Brokaw of NBC said, "That's not 'an egg' on our faces; that's 'an omelet.'"[2]

Executives at Fox News, the first to call Florida for Bush, were on the defensive not only for their mistaken call but because Bush's cousin John Ellis was in charge of the analysts that called the state, placing him in a clear conflict of interest. Also troubling were reports that Ellis was on the phone with both the candidate, George W. Bush, governor of Texas, and his brother Jeb Bush, governor of Florida, throughout the evening, presumably sharing exit poll data with his cousins.

Republicans had their own complaints about the networks. The networks projecting Gore as having carried Florida before the polls had closed in western Florida prompted Republicans to charge that the networks had depressed turnout in the most Republican part of the state. Since the 1980 election, the networks generally followed the practice of not calling a state before the polls had closed in that state, and the embarrassment of the 2000 election night will likely reinforce that practice in the future. Republican Representative Billy Tauzin, who chairs the House Commerce Subcommittee on Telecommunications, believed that election night coverage was biased toward Gore and suggested that networks were reluctant to call states for Bush in hopes that Bush supporters would be discouraged and not vote.

Election night projections were not the only controversy about the role of the media in the 2000 elections. Republicans charged a clear media bias in favor of Democrats, especially Al Gore. Democrats, not surprisingly, saw the media as overlooking or downplaying Bush's mistakes.[3] Democrats thought journalists favored Bush and Gore in roughly the same proportions, while Republicans overwhelmingly thought reporters favored Gore.[4]

In 2002, the media exit polls failed completely. On election day, the networks that sponsor the Voter News Service (VNS), which conducts the media exit polling, announced that they would not be releasing exit poll numbers nor would they be projecting winners. Following the 2000 election and the controversy over the Florida exit polling, VNS invested in new computers and software and developed new models to projects winners. They gathered data on election day but did not have confidence in their ability to accurately predict contests. Viewers on election night 2002 thus got what many had wanted, a night with only local exit polling. The absence of exit polling data, however, meant it was hard to assess the national mood and which types of people actually voted.

Media coverage of the 2000 election and its aftermath in Florida demonstrates the public's tremendous appetite for instant news and analysis, at least when it comes to a crisis or major controversy. Americans spend on average an hour a day consuming news, and the older they are, the more time they devote to it.[5] Yet people are quick to criticize the media. Writes journalist James Fallows, "Americans have never been truly fond of their press. Through the last decade, however, their disdain for the media establishment has reached new levels. Americans believe that the news media have become too arrogant, cynical, scandal-minded, and destructive."[6]

How often have you or your friends blamed the media for being biased, criticized the frenzy that surrounds a particular story, or denounced the "if it bleeds, it leads" mentality of nightly television news? Yet the content and style of news coverage is driven by market research in which viewers and readers are asked what they want to see reported and how they want it presented. Advertising revenue is closely linked to the number of readers or viewers a media outlet has.

Media bashing has become something of a national pastime. People often blame the media for many of our ills—increasing tension between the races, biased attacks on public officials, sleaze and sensationalism, increased violence in our society—and for being more interested in making money than in conveying information. Many in the media even agree with these charges.[7] But complaints about the media may simply be a case of criticizing the messenger in order to avoid dealing with the message. Comments like "It's the media's fault that we have lost our social values" or "The media's preoccupation with the private lives of politicians turns Americans off to politics" are overly broad assertions. Americans tend to blame far more problems on the media than are warranted.

The Influence of the Media on Politics

The media, in particular the print media, have been called the "fourth estate," and the "fourth branch of government."[8] Evidence that the media influence our culture and politics is plentiful. The **mass media**—newspapers and magazines, radio, television (broadcast, cable, and satellite), films, recordings, books, and electronic communication—are the means of communication that reach the mass public.[9] The **news media** are the mass media vehicles that emphasize the news, although the distinctions between entertainment and news are sometimes blurred. News programs often have entertainment value, and entertainment programs often convey news. Programs in this latter category include TV newsmagazines such as *60 Minutes, 20/20, Dateline,* and talk shows with hosts like Larry King, Oprah Winfrey, and Jon Stewart.

By definition, the mass media disseminate messages to a large and often heterogeneous audience. Because they must have broad appeal, their messages are often simplified, stereotyped, and predictable. The mass media make money by appealing to large numbers of people. But do large audiences equal political clout? Two factors are important in answering this question: the media's pervasiveness and their role as a linking mechanism between politicians and government officials and the public.

mass media
Means of communication that reach the mass public, including newspapers and magazines, radio, television (broadcast, cable, and satellite), films, recordings, books, and electronic communication.

news media
Media that emphasizes the news.

For over forty years, Americans have been getting their news primarily from television. Whenever there is a crisis, most people turn first to television for information. No event in recent history has done more to underscore the importance of television as the primary source of news in contemporary U.S. society than the terrorist attacks that took place on September 11, 2001.

Where do Americans get their news? Until 1960, most people got their news from newspapers. Today, although many people use several sources, they rely primarily on television. Whenever there is a crisis—the terrorist attacks on the World Trade Center in New York and the Pentagon in Washington, D.C., on September 11, 2001, is the ultimate example—people are glued to their TV sets.

The World Wide Web is becoming an increasingly important source of news for Americans, taking its place alongside print, radio, and television. The number of Americans going online for news is growing dramatically and promises to become even more important as candidates and issue advocates pay increasing attention to the Web as a way to get their messages to the voting public.[10] Using the Web as a news source permits the user to obtain information on only the topics or issues desired and from multiple sources. It also means the user can access the news from multiple locations and at convenient times.

The Pervasiveness of Television

Television has changed American politics more than any other invention. Most Americans watch some kind of television news every day. The average American watches television $4\frac{1}{2}$ hours a day, and most homes have more than two sets.[11] Television provides instant access to news from around the country and the globe, permitting citizens and leaders alike to observe, firsthand, a kidnapping in Southern California or a refugee crisis in Indonesia. This instant coverage increases the pressure on world leaders to respond quickly to crises, permits terrorists to gain widespread coverage of their actions, and elevates the role played by the president in both domestic and international politics.

The growth of around-the-clock cable news and information shows is one of the most important developments in recent years. Until the late 1980s, the network news programs on CBS, NBC, and ABC captured more than 90 percent of the audience for television news at set times in the morning and early evening hours. Owing to the rise of cable television and the advent of the Web, the broadcast networks now attract only about 50 percent of the viewing public, and more than half of the public are regular viewers of

President Bush surrounded by rescue workers at the scene of the World Trade Center disaster. Using a bullhorn to address the crowd and, indeed, the world, Bush projected an image of leadership and compassion by effectively manipulating the reins of the mass media.

CNN, CNBC, MSNBC, or Fox News.[12] In fact, cable news viewership was 44 percent higher in the first half of 2002 than it was in 2001.[13]

Satellites, cable television, computers, and videocassette recorders (VCRs) make vast amounts of political information available 24 hours a day. These technologies eliminate the obstacles of time and distance and increase the volume of information that can be stored, retrieved, and viewed. They have also reduced the impact of single sources of broadcast or cable news. Competition from cable stations for viewing has put pressure on broadcast networks to remain profitable, which has meant reduced budgets for news coverage and a tendency to look for ways of boosting the entertainment value of broadcast news.

One of the biggest changes in American electoral politics of the last half-century is that most voters now rely more on television commercials for information about candidates and issues and less on news coverage. Although debates and speeches by candidates generate coverage, the more pervasive battleground for votes is radio and TV ads. As a result, electoral campaigns now focus on image and slogans rather than on substance. Successful candidates must be able to communicate with voters through this medium. To get their message across to TV audiences, politicians increasingly rely on media advisers to define their opponent as well as themselves. These consultants also seek positive news coverage, but in many congressional campaigns, news coverage is fleeting.

The amount of television news devoted to politics has been declining and now constitutes less than one minute per half-hour broadcast.[14] A major effort to get local television stations to devote a few minutes to candidate debate in their nightly local news ended up with stations averaging 45 seconds a night, or as one observer put it, just enough time to "let candidates clear their throats."[15] In large urban areas, it is rare for viewers to see stories about their member of Congress, in part because there are several congressional districts in that media market. Newspapers do a better job of covering politics and devote more attention to it.

Interest groups advocating public policies—health care reform, trade agreements, opposition to affirmative action—also use paid advertising on television and radio to influence voters' choices on election day. This **issue advertising** permits groups to spend unlimited amounts of money so long as they do not explicitly call for the election or defeat of a candidate, as explained in our discussion of issue advocacy in Chapter 6. Interest groups have mounted expensive advertising campaigns on health care reform and gun legislation in an effort to sway votes in Congress, and in the weeks before recent general elections, they have spent millions to influence voters. In referendum elections, advertising is the most important source of information in voter decision making.[16] Passage of campaign finance reform in 2002 will likely only increase the amount of issue advocacy, especially through the mail and on the telephone. One part of the new law bans issue advocacy on television or radio that mentions a candidate by name in the two months before a general elections or one month before a primary election. If this provision withstands court challenge, it will force more and more interest group electioneering to the mail and telephone.

The Persistence of Radio

Television and the newer media have not displaced radio. On the contrary, radio continues to reach more American households than television does. Only one household in 100 does not have a radio, compared with four in 100 without a TV. Nine out of ten Americans listen to the radio every day.[17] Many Americans consider the radio an essential companion when driving. Americans get more than "the facts" from radio. They also get analysis and opinion from their favorite commentators and talk show hosts.

The Continuing Importance of Newspapers

Despite vigorous competition from radio and television, Americans still read newspapers. Daily newspaper circulation has been declining for the past 20 years to about 56 million nationwide—or about one copy for every four people.[18] The circulation figures for newspapers reflect a troubling decline in readership among younger persons: About 30 percent fewer young people read newspapers on a regular basis.[19]

issue advertising
Promoting a particular position or an issue paid for by interest groups or individuals but not candidates. Much issue advocacy is often electioneering for or against a candidate and, until 2004, had not been subject to any regulation.

In addition to metropolitan and local newspapers, we now have national ones. Created in 1982 by the Gannett Corporation, *USA Today,* with a circulation of more than 2.2 million, recently replaced the *Wall Street Journal* as America's top-circulating newspaper.[20] The *Wall Street Journal,* with a circulation of nearly 1.8 million, has long acted as a national newspaper specializing in business and finance. The *New York Times* has a national edition that is read by more than 1 million people.

The World Wide Web

From its humble beginnings as a Pentagon research project in the 1970s, the Web has blossomed into a global phenomenon. There are now more than 1 billion documents on the Web,[21] and more than 15 million unique domains have been registered worldwide. The Web opens up resources for citizens in dramatic ways. One study found that nearly half of Americans go online to search for news on a particular topic; somewhat smaller proportions go online for updates on stock quotes and sports scores. Fewer people use the Web as their primary source of news—29 percent.[22] Web users can also interact with other people or politicians about politics through electronic mail and chat rooms.

The Web is already a well-established means for accessing news. Many media (private and broadcast) outlets now have Web sites with 24-hour news, weather, and sports updates. An example of a Web-based news source is the Drudge Report. During the Clinton presidency, the Drudge Report was the first to break the story of President Clinton's affair with White House intern Monica Lewinsky.

The Web provides an inexpensive way to communicate with volunteers, contributors, and voters and promises to become an even larger component of campaigns in the future. Candidates maintain home pages where voters can learn about office seekers or ballot referendums. Former Minnesota governor Jesse Ventura and presidential primary contender John McCain effectively used the Web to get the word out to supporters about campaign events.

Extensive use of computers by young children has left them vulnerable to sexual predators and commercial fraud, opening the issue of whether government regulation is needed. Parental supervision remains the best protection.

Critics' Choices and Public's Picks

The *Columbia Journalism Review,* a well-respected journal, conducted a survey among 100 American newspaper editors from both small and large papers to decide the nation's top papers. Factors such as extent of local coverage, representation of the paper's community, investigative reporting, and effective design layout were weighed in the editors' choice. Compare their evaluations with the top ten in terms of circulation. (Daily circulation is given in parentheses.)

Critics' Choices	Public's Picks (Circulation)
1. *New York Times*	1. *USA Today* (2,241,677)
2. *Washington Post*	2. *Wall Street Journal* (1,780,605)
3. *Wall Street Journal*	3. *New York Times* (1,109,371)
4. *Los Angeles Times*	4. *Los Angeles Times* (972,957)
5. *Dallas Morning News*	5. *Washington Post* (759,864)
6. *Chicago Tribune*	6. *New York Daily News* (734,473)
7. *Boston Globe*	7. *Chicago Tribune* (621,305)
8. *San Jose Mercury News*	8. *Newsday* (577,354)
9. *St. Petersburg Times*	9. *Houston Chronicle* (551,854)
10. *Baltimore Sun*	10. *New York Post* (533,860)

Sources: "America's Best Newspapers," *Columbia Journalism Review,* November/December 1999, p.14; and Audit Bureau of Circulations, at abcas1.accessabc.com/ecirc.

Candidates are now using the Web for fund raising. Once a candidate gains recognition, as McCain did after his victory in the New Hampshire presidential primary campaign, it is possible to raise money quickly and inexpensively via the Web. In fact, in 2000, McCain collected twice as much money over the Web as Gore and Bush.[23]

The Changing Role of the American News Media

At the time of the ratification of the Constitution, newspapers consisted of a single sheet, often printed irregularly by store owners to hawk their services or goods. Newspapers rarely stayed in business more than a year, due to delinquent subscribers and high costs.[24] But the framers understood the important role the press should play as a watchdog of politicians and government, and they included freedom of the press in the Bill of Rights.

Political Mouthpiece

The new nation's political leaders, including Alexander Hamilton and Thomas Jefferson, recognized the need to keep voters informed. Political parties as we know them did not exist, but the active role of the press in supporting the Revolution had fostered a growing awareness of the political potential of newspapers. Hamilton recruited staunch Federalist John Fenno to edit and publish a newspaper in the new national capital of Philadelphia. Jefferson responded by attracting Philip Freneau, a talented writer and editor and a loyal Republican, to do the same for the Republicans. (Jefferson's Republicans later became the Democratic party.) The two papers became the nucleus of a network of competing partisan newspapers throughout the nation.

Although the two newspapers competed in Philadelphia for only a few years, they served as a model for future partisan newspapers. The early American press served as a mouthpiece for political leaders. Its close connection with politicians and political parties offered the opportunity for financial stability—but at the cost of journalistic independence.

Financial Independence

During the Jacksonian era of the 1820s and 1830s, the right to vote was extended to all white adult males through the elimination of property qualifications. The press began to shift its appeal away from elite readers and toward large masses of less educated and less politically interested readers. The rising literacy rate reinforced this popularization of newspapers. These two forces—increased political participation by the common people and the rise of literacy among Americans—began to alter the relationship between politicians and the press.

Some newspaper publishers began to experiment with a new way to finance their newspapers. They charged a penny a paper, paid on delivery, instead of the traditional annual subscription fee of $8 to $10, which was beyond the ability of most readers to pay. The "penny press," as it was called, expanded circulation and put more emphasis on advertising, enabling newspapers to become financially independent of the political parties.

The changing finances of newspapers also affected the definition of news. Before the penny press, all news was political—speeches, documents, editorials—directed at politically interested readers. The penny press reshaped the definition of news as it sought to appeal to less politically aware readers with human interest stories and reports on sports, crime, public trials, and social activities.

"Objective Journalism"

By the early decades of the twentieth century, many journalists began to argue that the press should be independent of the political parties. *New York Tribune* editor Whitelaw Reid eloquently expressed this sentiment: "Independent journalism! That is the watchword of the future in the profession. An end of concealments because it would hurt the party; an end of one-sided expositions . . . ; an end of assaults that are not believed fully just but must be made because the exigency of party warfare demands them."[25]

MAINE EXPLOSION CAUSED BY BOMB OR TORPEDO?

The New York World a day after

As the nineteenth century progressed, literacy grew among the U.S. masses and more people began to get their news from newspapers. The popularization of the print media forced politicians and public officials to devote growing attention to their relationship with the press.

Journalists began to view their work as a profession and established professional associations with journals and codes of ethics. This professionalization of journalism reinforced the notion that journalists should be independent of partisan politics. Further strengthening the trend toward objectivity was the rise of the wire services, such as the Associated Press and Reuters, which deliberately remained politically neutral so as to attract more customers.

The Impact of Broadcasting

Radio and television nationalized and personalized the news. People could follow events as they were happening and not have to wait for the publication of a newspaper. From the 1920s, when radio networks were formed, radio carried political speeches, campaign advertising, and coverage of political events such as national party conventions.[26] Radio provided a means to bypass the screening of editors and reporters, since politicians could now speak directly to listeners. It also increased interest in national and international news because events outside a listener's local area could be followed as if one were actually there.

President Franklin Roosevelt used radio with remarkable effectiveness. Before 1933, most radio speeches were formal orations, but Roosevelt spoke to his audience on a personal level, seemingly in one-on-one conversations. These "fireside chats" established a standard still followed today. When Roosevelt began speaking over the microphone, he would visualize a tiny group of average citizens in front of him. Roosevelt "would smile and light up as though he were actually sitting on the front porch or in the parlor with them."[27]

Television added a dramatic visual dimension, which contributed to rising audience interest in national events and permitted viewers to witness lunar landings and the aftermath of political assassinations, as well as more mundane news events. By 1963, the two largest networks at the time, CBS and NBC, had expanded their evening news programs from 15 to 30 minutes. Today news broadcasting has expanded to the point that many local stations provide 90 minutes of local news every evening as well as a half-hour in the morning and at noon. Programs such as *20/20* and other newsmagazine shows are among the most popular in the prime-time evening hours.

Cable television brought round-the-clock news coverage. During the Clinton impeachment hearings and the 2000 Florida ballot-counting controversy, American cable news was watched at home and around the world for its instantaneous coverage. C-SPAN

Franklin D. Roosevelt was the first president to recognize the effectiveness of radio to reach the public. His fireside chats were the model for later presidents.

now provides uninterrupted coverage of congressional deliberations, the courts, and state and local governments.

Investigatory Journalism

Contemporary news reporters do more than convey the news; they investigate it, and their investigations often have political consequences. Notable examples of influential investigatory reporters include Seymour Hersh of the *New York Times,* who exposed what became known as the *Pentagon Papers,* revealing how the United States became involved in the Vietnam War; Robert Woodward and Carl Bernstein of the *Washington Post,* who played an important role in uncovering the Watergate conspiracy; Nina Totenberg of National Public Radio, whose reporting on sexual harassment charges against Clarence Thomas helped force the Senate Judiciary Committee to extend the hearings on his confirmation to the U.S. Supreme Court; and Michael Isikoff of *Newsweek,* who broke the story of Bill Clinton's alleged perjury involving sexual misconduct with Monica Lewinsky.

Media Conglomerates

Australian-born Rupert Murdoch owns the Fox Network, dozens of U.S. television stations, magazines, publishing organizations, and movie studios.

If a few owners corner the market on newspapers and television stations, is the free flow of information to the public endangered? As in other sectors of the economy, media companies have merged and created large conglomerates. When television was in its infancy, radio networks and newspapers were among the first to purchase television stations. These mergers established cross-ownership patterns that persist today. The Gannett Corporation, for example, owns 87 daily newspapers and 21 television stations and cable television systems—assets that provide news coverage to nearly 17 percent of the United States.[28] The *Chicago Tribune* substantially expanded its reach of newspapers and television stations in 2000 when it paid $6 billion for Times-Mirror, publisher of the *Los Angeles Times* and ten other newspapers, 22 TV stations, four radio stations, and a growing online business.[29] The Federal Communications Commission (FCC) and the courts are reinforcing the trend toward media conglomeration by relaxing and striking down regulations that limit cable and television network ownership by the same company.[30]

Local firms used to own the local newspapers, radio, and television stations. Today large conglomerates, some of them foreign, have acquired ownership of many newspapers and broadcasting stations. The merger of the Disney organization with ABC/Capital Cities, approved early in 1996, cost Disney $19 billion but gave it control not only of the ABC television network but also ESPN, the cable sports station. Months later, the Westinghouse Company bought the CBS television network for $7.5 billion,[31] and CBS merged with Viacom in May 2000 at a cost estimated at $50 billion. Time Warner purchased Turner Broadcasting System in late 1996 for reportedly just under $7 billion,[32] and it, in turn, was purchased by America Online (AOL) for $165 billion in 2000. The foremost example of foreign involvement in our news media is Australian Rupert Murdoch, founder of the Fox network, who owns 22 television stations in the United States, the Family Channel, and 20th Century-Fox. Murdoch also owns HarperCollins publishers and *TV Guide,* which has the largest magazine circulation in America.

When reporting national news, local outlets depend heavily on news that is gathered, edited, and distributed by national organizations like United Press International and the Associated Press. As a result, some people contend that information these days is more diluted, homogenized, and moderated than it would be if the newspapers and broadcast stations were locally owned and the news was gathered and edited locally.[33]

Regulation of the Media

Regulation of the broadcast media has existed in some form since their inception. Because of the limited number of television and radio frequencies, the national government oversees matters like licensing, financing, and even content. One such regulation required "fairness" in news programming.[34] As written into law and interpreted by the FCC, the **fairness doctrine** imposed an obligation on radio and television license holders to ensure

fairness doctrine
Federal Communications Commission policy that required holders of radio and television licenses to ensure that different viewpoints were presented about controversial issues or persons; largely repealed in 1987.

IN COMPARATIVE PERSPECTIVE

The Media's Role in Keeping Government Honest

The United Nations has declared that all citizens of the world have an unqualified right to freedom of opinion and expression, which includes the right to seek, receive, and impart information through any medium, regardless of national boundaries. Nations vary greatly in the degree to which they guarantee this right, however. Some, such as Cambodia, Singapore, North Korea, Cuba, Kazakhstan, Turkey, and China, limit freedom of the press through a mix of intimidation, censorship, and even murder. Pakistan, Jordan, and other countries have strict contempt laws and severely limit the press, while others, such as Venezuela, Kuwait, and Kenya, impose more limited constraints through government ownership of the media. The United States is one of 30 nations that can be judged as having a truly free press; others include Norway, Canada, Germany, Japan, the United Kingdom, France, Hungary, South Korea, and Brazil.

Although citizens in most western democracies believe a free press plays an important watchdog role, significant numbers also believe that the media are not free to report the truth about political and national issues. Respondents in Italy, Germany, and France believe the greatest threat to a free press comes from political parties, while citizens in Mexico, the United Kingdom, the United States, and Canada believe the greatest threat comes from government.

SOURCE: Times-Mirror Center for the People and the Press, *Mixed Message About Press Freedom on Both Sides of the Atlantic* (Times-Mirror Center, 1994).

that differing viewpoints were presented regarding controversial issues or persons. With the advent of cable television and the Reagan administration's antiregulatory campaign, much of the fairness doctrine was repealed in 1987, and the final remnants of it were repealed in 2000. Will broadcasters provide fair and balanced news coverage in the absence of regulation? Proponents of deregulation who pushed for repeal think so.[35]

Mediated Politics

When dramatic events like the terrorist attacks on the World Trade Center and the Pentagon on September 11, 2001, occur, we realize the power television has in bringing world events into our lives. Osama bin Laden, the purported mastermind behind the attacks, understood the power of the media both inside and outside the United States, as evidenced by his release of videotapes of himself through the Al-Jazeera network in the Middle East in the weeks and months after the attacks.

The pervasiveness of newspapers, magazines, radio, and television places the individuals who determine what we read, hear, and see in a position of great influence because they can reach so much of the American public so quickly. With a large population scattered over a continent, both the reach and the speed of the modern media elevate the importance of the people in charge of them.

Political parties and interest groups have long been political mediators that help organize the world of politics for the average citizen. Their role is less important today because the media now serve that function and political parties have largely lost control over the nominating process (see Chapters 7 and 9). Greater attention is now given to judging candidates not so much in terms of party affiliation and platform but in terms of character and competence. The press, not the parties, performs this evaluative function.

The news media have also assumed the role of "speaking for the people." Journalists report what "the people" want and think, and then they tell the people what politicians and policy makers are doing about it. Politicians realize how dependent they are on the media for getting their message out to voters, and they are well aware that a hostile press can hurt them. That explains why today's politicians spend so much of their time developing good relations with the press.

Children Changing Parents' Political Awareness

Most often parents teach children political values, but sometimes children become the teachers. At least that is what a recent study by Michael McDevitt and Steven H. Chaffee concluded. McDevitt and Chaffee studied students in kindergarten through twelfth grade who were participating in Kids Voting USA, a civics curriculum in public schools in San Jose, California. Not only did the program increase political awareness in children, but the political effects "trickled up" to their parents as well. Families watched more news programs and demonstrated greater knowledge of candidates and issues. Furthermore, child-parent interaction and discussion about politics increased substantially. Families from low socioeconomic backgrounds were especially affected by this civics curriculum. These findings are surprising for two reasons. First, people in lower socioeconomic settings, where politics is assumed to be less frequently discussed, respond readily to political stimulus, and second, public school programs may have a greater effect on children and their parents than was previously thought.

SOURCE: Thomas J. Johnson, Carol E. Hays, and Scott P. Hays, eds., *Engaging the Public* (Rowman & Littlefield, 1998).

political socialization
The process by which we develop our political attitudes, values, and beliefs.

selective exposure
The process by which individuals screen out messages that do not conform to their own biases.

selective perception
The process by which individuals perceive what they want to in media messages.

The Media and Public Opinion

The ability of television to present images and communicate events has influenced American public opinion. Television footage of the violence done to blacks during the civil rights revolution of the 1950s and 1960s made the issue more real and immediate. News coverage of the war in Vietnam galvanized the antiwar movement in the United States because of the horrible images news shows brought into people's homes. The testimony of White House staff before the Senate Watergate and later House Judiciary committees intensified the crisis of confidence in the Nixon administration. The repeated television coverage of the terrorist attacks on the World Trade Center and Pentagon left an indelible impression on all who saw them.

For a long time, analysts tended to play down the influence wielded by the media in American politics relative to the influence wielded by political leaders. The impact of Franklin D. Roosevelt's fireside chats came to symbolize the power of the politician over that of the news editor. Roosevelt spoke directly to his listeners over the radio in a way and at a time of his own choosing, and no network official was able to block or influence that direct connection. President John Kennedy's use of the televised press conference represented a similar direct contact with the public. President Ronald Reagan was nicknamed the "Great Communicator" because of his ability to talk persuasively and often passionately about public policy issues with the people through television.

However, broadcasters and journalists are now so important to the political process that elected officials and politicians spend considerable time trying to learn how to use them to their advantage. Presidential events and "photo opportunities" are planned with the evening news and its format in mind.[36] Members of Congress use Capitol Hill recording studios to tape messages for local television and radio stations. White House press briefings are frequently included in the evening news.

Factors That Limit Media Influence on Public Opinion

People are not just empty vessels into which politicians and journalists pour information and ideas. How people interpret political messages depends on a variety of factors: political socialization, selectivity, needs, and the individual's ability to recall and comprehend the message.

POLITICAL SOCIALIZATION   The media, particularly television, although not as important as family, play a role in socializing, influencing our values and attitudes.[37] The media shape public perceptions and knowledge. Television, with its concreteness and drama, has an emotional impact that print cannot hope to match.[38] Television cuts across age groups, educational levels, social classes, and races. Newspapers provide more detail about the news and often contain contrasting points of view, at least on the editorial pages, that help inform the public.

We develop our political attitudes, values, and beliefs through an education process that social scientists call **political socialization**.[39] (See Chapters 4 and 8 for more detail on this process.) Face-to-face contacts with friends and business associates (*peer pressure*) often have far more impact than the impersonal television or newspaper. Strong identification with a party also acts as a powerful filter.[40] A conservative Republican from Arizona might watch the "liberal eastern networks" and complain about their biased news coverage while sticking to her own opinions. A liberal from New York will often complain about right-wing talk radio, even if he listens to it some nights on the way home from work.

SELECTIVITY   People practice **selective exposure**—screening out messages that do not conform to their own biases. They subscribe to newspapers or magazines that support their views. People also practice **selective perception**—perceiving what they want to in media messages.[41] One dramatic example was the differing reactions of

Democrats and Republicans to reports of President Clinton's sexual misconduct with Monica Lewinsky, a former White House intern, and the possibility that he encouraged her to lie under oath. In the first weeks after the story broke, Republicans were four times more likely than Democrats to believe that Clinton had been sexually involved with Lewinsky.[42] More than two-thirds of Republicans and Democrats agreed that Clinton committed perjury before the grand jury, but they had dramatically different opinions on whether Clinton should remain in office. Nearly two-thirds of Republicans wanted Clinton out of office, while 63 percent of Independents and 87 percent of Democrats felt that Clinton should continue as president.[43]

NEEDS   People read newspapers, listen to the radio, or watch television for very different reasons, often out of habit or because they want information.[44] People who seek information and cultivate an interest in politics are affected by what they read and see differently from those who use media primarily for entertainment.[45] For those seeking entertainment, gossip about politicians' peccadilloes is more important than those politicians' opinions or voting patterns. Members of the broader audience are also more likely to pay attention to news that directly affects their lives, such as interest rate changes or the price of gasoline.[46]

RECALL AND COMPREHENSION   Still another limitation of media influence on public opinion is the extent to which the audience can recall the stories or comprehend their importance. Candidates and officials send out vast amounts of information designed to influence what people think and do, and especially how they vote, but people forget or fail to comprehend much of it.[47] The fragmentary and rapid mode of presentation of television news contributes to the problem. Most television news stories, for example, last less than 90 seconds.

Given the abundance of information available about politics and government, it is not surprising that most people pick and choose which media source—television, radio, newspapers, cable, the Web—they pay attention to and which news stories they consider important.[48] The best predictor of retention of news stories is political interest. People tend to fit today's news stories into their general assumptions or beliefs about government, politicians, or the media itself.

AUDIENCE FRAGMENTATION   With the growth of cable television and new media like the Web, the influence of any one media source is weakened. Because people are scattered across a larger number of press outlets and these outlets cover politics in varied ways, the impact of the press will be more disparate. People can now tailor their news to their preferred point of view. Fragmentation of the media audience tends to counteract the impact of media conglomeration. As media giants move to both cable and broadcast (NBC, CNBC, MSNBC, for example), the trends may converge.

Are the Media Biased?

Americans tend to blame the media for lots of things. Conservatives complain, "The media are too liberal." Radio talk show host Rush Limbaugh even once said, "They all just happen to believe the same way. . . . They are part of the same culture as Bill Clinton."[49] Extreme liberals contend that the ruling class controls the mainstream press, and they charge that government propaganda distorts the facts. Conservatives say the press is too liberal in its selection of news covered and the interpretation of events. Liberals point to newspaper endorsements of Republican presidential candidates to support their claim that newspapers are biased in favor of conservative policies and candidates.

Newspapers, magazines, and television stations are business corporations concerned about profits. They work to boost circulation and ratings and must please their advertisers, sponsors, and stockholders. Reporters and editors pride themselves on impartial reporting of the facts.[50] Yet some liberal critics contend that the media

"Hey, do you want to be on the news tonight or not? This is a sound bite, not the Gettysburgh Address. Just say what you have to say, Senator, and get the hell off."

Pick Your Own News— Good for Democracy?

The future of news is here. With the advent of media sources on the Web, people no longer have to wait for the newspaper to check the weather, the stock market, or their favorite sports team's scores. The ease of accessing information online is made even easier by e-mail accounts from sources like www.nytimes.com, www.washingtonpost.com, and www.usatoday.com. Often at no cost, you can sign up for only the news you want from the sources you want and receive it daily via e-mail. Although this abundance of news sources may appear to have only positive consequences, one legal scholar fears it may have negative effects on democracy. Cass Sunstein, in his book *Republic.com,* asserts that there are limitations to citizens' ability to sort their news along personal preferences. Democracy, Sunstein maintains, depends on shared experiences and requires citizens to be exposed to topics and ideas that they would not have chosen in advance. When we exclude other opinions and ideas from our news diet, there may be a danger of dissolving our shared culture and creating louder and ever more extreme echoes of our own voices.

SOURCE: Cass R. Sunstein, *Republic.com* (Princeton University Press, 2001).

reflect a conservative bias not only in what they report but also in what they choose to ignore. Political scientist Michael Parenti states that journalists "rarely doubt their own objectivity even as they faithfully echo the established political vocabularies and the prevailing politico-economic orthodoxy."[51]

Newspapers and television management go to some lengths to insulate reporters from their advertising and business operations, in part to reduce criticism about favorable treatment of large advertisers or the corporate owners. When the management of the *Los Angeles Times* attempted to foster closer relations between the business and news divisions, it was criticized for insensitivity to this concern.[52] Another internal check on media bias is the fact that news coverage involves many reporters and a host of editors, all of whom have input into what is covered and how it is presented.

Some commentators have suggested that a possible bias flows from the fact that reporters and editors become too friendly with the people and organizations they write about. David Broder of the *Washington Post* voices his concern about the confusion of roles by journalists who have served in government. According to Broder, a line should divide objective journalism from partisan politics, but many members of the print and television media have crossed this line. Broder opposes the idea of journalists' becoming government officials and vice versa.[53] Others argue that journalists with previous government service have close working relationships with politicians and can give us a valuable perspective on government without losing their professional neutrality.

A frequent criticism is the media's alleged political bias, whether liberal or conservative. But to whom are these critics referring? To reporters, writers, editors, producers, or owners of TV stations and newspapers? Do they assume that a journalist's personal politics will be translated into biased reporting? And does the public think so? Journalists are usually more liberal than the population as a whole; editors tend to be a bit more conservative than their reporters are; and media owners are more conservative still. Slightly more than half of all journalists classify themselves as liberals, compared with only about one-fourth of the general public (see Table 10-1).[54] Elite journalists—those who work for national news media organizations—tend to share a similar culture: cosmopolitan, urban, upper-class. Their approach to the events and issues they cover is governed by their common worldview, which may be derived from their professional training.[55] The result, some critics contend, is that elite journalists give greater weight to the side of issues that corresponds to their own version of reality.[56]

One bias of the media that does not have a particular partisan or ideological slant is the bias toward sensationalism. Scandals of all types happen to liberals and conservatives,

TABLE 10-1   The Politics of Journalists and the Public

	Washington-Based Reporters	Newspaper Editors (National)	Public
Party Identification			
Democrat	50%	31%	34%
Republican	4	14	28
Independent	37	39	25
Other	9	7	8
Self-Described Ideology			
Liberal	61	32	20
Moderate	30	35	34
Conservative	9	25	27

SOURCE: The Roper Center, *The Public Perspective,* October–November 1996, p. 8, based on a Media Studies Center/Roper Center survey of 1,200 persons conducted in September 1995.

Republicans and Democrats. Once the province of tabloids like the *National Enquirer,* stories about scandal have recently become commonplace in the mainstream media. For years, the media have seemed to gravitate to stories involving celebrities, sex, or both. From the O. J. Simpson murder trial to the coverage of a missing intern who had been involved in an affair with a congressman, we have seen what some observers have called a media "feeding frenzy."[57] The intense and unrelenting focus on the scandal involving former President Bill Clinton and White House intern Monica Lewinsky is a clear example of the media's fondness for sensational coverage.

Newspapers and television news often set a tone of dissatisfaction with the performance of the national government and cynicism about politics and politicians. A critical tone may be an inevitable element of the mind-set of the press, but to whose benefit does that critical tone work? The media are accused of having an anti-religion bias, a bias in favor of young viewers, and a bias fostering continuing crises.[58] The question is not whether the press is biased but whether a press bias—whatever the direction—seeps into the content of the news. The answer to that question is still not settled.

Public Opinion

Two important influences of print and broadcast media on public opinion are *agenda setting* and *issue framing.*

AGENDA SETTING   By calling public attention to certain issues, the media help determine what topics will become subjects of public debate and legislation.[59] However, the agenda-setting function of the media is not uniformly pervasive. The audience and the nature of the issue limit it.[60] According to former Vice President Walter Mondale, "If I had to give up . . . the opportunity to get on the evening news or the veto power, . . . I'd throw the veto power away. [Television news] is the President's most indispensable power."[61] Ronald Reagan, more than any president before him, effectively used the media to set the nation's agenda. Reagan and his advisers carefully crafted the images and scenes of his presidency to fit television. Thus television became an "electronic throne."

Communicating through the media works especially when it is natural and unscripted. When President Bush first visited the scene of the demolition of the World Trade Center in New York City, taking a bullhorn, he said, "I can hear you. The rest of the world hears you, and the people who knocked these buildings down will hear all of us soon."[62] This action projected leadership and empathy on the part of the president.

You Decide • Thinking It Through

HOW SHOULD THE MEDIA REPORT SEX SCANDALS?

You Decide... Early in the 1992 presidential campaign, Bill Clinton's press coverage turned negative as reports circulated in the *Star,* a supermarket tabloid, that he and Gennifer Flowers, a former Arkansas state employee, had had a 12-year-long extramarital affair. Clinton, with Mrs. Clinton by his side, denied the Flowers account in an interview on *60 Minutes,* a CBS-TV news program, on Superbowl Sunday. Because Flowers had been paid for her story by the *Star,* some people discounted the story. Others were doubtful that tabloid papers like the *Star* ever print anything close to the truth. Despite the existence of tapes that appeared to confirm Flowers's account, the press essentially dropped the story. The reverse was true for Democratic Congressman Gary Condit of California, who in an August 2001 interview on ABC-TV's *PrimeTime Live* refused to comment about his alleged sexual involvement with constituent and Federal Bureau of Prisons intern Chandra Levy. Condit's silence, coupled with Levy's disappearance and possible death, seemed to intensify media coverage.

After winning the presidency, Clinton was dogged by a series of accusations of unwanted sexual advances toward Paula Jones and Kathleen Willey and of a consensual affair with Monica Lewinsky. In a transcript of his deposition in the Jones sexual harassment suit, Clinton admitted having an affair with Gennifer Flowers. This raised anew questions of how the media had reported the original accusations. Regarding the Chandra Levy story, after the events of September 11, 2001, the press shifted its focus to the war on terror and away from the Condit story. After six terms of service, the California Congressman lost the March 2002 Democratic primary and blamed media coverage for ruining his political career. Did the press handle those stories properly?

Thinking It Through... Some people dismiss reporting on sex scandals as sensationalistic and unrelated to governing. Others, like Larry Sabato, a political scientist who has written on the media, disagree. Sabato says the press "didn't reveal what most of them knew then about Clinton and all the other women. If the press had done its job in '92, the country would not be facing this horrible dilemma in '98."*

The question of how to report sexual misbehavior by political candidates is unresolved. It is debatable whether such matters ought to be reported at all. Some people, including some reporters, think sex scandals are not important. The public wants to know whether candidates meet high standards of personal conduct, but they react negatively to coverage that is too aggressive. Public reaction to the explicit details of the Star report is instructive: 84 percent of the public wanted to know the conclusions of the investigation, but 70 percent felt that Congress should have omitted the details of the sexual encounters.†

*Larry J. Sabato, quoted in William Power, "News at Warp Speed," National Journal, January 31, 1998, p. 220.

†Frank Newport, "Initial Reaction Mixed on Delivery of Star Report to Congress," September 12, 1998, at www.gallup.com/poll_archives/980912.htm.

ISSUE FRAMING   Politicians, like everybody else, try to frame issues to win arguments, and they try to influence the "spin" the media will give to their actions or issues. Examples abound. Opponents of U.S. intervention in Bosnia tried to portray such action as another Vietnam. Objectors to permanent normal trade relations with China framed the granting of that status as a human rights travesty. When Bill Clinton wanted to forestall a Republican tax cut, he decried the resulting need to dip into the budget surplus to "rescue Social Security." People who favor abortion define the issue as one of freedom of choice; those who oppose it define it as murder. In referendum campaigns, the side that wins the battle of interpreting what the referendum is about wins the election.[63]

In the 2002 election, voters indicated that the economy and jobs were the most important issues, followed by education. Surprisingly, they did not say that Social Security, prescription drugs, or corporate mismanagement were important. All of these issues had received a lot of attention in the news and were the subjects of broadcast ads and political mail.

The Media and Elections

News coverage of campaigns and elections is greatest in presidential contests, less in statewide races for governor and U.S. senator, and least for other state and local races. Generally, the more news attention given the campaign, the less likely voters are to be swayed by any one source. Hence news coverage is likely to be more influential in a city council contest than in an election for president or the Senate. For most city elections, there are only one or two sources of information about what candidates say and stand for; for statewide and national contests, there are multiple sources.

Diversification of the news media lessens the ability of any one medium to influence the outcome of elections. Newspaper publishers who were once seen as key figures in state and local politics are now less important because politicians and their media advisers are no longer so dependent on newspapers and other news media to communicate their messages. Candidates can use ads on radio and television, direct mail, phone, the Web, and cable television to communicate with voters.

"I'm still undecided—I like Leno's foreign policy, but Letterman makes a lot of sense on domestic issues."

Choice of Candidates

The extensive use of television has made being "good on television"—looking and sounding good—much more important. It has also fostered growth in the political consulting industry and made visibility the watchword in politics. Television greatly affects the public's idea of what traits are important in a candidate. A century ago, successful candidates needed a strong pair of lungs; today it is a telegenic appearance, a pleasing voice, and no obvious physical impairments. Back in the 1930s, the press chose not to show Franklin Roosevelt in his wheelchair or using braces, whereas today the country knows every intimate detail of the president's health. The importance of the public's perception of these traits is evident in the ridicule often directed at candidates. In 2000, George W. Bush was lampooned for his inability to answer reporters' questions on foreign affairs, and Al Gore was the subject of jokes for following a consultant's advice to bring out the more domineering side of his personality.

Although the media insist that they pay attention to all candidates who have a chance to win, they also influence who gets such a chance. Consequently, candidates have to come up with creative ways to attract media attention. Paul Wellstone, in his 1996 Minnesota Senate campaign, said in his advertisements that he did not have much money to pay for ads, so he would have to talk fast to cram what he had to say into fewer commercials. His witty commercial became a news event itself—it got Wellstone additional coverage.

In the 2000 elections, three U.S. Senate candidates in states bordering Canada organized bus trips to Canada for people to purchase prescription drugs at Canadian prices, which were sharply lower than in the United States. Montana Senate candidate Brian Schweitzer called his excursions "The Run for the Border" and generated substantial positive media coverage for his campaign through the tactic.[64]

The choice of candidates was especially important in two competitive U.S. Senate races in 2002. In New Jersey, incumbent Democrat Robert Torricelli, under attack for ethics problems, dropped out of the race. The Democrats substituted former U.S. Senator Frank Lautenberg for Torricelli. Lautenberg was elected. In Minnesota, Democratic incumbent Paul Wellstone died in an airplane accident eleven days before the election. The Minnesota Democrats then nominated former Vice President Walter Mondale, who lost to Republican Norm Coleman.

Campaign Events

Candidates schedule events—press conferences, interviews, and "photo ops"—in settings that reinforce their verbal messages and public image. Many events organized by campaigns fail to receive attention from reporters because of competing news stories and a sense that the events were staged primarily to generate news coverage.

An Internet Town Meeting?

With the Web, citizens now have the opportunity to interact with each other on a wide range of political topics. In this sense, the Web is something like a town meeting, but without people leaving their homes or offices. In chat rooms on the World Wide Web, people express ideas and respond to each other's opinions. Examples of chat rooms include Abortion Chat, Democrat Chat, Environment Chat, Republican Chat, and Congress Chat. Most chat rooms offer group discussions in which anyone in the group can read and send messages, but some chat rooms also permit private messages to be sent.

As with town meetings, politicians can learn about public sentiment via the Web. They can participate in a chat room or read postings on the Web in what is called Usenet. Reading messages posted on Usenet permits politicians to gauge public opinion and tap in to particular segments of the population. But because those who use the Web are not a representative sample of the general public, politicians should be wary not to generalize from the opinions expressed through this medium.

The party national convention used to capture national attention. However, since candidates are now selected in party primaries, the conventions no longer provide much suspense or make news except perhaps over who will be the vice presidential nominee. This is one reason why the networks have dramatically cut back their coverage of presidential nominating conventions. In 1952, the average television set was tuned to the political conventions for 26 hours, or an average of more than three hours a night for the eight nights of convention coverage.[65] During the 2000 presidential conventions, by contrast, the major networks provided only one or two hours of prime-time coverage each evening. Political parties have sought, in vain, to regain audience interest by relying on "movie stars, entertainment routines, and professionally produced documentaries to spice up their conventions."[66]

Technology

Although the expense associated with television has contributed to the skyrocketing costs of campaigning, it has also made politics more accessible to more people. Thanks to satellites, candidates can conduct local television interviews without actually traveling to local studios. Specific voter groups can be targeted through cable television or low-power television stations that reach homogeneous neighborhoods and small towns. Videocassettes with messages from the candidates further extend the campaign's reach.[67] All serious candidates for Congress and governor in 2000 and 2002 made themselves and their positions available through a home page on the World Wide Web.

Image Making and Media Consultants

Candidates recognize that their messages about issues are often ignored. The press tends to emphasize goofs and gossip or tension among party leaders. Candidates in turn try to spin the news. Attempts to shape the news and to portray candidates in the best possible light are not new. Presidential campaign sloganeering such as "Tippecanoe and Tyler Too" in 1840 and "Abe the Rail Splitter" in 1860 conveyed the candidate's image. Radio, television, and the Web have expanded the ability to project images, and that expansion has in turn affected candidates' vote-getting strategies and their manner of communicating messages. Television is especially important because of the power of the visual image.

Television has contributed to the rise of new players in campaign politics: *media consultants,* campaign professionals who provide candidates with advice and services on media relations, advertising strategy, and opinion polling.[68] For example, candidates regularly receive consultants' advice on what colors work best for them, especially on television. Male U.S. Senators often appear in light blue shirts with red ties, sometimes called "power ties." A primary responsibility of a campaign media consultant is to present a positive image of the candidate and to reinforce negative images of the opponent.

Some media consultants have been credited with propelling candidates to success. Dick Morris was seen as important to Clinton's resurgence after the 1994 congressional election defeats, until he had to resign from the campaign following a personal scandal. Republican consultants Mike Murphy and Jim Innocenzi and Democratic consultants Dawn Laguens and Carter Eskew have acquired powerful reputations. But media consultants have also been blamed for the negativity of recent presidential campaigns.

Media consultants have taken over the role formerly played by party politicians. Before World War II, party professionals groomed candidates for office at all levels. Such leaders made judgments about possible candidates on the basis of their chances of victory and observation of the candidates' performance under fire, decisiveness, conviction, political skill, and other leadership qualities. Party professionals advised candidates which party and interest group leaders to placate, which issues to stress, and which topics to avoid.

Today consultants coach candidates about television technique, appearance, and subject matter. Consultants report the results of *focus groups* (small sample groups of people who are asked questions about candidates and issues in a discussion setting) and *public opinion polls,* which in turn determine what the candidate says and does. Some critics allege that political consultants have become a new "political elite" who can virtually choose candidates by determining in advance which men and women have the right images or at least images that can be restyled for the widest popularity.[69] But political consultants who specialize in media advertising and image making realize their own limitations in packaging candidates. As one media consultant put it, "It is a very hard job to turn a turkey into a movie star; you try instead to make people like the turkey."[70]

The Media and Voter Choice

As television has become increasingly important to politics, and as the political parties have been weakened with such reforms as primary elections, news coverage of candidates has taken on added significance. Although some critics think reporters pay too much attention to candidates' personality and background, others say character and personality are among the most important characteristics for readers and viewers to know about. What is not in dispute is the central role the news media play in our democratic process.

THE HORSE RACE   What voters know about candidates is based largely on what they see on television, read in newspapers, and hear on the radio. Journalists are more likely to comment on a candidate's standing in the polls compared to other candidates—what is sometimes called the **horse race**—than they are about policy issues.[71] "Many stories focus on who is ahead, who is behind, who is going to win, and who is going to lose, rather than examining how and why the race is as it is."[72] Reporters focus on the tactics and strategy of campaigns because they perceive that the public is interested and influenced by such coverage.[73] The media's propensity to focus on the "game" of campaigns displaces coverage of issues.

NEGATIVE ADVERTISING   Political advertising always contained negative remarks about opponents, but recent campaigns have taken on an increasingly negative tone. A rule of thumb in the old politics was to ignore the charges of the opposition and thus to accord one's rival no importance or standing. That practice has changed as today's candidates trade charges and countercharges.

Voters say they are turned off by the attack style of politics, but the widespread perception among campaign consultants is that negative campaigning works. This seeming inconsistency may be explained by evidence suggesting that campaigns that foster negative impressions of the candidates contribute to lower turnout.[74] Negative advertising may thus discourage some voters who would be inclined to support a candidate (a phenomenon known as *vote suppression*) while reinforcing the inclination of committed supporters to come out to vote.

INFORMATION ABOUT ISSUES   In recent elections, the media have experimented with a more issues-centered focus, what has been called *civic journalism.* With funding from charitable foundations, some newspapers have been identifying the concerns of community leaders and talking to ordinary voters and then writing campaign stories from their point of view.[75] Some newspaper editors and reporters disagree with this approach; they believe the media should stick to responding to newsworthy events. Advocates of civic journalism counter that important concerns of the community are often overshadowed by news events like murders and violence.

A candidate's image often takes precedence over that candidate's message in the mass media. This was as true in the mid-nineteenth century as it is today. This is why image makers and media consultants have been in such high demand for so long. On the top, we see a portrait of Abraham Lincoln as "Abe the Rail Splitter." On the bottom, we see George W. Bush playing a game of golf. It is striking to see the contrast between how Lincoln wanted to portray himself publicly and how Bush wants to be portrayed.

horse race
A close contest; by extension, any contest in which the focus is on who is ahead and by how much rather than on substantive differences between the candidates.

MAKING A DECISION   Newspapers and television seem to have more influence in determining the outcome of primaries than of general elections,[76] probably because voters are less likely to know about the candidates and have fewer clues about how they stand in a primary. By the time of the November general election, however, party affiliation, incumbency, and other factors moderate the impact of media messages. The mass media are more likely to influence undecided voters who, in a close election, can determine who wins and who loses.

ELECTION NIGHT REPORTING   Does TV coverage on election night affect the outcome of elections? Election returns from the East come in three hours before the polls close on the West Coast. Because major networks often project the presidential winner well ahead of poll closings in western states, some western voters have been discouraged from voting. As a result, voter turnout in congressional and local elections has been affected. In a close presidential election, however, such early reporting may well stimulate turnout because voters know their vote could determine the outcome. In short, it is only in elections in which one candidate appears to be winning by a large margin that television reporting makes voters believe their vote is meaningless.[77]

The Media and Governance

The press rarely follows the policy process to its conclusion. Rather, it leaves the issue at the doorstep of public officials. By the time a political issue reaches the stages of policy formulation and implementation, the press has moved on to another issue. When policies are being formulated and implemented, decision makers are at their most impressionable, yet the press has little impact at this stage.[78]

Lack of press attention to policy implementation explains in part why we know less about how bureaucrats go about their business than we do about heated legislative debates or presidential scandals. Only in the case of a policy scandal, such as the lax security surrounding nuclear secrets at Los Alamos, does the press take notice. "Most executives would be satisfied with a press strategy of no surprises. All their press officers need do to be doing their job is provide a rudimentary early warning system [for crises] and issue routine announcements."[79]

TABLE 10–2   Presidential News Conferences with White House Correspondents

President	Average per Month	Total Number
Herbert Hoover (1929–1933)	5.6	268
Franklin D. Roosevelt (1933–1945)	6.9	998
Harry Truman (1945–1953)	3.4	334
Dwight Eisenhower (1953–1961)	2.0	193
John Kennedy (1961–1963)	1.9	64
Lyndon Johnson (1963–1969)	2.2	135
Richard Nixon (1969–1974)	0.5	37
Gerald Ford (1974–1977)	1.3	39
Jimmy Carter (1977–1981)	0.8	59
Ronald Reagan (1981–1989)	0.5	44
George Bush (1989–1993)	3.0	142
Bill Clinton (1993–2001)	2.0	192
George W. Bush (2001–2004)	1.9	82

SOURCE: *Weekly Compilation of Presidential Documents*, vol. 31, *Annual Index* (p. C12); personal communication, White House Press Office, December 27, 2000 and www.whitehouse.gov.

Some media critics contend that the media's pressuring policy makers to provide immediate answers forces them to make untimely decisions. Foreign policy may be in particular danger from such quick responses:

> If an ominous foreign event is featured on TV news, the president and his advisers feel bound to make a response in time for the next evening news broadcast. . . . If he does not have a response ready by the late afternoon deadline, the evening news may report that the president's advisers are divided, that the president cannot make up his mind, or that while the president hesitates, his political opponents know exactly what to do.[80]

Political Institutions and the News Media

Presidents have become the stars of the media, particularly television, and have made the media their forum for setting the public agenda and achieving their legislative aims. Presidential news conferences command attention (see Table 10-2). Every public activity, both professional and personal, is potentially newsworthy; a presidential illness can become front-page news, as can presidential vacations and family pets.

A president attempts to manipulate news coverage to his benefit. Speeches are used to set the national agenda or spur congressional action. Travel to foreign countries usually boosts popular support at home, thanks to the largely favorable news coverage. Better yet for the president, most coverage of the president—either at home or abroad—is favorable to neutral.[81] President Clinton's trip to Israel during the height of the furor surrounding his impeachment may have helped distract attention from his domestic problems in both senses of that word.

Congress is a fragmented body usually unable to act quickly. It is also more likely to get negative coverage than either the White House or the Supreme Court. Unlike the executive branch, it lacks an ultimate spokesperson, a single individual who can speak for the whole institution.[82] Congress does not make it easy for the press to cover it. Whereas the White House engages in attentive care and feeding of the press corps, Congress does not arrange its schedule to accommodate the media; floor debates, for example, often compete with committee hearings and press conferences.[83] Singularly dramatic actions rarely occur in Congress; the press therefore turns to the president to describe federal government activity on a day-to-day basis and treats Congress largely as a foil to the president. Most coverage of Congress is of its reaction to the initiatives of the president.[84]

The federal judiciary is least dependent on the press. The Supreme Court does not rely on public communication for political support. Rather, it relies indirectly on public opinion for continued deference to or compliance with its decisions.[85] The Court does not allow television cameras to cover oral arguments, rarely allows audiotaping, and has no reporters present when it votes. The Court has strong incentives to avoid the perception of manipulating the press, so it retains an image of aloofness from politics and public opinion. The justices' manipulation of press coverage is far more subtle and complex than that of the other two institutions.[86] For example, the complexity of the Supreme Court's decision in 2000's Florida vote recount case, with multiple dissents and concurrences and no press release or executive summary, made broadcast reporting on the decision difficult.

The news media's most influential role may be at the local level.[87] Most of us have multiple sources for finding out what is happening in Washington that act as a check on the biases and limitations of reporters who cover national government and policy. But when it comes to finding out about the city council, the school board, or the local water district, most of us are dependent on the work of a single reporter. Consequently, the media's influence is much greater when there are fewer news sources.

Not all who think the media are powerful agree that their power is harmful. After all, they argue, the media perform a vital educational function. Almost 70 percent of the public thinks the press is a watchdog that keeps government leaders from doing bad things.[88] At the very least, the media have the power to mold the agenda of the day; at most, in the words of the late Theodore White, they have the power to "determine what people will talk and think about—an authority that in other nations is reserved for tyrants, priests, parties, and mandarins."[89]

Summary

1. The news media include newspapers, magazines, radio, television, films, recordings, books, and electronic communications, in all their forms. These means of communication have been called the "fourth branch of government."

2. The news media are a pervasive feature of American politics and generally help define our culture. The rise of new communications technologies has made the media more influential throughout American society. The news media serve as a link between politicians and government officials and the public.

3. Our modern news media emerged from a more partisan and less professional past. Autonomy of the media from political parties is one of the important changes. Now journalists strive for objectivity and see themselves as important to the political process. They also engage in investigative journalism.

4. Broadcasting on radio and television has changed the news media, and most Americans use television and radio as primary news sources. The role of corporate ownership of media outlets, especially media conglomerates, raises questions about media competition and orientation.

5. The influence of the mass media over public opinion is significant but not overwhelming. People may not pay much attention to the media or may not believe everything they read or see or hear. They may be critical or suspicious of the media and hence resistant to it. People tend to filter the news through their political socialization, selectivity, needs, and ability to recall or comprehend the content of the news.

6. The media are criticized as biased both by conservatives (who charge that the media are too liberal) and by liberals (who claim that the media are captives of corporate interests and major advertisers). Little evidence exists of actual, deliberate bias in news reporting.

7. A major effect of mass media news is agenda setting—determining what problems will become salient issues for people to form opinions about and to discuss. The media are also influential in defining issues for the general public.

8. Presidential campaigns are dominated by media coverage both before and after the national convention. One effect of media influence is that most people seem more interested in the contest as a game or "horse race" than as an occasion for serious discussion of issues and candidates. Another effect has been the rise of image making and the media consultant.

9. The press serves as both observer and participant in politics, as a watchdog, agenda setter, and check on the abuse of power, but it rarely follows the policy process to its conclusion.

Key Terms

mass media

news media

issue advertising

fairness doctrine

political socialization

selective exposure

selective perception

horse race

Further Reading

STEPHEN ANSOLABEHERE AND SHANTO IYENGAR, *Going Negative: How Attack Ads Shrink and Polarize the Electorate* (Free Press, 1996).

SIMONE CHAMBERS AND ANNE COSTAIN, EDS., *Deliberation, Democracy, and the Media* (Rowman & Littlefield, 2000).

TIMOTHY E. COOK, *Making Laws and Making News: Press Strategies in the U.S. House of Representatives* (Brookings Institution, 1990).

TIMOTHY E. COOK, *Governing with the News: The News Media as a Political Institution* (University of Chicago Press, 1998).

RICHARD DAVIS, *The Web of Politics: The Web's Impact on the American Political System* (Oxford University Press, 1999).

RICHARD DAVIS AND DIANA MARIE OWEN, *New Media and American Politics* (Oxford University Press, 1998).

ROBERT M. ENTMAN AND W. LANCE BENNETT, EDS., *Mediated Politics: Communication in the Future of Democracy* (Cambridge University Press, 2000).

JAMES FALLOWS, *Breaking the News: How the Media Undermine American Democracy* (Pantheon Books, 1996).

DORIS A. GRABER, *Processing Politics: Learning from Television in the Web Age* (University of Chicago Press, 2001).

DORIS A. GRABER, *Mass Media and American Politics*, 6th ed. (CQ Press, 2002).

RODERICK P. HART, *Campaign Talk: Why Elections Are Good for Us* (Princeton University Press, 2000).

STEPHEN HESS, *Live from Capitol Hill: Studies of Congress and the Media* (Brookings Institution, 1991).

PHYLISS KANISS, *Making Local News* (University of Chicago Press, 1991).

HOWARD KURTZ, *Spin Cycle: Inside the Clinton Propaganda Machine* (Free Press, 1998).

PAUL J. LAVRAKAS AND MICHAEL W. TRAUGOTT, *Election Polls, the News Media, and Democracy* (Chatham House, 2000).

S. ROBERT LICHTER, STANLEY ROTHMAN, AND LINDA S. LICHTER, *The Media Elite* (Adler & Adler, 1986).

PIPPA NORRIS, *A Virtuous Circle: Political Communications in Post-Industrial Societies* (Cambridge University Press, 2000).

MARTIN PLISSNER, *The Control Room: How Television Calls the Shots in Presidential Elections* (Free Press, 1999).

TOM ROSENSTEIL, *Strange Bedfellows: How Television and the Presidential Candidates Changed American Politics, 1992* (Hyperion, 1993).

LARRY J. SABATO AND S. ROBERT LICHTER, *Peepshow: Media and Politics in an Age of Scandal* (Rowman & Littlefield, 2000).

DAVID A. SCHULTZ, ED., *It's Show Time: Media, Politics, and Popular Culture* (Lang, 2000).

JAMES A. THURBER, CANDICE J. NELSON, AND DAVID A. DULIO, EDS., *Crowded Airwaves: Campaign Advertising in Elections* (Brookings Institution, 2000).

DARRELL M. WEST, *Air Wars: Television Advertising in Election Campaigns, 1952–1992* (CQ Press, 1993).

CONGRESS
The People's Branch

T HE UNITED STATES CONGRESS IS ONE OF

THE MOST PRAISED YET MOST CRITICIZED

POLITICAL INSTITUTIONS IN THE WORLD. ON THE

one hand, it is one of the world's most representative and democratic institutions, admired
for its openness and deliberateness. On the other hand, it is criticized relentlessly for its
inefficiency and unresponsiveness. Citizens think members of Congress do not understand
their needs, place the concerns of special interests ahead of those of their regular constituents, and will say anything to get reelected and then do pretty much whatever they
want. Sixty-two percent of participants in one national survey complained that "Congress creates more problems than it solves."[1]

These two views of Congress came into sharp focus in 2001. The year started out
with Republicans holding a slim majority in the House and the two parties tied in the Senate. The prospects for making laws worsened when Senator James Jeffords (R.-Vt.) left the
Republican party in May, giving the Democrats a 50-to-49 majority in the Senate and
the power to derail almost any legislation that President George W. Bush and his Republican congressional allies wanted. As a result, 2001 proved to be one of the least active
legislative years in modern congressional history.

The success of any one-year session of Congress cannot be measured in the number of
laws enacted, however. The framers understood that Congress could sometimes be quite successful by *not* passing any laws at all. Having given each branch of government its own list of
checks and balances against the other two branches, the framers expected that the odds against
action would be high. The framers did not want Congress to defeat all legislation, however. In
giving Congress a long list of carefully prescribed legislative powers in Article I, Section 1, of
the Constitution, the framers clearly expected Congress to address foreign and domestic threats.

That is certainly what the divided Congress did after the events of September 11,
2001. Congress moved quickly to authorize the president to use military force against terrorism abroad and expand the government's authority to strengthen homeland security.

After the attacks on September 11, 2001, the National Guard provided additional security at the Capitol and at other sites throughout Washington, D.C.

The most significant law was the United and Strengthening America by Providing Appropriate Tools Required to Intercept and Obstruct Terrorism, or the USA PATRIOT Act, which gave the president the new power to detain immigrants indefinitely without charging them with a crime while providing $75 billion for homeland security initiatives. Between September 11 and October 31, Congress enacted 40 bills that were signed into law by the president, more than doubling the number of bills it had enacted in the nine months before.

Because the framers created a system of shared powers, Congress and the president often agree to disagree, postponing action on important issues until compromise can be reached. That may be frustrating to the nation, especially when the public favors action, and may create the image of a "do-nothing" Congress, but it fits perfectly with the framers' intention to protect the nation from the passions of the moment. Congress protects the nation by both passing and defeating legislation.

In this chapter, we examine the politics of representation and how Congress organizes itself to do its work of making laws and representing the people. We also look at how this highly public, open, and political institution cannot avoid provoking conflicts that sometimes lead to bitter clashes with the White House and other rivals for influence in the shaping of U.S. public policies.

Congressional Elections

There is only one Congress described in the Constitution, but there are two very different electoral calendars for entering office. Each of the 435 members of the House of Representatives is elected to a two-year term in even-numbered years, while only a third of the Senate's 100 members are chosen for six-year terms every two years. The number of House members was finally capped at 435 when Congress ordered states to stop drawing new districts in 1910.

There are also somewhat different requirements for becoming members of the House and Senate. At minimum, members of the House must be 25 years old and have been citizens for seven years, whereas senators must be 30 years old and have been citizens for nine years. House and Senate candidates must be residents of the states from which they are elected.

By setting the Senate's requirements higher and giving its members a six-year term, the framers hoped the Senate would act as a check against what they saw as the less predictable House. Concerned about the "fickleness and passion" of the House of Representatives, James Madison in particular saw the Senate as "a necessary fence against this danger."[2]

The framers did not limit the number of terms a House member or senator could serve. The term limits imposed by the Articles of Confederation had forced several talented members out of office, leaving the Continental Congress less effective and souring the framers on the idea.[3]

Regardless of differences between the two houses of Congress, representatives and senators are all politicians who enter office by winning an election. Ironically, it is often good politics for them to deny that they are politicians and to lead the charge against the institution in which they serve. The willingness of "House members to stand and defend their own votes or voting record contrasts sharply with their disposition to run and hide when a defense of Congress might be called for," writes political scientist Richard F. Fenno Jr. "Members of Congress run *for* Congress by running *against* Congress. The strategy is ubiquitous, addictive, cost-free, and foolproof. . . . In the short run, everybody plays and nearly everybody wins. Yet the institution bleeds from 435 separate cuts."[4]

Where Representatives and Senators Are Elected

Members of the House and Senate represent different populations. According to the Constitution, every state has two U.S. senators, each of whom represents the entire state.

Seats in the House of Representatives are distributed or apportioned among the states according to population. There are 435 House districts, each composed of about 650,000 people. No matter how small its population, every state is guaranteed at least one House member.

The word "gerrymander" comes from the name of the governor of Massachusetts, Elbridge Gerry, and the salamander-shaped district that was created to favor his party in 1811.

The exact apportionment among the states is determined by a national census of the population that is required by the Constitution every ten years. As a result of the 2000 census, Congress had to reallocate seats based on population shifts through a process called **reapportionment**. New York and Pennsylvania lost two House seats; Ohio, Indiana, Illinois, Wisconsin, and Michigan all lost one seat. Florida, Georgia, Texas, and Arizona gained two seats; Colorado, Nevada, North Carolina, and California gained one seat each.

While census figures dictate how House districts are apportioned across the nation, each state determines where those districts lie within its own boundaries. State legislatures nearly always control this **redistricting** process, subject to final approval by the governor. Not surprisingly, the majority party in the legislature often draws the new map to increase the number of House districts that its own candidates are likely to win. In extreme cases, this process is known as **gerrymandering**, after Governor Elbridge Gerry who approved a Massachusetts redistricting plan that created a salamander-shaped district drawn for distinctly partisan purposes following the 1810 census. Most of the redistricting that followed the 2000 census protected House incumbents, reducing the number of districts considered too close to call in the 2002 election.[5]

Partisan gerrymandering, except in the most extreme cases, is entirely legal. The U.S. Supreme Court has ruled that only a plan that eliminates the minority party's influence statewide is unconstitutional.[6] This is such a tough standard to meet that only one partisan gerrymandering challenge filed after the 1990 census was successful. In that case, North Carolina Republicans were able to show that Democrats had so manipulated the state judicial election districts for so long that only one Republican superior court judge had been elected in the state since 1900.[7]

State legislatures may also draw districts in which a majority of voters are members of minority groups. Such racial gerrymandering is legal unless the legislature considered race and ignored traditional redistricting concerns, such as keeping communities together and reelecting incumbents.[8] Furthermore, a party attacking a majority-minority district must show that the legislature could have achieved the same political result with a significantly different racial balance. A challenge to a North Carolina congressional district failed because Republicans could not show that the district could include more white voters and still be drawn as favorably to Democratic interests.[9]

The principle of equal representation does not apply to the Senate. Because each state has two senators regardless of population, the Senate represents constituencies that are more rural, white, and conservative than would be the case if the one-person, one-vote norm applied to Senate elections.

Such disparities make the Senate the most malapportioned elected legislature in the democratic world, giving the advantage to residents of the smaller states. Frances Lee and Bruce Oppenheimer concluded that the size of a state's population affects senator-constituent relationships, fund raising and elections, strategic behavior within the Senate, and ultimately policy decisions.[10] Retired U.S. Senator Daniel Patrick Moynihan (D.-N.Y.), who knew firsthand how citizens of larger states fared less well in U.S. Senate policy battles, predicted that "some time in the next century the United States is going to have to address the question of apportionment in the Senate,"[11] but the prospects for changing the two-senators-per-state constitutional rule are highly unlikely in the near future.

Predicting Congressional Elections

The outcome of any congressional election depends on many factors, including campaign financing, local and national policy issues, and each candidate's skills. But all congressional elections start with the nature of the seat at stake. Some House campaigns involve a **safe seat**—one that is predictably won by one party or the other. Others involve a competitive seat that draws strong candidates from both major parties,

Freshmen House of Representatives of the 108th Congress, who took office in January 2003, on the steps of the U.S. Capitol for their "class" picture.

reapportionment
The assigning by Congress of congressional seats after each census. State legislatures reapportion state legislative districts.

redistricting
The redrawing of congressional and other legislative district lines following the census, to accommodate population shifts and keep districts as equal as possible in population.

gerrymandering
The drawing of legislative district boundaries to benefit a party, group, or incumbent.

safe seat
An elected office that is predictably won by one party or the other, so the success of that party's candidate is almost taken for granted.

State campaigns such as this one for incumbent U.S. Senator Jean Carnahan, Democrat from Missouri, are important as Democrats and Republicans both struggle to gain control of the Senate. Carnahan lost to Republican Jim Talent.

while still others involve an open seat that has been vacated by a sitting member who retires or runs for higher office.

Because only a third of the Senate stands for election every two years, Senate elections tend to be highly competitive and better financed than House elections. They also tend to turn on national, not local, issues, particularly in states with substantial media coverage. Although contests in large states often involve the largest amounts of money, even small states such as South Dakota, where former Senate Majority Leader Tom Daschle lives, can play host to very expensive campaigns.

In contrast, House elections tend to be local affairs. Although current members of Congress are sometimes judged by what they did in Washington, particularly when nationally visible issues such as Medicare, the economy, or education are on voters' minds, most citizens feel favorable toward their own member of Congress, even when they do not recognize their member's name and are harshly critical of Congress as a whole.

The last thing most candidates want to do is "nationalize" an election. They would much rather have the campaign be about how well they served the local community through constituent service.

The 2004 Congressional Elections

The 2004 congressional elections are best understood for what did not happen rather than for what did. Despite Democratic hopes for a surge in House seats and Republican hopes for a dramatic gain, the House campaigns produced a shift of only four seats for a balance of at least 231 to 201, with one independent and two races undecided as of mid November.

Also, despite Democratic hopes for a gain of enough Senate seats to recapture a majority and despite Republican hopes for a gain of enough seats to create the 60 votes needed to prevent filibusters, which are discussed later in this chapter, the Senate campaigns produced a net gain of four Republican seats for a balance of 55 to 44, with one independent who usually votes with the Democrats.

The elections were hardly uneventful, however, particularly in the Senate, where the Democrats had 19 seats to defend and the Republicans had 15. Republicans took six seats from the Democrats, including the seat held by Senate minority leader Tom Daschle (D.-S.D.), who was defeated by 8,000 votes in the most expensive Senate race in the nation, and the last five Southern seats still held by Democrats, four of which were vacated through Democratic retirements. In turn, Democrats took two seats from the Republicans, including the Illinois seat won by Barack Obama, who had established a national presence with his keynote address at the Democratic National Convention in July 2004, and the Colorado seat occupied by Native American Ben Nighthorse Campbell, who had entered the Senate a Democrat but who retired after having switched to the Republican party.

THE RESULTS   Beyond the Daschle upset and several tight contests in both chambers, the congressional elections produced little overall turnover. Voters reelected 18 of the 19 Senate incumbents who ran, and 394 of the 403 House incumbents who ran. Even including the four Texas **incumbents** who lost, 98.2 percent of incumbents won reelection, marking the third highest rate in fifty years; without the Texans, the rate hit 99.2 percent.

Indeed, many Senators and Representatives faced token opposition at best. Even before the election, only 9 of the 33 Senate seats up for election were rated as competitive, six of which involved an open seat where an incumbent had retired; while 371 House districts were rated as "safe," including 28 Democrats and 34 Republicans who ran unopposed. "In more than half the states with Senate races, voters are being denied the experience of seeing their senators seriously tested on their records or their plans," *Washington Post* veteran columnist David Broder wrote just before election day, "The situation in the House of Representatives is similar—but worse." (See David Broder, "What Democracy Needs: Real Races," *The Washington Post*, October 31, 2004, p. B07.) As if to prove the point, four of the nine incumbents who were defeated came from Texas, where two of the losing Democratic incumbents were matched up against Republican incumbents in newly-created districts.

Much of the incumbency advantage involved campaign financing. According to the nonpartisan Campaign Finance Institute, candidates for the 435 House seats spent nearly $450 million in 2004, while candidates for the 33 Senate seats spent nearly $225 million. On average, the House campaigns cost more than $1 million per seat, up almost 20 percent from the winners in 2002, while the Senate campaigns cost more than $6.5 million, up nearly 50 percent from 2002 and almost 60 percent from 1998 when the same 33 seats were last up for election (see Campaign Finance Institute, "House Winners Average $1 Million for the First Time; Senate Winners Up 47%," news release, Washington, D.C., November 5, 2004).

More importantly, winners outspent their challengers by large margins. House incumbents who were reelected by 60 percent or more of the vote outspent their challengers by four to one, or $900,000 to $170,000; while Senate incumbents who won by similar margins outspent their challengers by a margin of five to one, or $4.9 million to $900,000. As of September 30, 2004, incumbent Senator George Voinovich (R.-Ohio) had $4.2 million in cash on hand against an opponent with just $93,000, while incumbent senator and future minority leader Harry Reid (D.-Nev.) had $3.3 million in hand against an opponent with just $15,000.

Given its national importance to both Democrats and Republicans, South Dakota had the most expensive Senate campaign at $33 million. But high spending was not always tied to competitiveness. Despite the lack of strong opposition, New York had the second most expensive Senate campaign at $28 million, followed by California at $23 million, and Pennsylvania at $20 million.

Texas had the most expensive House race at $8.4 million in a Dallas-Fort Worth contest between two incumbents, Democrat Martin Frost and Republican Pete Sessions, which Sessions won, while South Dakota came in with the second most expensive contest at almost $6 million as Democrat Stephanie Herseth outlasted Republican Larry Diedrich in a rematch of their special election battle only six months earlier.

Congressional Election Results, 2004

	2000	2004
Senate		
Republican	51	55
Democrat	48	46
Independent	1	1
House		
Republican	227	231
Democrat	205	201
Independent	1	1
Undecided/Vacant*	2	2

*Two House seats were still undecided when this edition went to press.

incumbent
The current holder of an office.

Why Do Incumbent Members of Congress Usually Win?

- They enjoy better name recognition, and to be known at all is generally to be known favorably. Challengers are almost always less well known.

- They enjoy free mailings to every household in the state or district. These mailings—which often resemble campaign brochures—portray members as hardworking and influential.

- They have greater access to the media.

- They raise campaign money more easily than challengers, because lobbyists and political action committees (PACs) seek their ears and their favors. Also, many campaign contributors know that incumbents are more likely than challengers to get reelected, so they give to the candidates they are fairly certain will win. (PACs in recent elections have given as much as $8 out of every $10 to incumbents.)

- They have usually had more campaign experience, and they can claim to have had more experience in Congress and in Washington. And they are usually better campaigners.

- They have staffs to help with casework and constituency services for the folks back home.

- They take credit for federal money that gets allocated to their region.

- They are in a better position than challengers to take advantage of government research staffs, new government studies, and even classified information.

None of these factors can guarantee a member's reelection, yet skillful use of them makes it difficult to unseat an incumbent who is perceived as doing an adequate job.

Although incumbency and the campaign money that goes with it help explain the 2004 results, there were a number of unpredictable contests in which candidate conduct contributed to the uncertainty. In the Senate elections, Illinois Democrat Obama won his seat after the initial Republican candidate quit following reports that he had taken his wife to a sex club in Paris; Kentucky Republican incumbent and former major league Hall-of-Fame pitcher, Jim Bunning, survived despite having described his opponent as resembling one of Iraqi dictator Saddam Hussein's sons; Oklahoma Republican candidate Tom Colburn won his election after saying that physicians who perform abortions should be subject to the death penalty; and Alaska Republican Lisa Murkowski won her first election after having been appointed to her seat by her father, who was governor at the time. (For a complete summary of the 2004 congressional campaigns, see *Congressional Quarterly Weekly,* November 6, 2004.)

In the House, Illinois Democratic challenger Melissa Bean defeated the dean of the Republican majority, Philip Crane, who had been in the House since 1969 when she was just seven years old; while a Colorado Democrat and brother of the state's new senator won an open seat once held by a Republican.

If there was a single winner in the elections, it was House majority leader Tom DeLay, who designed the Texas redistricting strategy that gave the Republicans the four added seats. DeLay positioned himself as the heir-apparent when the current Speaker of the House, J. Dennis Hastert, retires. DeLay is not without enemies, however, and may yet face an indictment surrounding allegations that he directed corporate funding into the 2002 Texas state legislative campaigns that produced the new majority stemming from the redistricting.

GOVERNING IN THE NEW CONGRESS   The Senate clearly emerged as the new battleground in governing. Several of the new Republican senators are deeply conservative and have promised to bring issues such as abortion and gay marriage to the floor for votes as soon as possible, while veterans in both chambers have already signaled their intention to press for Democratic concessions on social and economic issues. "I earned capital in the campaign, political capital, and now I intend to spend it," President Bush said in November 2004, and he clearly hopes that his dual majorities in Congress will do much of the spending.

However, as Democrats learned when they had similar majorities in both chambers, 55 votes in the Senate is still five votes shy of the 60 needed to shut down filibusters and 11 short of the number needed to ratify treaties.

The Structure and Powers of Congress

The framers made two critical decisions early in the Constitutional Convention. First, they agreed to create a legislature as the first branch of government. Next, they divided that legislature into two chambers, the House of Representatives and the Senate. In doing so, the framers created one of the single most important obstacles to making laws. Worried about the tendency for the legislative branch to dominate government, they diluted the power of Congress by creating two chambers "as little connected with each other as the nature of their common functions and their common dependence on the society will admit."[12] Not only would Congress be balanced by the presidency and judiciary, but it would also be balanced against itself.

A Divided Branch

Bicameralism remains the most important organizational feature of the U.S. Congress. Each chamber has its own place to meet in separate wings of the Capitol Building (see Figure 11-1); each has offices for its members on separate ends of Capitol Street; each has its own committee structure, its own rules for considering legislation, and its own record of proceedings (even though the records are published together as the *Congressional Record*); and each sets the rules governing its own members (each establishes its own legislative committees, for example).[13]

Bicameral legislatures were common in most of the colonies, and the framers believed that the arrangement was essential for preventing strong-willed majorities from oppressing individuals and minorities.[14] As James Madison explained in *The Federalist*, No. 51, "In order to control the legislative authority, you must divide it." (*The Federalist*, No. 51, is

bicameralism
The principle of a two-house legislature.

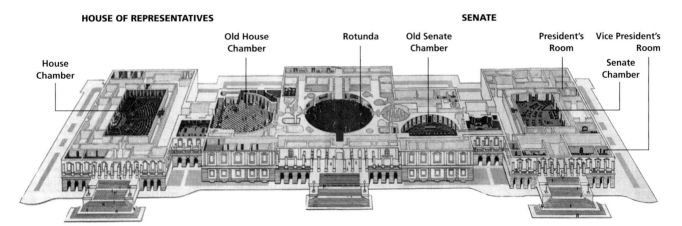

| HOUSE OF REPRESENTATIVES | | | | SENATE | | |

FIGURE 11–1   **The Capitol Building.**

Congress Performs Seven Important Functions

1. *Representation:* expressing the diversity and conflicting views of the regional, economic, social, racial, religious, and other interests in the United States

2. *Lawmaking:* enacting measures to help solve substantive problems

3. *Consensus building:* engaging in the bargaining process by which these interests are reconciled

4. *Overseeing the bureaucracy:* ensuring that laws and policies approved by Congress are faithfully carried out by the executive branch and accomplish what was intended

5. *Policy clarification:* identifying and publicizing issues

6. *Investigation:* investigating the operation of government agencies, including the White House; responsibility includes impeachment processes

7. *Approval:* for the Senate, confirming presidential appointees by a majority vote and ratifying treaties by a two-thirds vote

TABLE 11–1   Differences Between the House of Representatives and the Senate

House	Senate
Two-year term	Six-year term
435 members	100 members
Smaller constituencies	Larger constituencies
Less personal staff	More personal staff
Equal populations represented	States represented
Less flexible rules	More flexible rules
Limited debate	Extended debate
More policy specialists	Policy generalists
Less media coverage	More media coverage
Less prestige	More prestige
Less reliance on staff	More reliance on staff
More powerful committee leaders	More equal distribution of power
Very important committees	Less important committees
20 major committees	20 major committees
Nongermane amendments (riders) not allowed	Nongermane amendments (riders) not allowed
Important Rules Committee	Special treaty ratification power
Some bills permit no floor amendments (closed rule)	Special "advise and consent" confirmation power
	Filibuster allowed

reprinted in the Appendix.) Although the Seventeenth Amendment to the Constitution (1913) provided for direct election of U.S. senators (senators were originally chosen by state legislatures), the two chambers remain very different (see Table 11-1).

Defenders of bicameralism point to its moderating influence on partisanship or possible errors in either chamber. This constitutionally mandated structure also guarantees that many votes will be taken before a policy is finally approved. The arrangement also provides more opportunities for bargaining and allows legislators with different policy goals a role in the shaping of national laws.

The Powers of Congress

The framers gave the longest list of **enumerated powers** to Congress. Because the Revolutionary War had been sparked by unfair taxation, the framers listed the power "to lay and collect Taxes" as the very first duty of Congress. They then gave Congress the power to borrow and coin money, regulate citizenship, build post offices and postal roads, and establish the lower courts of the federal judiciary, meaning every court below the Supreme Court. The framers also gave Congress the power to protect the nation against foreign threats by declaring war, raising armies, and building navies and the power to protect the nation from domestic threats by regulating commerce and immigration.

Just in case the list was not enough to allow Congress to do its job, the framers gave Congress the catchall power to "make all Laws which shall be necessary and proper for carrying into Execution the foregoing Powers, and all other Powers vested by this Constitution in the Government of the United States, or in any Department or Officer thereof." This clause is sometimes called the *elastic clause* because it stretches to cover much of what Congress might do. The Constitution also gave Congress complete authority to set its own rules for its proceedings.

Finally, the Constitution gave Congress several nonlegislative functions, such as participating in the process of constitutional amendment and impeachment (given to the House) and trying an impeached federal officer (given to the Senate). The Constitution

enumerated powers
The powers explicitly given to Congress in the Constitution.

stipulates that the grounds for impeachment that can lead to the removal from office of a president or vice president or other federal officers, including federal judges, are the commission of "High Crimes and Misdemeanors" (never clearly defined). The House sits to determine whether or not an official's actions reach the level of impeachable offenses, and if so, it can impeach by a majority vote. The Senate sits as a court to decide if the impeached official should be convicted and whether the nature of the offense warrants removal from office. A two-thirds vote is needed to convict; thus a minority of just 34 senators can block the conviction of an impeached official.

As the impeachment power shows, the Constitution gives different duties to each chamber. The Senate has the power to confirm many presidential nominations. The Senate must also play a crucial "advise and consent" role in making treaties—formal agreements between the United States and other countries. All treaties must be approved by a two-thirds vote in the Senate before they can be ratified by the president.

The House has some of its own responsibilities, too, but they are not as important as those given to the Senate. For example, although all revenue bills must originate in the House, this practice does not give the House much advantage, because the Senate can freely amend spending bills even to the point of changing everything except the title.

Despite its position as the first branch of government and its substantial powers, Congress has difficulty keeping pace with its great rival, the presidency. The president's national security responsibilities, preparation of the budget, media visibility, and agenda-setting influence have all enhanced the position of the presidency relative to Congress.

Republican Dennis Hastert, Speaker of the House of Representatives.

Managing Congress

Today's Congress bears the unmistakable imprint of the bicameralism created more than 200 years ago. The Senate prides itself on being an incubator of ideas, a place in which individual members can take the floor to defend an intense minority and delay action until at least 60 senators vote to end the debate; the House prides itself on being the voice of the people.

The two chambers are no more complex, however, than the society they have come to represent and the executive branch they must oversee. It was far easier to control the 59 House members and 22 senators who represented white male property owners in 1789 when the First Congress was gaveled to order than it is to control the 435 House members and 100 senators who represent the diverse United States of today. It was far easier to write legislation for the tiny government in 1789 than for today's $2 trillion behemoth. In the 1790s, a handful of permanent committees could handle the entire task of making the laws and checking government.

Leading the House of Representatives

The organization and procedures in the House are different from those in the Senate, largely because the House is more than four times larger than the Senate. A larger membership requires more rules, which means that *how* things are done affects *what* is done. The House assigns different types of bills to different calendars. For instance, financial measures—tax or appropriations bills—are put on a special calendar for quicker action.

The House has other ways to speed up lawmaking, including electronic voting. Ordinary rules may be suspended by a two-thirds vote, or immediate action may be taken by *unanimous consent* of the members on the floor. By acting as a *committee of the whole,* the House is able to operate more informally and more quickly than under its regular rules. A *quorum* in the committee of the whole requires only 100 members, rather than a majority of the whole chamber, and voting is quicker and simpler. Members are limited in how long they can speak, and debate may be cut off simply by majority vote.

THE SPEAKER OF THE HOUSE   The **Speaker** is the presiding officer in the House of Representatives.[15] The Constitution mandates that the House of Representatives shall choose its Speaker, yet it does not say anything about the duties or powers of the office. The Speaker is

Speaker
The presiding officer in the House of Representatives, formally elected by the House but actually selected by the majority party.

The Changing Face of Congress

Although the Constitution does not mention race, gender, or wealth among the qualifications for office, the framers expected members of Congress to be white male property owners. After all, women and slaves could not vote, let alone hold office.

The framers would therefore be surprised at the face of Congress today. Recent Congresses have had record numbers of women and minorities, including the first African American woman in the Senate, Carol Moseley-Braun (D.-Ill.), and the first Native American, Ben Nighthorse Campbell (R.-Colo., still in office). The Congress that was sworn into office in 2001 had the largest number of women (59 in the House and 13 in the Senate) and racial and ethnic minorities (63 in the House and 3 in the Senate). Where minorities seem unable to gain ground is in the Senate, where the number has been stuck at four or less for almost three decades and moved down in 1998 when Moseley-Braun was defeated for reelection.

The changing face of Congress reflects the growing effectiveness of women and minority candidates in running for office. Campaigning as the ultimate outsiders, for example, women candidates offer an option to voters who see Congress as out of touch with ordinary Americans. Voters also judge women to be more honest than men by 5 to 10 percentage points, more caring by 5 points, and less tied to special interests.

The changing face of Congress also reflects changes in who gets to vote. The Voting Rights Act of 1965 allowed millions of African Americans to register and vote in the South. In Mississippi,

Women senators pose before a book-signing for their book Nine and Counting The Women of the Senate.

for example, only 14 percent of African Americans were registered to vote in 1960. By 1968, the number had increased to 64 percent. As the number of African American voters increased, so did the number of African American legislators.

The face of Congress may be changing, but its pocketbook and occupational history definitely are not. Almost one-third of the senators who served in the 106th Congress were millionaires, and more than half were lawyers. Moreover, old customs die hard. Even with the Democratic senator from Washington, Patty Murray, sitting on his Appropriations Committee, Chairman Robert Byrd still addressed committee members as "Gentlemen." However, with new sources of campaign funds for women and minority candidates and a growing list of election victories, the Senate and House are likely to continue changing.

Women and minorities have changed the policy agenda of Congress. Women legislators are more likely than men to oppose nuclear power and limits on abortion, for example, while minority members tend to be much more supportive of expanded government spending on cities and the poor. Both groups are more likely to support equal rights for women and minorities and are generally more liberal on the economic and social issues that come before Congress.

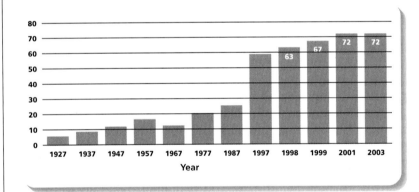

Number of Women in U.S. Congress.

SOURCE: Rutgers University Center for the American Woman and Politics. Adapted from the *Washington Post*, October 12, 1998, p. 10. Updated by the authors.

formally elected by the entire House yet is actually selected by the majority party. As the highest-ranking officer in Congress, the Speaker represents the legislative branch on ceremonial occasions. The Speaker is second in the line of succession to the presidency (after the vice president) in case of the death, resignation, or impeachment of the president and must keep the White House informed about his or her whereabouts.

The routine powers of the Speaker include recognizing members who wish to speak, ruling on questions of parliamentary procedure, and appointing members to temporary committees, not the major committees that help make the laws. In general, the Speaker today directs business on the floor of the House. More significant, of course, is the Speaker's political and behind-the-scenes influence.

When the Republicans won control of the House in 1994, they elected Representative Newt Gingrich of Georgia as Speaker. As the first Republican Speaker in 40 years, he was a novelty in Washington. "I had set out to do a very unusual job," said Gingrich, as "part revolutionary, part national political figure, part Speaker, part intellectual."[16]

Gingrich established his authority—reorganizing House committees, naming committee chairs, bypassing the seniority rule to appoint his allies to leadership posts, reorganizing House committees, and reducing perks and committee staffs. He pushed through some of the legislation outlined in the long list of campaign promises called the "Contract with America." He delegated considerable power to fellow Republican leaders yet claimed for himself the main role as spokesperson for major policy initiatives. He published books detailing his ideas about government and his party,[17] and he cheerfully took on the White House and the national press.

After a long investigation into the Speaker's use of tax-exempt funds, the House Ethics Committee concluded that Gingrich had violated certain standards of conduct. He insisted that there was little overlap between his political activities and his nonpartisan educational endeavors, but the committee recommended, and the House of Representatives quickly passed, a reprimand of Gingrich and imposed a fine of $300,000 for misusing charitable deductions for political purposes and for misleading the House Ethics Committee. This was an unprecedented rebuke for a Speaker.

Following his party's poor showing in the midterm election of 1998, Gingrich retired both as Speaker and as a member of Congress. Republicans soon selected Illinois Representative J. Dennis Hastert as Speaker. Hastert, a former high school teacher and wrestling coach, had served for six years in the Illinois state legislature and 12 years in the U.S. House of Representatives before becoming Speaker of the House. "It's a calling that I have not sought," said Hastert about the Speakership. "However, it is a duty that I cannot ignore."[18] Hastert displays a low-key, quiet self-confidence that has pleased most Republicans and has earned praise from Democrats.[19] He has been particularly effective in holding Republicans together on key party votes in the chamber while drawing extra votes from Democrats who belong to the "Blue Dog" coalition, a group of mostly southern conservatives.

OTHER HOUSE OFFICERS   The Speaker is assisted by the **majority leader**, who helps plan party strategy, confers with other party leaders, and tries to keep members of the party in line. The minority party elects the **minority leader**, who usually steps into the Speakership when his or her party gains a majority in the House. (These positions are also sometimes called majority and minority *floor leaders*.) Assisting each floor leader are the party **whips**. (The term comes from *whipper-in,* the huntsman who keeps the hounds bunched in a pack during a fox hunt.) The whips serve as liaisons between the House leadership of each party and the rank-and-file. They inform members when important bills will come up for a vote, prepare summaries of the bills, do nose counts for the leadership, exert pressure (sometimes mild and sometimes heavy) on members to support the leadership, and try to ensure maximum attendance on the floor for critical votes.

At the beginning of the session and occasionally afterward, each party holds a **party caucus** of all its members (called a *conference* by the Republicans) to elect party officers, approve committee assignments, elect committee leaders, discuss important legislation, and perhaps try to agree on party policy.

THE HOUSE RULES COMMITTEE   The House has a powerful Rules Committee that regulates the time of floor debate for each bill and sets limitations on floor amendments. By refusing to grant a *rule,* which describes the conditions of debate, the Rules Committee can delay consideration of a bill. A **closed rule** prohibits amendments altogether or provides that only members of the committee reporting the bill may offer amendments; closed rules are usually reserved for tax and spending bills. An **open rule** permits debate within the overall time allocated to the bill.

U.S. Senate minority leader Tom Daschle making a point on NBC's Meet the Press.

majority leader
The legislative leader selected by the majority party who helps plan party strategy, confers with other party leaders, and tries to keep members of the party in line.

minority leader
The legislative leader selected by the minority party as spokesperson for the opposition.

whip
Party leader who is the liaison between the leadership and the rank-and-file in the legislature.

party caucus
A meeting of the members of a party in a legislative chamber to select party leaders and to develop party policy. Called a *conference* by the Republicans.

closed rule
A procedural rule in the House of Representatives that prohibits any amendments to bills or provides that only members of the committee reporting the bill may offer amendments.

open rule
A procedural rule in the House of Representatives that permits floor amendments within the overall time allocated to the bill.

Senator Bill Frist of Tennessee, Republican majority leader.

From the New Deal era in the mid-1930s until the mid-1960s, a coalition of Republicans and conservative Democrats used the Rules Committee to block significant legislation on civil rights, health care, and poverty. Liberals denounced it as unrepresentative, unfair, and dictatorial. More recently, the Rules Committee membership has come to reflect the views of the general makeup of the majority party. It has become much less an independent obstacle to legislation and more a place to design rules that help advance the general goals of the majority party.

Leading the Senate

The Senate has the same basic committee structure, elected party leadership, and decentralized power as the House, but because the Senate is a smaller body, its procedures are more informal, and it permits more time for debate. It is a more open, fluid, and decentralized body now than it was a generation or two ago. Indeed, it is often said that the Senate has 100 separate power centers and is so splintered that the party leaders have difficulty arranging the day-to-day schedule.[20]

The Senate is led by the Senate majority leader, who is elected by the majority party in the Senate. When the majority leader is from the president's party, the president is the party's most visible leader. However, when the majority leader and the president are from different parties, the majority leader is considered his or her party's national spokesperson.

As the Senate's power broker, the majority leader has the right to be the first senator heard on the floor. In consultation with the Senate minority leader, the majority leader controls the Senate's agenda and recommends committee assignments for members of the majority party. But the position confers less authority than the Speakership in the House, and its influence depends on the person's political and parliamentary skills and on the national political situation.[21] Senate majority leaders have to be persuaders and negotiators, not only working closely with the minority leader but also working with a number of powerful majority and minority senators and the White House.

Nevertheless, the majority leader does have substantial influence over the legislative agenda in the Senate. Senator Lott proved this point in the session of Congress immediately following the 2002 election. Although his party was not technically in the majority until the new Congress was sworn into office in January 2003, Lott worked with the president to make sure that the new Department of Homeland Security became law. (Chapter 14 provides more details on the new department.)

A 50–50 Split

Following the extraordinarily close outcome of the 2000 election, the Senate voted to grant Democrats and Republicans an equal number of seats on all committees and an even share of the money to run them. . . .

Senator Trent Lott, the former Republican leader, and Senator Tom Daschle, the Democratic leader, negotiated the proposal over several weeks and presented it to their respective parties, hailing it as a formula for bipartisanship.

A reluctant Republican conference signed off on the proposal after two days of discussion, realizing it was the best deal they could secure under the circumstances, Mr. Lott said.

"It's going to force us to work together more than we have in the past," Mr. Lott said. "No doubt. I don't think that's bad. I think this is a framework for bipartisanship."

. . . Neither party got everything it wanted, although Republicans were forced to bend the most. While Republicans retained control of the Senate because the Constitution gave the vice-president the right to break the votes, they were forced to share control of their committees, though they kept the chairmanships.

The resolution called for an equal division of committee assignments and an equal share of money between the two parties to run the committees, which meant Democrats could hire more policy experts and buy more computers. In the past, Republicans held a one-third advantage in staff, office space, and money.

Even though the 50–50 tie was broken when Senator James Jeffords of Vermont left the Republican party to become an independent in May 2001, the two parties agreed to abide by the power-sharing agreement throughout the rest of the 107th Congress. Senator Daschle did become majority leader, and Democrats took over all the committee chairmanships, but Republicans retained their staffs and office space.

SOURCE: Lizette Alvarez, "Senate to Divide Power and Money Equally in Panels," *New York Times,* January 6, 2001, p. 1.

Lott was not to be majority leader for long, however. He soon became embroiled in a controversy surrounding remarks he made at the 100th birthday party for retiring South Carolina Senator Strom Thurmond. In congratulating Thurmond for his forty-eight years of Senate service, Lott remarked that the nation would have been better off had Thurmond won the presidency as the candidate of the independent Dixiecrat Party in 1948. The Dixiecrat Party was formed to oppose racial integration, and fought civil rights throughout the 1950s and into the 1960s. Lott was forced to resign his post on December 20, 2002, and was replaced by Tennessee Senator Bill Frist, a former heart surgeon who had been in the Senate for just eight years.

Party machinery in the Senate is similar to that in the House. There are party caucuses (conferences), majority and minority floor leaders, and party whips. Each party has a *policy committee,* composed of party leaders, which is theoretically responsible for the party's overall legislative program. In the Senate, the party policy committees assist the leadership in monitoring legislation and provide policy expertise. Unlike the House party committees, the Senate's party policy committees are formally provided for by law, and each has a regular staff and a budget. Although the Senate party policy committees have some influence on legislation, they have not asserted strong legislative leadership or managed to coordinate policy.

The president of the Senate (the vice president of the United States) also has little influence over Senate proceedings. A vice president can vote only in case of a tie. The Senate elects a **president pro tempore**, usually the most senior member from the majority party, who acts as chair in the absence of the vice president. Presiding over the Senate on most occasions is a thankless chore, so the president pro tempore regularly delegates this responsibility to junior members of the chamber's majority party.

Despite these various leaders and offices, the Senate is far less structured than the House. It has always operated under rules that vest great power in the individual senator. Extended debate allows senators to hold the floor as long as they wish unless a supermajority of 60 colleagues votes to end debate. Moreover, the Senate's rules allow individual senators to offer amendments on virtually any topic to a pending bill, allowing them to amend a bill to death.[22]

One relatively recent expression of this individualism is a practice called the **hold**. A hold is a procedure allowing any senator to block temporarily the consideration of either a legislative bill or a presidential nomination. Found nowhere in the Constitution or in Senate rules, the hold has "evolved as a courtesy for senators who could not be present when a vote was scheduled or who needed time to bone up on a subject before the floor debate began."[23] But since the early 1990s, the hold has expanded beyond its past purposes and is now often a tactic used to kill a bill or nomination.

Although successful Senate leadership still depends on personal relationships, individual members have become more partisan in recent decades. "Senators known for compromise, moderation and institutional loyalty," observe political scientists Nicol Rae and Colton Campbell, "have been replaced with more ideological and partisan members who see the chamber as a place to enhance their party fortunes."[24] Partisanship in the Senate was vehement during the Bill Clinton impeachment proceedings and to a lesser extent in the confirmation battle of George W. Bush's nominee John Ashcroft as his attorney general.

THE FILIBUSTER   Because of its smaller size and looser rules, debate is more open in the Senate. A senator who gains the floor may go on talking until he or she relinquishes the right to talk voluntarily or through exhaustion. This right to unlimited debate, known as the **filibuster**, may be used by a small group of senators to delay Senate proceedings by talking continuously so as to postpone or prevent a vote. At one time, the filibuster was a favorite weapon of southern senators intent on blocking civil rights legislation. More recently, the filibuster has been used for a wider range of issues. In 1993, Republicans used a filibuster to kill President Clinton's economic stimulus package and Democrats considered filibusters to derail the Ashcroft confirmation and parts of the Bush tax plan.

A filibuster, or the threat of a filibuster, is typically most potent at the end of a congressional session, when a date has been fixed for adjournment, because it could mean that many bills that have otherwise made it through the legislative process will die for lack of a floor vote. The knowledge that a bill might be subject to a filibuster is often enough to

"Listen, pal! I didn't spend seven million bucks to get here so I could yield the floor to you."

president pro tempore
Officer of the Senate selected by the majority party to act as chair in the absence of the vice president.

hold
A procedural practice in the Senate whereby a senator temporarily blocks the consideration of a bill or nomination.

filibuster
A procedural practice in the Senate whereby a senator refuses to relinquish the floor and thereby delays proceedings and prevents a vote on a controversial issue.

As part of her confirmation process, Labor Secretary Elaine Chao answered questions for congressional committee members on Capitol Hill.

force a compromise satisfactory to its opponents. Sometimes the leaders, knowing that a filibuster will tie up the Senate and keep it from enacting other needed legislation, do not bring a controversial bill to the floor.

A filibuster can be defeated. Until 1917, the Senate could terminate a filibuster only if every member agreed. That year, however, the Senate adopted its first debate-ending rule, or **cloture.** The rule specifies that the question of curtailing debate must be put to a vote two days after 16 senators sign a petition asking for cloture. If three-fifths of the total number of the Senate (60 of the 100 members) vote in favor of cloture, no senator may speak on the measure under consideration for more than one hour. Once invoked, cloture requires that the final vote on the measure be taken after no more than 30 hours of debate.

There has been an increase in the use and threat of filibusters in recent years, and these tactics have often been used for partisan and parochial purposes. Indeed, as noted, senators usually anticipate a filibuster on controversial measures, and the threat is often sufficient to force the majority to compromise and modify its position.[25] Both parties have learned to use the filibuster when they are in the minority. The Senate has averaged a few dozen filibusters in recent years, and nearly 50 cloture votes were held in 1999–2000.[26]

THE POWER TO CONFIRM   The Constitution leaves the precise practices of the confirmation process somewhat ambiguous: "The President . . . shall nominate, and by and with the Advice and Consent of the Senate, shall appoint Ambassadors, other public Ministers and Consuls, Judges of the Supreme Court, all other officers of the United States." The framers of the Constitution regarded the confirmation process—the Senate's "advise and consent" power—as an important check on executive power. Alexander Hamilton viewed it as a way for the Senate to prevent the appointment of "unfit characters."

As with other legislative business, the confirmation process starts in committees, with the relevant committee that oversees the particular function or activity involved. For example, the Judiciary Committee considers federal judges and Supreme Court nominees; the Foreign Relations Committee considers ambassadorial appointments. Nominees appear before the committee to answer questions, and they typically meet individually with key senators before the hearing.

Presidents have never enjoyed exclusive control over hiring and firing in the executive branch. The Senate jealously guards its right to confirm or reject or even delay major appointments; during the period of strong Congresses after the Civil War, presidents had to struggle to keep their power to appoint and dismiss. But for most of the past century, presidents have gained a reasonable amount of control over top appointments, in part because a growing number of people in and out of Congress believe that chief executives without compatible cabinet-level appointees of their choice cannot be held accountable. The Senate's advise and consent powers sometimes force presidents to make compromises, plainly constraining their ability to use the presidential appointment power.

The Senate's role in the confirmation process was never intended to prevent a president from taking political considerations into account when appointments are made but rather was designed to use the political judgment of senators as a safeguard against weak or ill-advised nominees. When the Senate was Democratic and the White House Republican, conservatives complained that the Senate was interfering with the executive power of the president by rejecting nominees because of their political beliefs. Yet when the Republicans controlled the Senate and the Democrats the White House, it was the liberals who made the same complaint.

In recent years, the Senate has taken a tough stand on some presidential appointments and spent more time evaluating and screening presidential nominations. The Senate rejected several nominees of Presidents Ronald Reagan and George Bush, and Presidents Bill Clinton and George W. Bush withdrew nominees in the face of Senate opposition.

By a tradition called **senatorial courtesy**, a president confers with the senator or senators in his own political party from the state where an appointee is to work. Occasionally, a president has to take into account the views of a politically powerful senator in the

cloture
A procedure for terminating debate, especially filibusters, in the Senate.

senatorial courtesy
Presidential custom of submitting the names of prospective appointees for approval to senators from the states in which the appointees are to work.

opposition party. A nomination is less likely to secure Senate approval against the objection of these senators, especially if these senators are members of the president's party. Thus for nearly all district court judgeships and a variety of other positions, senators can exercise what is in fact a veto that can be overridden only with difficulty. Further, it is usually exercised in secret and subject to little accountability. Since this form of patronage or influence is sufficiently important to senators, it is likely to continue.

As noted earlier, a controversial practice has emerged in recent years that allows an individual senator to request of the Senate leadership that a hold be placed on a nomination. The hold is requested to permit that senator to meet with the nominee, to gain more information about the nominee, or similar purposes. Despite presidential protests, such holds have become more frequent and are used to delay an appointment, to extract concessions from the president or other senators, or sometimes even to kill a nomination.

It is useful to note a distinction between *judicial* appointments, especially those to the Supreme Court, and *executive branch* or *administrative* appointments. The Senate plays a greater role in judicial appointments because federal judges serve for life and constitute an independent and vital branch of the government.[27] When it comes to cabinet-level positions in the executive branch, it is assumed that a president ought to be able to choose who will carry out the general views of the White House; in contrast, a president is not expected to enjoy partisan loyalty from individuals nominated to the bench.

Congressional Committees

It is sometimes said that Congress is a collection of committees that come together in a chamber every once in a while to approve one another's actions. Congress has long relied on committees to get its work done. Woodrow Wilson, a political science professor before he became president, expressed a similar thought: "Congress in session is Congress on display. Congress in committee is Congress at work."[28] More precisely, Congress in subcommittee is Congress at work, because the initial struggle over legislation takes place in subcommittees.[29]

TABLE 11–2   Congressional Standing and Select Committees

House	Senate	Joint Committees
Agriculture	Agriculture, Nutrition, and Forestry	Economics
Appropriations	Appropriations	Printing
Armed Services	Armed Services	Taxation
Budget	Banking, Housing, and Urban Affairs	On the Library
Education and the Workforce	Budget	
Energy and Commerce	Commerce, Science, and Transportation	
Financial Services	Energy and Natural Resources	
Government Reform	Environment and Public Works	
House Administration	Finance	
International Relations	Foreign Relations	
Judiciary	Governmental Affairs	
Resources	Health, Education, Labor, and Pensions	
Rules	Indian Affairs	
Science, Space, and Technology	Judiciary	
Select Intelligence	Rules and Administration	
Small Business	Select Ethics	
Standards of Official Conduct	Select Intelligence	
Transportation and Infrastructure	Small Business	
Veterans' Affairs	Special Aging	
Ways and Means	Veterans' Affairs	

Congressional members of the House Energy Subcommittee meet to investigate the accounting scandal associated with the Enron Corporation.

TYPES OF COMMITTEES   In theory, all congressional committees are created anew in each new Congress. In reality, however, most continue with little change from Congress to Congress. **Standing committees** are the most durable and are the sources of most bills, while **special or select committees** come together to address temporary priorities of Congress such as aging or taxes and rarely author legislation. **Joint committees** have members from both the House and the Senate and exist either to study an issue of interest to the entire Congress or to oversee congressional support agencies such as the Library of Congress or the U.S. Government Printing Office. Almost all standing committees have subcommittees that help handle the legislative workload.

Of the various types of committees, standing committees are the most important for making laws and representing constituents, and they fall into four types: authorizing, appropriations, rules, and revenue. As Table 11-2 shows, there are more than three dozen standing committees in the House and Senate.

Authorizing committees pass the laws that tell government what to do. The House and Senate education and labor committees, for example, are responsible for setting the rules governing the Pell Grant student loan program, including who can apply, how much they can get, where the loans come from, and how defaults are handled. Simply stated, authorizing committees make the most basic decisions about who gets what, when, and how from government. In 1999–2000, there were 15 authorizing committees in the House and 17 in the Senate. The number of committees remained unchanged in 2003–2004.

Authorizing committees are also responsible for oversight of the federal bureaucracy. Some of this oversight is designed to ask whether programs are working well, and some is designed to reduce fraud, waste, or abuse in an agency of government. The amount of congressional oversight is increasing. Political scientist Joel Aberbach found, for example, that just 8 percent of all legislative hearings focused on oversight in 1961, compared to over 25 percent just two decades later.[30]

Appropriations committees make decisions about how much money government will spend on its programs and operations. Although there is just one appropriations committee in each chamber, each appropriations committee has one subcommittee for each of the 13 appropriations bills that must be enacted each year to keep government running. Because they decide who gets how much from government, these subcommittees have great power to undo or limit decisions by the authorizing committees. The House and Senate authorizing committees may have authorized Pell Grants to rise as high as $3,700 a year in 1992, but the appropriations subcommittees on education provided enough money for grants of only $2,300. It was not until 1998 that the money finally caught up with the authorization, in part because the Pell Grant authorization fell to $3,300.

Rules and administration committees determine the basic operations of the two houses—for example, how many staffers individual members get. Again because of the number of members it must control, the House Rules Committee is more powerful than its twin in the Senate. As noted earlier, the House Rules Committee has special responsibility for giving each bill a rule, or ticket, to the floor of the House and determines what, if any, amendments to a bill will be permitted.

Revenue and budget committees deal with raising the money that appropriating committees spend while setting the broad targets that shape the federal budget. The House Ways and Means Committee is arguably the single most powerful committee in Congress, for it both raises and authorizes spending. As the only committee in either chamber that can originate tax and revenue legislation, it is also responsible for making basic decisions on the huge Social Security and Medicare programs.

CHOOSING COMMITTEE MEMBERS   Control and staffing of standing committees are partisan matters. The chair and a majority of each standing committee come from the majority party. The minority party is represented on each committee roughly in proportion

standing committee
A permanent committee established in a legislature, usually focusing on a policy area.

select or special committee
A congressional committee created for a specific purpose, sometimes to conduct an investigation.

joint committee
A committee composed of members of both the House of Representatives and the Senate; such committees oversee the Library of Congress and conduct investigations.

to its membership in the entire chamber, except on some powerful committees on which the majority may want to enhance its position.

Getting on a politically advantageous committee is important to members of Congress. A representative from Kansas, for example, would rather serve on the Agriculture Committee than on the Banking and Financial Services Committee. Members usually stay on the same committees from one Congress to the next, although junior members who have had less desirable assignments often seek better committees when places become available.

The House and Senate choose committee members in different ways. Republicans in the House choose committee members through their Committee on Committees, which is composed of one member from each state that has Republican representation in the House. Because each member has as many votes in the committee as there are Republicans in the delegation, the group is dominated by senior members from the large state delegations. Democrats in the House choose committee members through the Steering and Policy Committee of the Democratic caucus in negotiation with senior Democrats from the state delegations.

Veteran party members also dominate the Senate assignment process, where both parties have small Steering Committees that make committee assignments. In making assignments, leaders are guided by various considerations: how talented and cooperative a member is, whether his or her region is already well represented on a committee, and whether the assignment will aid in reelecting the member. Sometimes fierce battles erupt within these committees, reflecting ideological, geographical, and other differences.

One way Congress copes with its legislative workload is to organize its committees and subcommittees by subject matter. This specialization allows members to develop technical expertise in specific areas and to recruit skilled staffs. Thus Congress is often able to challenge experts from the bureaucracy. Interest groups and lobbyists realize the great power a specific committee has in certain areas and focus their attention on its members. Similarly, members of executive departments are careful to cultivate the committee and subcommittee chairs and members of "their" committees. The connections among a committee, an interest group, and an executive branch agency can be so strong that it is sometimes referred to as an *iron triangle.*

How each chamber in Congress uses committees is critical in its role as a partner in policy making, both with the other house and with the executive branch. In recent years, progress has been made in opening hearings to the public and improving the quality of committee staffs, but it is difficult to restructure committee jurisdictions so that they do not overlap. Consequently, a dozen different committees deal with energy, education, and the war on drugs. Efforts to make the committee system more efficient are often considered threats to the delicate balance of power within the chamber.

THE ROLE OF SENIORITY   Forty years ago, committee chairs determined the workload of committees, hired and fired staff, formed subcommittees, and assigned them jurisdictions, members, and aides. Chairs also managed the most important bills assigned to their committees. Since the mid-1970s, however, junior members have insisted on being given more authority. Subcommittee chairs have also become more independent. In recent years, there have also been moves to strengthen the powers of the party leaders and caucuses at the expense of committee chairs.

Most chairs are selected on the basis of the **seniority rule**; the member of the majority party with the longest continuous service on the committee becomes chair upon the retirement of the current chair or a change in the party in control of Congress. The seniority rule gives power to representatives who come from safe districts where one party is dominant and a member can build up years of continuous service. Conversely, the seniority rule lessens the influence of states or districts where the two parties are more evenly matched and where there is more turnover.

Although it is not uncommon for the party leadership to reward a junior member with a prestigious committee assignment, seniority has long been respected in Congress

seniority rule
A legislative practice that assigns the chair of a committee or subcommittee to the member of the majority party with the longest continuous service on the committee.

for several reasons: It encourages members to stay on a committee, it encourages specialization and expertise, and it reduces the interpersonal politics that would arise if several members of a committee sought to become chair. Under new rules adopted in the mid-1990s, however, both House and Senate Republicans agreed to limit committee chairs to serving no more than three consecutive terms.[31] Those rules resulted in significant turnover in the House following the 2002 election.

INVESTIGATIONS AND OVERSIGHT   Committees do more than produce legislation. They also have two additional roles in making government work.

The first is the power to *investigate*. Congress conducts investigations to determine if legislation is needed, to gather facts relevant to legislation, to assess the efficiency of executive agencies, to build public support, to expose corruption, and to enhance the image or reputation of its members.[32] Hearings by standing committees, their subcommittees, or special select committees are an important source of information and opinion. They provide an arena in which experts can submit their views.

The second is the *oversight* power—the responsibility to question executive branch officials to see whether their agencies are complying with the wishes of the Congress and conducting their programs efficiently. Authorization committees regularly hold oversight hearings, and appropriations committees, exercising "the congressional power of the purse," often use appropriations hearings to communicate committee members' views about how agency officials should conduct their business. Cabinet members and agency heads have been known to dread the loaded questions of hostile members of Congress and to hate having to watch themselves on the evening news trying to explain why their agency made some mistakes.

THE SPECIAL ROLE OF CONFERENCE COMMITTEES   Given the differences between the House and the Senate, it is not surprising that the version of a bill passed by one chamber may differ substantially from the version passed by the other. Only if both houses pass an absolutely identical measure can it become law. Most of the time, one house accepts the language of the other, but about 10 to 12 percent of all bills passed, usually major ones, must be referred to a **conference committee**—a special committee of members from each chamber that settles the differences between versions.[33] Both parties are represented, but the majority party has more members.

The proceedings of a conference committee are usually an elaborate bargaining process. When the revised bill is brought back to the two chambers, the conference report can be accepted or rejected (often with further negotiations ordered), but it cannot be amended. Conference members of each chamber must convince their colleagues that any concessions made to the other chamber were on unimportant points and that nothing basic to the original version of the bill was surrendered.

Conference committees have considerable leeway in reaching agreement, prompting President Ronald Reagan to note, "You know, if an orange and an apple went into conference consultations, it might come out a pear."[34] Ordinarily, members are expected to end up somewhere between the different versions. On matters for which there is no clear middle ground, members are sometimes accused of exceeding their instructions and producing an entirely new bill. For this reason, the conference committee has been called a "third house" of Congress and one of the most significant congressional institutions.[35]

It is not clear whether the House or the Senate wins more often in conference committees. On the surface, it appears that the Senate's version wins more often, but this is partly because the Senate often acts on its legislation after the House. But by approving the initial bill first and thereby setting the agenda on an issue, the House often has more of an impact on the final outcome than the Senate.

CAUCUSES   In contrast to conference committees, which are appointed by the House and Senate leadership to perform a specific legislative role, caucuses are best defined as informal committees that allow individual members to promote shared legislative interests.

conference committee
Committee appointed by the presiding officers of each chamber to adjust differences on a particular bill passed by each in different form.

There are caucuses for House members only, for senators only, and for members of both chambers together. By the 1990s, according to one count, House members actually served on more informal caucuses than on committees and subcommittees.[36]

The growing diversity of the caucuses parallels the rest of society. They include the Black Caucus, Hispanic Caucus, Women's Issues Caucus, Rural Health Caucus, Children's Caucus, Cuba Freedom Caucus, Pro-Life Caucus, Homelessness Task Force, Urban Caucus, and Ethiopian Jewry Caucus. The diversity also parallels the fragmentation of interest groups, with caucuses on nearly every business and public interest issue—including steel, beef, wheel bearings, the Internet, mushrooms, mining, gas, sweeteners, wine, footwear, soybeans, animal rights, Chesapeake Bay, clean water, drug enforcement, adoption, the arts, energy, military reform, AIDS, and antiterrorism. There are also caucuses composed of friends of the Caribbean Basin, animals, human rights monitors, and Ireland.

The Job of the Legislator

Membership in Congress was once a part-time job. Members came to Washington for a few terms, averaged less than five years of continuous service, and returned to their careers. Congressional pay was low, and Washington was no farther than a carriage ride from home.[37]

Congress started to meet more frequently in the late 1800s, pay increased, and being a member of Congress became increasingly attractive.[38] In the 1850s, roughly one-half of all House members retired or were defeated at each election; by 1900, the number who left at the end of each term had fallen to roughly one-quarter; by the 1970s, the number had fallen to barely a tenth. Even in the 1994 congressional elections, when Republicans won the House majority for the first time in 40 years, 90 percent of House incumbents who ran for reelection won.[39] In 2002, 98 percent of House incumbents were reelected.

By the 1950s, being a member of Congress had become a full-time job and a long-term career. Members came to Washington to stay and began to exploit the natural advantages that come with running for reelection as an incumbent: name recognition, service to citizens back home, copious campaign funding, nearly unlimited access to the media, and free postage under the *franking privilege* for mailings back home. In 1954, for example, members of Congress sent 44 million pieces of mail back home. By 1992, the number had increased more than tenfold to nearly 460 million.[40]

The workday also got longer. According to a 1998 survey, most members reported that they worked more than 70 hours a week, dividing their time among committee and subcommittee hearings, floor debates, meetings with citizens and interest groups, and raising money for the next election. Members do not seem to think the job is too tough, at least not the 402 members who ran for reelection in 1998. Nor has job satisfaction declined: 96 percent of members reported that they were very or mostly satisfied with their jobs in 1998, and only 15 percent said the job had gotten less satisfying since they first entered Congress. There appears to be little softening of interest in holding these jobs, despite the high levels of public distrust in Congress as an institution.[41]

As members of Congress became attached to their careers, they began to abandon many of the norms that once guided their behavior in office.[42] The old norms were simple. Members were supposed to specialize in a small number of issues (the norm of specialization), defer to members with longer tenure in office (the norm of seniority), never criticize anyone personally (the norm of courtesy), and wait their turn to speak and introduce legislation (the norm of apprenticeship). As longtime House Speaker Sam Rayburn once said, new members were to go along in order to get along, and to be seen and not heard.

The new norms are equally simple. New members are no longer willing to wait their turn to speak or introduce legislation and now have enough staff to make their opinions known on just about any issue at just about any point in the legislative process. Although the norm of courtesy still lives on as members refer to each other with great respect, the new congressional career allows little time for the old norms of specialization, seniority, and apprenticeship. Members must take care of themselves first.

Legislators as Representatives

Congress has a split personality. On the one hand, it is a *lawmaking institution* that writes laws and makes policy for the entire nation. In this capacity, all the members are expected to set aside their personal ambitions and perhaps even the concerns of their own constituencies. Yet Congress is also a *representative assembly,* made up of 535 elected officials who serve as links between their constituents and the national government (see Table 11-3). The dual roles of making laws and responding to constituents' demands force members to balance national concerns against the specific interests of their states or districts.

Individual members of Congress perceive their roles differently. Some believe they should serve as **delegates** from their districts. These legislators believe it is their duty to find out what "the folks back home" want and act accordingly. Other members see their role as that of **trustee**. Their constituents, they contend, did not send them to Congress to serve as mere robots or "errand runners." They act and vote according to their own view of what is best for their district or state as well as the nation.

Most legislators shift back and forth between the delegate and trustee roles, depending on their perception of the public interest, their standing in the last and next

delegate
An official who is expected to represent the views of his or her constituents even when personally holding different views; one interpretation of the role of the legislator.

trustee
An official who is expected to vote independently based on his or her judgment of the circumstances; one interpretation of the role of the legislator.

TABLE 11–3   Profile of the 108th Congress, 2003–2005

	Senate (100)	House (435)
Party Affiliation		
Republican	51	229
Democratic	48	205
Independent	1	1
Sex		
Male	86	373
Female	14	62
Religion		
Catholic	25	124
Jewish	11	26
Protestant	63	278
Other	1	7
Average Age	60	54
Racial/Ethnic Minorities	3	64
Occupational Field		
Law	60	161
Education	12	88
Business, banking	25	165
Agriculture	5	26
Journalism	6	11
Engineering	1	8
Real estate	3	30

SOURCE: *Congressional Quarterly Weekly,* January 25, 2003, pp.190–193

elections, and the pressures of the moment. Most also view themselves more as free agents than as instructed delegates for their districts. And recent research suggests that they often are free, since about 50 percent of citizens are unaware of how their representatives voted on major legislation and often believe their representative voted in accordance with constituent policy views. Still, nearly everyone in Congress spends a lot of time building constituency connections, mending political fences, reaching out to swing voters, and worrying about how a vote on a controversial issue will "play" back home.[43]

Legislators as Lawmakers

About 5,000 bills are introduced in the House every two years and as many as 3,000 in the Senate. Members of Congress cast as many as 1,000 votes each year.[44] When they vote, members of Congress are influenced by their own philosophy and values, their perceptions of their constituents' interests, the views of their trusted colleagues and staff, their partisan ties, and party leaders, lobbyists, and the president.

POLICY AND PHILOSOPHICAL CONVICTIONS Members are influenced by their ideological beliefs most of the time. Their experiences and their attitudes about the role of government shape their convictions and help explain a lot of the differences in voting patterns.[45] A liberal on social issues is also likely to be a liberal on tax and national security issues. On controversial issues such as Social Security reform, tax cuts, or defense spending, knowing the general philosophical leanings of individual members provides a helpful guide both to how they make up their minds and how they will vote.

In 2003, the widely respected weekly report *National Journal,* rated Barbara Boxer (D.-Calif.) as the most liberal senator and Pat Roberts (R.-Kansas) as the most conservative; and they rated John Conyers (D.-Mich.) and Pete Stark (D.-Calif.) as the most liberal representatives, while 13 members of the House tied as the most conservative.[46] Although Democrats are more likely to be liberals and Republicans more likely to be conservatives, there are centrists in both parties. Almost all of the most liberal Democrats in the House and Senate come from western states, while almost all of the most conservative Republicans come from southern states.

Ideology is not all-powerful, however. In 2001, for example, many liberal Democrats joined conservative Republicans to support the USA PATRIOT Act, which expanded the government's power to detain immigrants, while conservative Republicans returned the favor by voting for a multibillion-dollar aid package for rebuilding the terrorist-damaged part of New York City.

VOTERS Rarely does a legislator consistently and deliberately vote against the wishes of the people back home, but a paradox is evident here. Members of Congress sometimes think that what they do and how they vote make a lot of difference to voters back home, even though most voters do not follow Congress closely.[47] Aside from periodic polls, members hear most often from the **attentive public**—citizens who follow public affairs carefully—rather than the general public. Nearly 70 percent of constituents say they have not visited, faxed, phoned, e-mailed, or written their member of Congress in the past four years.[48] Still, members of Congress are generally concerned about how they will explain their votes, especially as election day approaches. Even if only a few voters are aware of their stand on a given issue, this group might make the difference between victory and defeat.

COLLEAGUES Legislators are often influenced by the advice of their close friends in Congress. Their busy schedules and the great number of votes force them to depend on the advice of like-minded colleagues. In particular, they look to respected members of the committee who worked on a bill.[49] Legislators find out how their

Congresswoman Connie Morella recognizes, as all members of Congress do, the importance of staying in touch with constituents back home. Nevertheless, Morella was defeated in 2002.

attentive public
Those citizens who follow public affairs carefully.

PEOPLE DEBATE
DISSENT IN WAR

In the weeks and months following the events of September 11, 2001, several members of the Bush administration argued that criticism of the war on terrorism was unpatriotic. No one was harsher toward the critics than the head of the Department of Justice, Attorney General John Ashcroft, a former senator from Missouri. He made his case against criticism before the Senate Judiciary Committee on December 6. Noting that December 7, 2001, was the sixtieth anniversary of the attack on Pearl Harbor, the chairman of the committeee, Democrat Patrick Leahy of Vermont, defended Congress's right to ask questions.

Ashcroft

Since those first terrible hours of September 11, America has faced a choice that is as stark as the images that linger of that morning. One option is to call September 11 a fluke, to believe it could never happen again, and to live in a dream world that requires us to do nothing differently. The other option is to fight back, to summon all our strength and all of our resources and devote ourselves to better ways to identify and disrupt and dismantle terrorist networks. . . .

The terrorist enemy that threatens civilization today is unlike any we have ever known. It slaughters thousands of innocents—a crime of war and a crime against humanity. It seeks weapons of mass destruction and threatens their use against America. No one should doubt the intent or the depth of its continuing destructive hatred. . . .

In all of these ways and more, the Department of Justice has sought to prevent terrorism with reason, careful balance, and excruciating attention to detail. Some of our critics, I regret to say, have shown less affection for detail. Their bold declaration of so-called facts have quickly dissolved upon inspection into vague conjecture. Charges of kangaroo courts and shredding the Constitution give new meaning to the term "fog of war."

Since lives and liberties depend on clarity, not obfuscation, and on reason, not hyperbole, let me take this opportunity to be clear. Each action taken by the Department of Justice, as well as the war crimes commissions considered by the president and the Department of Defense, is carefully drawn to target a narrow class of individuals: terrorists. Our legal powers are targeted at terrorists. Our investigation is focused on terrorists. Our prevention strategy targets the terrorist threat. . . .

We need honest, reasoned debate, not fear-mongering. To those who pit Americans against immigrants and citizens against noncitizens, to those who scare peace-loving people with phantoms of lost liberty, my message is this: Your tactics only aid terrorists, for they erode our national unity and diminish our resolve. They give ammunition to America's enemies and pause to America's friends. They encourage people of goodwill to remain silent in the face of evil.

Attorney General John Ashcroft holds up an al-Qaeda training manual before the Senate Judiciary Committee to justify the Bush administration's position on the war on terrorism.

Patrick Leahy

Today, just as 60 years ago, government at every level is under great pressure to act. Our system is intended to help make sure that what we do keeps us on a heading that achieves our goals while holding true to our constitutional principles.

The Constitution does not need protection when its guarantees are popular, but it very much needs our protection when events tempt us to, just this once, go beyond the Constitution. The need for congressional oversight and vigilance is not, as some mistakenly describe it, to protect terrorists. It is to protect ourselves as Americans and protect our American freedoms that you and I and everybody in this room cherish so much.

Every single American has a stake in protecting our freedoms. It's to make sure that we keep in sight at all times a line that separates tremendous government power on the one hand and the rights and liberties of all Americans on the other hand. It's to make sure that our government has good reason before snooping into our bank records, our tax returns, our e-mails, or before the government listens in as we talk with our attorneys. It's to make sure that no one official, however well intentioned, decides when that line is to be crossed without good reason for that decision.

Now, whether the administration's recent actions are popular or unpopular at the moment, that's not the issue. As the oversight committee for the Department of Justice, we accept our responsibility to examine it. That's our role under the Constitution. That's our duty. We are sworn to do that. We will not shrink from that duty.

But so, too, is congressional oversight important in helping to maintain public confidence in our system of laws. In our society, unlike in so many other nations, when a judge issues an order, it's respected and carried out because the public has faith in our system and its laws. The division of power and the checks and balances built into our system help sustain and earn the public's confidence in the actions taken by the government. The consent of the governed that's at the heart of our democracy makes our law effective and sustains our society. . . .

It's never easy to raise questions about the conduct of the executive branch when our military forces are engaged in combat, even when questions do not concern our military operations. The matters we are examining concern homeland security and

Voicing concerns regarding the right to privacy, Senator Partick Leahy holds up a copy of the Constitution during a Senate Judiciary Committee meeting in which members questioned Attorney General John Ashcroft on policy issues in the fight against terrorism.

our constitutional rights and preserve the limits on governmental authority that form the foundation of our constitutional democracy. These are questions that go to the heart of what America stands for, to its people and to the world, especially to show them what we are and what we do when we are put to the test, a test that we've been put to far more than most of us can remember. . . .

None of us in elected or appointed positions in government has a monopoly on wisdom or patriotism. Under our system, none of us has a monopoly on authority. . . . We can be both tough on terrorists and true to the Constitution. It is not an either-or choice.

1. Do questions about the conduct of a war undermine morale of the armed services? If so, what might be done to reassure the troops that such debate is not unpatriotic?

2. Are there ways of conducting congressional oversight during national emergencies that might be less troublesome to an administration?

3. Should Congress ban criticism of an administration during the first weeks of a national emergency such as a war?

U.S. Senator James Jeffords of Vermont, on the steps of the Capitol with prominent Democrats the day before he left the Republican party to become an Independent. Jeffords's decision gave the Democrats control of the Senate until 2003. He left the Republican party because he believed it had grown too conservative and was putting undue pressure on him to vote the party line.

friends stand on an issue, listen to the party leadership's advice, and take the various committee reports into account. Sometimes members are influenced to vote one way merely because they know a colleague is on the other side of the issue. For some legislators, the state delegation (senators and representatives from their home state) reinforces a common identity.

A member may also vote with a colleague in the expectation that the colleague will later vote for a measure about which the member is concerned—called **log rolling**. Some vote trading takes place to build coalitions so that members can "bring home the bacon" to their constituents. Other vote trading reflects reciprocity in congressional relations or deference to colleagues' superior information or expertise.

CONGRESSIONAL STAFF   Representatives and senators used to be at a distinct disadvantage in dealing with the executive branch because they were overly dependent on information supplied by the White House or lobbyists. The complexity of the issues and increasingly demanding schedules created pressures for additional staff. Congress responded and gradually expanded its staffs, and this expansion has strengthened the role of Congress in the public policy process.

Because both chambers have roughly equal amounts of money for staff, Senate members and committees have much larger staffs than their House counterparts. About one-third of the House of Representatives staff and one-fourth of the Senate staff are based back home, where they help their bosses communicate with voters and provide constituency services and casework. (Helping people with a misplaced Social Security check or helping them qualify for veterans' benefits are examples of casework provided by congressional offices.) Much of the work done in district offices is akin to a continuous campaign effort: generating favorable publicity, arranging for local appearances and newspaper interviews, scheduling, and contacting important civic and business leaders in the region.

Members rely heavily on the advice of congressional staffers. Staff members draft bills, do research, and are often involved in negotiating and coalition building. Staff specialists in policy areas sometimes deal on a day-to-day basis with their counterparts in the executive branch departments and with interest groups. With their direct access to the members of Congress they serve, these staff aides are often among the most influential people in Washington.

PARTY   Members generally vote with their party. Whether as a result of party pressure or natural affinity, on major bills there is a tendency for most Democrats to be arrayed against most Republicans. Partisan voting has increased in the House since the early 1970s and has intensified even more since the 1994 elections. Indeed, party-line voting has been greater in recent years than at any time in recent decades. Party differences are stronger over domestic, regulatory, and welfare reform measures than over foreign policy or civil liberties issues. Ninety-eight percent of House Republicans, for example, voted to impeach Bill Clinton in a historic vote in late 1998; the same percentage of House Democrats voted *against* impeachment.

Congressional redistricting has helped increase partisanship in congressional voting. "Advances in computer-driven mapping capabilities have made an art form of the old-fashioned gerrymandering that occurs where congressional districts are redrawn after each decennial census." Party operatives in the states can with great precision draw district lines to create relatively safe Democratic or Republican districts, "increasing the number of secure members answerable to only their own party's primary votes."[50]

As redistricting efforts in many states have ensured more safe seats, the House of Representatives has more members who are not inclined to compromise or be moderate. Consequently, House Republicans have become more politically conservative and House Democrats more confirmedly liberal. The House is more politically partisan than the

logrolling
Mutual aid and vote trading among legislators.

Senate not because of personalities but largely because of these constitutional-political procedures. House districts are also likely to be composed of similar kinds of voters, while states as a whole tend to be more diverse.

Party leaders in both chambers do their best to get their members to vote together. Republican leaders claim that cohesive voting is the only way Republicans can implement their party platform and satisfy the majorities who elected them in recent years. Senators are usually more independent, so party leaders in the Senate have a harder time maintaining party discipline than leaders in the House do.

INTEREST GROUPS   Interest groups, acting through their lobbyists and political action committees (PACs), make substantial contributions to congressional elections. These PACs give disproportionately to incumbents; at least 70 percent of PAC contributions have gone to incumbents in recent years.[51] In addition to their role as financiers of elections, interest groups provide important information for making laws.

Interest groups not only watch and try to influence national legislators but also monitor one another. If a member of Congress tries to insert a "special interest" measure into an appropriations bill that is especially favorable to a particular interest, for example, opposing interest groups are almost certain to lobby for the measure's defeat. "The result," says Senator Joe Lieberman of Connecticut, "is that everyone on Capitol Hill is keeping a close eye on everyone else, creating a self-adjusting system of checks and balances."[52]

Interest groups can also be effective when they mobilize grassroots activists and rally various constituencies to lobby their home state members of Congress. For example, higher education lobbying groups have effectively mobilized students and educators to write and call members of Congress on behalf of student aid and related provisions in various measures before Congress.[53] And tobacco companies spent large sums to fight taxes on cigarettes. Although most members of Congress reject the popular perception that interest groups "buy" their votes, political contributions certainly do influence the parties and help provide access to members of Congress.

THE PRESIDENT   Through effective use of their constitutional and political powers, presidents are usually partners with Congress in the legislative process. In fact, the president is often the single most important (though not always decisive) force in determining the course of legislation.

Members of Congress, however, are invariably reluctant to admit that they are influenced by pressure from the White House. On domestic issues, legislators generally say they are more likely to be influenced by their own convictions or by their constituents than by what the White House wants. But presidents and their aides work hard to influence public opinion and to win members over to the president's point of view. For example, despite a Democratic majority in the Senate and a razor-thin Republican majority in the House, George W. Bush won an impressive 87 percent support from Congress on the 120 votes on which he took a clear position in 2001. That was the best success mark since 1965, when Lyndon Johnson won 93 percent of the key votes.[54] Bush did it in part by taking fewer strong positions on legislation. Whereas Bill Clinton took a position on an average of 86 House votes a year during his eight years in office, Bush took a position on only 43 House bills in 2001. Moreover, when Bush did take a position, it was mostly in favor of bills that Congress was about to pass.

For a variety of reasons, especially because of the tendency of the nation to rally around the president in time of foreign crisis, presidents have more influence on how members of Congress vote on foreign policy or national security issues than on domestic policy.[55] President George W. Bush benefited from a bipartisan coalition that passed the resolution authorizing the use of military force against terrorist forces in Afghanistan, for example.

The Legislative Obstacle Course

Congress operates under a system of multiple vetoes. The framers intentionally dispersed powers so that no would-be tyrant or majority could accumulate enough authority to oppress the nation. Follow a bill through the legislative process, and this dispersal of power is clear (see Figure 11-2). The procedures and rules of the Senate differ somewhat from those of the House, but in each chamber, power is fragmented and decentralized.

How Ideas Become Bills

Members introduce bills for different reasons. Although many bills are introduced to help win reelection or higher office, members of Congress do care about the national interest. As Democratic representative Tim Penny of Minnesota said of his decision to run for

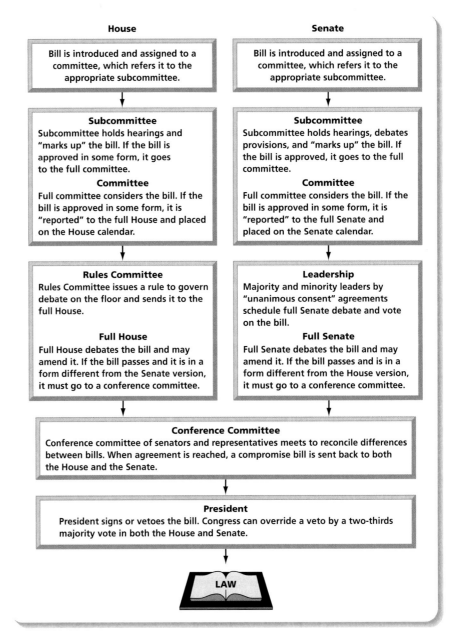

FIGURE 11–2   How a Bill Becomes a Law.

Congress, "I was young and idealistic. . . . I wanted to show people that government can work and that partisanship doesn't have to be the dominant force in politics, that interest groups don't have to be a deciding factor on every vote."[56]

Members also care about making a personal difference. "Politicians are human beings," said Massachusetts representative Joe Kennedy II, whose father was assassinated with a handgun during the 1968 presidential campaign and whose cousin suffered from bone cancer. "When there is a degree of very personal pain that one feels toward an issue—it might be gun control or my uncle's interest in fighting cancer—commitment level is higher and your willingness to compromise is lower."[57]

How Bills Become Laws

The odds against a bill's becoming a law are great, but Congress still produces an extraordinary amount of legislation. In 2001, a typical year, members of Congress introduced a total of 5,500 bills. Of those, committees in one or the other chamber sent nearly 400 to the floor for further consideration, of which the Senate passed 115 and the House passed 390; 136 of those were approved by both chambers and signed into law. Congress is obviously very selective about what becomes law.

A bill must win many small contests on the way to final passage. There are four broad steps from beginning to end: (1) introduction, which involves putting a formal proposal before the House or the Senate; (2) committee review, which involves holding a hearing and "marking up" the bill; (3) floor debate and passage, which means getting on the legislative calendar, passing once in each chamber, surviving a conference to iron out any differences between the House and Senate versions, and passing once again in each chamber; and (4) presidential approval.

INTRODUCING A BILL   House members introduce a bill by placing it into a mahogany box (called the hopper) on a desk at the front of the House chamber; senators introduce a bill by either handing it to the clerk of the Senate or by presenting it to their colleagues

How to Kill a Bill

The complexity of the congressional system provides a tremendous built-in advantage for opponents of any measure. Multiple opportunities to kill a bill exist because of the dispersion of influence. At a dozen or more points, a bill may be stopped or allowed to die (inaction is the same as killing a bill). Sponsors of a bill must win at every step; opponents need to win only once. Whether good or bad, a proposal can be delayed or rejected by any one of the following:

1. The House subcommittee and its chair
2. The chair of the House standing committee
3. The House standing committee and its leaders
4. The House Rules Committee
5. The majority of the House
6. The Senate subcommittee and its chair
7. The Senate standing committee
8. The majority of the Senate
9. The floor leaders in both chambers
10. A few senators, in the case of a filibuster
11. The House-Senate conference committee, if the chambers disagree
12. The president (by veto)

in a floor speech. In the more informal Senate, members sometimes short-circuit the formalities by offering a bill as an amendment to pending legislation. A bill that comes from the House is always designated H.R. (House of Representatives) followed by its number, and a bill from the Senate is always designated S. (Senate) followed by its number. Although presidents often recommend legislation to Congress, all bills must be introduced by a member of the House or Senate.

COMMITTEE REVIEW   Once a bill is introduced in either chamber, it is "read" into the record as a formal proposal and referred to the appropriate committee—tax bills to Ways and Means or Finance; farm bills to Agriculture; technology bills to Science, Space, and Technology; small business to Small Business; and so forth. The parliamentarian in each chamber decides where to send each bill.

The Referral Decision   Although most bills are referred to a single committee, particularly complex bills may be referred simultaneously or sequentially to multiple committees. President Bush's proposed department of homeland security bill was so complicated and touched so many agencies that it was managed by a temporary special committtee in the House. The bill was referred to at least ten committees, including Judiciary, Ways and Means, and Government Reform, all of which held hearings on specific provisions of the largest government reorganization since the Department of Defense was created in 1947. The bill went into the House as a 35-page proposal and came out almost 500 pages long. Committees and their subcommittees are responsible for building a legislative record in support of a given bill. This *legislative record* also helps the president and federal courts interpret what Congress wants.

BELOW THE BELTWAY

Markup Once a committee or subcommittee decides to pass the bill, it "marks it up" to clean up the wording or amend its version of the bill. The term *markup* refers to the pencil marks that members make on the final version of the bill. Once markup is over, the bill must be passed by the committee or subcommittee and forwarded to the next step in the process. If it is passed by a subcommittee, for example, it is forwarded to the full committee; if it is passed by a full committee, it is forwarded to the full chamber.

Discharge Although most bills die in committee without a hearing or further review, a bill can be forced to the floor of the House through a **discharge petition** signed by a majority of the membership. In 2002, for example, House members were able to collect enough signatures to discharge the Rules Committee on a campaign finance reform bill that had been stalled for six months. Because most members share a strong sense of reciprocity, or mutual respect, toward the work of other committees, few discharge petitions are successful. The Senate does not use discharge petitions.

FLOOR DEBATE AND PASSAGE Once reported to the full chamber directly from committee in the Senate or through the Rules Committee in the House, a bill will either be scheduled for floor action or dropped entirely, depending on the party leadership and the amount of time left in the session. The busiest time of the year occurs just before the end of a session, usually in late September or early October, when bills must be passed or die.

In the Senate, it is not uncommon for members to propose **riders**, or amendments, that are unrelated to the bill on which they want to ride. Senators use riders to force the president to accept legislation attached to a bill that was otherwise popular, because the president has to either accept the *entire* bill or to veto it. The number of riders attached to appropriations bills has increased in recent years. Republicans in both the House and the Senate skirmished with President Clinton by adding riders concerning restrictions on abortion, enforcement of environmental laws, and the right of nonprofit groups that receive federal grants to lobby.[58]

Except for tax bills, the House and Senate discuss bills simultaneously rather than waiting for one to act first. If only one chamber passes a bill at the end of that congressional term, it dies. If both houses pass bills on the same subject but there are differences between the bills—and there often are—the two versions must go to a conference committee for *reconciliation*. If a bill does not make it through both chambers in identical form in the same two-year Congress, it must begin the entire process again in the next Congress.

When a bill has passed both houses in identical form, it goes to the president, who may *sign* it into law or *veto* it. If Congress is in session and the president waits ten days (not counting Sundays), the bill becomes law *without* his signature. If Congress has adjourned and the president waits ten days without signing the bill, it is defeated by what is known as a **pocket veto**. After a pocket veto, the bill is dead. Otherwise, when a bill is vetoed, it is returned to the chamber of its origin by the president with a message explaining the reasons for the veto. Congress can vote to **override** the veto by a two-thirds vote in each chamber, but assembling such an extraordinary majority is often difficult.

The Importance of Compromise

Since it takes a majority vote in two chambers of Congress and the signature of the president before a bill becomes a law, sponsors of new legislation have to be willing to compromise. One tactical decision at the start is whether to push for action in the Senate first, in the House first, or in both simultaneously. For example, if it appears that the Senate is not likely to approve a bill, its sponsors may seek passage in the House

discharge petition
Petition that, if signed by a majority of the members of the House of Representatives, will pry a bill from committee and bring it to the floor for consideration.

rider
A provision attached to a bill—to which it may or may not be related—in order to secure its passage.

pocket veto
A veto exercised by the president after Congress has adjourned; if the president takes no action for ten days, the bill does not become law and is not returned to Congress for a possible override.

override
An action taken by Congress to reverse a presidential veto that requires a two-thirds majority in each chamber.

You Decide / Thinking It Through

HOW WOULD YOU "REFORM" CONGRESS?

You Decide... There have been many ideas over the years for making Congress more efficient and accountable, from radical reforms such as switching to a European-style parliamentary system to more modest restrictions on campaign financing and time spent in Washington. Which of these proposed reforms do you think should be adopted to improve Congress?

- Move to a European-style parliamentary system.
- Extend House terms to four years.
- Limit House and Senate tenure in office to no more than 12 years.
- Provide for public financing of campaigns and ban campaign contributions.
- Permit only people who live in a district or state to contribute to candidates for Congress.
- Sharply reduce the number of committees and subcommittees.
- Strengthen the power and resources of the party leaders.
- Reduce the size of congressional staffs.
- Have shorter sessions for Congress so that members can spend more time in their districts.

Thinking It Through... No reform is neutral in its effects. Some groups would benefit more than others from the passage of each reform proposal, and most reforms also have unanticipated consequences that would create more problems than they solve. In addition, some reforms would require amendments to the Constitution, while others might actually succeed in making Congress more efficient and therefore more responsive to short-term shifts in public opinion.

and hope that a sizable victory there will spur the Senate into action. Another tactic concerns the committee that will consider a bill. Normally, referral to a committee is automatic, but sometimes sponsors have discretion. A bill that involves more than one jurisdiction can be written in such a way that it may go to a committee that will look on it more kindly.[59]

Congress: An Assessment and a View on Reform

More than two centuries after its creation, Congress is a larger, more vital, and very different kind of institution from the one the framers envisioned. Yet most of its major functions remain the same, and their effective exercise is crucial to the health of our constitutional democracy. Even in the twenty-first century, we still look to Congress to make laws, raise revenues, represent citizens, investigate abuses of power, and oversee the executive branch.

Although most incumbents are easily reelected, most campaign constantly to stay in office, creating what some observers have called the "permanent campaign." Members appear driven by their desire to win reelection, so that much of what takes place in Congress seems mainly designed to promote reelection. These efforts usually pay off for members of Congress: Most who want to get reelected do. At the same time, these efforts also pay off for our democracy. Members' concern with reelection fosters *accountability* and the desire to please the voters.

The permanent campaign clearly hinders legislative progress. In an institution where most members act as individual entrepreneurs and consider themselves leaders, the task of providing institutional leadership is increasingly difficult. With limited resources, and only sometimes aided by the president, congressional leaders are asked to bring together a diverse, fragmented, and independent institution. The congressional system acts only when majorities can be achieved. That the framers accomplished their original objective—creating a body that would not move with imprudent haste—has been generally well realized.

Americans often characterize Congress as a bickering, timid, ignorant, selfish, or narrow-minded institution. But they also admire the stamina and civic responsibility of their own member of Congress. Individual members of Congress are almost always more popular than the institution. Public approval of Congress as an institution fluctuates between 35 and 50 percent, while the typical member of Congress enjoys a 60 to 65 percent approval rating. One explanation may be that people judge individual members primarily on how well they serve the interests of their states and districts and on their personal appeal.

Some of the criticism of Congress is justified. However, critics usually forget that our national legislature is particularly exposed, and some of our expectations of it are unrealistic. First, Congress does nearly all its work directly in the public eye, even more so now that it is televised live on C-SPAN. Unfortunate incidents—quarrels, name-calling, evasive actions, inaccurate statements, ethical lapses—that might be hushed up in the executive or judicial branches are observed and duly reported by the media.

Second, Congress by its nature is controversial and argumentative. Its 535 members are found on all sides—sometimes half a dozen sides—of every important question. Moreover, during the 1990s, Congress raised taxes and cut services; closed military bases; reduced spending for welfare, the arts, and many research programs; shut down the government for a number of weeks; and impeached a generally well-liked president—none of which is a recipe for popularity.

Criticisms of Congress

Criticisms of Congress are easy to recite, if only by paying attention to what members of Congress say about their own institution. Members long ago figured out that Americans love their own incumbents but have a steady distrust of Congress as a whole.

CONGRESS IS INEFFICIENT   Some experts argue that House and Senate procedures are simply not suited to the needs of a modern Information Age nation. Some of this criticism is exaggerated. Evaluating procedure and structure is difficult to separate from evaluating policy, about which everyone has an individual preference. Congress deals with an enormous number of complex measures. Many procedures expedite the handling of bills, and the committee and subcommittee system is a reasonable device for hearing arguments and compiling information.

Still, the question of efficiency remains. Study groups inside and outside Congress have urged the chambers to reduce the number of committee assignments, establish better information systems, centralize more power in leadership positions, and strengthen majority rule. Congress has done many of these things recently, yet the pace of legislation has not improved.

CONGRESS IS UNREPRESENTATIVE   The complaint is often made that Congress represents constituents' interests over the national interest. Defenders of Congress respond that representing their districts is precisely what Congress was designed to do. Legislators are described as being obsessed with staying in office—indeed, as concentrating solely on winning reelection—often at the expense of critical national issues such as Social Security, drug abuse, foreign policy, and trade.

On Tuesday, September 11, 2001, the leadership of the House of Representatives and the Senate gathered on the steps of the Capitol with other congressional members in a gesture of unity after the terrorist attacks.

Congress is supposed to reflect geographical and narrow interests, to register the diversity of the United States. In *The Federalist,* No. 57, James Madison wrote: "Who are to be the electors of the Federal Representatives? Not the rich more than the poor; not the learned more than the ignorant; not the haughty heirs of distinguished names more than the humble sons of obscure and unpropitious fortune."[60] Yet as the costs of campaigning increase and as the majority of elected officials continue to come from the upper and upper-middle classes, we do have to ask whether ours is the open, representative, responsive, and responsible legislative system we can point to with pride as a model for those in other parts of the world who yearn for constitutional democracy. Simply asked, can a Congress composed of so few women and minority members represent the nation's diverse population?

CONGRESS IS UNETHICAL   Some critics claim we have "the best Congress money can buy."[61] Many people—including Republican Senator John McCain of Arizona, who made this charge a central theme in his bid for the 2000 presidential nomination—allege that special interests and single-issue groups are stronger than ever and that they are able to delay or block proceedings in Congress. Even with reform of the current system to ban "soft," or unregulated, money, members of Congress will still have to seek financing from wealthy individuals and political action committees whose primary purpose is to seek support for pet legislation.

In response to occasional scandals, both houses have passed ethics codes and created ethics subcommittees. These codes require public disclosure of income and property holdings by legislators, key aides, and spouses. They also ban most gifts of over $100 to a legislator, a staff member, or a legislator's family from a registered lobbyist, an organization with a political action committee, a foreign government, or a business with an interest in legislation before Congress. But valuable as these changes have been, they have apparently failed to improve the image of Congress.[62]

Defenders of Congress insist that these charges are overstated. They say money would hardly influence the three dozen or more millionaires who are members of the Senate and the hundred or so members of the House who are well-off financially. Defenders of Congress also point out that some members of Congress regularly turn down certain types of campaign contributions.

CONGRESS LACKS COLLECTIVE RESPONSIBILITY   Some critics see the main problem in Congress as the dispersion of power among committee and subcommittee leaders, elected party officials, factional leaders, informal caucus leaders, and other legislators. It is a "nobody's in charge" system. This dispersion of power means that to get things done, congressional leaders must bargain and negotiate. The result of this "brokering" system is that laws may be watered down, defeated, delayed, or written in vague language. According to some critics, too much leeway is given to unelected bureaucrats to develop the regulations that will implement the legislation. Accountability is confused, responsibility is eroded, and well-organized special interests that know how to work the system have an unfair advantage.

A Defense of Congress

Making fun of Congress has been a national pastime for generations. The humorist Will Rogers told some of his best jokes during the 1930s and 1940s at the expense of Congress, just as Jay Leno and David Letterman do today—Leno once defined "politics" as as a combination of the word *poli,* meaning "many," and *ticks,* meaning "bloodsucking insects." Cartoonists love Congress for its unfailing ability to put its worst foot forward. Even members of Congress often run against Congress when they are at home in their districts.

The challenge to reconcile the need for executive energy with republican liberty is still part of the constitutional landscape today. The history of constitutional democracy has always been the search for limitations on absolute power and for techniques of sharing power. Our American style of constitutionalism and separation of powers often means a slow-moving and sometimes inefficient decision-making system. It means a system that often hinders rather than facilitates leadership, a system that invites contention, division, debate, delay, and political conflict. Critics call this gridlock or deadlock or even paralysis. Defenders of Congress prefer to call it the world's greatest deliberative body. They point out that the framers of the U.S. Constitution took great efforts to insulate policy-making processes from the momentary fancies of the people.

Newly elected presidents and members of Congress always arrive in Washington enthusiastically ready to enact the people's wishes. But they find that governing is invariably tougher and slower than they expected because government deals with complex issues about which there is often little consensus. Building policy majorities is hard because complex problems generate complex solutions, and the structure of Congress requires supermajorities to agree to serious changes. Thus the president's veto, the filibuster, and the use of holds and legislative riders all make consensus more difficult to find.

Criticism of Congress—its alleged incompetence, its overresponsiveness to organized interests, its inefficiencies, its partisan character—is difficult to separate from the context of policy preferences and democratic procedures. Sometimes criticism tells us more about the critic than it does about the effectiveness of Congress. Constitutional democracy is not the most efficient form of government. Congress was never intended to act swiftly; it was not created to be a rubber stamp or even a cooperative partner for presidents. Its greatest strengths—its diversity and deliberative character—also weaken its position in dealing with the more centralized executive branch. Its members will rarely be fast on their feet. Not surprisingly, the 535 members, divided into two houses, two parties, dozens of committees, and nearly 200 subcommittees, often have a difficult time arriving at a common strategy to make the laws.

The framers would not be troubled by the lack of action, however. By dividing power, they hoped to control it. The odds against action are high precisely because the framers did not want Congress to become too quick to oppress the public.

RUNNING FOR CONGRESS

Deciding to run for Congress involves a variety of calculations. Potential candidates need to decide whether they want to take on an entrenched incumbent (difficult), run for an open seat (easier), or take on a vulnerable incumbent (easier still). They also need to ask whether they have enough funding, name recognition, and campaigning ability to mount a credible campaign, and whether their beliefs fit the prevailing opinions of their district. Once they have made the decision to run, candidates must also decide where to spend their money, how to spend their time, and what issues to emphasize. As the simulation on running for Congress shows, winning against incumbents is not easy, which helps explain why so many incumbents are reelected.

Go to PoliSim "Running for Congress."

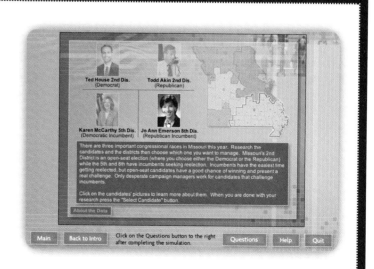

Summary

1. Congress plays a crucial role in our system of shared powers, controlling key decisions and constraining presidents. Yet over time, Congress has lost some influence as the presidency has gained influence. In recent decades, however, Congress has become more capable as a policy-making competitor for presidents. Redistricting and reapportionment have shaped a Congress that somewhat more accurately reflects the population.

2. The most distinctive feature of Congress is its bicameralism, which the framers intended as a moderating influence on partisanship and possible error. Each chamber has a few distinctive functions. The organization and procedures of the two houses also differ slightly, as do their political environments.

3. Congress performs these functions: representation, lawmaking, consensus building, overseeing the bureaucracy, policy clarification, and investigating. The Senate also confirms or denies presidential appointments and participates in the ratification of treaties.

4. Congress manages its workload through a leadership system that is different in both chambers. The House is led by the Speaker, a majority and a minority leader, and whips in each party, while the Senate is led by a majority and a minority leader. The Senate is more difficult to lead because of its greater individualism, which is sometimes expressed through the use of holds and filibusters to control the legislative process.

5. Most of the work in Congress is done in committees and subcommittees. Congress has attempted in recent years to streamline its committee system and modify its methods of selecting committee chairs. Seniority practices are still generally followed. Subcommittees are important. They can prevent or delay legislation from being enacted. But there are numerous other stages where bills can be killed, making it easier to stop legislation than to enact it.

6. As a collective body, Congress must attempt to accomplish its tasks even as most of its members serve as delegates or trustees for their constituents. When they vote, members are influenced by their philosophy and values, their perceptions of constituents' interests, and the views of trusted colleagues and staff, partisan ties and party leaders, lobbyists, and the president.

7. The members of Congress do an excellent job of representing the values and views of most of their constituents. But they are cautious about enacting proposed measures by their own colleagues or the legislative agenda put forward by presidents. Most proposed legislation dies for lack of majority support.

8. Members of Congress are motivated by the desire to win reelection, and much of what Congress does is in response to this motive. Members work hard to get favors for their districts, to serve the needs of constituents, and to maintain a high visibility in their districts or states. Incumbents have advantages that help explain their success at reelection: They have greater name recognition, they have large staffs, they are much better able to raise campaign money, and they have greater access to the media.

9. A bill becomes a law through a process that involves many opportunities for defeat. Although all formal bills are referred to committees for consideration, very few receive a hearing, even fewer are marked up and sent to the floor, and even fewer still are enacted by both chambers and signed into law by the president. In addition, the legislative obstacle course sometimes involves filibusters, riders, holds, and the occasional override of a presidential veto.

10. Individual members of Congress are more popular than the institution. Congress is criticized for being inefficient, unrepresentative, unethical, and lacking in collective responsibility. Yet criticisms of Congress are difficult to separate from the context of policy preference and democratic procedures. Congress's greatest strengths—its diversity and its deliberative character—also contribute to its weaknesses.

Key Terms

reapportionment	majority leader	filibuster	delegate
redistricting	minority leader	cloture	trustee
gerrymandering	whip	senatorial courtesy	attentive public
safe seat	party caucus	standing committee	logrolling
incumbent	closed rule	select or special committee	discharge petition
bicameralism	open rule	joint committee	rider
enumerated powers	president pro tempore	seniority rule	pocket veto
Speaker	hold	conference committee	override

Further Reading

JOEL D. ABERBACH, *Keeping a Watchful Eye: The Politics of Congressional Oversight* (Brookings Institution, 1990).

E. SCOTT ADLER, *Why Congressional Reforms Fail: Reelection and the House Committee System* (University of Chicago Press, 2002).

SARAH A. BINDER AND STEVEN S. SMITH, *Politics or Principles? Filibustering in the United States Senate* (Brookings Institution, 1997).

BILL BRADLEY, *Time Present, Time Past: A Memoir* (Knopf, 1996).

DAVID W. BRADY AND CRAIG VOLDEN, *Revolving Gridlock: Politics and Policy from Carter to Clinton* (Westview Press, 1998).

ADAM CLYMER, *Edward M. Kennedy: A Biography* (Morrow, 1999).

ROGER H. DAVIDSON AND WALTER J. OLESZEK, *Congress and Its Members,* 8th ed. (CQ Press, 2002).

CHRISTOPHER J. DEERING AND STEVEN S. SMITH, *Committees in Congress,* 3d ed. (CQ Press, 1997).

LAWRENCE C. DODD AND BRUCE J. OPPENHEIMER, EDS., *Congress Reconsidered,* 5th ed. (CQ Press, 1993).

RICHARD F. FENNO JR., *Home Style: House Members in Their Districts* (Little, Brown, 1978).

RICHARD F. FENNO JR., *Learning to Govern: An Institutional View of the 104th Congress* (Brookings Institution, 1997).

RICHARD F. FENNO JR., *Senators on the Campaign Trail: The Politics of Representation* (University of Oklahoma Press, 1996).

MORRIS P. FIORINA, *Congress: Keystone of the Washington Establishment,* 2d ed. (Yale University Press, 1989).

PAUL HERRNSON, *Congressional Elections,* 3d ed. (CQ Press, 2000).

JOHN R. HIBBING AND ELIZABETH THEISS-MORSE, *Congress as Public Enemy: Public Attitudes Toward American Political Institutions* (Cambridge University Press, 1995).

GODFREY HODGSON, *The Gentleman from New York: Daniel Patrick Moynihan* (Houghton Mifflin, 2000).

LINDA KILLIAN, *The Freshmen: What Happened to the Republican Revolution?* (Westview Press, 1998).

FRANCES E. LEE AND BRUCE I. OPPENHEIMER, *Sizing Up the Senate: The Unequal Consequences of Equal Representation* (University of Chicago Press, 1999).

JOSEPH I. LIEBERMAN, *In Praise of Public Life* (Simon & Schuster, 2000).

TOM LOFTUS, *The Art of Legislative Politics* (CQ Press, 1994).

JANET M. MARTIN, *Lessons from the Hill: The Legislative Journey of an Education Program* (St. Martin's Press, 1993).

DAVID R. MAYHEW, *America's Congress: Actions in the Public Sphere, James Madison Through Newt Gingrich* (Yale University Press, 2002).

BARBARA MIKULSKI ET AL., *Nine and Counting: The Women of the Senate* (Morrow, 2000).

WALTER J. OLESZEK, *Congressional Procedures and the Policy Process,* 4th ed. (CQ Press, 1995).

NORMAN J. ORNSTEIN, THOMAS MANN, AND MICHAEL MALBIN, *Vital Statistics on Congress, 2000–2002* (AEI Press, 2002).

RONALD M. PETERS JR., ED., *The Speaker: Leadership in the U.S. House of Representatives* (CQ Press, 1995).

DAVID E. PRICE, *The Congressional Experience: A View from the Hill* (Westview Press, 1993).

NICOL RAE AND COLTON CAMPBELL, EDS., *New Majority or Old Majority: The Impact of Republicans on Congress* (Rowman & Littlefield, 1999).

WARREN B. RUDMAN, *Combat: Twelve Years in the U.S. Senate* (Random House, 1996).

BARBARA SINCLAIR, *Unorthodox Lawmaking: New Legislative Processes in the U.S. Congress,* 2d ed. (CQ Press, 2000).

DARVELL M. WEST, *Patrick Kennedy: The Rise to Power* (Prentice Hall, 2001).

12
CHAPTER

THE PRESIDENCY
The Leadership Branch

THE FRAMERS BOTH ADMIRED AND FEARED CENTRALIZED LEADERSHIP. ON THE ONE HAND, THEY REALIZED THE COUNTRY NEEDED A more effective national government led by a single executive. On the other hand, they were suspicious of the potential abuses of power invested in just one person. Having lived under the tyranny of the English monarchy, they had every right to worry. They wanted to have a president powerful enough to lead the nation during periods of domestic and international crisis but wanted checks on that power.

Americans saw both sides of this presidency in the moments following September 11, 2001. Acting as commander in chief, President George W. Bush moved quickly to mobilize the nation's military to address the crisis, ordering all air travel to an immediate halt and putting the military on the highest alert. He also ordered the federal government to begin hunting down the terrorists both at home and abroad.

He acted quickly as well to reassure the nation and the world that the United States would not be bowed by the attacks. He addressed the public three times on September 11, once just after the two airplanes crashed into the World Trade Center towers in New York City, a second time on his way back to Washington from Barksdale Air Force Base in Louisiana, and a third time on national television that evening. "The functions of our government continue without interruption," he told the nation that night. "Federal agencies in Washington, which had to be evacuated today, are reopening for essential personnel tonight and will be open for business tomorrow. Our financial institutions remain strong, and the American economy will be open for business as well."

Bush also recognized that the Constitution did not give him the power to act alone for long. He immediately asked the senior leadership of Congress to start drafting legislation to authorize military action against the terrorists and strengthen government's power to protect the nation's borders. He also acted to lower public expectations of a quick victory in the war against terrorism. Appearing before a joint session of Congress on September 20, he told the nation, "This war will not be like the war against Iraq a decade ago with a decisive liberation of territory and a swift conclusion. It will not look like the air war above Kosovo two years ago, where no ground troops were used and not a single American was lost in combat."

Americans responded by rallying around the president with record approval levels. Only 51 percent of Americans said they approved of the job Bush was doing on September 10, compared to 90 percent by September 22.[1] Bush maintained that high level of support throughout the final quarter of 2001. He also enjoyed an average of 65% approval throughout 2002.

Americans were not willing to give the president a free hand to combat terrorism, however. A substantial minority worried that new antiterrorism laws would restrict civil liberties, and many wanted the president to boost the ailing economy. Moreover, although most Americans also said they favored the use of force against nations that harbor terrorists, a majority also said that the United States should only proceed with the support of its allies. In other words, Americans supported the president, but only within limits.[2]

This chapter will explore the presidential balancing act in more detail. We will start by reviewing the structure and powers of the presidency, ask what Americans expect from the president, examine how presidents manage the presidency, outline the presidential job description, and conclude with a discussion of the ingredients of presidential greatness.

The Structure and Powers of the Presidency

Just as the Constitution gives Congress the lawmaking power of the United States in the first sentence of Article I, it gives the president the executive power in the first sentence of Article II. The executive power includes everything from the president's role as commander in chief of the Army and Navy of the United States to broad responsibility for the faithful execution of the nation's laws. It also provides the basic authority the president needs to oversee the federal bureaucracy, develop recommendations for spending money, and select the senior appointees of government.

Having given this executive responsibility to a single individual, the framers insulated the presidency from public passions. To this day, presidents are not elected by the public, for example, but by electors who are selected in winner-take-all systems in all but two states, Maine and Nebraska. As a result, presidents often claim to speak for the entire nation, not a single district or state.

At the same time, the framers created a presidency of limited powers. They wanted a presidential office that would steer clear of parties and factions, enforce the laws passed by Congress, handle communications with foreign governments, and help states put down disorders. They wanted a presidency strong enough to match Congress yet not so strong that it would overpower Congress.

Divided Powers

American government was designed to combine both shared powers and divided powers. The framers wanted disagreement as well as cooperation because they assumed that the checks and balances within the government would prevent the president and Congress from "ganging up" against the people's liberties. Having three branches of national government—legislative, executive, and judicial—does not by itself create a pure system of separated powers; England has different branches performing these functions. The United States is different in that the president, Senate, House of Representatives, and judiciary are independent from one another yet share power in making decisions about public policy.

The United States is a rarity among major world powers because it is neither a parliamentary democracy nor a wholly executive-dominated government. Our Constitution plainly invites both Congress and the president to set policy and govern the nation. Leadership and

IN COMPARATIVE PERSPECTIVE

Types of Presidential Systems

The United States is among a very few democracies in which a strong presidential system has coincided with democratic rule. Elsewhere, democratic presidential regimes have often given way to authoritarian presidential rule.

Most democracies are based on a *parliamentary* system of government (as in Australia, Britain, and Israel) that confers full powers on a bicameral parliament, which then delegates executive powers to a handful of its members. These officials, the head of government (called the prime minister, premier, or chancellor), and cabinet ministers make up what is known as "the government." The government serves only so long as it maintains the confidence of a majority in the lower house of parliament. If parliament indicates its loss of support for the government by a vote of censure, by a vote of no confidence, or by defeating a major piece of government-sponsored legislation, the government resigns, either to allow a new government to be formed or to call for new parliamentary elections. In parliamentary systems, the head of state (usually a president elected by parliament but sometimes, as in Britain, a hereditary monarch) has only ceremonial responsibilities.

In a wave of democratizations over the past decade, a number of countries have experimented with a mixed presidential-parliamentary system. Based on the French Fifth Republic (established in 1958), the mixed system includes a popularly elected presidency that has extensive powers of its own, notably in foreign and defense matters, *and* a prime minister and cabinet accountable to parliament. This mixed presidential-parliamentary system has been adopted in Russia, Poland, the Czech Republic, and several other new democracies.

There is a lively debate on which pattern of government—presidential, parliamentary, or mixed—is most conducive to democracy. Some observers fear that powerful presidents are a source of authoritarianism. Others claim that a strong president is needed to give leadership and coherence to the often fragmented parliaments in newer democracies. Still others see the solution in some kind of hybrid.

It is true that historically, most presidential regimes have given way to dictatorships. But in many of these cases, the causes for the failure of democracy were less with the specific institutions than with the attitudes and commitments of the people and their leaders. It is unlikely that any single set of institutions can create or perpetuate democratic government. The presence of democratic values is more important in building and maintaining democracy than the existence of a particular institutional arrangement.

---

policy change are encouraged only when Congress and the president, and sometimes the courts along with them, concur on the desirability of new directions.

A president and members of Congress are legitimate participants in a whole range of policy activities. Triumphs for a president acting alone in a system of separated powers are rare. "Whenever powers are shared, attention must be devoted to the other decision makers," writes political scientist Charles O. Jones. "How do they view the problem? What are their present commitments? On what basis will they compromise? The test in a separated system is not simply one of presidential success. It is rather one of achievement by the system, with presidents and members of Congress inextricably bonded and similarly judged."[3]

The politics of shared power has often been stormy; we treat that subject in detail in the next chapter. But making a system of separated powers work is not easy either. A president is usually helped when majorities of his party are in control of Congress, which can join together what the framers separated. In recent decades, however, **divided government**, in which one party controls the executive branch and the other the legislative branch, has been the norm.

Democrat Bill Clinton served his last six years with a Congress controlled by Republicans. Republican George W. Bush was elected in 2000 with a slim majority of Republicans in the House of Representatives and a U.S. Senate soon controlled by a razor-thin Democratic majority. Thus for all practical purposes, divided government endures, forcing presidents to govern from the center of the ideological spectrum. President Bush, like others before him, reached out to moderates in the other party for support, yet he too found that divided government inevitably entails compromise and a certain amount of gridlock. We will examine the problem of gridlock between Congress and the presidency again in Chapter 13.

divided government
Governance divided between the parties, especially when one holds the presidency and the other controls one or both houses of Congress.

Defining the Presidency

The framers' most important decision about the presidency was also their first. Meeting on June 1, 1787, the Constitutional Convention decided that there would be a single executive. Despite worries that a single president might lay the groundwork for a future monarchy, the framers also believed that the new government needed energy in the executive. They were willing to increase the risk of tyranny in return for some efficiency.

Once past this first decision, the framers had to decide just how independent that executive would be from the rest of the national government, which in turn meant finding an appropriate method of selection or election. Had they wanted Congress to select the president from among its members, the framers would have created a **parliamentary system** of government that would look more like the English system.

The convention was initially divided on how the president would be selected. A small number of delegates favored direct election by the people, which Pennsylvania's James Wilson thought would ensure that the president was completely independent of Congress. Convinced that the nation was too diverse to handle direct election and afraid that states might join together to support regional candidates who would favor their part of the country, the delegates never seriously considered direct election. A larger number of delegates favored selection by Congress, tying the president more closely to the legislative branch.

Eventually, the framers compromised on the creation of an electoral college: Voters would cast their ballots for competing slates of electors, who would in turn cast their electoral votes for president. It might be called a form of indirect direct election. The framers also gave the executive a four-year term of office, further balancing the House (two-year term) and Senate (six-year term). Although they were silent on the number of terms a president could serve, the nation's first president, George Washington, quickly established the two-term precedent, which held until Franklin Roosevelt's historic four-term presidency from 1932–1945. The Twenty-Second Amendment to the Constitution, ratified in 1951, restored Washington's precedent by limiting presidents to two terms.

The framers also created the position of vice president just in case the president left office before the end of the term. With little debate, the founders decided to give the vice president the power to break tie votes in the Senate. Otherwise, the vice president has no constitutional duties but to wait for the president to be incapacitated or otherwise unable to discharge the powers and duties of the presidency.

parliamentary system
A system of government in which the legislature selects the prime minister or president.

The Bush–Gore election in 2000 was so close that the role of the electoral college was brought into focus for the first time in years. On December 18, 2000, Alabama's nine Republican electors cast their votes for President-elect Bush.

The framers also established three simple qualifications for both offices. Under the Constitution, the president and vice president must be (1) at least thirty-five years old; (2) a natural-born citizen of the United States, as opposed to an immigrant who becomes a citizen by applying to the U.S. government for naturalization; and (3) have lived in the United States for fourteen years. The citizenship and residency requirements were designed to prevent a popular foreign-born citizen from capturing the office.

The Presidential Ticket

With this basic structure in place, the framers had to decide how the vice president would be selected. Once again, they created a remarkable electoral arrangement: The candidate who received the most electoral college votes would become president, and the candidate who came in second would become vice president.

It did not take long for the framers to discover the problem with this runner-up rule. The 1796 election produced Federalist President John Adams and Democratic-Republican Vice President Thomas Jefferson. Because the two disagreed so sharply about the future of the country, Jefferson was rendered virtually irrelevant to government.

This rule created a constitutional crisis in 1800. The election could not have been more important, for it occurred during a time of rising public anger about the nation's direction. With the Federalist party fading quickly in the wake of the Alien and Sedition Acts and growing anti-British sentiments, two Democratic-Republicans, Thomas Jefferson and Aaron Burr, emerged from the 1800 election with exactly 73 electoral votes each, leaving Federalist John Adams behind with just 63. With the election now thrown to the House of Representatives under the Constitution's tie-breaking rules, the nation teetered on the edge of a constitutional crisis for 36 ballots before Jefferson was finally elected. His vice president was none other than Aaron Burr, the candidate whom he had just defeated.

The problem was solved under the Twelfth Amendment, which was ratified in 1804. Under the new process, electors are allowed to cast two votes, one for president and one for vice president, thereby encouraging the two candidates to run together as a **presidential ticket**.

Presidential Powers

Article II of the Constitution begins even more simply than Article I: "The executive Power shall be vested in a President of the United States of America." Some experts argue that the executive power covers almost everything not granted to the legislature or judiciary, while others believe that the president's relatively short list of enumerated powers suggests that the framers wanted a more limited executive.[4] Although short, Article II does address foreign threats and the day-to-day operations of government, establishing the president's authority to play three central roles in the new government: (1) commander in chief, (2) diplomat in chief, and (3) administrator in chief.

COMMANDER IN CHIEF   The Constitution explicitly requires the president to be commander in chief of the army and navy. It is a fundamental expression of the president's role in protecting the nation as a whole. The framers saw the president as the commander in chief but were divided over which branch would both declare and make war.[5] The framers initially agreed that Congress would make war, raise armies, build and equip fleets, enforce treaties, and suppress and repel invasions but eventually changed the phrase "make war" to "declare war." But unlike the English king of their time, the framers limited the presidential war power by granting to Congress some responsibility over the military, including the power to appropriate money for the purchase of arms and military pay.

DIPLOMAT IN CHIEF   Article II also makes the president negotiator in chief of treaties with foreign nations. Presidents can also make **executive agreements** with foreign nations. Unlike treaties, which last beyond the end of any given administration or Congress, executive agreements generally expire at the end of an administration and must be renewed by the next president.

presidential ticket
The joint listing of the presidential and vice presidential candidates on the same ballot as required by the Twelfth Amendment.

executive agreements
Agreements between the U.S. president and the leaders of other nations that do not require Senate approval.

President Bush meets with his National Security advisors in the Situation Room of the White House soon after September 11, 2001.

ADMINISTRATOR IN CHIEF   In giving the president the power to both appoint officers of government (heads of departments and agencies) and require them to report in writing, Article II clearly makes the president the head of the federal bureaucracy.

Until 1973, the president's communications with the bureaucracy were generally treated as confidential. The other two branches of government accepted this concept of **executive privilege** until they learned that President Richard Nixon had secretly recorded conversations involving the cover-up of his role in the 1972 burglary of the Democratic party headquarters, which were located in the Watergate Hotel. When a federal prosecutor asked the president to release all tapes dealing with his role in the Watergate scandal, Nixon claimed that executive privilege gave the president the right to withhold executive communications if he asserted that the release of such communications would jeopardize national welfare and security.

A unanimous Supreme Court resolved the dispute in *United States* v. *Nixon*, ruling that presidents did indeed have a constitutionally valid right to claim executive privilege, especially when the release of sensitive military or diplomatic information might harm the nation.[6] However, in the case of the secret White House tapes, the Court also ruled there is no "absolute unqualified Presidential privilege of immunity from judicial process under all circumstances." In other words, executive privilege is a limited power, particularly in criminal cases where presidential communications have a direct bearing on a case. Nixon was ordered to provide the tapes to the judiciary, which he promptly did. The tapes proved that he had been involved in the cover-up, and he soon resigned from office.

ADDITIONAL EXECUTIVE POWERS   Alongside these enumerated roles of commander, diplomat, and administrator in chief, the Constitution also gives the president the power to grant pardons to individuals convicted of federal, but not state, crimes, thereby providing a check against the judiciary.

Presidents are also responsible to take care that the laws are faithfully exercised under **take care clause**. Located near the end of Article II is the simple statement that the president "shall take Care that the Laws be faithfully executed." This clause makes the president responsible for implementing the laws that Congress enacts, even ones that are enacted through the override of a presidential veto.

executive privilege
The right to keep executive communications confidential, especially if they relate to national security.

take care clause
The constitutional requirement (in Article II, Section 3) that presidents take care that the laws are faithfully executed, even if they disagree with the purpose of those laws.

The Pardon Power

Article II, Section 2, of the U.S. Constitution provides that the president shall have the power to grant "Reprieves" and "Pardons" for offenses against the United States, except in cases of impeachment. This authority, the roots of which can be traced directly to the royal authority of the king of England, is probably the most imperial and often the most delicate power a president exercises. The pardon power is generally a tool of mercy, an instrument to correct miscarriages of justice and to restore full civil rights to those who have served their sentences and are expected to be law-abiding.

The pardon power permits a president to be merciful, but it can also be used strategically when a pardon can restore peace and stability. George Washington used this power to help end the Whiskey Rebellion. Presidents Abraham Lincoln and Andrew Johnson used it to provide amnesty to Confederate leaders and soldiers. Presidents Gerald Ford and Jimmy Carter used it for Vietnam War draft evaders. President Ford also used it to pardon Richard Nixon, one of the most controversial exercises of the pardon power. On his final day in office, Clinton pardoned his half-brother, one of his former business partners, one of his former cabinet members, and a fugitive commodities trader, Marc Rich, whose ex-wife was a major contributor to Clinton's campaigns and presidential library.

Presidents sometimes use the take care clause to claim **inherent powers**, meaning powers they believe are essential to protecting the nation. Although Jefferson drew on this broad notion in making the Louisiana Purchase in 1804, Abraham Lincoln extended the concept at the beginning of the Civil War in 1861 to suspend the rights of prisoners to seek judicial review of their cases, impose a blockade of Confederate shipping, and expand the size of the army beyond authorized ceilings, all without prior congressional approval as required under the Constitution's lawmaking power.

THE LAWMAKING POWER   Although Congress is the legislative branch of government, presidents have exploited their constitutional powers to become the most influential actors in the legislative process. Presidents have a particularly important role in setting the agenda of issues that Congress will address. This agenda-setting role centers on the Article II requirement that the president "from time to time give to the Congress Information of the State of the Union, and recommend to their Consideration such Measures as he shall judge necessary." Over the years, the phrase "from time to time" has evolved to mean a constant stream of presidential messages, as well as the annual **State of the Union Address**.

The president also has the power to convene Congress in extraordinary circumstances and recommend "such Measures as he shall judge necessary and expedient." Those suggestions can range from simple ideas presented in a letter or news conference to the proposals President George W. Bush made in his speech before a joint session of Congress following September 11, 2001.

George W. Bush won the 2004 election with 286 electoral votes and 51% of the popular vote.

Presidential Succession

Having decided how a president would enter office, the framers also decided how a president would leave. In addition to impeachment, reelection defeat, retirement, resignation, or death, the Constitution now contains two other ways to remove a president from office. Under the Twenty-Second Amendment, presidents must leave office after completion of two elected terms in office.

Under the Twenty-Fifth Amendment, presidents can be forced from office temporarily if the vice president and a majority of either Congress or the president's own cabinet secretaries declares that the president is unable to discharge the powers and duties of the office. In such a case, the vice president becomes the acting president until the duly elected president returns to office. The amendment also allows a president to appoint a new vice president in the event of the vice president's own resignation, death, impeachment, or rise to the presidency.

The framers gave Congress exclusive power to remove the president through the **impeachment** process. Recall from Chapter 11 that the House must draft articles of impeachment that charge the president with treason, bribery, or other high crimes and misdemeanors. Once approved through a majority vote, the articles form the basis for a trial before the full Senate, which can convict the president on a two-thirds vote. Conviction results in immediate removal from office.

Impeachment has been used only twice, once in 1868 against Andrew Johnson and a second time in 1998 against Bill Clinton. Both Senate trials resulted in acquittals. Richard Nixon resigned from office in 1974 facing impeachment for his role in the Watergate cover-up.

The Evolution of Presidential Power

The formal powers the U.S. Constitution vests in a president have not been changed for more than 200 years. But the influence of modern presidents is considerably greater today than it was two centuries ago. The power and influence of any given president are partly the consequences of the president's character and energy, combined with the needs of the time, the party balance in Congress, the values of the citizenry, and the challenges to our nation's survival.

inherent powers
Powers that grow out of the very existence of government.

State of the Union Address
The president's annual statement to Congress and the nation.

impeachment
Formal accusation against a public official, the first step in removal from office.

The Chain of Succession

The Constitution leaves succession after the vice president up to Congress. This is the line of succession established by Congress in 1947 and by the Twenty-Fifth Amendment. Note that the constitutional qualifications still apply. For example, if the secretary of state was born in a foreign country of parents who were not U.S. citizens, he or she would be bypassed in this line.

1. Vice President

2. Speaker of the House of Representatives

3. Senate President Pro Tempore

4. Secretary of State

5. Secretary of the Treasury

6. Secretary of Defense

7. Attorney General

8. Secretary of the Interior

9. Secretary of Agriculture

10. Secretary of Commerce

11. Secretary of Labor

12. Secretary of Health and Human Services

13. Secretary of Housing and Urban Development

14. Secretary of Transportation

15. Secretary of Energy

16. Secretary of Education

17. Secretary of Veterans Affairs

18. Secretary of Homeland Security

In response to the terrorist attacks on September 11, 2001, President Bush used his presidential authority to appoint former Pennsylvania Governor Tom Ridge the Director of Homeland Security. Ridge was later appointed as the first Secretary of the Department of Homeland Security.

By and large, the history of presidential power is one of steady, if uneven, growth. Of the individuals who have filled the office, about one-third have enlarged its powers. Andrew Jackson, Abraham Lincoln, and both Roosevelts, for example, redefined both the institution and many of its powers by the way they set priorities and responded to crises.

Two centuries of national expansion and crises have increased the influence of the president beyond the framers' design. As we saw in Chapter 11, the complexity of Congress's decision making procedures, its unwieldy numbers, and its constitutional responsibilities make it a more public, deliberative, and divided institution than the presidency. When crises occur, Congress traditionally holds debates and, almost as predictably, delegates authority to the president, charging the executive branch to take whatever actions are deemed necessary. Or Congress has allowed presidents to take charge, as it essentially did in the 1990s in response to presidential calls for U.S. involvement in Kuwait, Somalia, Haiti, Iraq, and Yugoslavia. It also expected the president to take charge in the moments following September 11, 2001.

In the history of presidential–Supreme Court relations, the nation's highest court has generally favored an expansive interpretation of presidential power. The Court has on occasion halted a presidential action or ruled a presidential decision unconstitutional, but it has more frequently given legitimacy to the growth of presidential power.

Several factors have strengthened the presidency in recent decades. The danger of war and the destructive potential of new weaponry plainly increased the president's influence. The cold war—with its enormous standing armies, nuclear weapons, and widespread intelligence and alliance operations—invited presidential leadership in national security matters.

The end of the cold war period has not reduced the need for presidential leadership, however. As the events of September 11, 2001, and the Middle East uprising in early 2002 showed, the world is just as dangerous as it was at the height of the cold war—perhaps even more so. As weapons of mass destruction become more easily available, the president's role in protecting the nation from terrorism has become much more pronounced.

The growth of federal involvement in economic and social issues and the increasing complexity of public policies have increased presidential responsibility and contributed to the growth of agencies reporting directly to the White House. Problems not easily delegated to any one department often get pulled into the White House. When new programs involve several federal agencies, someone near the president is often asked to reconcile conflicts and set a consistent policy. White House aides, with some justification, claim that the presidency is the only place in government where it is possible to establish and coordinate national priorities. Presidents set up central review and coordination units that help formulate new policies, settle jurisdictional disputes among departments, and provide access for the well-organized interest groups that want their views to be given weight in decision making.

That is precisely what George W. Bush did in creating the new White House Office of Homeland Security immediately after the attacks on New York City and Washington. The new office, which was headed by former Pennsylvania Governor Tom Ridge, was given responsibility for coordinating the federal government's response to terrorism. Ridge was made a member of the president's cabinet and given authority to create a new alert system to inform the nation of terrorist threats.

Some experts believe that presidential influence has declined in recent years, in part because of political scandals such as Watergate (Nixon), Iran-Contra (Reagan), and Whitewater and Monica Lewinsky (Clinton). The near impeachment of Richard Nixon and the impeachment of Bill Clinton are cited as having decreased respect for the presidency. The closeness of the 2000 presidential election, the questions surrounding the Florida recount in it, and the confusing court decisions about vote counting seemed likely to limit Bush's influence. As noted earlier, however, the events of September 11

Election 2004: An Analysis

George W. Bush started the 2004 campaign with a long list of liabilities. His public approval rating was falling; the economy was still sluggish; the war in Iraq was anything but the "mission accomplished" that the president had celebrated the previous May; and Democrats were well-funded, highly motivated, and still angry about the 2000 election, which Bush had won in the courts, not in the popular vote count.

Yet, Bush also had significant assets. He was a likable wartime president with a stubborn commitment to the war in Iraq. Bush also had all the prerequisites of the presidency, including Air Force One, a powerful political machine, some of the cleverest political strategists in the country, and a plainspoken persistence that just might appeal to undecided voters. If Bush could get all of his supporters to the polls, shift the public's focus from the economy to terrorism, and win enough of the swing voters who had voted for Vice President Al Gore in 2000, he just might be able to win.

Bush also needed the right opponent. If Democrats nominated someone with just enough inconsistency in his record and just enough mistakes in his strategy, the president might be able to argue that he was the safer choice in an uncertain world. If Bush could make the 2004 election a referendum on his opponent, not on his record, he might erase the doubts about his own record on jobs, the war in Iraq, and health care.

Remarkably, Bush did all of the above and more. Despite pink slips for workers in "battleground" states such as Ohio and Pennsylvania, rising Medicare premiums for the elderly, worries about a draft for the young, and rising casualties and a prison-abuse scandal in Iraq, Bush won both the electoral and popular vote on Tuesday, November 2, 2004. With Bush's 286–252 electoral margin, and a 4-million popular-vote cushion, there would be no repeat of the agonizing recount that had paralyzed the country in 2000.

Yet, if Bush's victory was firm, it was also surprisingly familiar. Although Bush earned 9 million more votes in 2004 than 2000, only three states actually switched sides: New Hampshire "flipped" from the Republican to the Democratic column, while Iowa and New Mexico flipped from the Democratic column to the Republican. The other 47 states remained exactly where they had been four years earlier, with the Republican "red" states concentrated in the South and Midwest and most of the Democratic "blue" states in the Northeast and on the West Coast.

Moreover, Bush and Kerry did well in 2004 exactly where Bush and Vice President Al Gore had done well in 2000. Bush ran ahead of Kerry among men; older Americans; whites; Republicans; and white, born-again Christians; while Kerry ran ahead of Bush among women, younger Americans, minority voters, Democrats, and gays.

The obvious question is what changed. Simply put, how did George W. Bush win?

A first answer is that Bush's supporters were more committed than Kerry's, in part because the Bush campaign was able to rally religious conservatives who had stayed home in 2000. Anti-gay-marriage initiatives were on the ballot in eleven states, including Ohio, which some pundits argue brought large numbers of passionate conservatives to the polls.

However, Bush's winning margin did not come from these groups alone. Of the 9 million votes that Bush gained between 2000 and 2004, the largest share came from two groups that were distinctly non-evangelical and not opponents of gay marriage. His share of the vote among white women surged from 49 percent in 2000 to 55 percent in 2004, and among Hispanic/Latino voters from 36 percent to 44 percent. Put together, the gains produced exactly 3.5 percent of the popular vote, or roughly the 4 million votes that gave Bush the deciding margin.

A second answer is that Bush was a much better candidate than John Kerry. He was always judged the more likeable candidate—although voters had significant concerns about his policies, particularly his management of the economy and the war in Iraq, they saw him as more approachable. Kerry never fully connected with the public as an individual—he was generally viewed as distant, even snobbish.

It is no surprise, for example, that Bush ran well among 91 percent of voters who said they cared most about each candidate's religious faith. But Bush also won 70 percent who wanted an honest, trustworthy president; 87 percent of those who wanted a strong leader; and 79 percent who wanted a president who takes a clear stand on issues. Although Kerry ran well among those who wanted a president that cares about people, his greatest strength came from those who wanted an intelligent leader who would bring change to the country.

A third answer is simply that Bush ran a better campaign. In spite of all the bad news coming into the campaign from Iraq, the Bush campaign kept Kerry on the defensive. Bush operatives were particularly effective in exploiting Kerry's own statements and creating an image of him as a "flip flopper" who could not be trusted to run the nation during war.

A fourth and final answer involves issues. When asked what issue most influenced their vote, 22 percent of Americans referred to moral issues such as abortion and gay marriage; another 20 percent said the economy and jobs; 19 percent said terrorism; 15 percent said the war in Iraq; and 8 percent said health care. Bush won 80 percent of the votes among those who focused on moral issues and 86 percent of the votes among those who focused on terrorism, while Kerry did exceptionally well among the rest.

No matter how close the actual results, Bush began preparing for his second term as if he had won a sweeping mandate. The fact that Republicans picked up seats in the Senate and House gave him additional ammunition for the case.

But claiming a mandate and having one are two different things. Second-term presidents have very little time to set the legislative agenda, in part because the modern campaign system forces candidates in both parties to start planning for the next election early. Because Bush refused to pick an heir-apparent as his vice presidential running mate, Republicans were already lining up for the 2008 election even before the 2004 election was over.

SOURCE: Adam Nagourney, "Bush Celebrates Victory," *The New York Times,* November 4, 2004, p. A1.

vaulted Bush to record levels of public approval and erased most doubts about both his ability and his legitimacy as president.

Although we may dislike and even condemn individual presidents, public attitudes toward the institution of the presidency remain positive. We want to believe in our presidents; we want them to provide unifying leadership. Perhaps this is peculiarly the case in America, where we have no royal family, no established church, and no other common source of ceremonial leadership.

Bush v. Kerry	Bush	Kerry
Men	55%	44%
Women	48	51
18–29 years old	45	54
30–44 years old	53	46
45–59 years old	51	48
60 years old or over	54	46
White	58	41
Black	11	88
Hispanic/Latino	44	53
Asian	44	56
Republican	93	6
Independent	48	49
Democrat	11	89
White evangelical or born again Christian	78	21
Gay, lesbian, or bisexual	23	77

SOURCE: "Survey of Voters: Who They Were...,"
The New York Times, November 4, 2004, p. 4.

What Americans Expect of Their Presidents

The framers designed the presidency hoping that George Washington would be the first to occupy the post. Washington commanded the public's trust and respect and was unanimously elected as the first president of the new Republic in 1789. He understood that the people needed to have confidence in their fledgling government, a sense of continuity with the past, and a time of calm and stability free of emergencies and crises. He also knew that the new nation faced both domestic and foreign threats to its future.

If presidents act too forcefully in response to threats, however, they are often accused of acting like dictators, especially by their political opponents. At the same time, if they respond too meekly, they are criticized for being weak or passive and, even more likely, blamed for whatever happens to be wrong with the country. People who like what a president is doing are champions of presidential leadership; people who disapprove of what a president is doing point to the dangers of dictatorship. Regardless of their views, Americans want their presidents to be honest, dignified, and trustworthy. See Table 12-1 for a list of information Americans want about their presidential candidates.

Voters often place as much emphasis on a presidential candidate's character and integrity as they do on a candidate's political philosophy and past experience. Such emphasis is not misguided. Presidents have enormous influence, especially in times of crisis. They recruit the people who run the executive departments and serve on our courts, and thus they have much to do with governmental performance and ethics. Hence it is important to weigh their character, allegiance to constitutional and democratic values, and ability to manage their emotions and turn them to constructive purposes.[7]

Concerns about presidential character are as old as the presidency itself. In 1800, for example, religious leaders denounced Thomas Jefferson from their pulpits as "godless," and in the 1820s, Andrew Jackson was pilloried as a barbarian and an adulterer.

The election of 1884 provides a fascinating case study of character in politics. In that election, Democratic candidate Grover Cleveland was charged with fathering a child out of wedlock. Cleveland took responsibility and agreed to pay for the child's upbringing. Not surprisingly, this became a hot issue for his opponent, James G. Blaine. The dilemma was that while Cleveland's private life raised doubts, he was responsible in his political and professional life. Blaine, on the other hand, had an "upright" private life but was less well regarded for his political integrity. Voters elected Cleveland.

Bill Clinton had major character flaws, yet his political supporters hoped, sometimes in vain, that he would avoid reckless behavior and concentrate on the policy initiatives they favored. Clinton was impeached by the House of Representatives and nearly removed from office by the Senate for lying under oath about his relationship with a White House intern. What was remarkable was that an unusually large number of Americans (often 60 percent or more) continued to approve of Clinton's handling of the job of the presidency while disapproving of his personal behavior. Most people apparently judged Clinton on how well the economy did, on traditional "peace and prosperity" measures, and on his adroit political and communication skills rather than on his personal morals.

Americans want presidents they can trust, individuals who have a basic respect for others, as well as a commitment to serve the public interest. A sense of decency, integrity, and fair play will always be part of what is wanted in a president. Here, briefly, are some additional qualities Americans yearn for in an ideal president.

- *Courage:* Americans want a leader who takes firm stands on issues, is concerned about the average citizen, and places the country's interests ahead of politics. A president should have the intellectual courage to take risks and do what is right, even when it is not popular or easy; the willingness to serve all the people, not just those who supported his candidacy; and the perseverance not to give up after initial legislative or political defeats.

- *Experience:* Americans want presidents who have proven competence in understanding complex policy issues. Presidents need to be skilled at bringing people together to solve intricate policy problems.

- *Political ability:* Presidents need an understanding of the role of politics in governing and the ability to be an effective politician working with people of all political viewpoints. The job requires an ability to build coalitions, generate public support, and manage the media.

- *A sense of history and constitutionalism:* Americans want a president to have a great respect for the U.S. Constitution and American values, exhibiting a solid grasp of how governments and markets work and of diplomacy and trade.

- *Vision:* The ideal president should have ideas and programmatic plans to make the country stronger. We ask presidents to clarify options and help set the nation's policy agenda. A president must be able to see the big picture and articulate clear goals in areas such as economic opportunity, civil rights, equality, education, trade, nuclear proliferation, terrorism, and equality.

- *Listening and teaching skills:* Our best presidents both listen to us and lead us. They must know how to teach the nation what is right yet be able to hear what the public is ready to accept. We want presidents who give us a sense not only of who they are but, even more important, of who we are and what kind of nation we might become.

- *Communication skills:* Ideas and wisdom are of little use if a president cannot motivate and rally the public and empower constituencies to act. Presidents have to develop impressive speaking and media management skills.

- *Morale-building skills:* The presidency is more than just a constitutional or political office; it has to help us navigate through crises and transitions and unify us when we experience national setbacks and tragedy. At their best, presidents remind us of our mutual obligations, shared beliefs, and the trust and caring that bind us together. Americans understandably yearn for presidents like George Washington and Abraham Lincoln, who can bring us together and challenge us to be better.

Americans often exaggerate the president's capacity to change the course of events.[8] They often ask too much of our presidents. They want vision, character, competence, intelligence, honesty, stamina, inspiration, sound judgment, wisdom, and, of course, political beliefs in line with their own. But presidents are only human and cannot be expected to be all things to all people.

TABLE 12–1 What Americans Want to Know About Their Presidential Candidates

Percentage of Americans who said it is very important to know the following about a presidential candidate:

Reputation for honesty	82%
Ability to connect with people	71
Past voting record	58
Major campaign contributions	37
Church involvement	25
Clubs and organizations	24
Spouse's personal qualities	21
Experiences growing up	20
Military background	19
Spouse's professional life	15
Personal finances	13
Children	8

SOURCE: Pew Research Center for the People and the Press, "Candidate Qualities May Trump Issues in 2000," October 1999, p. 1.

Roles Assumed by the President

Presidents are asked to perform roles not explicitly defined in the Constitution. We want the chief executive to be an international peacemaker as well as a national morale builder, a politician in chief as well as a commander in chief. We want the president to be the architect of a new world order, or at least a peaceful world order, who negotiates favorable trade pacts with major trading partners. In addition to the obvious leadership responsibilities a president has in foreign policy, economics, and domestic policy, a variety of broad functional kinds of leadership are expected of a president. These policy areas and functions permit us to develop a presidential job profile (see Table 12-2).

Presidents as Crisis Managers

The framers designed the president's job as commander in chief as a limited role. Congress, not the president, declares war, makes the rules for the Army and Navy, and controls the funding of wars. Yet the president is still in charge of the military as commander in chief.

TABLE 12-2   A Presidential Job Description

Area	Examples of Policy Responsibilities		
	Foreign Policy	Economic Policy	Domestic Policy
Crisis management	Bush's authorizing the war on Afghanistan	G. W. Bush's 2001 Tax Rebates	Initiating federal disaster relief
Symbolic and morale-building leadership	G. W. Bush's visit to Mexico to celebrate trade and friendship	Response to Enron scandal	Visiting flood and disaster victims
Recruitment of top officials	Selecting the Chairman of Joint Chiefs of Staff chair	Appointing Donald Evans as secretary of commerce	Nominating Supreme Court justices
Priority setting and problem clarification	Working with United Nations on peacekeeping priorities	Outlining tax-cut or revenue-producing programs	Setting priorities in environmental protection and health care
Legislative and political coalition building	Negotiating with Congress on new members of NATO	Working out a tax cut with Congress	Bush's efforts to pass homeland security legislation
Program implementation, administration, and oversight	Hosting Middle East peace talks	Monitoring homeland security	Appraising the impact of federal social programs

The president's role is based on the principle of *civilian control over the military,* a central condition of a constitutional democracy.[9] Civilian control means that all soldiers and sailors, from the newest recruit to every general and admiral, take their orders from and owe their allegiance to the one person elected by all the people. The professional military, no matter what their own personal political views and values, take their military orders from the president and his chief civilian agent, the secretary of defense.

Presidents are expected to be crisis managers in the domestic sphere as well. Presidents or their surrogates in the cabinet are often the first on the scene in national disasters such as hurricanes and floods and are expected to play a significant role in reassuring the nation after accidents such as the Challenger space shuttle explosion in 1986 or the Oklahoma City bombing in 1995.

Presidents as Morale Builders

As chief of state, the president must project a sense of national unity and authority as the country's chief ceremonial leader. The framers of the Constitution did not fully anticipate the symbolic and morale-building functions a president must perform. Certain magisterial functions, such as receiving ambassadors and granting pardons, were conferred. But over time, the presidency has acquired enormous symbolic significance.

Presidents are the nation's number one celebrities; almost anything they do is news. Presidents command attention merely by jogging, fishing, golfing, or going to church. By their actions, presidents can arouse a sense of hope or despair, honor or dishonor.

The morale-building job of the president involves much more than just ceremonial cheerleading or quasi-chaplain duties. Presidential leadership, at its finest, radiates national self-confidence and helps unlock the possibility for good that exists in the nation. Our best leaders have been able to provide this special and often intangible element. That is certainly what George W. Bush intended in the days and weeks that followed September 11, 2001. By his words and deed, he sought to simultaneously calm the nation and warn the rest of the world that the United States would not tolerate further terrorist attacks.

Presidents as Recruiters

Presidents make more than 7,000 political appointments, including hundreds of federal judgeships, top positions in the military and diplomatic service, and at least 500 executive branch positions subject to Senate confirmation. Effective presidents shrewdly use their appointment powers not only to reward campaign supporters and enhance ties to Congress but also to communicate priorities and policy directions. Moreover, the White House in recent decades has often placed campaign aides in key deputy positions to ensure loyalty to the White House.[10]

The president must also try to keep the most talented of these officials in government as long as possible. Many able people come to top positions in the cabinet or sub-cabinet and stay for just two or three years. Among the reasons for these short terms is that top federal posts do not pay as much as similar positions in the private sector, and living in Washington is expensive.[11]

Presidents have a lasting impact beyond their terms of office by their power to nominate federal judges. For example, President Dwight Eisenhower's nomination of Earl Warren to be chief justice of the United States was one of his most significant decisions in the area of domestic policy. Warren served for more than 15 years and presided over vast changes in civil rights and civil liberties. President Clinton nominated hundreds of federal judges, including Supreme Court justices Ruth Bader Ginsburg and Stephen Breyer, who are likely to have long-term effects. In a similar way, the selection of a secretary of state, a top economic adviser, a secretary of the treasury, a Federal Reserve Board member, or a top White House aide can have a substantial impact on long-term national policy. But Supreme Court appointments, because they are lifetime positions, overshadow almost all the others.

Various financial disclosure and conflict-of-interest requirements, imposed on presidential appointees as a result of the Ethics in Government Act of 1978, discourage some potential appointees from accepting government jobs. They must fill out at least four different forms, which together include more than 200 separate questions about their personal and employment history, and they must testify at sometimes complicated, time-consuming, confusing, and embarrassing congressional hearings.[12]

President Bush with Russian President Vladimir Putin. Presidential responsibilities include meeting with foreign leaders to establish communication and the exchange of ideas.

Presidents as Priority and Agenda Setters

By custom and circumstance, presidents are now responsible for proposing initiatives in foreign policy and economic growth and stability. This was not always the case. But beginning with Woodrow Wilson, and especially since the New Deal, a president has been expected to propose reforms to ensure domestic progress. New ideas are seized on by a presidential candidate searching for campaign issues, and they are later refined and implemented by the executive office staff, by special presidential task forces, and by Congress.[13]

NATIONAL SECURITY POLICY   The framers foresaw a special need for speed and unity in dealing with other nations. As a result, presidents generally have more leeway in foreign policy and military affairs than they have in domestic matters. The Constitution vests in a president command of the two major instruments of foreign policy—the diplomatic corps and the armed services. It also gives the chief executive responsibility for negotiating treaties and commitments with other nations, although the Senate must consent to treaty ratifications, and almost all international agreements require congressional action for their implementation.

Congress has granted presidents discretion in initiating foreign policies, for diplomacy frequently requires quick action. The Supreme Court has upheld strong presidential authority in this area. In *United States* v. *Curtiss-Wright* (1936), the Court referred to the "exclusive power of the president as the sole organ of the federal government in the field of international relations—a power which does not require as a basis for its exercise an act of Congress, but which, of course, like every other governmental power, must be exercised in subordination to the applicable provisions of the Constitution."[14] These are sweeping and much-debated words.[15] Still, a determined Congress that knows what it wants does not lack power in foreign relations. Congress must authorize and appropriate the funds that back up the president's policies abroad.

ECONOMIC POLICY   Ever since the New Deal, presidents have been expected to promote policies to keep unemployment low, fight inflation, keep taxes down, and promote economic growth and prosperity. The Constitution did not specify these duties for the executive, yet presidents know that when the nation is not prosperous and jobs are scarce, they may suffer the fate of Herbert Hoover, who was denounced for his inaction at the beginning of the Great Depression. The growth and complexity of economic problems since the Depression of the 1930s have placed more economic responsibility in the president's hands. The delicate balancing required to keep a modern economy operating means that presidents must make key fiscal and budgetary policy decisions.[16] The presidential elections in 1980 and 1992 turned largely on the economy, and the election of 2000 involved a debate about which candidate would be better able to keep the economic boom going.

Although presidents sometimes get their economic advice elsewhere, their chief advisers on economic policy are the secretary of the treasury, the three members of the Council of Economic Advisers, and the director of the Office of Management and Budget. The chair of the Federal Reserve Board of Governors is also an influential, if independent, adviser on the economy.

DOMESTIC POLICY   Some experts believe that a leader is one who knows where the followers are. Abraham Lincoln did not invent the antislavery movement. John Kennedy and Lyndon Johnson did not begin the civil rights movement. Bill Clinton was not the first leader to notice the unfairness of health care and welfare policies, nor was George W. Bush the first to note the skyrocketing price of prescription drugs. But they all, in their respective times, became embroiled in these controversies, for a president cannot long ignore what divides or inspires a nation.

At the same time, presidents sometimes take highly unpopular positions for the good of the country. The vast majority of Americans opposed Harry Truman's decision to integrate the armed services, and many southerners bolted the Democratic party when Lyndon Johnson demanded action on civil rights. Similarly, many Americans opposed George W. Bush's 2001 decision to limit fetal research, which he believed might increase abortion.

Presidents as Legislative and Political Coalition Builders

Presidents must build political coalitions if they are to have any chance of winning passage of their legislative programs. As candidates, they make promises to the people and assemble an electoral coalition of supporters. To get things done and to get reelected, however, they must work with interest groups and people who have differing loyalties and responsibilities. Inevitably, presidents become embroiled in legislative, bureaucratic, and lobbying politics, and their approval ratings often suffer as a consequence.

Despite their formal powers, presidents spend most of their time *persuading* people. As Richard Neustadt argues, the power to persuade is the president's chief resource, and that power comes through bargaining.[17] Bargaining, in turn, comes primarily through getting others to believe it is in their self-interest to cooperate. Presidents and their aides spend a lot of time dispensing favors to various members of Congress from whom they are seeking votes and political support. Hence the skill of a president in communicating and winning others over is the necessary energizing factor in moving the institutions of the national government to action.

Presidents often clash with Congress, as we shall discuss in the next chapter, yet they cooperate and collaborate just as often, if not more so. Plainly, working with Congress is a major part of the job of being president.

Presidents and the Public

The press conference is an example of how a president can employ the machinery of communication to build legislative and political coalitions. Years ago, press conferences were rather casual affairs. Franklin Roosevelt ran his press meetings as informal get-togethers and was a master at withholding information as well as giving it. Under Harry Truman, the conference became an institutionalized part of the presidential communications apparatus. John Kennedy authorized live telecasts of press conferences and used them frequently for direct communication with the people. Ronald Reagan and Bill Clinton effectively used five-minute Saturday afternoon radio chats to communicate their views, ask for support, and win Sunday morning media coverage.

Presidents regularly commission polls to find out how they are doing. They want to learn about the public's views, estimate the strength and direction of its thinking, and respond to it. Public opinion can be unstable and unpredictable. Richard Nixon dropped nearly 40 percentage points in public approval during the Watergate scandal. Most presidents lose support the longer they are in office. Dissatisfaction sets in, interest groups grow impatient, unkept promises must be accounted for, and the president gets blamed for things that go wrong.

There are exceptions to this rule, however. Bill Clinton surprisingly retained and even gained popularity the longer he was in office. Indeed, the more personal trouble Clinton got into, the more his public approval ratings went up—even after he was impeached by the U.S. House of Representatives. The Clinton years of "peace, prosperity, and moderation" kept his approval ratings high.[18] George W. Bush also gained popularity in his first year. Having started his presidency with a 57 percent approval rating, Bush soared after September 11, then began to falter in March 2002 as Americans began to question his response to a succession of suicide bombings in Israel.

President John F. Kennedy understood the importance of direct communication with the American people and often addressed the public with television broadcasts.

Presidents as Party Leaders

As chief of government, each president is called on to act as partisan political leader. Most presidents since Thomas Jefferson have been party leaders, and generally the more effective the president, the more use he has made of party support. Woodrow Wilson, the two Roosevelts, and Ronald Reagan fortified their executive and legislative influence by mobilizing support within their party. Reagan, Clinton, and George W. Bush were uncommonly effective fund raisers for their political parties. In doing so, they were able to build needed connections within their political parties and overcome at least some of the gridlock in Congress.

Going Public

One of the ways in which presidents mold public opinion is to "go public" about their contests with Congress. One way to build a fire on Capitol Hill in favor of the president's program is to light a match in the congressional districts. Although presidents have been communicating with the public from the very beginning of the Republic, today's presidents are communicating much more often and for a very different purpose: to focus public pressure on Congress.

Presidents are going public more frequently. They are making more prime-time television appearances, giving more speeches, and spending more time outside of Washington in efforts to influence the country. According to political scientist Samuel Kernell, the number of major and minor presidential addresses has grown from just a dozen or so in the first three years of the Hoover administration (1929–1931) to well over 100 in the first three years of the Bush presidency almost 60 years later. The greatest growth came in the number of minor addresses before specialized audiences—trade associations, college graduations, advocacy groups.

At the same time, presidents have been spending less time holding press conferences. Whereas Franklin Roosevelt averaged almost seven press conferences a month during his dozen years in office, Reagan, Bush, and Clinton averaged barely one a month. Presidents would much rather be interviewed by local reporters outside Washington than by members of the hardened White House press corps, much rather give exclusive interviews to a sympathetic interviewer such as ABC's Barbara Walters than face a roomful of unpredictable reporters, and much rather use live satellite feeds to remote stations to get their message across than deal with the *Washington Post, New York Times,* or *Wall Street Journal.* (Presidential press conferences are covered in more detail in Chapter 10.)

Going public clearly fits with changes in the electoral process. Presidents now have the staff, the technology, and the public opinion research to tell them how to target the message and the nearly instant media access to go public easily. And as elections have become more image-oriented and candidate-centered, presidents have the incentive to use these tools to operate a permanent White House campaign. Unable to count on their party to deliver the voters, presidents go public because it is one of the few strategies that promise success. Presidents are still welcome to bargain and persuade, to focus congressional attention and twist arms, but members of Congress may pay attention only when pressure is coming from the voters back home.

Source: Jeffrey Tulis, *The Rhetorical Presidency* (Princeton University Press, 1987); Samuel Kernell, *Going Public* (CQ Press, 1993)

Despite their best efforts, presidents are often led by their party, or at least constrained by it, as much as they lead it. Although presidents do name the head of their national party committees and play an important role in recruiting candidates for congressional campaigns, no president has ever wholly dominated his party.[19]

Managing the Presidency

Without help, presidents not could manage crises, build morale, set priorities and agendas, build legislative and political coalitions, mold public opinion, lead their parties, and otherwise take care that the laws are faithfully executed. Although some of that help comes from their *inner circle,* which is composed of their closest advisers including the first lady, presidents could not do jobs without a vast array of support that extends well beyond 1600 Pennsylvania Avenue to include the executive branch as a whole.

The White House Staff

Presidents have come to rely heavily on their personal staffs. Nowhere else—not in Congress, not in the cabinet, not in the party—can presidents find the loyalty and single-mindedness that often develops among their closest White House aides.[20] Cabinet heads are often perceived as staunch advocates of their departments and the constituencies their departments serve and so cannot be assumed to give objective advice. By contrast, presidents presume that their aides will provide them with sound and unbiased policy guidance. But there are sometimes substantial costs to listening only to one's closest associates.

THE WHITE HOUSE ORGANIZATION The number of employees in the presidential entourage grew steadily from the early 1900s through the early 1990s. Today a White House staff of about 400 operates at a slight reduction from previous years. This staff is headed by the **chief of staff**, who is considered the president's most loyal assistant. The White House staff also includes the president's chief lawyer, speechwriters, legislative liaison staff, and press secretary. The chief of staff supervises all other White House staff and is considered a member of the president's inner circle.

Most of these advisers have offices in the West Wing of the White House or the Old Executive Office Building. Once used to house all the federal departments in the early 1800s, the Old Executive Office Building now holds mostly presidential and vice presidential staff. These staffers must be available to brief the president on a moment's notice and often serve as a buffer between the president and the heads of the departments and agencies:

> Political staffers who have made it to the West Wing have achieved a rare condition of the soul: They do not wish to be anybody else, do not wish to be anywhere else. This is as good as it gets for people in politics who do not have it in them to run for public office themselves. Real proximity to real power produces a special high, one made up of equal parts self-congratulation (I have finally made it) and anxiety (They'll figure out I'm really an incompetent nobody and come and take it all away). If parasites could fear, this is what their fear would be: expulsion from the host.[21]

White House staff sometimes insist they are simply the eyes and ears of the president, that they make few important decisions, and that they never intrude between the chief executive and the heads of departments. But the inevitable emergence of a few strong White House advisers such as Karl Rove and Karen Hughes in the Bush White House renders this traditional picture inaccurate.[22]

RUNNING THE WHITE HOUSE Over the past three decades, presidents have used three very different models for running the White House staff: competitive, collegial, and hierarchical. Among modern presidents, Franklin Roosevelt and Lyndon Johnson both used the competitive approach, a "survival of the fittest" situation in which the president allows aides to fight each other for access to the Oval Office. Johnson sometimes gave different staffers the same assignment, hoping that the competition would produce a better final decision.

chief of staff
The head of the White House staff.

In contrast, John Kennedy, Jimmy Carter, and Bill Clinton all used the collegial approach, in which presidents encourage aides to work together toward a common position. It is a much friendlier way to work than the competitive approach but may have the serious drawback of producing what some social psychologists call *groupthink*. Groupthink is the tendency of small groups to stifle dissent in the search for common ground.[23]

Finally, Dwight Eisenhower, Richard Nixon, Ronald Reagan, and George H. W. Bush all used the hierarchical model, in which presidents establish tight control over who does what in making decisions. A hierarchy is a form of organization that looks very much like a pyramid: one leader at the top, two right underneath, three or more right underneath those two, and so on down the organization. The chief advantage of a hierarchy is in reducing the number of people the leader has to deal with—the tighter the hierarchy, the fewer the contacts. Most hierarchies depend on a "gatekeeper" near the very top, usually the chief of staff, to enforce tight control over access to the leaders.

George W. Bush has used a hierarchical approach in organizing the White House. He uses clear lines of authority to minimize chaos and expects his staff to be loyal above all else. Most decisions have been made through tightly controlled discussions led by the president, his top staff aides, or Vice President Cheney.

The Executive Office of the President

Created in 1939, the **Executive Office of the President** consists of the Office of Management and Budget, the Council of Economic Advisers, and several other staff units (see Figure 12-1). It also contains the White House staff.

The **Office of Management and Budget (OMB)** is the central presidential staff agency. Its director advises the president in detail about the hundreds of government agencies—how much money they should be allotted in the budget and what kind of job they are doing. OMB seeks to improve the planning, management, and statistical work of the agencies. It makes a special effort to see that each agency conforms to presidential policies in its dealings with Congress; each agency has to clear its policy recommendations to Congress through OMB first.[24]

Through the long budget preparation process, presidents use OMB as a way of conserving and centralizing their own influence. A budget is more than just a financial plan because it reflects power struggles and indicates national priorities (and wishful thinking). To the president, the budget is a means of control over administrators who may be trying to join ranks with other politicians or interest groups to thwart presidential priorities.

Executive Office of the President
The cluster of presidential staff agencies that help the president carry out his responsibilities. Currently the office includes the Office of Management and Budget, the Council of Economic Advisers, and several other units.

Office of Management and Budget (OMB)
Presidential staff agency that serves as a clearinghouse for budgetary requests and management improvements for government agencies.

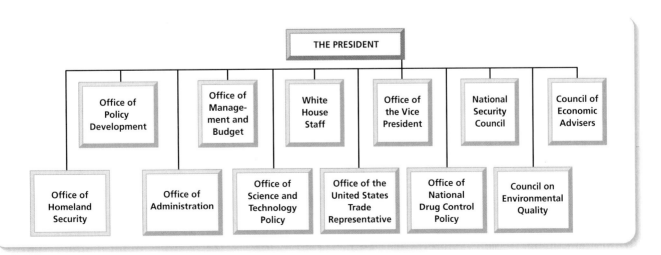

FIGURE 12–1   Executive Office of the President.

SOURCE: *United States Government Manual, 2000–2001* (Government Printing Office, 2000), p. 87.

The Cabinet

It is hard to find a more unusual institution than the president's **cabinet**. The cabinet is not specifically mentioned in the Constitution, yet since George Washington's administration, every president has had one. Washington's consisted of his secretaries of state, treasury, and war, plus his attorney general.

SELECTING THE CABINET   Selecting the cabinet today is the first major job for the president-elect. The cabinet consists of the president, the vice president, the heads of the 15 executive departments, and a few others a president considers cabinet-level officials. The cabinet has always been a loosely designated body, and it is not always clear who belongs in it. In recent years, certain executive branch administrators and White House counselors have been accorded cabinet rank. Nineteen officials have cabinet status in the George W. Bush administration, including the 15 cabinet secretaries, the vice president, the chief of staff, and the director of Homeland Security.

George W. Bush recruited a notably diverse cabinet that included three women, two African Americans, two Asian Americans, and one Hispanic. His key appointments at Defense, State, and Treasury had all served extensively in previous Republican administrations. One of his nominees, Linda Chavez, had to withdraw when a controversy developed over her having housed and employed an undocumented alien. Bush's attorney general nominee, former Missouri governor and U.S. senator John Ashcroft, won confirmation by a 58-to-42 vote after heated hearings and debates over some of his political beliefs and voting history.

CABINET GOVERNMENT   Cabinet government is generally defined as a system of advice in which the voice of individual cabinet members is of major importance. As such, cabinet government does not exist in the United States.[25] In fact, an American president is not required by the Constitution to form a cabinet or to hold regular meetings. Presidents John Kennedy, Lyndon Johnson, and Richard Nixon all preferred small conferences with individuals specifically involved in a problem and rarely held cabinet meetings. Kennedy saw no reason, for example, to discuss Defense Department matters with his secretaries of agriculture and labor, and he thought cabinet meetings wasted valuable time. Both Jimmy Carter and Ronald Reagan tried to revive the cabinet, and both met often with their cabinets during their first two years. But the longer they remained in office, the less frequently they met with their cabinets as a whole.

cabinet
Advisory council for the president, consisting of the heads of the executive departments, the vice president, and a few other officials selected by the president.

President George W. Bush with his cabinet.

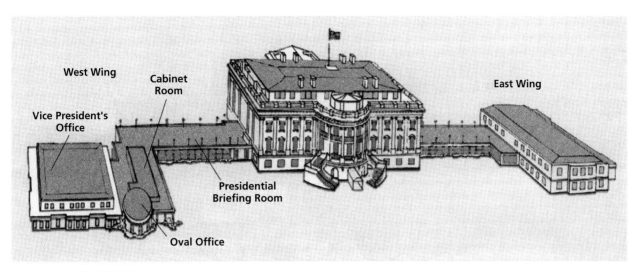

FIGURE 12–2   The White House.

Bill Clinton, like those he followed, seldom called for full cabinet meetings, holding just 18 such meetings in his first term and even fewer during his second.[26] George W. Bush has also shown limited interest in full cabinet meetings, preferring to assemble small groups of cabinet members on an as-needed basis.

Presidential advisers and the heads of various White House–based cabinet-level councils, such as the National Security Council and the Office of Management and Budget, have gained equal or even superior status to many cabinet secretaries. This shift occurred in part because these advisers are physically located in or next door to the White House (see Figure 12-2). Further, presidents are aware that some cabinet members adopt narrow "advocate" views: the Agriculture Department secretary is a strong advocate for the farmers; the Housing and Urban Development Department secretary is an ambassador for the housing industry and, to some extent, also for big city mayors; and so on through much of the cabinet, especially in departments occupied primarily with domestic policy matters.

CABINET DIFFERENCES   Cabinet departments vary by staff size (the Department of Defense has nearly a million employees, while the Department of Education has barely 5,000) and budget (the Department of Health and Human Services had a budget of well over $400 billion in 2002, while the Department of State barely hit $6 billion).

The departments also vary in their influence with the White House. Presidents tend to pay the greatest attention to the oldest and most visible of the departments: Defense, Justice, State, and Treasury. These four departments are often called the *inner cabinet* because they are so important to the president's foreign and domestic success. The economy (Treasury), crime (Justice), and international affairs (State and Defense) are rarely far from the top of the president's list of policy concerns. Presidents almost always appoint very close allies to the inner cabinet posts, even if those allies do not always have the best credentials for the jobs.

The other departments are generally called the *outer cabinet,* largely because they are more distant from the day-to-day worries that occupy the president and White House staff. The Department of Veterans Affairs, for example, is rarely in the headlines, even though its 250,000 full- and part-time employees make it the second-largest department in the federal bureaucracy.

The Vice Presidency

Despite Vice President Dick Cheney's visible role today, the vice presidency has not always been an important job. For most of American history, the vice president was at best seen as an insignificant officer and at worst a political rival who sometimes connived against the president. The office was often dismissed as a joke. One reason for

PEOPLE IN POLITICS

HILLARY CLINTON

The president's inner circle of close advisers has always included the first lady to some extent. Eleanor Roosevelt was particularly visible as an advocate for a strong national government during the economic depression of the 1930s. In recent decades, however, the first lady has steadily become much more prominent as a policy adviser to the president, in part because the media have become so aggressive in covering the White House. Lady Bird Johnson was a tireless and persuasive advocate for the beautification of America, Betty Ford for cancer research, Rosalyn Carter for the Equal Rights Amendment, Nancy Reagan for drug control, and Barbara Bush for literacy programs. Hillary Clinton clearly drew on these role models in setting her own White House course.

What made Hillary Clinton different from her predecessors was her highly visible role in actually shaping important presidential proposals. As head of the president's health care reform task force, she played a major role in designing a top legislative initiative and soon emerged as a key player on a host of other issues. She clearly had the experience and the credentials for the job: She attended Wellesley College, where she was elected president of the student body; graduated first in her class at Yale Law School, just ahead of the future president; and was headed for a career in law and public service long before her husband entered public life.

Clinton's image was not all positive, however. Her role in the Whitewater real estate development and her alleged failure to answer specific questions about it caused concern. She became the first first lady to be subpoenaed to testify before a grand jury, and she, along with her husband, was questioned by a federal independent counsel.

Hillary Clinton was hailed by some as a first lady for our times and a model for contemporary women who choose to have both a career and a family. But she was also criticized in the press, satirized in the novel *Primary Colors,* and ridiculed by opposition politicians and pundits. She stood by her husband throughout the Monica Lewinsky scandal and energized Democratic opposition to her husband's impeachment. In 2000, she won election as a U.S. senator from New York.

The high-profile Hillary Clinton model of service as first lady is unlikely to become the standard. Laura Bush, a former school librarian, prefers a lower-profile role. One of her keen interests is promoting reading and celebrating books and authors. When her husband was governor of Texas, she founded an annual book festival for Texas public libraries. She is likely to sponsor similar programs as first lady. And she has made it clear that she will not be involved in policy development. She has an office in the White House, but unlike Hillary Clinton's, it is in the East Wing rather than the high-status West Wing.

First Lady Hillary Clinton welcomes future First Lady Laura Bush to the White House on December 18, 2000.

the vice president's posture as an outsider was that presidential nominees usually chose running mates who were geographically, ideologically, demographically, and in other ways likely to "balance the ticket."

Inevitably, vice presidents are "backup equipment" in case something happens to the president. They can head up any number of councils, visit any number of countries, and still not be much involved in the day-to-day operations of the presidency.

This does not mean that vice presidents cannot be influential in their administrations. President Jimmy Carter included Walter Mondale in the daily processes of decision making in the White House; President Ronald Reagan sometimes included George Bush in a similar way; President Clinton used Al Gore as an important adviser and confidant on domestic as well as foreign policy matters and key appointments. All of these vice presidents had an office in the West Wing of the White House, weekly private lunches with their president, and access to all of the information flowing into the Oval Office.

George W. Bush selected Dick Cheney as his vice president in large part because Cheney's prior experience in Congress, in the White House, and in the cabinet brought credibility to the Bush campaign. His previous government positions strengthened Bush's ability to govern if the ticket won the White House. After the election, Cheney headed up the presidential transition team, recruiting senior administrators and shaping the legislative agenda. Cheney became perhaps more important than any previous vice president. Having served as secretary of defense during the 1991 Gulf War, Cheney was also central to the decisions made after September 11, 2001.

Although the sorts of tensions between president and vice president that existed in the past rarely affected Clinton and Gore or Bush and Cheney, tension between a president and a vice president is natural. After all, except for the vice president, everybody who works closely with a president can be fired. It is almost certain that vice presidents will continue to have an undefined ad hoc set of assignments, subject more to the goodwill and mood of the president than to any fixed description.[27]

Vice President Dick Cheney.

Holding Presidents Accountable

The United States has had great presidents, yet it has also had ineffective and flawed presidents. We have no foolproof way to guarantee that our presidents will possess the leadership skills and moral character the job requires. Our constitutional structure and political system have successfully held presidents accountable.

Accountability refers to a president's responsiveness to the will of the majority and taking responsibility for his own actions. Accountability implies as well that important presidential decisions will be explained to the public to allow citizens to evaluate how well the president is handling the assignments of the office. Let us examine some of the ways in which presidents are constrained and held to account.

Reelection and Legacy

Presidents want to win reelection because reelection is a validation of their first term as well as an opportunity for them to continue to implement their agenda. To win reelection, a president has to win the approval of large numbers of attentive citizens. It is in this sense that elections hold a president to account after four years in office.

But even midterm congressional elections also serve as a check on presidents. For example, Lyndon Johnson, Gerald Ford, and Bill Clinton all suffered major losses in their party's ranks in Congress in the midterm elections of 1966, 1974, and 1994, respectively. These losses sent a stark message to the White House and affected how these presidents behaved. In Clinton's case, the 1994 midterm elections forced him to move to the political center on issues such as welfare reform. The 2002 midterm elections acted as both an accelerator and a check on President Bush's agenda. The elections gave the president's party control of the House, Senate, and White House, thereby assuring faster action on the president's legislative concerns. But the margin in the Senate was far short of the 60 votes he needed to assure a filibuster-proof Senate. Although a Republican Senate gave a higher probability of legislative success, his majority contained enough moderates, such as Maine's Susan Collins and Olympia Snowe, Rhode Island's Lincoln Chafee, Oregon's Gordon Smith, and Pennsylvania's

Presidents Clinton, Bush, Reagan, Carter, and Ford, and their wives, attending the memorial service for former President Richard Nixon.

Arlen Specter, that he could not even be sure of a majority on environmental and social issues.

Every president also wants to leave a legacy that will be viewed positively by historians and later generations. Thus presidents are usually inclined to do what is right in the hope of being judged successful and effective by future generations.

Congress and the President

Chapter 13 will examine the special relationship between Congress and the president. For now, it is important to remember that the framers gave Congress important checks on presidential power. Congress was given the power to make the laws, raise revenues, appropriate money, investigate and oversee the bureaucracy, and even override a presidential veto. Congress was also given the authority to reject presidential nominees to the executive departments, to the courts, and to diplomatic posts. And Congress was given the authority to remove a president from office.

The Supreme Court and the President

The framers of the Constitution intended the Supreme Court to serve as a check on the potential abuses of power by presidents. The Court, they hoped, would consist of wise and well-educated statesmen who would strive to preserve the Constitution, especially from legislative and executive wrongdoing. Most of the framers believed that the Supreme Court would work hand in hand with the executive. Some even viewed the courts as an executive department, involved in executing, interpreting, and applying the laws. But presidents and the courts have had their share of clashes.

The Media and the President

There is a natural tension between the president and the media no matter who is in office. This ongoing struggle is inherent in a constitutional democracy. Exposés of campaign contribution scandals and the Monica Lewinsky affair in the 1990s fortified the media's role in bringing these events to public attention.

A free press is a basic check on presidential power. Much as presidents want their initiatives publicized and praised, reporters and commentators believe they should pro-

SHOULD PRESIDENTS BE LIMITED TO TWO TERMS IN OFFICE?

You Decide... Before he left office, former President Ronald Reagan called for the repeal of the Twenty-Second Amendment to the Constitution, the one that limits a president to two terms. Why do you think he opposed the amendment? What additional reasons could be put forth to persuade people to repeal this relatively new (1951) provision in the Constitution? What are the best reasons for retaining the Twenty-Second Amendment?

Thinking It Through... Reagan felt that the people should be able to reelect a president as many times as they want, just as they now reelect House and Senate members. He also hinted that the Twenty-Second Amendment might weaken a president late in his second term by making him a lame duck, less powerful because everyone knows he will not be around in a year or so. Advocates of repeal also say we may sometimes need to keep a veteran president in office during a crisis period, much as we retained Franklin Roosevelt in 1940. Others say eight years may not be enough time to resolve certain major problems.

The Twenty-Second Amendment is not only a limit on the incumbent but also on the electorate, the first since the ratification of the Constitution to restrict the power of the electorate rather than expand it. It is based, advocates of repeal suggest, on the assumption that the voters cannot be trusted.

Those who favor keeping the Twenty-Second Amendment cite these reasons: First, the presidency is so powerful today that we need the Twenty-Second Amendment as an additional check against abuse of this power. Second, the amendment encourages both parties to seek out effective candidates to succeed to office and discourages dependence on a single ruler. Third, few leaders are likely to have the health, the intellectual energy, and the new ideas needed to perform the demanding responsibilities of the presidency beyond eight years in office. Finally, Americans have always believed in citizen-leaders rather than career politicians, and this amendment encourages this ideal.

---

vide a context in which presidential statements can be understood. Hence the media not only tell people what a president says but often try to explain what the statements mean. Because the media—especially television—are viewed as more trustworthy and believable than some other national institutions, most Americans, most of the time, believe what they hear and see on television.

That is why the White House works so hard to shape what the media report. Communicators such as Franklin Roosevelt, John Kennedy, and Ronald Reagan often put their own spin on the news and court the scores of media representatives stationed at the White House.[28] Out-of-town editors are invited in for special briefings, and an extra effort is made to get the president out of Washington for meetings with local and regional media representatives, who are generally viewed as less critical than Washington-based media. White House media experts devise ways to get the president's point of view out to the public, to get the president on prime-time television, and to arrange for flattering photo opportunities.

Public Opinion and Presidential Accountability

Presidents are influenced by their anticipation not only of the next election but also of tomorrow's headlines and editorials, next week's public opinion polls, and next month's congressional hearings. They are subjected to a barrage of polls that judge their day-to-day or even minute-to-minute actions. In many ways, the time frame for presidential decision making and problem solving has been dramatically shortened. Issues cannot ripen,

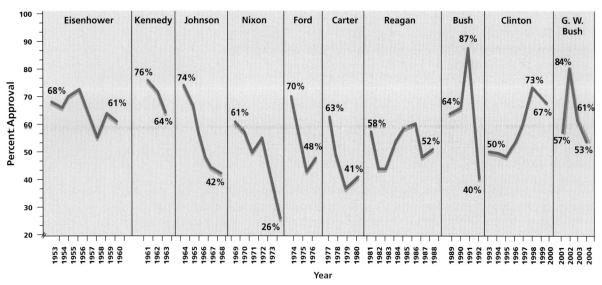

FIGURE 12-3   Presidential Approval Ratings, 1945–2004.

SOURCE: Gallup Organization, at www.gallup.com.

and problems cannot be debated, discussed, and analyzed over several days. Round-the-clock television newscasts and immediate Internet news analyses may indeed be holding presidents to instant accountability.

The fact that a president's approval is higher at the beginning of the term and lower at the end does not mean it can never go up in between. When drawn on a chart, the general decline is often interrupted by occasional jumps in approval during foreign crises. These **rally points** are particularly strong when a military action, such as an invasion or a bombing, is both short and successful. Gerald Ford's approval rating jumped 11 percent after he sent special troops to rescue the crew of the merchant ship *Mayagüez*, which had been seized by the Cambodian government; George W. Bush's ratings jumped dramatically following the September 11 terrorist attacks (see Figure 12-3).

Not all rally points involve foreign crises. Clinton's approval rose after the Oklahoma City bombing in 1995 in large part because Americans turned to him for leadership in the crisis. Presidential approval can also rise during periods of great national pride. Reagan's public approval (and reelection chances) jumped during the 1984 Olympic Games as the United States won one gold medal after another, in part because the Soviet Union and its eastern European allies boycotted the event.

Rally points often evaporate quickly once the crisis eases. George H. W. Bush's public approval hit 87 percent at the height of the Gulf War in 1991, only to plummet to 40 percent 18 months later. The Gulf War turned out to be rather like a television miniseries that slowly faded from memory as the season wore on.

Experts are not exactly sure what people mean when they say they "approve" of a president's job performance. People respond to presidents at least as much through emotions as they do through a rational understanding of the government's performance or a president's precise position on issues. But we do know that positive economic success helps a president's standing in the polls. Major nationally televised addresses also give a president a boost in public approval. Similarly, short successful wars and diplomatic breakthroughs at least temporarily improve a president's public approval. A president's favorable standing in the polls may help win congressional backing of White House policy measures; legislative victories, in turn, probably help enhance a president's standing in the polls.[29]

Ultimately, no safeguard can hold a wayward president or a corrupt White House aide completely accountable. Our framers designed a constitutional system that does not depend on our finding angels to run the government. It assumes that presidents, even good ones, need checks on their powers. James Madison's advice remains crucial: "A dependence on the people is, no doubt, the primary control of the government, but experience has taught mankind

rally point
A rise in public approval of the president that follows a crisis as Americans "rally 'round the flag" and the chief executive.

the necessity of auxiliary precautions," or checks (see *The Federalist*, No. 51, in the Appendix of this book). Americans must vigilantly maintain the effectiveness of these "auxiliary precautions"—Congress, political parties, the courts, the press, the Bill of Rights, and concerned citizens' groups—to ensure a properly balanced and constitutional presidency.

Judging Presidential Greatness

One of the paradoxes of presidential greatness is that we yearn for the democratic "common person" and simultaneously for a leader who is uncommon, charismatic, visionary, and heroic. Political scientist Harold J. Laski once suggested, "He must have 'common opinions.' But it is equally important that he be an 'uncommon man.' The public must see themselves in him, but they must, at the same time, be confident that he is something bigger than themselves."[30]

At least according to the occasional rankings of great and near-great presidents by historians and political scientists, the great presidents stretched the Constitution and strengthened the presidency to bring about change. Sometimes this is called the "doctrine of necessity"—doing what needs to be done. Thus the presidents considered "great" were often those who gave Congress the hardest time. They sometimes exercised powers that were thought to be solely or primarily congressional. Some of the presidents regularly challenged Congress and the Supreme Court as well.

There are several sources of greatness. President Washington, more than any other person, converted the paper notions outlined in the Constitution into an enduring, practical governing process. With extraordinary character, he set the precedents that balanced self-government and leadership, chief of state and chief executive, constitutionalism and statesmanship.

Thomas Jefferson, a genius in his generation, was a skilled organizer and a resourceful party leader and chief executive. He made mistakes, yet he adapted the presidency to the new realities of his day. His expansions of territory with the Louisiana Purchase, his sponsorship of the Lewis and Clark expedition, and similar bold ventures assures him a revered status among presidents.

President Lincoln is remembered for saving the Union and is revered as the nation's foremost symbol of democracy and tenacious leadership in the nation's ultimate crisis. President Franklin Delano Roosevelt is viewed as guiding the nation through its worst economic crisis and for leading the "greatness generation" to victory in World War II. George W. Bush may yet be remembered for his steadfastness in calming the nation after September 11, 2001.

These presidential accomplishments are part of the legend of America. Yet this heroic view of presidents raises a good many questions. If presidents alone were responsible for these and similar feats, it is little wonder that our expectations are so high concerning what current and future presidents should accomplish.

In fact, a variety of people and institutions contributed to the achievements credited to past presidents. History seldom adequately honors the reformers and leaders who provided behind-the-scenes leadership. The best presidents surround themselves with talented advisers and administrators. Great leadership depends on situation, resources, opportunity, and teams of leaders. Being at the right place at the right time also helps.

Many of the great presidents made mistakes, sometimes great mistakes. And the great presidents typically look better some years later than they did while they were at the helm. Harry Truman is a prime example of a presidential leader who was viewed as a lesser light while in office but was later recognized as great.

The nation can learn from those presidents judged as failures. Experts rank some presidents at or near the bottom because of political corruption while placing others near the bottom because they lacked a compelling program, vision, political skill, or integrity. Although Richard Nixon was respected for his foreign policy initiatives, especially for his recognition of the People's Republic of China, he is nonetheless viewed as one of the lesser presidents because he lied to the American public, plotted a cover-up of illegal and unconstitutional activities, resigned in disgrace, and, in the eyes of many, sullied the dignity of the Oval Office.

It is too early to guess where George W. Bush will be regarded. His early response to September 11 was steady and reassuring. But a place in history is based on an entire presidency evaluated years, even decades, after the president has left office. By remembering that there is a future accounting, presidents can find some inspiration for making the hard and sometimes unpopular choices that have led to greatness among their predecessors. Thus the judgment of history may be one of the most important sources of accountability that the nation has on its presidents.

PRESIDENTIAL GREATNESS: HOW DO WE JUDGE THEM?

Presidents rise and fall in the historical rankings based on a number of factors. Some rise because they led the nation through periods of intense domestic or international crisis; others rise because they had a distinctive vision of where the nation should go on issues such as civil rights, social policy, or the economy. Rankings also involve at least some assessment of how presidents did as political and morale leaders of the nation. Some fall because of political or personal scandal, others because they failed to grapple with a big issue such as national health insurance or economic crisis. In the end, rankings involve the overall measure of a president's impact in meeting the public's expectations.

Go to PoliSim "Presidential Greatness: How Do We Judge Them?"

Summary

1. The framers created a presidency with limited powers. To enact government business, the president must cooperate with Congress, but powers are divided among the branches, and the politics of shared power has often been stormy. In general, however, the role and influence of presidents have increased over the course of the nation's history.

2. The framers gave the president three central roles in the new government: commander in chief, diplomat in chief, and administrator in chief. Presidents have expanded their powers in several ways over the decades. Crises, both foreign and economic, have enlarged these powers. When there is a need for decisive action, presidents are asked to supply it. Congress, of course, is traditionally expected to share in the formulation of national policy. Every president must learn anew the need to work closely with the members of Congress.

3. Every four years, Americans try to select the candidate whom they think will be an honest and effective president who will propose solutions to the nation's toughest problems. We expect far more than is reasonable, but ideally we want someone as good as Washington, Lincoln, or Franklin Roosevelt.

4. Presidents must act as crisis-managing, morale-building, personnel-recruiting, priority-setting, coalition-building, public opinion–molding party and managerial leaders. No president can divide the job into tidy compartments. Ultimately, these responsibilities overlap.

5. Presidents perform these roles with the assistance of a White House staff composed of roughly 400 individuals and a cabinet of department secretaries that oversees the civil servants. The vice president is also involved in helping the president manage government.

6. Presidential power is usually exercised for important and noble ends, yet it can also on occasion be abused. Presidents, however, are held to account by a variety of checks and balances, including elections and the future judgment of history, Congress, the courts, the media, and public opinion.

7. Presidential greatness is often talked about but hard to define. Nearly everyone considers Lincoln, Washington, and Franklin Roosevelt as outstanding presidents. Presidents are viewed as great when they brought about desirable progress and guided the nation through crises.

Key Terms

divided government
parliamentary system
presidential ticket
executive agreements

executive privilege
take care clause
inherent powers
State of the Union Address

impeachment
chief of staff
Executive Office of the
   President

Office of Management and Budget
   (OMB)
cabinet
rally point

Further Reading

DAVID GRAY ADLER AND LARRY N. GEORGE, EDS., *The Constitution and the Conduct of American Foreign Policy: Essays on Law and History* (University Press of Kansas, 1996).

PAUL BRACE AND BARBARA HINCKLEY, *Follow the Leader: Opinion Polls and the Modern Presidents* (Basic Books, 1992).

JOHN P. BURKE AND MICHAEL NELSON, *The Institutional Presidency: Organizing and Managing the White House from FDR to Clinton,* 2d ed. (Johns Hopkins, 2000).

THOMAS E. CRONIN, ED., *Inventing the American Presidency* (University Press of Kansas, 1989).

THOMAS E. CRONIN AND MICHAEL A. GENOVESE, *The Paradoxes of the American Presidency* (Oxford University Press, 1998).

TERRY EASTLAND, *Energy in the Executive* (Free Press, 1992).

MICHAEL A. GENOVESE, *The Power of the American Presidency, 1989–2000* (Oxford University Press, 2000).

DAVID GERGEN, *Eyewitness to Power: The Essence of Leadership, Nixon to Clinton* (Simon & Schuster, 2000).

STEPHEN HESS, *Organizing the Presidency,* 2d ed. (Brookings Institution, 2003).

FRED GREENSTEIN, *The Presidential Difference* (Free Press, 2000).

ERWIN C. HARGROVE, *The President as Leader: Appealing to the Better Angels of Our Nature* (University Press of Kansas, 1998).

CHARLES O. JONES, *Passages to the Presidency: From Campaigning to Governing* (Brookings Institution, 1998).

GARY KING AND LYN RAGSDALE, *The Elusive Executive: Discovering Statistical Patterns in the Presidency,* 2d ed. (CQ Press, 2002).

MARK LANDY AND SIDNEY M. MILKIS, *Presidential Greatness* (University Press of Kansas, 2000).

LEONARD W. LEVY AND LOUIS FISHER, EDS., *Encyclopedia of the American Presidency* (Simon & Schuster, 1994).

JOHN A. MALTESE, *Spin Control: The White House Office of Communications and the Management of the Presidential News* (University of North Carolina Press, 1992).

SIDNEY M. MILKIS, *The President and the Parties: The Transformation of the American Party System Since the New Deal* (Oxford University Press, 1993).

SIDNEY M. MILKIS AND MICHAEL NELSON, *The American Presidency: Origins and Development, 1976–1998,* 3d ed. (CQ Press, 1999).

MICHAEL NELSON, ED., *The Presidency and the Political System,* 6th ed. (CQ Press, 2000).

RICHARD E. NEUSTADT, *Presidential Power and the Modern Presidents* (Free Press, 1991).

HUBERT S. PARMET, *George Bush: The Life of a Lone Star Yankee* (Scribner, 1998).

STEPHEN PONDER, *Managing the Press: Origins of the Media Presidency* (Palgrave, 2000).

BRADLEY H. PATTERSON, JR., *The White House Staff: Inside the West Wing and Beyond* (Brookings Institution, 2000).

JAMES P. PFIFFNER, *The Strategic Presidency: Hitting the Ground Running,* 2d ed. (University Press of Kansas, 1996).

GLENN A. PHELPS, *George Washington and American Constitutionalism* (University Press of Kansas, 1993).

LYN RAGSDALE, *Vital Statistics on the Presidency,* rev. ed. (CQ Press, 1998).

SHELLEY LYNNE TOMKINS, *Inside OMB: Politics and Process in the President's Budget Office* (Sharpe, 1998).

KENNETH T. WALSH, *Feeding the Beast: The White House Versus the Press* (Random House, 1996).

SHIRLEY ANNE WARSHAW, *Powersharing: White House–Cabinet Relations in the Modern Presidency* (State University of New York Press, 1996).

13

CHAPTER

CONGRESS
AND THE
PRESIDENT

P

RESIDENT GEORGE W. BUSH CAME TO THE WHITE HOUSE IN 2001 WITH DAUNTING CHALLENGES AND A "WEAK HAND." AS VETERAN *Washington Post* reporter David Broder noted just before the president's inauguration, Bush enjoyed "no majority. No mandate. Not even broad agreement that he deserved the prize that fell into his hands when the Supreme Court, itself deeply divided, ordered the ballot recounts in Florida must halt."[1] This is hardly the way a president wants to begin a presidency.

Despite the obstacles, George W. Bush pursued an aggressive legislative agenda including proposals for a major tax cut, increased spending on education and military pay, a new energy plan, and prescription drug coverage for Medicare recipients, among other things. He had campaigned on these issues, even though he understood that he might have to scale back some of his plans in order to win bipartisan support. But he understood, too, that the American people expect presidents to set the nation's policy agenda and that elections, even with unclear mandates, are part of the process of bringing about changes in public policy.

Presidents rarely act alone, however. Although they can use executive orders to accomplish some limited policy goals, they must win congressional support for large-scale initiatives of the kind Bush supported. Winning that support is never easy, even for presidents who have won decisive election victories. Members of the opposing party in Congress have their own agendas. Even members of the president's own party in Congress can pose a challenge to presidential plans. That was the case when Republican Senator John McCain came out in support of campaign finance reforms that Bush openly opposed. That was also the case when the Democrats took control of the Senate in the wake of Senator James Jefford's decision to bolt the Republican party. With the economy weakening and Democrats in control, Bush had to fight hard for victories on his tax cuts and education plan. Although the events of September 11, 2001, strengthened his case for in-

Presidents are sometimes opposed by members of their own party, as George W. Bush was by Senator John McCain, his former opponent in the presidential campaign, on the matter of campaign finance reform.

creased military spending, even record levels of public approval did not translate into legislative support on his energy plan. Democrats defeated his proposal for oil drilling in the Alaskan wilderness in April 2002, for example.

Tensions between Congress and presidents go back to the origins of American government. Alexander Hamilton, General George Washington's chief aide, complained about the deadlock rooted in the design of the Continental Congress more than 200 years ago. Yet it was the intention of the framers of the U.S. Constitution to create a government of sharply limited powers and separated institutions that would both share and compete for power. The framers saw the separation of powers not necessarily as a weakness but as a source of strength and especially as a way to ensure deliberation and to prevent tyranny.

The popular assumption is that a president essentially guides Congress in most of its lawmaking activity. But the reality is often different. The decentralized nature of Congress, the independent and entrepreneurial mode of legislators, and the institutional responsibilities and pride of Congress all work to weaken a president's legislative influence.

As Bill Clinton and George W. Bush found out, members of Congress take the measure of the new president as soon as the oath of office is taken, if not before. Will the president reach out and try to cooperate with Congress? Will the president overreach and push too fast—as Clinton did with his health care proposal? Will the president be highly partisan or bipartisan? Will the president try to intimidate and coerce reluctant legislators?

The framers did not intend Congress and the presidency to be in constant stalemate, however. Even as they protected the people from government, they wanted government to protect the people from foreign and domestic threats. That is precisely what Congress and Bush did in the wake of September 11. They came together quickly to authorize military action and draft a long list of new laws to rebuild homeland security and prosecute terrorists. Although they could not agree on a plan to stimulate the ailing economy, the two branches clearly put the nation's security above partisan politics.

In this chapter, we take a deeper look at our complicated system of separate branches, which of necessity must find ways to work together. What did the framers intend? What has evolved over the years? Why do members of Congress often see things differently from the way presidents do? What are some of the ongoing controversies between the two branches? What are some of the ways presidents try to win congressional support? And how does the president set the policy agenda?

Separate but Equal Branches

The framers of the Constitution saw Congress as the central, if not dominant, branch of government. Congress would have the power of the purse, in addition to extensive supervision of interstate and foreign commerce and the currency. Congress would also play a crucial role in military and foreign policy matters since only Congress could declare war and only the Senate could approve treaties. And Congress was granted the all-important power to make laws "which shall be necessary and proper" for carrying out its specified powers.

America's first presidents deferred to Congress on many issues, but gradually presidents began to play a more assertive role in the legislative process. A stronger executive gradually evolved to provide balance and leadership. Some of the more ambitious chief executives, such as Thomas Jefferson, used the newly formed political parties to exert influence in Congress. Others, such as Andrew Jackson, marshaled public opinion to gain influence with Congress. Still others, such as Abraham Lincoln and Franklin Roosevelt, gained additional powers during national crises. In between these strong presidents were less assertive or weaker chief executives. Thus an institutional ebb and flow characterized the relationship between Congress and presidents. What was designed in many ways as a congressionally centered system evolved by the mid-twentieth century into a system centered around the presidency.

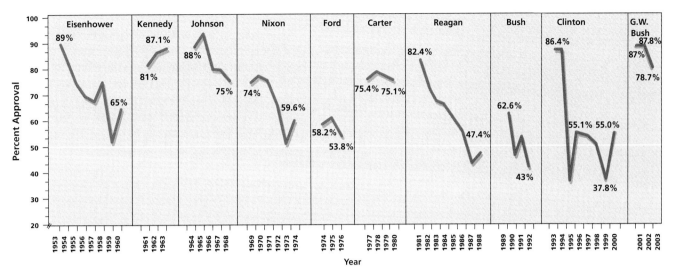

FIGURE 13-1 **Presidential Legislative Support from Congress, 1953–2003.**

SOURCE: *Congressional Quarterly Weekly,* January 12, 2002, p. 110.

Note: Percentages represent average scores for both chambers of Congress.

But Congress can impose its will on presidents, as Ronald Reagan found out when Congress rejected his strongly argued plea for millions in military aid to the Contra rebels in Nicaragua and Bill Clinton discovered when Congress refused to enact his health care reform measures and the Senate failed to ratify the Comprehensive Test Ban Treaty. George W. Bush learned that Congress had its own opinions on public policy when the Senate rejected his plan for stimulating the economy in late 2001. Virtually every president has also faced setbacks in dealing with the Senate on confirmation of nominees to the cabinet or the courts. Even a presidential veto is not a guarantee of influence. Richard Nixon vetoed the Congressional Budget and Impoundment Control Act in 1974, only to be overridden by an angry Congress. Presidential scholar George Edwards, who carefully examined major legislative measures proposed by recent presidents, finds that fewer than half of these measures become law (see Figure 13-1). Thus at least some of the time, presidents fail to win congressional backing even on their most cherished measures.[2]

The separation of powers and divided government can be obstacles to the passage of legislation, yet they are not necessarily barriers to good public policy making. Indeed, a certain amount of delay and the need for compromise often make for better public policy than bills rushed through Congress with minimal debate. And despite all the media attention highlighting their disagreements, Congress and the president often cooperate. Even when the two institutions are divided between the two major parties, bills get passed and become law, appointments are confirmed, budgets are enacted, and the government receives both the funding and the general direction it needs to get work done.

Sources of Discord

Many of the barriers to legislative success are embedded in the Constitution itself, which divided power between Congress and the presidency and then divided it again between the House and the Senate. Power gets divided further when these institutions are controlled by different parties and when the American public gives greater support to one branch or the other. Together, the sources of discord increase the odds against passing a bill.

Constitutional Ambiguities

Article I of the Constitution grants Congress "all legislative Powers" but limits those powers to those "herein granted." It then sets forth in some detail the powers vested in Congress. In contrast, Article II vests in the president "the executive Power" without limiting it to such powers as are "herein granted" and then proceeds to describe those powers in very general terms.

Some scholars and most presidents have argued that Article II gives each president a general and undefined power to act to promote the well-being of the United States, subject only to precise constitutional limits. Therefore, they contend, a president is *not* limited to the specific powers spelled out in the Constitution, as Congress is, but has all the executive powers of the United States. Other scholars and many members of Congress contend that the president either has no such inherent power or has it only in extraordinary circumstances.[3]

Whatever the intent of the Constitution, the president has often exercised powers not expressly granted by it. These powers have been given a variety of names: *implied, inherent,* or *emergency powers.* For example, Bill Clinton worked out a way to lend Mexico billions of dollars in 1995 to stabilize its currency, even though Congress had essentially refused to do so. Similarly, George W. Bush ordered the armed services to start preparing for the war in Afghanistan well ahead of congressional authorization. Actions like these prompt many in Congress to criticize presidents, even if they believe that in certain emergencies a president must act promptly without clear constitutional or statutory support.

COMPETING CONSTITUENCIES　The Constitution also guarantees that Congress and the president will represent different constituencies. Members of Congress represent state and local districts, and hence they reflect specific geographic, ethnic, and economic interests. James Madison and other framers of the Constitution anticipated that legislators would often be pressured by local and state interests to adopt a narrow or parochial view, as opposed to a national view, on certain policy issues, and presidents and their aides often think Madison was right. Members of Congress, of course, see sensitivity to state and local concerns as essential to their job as representatives and to their prospects for reelection. As a result, members of Congress—even those from the president's own party and own region—may look at problems and solutions somewhat differently from the way the president does. The president is expected to assume a national perspective.

COMPETING CALENDARS　The Constitution also ensures that Congress and the president will not share the same terms of office. Presidents serve for four years with a chance of reelection to a second term; senators have the luxury of six-year terms; members of the House of Representatives are elected to two-year terms. Different constituencies and lengths of service make these national officials responsive to different moods and points of view. Different electoral forces are at work in different election years. A majority of the voters can win control over only part of the national government at a time, and this arrangement, too, was by design.

Presidents often act quickly to shape national priorities in their first months following the flush of their electoral victory, to win support for their agendas before a possible decline in public approval. Congress, by contrast, usually moves more slowly "because it represents a vast array of local interests."[4] Another obvious difference in the speed of their two branches has to do with numbers: There is one president, but there are 435 members of the House and 100 senators.

COMPETING CAMPAIGNS　Finally, the Constitution ensures that Congress and the president will run different kinds of election campaigns. Most members of Congress finance their election campaigns with only minimal assistance from their national political party.

They customarily respond to local conditions and run their campaigns independently of their party's presidential candidate or national platform. And changes in the electorate in recent years that enhance an incumbent's chances of reelection weaken the connection between the president and fellow partisans in Congress.

Members of the president's party have typically run well ahead of their president in elections in their home districts, and thus they are less fearful of punishment for ignoring occasional party appeals for loyalty. They are more likely to go along with the president when a measure converges with their own political philosophy and is in the interest of their home district or state. Although parties have become vigorously partisan within Congress, especially in the House of Representatives, there are always several independent thinkers who will at times—sometimes crucial times for the White House—go their own way rather than cooperate with the White House, even when the president is a member of the same party.[5]

Nevertheless, party is the most reliable predictor of how members of Congress will vote. Congress was deeply divided along party lines on the Clinton impeachment, for example, and party discipline has been strong during the first two years of the Bush presidency.

Members of the 1972 Senate Select Committee on Watergate. During the Watergate hearings involving Republican President Richard Nixon, some Republican senators did not support the president.

Divided Government

The Constitution is not the only source of discord between the branches, however. Since 1952, there have been frequent divisions in party control of Congress and the presidency. Seven of the last ten presidents (Republicans Dwight Eisenhower, Richard Nixon, Gerald Ford, Ronald Reagan, George H. W. Bush, George W. Bush, and Democrat Bill Clinton) had to deal with divided government during their terms in office, while only three (Democrats John Kennedy, Lyndon Johnson, and Jimmy Carter) had unified government. Even with unified government, however, Kennedy and Carter had extraordinary difficulty winning passage of prized programs.

Many people believe that presidents will generally enjoy more success in Congress when their party has clear control of both houses in Congress. "Unified party control is necessary, the argument goes, for ensuring that the two branches share common policy and electoral motivations," writes political scientist Sarah Binder. "Under divided government, competing policy views and electoral incentives are sure to make legislative compromise unlikely."[6] Both parties seek a record that will enhance their election chances. This has been the case in recent decades, yet divided government is only one of many reasons that presidents fail to win the cooperation they would like to get from Congress.

Public Support

Americans have generally held the presidency in higher esteem than Congress in recent years (see Figure 13-2). Ratings of the two institutions not only rise and fall at different rates, but the president's approval is always higher. Thus Bush's approval rose 37 percentage points following September 11, while Congress's rose just 22 points. Greater prestige for the presidency can give the president a slight edge in battles with Congress, particularly if presidents can tie the prestige of their office to a particular issue such as the war on terrorism.

Congress may be viewed by many people as slow or inefficient, in part because it has to represent local interests and respond to particular constituencies.[7] Yet when presidents decline in popularity, as Nixon did after the Watergate scandal, Americans turn to Congress to hold the president and the presidency accountable.

Operating Majorities

Americans are often frustrated that presidents and Congress seem to have so many ways to defeat legislation that has strong public support, such as national health insurance or increases in the minimum wage. After all, they are taught that American government operates on the principle of majority rule.

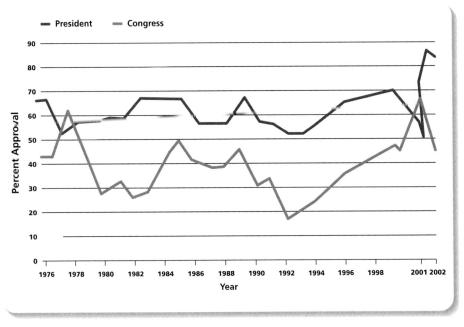

FIGURE 13–2   Presidential and Congressional Approval Ratings, 1976–2002.

SOURCE: Gallup Poll; CBS News/*New York Times* Poll; NBC News/*Wall Street Journal* Poll. Updated by the authors.

The reality is that the Senate's filibuster power, the president's veto authority, and the Senate's treaty approval responsibilities sometimes make *supermajorities* necessary. (At least 60 votes in the Senate are needed to end a filibuster, at least two-thirds of the senators present must concur on a proposed treaty, and a two-thirds supermajority vote in both the Senate and the House is needed to override a presidential veto of a proposed law.) The filibuster in the Senate has become more common in recent years. The filibuster effectively gives a veto to any 40 senators whose states may represent as little as 10 percent of the population and whose views might not be especially centrist. Similarly, these realities make it harder for presidents to gain acceptance for their programs.

They also frustrate members of Congress: "The harsh reality that new members discover is that developing supermajority coalitions around complex issues is difficult," write political scientists David Brady and Craig Volden. "Policy gridlock is the result of not being able to build such coalitions without violating the trust of the folks back home."[8]

In short, competing constituencies, competing calendars, competing campaigns, and sometimes divided party control all help explain why members of Congress view their responsibilities and their political needs differently from the way presidents view theirs. It is sometimes astonishing that they get along at all.

The Ebb and Flow of Power Between the Branches

The past few decades have been packed with political and legal controversies, ranging from the proper use of the warmaking power to the intensely partisan politics when Bill Clinton was impeached. Some of these disputes were resolved in the courts, some were worked out between Congress and the administration, and others persist as disputes between the branches.

The War Power

The Constitution divided the war power between the president and Congress. Article I states that Congress has the power to declare war, but Article II gives the president the power to wage war as commander in chief.

James Madison and his colleagues recognized that declaring war was both one of the most important powers of government and one of the most easily abused. Writing as a young member of Congress, Abraham Lincoln expressed the founders' intent as follows:

> The provision of the Constitution giving the war-making power to Congress was dictated, as I understand it, by the following reasons. Kings had always been involving and impoverishing their people in wars, pretending generally, if not always, that the good of the people was the object. This our convention understood to be the most oppressive of all kingly oppressions, and they resolved to so frame the Constitution that no one man should hold the power of bringing this oppression upon us.[9]

Yet in the past few decades, U.S. presidents have used military force in many parts of the world, including Korea, Vietnam, Grenada, Panama, the Persian Gulf, and Kosovo, all without asking Congress for a declaration of war. Although Presidents George Bush, Bill Clinton, and George W. Bush all sought and received congressional approval before they committed troops to actual hostilities in the Persian Gulf, over Kosovo, and in Afghanistan, respectively, they readied those actions without permission.

Presidents defend such action by arguing that they are better informed than Congress. They also argue that presidents need the flexibility and secrecy to respond quickly to military threats to the nation's security interests. One State Department official described the president's warmaking authority as follows: "The Constitution leaves to the President the judgment to determine whether the circumstances of a particular armed attack are so urgent and the potential consequences so threatening to the security of the U.S. that he should act without formally consulting the Congress."[10]

Presidents and some scholars also blame Congress for abdicating its constitutional authority to the presidency. Constitutional scholar Louis Fisher holds that Congress has repeatedly abdicated its fundamental war powers to the president. The framers knew what monarchy looked like and rejected it, writes Fisher. "Yet especially in matters of the war power, the United States is re-creating a system of monarchy while it professes to champion democracy and the role of law abroad."[11] Fisher calls on members of Congress to reeducate themselves on their constitutional prerogatives.

Congress tried to reassert its role and authority in the use of military force at the end of the Vietnam War. In 1973, Congress enacted the War Power Resolution over Richard Nixon's veto. The law, which is still in place, declares that a president can commit the armed forces of the United States only (1) after a declaration of war by Congress, (2) by specific statutory authorization, or (3) in a national emergency created by an attack on the United States or its armed forces. After committing the armed forces under the third circumstance, the president is required to report to Congress within 48 hours. Unless Congress declares war, the troop commitment must be ended within 60 days.

This resolution signaled a new determination by Congress to take its prerogatives seriously, yet presidents have generally ignored it. And many leading scholars now believe that this earnest and well-intentioned effort by Congress to reclaim its proper role actually gave away more authority than previous practices had already done. They say it was ill conceived and badly written, full of tortured ambiguity and self-contradiction. "The statute further subordinates Congress to presidential war initiatives and should be repealed in its entirety."[12]

Most observers believe the United States is best served when both president and Congress are fully engaged partners in foreign and defense policy making. Congressman Lee Hamilton sums up the virtues of joint action by these rival branches: "I believe that a partnership, characterized by creative tension between the president and the Congress, produces a foreign policy that better serves the American national interest—and better reflects the values of the American people—than policy produced by the president alone."[13] In recent years, that tension has produced congressional authorizations for the use of force but not formal declarations of war.

The Appointment and Confirmation Powers

The Constitution gives the Senate a crucial role in approving key presidential nominees, including department secretaries, senior military officials, and ambassadors. Senators normally defer to presidents, especially newly elected ones, on their executive appointees but often disagree on judicial appointees, in part because judges serve for life terms, whereas executive appointees leave with the president. Moreover, individual senators actually play a role in selecting district court nominees for their states. As former Judiciary Committee chairman and Republican Senator Orrin Hatch of Utah writes, "Senators from the states where the judgeship is located are the ones who usually exercise the power to oppose nominees, since they represent the citizens who will be subject to the decisions of that nominee."[14]

The Senate has rejected only nine cabinet members over the past 200 years (see Table 13-1) and 28 of 145 nominees for the U.S. Supreme Court. However, it has rejected a great many nominees for lower federal offices and courts.[15] George W. Bush's first nominee for secretary of labor, Linda Chavez, withdrew from the confirmation process even before the president was sworn into office when she was accused of housing and employing an illegal alien.

Senate Democrats also blocked consideration of two controversial Bush appointees late in 2001. Unable to convince the Democrats to confirm Eugene Scalia, son of Supreme Court Justice Antonin Scalia, and Otto Reich, a crucial link to Cuban Americans in Florida, Bush put both men into office using *recess appointments*. Under this power, the president is allowed to appoint an individual to a Senate-confirmed position if the Senate is not in session. Such appointments are valid only until the end of the congressional session that begins in the year following the recess appointment.

While the Senate confirms the vast majority of presidential nominees for judicial or executive branch positions, the process is fraught with delay. It begins with 60 pages of forms, most of which have to be filled out on a typewriter, and continues with a detailed investigation by the Federal Bureau of Investigation and the Office of Government Ethics, as well as another packet of forms from the Senate. Roughly half of the appointees in the 1980s and 1990s said they sought outside help to navigate the process, and one in six spent more than $5,000 to deal with the forms.[16] Because the White House and Senate can handle only a small number of nominations at a time, some of the current administration's first appointees had to wait more than a year for confirmation. The White House also reported difficulty in getting candidates to enter the burdensome appointments process.

TABLE 13–1   Cabinet Nominees Rejected by the Senate

Nominee	Position	President	Year	Vote
Roger B. Taney	Secretary of the Treasury	Jackson	1834	18–28
Caleb Cushing	Secretary of the Treasury	Tyler	1843	19–27
Caleb Cushing	Secretary of the Treasury	Tyler	1843	10–27
Caleb Cushing	Secretary of the Treasury	Tyler	1843	2–29
David Henshaw	Secretary of the Navy	Tyler	1844	6–34
James M. Porter	Secretary of War	Tyler	1844	3–38
James S. Green	Secretary of the Treasury	Tyler	1844	—*
Henry Stanbery	Attorney General	A. Johnson	1868	11–29
Charles B. Warren	Attorney General	Coolidge	1925	39–41
Charles B. Warren	Attorney General	Coolidge	1925	39–46
Lewis L. Strauss	Secretary of Commerce	Eisenhower	1959	46–49
John Tower	Secretary of Defense	Bush	1989	47–53

*Not recorded.

Many of George W. Bush's judicial nominees waited months for Senate review. The president also suffered a stinging defeat on the nomination of Charles Pickering for the federal Fifth Circuit Court of Appeals. Although Pickering was already a federal district court judge at the time of the nomination, civil rights, abortion rights, and organized labor groups opposed his elevation to the circuit court post, arguing that he was too conservative for the higher post. The Senate Judiciary Committee refused to report his nomination to the full Senate for a vote in March 2002, and his nomination died in committee.

Most senators believe that presidents deserve to have members of their cabinet who generally agree with them. Thus senators do not ordinarily object to nominees because of differences in party ideology. Yet when former U.S. Senator John Ashcroft was nominated to be attorney general in 2001, many senators opposed the nomination because of his positions on abortion and civil rights matters. Democrats sharply criticized his nomination. Nonetheless, he was confirmed by a vote of 58 to 42.

The confirmation provision in the Constitution has fulfilled most of the intentions of the framers, and the nation has been well served by most individuals who have come through the process. The process has sometimes deterred the appointment of people who hold especially strident political views. The Senate's role in the confirmation process was never intended to eliminate politics but rather to use politics as a safeguard. Perhaps in recent years more than ever, senators have used this process to make their political and policy views known to prospective appointees as well as to the White House. This is as true for liberal senators such as Ted Kennedy or Joe Biden as it is for conservatives like Jesse Helms and Orrin Hatch.

The Senate Judiciary Committee refused to support Bush's nominee, U.S. District Court Judge Charles Pickering, for nomination to the Senate for the federal Fifth Circuit Court of Appeals.

Executive Privilege

The presidential claim of **executive privilege** is yet another area of controversy between presidents and Congress. The Constitution does not authorize presidents to withhold information because Congress and the public need information to do their jobs. However, courts have recognized that presidents can keep secret some limited and narrowly defined kinds of information, especially information that would jeopardize national security if released.

Some experts argue that executive privilege has no constitutional basis.[17] Yet presidents have withheld documents from Congress at least as far back as 1792, when President George Washington temporarily refused to share sensitive documents with a House committee studying an Indian massacre of federal troops. Although he later shared the information with Congress, Washington set the precedent for the use of executive privilege. Thomas Jefferson and the primary author of the Constitution, James Madison, also withheld information during their presidencies.

Most scholars, the courts, and even members of Congress agree that a president does have the implicit, if not constitutionally explicit, right to withhold information that could harm the nation's security. Presidents must keep secrets, including the date and place of military actions and communications with their highest advisers.

Although the formal term "executive privilege" was first used in the 1950s during the Eisenhower administration, Richard Nixon created the controversy over the term.[18] In an effort to hide his own role in the Watergate scandal, President Nixon refused to release secret tapes of the meetings that followed the failed burglary of Democratic party headquarters in the Watergate building. He and his lawyers went so far as to claim that the decision to invoke executive privilege was not subject to review by Congress or the courts.

In a complicated decision, the Supreme Court acknowledged for the first time that presidents do indeed have the power to claim executive privilege if the release of certain information would be damaging to the nation's security interests. At the same time, the Court held that such claims are not exempt from review by the courts and that national security was not threatened in the Watergate case, and so the Court ordered that Nixon had to yield his tapes, effectively dooming his presidency.[19]

executive privilege
The right to keep executive communications confidential, especially if they relate to national security.

The Impeachment of Bill Clinton

In all of our history, only two presidents have been impeached—Andrew Johnson in 1868 and Bill Clinton in 1998. Richard Nixon was about to be impeached in 1974 when he abruptly resigned from office.

The Clinton impeachment hearings dramatized the House Judiciary Committee and its role in establishing whether an impeachment is justified. Nationally televised debates by the full House of Representatives were heated and partisan. Opinion polls showed the public solidly opposed to impeachment and removal from office, yet House Republicans remained unified in the effort to impeach. Two articles of impeachment were passed by the House of Representatives: for perjury before a federal grand jury (228 to 206) and for obstruction of justice (221 to 212). Most House Republicans voted for impeach-

The House Judiciary Committee investigated charges that President Clinton had lied about his relationship to Monica Lewinsky to determine if they warranted impeachment. After a long and angry argument between Republican and Democratic members, two articles of impeachment were passed by the House of Representatives, and the matter was turned over to the Senate for trial.

ment, and most House Democrats voted against the articles of impeachment. The matter was then turned over to the Senate.

The proceedings in the Senate were in marked contrast to the House deliberations. They were more formal, less heated, and in the end less partisan. Representatives from the House Judiciary Committee acted as the prosecutors, while lawyers for the president defended Bill Clinton. It would have taken a two-thirds majority, or 67 votes in the Senate, to convict Clinton, but only 45 senators voted to convict him on perjury charges; 10 Republicans defected to join 45 Democrats in voting "not guilty." Fifty senators (all Republicans) voted to convict Clinton on the obstruction of justice charges, while 5 Republicans joined all 45 Democrats in voting "not guilty."

In the end, it was the office of the presidency that saved the president. Republicans argued that when Clinton chose not to tell the truth, he put himself above the law and his oath of office. Democrats agreed that the president's conduct was wrong, boorish, indefensible, and reprehensible, but they did not believe that what Clinton did threatened the Republic. The president's legal team argued convincingly that Clinton's wrongdoings in the Monica Lewinsky affair were simply not fit subjects for impeachment. To remove a president on this basis, they contended, would lower the impeachment bar too far and create an unhealthy precedent.

Some scholars believe this whole process was very damaging for the presidency and perhaps, too, for Congress. But most observers realized that national institutions are resilient and fulfill their assigned responsibilities. Most people also believe that the Constitution prevailed.

One lesson of the Clinton impeachment process is that an impeachment conducted primarily along partisan lines is unlikely to succeed under our constitutional system of checks and balances. A second lesson is that impeachment was designed primarily to punish crimes against the state, against the system of government itself.

Twenty years later, Congress requested a number of documents concerning the Clinton administration's foreign policy toward Haiti. The White House refused, claiming that the documents contained sensitive national security information. Although Congress eventually decided not to pursue the issue in the federal courts, it remains dissatisfied about the lack of cooperation in this and similar incidents. The Clinton administration claimed executive privilege on at least a dozen occasions, often in cases related to various independent counsel investigations of Clinton or cabinet members.[20] Executive privilege cannot be asserted in either congressional or judicial proceedings when the issue is basically one of refusing to cooperate in investigations of personal wrongdoing.

Presidents and members of Congress will continue to differ over the way executive privilege is exercised. There is no way this matter can be settled once and for all. It is a matter that will be revisited in each administration and tested by presidents and by the legislative branch. On occasion, courts will try to settle the ongoing dispute about the limits and conditions under which a president can invoke this well-established, if sometimes abused, presidential practice.

Executive Orders

executive order
Directive issued by a president or governor that has the force of law.

Executive orders, though not provided for in the Constitution, have become a generally accepted presidential practice. An **executive order** is a presidential directive that has the force of law. It can be challenged in the courts, and it can be overturned by subsequent presidents. Most executive orders are reasonable modifications or specific implementations of past legislation. But some presidential executive orders have antagonized members of Congress and led to charges that presidents were usurping the lawmaking functions assigned to Congress. According to past Supreme Court decisions, executive orders are generally accepted as the supreme law of the land unless they are in conflict with the Constitution or a federal law.

Beginning with George Washington, presidents have issued more than 13,000 executive orders. These orders have been used to declare American neutrality in the war between France and England (1793), the internment of Japanese Americans during World War II, and Bill Clinton's protection of large tracts of federal land as "national monuments" in Arizona, Colorado, Oregon, Utah, and Washington. President George W. Bush used an executive order in October 2001 to create the Office of Homeland Security with broad authority to coordinate information on potential threats to the nation. Under the order, the new office developed the Homeland Advisory Alert System, which warns the nation to pay heightened attention to threats.

Presidents sometimes use executive orders as a way to circumvent a Congress that is unfriendly to their initiatives or when traditional avenues are denied to the White House. Clinton used this power extensively (on more than 350 occasions), strategically, and across many types of policy. He set a standard that George W. Bush and other successors will follow, especially when Congress is controlled by the opposition party.[21]

The president's power to shape public policy through executive orders has grown along with the expansion of other executive branch responsibilities. While some of these responsibilities have been delegated to presidents by Congress, presidents have also assertively assumed additional authority on their own. Courts can, but seldom do, strike down executive orders. As a result, presidents have to exercise this power responsibly. "Should they go too far or fast, or move into the wrong areas at the wrong time, they would find that there are heavy political costs to be paid. . . . It is a matter of strategy. Presidents have to calculate . . . the costs as well as the benefits. . . . They have to pick their spots. But they will constantly be on the lookout, ready to move, and quite capable of moving if that is what they decide to do.[22]

Presidents rarely view their job as merely implementing laws passed by Congress. Because the laws passed by Congress usually have not been written with all the details specified, considerable discretion is left to presidents and the agencies of the executive branch. And most presidents view themselves as an authority in their own right, not subordinates to Congress but coequal with it.

The Veto Power

The Constitution provides that bills passed by the U.S. House of Representatives and Senate "shall be presented to the President of the United States," and the president can then approve the measure or issue a **veto**. If a bill is vetoed by a president, it can be enacted only if the veto is overridden, which requires a two-thirds vote in each chamber of Congress.

A variation of the veto is the **pocket veto**. In the ordinary course of events, if a president does not sign or veto a bill within ten days after receiving it (not counting Sundays), the bill becomes law without the president's signature. But if Congress adjourns within the ten days, the president, by taking no action, can kill the bill.

The power of a veto lies in the difficulty of overriding a president's decision. Recall that two-thirds of both houses must vote to overturn a veto. Historically, Congress has overridden fewer than 10 percent of presidents' regular vetoes (see Table 13-2). This requirement gives presidents a vital bargaining chip in the legislative process, where the mere threat of a veto, announced publicly or through legislative aides, can strengthen a president's hand in persuading Congress to accommodate his wishes. A president may also threaten to veto a bill that Congress wants unless action is taken on another bill that the president wants. Powerful though it is, the veto is essentially a negative weapon, more useful to presidents who want to block legislation than for those who seek programmatic changes.

Because the Constitution is straightforward about the veto power, its regular use by presidents stirs little controversy. Franklin Roosevelt holds the record with 635 vetoes, Ronald Reagan issued 78 vetoes in his two terms, and Bill Clinton vetoed only 37 times in his eight years. In late 1999, Clinton vetoed a Republican-backed appropriations bill

veto
Rejection by a president or governor of legislation passed by a legislature.

pocket veto
A veto exercised by the president after Congress has adjourned; if the president takes no action for ten days, the bill does not become law and is not returned to Congress for a possible override.

TABLE 13–2   Presidential Vetoes, 1789–2002

	Regular Vetoes	Pocket Vetoes	Total Vetoes	Vetoes Overridden
Washington	2	0	2	0
J. Adams	0	0	0	0
Jefferson	0	0	0	0
Madison	5	2	7	0
Monroe	1	0	1	0
J. Q. Adams	0	0	0	0
Jackson	5	7	12	0
Van Buren	0	1	1	0
W. Harrison	0	0	0	0
Tyler	6	4	10	1
Polk	2	1	3	0
Taylor	0	0	0	0
Fillmore	0	0	0	0
Pierce	9	0	9	5
Buchanan	4	3	7	0
Lincoln	2	5	7	0
A. Johnson	21	8	29	15
Grant	45	49*	94*	4
Hayes	12	1	13	1
Garfield	0	0	0	0
Arthur	4	8	12	1
Cleveland (both terms)	346	238	584	7
B. Harrison	19	25	44	1
McKinley	6	36	42	0
T. Roosevelt	42	40	82	1
Taft	30	9	39	1
Wilson	33	11	44	6
Harding	5	1	6	0
Coolidge	20	30	50	4
Hoover	21	16	37	3
F. Roosevelt	372	263	635	9
Truman	180	70	250	12
Eisenhower	73	108	181	2
Kennedy	12	9	21	0
L. Johnson	16	14	30	0
Nixon	26	17	43	7
Ford	48	18	66	12
Carter	13	18	31	2
Reagan	39	39	78	9
Bush, G.H.W.	29	17	44	1
Clinton	36	1	37	2
Bush, G. W.	0	0	0	0
Total	1,484	1,069	2,551	106

SOURCE: U.S. Senate Historical Office, Senate Library, January 2002.

*Includes one pocket veto in which the bill was not placed before the president for signature.

and threatened to veto it again and again until Congress made major compromises with him. His use of the veto worked; Congress eventually went along on about two-thirds of the spending items that Clinton wanted.

The Budget and Spending Powers

Battles over budgets and spending have been at the heart of national politics since the beginning of the Republic. The Constitution explicitly gives Congress the power to appropriate money; presidents are charged with implementing and administering the spending.

Congress dominated the budget-making process until 1921, when it approved the Budget and Accounting Act. That law mandated that the president submit annual budgets to Congress, and it established the Bureau of the Budget, which in 1970 became the Office of Management and Budget. Although the 1921 act also created the General Accounting Office as an auditing and oversight arm of Congress, presidents have played an increasingly powerful role in shaping the federal budget.

President Nixon, however, overplayed his hand when his White House developed legal theories that justified a bold change in the traditional definition of **impoundment**. Under the traditional definition, presidents were allowed to change the purpose of a spending bill to accommodate emergencies such as war or international crisis. Under the Nixon definition, impoundment was broadened to allow changes in a spending bill based on the president's ideology. Nixon claimed that the Democratic Congress was appropriating too much money, which created unacceptably high budget deficits. Congress responded that Nixon was using impoundment to set policy in explicit violation of the Constitution. In 1974, Congress approved the Congressional Budget and Impoundment Control Act, which sharply curtailed the president's use of impoundment. Enacted over Nixon's veto, the law gave Congress new powers to control its own budget process, created the Congressional Budget Office (CBO) to give the institution its own sources of economic and spending forecasts, and required the president to submit detailed requests to Congress for any proposed *recission* (cancellation) of congressional appropriations.

Every budget cycle witnesses a new round of clashes between the branches. In recent years, Congress has almost always failed to pass all of the appropriations bills by the beginning of the fiscal year. Instead, the two branches have relied on *continuing resolutions,* proclamations extending the authority for federal spending a few days, weeks, or months. This has often led to confusion, bickering, and in 1995 an especially bruising showdown between the Newt Gingrich–led Republican Congress and the Clinton Democratic White House that resulted in two shutdowns of the federal government. Despite these clashes, Congress in 1996 voted to give the president greater budget power through the **line item veto**. Presidents would now be allowed to strike out specific sections of an appropriations bill while signing the rest into law. Although this power is common in state government, the Supreme Court declared it unconstitutional at the federal level in 1997. According to the Supreme Court, Congress cannot delegate such decisions to the president.

George W. Bush came to the presidency when budgets were in balance and the country was enjoying impressive surpluses, but he promptly asked Congress to enact a $2 trillion tax cut. With the economy slowing down, revenues dropping, and the costs of homeland security rising, the federal government slipped back into deficit by the end of 2001.

Even without the economic slowdown and events of September 11, the hard-to-control parts of the national budget such as Social Security continue to grow, and the two parties have strongly competing views about the size of tax cuts, whether defense spending should be increased, the role of the surplus to help finance Social Security and Medicare, and the timetable for paying down the national debt. Executive-legislative struggles over budget policy remain a constant in the nation's capital.

impoundment
Presidential refusal to allow an agency to spend funds authorized and approved by Congress.

line item veto
Right of an executive to veto parts of a bill approved by a legislature without having to veto the entire bill.

President Bush hugs Senate Majority Leader Tom Daschle after his speech to the joint houses of Congress on September 20, 2001. Partisan politics were put aside in the first months after the terrorist attacks.

Building Coalitions

The American system of separation of powers and the nature of our party system ordinarily require that presidents build bipartisan coalitions if they want to get legislation approved by Congress. This is not an easy task in a country so large and diverse and in a Congress that, as we have noted, is highly decentralized and designed more for deliberation than collaboration.

Lessons from recent presidencies have led scholars to agree that presidents have to win the support of the American people if they are to win the support of Congress. Political scientist George Edwards summarizes the realities:

1. Members of Congress are responsive to public opinion.
2. Public support is crucial to the president's success.
3. Presidents must not only earn public support with their performance in office but must also actively take their case to the people. Moreover, they must do it not only at reelection time but all the time.
4. Through the permanent campaign, the White House can persuade or even mobilize the public.[23]

Presidents use State of the Union Addresses, news conferences, and travel around the country in an effort to win political support for their programs. Presidents also spend considerable time meeting with reporters, editors, and publishers, both individually and in groups, to make the case for their legislative priorities. John Kennedy, Ronald Reagan, and Bill Clinton are considered to have been effective communicators. But careful analysis of their ability to sway the public suggests that they were able to influence the public for only brief periods and usually on foreign policy matters or during short-term crises.[24]

Presidential efforts to rally public support for White House initiatives are inevitably aimed at building coalitions in Congress. A president's efforts at public relations are greatly helped, of course, if the president's party controls Congress. Presidents are almost twice as likely to win approval of significant White House–endorsed legislation with their party in control of Congress than in a divided government.[25] Even when presidents have high public approval on foreign policy, which George W. Bush did in the wake of September 11, they may find it difficult to focus public attention on domestic concerns.

Ultimately, presidents must deal with the Congress they inherit. Presidents go to considerable lengths to reward their allies and to entice potential supporters to cross over and support at least some of the their legislative proposals. Sometimes this reaching out involves incorporating opponents' policy suggestions into the president's larger program. Sometimes a president will meet one-on-one with a key member and personally lobby the legislator.

White House aides are specifically assigned to build coalitions in both chambers of Congress. These aides spend a lot of time on Capitol Hill, talking with party and committee leaders and serving as ambassadors from the White House to various supporters and would-be supporters who could make the difference in whether a president's legislative program succeeds or fails.[26]

An ambitious agenda is difficult to pass in good times, but in a divided government, legislative victories are much harder to achieve. Clinton co-opted several Republican issues, such as welfare reform, crime measures, and deficit reduction initiatives, and enjoyed success on these issues but struggled to win passage of large-scale reforms such as national health insurance.

George W. Bush faced a similar challenge as he set about to build political coalitions in Congress. He had enjoyed success in his bipartisan efforts in Texas, where he had served as a popular governor for six years, but as president found that campaign promises such as school vouchers invited Democratic opposition. Although he set a near record in congressional support in his first full year and won strong support for his war on terrorism, he was unable to win passage of his economic stimulus package and felt compelled to sign a campaign finance reform that his party had opposed.

The President's Agenda

Presidents have long had a substantial, if not always dominant, role in shaping what Congress does. Their primary vehicle for doing so is the president's agenda, which is an informal list of legislative priorities. Whether through State of the Union Addresses or other messages and signals, presidents make clear what they think Congress should do.[27]

It is one thing to proclaim a presidential priority, however, and quite another to actually influence congressional action. As Richard Neustadt argued in *Presidential Power,* the president's constitutional powers provide very little actual influence. According to Neustadt, a president's constitutional powers add up to little more than a job as America's most distinguished office clerk. It is a president's "power to persuade" that spells the difference between being a clerk and being a national leader.[28] Lyndon Johnson, who was one of the nation's most persuasive presidents, may have said it all in a single sentence: "You can tell a man to go to hell, but you can't make him go."[29] This power to persuade rests in the resources presidents bring to office and the skills they use in making the most of those resources.

Presidential Resources for Making and Influencing Policy

Two kinds of resources shape a president's agenda and its ultimate impact on Congress. The first involves the political resources needed to convince Congress to support the president, and the second involves the decision-making resources that help presidents decide what they want.

POLITICAL RESOURCES   A president's external influence comes from three sources: (1) the mandate provided by his election, (2) his level of public approval, and (3) the number of seats his party occupies in Congress. New presidents usually begin with at least some of each. As Democratic Vice President Walter Mondale once explained the concept, "A president, in my opinion, starts out with a bank full of goodwill and slowly checks are drawn on that, and it's very rare that it's replenished. It's a one-time deposit."[30]

Presidents who enter office with a large electoral margin, high public approval, and a party majority in Congress often claim a **mandate** to govern. The winner-take-all nature of the electoral college system tends to make the president's popular vote look larger than it truly is. In 1984, for example, Ronald Reagan set the modern record by winning every state but Massachusetts and the District of Columbia, rolling up 98 percent of the electoral votes by winning only 59 percent of the popular vote.

Mandates also reside in public approval for either the president or some policy issue. In 2000, for example, George W. Bush claimed a mandate for a tax cut, arguing that the issue was at the core of much of his public support. The fact that his 2000 opponent had also argued for a tax cut, albeit a much smaller one targeted more to lower-income Americans, also helped Bush make the case for a mandate.

Finally, mandates can come from a dramatic increase in party seats in Congress, particularly when presidents can prove that their popular vote totals created electoral coattails that pulled members of their party into office. Such coattails are said to exist when the president receives more votes in a district than the member representing that district. In 1964, for example, Johnson won the popular vote in 375 of the nation's 435 House districts, showing the breadth of his popular support. But he received more votes than the winning House candidate in only 134 of the 375, suggesting that his coattails were much shorter than he claimed.

With strong public support for his legislative agenda and the largest Democratic congressional majority in recent history, Johnson started his term with the largest "goodwill bank account" of any modern president. Reagan entered with significant public approval, too, and was reelected with a huge electoral margin but suffered from a lack of congressional support. Although Republicans had captured the Senate in 1980, Democrats retained the House, creating divided government both inside Congress and with the presidency.

Divided government is not always a recipe for legislative stalemate, however. Some of the nation's most significant policy proposals have been enacted into law

mandate
The perceived level of support for a president's policy priorities.

under divided party control. Political scientist David Mayhew even makes the argument that party control has not made a noticeable difference in the passage of particularly significant laws.[31]

PERSONAL RESOURCES   Presidents can hardly claim mandates or invest their political resources if they do not have the time, energy, and information to set the policy agenda or the political skills to focus congressional attention on their priorities. The first two of these personal resources, time and energy, run out over the course of the term and are difficult to replace. Presidents have only so much time to make their mark. Since they can only serve for two consecutive terms under the Twenty-Second Amendment, they must make every day count.

Presidents have only so much energy to give to the job. One need only compare pictures of presidents at the start and end of their terms to see the impact of the long hours and constant stress.

The third personal resource, information, actually increases over time as presidents learn the job. The presidency is the nation's most intense course in American government. One way presidents can increase their learning is to take "prerequisites" before entering office—holding other executive offices, such as the vice presidency or a governorship, that are similar to the presidency or studying issues as a senator or member of the House that are central to the president's constitutional duties.

The final personal resource involves the ability to focus congressional attention on the president's agenda through legislative timing and lobbying. Timing involves a president's ability to win congressional attention at key points in the legislative process, while lobbying involves the president's personal skill at persuading individual members of Congress.[32] Lobbying can involve everything from invitations to special White House events to "horse trades" on pet projects that members of Congress want.

Whatever the tactic, lobbying is designed to let the public and Congress know what the president wants, to make sure the list of priorities is not too long, and to keep the pressure on. Presidents who focus attention can make their political resources go farther.

Policy-Making Cycles

The pressure to move quickly is shaped by two cycles. The first is called the *cycle of decreasing influence:* Presidents tend to lose public and congressional support over time.

Presidential Lobbying Tools

- *Leadership meetings:* Inviting key leaders to the White House for an exchange of ideas and "educational" efforts
- *Bill-signing ceremonies:* Inviting supporters to the White House for official bill-signing celebrations
- *Social events:* Inviting members to state dinners or celebrity or medal presentations
- *Patronage:* Appointing the friends and political supporters of key members of Congress to various federal positions
- *Campaign aid:* Rewarding a legislator with a presidential fund-raising appearance or a presidential visit during a campaign
- *Constituency favors:* Providing presidential photographs, personal letters, White House tours, and souvenirs for a member's VIP constituents

SOURCE: Cary R. Covington and Kedron Bardwell, "Helping Friends or Wooing Enemies? How Presidents Use Favors to Build Support in Congress," paper presented at the annual meeting of the American Political Science Association, Boston, September 3–6, 1998.

The second is called the *cycle of increasing effectiveness:* Presidents almost always get better at their job over time.

The cycle of decreasing influence reflects the erosion of political resources as time goes on. At least since 1960, presidential approval tends to be at its highest at or near the start of the first term, falling more or less steadily over the next two years, almost always surging in the fourth year with the presidential campaign and, if the president is reelected, falling again from the fifth year on.[33]

The fact that a president's approval is usually higher at the beginning of the term and lower at the end does not mean it cannot go up in between. As shown in Figure 12-3 in the previous chapter, the general decline is often interrupted by occasional jumps in approval. Presidents almost always get a boost from American military action abroad, even if the action fails. Kennedy got a 5 percent boost in public approval following the failed Bay of Pigs invasion.

Alongside the decline in public approval, presidents almost always lose seats in the House of Representatives in the midterm elections. Indeed, there have been only two elections since 1862 in which the president's party has gained seats in the House. The worst of the recent defeats came in 1994, when Clinton's Democrats lost 52 seats, eclipsing the 1974 election that followed the Watergate scandal, when Republicans lost 48 seats. Much as members of Congress try to make campaigns about local issues, the midterm elections sometimes allow the public to hold a referendum on the president. Because presidents rarely accomplish all that they promise, losses are inevitable. Although President Bush defied these odds in 2002, he still had very narrow majorities in both chambers.

Even as presidents tend to lose influence over time, they begin to benefit from the cycle of increasing effectiveness. They steadily become better at their job. Just as students in an American government course should know more at the end than at the beginning, presidents know more in the fourth year of their term than in the first. Presidents should become more effective at using their powers over time. They may have less resources to work with, but should be able to make the most of what they have.

WHEN IS THE BEST TIME FOR THE PRESIDENT TO ACT?

You Decide... First-term presidents are almost always more popular with the public on the first day of their term than at the end. Their party is also likely to lose seats in Congress in the first midterm elections. That is why so many presidents enter office believing that they must "move it or lose it," meaning that they must get as much from Congress as they can in the first few months before their political capital declines. Kennedy, Nixon, Carter, Reagan, and both Bushes all sent their most important proposals to Congress within weeks of their inaugurations, and Clinton was roundly criticized for waiting until his first autumn to press Congress for passage of a national health care bill.

Thinking It Through... According to the cycles of decreasing influence and increasing effectiveness, the best time for presidents to win action on their legislative agendas also happens to be the time when they know the least about their job. Presidents are acutely aware that their honeymoon with Congress and the public is short and that they must get their priorities to Congress early or risk defeat. This may lead to significant policy mistakes as presidents try to take advantage of limited mandates from the public. That may have been what happened in 1981, for example, when Ronald Reagan won passage of deep budget and tax cuts that doomed the federal budget to nearly two decades of deficits; that may well be the result of the George W. Bush tax cut in 2001 as well.

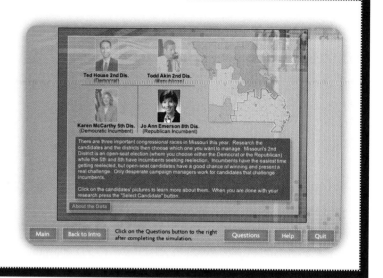

WHO'S GOT THE POWER?

Winning a foreign policy battle in the House and Senate involves timing, effective communication, and available options. It also involves the presence or absence of international crisis, the nation's ability to respond, the military's readiness, diplomatic skills, and the weight of history. As this simulation shows, presidents have several choices when such a crisis occurs. They can intensify their lobbying of the Senate, change policies entirely, or go over the head of the Senate to the American people for support.

Go to PoliSim "Who's Got the Power?"

Summary

1. The framers of the U.S. Constitution created a presidency that must win cooperation from Congress to get the work of government done. Lawmaking and policymaking powers are divided, and the politics of shared power has often been stormy. In general, however, Congress and presidents somehow find ways to collaborate and solve problems.

2. The relationship between a president and Congress is the most important one in the American political system, and while presidents spend great energy courting the media and appealing to the public, they do so in large part to gain support in Congress. A president may not like it, but sustained cooperation from majorities in Congress is a necessity.

3. Several factors can cause conflict in our system of separated institutions sharing power. Among them are constitutional ambiguities, different constituencies, varying terms of office, divided party control of the different branches, and fluctuating support of the president or Congress.

4. The media may exaggerate presidential tensions or disputes with Congress, yet clashes between the branches over presidential nominations, vetoes, budget proposals, military actions, and the exercise of executive privilege and executive orders are inevitable. These and other political realities are part of the continuing struggle that shapes presidential-congressional relations.

5. Presidential powers have increased over the past 60 years in good part because of grants of power by Congress to the presidency. Many of these powers have come in military and foreign policy areas and are due to the increased role of the United States in global affairs.

6. The framers created a presidency of limited powers, yet the role and leadership responsibilities of presidents increased as a result of national security and economic emergencies throughout the past several generations and because of the nation's world leadership responsibilities in this era. Congress usually tries to assert itself and serve as a reasonable and responsible check on the exercise of presidential power. It is sometimes effective and sometimes less effective in this role; yet no president can ever take congressional support for granted, and presidents can always expect at least suspicion if not hostile actions from the opposition party in Congress.

7. The president's policy agenda is shaped by political and personal resources. Presidents tend to lose influence over the course of office as their public approval and party support in Congress fall. At the same time, they also become more effective at their job as they learn more about one of the most difficult positions in the world.

Key Terms

executive privilege	veto	impoundment	mandate
executive order	pocket veto	line item veto	

Further Reading

DAVID GRAY ADLER AND MICHAEL A. GENOVESE, EDS., *The Presidency and the Law: The Clinton Legacy* (University Press of Kansas, 2002).

JON BOND AND RICHARD FLEISHER, EDS., *Polarized Politics: Congress and the President in a Partisan Era* (CQ Press, 2000).

DAVID W. BRADY AND CRAIG VOLDEN, *Revolving Gridlock: Politics and Policy from Carter to Clinton* (Westview Press, 1998).

JAMES MACGREGOR BURNS AND GEORGIA SORENSON, *Dead Center: Clinton-Gore Leadership and the Perils of Moderation* (Scribner, 1999).

CHARLES M. CAMERON, *Veto Bargaining: Presidents and the Politics of Negative Power* (Cambridge University Press, 1999).

STEPHEN CARTER, *The Confirmation Mess: Cleaning Up the Federal Appointment Process* (Basic Books, 1994).

MORRIS P. FIORINA, *Divided Government,* 2d ed. (Allyn & Bacon, 1996).

LOUIS FISHER, *Congressional Abdication on War and Spending* (Texas A&M Press, 2000).

LOUIS FISHER, *The Politics of Shared Power: Congress and the Executive,* 4th ed. (Texas A&M Press, 1998).

CHARLES O. JONES, *The Presidency in a Separated System* (Brookings Institution, 1994).

PAUL C. LIGHT, *The President's Agenda: Domestic Policy Choice From Kennedy Through Clinton* (Johns Hopkins University Press, 1999).

DAVID R. MAYHEW, *Divided We Govern: Party Control, Lawmaking, and Investigations, 1946–1990* (Yale University Press, 1991).

MARK PETERSON, *Legislating Together* (Harvard University Press, 1994).

RICHARD A. POSNER, *An Affair of State: The Investigation, Impeachment, and Trial of President Clinton* (Harvard University Press, 1999).

MARK J. ROZELL, *Executive Privilege: The Dilemma of Secrecy and Democratic Accountability,* 2d ed. (University Press of Kansas, 2000).

ARTHUR M. SCHLESINGER JR., *The Imperial Presidency* (Houghton Mifflin, 1972).

ROBERT J. SPITZER, *The Presidential Veto: Touchstone of the American Presidency* (State University of New York Press, 1988).

JAMES A. THURBER, ED., *Rivals for Power: Presidential-Congressional Relations* (CQ Press, 1996).

EMILY FIELD VAN TASSEL AND PAUL FINKELMAN, EDS., *Impeachable Offenses: A Documentary History from 1787 to the Present* (CQ Press, 1999).

SEE ALSO *Legislative Studies Quarterly* and *Presidential Studies Quarterly.*

THE FEDERAL BUREAUCRACY
The Real Power?

H

ARDLY A MOMENT GOES BY WHEN AMERICANS ARE NOT AFFECTED BY SOMETHING THE FEDERAL GOVERNMENT does. Our food is safer, cars are more fuel-efficient, health care is better, college is more accessible, air is cleaner, streets are smoother, and water is purer all because of federal rules.

Despite its reach, and perhaps because of it, Americans have a love-hate relationship with the federal government. We want more of virtually everything government delivers, from Social Security to national parks, from food and drug inspections to home loans, yet we often complain that government is too big. A majority of Americans believe that the federal government creates more problems than it solves and that it controls too much of daily life.[1]

When crisis comes, however, Americans often rally around the federal government as the nation's first line of defense. This is certainly what happened immediately after September 11, 2001. Confidence in the president and vice president rose dramatically in the days following the terrorist attacks on New York City and Washington, as did confidence in elected officials such as members of Congress. But confidence in presidential appointees and federal workers also soared. In July 2001, only 12 percent of Americans held a highly favorable opinion of presidential appointees and government workers. By October, 26 percent of Americans had a very favorable opinion of presidential appointees, and 20 percent felt the same about government workers.[2]

Despite this greater confidence in federal leaders and workers, Americans retained their traditional skepticism about big government. Interviewed three weeks after the 2001 terrorist attacks, 70 percent of Americans assumed that most federal employees chose to work for the government because of the job security, and 68 percent cited the salary and benefits. Even at a time when Americans accepted the need for a strong federal government, they doubted the basic motivations of the people who work for it.[3]

Red Tape

The term "red tape" comes from the ribbon that English civil servants once used to tie up and bind legal documents. Today, along with death and taxes, we think of red tape as inevitable. We are annoyed when we have to wait in lines while officials check files or consult with their supervisors. We are furious when officials lose important documents. Red tape often takes the form of an official's infuriating adherence to rigid procedures. We may view it as a hopeless tangle of rules and regulations that keep public servants from doing anything but stamping and shuffling papers.

But these same rules and regulations help ensure that public servants act impartially. In other words, red tape stems from our desire not to give public servants too much discretion and to hold them accountable. After all, they are spending our money. Remember, too, that one person's red tape is another person's prudent system or proper cautiousness.

bureaucrat
A career government employee.

bureaucracy
A professional corps of officials organized in a pyramidal hierarchy and functioning under impersonal, uniform rules and procedures.

What goes up, at least in trust in government, must eventually come down. As the intense emotions of September 11 faded, so did the newfound trust in government. By May 2002, the number of Americans who trusted the federal government to do the right thing "just about always or most of the time" had fallen from 57 percent in October to 40 percent. Although that number was still above its pre–September 11 level of just 29 percent, trust in government was well on the way back to normal.

In this chapter, we explain who the bureaucrats are and examine the origins, functions, and realities of our national public bureaucracy. We also explore how elected officials are trying to make the bureaucracy leaner, more responsive, and more accountable to the American people. It is important to examine whether our bureaucracy and its methods are stifling innovation, productivity, and common sense.

Defining the Federal Bureaucracy

Whether they are called **bureaucrats** or federal employees, more than 2.7 million Americans work in the executive branch, in the 14 cabinet-level departments, and in the more than 50 independent agencies embracing about 2,000 bureaus, divisions, branches, offices, services, and other subunits of government. Six big agencies—the Departments of the Army, the Navy, and the Air Force (all three in the Department of Defense), the Department of Veterans Affairs, the Department of Homeland Security, and the U.S. Postal Service—tower over the others in size. Most agencies are directly responsible to the president, yet some, like the Postal Service, are partly independent. Agencies exist by act of Congress; legislators can abolish them either by passing a new law or by withholding funds.

The terms "bureaucrat" and "bureaucracy" date from the early nineteenth century. Originally, the word "bureau" referred to a cloth covering the desks of French government officials in the eighteenth century and eventually came to be applied to the desk itself. The term was soon linked with the suffix "-ocracy" (as in "democracy" or "aristocracy") to describe government (essentially, "rule by people at desks"). A century ago, **bureaucracy** was regarded as a rational, efficient method of organization. The term typically refers to the whole body of unelected and unappointed government officials in the executive branch who work for presidents and their political appointees. In this chapter, we use the terms "bureaucracy" and "bureaucrat" in this neutral sense, although in popular use, these terms may have negative connotations.

Bureaucracies are public or private organizations that are large and hierarchical, with each employee accountable to a superior through a chain of command. They provide each employee with a defined role or responsibility, base their decisions on impersonal rules, and hire and promote employees according to job-related skills.[4] Bureaucracies in the modern sense exist to provide predictability and efficiency and to minimize the arbitrary practices that so often characterized rule under dictators and monarchs.

In a large, complex society, bureaucracy is virtually inevitable. Most of us will work in a bureaucracy at some point in our lives. Some of those bureaucracies will be giant private companies such as IBM or General Electric, others will be nonprofit agencies such as the Salvation Army or the Red Cross, and still others will be in government. Governmental bureaucracies pose special challenges because they report to competing political institutions and must function within our constitutional democracy of shared powers and multiple checks and balances.

How Is the Federal Government Organized?

Because the federal bureaucracy was created one organization at a time over more than 200 years, no two government departments or agencies are quite alike. Some, such as the Department of Defense, are collections of huge agencies in their own right. The Defense Department contains the Departments of the Army, Navy, and Air Force,

The Changing Face of the Federal Government

One way to make the federal bureaucracy more accountable to the public is to make it look more like the public. By creating a representative bureaucracy, at least in terms of race and gender, the federal government can strengthen its connection to the people it serves.

The federal government is clearly more representative of the public now than it was in the 1950s, when most of its employees were white and most women were clerk-typists. Women now occupy 45 percent of all federal jobs; minorities occupy nearly 30 percent.

Even though the number of women and minorities in the federal work force is at an all-time high, they still face barriers in rising to the top. First, women and minorities are not equally represented in all departments and agencies. Women and minorities tend to concentrate in departments with strong social service missions such as Education, Health and Human Services, Housing and Urban Development, and Veterans Affairs (which runs the VA hospital system, with its mostly female nursing corps), all of which have more than 50 percent women employees. Military and technical departments such as Defense, Energy, NASA, and Transportation have far fewer women. Health and Human Services has 65 percent women, while Transportation has just 25 percent; 50 percent of the Department of Education's employees are minorities, compared to just 16 percent of Agriculture's.

Second, women and minorities are not represented at all levels of the federal bureaucracy. In 2000, women held only 35 percent of the professional and administrative jobs, where the higher-paying management posts are, but 70 percent of the lower-paying technical and clerical positions. Minorities were also heavily represented in the lower-paying jobs. Together, women and minorities held almost half the jobs at the bottom level of the federal pay system in 2000 and just 10 percent of the posts at the top.

Education Department employee Claudia Gaines and Education Secretary Rod Paige work with a fourth grade student during National Volunteer Week.

The Face of the Federal Work Force

Gender	
Men	55%
Women	45
Race	
White	70
African American	17
Hispanic	7
Asian and Pacific Islander	5
American Indian	2
Education	
High school or some college	60
College graduate	40

SOURCE: Office of Personnel Management, *The Fact Book, 2000 Edition* (Government Printing Office, 2002).

---

each with its own separate duties (as if to confirm how Congress sometimes divides responsibilities, the Army has its own air corps, and the Navy has its own army, the Marines). Others, such as the Department of Education, are tiny by comparison. Whereas the Department of Defense employees more than 600,000 civilian employees and 1.4 million uniformed military personnel, the Department of Education employs just 5,000 civilians.

FORMAL ORGANIZATION   Public administration scholars classify the organizations of government into four broad categories: (1) *departments*, (2) *independent agencies*, (3) *independent regulatory commissions*, and (4) *government corporations*.

Departments tend to be the largest federal organizations of all and have the broadest missions. **Independent agencies** tend to be smaller and have more focused responsi-

department
Usually the largest organization in government; also the highest rank in federal hierarchy.

independent agency
A government entity that is independent of the legislative, executive, and judicial branches.

Executive Branch Departments

Date indicates when the department was established.

Department of State (1789)

Department of the Treasury (1789)

Department of Defense (1947; originally War, 1789)

Department of Justice (1789)

Department of the Interior (1849)

Department of Agriculture (1862)

Department of Commerce (1913; originally Commerce and Labor, 1903)

Department of Labor (1913; originally Commerce and Labor, 1903)

Department of Health and Human Services (1979; originally Health, Education and Welfare, 1953)

Department of Housing and Urban Development (1965)

Department of Transportation (1966)

Department of Energy (1977)

Department of Education (1979)

Department of Veterans Affairs (1989)

Department of Homeland Security (2002)

independent regulatory commission
A government agency or commission with regulatory power whose independence is protected by Congress.

government corporation
A government agency that operates like a business corporation, created to secure greater freedom of action and flexibility for a particular program.

bilities. **Independent regulatory commissions** are similar to agencies but are designed to be free from partisan control. Finally, **government corporations** are designed to operate much like private businesses.

Departments   Cabinet departments are the most visible organizations in the federal bureaucracy. Today's 15 departments of government employ more than 70 percent of all federal civil servants and spend 93 percent of all federal dollars. Thirteen of the departments are headed by secretaries; the fifteenth, the Justice Department, is headed by the attorney general.

Measured by total employees, the largest department by far is the Department of Defense, which contains what were once the separate departments of the Air Force, Army, and Navy. Next in size are the Department of Veterans Affairs, which administers programs to help veterans return to civilian life after service; the Department of Homeland Security, which was created to protect the nation from terrorism; the Department of the Treasury, which manages the economy and raises revenues through the Internal Revenue Service; and the Department of Justice, which enforces the laws through the federal courts and investigates crime through the Federal Bureau of Investigation. Measured by budget, the Department of Health and Human Services comes first, followed by Defense.

The greatest expansion in the number of departments occurred between 1945 and 1990: Health, Education, and Welfare (HEW) was created in 1953; Housing and Urban Development (HUD) in 1965; Transportation in 1966; Energy in 1977; and Veterans Affairs (VA) in 1989. HEW was divided in 1979 to create two new departments, Health and Human Services and Education.

These 14 departments represent two very different approaches to department building. One approach is to use a department to collect a number of related programs under one broad umbrella, or conglomerate. The Department of Homeland Security was created by combining elements of twenty-two separate agencies, including the Coast Guard, Immigration and Naturalization Service, Customs Service, Federal Emergency Management Agency, Secret Service, and the Animal Plant Health and Inspection Service. The Departments of Agriculture, Health and Human Services, Commerce, and Defense also reflect a conglomerate approach.

The other approach is to use a department to give added visibility to a popular issue such as education, housing, or energy or to a large group of Americans such as the elderly or workers. These departments are not conglomerates but highly specialized voices for a specific group of Americans. Not surprisingly, these departments are often closely tied to interest groups. Congress created the Department of Veterans Affairs in 1989 under pressure from veterans' groups such as the American Legion, who wanted their own advocate in the president's cabinet. It was hardly the first time that Congress yielded to such pressure. One can easily argue that the Departments of Agriculture, Commerce, Education, and Labor were all created in response to interest group pressure, making them *clientele agencies* that owe much of their survival to the strength of the constituency groups.

Independent Regulatory Commissions   Size and age are not the only ways to compare units within the federal bureaucracy. Power, or impact on daily life, is also important. Indeed, when Americans complain about bureaucracy being on their backs, they are often talking about the federal government's independent regulatory commissions.

Yet that is exactly why Congress and the president created the federal government's independent regulatory commissions. All were designed to "get on the backs" of people and corporations, whether to protect consumers (the Consumer Product Safety Commission), regulate stock markets (the Securities and Exchange Commission), oversee federal election laws (the Federal Election Commission), monitor television and radio (the Federal Communications Commission), regulate business (the Federal Trade Commission), control the supply of money (the Federal Reserve Board), or watch over nuclear power plants (Nuclear Regulatory Commission).

The commissions may be small in budget and employees (just $70 million and 1,200 employees for all the independent commissions combined), but their influence over American life is large. Many experts contend that the Federal Reserve Board chair is the second most influential person in making economic policy, and others would argue that the current chair, Alan Greenspan, is the most important leader in influencing public confidence about the economy.[5]

Although independent regulatory commissions are part of the federal bureaucracy, they have a measure of independence from both Congress and the president through their leadership structure. By definition, these commissions are headed not by a single executive but by a small number of commissioners who are appointed by the president, with Senate confirmation, for fixed terms of office. Unlike other presidential appointees, commissioners cannot be removed from office without cause, which is defined by law to mean "inefficiency, neglect of duty, or malfeasance in office." As a result, independent regulatory commissions are less responsive to political pressure from either end of Pennsylvania Avenue.

Independent commissions are not completely independent. Their annual budgets must be approved by Congress, and their decisions are subject to judicial review. The collapse of the Enron Corporation in 2002 prompted a congressional investigation of the Securities and Exchange Commission, which is responsible for overseeing the honesty of publicly traded companies.

Nevertheless, most independent regulatory commissions operate with great freedom and public support. Any effort to reduce the independence of the Federal Reserve Board, Securities and Exchange Commission, or Federal Communications Commission would be seen as a threat to the economic vitality of the nation.

Independent Agencies   The word "independent" means at least two things in the federal bureaucracy. Applied to a regulatory commission, it means that the agency is outside the president's control. Applied to an agency or administration, it merely means "separate" or "standing alone." Whereas independent regulatory commissions do not report to the president, independent agencies do.

The Federal Reserve Board meets in Washington, D.C. under the seal of the U.S. Supreme Court.

Principles of Bureaucratic Management

Followers of the noted German sociologist Max Weber contended that a properly run bureaucracy could be a model of efficiency based on rational and impartial management.* President Woodrow Wilson, when he was a Princeton University professor, adopted many of these views in his writing. Politics and public administration, he said, should be carefully separated. Leave politics to Congress and management to administrators who adhere to the laws passed by Congress.

According to the textbook model, bureaucrats should be closely controlled by established rules and regulations. Although this is not always true in practice, it is generally the case. Administrators are not free to make any rules they wish or to decide disputes any way they please. Several kinds of limitations exist:

- The legislative power of Congress compels agencies to interpret and apply laws as Congress would wish. Congress can amend a law to make its intent clearer, conduct oversight hearings and investigations, or restrict appropriations.

- Congress has closely regulated the procedures to be followed by regulatory agencies. Under the Administrative Procedures Act of 1946, agencies must publicize their procedures and organization, give advance information of proposed rules to interested persons, allow such persons to present written information and

arguments, and allow parties appearing before the agency to be accompanied by counsel and to cross-examine witnesses.

- Under certain conditions, final actions of agencies may be appealed to the courts.

- Some federal agencies are created for the specific purpose of overseeing and limiting their fellow agencies. Examples are the Office of Management and Budget (OMB), which is supervised by the White House, and the General Accounting Office (GAO), which is supervised by Congress.

- Administrators must keep in mind the demands of professional ethics, the advice and criticism of experts, and the attitudes of Congress, the president, interest groups, political parties, and citizens. In the long run, these informal safeguards may be the most important of all.

This textbook model remains influential because it reflects reality. Laws of Congress, although not the whole story, are an important part of it. Federal agencies and career servants are creatures of the enabling laws under which they work.

*For an examination of Max Weber's ideas on bureaucracy, see Brian Fry, *Mastering Public Administration: From Max Weber to Dwight Waldo* (Chatham House, 1989).

As a general rule, independent agencies are small federal bureaucracies that serve specific groups of Americans or work on specific problems. Becoming an agency is often the first step toward becoming a department. As noted, the Department of Veterans Affairs is basically the same organization that once existed as the Veterans Administration. The Department of Transportation was created as an umbrella for the old Federal Aviation Administration, the Federal Railroad Administration, and the Federal Highway Administration.

Independent agencies are usually headed by an administrator, which is the second most senior title in the federal bureaucracy behind secretary or attorney general. There are roughly 60 such agencies today, including the Environmental Protection Agency (EPA), the Central Intelligence Agency (CIA), the National Aeronautics and Space Administration (NASA), the National Security Agency (NSA), and the Small Business Administration (SBA).

Although independence increases each agency's ability to focus on its mission, independence also weakens its willingness to cooperate. The spread of independent agencies can also increase confusion about who is responsible for what in the federal government. In 2002, for example, the future secretary of homeland security, former Pennsylvania Governor Tom Ridge, complained about the dozens of agencies involved in guarding the nation's borders: "There is no line of accountability," he said. "As you take a look at twenty-first-century borders, you have got to have somebody in charge."[6]

Ridge was worried about more than just FEMA and the CIA, however. He was also concerned about agencies that exist within federal departments, such as the Immigration and Naturalization Service, which is part of the Justice Department; the Customs Service, which is part of Treasury; and the Coast Guard, which is part of Transportation. Those agencies have long behaved as if they are independent of their departments.

As noted, independent agencies do not have to be small. NASA, for example, has an annual budget of over $11 billion and a work force of more than 23,000 employees, not to mention the private contract employees who help put the space shuttle into orbit. NASA's budget ranks it ahead of four cabinet departments (Justice, Interior, State, and Commerce).

Moreover, independent agencies can be more important to the president than some cabinet departments. There are times, for example, when the director of the CIA or the administrator of EPA gets a higher place on the president's agenda than the secretary of HUD or Agriculture, particularly when an issue such as international spying or global warming is in the headlines. And both usually have a seat at the cabinet's conference table. Although being a cabinet secretary certainly conveys some visibility, it is no guarantee that the president or Congress will pay more or less attention.

It is useful to note that independent agencies are not the only government organizations that call themselves agencies. There are a number of highly visible agencies that actually exist within departments, including the Forest Service (located in the Agriculture Department), the National Park Service (located in the Department of the Interior), the Occupational Safety and Health Administration (located in the Labor Department), and the Census Bureau (located in the Commerce Department). What makes these agencies different from the independent agencies is that they do not report to the president directly but do so through a cabinet secretary.

Government Corporations   Perhaps the least understood organizations in the federal bureaucracy, government corporations are intended to act more like businesses than like traditional government departments and agencies. Because they are designed to make money through the sale of services such as rail tickets or stamps, they are generally given more freedom from the assorted rules that control what agencies do, such as hiring and firing employees quickly, purchasing goods and services, and accounting for spending.[7]

Yet no two government corporations are alike. The term is so loosely used that no one knows exactly how many corporations the federal bureaucracy has. What experts do know is that the number is between 31 and 47, including the Corporation for Public

Broadcasting (which runs PBS television), the U.S. Postal Service, the National Railroad Passenger Association (better known as Amtrak), and Americorps (which runs a national service program created by the Clinton administration), along with a host of financial enterprises that make loans of one kind or another. Once again, the fact that these organizations are not departments does not mean they are small or insignificant. The U.S. Postal Service employs almost 800,000 people, making it the second-largest organization in the federal bureaucracy. It also lost $1.5 billion in 2002, bringing the amount of money it has borrowed from the federal government to more than $12 billion.

INFORMAL ORGANIZATIONS   To study a formal organization is only to begin to understand how bureaucracy works, for we also need to understand the informal organization (see Figure 14-1). Bureaucrats differ in attitudes, motives, abilities, experiences, and political clout, and these differences matter. Leadership in an organization is exercised in a variety of places; some officials may have considerably more influence than others with the same formal status. Further, loyalties of officials cut across the formal aims of the agency.

Informal organization can have a significant effect on administration. A subordinate official in an agency may be especially close to the chief because they went to the same college or because they play racquetball together or because the subordinate knows how

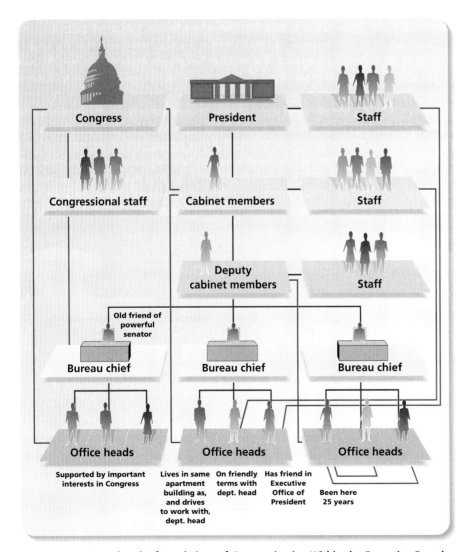

FIGURE 14–1   **Formal and Informal Lines of Communication Within the Executive Branch.**

to ingratiate himself with the chief. A staff official may have tremendous influence, not because of formal authority but because of experience, fairness, common sense, and personality. If an agency is headed by a chief who is weak or unimaginative, a vacuum may develop that encourages others to take over. Such informal organization and communication, cutting across regular channels, are inevitable in any organization—public or private, civilian or military.

Who Leads the Bureaucracy?

Every department and agency of the federal bureaucracy is headed by a presidential appointee, who is either subject to confirmation by the Senate or appointed on the sole authority of the president. As political officers, presidential appointees serve at the pleasure of the president and generally leave their posts at the end of that president's term in office. There are roughly 4,000 presidential appointees in the federal government, including 600 administrative officers who are subject to Senate confirmation, and another 2,400 who serve entirely "at the pleasure of the president." The president also appoints roughly 1,000 U.S. marshals, U.S. attorneys, and ambassadors to foreign nations.

In turn, presidential appointees work closely with the 7,000 members of the **Senior Executive Service**, which contains the most senior career officers of the federal bureaucracy. As career professionals, senior executives continue in their posts regardless of who happens to be president and are selected on the basis of merit, not political history or campaign contributions. Although presidents and their appointees do have some authority to transfer senior executives from office to office, they have no influence over who gets chosen to be a member of the Senior Executive Service.

Together, these two types of executives, political and career, constitute the leadership corps of the federal bureaucracy. The number has grown dramatically over the past three decades as the federal government has "thickened" with more layers of leadership and more leaders at each layer.[8]

Some political scientists argue that Congress created the pressure for thickening by creating highly complex programs that demand close supervision, while others believe that thickening is driven in part by a competition for power among competing organizations. According to this *theory of public bureaucracy,* bureaucratic organizations constantly seek to enhance their power, whether by creating new titles, adding more staff, or increasing their budgets.[9] Regardless of the explanation, the way to control thickening is to make sure that every new title is carefully considered before it is used.

Senior Executive Service
Established by Congress in 1978 as a flexible, mobile corps of senior career executives who work closely with presidential appointees to manage government.

In November 1995, the vast bureaucracy of the federal government shut down for lack of funds.

How Did the Bureaucracy Evolve?

The federal bureaucracy started out very small. As public administration scholar Leonard White once wrote, the entire federal bureaucracy of 1790 consisted of nothing more than a "foreign office with John Jay and a couple of clerks to deal with correspondence from John Adams in London and Thomas Jefferson in Paris; . . . a Treasury Board with an empty treasury; . . . a 'Secretary at War' with an authorized army of 840 men; . . . [and] a dozen clerks whose pay was in arrears."[10]

Creating the first departments was not without controversy, however. Congress not only wanted to restrict the president's removal power for all officers but also sought to continue the Constitutional Convention debate over who should run the Department of the Treasury. Having lost the power to appoint the secretary in the last days of the convention, the first Senate pressed to have the new department headed by a board rather than a single secretary and briefly succeeded in requiring the secretary to submit all financial plans to Congress for approval. The Senate's proposals would have sharply limited the president's authority to execute the laws and were eventually defeated on close votes. (See Table 14-1 for measures of the federal government's size since 1940.)

Once past the legislative disputes, the first three departments came into being smoothly. Washington made excellent first appointments: Thomas Jefferson to the Department of State, Alexander Hamilton to the Department of the Treasury, and Henry Knox to the War Department. All three were easily confirmed and quickly went about the business of running their departments. At roughly the same time, Congress also created the Post Office Department and allowed for the appointment of a U.S. attorney general.

Even though the federal bureaucracy was but the tiniest fraction of its current size, it was not long before presidential candidates began promising smaller government. Indeed, Jefferson made waste in government a centerpiece of his first Inaugural Address in 1801, promising "a wise and frugal government, which shall restrain men from injuring one another, shall leave them otherwise free to regulate their own pursuits of industry and improvement, and shall not take from the mouth of labor what it has earned." Jefferson

TABLE 14–1   Measuring the Size of Government, 1940–2005

Year	Employment (in thousands)	Budget (in billions of current dollars)	Budget (in 1996 dollars)	Budget as a Percentage of Gross Domestic Product
1940	699	$ 9.5	$ 94.3	9.9%
1945	3,370	92.7	804.1	43.7
1950	1,439	42.6	312.5	16.0
1955	1,860	68.4	431.3	17.8
1960	1,808	92.2	493.0	18.3
1965	1,901	118.2	575.6	17.6
1970	2,203	195.6	761.6	19.9
1975	2,149	332.3	909.3	22.0
1980	2,161	590.9	1,092.5	22.3
1985	2,252	946.4	1,304.7	23.9
1990	2,250	1,253.2	1,483.6	21.9
1995	2,018	1,788.8	1,551.5	21.9
2000	1,784	1,788.8	1,659.5	18.2
2005 (estimated)	—	2,168.7	1,782.8	16.6

SOURCE: Office of Management and Budget, *Budget of the U.S. Government, Fiscal Year 2003, Historical Tables* (Government Printing Office, 2002).

wanted a government that taxed lightly, paid its debts on time and in full, and sought "economy in the public expense." Jefferson set aside his promise long enough to make the Louisiana Purchase, which doubled the size of the nation and laid the groundwork for a vast expansion of America's economy.

Unfortunately, Jefferson's purchase also set off a wave of corruption at the federal government's General Land Office, where corrupt federal clerks reserved the best pieces of land to sell for themselves. The corruption eventually ignited the western anger that swept Andrew Jackson—and a new era in two-party competition—into office in 1828. Jackson soon introduced a **spoils system** into government—as in "to the victor belong the spoils." This system was based on the theory that party loyalists should be rewarded and that government would be effective and responsive only if supporters of the president held most key federal posts. Besides, it was assumed that government should not be complicated; anybody should be able to do the job. With each new president came a full turnover in the federal service.

Later in the nineteenth century, however, a sharp reaction set in against the spoils system. In response to abuses such as bribery and poor performance, and most immediately to the assassination of President James Garfield in 1881 by a disappointed office seeker, Congress passed the Pendleton Act. It set up a limited **merit system** based on a testing program for evaluating candidates. Federal employees were to be selected and retained according to their "merit," not their party connections or loyalty. Federal service was placed under the control of a three-person bipartisan board called the Civil Service Commission, which functioned from 1883 to 1978.[11]

By the 1950s, coverage under the merit system had grown from 10 percent of all federal employees, when it was first established, to about 90 percent. In 1978, the Civil Service Reform Act abolished the Civil Service Commission and split its functions between two new agencies. This split was made to eliminate the possible conflict of interest in an agency that recruits, hires, and promotes employees and also passes judgment on employee grievances about fairness and discrimination.

Today, the **Office of Personnel Management (OPM)** administers civil service laws, rules, and regulations. The independent Merit Systems Protection Board is charged with protecting the integrity of the federal merit system and the rights of federal employees. It conducts studies of the merit system, hears and decides charges of wrongdoing, considers employee appeals against adverse agency actions, and orders corrective and disciplinary actions against an agency executive or employee when appropriate. (A sampling of current federal job offerings can be found at www.usajobs.opm.gov.)

Working for Government

By any measure, the federal government is large. As already noted, it employs nearly 2.7 million civilian federal workers and 1.4 million uniformed military personnel. It also employs nearly 1 million postal workers, 5.6 million employees under federal government contracts, and 2.6 million whose salaries are covered by federal research and construction grants. The federal government will spend almost $1.8 trillion in fiscal year 2002.[12]

Yet large as it is, the federal government is actually smaller today by some measures than it was at the end of World War II in 1945. Although its budget is certainly much larger in absolute numbers, the budget is smaller as a percentage of gross domestic product, which is a measure of the size of the economy.

Moreover, despite its considerable girth in total employees, the federal government is composed of many small parts that administer thousands of different programs. Parts of 22 agencies and their 170,000 employees were merged into the new Department of Homeland Security (see Figure 14–2), for example, but almost 50 other agencies involved in homeland security were left out of the organization. That number includes law enforcement agencies such as the Federal Bureau of Investigation, which is responsible for

spoils system
A system of public employment based on rewarding party loyalists and friends.

merit system
A system of public employment in which selection and promotion depend on demonstrated performance rather than political patronage.

Office of Personnel Management (OPM)
Agency that administers civil service laws, rules, and regulations.

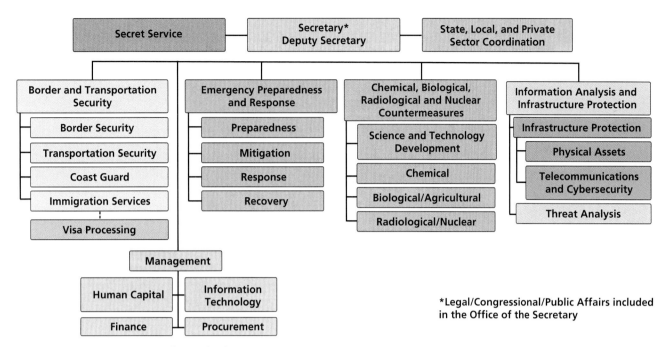

FIGURE 14–2   **The Department of Homeland Security.**

tracking down suspected terrorists within the United States, as well as health agencies such as the National Institutes of Health and Centers for Disease Control, which are responsible for investigating biological agents that might be used in a terrorist attack and vaccinating citizens against diseases such as smallpox.

Consider the Centers for Disease Control and Prevention (CDC) in Atlanta. It does much more than research on bioterrorism. The CDC was created by Congress in 1946 and remains headquartered in Atlanta, where its predecessor, the Communicable Disease Center, had been located, close to the sources of mosquito-borne malaria, which it was originally created to fight.

The CDC is responsible for a variety of federal programs, including disease detection and prevention. The federal role in vaccinating children against life-threatening diseases dates back to the 1950s when Congress enacted the Poliomyelitis Vaccination Assistance Act to cover the cost of free vaccines against the deadly childhood disease. It then passed the Vaccination Assistance Act in 1961 to help state governments immunize all children against polio, diphtheria, whooping cough, and tetanus by the age of five.

The CDC continues to manage the vaccination program today, which has produced a stunning return on investment. Every dollar spent immunizing children against measles, mumps, and rubella saves $21 in future health costs, for example, and every dollar spent on vaccinations for diphtheria, pertussis (whooping cough), and tetanus saves $29.

The CDC and its 8,000 employees do more than operate the national vaccination program, however. They also conduct deep research on some of the nation's most troubling health issues, which has led to significant reductions in heart disease and significant gains in cancer survival rates. The CDC's disease detectives have been at the forefront of identifying a host of mystery illnesses, including the respiratory disease that attacked attendees at an American Legion convention in 1968 (Legionnaire's disease), toxic shock syndrome in 1980, and hepatitis C in 1989, while tracking down the causes of major health disasters, including the outbreak of food poisoning at Jack-in-the-Box hamburger outlets in Washington State in 1993 and the emergence of a new strain of flu in 1997.

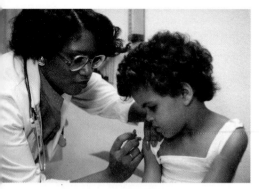

The Centers for Disease Control (CDC) has been very successful in educating the public about the importance of immunization for children.

Myths About Government

Americans believe a number of myths about the federal bureaucracy. Polls show that many of us think that most federal employees work in Washington, D.C., and that the federal government spends much more on welfare and assistance for the poor than it does on Social Security or defense.

The realities are much different:

• Only about 15 percent of the career civilian employees work in the Washington area. The vast majority are scattered throughout the country and around the world.

• More than 25 percent of the civilian employees work for the Army, the Navy, the Air Force, or some other defense agency; another 30 percent work for the U.S. Postal Service.

• Welfare may consume a sizable portion of the U.S. budget, yet the federal bureaucracy that administers it is relatively small. Fewer than 10 percent of the bureaucrats work for welfare agencies such as the Social Security Administration or the Department of Veterans Affairs.

• Federal civilian employees are more broadly representative of the nation than legislators or politically appointed executives in terms of social origin, education, religion, and other background factors.

• Thousands of different personnel skills are represented in the federal government; however, most federal employees are white-collar workers: secretaries, clerks, lawyers, inspectors, engineers.

Most bureaucrats are honest professionals and experts at their business. Presidents, Congress, and other elected officials sometimes ignore the bureaucracy's advice at their peril. Yet bureaucracies can also hide incompetence and produce delays in processing information. In June 2002, for example, Americans learned that the Federal Bureau of Investigation had received several clear warnings about the use of airplanes in suicide attacks before September 11, 2001, but failed to make the connections that might have led investigators to the plotters of the attacks.

The Hiring Process

Today's civil service system was designed to reduce political corruption by promoting merit in the hiring process. But hiring on the basis of merit is not the only way government seeks to reduce corruption. It regulates the hiring process to make sure that merit is the only basis for employment and regulates what federal employees can and cannot do by way of political participation.

As noted, the Office of Personnel Management is responsible for recruiting, examining, and appointing government workers. It advertises for new employees, prepares and administers oral and written examinations throughout the country, and compiles a roster of names of those who pass the tests. OPM delegates to the individual agencies the responsibility for hiring new personnel, subject to its standards. Individual agencies may promote people from within or transfer a civil servant from another agency in the government. If, however, they wish to consider an "outsider," they request that OPM certify possible candidates from its roster of applicants. OPM typically certifies the top three applicants for the opening, and the agency normally selects one of these. However, the agency can decide to make no appointment or to request other applicants if it thinks none of the three is suitable.

These procedures are intended to protect the merit principle and to meet agencies' needs for qualified personnel. In practice, the two objectives sometimes come into conflict. Trade-offs have to be made, particularly between central control by OPM and delegation of discretionary authority to the agencies. And sometimes the pursuit of both objectives is undermined by other goals, such as giving military veterans extra credit in the hiring process.

Regulating the Civil Service

In 1939, Congress passed the Act to Prevent Pernicious Political Activities, usually called the **Hatch Act** after its chief sponsor, Senator Carl Hatch of New Mexico. The act was designed to neutralize the danger of a federal civil service being able to shape, if not dictate, the election of presidents and members of Congress. In essence, the Hatch Act permitted federal employees to vote in government elections but not to take an active part in partisan politics. The Hatch Act also made it illegal to dismiss federal officials below cabinet and subcabinet rank for partisan reasons.[13]

In 1993, Congress, with the encouragement of the Clinton administration, overhauled the Hatch Act and made many forms of participation in partisan politics permissible. The revised Hatch Act still bars federal officials from running as candidates in partisan elections, but it does permit most federal civil servants to hold party positions and involve themselves in party fund raising and campaigning. This new law was welcomed by those who believed the old Hatch Act discouraged political participation by 3 million individuals who might otherwise be vigorous political activists.[14]

The new Hatch Act spells out many restrictions on federal bureaucrats; they cannot raise campaign funds in their agencies, and those who work in such highly sensitive federal agencies as the CIA, FBI, Secret Service, and certain divisions of the IRS are specifically barred from nearly all partisan activity. Those who work in the U.S. military have stricter rules regulating their political involvement. The rules for federal civilian employees specify that they

May register and vote as they choose

May assist in voter registration

May express opinions about candidates and issues

May participate in campaigns as off-duty activities

May contribute money to political organizations or attend political fund-raising functions

May wear or display political badges, buttons, or stickers

May attend political rallies and meetings

May join political clubs or parties

May seek and hold positions in political parties

May campaign for or against referendum questions, constitutional amendments, and municipal ordinances

May not be candidates for public office in partisan elections

May not use official authority to interfere with or affect the results of an election

May not collect contributions or sell tickets to political fund-raising functions from subordinate employees

May not solicit funds or discourage the political activity of any person who has business before the employee's office

May not solicit funds or discourage political activity by any person who is the subject of an ongoing audit, investigation, or enforcement action

The Role of Government Employee Unions

Since 1962, federal civilian employees have had the right to form unions or associations that represent them in seeking to improve government personnel policies, and about one-third of them have joined such unions. Some of the most important unions representing federal employees today are the American Federation of Government Employees, the National Treasury Employees Union, the National Association of Government Employees, and the National Federation of Federal Employees.

Hatch Act
Federal statute barring federal employees from active participation in certain kinds of politics and protecting them from being fired on partisan grounds.

Unlike unions in the private sector, federal employee unions lack the right to strike and are not able to bargain over pay and benefits. But they can attempt to negotiate better personnel policies and practices for federal workers, they can represent federal bureaucrats at grievance and disciplinary proceedings, and they can lobby Congress on measures affecting personnel changes. They can also vote in elections. This is why members of Congress from districts that have large numbers of federal workers often sit on the House and Senate civil service subcommittees.

These rules and regulations cannot ensure merit if talented Americans do not apply for federal jobs in the first place. Unfortunately, the federal government is viewed by many young Americans as an employer of last resort, partly because of lower wages paid by government, compared to the private sector. There is a pay gap of 25 to 30 percent between comparable federal and private jobs.[15] Moreover, unlike the private sector, the federal government provides few sizable financial rewards for good performance.

The Bureaucracy's Job

Whatever their size or specialty, all federal organizations share one job: to implement the laws. **Implementation** covers a broad range of bureaucratic activities, from writing checks at the Social Security Administration to inspecting job sites at the Occupational Health and Safety Administration, swearing in new citizens at the Immigration and Naturalization Service, or monitoring airline traffic at the Federal Aviation Administration. Some agencies implement the laws by spending money, others by raising revenues or by issuing rules that govern what private citizens and businesses do, and still others by collecting information or conducting research. Whatever tool government uses, implementation is the act of converting a law into action.

Because Congress and the president could never pass laws that are detailed enough to execute themselves, they give federal departments and agencies a certain amount of **administrative discretion** to implement the laws in the most efficient and effective manner possible. This freedom often varies from agency to agency, depending on both past performance and congressional politics. Political scientist Theodore Lowi believes that Congress often gives the federal bureaucracy vague directions because it is unable or unwilling to make the tough choices needed to resolve the conflicts that arise in the legislative process. Congress gets the credit for passing a law, while the federal bureaucracy gets the challenge of implementing an unclear law.[16]

Whether a law is clear or ambiguous, most agencies implement the law through two means: administrative *regulations,* which are formal instructions for either running an agency or for controlling the behavior of private citizens and organizations, or *spending,* which involves the transfer of money to and from government.

Making Regulations

Regulations, or rules, are designed to convert laws into action. They tell people what they can and cannot do, as well as what they must or must not do. It is an Agriculture Department rule that tells meat and poultry processors how to handle food, an Environmental Protection Agency rule that tells automobile makers how much gasoline mileage their cars must get, a Social Security Administration rule that tells Americans how long they must work before they are eligible for a federal retirement check, an Immigration and Naturalization Service rule that tells citizens of other nations how long they can stay on a student visa, and a Justice Department rule that tells states what they must do to ensure that every eligible citizen can vote. Although all these rules can be traced back to legislation, they provide the details that most laws leave out.

Rules are drafted and reviewed through a quasi-legislative **rule-making process** that is governed by the Administrative Procedure Act. Enacted in 1946 to make sure that all rules are made visible to the public, the act requires that all proposed rules be published

implementation
The process of putting a law into practice through bureaucratic rules or spending.

administrative discretion
Authority given by Congress to the federal bureaucracy to use reasonable judgment in implementing the laws.

regulations
The formal instructions that government issues for implementing laws.

rule-making process
The formal process for making regulations.

in the *Federal Register.* Publication in the federal government's newspaper marks the beginning of what is known as the "notice and comment" period in which all parties affected by the proposed regulation are encouraged to make their opinions known to the agency. Because rules have the force of law and can become the basis for legal challenges, the process can take years from start to finish and can involve thousand of pages of records. Some agencies even hold hearings and take testimony from witnesses in the effort to build a strong case for a particularly controversial rule.

The rule-making process does not end with final publication and enforcement. All rules are subject to the same judicial review that governs formal laws, thereby creating a check against potential abuse of power when agencies exceed their authority to faithfully execute the laws.

Spending Money

The federal bureaucracy also implements laws through spending, whether by writing checks to more than 35 million Social Security recipients a year, buying billions of dollars' worth of military equipment, or making grants to state governments and research universities. Viewed in relative terms as a percentage of gross domestic product (GDP), federal spending more than doubled over the past half-century but has recently begun to shrink in the wake of the end of the cold war in 1989. Viewed in constant dollars to adjust for inflation, however, federal spending continues to rise each year, driven in part by the cost of caring for a rapidly aging population.

Whether the federal budget is getting bigger or smaller depends on what measure one picks. Not surprisingly, conservatives often use constant dollars to argue for cuts, while liberals often use percentage of GDP to justify increases.

Most of this spending goes to what political scientists and budget experts call **uncontrollable spending**, defined as spending for (1) programs in which financial payments are required for all Americans who are eligible, such as Social Security for older Americans, college loans for poor students, or help for the victims of natural disasters such as floods and hurricanes (in these programs, everyone who is eligible and applies automatically gets the help), and (2) programs that require more federal spending each year automatically through cost-of-living increases or interest on the national debt.

Uncontrollable spending sharply limits the amount of the federal budget that is actually subject to debate in any given year (see Figure 14-3). Even funding for programs such as defense, which is technically subject to yearly control, may be almost impossible to cut without controversy, leaving even less room for reducing the budget.

The largest share of uncontrollable spending comes from Social Security and Medicare, which are guaranteed to any American who has paid taxes into the program for enough years. The aging of the American population means that more older people than ever will qualify for Social Security and Medicare, so uncontrollable spending will almost certainly rise over the next few decades.

A much smaller share of the uncontrollable budget involves welfare for the poor, which is linked to economic performance. More unemployment, for example, means more federal unemployment insurance; more poverty means more food stamps, job training, Temporary Assistance to Needy Families, and other income support programs. It is important to note, however, that welfare for the poor is not the only welfare in the federal budget. American businesses receive a substantial amount of welfare, too, including tax breaks for companies that manufacture prescription drugs in Puerto Rico, farmers who raise sugar cane in Florida, and mining companies that extract minerals from U.S. land.

What makes these uncontrollable programs similar is that they guarantee benefits to anyone eligible; hence these programs are often called **entitlements.** All told, these automatic programs cost the federal government more than $800 billion in 1999–2000, accounting for over half of the federal government's $1.8 trillion budget.

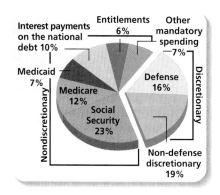

FIGURE 14–3   How the Federal Government Spends Its Money, 2003.

SOURCE: Office of Management and Budget, *Budget of the U.S. Government, Fiscal Year 2003, Historical Tables* (Government Printing Office, 2002).

uncontrollable spending
The portion of the federal budget that is spent on programs, such as Social Security, that the president and Congress are unwilling to cut.

entitlements
Programs such as unemployment insurance, disaster relief, or disability payments that provide benefits to all eligible citizens.

IN COMPARATIVE PERSPECTIVE

Comparing the Size of Governments

There are two ways to compare the size of government work forces around the world. The first is to compare the total number of government employees as a percentage of the entire work force; the second is to compare the total amount of money spent on government salaries as a percentage of gross domestic product (GDP). The Scandinavian nations of Denmark, Norway, and Sweden have long been the world's biggest government employers in relative terms, mainly because they offer such extensive government services. In contrast, most Asian nations, including Japan, South Korea, and Hong Kong, are among the world's smallest employers, again mainly because they have such low levels of government activity.

The problem with using these two measures is that many governments use contracts and grants to private companies and nonprofit agencies to purchase goods and services on behalf of government. Although the employees who deliver those goods and services are not technically government employees, they can be considered part of the shadow of government. In the United States, for example, the true size of the federal work force is roughly 13 million people, including contractors, grantees, and state and local government employees who implement mandates on behalf of the federal government, moving government employment closer to 20 percent of the economy.

Even though the U.S. government is relatively small when measured against other nations, Americans are more likely to view government as wasteful and inefficient. According to a six-nation survey conducted in 1997, 64 percent of Americans agreed that anything run by government is likely to be wasteful and inefficient, compared to 52 percent of the British, 51 percent of Germans, and just 40 percent of the Spanish. Only the French and Italians were as harshly critical.

Relative Size of Civil Service Employment and Overall Public Sector Compensation

Nation	National Government Employment as a Percentage of Total Employment	National Government Salaries as a Percentage of Gross Domestic Product
Australia	15%	8%
Canada	19	19
France	25	13
Spain	15	12
Sweden	31	16
United Kingdom	14	11
United States	13	8

SOURCE: Organization of Economic Cooperation and Development, 2000, at www.oecd.org/publications/figures/e_36-37_public_sector.pdf. Data are for 1996–1997.

The uncontrollable budget is not growing just because more people are eligible for entitlements, however. Many of these entitlements are subject to **indexing**—that is, they grow automatically with inflation, regardless of how the economy is doing. Indexing affects a growing list of federal programs, again leaving Congress and the president little control over year-to-year increases. The number of programs indexed to automatic cost-of-living adjustments (COLAs) grew from 17 in 1966 to almost 100 by 2000.[17]

Holding the Bureaucracy Accountable

Every president enters office promising to make the federal bureaucracy work better. Indeed, Jimmy Carter, Ronald Reagan, Bill Clinton, and George W. Bush all made bureaucratic reform a central part of their presidential campaigns. Carter promised to create a government as good as the American people, Reagan promised to reduce waste in government, Clinton and Vice President Al Gore promised to reinvent government, and Bush promised to make government more friendly to citizens.

Yet presidents leave office frustrated by their lack of success. As political scientist James Q. Wilson noted, "Presidents see much of the bureaucracy as their natural enemy and always are searching for ways to bring it to heel."[18] And presidents are not the only ones who want to control the bureaucracy. Congress, too, clearly worries about making bureaucracy work better. Together, both complain that the federal bureaucracy can be more accountable to interest groups and itself than either branch.

indexing
Providing automatic increases to compensate for inflation.

PEOPLE IN POLITICS

JAMES LEE WITT

James Lee Witt faced a tough choice on his first day as President Clinton's new administrator of the Federal Emergency Management Agency (FEMA) in 1993. As the head of the federal government's primary organization for helping Americans cope with disasters, his agency was on the verge of collapse. One senator characterized FEMA as "the sorriest bunch of bureaucratic fools I've ever known"; another described its response to the devastation of Hurricane Andrew in August 1992 as "pathetically sluggish"; still another had introduced legislation to abolish the agency.

The agency had been created in 1979 to bring some sense to the federal government's emergency relief efforts, which were spread across a half dozen other departments and agencies. With the power to draw on nearly 6,500 full-time, temporary, and reserve employees and with roughly $4 billion to provide in loans and disaster relief, FEMA was designed to serve as a single point of contact for victims of everything from tornadoes to droughts, blizzards, earthquakes, and hurricanes.

Unfortunately, FEMA was known more for its red tape than for its speed. Witt began rebuilding the agency by creating three primary divisions under his direct control: one that would be in charge of all response and recovery efforts, a second that would work with high-risk areas to reduce the damage from future disasters, and a third that would prepare communities to provide immediate assistance in the first hours after a disaster strikes.

The reorganization did more than focus the agency on reducing the loss of life and property. It also reduced the number of administrative layers between the top of the agency and its bottom, while giving its employees greater authority to make the quick judgments to help disaster victims without fear of second guessing by middle-level managers. Furthermore, Witt communicated the message that every employee had a role in the agency's mission.

Witt also changed the basic orientation of the agency to put the emphasis on getting help to victims fast and demanded that FEMA's performance be measured first by speed of action and second by citizen satisfaction. FEMA became faster and more responsive as a result. By 1999, disaster victims were getting their relief checks just eight days after filing their applications, down from an average of 20 days in 1992, and nine out of ten disaster aid recipients gave the agency favorable marks.

Witt also launched a new effort to reduce the costs of disasters by relocating homes, even entire communities, from flood plains; designing earthquake-resistant homes and buildings; and making citizens who insist on staying in harm's way absorb a greater share of the disaster costs.

Although Witt was gone from FEMA by 2001, his agency was one of the first on the scene following the World Trade Center tragedy on September 11. The agency moved quickly to help victims of the disaster secure loans and relief and become the hub of the federal rescue effort. Having been known for its mediocre staff in the early 1990s, FEMA had within a decade become the "gold standard" for responsiveness.

Director of FEMA, James Lee Witt, in Moore, Oklahoma after a tornado ripped through the town.

Why Presidents Like to Reorganize the Bureaucracy

- To shake up an organization to increase managerial control
- To simplify or streamline the bureaucracy or a specific agency
- To reduce costs by lessening overlap, duplication, and waste
- To give a higher priority to an existing issue
- To improve program effectiveness by bringing similar programs together
- To improve policy integration by placing competitive or conflicting interests within a single organization
- To downgrade the importance of a program to weaken it
- To increase power over an unresponsive agency by creating more control through presidential appointees

Accountability to the President

Modern presidents invariably contend that the president should be in charge, for the chief executive is responsive to the broadest constituency. A president, it is argued, must see that popular needs and expectations are converted into administrative action. When the nation elects a conservative president who favors cutbacks in federal programs and less governmental intervention in the economy, his policies must be carried out by the bureaucracy. The voters' wishes can be translated into action only if the bureaucrats support presidential policies.

Yet under the American system of checks and balances, the party winning a presidential election does not acquire total control of the national government. Under our Constitution, the president is not even the undisputed master of the executive structure. Presidents come into an ongoing system over which they have little control and within which they have little leeway to make the bureaucracy responsive.

Still, the president has some control over the bureaucracy through the powers of appointment, reorganization, and budgeting. More specifically, a president can attempt to control the bureaucracy by appointing or promoting sympathetic personnel, mobilizing public opinion and congressional pressure, changing the administrative apparatus, influencing budget decisions, using extensive personal persuasion, and if all else fails, shifting a bureaucracy's assignment to another department or agency (although such a shift requires tacit if not explicit congressional approval).[19]

Presidents appoint about 4,000 people to top positions within the executive branch; however, many of these are confidential assistants or special aides to cabinet officers who require Senate confirmation and are not exclusively a president's choice. Some critics suggest that a president's hand could be strengthened if the chief executive were able to make two or three times as many political appointments, while others argue that the large number of appointees, and the cumbersome appointments process that goes with it, weakens the president's ability to control the front lines of government.

Accountability to Congress

Congress has a number of ways to exercise control over the bureaucracy, whether by establishing agencies, formulating budgets, appropriating funds, confirming personnel, authorizing new programs or new shifts in direction, conducting investigations and hearings, or even terminating agencies.

Much of this authority is used to help constituents as they battle federal red tape. Members of Congress earn political credit by interceding in federal agencies on behalf of their constituents. Still, Congress deserves at least some of the blame for having created the red tape in the first place, whether by enacting pet programs, refusing to give federal agencies greater flexibility, delaying presidential appointments, or placing limits on bureaucratic discretion to protect some constituents but not others. Moreover, by demanding special attention for their constituents, members of Congress may undermine the fairness of the entire process. Like cutting into line at a movie theater, they slow the progress for everyone but the special few who get their attention.

The brutal fact is that only a small minority of our 535 members of Congress would trade the present bureaucratic structure for one that was an efficient, effective agent of the general interest—the political payoffs of the latter are lower than those of the former. Congressional talk of inefficient, irresponsible, out-of-control bureaucracy is typically just that—talk—and when it is not, it usually refers to agencies under the jurisdiction of other legislators' committees. Congress can abolish or reorganize an agency. Congress can limit or expand an agency's jurisdiction or allow its authority to lapse entirely. Congress can slash an agency's appropriations. Congress can investigate. Congress can do all these things, but individual members of Congress generally find reasons not to do so.[20]

It is not Congress as a whole that shares direction over the bureaucracy with the president. More accurately, individual members and committees specialize in the appropriations and oversight processes. They oversee policies of a particular cluster of agencies—often the agencies serving constituents in their own districts. Some legislators stake out a claim over specific areas. Members of Congress, who see presidents come and go, come to think they know more about particular agencies than the president does (and often they do). Some congressional leaders prefer to seal off "their" agencies from presidential direction and maintain their influence over public policy. Sometimes their power is institutionalized; the Army Corps of Engineers, for example, is given authority by law to plan public works and report to Congress without going through the president.

Accountability Through Oversight

Congress and the president spend a great deal of energy monitoring the federal bureaucracy. The hope is that **oversight**, the process of monitoring day-to-day activities, will somehow encourage agencies to perform better or at least deter them from worse performance.

Presidents have a number of tools for keeping a watchful eye. They can put loyal appointees, such as Attorney General John Ashcroft, into the top jobs at key agencies; they can direct White House aides, such as homeland security chief Tom Ridge or Vice President Dick Cheney, to oversee the work of certain agencies; and they can always call cabinet meetings to learn more about what is happening in the bureaucracy.

However, presidents tend to use the Office of Management and Budget for most routine oversight. Departments and agencies must get the president's approval before testifying before Congress on pending legislation, making legislative proposals, or answering congressional inquiries about their activities. Under this **central clearance** system, OMB forwards communications to Congress in three categories: "in accordance" with the president's program (reserved for the president's top priorities), "consistent with" the president's program (indicating the president's second-tier priorities), or "no objection." If the president objects to any communication, OMB simply does not forward the legislation to Congress. OMB also conducts oversight on all federal departments and agencies as it assembles the president's budget plan.

Congress also has a number of tools for overseeing the federal bureaucracy, not the least of which consists of the individual members of Congress themselves, who are free to ask agencies for detailed information on just about any issue. However, most members and committees tend to use the General Accounting Office or the Congressional Budget Office (both discussed in Chapter 11) to conduct a study or investigation of a particular program.

Congress uses these and other sources of information as a basis for committee and subcommittee hearings on specific agencies or programs. Today, Congress holds more oversight hearings than ever before. In the 1960s, for example, both chambers held a total of 157 days of oversight hearings per two-year Congress; by the early 1980s, the number had more than tripled, to 587 days. The greatest increase occurred in the 1970s, fueled in part by the increasing number of legislative committees and subcommittees. More committees and more staff meant more time and energy to hold oversight hearings.[21]

Together, Congress and the president conduct two basic types of oversight. One is what can be called "police patrol" oversight, in which the two branches watch the bureaucracy through a routine pattern. They read key reports, watch the budget, and generally pay attention to how the departments and agencies are running. If they happen to see a "crime" in progress, all the better. But the general goal of the patrol is to deter problems before they arise. The other can be called "fire alarm" oversight, in which the two branches wait for citizens, interest groups, or the press to find a major problem and pull the alarm. The media play a particularly important role in such oversight, often uncovering a scandal before a routine "police patrol" can spot it.[22]

The Problem of Self-Regulation

Career administrators are in a good position to know when a program is not operating properly and what action is needed. But many Americans believe that federal employees, whether selected on merit or not, fail to make things better. The problem is that many bureaucrats often learn by hard experience that they are more likely to get into trouble by

Cabinet members, such as Attorney General John Ashcroft, often have to answer questions Congress has regarding the bureaucratic and financial needs of their particular department.

oversight
Legislative or executive review of a particular government program or organization. Can be in response to a crisis of some kind or part of routine review.

central clearance
Review of all executive branch testimony, reports, and draft legislation by the Office of Management and Budget to assure that each communication to Congress is in accordance with the president's program.

"Think of it. Presidents come and go, but WE go on forever!"

Berry's World. Reproduced by permission of Newspaper Enterprise Association, Inc.

attempting to improve or change programs than if they just do nothing. Hardening of administrative arteries is more likely, some critics say, than administrative aggressiveness.

Often the fiercest battles in Washington are not over principles or programs but over jurisdictional boundaries, personnel cuts, and fringe benefits. Career employees come to believe that the expansion of their organization is vital to the public interest. They sometimes become more skillful at building political alliances to protect their own organization than at building political alliances to ensure their programs' effectiveness.

Career administrators usually try hard to be nonpartisan, yet they are inevitably involved in politics. Some of them have more bargaining and alliance-building skills than the elected and appointed officials to whom they report. In one sense, agency leaders are at the center of action in Washington. Over time, administrative agencies may come to resemble entrenched pressure groups in that they operate to advance their own interests. The FBI is a good example; it is always seeking more funds, new projects, and as much independence as possible from the Justice Department in which it is located.

The growth of federal programs from the 1930s through the 1970s brought an increase in the number of policy aides on Capitol Hill, of Washington law firms that specialize in assisting clients who are interested in policy development, and of lobbyists (some say at least 40,000) who work with Congress and the federal bureaucracy to advance various economic and professional interests.

Special-interest groups that perceive real or potential harm to their interests cultivate the bureau chiefs and agency staffs who have jurisdiction over their programs. They also work closely with the committees and subcommittees of Congress that authorize, appropriate, and oversee programs run by these key bureaucracies. Recognizing the power of interest groups, bureau chiefs frequently recruit them as allies in pursuing common goals. What these bureau officials have in common with interest groups and their allies in Congress is a shared view that more money should be spent on federal programs run by the bureau in question. These alliances among bureaucrats, interest groups, and subcommittee members and their staffs on Capitol Hill are sometimes described as *iron triangles,* a topic discussed in Chapter 6.

The executive branch is not necessarily the smooth-operating hierarchy it is made to appear on an organization chart. The president, cabinet members, and their politically appointed undersecretaries and assistant secretaries have their work cut out for them as they try to impose their will on the permanent civil service. Bureaucrats, with their strong allies in Congress and the interest groups, often resist change and direction from their appointed or elected political "superiors."[23]

Despite these and other flaws, Americans still get substantial value from the federal bureaucracy. They may complain about the red tape and all the bureaucrats in Washington, but the federal bureaucracy continues to make progress in solving some of the most difficult problems of modern governance. A devastated Europe was rebuilt after World War II and now stands as a major economic competitor to the United States; veterans of World War II, Korea, Vietnam, and the Gulf War were able to get back to their ordinary lives through the G.I. Bill; and the United States landed a man on the moon and brought him safely back to earth and repeated the feat five times before the Apollo program ended in 1972. The list of objective success goes on and on:

- Poverty among older Americans has fallen to modern lows.
- The United States won the cold war.
- African American voting rates have increased with each passing election.
- Air and water quality have improved.
- The interstate highway system was built and is still expanding.
- More women are graduating from college and professional school, and more are competing in college sports.
- Food and drugs have become safer, and the drug approval process has become faster.

- More poor children are getting a head start in preschool.
- The air traffic control system is handling record amounts of traffic.
- More pregnant women are receiving proper medical care.
- Home ownership rates have risen to their highest levels ever.
- Americans are living longer.
- Polio and tuberculosis have been virtually eliminated.
- The Internet (originally developed by the Defense Department) has revolutionized communications.
- Poor children have greater access to health care.
- Welfare rates have fallen.
- Crime rates have fallen.
- More Americans are completing high school and attending college.

SHOULD THERE BE RANDOM DRUG TESTS OF FEDERAL WORKERS?

You Decide... Recent statistics indicated that roughly 14 million Americans use illegal drugs, including 10 million who use marijuana and over 6 million who have tried ecstasy. This drug use costs the nation tens of billions in heath costs, lost productivity, criminal justice expenses, and neighborhood decay. Drug use by federal employees can be particularly damaging, whether they are air traffic controllers, intelligence analysts, health researchers, or passenger and baggage screeners. And it can cause the same sort of lost productivity in agencies such as the Social Security Administration, the Internal Revenue Service, or NASA. Do the consequences of illegal drug use justify random, unannounced drug tests for civil servants?

Thinking It Through... Unannounced drug testing raises serious Fourth Amendment questions. The idea that a group of people should be subjected to random searches without reasonable individual cause has been resisted since the outset of our life as a nation. When Congress, the president, or the head of a federal agency requires testing as a condition of employment, even if evidence of drug use would not be used to dismiss employees, skeptical judges must be persuaded that the testing is not an "unreasonable search and seizure."

The Supreme Court ruled in two 1989 decisions involving railway workers and U.S. Customs Service employees that mandatory blood and urine tests may be required for certain workers without a showing of "individualized suspicion." The cases dealt with postaccident testing of railway personnel on duty at the time of a major accident and with customs officials who carry firearms, handle classified information, or intercept drugs. Writing for the Court in the railway workers' case, Justice Anthony Kennedy said the government's interest in testing even without a showing of individual suspicion is compelling. Employees subject to the tests discharge duties fraught with such risks of injury to others that even a momentary lapse of attention can have disastrous results.

Drug testing of all federal employees, or even only those in policy-making positions, presents difficult constitutional issues. Supporters of privacy rights and civil liberties are uncomfortable with carrying this policy too far. Drug testing, some concede, may be necessary for certain individuals if public safety is genuinely involved, but it is not needed and would be an unconstitutional deprivation of privacy rights under the Fourth Amendment as a general policy.

Among its proposed reforms of the bureaucracy, Congress wanted to end support of public broadcasting, claiming that programs like Sesame Street could support themselves on commercial television. The public, however, disagreed, and Big Bird, the Grouch, and other childhood favorites still receive government subsidies.

Not every federal endeavor has produced success. Too many American children still go to bed hungry, too many people are still homeless, too many workers are unable to make ends meet with minimum-wage jobs, and too many citizens have too little access to health care. But if the mark of a great society is what it asks its government to achieve, Americans can be proud of the federal bureaucracy today.

BUREAUCRACY: A PLACE WHERE IDEALS MEET REALITY

The more senior the position in government, the more difficult the policy choices. In this simulation, the assistant director of the Census Bureau must make a series of choices regarding the future of the agency. Each memo produces consequences and feedback, sometimes positive, other times negative.

Go to PoliSim "Bureaucracy: A Place Where Ideals Meet Reality."

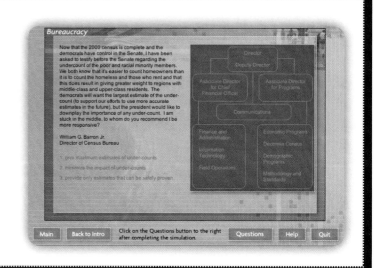

Summary

1. The chief characteristics of bureaucracy are continuity, predictability, impartiality, standard operating procedures, and "red tape." Our bureaucratic agencies reflect the ways in which our political system attempts to identify our most important national goals and how policies are implemented.

2. Most of the 2.7 million civilian employees of the federal government serve under a merit system that protects their independence of politics. They work in one of the 15 cabinet departments or else in any of innumerable government corporations, independent agencies, and independent regulatory boards or commissions.

3. The federal government's Office of Personnel Management sets policy for recruiting and evaluating federal workers. Various restrictions on federal workers prevent them from running for political office or engaging in political fund-raising activities. The federal bureaucracy generally prizes continuity, stability, and following the rules more than risk taking or innovation.

4. The bureaucracy generally uses regulations or spending to implement the laws. The rule-making process is governed by the Administration Procedure Act, while the spending process is governed by the federal budget. Most of the federal budget is uncontrollable, whether because of indexing to inflation or because Congress and the president are unwilling to cut highly popular programs such as Social Security.

5. The American bureaucracy has at least two immediate bosses: Congress and the president. It must pay considerable attention as well to the courts and their rulings and to well-organized interest groups and public opinion. In many ways, the bureaucracy is a semi-independent force—a fourth branch of government—in American politics.

6. Debates and controversy over big government and big bureaucracy and over how to reorganize and eliminate waste in them are never-ending. Compared with many other nations and their centralized bureaucracies, the hand of bureaucracy rests more gently and less oppressively on Americans than on citizens elsewhere.

Key Terms

bureaucrat
bureaucracy
department
independent regulatory
    commission
independent agency

government corporation
Senior Executive Service
spoils system
merit system
Office of Personnel Management
    (OPM)

Hatch Act
implementation
administrative discretion
regulations
rule-making process
uncontrollable spending

entitlements
indexing
oversight
central clearance

Further Reading

JOEL D. ABERBACH, *Keeping a Watchful Eye: The Politics of Congressional Oversight* (Brookings Institution, 1990).

DAN BAUM, *Smoke and Mirrors: The War on Drugs and the Politics of Failure* (Little, Brown, 1996).

ROBERT D. BEHN, *Rethinking Democratic Accountability* (Brookings Institution, 2001).

BARRY BOZEMAN, *Bureaucracy and Red Tape* (Prentice Hall, 2000).

SHELLEY L. DAVIS, *Unbridled Power: Inside the Secret Culture of the IRS* (HarperBusiness, 1997).

JOHN J. DI IULIO JR., ED., *Deregulating the Public Service: Can Government Be Improved?* (Brookings Institution, 1994).

JAMES W. FESLER AND DONALD F. KETTL, *The Politics of the Administrative Process* (Chatham House, 1991).

JANE E. FOUNTAIN, *Building the Virtual State: Information Technology and Institutional Change* (Brookings Institution, 2001).

CHARLES T. GOODSELL, *The Case for Bureaucracy*, 3d ed. (Chatham House, 1994).

AL GORE, *The Best Kept Secrets in Government: How the Clinton Administration Is Reinventing the Way Washington Works* (Random House, 1996).

AL GORE, *Creating a Government That Works Better and Costs Less: The Report of the National Performance Review* (Plume-Penguin, 1993).

PHILIP K. HOWARD, *The Death of Common Sense: How Law Is Suffocating America* (Random House, 1994).

RONALD N. JOHNSON AND GARY D. LIBECAP, *The Federal Civil Service System and the Problem of Bureaucracy* (University of Chicago Press, 1994).

HERBERT KAUFMAN, *The Administrative Behavior of Federal Bureau Chiefs* (Brookings Institution, 1981).

DONALD F. KETTL, *The Global Public Management Revolution* (Brookings Institution, 2001).

DONALD F. KETTL, *Reinventing Government: A Fifth-Year Report Card* (Brookings Institution, 1998).

ANDREW KOHUT, ED., *Deconstructing Distrust: How Americans View Government* (Pew Research Center for the People and the Press, 1998).

PAUL C. LIGHT, *The New Public Service* (Brookings Institution, 1999).

PAUL C. LIGHT, *Thickening Government: Federal Hierarchy and the Diffusion of Accountability* (Brookings Institution, 1995).

PAUL C. LIGHT, *The Tides of Reform: Making Government Work, 1945–1995* (Yale University Press, 1997).

AREND LIJPHART, *Patterns of Democracy: Government Forms and Performance in Thirty-Six Countries* (Yale University Press, 1999).

DAVID OSBORNE AND TED GAEBLER, *Reinventing Government: How the Entrepreneurial Spirit Is Transforming the Public Sector* (Addison-Wesley, 1992).

DAVID OSBORNE AND PETER PLASTRIK, *Banishing Bureaucracy: The Five Strategies for Reinventing Government* (Addison-Wesley, 1997).

JAMES Q. WILSON, *Bureaucracy: What Government Agencies Do and Why They Do It* (Basic Books, 1989).

Four useful journals are the *Journal of Policy Analysis and Management,* the *National Journal, Public Administration Review,* and *Government Executive.*

15
CHAPTER

THE JUDICIARY
The Balancing Branch

OREIGN VISITORS ARE OFTEN AMAZED AT THE POWER OF AMERICAN JUDGES. IN 1834, AFTER HIS VISIT TO THE UNITED STATES, FRENCH aristocrat Alexis de Tocqueville wrote: "If I were asked where I place the American aristocracy, I should reply without hesitation . . . that it occupies the judicial bench and bar. . . . Scarcely any political question arises in the United States that is not resolved, sooner or later, into a judicial question."[1] A century later, British political scientist Harold J. Laski observed, "The respect in which federal courts and, above all, the Supreme Court are held is hardly surpassed by the influence they exert on the life of the United States."[2] In recent decades, national courts in Europe and elsewhere have likewise asserted their power, and there is an emerging trend toward the "globalization of judicial power."[3]

Why do judges play such a central role in our political life? As discussed in Chapter 2, Chief Justice John Marshall in 1803 successfully claimed for judges the power of **judicial review**, that is, the power to authoritatively interpret the Constitution. Only a constitutional amendment or a later Supreme Court can modify the Court's doctrine. Justice Felix Frankfurter suggested tersely: "The Supreme Court is the Constitution."

Judges—and not just those on the Supreme Court—are also asked to resolve disputes involving billions of dollars, decide conflicts among competing interest groups, supervise the criminal justice system, and make rules affecting the lives of millions of people. They not only settle legal conflicts but in some cases have overseen the operation of schools, prisons, mental hospitals, and complex businesses. Sometimes they decide the details of how these institutions should be run. Still, the scope and nature of judicial power limit the role of judges.

The Scope of Judicial Power

The American judicial process rests on an **adversary system**. A court of law is a neutral arena in which two parties argue their differences and present their points of view before an impartial arbiter. The adversary system is based on the *fight theory,* which holds that arguing over law and evidence, which may or may not arrive at the truth, guarantees fairness in the judicial system.[4] The adversary system thus imposes restraints on the exercise and scope of judicial power.

Judicial power is essentially *passive* and *reactive.* Judges cannot instigate a case. Moreover, not all disputes are within the scope of judicial power. Judges decide only **justiciable disputes**—lawsuits that grow out of actual controversies and are capable of judicial resolution. Judges do not use their power unless there is a real case or controversy. It is not enough for a judge merely to have a general interest in a subject or to believe that a law is unconstitutional.

The party bringing a lawsuit (the *plaintiff*) must have *standing to sue;* this means that the plaintiff must have sustained or be in immediate danger of sustaining a direct and personal injury. Plaintiffs may not raise hypothetical issues; they must have a real dispute and opposing interests with another party. Traditionally, individuals had to show an actual monetary damage in order to gain standing to sue. But in recent decades, the Supreme Court has granted standing to individuals who claim nonmonetary injuries that are shared by others. In a classic statement, the Court observed, "Aesthetic and environmental well-being, like economic well-being, are important ingredients of the quality of life in our society, and the fact that particular environmental interests are shared by the many rather than the few does not make them less deserving of legal protection through the judicial process."[5] Individuals still must claim a personal injury—the violation of a constitutional or other legal right—and show a "personal stake in the outcome." But they may now bring suits over environmental damages, defective consumer products, and other matters that affect interest groups and large numbers of people.[6]

A related and increasingly important development is the use of **class action suits**, in which a small number of persons represent all other people similarly situated—a suit on behalf of all students in a university, for example, or all persons who smoke a particular brand of cigarettes. "Would-be class action litigants must show that they are proper representatives for the class of persons they seek to champion [and] that the types of issues they wish to raise are common to the class, and they must be able to demonstrate how a remedy can be formed that will meet the needs of the class."[7] These lawsuits may force major changes in public policy—governing, for example, the operation of prisons—and business practices, such as the marketing of defective or harmful products. In recent years, tobacco companies, drug manufacturers, and financial institutions have confronted a series of class action lawsuits and been ordered to pay damages.

When individuals sue each other over a traffic accident, for instance, they file suits under *civil law* and seek monetary awards for the injuries they suffered or the damages to their property. The government may also bring civil lawsuits against individuals and business. But only the government may prosecute individual crimes, such as carjacking and robbery, as defined in state and federal *criminal law.* As discussed further in Chapter 17, persons accused of crimes are guaranteed certain rights in the Bill of Rights and must be accorded the due process of law, but if convicted, they face imprisonment, and for murder, they may be sentenced to death.

Judges decide cases; they do not prosecute persons for allegedly committing crimes. *Prosecutors* decide whether to charge an offense and which offense to charge. They have largely unreviewable discretion, so long as they have probable cause to believe that the accused has committed an offense.[8] Prosecutors negotiate with the lawyers for **defendants** (those accused of an offense) and often work out a **plea bargain**, whereby defendants agree to plead guilty to a lesser offense to avoid having to stand trial and face a sentence for a more serious offense. Prosecutors also make recommendations to judges about what sentences to impose.

judicial review

The power of a court to refuse to enforce a law or government regulation that in the opinion of the judges conflicts with the U.S. Constitution or, in a state court, the state constitution.

adversary system

A judicial system in which the court of law is a neutral arena where two parties argue their differences.

justiciable dispute

A dispute growing out of an actual case or controversy and that is capable of settlement by legal methods.

class action suit

Lawsuit brought by an individual or a group of people on behalf of all those similarly situated.

defendant

In a criminal action, the person or party accused of an offense.

plea bargain

Agreement between a prosecutor and a defendant that the defendant will plead guilty to a lesser offense to avoid having to stand trial for a more serious offense.

Types of Laws

Statutory Law

Law that comes from authoritative and specific lawmaking sources, primarily legislatures but also including treaties and executive orders.

Common Law

Judge-made law that originated in England in the twelfth century, when royal judges traveled around the country settling disputes in each locality according to prevailing custom. The common law continues to develop according to the rule of *stare decisis,* which means "let the decision stand." This is the rule of precedent, which implies that a rule established by a court is to be followed in all similar cases.

Equity Law

Law used whenever common law remedies are inadequate. For example, if an injury done to property may do irreparable harm for which money damages cannot provide compensation, under equity a person may ask the judge to issue an injunction ordering the offending person not to take the threatened action. If the wrongdoer persists, he or she may be punished for contempt of court.

Constitutional Law

Statements interpreting the U.S. Constitution that have been given Supreme Court approval.

Admiralty and Maritime Law

Law applicable to cases concerning shipping and waterway commerce on the high seas and on the navigable waters of the United States.

Administrative Law

Law relating to the authority and procedures of administrative agencies as well as to the rules and regulations issued by those agencies.

Criminal Law

Law that defines crimes against the public order and provides for punishment. Government is responsible for enforcing criminal law, the great body of which is enacted by states and enforced by state officials in state courts. The criminal caseload of federal judges is growing.

Civil Law

Law that governs the relations between individuals and defines their legal rights. However, the government can also be a party to a civil action. Under the Sherman Antitrust Act, for example, the federal government may initiate civil as well as criminal action to prevent violations of the law.

On the federal level, the job of prosecution falls to the Department of Justice: the attorney general, the solicitor general, the 94 U.S. attorneys, and some 1,200 assistant attorneys. The president, with the consent of the Senate, appoints a U.S. attorney for each district court. U.S. attorneys serve four-year terms but may be dismissed by the president at any time. These appointments are of great interest to senators, who exercise significant influence over the selection process. Because U.S. attorneys are almost always members of the president's political party, it is customary for them to resign if the opposition party wins the White House.

The attorney general, in consultation with the U.S. attorney in each district, appoints assistant attorneys. Some districts have only one; the largest, the Southern District of New York, has more than 65. These attorneys, working with the U.S. attorney and assisted by the Federal Bureau of Investigation and other federal law enforcement agencies, begin proceedings against those alleged to have broken federal laws. They also represent the United States in civil suits.

Jurisdiction of the Federal Courts

Federal courts can hear and decide cases or controversies in law and equity in the following circumstances:

- If they arise under the Constitution, a federal law, or a treaty

- If they arise under admiralty and maritime laws

- If they arise because of a dispute involving land claimed under titles granted by two or more states

- If the United States is a party to the case

- If a state is a party to the case (but not if a suit was begun or prosecuted against a state by an individual or a foreign nation)

- If they are between citizens of different states (Congress has chosen to limit this *diversity jurisdiction* of federal courts, as it is called, to cases in which the amount in controversy exceeds $50,000)

- If they affect the accredited representatives of a foreign nation

public defender system
Arrangement whereby public officials are hired to provide legal assistance to people accused of crimes who are unable to hire their own attorneys.

political question
A dispute that requires knowledge of a nonlegal character or the use of techniques not suitable for a court or explicitly assigned by the Constitution to Congress or the president; judges refuse to answer constitutional questions that they declare are political.

writ of habeas corpus
A court order requiring explanation to a judge why a prisoner is being held in custody.

The state and federal governments provide lawyers for poor defendants in criminal trials. Traditionally, private attorneys have been appointed to provide assistance, but many state and federal courts employ a **public defender system**. Salaried public defenders operate in the federal courts under the general supervision of the Administrative Office of the United States Courts. The Judicial Conference of the United States, consisting of circuit and district court judges from around the country, has said that the most important problem confronting the public defender program is lack of money. The Legal Services Corporation also provides financial assistance to 323 organizations that furnish legal help to the poor in noncriminal legal matters.

Courts cannot resolve all disputes. Some raise **political questions** that would require the use of methods not suitable for a court, for which there is no legal remedy, or which the Constitution explicitly assigns to Congress or the president to decide. Such is the case with many questions arising from the conduct of foreign affairs. Which of two competing state governments is the proper one? Which group of officials of a state or foreign nation should the United States recognize as the government?[9] When the president sends the military into international conflicts without congressional authorization, has the constitutional provision that only Congress may "declare war" been violated? These are political questions.

The political question doctrine is admittedly circular, and the Supreme Court ultimately decides what is and is not a "political question." In 2000, for instance, most observers thought that the Supreme Court would refuse to allow itself or the federal courts to become involved in deciding which votes from Florida should be counted in the presidential election. There is hardly anything more political than this, and the Constitution specifically charges Congress with the responsibility for counting electoral votes. Nonetheless, the Supreme Court accepted the case in *Bush* v. *Gore*, deliberated promptly, and by a bare 5-to-4 majority stopped the recount of votes; the four dissenters contended that the matter should have been left to the political branches to decide.[10] In short, as political scientist John Roche observed, "Political questions are matters not soluble by the judicial process; matters not soluble by the judicial process are political questions. As an early dictionary explained, 'violins are small cellos, and cellos are large violins.'"[11]

Judicial Federalism: State and Federal Courts

Most countries have a single, unitary judiciary, but the United States has a dual judicial system of federal and state courts. Alongside the federal judiciary, each state maintains a judiciary of its own, and many large municipalities have judicial systems as complex as those of the states. Within both federal and state systems, judicial power is further divided between trial courts (and other lesser courts such as traffic courts) and one or more levels of appellate courts, which hear appeals from the lower courts.

The federal and state court systems are related, but not in a superior-inferior hierarchy. State courts primarily interpret and apply their state constitutions and law. When their decisions are based solely on state law, their rulings may not be appealed to or reviewed by federal courts. Only decisions that raise a federal question, involving the application of the Bill of Rights or other federal law, are federal courts able to review. Federal courts have **writ of habeas corpus** jurisdiction (the power to release persons from custody if a judge determines that they are not being detained constitutionally) and may review criminal convictions in state courts for violations of the federal constitutional and legal rights of the accused. Except for habeas corpus jurisdiction, the Supreme Court is the only federal court that may review state court decisions, and only in cases involving a conflict with federal law. Other than the original jurisdiction the Constitution vests directly in the Supreme Court, no federal court has any jurisdiction except that granted to it by an act of Congress. Congress also determines whether the judicial power of the United States is exercised exclusively by federal courts or concurrently by both federal and state courts.

Most litigation occurs in state courts, which annually face tens of millions of civil and criminal cases. The type of litigation in state courts also tends to differ from that in federal courts. Apart from criminal cases, the largest portion of state court cases involves economic issues—state regulation of public utilities, zoning and small business, labor relations, natural

Types of Courts

Examples of Special Article III (Constitutional) Courts

In addition to courts of general jurisdiction, Congress has created constitutional courts with special jurisdiction.

United States Court of International Trade (formerly U.S. Customs Court)

Consists of nine judges who review rulings of customs collectors and conflicts arising under various tariff and trade laws.

Foreign Intelligence Surveillance Court

Composed of seven district court judges appointed by the chief justice. They serve on a regular rotation and meet in secret to hear requests from the Department of Justice acting on behalf of the National Security Agency, the Federal Bureau of Investigation, and other intelligence agencies that engage in electronic surveillance and physical searches of the homes and offices of foreign agents.

Examples of Article I (Legislative) Courts

United States Court of Claims

Consists of 16 judges appointed for 15-year terms who have jurisdiction over all property and contract damage suits against the United States.

United States Court of Appeals for the Armed Forces

Consists of five civilian judges appointed for 15 years each by the president with the consent of the Senate. This court, created by Congress under its grant of authority to make the rules and regulations for "land and naval forces," applies military law, which is separate from the body of law that governs the rest of the federal court system.

Bankruptcy Judges

Almost 300 judges appointed by the courts of appeals to serve as adjuncts to the federal district courts for terms of 14 years each. These judges handle bankruptcy matters subject to review by federal district judges.

United States Court of Veteran Appeals

Consists of two to six judges who hear appeals from certain administrative decisions of the Veterans' Administration.

resources, energy, and the environment. Litigation varies from state to state as well, depending on the size of the population, urbanization, and the economy.[12] (For more information on state courts and links to state court Web sites, go to the site of the National Council of State Courts at www.ncsconline.org.)

The Federal Judicial System

"The judicial Power of the United States," says Article III of the Constitution, "shall be vested in one supreme Court, and in such inferior Courts as the Congress may from time to time ordain and establish." Courts created to carry out this judicial power are called *Article III* or *constitutional courts.* Congress may also establish *Article I* or *legislative courts*—courts, for instance, to handle bankruptcies and veterans' appeals—to carry out the legislative powers the Constitution has granted to it. The main difference between a legislative and a constitutional court is that the judges of a legislative court need not be appointed to "hold their Offices during good Behavior" and may be assigned other than purely judicial duties, such as supervising tax collections. Article III judges basically have lifetime appointments, subject only to removal by impeachment; only 11 federal judges have been impeached by the House of Representatives and seven convicted and removed by the Senate.[13]

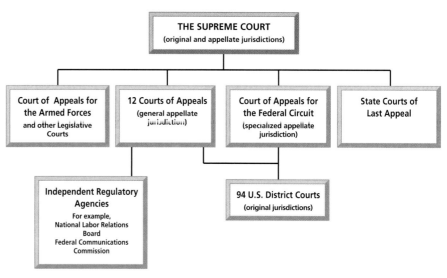

FIGURE 15–1   Structure of the Federal Courts.

The Constitution requires a Supreme Court. It is a necessity if the national government is to have the power to make and enforce laws that take precedence over those of the states. The lack of such a court to maintain national supremacy, ensure uniform interpretation of national legislation, and resolve conflicts among the states was one of the glaring defects of government under the Articles of Confederation.

Congress decides whether there will be other courts in addition to the Supreme Court. The First Congress divided the nation into circuits (geographical areas) and created lower courts for each. Today the hierarchy of federal courts of general jurisdiction consists of district courts, courts of appeals, and the Supreme Court (see Figure 15-1). In cases affecting ambassadors, other public ministers, and consuls and in cases in which a state is a party, the Supreme Court has **original jurisdiction**, the authority of a court to hear a case "in the first instance." In all other cases, the Supreme Court has **appellate jurisdiction**—power to review decisions of other courts and agencies—as determined by Congress.

District Courts

Although the Supreme Court and its justices receive most of the attention, the workhorses of the federal judiciary are the district courts in the states, the District of Columbia, and U.S. territories. In 2002, they heard more than 250,900 civil cases and 62,700 criminal cases.[14]

Each state has at least one federal district court. Larger states have as many as the demands of judicial business and the pressure of politics require, although no state has more than four. There are 665 judgeships in 94 district courts, located in each of the 50 states, the District of Columbia, and the Commonwealth of Puerto Rico. Each federal circuit has at least one district court judge but may have as many as 99.

District courts are the trial courts of original jurisdiction. They are the only federal courts that regularly employ **grand juries**, which are used to secure criminal indictments, and **petit juries**, used in trials. When cases tried before district judges involve citizens of different states, judges apply the appropriate state laws. Otherwise, district judges are concerned with federal laws. For example, they decide cases involving crimes against the United States—suits under the national revenue, postal, patent, copyright, trademark, bankruptcy, and civil rights laws.[15]

District judges normally sit separately and hold court by themselves; however, they sit in three-judge panels in cases involving reapportionment and voting rights. They are appointed by the president, subject to confirmation by the Senate, and hold office for life. District judges appoint and are assisted by clerks, bailiffs, stenographers, law clerks, court reporters, and probation officers.

original jurisdiction
The authority of a court to hear a case "in the first instance."

appellate jurisdiction
The authority of a court to review decisions made by lower courts.

grand jury
A jury of 12 to 23 persons who, in private, hear evidence presented by the government to determine whether persons shall be required to stand trial. If the jury believes there is sufficient evidence that a crime was committed, it issues an indictment.

petit jury
A jury of 6 to 12 persons who determine guilt or innocence in a civil or criminal action.

District court judges also appoint **magistrate judges**, who are increasingly important because of rising caseloads. After being screened by panels composed of residents of the judicial districts, full-time magistrates are appointed for eight-year renewable terms and part-time magistrates for four-year renewable terms. There are 429 full-time and 76 part-time federal magistrate judges. Magistrates look and act like judges. Most wear robes and since 1990 are addressed as "Judge." They issue arrest warrants, hold hearings to determine whether arrested persons should be held for action by the grand jury, and if so, set bail. They hear motions subject to varying kinds of review by their district judges. They preside over civil trials—jury and nonjury—with the consent of both parties and over nonjury trials for petty offenses with the consent of the defendants. Under the supervision of the district judge, and with the consent of the accused, a magistrate may preside over the selection of a jury for a felony trial.[16]

Courts of Appeals

The decisions of federal district courts may be appealed and reviewed by federal **courts of appeals**, although reapportionment and voting rights cases decided by three-judge panels are taken directly to the Supreme Court. District judges are bound by the precedents of higher courts, but they have considerable discretion in applying them. Courts of appeals are located geographically in 11 *judicial circuits* that include all the states and U.S. territories (see Figure 15-2). A twelfth is located in the District of Columbia and hears the largest number of cases challenging federal statutes, regulations, and administrative decisions. The thirteenth appellate court is the Court of Appeals for the Federal Circuit, which is located in the District of Columbia and has national jurisdiction, though it deals primarily with appeals in patent, copyright, and international trade cases. The largest circuit is the ninth, with 28 circuit judges and 99 district judges. It is geographically the size of western Europe and contains 20 percent of the U.S. population.

Each circuit court of appeals consists of 6 to 28 permanent judgeships (179 in all). These courts normally hear cases in panels of three judges. But in especially important and controversial cases, all judges may be present; that is, they sit *en banc*. They annually hear more than 50,000 appeals.

Although courts of appeals have only appellate jurisdiction, they are powerful policy makers. Fewer than 1 percent of their decisions are appealed to the Supreme Court. As the policy-making role of federal courts has become a prominent political issue, more

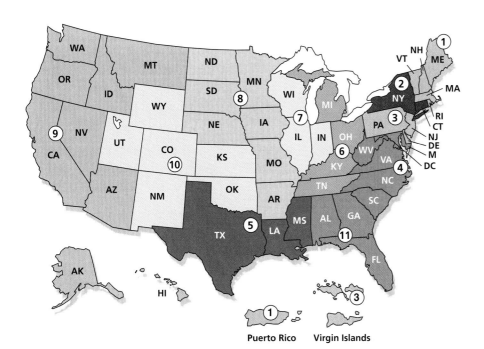

FIGURE 15–2   The Eleven U.S. Circuit Courts of Appeals.

magistrate judge
An official who performs a variety of limited judicial duties.

court of appeals
A court with appellate jurisdiction that hears appeals from the decisions of lower courts.

attention has focused on these courts and the judges who serve on them.[17] One current controversy involves the growing failure of appellate courts to publish their opinions, due to their growing caseloads, and whether unpublished opinions are binding precedents.[18] Another controversy revolves around whether the number of judges should be increased to keep pace with rising caseloads. (For more information about the federal judiciary, go to the Web site of the Administrative Office of the U.S. Courts at www.uscourts.gov.)

The Politics of Appointing Federal Judges

The selection of federal judges has always been a significant part of the political process. It makes a difference who serves on the federal courts. As the courts play an even more important role in the political process and as more and more interests—African Americans and women, for example—participate in that process, judicial selection politics has come front and center on the political stage.

The president selects federal judges with the advice and consent of the Senate. Political reality imposes constraints on the president's discretion, so the selection of a federal judge is actually a complex bargaining process. The principal figures involved are the candidates, the president, and the "subpresidency for judicial selection,"[19] consisting of key members of the Department of Justice, U.S. senators, the American Bar Association, party leaders, and, increasingly, interest groups. In addition, recent presidents have inserted the White House much more directly into the process than their predecessors did.

Department of Justice officials and key White House staff meet often to review proposed candidates. Since the Reagan administration, the assistant attorney general in charge of the Office of Legal Policy in the Department of Justice oversees the screening of potential judicial nominees. After candidates' backgrounds and judicial philosophies have been checked, they are discussed by a White House working group that includes the legal counselor to the president and the attorney general. This group recommends to the president whom to nominate to the federal bench. (For more information about the Office of Legal Policy and current judicial nominations, go to its Web site at www.usdoj.gov/olp.)

In practice, before the White House submits names of nominees for the federal district and appeals courts, it observes the practice of **senatorial courtesy**—the custom of submitting the names of prospective appointees for approval to the senators from the states in which the appointees are to work. If negotiations are deadlocked between the senators or between the senators and the Department of Justice, a seat may stay vacant for years.[20] The custom of senatorial courtesy does not apply to Supreme Court appointments, since they have national jurisdiction; nevertheless, President Clinton consulted with Republican Senator Orrin Hatch, who at the time chaired the Senate Judiciary Committee because the Senate was controlled by Republicans, so as to avoid a confirmation battle over his nominees to the Supreme Court.

In addition, liberal interest groups, such as People for the American Way and the Alliance for Justice, as well as conservative groups, such as the Heritage Foundation and a coalition of 260 conservative organizations called the Judicial Selection Monitoring Project, monitor potential judicial candidates. These organizations used to wait until after the president sent the name of a nominee to the Senate, but now they are active in the preliminaries, making known their views even before the names of nominees are released to the public or sent to the Senate Judiciary Committee.

The American Bar Association's Standing Committee on the Federal Judiciary once played a special role in evaluating candidates. Presidents were hesitant to submit for Senate confirmation a candidate rated "not qualified" by the ABA. In recent years, conservative groups mounted an attack on the ABA's role, contending that it reflects a liberal bias and has given low ratings to some conservative nominees. In response to this criticism, shortly after taking office in March 2001, President George W. Bush announced that the ABA would no longer be asked to evaluate judicial candidates before nomination. But Democratic senators on the Judiciary Committee continue to receive the ABA's evaluations of judicial nominees.

senatorial courtesy
Presidential custom of submitting the names of prospective appointees for approval to senators from the states in which the appointees are to work.

Confirmation Politics

Examination of recent nomination battles highlights the interplay of party, race, gender, ideology, and judicial philosophy in the process of selecting and confirming a Supreme Court justice.

The Bork Battle

Robert Bork.

When Justice Lewis F. Powell Jr., who cast the pivotal vote on such critical issues as affirmative action and abortion, announced his retirement as he neared 80 years of age at the end of the term in July 1987, President Reagan quickly nominated Judge Robert Bork, a member of the Court of Appeals for the District of Columbia and a noted jurist and legal scholar. Despite Bork's controversial writings on many current constitutional issues, his scholarly and legal qualifications made it appear initially that he would be confirmed. However, his nomination so offended women's and civil rights organizations that they organized a campaign to block Bork's confirmation. After almost four months of national debate, 12 days of acrimonious questioning by the members of the Senate Judiciary Committee, and 23 hours of debate on the Senate floor, the Senate voted 58 to 42 against Bork's confirmation.

The Souter Solution

David Souter.

The political bruises resulting from the Bork confirmation proceedings were traumatic. Political pundits speculated that in the future, presidents would seek noncontroversial candidates for the Supreme Court. This prediction came true in 1990 with George Bush's nominee to replace William J. Brennan Jr., leader of the liberal bloc on the Supreme Court. President Bush chose David Souter, a member of the New Hampshire Supreme Court. Educated at Harvard and Oxford, he had written no law articles, made practically no speeches, and lived the secluded life of a sitting judge. When he appeared before the Judiciary Committee, Souter steadfastly refused to answer any questions that might reveal his orientation on abortion and privacy issues, to the frustration of the Senate Democrats. He was confirmed by an overwhelming vote. He became one of the more liberal judges.

The Thomas Tangle

When Justice Thurgood Marshall retired in 1991, President Bush sent to the Senate the name of a controversial jurist, Judge Clarence Thomas, then sitting on the Court of Appeals for the District of Columbia. Thomas is a conservative African American. Prior to his brief service on the Court of Appeals, he had served as chair of the Equal Employment Opportunity Commission (EEOC) and in the Office of Civil Rights. During five days of grueling questions about his constitutional views, Judge Thomas, like his predecessor, refused to respond. The Senate Judiciary Committee narrowly recommended his confirmation.

Clarence Thomas.

Two days before the Senate was due to vote on his confirmation, documents leaked to the press revealed that a former associate of Judge Thomas, Anita Hill, had accused him of sexually harassing her when she worked for him in the Department of Education and the EEOC. Women's and liberal groups exploded in outrage. There followed three days of dramatic and emotion-charged hearings telecast to the nation in which Judge Thomas categorically denied the charges presented persuasively by his accuser. Panels of witnesses pro and con came forward to testify. Thomas was confirmed by the Senate 52 to 48, one of the closest confirmation votes for a Supreme Court justice.

The Clinton Choices

Almost as soon as President Bill Clinton took office, Justice Byron White announced he would leave the Court at the end of its 1992–1993 term. It was clear that with this appointment, Clinton could arrest the Court's conservative drift and fulfill his campaign pledge to appoint justices committed to protect the right of privacy—that is, to preserve a woman's freedom to choose an abortion.

After several months of deliberation, including the embarrassingly public consideration of other candidates, President Clinton nominated Ruth Bader Ginsburg. Judge Ginsburg was a 13-year veteran of the Court of Appeals for the District of Columbia, to which President Carter had appointed her. On the Court of Appeals, she had earned a reputation for fairness and moderation. She was readily confirmed by the Senate and took her seat for the opening of the 1993–1994 term.

Clinton had a second opportunity when Harry A. Blackmun, at age 85, announced his intention to leave the Court during the spring of 1994. Blackmun, best known for writing the opinion in *Roe* v. *Wade,* was thought at first to be a judicial conservative, but by the time of his retirement, he had become the most liberal member of the Court. President Clinton nominated Stephen G. Breyer, chief judge of the First Circuit, a noncontroversial judicial moderate. Justice Breyer, a graduate of Stanford University, Oxford, and Harvard Law School, had served as Supreme Court law clerk for Justice Arthur Goldberg and was a member of the faculty at Harvard Law School before being appointed by President Carter as a federal appeals court judge. After a cordial hearing before the Senate Judiciary Committee in July 1994, Breyer was easily confirmed by the Senate.

Ruth Bader Ginsberg.

Stephen G. Breyer.

Senate: Advice and Consent

The normal presumption is that the president should be allowed considerable discretion in the selection of federal judges. Despite this presumption, the Senate takes seriously its responsibility in confirming judicial nominations, especially when the party controlling the Senate is different from that of the president, as has been the case in recent years.

When the Senate receives the name of a judicial nominee, it sends the nomination to the Judiciary Committee for consideration. Before the committee holds a hearing on the nominee, it sends to the senators of the nominee's home state a letter—called a "blue slip" because of its color—asking whether they approve. If one of the senators declines to return the slip, the nomination is dead, and no hearing will be held. During the last two years of Clinton's presidency, Republican senators delayed and defeated confirmation of many of his judicial nominees in this way. With Democrats in control of the Senate during his first two years, they retaliated and stalled the confirmation of a number of President George W. Bush's nominees.[21] If both home-state senators approve of a nominee, the committee holds a hearing, votes on the nominee, and sends its recommendation to the full Senate for consideration and confirmation based on a majority vote.

Prior to 1955, the common practice was for the Senate to look into candidates' qualifications and background but not to interview the person. But since then, the committee has asked judicial nominees a wide range of questions, since their judicial and political philosophy is a major factor in determining how they might vote on particular cases and controversies. Except for Robert Bork, nominated by President Ronald Reagan in 1987, most judicial nominees have refused to answer questions that might reveal how they would decide a case. But Judge Bork had written so many articles, made so many speeches, and decided so many cases that he thought he had to clarify his constitutional views. His candor may well have contributed to the Senate's rejection of him, and that has made subsequent nominees even more reluctant to respond to similar questions.

Until recently, most judicial appointments, especially those for the lower federal courts, were processed without much controversy. However, "now that lower court judges are more commonly viewed as political actors, there is increasing Senate scrutiny of these nominees."[22] The battle over judicial confirmations ordinarily takes place before the Senate

---

TABLE 15–1   Party Affiliation of District Judges and Court of Appeals Judges Appointed by Presidents

President	Party	Appointees from Same Party
Roosevelt	Democrat	97%
Truman	Democrat	92
Eisenhower	Republican	95
Kennedy	Democrat	92
Johnson	Democrat	96
Nixon	Republican	93
Ford	Republican	81
Carter	Democrat	90
Reagan	Republican	94
G.H.W. Bush	Republican	89
Clinton	Democrat	88
G. W. Bush	Republican	93

SOURCE: Sheldon Goldman, "Judicial Selection Under Clinton: A Midterm Examination," *Judicature* (May–June 1995), p. 280; Sheldon Goldman and Elliot Slotnick, "Clinton's Second Term Judiciary: Selection Under Fire," *Judicature* (May–June 1999), updated to June 8, 2002, by the Federal Judicial Center, at air.fjc.gov/history_judges_frm.html.

Judiciary Committee. The Senate usually goes along with the recommendations of its Judiciary Committee without much debate, although floor debates are not all that rare. Overall, the Senate has refused to confirm 29 of the 138 presidential nominations for Supreme Court justices.[23]

The Role of Party, Race, and Gender

Presidents so seldom nominate judges from the opposing party (around 90 percent of judicial appointments since the time of Franklin Roosevelt have gone to candidates from the president's party) that partisan considerations are taken for granted, and partisan affiliation is rarely mentioned (see Table 15-1). Today more attention is paid to other characteristics, such as race and gender.[24]

President Jimmy Carter, who had no opportunity to make an appointment to the Supreme Court, selected more African Americans, Hispanics, and women for the lower federal courts than all other prior presidents combined—40 women, 37 African Americans, and 16 Hispanics. President Ronald Reagan, although the first to appoint a woman to the Supreme Court, appointed fewer minority members or women than Carter did, perhaps in part because fewer minorities and women could pass the Reagan administration's ideological screening.[25] Twenty percent of George Bush's appointees were women, 7 percent African Americans, and 4 percent Hispanics.[26]

Bill Clinton promised to appoint federal judges who would be more representative of the ethnic makeup of the United States. "We don't have litmus tests or judicial-philosophy tests," insisted Assistant Attorney General Eleanor Dean Acheson, who oversaw judicial selection during the Clinton administration, "but I do think we've put people on the bench who are interested in people and their problems"[27] and brought diversity to the federal bench. Clinton lived up to his pledge; he named more women and minorities to the bench than his predecessors had (see Figure 15-3).

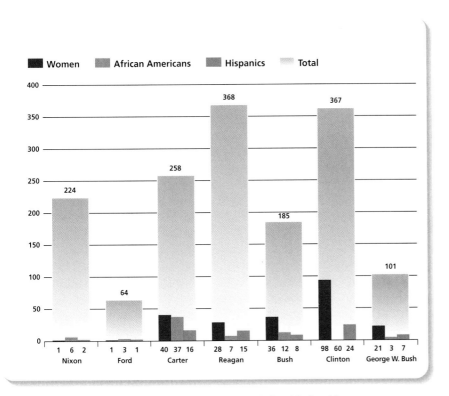

FIGURE 15–3   Female and Minority Appointments to Federal Judgeships.

SOURCE: Sheldon Goldman, Elliot Slotnick, Gerard Gryski, and Gary Zuk, "Clinton's Judges," *Judicature* 84, March–April 2001:228–254. Updated through December 2002, based on data from the Office of Legal Policy, at www.usdoj.gov/olp.

PEOPLE IN POLITICS

JUSTICE SANDRA DAY O'CONNOR

Appointed to the Supreme Court by Republican President Ronald Reagan in 1981, Justice Sandra Day O'Connor is the first woman to serve on the high bench. Along with her brother, she recently published an autobiography, *Lazy B*, recounting her growing up on a large cattle ranch in Arizona.* After graduating at the top of her class from Stanford Law School, she found it difficult to find a job in her home state. She eventually entered politics,

serving first as assistant attorney general and then winning election to the Arizona state senate, where she served until her appointment to a state trial court and later an intermediate court of appeals.

On the Supreme Court, Justice O'Connor is conservative but less hard-line than the other Reagan appointees. She casts the deciding vote on controversial issues such as abortion, affirmative action, minority-majority voting districts, and

some disputes involving the separation of church and state.

Because Justice O'Connor is at the center of the Rehnquist Court and casts so many deciding votes, if she retires during President George W. Bush's term in office and Democrats are in control of the Senate, a controversy over the appointment of her successor may arise.

*Sandra Day O'Connor and H. Alan Day, *Lazy B: Growing Up on a Cattle Ranch in the American Southwest* (Random House, 2002).

George W. Bush appointed a number of women and minorities in his first year in office but fewer in his second, and the Democratic majority on the Senate Judiciary Committee stalled many of his more conservative judicial nominees. Splitting along party-line votes of 10 to 9, the committee rejected his nomination of Judge Charles W. Pickering and Pricillia Owen to the Court of Appeals for the Fifth Circuit and refused to send their nominaton to the full Senate for a vote on their confirmation.

The Role of Ideology

Finding a party member is not enough; presidents want to pick the "right" kind of Republican or "our" kind of Democrat to serve as judges. By and large, they have been able to achieve this goal. Judges picked by Republican presidents tend to be judicial conservatives (with some notable exceptions, such as President Dwight Eisenhower's appointments of Chief Justice Earl Warren and Justice William J. Brennan Jr., President Gerald Ford's appointment of Justice John Paul Stevens, and President George Bush's appointment of Justice David H. Souter). Judges picked by Democratic presidents are more likely to be liberals. Both of these orientations are tempered by the fact that judges must go through a senatorial confirmation process that during recent administrations has been rigorous and driven by opposition to the White House.[28]

President Ronald Reagan's two terms made it possible for him to join Presidents Franklin D. Roosevelt and Dwight D. Eisenhower as the only presidents in the last century to appoint a majority of the federal bench. All told, Reagan appointed 368 lifetime judges. His administration acted carefully to nominate only those whose views about the role of the courts and constitutional issues were consistent with Reagan's own.[29] Not only were a large number of judicial conservatives appointed, but many of them—because they were comparatively young—will continue to have an effect on judicial policy well into the twenty-first century.

Because President George H. W. Bush was less committed to conservatism than Reagan, conservative organizations—the Heritage Foundation, the Pacific Legal Foundation, and the Federalist Society—focused more attention on his judicial nominees. Bush appointed 148 district judges, 37 appellate judges, and two Supreme Court justices—David Souter and Clarence Thomas. It turned out that his appointees, with the exception of Justice Souter, were among the most conservative in recent history.[30] His appointment of Justice Thomas helped consolidate the Court's "turn to the right."[31]

President Clinton gave Democratic senators "clear guidelines about the kind of judges he wants"[32]—competent professionals who would bring diversity to the bench. But after the Republicans took control of the Senate in 1994, Clinton instructed his advisers to consult closely with Republican Senator Orrin Hatch, chair of the Senate Judiciary Committee. Clinton abandoned or declined to nominate several judicial candidates opposed by conservative interest groups and had to reach compromises with Republican senators. In his second term, Clinton faced increasing opposition from the Republican-controlled Senate, which slowed down confirmations to such an extent that Chief Justice Rehnquist, in his annual reports on the federal judiciary, scolded the Senate for jeopardizing the ability of the federal courts to do their work. Despite the slowdown in Senate confirmations, by the time Clinton left office, he had named 367 of the 849 authorized federal judges and appointed a large number of women and minorities.[33]

President George W. Bush likewise confronted increasing difficulties over his judicial nominees from the Democratic-controlled Senate. After the defeat of two of his nominees and the Senate's refusal to process several others, in 2002 he vowed to make federal judgeships a campaign issue in the hope of regaining a Republican majority in the Senate. As he put it, "We've got to get good, conservative judges appointed to the bench and approved by the United States Senate."[34]

The Role of Judicial Philosophy

What about a candidate's judicial philosophy? Does a candidate believe that judges should interpret the Constitution to reflect what the framers intended and what its words literally say; that is, does the candidate believe in **judicial self-restraint**? Or does the candidate believe that the Constitution should be adapted to reflect current conditions and philosophies; that is, does the candidate believe in **judicial activism**?

Throughout most of our history, federal courts have been more conservative than Congress, the White House, or state legislatures. Prior to 1937, judicial self-restraint was the battle cry of liberals who objected to judges' interpreting the due process clauses of the Fifth and Fourteenth Amendments to strike down many laws passed to protect labor and women and to keep the national and state governments from regulating the economy. These judges broadly construed the words of the Constitution to prevent what they thought to be unreasonable regulations of property.

With Presidents Richard Nixon, Ronald Reagan, George H. W. Bush, and George W. Bush, however, the judicial shoe was on the other foot, and it was conservatives who were advocates of judicial self-restraint. What is needed, they argued, are judges who will let Congress, the president, and the state legislatures regulate or forbid abortions, permit prayer in public schools, impose capital punishment, and not hinder law enforcement.

Still, it would be wrong to assume that judicial philosophy is nothing more than another way to argue about political ideology. Some conservatives, for example, favor judicial activism because they want current judges to reverse the last half-century of precedents on civil rights and to protect property rights from government regulation. The conservative majority on the Rehnquist Court has invited criticisms from liberals for its judicial activism in overturning precedents and striking down state and federal laws promoting affirmative action, for example, and invalidating congressional enactments for infringing on states' rights. In these areas, liberals favor judicial restraint because they believe that judges should defer to the democratic process and that democratic self-governance will flourish if judges stay out of such policy debates.

Hence the debate over the role of the Supreme Court and the federal judiciary today is less about activism and restraint than about competing conceptions of the proper balance between government authority and individual rights, between the power of democratically accountable legislatures and that of courts and unelected judges. The debate is also about whether and on what basis judges should make law.

judicial self-restraint
Philosophy proposing that judges should interpret the Constitution to reflect what the framers intended and what its words literally say.

judicial activism
Philosophy proposing that judges should interpret the Constitution to reflect current conditions and values.

Do Judges Make Law?

"Do judges make law? 'Course they do. Made some myself."[35] That was the candid response of New Hampshire Justice Jeremiah Smith. Most judges are less candid. Judges obviously make law, but to admit it is somehow disturbing. Such statements do not conform to popular notions of what judges do.

Why do people think judges should not make law? Many people equate a judge's role with that of a referee in a prizefight, because of their role in trials and the adversary system. We expect referees to be impartial and disinterested, treating both parties as equals. We expect them to apply rules, not make them. Laws are not made, however, in the same way as the rules of a sport, and therein lies the answer to our question. Not only *do* judges make law, but they *must.*

Legislatures make law by enacting statutes, but judges must apply the statutes to concrete situations. Statutes are drawn in broad terms: Drivers shall act with "reasonable care"; no one may make "excessive noise" in the vicinity of a hospital; employers must maintain "safe working conditions." Such broad terms must be used because legislators cannot know exactly what will happen in every circumstance. Courts must judge their application in concrete cases. In the words of Justice Felix Frankfurter, "Legislatures make law wholesale, judges retail."[36]

The problems of interpreting and applying law are intensified when judges are required—as American judges are—to apply our more than 212-year-old Constitution. The Constitution is full of generalizations: "due process of law," "equal protection of the laws," "unreasonable searches and seizures," "Commerce . . . among several States." Recourse to the intent of the framers or to the words of the Constitution may not help judges facing cases involving thermal imaging, multinational corporations, the Internet, or birth control.

Adherence to Precedent

Just because judges make policy, they are not free to do whatever they wish. They are subject to a variety of limits on what they decide—some imposed by the political system of which they are a part and some imposed by higher courts and the legal profession. Among these constraints is the policy of **stare decisis**, the rule of precedent.

Stare decisis pervades our judicial system and promotes certainty, uniformity, and stability in the law. Judges are expected to abide by previous decisions of their own courts and by rulings of superior courts. Although adherence to precedent is the norm, the doctrine of *stare decisis* is not very restrictive.[37] Judges may distinguish between precedents because of differences in the context of cases, and many questions of law have conflicting precedents that can be used to support a decision for either party.

The doctrine of *stare decisis* is even less controlling in the field of constitutional law. Because the Constitution itself, rather than any one interpretation of it, is binding, the Court can *reverse* a previous decision it no longer wishes to follow, as it has done hundreds of times. Supreme Court justices are therefore not seriously restricted by *stare decisis.* Liberal Justice William O. Douglas, for one, maintained that *stare decisis* "was really no sure guideline because what did the judges who sat there in 1875 know about, say, electronic surveillance? They didn't know anything about it."[38] Chief Justice William H. Rehnquist is no less candid in holding that precedents dealing with civil rights that were handed down on a 5-to-4 vote should always be open for reconsideration, since they were decided by only a bare majority of the Court. Since 1789, the Supreme Court has reversed 217 of its own decisions and overturned more than 164 acts of Congress, more than 959 pieces of state legislation and state constitutional provisions, and more than 114 city ordinances.[39]

Judicial Longevity and Presidential Tenure

Ideology and judicial philosophy affect not only presidents' nominations for the federal courts but also when sitting judges choose to retire. Because federal judges serve for life, they may be able to schedule their retirement to allow a president whose views they approve to nominate their successors. Chief Justice Roger B. Taney stayed on the bench long after his health began to fail to prevent President Abraham Lincoln from nominating a Republican.

stare decisis
The rule of precedent, whereby a rule or law contained in a judicial decision is commonly viewed as binding on judges whenever the same question is presented.

In 1929, Chief Justice William Howard Taft wrote: "I am older and slower and less acute and more confused. However, as long as things continue as they are, and I am able to answer in my place, I must stay on the court in order to prevent the Bolsheviki [Herbert Hoover, a conservative Republican, was in the White House] from getting control."[40]

Although Chief Justice Warren Burger denied that he retired in 1986 in order to permit President Ronald Reagan to replace him with a conservative, his retirement gave Reagan an opportunity to rejuvenate the conservative wing of the Court by promoting William H. Rehnquist to the chief justiceship. Reagan then picked another conservative, Antonin Scalia, to take the seat vacated by Rehnquist. Liberal Supreme Court Justices William J. Brennan Jr. and Thurgood Marshall held on to their seats well into their eighties, and many assumed that they were doing so in the hope that they might be able to stay on the Court until a president more congenial to their views might be in the White House. They did not make it. Republican President George H. W. Bush, rather than a Democrat, appointed their successors. It should be noted, however, that personal and institutional factors other than partisan concerns are the main reason justices retire.[41]

Reform of the Selection Process

The televised confirmation hearings of Robert Bork in 1987 and Clarence Thomas in 1991, which were lengthy and embattled, aroused considerable criticism from both liberals and conservatives and called forth widespread complaints that "something is wrong with the process." Subsequently, several task forces and studies recommended that attempts be made to constrain the partisan politics surrounding the confirmation process for Supreme Court justices and lower federal court judges. They proposed that "Supreme Court nominees should no longer be expected to appear as witnesses during the Senate Judiciary Committee's hearings on their confirmation" and that the Senate should return to the practice of judging nominees on their written record and on the testimony of legal experts.[42] A bipartisan commission on judicial selection from the Miller Center of Public Affairs at the University of Virginia recommended that the time between nominations and Senate confirmation be shortened.[43] But the problems of delaying and blocking confirmation of judicial nominees remain, as both Presidents Clinton and George W. Bush found, particularly when the Senate is controlled by the party in opposition to the president.[44]

The politics of judicial selection may shock those who like to think judges are picked strictly on the basis of legal merit and without regard for ideology, party, gender, or race. But as a former Justice Department official observed, "When courts cease being an instrument for political change, then maybe the judges will stop being politically selected."[45] Moreover, as another scholar put it, "Supreme Court Justices have always been appointed for political reasons by politicians, and their confirmation process has always been dictated by politicians for political purposes. . . . In fact," he concluded, "not despite the politicization of the appointment and confirmation process, but because of it, the Supreme Court has endured as a flexible, viable force in the American democracy for over 200 years."[46]

CHANGING THE NUMBERS   One of the first actions a political party takes after gaining control of the White House and Congress is often to increase the number of federal judgeships. With divided government, however, when one party controls Congress and the other holds the White House, a stalemate is likely to occur, and relatively few new judicial positions will be created. During Andrew Johnson's administration, Congress went so far as to reduce the size of the Supreme Court to prevent the president from filling two vacancies. After Johnson left the White House, Congress returned the Court to its former size to permit Ulysses S. Grant to fill the vacancies.

In 1937, President Franklin Roosevelt proposed an increase in the size of the Supreme Court by one additional justice for every member of the Court over the age of 70, up to a total of 15 members. Ostensibly, the proposal was aimed at making the Court more efficient. In fact, Roosevelt and his advisers were frustrated because the Court had declared much of the early New Deal legislation unconstitutional. Despite Roosevelt's

PEOPLE DEBATE
BUSH V. GORE AND THE 2000 PRESIDENTIAL ELECTION

In the 2000 election, the Supreme Court played a decisive role in determining who won the presidency when in a 5-to-4 ruling it halted the manual recounting of ballots in Florida. After an automatic recount required under Florida law, George W. Bush's lead in the popular vote was 327 votes. The winner of Florida's 25 electoral votes was certain to decide the election. The issue before the Court was whether manual recounts should proceed as ordered by the Florida Supreme Court in counties where the Gore campaign had asked for them and what the standard for the recount should be. The state supreme court had not specified a standard. Governor George W. Bush appealed the Florida court's decision to the U.S. Supreme Court. One day after hearing oral arguments at 10:00 p.m., on December 12, the Court handed down its ruling.

The Majority's Position

A majority of the justices ruled that the manual recounts violated the equal protection clause by applying different standards for counting the ballots in different counties. Chief Justice Rehnquist and Justices O'Connor, Kennedy, Scalia, and Thomas also held that there was not time to remedy the problem before a congressional deadline of December 12 for forwarding electoral votes to Congress. The majority argued:

The right to vote is protected in more than the initial allocation of the franchise. Equal protection applies as well to the manner of its exercise. Having once granted the right to vote on equal terms, the State may not, by later arbitrary and disparate treatment, value one person's vote over that of another....

The recount mechanisms implemented in response to the decisions of the Florida Supreme Court do not satisfy the minimum requirement for non-arbitrary treatment of voters necessary to secure the fundamental right.... The formulation of uniform rules to determine intent based on these recurring circumstances is practicable and, we conclude, necessary.... The want of those rules here has led to unequal evaluation of ballots in various respects....

It is obvious that the recount cannot be conducted in compliance with the requirements of equal protection and due process without substantial additional work. It would require not only the adoption (after opportunity for argument) of adequate statewide standards for determining what is a legal vote, and practicable procedures to implement them, but also orderly judicial review of any disputed matters that might arise.

popularity, his "court-packing scheme" aroused intense opposition. Roosevelt's proposals to change the Court's size failed. He lost the battle but won the war, as the Court began to sustain some important New Deal legislation, and subsequent retirements from the bench enabled him to make eight appointments to the Court.

CHANGING THE JURISDICTION   Congressional control over the structure and jurisdiction of federal courts has been used to influence the course of judicial policy making. Although unable to get rid of Federalist judges by impeachment, the Jeffersonians abolished the circuit courts created by the Federalist Congress just before they lost control. In 1869, radical Republicans in Congress altered the Supreme Court's appellate jurisdiction in order to snatch from the Court a case it was about to review involving the constitutionality of some Reconstruction legislation.[47]

Each year, a number of bills are introduced in Congress to eliminate the jurisdiction of federal courts over cases relating to abortion, school prayer, and school busing

The Dissenters' View

The four dissenters disputed the majority's claim that the U.S. Supreme Court had jurisdiction to decide the case. Justices Stevens, Souter, Ginsburg, and Breyer also argued that while equal protection may have been an issue, there were alternatives to simply ending the recounts altogether. In Justice Stevens's words:

The federal questions that ultimately emerged in this case are not substantial. . . . Article II provides that "each State shall appoint, in such Manner as the Legislature thereof may direct, a Number of Electors." The legislative power in Florida is subject to judicial review pursuant to Article V of the Florida Constitution, and nothing in Article II of the Federal Constitution frees the state legislature from the constraints in the state constitution that created it. . . .

It hardly needs stating that Congress, pursuant to [Section] 5 did not impose any affirmative duties upon the States that their governmental branches could "violate." Rather, [Section 5 of the Electoral Count Act of 1887, guaranteeing a "safe harbor" for electoral votes receiving certification by December 12,] provides a safe harbor for States to select electors in contested elections "by judicial or other methods" established by laws prior to the election day. Section 5, like Article II, assumes the involvement of the state judiciary in interpreting state election laws and resolving election disputes under those laws. Neither [Section] 5 nor Article II grants federal judges any special authority to substitute their views for those of the state judiciary on matters of state law.

In a separate dissenting opinion, Justice Breyer further argued:

I agree that, in these very special circumstances, basic principles of fairness may well have counseled the adoption of a uniform standard to address the problem. . . . Nonetheless, there is no justification for the majority's remedy, which is simply to reverse the lower court and halt the recount entirely. An appropriate remedy would be, instead, to remand this case with instructions that, even at this late date, would permit the Florida Supreme Court to require recounting all undercounted votes in Florida, . . . and to do so in accordance with a single-uniform substandard.

1. Should the Supreme Court have decided this case or dismissed it as a "political question" for other branches to decide?

2. How do you square the majority's holding that a "uniform rule" for counting votes is required with its usual defense of federalism and states' rights?

3. Was the majority wrong to hold that there was no remedy available and to stop the recount of ballots?

or to eliminate the appellate jurisdiction of the Supreme Court over such matters. These attacks on federal court jurisdiction spark debate about whether the Constitution gives Congress authority to take such actions. And Congress has not yet decided to do so, because it would amount to a fundamental shift in the relationship between Congress and the Supreme Court. As one scholar concluded, "History suggests the public has seen such attempts for precisely what they are, as attacks on judicial independence, and such attacks have been resisted."[48]

The Supreme Court and How It Operates

The Supreme Court's term runs from the first Monday in October through the end of June. The justices listen to oral arguments for two weeks each month from October to April and then adjourn for two weeks to consider the cases and to write opinions. By agreement,

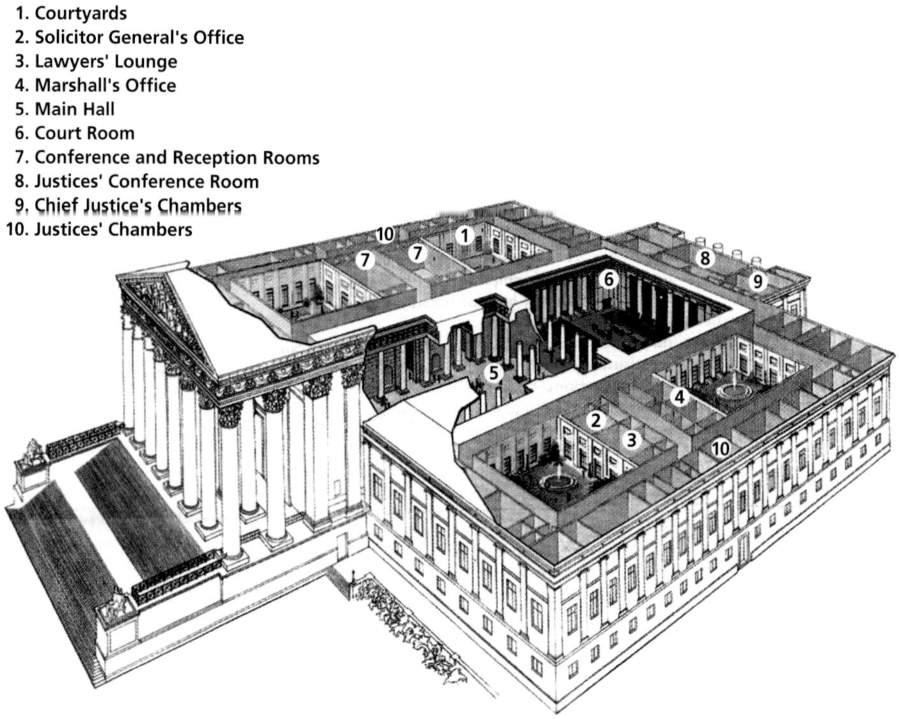

1. Courtyards
2. Solicitor General's Office
3. Lawyers' Lounge
4. Marshall's Office
5. Main Hall
6. Court Room
7. Conference and Reception Rooms
8. Justices' Conference Room
9. Chief Justice's Chambers
10. Justices' Chambers

FIGURE 15–4   The Supreme Court Building.

six justices must participate in each decision. Cases are decided by a majority vote. In the event of a tie vote, the decision of the lower court is sustained, although on rare occasions it may be reargued.

At 10:00 A.M. on the days when the Supreme Court sits, the eight associate justices and the chief justice, dressed in their robes (Chief Justice Rehnquist has four gold stripes on each sleeve of his robe),[49] file into the courtroom. As they take their seats—arranged according to seniority, with the chief justice in the center—the clerk of the Court introduces them as the "Honorable Chief Justice and Associate Justices of the Supreme Court of the United States." Those present in the courtroom, asked to stand when the justices enter, are seated, and counsel take their places along tables in front of the bench. The attorneys for the Department of Justice are at the right. The other attorneys are dressed conservatively; sport coats are not considered proper. Dress and ceremony are all part of the high ritual of the Court (see Figure 15-4).

The Powers of the Chief Justice

The chief justice of the United States is appointed by the president upon confirmation by the Senate, like other federal judges. Yet because the chief justice heads the entire federal judiciary, this method of appointment gives him (in our history, all have been men) greater visibility than if selected by rotation of fellow justices, as is the practice in the state supreme courts, or by seniority, as is the practice in the federal courts of appeals. The chief justice has special administrative responsibilities in overseeing the operation of the judiciary, such as assigning judges to committees, responding to proposed legislation that affects the judiciary, and delivering the Annual Report on the State of the Judiciary.

But within the Supreme Court, the chief justice is only "first among equals," even though periods in Court history are often named after the chief justice. As Chief Justice Rehnquist said when he was still an associate justice, the chief deals not with "eight subordinates whom he may direct or instruct, but eight associates who, like him, have tenure during good behavior, and who are as independent as hogs on ice."[50] As political scientist David Danelski observed, "The Chief Justiceship does not guarantee leadership. It only offers its incumbent an opportunity to lead." Yet the chief justice "sets the tone, controls

You Decide — Thinking It Through

DOES THE NUMBER OF FEDERAL JUDGES NEED TO BE INCREASED IN ORDER TO ENSURE ACCESS TO JUSTICE?

You Decide... The Committee on Long-Range Planning of the Judicial Conference of the United States has studied the increasing caseload of federal courts and projects a continued growth in cases and a need for more judges:

Year	District Court Caseloads	Judges	Circuit Court Caseloads	Judges
1950	91,005	224	2,830	65
1960	87,421	245	3,899	68
1970	125,423	401	11,662	97
1980	196,757	516	23,200	132
1990	264,409	575	40,898	156
2000	386,200	940	84,800	430
2010	642,500	1,510	171,600	840
2020	1,109,000	2,530	325,100	1,580

SOURCE: Committee on Long-Range Planning, Judicial Conference of the United States, *Proposed Long-Range Plan for the Federal Courts* (Judicial Conference of the United States, 1995), pp. 14–15.

Thinking It Through... Politicians and judges disagree over whether the number of judges should be increased. Some warn of the bureaucratization of the judiciary and the fragmentation of federal law. Others argue that if the number is not increased, citizens will confront lengthy delays and a denial of access to justice.

Second Circuit Judge Jon O. Newman argues that the number of judges should not rise above 1,000 because there would be a drop in the quality of judges, increased bureaucracy, inefficiency in large appellate courts, and a fragmentation of federal law. He and others recommend shifting to state courts cases involving routine traffic accidents, drug possession, tax, and other civil litigation.*

By contrast, Ninth Circuit Judge Stephen Reinhardt contends that freezing the size of the bench would be elitist. An increase in the number of judges would ensure access to justice for the poor, minorities, and other disadvantaged people. He maintains that large federal courts can and do work well.†

*Jon O. Newman, "1,000 Judges: The Limit for an Effective Judiciary," Judicature 76 (June–July 1993), p. 187.

†Stephen Reinhardt, "Whose Federal Judiciary Is It Anyway?" Loyola of Los Angeles Law Review 27 (1993), p. 1.

the conference, assigns the most opinions, and usually, takes the most important, nation-changing decisions for himself."[51]

The ability of the chief justice to influence the Court has varied considerably.[52] Chief Justice Charles Evans Hughes ran the conferences like a stern schoolmaster, keeping the justices on the point, moving the discussion along, and doing his best to work out compromises in order to achieve unanimous decisions, which carry greater weight. Chief Justice Harlan F. Stone, by contrast, encouraged justices to state their own points of view and let the discussions wander. Chief Justice Warren Burger was not very successful in leading conferences. He devoted much of his time to judicial reform, speaking to bar associations and trying to build political support for modernizing the judicial process.

William H. Rehnquist had 15 years of Court experience prior to his elevation to chief justice. He "has not utilized his position as Chief Justice to shape the decisions of the Court."[53] However, as the Reagan-Bush justices became a majority, his constitutional views on federalism and affirmative action, formerly expressed in his dissenting opinions, became the opinions of the Court.[54]

Chief Justice William Hubbs Rehnquist presided at the Senate hearing on the impeachment of President Clinton.

Which Cases Reach the Supreme Court?

When citizens vow to take their cases to the highest court of the land even if it costs their last penny, they underestimate the difficulty of securing Supreme Court review and misunderstand the Court's role. The rules for appealing a case are established by the Supreme Court and Congress. Until 1988, when Congress enacted the Act to Improve the Administration of Justice, the Supreme Court was obliged by law to review a large number of appeals. Today, however, almost all appeals come to the Court by means of a discretionary **writ of certiorari**, a formal petition used to bring a case before the Court that may be denied. Since the Supreme Court's docket is now largely discretionary, it has the power to set its own agenda and to select which cases it wishes to review. As a result, the justices decide fewer than 100 of the 9,000 cases appealed to them annually. That is half the number of cases decided annually two decades ago (see Figure 15-5).[55]

The crucial factor in determining whether the Supreme Court reviews a case is its importance to the operation of the governmental system as a whole. The Supreme Court will review a case only if the claim involves a substantial question of federal law that has broad public significance—what kinds of affirmative action programs are permissible, whether individuals have a right to doctor-assisted suicide, or under what conditions women may have abortions. The Court also tends to review cases in which rulings among the courts of appeals are in conflict, and by deciding a case, the Supreme Court establishes which ruling is to be followed. Or a case may raise a constitutional issue on which a state supreme court has presented an interpretation with which the Court disagrees.

The Court grants cases based on the *rule of four*. If four justices are sufficiently interested in a petition for a writ of certiorari, it will be granted and the case brought up for review. The justices' law clerks read the petitions and write a memorandum on each, recommending whether a review should be granted. These memos circulate to all the justices except Justice John Paul Stevens, whose law clerks review the petitions for him, and he reads a few of them himself.[56]

Denial of a writ of certiorari does not mean that the justices agree with the decision of the lower court, nor does it establish precedent. Refusal to grant a review may indicate all kinds of possibilities. The justices may wish to avoid a political "hot potato," or the Court may be so divided on an issue that it is not yet prepared to take a stand, or it may want to let an issue "percolate" in the federal courts so that the Court may benefit from their rulings before it decides. The Court tends to take cases on which two or more appellate courts have rendered conflicting rulings on an issue, in order to resolve their conflict and to provide uniformity to the law.[57]

writ of certiorari

A formal writ used to bring a case before the Supreme Court.

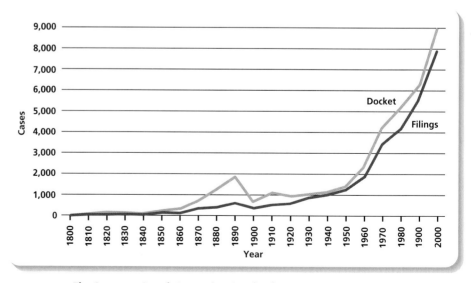

FIGURE 15–5   The Supreme Court's Increasing Caseload.

After a case is granted review, each side prepares written *briefs* presenting legal arguments, relevant precedents, and historical background for the justices and their law clerks to study and on the basis of which to render their decisions.

The Role of the Law Clerks

Beginning in the 1920s and 1930s, federal judges began hiring the best recent graduates of law schools to serve as clerks for a year or two. As the judicial workload increased, more law clerks have been appointed. Today each Supreme Court justice is entitled to four clerks. These are young people who have graduated from a leading law school and have previously clerked for a federal or state court.

Each justice picks his or her own clerks and works closely with them throughout the term. Clerks screen writs of certiorari and prepare draft opinions for the justices. Some observers and former law clerks claim that the justices now depend too much on their clerks and that the Court is "clerk-driven."[58] As the number of law clerks and computers has increased, so has the number of concurring and dissenting opinions, and today's opinions are longer and have more footnotes and elaborate citations of cases and law review articles. This is the result of the greater number of law clerks and the fact that the justices' chambers operate like "nine little law firms," often practicing law against each other.[59]

The Solicitor General

Attorneys in the Department of Justice and from other federal agencies participate in more than half of the cases that the Supreme Court agrees to decide and therefore play a crucial role in setting its agenda. Of special importance is the *solicitor general* (SG), who represents the federal government before the Supreme Court and is sometimes called the "tenth justice."[60]

When the SG petitions the Supreme Court to review a decision of a lower court, the Court is likely to do so. That is in part because no appeal may be taken on behalf of the United States to any appellate court without the approval of the solicitor general. Hence the SG's office may pick which cases to appeal. Although an appointee of the president, the SG has considerable independence from the White House. The SG also relies on deputy attorneys general, who are experienced career attorneys and enjoy a reputation for the high quality of their work.

The solicitor general also files **amicus curiae** (Latin for "friend of the court") **briefs** in cases in which the federal government is not a party. The practice of filing *amicus curiae* briefs guarantees that the Department of Justice is represented if a suit questions the constitutionality of an act of Congress or the executive branch. The solicitor general may also use these briefs to bring to the Court's attention the views of the current administration.[61] On occasion, though, solicitors general appear to compromise their independence, as during the administrations of Ronald Reagan and George H. W. Bush, in too aggressively asking the Court to overturn precedents.[62] Still, when the SG appears before the Supreme Court, only respectful formal attire is worn—dark vest, tails, and striped pants. (Briefs filed by the solicitor general may be found on the Web at www.usdoj.gov/osg.)

Amicus Curiae Briefs

Individuals, interest groups, and organizations may also file *amicus curiae* briefs if they claim to have an interest in the case and to have information of value to the Court.[63] An *amicus* brief may help the justices by presenting arguments or facts that the parties to the case have not raised. In recent decades, interest groups have increasingly filed such briefs in an effort to influence the Court and to counter the positions of the solicitor general and the government.

In *Webster* v. *Reproductive Health Services,* dealing with a Missouri law regulating abortions and asking the Court to reverse *Roe* v. *Wade,* 78 *amicus* briefs were filed.[64] In *United States* v. *Lopez,* which challenged congressional authority to ban guns in and around schools, more than 40 parties filed a dozen *amicus* briefs. Ohio, New York, and the District of Columbia argued in favor of federal power, as did associations of police and school officials. On the other side were some conservative public interest firms, the National Governors Association, and the National League of Cities.[65]

amicus curiae brief
Literally, a "friend of the court" brief, filed by an individual or organization to present arguments in addition to those presented by the immediate parties to a case.

Interest groups may file *amicus curiae* briefs before the Supreme Court grants a writ of certiorari in order to encourage the Supreme Court to review the case. Their doing so enhances the probability that the Court will take the case for review but has almost no influence on how the case is decided.[66] More typically, these briefs are filed after the Court has granted a case review to urge the Court to reach a particular decision.

Oral Arguments

Once the justices receive printed briefs from each side, a case is set for oral arguments—usually in three to four months. Lengthy oratory before the Supreme Court, once lasting for several days, is a thing of the past. As a rule, counsel for each side is now allowed only 30 minutes. Lawyers use a lectern with two lights: A white light flashes five minutes before time is up; when the red light goes on, the lawyer must stop, even in the middle of a sentence.

The entire procedure is informally formal. Sometimes, to the annoyance of attorneys, justices talk among themselves or consult briefs or books during oral arguments. Other times, if justices find a presentation particularly bad, they will tell the attorneys so. Justices freely interrupt the lawyers to ask questions and request additional information. In recent years, "the justices seem barely able to contain themselves, often interrupting the answer to one question with another query."[67] Hence the 30-minute limit is problematic, especially when the solicitor general participates, since his 10 minutes come out of the time of the two parties before the Court.

If a lawyer is having a difficult time, the justices may try to help out with a question. Occasionally, justices bounce arguments off a hapless attorney and at one another. Justice Antonin Scalia is a harsh questioner. "When Scalia prepares to ask a question, he doesn't just adjust himself in his chair to get closer to the microphone like the others; he looks like a vulture, zooming in for the kill. He strains way forward, pinches his eyebrows, and poses the question, like '. . . do you want us to believe?'"[68] Justice Ruth Bader Ginsburg is a particularly persistent questioner, frequently rivaling Justice Scalia in asking the most questions.[69] Justice Clarence Thomas almost never asks a question. Justice David Souter has a thick New England accent. He once asked an attorney during oral arguments in an affirmative action case, "What's the floor?" The attorney hemmed and hawed until, with a smile, Souter explained he meant, "What's the flaw?"[70] (Oral arguments in landmark cases may be listened to on the Web by going to www.oyez.nwu.edu.)

Behind the Curtains: The Conference

On Wednesday afternoons and Fridays, the justices meet in private conference. They have heard the oral arguments and studied the briefs. Each brings to the meeting a red leather book in which the cases and the votes of the justices are recorded. These conferences are held in secret. They are usually a collegial but vigorous give-and-take.

The chief justice presides, usually opening the discussion by stating the facts, summarizing the questions of law, and suggesting how to dispose of each case. Each justice, in order of seniority, then gives his or her views and conclusions. Chief Justice Rehnquist tries to see to it that "everybody [speaks] once before the vote is taken."[71] Recently, the justices have not bothered with formal votes because their votes are clear from their discussion of the case.[72]

Opinions

The Supreme Court announces and explains its decisions in **opinions of the Court**. Opinions generally state the facts, present the issues, and explain the reasoning of the Court. These opinions are the Court's principal method of expressing its views to the world. Their primary function is to instruct judges of state and federal courts how to decide similar cases in the future.

Opinions of the Court are delivered by a justice but do not reflect his or her thinking alone. They must explain the reasoning of the majority of the justices. Consequently, opinions of the Court are negotiated documents that require the author to compromise and at times bargain with other justices to attain agreement on an opinion.[73]

opinion of the court
An explanation of a decision of the Supreme Court or any other appellate court.

Then it went to the U.S.
Supreme Court.

Patrick Oliphant, © Universal Press Syndicate.
Reprinted with permission. All rights reserved.

Judicial opinions may also be directed at Congress or at the president. If the Court regrets that "in the absence of action by Congress, we have no choice but to . . . " or insists that "relief of the sort that petitioner demands can only come from the political branches of government," it is asking Congress to act.[74] Justices also use opinions to communicate with the public. A well-crafted opinion may increase support for a policy the Court favors.

ASSIGNING OPINIONS   When voting with the majority, the chief justice decides who will draft the opinion of the Court. When the chief justice is in the minority, the senior justice among the majority makes the assignment. The justice assigned to write the opinion must give persuasive reasons for the outcome, for no vote in conference is final until the opinion of the Court has been agreed to. Justices are free to change their minds if not persuaded by draft opinions.

A justice is free to write a **dissenting opinion** if desired. Dissenting opinions are, in Chief Justice Charles Evans Hughes's words, "an appeal to the brooding spirit of the law, to the intelligence of a later day."[75] Dissenting opinions are quite common, as justices hope that some day these dissenting opinions will command a majority of the Court. If a justice agrees with the majority on how the case should be decided but differs on the reasoning, that justice may write a **concurring opinion**.

CIRCULATING DRAFTS   Writing the opinion of the Court is an exacting task. The document must win the support of at least four—and more, if possible—intelligent, strong-willed persons. Assisted by the law clerks, the assigned justice writes a draft and sends it to colleagues for comments. If the justice is lucky, the majority will accept the draft, perhaps with only minor changes. If the draft is not satisfactory to the other justices, it must be redrafted and recirculated until a majority reaches agreement.

The two weapons justices can use against their colleagues are their votes and the threat of writing dissenting opinions attacking the majority's opinion. Especially if the Court is closely divided, one justice may be in a position to demand that a certain point or argument be included in, or removed from, the opinion of the Court as the price of his or her vote. Sometimes such bargaining occurs even though the Court is not closely divided. An opinion writer who anticipates that a decision will invite critical public reaction may want a unanimous Court and will therefore compromise to achieve unanimity. For this reason, the Court delayed declaring school segregation unconstitutional, in *Brown* v. *Board of Education,* until unanimity was secured.[76] The justices understood that any sign of dissension on the bench on this major social issue would be an invitation to evade the Court's ruling.

RELEASING OPINIONS TO THE PUBLIC   In the past, justices read their entire opinions from the bench on "opinion days." Now they give only brief summaries of the decision and their opinions. Copies are immediately made available to reporters and the public and published in the official *United States Supreme Court Reports.* Since April 2000, the Court has made its opinions available on its Web site (www.supremecourtus.gov).

dissenting opinion
An opinion disagreeing with the majority in a Supreme Court ruling.

concurring opinion
An opinion that agrees with the majority in a Supreme Court ruling but differs on the reasoning.

Finding Supreme Court Opinions

The decisions and opinions of the Supreme Court are published in its official reports. References to cases are in the following format: *Gitlow v. New York,* 268 U.S. 652 (1925). This means that the case of the petitioner, Gitlow, against the respondent, the state of New York, can be found in volume 268 of *United States Supreme Court Reports* on page 652, and it was decided in 1925.

On the Internet, recent decisions may be found on the Supreme Court's Web site, www.supremecourtus.gov. These and other federal and state court decisions may also be located at Findlaw's site, www.findlaw.com, or through links on our Web site, www.prenhall.com/burns.

In this and the next several chapters, we discuss the Court's rulings at length because to talk about the Constitution and the Bill of Rights is to talk about Supreme Court decisions. Many of these decisions are cited in the notes at the back of the book so that you may look them up.

After the Court Decides

Victory in the Supreme Court does not necessarily mean that winning parties get what they want. The Court does not implement its own decision but *remands* the case, sending it back to the lower court with instructions to act in accordance with its opinion. The lower court often has considerable leeway in interpreting the Court's mandate as it disposes of the case.

Decisions whose enforcement requires only the action of a federal agency usually become effective immediately. Thus when the Supreme Court held that President Richard M. Nixon had to turn over confidential White House materials,[77] the president promptly complied.

The impact of a particular Supreme Court ruling on the behavior of individuals who are not immediate parties to a lawsuit is more uncertain. The most important rulings require a change in the behavior of thousands of administrative and elected officials. Sometimes Supreme Court pronouncements are simply ignored. For example, despite the Court's holding that it is unconstitutional for school boards to require students to pray within a school, some schools continue this practice.[78] And for years after the Supreme Court held public school segregation unconstitutional, many school districts remained segregated.[79]

The most difficult Supreme Court decisions to implement are those that require the cooperation of large numbers of officials. For example, a Supreme Court decision announcing a new standard for warrantless searches is not likely to have an impact on the way police make arrests for some time, since not many police officers subscribe to *United States Supreme Court Reports.* The process is more complex. Local prosecutors, state attorneys general, chiefs of police, and state and federal trial court judges must all participate to give meaning to Supreme Court decisions. The Constitution may be what the Supreme Court says it is, but a Supreme Court opinion, for the moment at least, is what a trial judge or police officer or prosecutor or school board or city council says it is.

Judicial Power in a Constitutional Democracy

An independent judiciary is one of the hallmarks of a free society. As impartial dispensers of equal justice under the law, judges should not be dependent on the executive, the legislature, parties to a case, or the electorate. But judicial independence, essential to protect judges in their role as legal umpire, encounters problems when a democratic society decides—as ours has—also to allow these same judges to make policy. Perhaps in no other society do the people resort to litigation as a means of making public policy as much as they do in the United States. For example, the National Association for the Advancement of Colored People (NAACP) turned to litigation to get relief from segregation practices in the 1930s, 1940s, and 1950s. More recently, an increasing number of women's organizations, environmental groups, and religious and conservative organizations have also turned to the courts.[80]

The involvement of courts in politics exposes the judiciary to political criticism. Throughout our history, the Supreme Court has been attacked for engaging in "judicial legislation." This is nothing new. Yet the active role of the federal courts on behalf of liberal causes since 1937 and Republican attacks on that role have returned these issues to the forefront of public debate.

Whereas in earlier times judges occasionally told public officials what they could *not* do, today they often tell them what they *must* do. For example, federal judges, responding to class action complaints, have told Congress, state legislatures, and local officials that they must provide attorneys for the poor, ensure adequate care for mental patients, modernize prisons, and even break up the telephone system. Often judges retain jurisdiction for years as they preside over the implementation of the decrees they have issued.[81] Judges have always been policy makers; that role is not a matter of choice but flows from the roles they play in deciding cases.

The Great Debate over the Proper Role of the Courts

Some people contend that the courts have a duty to protect the interests of the public. Defenders of this *activist* judicial role argue that if Congress, the White House, and the state legislatures are unwilling or unable to resolve pressing problems when people are denied justice and their constitutional rights, then the courts must address those problems. The Supreme Court, they say, should be "a leader in a vital national seminar that leads to the formulation of values for the American people."[82]

Critics of judicial activism contend that for the past half-century, the federal courts, in their zeal to protect people, have become unhinged from their political moorings in the political and constitutional system. Even if courts make the "right" decisions, these critics argue, it is still not right for them to take over the legislative function of elected representatives. Courts should exercise self-restraint.

Others claim that the debate between those who favor judicial activism and those who favor judicial restraint oversimplifies the choices. Judges, they argue, should take a leadership role in some areas but a restrained role in others. They stand with Chief Justice Harlan F. Stone, who argued that courts have a special duty to intervene (1) whenever legislation restricts the political process by which decisions are made or (2) whenever legislation restricts the rights of "discrete and insular minorities" and (3) when guarantees of the Bill of Rights are violated. In all other areas, the political process should be allowed to work, and judges should not set aside legislation or interfere with administrative agencies merely because they would prefer some other policy or even some other interpretation of the Constitution.[83]

The People and the Court

Whether judges are liberal or conservative, defer to legislatures or not, try to apply the Constitution as they think the framers intended, or interpret it to conform to current values, there are linkages between what judges do and what the people want done. The linkages are not direct, and the people never speak with one mind, but these linkages are the heart of the matter.[84] In the first place, the president and the Senate are likely to appoint justices whose decisions reflect their values. Therefore, elections matter, because the perspectives of the people who nominate and confirm the judges are reflected in the composition of the courts. For instance, in 1992, the Supreme Court, by a 5-to-4 vote in *Planned Parenthood* v. *Casey,* refused to overturn *Roe* v. *Wade* and upheld its core holding—that the Constitution protects the right of a woman to an abortion—although upholding state regulations that do not "unduly burden" that right.[85] This close vote on abortion made it clear that presidential elections could determine whether that right would continue to be protected, depending on whether there are retirements from the bench and new appointments to the Court.

Scholars debate how public opinion influences what judges decide, whether it is direct or indirect through presidential selection and Senate confirmation of judges, but there is little question that there is a correlation between public opinion and judicial decisions.[86] Judicial opinions that reflect what the people want have the greatest survival value. When a new political coalition takes over the White House or Congress, the old regime may stay on in the federal courts. New electoral coalitions eventually take over the federal courts, and before long, new interpretations of the Constitution reflect the dominant political ideology.[87]

Judges have neither armies nor police to execute their rulings. Although Congress cannot reverse Supreme Court decisions that relate to constitutional interpretations, and only six Supreme Court decisions have been reversed by formal constitutional amendment, the political system alters judicial policy in more subtle ways. Decisions are binding on the parties to a particular case, but the policies that result from judicial decisions are effective and durable only if they are supported by the electorate. To win a favorable Supreme Court decision is to win something of considerable political value.

"American courts are not all-powerful institutions."[88] If the Court's policies are too far out of step with the values of the country, the Court is likely to be reversed. In Chief Justice William H. Rehnquist's words, "No judge worthy of his salt would ever cast his vote in a particular case simply because he thought the majority of the public wanted him to vote that way, but that is quite a different thing from saying that no judge is ever influenced by the great tides of public opinion that run a country such as ours."[89]

"Do you ever have one of those days when nothing seems constitutional?"

The Wall Street Journal, August 3, 1998. By permission of Cartoon Features Syndicate.

"The people" speak in many ways and with many voices. The Supreme Court also hands down rulings on controversies—abortion, affirmative action, and the 2000 presidential election—on which the public is deeply divided. And the justices are often likewise split in deciding those cases. The Supreme Court—and the other courts—thus generally represent and reflect the competing values of the people. Whether they agree or disagree with particular rulings, the public generally holds the Supreme Court in high regard. Notably, the Court's public approval rating remained high and virtually unchanged after its controversial decision in *Bush* v. *Gore* (2000), contrary to predictions by the four dissenting justices and critics that the Court's reputation would be badly damaged by the bare majority's ruling assuring George W. Bush's election.[90]

Although the Court is not the defenseless institution portrayed by some commentators, and its decisions are as much shapers of public opinion as reflections of it, ultimately the power of the Supreme Court in a constitutional democracy rests on retaining the support of most of the people most of the time. The Court's power rests, as Chief Justice Edward White observed, "solely upon the approval of a free people."[91] No better standard for determining the legitimacy of a governmental institution has been discovered.

Summary

1. The American judicial process is based on the adversary system. Judges in the United States play a more active role in the political process than they do in most other democracies. Unlike other countries, the United States has a dual judiciary—federal and state court systems. In both federal and state courts, individuals must have standing to sue and must assert a personal injury. Courts decide only justiciable disputes—actual cases or controversies—and not political questions.

2. Except for the Supreme Court, federal courts are established by and receive their jurisdiction directly from Congress, which must decide the constitutional division of responsibilities among federal and state courts. District courts are the trial courts of the federal judicial system, and their decisions may be reviewed by courts of appeals. Federal judges apply federal criminal and civil law but in doing so exercise discretion. Their decisions are subject to reversal by the Supreme Court, which resolves conflicts and tries to promote stability and uniformity in the law.

3. The Supreme Court has almost complete control over the cases it chooses to review as they come up from the state courts, the courts of appeals, and district courts. Law clerks and the solicitor general play important roles in determining the kinds of cases the Supreme Court agrees to decide. Its nine justices dispose of thousands of cases, but most of their time is concentrated on the fewer than 100 cases per year that they accept for review. The Court's decisions and opinions establish guidelines for lower courts and the country.

4. Partisanship and ideology are important factors in the selection of federal judges, and these factors ensure a linkage between the courts and the rest of the political system, so that the views of the people are reflected, even if indirectly, in the work of the courts. In recent decades, candidates for the presidency and the Senate have made judicial appointments an issue in their election campaigns.

5. The president's judicial nominees must be confirmed by the Senate, and the confirmation process tends to be stalled or to erupt into bitter political battles when the majority of the Senate and the president are from opposing political parties.

6. A continuing concern of major importance is the reconciliation of the role of judges—especially those on the Supreme Court—as independent and fair dispensers of justice with their vital role as interpreters of the Constitution. This is an especially complex problem in our democracy because of the power of judicial review and the significant role courts play in making public policy.

7. The debate about how judges should interpret the Constitution is almost as old as the Republic. More than 212 years after the Constitution was adopted, the argument between those who contend that judges should interpret the document literally and those who believe they cannot and should not remains in the headlines. Both liberals and conservatives have attacked judicial activism and urged judicial self-restraint.

Key Terms

judicial review
adversary system
justiciable dispute
class action suit
defendant
plea bargain

public defender system
political question
writ of habeas corpus
original jurisdiction
appellate jurisdiction
grand jury

petit jury
magistrate judge
court of appeals
senatorial courtesy
judicial self-restraint
judicial activism

stare decisis
writ of certiorari
amicus curiae brief
opinion of the court
dissenting opinion
concurring opinion

Further Reading

HENRY J. ABRAHAM, *Justices, Presidents, and Senators: A History of U.S. Supreme Court Appointments from Washington to Clinton* (Rowman & Littlefield, 1999).

ROBERT A. CARP AND RONALD STIDHAM, *The Federal Courts* (CQ Press, 2001).

CORNELL CLAYTON AND HOWARD GILMAN, EDS., *Supreme Court Decision Making: New Institutionalist Approaches* (University of Chicago Press, 1999).

CLARE CUSHMAN, *The Supreme Court Justices: Illustrated Biographies, 1789–1995,* 2d ed. (CQ Press, 1996).

DEL DICKSON, *The Supreme Court in Conference, 1940–1995* (Oxford University Press, 2001).

LEE A. EPSTEIN, JEFFREY A. SEGAL, HAROLD SPAETH, AND THOMAS WALKER, EDS., *The Supreme Court Compendium,* 2d ed. (CQ Press, 2001).

HOWARD GILLMAN, *The Votes That Counted: How the Court Decided the 2000 Presidential Election* (University of Chicago Press, 2001).

SHELDON GOLDMAN, *Picking Federal Judges: Lower Court Selection from Roosevelt Through Reagan* (Yale University Press, 1997).

KERMIT L. HALL, ED., *The Oxford Companion to the Supreme Court of the United States* (Oxford University Press, 1992).

PETER IRONS, *A People's History of the Supreme Court* (Viking, 1999).

LISA KLOPPENBERG, *Playing It Safe: How the Supreme Court Sidesteps Hard Cases and Stunts the Development of the Law* (New York University Press, 2001).

FORREST MALTZMAN, JAMES F. SPRIGGS III, AND PAUL WAHLBECK, *Crafting Law on the Supreme Court: The Collegial Game* (Cambridge University Press, 2000).

ROBERT G. MCCLOSKEY, *The American Supreme Court,* 3d ed. (University of Chicago Press, 2001).

DAVID M. O'BRIEN, ED., *Judges on Judging: Views from the Bench,* 2d ed. (Chatham House, 2003).

DAVID M. O'BRIEN, *Storm Center: The Supreme Court in American Politics,* 6th ed. (Norton, 2003).

J. W. PELTASON, *Federal Courts in the Political Process* (Doubleday, 1955).

TERRI JENNINGS PERETTI, *In Defense of a Political Court* (Princeton University Press, 1999).

GERALD N. ROSENBERG, *The Hollow Hope: Can Courts Bring About Social Change?* (University of Chicago Press, 1991).

C. K. ROWLAND AND ROBERT A. CARP, *Politics and Judgment in Federal District Courts* (University Press of Kansas, 1996).

PETER RUSSELL AND DAVID M. O'BRIEN, EDS., *Judicial Independence in the Age of Democracy: Critical Perspectives from Around the World* (University Press of Virginia, 2001).

ELLIOT E. SLOTNICK, *Judicial Politics: Readings from* Judicature, 2d ed. (American Judicature Society, 1999).

DONALD R. SONGER AND SUSAN B. HAIRE, *Continuity and Change on the United States Courts of Appeals* (University of Michigan Press, 2000).

DAVID ALISTAR YALOF, *Pursuit of Justices: Presidential Politics and the Selection of Supreme Court Nominees* (University of Chicago Press, 1999).

16
CHAPTER

FIRST AMENDMENT FREEDOMS

"CONGRESS SHALL MAKE NO LAW," DECLARES THE FIRST AMENDMENT, "RESPECTING AN ESTABLISHMENT OF RELIGION, OR PROHIBITING the free exercise thereof, or abridging the freedom of speech, or of the press, or the right of the people peaceably to assemble, and to petition the Government for a redress of grievances." In this one sentence, our Constitution lays down the fundamental principles of a free society: freedom of conscience and freedom of expression. These freedoms are essential to our individual self-determination and to our collective self-governance—to government by the people. Yet they are also vulnerable during times of war and now with recent security measures put into place to combat international terrorism.[1]

These freedoms were not constitutionally guaranteed, though, until the addition in 1791 of the first ten amendments, the Bill of Rights. For that reason, we begin this chapter by discussing the rights in the original Constitution and in the Bill of Rights as applied to both the national and state governments before turning to the "first freedoms" of religion, speech, press, and assembly.

Rights in the Original Constitution

Even though most of the framers did not think a bill of rights was necessary, they considered certain rights important enough to be spelled out in the Constitution. These rights included the writ of habeas corpus and protection against *ex post facto* laws and bills of attainder.

Foremost among constitutional rights is the **writ of habeas corpus**. Literally meaning "produce the body," this writ is a court order directing any official having a person in custody to produce the prisoner in court and explain why the prisoner is being held. As originally used, the writ was merely a judicial inquiry to determine whether a person in custody was being held as the result of the action of a court with proper jurisdiction. But over the years, it developed into a remedy for any illegal confinement. People being held

Rights in the Original Constitution

1. Habeas corpus

2. No bills of attainder

3. No *ex post facto* laws

4. No titles of nobility

5. Trial by jury in national courts

6. Protection for citizens as they move from one state to another, including the right to travel

7. Protection against using crime of treason to restrict other activities; limitation on punishment for treason

8. Guarantee that each state has a republican form of government

9. No religious test oaths as a condition for holding a federal office

writ of habeas corpus
Court order requiring explanation to a judge why a prisoner is being held in custody.

ex post facto law
Retroactive criminal law that works to the disadvantage of an individual; forbidden in the Constitution.

bill of attainder
Legislative act inflicting punishment, including deprivation of property, without a trial, on named individuals or members of a specific group.

due process clause
Clause in the Fifth Amendment limiting the power of the national government; similar clause in the Fourteenth Amendment prohibiting state governments from depriving any person of life, liberty, or property without due process of law.

can appeal to a judge, usually through an attorney, stating why they believe they are held unlawfully and should be released. The judge then orders the jailer or a lower court to show cause why the writ should not be issued. If a judge finds a petitioner is detained unlawfully, the judge may order the prisoner's immediate release. Although state judges lack jurisdiction to issue writs of habeas corpus to find out why federal authorities are holding persons, federal district judges may do so to find out if state and local officials are holding people in violation of the Constitution or national laws.

In recent years, the use of the writ of habeas corpus by federal courts to review convictions by state courts has been widely criticized. Some people believe the writ has been abused by state prisoners to get an endless and expensive round of reviews, which sometimes lead to convictions' being set aside by a federal judge after the matter has been reviewed by two or more state courts. Partly because of concerns about maintaining the principles of federalism and partly because of the growing caseloads of federal courts, the Supreme Court and Congress have severely restricted the habeas corpus jurisdiction of federal judges. The Antiterrorism and Effective Death Penalty Act of 1996, for example, restricts the number of times a person may be granted a habeas corpus review, stops appeals for most habeas petitions at the level of the U.S. Court of Appeals, and calls for deference by federal judges to the decisions of state judges unless they are clearly "unreasonable."[2]

An *ex post facto* **law** is a retroactive criminal law making a particular act a crime that was not a crime when an individual committed it, increasing punishment for a crime after the crime was committed, or lessening the proof necessary to convict for a crime after it was committed. This constitutional prohibition does not prevent the retroactive application of laws that work to the benefit of an accused person—a law decreasing punishment, for example—or prevent the retroactive application of civil law, such as an increase in income tax rates applied to income already earned.

Bills of attainder are legislative acts inflicting punishment, including deprivation of property, on named individuals or members of a specified group without a trial. For example, when Congress adopted a rider to an appropriations bill denying payment of the salaries of three federal employees for "disloyalty," the Supreme Court struck down the rider for being a bill of attainder.[3]

The Bill of Rights and the States

Although it was the framers who wrote the Constitution, in a sense it was the American people who drafted our basic charter of rights. The Constitution drawn up in Philadelphia included guarantees of a few basic rights but lacked a specific bill of rights similar to those in most state constitutions. The Federalists argued that the Constitution established a limited government that would not threaten individual freedoms, and therefore a bill of rights was unnecessary. The Antifederalists were not persuaded, and the omission aroused widespread suspicion. As a result, to persuade delegates to the state ratification conventions to vote for the Constitution, the Federalists promised to correct this deficiency. In its first session, the new Congress made good on that promise by proposing 12 amendments, ten of which were promptly ratified and became part of the Constitution.[4]

Note that the Bill of Rights applies *only to the national government*, not state governments.[5] Why not the states? The framers were confident that citizens could control their own state officials, and most state constitutions already had bills of rights. It was the new and distant central government the people feared. As it turned out, those fears were largely misdirected. The national government has generally shown less tendency to curtail civil liberties than state and local governments have.

When the Fourteenth Amendment, which applies to the states, was adopted in 1868, supporters contended that its **due process clause**—which states that no person shall be deprived by a state of life, liberty, or property without due process of law—limits states in precisely the same way the Bill of Rights limits the national government. At least, they argued, freedom of speech is protected by the Fourteenth

Key Concepts

At the outset, it is helpful to clarify certain terms—*liberties, rights, freedoms,* and *privileges*—that are often used interchangeably in discussions of rights and freedoms. We offer the following definitions.

Civil liberties The freedoms of all persons that are constitutionally protected against governmental restraint; the freedoms of conscience, religion, and expression, for example, which are secured by the First Amendment. These civil liberties are also protected by the due process and equal protection clauses of the Fifth and Fourteenth Amendments.

Civil rights The constitutional rights of all persons, not just citizens, to due process and the equal protection of the laws; the constitutional right not to be discriminated against by governments because of race, ethnic background, religion, or gender. These civil rights are protected by the due process and equal protection clauses of the Fifth and Fourteenth Amendments and by the civil rights laws of national and state governments.

Rights of persons accused of crimes The rights of all persons, guilty as well as innocent, to protection from abusive use by the government of the power to prosecute and punish persons accused of vio-

lating criminal laws. These rights are [...] Sixth, Eighth, and Fourteenth Amendme[...]

Political rights The rights of citizens to particip[...] of governance flowing from the right to vote. Th[...] Fifth, secured by the Fourteenth, Fifteenth, Nineteenth, and [...] Third Amendments.

Legal privileges Privileges granted by governments to which we have no constitutional right and which may be subject to conditions or restrictions; for example, the right to welfare benefits or to a driver's license. But once such privileges are granted, we may have a legal right to them, and they cannot be denied except for "reasonable reasons" and by appropriate procedures.

Common law Judge-made law based on the interpretation and application of legal principles—the principle of freedom of speech, for example. Australia, England, and the United States are *common law* countries, in contrast with *civil law* countries on the European Continent.

Civil law Law evolved from Roman law and based on codes that are strictly applied by judges. *Civil law* also applies to disputes between individuals and the government that carry no criminal penalties.

Amendment. But for decades, the Supreme Court refused to interpret the Fourteenth Amendment in this way. Then in *Gitlow* v. *New York* (1925), the Court announced that it assumed "that freedom of speech and of the press—which are protected by the First Amendment from abridgment by Congress—are among the fundamental personal rights and 'liberties' protected by the due process clause of the Fourteenth Amendment from impairment by the States."[6]

Gitlow v. *New York* was a revolutionary decision. For the first time, the U.S. Constitution protected freedom of speech from abridgment by state and local governments. In the 1930s and continuing at an accelerated pace during the 1960s, through the **selective incorporation** of provision after provision of the Bill of Rights into the due process clause, the Supreme Court applied the most important of these rights to the states.[7] Today the Fourteenth Amendment imposes on the states all the provisions of the Bill of Rights except those of the Second and Third Amendments, the Fifth Amendment provision for indictment by a grand jury, the Seventh Amendment right to a jury trial in civil cases, and the Ninth and Tenth Amendments (see Table 16-1).

Selective incorporation of most provisions of the Bill of Rights into the Fourteenth Amendment is probably the most significant constitutional development since the writing of the Constitution. It has profoundly altered the relationship between the national government and the states. It made the federal courts, under the guidance of the Supreme Court of the United States, the most important protectors of our liberties.

Recently, however, there has been a renewal of interest in state constitutions as independent sources of additional protections for civil liberties and civil rights.[8] Advocates of what has come to be called the *new judicial federalism* contend that the U.S. Constitution should set minimum but not maximum standards to protect our rights. State bills of rights sometimes provide more protection of rights—the rights to equal education and personal privacy, for instance—than the national Bill of Rights or the Supreme Court's rulings on its guarantees. Despite the revival of interest in state bills of rights, the U.S. Supreme Court and the national Bill of Rights remain the dominant protectors of civil liberties and civil rights.

selective incorporation
The process by which provisions of the Bill of Rights are brought within the s[...] e of the Fourteenth Amendment and [...] plied to state and local governme[...]

"...ust" Mottos "...hools"

...fervor ignited in the after... ...the terrorist attacks of Septem-... ...2001, fueled a movement to post ...motto "In God We Trust" in public school classrooms across the country. Before the attacks, only Mississippi had enacted a law requiring the posting. But three months afterward, Michigan adopted the requirement as part of its homeland security legislation. South Carolina, Utah, and Virginia, among other states, are considering similar legislation.

The American Family Association, a fundamentalist Christian organization, began a campaign in 1999 to get states to require the display of the national motto in public schools. The American Civil Liberties Union has fought the effort, claiming that it is simply a way to promote religion in schools and that it violates the First Amendment. The motto "In God We Trust" was adopted in 1956, during the cold war, and replaced *E Pluribus Unum* ("From Many, One").

SOURCE: Debbie Howlett, "'In God We Trust' Pressed for Schools," *USA Today*, February 20, 2002, A3.

TABLE 16–1 Selective Incorporation and the Application of the Bill of Rights to the States

Right	Amendment	Year
Public use and just compensation for the taking of private property by the government	5	1897
Freedom of speech	1	1925
Freedom of the press	1	1931
Fair trial	6	1932
Freedom of religion	1	1934
Freedom of assembly	1	1937
Free exercise of religion	1	1940
Separation of religion and government	1	1947
Right to a public trial	6	1948
Right against unreasonable searches and seizures	4	1949
Freedom of association	1	1958
Exclusionary rule	4	1961
Ban against cruel and unusual punishment	8	1962
Right to counsel in felony cases	6	1963
Right against self-incrimination	5	1964
Right to confront witness	6	1965
Right of privacy	1,3,4,5,9	1965
Right to an impartial jury	6	1966
Right to a speedy trial and compulsory process for obtaining witnesses	6	1967
Right to a jury trial in nonpetty cases	6	1968
Protection against double jeopardy	5	1969

Freedom of Religion

The first words of the First Amendment are emphatic and brief: "Congress shall make no law respecting an establishment of religion, or prohibiting the free exercise thereof." Note that there are *two* religion clauses: the *establishment* clause and the *exercise* clause. The Supreme Court has struggled to reconcile these two clauses, both of which are cast in absolute terms, and either of which, if expanded to a logical extreme, would clash with the other. Does a state scholarship for blind students given to a college student who decides to attend a college to become a minister violate the establishment clause by indirectly aiding religion? Or would denying the scholarship violate the student's free exercise of religion? The Supreme Court has held that giving such benefits does not violate the establishment clause.[9]

The Establishment Clause

In writing what has come to be called the **establishment clause**, the framers were reacting to the English system, wherein the crown was the head not only of the government but also of the established church—the Church of England—and public officials were required to take an oath to support the established church as a condition of holding office. The establishment clause goes beyond merely separating government from religion by forbidding the establishment of a state religion. It is designed to prevent three evils: government sponsorship of religion, government financial support of religion, and government involvement in religious matters. However, the clause does not prevent governments from "accommodating" religious needs. To what extent and under which conditions governments may accommodate these needs are at the heart of much of the debate in the Supreme Court and the country over interpreting the clause.

establishment clause
Clause in the First Amendment that states that Congress shall make no law respecting an establishment of religion. It has been interpreted by the Supreme Court as forbidding governmental support to any or all religions.

Controversies over the establishment clause are not easy to resolve. They stir deep feelings and frequently divide the justices among themselves. The prevailing interpretation stems from the decision in *Everson* v. *Board of Education of Ewing Township* (1947) that the establishment clause creates a "wall of separation" between church and state and prohibits any law or governmental action designed to specifically benefit any religion, even if all religions are treated the same.[10] That decision, though, was decided by a bare majority and upheld state support for transportation of children to private religious schools as a "child benefit."

The separation of church and state was further elaborated in *Lemon* v. *Kurtzman* (1971), which laid down a three-part test: (1) A law must have a secular legislative purpose, (2) it must neither advance nor inhibit religion, and (3) it must avoid "excessive government entanglement with religion."[11] This so-called *Lemon test* is often, but not always, used because the justices remain divided over how much separation between government and religion is required by the First Amendment.

Another test, championed by Justice Sandra Day O'Connor, is the *endorsement test*. Justice O'Connor believes that the establishment clause forbids governmental practices that a reasonable observer would view as endorsing religion, even if there is no coercion.[12] The endorsement test has been honed in a series of decisions as the Court struggled with the question of whether governments may allow religious symbols to be displayed on, in, or near public properties and in public places. For example, the Court concluded that when a nativity scene was displayed in a shopping district together with Santa's house and other secular and religious symbols of the Christmas season, there was little danger that a reasonable person would conclude that the city was endorsing religion.[13] But the Constitution does not permit a city government to display the nativity scene on the steps of the city hall, because in this context, the city gives the impression that it is endorsing the display's religious message.[14]

The Court's three most conservative justices—Chief Justice William Rehnquist and Justices Antonin Scalia and Clarence Thomas—support a *nonpreferentialist test*.[15] They believe the Constitution prohibits favoritism toward any particular religion but does not prohibit government aid to *all* religions. In their view, government may accommodate religious activities and even give nonpreferential support to religious organizations so long as individuals are not legally coerced into participating in religious activities and religious activities are not singled out for favorable treatment.[16]

By contrast, the more liberal justices—Justices David H. Souter, John Paul Stevens, Ruth Bader Ginsburg, and Stephen Breyer—usually maintain that there should be *strict separation* between religion and the state.[17] They generally hold that even indirect aid for religion, such as scholarships or teaching materials and aids for students attending private religious schools, crosses the line separating the government from religion.

Applying these generalizations, we find that the establishment clause forbids states—including state universities, colleges, and school districts—from introducing devotional exercises into the public school curriculum, including school graduations and events before football games.[18] However, the Supreme Court has not, as some people assume, entirely prohibited prayer in public schools. It is not unconstitutional for students to pray in a school building. What is unconstitutional is sponsorship or encouragement of prayer *by public school authorities*.[19] Devotional reading of the Bible, recitation of the Lord's Prayer, and posting of the Ten Commandments on the walls of classrooms in public schools have also been ruled to be unconstitutional. A state may not forbid the teaching of evolution or require the teaching of "creation science"—the belief that human life did not evolve but rather was created by a single act of God.[20]

Tax exemptions for church properties, similar to those granted to other nonprofit institutions, are constitutional. State legislatures and Congress may also hire chaplains to open each day's legislative session—a practice that has continued without interruption since the first session of Congress. But if done in a public school, this practice would be unconstitutional. Apparently, the difference is that legislators, as adults, are not "susceptible to religious indoctrination or peer pressure."[21] Also, as the joke goes, legislators need the prayer more.

In this classroom at Pearl Upper Elementary School in Pearl, Mississippi, the controversial "In God We Trust" motto is on display. Before September 11, 2001, Mississippi was the only state to require the display of this motto; however, since this time, Michigan adopted the requirement as well and several other states are considering similar legislation.

Vouchers and State Aid for Religious Schools

A troublesome area involving the separation of religion and government has revolved around states' providing financial assistance to parochial and other religious schools. The Supreme Court has tried to draw a line between permissible tax-provided aid to school-children and impermissible aid to religion.

At the college level, the problems are relatively simple. Tax funds may be used to construct buildings and operate educational programs at church-related schools as long as the money is not spent directly on buildings used for religious purposes or on teaching religious subjects. Even if students choose to attend religious schools and become ministers, government aid to these students is permissible, because such aid has a secular purpose. Its effect on religion is the result of individual choice "and it does not confer any message of state endorsement of religion."[22]

At the level of elementary and secondary schools, however, the constitutional problems are more complicated. Here the secular and religious parts of institutions and instruction are much more closely interwoven. Also, students are younger and more susceptible to indoctrination, so the chances are greater that aid to church-operated schools aids religion in violation of the establishment clause.

Despite the constitutional obstacles, some states have provided tax credits or deductions for parents who send their children to private, largely religious-run schools. Such deductions or credits available *only* to parents of children attending nonpublic schools are unconstitutional, but allowing taxpaying parents to deduct or take a credit from their state income taxes for what they paid for tuition and other costs to send their children to school—public or private—is constitutional, even if most of the benefit goes to those sending their children to private religious schools.[23]

The Supreme Court has also approved using tax funds to provide students who attend primary and secondary church-operated schools (except those that deny admission because of race or religion) with textbooks, standardized tests, lunches, transportation to and from school, diagnostic services, sign language interpreters, and teachers for remedial and enrichment classes, as well as computers and software for both public and parochial schools.[24]

One hot controversy that the Supreme Court avoided for years involved whether states may also use tax money to give parents **vouchers** for the tuition of children to attend schools of their choice, including religious schools. Maine and Vermont have long had voucher programs for students living in rural areas. But Cleveland, Milwaukee, and the state of Florida experimented with voucher programs, permitting the payment of tuition at religious schools, that faced challenges in the courts.[25] Opponents argue that such programs violate the establishment clause, while supporters counter that they do not and argue that the denial of vouchers for attending religious schools violates the free exercise clause and denies parents the freedom of school choice in opting out of dysfunctional public schools.

The Supreme Court finally addressed the constitutionality of voucher programs in *Zelman v. Simmons-Harris* (2002),[26] and by a 5-to-4 vote found Ohio's program to be neutral and permissible. Ohio's law provides low-income families in Cleveland with vouchers of up to $2,250 per child to put toward the cost of their children's attending public or private schools outside of the failing inner-city school district, and 96 percent of the vouchers went to religious schools. As a result of this ruling, there may be increased pressure on state legislatures and school boards to adopt voucher programs.

The Free Exercise Clause

The right to hold any or no religious belief is one of our few absolute rights. The **free exercise clause** affirms that no government has authority to compel us to accept any creed or to deny us any right because of our beliefs or lack of them. Requiring religious oaths as a condition of public employment or as a prerequisite to running for public office is unconstitutional. In fact, the original Constitution states, "No religious Test shall ever be required as a Qualification to any Office or public Trust under the United States" (Article VI).

vouchers
Money provided by the government to parents for payment of their children's tuition in a public or private school of their choice.

free exercise clause
Clause in the First Amendment that states that Congress shall make no law prohibiting the free exercise of religion.

Although carefully protected, the right to practice a religion has had less protection than the right to hold particular beliefs. Prior to 1990, the Supreme Court carefully scrutinized laws allegedly infringing on religious practices and insisted that the government provide some compelling interest to justify actions that might infringe on somebody's religion. In other words, the First Amendment was thought to throw a "mantle of protection" around religious practices, and the burden was on the government to justify interfering with them in the least restrictive way.

Then, in *Employment Division* v. *Smith* (1990), the Rehnquist Court significantly altered the interpretation of the free exercise clause by discarding the compelling governmental interest test for overriding the interests of religious minorities.[27] As long as a law is generally applicable and does not single out and ban religious practices, the law may be applied to conduct even if it burdens a particular religious practice.

The ruling in *Employment Division* v. *Smith* was controversial and led Congress to enact the Religious Freedom Restoration Act of 1993 (RFRA), which aimed to override the *Smith* decision and to restore the earlier test prohibiting the government—federal, state, or local—from limiting a person's exercise of religion unless the government demonstrates a compelling interest that is advanced by the least restrictive means. Congress asserted its power to pass the RFRA because the Fourteenth Amendment gives it the authority to enforce rights secured by that amendment, including the right to free exercise of religion.

Reverend Anthony Cummins, pastor of St. Peter the Apostle Church, in front of his church in Boerne, Texas, after a battle with city officials who denied the church permission to build an addition to the historic structure.

However, when the Catholic archbishop of San Antonio was denied a building permit in 1997 to enlarge a church in Boerne, Texas, because the remodeling did not comply with the city's historical preservation plan, he claimed that the city's denial of a building permit interfered with religious freedom as protected by the Religious Freedom Restoration Act. The Supreme Court then ruled the RFRA to be unconstitutional because Congress was attempting to define, rather than enforce or remedy, constitutional rights and was thereby assuming the role of the courts, which contradicted "vital principles necessary to maintain separation of powers and the federal balance."[28]

Tensions between the establishment and free exercise clauses have recently become more prominent. On the one hand, the University of Virginia denied a Christian student group funds to pay for the printing of its newspaper, *Wide Awake,* because it interpreted the establishment clause to forbid allocating student fee money to a newspaper that "primarily promotes a belief in or about a deity." The students argued that the university deprived them of their freedom of speech, including religious speech, and the Supreme Court agreed with the students.[29] On the other hand, some Christian students at the University of Wisconsin objected to the use of mandatory student activity fees for funding groups they deemed offensive and contrary to their religious beliefs. They argued that they should be exempt from paying that portion of their fees, but the Supreme Court rejected their claim.[30]

Free Speech and Free People

Government by the people is based on every person's right to speak freely, to organize in groups, to question the decisions of the government, and to campaign openly against them. Only through free and uncensored expression of opinion can government be kept responsive to the electorate and political power transferred peacefully. Elections, separation of powers, and constitutional guarantees are meaningless unless all persons have the right to speak frankly and to hear and judge for themselves the worth of what others have to say. As Justice Oliver Wendell Holmes observed, "The best test of truth is the power of the thought to get itself accepted in the competition of the market. . . . That at any rate is the theory of our Constitution. It is an experiment, as all life is an experiment."[31]

Free speech is not simply the personal right of individuals to have their say; it is also the right of the rest of us to hear them. John Stuart Mill, whose *Essay on Liberty* (1859) is the classic defense of free speech, put it this way: "The peculiar evil of silencing the expression of opinion, is that it is robbing the human race. . . . If the opinion is right, they are deprived of the

Police arrest Scott Tyler of Chicago after he set fire to an American flag on the steps of the Capitol building in Washington. The Supreme Court ruled that freedom of speech even covers "symbolic speech" like burning the U.S. flag.

opportunity of exchanging error for truth; if wrong, they lose what is almost as great a benefit, the clearer perception and livelier impression of truth, produced by its collision with error."[32]

Americans overwhelmingly support the principle of freedom of expression in general. Yet some who say they believe in free speech draw the line at ideas they consider dangerous or when speech attacks them or is critical of their race, religion, or ethnic origin. But what is a dangerous idea? Who decides? In the realm of political ideas, who can find an objective, eternally valid standard of right? The search for truth involves the possibility—even the inevitability—of error. The search cannot go on unless it proceeds freely in the minds and speech of all. This means, in the words of Justice Robert Jackson, that "freedom to differ is not limited to things that do not matter much. That would be a mere shadow of freedom. The test of its substance is the right to differ as to things that touch the heart of the existing order."[33]

Even though the First Amendment explicitly denies Congress the power to pass any law abridging freedom of speech, the amendment has never been interpreted in absolute terms. Like almost all rights, the freedoms of speech and of the press are limited. In discussing the constitutional power of government to regulate speech, it is useful to distinguish among *belief, speech,* and *action.*

At one extreme is the right to *believe* as we wish. Despite occasional deviations in practice, the traditional American view is that government should not punish a person for beliefs or interfere in any way with freedom of conscience. At the other extreme is *action,* which is usually subject to governmental restraint. As has been said, "The right to swing your fist ends where my nose begins."

Speech stands somewhere between belief and action. It is not an absolute right, like belief, but neither is it as exposed to governmental restraint, like action. Some kinds of speech—libel, obscenity, fighting words, and commercial speech—are not entitled to constitutional protection in all circumstances. Many problems arise in distinguishing between what does and does not fit into the categories of nonprotected speech. People disagree, and it usually falls to the courts to decide and to defend the free speech of individual and minority dissenters.

Judging: Drawing the Line

Plainly, questions of free speech require that judges weigh a variety of factors: What was said? In what context? How was it said? Which level of government is attempting to regulate the speech—a city council speaking for a few people, or Congress, speaking for many? (The Supreme Court is much more deferential to acts of Congress than to those of a city council or state legislature.) How is the government attempting to regulate the speech—by prior restraint (censorship) or by punishment after the speech? Why is the government doing so—to preserve the public peace or to prevent criticism of the people in power? These and scores of other considerations are involved in the never-ending process of determining what the First Amendment permits and what it forbids.

Historical Constitutional Tests

It is useful to start with the three constitutional tests developed in the first part of the twentieth century: the bad tendency test, the clear and present danger test, and the preferred position doctrine. Although they are no longer applied, they provide a background for the current judicial approach to governmental regulation of speech and to the courts' expanding protection for free speech.

THE BAD TENDENCY TEST   This test was rooted in English common law. According to the **bad tendency test,** judges presumed it was reasonable to forbid speech that has a tendency to corrupt society or cause people to engage in illegal acts. The test was abandoned because it swept too broadly and ran "contrary to the fundamental premises underlying the First Amendment as the guardian of our democracy."[34] Some legislators still appear to hold this position today, and it also seems to be the view of some college students, who want to see their institution punish student colleagues or faculty who express "hateful" or "offensive" ideas.

bad tendency test
Interpretation of the First Amendment that would permit legislatures to forbid speech encouraging people to engage in illegal action.

You Decide   Thinking It Through

SHOULD THE BILL OF RIGHTS BE AMENDED
TO PROHIBIT FLAG BURNING?

You Decide... The American flag arouses patriotic emotions in Americans, many of whom fought and saw friends die under that banner. It is understandable that they would be angry to see that flag burned by protesters. Do you think the Constitution should be amended to give Congress the right to prohibit desecration of the American flag? Or would a constitutional amendment to prohibit flag burning be an unconstitutional violation of free speech?

Thinking It Through... On June 21, 1989, the Supreme Court, in *Texas* v. *Johnson,* decided by a 5-to-4 vote that the First Amendment protects the act of burning the flag as freedom of expression. President George H. W. Bush denounced the decision and called for a constitutional amendment that would nullify it. Congress responded by passing a federal law that would make it a crime to burn or deface the flag, whatever one's purposes or intent. In June 1990, the Supreme Court declared that law unconstitutional in *United States* v. *Eichman.*

An amendment to the Constitution would give Congress the power to prohibit flag desecration. Public opinion polls show strong support for it. Forty-nine state legislatures have already indicated they would ratify such an amendment, far more than the 36 needed. A Senate majority has several times voted in favor of such an amendment but has fallen short of the two-thirds majority needed to pass a constitutional amendment.

Before you decide, you might want to read the opinions of the Supreme Court justices in *Texas* v. *Johnson,* 491 U.S. 397 (1989), and *United States* v. *Eichman,* 496 U.S. 310 (1990). You may listen to the oral arguments in these cases by going to the Oyez Web site at www.oyeznwu.edu.

THE CLEAR AND PRESENT DANGER TEST   This is perhaps the most famous test. The **clear and present danger test** was formulated by Justice Oliver Wendell Holmes Jr. in *Schenck* v. *United States* (1919) as an alternative to the bad tendency test. In the words of Justice Holmes, "The question in every case is whether the words are used in circumstances and are of such a nature as to create a clear and present danger that they will bring about substantive evils that Congress has a right to prevent."[35] A government should not be allowed to interfere with speech unless it can prove, ultimately to a skeptical judiciary, that the particular speech in question presents an immediate danger—for example, speech leading to a riot, the destruction of property, or the corruption of an election.

Supporters of the clear and present danger test concede that speech is not an absolute right. Yet they believe free speech to be so fundamental to the operations of a constitutional democracy that no government should be allowed to restrict speech unless it can demonstrate a close connection between the speech and an imminent lawless action. To shout "Fire!" falsely in a crowded theater is the most famous example of unprotected speech.

THE PREFERRED POSITION DOCTRINE   This was advanced in the 1940s when the Court applied all of the guarantees of the First Amendment to the states. The **preferred position doctrine** came close to the position that freedom of expression—the use of words and pictures—should rarely, if ever, be curtailed. This interpretation of the First Amendment gives these freedoms, especially freedom of speech and of conscience, a preferred position in our constitutional hierarchy. Judges have a special duty to protect these freedoms and should be most skeptical about laws trespassing on them. Once that judicial responsibility was established, judges had to draw lines between nonprotected and protected speech, as well as between speech and nonspeech.

clear and present danger test
Interpretation of the First Amendment that holds that the government cannot interfere with speech unless the speech presents a clear and present danger that it will lead to evil or illegal acts. To shout "Fire!" falsely in a crowded theater is Justice Oliver Wendell Holmes's famous example.

preferred position doctrine
Interpretation of the First Amendment that holds that freedom of expression is so essential to democracy that governments should not punish persons for what they say, only for what they do.

Nonprotected and Protected Speech

Today the Supreme Court holds that only four narrow categories of speech—*libel, obscenity, fighting words,* and *commercial speech*—are **nonprotected speech** because they lack social redeeming value and are not essential to democratic deliberations and self-governance.

The fact that nonprotected speech does not receive First Amendment protection does not mean that the constitutional issues relating to these kinds of speech are simple. How we prove libel, how we define obscenity, how we determine which words are fighting words, and how much commercial speech may be regulated remain hotly contested issues.

Libel

At one time, newspaper publishers and editors had to take considerable care about what they wrote for fear they might be prosecuted for **libel**—published defamation or false statements—by the government or sued by individuals. Today, through a progressive elevation of constitutional standards, it has become more difficult to win a libel suit against a newspaper or magazine.

Seditious libel—defaming, criticizing, and advocating the overthrow of government—was once subject to criminal penalties but no longer is. Seditious libel was rooted in the common law of England, which has no First Amendment protections. In 1798, only seven years after the First Amendment had been ratified, Congress enacted the first national law against **sedition**, the Sedition Act of 1798. Those were perilous times for the young Republic, for war with France seemed imminent. The Federalists, in control of both Congress and the presidency, persuaded themselves that national safety required some suppression of speech. But popular reaction to the Sedition Act helped defeat the Federalists in the elections of 1800, and the Sedition Act expired in 1801. The Federalists had failed to grasp the democratic idea that a person may criticize the government, oppose its policies, and work for the removal of the individuals in power yet still be loyal to the nation. They also failed to grasp the distinction between *seditious speech* and *seditious action*—conspiring to commit and engaging in violence against the government, which can be prosecuted and punished.

Another attempt to limit political criticism of the government was the Smith Act of 1940. That law forbade advocating the overthrow of the government, distributing material advocating the overthrow of government by violence, and organizing any group having such purposes. In 1951, during the cold war, the Supreme Court agreed that the Smith Act could be applied to the leaders of the Communist party who had been charged with conspiring to advocate the violent overthrow of the government.[36]

Since then, however, the Court has substantially modified constitutional doctrine, giving all political speech First Amendment protection. In *New York Times* v. *Sullivan* (1964), seditious libel was declared unconstitutional.[37] Now neither Congress nor any government may outlaw mere advocacy of the abstract doctrine of violent overthrow of government: "The essential distinction is that those to whom the advocacy is addressed must be urged to do something now or in the future, rather than merely to believe in something."[38] Moreover, advocacy of the use of force may not be forbidden "except where such advocacy is directed to inciting or producing imminent lawless action and is likely to incite or produce such action."[39]

In the landmark ruling in *New York Times* v. *Sullivan* and subsequent cases, the Supreme Court established guidelines for libel cases and severely limited state power to award monetary damages in libel suits brought by public officials against critics of official conduct. Neither public officials nor public figures can collect damages for comments made about them unless they can prove with "convincing clarity" that the comments were made with "actual malice." *Actual malice* means not merely that the defendant made false statements but that the "statements were made with a knowing or reckless disregard for the truth."[40]

Public figures cannot collect damages even when subject to outrageous, clearly inaccurate parodies and cartoons. Such was the case when *Hustler* magazine printed a

nonprotected speech
Libel, obscenity, fighting words, and commercial speech, which are not entitled to constitutional protection in all circumstances.

libel
Written defamation of another person. Especially in the case of public officials and public figures, the constitutional tests designed to restrict libel actions are very rigid.

sedition
Attempting to overthrow the government by force or to interrupt its activities by violence.

parody of the Reverend Jerry Falwell; the Court held that parodies and cartoons cannot reasonably be understood as describing actual facts or actual events.[41] Nor does the mere fact that a public figure is quoted as saying something that he or she did not say amount to a libel unless the alteration in what the person said was made deliberately, with knowledge of its falsity, and "results in material change."[42]

Constitutional standards for libel charges brought by private persons are not as rigid as those for public officials and figures. State laws may permit private persons to collect damages without having to prove actual malice if they can prove the statements made about them are false and were negligently published.[43]

Obscenity and Pornography

Obscene publications are not entitled to constitutional protection, but members of the Supreme Court, like everybody else, have great difficulty in defining obscenity. As Justice Potter Stewart put it, "I know it when I see it."[44] Or, as the second Justice John Marshall Harlan explained, "One man's vulgarity is another man's lyric."[45]

In *Miller* v. *California* (1973), the Court finally agreed on a constitutional definition of **obscenity**. A work may be considered legally obscene if (1) the average person, applying contemporary standards of the particular community, would find that the work, taken as a whole, appeals to a prurient interest in sex; (2) the work depicts or describes in a patently offensive way sexual conduct specifically defined by the applicable law or authoritatively construed; and (3) the work, taken as a whole, lacks serious literary, artistic, political, or scientific value.[46]

Before *Miller,* the distinction between *pornography* and *obscenity* was not clear. The *Miller* standard clarified that only hard-core pornography is constitutionally unprotected. X-rated movies and adult theaters that fall short of the constitutional definition of obscenity are entitled to some constitutional protection, but less protection than political speech, and they are subject to greater government regulation. Cities may, as New York City has done, also regulate where adult theaters may be located by zoning laws,[47] and they may ban totally nude dancing in adult nightclubs.[48] Under narrowly drawn statutes, state and local governments can also ban the sale of "adult" magazines to minors, even if such materials would not be considered legally obscene if sold to adults.

The Court has also held that *child pornography*—sexually explicit materials either featuring minors or aimed at them—is not protected by the First Amendment.[49] Just as the government may protect minors, so apparently may it protect members of the armed forces. The Supreme Court left standing a ruling of a lower court upholding an act of Congress forbidding the sale or rental on military property of magazines or videos whose "dominant theme" is to portray nudity "in a lascivious way."[50]

Pressure for regulating pornography came primarily from political conservatives and religious fundamentalists concerned that it undermines moral standards. More recently, some feminists have joined them, arguing that pornography is degrading and perpetuates sexual discrimination and violence. They argue that just as sexually explicit materials featuring minors are not entitled to First Amendment protection, so should there be no protection for pornographic materials. They contend that pornography promotes the sexual abuse of women and maintains the social subordination of women as a class. Some feminists define pornographic materials more broadly than the Court has and would include sexually explicit pictures or words that depict women as sexual objects enjoying pain and humiliation or that present abuse of women as a sexual stimulus for men.[51]

Not all feminists favor antipornography ordinances, yet those who do have been joined by social conservatives, and thus a new battle over pornography continues to be fought. For this new antipornography coalition to be successful, a substantial alteration in constitutional doctrine will be required. Unlike the Canadian Supreme Court, which redefined obscenity to include materials that degrade women,[52] the U.S. Supreme Court does not appear willing to substantially change current doctrine.

Hustler *publisher Larry Flynt agrees to a plea bargain in which obscenity charges were dropped and a fine imposed if Flynt removed X-rated videos from a downtown store.*

obscenity
Quality or state of a work that taken as a whole appeals to a prurient interest in sex by depicting sexual conduct in a patently offensive way and that lacks serious literary, artistic, political, or scientific value.

IN COMPARATIVE PERSPECTIVE

Hate Speech in Canada

Although the Supreme Court of Canada, in interpreting the nation's Charter of Rights, generally follows the rulings on freedom of speech of the Supreme Court of the United States, it refused to do so with respect to hate speech. Whereas the U.S. Supreme Court held that the First Amendment bars making hate speech a crime,* the Canadian Supreme Court upheld a law making it a crime to express "hatred against any indentifiable group . . . distinguished by colour, race, religion, or ethnic origin."

James Keegstra.

James Keegstra, a high school teacher, was convicted of communicating anti-Semitic teachings to his students. His conviction, however, was overturned by an appeals court on the ground that the law punishing hate speech violated the Charter's guarantee of freedom of expression. In reversing the lower court and upholding Keegstra's conviction and Canada's hate speech law, the Supreme Court observed:

> The international commitment to eradicate hate propaganda and, most importantly, the special role

given equality and multiculturalism in the Canadian Constitution necessitate a departure from the view, reasonably prevalent in America at present, that the suppression of hate propaganda is incompatible with the guarantee of free expression. . . .

At the core of freedom of expression lies the need to ensure that truth and the common good are attained, whether in scientific and artistic endeavors or in the process of determining the best course to take in our political affairs. . . . Nevertheless, the argument from truth does not provide convincing support for the protection of hate propaganda. Taken to its extreme, this argument would require us to permit the communication of all expression, it being impossible to know with *absolute* certainty which factual statements are true, or which ideas obtain the greatest good. . . . There is very little chance that statements intended to promote hatred against an identifiable group are true, or that their vision of society will lead to a better world. To portray such statements as crucial to truth and the betterment of the political and social milieu is therefore misguided.†

*R.A.V. v. St. Paul, 505 U.S. 377 (1992).

†Regina v. Keegstra, 3 S.C.R. 697 (1990).

Fighting Words

Fighting words were held to be constitutionally unprotected because "their very utterance may inflict injury or tend to incite an immediate breach of peace."[53] That the words are abusive, offensive, and insulting or that they create anger, alarm, or resentment is not sufficient. Thus a four-letter word worn on a sweatshirt was not judged to be a fighting word in the constitutional sense, even though it was offensive and angered some people.[54] In recent years, the Court has overturned convictions for uttering fighting words and struck down laws that criminalized "hate speech"—insulting racial, ethnic, and gender slurs.[55]

Commercial Speech

Commercial speech—such as advertisements and commercials—used to be unprotected because it was deemed to have lesser value than political speech. But in recent years, the Court has reconsidered and extended more protection to commercial speech, as it has to fighting words. In *44 Liquormart, Inc., v. Rhode Island* (1996), for instance, the Court struck down a law forbidding the advertising of the price of alcoholic drinks.[56] It now appears that states may forbid and punish only false and misleading advertising, along with advertising the sale of anything illegal—for example, narcotics. Although the Supreme Court has not specifically removed it from the nonprotected category, the Court has interpreted the First, Fifth, and Fourteenth Amendments so as to provide considerable constitutional protection for commercial speech.

fighting words
Words that by their very nature inflict injury on those to whom they are addressed or incite them to acts of violence.

commercial speech
Advertisements and commercials for products and services; they receive less First Amendment protection, primarily to discourage false and misleading ads.

Protected Speech

Apart from these four categories of nonprotected speech, all other expression is constitutionally protected, and courts strictly scrutinize government regulation of such speech. The Supreme Court uses the following doctrines to measure the limits of governmental power to regulate speech.

PRIOR RESTRAINT   Of all the forms of governmental interference with expression, judges are most suspicious of those that impose **prior restraint**—censorship before publication. Prior restraints include governmental review and approval before a speech can be made, before a motion picture can be shown, or before a newspaper can be published. Most prior restraints are unconstitutional, as the Court has said: "Any system of prior restraints of expression comes to this Court bearing a heavy presumption against its constitutional validity."[57] About the only prior restraints approved by the Court relate to military and national security matters—such as the disclosure of troop movements[58]—and to high school authorities' control over student newspapers.[59] Student newspapers at colleges and universities receive the same protections as other newspapers because they are independent and financially separate from the college or university.

VOID FOR VAGUENESS   Laws must not be so vague that people do not know whether their speech would violate the law and hence are afraid to exercise protected freedoms. Laws must not allow the authorities who administer them so much discretion that they may discriminate against people whose views they dislike. For these reasons, the Court strikes down laws under the void for vagueness doctrine.

LEAST DRASTIC MEANS   Even for an important purpose, a legislature may not pass a law that impinges on First Amendment freedoms if other, less drastic means are available. To illustrate, a state may protect the public from unscrupulous lawyers, but it may not do so by forbidding attorneys from advertising their fees for simple services. The state could adopt other ways to protect the public from such lawyers that do not impinge on their freedom of speech; it could, for example, provide for the disbarment of lawyers who mislead their clients.

CONTENT AND VIEWPOINT NEUTRALITY   Laws concerning the time, place, or manner of speech that regulate some kinds of speech but not others or that regulate speech expressing some views but not others are much more likely to be struck down than those that are content-neutral or viewpoint-neutral, that is, laws that apply to *all* kinds of speech and to *all* views. For example, the Constitution does not prohibit laws forbidding the posting of handbills on telephone poles. Yet laws prohibiting only religious handbills or only handbills advocating racism or sexism would in all probability be declared unconstitutional because they would relate to the kinds of handbills or what is being said rather than to all handbills regardless of what they say.

The lack of viewpoint neutrality was the grounds for the Court's striking down a St. Paul, Minnesota, ordinance that prohibited the display of a symbol that would arouse anger on the basis of race, color, creed, religion, or gender. The ordinance was not considered viewpoint-neutral because it did not forbid displays that might arouse anger for other reasons, for example, because of political affiliation.[60]

Freedom of the Press

Courts have carefully protected the right to publish information, no matter how journalists get it. But some reporters, editors, and others argue that this is not enough. They insist that the First Amendment gives them the right to ignore legal requests and to withhold information. They also contend that the First Amendment gives them a *right of access,* a right to go wherever they need to go to get information.

prior restraint
Censorship imposed before a speech is made or a newspaper is published; usually presumed to be unconstitutional.

Does the Press Have the Right to Withhold Information?

Although most reporters have challenged the right of public officials to withhold information, they claim the right to do so themselves, including the right to keep information from grand juries and legislative investigating committees. Without this right to withhold information, reporters insist, they cannot assure their sources of confidentiality, and they will not be able to get the information they need to keep the public informed.

The Supreme Court, however, has refused to acknowledge that reporters, and presumably scholars, have a constitutional right to ignore legal requests such as subpoenas and to withhold information from governmental bodies.[61] It is up to Congress and the states to provide such privileges for news reporters, and many states have passed *press shield laws* providing some protection for reporters from state court subpoenas.

Does the Press Have the Right to Know?

The press has argued that if reporters are excluded from places where public business is conducted or are denied access to information in government files, they are not able to perform their traditional function of keeping the public informed. In similar fashion, some reporters argue that they may enter facilities such as food markets, child care centers, and homes for the mentally ill, even using false identities, to expose racial discrimination, employment discrimination, and financial fraud. The Supreme Court, however, has refused to acknowledge a constitutional right of the press to know, although it did concede that there is a First Amendment right for the press, along with the public, to be present at criminal trials.[62]

Although they have no constitutional obligation to do so, many states have adopted *sunshine laws* requiring government agencies to open their meetings to the public and the press. Congress requires most federal executive agencies to open hearings and meetings of advisory groups to the public, and most congressional committee meetings are open to the public. Federal and state courtroom trials are also open, but judicial conferences, in which the judges discuss how to decide the cases, are not.

Congress has authorized the president to establish a classification system to keep some public documents and governmental files secret, and it is a crime for any person to divulge such classified information. So far, however, although they have been threatened, no newspapers have been prosecuted for doing so.

The Freedom of Information Act (FOIA) of 1966, since amended, liberalized access to nonclassified federal government records. This law makes the records of federal executive agencies available to the public, with certain exceptions, such as private financial transactions, personnel records, criminal investigation files, interoffice memorandums, and letters used in internal decision making. If federal agencies fail to act promptly on requests for information, applicants are entitled to speedy judicial hearings. The burden is on an agency to explain its refusal to supply material, and if the judge decides the government has improperly withheld information, the government has to pay the legal fees. Since the inception of FOIA, more than 250,000 people have requested information, and more than 90 percent of these requests have been granted.

President Bill Clinton issued an executive order calling for automatic declassification of almost all government documents after 25 years. Any person who wants access to documents that are not declassified can appeal to an Interagency Security Classification Appeals panel, which has a record of ruling in favor of releasing documents. The Electronic Freedom of Information Act of 1996 requires most federal agencies to put their files online and to establish an index of all their records. The National Aeronautics and Space Administration (NASA) has done the most of the federal agencies (see www.nasa.gov). One of the most frequent requests to NASA's Electronic Reading Room is for documents relating to unidentified flying objects (UFOs).

Free Press Versus Fair Trials

When newspapers and television report in vivid detail the facts of a crime, interview prosecutors and police, question witnesses, and hold press conferences for defendants and their attorneys—as in the O. J. Simpson murder and Oklahoma City bombing cases—they may so inflame the public that finding a panel of impartial jurors and conducting a fair trial is difficult. In England, strict rules determine what the media may report, and judges do not hesitate to punish newspapers that comment on pending criminal proceedings. In the United States, in contrast, free comment is protected. Yet the Supreme Court has not been indifferent to protecting persons on trial from inflammatory publicity. Judges may impose "gag orders" on lawyers and jurors, but not reporters, restraining them from talking about an ongoing trial, and new trials may be ordered as a remedy for prejudicial publicity. Trials may, on rare occasions, be closed to the press and the public. Although federal rules of criminal procedure forbid radio or photographic coverage on criminal cases in federal courts, most states permit televising courtroom proceedings, and court TV programs have become very popular.

Other Media and Communications

When the First Amendment was written, freedom of "the press" referred to leaflets, newspapers, and books. Today the amendment protects other media as well—the mails, motion pictures, billboards, radio, television, cable, telephones, fax machines, and the Internet. Because each form of communication entails special problems, each needs a different degree of protection.

The Mails

More than 80 years ago, Justice Oliver Wendell Holmes Jr. wrote in dissent, "The United States may give up the Post Office when it sees fit, but while it carries it on, the use of the mails is almost as much a part of free speech as is the right to use our tongues."[63] In 1965, the Court adopted Holmes's view by striking down an act that had directed the postmaster general to detain foreign mailings of "communist political propaganda" and to deliver these materials only upon the addressee's request.[64] The Court has also set aside federal laws authorizing postal authorities to exclude from the mails materials they consider obscene.

Although government censorship of mail is unconstitutional, household censorship is not. The Court has sustained a law giving householders the right to ask the postmaster to order mailers to delete their names from certain mailing lists and to refrain from sending any advertisements that they believe to be "erotically arousing or sexually provocative."[65] Moreover, Congress may forbid—and has forbidden—the use of mailboxes for any materials except those sent through the United States mails.

Handbills, Sound Trucks, and Billboards

Religious and political pamphlets, leaflets, and handbills have been historic weapons in the defense of liberty, and their distribution is constitutionally protected. So, too, is the use of their contemporary counterparts, sound trucks and billboards. A state cannot restrain the distribution of leaflets merely to keep its streets clean,[66] but it may impose reasonable restrictions on their distribution so long as they are neutrally enforced, without regard to the content.

Motion Pictures and Plays

Prior censorship of films to prevent the showing of obscenity is not necessarily unconstitutional; however, laws calling for submission of films to a government review board are constitutional only if there is a prompt judicial hearing. The burden is on the government to prove to the court that the particular film in question is obscene. Prior censorship of films by review boards was once common, but no longer. Live performances, such as plays and revues, are also entitled to constitutional protection.[67]

At a press conference, Howard Stern defends his use of raunchy language and subject matter that led to the FCC fining the Infinity Broadcasting network.

Broadcast and Cable Communications

Television remains an important means of distributing news and appealing for votes, though the Internet has gained popularity. Yet of all the mass media, broadcasting receives the least First Amendment protection. Congress has established a system of commercial broadcasting, supplemented by the Corporation for Public Broadcasting, which provides funds for public radio and television. The Federal Communications Commission (FCC) regulates the entire system by granting licenses and making regulations for their use.

The First Amendment would prevent censorship if the FCC tried to impose it. The First Amendment does not, however, prevent the FCC from imposing sanctions on stations that broadcast indecent or filthy words, even if they are not legally obscene.[68] The FCC did precisely that when it fined Infinity Broadcasting for indecent remarks by "shock jock" Howard Stern. Nor does the First Amendment prevent the FCC from refusing to renew a license if, in its opinion, a broadcaster does not serve the public interest.

The Supreme Court allows more governmental regulation of broadcasters than of newspaper and magazine publishers because space on the airwaves was limited. However, technological advances such as cable television, videotapes, and satellite broadcasting have opened up new means of communication and brought competition to the electronic media. Recognizing these changes, Congress passed the Telecommunications Act of 1996, allowing telephone companies, broadcasters, and cable TV stations to compete with one another. In adopting the act, Congress did not abandon all government regulation of the airways. On the contrary, the act calls for many new regulations—for example, requiring that all new television sets sold in the United States be equipped with V-chips that allow viewers to block programs containing violent or sexual material.

The Court has upheld a congressional requirement that cable television stations must carry the signals of local broadcast television stations.[69] The Court has also held that Congress may authorize cable operators to refuse access to leased channels for "patently offensive" programs. The Court, however, struck down congressional requirements that if a cable operator allows such offensive programming, it must be blocked and unscrambled through special devices. In *United States* v. *Playboy Entertainment Group* (2000), the Court underscored the greater protection for cable than for broadcast television. Whereas broadcast television may be required to provide programming for children and not air violence at certain times, the Court held that such rules do not apply to cable television because unwanted programming can be blocked by homeowners.[70]

Telecommunications and the Internet

Millions of Americans log on to the Internet to buy books, clothing, jewelry, airplane tickets, stocks, and bonds. Because the Internet has become a commercial marketplace and a major channel for communication, Congress is struggling with issues raised by cyberspace communication. Although Congress has imposed a moratorium on state taxation of commercial transactions on the Internet, debate continues over whether the national government should preempt state taxation. How do existing laws against copyright piracy apply to the World Wide Web? Should there be national regulation of junk e-mail, or can state laws take care of the problem? In what ways may Congress regulate indecent and obscene communications on the Web? Should Congress try to protect the privacy of those who use the Web? (For more information about privacy and developments on the Web, go to the Electronic Privacy Information Center at www.epic.org.)

As Congress and the state legislatures begin to deal with these and other new problems, legislators and judges will have to apply traditional constitutional principles to new technologies and means of communication. The Court distinguishes between a limited ban on indecent messages on radio and broadcast television and those on telephones, cable television, and the Internet. Radio and broadcast messages are readily available to children and can intrude into the privacy of the home without prior warning. By contrast, telephone messages may be blocked, and access by minors is more readily restricted.[71] In

Regulating Decency on the Internet

The Communications Decency Act of 1996 made it a federal crime to use the Internet to knowingly transmit obscene or indecent and "patently offensive" words or pictures to minors. The constitutionality of the law was immediately challenged by the American Civil Liberties Union (ACLU), which contended that "the government cannot reduce the adult population to reading or viewing only what is appropriate for children." In defending the law, the Department of Justice countered, "The Internet threatens to give every child a free pass into the equivalent of every adult bookstore and every adult video store in the country."

In *Reno* v. *ACLU* (1997), the Supreme Court struck down the provisions against transmission of indecent communications and agreed with a lower court that the Internet, "as the most participatory form of mass speech yet developed, deserves the highest protection from government intrusion."* Cyberspace, the Supreme Court concluded, is a unique medium that should receive broad First Amendment protection like books and magazines. The Internet, unlike broadcasting, is not a scarce commodity and should not be subject to the same kind of regulation as the broadcast industry. Moreover, the Internet is not as invasive as radio and television and should be given the same constitutional protection as the print media.

In 1996, Congress also enacted the Child Pornography Prevention Act, making it a federal crime to create or distribute "virtual child pornography" generated by computer images of young adults rather than actual children. When that law was challenged, the Supreme

Court struck it down as unconstitutionally broad. The law went beyond punishing child pornography, which is a crime because actual children are involved, the Court ruled, and had the potential to chill clear artistic and literary expression.†

In response to *Reno* v. *ACLU,* Congress passed the Child Online Protection Act of 1998 (COPA), which made it a crime for a commercial Web site to knowingly make available to anyone under the age of 17 sexually explicit material considered "harmful to minors" based on "community standards." That law was challenged on the grounds that it would give conservative communities a veto over sexual content on the Web. The Supreme Court disagreed but held that the law may not go into effect until lower courts have addressed other questions about COPA's impact on free speech.‡

In 2002, a federal appellate court also invalidated the Children's Internet Protection Act of 2000, which required public schools and libraries to use electronic filters on computers to block access to pornographic Web sites. The court found that the technology inadvertently blocked access to legitimate sites and hence violated the First Amendment.§

*Reno v. *ACLU,* 521 U.S. 844 (1997).

†Ashcroft v. *Free Speech Coalition,* 122 S.Ct. 1389 (2002).

‡Ashcroft v. *ACLU,* 122 S.Ct. 1389 (2002).

§Robert O'Harrow, "Internet Filtering Overruled, "*Washington Post,* June 1, 2002, A1.

its first ruling on First Amendment protection for the Internet, *Reno* v. *American Civil Liberties Union* (1997), the Court struck down provisions of the Communications Decency Act of 1996 that had made it a crime to send obscene or indecent messages to anyone under 18 years of age. In doing so, the Court emphasized the unique character of the Internet, holding that it is less intrusive than radio and broadcast television.[72]

Freedom of Assembly

In the fall of 1998, Khallid Abdul Muhammad, a known racist and anti-Semite, organized the "Million Youth March" in New York City. Mayor Rudolph Giuliani denied a permit for the march on grounds that it would be a "hate march." A federal appeals court upheld a lower court ruling that denial of the permit was unconstitutional; however, the three-judge panel placed restrictions on the event, limiting its duration to four hours and scaling it back to a six-block area. The march proceeded, surrounded by police in riot gear who broke up the demonstration after Muhammad delivered a vitriolic speech against police, Jews, and city officials.[73]

It took judicial authorities to defend the rights of these unpopular speakers and marchers, but it is not always the "bad guys" whose rights have to be protected by the courts. It also took judicial intervention in the 1960s to preserve for Martin Luther King Jr. and those who marched with him the right to demonstrate in the streets of southern cities on behalf of civil rights for African Americans.

Such incidents present a classic free speech problem. It is almost always easier, and certainly politically more prudent, to maintain order by curbing public demonstrations by unpopular groups. However, if police did not have the right to order groups to disperse, public order would be at the mercy of those who resort to street demonstrations to create tensions and provoke street battles.

Free Speech on the Steps of the U.S. Capitol

In June 2002, a federal appellate court struck down a 30-year-old ban on protests and demonstrations on the sidewalks and entrances on the east side of the U.S. Capitol. Although the case

Protests held on the steps of the U.S. Capitol, like this large demonstration against the war in Vietnam and neighboring countries, were prohibited by law for 30 years until June 2002, when a federal appellate court struck down the ban as a violation of the right to freedom of speech.

originated before the terrorist attacks of the preceding September, the government contended that increased security concerns justified the prohibition. Attorneys for the Department of Justice argued that "if this country has learned anything at all from September 11, we learned that the unthinkable can happen, the unimaginable, in fact, can be imagined by someone, and a terrible toll that can stab the heart of our nation can be exacted by a small group of people."

The appellate court rejected the government's argument that increased security needs outweigh the value of free speech. The case originated when an artist, Robert Lederman, was arrested on the steps of the Capitol in 1997 for handing out leaflets protesting restrictions on sidewalk artists in New York City.

The U.S. Capitol, said the appellate court, is "a centerpiece of democracy," in rejecting "the proposition that demonstrations of any stripe pose a greater security risk to the Capitol building and its occupants than do pedestrians, who may come and go anonymously, travel in groups of any size, carry any number of bags and boxes, and linger as long as they please." The government may regulate the size and manner of protests in public places, but an absolute ban is a "serious loss to speech," concluded the court, "for a disproportionately small government gain."

SOURCE: Neely Tucker, "Capitol Ban on Protests Nullified," *Washington Post*, June 1, 2002, p. A1.

A current controversy surrounds Attorney General John Ashcroft's decision in 2002 to allow law enforcement agents to go undercover to monitor activities and assemblies in any public place—including mosques, churches, and chat rooms on the Internet—in combating international terrorism. He thereby abandoned the Department of Justice's guidelines adopted in 1976 after Congress discovered that FBI agents were conducting surveillance and had infiltrated the civil rights movement and other groups engaged in lawful activities, as well as closely monitored King and other leaders. In response to criticisms that the new guidelines infringed on the freedoms of assembly and association, Ashcroft stressed that FBI agents would be limited to investigating terrorist activities.

Public Forums and Time, Place, and Manner Regulations

The Constitution protects the right to speak, but it does not give people the right to communicate their views to everyone, in every place, at every time they wish. No one has the right to block traffic or to hold parades or make speeches in public streets or on public sidewalks whenever he or she wishes. Governments may not censor what can be said, but they can make "reasonable" *time, place,* and *manner* regulations for protests or parades. The Supreme Court has divided public property into three categories: public forums, limited public forums, and nonpublic forums. The extent to which governments may limit access depends on the kind of forum involved.

Public forums are public places historically associated with the free exercise of expressive activities, such as streets, sidewalks, and parks. Courts look closely at time, place, and manner regulations that apply to these traditional public forums to ensure that they are being applied evenhandedly and that action is not taken because of what is being said rather than how and where or by whom it is being said.[74]

Other kinds of public property, such as rooms in a city hall or in a school after hours, may be designated as *limited public forums,* available for assembly and speech for

New York City police in riot gear formed a human wall in front of the Million Youth March and charged the stage after Khallid Abdul Muhammad, organizer of the rally, urged the audience to riot and kill.

Security Versus Civil Liberties

Judge Richard A. Posner.

In the aftermath of the terrorist attacks of September 11, 2001, Congress enacted the USA Patriot Act and President George W. Bush and Attorney General John Ashcroft issued new guidelines giving law enforcement expanded powers. Some people of Middle Eastern and Asian descent, along with civil libertarians, counter that the government is going too far in curbing basic freedoms in waging war against international terrorism. In an insightful yet provocative essay, Judge Richard A. Posner places the need for balancing security and civil liberties into legal and historical perspective.

In the wake of the September 11 terrorist attacks have come many proposals for tightening security; some measures to that end have already been taken. Civil libertarians are troubled. They fear that concerns about national security will lead to an erosion of civil liberties. They offer historical examples of supposed overreactions to threats to national security. They treat our existing civil liberties—freedom of the press, protections of privacy and of the rights of criminal suspects, and the rest—as sacrosanct, insisting that the battle against international terrorism accommodate itself to them.

I consider this a profoundly mistaken approach to the question of balancing liberty and security. The basic mistake is the prioritizing of liberty. It is a mistake about law and a mistake about history. Let me begin with law. What we take to be our civil liberties—for example, immunity from arrest except upon probable cause to believe we've committed a crime, and from prosecution for violating a criminal statute enacted after we committed the act that violates it—were made legal rights by the Constitution and other enactments. The other enactments can be changed relatively easily, by amendatory legislation. Amending the Constitution is much more difficult. In recognition of this the Framers left most of the constitutional provisions that confer rights pretty vague. The courts have made them definite.

Concretely, the scope of these rights has been determined, through an interaction of constitutional text and subsequent judicial interpretation, by a weighing of competing interests. I'll call them the public-safety interest and the liberty interest. Neither, in my view, has priority. They are both important, and their relative importance changes from time to time and from situation to situation. The safer the nation feels, the more weight judges will be willing to give to the liberty interest. The greater the threat that an activity poses to the nation's safety, the stronger will the grounds seem for

seeking to repress that activity, even at some cost to liberty. This fluid approach is only common sense. . . .

It will be argued that the lesson of history is that officials habitually exaggerate dangers to the nation's security. But the lesson of history is the opposite. It is because officials have repeatedly and disastrously underestimated these dangers that our history is as violent as it is. Consider such underestimated dangers as that of secession, which led to the Civil War; of a Japanese attack on the United States, which led to the disaster at Pearl Harbor; of Soviet espionage in the 1940s, which accelerated the Soviet Union's acquisition of nuclear weapons and emboldened Stalin to encourage North Korea's invasion of South Korea; of the installation of Soviet missiles in Cuba, which precipitated the Cuban missile crisis; of political assassinations and outbreaks of urban violence in the 1960s; of the Tet Offensive of 1968; of the Iranian revolution of 1979 and the subsequent taking of American diplomats as hostages; and, for that matter, of the events of September 11.

It is true that when we are surprised and hurt, we tend to overreact—but only with the benefit of hindsight can a reaction be separated into its proper and excess layers. In hindsight we know that interning Japanese-Americans did not shorten World War II. But was this known at the time? If not, shouldn't the Army have erred on the side of caution, as it did? Even today we cannot say with any assurance that Abraham Lincoln was wrong to suspend *habeas corpus* during the Civil War, as he did on several occasions, even though the Constitution is clear that only Congress can suspend this right. (Another of Lincoln's wartime measures, the Emancipation Proclamation, may also have been unconstitutional.) . . .

Lincoln's unconstitutional acts during the Civil War show that even legality must sometimes be sacrificed for other values. We are a nation under law, but first we are a nation. I want to emphasize something else, however: the malleability of law, its pragmatic rather than dogmatic character. The law is not absolute, and the slogan *"Fiat iustitia ruat caelum"* ("Let justice be done though the heavens fall") is dangerous nonsense. The law is a human creation rather than a divine gift, a tool of government rather than a mandarin mystery. It is an instrument for promoting social welfare, and as the conditions essential to that welfare change, so must it change.

Judge Richard A. Posner was appointed by President Ronald Reagan to the U.S. Court of Appeals for the Seventh Circuit. He clerked for liberal Justice William J. Brennan before teaching at the University of Chicago School of Law.

SOURCE: Reprinted from Richard A. Posner, "Security Versus Civil Liberties," *Atlantic Monthly,* December 2001, pp. 46–48.

limited purposes, for a limited amount of time, and even for a limited class of speakers (such as only students, only teachers, or only employees), provided the distinctions between the people allowed access and those excluded are not biased.

Nonpublic forums include public facilities such as libraries, courthouses, prisons, schools, swimming pools, and government offices that are open to the public but are not public forums. As long as people use such facilities within the normal bounds of conduct, they may not be constitutionally restrained from doing so. However, people may be excluded from such places as a government office or a school if they engage in activities for which the facilities were not created. They have no right to interfere with programs or try to take over a building—especially facilities such as a university president's office—in order to stage a political protest.

Does the right of peaceful assembly include the right to violate a law nonviolently but deliberately? We have no precise answer, but in general, **civil disobedience**, even if peaceful, is not a protected right. When Martin Luther King Jr. and his followers refused to comply with a state court's injunction forbidding them to parade in Birmingham without first securing a permit, the Supreme Court sustained their conviction, even though there was serious doubt about the constitutionality of the injunction and the ordinance on which it was based.[75]

More recently, the First Amendment right of antiabortion protesters to picket in front of abortion clinics has come into conflict with a woman's right to go to an abortion clinic. Protesters have often massed in front of clinics, shouting at employees and patrons and blocking entrances to the clinic. The Supreme Court has struck down provisions that prohibit protesters from expressing their views. But the Court has upheld injunctions that keep antiabortion protesters outside of a buffer zone around abortion clinics and also upheld injunctions that were issued because of prior unlawful conduct by the protesters. The proper constitutional test for such injunctions is "whether the challenged provisions . . . burden no more speech than necessary to serve a significant government interest," such as public safety or the right of women to go into such a clinic.[76]

The combination of First Amendment guarantees for rights and freedoms and their judicial enforcement is one of the basic features of our government and political system. As Supreme Court Justice Robert H. Jackson wrote:

> The very purpose of [the] Bill of Rights was to withdraw certain subjects from the vicissitudes of political controversy, to place them beyond the reach of majorities and officials and to establish them as legal principles to be applied by the courts. One's right to life, liberty, and property, to free speech, a free press, freedom of worship and assembly, and other fundamental rights may not be submitted to vote: they depend on the outcome of no elections.[77]

The connection between constitutional limitations and judicial enforcement is an example of the "auxiliary precautions" James Madison believed were necessary to prevent arbitrary governmental action. Citizens in other free nations rely on elections and political checks to protect their rights; in the United States, we also appeal to judges when we fear our freedoms are in danger.

civil disobedience
Deliberate refusal to obey a law or comply with the orders of public officials as a means of expressing opposition.

CIVIL LIBERTIES: THE GREAT BALANCING ACT

The war against international terrorism has highlighted the politics of rights in balancing freedom and security. In this simulation, you judge the constitutionality of state and local policies affecting civil rights and civil liberties and find out the political implications as well as how liberals, conservatives, and centrists would decide.

Go to PoliSim "Civil Liberties: The Great Balancing Act."

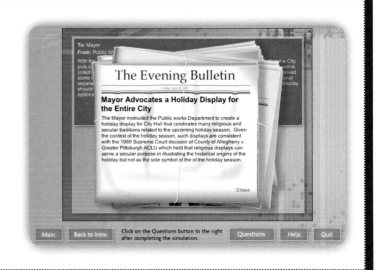

Summary

1. The Constitution protects our right to seek a writ of habeas corpus and forbids *ex post facto* laws and bills of attainder.

2. First Amendment freedoms—freedom of religion, of speech, of the press, and of assembly and association—are at the heart of a healthy constitutional democracy.

3. Since World War I, the Supreme Court has become the primary branch of government for giving meaning to these constitutional restraints. And since 1925, these constitutional limits have been applied not only to Congress but to all governmental agencies—national, state, and local.

4. The First Amendment forbids the establishment of religion and also guarantees the free exercise of religion. These two freedoms, however, are often in conflict with each other and represent conflicting notions of what is in the public interest.

5. The Supreme Court holds that there are only four categories of nonprotected speech—libel, obscenity, fighting words, and commercial speech. All other speech is protected under the First Amendment, and government may regulate that speech only when it has a compelling reason and does so in a content-neutral way.

6. Over the years, the Supreme Court has taken a pragmatic approach to First Amendment freedoms. It has refused to make them absolute rights above any kind of governmental regulation, direct or indirect, or to say that they must be preserved at whatever price. But the justices have recognized that a constitutional democracy tampers with these freedoms at great peril. They have insisted on compelling justification before permitting these rights to be limited. How compelling the justification is, in a free society, will always remain an open question, but is especially difficult during times of war.

Key Terms

writ of habeas corpus	establishment clause	preferred position doctrine	fighting words
ex post facto law	vouchers	nonprotected speech	commercial speech
bill of attainder	free exercise clause	libel	prior restraint
due process clause	bad tendency test	sedition	civil disobedience
selective incorporation	clear and present danger test	obscenity	

Further Reading

STUART BIEGEL, *Beyond Our Control? Confronting the Limits of Our Legal System in the Age of Cyberspace* (MIT Press, 2001).

LEE BOLLINGER AND GEOFFREY R. STONE, EDS., *Eternally Vigilant: Free Speech in the Modern Age* (University of Chicago Press, 2002).

JAMES MACGREGOR BURNS AND STEWART BURNS, *A People's Charter: The Pursuit of Rights in America* (Knopf, 1991).

JESSE CHOPER, *Securing Religious Liberty: Principles for Judicial Interpretation of Religion Clauses* (University of Chicago Press, 1995).

STEPHEN M. FELDMAN, ED., *Law and Religion: A Critical Anthology* (New York University Press, 2000).

MIKE GODWIN, *Cyber Rights: Defending Free Speech in the Digital Age* (Times Books, 1998).

ROBERT JUSTIN GOLDSTEIN, *Flag Burning and Free Speech: The Case of Texas v. Johnson* (University Press of Kansas, 2002).

NAT HENTOFF, *Living the Bill of Rights: How to Be an Authentic American* (HarperCollins, 1998).

LAWRENCE LESSIG, *Code and Other Laws of Cyberspace* (Basic Books, 1999).

LEONARD W. LEVY, *Emergence of a Free Press* (Oxford University Press, 1985).

LEONARD W. LEVY, *The Establishment Clause: Religion and the First Amendment* (Macmillan, 1986).

ANTHONY LEWIS, *Make No Law: The Sullivan Case and the First Amendment* (Random House, 1991).

CATHARINE A. MACKINNON, *Only Words* (Harvard University Press, 1993).

ALEXANDER MEIKLEJOHN, *Political Freedom: The Constitutional Powers of the People* (Harper & Row, 1965).

JOHN STUART MILL, *Essay on Liberty,* in *The English Philosophers from Bacon to Mill,* ed. Arthur Burtt (Random House, 1939), pp. 949–1041.

JOHN T. NOONAN JR., *The Lustre of Our Country: The American Experience of Religious Freedom* (University of California Press, 1998).

DAVID M. O'BRIEN, *Constitutional Law and Politics: Civil Rights and Civil Liberties,* 5th ed. (Norton, 2003).

SHAWN FRANCIS PETERS, *Judging Jehovah's Witnesses: Religious Persecution and the Dawn of the Rights Revolution* (University Press of Kansas, 2002).

J. W. PELTASON AND SUE DAVIS, *Understanding the Constitution,* 15th ed. (Harcourt, 2000).

FRANK S. RAVITCH, *School Prayer and Discrimination: The Civil Rights of Religious Minorities and Dissenters* (Northwestern University Press, 1999).

NADINE STROSSEN, *Defending Pornography: Free Speech, Sex, and the Fight for Women's Rights* (Scribner, 1995).

17
CHAPTER

RIGHTS TO LIFE, LIBERTY, AND PROPERTY

T HE TERRORIST ATTACKS OF SEPTEMBER 2001 ARE FORCING US TO RETHINK THE BALANCE BETWEEN LIBERTY AND SECURITY. Neither is likely to be taken for granted again. We are all affected by measures to strengthen homeland security—whether in schools; at concerts; traveling in airports, on trains, or on public streets; or in our homes. Yet we are still the freest people in the world. And we need to remember how fortunate we are to live in a society that values *due process*—established rules and regulations that restrain persons in government who exercise power. Such procedures are not available to citizens in Iraq, China, much of Africa and South America, and elsewhere in the world.

Public officials in the United States do have great power. Under certain conditions, they can seize our property, put us in jail, and—in extreme circumstances—even take our lives. The framers of our Constitution recognized that it is necessary—but dangerous—to give power to those who govern. It is so dangerous that we do not depend on the ballot box alone to keep our officials from becoming tyrants. Because political power can threaten our liberty, we parcel it out in small chunks and surround it with restraints. No single official can decide to take our lives, liberty, or property. Officials must act according to the rules. If they act outside the scope of their authority or contrary to the law, they can be restrained, dismissed, or punished. These rights to due process are the precious rights of all who live under the American flag—rich or poor, young or old, man or woman, and regardless of race, religion, or color.

In this chapter, we look at the rights of all persons to due process, but before we do, let us look at the precious freedoms and rights that flow from citizenship.

Requirements for Naturalization

An applicant for naturalization must:

1. Be over age 18.

2. Be lawfully admitted to the United States for permanent residence and have resided in the United States for at least five years and in the state for at least six months.

3. File a petition of naturalization with a clerk of a court of record (federal or state) verified by two witnesses.

4. Be able to read, write, and speak English.

5. Possess a good moral character.

6. Understand and demonstrate an attachment to the history, principles, and form of government of the United States.

7. Demonstrate that he or she is well disposed toward the good order and happiness of the country.

8. Demonstrate that he or she does not now believe in, nor within the last ten years has ever believed in, advocated, or belonged to an organization that supports opposition to organized government, overthrow of government by violence, or the doctrines of world communism or any other form of totalitarianism.

For more information about immigration and naturalization, go to the Web site of the Federation for American Immigration Reform, at www.fairus.org.

naturalization
A legal action conferring citizenship on an alien.

dual citizenship
Citizenship in more than one nation.

right of expatriation
The right to renounce one's citizenship.

Citizenship Rights

Every nation has rules that determine nationality and define who is a member of, owes allegiance to, and is a subject of the nation. But in a constitutional democracy, citizenship is an *office,* and like other offices, it carries with it certain powers and responsibilities. How citizenship is acquired and retained is therefore a matter of considerable importance.

How Citizenship Is Acquired and Lost

The basic right of citizenship was not given constitutional protection until 1868, when the Fourteenth Amendment was adopted; prior to that, each state determined citizenship. The Fourteenth Amendment states, "All persons born or naturalized in the United States, and subject to the jurisdiction thereof, are citizens of the United States and of the State wherein they reside." This means that all persons born in the United States, except children born to foreign ambassadors and ministers, are citizens of this country regardless of the citizenship of their parents. (Congress has defined the United States for this purpose to include Puerto Rico, Guam, the Northern Marianas, and the Virgin Islands.) A child born to an American citizen living abroad or who has an American citizen as a grandparent is an American citizen if either the parent or grandparent has lived in the United States for at least five years, including two of which were after age 14. Although the Fourteenth Amendment does not make Native Americans citizens of the United States and of the states in which they live, Congress did so in 1924.

NATURALIZATION   Citizenship may also be acquired by **naturalization**, a legal action conferring citizenship on an alien. Congress determines naturalization requirements. Today, with minor exceptions, nonenemy aliens over age 18 who have been lawfully admitted for permanent residence and who have resided in the United States for at least five years and in the state for at least six months are eligible for naturalization. Any state or federal court in the United States or the Immigration and Naturalization Service (INS) can grant citizenship. The INS, with the help of the Federal Bureau of Investigation (FBI), makes the necessary investigations.

Any person denied citizenship after a hearing before an immigration officer may appeal to a federal district judge. Citizenship is granted if the judge is satisfied that the applicant has met all the requirements after reviewing the FBI check that no disqualifying felony conviction has been found. The applicant renounces allegiance to his or her former country, swears to support and defend the Constitution and laws of the United States against all enemies, and promises to bear arms on behalf of the United States when required to do so by law. Those whose religious beliefs prevent them from bearing arms are allowed to take an oath swearing that if called to duty, they will serve in the armed forces as noncombatants or will perform work of national importance under civilian direction. The court or INS then grants a certificate of naturalization.

Naturalized citizenship may be revoked by court order if the government can prove that citizenship was secured by deception. But citizenship cannot be taken from people because of what they have done—for example, for committing certain crimes, voting in foreign elections, or serving in foreign armies. In addition, citizenship, however acquired, may be renounced voluntarily. Even so, the government must prove that the citizen "not only voluntarily committed the expatriating act prescribed in the statute, but also intended to relinquish his citizenship."[1]

DUAL CITIZENSHIP   Because each nation has complete authority to decide for itself the definition of nationality, it is possible for a person to be considered a citizen by two or more nations. **Dual citizenship** is not unusual, especially for people from nations that do not recognize the right of individuals to renounce their citizenship, called the **right of expatriation**. (One of the issues of the War of 1812 was that England did not recognize sailors born in England as having abandoned their English citizenship on becoming naturalized American citizens.) Children born abroad to American citizens may also be citizens of the nation in which they were born. Children born in the United States of parents from a foreign nation may also be citizens of their parents' country.

Among the nations that allow dual citizenship are Canada, Mexico, France, and the United Kingdom. One expert estimates that based on the number of American children born to foreign-born parents, the number of Americans eligible to hold citizenship in another country grows by about 500,000 a year.[2] Moreover, with more than 7 million Mexican-born immigrants in the United States and their American-born children now becoming eligible to apply for Mexican citizenship, the number of dual citizens in the United States is on the rise. Dual citizenship carries negative as well as positive consequences; for example, a person with dual citizenship may be subject to national service obligations and taxes in both countries.

Proud naturalized citizens are sworn in at an emotional ceremony.

Rights of American Citizens

An American becomes a citizen of one of our states merely by residing in that state. *Residence* as understood in the Fourteenth Amendment means the place one calls home. The legal status of residence should not be confused with the fact of physical presence. A person may be living in Washington, D.C., but be a citizen of California—that is, consider California home and vote in that state.

Most of our most important rights flow from *state* citizenship. In the *Slaughter-House Cases* (1873), the Supreme Court carefully distinguished between the privileges of U.S. citizens and those of state citizens.[3] It held that the only privileges of national citizenship are those that "owe their existence to the Federal Government, its National Character, its Constitution, or its laws." These privileges have never been completely specified, but they include the right to use the navigable waters of the United States and to protection on the high seas, to assemble peacefully and petition for redress of grievances, to vote if qualified to do so under state laws and have one's vote counted properly, and to travel throughout the United States.

In times of war, the rights and liberties of citizenship are tested and have been curbed. Although the Supreme Court overruled President Abraham Lincoln's use of military courts to try civilians during the Civil War,[4] it upheld the World War II internment of Japanese Americans in "relocation camps" and never questioned their loyalty or the government's argument that they posed a threat to national security. The Supreme Court drew a distinction between the rights of citizenship during peacetime and wartime, observing that, "hardships are part of war, and war is an aggregation of hardships. All citizens alike, both in and out of uniform, feel the impact of war in greater or lesser measure. Citizenship has it responsibilities as well as its privileges, and in time of war the burden is always heavier."[5] The Supreme Court also approved the use of military tribunals to try captured foreign saboteurs[6] but held that citizens may not be subject to courts-martial or denied the guarantees of the Bill of Rights.[7] For that reason, John Walker Lindh, the young American captured fighting with the Taliban in Afghanistan, was accorded the assistance of counsel and tried in court. However, in his war against international terrorism, President George W. Bush issued orders declaring U.S. citizens "enemy combatants," for plotting with the al Qaeda network and other terrorists to deploy radioactive "dirty bombs" in the United States, and authorized their detention in military compounds, without counsel or trial in a court of law.[8] His orders are controversial and likely to be challenged in the courts and reviewed by the Supreme Court.[9]

THE RIGHT TO LIVE AND TRAVEL IN THE UNITED STATES   This right, which is not subject to any congressional limitation, is perhaps the most precious aspect of American citizenship. Aliens have no such right. They may be stopped on the high seas or at the borders and turned away if they fail to meet the terms and conditions stipulated by Congress for admission. Today millions of people around the world yearn to come and live in the United States, but only American citizens have a constitutionally guaranteed right to do so.

THE RIGHT TO TRAVEL ABROAD   The right to international travel can be regulated within the bounds of due process. Under current law, it is unlawful for citizens to leave or enter the United States without a valid passport (except as otherwise provided by the president, as has been done for travel to Mexico, Canada, and parts of the Caribbean). Travel to Cuba is forbidden unless special permission is granted, as has increasingly been done for journalists, artists, scholars, and politicians.

Rethinking the Second Amendment

The Second Amendment states, "A well regulated Militia, being necessary to the security of a free State, the right of the people to keep and bear Arms, shall not be infringed." In its principal ruling on the amendment, upholding the National Firearms Act of 1934, the Supreme Court ruled that it does not guarantee a private right to possess firearms but instead was designed to ensure the effectiveness of the militia, because when it was adopted there was no permanent U.S. military.* Until the presidency of George W. Bush, every Department of Justice took the same position, that the Second Amendment does not confer a "right to bear arms."

Attorney General John Ashcroft, however, reversed the policy of the Department of Justice in taking the position that "the text and original intent of the Second Amendment clearly protect the right of individuals to keep and bear arms." He conceded that the right to bear arms remains subject to "reasonable restrictions" and regulations. Still, the Department of Justice is defending this new policy in several cases, and the Supreme Court may well have to rule again on the matter.†

*United States v. Miller, 307 U.S. 174 (1939).

†Jack Rakove, "Faulty Rethinking of the 2nd Amendment," New York Times, May 12, 2002, p. WK15.

Immigrants arriving at Ellis Island in 1900 came with high hopes but few material possessions.

Rights of Aliens

During periods of suspicion and hostility toward aliens, the protections of citizenship are even more precious. True, the Constitution protects many rights of *all persons,* not just of American citizens; for example, neither Congress nor the states can deny to aliens the right of freedom of religion or the right of freedom of speech. Nor can any government deprive any person, unless deemed an "enemy combatant," of the due process of the law or equal protection under the laws.

However, Congress may deny or limit welfare and many other kinds of benefits to aliens. Congress has denied most federally assisted benefits to illegal immigrants and has permitted states to deny them many other benefits, making an exception only for emergency medical care, disaster relief, and some nutrition programs. While states have considerable discretion over what benefits they give to aliens, the Supreme Court has held that states cannot constitutionally exclude children of undocumented aliens from the public schools or charge their parents tuition.[10]

Admission to the United States

President Franklin Roosevelt, reminding us of our heritage as a haven for people fleeing religious and political persecution, opened his address to a convention of the Daughters of the American Revolution with the salutation, "Fellow immigrants and revolutionaries." Some Americans, however, are concerned that admitting so many people from abroad will dilute American traditions and values. Throughout our history, debates have flared among those wishing to open our borders and those wishing to close them.

Aliens do not have a constitutional right to enter the United States. Congress has wide discretion in setting the numbers, terms, and conditions under which aliens can enter and stay in the United States. The Immigration Act of 1965, as amended in 1990 and 1996, sets an annual ceiling of 675,000 nonrefugee aliens allowed to come here as permanent residents, but when refugees and other exempt categories are added, about 800,000 people enter the United States each year. The law also sets an annual limit on immigrants from any single country. Preference is given for family reunification and to people who have special skills or who are needed to fill jobs for which U.S. workers are not available. Another provision allows for the admission of "millionaire immigrants" who are willing and able to invest a substantial sum to create or support a business in the United States that will provide jobs for Americans. There have been few takers for admission under this provision. There is also a "diversity" category to provide visas for 55,000 immigrants from 34 countries whether or not they have relatives living in the United States. These visas are drawn annually by lottery from a pool of qualified applicants.

In addition to regularly admitted aliens, political refugees are admitted. In recent years, more than 100,000 were admitted annually, but the Bush administration decreased the number to 70,000 in 2002.[11] *Political refugees* are people who have well-founded fears of persecution in their own countries based on their race, religion, nationality, social class, or political opinion. People admitted as political refugees can apply to become permanent residents after one year. The attorney general, acting through the Immigration and Naturalization Service, may also grant *asylum* to applicants who have well-founded fears of persecution in the country to which they would be returned, based on their race, religion, nationality, membership in a particular social group, or political opinion. It is not enough, however, that applicants face the same terrible conditions that all other citizens of their country face or that they wish to escape bad economic conditions. They must show specific danger of persecution.

The Immigration and Naturalization Service may turn back at the border persons seeking asylum if it considers their requests insubstantial; it may even hold them in detention camps. The president may order the Coast Guard—as Presidents George H. W. Bush and Bill Clinton did with respect to Haitian and Cuban refugees—to stop people on the high seas before they enter the territorial waters of the United States and return them to the country from which they have fled without determining whether they qualify as refugees.[12]

HOW SHOULD THE UNITED STATES GOVERNMENT DEAL WITH UNDOCUMENTED ALIENS?

You Decide... An estimated 2.3 to 2.4 million undocumented aliens—mostly from Mexico and other nations in Central and South America and a few from Canada and Poland—illegally cross our borders, not because they fear political persecution, but because they see greater economic opportunity in the United States. Even though most undocumented immigrants from Mexico return to Mexico after only two years and well over half return within ten years, undocumented aliens present a big political problem. How should the United States' government deal with this problem?

Thinking It Through... The inability to keep illegal aliens out of the country is not a question of constitutional power, for Congress has complete power over the admission of aliens. Rather, the problems are political and practical. Although Congress has authorized an increase in the number of border patrol guards and funded additional fencing of the California-Mexico border, there are thousands of miles of borders. Moreover, it is difficult to track down undocumented aliens once inside the United States and then expel them in a fashion consistent with the practices and policies of a free society.

Congress faces conflicting pressures: from Hispanic groups concerned that making it illegal to hire undocumented workers will make employers hesitate to hire any Hispanics, from employers who do not want to keep costly records and investigate the legal status of everybody they hire, from employers of farm workers who want to be sure they will have enough laborers to pick seasonal crops, from American workers who do not want undocumented workers being used to keep wages low, and from city and local governmental officials who have to find the funds to provide social services for undocumented aliens.

The United States government tends to consider immigration policy a purely internal matter. In California and some other states, there are strong anti-immigration pressures. Immigration policy clearly affects our relations with other nations, especially with Mexico, as the lengthy negotiations over the North American Free Trade Agreement (NAFTA) demonstrated. Although we view immigration policy as a matter of national sovereignty, Mexicans see it as a matter that directly affects them and have advocated "open borders."

Nonetheless, many people are still willing to risk great danger to get here and suffer detention once they arrive, just for the chance of being granted asylum. According to the 2000 census, an estimated 115,000 immigrants from the Middle East alone are here illegally.[13]

Once in the United States, aliens are subject to the full range of obligations, including the payment of taxes. Aliens are counted in the census for the purpose of apportioning seats in the U.S. House of Representatives. Legally admitted aliens may be detained and deported for a variety of reasons—for example, conviction of crimes involving immoral acts, turpitude, incitement of terrorist activity, illegal voting in elections, and conviction of domestic violence. In the months following the September 2001 terrorist attacks, over 1,100 people were detained for questioning and their identities not disclosed, and approximately 5,000 more people of Middle Eastern descent were questioned voluntarily.[14]

Property Rights

Constitutional Protection of Property

Property does not have rights. People do. People have the right to own, use, rent, invest in, buy, and sell property. Historically, the close connection between liberty and ownership of property, between property and power, has been emphasized in American political thinking and American political institutions. A major purpose of the framers of the Constitution was to establish a government strong enough to protect people's rights to use and enjoy their property. At the same time, the framers wanted to limit government so it could not endanger that right. As a result, the framers included in the Constitution a variety of clauses protecting **property rights**.

Of special concern to the framers were the efforts of some state legislatures to protect debtors at the expense of their creditors by issuing paper currency and setting aside private contracts. To prevent these practices, the legal tender and contract clauses in the Constitution forbid states from making anything except gold or silver legal tender for the payment of debts and from passing any "Law impairing the Obligation of Contracts."

The **contract clause** (Article I, Section 10) was designed to prevent states from extending the period during which debtors could meet their payments or otherwise get out of contractual obligations. The framers had in mind an ordinary contract between private persons. However, beginning with Chief Justice John Marshall (1801–1835), the Supreme Court expanded the coverage of the clause to prevent states from taking away privileges previously conferred on corporations. In effect, the contract clause was used to protect property and to maintain the status quo at the expense of a state's power.

In the late nineteenth century, however, the Supreme Court gradually began to restrict the coverage of the contract clause and to subject contracts to what in constitutional law are known as **police powers**—the powers of states to protect the public health, safety, and welfare of their residents. By 1934, the Supreme Court actually held that even contracts between individuals—the very ones the contract clause was intended to protect—could be modified by state law to avert social and economic catastrophe.[15] Although the contract clause is still invoked occasionally to challenge state regulation of property, it is no longer a significant limitation on governmental power.

What Happens When the Government Takes Our Property?

Both the national and state governments have the power of **eminent domain**—the power to take private property for public use—but the owner must be fairly compensated. This limitation, contained in the Fifth Amendment, was the first provision of the Bill of Rights to be enforced as a limitation on state governments as well as on the national government.[16]

What constitutes a "taking" for purposes of eminent domain? Ordinarily, but not always, the taking must be direct, and a person must lose title and control over the property. Sometimes, especially in recent years, the courts have found that a governmental taking has gone "too far," and the government must pay compensation to its owners, even when title is left in the name of the owners.[17] These are called **regulatory takings**. Thus if a government creates landing and takeoff paths for airplanes over property adjacent to an airport, making the land completely unsuitable for its original use (say, raising chickens), compensation is warranted.[18] The government may, however, impose land use and environmental regulations, temporarily prohibiting the development of a property, without compensating the owners.[19]

"Just compensation" is not always easy to define. When there is a dispute over compensation, the courts make the final resolution based on the rule that "the owner is entitled to receive what a willing buyer would pay in cash to a willing seller at the time of the taking."[20] An owner is not entitled to compensation for the personal value of an old, broken-down house that is loved dearly—just the value of the old, broken-down house.

Due Process Rights

Perhaps the most difficult parts of the Constitution to understand are the clauses in the Fifth and Fourteenth Amendments forbidding the national and state governments to deny any person life, liberty, or property without "due process of law." Cases involving these clauses have resulted in hundreds of Supreme Court decisions. Even so, it is im-

property rights
The rights of an individual to own, use, rent, invest in, buy, and sell property.

contract clause
Clause of the Constitution (Article I, Section 10) originally intended to prohibit state governments from modifying contracts made between individuals; for a while interpreted as prohibiting state governments from taking actions that adversely affect property rights; no longer interpreted so broadly and no longer constrains state governments from exercising their police powers.

police powers
Inherent powers of state governments to pass laws to protect the public health, safety, and welfare; the national government has no directly granted police powers but accomplishes the same goals through other delegated powers.

eminent domain
Power of a government to take private property for public use; the U.S. Constitution gives national and state governments this power and requires them to provide just compensation for property so taken.

regulatory taking
Government regulation of property so extensive that government is deemed to have taken the property by the power of eminent domain, for which it must compensate the property owners.

possible to explain *due process* precisely. In fact, the Supreme Court has refused to give due process a precise definition and has emphasized that "due process, unlike some legal rules, is not a technical conception with a fixed content unrelated to time, place and circumstances."[21] We define **due process** as rules and regulations that restrain those in government who exercise power. There are, however, basically two kinds of due process: procedural and substantive.

Procedural Due Process

Traditionally, **procedural due process** refers not to the law itself but to the *way in which a law is applied.* To paraphrase Daniel Webster's famous definition, the due process of law requires a procedure that hears before it condemns, proceeds upon inquiry, and renders judgment only after a trial or some kind of hearing. Originally, procedural due process was limited to criminal prosecutions, but it now applies to most kinds of governmental proceedings. It is required, for instance, in juvenile hearings, disbarment proceedings, proceedings to determine eligibility for welfare payments, revocation of drivers' licenses, and disciplinary proceedings in state universities and public schools.

A law may also violate the procedural due process requirement if it is too vague or if it creates an improper presumption of guilt. A vague statute fails to provide adequate warning and does not contain sufficient guidelines for law enforcement officials, juries, and courts.

The liberty that is protected by due process includes "the right of the individual to contract, to engage in any of the common occupations of life, to acquire useful knowledge, to marry, to establish a home and bring up children, to worship God according to the dictates of his own conscience, and generally to enjoy those common law privileges long recognized as essential to the orderly pursuit of happiness by free men."[22] The property protected by due process includes a variety of rights that may be conferred by state law, such as certain kinds of licenses, protection from being fired from some jobs except for just cause (for example, incompetence) and according to certain procedures, and protection from deprivation of certain pension rights.

The USA PATRIOT Act of 2001

Enacted in response to the terrorist attacks of September 11, 2001, the USA PATRIOT Act authorizes:

- Monitoring of international students

- Roving wiretaps—wiretaps on any telephone used by a person suspected of terrorism; key-logger devices, which register every stroke made on a computer; and Internet wiretaps

- Police searches of private property without prior notification of the owners and without a search warrant

- A lower standard for judicial approval of wiretaps for individuals suspected of terrorist activities

- The attorney general's designating certain domestic groups as terrorist organizations and blocking the entry into the country of foreigners aligned with them

- The Central Intelligence Agency's investigating Americans suspected of having connections to terrorism

- Treasury Department monitoring of financial transactions—bank accounts, mutual funds, and brokerage deals—and medical and other electronic records

- The detention and deportation of foreigners suspected of having connections to terrorist organizations

Note: The full title of the law is the Uniting and Strengthening America by Providing Appropriate Tools Required to Intercept and Obstruct Terrorism (USA PATRIOT) Act of 2001.

due process
Established rules and regulations that restrain people in government who exercise power.

procedural due process
Constitutional requirement that governments proceed by proper methods; places limits on how governmental power may be exercised.

Substantive Due Process

Procedural due process places limits on *how* governmental power may be exercised; **substantive due process** places limits on *what* a government may do. Procedural due process mainly limits the executive and judicial branches because they apply the law and review its application; substantive due process mainly limits the legislative branch because it enacts laws. Substantive due process means that an "unreasonable" law, even if properly passed and properly applied, is unconstitutional. It means that there are certain things governments *should not be allowed to do.*

Before 1937, substantive due process was used primarily to protect the right of employers to make contracts with employees freely, without government interference.[23] During this period, the Supreme Court was dominated by conservative jurists who considered almost all social welfare legislation unreasonable. They used the due process clause to strike down laws setting maximum hours of labor, establishing minimum wages, regulating prices, and forbidding employers to fire workers because they joined a union.

Since 1937, the Supreme Court has largely refused to apply the doctrine of substantive due process in reviewing laws regulating business enterprises and economic interests. The Court now believes that deciding what constitutes reasonable regulation of business and commercial life is a legislative, not a judicial, responsibility. As long as the justices find a conceivable connection between a law regulating business and the promotion of the public welfare, the Supreme Court will not interfere with laws passed by Congress or state legislatures.

This does not mean, however, that the Court has abandoned substantive due process. On the contrary, substantive due process has taken on new life as a protector of civil liberties, especially the right of privacy. Substantive due process has deep roots in concepts of natural law and a long history in the American constitutional tradition. For most Americans most of the time, it is not enough merely to say that a law reflects the wishes of the popular or legislative majority. We also want our laws to be just, and we continue to rely heavily on judges to decide what is just.

Privacy Rights

The most important extension of substantive due process in recent decades has been its expansion to protect the right of privacy, especially marital privacy. Although there is no mention of the right of privacy in the Constitution, in *Griswold* v. *Connecticut* (1965), the Supreme Court pulled together elements of the First, Third, Fourth, Fifth, Ninth, and Fourteenth Amendments to recognize that personal privacy is one of the rights protected by the Constitution.[24]

There are three aspects of this right: (1) the right to be free from governmental surveillance and intrusion, especially in marital matters; (2) the right not to have private affairs made public by the government; and (3) the right to be free in thought and belief from governmental regulations.[25]

Abortion Rights

The most controversial aspect of constitutional protection of privacy relates to the extent of state power to regulate abortions. In *Roe* v. *Wade* (1973), the Supreme Court ruled that (1) during the first trimester of a woman's pregnancy, it is an unreasonable and therefore unconstitutional interference with her liberty and privacy rights for a state to set any limits on her choice to have an abortion or on her doctor's medical judgments about how to carry it out; (2) during the second trimester, the state's interest in protecting the health of women becomes compelling, and a state may make a reasonable regulation about how, where, and when abortions may be performed; and (3) during the third trimester, when the fetus becomes capable of surviving outside the womb, the state's interest in protecting the unborn child is so important that the state can prohibit abortions altogether, except when necessary to preserve the life or health of the mother.[26]

substantive due process
Constitutional requirement that governments act reasonably and that the substance of the laws themselves be fair and reasonable; places limits on what a government may do.

The *Roe* decision led to decades of heated public debate and attempts by Presidents Ronald Reagan and the first George Bush to select Supreme Court justices who might be expected to reverse it. Nonetheless, *Roe* v. *Wade* was reaffirmed in *Planned Parenthood* v. *Casey* (1992). A bitterly divided Rehnquist Court, by a five-person majority (O'Connor, Kennedy, Souter, Blackmun, and Stevens), upheld the view that the due process clauses of the Constitution protect a woman's liberty to choose an abortion prior to viability. The Court, however, held that the right to have an abortion prior to viability may be subject to state regulation that does not "unduly burden" it. In other words, states may make "reasonable regulations" on how a woman exercises her right to an abortion so long as they do not prohibit any woman from making the ultimate decision on whether to terminate a pregnancy before viability.[27]

Applying the undue burden test, the Court has held, on the one hand, that states can prohibit the use of state funds and facilities for performing abortions; states may make a minor's right to an abortion conditional on her first notifying at least one parent or a judge; and states may require women to sign an informed consent form and to wait 24 hours before having an abortion. On the other hand, a state may not condition a woman's right to an abortion on her first notifying her husband. The Court also struck down Nebraska's ban on "partial birth" abortions in *Stenberg* v. *Carhart* (2000) because it completely forbade one kind of medical procedure and provided no exception for when a woman's life is at stake and thus imposed an "undue burden" on women.[28]

Sexual Orientation Rights

Although there is general agreement on how much constitutional protection is provided for marital privacy, in *Bowers* v. *Hardwick* (1986), the Supreme Court refused to extend such protection to relations between homosexuals.[29] By a 5-to-4 vote, the Court refused to declare unconstitutional a Georgia law that made consensual sodomy a crime. That homosexual sodomy occurs in the privacy of the home, said the majority, does not matter. But a number of state supreme courts, including that in Georgia, found greater privacy protection in their state constitutions than the U.S. Supreme Court found in the U.S. Constitution. In 1999, the Vermont state supreme court held that same-sex couples must be given the same benefits and protections as married couples,[30] and the state legislature enacted a law recognizing the "civil unions" of homosexuals. In 2002, California likewise passed a law giving homosexual couples the same rights and benefits as married heterosexuals; still, 13 states have laws outlawing homosexual behavior.[31]

In *Boy Scouts of America* v. *Dale* (2000), again by a 5-to-4 vote, the Supreme Court held that a New Jersey public accommodations law could not be applied to keep the Boy Scouts from excluding gays from being Scout leaders.[32] The Court majority concluded that the Boy Scouts is a private association and as such has a right to exclude people whose beliefs and conduct are inconsistent with the Scouts' views and mission.

The U.S. Supreme Court, in *Romer* v. *Evans* (1996), struck down an initiative amending the Colorado constitution that prohibited all legislative, executive, or judicial action designed to protect homosexuals at any level of state or local government. Although the Court did not rule on the basis of substantive due process, it held this provision to violate the equal protection clause because it lacked a rational basis and simply represented a prejudice toward a particular group of people. Justice Antonin Scalia in dissent accused the Court of taking sides in "the cultural wars through an act not of judicial judgment but of political will."[33]

Because of the strong emotions on both sides of this issue, the right of privacy as an element of substantive due process is one of the developing edges of constitutional law, one about which people both on and off the Court have strong disagreements. How the Supreme Court handles privacy issues has become front-page news.

The battle over abortion has been fought in the courts and on the streets, and has been a key issue in recent presidential elections. Republicans anticipate that George W. Bush will appoint justices to the U.S. Supreme Court who will reverse Roe v. Wade.

Rights of Persons Accused of Crimes

Despite what you sometimes see in television police dramas, law enforcement officers have no general right to break down doors and invade homes. They are not supposed to search people except under certain conditions, and they have no right to arrest them except under certain circumstances. They also may not compel confessions, and they must respect other procedural guarantees aimed at ensuring fairness and the rights of the accused. Persons accused of crimes are guaranteed these and other rights under the Fourth, Fifth, Sixth, Eighth, and Fourteenth Amendments.

Freedom from Unreasonable Searches and Seizures

According to the Fourth Amendment, "The right of the people to be secure in their persons, houses, papers, and effects, against unreasonable searches and seizures, shall not be violated, and no Warrants shall issue, but upon probable cause, supported by Oath or affirmation, and particularly describing the place to be searched, and the persons or things to be seized."

Protection from unreasonable searches and seizures requires police, if they have time, to obtain a valid **search warrant**, issued by a magistrate after the police indicate under oath that they have *probable cause* to justify its issuance. Magistrates must perform this function in a neutral and detached manner and not serve merely as rubber stamps for the police. The warrant must specify the place to be searched and the things to be seized. *General search warrants*—warrants that authorize police to search a particular place or person without limitation—are unconstitutional. A search warrant is usually needed to search a person in any place he or she has an "expectation of privacy that society is prepared to recognize as reasonable," for example, in a hotel room, a rented home, or a friend's apartment.[34] In short, the Fourth Amendment protects people, not places, from unreasonable governmental intrusions.[35]

Police may make reasonable *warrantless searches* in *public places* if the officers have probable cause, or at least a reasonable suspicion, that the persons in question have com-

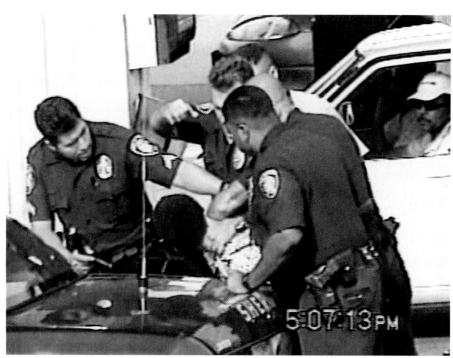

search warrant
A writ issued by a magistrate that authorizes the police to search a particular place or person, specifying the place to be searched and the objects to be seized.

Police brutality against minorities is a widespread problem throughout the United States and serves as a painful reminder that not all U.S. citizens are treated equally under the law. Here police in Inglewood, California are shown viciously beating 16-year-old Donovan Jackson in July 2002 after his father was pulled over for a routine traffic stop.

mitted or are about to commit crimes. No later than two days after making such an arrest, the police must take the arrested person to a magistrate so that the magistrate—not just the police—can decide whether probable cause existed to justify the warrantless arrest.[36] Probable cause, however, does not, except in extreme emergencies, justify a warrantless arrest of people in their own homes.

Under the common law, police officers apprehending a fleeing suspected felon can use weapons that might result in the felon's serious injury or even death. But the Fourth Amendment places substantial limits on the use of what is called *deadly force.* It is unconstitutional to shoot at an apparently unarmed, fleeing suspected felon unless the officer has probable cause to believe that the suspect poses a significant threat of death or serious injury to the officer or others. Also, when feasible, the officer must first warn the suspect, "Halt or I'll shoot."

Not every time the police stop a person to ask questions or to seek that person's consent to a search is there a seizure or detention requiring probable cause or a warrant. If the police just ask questions or even seek consent to search an individual's person or possessions in a noncoercive atmosphere, there is no detention. "So long as a reasonable person would feel free 'to disregard the police and go about his business,' the encounter is consensual and no reasonable suspicion is required." But if the person refuses to answer questions or consent to a search, and the police, by either physical force or a show of authority, restrain the movement of the person, even though there is no arrest, the Fourth Amendment comes into play.[37] For example, if police approach people in airports and request identification, this act by itself does not constitute a detention. The same is true if police ask bus passengers for consent to search their luggage for drugs. But if the police do more, especially after consent is refused, then their actions require them to have some objective justification for the search beyond mere suspicion.[38]

The Supreme Court also upheld, in *Terry* v. *Ohio* (1968), a *stop and frisk* exception to searches of individuals when officers have reason to believe they are armed and dangerous or have committed or are about to commit a criminal offense. The *Terry* search is limited to a quick pat-down to check for weapons that might be used to assault the arresting officer, to check for contraband, to determine identity, or to maintain the status quo while obtaining more information.[39] If an officer stops and frisks a suspect to look for weapons and finds criminal evidence that might justify an arrest, the officer can make a full search.[40] Police and border guards may also conduct *border* searches—searches of persons and the goods they bring with them at border crossings.[41] The border search exception also permits officials to open mail entering the country if they have "reasonable cause" to suspect it contains merchandise imported in violation of the law.[42]

There are several other exceptions to the general rule against warrantless searches and seizures of what is found by police and customs officials. The most important are the following.

1. *The Plain-View Exception.* The plain-view exception permits officers to seize evidence without a warrant if they are lawfully in a position from which the evidence can be viewed, it is immediately apparent to them that the items they observe are evidence of a crime or are contraband, and they have probable cause to believe—a reasonable suspicion will not do—that the evidence uncovered is contraband or evidence of a crime.[43]

2. *Exigent Circumstances.* Searches are permissible when officers do not have time to secure a warrant before evidence is destroyed, when a criminal escapes capture, or when there is need "to protect or preserve life or avoid serious injury." An example is that firefighters and police may enter a burning building without a warrant and may remain there for a reasonable time to investigate the cause of the blaze after the fire has been extinguished. However, after the fire has been put out, the emergency is not to be used as an excuse to make an exhaustive, warrantless search for evidence.

Police may detain and search cars and their passengers if they have probable cause to believe the passengers may be involved in criminal activity.

Use of metal detectors and locker searches at schools does not require search warrants and other protections applied to police searches.

3. *The Automobile Exception.* If officers have probable cause to believe that an automobile is being used to commit a crime, even a traffic offense, or that it contains persons who have committed crimes, or that it contains evidence of crimes, they may stop the automobile, detain the persons found therein, and search them and any containers or packages found inside the car.[44] Once an automobile has been lawfully detained, the police officers may order the driver and passengers to get out of the car without violating the Fourth Amendment.[45]

4. *Foreign Agents.* Although never directly sustained by the Supreme Court, Congress has endorsed the presidential claim that a president can authorize warrantless wiretaps and physical searches of agents of foreign countries. Congress created the Foreign Intelligence Surveillance Court to approve such requests; this court, consisting of federal district judges, meets in secret. The USA PATRIOT Act of 2001 expanded the size of this court and lowered the basis for its approval of warrants in cases involving terrorism and permits searches for intelligence and just evidence of terrorist activities.

In addition, various administrative searches by nonpolice government agents, such as teachers and health officials, do not require search warrants. Rules governing the conduct of such administrative searches are more lenient than those for searches by police investigating crimes. Administrative searches conducted without grounds for suspicion of particular individuals have been upheld in certain limited circumstances.[46]

One recent troublesome area relates to **racial profiling**—the police practice targeting members of certain racial groups for street questioning or traffic stops on the assumption that members of these groups are likely to be engaged in illegal activities. African Americans and civil rights organizations have complained for years about the practice because police do not need probable cause to stop someone and because it encourages racial discrimination.[47] After the September 2001 terrorist attacks, Arab Americans complained about their being targeted by police.[48]

Another controversial practice is the recent expansion of compulsory, random drug testing. The Supreme Court has upheld the constitutionality of blood and urine tests of rail employees involved in train accidents, of federal employees, and of high school students engaged in interscholastic athletic competitions. But it struck down a Georgia law requiring candidates for designated state offices to certify that they had taken and passed a drug test because Georgia failed to show why this invasion of personal privacy was necessary.[49] In 2002, however, the Court on a 5-to-4 vote held that schools may require students who participate in extracurricular activities of any kind to submit to random drug tests.[50]

THE EXCLUSIONARY RULE   In *Mapp* v. *Ohio* (1961), the Supreme Court adopted a rule excluding from a criminal trial evidence that the police obtained unconstitutionally or illegally.[51] This **exclusionary rule** was adopted to prevent police misconduct. Critics of the exclusionary rule question why criminals should go free just because of police misconduct or ineptness,[52] but the Supreme Court has refused to abandon the rule. It has made some exceptions to it, however, such as cases in which police relied in "good faith" on a search warrant that subsequently turned out to be defective or granted improperly.[53]

THE RIGHT TO REMAIN SILENT   During the seventeenth century, certain special courts in England forced confessions from religious dissenters. The British privilege against self-incrimination developed in response to these practices. Because they were familiar with this history, the framers of our Bill of Rights included in the Fifth Amendment the provision that persons shall not be compelled to testify against themselves in criminal prosecutions. This protection against self-incrimination is designed to strengthen the fundamental principle that no person has an obligation to prove innocence. Rather, the burden is on the government to prove guilt.

racial profiling
Police targeting of racial minorities as potential suspects of criminal activities.

exclusionary rule
Requirement that evidence unconstitutionally or illegally obtained be excluded from a criminal trial.

The privilege against self-incrimination applies literally only in criminal prosecutions. But it has always been interpreted to protect any person subject to questioning by any agency of government, such as a congressional committee. It is not enough, however, to contend that answers might be embarrassing or might lead to loss of a job or even to civil suits; persons must have a reasonable fear that their answers might support a criminal prosecution against them.

Sometimes authorities would rather have information from witnesses than prosecute them. Congress has established procedures so that prosecutors and congressional committees may secure a grant of **immunity** for such a witness. When immunity has been granted, a witness no longer has a constitutional right to refuse to testify, and the government cannot use the information derived directly from the compelled testimony in any subsequent prosecution, though the witness may still be prosecuted for crimes on the basis of other evidence.

THE *MIRANDA* WARNING   Police questioning of suspects is a key procedure in solving crimes. Roughly 90 percent of all criminal convictions result from guilty pleas and never reach a full trial. Police questioning, however, can easily be abused. Police officers sometimes forget or ignore the constitutional rights of suspects, especially those who are frightened and ignorant. Unauthorized detention and lengthy interrogation to wring confessions from suspects, common practice in police states, were not unknown in the United States.

Federal and state laws require police officers to take people they have arrested before a magistrate promptly so that the magistrate may inform them of their constitutional rights and allow them to get in touch with friends and seek legal advice. Despite these requirements, police were often tempted to quiz suspects first, trying to get them to confess before a magistrate informed them of their constitutional right to remain silent.

To put an end to such practices, the Supreme Court, in *Miranda* v. *Arizona* (1966), announced that no conviction could stand if evidence introduced at the trial had been obtained by the police during "custodial interrogation" unless suspects were notified that they have a right to remain silent and to have an attorney present during questioning by police, as well as have a lawyer appointed to represent them if they cannot afford to hire their own attorney.[54] If suspects answer questions in the absence of an attorney, the burden is on prosecutors to demonstrate that suspects knowingly and intelligently gave up their right to remain silent. Failure to comply with these requirements leads to reversal of a conviction, even if other evidence is sufficient to establish guilt.

Critics of the *Miranda* decision believe that the Supreme Court severely limited the ability of the police to bring criminals to justice. Over the years, the Court has modified the original ruling by allowing evidence obtained contrary to the *Miranda* guidelines to be used to attack the credibility of defendants who offer testimony at their trial that conflicts with their statements to the police. Congress tried to get around *Miranda* in the Crime Control and Safe Streets Act of 1968 by allowing confessions made in violation of *Miranda* to be used as evidence in federal courts. But in a decision handed down in June 2000, the Court reaffirmed the constitutionality of the *Miranda* doctrine. In an opinion by Chief Justice William H. Rehnquist, the Court held that the *Miranda* warning is not merely a rule of evidence to enforce the constitutional guarantee but is itself constitutionally required and applies in both state and federal courts.[55]

Fair Trial Procedures

Many people consider the rights of persons accused of a crime to be less important than other rights. But as Justice Felix Frankfurter observed, "The history of liberty has largely been the history of observance of procedural safeguards." Further, these safeguards have frequently "been forged in controversies involving not very nice people."[56] Nonetheless, they guarantee that all persons accused of crimes will have the right to representation by counsel and to a fair trial by an impartial jury.

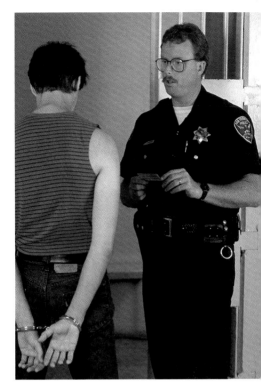

The Miranda *warning is read to a suspect by a police officer to inform him of his rights, such as the right to remain silent and the right to have an attorney present.*

immunity
Exemption from prosecution for a particular crime in return for testimony pertaining to the case.

The *Miranda* Warning

In *Miranda v. Arizona* (1966), the Supreme Court held that before questioning criminal suspects, the police must give them the following information:

- They have a right to remain silent.
- Anything they say may and will be used against them in a court of law.
- They have the right to presence of a lawyer during police questioning.
- If they cannot afford an attorney, one will be appointed for them.
- They have a right to terminate police questioning at any point.

grand jury
A jury of 12 to 23 persons who, in private, hear evidence presented by the government to determine whether persons shall be required to stand trial. If the jury believes there is sufficient evidence that a crime was committed, it issues an indictment.

indictment
A formal written statement from a grand jury charging an individual with an offense; also called a *true bill*.

plea bargain
Agreement between a prosecutor and a defendant that the defendant will plead guilty to a lesser offense to avoid having to stand trial for a more serious offense.

petit jury
A jury of 6 to 12 persons that determines guilt or innocence in a civil or criminal action.

THE RIGHT TO COUNSEL   If after questioning by police the suspect is arrested and charged with a crime, the Supreme Court has ruled that the accused has a constitutional right to counsel at every stage of the criminal proceedings—preliminary hearings, bail hearings, trial, sentencing, and first appeal. Communications between the accused and counsel are privileged. However, in cases of terrorism, under new guidelines issued by Attorney General John Ashcroft, police may listen in, undercover, on consultations between lawyers and detainees if "reasonable suspicion exists to believe that an inmate may use communications with attorneys or their agent to facilitate acts of terrorism."

INDICTMENT   Except for members of the armed forces and foreign terrorists, the national government cannot require anyone to stand trial for a serious crime except on the basis of a grand jury indictment or its equivalent; states are not required to use grand juries, and those that do not vest prosecutors with the power to seek indictments. A **grand jury** is concerned not with a person's guilt or innocence but merely with whether there is enough evidence to warrant a trial. The grand jury has wide-ranging investigatory powers and "is to inquire into all information that might bear on its investigations until it is satisfied that it has identified an offense or satisfied itself that none has occurred."[57] The strict rules that govern jury proceedings do not apply. The grand jury may admit hearsay evidence, and the exclusionary rule to enforce the Fourth Amendment does not apply. If a majority of the grand jurors agree that a trial is justified, they return what is known as a *true bill*, or **indictment**.

The Constitution guarantees the accused the right to be informed of the nature and cause of the accusation so that he or she can prepare a defense. After indictment for an offense, prosecutors and the attorney for the accused usually discuss the possibility of a **plea bargain** whereby the defendant pleads guilty to a lesser offense that carries a shorter prison sentence. Prosecutors, facing more cases than they can handle, like plea bargains because they save the expense and time of going to trial. Likewise, defendants are often willing to "cop a plea" for a lesser offense to avoid the risk of more serious punishment.

When defendants plead guilty, they are usually forever prevented from raising objections to their conviction. That is why, before accepting guilty pleas, the judge questions defendants to be sure their attorneys have explained the alternatives and they know what they are doing.

TRIAL   After indictment and preliminary hearings that determine bail and what evidence will be used as evidence against the accused, the Constitution guarantees a *speedy and public trial*. Do not, however, take the word "speedy" too literally. Defendants are given time to prepare their defense and in fact often ask for delays because delays can work to their advantage. In contrast, if the government denies the accused a speedy trial, not only is the conviction reversed but the case must also be dismissed outright.

Under the Sixth Amendment, the accused has a right to trial before a **petit jury** selected from the state and district in which the alleged crime was committed. Although federal law requires juries of 12 members, the Supreme Court has held that states may try defendants before juries consisting of as few as six persons. Conviction in federal courts must be by unanimous vote, but the Court has ruled that state courts may render guilty verdicts by nonunanimous juries, provided that such juries consist of six or more persons.[58]

An *impartial jury*, one that meets the requirements of due process and equal protection, consists of persons who represent a fair cross section of the community. Although defendants are not entitled to juries on which there must be individuals of their own race, sex, religion, or national origin, government prosecutors cannot strike people from juries because of race or gender, and neither can defense attorneys use what are called *peremptory challenges* to keep people off juries because of race, ethnic origin, or sex.[59]

During the trial, the defendant has a right to obtain witnesses in his or her favor and to have the judge subpoena witnesses to appear at the trial and testify. Both the accused and witnesses may refuse to testify on the grounds that their testimony would tend to incriminate themselves. If they testify, the prosecution has the right to cross-examine them, just as the accused has the right to confront and to cross-examine witnesses.

Sentencing and Punishment

At the conclusion of the trial, the jury recommends a verdict of guilty or not guilty. If the accused is found guilty, the judge hands down the sentence. The Eighth Amendment forbids the levying of excessive fines and the inflicting of cruel and unusual punishment.

In federal courts, judges follow the sentencing guidelines set down by the United States Sentencing Commission. Such sentences are not considered cruel and unusual. Many states have also established guidelines for sentencing by state courts.

THREE STRIKES AND YOU'RE OUT   Although the crime rate has actually been going down in the past few years, public concern about crime remains high. At the national and state level, presidents, governors, and legislators vie with one another to show their toughness on crime. California, Virginia, Washington, and a number of other states have "three strikes and you're out" laws, requiring a lifetime sentence without the possibility of parole for anyone convicted of a third felony. In some states, the felonies must be for violent crimes; in others, any three felonies will do. Scholars are skeptical that "three strikes and you're out" laws reduce crime, and constructing more jails to take care of aging felons requires great expenditures of public funds. Moreover, California's tough law for committing three felonies was struck down by a federal court for applying to a thief of videocassettes who received a sentence of 50 years to life. The Supreme Court will have to decide whether such "three strikes" laws violate the prohibition against cruel and unusual punishment.[60]

APPEALS AND DOUBLE JEOPARDY   After trial, conviction, and sentencing, defendants may appeal their convictions if they claim they have been denied some constitutional right or denied the due process and equal protection of the law. The Fifth Amendment also provides that no person shall be "subject for the same offense to be twice put in jeopardy of life or limb." **Double jeopardy** does not prevent punishment by the national and the state governments for the same offense or for successive prosecutions for the same

"The court finds itself on the horns of a dilemma. On the one hand, wiretap evidence is inadmissible, and on the other hand, I'm dying to hear it."

double jeopardy
Trial or punishment for the same crime by the same government; forbidden by the Constitution.

Military Tribunals and International Terrorists

Early in the war against al-Qaeda terrorists in Afghanistan, President George W. Bush issued an order, as commander in chief of the armed forces, that captured foreign terrorists would be detained indefinitely and tried in special secret military tribunals, without the possibility of appeal.

Bush's order invited a controversy because the "detainees" are not treated as "prisoners of war" according to international law. Under the Third Geneva Convention of 1949, prisoners of war are entitled to an indpendent and impartial trial, the assistance of counsel, and the right of appeal.

U.S. citizens may not be tried by military tribunals, and the Supreme Court overruled President Abraham Lincoln's use of military courts to try civilians during the Civil War.* U.S. citizens must be accorded the guarantees of the Bill of Rights, including a public trial and the right to counsel and to confront their accusers.†

During World War II, however, the Supreme Court approved President Franklin D. Roosevelt's use of military tribunals to try eight German soldiers captured in the United States for sabotaging bridges and utility plants. In the case of the "Nazi saboteurs," the Supreme Court ruled that the president has "the power . . . to carry into effect . . . all laws defining and punishing offenses against the law of nations, including those which pertain to the conduct of

war," and that power includes the authority "to seize and subject to disciplinary measures those enemies who in their attempt to thwart or impede our military effort have violated the law of war."‡ More controversially, the Supreme Court, by a 6-to-3 vote, upheld the internment of Japanese Americans in "relocation camps" after the attack on Pearl Harbor in 1941, even though there was no proof that any of the Japanese Americans were disloyal or engaged in sabotage.§

Based on these precedents, President Bush issued orders for the detention of foreign terrorists and U.S. citizens deemed "enemy combatants" because of their cooperation with international terrorists and threat to homeland security. But his orders are controversial and likely to be challenged in the courts.

*Ex Parte Milligan, 71 U.S. 2 (1866).

†Reid v. Covert, 354 U.S. 1 (1957).

‡Ex Parte Quirin, 317 U.S. 1 (1942).

§Korematsu v. United States, 323 U.S. 214 (1944).

Dan Eggan and Susan Schmidt, "Suspected al-Qaeda Operative Held as 'Enemy Combatant,'" *Washington Post,* June 11, 2002, p. A1; Laurence H. Tribe, "Citizens, Combatants, and the Constitution," *New York Times,* June 16, 2002, p. WK13.

The Death Penalty on Trial

As the number of death-row inmates and executions has grown, debate over the fairness and permissibility of capital punishment has spread. The American Bar Association (ABA) called for a halt to executions because the death penalty is administered in ways that deny fundamental due process and the equal protection of law. Christian televangelist Pat Robertson joined the ABA and Catholic bishops in calling for a moratorium on executions. Illinois Republican Governor George Ryan declared a moratorium on executions in his state because more death-row inmates were released from prison than executed in recent years because they had been wrongly convicted. He established a commission that recommended limiting the bases for imposing the death penalty and heightening review of those sentenced to death. In 2002, Maryland also suspended carrying out executions because of a report on racial bias. Prominent Republicans and Democrats also began questioning the system of imposing the death penalty.

The debate about the fairness of capital punishment was sparked by the increasing number of inmates who have been released because new DNA evidence proved their innocence—often after spending a decade or more on death row. DNA evidence is useful, however, only in cases of rape or murder when blood or tissue samples remain. A recent poll found that 92 percent of Americans say prison inmates convicted before the technology was available should be given the opportunity to submit to DNA tests now. (For more information, go to the Gallup Organization's Web site, at www.gallup.com.)

This debate has refocused the controversy by drawing into question the fairness of the entire process of capital punishment. Critics point out the seemingly randomness in imposing capital punishment. Public prosecutors seek the death penalty in less than 5 percent of all murder cases. Defendants often agree to plea bargains in return for life sentences. When murder trials are held, some juries refuse to impose death sentences. And of the criminals sentenced to death, some receive clemency or are pardoned.

A study of more than 4,500 capital cases found that more than two-thirds of all death sentences are overturned. Why? The primary

Illinois Governor George Ryan called a halt to executions in his state because of mishandling and inadequate defense of accused individuals who were later discovered to be innocent.

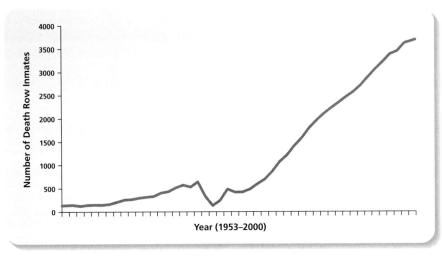

Death Row Inmates.

---

crime by two states. Nor does the double jeopardy clause forbid civil prosecutions, even after acquittal in a criminal trial for the same conduct.[61]

THE DEATH PENALTY   Capital punishment remains controversial. Japan and the United States are the only two industrialized countries to retain the death penalty. The 15 members of the European Union have outlawed capital punishment, and courts in South Africa and several central and eastern European countries have declared it unconstitutional and a denial of human dignity.

After a ten-year moratorium on executions in the late 1960s and early 1970s, the U.S. Supreme Court ruled that the death penalty is not necessarily cruel and unusual

Rubin "Hurricane" Carter was a boxer who was wrongly convicted of a murder in 1967 and spent 21 years on death row before he was exonerated and released.

reasons are that defense lawyers were incompetent, important evidence was overlooked by police, witnesses lied, or prosecutors withheld evidence from the defense. Besides the apparent randomness in who is sentenced to death and later executed, racial discrimination in the imposition of capital punishment is a major concern. Blacks who murder whites are much more likely to receive death sentences than whites who murder blacks or blacks who kill blacks.

The American public generally supports the death penalty, though support has slipped to 66 percent, the lowest point since 1978. Some people are morally opposed to capital punishment because of its finality; others maintain that it should be inflicted only on people who commit heinous murders; still others insist that it is too arbitrary and randomly imposed—or as Justice Potter Stewart put it, "Death sentences are cruel and unusual in the same way that being struck by lightning is cruel and unusual."*

SOURCE: Lori Montgomery, "Maryland Suspends Death Penalty," *Washington Post,* May 10, 2002; Barry Scheck, Peter Neufeld, and Jim Dwyer, *Actual Innocence: Five Days to Execution, and Other Dispatches from the Wrongly Convicted* (Doubleday, 2000); Harry Weinstein, "Death Penalty Is Overturned in Most Cases," *Los Angeles Times,* June 20, 2000, p. A1; *McCleskey* v. *Kemp,* 481 U.S. 279 (1987); Walter Berns, *For Capital Punishment: Crime and Morality of the Death Penalty* (Basic Books, 1979); Charles L. Black Jr., *Capital Punishment: The Inevitability of Caprice and Mistake* (Norton, 1974); Death Penalty Information Center, at www.deathpenaltyinfo.org.

*Potter Stewart, concurring in *Furman* v. *Georgia,* 408 U.S. 238 (1972).

SOURCE: U.S. Department of Justice, Bureau of Criminal Justice Statistics; Death Penalty Information Center. For more information, go to the Death Penalty Information Center, at www.deathpenaltyinfo.org.

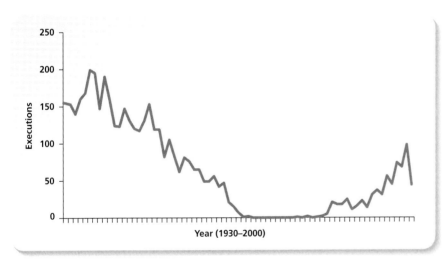

Executions in the United States.

punishment if it is imposed for crimes that resulted in a victim's death, if the procedures used by the courts "ensure that death sentences are not meted out wantonly or freakishly," and if these processes "confer on the sentencer sufficient discretion to take account of the character and record of the individual offender and the circumstances of the particular offense to ensure that death is the appropriate punishment in a specific case."[62]

The Rehnquist Court has made it easier to impose death sentences, cut back on appeals, and carry out executions. More states have added the death penalty (there are now 38), and the national government has increased the number of crimes for which the death penalty may be imposed. As a result, the number of persons on death row has increased dramatically. Since capital punishment was reinstated in 1976, more than 600 people have

Cruel and Unusual Punishment

The Eighth Amendment ban against cruel and unusual punishment limits government in three ways:

1. It limits the kinds and methods of publishment that may be imposed, prohibiting, for example, torture, intentional denial of medical care, inhumane conditions, unnecessary or wanton infliction of pain, and deliberate indifference to other needs of prisoners.*

2. It prohibits punishments grossly disproportionate to the severity of the crime.†

3. It limits the power of the government to decide what can be made a criminal offense. For example, the mere act of being a chronic alcoholic may not be made a crime because alcoholism is an illness. However, being drunk in public may be a criminal offense.

*Hudson v. McMillan, 503 U.S. 1 (1992); Farmer v. Brennan, 511 U.S. 825 (1994).

†Hutto v. Davis, 454 U.S. 370 (1982); Solem v. Helm, 463 U.S. 277 (1983).

been executed nationwide, and more than 3,700 are on death row. As the number of executions has increased, however, concerns have also grown about the fairness of how capital punishment is imposed. These concerns have been fueled by DNA tests that have established the innocence of a sizable number of those convicted of murder. Two states, Illinois and Maryland, have reimposed moratoriums on carrying out executions.[63]

The prohibition against cruel and unusual punishment also forbids punishments grossly disproportionate to the severity of the crime. In 2002, the Supreme Court overruled a prior ruling[64] and held that it is excessive and disproportionate to execute mentally retarded convicted murderers because they are not capable of understanding the seriousness of their offense. The Court noted that in recent years there has been a movement to bar executions of mentally retarded death-row inmates. And because 18 of the 38 states imposing capital punishment exempt the mentally retarded, the Court concluded that there was an emerging "national consensus" against executing mentally retarded inmates.[65]

How Just Is Our System of Justice?

Because the American system of criminal justice contains many guarantees for protecting the rights of the accused, critics often argue that due to these protections, justice is not done. Among the other criticisms are that the system is inefficient, biased, and unfair.

Too Many Loopholes?

Some observers argue that by overprotecting criminals and placing too much of a burden on the criminal justice system not to make any mistakes, we delay justice, encourage disrespect for the law, and allow guilty persons to go unpunished. Justice should be swift and certain without being arbitrary. But under our procedures, criminals may go unpunished because the police decide not to arrest them, the prosecutor decides not to prosecute them, the grand jury decides not to indict them, the judge decides not to hold them for trial, the jury decides not to convict them, the appeals court decides to reverse the conviction, the judge decides to release them on a writ of habeas corpus, or the president or governor decides to pardon, reprieve, or parole them if convicted. As a result, the public never knows whom to hold responsible when laws are not enforced. The police blame prosecutors, prosecutors blame the police, and they all blame the juries and judges.

Others take a different view and point out that there is more to justice than simply securing convictions. All the steps in the administration of criminal laws have been developed over centuries of trial and error, and each step has been constructed to protect ordinary persons from particular abuses by those in power. History warns against entrusting the instruments of criminal law enforcement to a single officer. For this reason, responsibility is vested in many officials.

Too Unreliable?

Critics who say that our system of justice is unreliable often point to trial by jury as the chief source of trouble. No other country relies as heavily on trial by jury as the United States. Jury trials are also time-consuming and costly. Trial by jury, critics argue, leads to a theatrical combat between lawyers who base their appeals on the prejudices and sentiments of the jurors. "Mr. Prejudice and Miss Sympathy are the names of witnesses whose testimony is never recorded, but must nevertheless be reckoned with in trials by jury."[66]

The jury system allows for what is called *jury nullification* when jurors ignore their instructions to consider only the evidence presented in court and vote for acquittal to express their displeasure with the law or the actions of prosecutors or police. Jury nullification has a long history. In colonial times, juries refused to convict colonists of political crimes against the king as a way to protest British rule. Before the Civil War, northern juries refused to convict people for helping runaway slaves. Before the 1970s, white southern juries sometimes refused to convict police for brutality against blacks.

Tribune Media Services.

Responding to growing public disenchantment with juries after a raft of unpopular verdicts, states have been rewriting the rules for the jury system. These changes include making it more difficult for people to be excused from jury service, allowing for nonunanimous decisions, limiting how long jurors can be sequestered, and exerting more control by judges over lawyers' statements to jurors in order to prevent appeals to jurors' emotions.

Defenders of the jury system reply that trial by jury provides a check by nonprofessionals on the actions of judges and prosecutors. There is no evidence that juries are unreliable; on the contrary, decisions of juries do not significantly differ from those of judges.[67] Moreover, the jury system helps educate citizens and enables them to participate in the application of their country's laws.

Too Discriminatory?

During the past several decades, the Supreme Court has worked particularly hard to enforce the ideal of equal justice under the law. Persons accused of crimes who cannot afford attorneys must be furnished them at government expense. If transcripts are required for appeals, such transcripts must be made available to those who cannot afford to purchase them. If appeals are permitted, the government must provide attorneys for at least one appeal of the decision of the trial court. Poor people cannot be imprisoned because of the inability to pay a fine. Nor, once sentenced, can poor people be kept in jail beyond the term of the sentence because they cannot afford to pay a fine. Even for civil proceedings—divorce proceedings, for example—fees cannot be imposed that deny poor people their fundamental rights, such as the right to obtain a divorce.

Unfair to Minorities?

One of the acute problems of our society is the tension between the police and the African American, Hispanic, and Middle Eastern communities congregated in inner cities. Many members of minorities believe they do not have equal protection under the law and that they are targeted by law enforcement officers. "Whether the stated belief is well founded or not," one political scientist observed, "is at least partly beside the point. The existence of the belief is damaging enough."[68]

Some blacks consider the police to be enforcers of white law. Studies proving prejudice on the part of some white police officers and examples of rough, even brutal, police treatment of blacks are ample evidence to support this viewpoint. One study in California found that "the rate of unfounded arrest was four times higher for African Americans than Anglos. Latino rates were double those of Anglos."[69] Police use of racial profiling, already a concern of blacks and Hispanics, has also became a concern of Muslims and whites.[70]

In recent decades, action has been taken to recruit more African Americans, Hispanics, and women as police officers, including appointment to command posts. In larger cities, there are now oversight boards including civilians to which complaints about police misconduct can be brought. **Community policing** is also being substituted in some cities for traditional police procedures. Police departments work with churches and other local community groups and take police out of patrol cars to walk the beat and work in neighborhoods. Community policing, when combined with working with community organizations to sponsor crime prevention programs, appears not only to reduce crime but also to improve minorities' confidence in the police.[71]

The Supreme Court and Civil Liberties

Judges play a major role in enforcing constitutional guarantees. Such reliance on judicial protection of our civil liberties focuses public attention on the Supreme Court. Yet only a small number of controversies are actually carried to the Supreme Court, and a Supreme Court decision is not the end of the judicial process. Lower court judges as well as police, superintendents of schools, local prosecutors, school boards, state legislatures, and thousands of others clarify the Court's doctrines.

Moreover, the Supreme Court can do little unless its decisions over time reflect a national consensus. As Supreme Court Justice Robert H. Jackson observed, "The attitude of a society and of its organized political forces, rather than its legal machinery, is the controlling force in the character of free institutions. Any court that undertakes by its legal processes to enforce civil liberties needs the support of an enlightened and vigorous public opinion."[72] Thus the Bill of Rights—and the other procedural and substantive liberties of our Constitution—cannot rest on a foundation merely of tradition. The preservation of these rights depends on wide, continuing, and knowledgeable public support.

Liberty and Doctor-Assisted Suicide

In the 1990 case of Nancy Cruzan, a college student who was left permanently brain-damaged in an automobile accident and kept alive with feeding tubes, the Supreme Court ruled that competent individuals have a constitutionally protected liberty interest in terminating such life support. Cruzan's parents had sued to discontinue her life support system, and the justices agreed that that was permissible if there is "clear and convincing evidence," as in a "living will," that an incompetent patient would have wanted to do so.*

Subsequently, a "right to die" movement emerged and maintains that individuals who are dying of cancer or AIDS, for example, also have a right to have doctors prescribe lethal drugs for them to take. Two federal appellate courts agreed, but the Supreme Court reversed those decisions and ruled that for now, the matter should be left for state legislatures to decide.†

In 1994 and 1997, voters in Oregon approved a "death with dignity" law, allowing doctors to prescribe "mentally competent and terminally ill" patients lethal doses of drugs. It is the only state to have such a law.

In 2001, Attorney General John Ashcroft, who is a staunch pro-life supporter and usually a defender of federalism, issued an order to the Drug Enforcement Agency to revoke the license of any doctor who prescribes such drugs, even under Oregon's law. When his order was challenged, a federal district court held that Ashcroft could not preempt the state law.‡

For more information, go to the Web site of the Death with Dignty National Center, at www.deathwithdignity.org.

*Cruzan by Cruzan v. Director, Missouri Department of Health, 497 U.S. 261 (1990).

†Washington v. Glucksberg, 521 U.S. 702 (1997); Vacco v. Quill, 521 U.S. 793 (1997).

‡Kevin Johnson, "Judge Upholds Oregon's Assisted-Suicide Law," USA Today, April 18, 2002, p. A3.

community policing
Assigning police to neighborhoods where they walk the beat and work with churches and other community groups to reduce crime and improve relations with minorities.

Summary

1. One of the basic distinctions between a free society and a police state is that in a free society, there are effective restraints on the way public officials, especially law enforcement officials, perform their duties. In the United States, the courts enforce these constitutional restraints.

2. The Constitution protects the acquisition and retention of citizenship. It protects the basic liberties of citizens as well as aliens, although in times of war, foreign saboteurs and terrorists may be detained and tried without the rights accorded citizens and other aliens.

3. The Constitution protects our property from arbitrary governmental interference, although debates about which interferences are reasonable and which are arbitrary are not easily settled. If private property is taken or rendered worthless by the government, just compensation must be paid to the owner.

4. The Constitution imposes limits not only on the procedures government must follow but also on the ends it may pursue. Some actions are out of bounds no matter what procedures are followed. Legislatures have the primary role in determining what is reasonable and what is unreasonable. However, the Supreme Court continues to exercise its own independent and final review of legislative determinations of reasonableness, especially on matters affecting civil liberties and civil rights.

5. The Supreme Court has pulled together elements from the First, Fourth, Fifth, Ninth, and Fourteenth Amendments to recognize a constitutionally protected right to personal privacy, especially with regard to marital privacy, including the right of a woman to choose an abortion.

6. The framers knew from their own experiences that in their zeal to maintain power and to enforce the laws, especially in wartime, public officials are often tempted to infringe on the rights of persons accused of crimes. To prevent such abuse, the Bill of Rights requires federal officials to follow detailed procedures in making searches and arrests and in bringing people to trial.

7. The Supreme Court continues to play a prominent role in developing public policy to protect the rights of the accused, to ensure that the innocent are not punished, and to guarantee that the public is protected against those who break the laws. The Court's decisions influence what the public believes and how police officers and others involved in the administration of justice behave. But the Court alone cannot guarantee fairness in the administration of justice.

Key Terms

naturalization
dual citizenship
right of expatriation
property rights
contract clause
police powers

eminent domain
regulatory taking
due process
procedural due process
substantive due process
search warrant

racial profiling
exclusionary rule
immunity
grand jury
indictment
plea bargain

petit jury
double jeopardy
community policing

Further Reading

JEFFREY ABRAMSON, *We, the Jury: The Jury System and the Ideal of Democracy* (Basic Books, 1994).

LIVA BAKER, *Miranda: Crime, Law and Politics* (Atheneum, 1983).

STUART BANNER, *The Death Penalty: An American History* (Harvard University Press, 2002).

ROBERT P. BURNS, *A Theory of the Trial* (Princeton University Press, 1999).

DAVID COLE, *No Equal Justice: Race and Class in the American Criminal Justice System* (New Press, 1999).

JOHN DENVIR, *Democracy's Constitution: Claiming the Privileges of American Citizenship* (University of Illinois Press, 2001).

GEORGE P. FLETHER, *Basic Concepts of Criminal Law* (Oxford University Press, 1998).

DAVID J. GARROW, *Liberty and Sexuality: The Right to Privacy and the Making of Roe v. Wade* (Macmillan, 1994).

ROGER HOOD, *The Death Penalty: A Worldwide Perspective*, 3d ed. (Oxford University Press, 2002).

KENNETH KARST, *Law's Promise, Law's Expression: Visions of Power in the Politics of Race, Gender, and Religion* (Yale University Press, 1993).

RANDALL KENNEDY, *Race, Crime, and the Law* (Pantheon, 1997).

ANTHONY LEWIS, *Gideon's Trumpet* (Random House, 1964).

JOHN R. LOTT JR., *More Guns, Less Crime: Understanding Crime and Gun Control Laws* (University of Chicago Press, 2000).

DAVID M. O'BRIEN, *Constitutional Law and Politics*: Vol. 2, *Civil Rights and Civil Liberties*, 5th ed. (Norton, 2003).

J. W. PELTASON and SUE DAVIS, *Understanding the Constitution*, 15th ed. (Harcourt, 2001).

WILLIAM H. REHNQUIST, *All the Laws but One: Civil Liberties in Wartime* (Knopf, 1998).

BARRY SCHECK, PETER NEUFELD, and JIM DWYER, *Actual Innocence: Five Days to Execution, and Other Dispatches from the Wrongly Convicted* (Doubleday, 2000).

MELVIN UROFSKY, *Lethal Judgments: Assisted Suicide and American Law* (University Press of Kentucky, 2000).

MARY E. VOGEL, *Coercion to Compromise: Plea Bargaining, the Courts, and the Making of Political Authority* (Oxford University Press, 2001).

WELSH S. WHITE, *Miranda's Waning Protections: Police Interrogation Practices After Dickerson* (University of Michigan Press, 2001).

EQUAL RIGHTS UNDER THE LAW

 WE HOLD THESE TRUTHS TO BE SELF-EVIDENT, THAT ALL MEN ARE CREATED EQUAL, THAT THEY ARE ENDOWED BY THEIR CREATOR WITH CERTAIN unalienable Rights, that among these are Life, Liberty, and the pursuit of Happiness." These ringing words of the Declaration of Independence affirm the precious rights of *equality* and *liberty* and appear to rate equality at least on a par with liberty. Although the Declaration does not specify equality of white, Christian, or Anglo-Saxon men (at that time "all men" meant white, property-owning Anglo-Saxon men), it took almost 200 years for that definition to be expanded to include all races, all religions, and all women as well as men. This creed of individual dignity and equality is nonetheless older than our Declaration of Independence; its roots go back into the teachings of Judaism and Christianity.

What about the Constitution? What does this historic document say about the framers' attitude toward liberty and equality? Although you will not find any reference to "equality" (the word never appears in the Constitution or in the Bill of Rights), we know the framers believed that all men—at least all white men—were equally entitled to life, liberty, and the pursuit of happiness. But like the Declaration, the Constitution referred only to "men" or "him," not to women, and none of its lofty sentiments applied to slaves, who enjoyed neither liberty nor equality.

The framers resolved their ambiguity about what kind of equality and for whom by creating a system of government designed to protect what they called *natural rights*. (Today we speak of *human rights*, but the idea is basically the same.) By **natural rights** the framers meant that every person has an equal right to protection against arbitrary treatment and an equal right to the liberties guaranteed by the Bill of Rights. These rights do not depend on citizenship; they are not granted by governments. They are the rights of *all people*.

The terms *civil liberties* and *civil rights* are often used interchangeably to refer to rights that are protected by the constitutions of constitutional democracies. *Civil liberties* is sometimes used more narrowly to refer to freedom of conscience, religion, and ex-

"When my distinguished colleague refers to the will of the 'people,' does he mean his 'people' or my 'people'?"

pression. *Civil rights* is used to refer to the right not to be discriminated against because of race, religion, gender, ethnic origin, or sexual orientation. Our Constitution provides two ways of protecting civil rights. First, it ensures that government officials do not discriminate against us; second, it grants national and state governments the power to protect these civil rights against interference by private individuals.

This chapter is concerned with both the protection of our rights from abuse *by government* and the protection *through government* of our right to be free from abuse by our *fellow citizens*. In this chapter, we focus on the struggles of African Americans, women, Hispanics, Asian Americans, and Native Americans to secure the basic civil rights to the vote, to an education, to a job, and to a place to live on equal terms with their fellow citizens.

Equality and Equal Rights

Americans are committed to equality. "Equality," however, is an elusive term. The concept for which there is the greatest consensus and that is most clearly written into the Constitution is that everybody should have *equality of opportunity* regardless of race, ethnic origin, religion, and, in recent years, gender and sexual orientation. Advancing the equality of opportunity has led to the historic struggles for civil rights in this country.

A variation of the concept of equal opportunity is *equality of starting conditions.* There is not much equal opportunity if one person is born into a well-to-do family, lives in a safe suburb, is well fed, and receives a good education, while another is born into a poor, broken family, lives in an inner-city neighborhood, and attends inferior schools. Thus, it is argued, if we are to have equality of opportunity in a meaningful sense, special opportunities must be provided for the disadvantaged through federal programs such as Head Start, which provides children from poor families with preschool experiences that prepare them for elementary school.

Traditionally, we have emphasized *individual* achievement, but in recent decades, some politicians and civil rights leaders have focused attention on the concept of *equality between groups.* When large disparities in wealth and advantage exist between groups—as between blacks and whites or between women and men—equality becomes a highly divisive political issue. Those who are disadvantaged tend to emphasize economic and social factors that exclude them from the mainstream. They champion programs like **affirmative action** that are designed to provide special help to people who have been disadvantaged due to their group memberships. Those who are advantaged, however, often act to maintain the status quo and downplay socioeconomic disparities. As a result, whether such programs promote or deny equality remains one of the most controversial current debates.

Finally, equality can also mean *equality of results.* One perennial debate, especially among college students, is whether social justice and genuine equality can exist in a nation in which people of one class have so much and others have so little and where the gap between them grows ever wider.[1] There is considerable support for guaranteeing a minimum floor—a "safety net"—below which no one should be allowed to fall. Yet Americans generally do not support an equality of results—that everybody should have the same amount of material goods—but instead tend to take the view that regardless of current economic status, a person should be able to expect that things will get better and that hard work and an entrepreneurial spirit will be rewarded.

The Quest for Equal Justice

To gain some perspective on the court decisions, laws, and other governmental actions relating to civil rights for women and minorities, we review here the political history and social contexts in which these constitutional issues arise. These issues involve not only court decisions, laws, and constitutional amendments, however. They encompass the entire social, economic, and political system. And although the struggles of all groups are interwoven, they are not identical, so we deal briefly and separately with each.

natural rights
The rights of all people to dignity and worth; also called *human rights.*

affirmative action
Remedial action designed to overcome the effects of past discrimination against minorities and women.

Racial Equality

Americans had a painful confrontation with the problem of race before, during, and after the Civil War (1861–1865). As a result of the northern victory, the Thirteenth, Fourteenth, and Fifteenth Amendments became part of the Constitution. During Reconstruction, Congress passed a series of civil rights laws to implement these amendments and established programs to provide educational and social services for the freed slaves. But the Supreme Court struck down many of these laws, and it was not until the 1960s that progress was again made toward ensuring African Americans their civil rights.

SEGREGATION AND WHITE SUPREMACY   Before Reconstruction programs had any significant effect, the white southern political leadership was restored to power, and by 1877, Reconstruction was ended. Northern political leaders abandoned African Americans to their fate at the hands of their former white masters; presidents no longer concerned themselves with the enforcement of civil rights laws, and Congress enacted no new ones. The Supreme Court either declared old laws unconstitutional or interpreted them so narrowly that they were ineffective. The Court also gave such a limited construction to the Thirteenth, Fourteenth, and Fifteenth Amendments that they failed to accomplish their intended purpose of protecting the rights of African Americans.[2]

White supremacy went unchallenged in the South, where most African Americans lived. They were kept from voting; they were forced to accept menial jobs; they were denied educational opportunities; they were segregated in public facilities.[3] African Americans were being lynched on an average of one every four days, and few whites raised a voice in protest.

During World War I, African Americans began to migrate to northern cities to seek jobs in war factories. Their relocation was accelerated in the 1930s by the Great Depression and in the 1940s by World War II. Although discrimination continued, more jobs became available, and social gains resulted. As migration of African Americans out of the rural South into southern and northern cities shifted the racial composition of cities, the African American vote became important in national elections. These changes created an African American middle class opposed to segregation as a symbol of servitude and a cause of inequality. By the middle of the twentieth century, urban African Americans were active and politically powerful citizens. There was a growing demand for the abolition of color barriers.

SLOW GOVERNMENT RESPONSE   By the 1930s, African Americans were resorting to lawsuits to challenge the doctrine of segregation. And after World War II, this civil rights litigation began to have a major impact. In the years that followed, the Supreme Court, beginning with the landmark 1954 ruling in *Brown* v. *Board of Education,* outlawed racially segregated public schools[4] and subsequently struck down most of the devices that had been used by state and local authorities to keep African Americans from voting.[5]

Presidents Harry S Truman and Dwight D. Eisenhower used their executive authority to fight segregation in the armed services and the federal bureaucracy. They directed the Department of Justice to enforce whatever civil rights laws were on the books, but Congress still held back. In the late 1950s, an emerging national consensus in favor of governmental action to protect civil rights plus the political clout of African Americans in the northern states began to have some influence on Congress. In 1957, Congress overrode a southern filibuster in the Senate and enacted the first federal civil rights laws since Reconstruction.

A TURNING POINT   Even after the Supreme Court declared racially segregated public schools unconstitutional, most African Americans still went to segregated schools, and there was widespread resistance to integration in the South. Many legal barriers in the path of equal rights had fallen, yet most African Americans still could not buy houses where they wanted, secure the jobs they needed, find educational opportunities for their children, or eat in a restaurant or walk freely on the streets of "white neighborhoods."

But times were changing. What had once been thought of as a "southern problem" was finally recognized as a national challenge. A massive social, economic, and political movement began to supplement the struggles in the courtrooms. It began in Montgomery,

Rosa Park's decision not to give up her seat on the bus in Montgomery, Alabama, sparked a boycott by African Americans who, for more than a year, refused to ride the segregated city buses.

Alabama, on December 1, 1955, when Rosa Parks refused to give up her seat to a white man in the front of a bus and as required by law was removed from the bus. The black community responded by boycotting city buses.

The boycott worked. It also produced a charismatic national civil rights leader, the Reverend Martin Luther King Jr. Through his doctrine of nonviolent resistance, King gave a new dimension to the struggle. By the early 1960s, new organizational resources came into existence in almost every city to support and sponsor "sit-ins," "freedom rides," "live-ins," and other nonviolent demonstrations. These measures were often met with violence, and some state and local governments failed to protect the victims or to prosecute the parties responsible for the violence.[6]

The simmering forces of social discontent boiled over in the summer of 1963. A peaceful demonstration in Birmingham, Alabama, was countered with fire hoses, police dogs, and mass arrests. More than a quarter of a million people converged on Washington, D.C., to hear King and other civil rights leaders speak while countless millions more watched them on television. By the time the summer was over, there was hardly a city, North or South, that had not had demonstrations, protests, or sit-ins. Some also had violence.

This direct action had some effect. Many cities enacted civil rights ordinances, more schools were desegregated, and President John F. Kennedy urged Congress to enact a comprehensive civil rights bill. Late in 1963, the nation's grief over the assassination of President Kennedy, who had become identified with civil rights goals, added political fuel to the drive for decisive federal action to protect civil rights.[7] President Lyndon B. Johnson made civil rights legislation his highest priority, and on July 2, 1964, after months of debate, he signed into law the Civil Rights Act of 1964, forbidding discrimination on the basis of race, color, religion, sex, or nationality.[8]

Fire fighters in Birmingham, Alabama, turned their hoses full blast on civil rights demonstrators in the 1960s. At times the water came with such force, even on children, that it literally tore the bark off fully grown trees.

RIOTS AND REACTION   By the early 1970s, the legal phase of the civil rights movement had largely come to a close, but as things got better, discontent grew. Millions of impoverished African Americans demonstrated growing impatience with the discrimination that remained. This volatile situation gave way to racial violence and disorders. In 1965, a brutal riot took place in Watts, a section of Los Angeles. In 1966 and 1967, the disorders spread in scope and intensity. The Detroit riot in July 1967, the worst such disturbance up to that time in modern American history, made clear the deep divisions between the races and the urgency of taking corrective action.[9]

"I Have a Dream . . . "

On August 28, 1963, the Reverend Martin Luther King Jr. addressed the throngs of participants in the March on Washington from the steps of the Lincoln Memorial. It is regarded as one of the great orations of the twentieth century.

Martin Luther King Jr.

Five score years ago, a great American in whose symbolic shadow we stand signed the Emancipation Proclamation. This momentous decree came as a great beacon light of hope to millions of Negro slaves who had been seared in the flames of withering injustice. It came as a joyous daybreak to end the long night of captivity. But one hundred years later, we must face the tragic fact that the Negro is still not free. One hundred years later, the life of the Negro is still sadly crippled by the manacles of segregation and the chains of discrimination. One hundred years later, the Negro lives on a lonely island of poverty in the midst of a vast ocean of material prosperity. One hundred years later, the Negro is still languishing in the corners of American society and finds himself an exile in his own land. So we have come here today to dramatize an appalling condition. . . .

I have a dream that one day this nation will rise up and live out the true meaning of its creed: "We hold these truths to be self-evident, that all men are created equal."

I have a dream that one day on the red hills of Georgia the sons of former slaves and the sons of former slave owners will be able to sit down together at the table of brotherhood.

I have a dream that one day even the state of Mississippi, a desert state sweltering with the heat of injustice and oppression, will be transformed into an oasis of freedom and justice.

I have a dream that my four little children will one day live in a nation where they will not be judged by the color of their skin but by the content of their character.

To listen to the entire speech, go to our Web site (www.prenhall.com/burns) or to the History and Politics Out Loud Web site, at www.hpol.org.

President Johnson appointed the special Advisory Commission on Civil Disorders in 1967 to investigate the origins of the riots and to recommend measures to prevent such disasters in the future. When the commission (called the Kerner Commission after its chair, Illinois Governor Otto Kerner) issued its report, it said in stark, clear language: "What white Americans have never fully understood—but what the Negro can never forget—is that white society is deeply implicated in the ghetto. White institutions created it, white institutions maintain it, and white society condones it." The basic conclusion of the commission was this: "Our nation is moving toward two societies, one black, one white—separate and unequal" and that "only a commitment to national action on an unprecedented scale" could change this trend.[10]

The commission made sweeping recommendations on jobs, education, housing, and the welfare system. But other events diverted attention from these recommendations: the Vietnam War; Watergate; the elections of Ronald Reagan and George Bush, who were reluctant to take governmental actions to enforce civil rights; and a growing skepticism about the effectiveness of governmental action generally.

The Clinton administration was more sympathetic toward the use of governmental power to deal with issues of inequality than its immediate predecessors, but because of budgetary constraints and Republican opposition to "big government" programs, it was largely unable to promote any major initiatives directly aimed at the problems of the inner cities. Still, civil rights leaders like the Reverend Jesse Jackson continue efforts to eliminate the vestiges of past racial discrimination. In the past decade, boycotts and lawsuits have been effective in persuading businesses and corporations to reach out and hire and promote more African Americans.

Susan B. Anthony and Elizabeth Cady Stanton
were the two most influential leaders of the
women's suffrage movement in the nineteenth century.

Women's Rights

The struggle for equal rights for women was intertwined with the battle to secure equal rights for African Americans. The Seneca Falls Women's Rights Convention (1848), which launched the women's movement, involved men and women who actively campaigned to abolish slavery and to secure the rights of African Americans and women. But as the Civil War approached, women were urged to abandon their cause and devote their energies to getting rid of slavery.[11] The Civil War brought the women's movement to a halt, and the temperance movement to prohibit the sale of liquor diverted attention away from women's rights as well. The Fourteenth and Fifteenth Amendments did not advance voting rights for women, even as they guaranteed that right to freed male slaves.

By the turn of the twentieth century, however, a vigorous campaign was under way for **women's suffrage**—the right to vote. The first victories came in western states, where Wyoming led the way. As a territory, Wyoming had given women the right to vote. When members of Congress in Washington grumbled about this "petticoat provision," the Wyoming legislators replied they would stay out of the Union 100 years rather than come in without women's suffrage. Congress gave in and admitted Wyoming to the Union. By the end of World War I, more than half the states had granted women the right to vote in some or all elections.

To many suffragists, this state-by-state approach seemed slow and uncertain. They wanted a decisive victory—a constitutional amendment that would force all states to allow qualified women to vote. Finally, in 1919, Congress proposed the Nineteenth Amendment. Opposition to granting voting rights to women was intertwined with opposition to granting voting rights to African Americans. Many southerners opposed the amendment because it gave Congress enforcement power, which might bring federal officials to investigate elections to ensure that the amendment was being obeyed—an interference that might call attention to how blacks were being kept from voting.

With the ratification of the Nineteenth Amendment in 1920, women won the right to vote, but they were still denied equal pay and equal rights, and they suffered numerous legal disabilities imposed by both national and state laws. In the 1970s and 1980s, the unsuccessful struggle to secure the adoption of the Equal Rights Amendment occupied much of the attention of the women's movement, but there are now other goals, and the political clout of women is mobilized behind issues that range from equal pay to world peace, sexual harassment, abortion rights, and election to office.[12]

Since the 1980s, the Supreme Court has been reluctant to expand the Fourteenth Amendment's protection against gender discrimination, though it did hold that Virginia could not create a separate military academy for women instead of admitting them into the all-male Virginia Military Institute, a 150-year-old state-run institution.[13]

The courts, however, have increasingly enforced the prohibition against sex discrimination in the 1964 Civil Rights Act and expanded it to forbid sexual harassment in the workplace. Ironically, that prohibition was put into the act in an effort by members of the House of Representatives to defeat passage of the legislation, which aimed primarily at ending racial discrimination.[14] As a result, it was initially not taken very seriously, and not until the 1980s did it apply to "quid pro quo" sexual harassment, in which an employer makes a person provide sexual favors as a condition of employment (in hiring, promotions, and firing).[15] Sexual harassment was then brought to national attention in 1991 by accusations made against Justice Clarence Thomas by Anita Hill, a law professor and former colleague, at the time of his Senate confirmation. Subsequently, the Supreme Court ruled that the law also applies to situations in which employees experience discrimination because they are forced to work in a "hostile environment." A hostile environment is defined as a workplace "permeated" with intimidation, ridicule, and insult that is severe and pervasive, and this includes same-sex harassment.[16]

Some women still complain of a "glass ceiling" in large corporations, preventing their advancement. But there is no denying that major progress has been made, with more and more women going to college and professional schools and into the media and

women's suffrage
The right of women to vote.

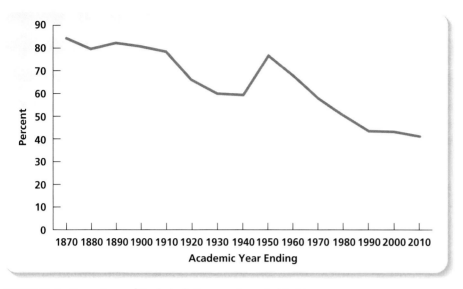

FIGURE 18–1   Percentage of Bachelor's Degrees Awarded to Men.

*Percent for 2010 is projected by the Pell Institute for the Study of Opportunity in Higher Education, National Center for Education Statistics.

Source: Michael A. Fletcher, "Degrees of Separation," *Washington Post,* June 25, 2002, p. A1.

business. Indeed, during the past three decades, the percentage of women graduating from colleges and universities has outpaced that of men (see Figure 18-1).

Hispanics

The struggle for civil rights has not been limited to women and African Americans. Each new wave of immigrants has been considered suspect by those who arrived earlier—all the more so if its members were not white or English-speaking. Formal barriers of law and informal barriers of custom combined to deny equal rights. But as groups established themselves—first economically and then politically—most of these barriers were swept away, and constitutionally guaranteed rights were asserted.

As we discussed in Chapter 5, most Hispanics—many of whose ancestors have been Americans for generations—are bilingual, speaking English as well as Spanish. However, because English may not be their first language, it has been difficult for some Hispanics to establish themselves educationally or to advance into the ranks of executives and professionals. Although not as visible as African Americans, Hispanics have suffered the same kinds of discrimination in employment, education, and accommodations.

Hispanic political clout has been unrealized because of internal political differences and because many Hispanics are not citizens or registered to vote. However, after California adopted Proposition 187 in 1994, which denied medical, educational, and social services to illegal immigrants, and Congress amended the federal welfare laws to curtail benefits to noncitizens, many immigrants rushed to become naturalized. In the 2000 election, both George W. Bush and Al Gore campaigned vigorously among Hispanics, and more voted in 2000 than in 1996, with big increases in California and Texas. Half of all Hispanic Americans live in those two states, and in 2001, California became the first big state in which whites are in the minority; Texas, the second most populous state, will become the second majority-minority state in 2004.[17]

Asian Americans

The term "Asian American" describes approximately 10 million individuals from many different countries and many different ethnic backgrounds. Most do not think of themselves as Asians but as Americans of Chinese, Japanese, Indian, Vietnamese, Cambodian, Korean, or other specific ancestry. They live chiefly in the western states, but their number has been increasing rapidly in New York and Texas.

In the war hysteria following the outbreak of World War II, Japanese Americans were rounded up and transported to internment camps.

Although Asian Americans are often considered a "model minority" because of their general success in education and business, the U.S. Civil Rights Commission found that "Asian-Americans do face widespread prejudice, discrimination and barriers to equal opportunity" and that racially motivated violence against them "occurs with disturbing frequency."[18]

CHINESE AMERICANS   The Chinese were the first Asians to come to the United States. Beginning in 1847, when young male peasants came here to get away from poverty and to work in mines, on railroads, and on farms, the Chinese encountered economic and cultural fears of the white majority, who did not understand them or their culture. In response, the Chinese seldom tried to assimilate but instead gravitated to "Chinatowns." Discriminatory immigration and naturalization restrictions, imposed beginning in 1882, were strengthened in later years and were not removed until the end of World War II.

Since that time, the Chinese have moved into the mainstream of American society, and they are beginning to run for and win local political offices. In 1996, Gary Locke, a Democrat and a graduate of Yale and Boston University Law School, was elected governor of Washington, the first Chinese American to become governor of a continental state. He won reelection in 2000.

JAPANESE AMERICANS   The Japanese first migrated to Hawaii in the 1860s and then to California in the 1880s. Most Japanese immigrants remained in the West Coast states. By the beginning of the twentieth century, they faced overt hostility. In 1905, labor leaders organized the Japanese and Korean Exclusion League, and in 1906, the San Francisco Board of Education excluded all Chinese, Japanese, and Korean children from neighborhood schools. Some western states passed laws denying the right to own land to aliens who were ineligible to become citizens—meaning aliens of Asian ancestry.

During World War II, anti-Japanese hysteria provoked the internment of West Coast Japanese—most of whom were loyal American citizens guilty of no crimes—in prison camps in California, Colorado, and some other states. During this time, the property of Japanese Americans was often sold at confiscatory rates, and many lost their businesses, jobs, and incomes. Following the war, the exclusionary acts were repealed. In 1988, President Ronald Reagan signed a law providing $20,000 restitution to each of the approximately 60,000 surviving World War II internees.

Major Civil Rights Laws

- **Civil Rights Act, 1957**   Makes it a federal crime to prevent persons from voting in federal elections.

- **Civil Rights Act, 1964**   Bars discrimination in employment or in public accommodations on the basis of race, color, religion, sex, or national origin; created the Equal Employment Opportunity Commission.

- **Voting Rights Act, 1965**   Authorizes the appointment of federal examiners to register voters in areas that have been discriminating.

- **Age Discrimination in Employment Act, 1967**   Prohibits job discrimination against workers or job applicants aged 40 through 65 and prohibits mandatory retirement.

- **Fair Housing Act, 1968**   Prohibits discrimination on the basis of race, color, religion, or national origin in the sale or rental of most housing.

- **Title IX, Education Amendment of 1972**   Prohibits discrimination on the basis of sex in any education program receiving federal financial assistance.

- **Rehabilitation Act, 1973**   Requires that recipients of federal grants greater than $2,500 hire and promote qualified handicapped individuals.

- **Fair Housing Act Amendments, 1988**   Give the Department of Housing and Urban Development authority to prohibit housing bias against the handicapped and families with children.

- **Americans with Disabilities Act, 1991**   Prohibits discrimination based on disability and requires that facilities be made accessible to those with disabilities.

- **Civil Rights Act, 1991**   Requires that employers justify practices that negatively affect women and minorities as job-related or show that no alternative practices would have a lesser impact. Also established a commission to examine the "glass ceiling" that keeps women from becoming executives and to make recommendations on how to increase promotion of women and minorities to management positions.

OTHER ASIAN AMERICANS   Like other Asian Americans, Koreans faced overt discrimination in jobs and housing, but a Korean middle class has been growing, with many Korean Americans becoming teachers, doctors, and lawyers. Others operate small family businesses such as dry cleaners, florist shops, service stations, and small grocery stores, often in inner cities.[19] As prosperous small businesspeople, they are often the target of the anger of the poor people whose neighborhoods they serve; many Korean stores in African American neighborhoods were destroyed in the 1992 Los Angeles riots.

When Filipinos first came to the United States in the early part of the twentieth century, they were considered American nationals because the Philippine Islands were an American possession. Nonetheless, they were denied rights to full citizenship and faced discrimination and even violence, including anti-Filipino riots in the state of Washington in 1928 and later in California, where nearly one-third of the approximately 1.5 million Filipinos live.[20] Their economic status has improved, but their influence in politics remains as small as their numbers.

The newest Asian arrivals consist of more than a million refugees from Vietnam, Laos, and Cambodia, who first came to the United States in 1975 and settled mostly in California. Although this group included middle-class people who left during the fall of Saigon following the end of the Vietnam War, it also consisted of large numbers of "boat people" who came to our shores without any financial resources. In a relatively short time, most established themselves economically. Although they are starting to have political influence, some remain socially and economically segregated.

Native Americans

Almost half of the more than 2 million Native Americans live on or near a *reservation*—a tract of land given to the tribal nations by treaty—and are enrolled as members of one of the 550 federally recognized tribes, including 226 groups in Alaska.[21] About 200 different Native American languages are spoken.

Native Americans speak of their tribes as "nations," yet they are not possessed of the full attributes of sovereignty. Rather, they are a separate people with power to regulate their own internal affairs, subject to congressional supervision. States are precluded from regulating or taxing the tribes or extending the jurisdiction of their courts over the tribes unless authorized to do so by Congress.[22] In recent years, Congress has stepped in to mediate growing tensions between Indian tribes who have used their sovereignty over reservations to operate gambling casinos and the states in which these reservations are located.

Sioux Indians took part in a 220-mile March of Memory to mark the 100th anniversary of the Battle of Wounded Knee, when U.S. troops opened fire and killed 200 men, women, and children.

The Evolution of Identity

Since 1860, the U.S. census has changed its classifications of race and ethnicity in light of the nation's growing diversity and political developments. Below are the categories used in the decennial counts from 1860 to 2000. Each new category is boldfaced at its first inclusion. For more information, see AmeriStat's Web site, at www.ameristat.org.

1860	1870	1880	1890	1900	1910	1920	1930	1940	1950
White	White	White	White	White	White	White	White	White	White
Black	Black	Black	Black	Black	Black	Black	Black	Black	Negro
Mulatto	Mulatto	Mulatto	Mulatto		Mulatto	Mulatto			
	Chinese	Chinese	Chinese	Chinese	Chinese	Chinese	Chinese	Chinese	Chinese
	Indian	Indian	Indian	Indian	Indian	Indian	Indian	Indian	American-Indian
			Quadroon						
			Octoroon						
			Japanese	Japanese	Japanese	Japanese	Japanese	Japanese	Japanese
						Filipino	Filipino	Filipino	Filipino
						Hindu	Hindu	Hindu	
						Korean	Korean	Korean	
							Mexican		
					Other	Other	Other	Other	Other

Tiger Woods, the prize-winning golfer, is proud of his diverse heritage. He is both African American and Asian (Thai.) He feels that ethnic background should not make a difference. It doesn't to him. As Woods says, "I am an American . . . and proud of it."

By acts of Congress, Native Americans are citizens of the United States and of the states in which they live. They have the right to vote. Native Americans living off reservations and working in the general community pay taxes just like everybody else; off reservations they have the same rights as any other Americans. If they are enrolled members of a recognized tribe, they are entitled to certain benefits created by law and by treaty. The Bureau of Indian Affairs of the Department of the Interior administers these benefits.

During the period of assimilation that began in 1887 and lasted until 1934, tribal governments were weak, some reservations were dissolved, and more than 100 tribes had their relationship with the federal government severed.[23] The civil rights movement of the 1960s created a more favorable climate for the concerns of Native Americans. Their goals were to reassert treaty rights and secure greater autonomy for the tribes. Under the leadership of the Native American Rights Fund (NARF), more Indian law cases were brought in the past several decades than at any time in our history.[24]

CHAPTER 18   *Equal Rights Under the Law*   459

1960	1970	1980	1990	2000
White	White	White	White	White
Negro	Negro/Black	Black/Negro	Black/Negro	Black/African American/Negro
Chinese	Chinese	Chinese	Chinese	Chinese
American-Indian	American-Indian	Indian	Indian	American Indian or Alaska Native
Japanese	Japanese	Japanese	Japanese	Japanese
Filipino	Filipino	Filipino	Filipino	Filipino
		Asian Indian	Asian Indian	Asian Indian
	Korean	Korean	Korean	Korean
Aleut		Aleut	Aleut	
Eskimo		Eskimo	Eskimo	
Hawaiian	Hawaiian	Hawaiian	Hawaiian	Native Hawaiian
Part Hawaiian				
		Vietnamese	Vietnamese	Vietnamese
		Guamanian	Guamanian	Guamanian or Chamorro
		Samoan	Samoan	Samoan
		Other Asian Pacific Islander	**Other Asian Pacific Islander**
Other	Other	Other	Other race	Some other race

ETHNICITY

1960	1970	1980	1990	2000
	Mexican	Mexican American	Mexican/Mexican American	Mexican/Mexican American
		Chicano	Chicano	Chicano
	Puerto Rican	Puerto Rican	Puerto Rican	Puerto Rican
	Central/South American			
	Cuban	Cuban	Cuban	Cuban
	Other Spanish	Other Spanish/Hispanic	Other Spanish/Hispanic	Other Spanish/Hispanic/Latino
	(None of these)	Not Spanish/Hispanic	Not Spanish/Hispanic	Not Spanish/Hispanic/Latino

As a result of the militancy of Native American leaders and a greater national consciousness of the concerns of minorities, most Americans are now aware that many Native Americans live in poverty. Native Americans "are in far worse health than the rest of the population, dying earlier and suffering disproportionately from alcoholism, accidents, diabetes, and pneumonia."[25] Although in recent years the rest of the United States has enjoyed less than 4 percent unemployment, many reservations continue to experience 50 to 60 percent unemployment. Some reservations lack adequate health care facilities, educational opportunities, decent housing, and jobs. Congress has started to compensate Native Americans for past injustices and to provide more opportunities for the development of tribal economic independence, and judges are showing greater vigilance in the enforcement of Indian treaty rights.

In 1986, Ben Nighthorse Campbell became the first Native American to be elected to Congress. He was elected as a Democrat from Colorado but became a Republican after being elected to the Senate in 1992, and then was reelected in 1998.

Equal Protection of the Laws: What Does It Mean?

The **equal protection clause** of the Fourteenth Amendment declares that no state (including any subdivision thereof) shall "deny to any person within its jurisdiction the equal protection of the laws." Although there is no parallel clause explicitly limiting the national government, the Fifth Amendment's **due process clause**, which states that no person shall "be deprived of life, liberty, or property, without due process of law," has been interpreted to impose the same restraints on the national government as the equal protection clause imposes on the states.

The equal protection clause applies only to the actions of *governments,* not to those of private individuals. If a discriminatory action is performed by a private person, it does not violate the Constitution, although it may violate federal and state laws. The equal protection clause does not, however, prevent governments from creating various classifications of people in its laws. What the Constitution forbids is *unreasonable* classifications. In general, a classification is unreasonable when there is no relation between the classes it creates and permissible governmental goals. A law prohibiting redheads from voting, for example, would be unreasonable. In contrast, laws denying persons under 18 the right to vote, to marry without the permission of their parents, or to apply for a license to drive a car appear to be reasonable (at least to most persons over 18).

Constitutional Classifications and Tests

One of the most troublesome constitutional questions is how to distinguish between constitutional and unconstitutional classifications. The Supreme Court uses three tests for this purpose: the *rational basis* test, the *strict scrutiny* test, and the *heightened scrutiny* test.

THE RATIONAL BASIS TEST   The traditional test to determine whether a law complies with the equal protection requirement places the burden of proof on the parties attacking the law. They must show that the law has no rational or legitimate governmental goals. For example, the Supreme Court has held that a state might deny unemployment benefits to residents who attend day school but make them available to those who attend night school. This classification of schools meets the rational basis test since it is reasonable to assume that students who go to school during the day are less likely to be available for employment than are those who go to school after work.[26]

SUSPECT CLASSIFICATIONS AND STRICT SCRUTINY   When a law is subject to strict scrutiny, the courts must be persuaded that there is both a "compelling public interest" to justify such a classification and no less restrictive way to accomplish this compelling purpose. The Court applies the strict scrutiny test to suspect classifications. A *suspect classification* is a class of people deliberately subjected to such unequal treatment in the past or relegated by society to a position of such political powerlessness as to require extraordinary judicial protection.[27]

Classifications based on race or national origin are always suspect. It does not make any difference if the laws are designed for supposedly benign purposes—that is, to help persons of a particular race or national origin. For example, the Supreme Court has held that laws that give preference for public employment based on race are subject to strict scrutiny.

QUASI-SUSPECT CLASSIFICATIONS AND HEIGHTENED SCRUTINY   To sustain a law under this test, the burden is on the government to show that its classification serves "important governmental objectives." Classifications based on gender are subject to heightened scrutiny. Not until 1971 was any classification based on gender declared unconstitutional. Before that time, many laws provided special protection for women—such as a Michigan law forbidding any woman other than the wife or daughter of a tavern owner to serve as a barmaid. As Justice William J. Brennan Jr. wrote for the Court, "There can be no doubt that our nation has had a long and unfortunate history of sex discrimination. Traditionally such discrimination was rationalized by an attitude of 'romantic paternalism' which in practical effect put women, not on a pedestal, but in a cage."[28]

equal protection clause
Clause in the Fourteenth Amendment that forbids any state to deny to any person within its jurisdiction the equal protection of the laws. By interpretation, the Fifth Amendment imposes the same limitation on the national government. This clause is the major constitutional restraint on the power of governments to discriminate against persons because of race, national origin, or sex.

due process clause
Clause in the Fifth Amendment limiting the power of the national government; similar clause in the Fourteenth Amendment prohibiting state governments from depriving any person of life, liberty, or property without due process of law.

Today the Court's view is that treating women differently from men (or vice versa) is forbidden when supported by no more substantial justification than "the role-typing society has long imposed upon women."[29] If the government's objective is "to protect members of one sex because they are presumed to suffer from an inherent handicap or to be innately inferior," that objective is illegitimate.[30] In recent years, the Supreme Court has struck down most laws brought before it that were alleged to discriminate against women but has tended to do so on the basis of federal statutes like the 1964 Civil Rights Act.

There is a continuing legal debate on whether or not schools in poorer districts should have the right to constitutional protection because these districts are not able to fund their public schools as successfully as wealthier districts.

POVERTY AND AGE   Just as racial minorities and women are entitled to special constitutional protection, it is argued, so should the poor and the elderly be protected. But the Supreme Court rejected the argument "that financial need alone identifies a suspect class for purposes of equal protection analysis."[31] However, state supreme courts in Texas, Ohio, and elsewhere have ruled that unequal funding for public schools as a result of "rich" districts spending more per pupil than "poor" districts violates their state constitutional provisions for free and equal education.[32]

Age is not a suspect class. Many laws commonly make distinctions based on age: to obtain a driver's license, to marry without parental consent, to attend schools, to buy alcohol, and so on. Many governmental institutions have age-specific programs: for senior citizens, for adult students, for midcareer persons. The Supreme Court has repeatedly refused to make age a suspect classification requiring extra judicial protection. As Justice Sandra Day O'Connor observed, "States may discriminate on the basis of age without offending the Fourteenth Amendment if the age classification in question is rationally related to a legitimate state interest."[33]

Congress, however, responding to "gray power," frequently treats age as a protected category. Congress has made it illegal for most employers to discriminate on the basis of advancing age. Except for a few exempt occupations, employers may not impose mandatory retirement requirements. Congress also attempted to extend the protections against age discrimination to cover state employees, but the Supreme Court ruled that Congress lacks the constitutional authority to open the federal courts to suits by state employees for alleged age discrimination. State employees are limited to recovering monetary damages under state laws in state courts.[34]

FUNDAMENTAL RIGHTS AND STRICT SCRUTINY   The Court also strictly scrutinizes laws impinging on *fundamental rights*. What makes a right fundamental in the constitutional sense? It is not the importance or the significance of the right that makes it fundamental but whether it is explicitly or implicitly *guaranteed by the Constitution*. Under this test, the rights to travel and to vote have been held to be fundamental, as well as First Amendment rights such as the right to associate for the advancement of political beliefs. Rights to an education, to housing, or to welfare benefits have not been deemed fundamental. Important as these rights may be, there are no constitutional provisions specifically protecting them from governmental regulation.

Proving Discrimination

Does the fact that a law or a regulation has a differential effect—what has come to be known as *disparate impact*—on persons of a different race or sex by itself establish that the law is unconstitutional? In one of its most important decisions, *Washington* v. *Davis* (1976), the Supreme Court said no.[35] "An unwavering line of cases" from the Supreme Court "hold that a violation of the Equal Protection Clause requires state action motivated by discriminatory intent; the disproportionate effects of state action are not sufficient to establish such a violation."[36] Or, as the Court said in another case, "the Fourteenth Amendment guarantees equal laws, not equal results."[37]

What do these rulings on disparate impact mean in practical terms? They mean, for example, that even when city ordinances permit only single-family residences and thus make low-cost housing projects impossible, they are not unconstitutional—even if their effect is to keep minorities from moving into the city—unless it can be shown that they were adopted with the *intent* to discriminate against minorities. For another example, preference for veterans in public employment does not violate the equal protection clause, even though its effect is to keep many women from getting jobs; the distinction between veterans and nonveterans was not adopted deliberately to create a sex barrier.

What is constitutional can nonetheless be illegal. For example, state laws creating legislative districts with no intent to discriminate against African Americans that in effect dilute their voting power are not unconstitutional. But in the Voting Rights Act of 1965, Congress made such laws illegal if the result is to dilute the voting power of African Americans, regardless of the laws' intent. The Voting Rights Act of 1965 tests the legality of state voting laws and practices by their *effects* rather than by the *intentions* of the legislatures that passed them.

Voting Rights

Under our Constitution, it is the states, not the federal government, that regulate elections and voting qualifications. However, Article I, Section 4, gives Congress the power to supersede state regulations as to the "Times, Places and Manner" of elections for representatives and senators. Congress has used this authority, along with its authority under Article II, Section 2, to set the date for selection of electors, to set age qualifications and residency requirements to vote in national elections, to establish a uniform day for all states to hold elections for members of Congress and presidential electors, and to give American citizens who reside outside the United States the right to vote for members of Congress and presidential electors in the states in which they previously lived.

Limitations on the states' power to set voting qualifications are contained in the Fourteenth Amendment (forbidding qualifications that have no reasonable relation to the ability to vote), the Fifteenth Amendment (forbidding qualifications based on race), the Nineteenth Amendment (forbidding qualifications based on sex), and the Twenty-Sixth Amendment (forbidding states to deny citizens 18 years of age or older the right to vote on account of age). These amendments also empower Congress to enact the laws necessary to enforce their provisions.

Protecting Voting Rights

In the 1940s, the Supreme Court began to strike down one after another of the devices that had been used to keep African Americans from voting. In the one-party South of the early decades of the twentieth century, the Democratic party would hold whites-only primaries, effectively disenfranchising black voters. In *Smith* v. *Allwright* (1944), the Court declared the **white primary** unconstitutional.[38] In 1960, the Court held that **racial gerrymandering**—the drawing of election districts to ensure that African Americans would be a minority in all districts—was contrary to the Fifteenth Amendment.[39] In 1964, the Twenty-Fourth Amendment eliminated the **poll tax**—payment required as a condition for voting—in presidential and congressional elections. In 1966, the Court held that the Fourteenth Amendment forbade the poll tax as a condition in any election.[40]

Officials seeking to deny African Americans the right to vote were forced to rely on registration requirements. On the surface, such requirements appeared to be perfectly proper, but it was the way they were administered that kept blacks from the polls. White election officers confronted African Americans trying to register while white police stood guard; white judges heard appeals of decisions made by registration officials. Officials often seized on the smallest error on an application form as an excuse to disqualify a black voter. In one parish in Louisiana, after four white voters challenged the registration of some black voters on the grounds that those voters had made an "error in spilling" [*sic*] in their applications, registration officials struck 1,300 out of approximately 1,500 black voters from the rolls.[41] After the 2000 presidential election, some black voters in several counties in Florida complained that they were discouraged from voting or that their votes were not counted.

white primary
Primary operated by the Democratic party in southern states that, before Republicans gained strength in the "one-party South," essentially constituted an election; ruled unconstitutional in *Smith* v. *Allwright* (1944).

racial gerrymandering
The drawing of election districts so as to ensure that members of a certain race are a minority in the district; ruled unconstitutional in *Gomillion* v. *Lightfoot* (1960).

poll tax
Payment required as a condition for voting; prohibited for national elections by the Twenty-Fourth Amendment (1964) and ruled unconstitutional for all elections in *Harper* v. *Virginia Board of Elections* (1966).

In many southern areas, **literacy tests** were used to discriminate against African Americans. Some states required applicants to demonstrate that they understood the national and state constitutions and that they were persons of good character. Although poor whites often avoided registering out of fear of embarrassment from failing a literacy test, the tests were more often used to discriminate against African Americans.[42] Whites were often asked simple questions; blacks were asked questions that would baffle a Supreme Court justice. "In the 1960s southern registrars were observed testing black applicants on such matters as the number of bubbles in a soap bar, the news contained in a copy of the *Peking Daily,* the meaning of obscure passages in state constitutions, and the definition of terms such as *habeas corpus.*"[43] In Louisiana, 49,603 illiterate white voters were able to persuade election officials they could understand the Constitution, but only two illiterate black voters were able to do so.

The Voting Rights Act of 1965

For two decades after World War II, under the leadership of the Supreme Court, many limitations on voting were declared unconstitutional, but this approach still did not open the voting booth to African Americans. Finally Congress acted. The Civil Rights Act of 1964 had hardly become law when events in Selma, Alabama, dramatized the inadequacy of depending on the courts to prevent racial barriers in polling places. Led by Martin Luther King Jr., a voter registration drive in Selma sparked arrests, marches on the state capital, and the murder of two civil rights workers. Still there was no dent in the color bar at the polls. Responding to events in Selma, President Lyndon Johnson made a dramatic address to Congress and the nation calling for federal action to ensure that no person would be deprived of the right to vote in any election for any office because of color or race. Congress responded with the Voting Rights Act of 1965.

Section 2 of the Voting Rights Act prohibits voting qualifications or standards that result in a denial of the right of any citizen to vote on account of race and color. Section 5 requires that states with a history of denying African Americans or Hispanic citizens the right to vote must clear with the Department of Justice changes in voting practice or laws that might dilute the voting power of these groups.[44] What precisely constitutes "dilution" and how it is to be measured are the subject of much litigation. Examples include changes in the location of polling places, changes in candidacy requirements and qualifications, changes in filing deadlines, changes from ward to at-large elections, changes in boundary lines of voting districts, and changes that affect the creation or abolition of an elective office and imposition by state political parties of fees for delegates to nominating conventions.[45]

Following the 1990 census, the Department of Justice pressured southern state legislatures to draw as many districts as possible in which minorities would constitute a majority of the electorate. Most of these districts tended to be Democratic, leaving the other congressional districts in these states heavily white and Republican. The lower federal courts sustained the Department of Justice's interpretation. As a result, there was a considerable increase in the number of congressional districts represented by minorities and Republicans.

The Supreme Court, however, in a series of cases beginning with *Shaw* v. *Reno* (1993), announced that although it was a legitimate goal for state legislatures to take race into account when they drew electoral districts in order to increase the voting strength of minorities, they could not make race the sole or predominant reason for drawing district lines. The Department of Justice, said the Supreme Court, was wrong in forcing states to create as many **majority-minority districts** as possible. A test case involved the North Carolina legislature's creation of a majority-minority district 160 miles long and in some places only an interstate highway wide. "If you drove down the interstate," said one legislator about this district, "with both car doors open, you'd kill most of the people in the district." North Carolina's reapportionment scheme, the Supreme Court declared, was so "irrational on its face that it can be understood only as an effort to segregate voters into separate voting districts because of their race." To comply with the Voting Rights Act, the Supreme Court explained, states must provide for districts roughly proportional to the minority voters' respective shares in the voting-age population.[46]

literacy test
Literacy requirement imposed by some states as a condition of voting, generally used to disqualify blacks from voting in the South; now illegal.

majority-minority district
A congressional district created to include a majority of minority voters; ruled constitutional so long as race is not the main factor in redistricting.

Thurgood Marshall (center), George C.E. Hayes (left), and James Nabrit Jr. (right) argued and won Brown v Board of Education of Topeka before the Supreme Court in 1954.

Since then the Court has expanded *Shaw* by clarifying that it was not meant to suggest that a "district must be bizarre on its face before there is a constitutional violation." Legislatures may be aware of racial considerations when they draw district lines, but when race becomes the overriding motive, the state violates the equal protection clause.[47] As a result, many southern states have had to redraw legislative districts. However, even when African American incumbents ran in these newly drawn districts with majority white electors, they were reelected.[48]

Education Rights

Until the Supreme Court struck down such laws in the 1950s, southern states had made it illegal for whites and blacks to ride in the same train cars, attend the same theaters, go to the same schools, be born in the same hospitals, or be buried in the same cemeteries. **Jim Crow laws**, as they came to be called, blanketed southern life. How could these laws stand in the face of the equal protection clause? This was the question raised in *Plessy* v. *Ferguson* (1896).

In the *Plessy* decision, the Supreme Court endorsed the view that governmentally imposed racial segregation in public transportation, and presumably in public education, did not necessarily constitute discrimination if "equal" accommodations were provided for the members of both races.[49] But the "equal" part of the formula was meaningless. African Americans were segregated in unequal facilities and lacked the political power to protest effectively. The passage of time did not lessen the inequalities. Beginning in the late 1930s, African Americans started to file lawsuits challenging the doctrine. They cited facts to show that in practice, "separate but equal" always resulted in discrimination against African Americans.

The End of "Separate but Equal": *Brown v. Board of Education*

At first, the Supreme Court was not willing to upset the separate but equal doctrine, but in *Brown* v. *Board of Education of Topeka* (1954), the Court finally reversed the *Plessy* doctrine as it applied to public schools by holding that "separate but equal" is a contradiction in terms. *Segregation is itself discrimination.*[50] A year later, the Court ordered school boards to proceed with "all deliberate speed to desegregate public schools at the earliest practical date."[51]

But many school districts moved very slowly, and in the 1960s, Congress and the president joined even more directly in the battle against school segregation. Title VI of the Civil Rights Act of 1964, as subsequently amended, stipulated that federal dollars under any grant program or project must be withdrawn from an entire school or institution of higher education that discriminates "on the ground of race, color, or national origin," gender, age, or disability, in "any program or activity receiving federal financial assistance."

From Segregation to Desegregation— but Not Yet Integration

School districts that had operated two kinds of schools, one for whites and one for blacks, now had an obligation to develop plans and programs to move from segregation to integration. For such school districts, desegregation would not be enough; they would have a duty to bring about integration. If they failed to do so on their own initiative, federal judges would supervise the school districts to ensure that they were doing what was necessary and proper to overcome the evils of segregation.

But since most whites and most African Americans continued to live in separate neighborhoods, merely removing legal barriers to school integration did not by itself integrate the schools. To overcome this residential clustering by race, some federal courts mandated busing across neighborhoods, moving white students to once predominantly black schools and vice versa. Busing students was not popular and triggered protests in many cities.

Jim Crow laws
State laws formerly pervasive throughout the South requiring public facilities and accommodations to be segregated by race; ruled unconstitutional.

The Supreme Court sustained busing only if it was to remedy the consequences of *officially* sanctioned segregation, **de jure segregation**. The Court refused to permit federal judges to order busing to overcome the effects of **de facto segregation**, segregation that arises as a result of social and economic conditions such as housing patterns.

Since *Brown* v. *Board of Education,* the federal government has intervened in more than 500 school desegregation cases. However, there has been no such judicial action for northern schools that have de facto segregation. As a result, many southern cities now have more integrated schools than large northern cities do. In both North and South, many school districts in central cities today are predominantly African American or Hispanic. This segregated pattern of schools is partly the result of "white flight" to the suburbs in the 1970s and 1980s and the transfer of white students to private schools to escape court-ordered busing. In more recent years, it is also due to higher birthrates and immigration among African Americans and Hispanics.[52]

After a period of vigorous federal court supervision of school desegregation programs, the Supreme Court has started to restrict the role of federal judges.[53] It has instructed some of them to restore control of a school system to the state and local authorities and to release districts from any busing obligations once a judge concludes that the authorities "have done everything practicable to overcome the past consequences of segregation."[54]

Political support for busing and for other efforts to integrate the schools has faded.[55] Many school districts have eliminated mandatory busing, with the result, according to one expert, that we may get "to a level of segregation we haven't seen since before the civil rights movement."[56] Some African American leaders, while still supporting desegregation efforts, are now more concerned about improving the quality of inner-city schools than desegregating them.

Residents of the Charlestown section of Boston took part in a "March Against Forced Busing" in May 1976.

Rights of Association, Accommodations, Jobs, and Homes

Association

As we have noted, the Fifth and Fourteenth Amendments apply only to governmental action, not to private discriminatory conduct. As Justice William O. Douglas said, our Constitution creates "a zone of privacy which precludes government from interfering with private clubs or groups. The associational rights which our system honors permit all-white, all-black, all-brown, and all-yellow clubs to be established. They also permit all-Catholic, all-Jewish, or all-agnostic clubs. . . . Government may not tell a man or a woman who his or her associates must be. The individual may be as selective as he desires."[57]

Families, churches, or private groups organized for political, religious, cultural, or social purposes are constitutionally different from large associations organized along other lines. For example, the Supreme Court has upheld the application of laws forbidding sex or racial discrimination by organizations such as the Jaycees, the Rotary Club, and large (in this case, more than 400 members) private eating clubs. Such associations and clubs are not small, intimate groups. Nor were they able to demonstrate that allowing women or minorities to become members would change the content or impact of their purposes.[58] In *Boy Scouts of America* v. *Dale* (2000), however, the Court held that the Boy Scouts may exclude homosexuals because of the organization's overall mission.[59]

Accommodations

In 1883, the Supreme Court had declared unconstitutional an act of Congress that made it a federal offense for any operator of a public conveyance, hotel, or theater to deny accommodations to any person because of race or color on the grounds that the Fourteenth Amendment does not give Congress such authority.[60] Since the 1960s, however, the constitutional authority of Congress to legislate against discrimination by private

de jure segregation
Segregation imposed by law.

de facto segregation
Segregation resulting from economic or social conditions or personal choice.

Native Americans and Welfare Reform

The 1996 welfare reform legislation, with its stricter work and job training requirements, is affecting Native American college enrollment, curriculum, and student services, according to a recent survey. The reservations on which most of the colleges are located have relatively high numbers of welfare recipients. . . . Given these needs, many states and tribes are turning to the colleges to provide remedial education and job training to reservation residents.

To examine the changes that have occurred since the welfare reform legislation was passed, the American Indian Higher Education Consortium (AIHEC) surveyed all 30 tribal colleges in the United States in spring 1998. . . .

The most obvious effects of the welfare reform provisions are on college enrollments. On the one hand, welfare recipients may get pushed out of higher education and into jobs; on the other, the new requirements may drive recipients who lack basic skills into basic adult education, GED, and vocational training programs.

Of the 18 colleges that responded, 11 colleges (61 percent) have seen enrollment changes that they believe are attributable to welfare reform. The reported shifts are varied: Four of the colleges mentioned increases in enrollment; three felt the enrollment changes have been mixed; one college said enrollment has declined; one college believed the students were getting younger; and two did not mention the direction of the enrollment changes. . . .

In addition to educating welfare recipients, the colleges are actively involved in helping them complete their transition into the labor force. For example, virtually all of the responding colleges (16, or 89 percent) work with local welfare agencies to coordinate their activities. Furthermore, seven of the colleges currently offer placement services for their students and graduates; two are planning to do so in the future; and two assist their students informally. These efforts continue despite an acute lack of available jobs.

According to recent Department of Commerce data, the average unemployment rate on reservations with tribal colleges is 28 percent and may be higher than 40 percent on some reservations. Some of the tribal colleges are following the paths of their students after graduation; 13 of the colleges said they currently track the employment or enrollment status of their graduates.

SOURCE: Alisa F. Cunningham, "Survey Reports Tribal Colleges' Response to Welfare Reform," *Tribal College Journal: Journal of American Indian Higher Education* (Winter 1998–1999), p. 36.

---

individuals is no longer an issue because the Court has broadly construed the **commerce clause**—which gives Congress the power to regulate interstate and foreign commerce— to justify action against discriminatory conduct by individuals. Congress has also used its power to tax and spend to prevent not only racial discrimination but also discrimination based on ethnic origin, sex, disability, and age.

TITLE II: PLACES OF PUBLIC ACCOMMODATION   For the first time since Reconstruction, the Civil Rights Act of 1964 authorized the massive use of federal authority to combat privately imposed racial discrimination. Title II makes it a federal offense to discriminate against any customer or patron in a place of public accommodation because of race, color, religion, or national origin. It applies to any inn, hotel, motel, or lodging establishment (except establishments with fewer than five rooms and occupied by the proprietor—in other words, small boardinghouses); to any restaurant or gasoline station that serves interstate travelers or serves food or products that have moved in interstate commerce; and to any movie house, theater, concert hall, sports arena, or other place of entertainment that customarily hosts films, performances, athletic teams, or other sources of entertainment that are moved in interstate commerce. Within a few months after its adoption, the Supreme Court sustained the constitutionality of Title II.[61] As a result, public establishments, including those in the South, opened their doors to all customers.

TITLE VII: EMPLOYMENT   Title VII of the 1964 Civil Rights Act made it illegal for any employer or trade union in any industry affecting interstate commerce and employing 15 or more people (and, since 1972, any state or local agency such as a school or university) to discriminate in employment practices against any person because of race, color, national origin, religion, or sex. Employers have an obligation to create workplaces that avoid

commerce clause
The clause of the Constitution (Article I, Section 8, Clause 3) that gives Congress the power to regulate all business activities that cross state lines or affect more than one state or other nations.

abusive environments. Related legislation made it illegal to discriminate against persons with physical handicaps, veterans, or persons over 40.

There are a few exceptions. Religious institutions such as parochial schools may use religious standards. Age, sex, or handicap may be considered where occupational qualifications are absolutely necessary to the normal operation of a particular business or enterprise—for example, hiring only women to work in women's locker rooms.

The Equal Employment Opportunity Commission (EEOC) was created to enforce Title VII. The commission works together with state authorities to try to bring about compliance with the act and may seek judicial enforcement of complaints against private employers. The attorney general prosecutes Title VII violations by public agencies. Not only do aggrieved persons have a right to sue for damages for themselves, but they can also do so for other persons similarly situated in a **class action suit**. The vigor with which the EEOC and the attorney general have acted has varied over the years, depending on the commitment of the president in office and the willingness of Congress to provide an adequate budget for the EEOC.[62]

Title VII was supplemented by a 1965 presidential executive order requiring all contractors doing work for the federal government, including universities, to adopt and implement affirmative action programs to correct "underutilization" of women and minorities. Such programs may not establish racial or ethnic quotas for minorities or women, but they may require contractors to establish timetables and goals; to follow open recruitment procedures; to keep records of applicants by race, sex, and national origin; and to explain why their labor force does not reflect the same proportion of persons in the appropriate labor market pools. Failure of contractors to file and implement an approved affirmative action plan may lead to loss of federal contracts or grants.

THE FAIR HOUSING ACT AND AMENDMENTS Housing is the last frontier of the civil rights crusade, the area in which progress is slowest and genuine change most remote.

> Segregated housing contributes mightily to a vicious circle that also includes educational and employment discrimination. . . . Because of poor schools for many minorities, they cannot find well-paying jobs. Without such jobs, they often cannot afford to live in nicer neighborhoods with decent housing. And because of their location in less desirable communities, good educational systems are less likely to be available.[63]

In 1948, the Supreme Court made racial or religious **restrictive covenants** (a provision in a deed to real property restricting its sale) legally unenforceable.[64] The 1968 Fair Housing Act forbids discrimination in housing, excluding from its protection what it called "Mrs. Murphy boardinghouses," housing owned by private individuals who own no more than three houses; dwellings that have no more than four separate living units in which the owner maintains a residence; and religious organizations and private clubs housing their own members on a noncommercial basis. For all other housing, the act forbids owners to refuse to sell or rent to any person because of race, color, religion, national origin, sex, or physical handicap or because a person has children. Discrimination in housing also covers efforts to deny loans to minorities.

The Department of Justice has filed hundreds of cases, especially those involving large apartment complexes, yet African Americans and Hispanics continue to face discrimination in housing. Some real estate agents continue to steer African Americans and Hispanics toward neighborhoods that are not predominantly white and to require larger rental deposits from minorities than from whites. Yet less than 1 percent of these discriminatory actions are complained about because they are so subtle that victims are often unaware that they are being discriminated against. However, the number of discrimination complaints received by the Department of Housing and Urban Development and local and state agencies has been increasing as the result of more aggressive enforcement.

Voluntary segregation obviously exists. "It's a fact of life that blacks like to live in black neighborhoods and whites like to live in white neighborhoods," according to Daniel Mitchell, who added, "Real estate agents generally like to bring customers to places they will like and where the agent can make a sale."[65] Whatever the reasons, housing segregation persists.

class action suit
Lawsuit brought by an individual or a group of people on behalf of all those similarly situated.

restrictive covenant
A provision in a deed to real property prohibiting its sale to a person of a particular race or religion. Judicial enforcement of such deeds is unconstitutional.

Many Americans believe that affirmative action is the best way to address the issue of past racial and ethnic quotas.

Affirmative Action: Is It Constitutional?

When white majorities were using governmental power to discriminate against African Americans, civil rights advocates cited with approval the famous words of the first Justice John Marshall Harlan: "Our Constitution is color-blind and neither knows nor tolerates class among citizens."[66] But by the 1960s, there was a new set of constitutional and national policy debates. Many people began to assert that government neutrality is not enough. If governments, universities, and employers stopped discriminating but changed nothing else, individuals previously discriminated against would still be kept from equal participation in American life. Because they had been so disadvantaged by past discrimination, they suffered disabilities not shared by white males in the competition for openings in medical schools, for skilled jobs, or for their share of government grants and contracts.

Remedies to overcome the consequences of past discrimination against African Americans, Hispanics, Native Americans, and women are known as *affirmative action* by supporters but as *reverse discrimination* by opponents. The Supreme Court's first major statement on the constitutionality of affirmative action programs came in a celebrated case relating to university admissions. Allan Bakke—a white male and a top student at Minnesota and Stanford universities, as well as a Vietnam War veteran—applied in 1973 and again in 1974 to the medical school of the University of California at Davis. In each of those years, the school admitted 100 new students, 84 in a general admissions program and 16 in a special admissions program created for minorities who had previously been underrepresented. Bakke's application was rejected each year while students with lower grade-point averages, test scores, and interview ratings were admitted under the special admissions program. After his second rejection, Bakke brought suit in federal court claiming he had been excluded because of his race, contrary to requirements of the Constitution and Title VI of the Civil Rights Act of 1964.

In *University of California Regents* v. *Bakke* (1978), the Supreme Court ruled the California plan unconstitutional.[67] But the Court also declared that affirmative action programs are not necessarily unconstitutional. A state university may properly take race and ethnic background into account as "a plus," as one of several factors in choosing students in order to achieve a diverse student body. The problem with the California plan was it created a *quota*—a set number of admissions from which whites were excluded solely because of race.

After *Bakke*: Refinements and Uncertainty

Following *Bakke*, the Court dealt with a variety of affirmative action programs, sustaining most but not all of them. As the justices continued to disagree on the application of the equal protection clause, opposition to such programs became more heated.

In *Richmond* v. *Croson* (1989), the Rehnquist Court struck down a regulation by the city of Richmond requiring nonminority city contractors to subcontract at least 30 percent of the dollar amount of their contracts to one or more minority business enterprises. Writing for the Court, Justice Sandra Day O'Connor called into question the validity of most government affirmative action plans and stated, "Race-sensitive remedial measures are to be justified only after a strong basis in evidence has established that remedial action is necessary to overcome the consequences of past discriminatory action."[68]

Since *Croson*, a bare majority of the Court has rejected the view that racial classifications, whether benign or hostile, should ever be subject to less than strict scrutiny by either the national or state and local governments.[69] And as we have noted, the Rehnquist Court is similarly opposed to the use of race as the sole criterion in the drawing of electoral district lines.[70]

The Court declined to review a decision by the Court of Appeals for the Fifth Circuit in *Hopwood* v. *Texas* (1996), striking down the University of Texas law school's affirmative action plan for admission of students.[71] The Court of Appeals for the Eleventh Circuit also struck down the University of Georgia's use of race, among other factors, in admissions.[72] In 2002, however, the Court of Appeals for the Sixth Circuit, in a 5-to-4 vote, upheld the University of Michigan Law School's program of promoting racial di-

Allan Bakke, who challenged the constitutionality of the University of California's affirmative action program.

versity in its admissions.[73] These conflicting decisions, along with some other lower court rulings, call into question the holding in *Bakke.* Until the Supreme Court clarifies the matter, as far as the U.S. Constitution is concerned, race—and presumably gender—may no longer be considered as a factor for admission to public universities and colleges in the Fifth Circuit (Texas, Louisiana, and Mississippi) and the Eleventh Circuit (Alabama, Florida and Georgia) but may be considered in the rest of the nation. It is nonetheless clear that the Supreme Court is closely scrutinizing programs that provide a preference based on race or ethnic origin or gender.

California's Proposition 209 and Other Plans

In 1995, the Regents of the University of California voted to eliminate race or gender as factors in employment, purchasing, contracting, or admissions. The following year, Californians voted overwhelmingly for Proposition 209 to amend the state constitution to forbid state agencies—including schools, colleges, and universities—to discriminate against or grant preferential treatment to any individual or group on the basis of race, sex, color, ethnicity, or national origin in public employment, public education, or public contracting, except where necessary to comply with a federal requirement.

Although Proposition 209 clearly forbids universities and other state agencies to take race and gender into account, it does not appear to make unconstitutional state-supported outreach programs designed to recruit more women and minorities to become scientists and engineers, nor does it prevent state universities from continuing outreach programs aimed at schools with large minority enrollments. In fact, although there was a drop in the percentage admitted in the last year before racial preferences were eliminated, due to such outreach programs the percentage of students admitted to the University of California from "underrepresented groups"—African Americans, Native Americans, and Hispanics—has gradually rebounded.[74] In 2001, the University of California's board of regents shifted policy to take into account the economic backgrounds and personal achievements, not just grades and SAT scores, of students applying for admission. As a result, in 2002–2003 the percentage of racial and ethnic minorities was almost back to previous levels, though still low at Berkeley, where Asian Americans make up more than 40 percent of the student body (see Figure 18-2).

Opponents of affirmative action had hoped that the adoption of Proposition 209 in California would start a national movement to restrict or eliminate affirmative action programs, and some federal programs designed to give women- and minority-owned businesses greater access to federal contracts were cut back. Under pressure from the Office of Civil Rights, some universities stopped offering scholarships based solely on race or ethnicity. But Congress has not moved to limit other federal affirmative action programs.

In the state of Washington, Initiative 200, almost identical to California's Proposition 209, called for abolishing preferential treatment in hiring and contracting. It received 58 percent of the popular vote, despite the fact that Governor Gary Locke and leading businesses outspent their opponents 3 to 1. Heartened by that victory, opponents of affirmative action moved toward putting the question before voters in other states, including Nebraska and Michigan.

California, Washington, Texas, Florida, and some other states have abandoned affirmative action programs and adopted the strategy of automatic admissions for a certain percentage of all high school graduates as a means of maintaining diversity in colleges and expanding educational opportunities for minorities. California offers admission to the top 4 percent of high school graduates, Texas offers admission to the top 10 percent, and Florida to the top 20 percent of every high school graduating class. The latter programs, though, have been sharply criticized for taking students from poor, inner-city schools who are not prepared to compete effectively in college with students from wealthier and more advantaged school districts.

Public support for affirmative action as measured in public opinion polls varies by race, social class, education, and life experience, but close inspection suggests that "whites and blacks are not separated by unbridgeable gaps on affirmative action issues, at least not

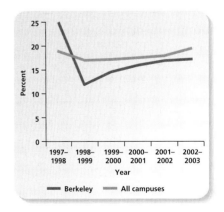

FIGURE 18–2 Percentage of First-Year Minority (Hispanic, Black, and Native American) Students at the University of California.

Source: "Affirmative Action," *Economist,* April 20, 2002, p. 30.

PEOPLE DEBATE
AFFIRMATIVE ACTION

For over 30 years, we have debated the appropriateness and constitutionality of affirmative action programs, as well as the goals and structure of those programs. Here are two contrasting views.

In Defense of Affirmative Action

Theodore M. Shaw

The goal of affirmative action is to break the cycle of discrimination and to enlarge opportunity for everyone. It is a moderate, effective remedy for exclusion, to achieve equality which is real and not illusory. As Justice Harry Blackmun has eloquently stated, "In order to get beyond racism, we must first take racism [and sexism] into account."

Affirmative action is not a single, rigid concept, but rather a mosaic of actions designed to eliminate artificial barriers and to allow merit to shine through. The particular affirmative measures utilized will vary in different circumstances, flexibly addressing the problem at hand.

Affirmative action does not mean admitting or hiring unqualified or less meritorious candidates. However, it may mean refining our definitions of merit. Affirmative action recognizes that we have not achieved the ideal of either merit selection or a colorblind and genderblind society. In addition to invidious discrimination based on race, ethnicity, and gender, our employment and contracting systems have always relied upon such non-merit-related criteria as nepotism, cronyism, and the "old boy network."

Affirmative action produces benefits for the entire community and nation. For example, as women have entered the medical profession and the United States Congress, more attention has been focused on crucial health needs of all women, such as breast cancer research.

Businesses have found that affirmative action is good for the bottom line. Productivity is improved in many instances, and a work force that reflects the diversity of the markets they serve allows businesses to compete more effectively. The Business Roundtable and the National Association of Manufacturers have repeatedly endorsed affirmative action.

We believe that there ought to be more opportunity for all poor and working-class people, who have been hurt by structural changes in our economy even while governmental and social policies much of the last 15 years have been tilted in favor of the rich, with the result that the wealthiest of Americans have become richer while the middle class has shrunk, and millions of people joined the ranks of the impoverished.

SOURCE: U.S. Congress, House of Representatives, Subcommittee on Employer-Employee Relations of the Committee on Economic and Educational Opportunities, 104th Cong., 1st Sess., *Hearings on Affirmative Action in Employment* (U.S. Government Printing Office, 1995), pp. 167–186.

insofar as college admissions decisions are concerned."[75] People's responses seem to depend to a significant degree on how the survey question is put. If the question asked is something like "Are you in favor of abolishing preferences in hiring or college admissions based on race or gender?" most people say yes. But if the question is something like "Do you favor affirmative action programs to increase the number of minorities in colleges or in jobs?" there is general support for such programs.

Clearly, the debate over the merits and constitutionality of affirmative action is not over. There are more decisions to come as the courts—and the nation—debate whether affirmative action is a vital tool to overcome decades of discrimination that needs to be "amended, not ended."

Equal Rights Today

Today, legal barriers have been lowered, if not removed, by civil rights legislation, executive orders, and judicial decisions. Important as these victories are, according to civil rights leader James Farmer, "They were victories largely for the middle class—those who

Toward Ending Preferences in Education and Employment

Brian W. Jones

I maintain that government-imposed preferential policies based upon race and gender, whether in the employment or education context, have outlived their usefulness, so to speak, and presently do a great deal more social harm than good. While 30 years ago such policies may have been an important tool for breaking down the systemic barriers to black entry into the economic mainstream, they have today, I think, reached the point of diminishing returns. . . .

The cost of preference policies can be measured in terms of: (1) the social discord created between preferred and non-preferred groups, and among the preferred groups; (2) the opportunity cost of mismatched minority talent and capital; (3) the economic cost to employers of complying with affirmative action mandates; (4) the injury done to innocents; and (5) the damage done to the constitutional ideal of equality.

Despite their significant social and economic cost, race and gender preferences in America are today justified essentially on two grounds: (1) the remediation of disadvantage caused by past discrimination; and (2) the desire to promote diversity.

Remediation of disadvantage was in fact the original moral claim of the proponents of affirmative action. . . . However, that justification today contains insuperable flaws. First, preferential policies today tend to benefit the least disadvantaged among and within preferred groups. Middle-class white women are now the primary beneficiaries of preferences, largely due to their relatively high level of education and cultural advantage.

The second justification for preferential policies is the notion of diversity. By diversifying the ranks of our employees, the theory goes, we will breed transracial familiarity and, consequently, harmoniously dynamic workplaces.

The anecdotal evidence suggests that both of these theories have been woefully inaccurate. Race relations in contexts where preference is writ large—college campuses and municipal employment, for example—have often become toxic as a result of increasing racial antagonism.

A truly constructive civil rights policy in America should focus on constructive efforts to confront the real underlying problems of performance in some of America's most distressed communities. A truly affirmative civil rights policy must concern itself with the hard work of improving the performance of disadvantaged individuals.

1. Do you think that affirmative action programs are defensible and desirable as remedies for past discrimination?
2. Are affirmative action programs aimed at promoting diversity in education and employment legitimate and worthwhile?

SOURCE: U.S. Congress, Senate, Committee on Labor and Human Resources, 104th Cong., 1st Sess., *Hearings on Affirmative Action and the Office of Federal Contract Compliance* (U.S. Government Printing Office, 1995), pp. 77–82.

could travel, entertain in restaurants, and stay in hotels. Those victories did not change life conditions for the mass of blacks who are still poor."[76]

As prosperous middle-class African Americans have moved out of inner cities, the remaining *underclass*, as they are coming to be called, has become even more isolated from the rest of the nation.[77] There are similar trends in Hispanic communities in Los Angeles, Dallas, and Houston.[78] Children are growing up on streets where drug abuse and crime are everyday events. They live in "separate and deteriorating societies, with separate economies, diverging family structures and basic institutions, and even growing linguistic separation within the core ghettos. The scale of their isolation by race, class, and economic situation is much greater than it was in the 1960s, with impoverishment, joblessness, educational inequality, and housing insufficiency even more severe."[79]

One of the difficulties is that as conditions have become better for many African Americans and Hispanics, the less fortunate see themselves as getting worse off; however, most Americans see conditions for minorities as improving. "Both perceptions will be correct. And the fact that both are correct in arriving at opposite perceptions of what is going on will itself lead to further misunderstanding."[80]

Despite the lack of improvement in social conditions, the push for integration has lessened:

> In fact, power on both sides of the color line is based to some extent on acceptance of segregation. On the black side of the color line, it is advantageous to keep African Americans within black electoral areas and keep black-controlled resources within black institutions; integrationist policies are often viewed as posing larger threats than they actually do. On the white side of the line, . . . some residents in outlying suburbs see critical advantages in their almost all-white and all middle-class status.[81]

Some contend that attention should be paid to the plight of the underclass and that instead of focusing on issues of race, what is needed is a focus on class differences and policies that provide jobs and improve education.[82] Others say there has to be a revival of the civil rights crusade, a restoration of vigorous civil rights enforcement, job training, and, above all, an attack on residential segregation.[83] In any event, it is clear that questions as to how best to provide equal opportunities for all citizens remain high on the national agenda.

TRAVEL THE CIVIL RIGHTS TIMELINE

This simulation lets you travel through a timeline of significant events in the struggles for civil rights of Native Americans, African Americans, Hispanic Americans, women, and the disabled. It provides links to speeches and biographies of leaders of each of those movements.

  Go to PoliSim "Travel the Civil Rights Timeline."

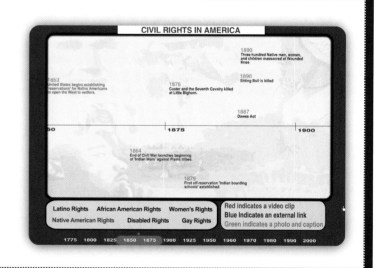

Summary

1. Americans are committed to "equality," an elusive term, with most support for equality of opportunity, some for equality of starting conditions, and some for equality of results.

2. Progress in securing civil rights for African Americans was a long time coming. After the Civil War, the national government briefly tried to secure some measure of protection for the freed slaves and to enforce the Thirteenth, Fourteenth, and Fifteenth Amendments and the civil rights laws passed to implement them. But when federal troops withdrew from the South in 1877, the national government withdrew from the field, and blacks were left to their own resources. Not for nearly a century did the national government take action to prevent racial segregation and discrimination against blacks.

3. The crusade for women's rights was born partly out of the struggle to abolish slavery. Similarly, the modern women's movement learned and gained power from the civil rights movements of the 1950s and early 1960s. The fate of these two social movements has long been intertwined. Women secured the right to vote in the Nineteenth Amendment.

4. Concern for equal rights under the law continues today for African Americans and women. Hispanics, Asian Americans, and Native Americans have also experienced discrimination.

5. The Supreme Court uses a three-tiered approach to evaluate the constitutionality of laws challenged as violating the equal protection clause. Laws touching economic concerns are sustained if they are rationally related to the accomplishment of a legitimate government goal. Laws that classify people because of sex or illegitimacy are subject by the courts to heightened scrutiny and are sustained only if they serve important governmental objectives. Strict scrutiny is used to review laws that touch fundamental rights or classify people because of race or ethnic origin. Such laws will be sustained only if the government can show a compelling public purpose.

6. A series of constitutional amendments, Supreme Court decisions, and laws passed by Congress have now secured the right to vote to all Americans aged 18 and over. Following the Voting Rights Act of 1965, the Justice Department can oversee practices in locales with a history of discrimination. Recent Supreme Court decisions have refined the lengths to which legislatures can go, or are obliged to go, in creating minority-majority districts.

7. *Brown v. Board of Education of Topeka* (1954) struck down the "separate but equal" doctrine that had justified segregated schools in the South, but school districts responded slowly. The Supreme Court demanded compliance, and some federal courts mandated busing children across neighborhoods to comply. Still, full integration has proved elusive, as "white flight" has left many inner cities, and their schools, predominantly black or Hispanic.

8. Discrimination in public accommodations was outlawed by the Civil Rights Act of 1964. This act also provided for equal employment opportunity. The Fair Housing Act of 1968 and its 1988 amendments prohibited discrimination in housing.

9. The desirability and constitutionality of affirmative action programs that provide special benefits to members of groups subjected to past discrimination divide the nation and the Supreme Court. Remedial programs tailored to overcome specific instances of past discrimination are likely to pass the Supreme Court's suspicion of race, national origin, and sex classifications. However, the courts must still clarify constitutional issues concerning preferential treatment in school admissions and hiring practices.

Key Terms

natural rights	due process clause	literacy test	de facto segregation
affirmative action	white primary	majority-minority district	commerce clause
women's suffrage	racial gerrymandering	Jim Crow laws	class action suit
equal protection clause	poll tax	de jure segregation	restrictive covenant

Further Reading

BARBARA R. BERGMAN, *In Defense of Affirmative Action* (Basic Books, 1996).

WILLIAM G. BOWEN AND DEREK BOK, *The Shape of the River: Long-Term Consequences of Considering Race in College and University Admissions* (Princeton University Press, 1998).

TAYLOR BRANCH, *Parting the Waters: America in the King Years, 1954–1963* (Simon & Schuster, 1988).

TAYLOR BRANCH, *Pillar of Fire: America in the King Years, 1963–65* (Simon & Schuster, 1998).

CLARE CUSHMAN, ED., *Supreme Court Decisions and Women's Rights* (CQ Press, 2000).

ARLENE M. DAVILA, *Latinos, Inc.: The Marketing and Making of a People* (University of California Press, 2001).

DAVID DENT, *In Search of Black America: Discovering the African American Dream* (Simon & Schuster, 2000).

JANET DEWART, ED., *The State of Black America* (National Urban League, published annually).

WILLIAM N. ESKRIDGE JR., *Gaylaw: Challenging the Apartheid of the Closet* (Harvard University Press, 2000).

BERNARD GROFMAN, ED., *Legacies of the 1964 Civil Rights Act* (University Press of Virginia, 2000).

JONATHAN GOLDBERG-HILLER, *The Limits to Union: Same-Sex Marriage and the Politics of Civil Rights* (University of Michigan Press, 2002).

ANDREW HACKER, *Two Nations: Black and White, Separate, Hostile, Unequal* (Scribner, 1992).

RANDALL KENNEDY, *Race, Crime, and the Law* (Pantheon, 1997).

PHILIP A. KLINKER AND ROGER M. SMITH, *The Unsteady March: The Rise and Decline of Racial Equality in America* (University of Chicago Press, 2000).

RICHARD KLUGER, *Simple Justice: The History of Brown v. Board of Education* (Knopf, 1976).

DAVID M. O'BRIEN, *Constitutional Law and Politics: Civil Rights and Civil Liberties*, 5th ed. (Norton, 2003).

GARY ORFIELD, SUSAN E. EATON, AND THE HARVARD PROJECT ON SCHOOL DESEGREGATION, *Dismantling Desegregation: The Quiet Reversal of Brown v. Board of Education* (New Press, 1996).

J. W. PELTASON, *Fifty-Eight Lonely Men: Southern Federal Judges and School Desegregation* (University of Illinois Press, 1971).

RUTH ROSEN, *The World Split Open: How the Modern Women's Movement Changed America* (Viking, 2000).

JOHN DAVID SKRENTNY, ED., *Color Lines: Affirmative Action, Immigration, and Civil Rights Options for America* (University of Chicago Press, 2001).

GIRARDEAU A. SPANN, *The Law of Affirmative Action: Twenty-Five Years of Supreme Court Decisions on Race and Remedies* (New York University Press, 1999).

PHILIPPA STRUM, *Women in the Barracks: The VMI Case and Equal Rights* (University Press of Kansas, 2002).

ROBERTO SURO, *Strangers Among Us: How Latino Immigration Is Transforming America* (Knopf, 1998).

STEPHEN THERNSTROM AND ABIGAIL THERNSTROM, *America in Black and White* (Simon & Schuster, 1997).

SUSAN F. VAN BURKLEO, "Belonging to the World": *Women's Rights and Constitutional Culture* (Oxford University Press, 2001).

MAKING ECONOMIC AND REGULATORY POLICY

T
HE 1996 TELECOMMUNICATIONS ACT AFFECTED THE U.S. ECONOMY ON TWO FRONTS. FIRST, IT BROUGHT NEW COMPETITION into the telephone industry by giving smaller companies such as Sprint and MCI a fighting chance to take on long-distance giants such as AT&T. Second, it created thousands of new jobs in an industry that had shown little growth. The market, not the federal government, would decide where phone companies would operate and what they could sell. Price and service, not federal regulation, would rule.

The act clearly succeeded on both fronts, at least for a while. Sprint and MCI not only grew, so did start-up companies such as WorldCom, Qwest Communications, and Global Crossing. WorldCom grew the fastest, purchasing MCI in 1998 and Sprint in 1999, but the industry as a whole did remarkably well even during the first few months of the 2001 economic downturn.

However, by mid-2002, it was clear that many of these companies had grown too fast and that at least one, WorldCom, had not grown as fast as it claimed. In June, WorldCom admitted that it had failed to report $3.8 billion in costs, which had falsely inflated its profits. Within days, the company announced plans to fire 17,000 employees in a desperate effort to stave off bankruptcy.

Although WorldCom had sown the seeds of its potential dimise through improper accounting, the rest of the industry was also in decline. One out of every ten jobs lost in the 2001–2002 economic downturn was in telecommunications, with no end in sight to the downsizing. Like the earlier deregulation of other industries discussed later in this chapter, the telecommunications deregulation produced a stunning rise in the number of companies, then a string of consolidations through mergers and acquisitions, and finally a collapse back to prederegulation levels.[1]

Telecommunications deregulation is just one of several types of economic policy that affect the overall performance of the U.S. economy. Presidents and Congress also influence the economy by spending money and collecting taxes, both of which influence the behavior of consumers, and the Federal Reserve Board sets the basic flow of money by setting interest rates. The goal of economic policy is to keep the economy on a steady course, even if that occasionally creates the kinds of wild market swings that buffeted WorldCom and the telecommunications industry.

The preceding chapters concentrated on the structure of our federal system and how government institutions are organized and operate. In this chapter and the two that follow, we focus on what the national government *does*—how voters, interest groups, and institutions (Congress, the White House, the executive branch, the courts) interact to promote the general welfare and provide for the common defense. We will be talking about making and implementing three different kinds of *public policy:* economic, social, and foreign policy.

Making Public Policy

The U.S. government has been making public policy since 1789. Having swept the election of 1788, the Federalists entered office with a long list of challenges, not the least of which was to create the first departments of government and pass the Bill of Rights. Both were clearly public policies. By creating the Departments of State, Treasury, and War, the government announced its intention to conduct foreign policy (State), manage the economic affairs of the nation (Treasury), and maintain a national defense (War). And by approving 12 of James Madison's 19 proposed amendments to the Constitution, the government signaled its intent to create the promised charter of rights that had been so important to ratification of the Constitution. Over time, these first successes provided a foundation for other public policies.

The Policy-Making Process

There are numerous approaches to the study of public policy making. The choice of which approach is most appropriate depends on what policies are being considered, the particular stage of the process selected for analysis, and the analyst's assumptions and political values. Nevertheless, the following distinct stages in the policy-making process can be identified.

1. Problem Identification

What is the problem? How and by whom is the problem defined? How does the problem fit with existing policy categories and priorities? Does the government need to help out, intervene, regulate, or make some kind of decision? Should the issue or problem even be placed on the government's agenda? What forces determine whether the problem will reach the attention of government officials? A variety of factors and people are involved in problem identification: events, crises, changes in expert opinion, changes in mass opinion, interest group agitation, and involvement by elected officials and their staffs.

2. Policy Formulation

What should be done? What alternatives should analysts consider? How should the alternatives be assessed? Who should be involved in the planning and design of the policy?

3. Policy Adoption

Who needs to act? What branch of government should get involved? What constitutional, legal, or political requirements must be met?

How specific or how general must the decision be? Should Congress or some regulatory body be asked to hold hearings on the matter and come up with recommendations? Or should the matter be turned over to the president, who can issue executive orders and deliver major addresses urging the public to comply?

4. Policy Implementation

Once adopted, how should the policy be carried out? At what level of government—federal, state, local, or all three—will the policy be most effectively implemented? How much money should be spent, where, and how? How can the policy be administered effectively? How and by whom will the implementation of the policy be defined? During this stage, policy is translated into practice.

5. Policy Evaluation

Is the policy working? How is the effectiveness of the policy measured? Who evaluates the policy? What are the consequences of policy evaluation and congressional oversight? On the one hand, program supporters and administrators tend to exaggerate the success of their favorite programs to justify the funds allocated to them. On the other hand, an agency may build in delays and deficiencies during evaluation to hide the real cost of its operations. Evaluation is never entirely nonpolitical; it is sometimes used by one party, branch of government, department, or agency against another.

It is tempting to imagine virtually everything the first members of Congress did in their new government as somehow more virtuous and rational than what has followed. After all, the first members included many of the Constitution's framers. Yet the reality is that the first public policies were as much a product of intense debate, even conflict and compromise, as any policies of today. The first members of Congress divided over many issues, not the least of which were seven proposed constitutional amendments that did not get the required two-thirds support in each chamber.

Despite their disagreements, the nation's first policy makers in Congress and the executive branch moved quickly to protect their young nation, finance the new government, and support veterans of the Revolutionary War. These policy makers clearly believed that the nation had to be more than just the sum of the 13 individual states. Otherwise, they never would have abandoned the Articles of Confederation. But building a sum greater than the parts meant more than patriotic slogans and a new flag. It also had to mean real policies that answered the problems of the day.

Today's policy-making process is much more complicated than anything the framers could have imagined. What were once vast tracts of empty land between Capitol Hill and the White House are now filled with office buildings that house a vast collection of interest groups, law firms, newspaper bureaus, government agencies, and think tanks, which may in turn have increased the odds of stalemate on issues such as prescription drug coverage where the vast majority of the public wants action.

It is also safe to suggest that there have never been more places where policy decisions get made, whether measured by the total number of congressional committees and subcommittees, White House units, government departments and agencies, or special task forces, commissions, and advisory boards. Those who wish to delay action have plenty of opportunities to do so at both ends of Pennsylvania Avenue, as well as in the federal courts.

But some matters of great importance never get on the public agenda. Matters like the growing income gap between the rich and the poor and the problems of our cities fail to get the attention some people think they deserve. Although some of these issues are resolved at the state and local level, "nondecisions" can occur at any level of government. The absence of government activity does not necessarily mean that government is without a policy in that area, for *inaction is itself a policy.* Inattention to an issue can be as important as decisive action.

Economic Policy

The federal government has been involved in economic policy since the end of the Revolutionary War. The framers wanted a government strong enough to promote free trade, protect patents and trademarks, and enforce contracts between individuals and businesses. And they wanted a government with enough funding that it could build the postal roads, bridges, railroads, and canals that would allow the young economy to grow.

Much as they worried about the state of the economy, the framers did not concentrate economic policy in any branch. Instead, they divided economic policy-making control between the the legislative and executive branches and between the House and the Senate. Article I, Section 8, of the Constitution gives Congress the power to borrow, coin, and print money yet requires that all bills for raising revenue originate in the House, while Article II, Section 2, gives the president the power to appoint the officers of government who would actually do the borrowing, coining, spending, and taxing yet requires that all officers be confirmed by the Senate. In a similar vein, Article I gives Congress the power to regulate commerce with foreign nations, among the states, and with Native American tribes, while Article II gives the president authority to negotiate the treaties and enforce the laws. Finally, Article I gives Congress the power to establish post offices and build postal roads, which were as important to the free movement of commerce in the 1700s as the highways, rails, and Internet are today, yet Article II gives the president the power to appoint executive officials such as the postmaster general of the United States.

By creating a national government of limited powers and providing constitutional guarantees to protect property from excessive regulation, the framers succeeded in protecting capitalism. More than two centuries later, the U.S. economy is the strongest in the world, and the federal government continues to safeguard the basic conditions needed for capitalism to thrive. Part of the government's role is to stay out of the way as individuals and businesses create wealth through new ideas and hard work, but part is to promote the national welfare through **fiscal policy**, which uses federal spending and taxation to stimulate or slow the economy, and **monetary policy**, which manipulates the supply of money that individuals and businesses have in their hands to keep the economy from swinging wildly from boom to bust. In addition, the federal government promotes economic growth and trade and controls many economic decisions through regulations against certain kinds of business, labor, and environmental practices.

These tools are designed to smooth the ups and downs of the normal *business cycle.* Economists tend to focus on four discrete stages of the cycle: (1) expansion, in which the economy produces new jobs and growth; (2) contraction, as the economy starts to slow down; (3) recession, in which the economy reaches a trough of low growth; and (4) recovery, in which the economy rebounds. The goal of effective economic policy today is to make sure the peaks are not too high and the troughs are not too low. In general, **inflation** in prices is considered the primary policy problem during expansion and recovery, and unemployment is the focus during contraction and recession.

The federal government exercises less control over the national economy than it does over social or foreign policy. Nevertheless, it keeps a firm hand on many of the gears and levers that guide not only the economy's general direction but the rate at which it moves. These controls are taxes, spending, and borrowing.

Fiscal Policy

Congress and the president make fiscal policy by taxing, borrowing, and spending money. Nothing reflects the growth of federal programs and the rise of big government more clearly than the increased spending by the national government. In 1933, the federal government spent only $4 billion, about $30 per capita. In 2003, the figure was $2.1 trillion, or about $7,700 per capita.

fiscal policy
Government policy that attempts to manage the economy by controlling taxing and spending.

monetary policy
Government policy that attempts to manage the economy by controlling the money supply and thus interest rates.

inflation
A rise in the general price level (and decrease in dollar value) owing to an increase in the volume of money and credit in relation to available goods.

Key Economic Measures

The Relationship Between Inflation and Unemployment.

*Estimated.

Economic policy is designed to smooth the ups and downs of the economic cycle and its two most noticeable impacts: inflation and unemployment. Inflation is usually measured by the Consumer Price Index (CPI), which shows how much more or less consumers are paying for the same "basket of goods" over time. The major components of the CPI are food, shelter, fuel, clothing, transportation, and medical care. Unemployment is measured simply by the percentage of able-bodied workers who are looking for jobs but cannot find them. It does not measure the number of able-bodied workers who have given up looking for work.

Inflation is considered part of economic expansion, while unemployment is considered a consequence of economic contraction. In theory, one rises as the other falls.

The Federal Budget

Today federal, state, and local governments spend an amount equal to about one-third of the income of all Americans. The national government is the biggest spender of all—it spends more than all state and local governments combined. Annual spending by the national government accounts for some 23 percent of the gross domestic product (GDP), or nearly one dollar out of every four spent in the U.S. economy. The national debt is about $3.6 trillion, and the United States pays $180 billion each year in interest payments on that debt (see Table 19-1).

WHERE THE MONEY COMES FROM   "In this world," Benjamin Franklin once said, "nothing is certain but death and taxes." Tax collecting is one of the oldest activities of government. Today the federal government gets most of its funds from personal and corporate income taxes. Other moneys come from borrowing, special fees and fines, grants and gifts, and administrative and commercial revenues.

Putting power over taxation into the hands of the people was a major achievement in the development of self-government. "No taxation without representation" has been a battle cry the world over. The Constitution clearly provided that Congress "shall have Power to lay and collect Taxes, Duties, Imposts, and Excises." **Tariffs** (import duties) and **excise taxes** (consumer taxes on specific kinds of merchandise) have to be levied uniformly throughout the United States.

Raising money is only one objective of taxation. Regulation and, more recently, promoting economic growth are other objectives. In a broad sense, all taxation regulates human behavior. For example, a **progressive tax**—under which people with high incomes pay larger fractions of their incomes than people with low incomes—has a leveling tendency on people's wealth.

In the federal budget for fiscal year 2002 (see Figure 19-1), federal receipts include the following:

1. *Individual income taxes.* Taxes on individuals' incomes account for about 48 percent of the federal government's tax revenue. Over the years, the income tax has grown increasingly complex as Congress responded to claims for differing kinds of exemptions and rates. Some members of Congress have advocated simplification or even elimination of the income tax in favor of a national sales tax.

2. *Corporate income taxes.* These taxes account for just under 10 percent of the national government's tax revenues. As late as 1942, revenue from corporate income taxes exceeded that from individual income taxes.

3. *Payroll receipts.* Payroll taxes are the second-largest and most rapidly rising source of federal revenue, accounting for 33.2 percent of all federal revenue, not including borrowing. Most people pay more in Social Security taxes than in federal income taxes. These are highly **regressive taxes**, meaning that low-income people generally pay larger fractions of their income than high-income people do.

4. *Excise taxes.* These taxes on liquor, tobacco, gasoline, telephones, air travel, and other so-called "luxury items" account for roughly 4 percent of federal revenue.

5. *Customs duties and tariffs.* Although no longer the main source of federal income, in recent years these taxes provided an annual yield of almost $20 billion.

6. *Borrowing.* Since World War II, the government has regularly resorted to borrowing money to finance itself. The government ran a deficit between 1969 and 1998, held a surplus for three years, and started running deficits again in 2002.

Ordinary people borrow money when they face emergency expenses. The same is true of governments. The **deficit** is the difference between the annual revenues raised and the expenditures of government, including the interest on past borrowing. The deficit is not to be confused with the **debt**, which is the total of our deficits, minus our surpluses, over the years.[2]

TABLE 19–1   Trends in the Gross Federal Debt

Year	Amount (billions)	Percentage of GDP
1950	$256.8	94.2%
1955	274.3	69.4
1960	290.5	56.1
1965	322.3	46.9
1970	380.9	37.7
1975	541.9	34.9
1980	909.0	44.3
1985	1,817.5	33.4
1990	3,206.5	56.4
1995	4,921.0	68.5
2000	5,686.3	59.4
2005*	7,206.9	58.0

*Estimated

SOURCE: Budget of the United States Government, 2002.

tariff
Tax levied on imports to help protect a nation's industries, labor, or farmers from foreign competition. It can also be used to raise additional revenue.

excise tax
Consumer tax on a specific kind of merchandise, such as tobacco.

progressive tax
A tax graduated so that people with higher incomes pay a larger fraction of their income than people with lower incomes.

regressive tax
A tax whereby people with lower incomes pay a higher fraction of their income than people with higher incomes.

deficit
The difference between the revenues raised annually from sources of income other than borrowing and the expenditures of government, including paying the interest on past borrowing.

debt
The accumulated total of federal deficits, minus surpluses, over the years.

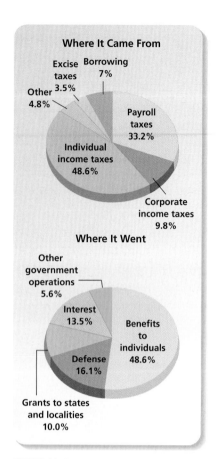

Where It Came From

FIGURE 19–1
The Federal Government Dollar.

SOURCE: U.S. Department of Commerce,
Statistical Abstract of the United States, 2002
(U.S. Government Printing Office, 2000),
Budget of the United States, 2003.

gross domestic product (GDP)
The total output of all economic activity in
the nation, including goods and services.

entitlements
Government programs, such as unemployment insurance, disaster relief, and
disability payments, that provide benefits to all eligible citizens.

During past military and economic crises, the federal government went heavily into debt; it engaged in deficit spending. But until the late 1990s, we also incurred
debts during periods of peace with a relatively healthy economy. The federal government borrowed $23 billion during World War I, about $13 billion during the Great
Depression of the 1930s, and $200 billion during World War II. In 2002, the total fed-
eral debt was about $3.5 trillion, while the federal budget was estimated to have a
deficit of $100 billion.

Borrowing costs money. The federal government borrows from investors who buy
Treasury notes, Treasury bills, and U.S. savings bonds. These investors include individuals (foreign and domestic), U.S. government accounts, banks, and other investors.

Americans might not be as troubled by the size of the debt if they understood two
characteristics of federal borrowing. First, the government owes roughly 90 percent of
the money to its own citizens rather than to foreign governments or investors, although
the amount owed to foreigners is growing. Second, the economic strength and resources
of the country are more significant than the size of the debt.

WHERE THE MONEY GOES   Much of the money the federal government takes in is
spent on benefit payments to individuals and national defense. Measured in absolute dollars spent in 2003, 49 percent of revenues went to required benefit payments for individuals (such as Social Security, Medicare, Medicaid, and other major social programs);
16 percent to national defense; 9 percent to interest on the national debt; 10 percent to
grant programs such as highways, medical research, and the environment; and 19 percent
to all other required operations and interest (again, see Figure 19-1).

The proportions do not change when spending is measured as percentage of the nation's **gross domestic product (GDP)**, which is an estimate of the total output of all U.S.
economic activity. Spending on domestic **entitlement** programs such as Social Security,
Medicare, and unemployment insurance to which qualified citizens are "entitled" by national legislation runs at about 11 percent of the GDP. Spending for defense is a little
more than 3 percent of GDP, payments on the deficit make up another 3 percent of GDP,
and nondefense discretionary spending comes to just over 3 percent.

Years ago, revenues and outlays were so small that federal tax and spending decisions had little impact on the overall economy. In today's $2.1 trillion federal budget,
even small changes in taxes and spending can alter the direction of the economy. However, because many federal programs are open to all eligible citizens, much of the federal budget is "uncontrollable." The most uncontrollable parts of the budget are Social
Security, Medicare, unemployment benefits, health benefits for the poor through Medicaid, and interest on the national debt.

The Budget Process

Before Congress enacted the Budget and Accounting Act of 1921, each executive
agency dealt with Congress on its own, requesting that Congress appropriate funds
for its activities with little or no presidential coordination. In 1921, the Bureau of the
Budget (changed to the Office of Management and Budget in 1970) was created in the
Treasury Department, and for the first time, the executive branch presented one budget to Congress.

THE EXECUTIVE BRANCH   The federal government's fiscal year begins on October 1.
The budget process begins nearly two years in advance, when the various departments and
agencies estimate their needs and propose their budgets to the president.[3] While Congress is debating the budget for the coming fiscal year, the agencies are making estimates
for the year after that (see Table 19-2). Agency officials take into account not only their
needs as they see them but also the overall presidential program and the probable reactions of Congress. Departmental budgets are detailed; they include estimates of expected needs for personnel, supplies, office space, and the like.

TABLE 19–2 Steps in the Budget Process, Fiscal Year 2004

February–December 2002	Executive branch agencies develop requests for funds, which are reviewed by the Office of Management and Budget and forwarded to the president for final decision.
December 2002	The formal budget documents are prepared.
January–February 2003	The budget is transmitted to Congress as a formal message from the president.
March–September 2003	Congress reviews the president's proposed budget, develops its own budget, and approves spending and revenue bills.
October 1, 2003	Fiscal year 2004 begins.
October 1, 2003–September 30, 2004	Executive branch agencies execute the budget provided in law.
October–November 2004	Data on actual spending and receipts for the completed fiscal year become available.

White House budget director Mitch Daniels testifying in Senate budget committee hearing.

The **Office of Management and Budget (OMB)**, a staff agency of the president, handles the next phase. OMB budget examiners review each agency's budget and reconcile it with the president's overall plans. OMB then holds informal hearings with every department and agency to give each one a chance to clarify and defend its estimates.

Once this give-and-take is over, the OMB director gives the president a single, consolidated set of estimates of both revenue and expenditures—the product of perhaps a year's work. The president takes several days to review these figures and make adjustments. The budget director also helps the president prepare a budget message that will stress key aspects of the budget and tie it to broad national goals. The president must submit the budget recommendations and accompanying message to Congress between the first Monday in January and the first Monday in February. The president's budget recommendations cover thousands of pages.

THE LEGISLATIVE BRANCH   Presidential submission of a budget proposal is only the beginning. Under our Constitution, Congress must appropriate the funds and raise the taxes. But the president also plays a role, since all appropriations and tax proposals are subject to a presidential veto. Thus the White House is an active participant in the congressional budget battles. When Congress acts on the budget, it does so by first approving the overall budget resolution. Then the actual appropriation of funds is detailed in 13 different bills, each of which is presented to the president for approval.

Congress adopted the Budget and Impoundment Control Act of 1974 to enhance its role in the budget process. This act specifies that the president must include proposed changes in tax laws, estimates of amounts of revenue lost through existing preferential tax treatments, and five-year estimates of the costs of new and continuing federal programs. The act also calls on the president to seek authorizing legislation for a program a year before asking Congress to fund it.

The 1974 Budget Act also created the **Congressional Budget Office (CBO)**, which gave Congress its own independent agency to prepare budget data and analyze budgetary issues. By February 15 of each year, CBO furnishes its analysis of the presidential recommendations to the House and Senate budget committees. CBO also provides Congress with biannual forecasts of the economy, analyzes alternative fiscal policies, prepares five-year cost estimates for bills proposed by congressional committees, and undertakes studies requested by committees. CBO also monitors the results of congressional action on individual appropriations and revenues against the targets or ceilings specified by legislation.

Office of Management and Budget (OMB)

Presidential staff agency that serves as a clearinghouse for budgetary requests and management improvements for government agencies.

Congressional Budget Office (CBO)

An agency of Congress that analyzes presidential budget recommendations and estimates the costs of proposed legislation.

The Disappearing Surplus

Americans received some stunning news in the summer of 1999: The federal government had its first budget surplus in more than 20 years. Although Congress and the president had set the process in motion with budget agreements in 1990, 1993, and 1997, the $5.6 trillion surplus showed up nearly three years ahead of schedule and much larger than expected.

The surplus is easy to explain. Controllable spending fell, due to declines in defense spending after the end of the cold war; uncontrollable spending did not rise as quickly, thanks to low unemployment and inflation; and revenues increased as the economy expanded.

Unfortunately, the budget outlook had worsened dramatically by 2002. President Bush's 2001 tax cut cost the federal government $1.35 billion in revenue, new defense and homeland security spending added roughly $500 billion in unanticipated spending, and the economic slowdown reduced revenue. The projected surplus increased

between January and March 2002 because of increased economic activity and lower unemployment. The impact of these changes can be seen in the table.

Spending the Surplus

Date	Key Event	Ten-Year Projected Surplus (trillions)
January 2001	—	$5.610
August 2001	$1.35 trillion tax cut	3.397
January 2002	September 11 attacks, economic slowdown	1.602
March 2002	Economic rebound	2.380

SOURCE: Alan Auerbach, William G. Gale, and Peter R. Orszag, *The Budget Outlook* (Brookings Institution, 2002).

Such budget reform efforts did not by themselves balance the budget, but they did set in place a discipline and a mind-set that moved toward balancing the budget. Equally if not more important was the economic boom of the 1990s, which generated huge tax revenues that helped achieve the first budget surpluses in 30 years.

The Politics of Taxing and Spending

In addition to raising funds to run the government, taxes also promote economic growth and reward certain types of behavior, such as owning a home, contributing to charities, and investing in high-risk but desirable (from a national standpoint) energy or housing ventures. Cynics suggest, too, that from a member of Congress's point of view, tax legislation has the additional and important function of raising campaign funds. As long as tax legislation is under consideration, lobbyists will be more inclined to contribute.[4]

Among people outside government, no one likes taxes, but nearly everyone realizes how necessary they are. There is considerable disagreement about the best type of tax. Some say a *progressive income tax* (also called a *graduated income tax*) is best because it is relatively easy to collect, hits hardest those who are most able to pay, and hardly touches those at the bottom of the income ladder. Others argue that *excise taxes* are the fairest because they are paid by people who spend money for luxury goods and thus obviously have money to spare. In addition, by discouraging people from buying expensive goods, excise taxes occasionally have a deflationary effect when prices are on the rise. However, excise taxes are more expensive to collect than income taxes. In some cases, such as the tax on tobacco, they may hit the poor the hardest. Excise taxes also face strong resistance from affected industries—tobacco, liquor, and airlines, for example.

The most controversial tax is a general **sales tax**, which is levied by almost all states on the sale of most goods, sometimes exempting food and drugs. Labor and liberal organizations see sales taxes as *regressive:* Because a sales tax is the same for all persons, these taxes are not related to a taxpayer's ability to pay, and poor persons pay a higher percentage of their income in sales taxes for the goods and services they buy than rich people do. Proponents of a national sales tax stress its potential anti-inflationary effect and point to its successful use in a number of states.

The sales tax is exclusively a state and local tax in the United States, but in Europe a similar tax, a **value-added tax (VAT)**, is used to raise revenues for central governments. The VAT differs from a sales tax in that it collects a tax on the increased value of a product *at*

sales tax
General tax on sales transactions, sometimes exempting food and drugs.

value-added tax (VAT)
A tax on increased value of a product at each stage of production and distribution rather than just at the point of sale.

IN COMPARATIVE PERSPECTIVE

Income Taxes in Various Countries

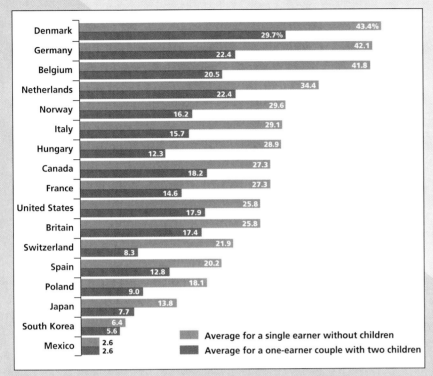

Percentage of Wages Full-Time Workers Pay in Income Taxes in Selected Countries.

SOURCE: "Tax Burdens," *Washington Post,* September 30, 2000, p. A14.

*Note: The rates include contributions to social insurance and retirement funds, less cash benefits paid, such as child allowances.

One way to compare nations is to ask how much citizens pay in income taxes. The higher the amount paid, the larger the national government is likely to be. Because income taxes are progressive in nature, they allow for the redistribution of income from wealthier households to low-income households. In theory, this redistribution reduces the amount of income inequality between the rich and poor. Some economists suggest, however, that high taxes of any kind reduce economic growth, thereby hurting all citizens, rich and poor. Though Americans complain about the taxes they pay, the United States actually ranks well down the list of Western democracies in its income tax rates. It makes up the difference through an across-the-board Social Security and Medicare tax on all workers, as well as state and local sales taxes.

each stage of production and distribution rather than just at the point of sale, as with a sales tax. A loaf of bread would thus have value added several times: The farmer would pay a value-added tax on the grain before selling to the miller, who would be taxed before selling to the baker, and so forth. The value-added tax is seen by some as a way to infuse a large amount of new revenue into the federal government. Opponents of the tax see it as regressive and increasing the tax burden. States see a federal VAT as invading their turf. Since it taxes consumption and not savings, a VAT could encourage savings and investment, both of which are vital to economic growth.

Tax Expenditures

Tax expenditures are a final type of fiscal policy that uses the tax code to provide special tax incentives or benefits to individuals and businesses for economic goals such as home ownership, retirement savings, and college education. These benefits, which now total more than $400 billion each year, come from special exclusions, exemptions, or reductions from gross income or from special credits, preferential tax rates, or deferrals of tax liability.

Tax expenditures are one means by which the national government carries out public policy objectives. For example, the government encourages investment in research and development by allowing such costs to be deducted from a company's taxes. Federal grants could also achieve this objective.

tax expenditure
Loss of tax revenue due to federal laws that provide special tax incentives or benefits to individuals or businesses.

Cutting Interest Rates

As the economy worsened in late 2000 and early 2001, the Fed began cutting interest rates to stimulate demand. In all, the Fed cut its federal funds rate 11 times in 2001, dropping the amount banks charge each other to borrow money from 6.5 percent in January to just 1.75 percent in December. Having moved rates to the lowest level in 40 years, the Fed decided to stop cutting for two reasons. First, there was not much room left to cut. If it cut all the way to zero, it would have no place to go. Second, Federal Reserve Board chair Alan Greenspan worried that too much cutting might produce a rebound in inflation.

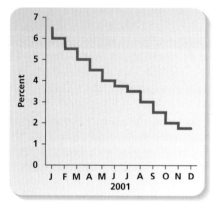

Interest Rate Cuts in 2001.

Note: In November 2002, the Fed cut interest rates by an additional .5 percent, bringing the total to just 1.25 percent.

Antitax protests erupted all over the country after Californians passed Proposition 13 in 1978, which placed strict limitations on state government revenues. California voters later enacted limits on state spending.

Critics assert that the rich get their "welfare" through such loopholes. This form of "welfare" does not require a visible appropriation of money plainly identified in the budget. However meritorious the objectives of tax expenditures are—encouraging home ownership, research and development, retirement savings—these tax benefits do not benefit all levels of society. In many instances, they lead investors to put their money into low-yield investments to obtain large tax benefits, which in turn pulls money out of more productive parts of the economy.

Monetary Policy

Monetary policy is the second way the national government manages the economy. The core element of **monetarism** is the idea that prices, incomes, and economic stability reflect growth in the money supply. Monetarists contend that money supply is the key factor affecting the economy's performance and that restrained yet steady growth in the money supply will encourage solid economic growth but not inflation.

The Federal Reserve System

Monetary policy is not made by either Congress or the president but by the Board of Governors of the **Federal Reserve System** (often simply called "the Fed"), specifically its Federal Open Market Committee. The members of that committee, some of the most powerful people in the United States, have a lot to say about how much interest you pay on the car you are buying and whether you refinance your home because of lower interest rates. They can stimulate the economy so that it could be easier for you to find a job or slow it down so that it could be harder. Who are these people with so much power, and how do they influence economic policy?

The Fed Board of Governors consists of a chair and six other members who are appointed by the president with the consent of the Senate to 14-year terms, with one member's term expiring every two years. These long, staggered terms are intended to insulate

monetarism
A theory that government should control the money supply to encourage economic growth and restrain inflation.

Federal Reserve System
The system created by Congress in 1913 to establish banking practices and regulate currency in circulation and the amount of credit available. It consists of 12 regional banks supervised by the Board of Governors. Often called simply *the Fed.*

How the Federal Reserve Board Controls Inflation

1. The Board of Governors *sets the discount rate,* the rate the Fed charges to lend money to banks. Raising rates is deflationary by increasing costs for money and credit; lowering rates is inflationary by decreasing the cost for money and credit.

2. The Fed's open market operations are its most flexible and important monetary policy tool. The Fed *buys or sells federal bonds.* Selling is deflationary by taking money and credit out of circulation; buying is inflationary by increasing money and credit in circulation. For example, if the Fed purchases $1 billion of government securities, the Fed pays for it by adding $1 billion to the reserve account that the security dealer keeps at the Fed, and the bank in turn credits the security dealer's account for that amount. As these funds are spent and respent, the stock of money and credit will increase by much more than the original $1 billion. If the Fed sells $1 billion, the amount is deducted from the security dealer's account, with less money flowing through the economy.

3. The Fed *sets reserve requirements for nationally chartered banks.* Raising reserves is deflationary by reducing the funds banks have available to lend; decreasing reserves is inflationary by increasing funds banks have available to lend. The Fed seldom changes reserve requirements because such changes can have a dramatic effect on institutions and the economy.

SOURCE: Federal Reserve System, at www.frbkc.org/infofrs/ifrsmain.htm.

members from politics as much as possible. They supervise 12 regional Federal Reserve banks, each headed by a president and governed by a nine-member board of directors chosen from the private banking business in that region.

The 12 members of the Federal Open Market Committee are all professional economists or bankers. Though their names are unfamiliar to most people, this group, which meets every six to eight weeks, decides how much money will be allowed to enter the economy, manages foreign currency operations, and regulates banks. It does this by buying and selling government securities, which can encourage either lower or higher interest rates. Other lenders closely watch the decisions of the Fed and typically make their interest rates consistent with Fed decisions. Because lenders make it either more or less expensive to borrow money, they influence a wide range of economic activity.

The chair of the Board of Governors, by tradition an economist, is appointed by the president to a four-year term. The current chair, Alan Greenspan, is one of the most influential national public policy officials. Greenspan was first appointed by President Ronald Reagan in 1987 and reappointed by Presidents George H. W. Bush and Bill Clinton. Greenspan's leadership had helped foster economic growth and was widely respected by financial leaders, factors that influenced Clinton's decision to reappoint him. The staff of the Federal Reserve System reports directly to the chair, not to the board, and the chair is the one who appears before Congress and the country to explain the policies of the Federal Reserve System. The chair heads the Federal Open Market Committee and is credited or blamed for the decisions made by the Fed.

Government and Economic Policy

Depression is a hard teacher, and the 1930s had a tremendous impact on American thinking about the role of government in the economy. The Great Depression that began in 1929 brought mass misery. "One vivid, gruesome moment of those dark days we shall never forget," wrote one observer. "We saw a crowd of some fifty men fighting over a barrel of garbage which had been set outside the back door of a restaurant. American citizens fighting for scraps of food like animals!"[5]

PEOPLE IN POLITICS

ALAN GREENSPAN, INFLATION BUSTER

Already regarded as one of the most important economic policy makers of the late twentieth century, Federal Reserve Board chair Alan Greenspan may well be remembered more for what he stopped than anything that he started. Simply stated, Greenspan spent the waning years of the twentieth century making sure that prices did not increase. Appointed to his post in 1987 by Ronald Reagan, Greenspan is best described as a monetarist who used the Fed to promote a single vision of economy policy: There is a limit to how fast the economy can grow without causing inflation.

No one knows for sure just where that break point is, but many of Greenspan's fellow monetarists believe that the economy cannot grow much faster than 2.5 percent per year without causing inflation. Whenever the economy got close to that mark during the 1990s, Greenspan engineered an increase in interest rates. The goal was never to slow the economy to a halt but rather to make sure that the economy grew at its true potential. Let it grow beyond that potential, Greenspan has long argued, and industries will run out of the workers or raw materials needed to sustain themselves, meaning that workers can charge more for their time and manufacturers can charge more for their products.

Greenspan is hardly the first chair of the Fed to press for higher interest rates, but he was the first to do so *before* inflation actually began. In other words, he is the Fed's first *proactive* chair. Colleagues at the Fed report that he has a gift for spotting early trends of future inflation.

Greenspan's commitment to preventing inflation knows no party lines. With the economy coming out of a recession in mid-1992, for example, Greenspan and his Fed colleagues hit the economic brakes on inflation by announcing an interest rate increase just before the Republican National Convention, contributing to President George H. W. Bush's defeat later that fall.

Although Greenspan is best known for his fight against inflation, he is a strong advocate of increasing the money flow to stimulate growth during recessions. Sworn in on August 11, 1987, Greenspan had been in office barely two months when the stock market had a meltdown, falling 508 points in what many observers described as a repeat of Black Thursday a half-century earlier. In contrast to the Fed's do-nothing reaction to the 1929 crash, Greenspan convinced his colleagues to flood the economy with desperately needed money, thereby ensuring that the 1987 drop would not trigger a recession. Four years later, he convinced the Fed to drop interest rates a full percentage point to pull the economy out of the 1991 recession. A decade later, in 2001, he worked to stimulate the economy through an unprecedented series of cuts in the federal interest rate.

Whether as an inflation fighter or a recession breaker, Greenspan is now one of the world's most watched economic leaders. Although he once joked that he had learned "to mumble with great incoherence" early on at the Fed, he also knew the power of words to slow the economy. In December 1996, for example, he wondered out loud whether the stock market was suffering from what he called "irrational exuberance," which prompted an immediate 145-point drop in the Dow Jones Industrial Average, the most widely followed stock indicator.

Greenspan finished his doctorate in economics in 1977, after leaving the Ford administration. He starts each day with a 2½-hour hot bath to sooth his ailing back. It is time he uses to read memos and analyze the latest economic data. "The unsung hero at the Fed is the assistant who has to read his waterlogged scribblings," says his wife, Andrea Mitchell, an NBC News correspondent. How interesting to think that the major architect of contemporary economic policy makes some of his toughest choices in the bathtub.

The Depression continued despite Franklin D. Roosevelt's New Deal economic agenda, which pumped new money into the economy, created hundreds of thousands of federally subsidized jobs, and established new regulations governing the financial markets. Faint signs of recovery could be seen in the mid-1930s, but a new recession in 1937 and 1938 indicated that the country was by no means out of the woods. Between 8 and 9 million people were jobless in 1939. Then came World War II, and unemployment seemed cured. Millions of people had more income, more security, and higher standards of living. Lord Beveridge in England posed a question that bothered many thoughtful Americans: "Unemployment has been practically abolished twice in the lives of most of us—in the last war and in this war. Why does war solve the problem of unemployment which is so insoluble in peace?"[6]

There were several theories about what the federal government could do to stimulate the economy at the time. Some economists urged the government to reduce spending, lower taxes, curb the power of labor, and generally leave business and the economy alone. This first theory is called **laissez-faire economics**.

Another group, deeply influenced by the work of English economist John Maynard Keynes,[7] recommended that when consumer spending and investment decline, government spending and investing should increase. Government must do the spending and investing during a recession because private enterprise will not or cannot. This second theory is called **Keynesian economics**. Roosevelt embraced Keynesian economics and pushed for much greater spending by the federal government as the answer to continued hard times.

Keynesian economics influences government management of the economy to this day. Yet politically, Keynesian economics presents a problem. It is much easier to increase spending and government programs than it is to curb them. As a result, deficit spending became a habit in this country for 50 years. To stimulate demand, the government spent more money than it took in. For many years, this policy was thought to be beneficial to the economy. It was also convenient politically. However, when the national debt soared, both Congress and the president searched for ways to balance the budget.

Promoting Economic Growth

Federal economic policy involves more than the effort to smooth the ups and downs of the business cycle. It also involves efforts to promote economic growth, often measured by the number of new jobs or businesses created. In doing so, it helps create jobs for individual Americans, which in turn produces higher revenues, which in turn produces either greater savings or more federal spending.

Promoting Business

The national government promotes a prosperous economy through its monetary and fiscal policies. It also provides various services to business and industry through an economic development infrastructure composed of several dozen departments and agencies, including the Departments of Agriculture and Commerce and the Small Business Administration.

The Department of Commerce is the most visible business promoter within the federal bureaucracy and is sometimes known as the nation's "service center for business." Its cabinet secretary, usually a person with an extensive business background, is a spokesperson for business interests. Historically, the department has been at the center of the government's efforts to promote economic growth and encourage business research and development.

The Department of Commerce also encourages innovation through the protection of intellectual property. Its Patent and Trademark Office (PTO) administers the patent system that Congress established "to promote the Progress of Science and useful Arts" under Article I of the Constitution. Each year, the PTO issues more than 100,000 patents to cover new and useful inventions that provide their owners certain exclusive rights for 17 years. The number of patents issued annually almost doubled during the economic expansion of the 1990s, but fell back during the 2001–2002 economic downturn.

The Department of Agriculture continues to provide ample support for farmers, including federal subsidies for corn, barley, oats, wheat, soybeans, cotton, and rice. Under a mix of programs that cost a record $32 billion in 2000 alone, the federal government either guarantees farmers a minimum price for their crops or pays a fee for not planting their fields. The department also provides a host of services to farmers, from education on how to generate higher yields to research on everything from blueberries to forest management. Although these payments were originally designed to help small family farmers, research by the Environmental Working Group, a Washington, D.C., advocacy group, showed that two-thirds of all payments from 1996 to 2000 went to just 10 percent of farmers, most of whom owned large tracts of land.[8]

laissez-faire economics
Theory that opposes governmental interference in economic affairs beyond what is necessary to protect life and property.

Keynesian economics
Economic theory based on the principles of John Maynard Keynes stating that government spending should increase during business slumps and be curbed during booms.

Speaking at the Chinese University of Finance and Economics in Beijing, U.S. Trade Representative Robert Zoellick makes a point while answering a student's question.

Promoting Trade

The United States experienced its first **trade deficit** in in more than a century when the amount of imports exceeded the value of exports in 1971. Since then, the nation has had trade deficits in the billions of dollars every year. Congress and the president are under continuing pressure from industry, unions, and regional political leaders to protect American jobs, companies, and communities from foreign competition. These pressures come not only from the textile and auto industries but also from glass, steel, shoes, lumber, electronics, book publishing, aluminum, farming, and domestic wine and spirit coalitions, to name just a few. These leaders claim that the trade deficit justifies the imposition of trade sanctions.

The problem, however, is not that the United States is importing too much but that it is exporting too little. German cars, Japanese radios, and Indonesian textiles are fine products; if other countries produce better cars or shoes at a lower price, free traders argue, the United States should buy from them and direct our labor and capital to areas in which it can do better.

The question is also whether U.S. products are given fair treatment by other nations. American agricultural products are denied entry into some countries and are subject to high tariffs in others. American automobile manufacturers complain of unfair restrictions imposed by the Japanese on our cars. Finally, some countries exploit the U.S. advantage in technology by slavishly copying our products and then selling them back to us or to other countries at a profit.

Another unfair trade practice is *dumping*—selling products below the cost of manufacturing or below their domestic price with the intention of driving other producers out of the market and then raising prices to profitable levels. Another practice is government *subsidizing* of certain industries. Some countries, for example, subsidize steel for export. Others require lengthy inspection procedures for imported goods. Japan has protected several of its industries—producers of automobiles, baseball bats, and even chopsticks, for example—by setting standards that are virtually impossible for U.S. manufacturers to meet. Japan also sets limits on rice imports.

In 1947, a group of countries formed a trade organization to negotiate free trade by lowering tariffs (taxes on imports that raises their price) and quotas (limits on the quantity of a particular product that may be imported) and other disadvantages countries face when trading. Today the **World Trade Organization** (**WTO**), based on the **General Agreement on Tariffs and Trade** (**GATT**), includes more than 130 countries, and its membership accounts for four-fifths of the world's trade. The WTO has negotiated agreements through eight rounds of trade negotiations (the most recent was called the Uruguay Round, named after the site of the initial conference).

The United States has tried to focus WTO and GATT negotiations on trade in agricultural items, foreign investment, and protection of technological innovations and intellectual property. Although U.S. imports and those of other countries still face many trade restrictions, the WTO and GATT have greatly helped lower tariffs and quotas and increase fair trade throughout the world. Many analysts maintain that GATT is one of the most successful innovations in the history of international relations and one of the contributing factors to the United States' economic success since the end of the cold war.[9]

Not everyone believes that free trade should be unlimited, however. Labor unions, environmentalists, and human rights advocates argue that U.S. trade policies spur the creation of low-wage jobs abroad and encourage child labor, pollution, and worker abuse.

The WTO became the center of intense debates and a street riot during its 1999 meeting in Seattle. Protesters rightly argued that the WTO has the power to override environmental and social legislation in member countries. If a country fails to comply with a WTO ruling, it faces strict fines that can cost hundreds of millions of dollars.

THE NORTH AMERICAN FREE TRADE AGREEMENT   In 1992, the United States, Canada, and Mexico signed the **North American Free Trade Agreement** (**NAFTA**), which formed the largest geographical free trade zone in the world, even surpassing the Euro-

trade deficit
An imbalance in international trade in which the value of imports exceeds the value of exports.

World Trade Organization (WTO)
International organization derived from the General Agreement on Tariffs and Trade (GATT) that promotes free trade around the world.

General Agreement on Tariffs and Trade (GATT)
An international trade organization with more than 130 members, including the United States and the People's Republic of China, that seeks to encourage free trade by lowering tariffs and other trade restrictions.

North American Free Trade Agreement (NAFTA)
Agreement signed by the United States, Canada, and Mexico in 1992 to form the largest free trade zone in the world.

pean Community's 15-country conglomerate. Although President George Bush signed NAFTA near the end of his presidency, the agreement could not become law until ratified by Congress. President Bill Clinton promoted NAFTA, even though many members of his own party were its most vigorous opponents. Congress passed NAFTA by a thin margin in a bipartisan vote in which the Democrats were the minority.

Though trade among the United States, Canada, and Mexico is not absolutely "free" or unimpeded, the agreement has had a tremendous impact on the economies of all three countries. Today Mexico is the United States' third most important trading partner, and the United States is Mexico's most important trading partner. Critics of NAFTA remain concerned because Mexican antipollution laws are significantly less stringent than those in the United States, and Mexican workers work for considerably lower wages. Both of these factors make relocation to Mexico attractive to many U.S. companies seeking to lower labor and pollution control costs.

Recent reports suggest that many of those lower-paid jobs in Mexico are now converted to even lower-paid jobs in China. Hourly wages in Tijuana, Mexico, range from $1.50 to $2.00, well below the U.S. minimum wage of $5.15 per hour but well above the 25 cents per hour paid in China. More than 500 low-wage assembly line factories in Mexico closed between 2000 and 2002, due largely to the migration of jobs in the global economy to Asia.[10]

REMOVING BARRIERS TO TRADE **Protectionism**—erecting barriers to protect domestic industry—sounds easy and workable as a solution to trade deficits, but trade deficits are symptomatic of more profound economic problems. Most economists favor free trade and strongly dislike protectionism because it prevents efficient use of resources and because consumers pay much more for protected products than they otherwise would. Tariffs merely divert attention from real solutions like increased productivity and capital investments and inevitably invite retaliation from foreign countries.

In the 1930s, many nations experienced high unemployment, low production, and general economic misery. The United States was no exception. In an effort to aid ailing American industries, Congress passed the Smoot-Hawley tariff, the highest general tariff the United States had ever had. Supporters hoped high tariffs on imported goods would increase the demand for goods produced in the United States and thus help get the country out of the Great Depression. The exact opposite occurred. Other nations retaliated with high tariffs on American goods. Demand fell, intensifying the Depression.

Later, Congress gave the president power to negotiate mutual tariff reductions with other nations, subject to certain restrictions, and by the early 1970s, tariffs on industrial products had been substantially reduced. Trade barriers are less severe today than they were back in the 1930s. But restrictions still exist. Certain tariffs, quotas on imported goods, and import regulations limit American consumption of foreign products. Most exist to protect American farmers, businesses, or workers in certain industries. Thus we have restrictions on clothing and textile imports, and these restrictions cost U.S. consumers a lot more than they benefit workers' wages.

The United States has generally supported increased trade and fewer trade barriers, yet many Americans worry that globalization will hurt the country. Free trade and globalization policies do not confer equal benefits on everyone. Inevitably, some workers will be worse off as a result of a freer international flow of goods and capital. All told, trade barriers cost U.S. consumers approximately $80 billion a year—equal to more than $1,200 per family.[11] At least some of these barriers helped save U.S. jobs, however, while protecting the environment and promoting human rights abroad.

U.S. economic policy in the future will probably be a combination of free trade and selective protectionism. Though protectionism shields highly visible industries from competition at home or abroad, such measures often constitute a kind of subsidy that protects one industry at the expense of another—and always at high cost to American consumers.

Even free trade advocates can occasionally find a reason, often political, for protectionism. In March 2002, for example, President George W. Bush imposed new tariffs

protectionism
Policy of erecting trade barriers to protect domestic industry.

United Steelworkers of America President Leo Gerard addresses steelworkers who came to Washington, D.C. to protest the problems globalization and free trade have created in their industry.

on steel imports in an effort to protect the ailing U.S. steel industry. By imposing tariffs ranging from 8 to 30 percent on ten different types of steel, Bush signaled big steel states such as Pennsylvania, Ohio, Michigan, Illinois, and West Virginia that he would honor his promise to help the industry battle low-priced imports from abroad.

There is no question that steel imports have hurt the U.S. industry. Nearly 50,000 jobs have been lost to bankruptcies since 1997 because of imports, and more than 300,000 jobs are at risk. Advocates of free trade and globabization would argue that the international economy is merely working its will, replacing an inefficient U.S. industry with more efficient foreign goods. But that does not put food on the steelworker's table—or votes in the ballot box for a protectionist president.

Regulating the Economy

The Constitution explicitly authorizes Congress to regulate commerce among the states and with foreign nations. In our earliest years, Congress used this regulatory power to impose or suspend tariffs on imports from other nations. In the nineteenth century, the federal government created a number of agencies to regulate the conduct of citizens and commercial enterprises with an eye toward promoting economic development. Among these were the Army Corps of Engineers (1824), the Patent and Trademark Office (1836), the Steamboat Inspecting Service (1837), and the Copyright Office of the Library of Congress (1870). In 1887, Congress created the Interstate Commerce Commission to deal with the widespread dissatisfaction over the practices of railroads.

Additional regulations came into existence to break up monopolies, to clean up meat-packing conditions such as those exposed in Upton Sinclair's *Jungle* (1906), to prevent the kind of pesticide contamination described in Rachel Carson's *Silent Spring* (1962), to correct the lack of auto safety documented in Ralph Nader's *Unsafe at Any Speed* (1965), and to respond to discrimination in employment on the basis of race, color, national origin, religion, sex, and age. More recently, regulations have been enacted to protect citizens from raw sewage in rivers, lead in paint and gasoline, toxins in the air, radon gas in homes, and asbestos, cotton dust, and hazardous products in the environment. Expenditures mandated by federal regulations are estimated to cost about $200 billion annually for environmental, health, and safety rules alone.[12]

In 1935, there were 4,000 pages of regulations in the *Federal Register* (a daily publication of proposed and existing federal regulations); there are now about 70,000 pages of regulations.[13] Both political parties say regulatory overkill threatens to overwhelm entrepreneurs and divert them from building vital, innovative companies. According to one estimate, "Regulations add as much as 33 percent to the cost of building an airplane engine and as much as 95 percent to the price of a new vaccine. Federal regulation also adds about $3,000 to the cost of a new car."[14] Once again, these regulations produce important benefits in the form of lower airplane noise, safer vaccines, and cleaner air.

The question is not whether there are both costs and benefits from regulation but whether the balance is right. Conservatives tend to overstate the costs of many regulations, while liberals tend to overstate the benefits.

Regulation Defined

In a broad sense, *regulation* is any attempt by the government to control the behavior of corporations, other governments, or citizens. **Regulation**, as we use the term, occurs when the government steps in and alters the natural workings of the open market to achieve some desired goal. Regulation by government interjects political goals and values into the economy in the form of rules that direct behavior in the marketplace. These rules have the force of law and are backed by the government's police powers.

There are no unregulated economies in the world. The United States operates in a competitive market economy in which wages, prices, the allocation of goods and services, and the employment of resources are generally regulated by the laws of supply and demand. The nation relies on private enterprise and market incentives to carry out most of our production and distribution.

Nevertheless, market economies have imperfections. Even opponents of regulation recognize that the market does not always solve every problem. Consider pollution. For a long time, no price was imposed on a business for using air and water to discharge toxic wastes. Therefore, market forces did not consider the social costs of its air and water pollution. When the market fails to set appropriate costs and benefits, pressures develop for the government to step in. The government can, for example, create regulations imposing penalties for air pollution. Market forces also do not encourage taking a bus instead of a car to work. If government enacted higher taxes on gasoline, our fuel costs would be brought more in line with Europe's. Such a policy would also reduce our dependence on Middle East oil and promote domestic energy production.

Types of Regulation

It is customary to talk of two general categories of regulation: economic and social regulation. *Economic regulation* generally refers to government controls on the behavior of businesses in the marketplace: the entry of individual firms into particular lines of business, the prices that firms may charge, the standards of service they must offer. Public utilities, transportation, and television are examples of regulated industries. As already noted, economic regulation began almost as early as the founding of the Republic and expanded in earnest in 1887, when the Interstate Commerce Commission was established; it continued in the twentieth century with the Federal Communications Commission, the Commodity Futures Trading Commission, and a host of regulatory agencies, boards, or commissions responsible for enforcing statutes in particular industries (see Table 19-3). In the twentieth century, regulatory bodies grew from five to about 80 regulatory organizations that employ about 100,000 people to enforce thousands of federal regulations.

The second type of regulation, *social regulation,* refers to government attempts to correct a wide variety of side effects, usually unintended, brought about by economic activity. Concern for worker health and safety and for environmental hazards has led to social regulation. Social regulation also includes the efforts by government to ensure equal rights in employment, education, and housing. Whereas economic regulation is usually organized along industry lines, social regulation cuts across these lines.

regulation
The attempt by government to control the behavior of corporations, other governments, or citizens through altering the natural workings of the open market to achieve some desired goal.

TABLE 19–3   Some Regulatory Agencies and Their Missions

Agency	Year Established	Primary Functions
Federal Trade Commission (FTC)	1914	Administers certain antitrust laws concerning advertising, labeling, and packaging to protect consumers from unfair business practices
Food and Drug Administration (FDA)	1931	Establishes regulations concerning purity, safety, and labeling accuracy of certain foods and drugs; issues licenses for manufacturing and distribution
Federal Communications Commission (FCC)	1934	Licenses civilian radio and television communication; licenses and sets rates for interstate and international communication
Animal and Plant Health Inspection Service	1953	Sets standards; inspects and enforces laws relating to meat, poultry, and plant safety
Environmental Protection Agency (EPA)	1970	Develops environmental quality standards; approves state environmental plans
Occupational Safety and Health Administration (OSHA)	1970	Develops and enforces worker safety and health regulations
Bureau of Alcohol, Tobacco and Firearms (ATF)	1972	Enforces laws and regulates legal flow of these materials
Consumer Product Safety Commission (CPSC)	1972	Establishes mandatory product safety standards and bans sales of products that do not comply
Nuclear Regulatory Commission (NRC)	1974	Licenses the construction and operation of nuclear reactors and similar facilities and regulates nuclear materials; licenses the export of nuclear reactors and the export and import of uranium and plutonium
National Nuclear Security Administration	2000	Monitors the nation's nuclear bomb-building laboratories; oversees the military's stockpile of nuclear weapons; protects the secrecy of U.S. weapons research
Transportation Security Administration (TSA)	2001	Controls passenger and baggage screening; regulates what passengers can carry; requires airlines to check bags through electronic screens; oversees all airport, land, and maritime security

The Environmental Protection Agency, the Consumer Product Safety Commission, and the Occupational Safety and Health Administration are regulatory agencies engaged in social regulation. In economic terms, producers regulated by social regulation must now pay for external costs that once were free, such as using rivers, landfills, or the atmosphere for waste disposal. These costs, however, are then passed along to the consumer, so the true cost of the product is more accurately reflected in its price. Some goods subsequently become too costly, and demand drops. Others become more popular (for instance, safe toys), and demand increases. The final goal of social regulation is the socially beneficial allocation of resources.

Congress has created two types of regulatory agencies: those within the executive branch and those that have a degree of independence from Congress and the president. Members of executive branch agencies serve at the pleasure of the president. Executive branch regulatory agencies include the Food and Drug Administration, the Office of Surface Mining, and the National Highway Traffic Safety Administration. Commissioners of independent regulatory agencies are appointed by the president and confirmed by the Senate, and they cannot be removed by a president except for cause. Independent agencies, usually headed by a board composed of seven members, include the Federal Communications Commission, the Equal Employment Opportunity Commission, and the Nuclear Regulatory Commission.

Regulating Business

During most of the nineteenth century, our national policy was to leave business pretty much alone. However, four major waves of regulatory legislation occurred in the twentieth century: at its start, in the 1910s, in the 1930s, and in the late 1960s through 1980. In each case, changing circumstances gave rise to the legislation.

Merger Mania

In recent years, thousands of mergers have taken place, many of them among competing companies: General Motors bought Hughes Aircraft, R. J. Reynolds absorbed Nabisco, GE and RCA merged with General Foods, Warner Communications merged with Time, and McDonnell-Douglas became part of Boeing. Airlines merged. Banks and financial services companies merged.

With a staff of 350 lawyers, the Antitrust Division of the Department of Justice investigates mergers and acquisitions to determine whether they violate the antitrust laws by unreasonably restraining interstate trade and commerce. If it so determines, it may seek to prevent the merger. The Antitrust Division also has authority to prosecute violators of the laws against price fixing, and it investigates and prepares cases to prevent anticompetitive bid rigging.

The Reagan and Bush administrations generally adopted a permissive policy toward mergers, and few were prevented. These Republican administrations assumed that most mergers were inherently good for the consumer and the economy. The Clinton administration was more vigorous in enforcing antitrust laws, yet the Justice Department's Antitrust Division and the Federal Trade Commission generally looked favorably on most mergers. The George W. Bush administration has been more encouraging of mergers, and approved the largest merger ever in 2001, the $111 billion merger of America Online and Time-Warner.

Top Ten Merger and Acquisition Deals

Acquirer	Acquisition	Year	Value (billions)
America Online	Time-Warner	2001	$111.0
Pfizer	Warner-Lambert	2000	89.7
Exxon	Mobil	1998	86.4
Travelers Group	Citicorp	1998	72.6
SBC Communications	Ameritech	1998	72.4
Bell Atlantic Corporation	GTE Corporation	2000	71.3
AT&T	TeleCommunications	1998	69.9
Vodaphone Group	AirTouch Communications	1999	65.9
NationsBank	BankAmerica Corporation	1998	61.6
Comcast	AT&T Broadband	2001	57.5

SOURCE: *The World Almanac and Book of Facts* (St. Martin's Press, 2002), p. 119.

Perhaps the number one responsibility of government regulation in our free market system is to maintain competition. When one company gains a **monopoly**, or several create an *oligopoly,* the market system operates ineffectively. The aim of **antitrust legislation** is to prevent monopolies, break up those that exist, and ensure competition. In the past, so-called natural monopolies, such as electric utilities and telephone companies, were protected by the government because it was assumed that in these fields competition would be grossly inefficient.

In the late nineteenth century, social critics and populist reformers believed that consumers were being cheated, especially in the oil, sugar, whiskey, and steel industries, where large monopolies, called **trusts**, stifled competition. People began to have mixed feelings about big business. Americans, who have often been impressed by bigness—the tallest skyscraper, the largest football stadium, the biggest steel mill—and the efficiency that often goes with bigness, became skeptical about giant enterprises.

In 1890, Congress responded by passing the Sherman Antitrust Act, which was designed "to protect trade and commerce against unlawful restraints and monopolies." Henceforth, persons making contracts, combinations, or conspiracies in restraint of trade in interstate and foreign commerce could be sued for damages, required to stop their illegal practices, and subjected to criminal penalties. However, the Sherman Antitrust Act had little immediate impact; presidents made few attempts to enforce it, and the Supreme Court's early interpretation of the act limited its scope.[15]

Congress added the Clayton Act to the antitrust arsenal in 1914. This act outlawed such specific abuses as charging different prices to different buyers in order to destroy a weaker competitor, granting rebates, making false statements about competitors and their products, buying up supplies to suppress competition, and bribing competitors' employees. In addition, *interlocking directorates* (having an officer or director in one corporation serve on the board of a competitor) were banned, and corporations were prohibited from acquiring stock in competing concerns if such acquisitions substantially lessened interstate competition. That same year, Congress

monopoly
Domination of an industry by a single company; also the company that dominates the industry.

antitrust legislation
Federal laws (starting with the Sherman Act of 1890) that try to prevent a monopoly from dominating an industry and restraining trade.

trust
A monopoly that controls goods and services, often in combinations that reduce competition.

established the Federal Trade Commission (FTC), run by a five-person board, to enforce the Clayton Act and prevent unfair competitive practices. The FTC was to be the "traffic cop" for competition.[16]

Regulating Labor

Government regulation of business is essentially restrictive. Most laws and rules curb business practices and steer private enterprise into socially useful channels. But regulation cuts two ways. In the case of American workers, most laws in recent decades have tended not to restrict labor but to confer rights and opportunities on it. Actually, many labor laws do not touch labor directly; instead they regulate relations with employers.

Federal regulations protect workers in the following important areas, among others:

1. *Public contracts.* The Walsh-Healy Act of 1936, as amended, requires that no worker employed under contracts with the national government in excess of $10,000 be paid less than the prevailing wage and that he or she be paid overtime for all work in excess of eight hours per day or 40 hours per week.

2. *Wages and hours.* The Fair Labor Standards Act of 1938 set a maximum workweek of 40 hours for all employees engaged in interstate commerce or in the production of goods for interstate commerce (with certain exemptions). Work beyond that amount must be paid for at $1\frac{1}{2}$ times the regular rate.

3. *Child labor.* The Fair Labor Standards Act of 1938 prohibits child labor (under 16 years of age, or under 18 in hazardous occupations) in industries that engage in or produce goods for interstate commerce.

4. *Industrial safety and occupational health.* The Occupational Safety and Health Act of 1970 created the first comprehensive federal industrial safety program. It gave the secretary of labor broad authority to set safety and health standards for companies engaged in interstate commerce.

During the first half of the twentieth century, labor's basic struggle was for the right to organize unions. For decades, trade unions had been held lawful by state legislatures, but the courts had chipped away at their status by legalizing anti-union devices. The most notorious was the **yellow-dog contract**, by which employers made new workers, as a condition of employment, promise not to join labor organizations. If labor organizers later tried to unionize the workers, the employers could apply for court orders to stop the organizers. In 1932, the Norris–La Guardia Act made yellow-dog contracts unenforceable and granted labor the right to organize. Under President Franklin D. Roosevelt, Congress enacted a series of laws to protect workers and their right to form trade unions.

The New Deal also opened a new era in union organizing. Under the 1935 National Labor Relations Act (usually called the Wagner Act), the federal government prohibited five types of anti-union employer action: (1) interfering with workers in their attempt to organize unions or bargain collectively, (2) supporting company unions (unions set up and dominated by the employer), (3) discriminating against members of unions, (4) firing or otherwise victimizing an employee for having taken action under the act, and (5) refusing to bargain with union representatives. The act prevents employers from using violence, espionage, propaganda, or community pressure to resist unionization.

Congress passed a major modification of the labor laws in 1947, the Labor-Management Relations Act, commonly called the Taft-Hartley Act. It remains the most important legislation regulating union activity in the United States:

- It outlaws the **closed shop** (a company that requires an employer to hire and retain only union members in good standing) and permits the **union shop** (a company in which new employees are obligated to join the union within a stated period of time).
- It makes it an unfair labor practice for unions to refuse to bargain with employers.

yellow-dog contract
Contract by an anti-union employer that forces new workers to promise they will not join a union as a condition of employment.

closed shop
A company with a labor agreement under which union membership is a condition of employment.

union shop
A company in which new employees must join a union within a stated time period.

- It allows limited use of the **labor injunction**, a court order forbidding specific individuals or groups to perform acts considered harmful to the rights or property of an employer or community.

- It permits states to outlaw union shops. *Right-to-work laws,* which states could now adopt, typically make it illegal for **collective bargaining** agreements—terms and conditions of employment negotiated by representatives of the union and the employer—to contain closed-shop, union shop, preferential-hiring, or any other clauses calling for compulsory union membership.

The Taft-Hartley Act set up machinery for handling disputes if a work stoppage threatens national health or safety. It has been invoked against strikes in vital sectors of the economy such as atomic energy, coal, shipping, steel, and telephone service. The president or the secretary of labor can attempt to mediate strikes without resorting to the act.

Regulating Markets

The stock market crash of 1929 did more than devastate the American economy and usher in the Great Depression. It also revealed deep problems in how stocks were sold to investors. Millions of new investors entered the stock market in the 1920s only to find out that the companies in which they had invested were virtually worthless.

Martha Stewart came under intense scrutiny in mid 2002 for selling nearly 4,000 shares of ImClone Systems stock one day before the price of the stock fell following bad news about the company's new cancer drug. The question is whether she had privileged information because of her friendship with the company's chief executive officer. Continuing concerns led to Stewart's resigning her position on the New York Stock Exchange.

WHAT IS INSIDER TRADING?

You Decide... The federal government has been regulating the stock markets since 1934, when the Securities and Exchange Commission was created. Although there is no legal definition of insider trading, the basic thrust of recent SEC rules is to promote maximum disclosure of all information that might affect investor decisions. Individuals with privileged, or secret, information that might affect a stock price are prohibited from using that information to benefit themselves.

Take the following quiz about what constitutes insider trading.

1. You are a taxi driver who overhears a . . . passenger . . . describe how his employer is about to receive approval for a new [cancer drug]. You tell your broker to buy 1,000 shares of the stock.

2. Your [stockbroker] tells you to sell stock in a company because he just received a call from that company's chief executive, who instructed him to dump all his [stock]. You sell the stock.

3. The same [stockbroker tells] you to sell [all your stock in that company] but does not say why. . . .

4. You play golf with [a new partner] who talks about [a] new product but gives no hint that he is associated with the company or where he received the information. You buy [some of the company's stock the next day].

5. A friend tells you that he is depressed because his wife has learned that she will probably be laid off . . . from her job . . . [because] her company has discovered deep financial problems . . . and will disclose them soon. . . . You call your broker and [sell all your stock in the company].

Thinking It Through... The answer to each question depends on whether the information is secret or not. You are not engaging in insider trading if you act on a conversation overheard in your taxi because you cannot be sure whether the passenger is telling the truth. You are if your broker gives you secret information on what the chief executive of a company is doing but not if your broker does not reveal the reason for the recommendation to sell. You are engaging in insider trading if you use information picked up on the golf course from someone you know is in a position to have privileged information and also if you take advantage of secret information given by your friend.

SOURCE: Steve Labation, "Is This Illegal?" *The New York Times,* June 30, 2002, p. 3-1.

labor injunction
A court order forbidding specific individuals or groups from performing certain acts (such as striking) that the court considers harmful to the rights and property of an employer or a community.

collective bargaining
Method whereby representatives of the union and employer determine wages, hours, and other conditions of employment through direct negotiation.

The fall of Enron, the nation's largest energy trading company, caused thousands of employees to lose their jobs as well as their pensions.

Prior to 1934, when the Securities and Exchange Commission (SEC) was created, investors had to determine whether a company was telling the truth about its stock. Since 1934, that responsibility has fallen to the SEC. Under the Securities Exchange Act of 1934 and a long list of later laws, companies that offer their stock for sale to the public must tell the truth about their businesses, which means full disclosure of all financial statements, as well as the stocks they are selling and the risks involved in investing.

At the same time, the act also required that anyone in the business of selling stocks, including brokers, dealers, and stock exchanges such as the New York Stock Exchange and Nasdaq, must treat investors fairly and honestly, putting investors' interests first. That means, for example, that individuals who know about a new stock offering in advance or have other inside information on events that might increase or decrease the value of a given stock are prohibited from using that information to benefit themselves.

Congress added to the long inventory of other laws to protect investors when it passed a corporate reform bill in 2002. The law was designed to prevent the kind of accounting games that led to the Enron collapse earlier in the year. The law strengthened the SEC, created a new oversight board to monitor accounting practices, and set new disclosure requirements on how corporations treat certain expenditures. Despite the public's concern about Enron, the bill was stalled in the Senate until the WorldCom scandal broke in June. The bill passed the Senate almost immediately after by a 97-to-0 vote.

Regulating the Environment

Air and water pollution vividly illustrates the regulatory dilemma. Critics of strict controls on air, water, and noise pollution say the pursuit of a clean environment increases costs of products and causes unemployment. They call attention, for example, to the disastrous economic consequences of the shutdown of companies for pollution violations. Until relatively recently, governments at all levels did little to protect the environment, and what little was done was by state and local governments. In recent decades, however, the national government has taken on new responsibilities, primarily because local governments failed to act.

Perhaps the most controversial environmental regulation involves **environmental impact statements,** which are used to assess the potential effects of new construction or development on the environment. Most projects using federal funds must file such statements. Since 1970, thousands of statements have been filed. Supporters contend that such statements point out major flaws in projects and can lead to cost savings along with greater environmental awareness. Critics claim that environmental impact reviews simply represent more government interference, paperwork, and delays in the public and private sectors.

Environmental impact statements are only one form of environmental regulation, however. The 1990 Clean Air Act, itself an amendment to the 1967, 1970, and 1977 acts of the same name, was designed to tighten controls on automobiles and the fuel they use. It required automakers to install pollution controls to reduce emissions of hydrocarbons and nitrogen oxides and set stiff standards for the kinds of gasoline that can be sold. The 1990 act stipulated that plants that emit any of 189 toxic substances have to cut those emissions to the average level of the 12 cleanest similar facilities. Plants posing a 1 in 10,000 risk of cancer to nearby residents by the year 2003 may be shut down. The act also promoted the phasing out of chlorofluorocarbons (CFCs) and other chemicals that harm the earth's protective ozone layer and may contribute to global warming.

The 1990 Clean Air Act has been called the most expensive piece of environmental legislation ever passed, with some estimates saying compliance will cost as much as $25 billion per year. But most people, including leaders in our nation's

environmental impact statement
A statement required by federal law from all agencies for any project using federal funds to assess the potential effect of the new construction or development on the environment.

basic industries, acknowledge that a healthy environment is essential to long-run economic growth.

Some economists suggest that the profit motive may be harnessed in the pursuit of pollution control. With this in mind, the EPA has pressed for new regulatory strategies that encourage market solutions for ecological problems: "Government sets broad limits on the amount of pollution allowed for a region or industry and allots permits to firms for their share of that total. Polluters can buy or sell these allowances, so that firms that can reduce a pollutant inexpensively will benefit by selling their allowances to dirtier neighbors."[17] Initial efforts along these lines have been successful, while saving billions.

Regulating the Global Environment

As globalization has expanded, so have the environmental challenges and hazards associated with that growth. Global temperatures are on the rise, suggesting the possibility that economic development and the burning of carbon-based fuels that goes with it may have created a blanket of carbon dioxide "greenhouse gases" that traps heat in the earth's atmosphere.

Concerns about the consequences of global warming led to negotiation of the Kyoto Protocol in 1997. Named for the Japanese city in which it was negotiated, this treaty required participating countries to make substantial cuts in greenhouse gas emissions year by year until 2012. Because not all nations participated in the negotiations and because the effort to control carbon-based fuels would slow the growth of less developed nations, the Kyoto Protocol immediately divided the world between North (developed countries) and South (less developed countries). Moreover, because the United States would be required to spend billions of dollars reducing the greenhouse gases from its cars and coal-fired electric plants, the Senate signaled its reluctance to participate, too. As of 2003, the Kyoto Protocol is stalled across the world, while nations in both North and South continue to pump carbon dioxide into their skies.

Global warming is only one of several environmental problems the world faces, however. Greenhouse gases may be on the rise, but the world's ozone layer, which protects humans from cancer-causing ultraviolet radiation, is thinning. Unlike global warming, the world has made considerable progress in limiting the major chemicals that cause ozone depletion.

Meeting of the United Nations Global Warming Conference in Kyoto, Japan in December 1997, which constructed the treaty known as the Kyoto Protocol.

The Deregulation Dilemma

One solution to criticism about government regulation has been **deregulation,** the reduction or complete abolishment of federal regulation in a particular sector of the economy. Deregulation has been tried in transportation, banking, and telecommunications, with both positive and negative results.

Deregulating Transportation

No industry has undergone more extensive deregulation than the transportation industry. Over the past generation, airlines, trucking, and railroads have been granted considerable freedom in conducting their operations. No deregulation effort was more visible to individual consumers than airline deregulation.

The federal government began regulating aviation when the Civil Aeronautics Board (CAB) was established by the federal government in 1938 to protect airlines from unreasonable competition by controlling rates and fares. Critics charged that airlines competed only in the frequency of flights and in the services they offered. Because there was no competition over price, consumers were forced to pay high rates for services they may not have desired. Others claimed that CAB regulation of fares kept them higher than they would have been under competitive conditions. It was also charged that airlines were too slow to open new routes under CAB supervision.

deregulation
A policy promoting cutbacks in the amount of federal regulation in specific areas of economic activity.

In light of these and other considerations, Congress in 1978 passed the Airline Deregulation Act. The CAB was abolished, and airlines were free to set whatever fares their markets would bear. Free entry and exit were allowed in all markets. One of the first results of deregulation was that rural and some medium-sized cities lost service because carriers found it more profitable to use their aircraft in busier markets. Airlines were raising fares on routes over which they had monopolies in order to subsidize lower fares on more competitive routes. Critics charged that safety precautions and maintenance suffered as a result of cutthroat competition and the ease with which new airlines could enter the market.

Although problems have been associated with airline deregulation, it has resulted in generally lower fares, greater choice of routes and fares in most markets, and more efficient use of assets by the industry.[18] Some airlines have been driven into bankruptcy and others have merged, but deregulation of the airlines has been judged a success by the surviving airlines and most observers of the industry. If an airline is overcharging passengers, a competitor will eventually steal those travelers away. Southwest Airlines is an example of a discount airline that took advantage of deregulation to take on larger airlines.[19] Deregulation has strengthened the industry by forcing companies to streamline their operations in order to survive in a competitive market. But recent mergers of major airlines have worsened the problems caused by deregulation and cancellation of service to rural and medium-sized cities in parts of states in the West, while the post–September 11 collapse in travel has pushed several airlines toward bankruptcy.

Deregulating Telecommunications

Airline deregulation may have been the most visible to consumers, but telecommunications deregulation may ultimately have the greatest impact on daily life, whether in the form of lower phone bills, easier access to the Internet, or better cellular technology. Unlike the deregulation of transportation, which came in a number of steps over time, deregulation of telecommunications came in a single, massive bill called the Telecommunications Act of 1996.

The act opened up large areas of telecommunications to companies that once were regulated both in the services they could provide and the prices they could charge. The main objective of the new law was to increase competition among phone, cable, and other communications companies. Telephone companies that were once divided into seven local "mini-Bell companies" were allowed to offer services outside their defined regions. Local telephone companies won the freedom to provide long-distance service, manufacture communications equipment, and offer video service in competition with cable television.

At the same time, local telephone companies opened their networks to competition for local telephone service from cable television and long-distance companies. In short, restrictions were removed so that cable television and local and long-distance telephone companies could effectively compete with one another.

Two controversial aspects of the Telecommunications Act of 1996 were regulation of Internet content and the advent of the V-chip to allow parents to block out television shows with objectionable content. However, the Supreme Court struck down the provisions making it a crime for any person knowingly to make indecent material accessible to minors on the Internet. The Court found the provision too vague and held that the Internet receives full protection under the First Amendment.[20] Although the debate continues on who will decide what is deemed violent or offensive, most surveys suggest that parents are unwilling or unable to use the V-chip to control their family viewing habits.[21]

Evaluating Regulatory Policy

Although the need for regulation, especially in areas affecting health and safety, is widely accepted, there are concerns about the negative consequences of regulation. A marked decrease in lead paint poisonings, the use of childproof bottle tops, and the banning of many cancer-producing pesticides are all positive outcomes. On the negative side, regulations generally increase the cost of products and may hamper some industries:

- *Regulation distorts and disrupts the operation of the market.* Some governmental intervention upsets the normal adjustment processes of the market and thus encourages higher prices, misallocation of resources, and inefficiency.

- *Regulation may discourage competition.* Some forms of regulation (often the kind desired by industry) actually have the reverse of their desired effect. This is especially true when the government grants operating licenses and charters to maintain a certain level of quality or stability in the market. Regulatory red tape has also been charged with discouraging entry into industries and driving small businesses out.

- *Regulation may discourage technological development.* If the reward for innovation is a new set of rules and a struggle for permission to use a new product, business may not find it worth the effort to innovate.

- *Regulatory agencies are often "captured" by the industries they regulate.* It is suggested that some regulatory bodies are controlled by the businesses they are supposed to be regulating. There is evidence, too, that some bureaucrats consider jobs in regulatory agencies as stepping-stones to lucrative careers in private industry, and the industries encourage this connection.

- *Regulation increases costs to industry and consumers.* Some critics estimate that government regulations cost every U.S. household $8,000 to $10,000 annually, while advocates argue that regulations return even more in health and safety.

- *Regulation has often been introduced without cost-benefit analysis.* Critics say too little attention is given to whether the benefits of a particular piece of regulation are great enough to justify its cost. Is it worth it to delay approval of new drugs while some who would benefit may die? Is it worth it to clean up 95 percent of automobile emissions if the cost is many times that of an 85 percent cleanup? How much should the nation spend to reduce cancer risk from hazardous waste?

- *Regulatory agencies may lack qualified personnel.* Critics of regulation, and some heads of regulatory agencies themselves, say regulators lack expertise. Regulatory agencies complain that they need larger budgets to do their job properly and attract more qualified staff. Critics argue, too, that government should not meddle in technological industries about which it knows little.

Deregulation appears to be working better in some areas than in others. In the area of drug deregulation, the results are mixed. The Food and Drug Administration, especially since the early 1980s, relaxed the requirements for introducing new medicines. People in the drug industry applaud these efforts. They argue that as a result of deregulation, the public gets better medicines faster and cheaper. Opponents contend, and with some evidence, that the accelerated approval process is endangering public health by prematurely allowing potentially hazardous drugs on the market. Conversely, many lifesaving medications are held back until lengthy testing is concluded.

In our federal system, the mere fact that the national government stops regulating an industry does not mean that the industry will be unregulated. On the contrary, sometimes 50 different state regulators take over, making it even more difficult for an industry to operate on a large scale. California, for example, has much tougher automobile emission rules than the national government. Variations in state regulations are the reason businesspeople themselves sometimes call for more, not less, national regulation; they would prefer one set of national guidelines to 50 different state ones.

In sum, the federal government is heavily involved in making economic and regulatory policies. It collects taxes, regulates the money supply, tries to prevent monopolies that would hurt consumers, and seeks to promote free trade. It does all this while trying to let the market, not government bureaucrats, shape the demand and price of products and services. Most Americans want their government to play only a limited role in the economy, but competing values such as fairness, equality, protecting the environment, and encouraging healthy competition inevitably encourage elected officials to take on certain balancing or referee responsibilities in order to promote the common good.

PoliSim

BALANCING THE NATION'S CHECKBOOK: WHAT CAN YOU GET FOR $4 TRILLION?

Imagine for a moment that you are the director of the Office of Management and Budget and have been directed to recommend budget cuts that are equal to the amount of revenue lost through the president's tax cuts. Each budget cut carries more than a dollar cost, of course. Each has some political impact on the president's approval and reelection. If the damage is too high, you will be out of a job long before the next election.

Go to PoliSim "Balancing the Nations Budget: What Can You Get for $4 Trillion?"

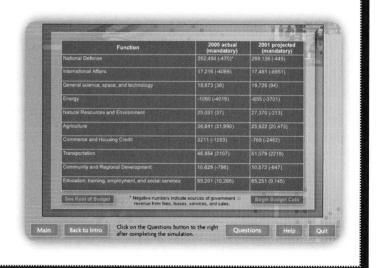

Function	2000 actual (mandatory)	2001 projected (mandatory)
National Defense	292,494 (-470)*	299,136 (-445)
International Affairs	17,216 (-4069)	17,461 (-6651)
General science, space, and technology	18,673 (36)	19,726 (94)
Energy	-1060 (-4019)	-655 (-3701)
Natural Resources and Environment	25,031 (37)	27,370 (-213)
Agriculture	36,641 (31,990)	25,922 (20,473)
Commerce and Housing Credit	3211 (-1263)	-788 (-2462)
Transportation	46,854 (2107)	51,079 (2219)
Community and Regional Development	10,629 (-796)	10,572 (-647)
Education, training, employment, and social services	59,201 (10,266)	65,251 (9,145)

See Rest of Budget   * Negative numbers indicate sources of government revenue from fees, leases, services, and sales.   Begin Budget Cuts

Main   Back to Intro   Click on the Questions button to the right after completing the simulation.   Questions   Help   Quit

Summary

1. The national government influences how wealth is produced and distributed primarily via fiscal policy (taxing and spending), monetary policy (control of the money supply), and regulatory policy.

2. Fiscal policy is implemented by the federal budget, which is annually negotiated between the president and Congress. Monetary policy is primarily under the control of the Federal Reserve System, which has considerable independence from both Congress and the president as it works to supply sufficient amounts of money and credit so that the economy will grow but not so much that it will lead to inflation.

3. Government's role in promoting growth and jobs is not new. It is as old as the Republic itself. The federal government has long been involved in promoting agriculture and concerned about the health of producers and consumers of farm commodities. Working through the Department of Commerce, it also promotes business. The national government is also involved in promoting trade and commerce with other nations. Our ability to buy from other nations and sell them our goods and services has much to do with the health of our economy.

4. Regulation, now a major activity of government, involves altering the natural workings of the open market to achieve some desired goal. Economic regulation aims to control the behavior of business in the marketplace. Social regulation aims to correct the unintended side effects of economic activity and to ensure equal rights in employment, education, and housing.

5. Regulation is a means of eliminating some of the abuses and problems generated by the private economy while avoiding government ownership and the risks of too much centralization. Regulation is an inevitable byproduct of a complex, industrialized, high-technology society.

6. The federal government regulates the economy in five ways. It maintains competition by preventing monopoly and oligopoly. It regulates labor to give workers the right to organize into unions. It regulates markets to protect investors. It regulates the environment to protect the public. And it is increasingly involved in regulating the global environment.

7. A deregulation movement designed to get the government out of the regulation of certain businesses has taken form over the past 30 years. Liberals sometimes favor deregulation if they believe it will foster more competition. Conservatives generally favor deregulation that will get federal regulators off their backs in areas such as safety, health, and environmental and consumer protection standards.

Key Terms

fiscal policy
monetary policy
inflation
tariff
excise tax
progressive tax
regressive tax
deficit
debt
gross domestic product (GDP)
entitlements

Office of Management and Budget (OMB)
Congressional Budget Office (CBO)
sales tax
value-added tax (VAT)
tax expenditure
monetarism
Federal Reserve System
laissez-faire economics
Keynesian economics

trade deficit
World Trade Organization (WTO)
General Agreement on Tariffs and Trade (GATT)
North American Free Trade Agreement (NAFTA)
protectionism
regulation
monopoly
antitrust legislation

trust
yellow-dog contract
closed shop
union shop
labor injunction
collective bargaining
environmental impact statement
deregulation

Further Reading

Jeffrey H. Birnbaum and Alan S. Murray, *Showdown at Gucci Gulch: Lawmakers, Lobbyists, and the Unlikely Triumph of Tax Reform* (Vintage, 1988).

Stephen G. Breyer, *Breaking the Vicious Circle: Toward Effective Risk Regulation* (Harvard University Press, 1993).

Gary Bryner, *Blue Skies, Green Politics: The Clean Air Act of 1990 and Its Interpretation,* 2d ed. (CQ Press, 1995).

Gary Burtless, Robert J. Lawrence, Robert E. Litan, and Robert J. Shapiro, *Globaphobia: Confronting Fears About Open Trade* (Brookings Institution, 1998).

Thomas W. Church and Robert T. Nakamura, *Cleaning Up the Mess: Implementation Strategies in Superfund* (Brookings Institution, 1993).

Robert W. Crandall and Harold Furchtgott-Roth, *Cable TV: Regulation or Competition?* (Brookings Institution, 1996).

Robert W. Crandall and Leonard Waverman, *Who Pays for Universal Service? When Telephone Subsidies Become Transparent* (Brookings Institution, 2000).

Robert W. Crandall et al., *An Agenda for Federal Regulatory Reform* (American Enterprise Institute/Brookings Institution, 1997).

Robert M. Entman, *Competition, Innovation, and Investment in Telecommunications* (Aspen Institute, 1998).

Thomas L. Friedman, *The Lexus and the Olive Tree: Understanding Globalization* (Anchor Books, 2000).

Al Gore, *Earth in the Balance: Ecology and the Human Spirit* (Houghton Mifflin, 1992).

William Greider, *Secrets of the Temple: How the Federal Reserve Runs the Country* (Simon & Schuster, 1987).

Philip K. Howard, *The Death of Common Sense: How Law Is Suffocating America* (Random House, 1994).

Cornelius M. Kerwin, *Rulemaking: How Government Agencies Write Law and Make Policy,* 2d ed. (CQ, 1998).

Robert Kuttner, *Everything for Sale: The Virtues and Limits of Markets* (Knopf, 1997).

Lawrence Lessig, *Code and Other Laws of Cyberspace* (Basic Books, 2000).

Calvin Mackenzie and Saranna Thorton, *Bucking the Deficit: Economic Policy-Making in America* (Westview Press, 1996).

Steven A. Morrison and Clifford Winston, *The Evolution of the Airline Industry* (Brookings Institution, 1995).

Peter G. Peterson, *Facing Up: Paying Our Nation's Debt and Saving Our Children's Future* (Simon & Schuster, 1994).

Allen Schick, *The Federal Budget: Politics, Policy, Process,* rev. ed. (Brookings Institution, 2000).

Joseph E. Stiglitz, *Globilization and Its Discontents* (Norton, 2002).

John Wargo, *Our Children's Toxic Legacy: How Science and Law Fail to Protect Us from Pesticides* (Yale University Press, 1997).

Bob Woodward, *Maestro: Greenspan's Fed and the American Boom* (Simon & Schuster, 2000).

Jeffrey Worshaw, *Other People's Money: Policy Changes, Congress, and Bank Regulation* (Westview Press, 1997).

Daniel Yergin and Joseph Stanislaw, *The Commanding Heights: The Battle Between Government and the Marketplace That Is Remaking the Modern World* (Simon & Schuster, 1998).

20
CHAPTER

MAKING SOCIAL POLICY

T HE PREAMBLE TO THE CONSTITUTION PROMISES THAT THE FEDERAL GOVERNMENT WILL DO MORE THAN CREATE A MORE PERFECT union, establish justice, ensure domestic tranquillity, provide for the common defense, and secure the blessing of liberty for posterity. It also promises that the federal government will promote the general welfare. Although the framers did not define each promise in detail, they clearly wanted the new government to have enough power to unite an increasingly divided Union, whether by building roads and bridges, opening post offices, or taking care of Revolutionary War veterans.

There have been times when one or more of the promises have been given greater attention. That was certainly the case immediately after the terrorist attacks of September 11, 2001, when Congress passed a series of laws to provide for the common defense against terrorism. But even during the weeks and months following the assault on New York City and Washington, the federal government continued to promote the general welfare through a host of programs such as Social Security and Medicare for the elderly, school lunches and preschool for poor children, and job training and insurance for the unemployed.

Congress also continued to work on major legislative initiatives to promote the general welfare through education. Congress had been working on major amendments to the 1965 Elementary and Secondary Education Act well before the September attacks. If Congress failed to act by December 31, 2001, the federal government would lose its authority to spend money on everything from special education to urban school aid. Not only did Congress renew the law, but Democrats and President Bush also reached a historic agreement in early December to expand the federal government's role in local education. Under the Leave No Child Behind Act of 2001, Congress provided billions of dollars in additional funding for poor, urban schools and for teacher training and recruitment. In return, local school systems had to test student performance annually, set

Orphanages run by religious orders provided for needy children. These orphans attended the Sisters of Charity of the Incarnate World Orphanage in Galveston, Texas, in the late 1890s.

higher standards for teachers, and close schools that fall short of state standards. Although states and localities still provided more than 90 percent of all school funding, the new law put important new strings on federal support.

Education was not the only social policy issue that had to be addressed in 2001–2002. Congress also worked on another round of welfare reform, moved forward on legislation to reorganize food safety agencies, debated the merits of human cloning, and considered, but rejected, several proposals to provide prescription drug coverage to older Americans. Through it all, the federal government continued to provide benefits to millions of Social Security recipients, health insurance to older Americans through Medicare, unemployment insurance to the thousands of Americans who lost their jobs in the 2001–2002 recession, and funding for school lunches for poor children.

This chapter will explore both how the federal government honors its promise to promote the general welfare today and how that promise has expanded over the past century. It will also examine three areas of social policy that are likely to be active over the next few years: health, education, and crime control.

The Role of Government in Social Policy

The nation has been debating the federal government's role in promoting the general welfare from the beginning of the Republic. Some Americans ask whether government should be involved at all in social policies such as child care, help for the needy, and job training, all of which were once thought of as purely private, religious, or charitable responsibilities. Others ask which level of government should be involved in specific issues such as education, welfare, and crime control, all of which were once thought to be solely state and local responsibilities. Today, these responsibilities are a large part of the agenda of our national government.

Public Versus Individual

Americans are sharply divided on how much government should do to care for the needy. Some Americans believe that people should take responsibility for their own mistakes even if that means they must live in poverty. They doubt government's ability to provide effective, efficient protection against misfortune and put their faith in the free market. They believe that the economy will provide opportunities for those with ambition and a willingness to work hard.

Other Americans believe that government must step in to help the needy through social programs such as job training, child care assistance, public housing, and other forms of aid. Although they too may doubt the efficiency of public solutions, they believe that the free market is often unfair, leaving some Americans behind because of their race, sex, lack of access to education, and so forth. They believe that government should provide a safety net against poverty, joblessness, and prejudice.

The two political parties tend to divide sharply in this debate. Republicans believe that the national government is part of the problem, not the solution, to poverty and other social ills by getting in the way of the free market. They tend to favor programs that create incentives for people to pull themselves out of poverty through hard work.

In contrast, Democrats are more likely to believe that only the national government has the resources and jurisdiction to provide adequate Social Security, help local governments improve the quality of education, and ensure that all Americans, rich and poor, have access to proper medical attention. They tend to favor programs that make sure all Americans are protected from the occasional failures of the free market system.

Public Versus Charity

The United States is a remarkably generous nation. Four out of ten Americans volunteer each year, and nine out of ten contribute to charity. Americans contributed over $400 billion in time and money to charity in 2001 alone. Some Americans believe that these contributions would increase dramatically if government would get out of the way. Others argue that charity can only treat the symptoms of poverty and other misfortunes, whereas only government can solve the underlying causes (see Table 20-1).

Once again, the two parties split on the issue. Republicans argue that the nation should rely more on charity and less on government. They point to the long history of charitable giving as positive proof that society as a whole will seek to remedy social problems without the higher taxes and big bureaucracy that come with government programs. They also note that charitable foundations also provide billions of dollars for programs designed to feed, house, educate, and provide health care to needy Americans.

Democrats believe the national government must provide a safety net for individuals and a minimum standard of living—a job, an education, health care, housing, and basic nutrition—for all citizens. They contend not only that compassion requires this minimum standard of living but also that social policy based on this premise is pragmatic. Without it, our cities would have far more homeless and hungry people, desperately trying to survive. Advocates of governmental solutions to social problems point to the inability of charitable giving to meet the needs of the poor, the elderly, and people who lack health insurance. They contend that the experience of the past half-century in the United States and other advanced industrial democracies has shown that national governmental support for housing, welfare, health care, and education is a necessity.

Both parties are right. Government and charity often work hand in hand in moments of need. After the terrorist attacks of September 11, 2001, even as Congress and the president were putting the finishing touches on a $40 billion package of assistance for New York and Washington, individual Americans were giving at record levels. Seventy percent of Americans reported that they gave money or blood in response to the tragedies. By December 1, Americans had contributed a total of $1.5 billion to help victims and their families. Roughly $1 billion went to the Red Cross's Liberty Fund and the United Way's September 11 Fund, and a quarter went to 50 other funds established to help the victims. New York Mayor Rudy Giuliani's Twin Towers Fund reported $113 million in receipts; the New York Firefighters 9-11 Disaster Fund, $90 million; the Robin Hood Relief Fund, $48 million; and the Uniformed Firefighters Association Widow's and Children's Fund, $29 million.[1]

National Versus State and Local

Finally, some Americans argue that state and local governments should solve social policy problems such as poverty, in part because states and localities know more about the specific needs in their communities. Others believe that only the national government can ensure that every American is protected against misfortune, in part because poor states and localities may not have the resources to provide as much help as their richer neighbors.

In recent years, Democrats and Republicans have resolved the debate in part by setting national standards that require all states and localities to provide minimum levels of help. In turn, state governors have been increasingly critical of *unfunded mandates* that require state action with little or no federal funding for implementation. The tendency of Congress to impose unfunded mandates forces state governments to raise taxes or reduce funding for other state programs. Governors argue that if Congress inaugurates a new program requiring states to take action, Congress should provide the federal funds to help pay for the state's costs to administer that program.

The Early History of Social Policy in the United States

Most Western governments expanded their social programs long before the United States did. Americans generally believed that people who could not succeed in a nation as big, rich, and open as the United States simply were not working hard enough. This commitment to *rugged individualism* meant that government, be it local, state, or national, played only a limited role in people's lives. Rather grudgingly, state governments in the early twentieth century extended relief to needy groups, especially the old, the blind, and the orphaned. But government aid was limited, and much reliance was placed on private charity.[2]

TABLE 20-1 Giving and Volunteering, 2000

Percentage of adults who volunteered	44%
Total number of adult volunteers	83.9 million
Average weekly hours per volunteer	3.6 hours
Total hours volunteered	15.5 billion hours
Estimate hourly value of volunteer time	$15.40
Total dollar value of volunteer time	$239.2 billion
Percentage of households that contributed to charity	89%
Average annual household contribution	$1,620
Total dollar value of individual giving	$170.1 billion

SOURCE: Independent Sector, *Giving and Volunteering in the United States, 2001* (Independent Sector, 2001).

On July 4, 1932 over 20,000 war veterans marched to the Capitol in Washington, D.C. to demand the passage of the Bonus Bill, which allowed the immediate payment of the Soldiers' Bonus.

This is not to suggest that the national government ignored domestic policy, however. From its founding, the national government took care of its military veterans. Indeed, with the Revolutionary War barely over, the Continental Congress established the nation's first programs to help soldiers who had been disabled in battle, as well as general retirement pensions at an amount equal to half pay for officers. Contrary to those who argue that government did not enter the social security arena until it created the Social Security system in 1935, the Continental Congress actually established the nation's first social security system well before the new government was even created.

Once established in the 1780s, that first social security system for veterans expanded slowly but steadily as the soldiers aged into disability and poverty. Americans could not stand to see their veterans in tattered clothing and felt obliged to provide support for the less fortunate. In 1818, for example, Congress expanded retirement benefits to cover all veterans of the Revolutionary War, whether officers or not, and created the first old soldiers' homes for poor veterans. In 1840, Congress expanded the veterans program again to provide financial relief to the widows of soldiers killed in battle.[3]

These early programs set two important precedents for contemporary domestic policy. First, they established the notion that some Americans would be automatically entitled to certain government benefits on the basis of an eligibility requirement such as service in the nation's armed forces. Thus veterans' relief was the nation's first **entitlements**, under which the government provides benefits to any citizen who is eligible. In the original program, only military officers met the eligibility requirement.

Second, these early programs also established government's right to restrict some benefits only to those citizens who could actually prove their need for help. Thus veterans' programs were early examples of what are now called **means-tested entitlements**, under which citizens must prove they are poor enough to deserve the government's help. In the original program, only poor veterans could go to old soldiers' homes.

Veterans' benefits are also important because they eventually came to cover huge numbers of Americans. As political scientist Theda Skocpol has noted, the Civil War triggered the largest expansion in veterans' benefits. The war involved 2.2 million Union soldiers who would later qualify for veterans' benefits. "By 1910, about 28 percent of all American men aged 65 or more, more than half a million of them, received federal benefits averaging $189 a year," writes Skocpol. "Over three hundred thousand widows, orphans, and other dependents were also receiving payments from the federal treasury."[4]

Because so many men served in the Civil War and because veterans' benefits were even more generous toward Spanish-American War and World War I veterans, veterans' benefits accounted for one-quarter of all federal spending by 1932. The numbers would have been even higher if Confederate soldiers had been entitled to benefits. However, Congress decided to leave their care to the former Confederate states and localities.

Types of Social Policy

Having entered the twentieth century with only a handful of federal domestic programs, most of which were built around helping veterans, the federal government left the century with a deep inventory of domestic programs. According to the *Catalog of Federal Domestic Assistance*, which lists every one of the federal government's 1,425 domestic funding programs in a searchable database (at www.cfda.gov), there are at least 38 separate programs for farmers, another 142 for colleges and their students, 148 for women, and 257 for children.

Social Policy Goals

Because most of these programs are restricted to one group of citizens only, they are often described as *categorical* aid. One only needs to type in a search term such as "students," "elderly," "children," "disabled," "workers," "farmers," "women," or "veterans" to see just how much help the federal government provides in each category. But regardless of category, federal domestic policy focuses on two broad goals.

entitlements
Programs such as unemployment insurance, disaster relief, or disability payments that provide benefits to all eligible citizens.

means-tested entitlements
Programs such as Medicaid and welfare under which applicants must meet eligibility requirements based on need.

The first goal is to protect citizens against poverty and personal misfortune, whether by providing relief for unemployed workers, health care for the elderly, emergency shelter for the homeless, or school lunches for poor children, almost all of which are available to citizens only on the basis of a means test. Although almost all Americans are covered by federal unemployment insurance through a payroll tax, only workers who have been laid off from their jobs through no fault of their own can qualify for benefits, and only then for a relatively brief period of time. (For an inventory of federal programs for helping workers, visit the Department of Labor Web site at www.workers.gov.)

The second goal of federal domestic policy is to raise the quality of life for all Americans, whether by improving air and water quality, building roads and bridges, regulating air traffic, fighting crime, or strengthening local schools through federal aid, almost all of which are available to all communities regardless of need. Almost all federal aid to the states is distributed on the basis of formula grants that allocate money on the basis of population, not need.

Most scholars trace the federal government's effort to protect citizens against economic and personal hard times to the Great Depression and the Social Security Act of 1935. Although there is no question that Franklin Roosevelt's New Deal agenda stimulated a remarkable expansion in the federal government's domestic policy role, there is also no question that federal, state, and local governments were helping citizens long before the Depression began.

Until about a century ago, the poor were divided into two groups: the worthy poor, meaning people who were in poverty through no fault of their own, and the unworthy poor, meaning people who were in poverty because of idleness or an unwillingness to work. As historian Joel Handler writes, this categorization emerged in the early 1800s as states began to place the worthy poor into separate government institutions such as schools for the blind and disabled. This movement was driven by a clear recognition that "those who were dependent by misfortune did not deserve the stigma of the unworthy poor."[5]

Types of Protection

By the early 1900s, however, public attitudes toward the poor had begun to change. Although the nation continued to distinguish between the worthy and unworthy poor, Congress and the president soon invented two very different types of federal programs to protect Americans against hardship, both of which continue to exist today.

The first type of help for the less fortunate is called **public assistance**, a term that is often used interchangeably with the word "welfare" to cover government aid for the poor. The first public assistance programs were actually created in the late 1800s when states established aid programs to help single, poor mothers and their children. Although these programs were often described as "mothers' pensions" to create the impression that the beneficiaries had earned the benefits through some contribution, they created a precedent for many of the federal government's later antipoverty programs.

Most of this assistance flows through noncontributory programs, meaning that recipients do not have to pay anything in advance to receive benefits. Most federal assistance programs also impose a means test on all applicants. As noted earlier, these tests require applicants to disclose all financial assets and income to prove that they fall below the poverty line, which is generally calculated as three times the amount of money an individual or family needs to purchase the food for a nutritious diet. Defined as such, the poverty level changes with the size of the family. The poverty level for an individual was set at roughly $9,200 in pretax income in 2001, while the level for a family of three (one parent and two children) was set at just over $14,250. As of 2001, more than 11 percent of Americans fell below the poverty line, with the highest concentration among children under 18 years of age (more than 16 percent) and African Americans (22 percent) and the lowest among people over 65 years of age (roughly 10 percent).

Public assistance in the United States today incorporates elements of job training; transportation subsidies; housing subsidies; free school lunches; food aid for poor families, pregnant mothers and their young children; and tax credits for low-income people (see Table 20-2). The national government also provides "corporate welfare" to favored industries such as agriculture

TABLE 20–2 **Federal Payments to Individuals, 2002**	
Public Assistance	
Medicaid	$145 billion
Supplemental Security Income	30 billion
Earned Income Tax Credit	28 billion
Food stamps	23 billion
Family support	22 billion
Foster care/adoption	6 billion
Day care	4.5 billion
Child nutrition	4 billion
September 11 assistance	1 billion
Other	7.4 billion
Total	1.06 trillion
Social Insurance Funding	
Social Security	$388 billion
Medicare	247 billion
Disability insurance	67 billion
Veteran's benefits	45 billion
Unemployment insurance	45 billion
Total	792 billion

SOURCE: Budget of the United States Government, 2002.

public assistance
Aid to the poor; "welfare."

Major Programs of the New Deal

- *Works Progress Administration (WPA)*—spent billions of dollars on local projects such as public housing, courthouses, and parks

- *Public Works Administration (PWA)*—built large permanent projects, such as dams and roads

- *Agricultural Adjustment Act (AAA)*—sought to stabilize farm income by providing price supports in return for limiting crop production

- *Civilian Conservation Corps (CCC)*—put people to work protecting natural resources on federal land

- *Tennessee Valley Authority (TVA)*—supervised the construction of dams and power plants on the Tennessee River to electrify and modernize the rural South

social insurance
Programs in which eligibility is based on prior contributions to government, usually in the form of payroll taxes.

and steel and "middle-class welfare" to college students, home buyers, and the citizenry as a whole in the form of college loans, tax deducations for home mortgages, and access to national parks and forests (supported by taxpayers but rarely used by poor people). However, the term "welfare" is generally used for public assistance to the needy, including the following forms:

Direct payments to single parents with young children, the unemployed, and the disabled

Vouchers that can be exchanged for food

Subsidies that reduce the cost of housing or the provision of public housing

Reduced cost or free access to public transportation, higher education, or job training

Subsidized medical care

In absolute numbers, most poor people are white. As a percentage within their own population, however, a larger proportion of African Americans and Hispanics are poor. Moreover, in both absolute and proportional terms, more women than men are poor. Indeed, some scholars refer to the relatively recent rise in poverty among women as the "feminization of poverty."[6] Women usually get paid less than men for doing the same work and tend to be employed in low-paying jobs. The official government figure is that women make 73 cents for every dollar earned by men.[7] Taking account of characteristics such as job experience, education, and other measures of productivity, economists find that wage discrimination costs women 89 to 98 cents for every dollar earned by men in the 27-to-33 age group.[8] Older women do not fare as well as younger women, largely because they are less likely to have worked and saved money over the years. Divorce adversely affects the living standard of women more than men, and women provide most of the child care.

The second type of protection against hardship is called **social insurance**, a term that refers to government programs that provide benefits to anyone who is eligible either because of past service (veterans, miners, merchant marines) or payments of some kind (payroll taxes for Social Security and Medicare, insurance premiums). Some social insurance programs, such as unemployment and disability insurance, provide benefits only to those in need, thereby acting like private automobile and life insurance, which pay off only when an accident or death occurs. Other social insurance programs, such as Social Security and Medicare, pay benefits regardless of wealth, thereby acting more like a private savings program or annuity, which pays off at a set point in time.

Many federal assistance programs involve partnerships with state governments. There are two reasons for the connection. First, except for veterans' policy, states have been responsible for protecting their citizens against hardship since the United States was formed. Second, states and local governments have the administrative agencies to stay in touch with recipients of aid, whether to make sure they are actually eligible for support or to provide services such as job training or school lunches.

Because states vary greatly in their generosity, most federal assistance is designed to set a minimum floor of support that individual states can raise on their own. The most generous states in the country tend to be located in the Northeast and West, where living costs tend to be higher and legislatures more liberal, while the least generous tend to be found in the South. In this way, states act as a check on the federal government's ability to raise benefits too far, frustrating those who believe that the federal government should set a uniform level of benefits for all citizens while ensuring the consent of the governed for helping those in need.

The Expansion of Social Policy in the Twentieth Century

The federal government's commitment to helping the poor and improving the quality of life expanded rapidly during the Great Depression that followed the stock market crash of 1929. The "social safety net" built by state and local governments and private charities simply could not meet the needs of the huge increase in the homeless, unemployed, and poor.

The New Deal

The most significant expansion of federal social policy occurred in the five years that followed Franklin Roosevelt's inauguration in 1933. That year, as part of Roosevelt's New Deal agenda, the federal government began making loans to states and localities to help the poor, and soon it launched a long list of programs to help older Americans (Social Security), the jobless (unemployment insurance), and the poor (Aid to Families with Dependent Children).

THE FIRST 100 DAYS   Before creating these signature New Deal programs, however, the Roosevelt administration moved quickly to help the needy. The first 100 days of the administration produced the most significant list of legislation ever passed in American history, including the Federal Emergency Relief Administration (FERA), established in May 1933 to give unemployed workers cash grants to get them through the summer, and the Civil Works Administration (CWA), created in November 1933 to provide millions of public jobs to help many of those same workers make it through the winter.

The WPA, part of President Roosevelt's New Deal, created jobs for thousands of workers during the Great Depression of the 1930s.

The list of "alphabet agencies" grew longer as the administration created a host of new programs to help the poor, including the Works Progress Administration (WPA), created in 1935 to provide semipermanent jobs for the millions of Americans still unable to find work as the Depression deepened, and the Civilian Conservation Corps (CCC), which found jobs for millions of young Americans in the national forests and parks. But the general point had been made: The federal government would have a role not just in rebuilding the economy but in providing a national safety net to catch those in need. It is little wonder, therefore, that scholars would describe the New Deal as the "big bang" of domestic policy.[9] Although the distinction between the worthy and unworthy poor still remained, joblessness was no longer defined as merely a problem of individual idleness.

Americans who had lost their jobs through no fault of their own would be entitled to help from a much more aggressive federal government. Between 1933 and 1945, for example, the WPA put 8.5 million Americans to work at a cost of $10 billion. All told, the WPA built 650,000 miles of roads, 125,000 public buildings, 8,200 parks, and 850 airports. The wages were hardly robust, however. The average WPA worker received just $55 a month, far below the $100 the federal government deemed a subsistence wage. The WPA was abolished during World War II when the economy finally rebounded.

HELP FOR OLDER AMERICANS   Once past the immediate crisis, the Roosevelt administration began designing the flagship programs of the New Deal. First on the list was **Social Security**, which was enacted in 1935 and stands today as the federal government's most popular social program. Social Security was designed to meet two goals: (1) to provide a minimum income floor for poor beneficiaries and (2) to ensure that benefits bear a relationship to the amount of payroll taxes a beneficiary actually paid. Supported by equal contributions from employers and employees, the program now covers more than 90 percent of the American work force.[10] The universal nature of Social Security is one reason it is politically so popular: Everyone benefits, regardless of need. As of 2002, the Social Security Administration issued checks to almost 50 million Americans every month, and three times that many working people contribute to the fund. Regardless of how much they paid in taxes or how long they worked, all beneficiaries who retired at age 65 in 2002 received a minimum benefit of $1,660 a month.

Social Security was expanded in 1939 to include financial support for survivors of workers covered by Social Security when the retired worker died, and in 1954, the program was again expanded to include support for disabled workers and the children of deceased or disabled workers. Benefit levels were raised repeatedly during the first 40 years of the program, often just before an election. The increases became so frequent and so costly that Congress finally indexed benefits to rise with inflation in 1975. Under legislation enacted in 1983, the Social Security retirement age will start to rise in 2003 and will reach 67 years of age by the year 2027. As of 2004, workers who retire at age 65 years and 4 months are eligible for full benefits, while workers who retire early at age 62 are eligible for a reduced amount.

Social Security
A combination of entitlement programs, paid for by employer and employee taxes, that includes retirement benefits, health insurance, and support for disabled workers and the children of deceased or disabled workers.

The Gray Panthers, an activist group made up of elderly Americans, often marches in support of numerous social issues, not only those causes that relate specifically to their needs.

Until the 1970s, growth in Social Security benefits was relatively noncontroversial, largely because "the costs were initially deceptively low," while the benefits increased steadily, making the system politically painless.[11] Since Social Security began, the program has experienced steady growth and is now the world's largest insurance program for retirees, survivors, and people with disabilities. In 2003, Social Security and Medicare expenditures totaled nearly $635 billion.

Social Security, unlike many welfare programs, is financed not from general taxes but from a trust fund into which taxes on employees and employers are placed—the Federal Insurance Contribution Act, commonly known as FICA. Over the years, Congress added benefits to the Social Security system without adding enough money to the trust fund to cover the added expense. In 1983, Congress was forced to put Social Security on a more sound financial foundation by raising the retirement age at which one qualifies for Social Security benefits, increasing Social Security taxes, and taxing 50 percent of the Social Security payments of upper-income individuals—a percentage that was raised to 85 percent in 1993.

Social Security taxes are now the largest tax paid by most Americans, and for three-quarters of Americans, their Social Security tax now exceeds their income tax. Employees had to pay a 7.65 percent tax on all wages up to $84,900 in 2002, which their employers had to match dollar for dollar. A single person with no dependents would have to earn $30,000 before paying more federal income tax than Social Security tax; families with two children would have to earn over $40,000 before their income tax would exceed their Social Security tax. Some experts believe that if Social Security expenditures are not controlled, more than half of every paycheck will be used to finance the program by 2040.[12]

Because people are living longer, the future financial stability of Social Security has become a major political issue. When the baby boomers retire, the number of people receiving benefits will increase in proportion to those contributing to the system. This increase would not be a problem if the money being contributed to Social Security by today's workers was put away for their eventual retirement. But much of the money taken from today's workers goes to pay for today's retirees. Social Security is thus a transfer program in which today's young workers finance the retirement of today's elderly. At some point, this reality is likely to foster intergenerational tension between workers and retirees.

The Social Security system is still running a surplus, meaning that the amount that is brought in through Social Security taxes is greater than the amount of money going out in benefits. The surpluses are invested in Treasury bonds, with the promise that they will

Social Security Programs

Old Age, Survivors, and Disability Insurance Trust Fund (OASDI)—established 1935

OASDI provides *retirement* benefits starting at age 65 and 4 months in 2004 (with reduced benefits available as early as 62). This is the largest and best known of the Social Security programs. But OASDI also provides *disability* benefits payable at any age to people who have enough Social Security credits and who have a severe physical or mental impairment that is expected to prevent them from doing "substantial" work for a year or more or who have a condition that is expected to result in death. Other members of the family of persons eligible for retirement or disability benefits may be entitled to *family* benefits. OASDI also provides *survivors'* benefits for certain family members of deceased persons who earned enough Social Security credits while working.

Medicare—established 1965

Medicare provides hospital insurance (Part A) and medical insurance (Part B). Generally, people who are over age 65 and getting

Social Security automatically qualify for Medicare, as do people who have been getting disability benefits for two years. Part A is funded by a portion of the Social Security taxes paid by people still working. It helps pay for inpatient hospital care, skilled nursing care, and other services. Part B is funded by monthly premiums paid by enrollees and from general revenues. It helps pay for doctors' fees, outpatient hospital visits, and other medical services and supplies.

Supplemental Security Income (SSI)—established 1972

Supplemental Security Income makes monthly payments to disabled persons or those over age 65 who have a low income and few assets. Levels of SSI support vary by state to reflect cost-of-living differences, and some states add money to that amount. Generally, people who get SSI also qualify for Medicaid, food stamps, and other assistance. SSI benefits are financed by general tax revenues.

SOURCE: Social Security Administration, at www.ssa.gov/pubs/10006.html.

be repaid with interest later. As the baby boomers retire and begin to collect Social Security, however, the bonds must be redeemed to pay benefits, and the program will start running annual deficits. Experts differ on when the next Social Security funding crisis will come, but there is little disagreement that something will have to be done to ensure the viability of Social Security for young people now paying into the system.[13]

Congress and the president have yet to reach agreement on how to fix the problem. There are only three possible solutions: cut benefits, raise taxes, or figure out some way to get a higher rate of return on the surplus. Congress could cut benefits by raising the retirement age to 70, for example, thereby delaying the age at which Americans could start withdrawing benefits, or raise payroll taxes to build up a larger surplus for the future, but both actions would be highly unpopular with the American public.

That is why Congress and the president have focused on ways to get a higher rate of return on the Social Security surplus. Treasury bonds may be safe, but they produce a very low annual yield. At least some reformers believe that some of the Social Security surplus should be invested in the stock market. The idea was particularly popular in the late 1990s and early 2000s during the stock market boom but was set aside temporarily when the stock market began to plunge in the spring of 2002. Americans are enthusiastic about investing their Social Security funds in the stock market when it is going up but not when it's falling.

HELP FOR THE UNEMPLOYED   Social Security was not the only strand of economic protection woven during the New Deal. The New Deal also produced the federal government's first unemployment insurance program, which was enacted as part of the 1935 Social Security Act. Under the program, which is administered by state governments but funded in part with federal unemployment taxes, eligible workers can receive benefits for up to 26 weeks in most states. In periods of high unemployment, the federal government also provides funds for extended benefits for a maximum of 39 weeks in most states.

The School Lunch Program

The school lunch program started during the New Deal as a way to put unemployed women to work. Soon the program had expanded as a way to help the ailing farm economy. The Federal Surplus Relief Corporation began purchasing surplus agriculture products for needy families in 1935 and launched the nation's first school lunch programs for poor children shortly thereafter.

By 1941, more than 5 million children were receiving free school lunches, consuming more than 450 million pounds of surplus pork, dairy products, and bread. Although the program was disbanded during World War II because of food shortages, it was restored under the 1946 National School Lunch Act. As President Harry Truman said at the signing ceremony, "No nation is any healthier than its children." He could have added many draftees had been rejected for service in World War II because of malnutrition.

Today, the school lunch program operates in nearly 100,0000 public and nonreligious private schools, providing low-cost or free lunches to 2 million children daily. The program also provides federal funding for snacks served in after-school programs to children through 18 years of age. Those lunches must meet the dietary guidelines issued by the federal government, which recommend that no more than 30 percent of an individual's calories come from fat.

The school lunch program set the stage for creation in 1964 of the food stamp program, which provides coupons to eligible low-income families that can be used to purchase food. In 2002, roughly 18 million Americans used food stamps at some time during the year to help them buy food. Roughly half of the Americans who benefit from the program are children.

Elementary school children stand in the cafeteria line for their lunch. Today, two million children receive some sort of aid to ensure they get lunch when at school.

PEOPLE DEBATE
RESTORING CONFIDENCE IN SOCIAL SECURITY

Although Social Security is arguably the most popular social policy in America, many young Americans do not believe they will ever see a penny in benefits. They worry that there will be no money left after the huge baby boom generation draws down the current surplus and have little confidence that there will even be a program by the time they retire. By 2010, the program will start spending more in benefits each year than it is scheduled to collect; by the 2030s, it will exhaust its surplus. In 1935, there were 46 taxpayers for each beneficiary; today there are just three; by 2030, there will be only two.

These trends have led Congress to consider options for increasing the yield on the current Social Security surplus. President Bush would allow individuals to invest up to 2 percent of their payroll savings taxes in private accounts of their own choosing. Even though he admitted that the stock market can, and even would, go down, Representative Nick Smith (R.-Mich.) agreed with the president, while Senator Richard Durbin (D.-Ill.) argued that taking money out of the Social Security system for individual retirement accounts would erode support for the program overall, regardless of how well or poorly those investments performed:

Nick Smith: Let the People Invest

Right now Social Security gives a wage earner, on average, a 1.7 percent return on the money they and their employer put in. So in 10 years we are looking at a situation where retirees will be receiving someplace maybe even closer to a 1 percent return because of Social Security taxes continually increasing, and the suggestion of expanding benefits is ever on the minds of this body. So the challenge before us certainly is: How are we going to keep Social Security solvent? What are the changes that can be made? How do we get better than a 1.1 percent return on that particular money?

If we can fix the problem today with a couple trillion dollars of that surplus and start getting a better return on the money that is invested, then we can keep Social Security solvent. . . . So I think there is some good justification for putting some of that money in accounts of individuals, to put it into the safe kind of investments where we can guarantee that it will earn more than what Social Security will pay under the current program, where we can guarantee, if you will, that individuals that decide that they want to stay with the old system will have that option, or they can have the option to . . . choose the different investments that they think will give them the maximum return on their investment. Now is a difficult time to maybe convince some people that they should have part of that investment in equities, in the stock market. Yet, if we just look at last month, last month there was almost a 3.5 percent increase in the money invested in the stock market. Since the 1890s, there has never been a 12-year period

HELP FOR THE POOR   The federal government became involved in protecting women and children against poverty when Congress passed the Infancy and Maternity Protection Act of 1921. Supported by many of the same women's groups that had just won ratification of the Nineteenth Amendment, which gave women the right to vote, the act gave the newly created federal Children's Bureau funds to encourage states to create new maternal, infant, and early childhood health programs. Although the act was allowed to expire in 1929, it set a precedent for future federal involvement in protecting families against poverty.

Congress moved much further when it passed the Aid to Families with Dependent Children (AFDC) program in 1935.[14] By its very name, AFDC tried to shift the

where there has been a loss of money invested in equities in the stock market. . . .

The real return of Social Security is less than 2 percent for most workers and shows a negative return for some compared to over 7 percent return in the marketplace for any . . . 15-year period. And the private investments are not only a greater return, but it is the security of knowing it is your money, not having politicians in the future reach into that pot and say, well, times are tough in America. We are going to have to reduce benefits or we are going to have to increase taxes on American workers.

SOURCE: *Congressional Record,* February 13, 2001.

Richard Durbin: Keep the Security in Social Security

What would happen if George Bush had his way? If we took 2 percent of the proceeds going into the Social Security trust fund and said they will no longer go into the trust fund but people will be allowed to invest them individually, what impact would that have? Frankly, it could have a very serious and, I think, a very negative impact. Keep in mind that the money being taken out of the payroll taxes each week in America goes to pay the current benefits of Social Security retirees. There is not some huge savings account that is blossoming. But basically we are talking about a pay-as-you-go system. If you take 2 percent away, you are still going to have the retirees needing their Social Security check. You are going to have to figure out some way to plug this gap. . . . I readily concede that over the last 8 years . . . the stock market has done very well. . . . It is naive to believe this will go on indefinitely. . . . To take your life savings, or take 2 percent of your payroll tax and Social Security, and put it in the stock exchange, you understand there are risks. . . . What if George Bush guesses wrong? What if people invest some part of their Social Security into the stock market, and the market goes down and they are losing money?. . . I happen to believe if the Bush privatization scheme goes through and it doesn't work, this Congress will be called on to come up with the money to bail out the families who guessed wrong in the stock market. . . . We are literally talking about a Social Security system that benefits tens of millions of Americans today and that many more Americans are counting on for the future. When people start talking about change in Social Security, I am very cautious.

SOURCE: *Congressional Record,* May 23, 2000.

1. Is the debate about privatization really about the performance of the stock market or about government's role in providing a financial safety net?

2. What would make you more confident about the future of Social Security?

3. Why do Democrats want all Americans to be part of the Social Security program even though poorer Americans benefit the most?

focus away from what the mother had or had not done to deserve poverty and onto the children who suffered whatever the cause, thereby reducing public opposition to expanded benefits. Under the program, states were given federal money to establish cash grants for poor families under two conditions: (1) States had to match the federal funds with some contribution of their own, and (2) states had to establish a means test for all families receiving benefits. AFDC was abolished in 1996 when Congress and the president created an entirely new program that required states to set time limits on public assistance, thereby creating a greater incentive for welfare recipients to find work.

President Lyndon Johnson's vision of a Great Society relied on the principle of government action to solve economic and social problems.

The Great Society

The second major expansion of social policy came in the 1960s with what became known as the Great Society. At a commencement speech at the University of Michigan in May 1964, President Lyndon Johnson described his vision of the Great Society:

> The Great Society rests on abundance and liberty for all. It demands an end to poverty and racial injustice. . . . But that is just the beginning. The Great Society is a place where every child can find knowledge to enrich his mind and to enlarge his talents. . . . It is a challenge constantly renewed, beckoning us toward a destiny where the meaning of our lives matches the marvelous products of our labors.[15]

Johnson's agenda was as broad as his rhetoric, and Congress enacted much of it in a fairly short period of time. Great Society programs dramatically increased the role of the federal government in education through a number of programs that exist today:

- *Food stamps.* The food stamp program gives poor families coupons that can be used to purchase the basics of a healthy, nutritious diet. The average benefit is about $75 per person per month.

- *Head Start.* Head Start is a preschool program designed to help poor children get ready for kindergarten. The program serves nearly 1 million children in 1,500 preschools around the country.

- *Medicaid.* **Medicaid** was created in 1965 to provide basic health services for poor families. The program is administered by state governments, which are responsible for determining eligibility, and covers everything from hospital care to family planning.

- *Supplemental Security Income.* The SSI program was created in 1972, to provide an extra measure of support for the elderly poor and the blind or disabled. The program provides monthly benefit checks ranging from just $1 to roughly $800 and is administered by the Social Security Administration.

- *Housing assistance.* The Department of Housing and Urban Development, which was created in 1965, administers a number of programs designed to help low-income families find affordable, safe housing, in part by giving property owners subsidies to make up the difference between what tenants can pay and what the local housing market will bear.

The Great Society also produced a vast new social insurance program to cover all hospital and most other health care costs for older Americans. Under **Medicare**, the federal government pays all of the reasonable costs of all inpatient hospital care, including drugs, surgery, and postoperative care, regardless of the beneficiary's personal wealth. Like Social Security, this insurance is "purchased" through payroll taxes, which are set aside solely for Medicare expenditures. Medicare beneficiaries are also entitled to purchase additional federal health insurance (under so-called Part B) to cover the costs of outpatient care, physician visits, and laboratory fees but not prescription drugs.[16] Medicare beneficiaries must also pay a deductible on all hospital stays and a monthly premium for the additional insurance.

Johnson was not the first modern president to propose a national health care program. Truman had offered a much more comprehensive program in the late 1940s, and Kennedy had forwarded the first version of Medicare immediately after his inauguration in 1961. The difference between 1961 and 1965 was the 1964 election, which brought 65 new Democrats to Congress, and the decision to focus exclusively on the elderly, which eased concerns about what conservatives called "socialized medicine." Final passage confirmed the federal government's ability to act once the public had given its consent.

The program faces two challenges in the future. First, Medicare does not cover the cost of prescription drugs, which can be prohibitively expensive for the elderly. By 2000, with the surplus growing with each forecast, both parties agreed that Medicare should be expanded to include prescription drugs. By 2002, with the surplus gone, Congress

Medicaid
Federal program that provides medical benefits for low-income persons.

Medicare
National health insurance program for the elderly and disabled.

Major Legislation of the Great Society

1964

- *Civil Rights Act*—set forth the most comprehensive civil rights protections since Reconstruction
- *Food Stamp Act*—expanded the New Deal program to improve nutrition among the poor
- *Economic Opportunity Act*—provided for job training, adult education, and loans to small businesses to attack the roots of unemployment and poverty
- *Nurses Training Act*—created grants for training nurses and the construction of nursing schools
- *Omnibus Housing Act*—added four federal housing programs to existing programs
- *Community Mental Health Centers Act*—created federal grants for staffing mental health centers

1965

- *Medicare*—provided health care benefits for the elderly, linked to Social Security
- *Medicaid*—provided health care benefits for the poor, linked to Aid to Families with Dependent Children
- *Elementary and Secondary Education Act*—established federal funding and programs in public education for disadvantaged children
- *Higher Education Act*—established federal funding for colleges and college students
- *Department of Housing and Urban Development Act*—created a new department with responsibility for low-rent housing and urban renewal programs
- *Older Americans Act*—created the Administration on Aging and provided grants to the states

- *Voting Rights Act*—enforced the right to vote in federal elections within the state voting process

1966

- *Child Nutrition Act*—expanded federal programs to reduce childhood hunger
- *Fair Packaging and Labeling Act*—expanded federal oversight of consumer labeling
- *Department of Transportation Act*—created a new department with responsibility for public transportation, including urban mass transit

1967

- *Wholesome Meat Act*—expanded the federal government's role in regulating meatpacking plants
- *Age Discrimination Act*—prohibited discrimination based on age

1968

- *Housing and Urban Development Act*—expanded federal housing and urban development programs
- *Open Housing Act*—prohibited discrimination in housing
- *Omnibus Crime Control and Safe Streets Act*—provided federal aid for local law enforcement, crime prevention, and corrections programs
- *Wholesome Poultry Act*—expanded the federal role in regulating the poultry industry

SOURCE: *Congress and the Nation, 1945–1964: A Review of Government and Politics* (CQ Press, 1965); *Congress and the Nation, 1965–1968: A Review of Government and Politics During the Johnson Years* (CQ Press, 1969).

had cooled on the idea. Second, even without prescription drug coverage, Medicare costs are rising much faster than revenues. Under current projections, those costs will exhaust payroll taxes sometime in the next 15 years and continue rising through the 2020s when the baby boomers reach the later stages of life. By 2030, Medicare will cost roughly twice as much as it does today, rising from an amount that is equal to 2.7 percent of gross domestic product in 2000 to 5.3 percent in 2040 and consuming roughly a third of the entire federal budget.

Like the New Deal, the Great Society was generally seen as a Democratic initiative. Many Republicans argued then, and many still argue now, that the Great Society went too far in expanding the federal government's role, not to mention its budget. The Great Society was cut dramatically under Ronald Reagan's 1981 budget and again when Republicans recaptured Congress in 1994.[17] Nevertheless, as Figure 20-1 shows, the New Deal and Great Society programs still account for a large share of the federal budget today.

Reforming Welfare

Republicans have not been the only critics of the New Deal and Great Society welfare programs. President Bill Clinton declared that "the era of big government is over"[18] in his 1996 State of the Union Address and soon acted on his promise to "end welfare as we know it."[19]

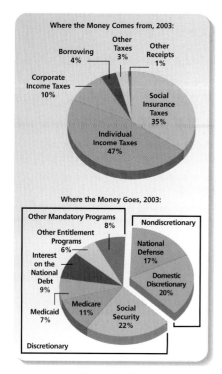

FIGURE 20–1   **The Federal Government Dollar: Where It Goes.**

SOURCE: Office of Management and Budget, *Budget of the United States Government, Fiscal Year 2003* (U.S. Government Printing Office, 2002).

Welfare Reform: Has It Worked?

There are several ways to measure the success of the 1996 welfare reform. One is simply to ask whether the number of welfare recipients has declined. The answer is absolutely clear as the table shows. In 2001, the number of welfare recipients was lower than it had been in more than three decades. As the authors of a 2002 study of welfare reform argue, "The welfare rolls have declined greatly, more mothers than ever are working, the average income of female-headed families is increasing, and poverty has dropped substantially."*

Yet merely reducing the number of welfare recipients is no guarantee that they either have good-paying jobs or are moving out of poverty. It is one thing to remove a recipient from the welfare rolls and quite another to get the person into a good job with decent benefits. Research suggests that most mothers who leave welfare make $7 to 8 per hour, well above the minimum wage. However, most mothers who leave welfare have other expenses, such as transportation and child care, that may or may not be covered by state or local assistance, and many who go to work lose their food stamps and Medicaid, which means they are more dependent on food banks and have to go without preventive health care.

Moreover, there appears to be a substantial minority of welfare recipients who simply cannot find jobs. Before the 1996 reforms, hard-to-employ recipients could stay on the welfare rolls year after year. Since 1996, everyone has a five-year time limit. Research shows that some recipients simply cannot move into work, because of addictions, disabled children, domestic violence, low levels of education, or a lack of work experience. Simply put, there may be some recipients who will simply never find or hold a job.

*Drawn from assorted chapters in Isabel V. Sawhill, R. Kent Weaver, Ron Haskins, and Andrea Kane, eds., *Welfare Reform and Beyond: The Future of the Safety Net* (Brookings Institution, 2002), p. 19.

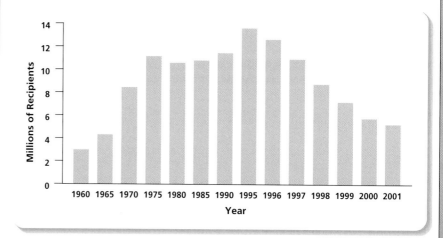

Number of Welfare Recipients.

SOURCE: Administration for Children and Families, Department of Health and Human Services, 2002, http://www.ocf.hhs.gov/news/welfare/index.htm.

Working with the new Republican congressional majority, Clinton won passage of the Personal Responsibility and Work Opportunity Reconciliation Act in 1996, which replaced AFDC with Temporary Assistance for Needy Families (TANF). Its name captures two themes of the new act—individuals should take more responsibility for themselves, and work, not welfare, is the goal of public assistance.

The burden of administering the new program was shifted entirely to the states. The federal government now gives *block grants* of money to the states and generally requires that the states match those funds. Federally funded public assistance is limited to five years over a person's lifetime; recipients must engage in work activities within two months of receiving benefits. States can exempt up to 20 percent of cases from the work

SHOULD THE FEDERAL GOVERNMENT ENCOURAGE WELFARE RECIPIENTS TO GET MARRIED?

You Decide... Although the 1996 welfare reform focused most on replacing welfare with work, it also ordered the federal government to promote marriage. Advocates argue that marriage improves the lives of both children and parents. Married adults, whether women or men, are happier, healthier, and wealthier than their unmarried peers and are more likely to give their children a healthier start. Some advocates even argue that more marriages would reduce health costs by reducing depression and crime.

The federal government can promote marriage in two ways. First, it can reduce the penalties it imposes on welfare recipients who get married. Under current law, for example, a single mother working full time at a minimum-wage job who marries stands to lose as much as $8,000 a year in cash and non-cash benefits. Second, it can promote marriage through advertising, counseling, or even cash grants for getting married to be paid out over a period of years.

Thinking It Through... Although the federal government has long engaged in activities designed to promote good social behavior, such as early childhood vaccinations, campaigns against smoking, the use of seat belts, and the 55-mile-an-hour speed limit, not all Americans believe that marriage is the answer to welfare. They note that domestic violence and child abuse occur almost as frequently among parents in married as in unmarried households. They also worry that government grants for marriage would promote a rash of false marriages designed to get the cash.

Most important, opponents believe that the best way to encourage marriage among welfare recipients is to find them good-paying jobs. They look to states such as Minnesota that have created strong welfare-to-work programs that do not punish married women for getting a job. Married women who entered Minnesota's Family Investment Program were a third more likely to still be married three years later than married women who stayed in the old welfare system. In theory, good-paying jobs lead to higher self-esteem, which leads to a sustainable marriage.

requirements and lifetime limits—an exemption intended for blind and disabled persons. The law originally excluded legal immigrants from many welfare programs, but at the strong urging of the governors, most welfare benefits were later restored to legal immigrants. To discourage persons on welfare from moving to states with more generous assistance payments, the law gave states the option of limiting welfare to newcomers from other states. This provision was declared unconstitutional by a federal district court judge, who said it "denies 'equal protection of the laws' to indigent families moving from one state to another."[20]

Besides confirming the fundamental American belief in rugged individualism, the 1996 welfare bill has significant ramifications for our federal system. This *devolution* of power to the states in the area of welfare is seen as a testing ground for the future. Depending on how well the states perform their new responsibilities, there may be a resurgence in the role played by the states in setting and implementing social policy. If the states are creative and successful in enacting welfare reform, other federal programs and powers may also be handed down to the states.

Since passage of welfare reform in 1996, the number of people on welfare has declined in every state except Hawaii. In fact, during the first three years, the number of families receiving welfare decreased nationally by 1.9 million, or 43 percent of the total number of families receiving welfare.[21]

Social Policy Challenges for the Future: Health, Education, and Crime

Social policy is clearly a major part of the federal government's agenda today. As Table 20-3 shows, human resource spending for programs such as Social Security, Medicare, Medicaid, and child nutrition has more than doubled since 1950. Spending is almost certain to rise in coming years as the baby boom generation enters retirement and starts to draw down the Social Security surplus and use Medicare. Moreover, the federal social policy agenda will almost certainly expand as Congress and the president respond to public pressure for action on health care, education, and crime control.

Health Care

Medicare is just one of the federal government's many health programs. It has been involved in reducing disease since 1887 when the federal government opened a one-room laboratory on Staten Island, New York, to study infectious diseases carried to the United States on passenger ships. In time, that one-room laboratory expanded into the National Institutes of Health (NIH), a conglomeration of 37 separate institutes on a 300-acre campus in Bethesda, Maryland.

The surgeon general of the United States is arguably the most visible health care official in government. As head of the Public Health Service (PHS), the surgeon general works closely with the NIH. Researchers in these institutes, working closely with experts in private laboratories, study causes and seek cures for serious diseases. Fellowships for health research are granted to able scientists and physicians. The NIH grants billions of dollars each year to support the research of university and other scientists and physicians. The PHS also administers grants to states and local communities to help improve public health. Another federal agency promoting health is the Food and Drug Administration (FDA).

There are dozens of other federal agencies that work to improve public health, however. The Centers for Disease Control and Prevention (CDC) in Atlanta is also intimately involved in preventing disease. The CDC and its 7,800 "disease detectives" have been at the forefront of identifying a host of mystery illnesses, including the respiratory disease that attacked attendees at an American Legion convention in 1968 (Legionnaire's disease), toxic shock syndrome in 1980, and hepatitis C in 1989, while tracking down the causes of major health disasters, including the outbreak of food poisoning at Jack-in-the-Box hamburger outlets in Washington State in 1993, the emergence of a new strain of flu in 1997, and the malicious use of a highly sophisticated strain of anthrax in 2001.

The CDC has a role in homeland defense by preparing the nation for a possible biological attack. That means preparing stockpiles of vaccines and pharmaceuticals that can be delivered to any site within 12 hours of an incident, monitoring disease outbreaks through a "sentinel" system that involves emergency rooms and infectious disease specialists across the country, and issuing guidelines on everything from mail handling to diagnosing new forms of biological or chemical attack. In late November 2001, the CDC purchased 155 million doses of smallpox vaccine to make sure the nation was protected against this deadly potential form of biological terrorism.

TABLE 20–3 Changing Priorities in the Federal Budget

Function	1950	1960	1970	1980	1990	2000	2005 (est.)
National defense	32%	52%	42%	23%	24%	15%	18%
Human resources	33	28	39	53	49	64	68
Physical resources	7	9	8	11	10	5	5
Interest on the debt	11	8	8	10	15	13	8

SOURCE: Budget of the United States, 2002.

Despite its success in making the nation healthier, the federal government faces two major health care challenges in the future: containing costs and expanding coverage.

THE RISING COST OF HEALTH CARE   Health care costs in the United States have nearly quadrupled, after controlling for inflation, since 1970.[22] Even as our economy has grown, the share of it devoted to health care has grown even faster. Pharmaceutical costs have soared, and the costs of children's vaccines have risen 1,000 percent in one decade.[23]

All Americans pay for the increasing costs. Employers directly pay a large share of the costs of health insurance; about 6 percent of employee compensation is the cost of health care.[24] Consumers also pay more for health care, whether through increased private insurance premiums, deductibles, or copayments for services. Finally, taxpayers pay for the increases through federal dollars that might otherwise go to other programs such as homeland security, college loans, or highway construction (see Figure 20-2).

The good news is that costs have risen in part because people live longer. Life expectancy increased by more than five years between 1970 and 1995. Most experts believe it will rise another year by 2010, in part because of advanced treatments, such as the "cocktail" of drugs for battling HIV-AIDS.[25] In 1900, only one out of every 25 Americans was over the age of 65. By 1950, the number was one in 12 and by 1985, one in nine. By 2030, it will be one in five. In 1900, the average American lived to age 47; by 2000, the average had increased to 79; by 2030, the number will be in the mid-eighties.

As people live longer, of course, they place greater demands on the health care system. New and advanced medical technology—life-support systems, ultrasound, sophisticated x-ray equipment, and genetic counseling—have all increased the costs of health care. They also place greater demands on other social policies such as Social Security.

The bad news is that some costs have nothing to do with saving lives or preventing disease. Some physicians claim that they have to perform procedures that may be medically unnecessary but are legally essential to reduce the risk of being sued by patients. These procedures are alleged to add up to billions in unnecessary costs, but they do not improve the quality of care provided to patients.[26] To avoid malpractice suits, for example, obstetricians may perform more than 300,000 unnecessary Caesarean sections each year.[27] Critics also accuse hospitals of charging high prices for items that are not used or not needed. Since few patients are knowledgeable enough to audit their hospital bills, insurance companies must monitor these expenses.

Physicians also complain about the high cost of malpractice insurance, nine times more costly in the United States than in Canada. Malpractice insurance costs for all physicians have more than doubled in a decade. A physician's insurance coverage routinely costs as much as $60,000 a year.[28] For specialists like obstetricians, premiums are 400 percent higher than for internists.[29]

Trial lawyers who represent people whose health was damaged or families of those whose lives were lost due to medical malpractice defend the huge punitive awards. They argue that physicians, like all professionals, have a responsibility to exercise sound professional judgment in their jobs, and when they do not, they should provide restitution to their victims.

Moreover, at least part of the cost crisis is avoidable. Medicare alone spends billions of dollars each year treating smoking-related diseases, and over the next 20 years, the costs to treat such diseases will continue to rise.[30] Other illnesses at least partly related to lifestyle include heart disease, liver disease, and AIDS. In an effort to recover some of the money spent treating illnesses related to cancer, states sued tobacco companies and won a $206 billion dollar settlement in 1998.[31] Much of this settlement money has gone to campaigns discouraging tobacco use, especially among young people.

COVERING THE UNINSURED   While most Americans have the best health care their money can buy, the nation has yet to develop a comprehensive insurance program for the approximately 44 million Americans who have no health insurance and are not covered by Medicaid.[32] Although some rely on public clinics, emergency room care, or charity, many people go without any health or dental care.[33] Many of the uninsured have jobs, but their employers do

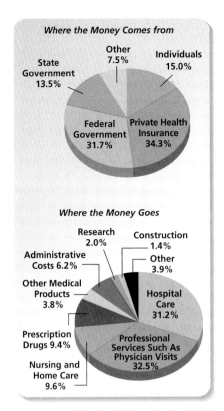

FIGURE 20–2   The Health Care Dollar, 2000.

SOURCE: Centers for Medicare and Medicaid Services, at http://www.cms.hhs.gov/statitics/nhe.

not provide health insurance, and because their incomes are above the poverty line, they do not qualify for Medicaid. Uninsured individuals usually seek care in hospital emergency rooms only when their illness has reached a critical stage. Postponing medical care drives up costs because critical care is much more expensive than preventive medicine or early treatment.

But it is not just the poor who are uninsured. People who change jobs may often go without coverage for several months before their new insurance takes effect. And people with serious medical conditions may find the insurance company unwilling to cover their expenses, claiming that the illness is a "preexisting condition." Some insurance companies set caps on their coverage, meaning that families coping with very expensive illnesses end up essentially uninsured.

Although there are many different proposals for health care reform, the essential approaches include a single-payer system, prepaid health plans, employer-mandated coverage, spending caps, individual responsibility, and medical savings accounts.

Single Payer.   Under a single-payer system, the national government, using broad-based taxes, covers the costs of health care and hospitalization and sets the rates. Like the system in Canada, such a plan would provide universal coverage and benefits to *all* Americans. No longer would people need to worry about the costs of catastrophic illnesses or a change in jobs that would exclude them from coverage. Proponents claim that the single-payer system would save billions of dollars in administrative expenses by reducing the number of insurers from about 1,200 to 1. Opponents of the single-payer system claim it would lead to a bureaucratic mess, with little incentive for innovation, cost control, or diversity of coverage. They further claim that the government would be put in the position of deciding which procedures to pay for and how to ration access to these procedures. As a result, they contend, Americans would lose not only quality in their health care but their freedom of choice as well.

Business leaders generally oppose single-payer coverage out of concern for costs and what the program would do to taxes and the federal budget. The American Medical Association, U.S. Chamber of Commerce, Health Insurance Association of America, and other interest groups representing health care providers oppose the single-payer system. Labor unions, some senior citizens groups, and most consumer groups advocate this type of plan.

Prepaid Health Plans.   Cost containment has been a frequent refrain of large corporations and consumer groups. In the 1970s and 1980s, business owners reduced benefits, increased payments by employees, and encouraged employees to join managed care plans called **health maintenance organizations (HMOs)** in which individuals or their employees pay a set amount for each person covered each year in return for health care and hospital coverage. During the 1980s and 1990s, HMO enrollment increased fourfold, from just under 10 million in 1980 to almost 80 million patients in 1999.[34] Most HMOs guarantee access, but many do not guarantee that a patient can see the same physician.

Because there are no national standards of heath care quality, consumer groups are pressing HMOs to improve treatment of specific conditions and are urging Congress and the president to enter the battle.[35] HMOs counter that they provide adequate care at reasonable costs and that national standards would drive up costs. Consumers want the reduced costs associated with HMOs but do not like the limitations on choice of physicians and the right to sue health plans or the lack of coverage for some procedures.[36]

The quality of HMO care and limitations on patient choice became political issues in the 2000 elections. Both parties endorsed competing variations of what they call a "patient's bill of rights." Such a bill of rights would permit a woman to see a gynecologist as her primary care physician, allow for review of the need for medical procedures, leave it to the doctor to determine the length of stay in the hospital, require coverage of emergency care a "prudent layperson" would deem necessary, and remove rules that deny doctors permission to talk to patients. George W. Bush called for granting HMO patients the right to appeal denials of care to an independent review panel, providing report cards on HMOs, giving women direct access to their obstetrician-gynecologist, and in some cases

health maintenance organization (HMO)
Alternative means of health care in which people or their employers are charged a set amount and the HMO provides health care and covers hospital costs.

being able to sue HMOs. Even though both presidential nominees called for expanded rights for HMO consumers, legislation on this matter after the election consistently stalled in both houses, due in part to an aggressive advertising campaign against the reforms that was funded by insurance companies and HMOs.

Employer-Mandated Coverage.   Currently more than 160 million Americans get some form of medical insurance as a benefit that goes with their job.[37] But many small businesses contend that they cannot afford to provide this benefit and stay in business. Some have estimated that the costs of health care for small businesses may be 10 to 40 percent higher than for large businesses. In businesses with fewer than 25 employees, only about one-third of the workers receive coverage directly from their employer.[38] Mandating coverage does not solve this problem, nor does it take care of individuals who do not have jobs.

It takes banks of computers for HMO employees to organize and run the bureaucracy of managed health care.

Proponents counter that the negative consequences can be mitigated through tax credits and government subsidies. They also point out that if all small businesses provide health insurance, none of them will be put at a disadvantage compared to other small businesses. As noted, the federal government allows businesses to deduct what they pay in health benefits to employees as a business expense and gives tax credits to low-income families to purchase coverage for their children.

Spending Caps.   Because the cost of providing health care each year consumes a larger and larger share of our gross domestic product, some have proposed that the national government impose an overall expenditure cap on health care that applies not only to public expenditures but to private ones as well. Supporters of a cap include some prominent Democrats. The American Hospital Association, American Medical Association, and Pharmaceutical Manufacturers Association vigorously oppose the idea. They argue that spending caps would limit research and development in medicine and deter talented young people from pursuing medical careers.

Individual Responsibility for Coverage.   Another reform proposal is to apply a free market approach to health care by abolishing *all* employer-provided benefits and encouraging individuals to buy health insurance on their own, in much the same way that individuals are responsible for purchasing their own automobile insurance. Those with low incomes, including people not now insured, would have tax credits or vouchers to assist in the purchase of insurance.

Advocates of such a market solution say that if individuals purchased their own insurance, they might pay more attention to costs and more closely monitor doctor and hospital fees. When higher wages are combined with tax credits, some individuals could end up with improved benefits tailored to their individual needs. Such a plan would also eliminate the need to impose price controls or pay for a large health care bureaucracy. It is unlikely, however, that employees would recover all they now spend on health care from their employers, so costs to individual consumers might increase. It is also unlikely that all uninsured persons who need government assistance could be taken care of without a tax increase to pay for it. Perhaps most important, such a proposal would run into so much political opposition that it presents an unlikely alternative.

Medical Savings Accounts.   In 1996, Congress authorized an experiment with **medical savings accounts.** Individuals may make tax-deductible contributions of $1,462 a year ($3,375 for a couple) to a special medical savings account that can be used to pay medical expenses.[39] Withdrawals for other purposes are taxable and subject to an early withdrawal penalty.

Supporters of medical savings accounts say that they will eventually lower health care costs by giving people the incentive to spend their own money more carefully. They also allow people to go to a doctor of their own choosing without prior approval from their insurance company. Opponents of medical savings accounts say that they amount to nothing more than a tax break for the wealthy and the healthy. Because of high deductibles, people may decide

medical savings account
Alternative means of health care in which individuals make tax-deductible contributions to a special account that can be used to pay medical expenses.

not to seek needed services and preventive care. Opponents also argue that because healthier people are more likely to sign up for medical savings accounts, sicker people pay higher insurance premiums. Older and less wealthy people will not be able to afford to invest in medical savings accounts, critics charge, and will be forced to depend on more expensive insurance.

Improving Education

Education has long been a state and local responsibility. Most children go to public schools run by local school boards and funded, at least partly, by property taxes. However, since local districts vary from areas with expensive homes to very poor neighborhoods, the funds available to local schools vary. Children from poor districts are much more likely to have lower-quality public schools than those from rich districts. Public schools vary in the quality of teacher preparation, student performance, dropout rates, and educational opportunities provided to minority students.

IN COMPARATIVE PERSPECTIVE

Health Care in Advanced Industrial Democracies

Advanced industrial democracies like Canada, Germany, Japan, the Netherlands, and the United Kingdom provide health care for their entire population either through national health insurance or a national health service. Although the United States outspends all these countries in terms of health expenditures as a percentage of gross domestic product (see chart), this high level of spending on health care does not mean that the United States has a healthier population. The nation's infant mortality rates, for instance, are among the worst of all industrialized countries, and the United States ranks below average for industrialized nations in male and female life expectancy at birth (see table).

The United States also differs from other countries in the extent to which health care costs are paid by public funds. Central or local governments fund approximately three-quarters of the cost of health care in most advanced industrial democracies.

In Canada, about 9 percent of the nation's GDP is devoted to health care spending, and all Canadians are covered by provincial health insurance. Canada's administration of health care is based on a publicly funded system, whereas the program in the United States is divided among public and private insurers. Canada's administrative costs per patient are only one-fourth the size of ours, and companies in the United States often pay three to five times more than Canadian companies to fund employee health and social benefits, including taxes collected by governments to pay for some of these benefits.

The Canadian health care system is not without its faults. Canadians are taxed at a much higher rate than Americans, in part to pay for the publicly funded system. In addition, patients may face delays in receiving services, especially for routine health problems and elective surgery. Doctors and nurses are also paid less in Canada, and thousands of them have moved to the United States, where salaries are much higher. Costs for health care are also increasing faster than the rate of inflation, and the Canadian federal and provincial governments have begun to cut back on funding certain services. Nevertheless, most Canadians express satisfaction with their health care system, and Canada manages to insure all of its people while spending far less per capita than the United States spends.

Infant Mortality and Life Expectancy Rates, 2000

Country	Infant Morality*	Life Expectancy† for Men (years)	Life Expectancy† for Women (years)
Japan	3.4	77.1	84.0
France	4.3	75.0	82.5
Germany	4.5	74.7	80.7
Switzerland	4.6	76.8	82.5
Canada	5.3	76.3	81.7
United Kingdom	5.8	75.0	79.8
United States	7.1	73.9	79.4

SOURCE: Organization for Economic Cooperation and Development, Health Data, 2002, www.oecd.org.

*Deaths of children under one year of age per 1,000 live births in a calendar year.

†Number of years a person born in 2002 can be expected to live.

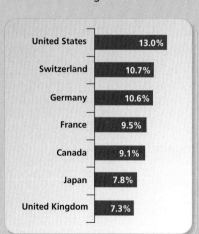

Total Health Care Expenditures as a Share of Gross Domestic Product, 1996.

SOURCE: Organization for Economic Cooperation and Development, Health Data, 2002.

This inequality is only part of the reason for federal involvement in education. The federal government's first involvement in education policy was with the Northwest Ordinance of 1785, in which Congress set aside one section in each township for support of a public school. In 1862, the Morrill Land Grant Act provided grants of land to states for universities specializing in the mechanical or agricultural arts. The U.S. Office of Education was established in 1867 to oversee these programs, but the scope of federal involvement was modest by today's standards. In 1944, Congress passed the G.I. Bill, which paid college or university tuition and living expenses for World War II veterans. The G.I. Bill helped provide a college education for approximately 20 million veterans. (Table 20-4 provides a breakdown of current federal funding for higher education.)

During the cold war, education became one part of the national defense. When the Soviet Union launched *Sputnik*—the first man-made satellite to orbit the earth—in 1957, Congress responded in 1958 by passing the National Defense Education Act to upgrade science, language, and mathematics courses.

In 1964, Congress created the Head Start program for preschool children plus college-level work-study programs. The following year, Congress passed the Elementary and Secondary Education Act (ESEA), which supplied educational materials for underprivileged public school students and provided funding for research on how to assist children from disadvantaged backgrounds. Yet even with this expanded role, the federal government today provides less than 10 cents of every dollar spent on education by state and local governments.[40] Still intact is local control over school construction, curriculum, teacher salaries, teacher standards, and governance.

The federal government has taken a keen interest, however, in dismantling state-imposed racial segregation in schools. As noted in Chapter 18, the Supreme Court's landmark 1954 decision in *Brown* v. *Board of Education of Topeka* held that maintaining "separate but equal" public schools is unconstitutional. This decision gave the federal government an added incentive to help states improve schools for poor and underprivileged students of all races and put added pressure on local school officials to end segregation.

College and university students also benefit from federal funding. Today, more than one-third of all college students receive some federal financial aid.[41] Pell grants for low-income students and low-interest guaranteed student loans continue to be the most available and most used subsidies for college expenses.

Americans ask more of their schools than just to educate their children. Schools have become one-stop social policy centers and are now a major means by which basic nutri-

TABLE 20–4 Federal Aid to Higher Education, 2000

Program	Funding	Percent of Total
Student Financial Aid	$13.8 billion	89%
Pell grants	7.6 billion	49
Other loans	4.5 billion	29
Other campus-based aid	1.7 billion	11
Nonfinancial Aid	1.8 billion	12
TRIO programs for disadvantaged students	650 million	4
GEAR-UP college readiness	200 million	1
Grants to schools of education for teacher training	200 million	1
Other	900 million	6

SOURCE: Louis Dickson Rice and Arthur Hauptman, "Moving Beyond Student Aid," *Brookings Conference Report No. 3,* July 2000, p. 1.

Sarah Brady campaigned tirelessly to get the Brady Handgun Violence Prevention Act passed. She became a vocal advocate for gun control after her husband, James Brady, President Ronald Reagan's White House Press Secretary, was shot on March 30, 1981. Brady was shot by John Hinckley Jr. during his failed assassination attempt on President Reagan.

tion is provided to millions of poor children. Schools screen at-risk children and attempt to get them medical and psychological assistance; they seek to socialize students into acceptable behaviors, often in the face of increasing violence in the surrounding neighborhoods; and they often reach out to families to provide basic help in parenting. The presence of police officers in most American high schools is relatively new and speaks to the problems of maintaining some minimal control over violence, drugs, and gangs.

Controlling Crime

Controlling crime is primarily a state and local matter. The federal government usually acts more as a banker than a police officer, providing grants to states and local governments to hire their own police officers, build more prisons, improve drug enforcement, and prosecute organized crime.

Crime is hardly unimportant to national politics, however. The federal government must enforce its own laws against everything from counterfeiting to pollution while protecting its borders and preventing drugs from flowing into the country.

Congress has intervened on such matters as gun control. Because guns are manufactured and transported across state lines, Congress has the power to regulate sales under the Constitution's commerce clause and has used it to ban the sale and ownership of semiautomatic weapons and assault rifles and set age minimums for the purchase of handguns (21 years of age) and long guns such as rifles and shotguns (18 years of age).

In 1993, for example, Congress passed landmark legislation imposing a waiting period on the purchase of handguns. Under the Brady Handgun Violence Prevention Act, federally licensed firearms dealers have five days to check with local law enforcement officials regarding the background of a potential purchaser. If local law enforcement officials fail to respond within five business days, the handgun can be sold. The National Rifle Association has been powerful enough to stop most other antigun legislation, even though such legislation has had the support of most police chiefs and most of the general public. The debate over gun control at the local, state, and national levels remains intense.

In 1994, Congress passed an omnibus anticrime bill that authorized over $30 billion in spending on federal crime initiatives. The money funded the hiring of as many as 100,000 new police officers and constructing new prisons and "boot camps" for juvenile offenders. The bill also added new assault rifle restrictions, made a long list of federal offenses punishable by death, imposed federal penalties and programs aimed at curbing domestic violence, and, with its "three strikes and you're out" provision, mandated life imprisonment upon conviction for a third violent felony.

The federal government enforces its laws primarily through the Department of Justice, which contains the Federal Bureau of Investigation (FBI). The FBI was created in 1908 and charged with gathering and reporting evidence in matters relating to federal criminal laws. In addition, the FBI provides investigative services on a cooperative basis to local law enforcement in fingerprint identification and laboratory services. Other law enforcement agencies of the federal government include the Drug Enforcement Agency, which is responsible for preventing the flow of illegal narcotics into the United States, patroling U.S. borders, and conducting joint operations with countries where drugs are produced, and the Bureau of Alcohol, Tobacco and Firearms, which monitors the sale of destructive weapons and guns inside the United States, regulates alcoholic beverage production, and oversees the collection of taxes on alcohol and tobacco.

Although the number of violent crimes decreased through the 1990s, it began rising in 2001, reinforcing the widespread perception that crime and violence are increasing and the federal government needs to step in. As a result, Congress has made more and more crimes federal ones and increased the severity of punishments for them. As more people are put in prisons, the costs for building and running them has increased dramatically.

Terrorism is clearly the federal government's top crime priority today. For its part, Congress passed a massive antiterrorism law in October 2001 and created the new Department of Homeland Security the following summer. For his part, the president created the Office of Homeland Security within the White House in October and ordered a complete reorganization of the Federal Bureau of Investigation in early 2002 to create a stronger focus on preventing terrorism. Under the USA PATRIOT Act of 2001 (the letters stand for Uniting and Strengthening America by Providing Appropriate Tools Required to Intercept and Obstruct Terrorism), for example, the federal government was given sweeping authority to conduct secret investigations of suspected terrorists, use "roving wiretaps" to intercept conversations on any phones that a suspect might use, and detain any noncitizens believed to be a national security risk for up to seven days without being charged with a crime.

Legislation has been proposed to require purchasers of guns at gun shows to undergo an identity check on whether they have a record of criminal activity.

The Politics of Social Policy

Despite the recent focus on terrorism and homeland security, social policy now dominates the agenda of American politics. Welfare, health care, education, and crime—and their costs—are today's political battleground between the parties and between contending interest groups. Education reform was at the forefront of the 2000 election; Social Security and prescription drug coverage played a role in the 2002 midterm elections.

Is Crime Rising?

According to the Federal Bureau of Investigation, the number of violent crimes went up in 2001, after nine years of decline. Murders were up 3.1 percent from 2000, robberies up 3.9 percent, arson up 2.0 percent, and car theft up 5.9 percent. Although some of the increase could be explained by the stagnating economy, experts predicted that crime is likely to rise well into the future because of at least three other factors.

First, state and local governments are releasing more prisoners, in part because of overcrowding in their jails and in part because sentences imposed during the crack cocaine epidemic of the 1980s are expiring. In 2000, for example, states and localities released more than 600,000 convicts, at least some of whom committed new crimes to feed old habits. Second, crime went down in the 1990s in large part because of a decline in the number of teenagers, who are the most likely segment of the population to commit crimes. Now that the number of teenagers is again rising, so is the crime rate. Third, some experts argue that persistent poverty in the nation's urban centers has generated a new kind of supercriminal that is more violent and active than the traditional felon.

As the number of crimes increases, the public will almost certainly put more pressure on the federal government to act. However, it is not clear what, if anything, the federal government can do to reduce crime caused by the trends we have described. Nor is it clear that toughened state laws have done much to deter crime. According to criminologist John J. Di Iulio, "given the abused, neglected, and otherwise severely at-risk life circumstances of most youth who go on to become serious offenders, and given estimates that as many as 60 percent of the most serious youth criminals are never caught or convicted, it is a profound mistake to think that violent crimes by and against juveniles can be prevented or controlled simply or mainly by increasing the punitiveness of the juvenile justice system, let alone by

incarcerating convicted juvenile felons in cells next to convicted adult felons."* Getting tough by treating juveniles as adults may be the least effective path to lower crime rates.

Instead of building more prisons, the federal government might make a bigger impact on crime through more spending on drug treatment. Drug treatment is available for barely half of the people who need it. The federal government could also put its funding behind mandatory treatment programs for prisoners, parolees, and convicted felons. As of now, the treatment system is largely voluntary, meaning that addicts can come or go as they please.

*John J. Di Iulio Jr., "Federal Crime Policy: Time for a Moratorium," *Brookings Review*, vol. 17 (Winter 1999), p. 21.

Changing Crime Rates, 1997–2001

	1997–1998	1998–1999	1999–2000	2000–2001
Violent Crime Index	−6.4%	−6.7%	−0.1%	+0.3%
Murder	−7.1	−8.5	−0.1	+3.1
Rape	−3.2	−4.3	+0.9	+0.2
Robbery	−10.4	−8.4	−0.4	+3.9
Aggravated assault	−4.8	−6.2	−0.1	−1.4
Burglary	−5.3	−10.0	−2.4	+2.6
Larceny	−4.8	−5.7	+0.2	+1.4
Car theft	−8.4	−7.7	+1.2	+5.9
Arson	−6.6	−3.6	+0.4	+2.0

SOURCE: Federal Bureau of Investigation, *Uniform Crime Reports*, June 24, 2002.

The nation long ago answered questions about whether the national government has a role in providing decent housing, adequate health care, and a solid education for all of its citizens. The answer—to use Ronald Reagan's phrase—is that government provides a "safety net" for those who cannot provide for themselves. But how to provide that net is very much debated. And what we can afford and are willing to pay for expanded social services is the problem. The policy battles of recent years have demonstrated that expensive national social policy programs are unlikely to pass. But a party or a president who ignores the social policy area is in political peril. Most voters expect public officials to improve education, reduce crime, save Social Security, and expand health care. Such an expansive agenda invites continued political debate and competition.

Summary

1. Conservatives advocate private solutions for most social problems, while liberals argue that it is the responsibility of government to provide a minimum standard of living—including a job, an education, health care, housing, and nutrition—for all citizens. Since the New Deal, some national government involvement in social programs has been widely accepted, although the extent of involvement has waxed and waned. Conservatives generally prefer state and local government action over federal programs.

2. Social Security, inaugurated in 1935 as part of the New Deal, is perhaps the most significant social legislation in U.S. history. Through a system of employee and employer taxes, retired workers and disabled individuals receive monthly payments and health benefits. With the country's changing demographic profile, strains on the system are likely to increase.

3. Welfare takes many forms, including direct payments to the poor, the unemployed, and the disabled; food stamps; job training; housing subsidies; free school lunches; tax credits; and subsidized medical care. Public assistance programs began with the New Deal and have grown ever since.

4. Welfare has long been criticized as creating disincentives to work, and many proposals have been put forward to make programs more effective and efficient. The most recent welfare reform, which became law in August 1996, transferred the administrative burden to the states, giving them more discretion over recipients and benefits while helping to fund welfare programs through block grants of federal money.

5. The federal government supports medical research and has increased its role in health care cost control and access as the country's mostly private health care system is beset by rising costs, increasing numbers of uninsured Americans, unnecessary procedures, endless paperwork, high litigation costs, avoidable illnesses, and limited access. A variety of proposals for reform are under consideration, including a single-payer system, prepaid health plans, employer-mandated coverage, spending caps, individual responsibility for coverage, and medical savings accounts.

6. Education continues to be primarily a state and local government function in the United States. The federal government plays an important role in funding public schools and pushing national goals for better education.

7. Crime control has been forced onto the national agenda by public perceptions of increases in crime and violence and by politicians eager to accuse opponents of being "soft on crime." Although crime rates declined from 1991 to 2000, they rose in 2001 and are expected to continue upward.

Key Terms

entitlements

means-tested entitlements

public assistance

social insurance

Social Security

Medicaid

Medicare

health maintenance organization (HMO)

medical savings account

Further Reading

ANNE MARIE CAMMISA, *From Rhetoric to Reform? Welfare Policy in American Politics* (Westview Press, 1998).

BARBARA EHRENREICH, *Nickled and Dimed: On (Not) Getting By in America* (Metropolitan Books, 2001).

FRANK FISCHER, *Evaluating Public Policy* (Nelson-Hall, 1995).

LAURENE A. GRAIG, *Health of Nations: An International Perspective on U.S. Health Care Reform* (CQ Press, 1993).

CHRISTOPHER JENCKS, *The Homeless* (Harvard University Press, 1994).

PAUL C. LIGHT, *Still Artful Work: The Continuing Politics of Social Security Reform* (McGraw-Hill, 1995).

THOMAS E. MANN AND NORMAN J. ORNSTEIN, EDS., *Intensive Care: How Congress Shapes Health Policy* (Brookings Institution, 1995).

DANIEL PATRICK MOYNIHAN, *Miles to Go: A Personal History of Social Policy* (Harvard University Press, 1996).

CHARLES MURRAY, *Losing Ground: American Social Policy, 1950–80* (Basic Books, 1984).

DAVID OSBORNE AND TED GAEBLER, *Reinventing Government: How the Entrepreneurial Spirit Is Transforming the Public Sector* (Addison-Wesley, 1992).

B. GUY PETERS, *American Public Policy: Promise and Performance,* 4th ed. (Chatham House, 1996).

FRANCES FOX PIVEN AND RICHARD A. CLOWARD, *Regulating the Poor: The Functions of Public Welfare* (Vintage, 1993).

THEDA SKOCPOL, *Social Policy in the United States: Future Possibilities in Historical Perspective* (Princeton University Press, 1995).

R. KENT WEAVER, *Ending Welfare as We Know It* (Brookings Institution, 2001).

MARGARET WEIR, ED., *The Social Divide: Political Parties and the Future of Activist Government* (Brookings Institution, 1998).

BOB WOODWARD, *Agenda: Inside the Clinton White House* (Simon & Schuster, 1994).

21
CHAPTER

MAKING FOREIGN AND DEFENSE POLICY

T HE EVENTS OF SEPTEMBER 11, 2001, CAUSED A FUNDAMENTAL SHIFT IN U.S. FOREIGN AND DEFENSE POLICY. IN AN INSTANT, old adversaries such as Pakistan, Russia, and Yemen became essential allies, and old friends such as Egypt and Saudi Arabia became question marks.[1]

Before September 11, for example, Pakistan was definitely an adversary. The United States was deeply worried about Pakistan's nuclear weapons program, angry at the military leaders who had replaced Pakistan's democratic government in 1999, and sharply critical of Pakistani support for militants fighting India's rule of the border state of Kashmir. The United States had cut off its foreign aid to Pakistan and had implemented strict prohibitions against trade.

After September 11, Pakistan needed to become a friend. Working through secret channels, the president demanded that Pakistan close its border with neighboring Afghanistan, cutting off an escape route for Osama bin Laden and his al-Qaeda network of terrorists. Pakistan not only complied but also declared its support for the U.S. war against terrorism, thereby muting criticism that the United States was waging war alone. In return, the United States lifted its prohibitions against trade, guaranteed $1 billion in aid, and agreed to help Pakistan reduce its huge international debt.

Relationships with other nations were not the only thing that changed as the United States moved against terrorism. Speaking before Congress only nine days after the attacks on New York City and Washington, D.C., President George W. Bush made clear his intent to treat any nation that harbors and supports terrorism as a hostile regime. Whereas the world was once divided into prodemocratic and antidemocratic nations, the new Bush Doctrine, as it quickly became labeled, seemed to put the world in two very different camps. One was composed of nations that agreed with the U.S. stance against terrorism, regardless of whether they were pro- or antidemocratic, while the other was composed of nations that gave even the slightest support to terrorism.

The question is whether the Bush Doctrine should preempt all the other U.S. foreign and defense priorities. Although the war against terrorism has reframed the international agenda, many traditional issues remain to be addressed, including trade, global warming, human rights, and reducing the threat of nuclear war. It is entirely possible that some nations will be on the right side in the war against terrorism but on the wrong side of opening their borders to trade, controlling weapons of mass destruction, or strengthening human rights.

Making foreign and defense policy involves hard choices between just such issues. Presidents must decide how hard to push on one issue before they will lose all influence over another, when to isolate a potential adversary such as Iran or Pakistan, and whether to use traditional diplomacy as a tool of implementation or the escalating force involved in economic sanctions and military action. They must also decide when the nation must act in concert with other nations, as the United States did with its North Atlantic Treaty Organization (NATO) allies in the war in Kosovo, or act unilaterally, as it mostly did in the war in Afghanistan.

This chapter will ask how the choices in making and executing foreign policy are changing in the wake of the 2001 terror attacks. We will first examine the foreign policy challenges before the nation today, including the new war against terrorism, then turn to the key actors in making foreign and defense policy, appraise the politics of making foreign and defense policy, and inventory the range of foreign and defense policy options. We will conclude with a more detailed assessment of defense policy.

Vital Interests in the Twenty-First Century

The framers of the U.S. Constitution did not have a grand strategy for using the basic tools of foreign and defense policy to preserve the nation and protect U.S. interests across the globe. Rather, they worried first about protecting the nation long enough to survive. Although the framers generally believed in free trade and hoped to protect their young nation from foreign threats, their general focus was on keeping the nation out of harm's way in Europe as it addressed its economic and domestic problems.

Toward these ends, the framers made three basic decisions that guide foreign policy to this day. First, they declared that foreign policy was a national, not state, responsibility. Even as the Constitution divided power between the president and Congress, Article I, Section 10 declares that no state shall enter into a treaty, alliance, or confederation with another nation, meaning that only the national government can conduct foreign policy.

Second, the framers concentrated the authority to make foreign and defense policy in the presidency. They gave the president sole authority to command the army and navy, make treaties, appoint ambassadors, and oversee the departments of government, thereby making the president both commander and diplomat in chief. The framers recognized that foreign policy could not be conducted by a collection of interests. The nation needed a single point of contact for representing what was then a very clearly defined national interest: survival.

Finally, having given the president authority to implement policy, the framers checked that power by giving Congress as a whole the power to declare war, raise an army and a navy, and make the rules of war and by giving the Senate the power to ratify all treaties by a two-thirds vote and confirm all ambassadors by a majority vote. Even as they made sure the national government could protect the United States against foreign threats through the use of armed force, they worried that a president might exploit that power to deny basic liberty. As John Jay argued in *The Federalist*, No. 4, "Absolute monarchs will often make war when their nations are to get nothing by it, but for purposes and objects merely personal, such as, a thirst for military glory." Madison was even more negative, arguing that war multiplies "the honours and emoluments of office" that the president enjoys, even as the 'laurels' that war produces grace the "executive brow." They wanted the decision to place American lives at risk to be made only when absolutely necessary.

Defining Vital U.S. Interests

In the broadest sense, the primary goal of U.S. foreign and defense policy goal is to protect the nation from harm, whether from other nations or individual terrorists, nuclear missiles, or suicide bombings. Over the past several generations, the United States has become involved in world affairs to a degree unprecedented in its history. Although much of this activity was due to the cold war against communism from 1945 to 1990, the sheer size and wealth of the United States makes it both a natural world leader and a target for extremism. There are other reasons as well. U.S. security and economic interests are inevitably tied to what happens in the rest of the world. Whether Americans like it or not, events far from home affect their life, liberty, and pursuit of happiness.

Balancing political, economic, and social values is critical in defining vital U.S. interests. Americans want peace, but not if it means that they must give up basic freedoms. Americans favor human rights, but not if it means less trade and fewer jobs. Americans support the general concept of a United Nations that represents all the nations of the world, but not if the United States must give up command of its own troops in U.N. missions. They want the United States to protect weaker nations against aggression, as long as not too many U.S. soldiers are put in harm's way. Where possible, they want to improve the standard of living in less developed nations and clean up the global environment, but they also want new markets for U.S. products, imports of raw materials, and adequate supplies of energy. The task of defining our interests requires extensive balancing of sometimes competing goals.

Making foreign and defense policy involves not simply defining U.S. interests but making tough choices about what to do, especially when resources are limited, risks are high, and U.S. objectives are sometimes in conflict. Policy making invariably involves deciding among options.

George W. Bush's national security adviser, Condoleezza Rice, outlined the priorities that the Bush White House believes will promote America's interests:

- To ensure that America's military can deter war, project power, and fight in defense of its interests if deterrence fails
- To promote economic growth and political openness by extending free trade and a stable international monetary system to all nations committed to these principles, including those in the Western Hemisphere, which has too often been neglected as a vital area of U.S. national interest
- To renew strong and intimate relationships with allies who share American values and can thus share the burden of promoting peace, prosperity, and freedom
- To focus U.S. energies on comprehensive relationships with the big powers, particularly Russia and China, that can and will mold the character of the international political system
- To deal decisively with the threat of rogue regimes and hostile powers, which is increasingly taking the form of the potential for terrorism and the development of weapons of mass destruction[2]

New Foreign Policy Challenges

"Gosh, I miss the Cold War," President Clinton said in 1993.[3] Many U.S. policy makers shared his view. It was not that they longed for the nuclear tensions of the 1960s or that they wanted to wage new wars in distant lands. Rather, they recognized that the world had become a far more complicated place for making foreign policy. Whereas the United States used to set its national interest in opposition to the Soviet Union, it must now think hard about where and how to engage. It must be clearer about the problems it wants to solve, the tools it has to deploy, and the ongoing implementation of its foreign policies.

Even small nations with limited resources can now have enormous influence on the rest of the world by building a single chemical, biological, or nuclear weapon. The Internet has made international borders virtually useless for stopping the flow of democratic ideas, while inexpensive air travel has made the movement of people much easier. As a result, the United States no longer has the power to simply declare a policy and assume that the rest of the world is listening. Even if the United States were to declare a new isolationism, citizens of other nations could easily visit the nation through the Internet or global financial markets.

The world is a much more unstable place than it was when the United States and Soviet Union faced off in the cold war. It was a war in which the two superpowers never fired a single bullet at each other but in which thousands of their soldiers died in wars trying to prevent the spread of communism (the wars in Korea and Vietnam) or expand their control (the 1979 Soviet invasion of Afghanistan).

But the U.S. victory over communism did not produce an instantly peaceful world. The elimination of totalitarian governments has led to the reemergence of ethnic nationalism in some areas of eastern Europe and the rise of fundamentalist governments in the Middle East and central Asia. Nations such as Yugoslavia and Czechoslovakia broke apart—the former with violence, the latter peacefully. The Middle East remains unsettled. Afghanistan turned from an ally of the United States in the fight against communism into a haven for the terrorists who planned the September 2001 attacks. And the "axis of evil" of Iraq, Iran, and North Korea, as Bush called it in early 2002, remain under totalitarian rule. In Africa, civil and national wars have resulted in the death of millions.

Primary Foreign Policy Goals

The United States has a long list of foreign and defense policy goals that span the globe. One day it might be working to promote peace between the Turkish and Greek governments over the tiny island of Cyprus; the next it might be arguing for free trade with South Vietnam, the restoration of democracy in Venezuela, or the release of hostages being held by rebels in the Philippines. Important though these day-to-day goals are, current U.S. foreign and defense policy is dominated by five major goals: winning the war on terrorism, controlling the spread of weapons of mass destruction, promoting U.S. trade, finding peace in the Middle East, and promoting democracy in the former Soviet Union. (Table 21-1 shows how public opinion on a number of foreign policy goals changed in the wake of the 2001 terrorist attacks.)

WINNING THE WAR ON TERRORISM   The United States was involved in fighting terrorism well before the 2000s. It began monitoring terrorist threats with the airplane hijackings of the 1970s, heightened its intelligence efforts after the 1993 World Trade Center bombings, and targeted Osama bin Laden and al-Qaeda after the August 1998 truck bombings of two U.S. embassies in Africa.

Nevertheless, the war against terrorism did not become a top foreign and defense priority until the September attacks showed just how determined terrorists such as bin Laden could be in bringing their terror to the United States. Suddenly, terrorism was not just something that happened to other nations.

TABLE 21-1 Changing Foreign Policy Goals Before and After September 11, 2001			
	Before	After	Change
Reduce spread of AIDS	73%	59%	-14%
Deal with world hunger	47	34	-13
Combat drug trafficking	64	55	-9
Promote U.S. business interests	37	30	-7
Ensure adequate energy supplies	74	69	-5
Promote democracy	29	24	-5
Help reduce world poverty	25	20	-5

SOURCE: Pew Research Center for the People and the Press, *Public Opinion in a Year for the Books* (Pew Research Center, 2002), p.12.

What Does Osama bin Laden Represent?

"We—with God's help—call on every Muslim who believes in God and wishes to be rewarded to comply with God's order to kill the Americans and plunder their money wherever and whenever they find it."* Thus did Osama bin Laden and his al-Qaeda network conclude their 1998 call for a *fatwa,* or holy war, against the United States in retaliation for its continued conflict with Iraq in the wake of the Persian Gulf War.

According to an unclassified Central Intelligence Agency fact sheet, bin Laden was born around 1955 in Saudi Arabia as the youngest son of a wealthy owner of a national construction company. He became involved in international politics in 1979 when he joined the Afghanistan guerrilla war against the Soviet Union and started giving money to the Afghan resistance in the mid-1980s. Bin Laden did not embrace the tra-

ditional East-West cold war divide. Rather, he saw himself as fighting for the liberation of Muslims from Western influence, forming his terrorist group, *al-Qaeda* (which means "the base" in Arabic), in 1988, promising to overthrow any and all governments in his path.

Bin Laden and his followers have never intended to fight their holy war on traditional terms. As he told ABC News in a November 7, 1998, interview, "We don't differentiate between those dressed in military uniforms or civilians. They are all targets in this *fatwa.*"† And if that means the use of chemical or nuclear weapons, so be it. As he told *Time* magazine, "Acquiring weapons for the defense of Muslims is a religious duty. If I have indeed acquired these weapons, then I thank God for enabling me to do so. And if I seek to acquire these weapons, I am carrying out a duty. It would be a sin for Muslims not to try to possess the weapons that would prevent the infidels from inflicting harm on Muslims."‡

As a "nonstate" terrorist, bin Laden represents a new kind of adversary to democracy. Before the 1990s, international terrorism was sponsored by nations such as Libya, Iran, and Iraq. Although Iraq may have a role in al-Qaeda's attacks, terrorism also involves a new generation of individual actors such as bin Laden who reject all forms of government as hostile to their cause. Bin Laden was just as ready to fight the Soviets as he was to challenge the United States.

Because he is not aligned with any government, bin Laden and others like him are less controllable and therefore more dangerous. Whereas the United States used a decade-long embargo to force the Libyan government finally to arrest the terrorists who bombed Pan Am Flight 103 over Lockerbie, Scotland, in 1988, it has no such power over individual terrorists such as bin Laden. The best the United States can do is to post multimillion-dollar rewards and hope that luck will lead to a capture.

*ABC News, *World News Tonight,* November 7, 1998.

†Ibid.

‡*Time,* January 11, 1999, vol. 53, no 1., p. 22.

The new war will have at least two phases, which are expected to last for years, even decades. In the short term, the war on terrorism focuses on law enforcement, better intelligence about threats, and the use of military force to attack terrorists. In the longer term, the war involves efforts to prevent terrorism by building healthy democracies in which terrorism cannot flourish; reducing the spread of weapons of mass destruction such as chemical, biological, radiological, and nuclear devices; and making sure that U.S. borders are secure.

Experts agree that the war on terrorism is going to be long and difficult. They also agree that the United States will almost certainly be attacked again. Indeed, the Bush administration's homeland security plan is designed around three broad goals that signal the great risk the nation faces: (1) to prevent specific acts of terrorism by tightening the borders, improving airline security, freezing the financial assets of individuals and groups that fund terrorism, reorganizing government, and prosecuting suspected terrorists; (2) to reduce the vulnerability of key domestic assets such as natural gas pipelines and nuclear power plants; and (3) to improve response and recovery time so that the victims of future terrorist attacks are helped as quickly as possible. The effort will almost certainly involve the further use of military force, whether against terrorist training bases or against the governments of countries such as Iraq that support terrorism. It will also involve aggressive prosecution of suspected terrorists such as Zacarias Moussaoui, who was arrested only weeks before the September 2001 attacks after offering cash for lessons on a Boeing 747 flight simulator.

Indian and Pakistani troops patrol the border in escalating numbers as religious and territorial differences over ownership of Kashmir bring the two countries closer to war. Tensions were reduced in part due to interventions by U.S. corporations that are dependent on India's high-tech workforce.

As noted at the start of this chapter, the war on terrorism is built around the Bush Doctrine. As Bush told a joint session of Congress on September 20, 2001, "From this day forward, any nation that continues to harbor or support terrorism will be regarded by the United States as a hostile regime. Every nation in every region now has a decision to make. Either you are with us, or you are with the terrorists." Bush restated the doctrine in even simpler terms before the United Nations in November: "There is no such thing as a good terrorist."

Unfortunately, it is one thing to declare a war on terrorism and quite another to identify and capture the terrorists. In many ways, terrorists have the advantage in an open society such as the United States. Short of curbing basic freedoms, there is only so much the nation can do to tighten its borders, police its streets, and prevent attacks. Even in Afghanistan, where the United States secured a quick victory in overthrowing the fundamentalist Taliban government that had harbored and supported terrorism, the United States could not be sure that it destroyed even a fraction of the network that planned the attacks on New York City and Washington, D.C. Unlike a traditional war, in which great armies battle head to head for supremacy, the war on terrorism must be fought one terrorist at a time.

CONTROLLING WEAPONS OF MASS DESTRUCTION   With the fall of the former Soviet Union and end of the cold war in 1990, the single greatest threat to U.S. security became the spread of weapons of mass destruction. India and Pakistan moved to the brink of nuclear war in the spring of 2002 over the disputed territory of Kashmir, North Korea continued its steady march toward developing its own nuclear arsenal, and several other so-called rogue nations such as Iraq continued to develop less sophisticated but still dangerous biological and chemical weapons such as anthrax, smallpox, and the 34 other toxins and microbes that the government considers the most dangerous in the world.

The October 2001 anthrax scare showed just how disruptive even a small terrorist action can be. In an attack apparently mounted by a single person, who was probably a U.S. citizen, a handful of anthrax-contaminated letters were sent by mail to several members of Congress, *NBC News* anchor Tom Brokaw, and the Florida offices of the *National Enquirer* tabloid, forcing post offices and office buildings to be shut down for weeks.

The world is working hard to reduce the spread of chemical, biological, and nuclear weapons. In 1992, for example, the United States, Russia, and a number of Western democracies agreed to curb the sale of materials and technology that could be used in the manufacture of nuclear weapons. This agreement was a direct result of concerns about Iraq's long-suspected nuclear weapons program, which was verified during inspections after the Gulf War of 1991. Although the accord established limits on the sale of materials or machinery that can be used either for peaceful purposes or for building nuclear bombs, experts still caution that "good intentions on export controls are often undermined by ignorance and greed."[4]

Even as they have worked to reduce access to the sophisticated technology needed to build a nuclear weapon, the United States and Russia are reducing their own stockpiles of nuclear weapons. In 2002, for example, Bush declared that the United States would reduce its nuclear arsenal over the next ten years from its current 7,200 warheads to between 1,700 and 2,200. Although the hoped-for number is still more than enough to destroy the world many times over, it reflects a broad agreement within the U.S. foreign policy community that Russia is no longer an enemy. Nevertheless, those warheads are still aimed at Russia and other republics of the former Soviet Union.[5]

The United States has also entered into a variety of agreements to restrict the use of biological and chemical materials. In 1972, a host of nations, including the United States and the Soviet Union, signed the Biological and Toxic Weapons Convention, which was widely hailed as the first international treaty to outlaw an entire class of weapons. Unfortunately, many of the signatories violated the treaty almost immediately. The Soviet Union, North Korea, and Egypt were developing biological weapons before the treaty was signed, and Iraq, South Africa, China, Iran, Libya, and Taiwan soon began work on their own programs. All had signed the treaty.

Twenty-one years later, in 1993, the United States, Russia, and an even larger number of other nations signed the Chemical Weapons Convention, which required all parties to declare and destroy their stocks of chemical weapons. This time the treaty worked, at least at first. Nine of the nations that signed the treaty declared that they did, indeed, have chemical weapons: Russia, China, Iran, Ethiopia, South Korea, India, Pakistan, Sudan, and Vietnam.

The United States almost failed to ratify the treaty, however. President Bill Clinton successfully waged a major legislative battle in 1997 against Senator Jesse Helms and many conservatives to win Senate ratification. Treaty supporters, such as former President George H. W. Bush and Senator John McCain (R.-Ariz.), contended that the security of our soldiers and citizens was at stake, while critics argued that the treaty amounted to unilateral disarmament because Libya, Iraq, Syria, and North Korea had not signed it. "How can a treaty that professes to address the problem of chemical weapons be credible unless it addresses the threat from the very countries, such as Syria and Iraq, that have actually deployed these weapons?"[6]

Despite these efforts, the United States has contingency plans to launch a "preemptive intervention" in nations like Iran, Iraq, Syria, Libya, or Algeria to keep an outlaw nation from developing weapons of mass destruction.[7] The Bush administration moved these contingency plans closer to execution in the summer of 2002 as it searched for a way to stop Iraq from continuing its support for terrorism.

PROMOTING U.S. TRADE   Even as the world has become more dangerous, it has become more interdependent and competitive economically. The United States has generally responded to this globalization with a basic policy of free trade, meaning a commitment to the free movement of goods across international borders.

Even nations that believe in free trade do not always honor the ideal, however. Many nations, including the United States, still protect certain industries through the use of import quotas (which restrict the amount of a particular product that can be purchased abroad) or export quotas (which restrict the amount of a product that can be sold). They also occasionally impose tariffs on particular imports to raise the price so that their own products are more attractive. Although such *protectionism* violates the basic concept of free trade, there may be good reasons to shield specific industries from global competition. The United States does not allow the export of technologies that can be used to build nuclear weapons, for example, and has long protected certain defense industries that would be essential should it ever be forced into another world war. The United States also uses trade as a tool to promote human rights and democratic reform.

This is precisely what happened in the battle over free trade with mainland China. On the one hand, China has a long history of violating basic human and democratic rights. On the other hand, China has one of the fastest-growing economies in the world. U.S. exports to China have tripled over the past decade, and imports from China have grown rapidly. This balancing effort reached a crescendo over President Clinton's request for **permanent normal trade relations (PNTR) status** for China, granting China the same favorable trade concessions and tariffs that its best trading partners receive.

The debate over China trade was so controversial that Congress refused to give President Clinton an extension of past "fast-track" authority to negotiate trade agreements. Under fast-track authority, which had been given to every president since Nixon but expired in 1994, Congress limited its own debate about trade agreements to a simple yes-or-no vote with no amendments. In 1998, however, Congress finally granted PNTR status to China. Four years later, it restored fast-track authority under the Trade Act of 2002, giving the Bush administration the opportunity to open new rounds of trade talks with Chile, Singapore, and South Africa.

FINDING PEACE IN THE MIDDLE EAST   The September 2001 attacks on the United States intensified the search for some formula for resolving the long conflict in the Middle East. If the United States was to win Arab support for any future attack on Iraq, as well

permanent normal trade relations (PNTR) status
Trade status granted as part of an international trade policy that gives a nation the same favorable trade concessions and tariffs that the best trading partners receive.

The Peace Corps

The Peace Corps is one of the nation's most important programs in promoting better understanding of the United States abroad. Established by the Peace Corps Act of 1961 in the Kennedy administration, the Peace Corps has a mission to encourage world peace and friendship, help other countries in meeting their social and development needs, and promote greater understanding between Americans and other peoples. Peace Corps volunteers are expected to serve in another nation for two years and become part of the community they are serving. Volunteers work on a variety of projects, such as teaching math and science, doing community development work, and improving water and sanitation systems.

The Peace Corps generally requires a college degree, experience, or a combination of both to apply. There is no age limit. In fact, about 10 percent of the 7,300 current volunteers are over 50 years old. The Peace Corps picks up the expenses and typically trains each volunteer in language and job skills for about three months prior to service abroad.

The Peace Corps operates in about 80 nations and has had funding of about $260 million a year. More than 170,000 Americans have been Peace Corps volunteers. Eight Peace Corps alumni have served in Congress. The Peace Corps is wholly separate from the State and Defense Departments and the intelligence agencies.

To would-be volunteers, the Peace Corps promotes itself as "the toughest job you'll ever love."

For more information, visit the Peace Corps website at, www.peacecorps.gov. For a useful study of the Peace Corps, see Elizabeth Cobbs Hoffman, *All You Need Is Love: The Peace Corps and the Spirit of the 1960s* (Harvard University Press, 1998).

as continued support for the war on terrorism from nations such as Saudi Arabia and Yemen, it had to address the demand for an independent Palestinian state in the territories captured by Israel during the 1967 Six-Day War and occupied since then.

A breakthrough nearly came in 1977 when Egyptian President Anwar el-Sadat traveled to Israel to announce his readiness to negotiate and Israeli President Menachem Begin traveled to Egypt to accept the offer. A year later, U.S. President Jimmy Carter invited both leaders to Camp David, the presidential retreat nestled in the Catoctin Mountains of Maryland. After 12 days of secret negotiations, Egypt agreed to acknowledge Israel's right to exist as an independent state, and Israel agreed to return the Sinai peninsula to Egyptian control. The agreement also laid the foundation for creation of an independent Palestinian state on the West Bank of the Jordan River that Israel had captured from Jordan in the Six-Day War.

Unfortunately, the fragile peace began to unravel almost immediately. Sadat was assassinated by militants in 1981; Israel invaded Lebanon a year later in an effort to destroy Yasser Arafat's Palestine Liberation Organization, which had been using the border nation as a staging ground for terrorist attacks on Israel. Once again, however, the United States used its foreign policy muscle to push both sides to negotiate. That pressure produced another round of secret negotiations, this time in Oslo, Norway, in 1991, which finally led to some tentative steps toward peace with Jordan and the creation of an independent Palestinian state, with Israel relinquishing many occupied areas to Palestinian control.

Much of that progress was lost in a wave of terrorist attacks on Israel that began with the Passover bombing in October 2001. Sponsored by militant Palestinian groups, the suicide bombings raised questions about Arafat's ability to govern and eventually led Israel to invade the refugee camps that provided shelter to the militants.

The rising tide of attack and counterattack put the United States in an extraordinarily difficult position. As a longtime ally of Israel, the United States supported Israel's use of force against the camps that sheltered the militants. Moreover, Israel Prime Minister Ariel Sharon used the language of the Bush Doctrine to justify his actions. However, the United States could not condone a renewed Israeli occupation of the Palestinian territories without weakening support for the war on terrorism among key Arab nations. The United States eventually resolved its dilemma by calling for Israel to withdraw while encouraging the Palestinian people to remove Arafat from power, but it found itself no closer to resolving the Palestinian question.

STRENGTHENING DEMOCRACY IN THE FORMER SOVIET UNION   The last thing the United States needs during its war on terrorism is a return to the cold war. Although the old Soviet Union will never reemerge, the transition from communism to capitalism has been a painful one in Russia and the other republics, so much so that many residents believe that the old communist system is preferable to the new democratic uncertainty.

The Communist party still survives in the nations that once made up the Soviet Union, in part because of economic chaos, organized crime, and food shortages. Americans want to help democracy take hold but worry about the ability of these nations to use the aid wisely. Foreign policy experts contend, however, that such investment is essential to help with the transition to a market economy and to encourage the gradual development of healthy constitutional democracies in that region.

The North Atlantic Treaty Organization is one part of the effort. With the end of the cold war, the mission, goals, and even membership of NATO have been redefined. In Bosnia, NATO forces conducted the alliance's first out-of-the-area military operation, and in 1997, NATO was expanded to include the former Warsaw Pact nations of Poland, the Czech Republic, and Hungary. By 2002, NATO was considering expansion to include Estonia, Latvia, and Lithuania and was even beginning to imagine a role for Russia.

The war on terrorism, controlling the spread of weapons of mass destruction, promoting trade, finding peace in the Middle East, and strengthening democracy in the former Soviet Union are not this nation's only foreign and defense policy goals, however. The United States is still concerned about reducing world poverty, promoting human rights,

Freedom in the World

Freedom House, a nonpartisan research organization, rates nations on the degree to which they embrace democratic freedoms such as freedom of the press and association, open elections, and civil liberties. Under its rating system, nations can be declared as free, partly free, or not free at all. Freedom House also monitors the number of nations that hold democratic elections.

	Free	Partly Free	Not Free	Democracies
1991–1992	76	65	42	91
1996–1997	79	55	53	118
2001–2002	85	59	48	128

SOURCE: Adrian Karaknycky, *The 2001–2002 Freedom House Survey of Freedom* (Freedom House, 2002), p. 9.

An increase in suicide bombings by Palestinians is a violent indication of the distance Palestine and Israel still have to travel to find a lasting peace. Israel responded with its own attack on terrorist bases in Palestine.

fighting the war on drugs, controlling population growth, and improving the global environment. But given a choice, terrorism is at the top of the U.S. foreign and defense policy agenda. At least for the time being, the United States appears ready to accept setbacks on other foreign and defense policy goals to win the war on terrorism.

The Foreign and Defense Policy Bureaucracy

As noted earlier in this chapter, presidents have primary responsibility for shaping foreign policy. Presidents can bargain, negotiate, persuade, apply economic pressure, threaten, or even use armed force. In addition, the agencies that carry out foreign policy report directly or indirectly to the president.

This does not mean the president has unfettered authority to act. Congress has the power to declare war, to appropriate funds for the armed forces, and to make rules that govern the armed forces. But the president is commander in chief of the armed forces and is authorized to negotiate treaties and receive and send ambassadors—that is, to recognize or refuse to recognize other governments. The Senate confirms U.S. ambassadorial appointments and gives consent (by a two-thirds vote) to treaty ratification. The courts have the power to interpret treaties, but by and large they have ruled that relations with other nations are matters for the executive to decide. The primacy of the executive in foreign policy is a fact of political life of all nations, including constitutional democracies.

Officially, the president's principal foreign policy adviser is the secretary of state, although others, such as the national security adviser or the vice president, are sometimes equally influential. The secretary of state administers the State Department, receives visits from foreign diplomats, attends international conferences, and usually heads the U.S. delegation in the General Assembly of the United Nations. The secretary also serves as the administration's chief coordinator of all governmental actions that affect our relations with other nations. In practice, the secretary of state delegates the day-to-day responsibilities for running the State Department and spends most of the time negotiating with the leaders of other countries.

The interdependence of foreign, economic, and domestic policies requires more than just one or two advisers. The conduct of foreign affairs is now the business of several major departments and agencies, including State, Defense, Treasury, Agriculture, Commerce, Labor, Energy, the Central Intelligence Agency (CIA), and the new Department of Homeland Security. The need for immediate reaction and full preparedness has transferred many responsibilities directly to the president and to a great extent to the senior White House aides who assist in coordinating information and advice. Yet no matter what the system for advice and coordination, there are always overlaps of responsibilities, redundancy, and competition among agencies.

Divided Opinions

Although these agencies are united by a common loyalty to the nation, their leaders often have intense disagreements over the direction of national policy. The Bush administration's foreign and defense team has been split between two very different images of the world, for example. In oversimplified terms, one side includes *neoconservatives,* or "hawks," such as Defense Secretary Donald Rumsfeld, Vice President Dick Cheney, and National Security Adviser Condoleezza Rice. These advisers believe that the United States has a moral obligation to confront evil wherever it resides. They also tend to be much more will ing to recommend the use of military force to protect vital U.S. interests. The other side includes *realists* such as Secretary of State Colin Powell. These advisers tend to see diplomacy as the first line of response in crisis and are suspicious of broad us-versus-them thinking of the kind embedded in the Bush Doctrine. They accept the world as it is and work with the realities as best they can to protect American interests.

Although the two sides showed uncommon solidarity in the months following the September 2001 terrorist attacks, they battled over the U.S. response to the Middle East crisis and the president's decision to label Iraq, Iran, and North Korea an "axis of evil" in his 2002 State of the Union Address. The neoconservatives supported Israel's hard-line response to the suicide bombings and applauded the axis-of-evil approach, while the

 ### The War in Afghanistan

The war in Afghanistan was the direct result of the terrorist attacks on the United States on September 11, 2001. By Thursday, September 13, Secretary of State Colin Powell had linked Osama bin Laden to the attacks. On Saturday, September 15, President Bush told American troops to "get ready" for a long war and also named bin Laden as a prime suspect in the attacks. The following Monday, the fundamentalist Taliban rulers of Afghanistan announced that they would not arrest bin Laden and extradite him to the United States for trial. In doing so, the Taliban sealed its fate.

The war in Afghanistan followed the following timeline.

October 7: The United States and Great Britain launch air strikes and cruise missile attacks on about 30 Taliban and al-Qaeda positions.

October 15: The most intensive daylight air strikes of the campaign are carried out; Secretary of State Powell travels to Pakistan to address criticism of U.S. actions.

October 19: The first U.S. special forces enter Afghanistan on an intelligence-gathering mission.

October 22: U.S. air strikes target front lines in support of Afghan Northern Alliance forces that have organized to fight the Taliban.

November 13: Northern Alliance troops capture Kabul, the traditional capital of Afghanistan; Taliban rule is effectively ended.

December 7: The last major city in Afghanistan falls to the Northern Alliance.

December 10: The U.S. embassy in Kabul is secured.

December 22: Hamid Karzai becomes the interim leader of Afghanistan pending democratic elections.

Although the war in Afghanistan was technically won when the Taliban fell, U.S. forces have continued to participate in attacks on suspected al-Qaeda and Taliban strongholds in the nation's mountainous terrain. It was not until January 4, 2002, that the first U.S. soldier was killed in combat. However, because the United States worked closely with Northern Alliance forces, it did not dispatch large numbers of soldiers to the war zone.

The war in Afghanistan was different from both the Persian Gulf War of 1991 and the 1999 air war in Kosovo. First, although the Americans and British fought together, there was no grand coalition of forces of the kind assembled in the Gulf War nor any request for help from NATO as in Kosovo. Second, the United States relied heavily on forces already fighting against the Taliban, especially the Northern Alliance. In doing so, the United States minimized the need for its own ground troops. U.S. forces pummeled Afghanistan with the latest in precision-guided weaponry, building on lessons learned in the skies above Iraq and Kosovo.

realists argued for a diplomatic settlement between Israel and the Palestinians and a more sophisticated campaign to isolate Iraq from the rest of the world.[8]

By early 2002, the split had emerged again as the administration faced charges that it was losing ground on a host of other foreign and defense policy goals, including immigration reform with Mexico, economic chaos in Central and South America, and human rights in Saudi Arabia. Friends of the administration, such as Brent Scowcroft, chairman of the president's own Foreign Intelligence Advisory Board, warned that the administration was in "real danger of being overextended," while critics such as former Clinton official James Steinberg opined that the Bush advisory team had not figured out "how to handle multiple foreign policy challenges."[9] The Bush Doctrine, which worked so well in defining a clear sense of mission immediately after September 11, 2001, appeared less useful in sorting through the growing backlog of other foreign and defense issues.

The split was particularly apparent in the Bush administration's high-profile planning for a possible attack on Iraq. Neoconservatives such as Rice argued that the United States had a moral obligation to remove Iraq's president, Saddam Hussein, from power. "This is an evil man who, left to his own devices, will wreak havoc again on his own population, his neighbors, and, if he gets weapons of mass destruction and the means to deliver them, on all of us," Rice told the British Broadcasting Corporation in August 2002. "There is a very powerful moral case for regime change. We certainly do not have the luxury of doing nothing."[10]

In contrast, the realists argued that the United States needed to consider the impact of such an attack on other foreign and defense policy goals. What would Egypt and Syria think? Would an attack reduce support for democratic reforms in Saudi Arabia? Would NATO support the effort? Could the United States reassemble the coalition that fought the Gulf War? Would the world view an attack as a way to deflect attention from the Palestinian dispute? Realists inside and outside the Bush administration argued that the attack could only be evaluated in the broader world context.

PREPARING THE NATION FOR WAR   The Bush administration eventually settled on a two-step process for addressing the dangers in Iraq. The first step was to announce a new U.S. policy called *pre-emption*. Under previous U.S. foreign policy, a president had never asked the nation to launch the first strike against an enemy. To the contrary, the United States had strongly opposed unprovoked attacks by other nations as a violation of international law. In 1981, for example, the United States had strongly condemned Israel for launching a pre-emptive attack against an Iraqi nuclear reactor being built in Osirak. Fears of Iraq prompted a change in policy, however. Appearing before the United Nations on September 12, 2002, exactly one year and one day after the terrorist attacks on New York City and Washington, D.C., President Bush claimed the right to attack any nation whose chemical, biological, or nuclear weapons threatened the United States either directly or through possible links to terrorists. As Bush explained, "Saddam Hussein's regime is a grave and gathering danger. To suggest otherwise is to hope against the evidence. To assume this regime's good faith is to bet the lives of millions and the peace of the world in a reckless gamble, and this is a risk we cannot take."

Bush then returned to Washington to ask the U.S. Congress to authorize the use of force against Iraq if Saddam Hussein would not voluntarily dismantle his weapons of mass destruction. Under the resolution, Congress was asked to authorize the use of U.S. armed forces to: defend the national security of the United States against the continuing threat posed by Iraq; and enforce all relevant United Nations Security Council resolutions against Iraq.

Under the proposed resolution, the president—and the president alone—would be given authority to order U.S. forces into action if he determined that "further diplomatic or other peaceful means alone" would not "adequately protect the national security of the United States. . . ."

The congressional debate was intense. Members of both parties expressed concerns about given such broad authority to the president to strike first against Iraq. Although virtually every member of Congress agreed that Iraq remained a significant threat to Middle East

National Security Advisor Condoleezza Rice meets with President George W. Bush at the presidential retreat in the Catoctin Mountains of Maryland, Camp David.

**Secretaries of the State
and the Presidents They Served**

George Marshall (Truman).

John Foster Dulles (Eisenhower).

Dean Rusk (Kennedy and Johnson).

Henry Kissinger (Nixon and Ford).

Cyrus Vance (Carter).

peace and that Saddam Hussein was fully capable of giving weapons of mass destruction to terrorists, many also worried that a pre-emptive strike against Iraq would prompt even more terrorism and might actually lead Hussein to launch any chemical, biological, and nuclear weapons he might have against Israel.

Despite these concerns, Congress passed the resolution on October 10, 2002 by sweeping majorities in both chambers. As Republican Representative Rob Simmons of Connecticut warned, "A gun only smokes after it has been fired, and that may be too late." In giving the president this unprecedented authority, Congress put the world on notice that the United States may strike first.

Realists within the Bush administration were able to win a significant second step, however. They obtained the president's support for a final diplomatic effort to secure a peaceful end to the crisis. With the president's support, the United States negotiated passage of a United Nation's resolution demanding a complete inventory of Iraq's weapons program by December 2002. In addition, the United Nations demanded unlimited inspections of all Iraqi weapons facilities. Iraq complied with both demands, claiming that it had no weapons of mass destruction, while apologizing to Kuwait for its 1990 invasion. In response, the Bush administration continued to argue that Iraq was lying to the international community and had moved large numbers of soldiers, sailors, and Air Force personnel into position for a strike on Iraq.

The National Security Council

The key coordinating agency for the president is the National Security Council (NSC). Created by Congress in 1947, it is intended to help presidents integrate foreign, military, and economic policies that affect national security. The NSC serves directly under the president. By law, it consists of the president, vice president, secretary of state, and secretary of defense. Recent presidents have sometimes included the director of the CIA, the White House chief of staff, and the national security adviser as nonstatutory members of the NSC.

The national security adviser, appointed by the president, has emerged as one of the most influential foreign policy makers, sometimes rivaling the secretary of state in influence. Presidents come to rely on these White House aides both because of their proximity (down the hall in the West Wing of the White House) and because they owe their primary loyalties to the president, not to any department or program. Each president has shaped the NSC structure and adapted its staff procedures to suit his personal preferences, but over the years, the NSC, as both a committee and a staff, has taken on a major role in making and implementing foreign policy. For her part, Condoleezza Rice has generally sided with the Bush administration's neoconservatives against the State Department and Colin Powell. In doing so, she has followed a time-honored path in which the NSC adviser is more an adversary of the State Department than an ally.

The State Department

The State Department is responsible for the diplomatic realm of foreign and defense policy. The department is organized around a series of "desks" representing different parts of the world and foreign policy missions. Among the State Department's main priorities are the following:

To promote peace and human rights

To negotiate with other nations and international organizations

To protect American citizens and interests abroad

To promote American commercial interests and enterprises

To collect and interpret intelligence

To represent an American presence abroad

To help U.S. citizens who are living or visiting other nations

To grant visitor visas to foreign citizens who wish to visit or study in the United States

It was in this last capacity that the State Department plays a significant role in homeland security. Many of the September 2001 attackers had entered the United States on student visas granted by the State Department's Bureau of Consular Affairs. Although their movements once in the United States were supposed to be monitored by the Justice Department's Immigration and Naturalization Service, the State Department was criticized for being too lax in granting visas to almost anyone with enough income to purchase an airline ticket.

An effective foreign policy is impossible to sustain by rhetoric alone or by noble intentions. As former Secretary of State Warren Christopher noted:

> Talk is cheap; leadership is not. Leadership in foreign policy requires resources: enough to keep our embassies open and our people trained; enough to maintain constructive relations with the world's great powers; enough to multiply our leverage through international institutions; enough to provide targeted aid to struggling democracies that can one day emerge as allies and export markets; enough to meet threats like terrorism and international crime.[11]

The State Department's budget of about $6 billion (not counting foreign aid) is the lowest of all the cabinet departments—only a fraction of the Department of Defense's much larger 2003 budget.[12] Considering the State Department's role and prestige, its staff of 25,000 worldwide is small, especially compared with the more than 2 million civilian and military personnel in the Department of Defense.

Its role is particularly impressive given recent cutbacks. The United States has closed at least 30 consulates and embassies over the past two decades, and many operate with obsolete technology and in antiquated and unsafe buildings. These cutbacks help explain the breakdowns in the visa issuance process. The State Department simply did not have enough employees to interview every applicant for a visa.

STAFFING THE DIPLOMATIC SYSTEM   American embassies are staffed largely by members of the U.S. Foreign Service. Although part of the State Department, the service represents the entire government and performs jobs for many other agencies. Its main duties are to carry out foreign policy as expressed in the directives of the secretary of state; gather political, economic, and intelligence data for American policy makers; protect Americans and American interests in foreign countries; and cultivate friendly relations with host governments and foreign peoples.

The Foreign Service is composed of officers, reserve officers, and staff officers. At its core are the foreign service officers, comparable to army officers in the military. They are a select, specially trained group expected to take assignments anyplace in the world on short notice. There are approximately 4,000 such officers; in recent years, fewer than 225 junior officers have won appointment each year. Approximately two-thirds of our U.S. ambassadors to about 160 nations come from the ranks of the Foreign Service. The others are usually political appointees, large donors, or friends of the president.

The Foreign Service is one of the most prestigious yet most criticized career services of the national government. Criticism sometimes comes as much from within as from outside. Critics claim that the organizational culture of the Foreign Service stifles creativity; attracts officers who are, or at least become, more concerned about their status than their responsibilities; and requires new recruits to wait 15 years or more before being considered for positions of responsibility. Like other federal agencies, most notably the Central Intelligence Agency and the Federal Bureau of Investigation, the Foreign Service has had great difficulty recruiting officers with significant Arabic-language skills, which clearly weakens the ability to interpret, let alone collect, intelligence on the terrorist networks that have emerged in the Middle East and central Asia.

Perhaps the greatest challenge for Foreign Service diplomats is how to function effectively in a high-tech world. Some have even suggested that diplomats posted in foreign countries are no longer needed to gather intelligence or to speak for the United States and that they should be replaced altogether and most of their work be conducted by e-mail, fax, and videoconferencing from Washington. Yet having a diplomat on the scene in Iran or Saudi Arabia who speaks Farsi and Arabic and who knows a country's major leaders personally is often a better method than relying on even the most sophisticated technologies, especially when making subtle judgments about a nation's political, economic, and military policies.[13]

Secretaries of the State and the Presidents They Served

George Shultz (Reagan).

James Baker (Bush).

Warren Christopher (Clinton).

Madeleine Albright (Clinton).

Colin Powell (Bush).

The Central Intelligence Agency

Effective foreign policy is dependent on accurate, timely information. Before our foreign policy makers can act on important issues, they have to know as much as possible about other countries: their possible reactions to a particular policy, their strengths and weaknesses, the character of their leaders, and, if possible, their strategic plans and intentions. The people who gather and analyze intelligence data are therefore among the most important advisers to policy makers.[14]

The Central Intelligence Agency, an outgrowth of the World War II Office of Strategic Services, was created in 1947 to coordinate the gathering and analysis of information that flows into various parts of the U.S. government from all over the world. In recent years, the CIA has had about 20,000 employees and has helped coordinate and integrate the intelligence work of the State Department's Bureau of Intelligence and Research, the Defense Intelligence Agency (which combines the intelligence operations of the Army, Navy, Air Force, and Marine Corps), the National Security Agency (which specializes in electronic reconnaissance and code breaking), the supersecret National Reconnaissance Office (which runs the U.S. satellite surveillance programs), the National Imagery and Mapping Agency, the Federal Bureau of Investigation, and a small intelligence operation run by the Departments of Energy and Treasury. Before the September 2001 attacks, these agencies spent about $30 billion a year on intelligence work.[15] After the attacks, all were slated for significant budget increases, including special funding to recruit specialists in Arabic languages.

Although most of the information the CIA gathers comes from open sources, the term "intelligence" conjures up visions of spies and undercover agents. Secret intelligence occasionally does supply crucial data. But it is not all glamour; much is routine. Intelligence work involves three basic operations: reporting, research, and dissemination. *Reporting* is based on the close and rigorous observation of developments around the world; *research* is the attempt to detect meaningful patterns out of what was observed in the past and to understand what appears to be going on now; *dissemination* means getting the right information to the right people at the right time.

ASSESSING THE CIA'S PERFORMANCE   The CIA has a mixed record in preventing foreign policy failures. Its analysts detected the military buildup by Iraq's Saddam Hussein in 1990, but their warnings about an invasion of Kuwait were too cautious and too late, according to later analyses.[16] Other intelligence disappointments include the failure to predict India's nuclear weapons test in 1998 and the faulty guidance that led a U.S. warplane to drop a bomb on the Chinese embassy in Belgrade in 2000.[17]

Moreover, the CIA appeared unable to catch spies in its own midst. In 1994, for example, the agency discovered that a senior CIA agent, Aldrich Ames, had been spying for the Soviets for the better part of a decade. Ames confessed to what is considered the worst betrayal of U.S. intelligence in the history of the CIA; it is estimated that at least 12 overseas agents or friendly sources were killed because of his deeds.

Such intelligence failures have made the CIA the target of frequent congressional investigation. The entire intelligence community, including the CIA, also came under fire in 2002 regarding its failure to piece together the knowledge it had about the September 2001 attacks on New York City and Washington, D.C. FBI agents in Phoenix and Minneapolis had raised concerns about flight training by suspected terrorists, and the CIA had at least some information about a coordinated terrorist attack by members of the bin Laden network. Even as some observers have argued that the CIA needs to be even more aggressive, others have called for less secrecy and more openness in foreign policy. According to former Senator Daniel Patrick Moynihan, the United States cannot conduct foreign policy without at least some secrecy. But a widely established culture of secrecy need not remain the tradition in diplomacy and national security operations. "A case can be made . . . that secrecy is for losers. For people who don't know how important information really is. The Soviet Union realized this too late," writes Moynihan. "Openness is now a singular, and singularly American, advantage. . . . It is time to dismantle government secrecy, this most pervasive of Cold War–era regulations. It is time to begin building the supports for the era of openness that is already upon us."[18]

Although the U.S. intelligence agencies have made mistakes over the years, most experts believe these agencies are essential. Political scientist Loch Johnson writes, "The likelihood that they contributed significantly to warding off a third world war has been enough to earn their keep."[19] Their analysis of complicated political and military developments in the Middle East, the Balkans, and North Korea has also proved strategically important. Nevertheless, since the attacks of September 11, 2001, the CIA has been under great pressure to improve its operations and has yet to convince Congress and the American public that it is up to the intelligence demands of a post–September 11 world.

The Department of Defense

The president, Congress, the National Security Council, the State Department, and the Defense Department all make overall defense policy and attempt to integrate U.S. national security programs, but the day-to-day work of organizing for defense is the job of the Defense Department. Its headquarters, the Pentagon, houses within its 17.5 miles of corridors 23,000 top military and civilian personnel. The offices of several hundred generals and admirals are there, as is the office of the secretary of defense, who provides civilian control of the armed services.

Although the Department of Defense has existed for more than half a century, its leaders are still working to ensure both strategic vision and practical coordination among the military services. Prior to 1947, there were two separate military departments—War and Navy. The difficulty of coordinating them during World War II led to demands for unification. In 1947, the Air Force, already an autonomous unit within the War Department, was made an independent department, and all three military departments—Army, Navy, and Air Force—were placed under the general supervision of the secretary of defense. The Unification Act of 1947 was a bundle of compromises between the Army, which favored a tightly integrated department, and the Navy, which wanted a loosely federated structure, but the act at least brought the military services onto a common organizational chart.

The committee known as the Joint Chiefs of Staff serves as the principal military adviser to the president, the National Security Council, and the secretary of defense. It includes the heads of the three armed services, plus the commandant of the Marine Corps, and the chair and vice chair of the Joint Chiefs. The president, with the consent of the Senate, appoints all the service chiefs to four-year nonrenewable terms. Note that the twice-

FBI Agent Coleen Rowley's testimony before the Senate Judiciary Committee on June 6, 2002, exposed communication problems between FBI field offices and FBI headquarters in Washington, D.C. Agent Rowley outlined how the FBI headquarters hindered the field office in Minneapolis in its investigation of a suspected terrorist before September 11, 2001.

The Pentagon, headquarters for the Defense Department, is the world's largest building. It has 17.5 miles of corridors and houses nearly 23,000 workers, who tell time by 4,200 clocks, consume 30,000 cups of coffee daily, and place 200,000 calls a day on 87,000 phones connected by 100,000 miles of cable.

Its significance as the center of U.S. defense policy made the Pentagon a prime target in the attacks on September 11, 2001. More than 150 civilian and military personnel were killed in the early morning attack.

renewable two-year term of the chair of the Joint Chiefs is part of the process of ensuring civilian control over the military.

Before 1986, the members of the Joint Chiefs of Staff were, collectively, very powerful. They advised the president and the secretary of defense. Because they functioned as a committee and could not act until unanimous agreement was reached, however, they often produced overly broad decisions. Critics therefore viewed much of the work of the Joint Chiefs as wasteful and even dangerous.

The Department of Defense Reorganization Act of 1986 shifted considerable power to the chair. Reporting through the secretary of defense, the chair now advises the president on military matters, exercises authority over the forces in the field, and is responsible for overall military planning. In theory, the chair of the Joint Chiefs can even make a military decision that the chiefs of the other services oppose. On paper at least, these other chiefs now serve the chair merely as advisers, and even the chair's deputy, the vice chair, outranks the other service chiefs. The chair has a mandate to encourage "jointness" in military education and in other spheres to integrate the services for maximum effectiveness. The chair of the Joint Chiefs today is the most powerful peacetime military officer in U.S. history. These changes clearly contributed to military success in the war in Afghanistan, where special operations forces and U.S. Marines worked closely with Navy and Air Force pilots to target precision-guided weapons on Taliban and al-Qaeda positions.

It is crucial to recognize, however, that the chair of the Joint Chiefs is *not* the head of the military. The chair and the Joint Chiefs are advisers to the secretary of defense and the president, but the president can, and on occasion has, disregarded their advice. A president must weigh military action or inaction against the larger foreign and security interests of the nation.

UNDERSTANDING THE DEFENSE BUREAUCRACY   It is common to hear criticisms of the "Pentagon machine" or the "national military establishment." The defense bureaucracy is, however, best understood—as is any bureaucracy—as something less than a monolith. Insiders often stress that this policy-making structure is best thought of as a *confederation* or a bargaining arena rather than a tight chain-of-command hierarchy. In fact, in recent years, strong sentiment has emerged for more centralized control and direction of the nation's defense bureaucracy.

Disputes among the military services involve more than professional jealousies. The technological revolution in warfare has rendered obsolete many concepts about military missions, thereby threatening the traditional roles of some of the services. In the past, it made sense to divide command among land, sea, and air forces. Today, defense research and development are constantly altering formerly established roles and missions, yet the individual services are reluctant to give up their traditional functions or to serve each other's crucial needs. The Navy, for example, is interested in waging sea warfare, not in running a freight service for the Army. Interservice rivalries erupt when the Army and Air Force quarrel over who should provide air support for ground troops. Each branch also supports weapons that bring it prestige. The Air Force and Navy dispute, for example, the effectiveness of land-based versus sea-based missiles.[20]

Whether strategic policies are worked out by the Defense Department, the White House, or Congress, the decisions result from a political process in which some measure of consensus is essential. The Joint Chiefs engage in the same type of vote trading used in Congress. On budget issues, the chiefs often endorse all the programs desired by each service. When forced to choose on an issue of policy, the chiefs have traditionally compromised among the different service positions rather than attempt to develop a position based on a unified military point of view.

The Department of Homeland Security

The new Department of Homeland Security plays a small but important role in foreign policy by policing U.S. borders. Created in late 2002, the department is composed of 22 agencies and a work force of 170,000 full-time civil servants. It includes the Border Patrol, the Coast Guard, the Customs Service, elements of the Immigration and Naturalization Service, and the Transportation Security Administration.

SHOULD THE UNITED STATES BUILD A MISSILE SHIELD?

You Decide... The United States has been trying to design a missile shield for 20 years. First proposed by President Ronald Reagan, the goal of his "Star Wars" system was simple: identify, intercept, and destroy incoming ballistic missiles before they enter the atmosphere above the United States. The idea mostly languished after the end of the cold war but regained momentum with the possibility that China, North Korea, and Iran were all developing long-range missiles capable of reaching the United States. The idea also gained support with the general fears that came with the terrorist attacks on New York City and Washington, D.C. According to the Pew Research Center for the People and the Press, 35 percent of Americans favored a missile defense system before those attacks, and 35 percent said the United States should not build the system at all. After the terrorist attacks, the number who favored a missile defense system increased to 49 percent, while the number who were opposed fell to 26 percent. Should we build the missile defense system or shouldn't we?

Thinking It Through... There are three potential problems with a missile shield. First, it would be extremely expensive to build. Estimates vary, but projections predict that it could cost $100 billion or more to implement. Second, it is extremely difficult to build. Although a shield makes sense in the abstract, the technical challenges are enormous. Experts argue that a shield could be easily defeated by launching thousands of decoys, all of which would have to be identified or destroyed to find the real missiles. Third, a missile shield would undermine the nuclear stability created by the concept of mutual assured destruction. Nations might be more likely to launch a nuclear strike against the United States in the hope of knocking down the missile shield. Moreover, a shield would violate the Anti-Ballistic Missile Treaty negotiated by the United States and Soviet Union in the 1970s, thereby inviting the Russians to embark on a new arms race. Some advocates of the shield have responded to these concerns by supporting a limited shield that could be used to destroy enemy missiles immediately after launch.

The department has two basic goals: to prevent the entry of terrorists into the country and to reduce the chances of a terrorist attack. It is responsible for screening all passengers and baggage on U.S. domestic flights (Transportation Security Administration), checking all cargo (Customs Service, Coast Guard), checking all visitors (Immigration Service), and patrolling the borders (Border Patrol, Coast Guard). It is also responsible for analyzing intelligence from the CIA, FBI, and other agencies to reduce vulnerability to terrorist attacks. Although the Bureau of Consular Affairs remains in the State Department, the secretary of homeland security now has primary responsibility for making sure that visas are not issued to potential terrorists.

Making Foreign and Defense Policy

Foreign policy flows through the same institutional and constitutional structures as domestic policy. Public opinion, interest groups, foreign countries, political parties, and Congress all affect the making of foreign policy. Yet these structures operate somewhat differently from the way they do in domestic affairs.

Public Opinion

In crisis situations such as the new war against terrorism, presidents and their military and intelligence advisers make the key decisions, often operating from a high-tech operations center in the basement of the White House. Yet even in these situations, presidents and their advisers know that their decisions will ultimately require support from the public and from Congress.

Sergeant First Class Nathan Ross Chapman, 31, was the first American casualty in Afghanistan after the start of the war on terrorism. Deaths, such as Chapman's, affect the general public more than specific foreign policy issues.

In normal situations, the public appears to consist of three subcategories. The largest, constituting perhaps as much as 75 percent of the adult population, is the *mass public.* This group knows little about the details of foreign affairs, despite the subject's importance. The mass public concerns itself with foreign affairs mainly in conflict situations, especially those involving the use of American troops abroad. The second group is the *attentive public,* constituting perhaps 15 to 20 percent of the population. It maintains an active interest in foreign policy. The *opinion makers* are the third and smallest public; as editors, teachers, writers, and political and business leaders, they transmit information and judgments on foreign affairs and mobilize the support of the other two publics.

Still, many Americans are indifferent or uninformed about foreign and defense policy. Foreign affairs issues are more remote than domestic issues. People have more firsthand information about unemployment, inflation, crime, and health care costs than about Japanese economic reform or Indonesian political problems. Most Americans have a poor sense of world geography and an even weaker grasp of geopolitics. Sometimes it seems that only when American soldiers or civilians overseas are killed does the mass public become directly concerned with foreign affairs. Whether ill-informed or not, Figure 21-1 shows that Americans do not believe the United States should be involved in all corners of the globe.

Even before September 11, 2001, Americans were better informed than many experts believed. "Contrary to a widely held assumption, their concern does not stop at the water's edge," writes Steven Kull.[21] A survey of American views on foreign and defense policy concludes that most Americans accept that the United States has serious obligations abroad.

Key Foreign Policy Concepts

- *Internationalism:* A foreign policy that recognizes that concern for trade, human rights, and international peace requires not only a strong military but also the willingness to intervene where vital U.S. interests are at stake. The goal is to create an international order consistent with American values.

- *Isolationism:* A foreign policy that curtails U.S. military aid and intervention abroad as much as possible. It was the dominant policy in this country during the nineteenth century and to some degree in the 1920s and 1930s. It was put forward again by Pat Buchanan during the 1996 and 2000 presidential elections.

- *Realpolitik:* A foreign policy based on practical and self-interest factors rather than on moral, idealistic, or theoretical considerations. Realists say the United States should intervene in world affairs only if its vital interests are in jeopardy or if a dispute involves overt outside aggression, not simply internal rebellion.

- *Containment:* A foreign policy aimed at halting the spread of communism, especially the influence of the former Soviet Union. This was the underlying foreign and national security policy of the United States between 1947 and 1990.

- *Deterrence:* After World War II, the nation's primary defense against nuclear attack was a strategy of *deterrence,* the ability to threaten massive retaliation on any nation that attacked us. Effective deterrence is commonly measured by the strength of survivable second-strike force. Thus the United States has maintained a large, diversified, and well-protected defense system so that a first strike by another nation would not cripple our ability to retaliate decisively. This strategy of *mutual assured destruction* (MAD) is still the core of American defense policy. Pentagon officials claim it works, even if it is costly. It has succeeded in achieving for the United States and our allies more than five decades of peace—twice as long as the period between World Wars I and II.

- *New World Order:* A vague and often confusing label pinned on the post–cold war period in which the United States presumably plays a vital role as the only remaining superpower in preserving peace, encouraging economic opportunity, and promoting human rights throughout the world.

Percentage of respondents identifying the country as vital to U.S. interests

More than 70%   51%–70%   41%–50%   40% or Less

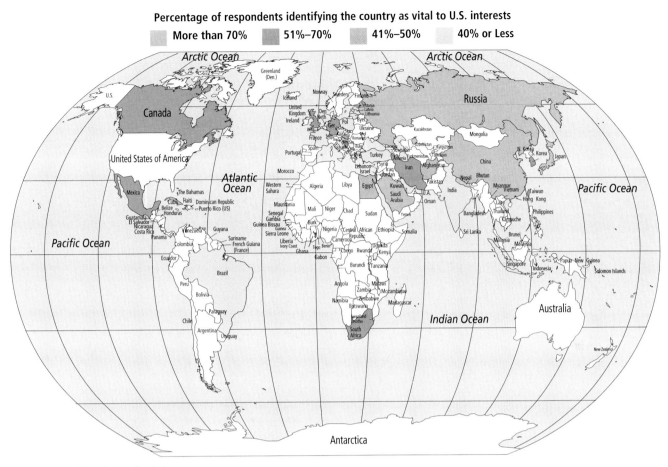

FIGURE 21–1   Public Views of U.S. Interests.

SOURCE: John E. Reilly, ed., *American Public Opinion and U.S. Foreign Policy, 1999* (Chicago Council on Foreign Relations, 1999), p. 13.

Americans were also more cautious about the world. Three months before the attacks, for example, 64 percent of Americans said that international terrorism was a "major threat" to the well-being of the United States; one month before the attacks, 53 percent said the world was a "more dangerous place" than it had been a decade earlier.[22]

Americans became even more engaged in the days and weeks following September 11, 2001. Ninety-six percent of Americans surveyed in mid-September said they were following news reports about the attacks closely. Another 77 percent said the United States should go to war with Afghanistan even if it meant taking heavy casualties. And 44 percent said military action to attack terrorism abroad was a wiser investment than building up the nation's defenses at home to prevent more attacks. As for the aims of military intervention, 57 percent said future attacks should be designed to prevent terrorism, compared to 22 percent who said military action should be used to punish those responsible for the September 11 attacks. As Table 21-2 shows, Americans became much more concerned about making foreign policy with the nation's allies in mind, in making sure the United States was in charge, and increasing defense spending.

Interest Groups

It is difficult to generalize about the impact of interest groups on American foreign policy. At times of international crisis, the president is usually able to mobilize public support so that interest groups find it difficult to exert much influence. As a general rule, special-interest groups with other than major economic interests rarely have a decisive role in the formulation of foreign policy.

TABLE 21–2 Views of Foreign Policy Before and After September 11, 2001

	Before	After
The United States should formulate foreign policy based on		
Mostly U.S. interests	38%	30%
Interests of allies	48	59
Neither or both	8	7
The U.S. leadership role should be		
Single leader or first among equals	38	45
Just one of leading nations	50	46
No leadership role	8	3
National defense spending should be		
Increased	32	50
Kept the same	44	41
Cut back	20	7

SOURCE: Pew Research Center for the People and the Press, *Public Opinion in a Year for the Books* (Pew Research Center, 2002), p. 12.

Ethnic interest groups, however, sometimes play an important role in foreign and defense policy decisions. As a nation of immigrants and the children and grandchildren of immigrants, our citizens often retain a special bond with their country of origin. Thus Irish Americans, Jewish Americans, Cuban Americans, African Americans, Asian Americans, Polish Americans, Greek Americans, Arab Americans, and Mexican Americans take a keen interest in decisions affecting Ireland, Israel, Cuba, South Africa, China, Poland, Greece, the Middle East, and Mexico. Such groups sometimes exert great pressures on policy makers to support (or in the case of Cuba, contest) the country to which they are emotionally linked. Congress listens.

Business groups also play a role in foreign and defense policy decisions. Defense contractors are heavily involved in decisions about defense spending and are heavy contributors to both presidential and congressional candidates. They lobby hard on behalf of their projects and often prevail despite the president's own opposition.

But defense contractors are not the only business interests involved in foreign and defense policy. Agricultural interests have lobbied successfully for expanded grain and food exports, the steel industry has lobbied successfully for import quotas on foreign steel, the entertainment industry has campaigned against piracy of music and film abroad, and the high-tech industry has pressed Congress to allow the immigration of more computer programmers.

Businesses may even have their own foreign policies. *New York Times* reporter Thomas L. Friedman wrote in August 2002 that General Electric, not General Powell, was responsible for reducing the nuclear tension between Pakistan and India over the disputed Kashmir region. According to Friedman, the U.S. high-tech economy has become dependent on millions of English-speaking, low-wage workers in India for everything from computer programming to troubleshooting. Not surprisingly, U.S. companies were angered when the State Department urged U.S. citizens to leave India because of the nuclear tension. They warned India that they would move their operations to other countries if the nation continued to threaten nuclear war. As Friedman wrote, "This was a real education for India's leaders in New Delhi, but, officials conceded, they got the message: loose talk about war or nukes could be disastrous for India. This was reinforced by another new lobby: the information technology ministers who now exist in every Indian state to drum up business."[23]

Foreign Nations

Most countries have embassies that lobby for their interests in Washington. In addition, some countries like Japan have built up a powerful network of lawyers, lobbyists, and Washington-based publicists who are retained by Japanese companies and trade associations, as well as by the Japanese government, to defend their extensive economic interests in the United States.[24] Lobbyists representing industrialized countries like South Korea, Taiwan, Singapore, Brazil, and Mexico have also expanded their Washington lobbying efforts to fight U.S. protectionism and import quotas on textiles, shoes, and other products. Such lobbying is legal provided that the lobbyists register and report their activities to Congress.

Foreign nations have occasionally tried to influence U.S. policy through less visible means. In 1996, for example, the fact that China and Indonesia had made large contributions to the Clinton-Gore reelection campaign came to light. Although the president vigorously denied any connection between the contributions and administration policy, the Democratic National Committee returned the money. In 2000, George W. Bush's inaugural committee returned a $100,000 gift in early 2001 to a donor who had questionable ties to foreign leaders.[25]

Political Parties

Political parties do not usually play a major role in shaping foreign and defense policy, for two reasons: (1) Many Americans still prefer to keep partisan politics out of foreign policy, and (2) parties usually take less clear and candid stands on foreign policy than they do on domestic policy. Party platforms often obscure the issues instead of highlighting them, and many members of Congress fail to follow any strict party line when it comes to foreign policy.

At the end of World War II, sentiment grew strong for a bipartisan approach to foreign policy. An ambiguous concept, **bipartisanship** in foreign affairs generally means (1) collaboration between the executive and the congressional leaders of both parties, (2) support of presidential foreign policies by both parties in Congress, and (3) downplaying major foreign policy differences in national elections and in presidential debates. Overall, bipartisanship is an attempt to remove the issues of foreign policy from partisan politics.

Not everybody agrees that bipartisanship is desirable. There is virtue, critics say, in debating contending ideas—such as foreign aid or the missile shield. Indeed, the bipartisanship that surrounded the early months of the war on terrorism started breaking down by early 2002 when then–Senate Majority Leader Thomas Daschle suggested that the war could not be considered a success until bin Laden was captured or killed. Although most Democrats remained reluctant to criticize the administration's handling of the war effort abroad, they were increasingly vocal about problems in restoring a sense of security at home. Democrats offered their own version of a homeland security department and were harshly critical of the CIA and FBI intelligence failures.

Congress

Although Congress seldom initiates foreign policy on its own, it has taken the lead on some trade and economic assistance questions and of course controls the power of the purse. In addition, Congress is authorized to define the limits of presidential warmaking powers.[26]

Individual members of Congress, however, are sometimes included within the circle of those who make foreign and defense policy decisions. Senator Jesse Helms, who retired in 2003, was a persistent opponent of foreign aid and the United Nations. Helms also used his power as an individual senator to prevent the confirmation of several key Bush administration appointees in 2001 until the president addressed his concerns about protecting the North Carolina textile industry from foreign imports.

Congress is a crucial link between policy makers and the public. Regardless of their party, members of Congress want a voice in foreign policy, or at least what some members call "meaningful consultation." After all, they represent the constituents who must

bipartisanship
A policy that emphasizes a united front and cooperation between the major political parties, especially on sensitive foreign policy issues.

Bill Clinton engaged in strenuous personal diplomacy in trying to work out an agreement between Israeli Prime Minister Ehud Barak and Chairman Yasser Arafat at Camp David in July 2000. Arafat turned it down, and Barak was later defeated by Ariel Sharon as the new prime minister of Israel.

fight the wars, pay the taxes, and bear the burdens of wartime. In the summer of 2002, for example, Republican Senator Richard Lugar asked for a full debate about the administration's plan for an attack on Iraq. "This is not an action that can be sprung on the American people," he said at the start of a Foreign Relations Committee hearing on the attack. Not all members of Congress felt so strongly about consultation, however. "What do they want us to say?" asked then Senate Minority Leader Trent Lott. "'Oh, Mr. Saddam Hussein, we're coming. . . . You can expect us . . . two weeks after Election Day. And by the way, here's the way we're coming. But before we do that, we'll have a huge debate so you'll know full well exactly what's going on.'"[27]

Making Foreign Policy in a Democracy

A democratic foreign policy is presumably one in which policy makers are known and are held accountable to the people. This is a tough test for any policy, yet it is especially tough for foreign policy because of the frequent need to act with speed and sometimes with secrecy, the generally low level of information among the general public, the anonymity of most foreign policy leaders, and the complexity of most international issues and strategic policy options. Still, the American public wants to be consulted and informed, and it wants its leaders held accountable.[28]

A constitutional democracy may not be able to keep leaders from making mistakes, but it can make sure that policy mistakes eventually become public. It is then that the safeguarding agencies of democracy—the opposition party, the press, and public opinion—play a crucial role in demanding accountability. The public's opposition to the Vietnam War eventually forced the United States to withdraw, for example, and its outrage over the genocide in Kosovo eventually forced the United States to intervene.

The temptation during times of crisis is to rally around the president and the flag in support of the country. But as noted elsewhere in this book, dissent is an essential element of maintaining accountability during such moments.

Foreign and Defense Policy Options

The United States can choose from a variety of options or tools for implementing foreign and defense policy, but it usually employs conventional diplomacy, foreign aid, economic sanctions, and military action, or some combination thereof. Whether these tools will work depends on whether they fit the particular strategic situation and whether the domestic conditions for pursuing such a strategy are favorable.

Conventional Diplomacy

Much of U.S. foreign policy is conducted by the Foreign Service and ambassadors in face-to-face discussions in Washington and other capitals, at the United Nations in New York and Geneva, at North Atlantic Treaty Organization or World Trade Organization meetings, and elsewhere around the world in regional or international organizations and world conferences. International summit meetings, with their high-profile pomp and drama, are another form of conventional diplomacy. Even though traditional diplomacy appears more subdued and somewhat less vital in this era of personal leader-to-leader communication by telephone, fax, and teleconferencing, it is still an important, if slow, process by which nations can gain information, talk about mutual interests, and try to resolve disputes.

Much of the conventional diplomacy carried out by the State Department may not produce important breakthroughs, yet it is difficult to measure the value of diplomatic representation. No price tag can be placed on close personal relations with foreign officials or on information gathered and arguments made to promote American interests around the world. Surely the closing of one embassy or the withdrawal from an international organization is unlikely to cause major setbacks for the United States, yet a less active diplomatic corps could mean a less effective foreign policy.

When relations between nations become strained, diplomatic relations are sometimes broken as a means of political coercion. When the United States breaks diplomatic ties, the consequences are more than merely symbolic. Doing so greatly restricts tourist and business travel to a country and in effect curbs economic as well as political relations with the nation.

Breaking diplomatic relations, however, is a next-to-last resort (force is the last resort), for such action undermines the ability to reason with a nation's leaders or to use other diplomatic strategies to resolve conflicts. The act also undermines our ability to get valuable information about what is going on in a nation and to have a presence in that nation.

THE ROLE OF THE UNITED NATIONS   The United Nations is one of the most important arenas for traditional diplomacy. Established in 1945 by the victors of World War II, the U.N. now has 189 nation members.

Despite its promise as a forum for world peace, the United Nations was mostly ineffective during its first 45 years. Critics contend that it either ducked crucial global issues or was politically unable to tackle them. During much of that time, the U.N. General Assembly, dominated by a combination of Third World and communist nations, was hostile to many U.S. interests. The General Assembly often became a talk shop, passing vague resolutions. More recently, the five permanent members of the U.N. Security Council—the United States, China, Russia (which replaced the Soviet Union), Britain, and France—have usually worked in harmony. Moreover, the U.N.'s assumption of responsibilities in the Persian Gulf War and its extensive peacekeeping missions in Cyprus and Lebanon won it respect. U.N. efforts in Cambodia and Somalia were less successful.

In addition, several of the specialized agencies of the United Nations—including the World Health Organization, the United Nations High Commission for Refugees, and the World Food Program—are considered major successes. But the review is much more mixed with respect to the U.N.'s peacekeeping efforts, of which it has conducted more than 50. Such a review suggests that these operations are plagued by inadequate and often underprepared personnel. "First-world countries with first-rate armies are usually unwilling to put their troops at risk," writes former United States Ambassador Dennis Jett. "Thus these operations are often left to third-world countries, and the United Nations sends some of the worst soldiers in the world off to situations where it can only hope they are not called on to actually do anything."[29]

Defenders of United Nations peacekeeping missions note that where the United States intervenes alone, the United States pays all the costs and runs all the risks. When the United Nations acts, the United States pays only 26 percent of the costs and others provide the vast majority of the troops. And most Americans, when surveyed, favor multilateral more than direct U.S. peacekeeping actions. Still, political leaders in the United States will continue to insist that the United Nations shows that the money it receives saves lives and secures peace and does so efficiently.

Nevertheless, the United Nations is still a work in progress. Critics across the ideological spectrum question whether it makes sense to give every U.N. member an equal vote in the General Assembly, regardless of its size, population, and contribution to the U.N. budget. Critics also worry about creating a standing U.N. army with a large contingent of U.S. troops under foreign command. Some U.S. officials call this situation "taxation without representation."

Foreign Aid

The United States offers aid to more than 100 countries directly and to other nations through contributions to various U.N. development funds. Since 1945, the United States has provided about $400 billion in economic assistance to foreign countries. In recent years, however, foreign aid spending has amounted to around $15 billion per year, or less than 50 percent of what it spent in inflation-adjusted dollars back in 1985.[30]

Most foreign aid goes to a few countries that the United States deems to be of strategic importance to our national security: Israel, Egypt, Ukraine, Jordan, India, Russia, South Africa, and Haiti. That list is sure to change in the future as the nation reallocates

The Israeli Army surrounds Yasser Arafat's compound. The failure to reach agreement produced a new round of deadly violence in the Middle East as Israeli forces sought some way to end a wave of suicide bombings across the nation.

Kofi Annan, secretary general of the United Nations.

its budget to nations central to the war on terrorism. However, regardless of which nation receives the aid, most foreign aid is actually spent in the United States, where it pays for the purchase of American services and products being sent to those countries. It thus amounts to a hefty subsidy for American companies and their employees.

Many Americans and members of Congress oppose foreign aid. A recent poll of American citizens found that only 9 percent supported increasing foreign aid, while 47 percent favored reducing it. Another 40 percent would keep it pretty much at the same level.[31] Few powerful interest groups or constituencies back foreign aid initiatives. State Department officials are invariably the biggest advocates of foreign aid. Presidents also recognize the vital role foreign aid plays in advancing U.S. interests. Successive presidents have all wanted to maintain the leverage with key countries that economic and military assistance provides. One of the major debates today is how much debt relief to provide for the world's poorest nations, some of which spend up to 50 percent of their budgets to service debt on old loans. The problem is particularly severe in Central and South America, where international debt has brought high inflation, unemployment, and civil unrest.

Despite these arguments, Congress invariably trims the foreign aid budget, responding in part to polls that show most Americans believe the United States spends more on foreign aid than it does on Medicare and other domestic priorities. Members of Congress often criticize foreign aid as a "Ghana versus Grandma" case. How, they say, can you give away taxpayers' money to some foreign country when we have poor older people who can't afford their prescription drugs and decent medical help?[32]

Critics also note that U.S. foreign aid has subsidized the most autocratic and most corrupt of dictators. And there are plenty of instances in which foreign aid money has been stolen or misspent. Defenders counter that some corruption is inevitable. "You can't engage in bone-poor countries that lack laws and independent journalists and elections, and expect American standards of transparency," writes Washington Post editorial writer Sebastian Mallaby. "Yes, many aid programs fail and will continue to do so. But you don't give up trying to educate and house people just because it's hard. And you don't give up on international engagement just because it's as daunting as it is important."[33]

IN COMPARATIVE PERSPECTIVE

Foreign Aid

By almost any measure of spending, the United States remains the world's last superpower, as well as one of its most generous neighbors. It spends more on defense than any nation in the world and contributes billions annually to foreign aid. In 2000, it spent more than $250 billion for defense and roughly $10 billion in foreign aid to other countries. Only Japan spent more on foreign aid, investing heavily in helping other Asian nations modernize their economies.

Absolute spending is not the only measure of foreign aid and military spending, however. Measured as a proportion of gross national income, which is an international measure of the size of a nation's economy, the United States has one of the Western world's smallest foreign aid budgets, while Denmark is the most generous in helping others. Although the United States still retains considerable international influence based on its military might, some experts argue that it could be more persuasive on other foreign policy issues if it increased its foreign aid budget.

Foreign Aid Spending, 2000

Nation	Total Spending (billions of U.S. dollars)	Percentage of Gross National Income
Denmark	$1.66	1.06%
Netherlands	3.10	0.84
Sweden	1.80	0.80
Norway	1.26	0.80
Switzerland	0.89	0.34
France	4.10	0.32
United Kingdom	4.50	0.32
Japan	13.50	0.28
Germany	5.03	0.27
Canada	1.74	0.25
Spain	1.19	0.022
Italy	1.38	0.13
United States	9.95	0.10

SOURCE: Organization for Economic Cooperation and Development, 2002.

Economic Sanctions

The United States has frequently applied economic pressure in response to a nation's unwillingness to abide by what we perceive to be international law or proper relations. Indeed, the United States has employed economic sanctions more than any other nation—over 100 times in the past 50 years. **Economic sanctions** entail a denial of export, import, or financial relations with a target country in an effort to change that country's policies. Economic sanctions imposed on South Africa doubtless helped end apartheid and encourage democracy in that nation. But sanctions imposed on Iraq and Cuba have not had much effect in dislodging those nations' dictatorial regimes. The United States imposed sanctions on India and Pakistan in 1998 when both nations began a round of nuclear testing, but because of economic distress both in Pakistan and among U.S. wheat growers, Congress and the president lifted most of the sanctions within months of imposing them.

In the first major offensive of the war on terrorism, American troops invaded Afghanistan.

The popularity of economic sanctions has risen and fallen over the years. They are especially unpopular among farmers and corporations that have to sacrifice part of their overseas markets to comply with government controls, and they rarely work as effectively as intended. Brookings Institution scholar Richard Haass claims, "Sanctions have caused humanitarian suffering (Haiti), weakened friendly governments (Bosnia), bolstered tyrants (Cuba), and left countries with little choice but to develop nuclear weapons (Pakistan)."[34] They can also be costly to U.S. businesses and workers while intensifying anti-American sentiment.

Senator Richard Lugar believes that sanctions seldom work unless they are multilateral rather than imposed by the United States alone.[35] Scholars suggest that when dealing with authoritarian regimes, the United States should direct sanctions at rulers, not the populace at large. "Iraqis are not our enemies. Nor are the Cubans," writes Gary Hufbauer. "Where the president imposes comprehensive sanctions on an authoritarian regime, he should view those sanctions as a prelude to the exercise of military force, not as a substitute for force. Unless we are prepared to remove bad governments with military force, we have no business heaping prolonged punishment on innocent people."[36]

Military Intervention

War is not merely an extension of diplomacy but rather the complete and total breakdown of diplomatic efforts. The United States has used military force in other nations on the average of almost once a year since 1789, although usually in short-term initiatives such as NATO's military activities in Bosnia and Kosovo and the war in Afghanistan. Of course, these may not be considered minor events by the target nations or by the American families who lose sons and daughters in these forays.

Military action by the United States is most successful when it involves small and even medium-sized countries (Grenada, Panama, Kuwait, Kosovo, and Afghanistan). But military intervention "often proves ineffective in the context of national civil wars (the United States in Vietnam; Israel in Lebanon)."[37] Lessons from past interventions are one reason Americans were reluctant to support, if not opposed to, U.S. military intervention in Haiti, Bosnia, and Kosovo. It also helps explain the public's general resistance to an attack on Iraq in 2002.

U.S. military efforts with its NATO allies in Kosovo sought to put an end to "ethnic cleansing" in that area. After an extensive air campaign, ground troops were able to force the withdrawal of Serbian military and police, permit the safe return of refugees, and secure stability in the province. President Clinton had been hesitant to use the military in a decisive way in Kosovo in large part because of the apparent opposition of the American people and Congress. And many in the military were also reluctant to commit forces to what they viewed as primarily a humanitarian initiative rather than a defense of America's vital national security interests. These opposing views prompted renewed debates about the conditions under which the United States should resort to military intervention.[38]

Not all military action is visible to the public or even the intended target. Covert activities are planned and executed to conceal the identity of the sponsor. The United States repeatedly engaged in covert operations during the cold war, including early intervention in

economic sanctions
Denial of export, import, or financial relations with a target country in an effort to change that nation's policies.

Public Diplomacy

In July 2002, President George W. Bush created the White House Office of Global Communications to address the question he asked before a joint session of Congress only a week after the terrorist attacks on New York City and Washington, D.C.: "Why do they hate us?" The office is designed to enhance America's image abroad, thereby countering the image of the United States as the "Great Satan," as some of its enemies describe it.

Bush was not the first president to worry about the U.S. image abroad. President Franklin Roosevelt created the Office of War Information early in World War II, which in turn established the Voice of America program to broadcast pro-American information into Nazi Germany. President Harry Truman followed suit early in the cold war with the Soviet Union by launching the Campaign of Truth, which eventually led to the creation of the United States Information Agency under President Dwight Eisenhower. Both agencies exist today and are being strengthened as part of the "new public diplomacy." In this case, the word "public" refers to citizens of other nations, not the United States.

Public diplomacy is a blend of age-old propaganda techniques and modern information warfare. It has three basic goals: (1) to cast the enemy in a less favorable light among its supporters, (2) to mold the image of a conflict such as the war in Afghanistan, and (3) to clarify the ultimate goals of U.S. foreign policy. The United States has tried to convince the people of Afghanistan that Osama bin Laden is the true enemy of the people, the war is not between Muslims and Western democracies, and the war is about preventing the deaths of innocent women and children in both Afghanistan and the United States. Public diplomacy is not a substitute for traditional information warfare such as jamming enemy radio broadcasts, destroying radio and television towers, and disseminating misleading information about the enemy. But it does strike at the heart of the hate that fuels terrorism.

SOURCE: P. W. Singer, "Winning the War of Words: Information Warfare in Afghanistan," *Brookings Analysis Paper No. 5* (October 2001).

Vietnam and Central America, as well as in Afghanistan, where it supported rebels fighting the Soviet invasion. But covert activities in Cuba, Chile, and elsewhere have backfired, and support for this strategy has cooled in the post–cold war era.[39] Ironically, U.S. covert aid to the Afghan rebels eventually led to the Soviet withdrawal, which in turn led to the establishment of the Taliban, which allowed Osama bin Laden and his followers to establish training bases in its territory. Obviously, covert action can produce entirely unintended consequences.

Special Problems in Defense Policy

The United States has a long history of military involvement in world affairs. Since 1945, more than 100,000 U.S. military personnel have died in undeclared wars; more than 400,000 have suffered battle injuries.[40] But Congress has formally declared war on only a few occasions. The war in Afghanistan was never formally declared, nor was the air war over Kosovo or the Gulf War. Although Congress passed joint resolutions supporting both engagements, the president moved military forces into position well before passage.

Americans believe that the United States should use its military power carefully. As noted earlier in this chapter, almost three out of five Americans said the United States should use military force to prevent future terrorism, compared to just one out of five who said it should use force to punish the terrorists. Even after the events of September 11, 2001, substantial numbers of Americans continued to believe that the United States should not send forces into regional conflicts when other means are available to achieve our objectives. Many also continued to believe that the United States should not intervene in conflicts without a broad public consensus at home and an alliance of nations abroad.

These views eventually led to the Powell Doctrine, formulated by General Colin Powell, the future secretary of state, when he served as chair of the Joint Chiefs of Staff in the late 1980s. The Powell Doctrine reflects the concerns of both average Americans and many senior military leaders. "When the United States goes to war," he said, "it should be for a clear purpose, only when our vital national security interests are threatened, and our goal should be overwhelming victory." Powell pointed out that "half-hearted warfare for half-baked reasons" is misguided defense policy.[41] As one analyst explained Powell's reasoning: "He argues that the people he calls 'K-mart parents'— working class Americans who tend to be the parents of soldiers—should understand why their children are being put at risk and should never doubt that the country will back them to the hilt."[42]

This doctrine involves far more than a simple contest between internationalism and isolationism; it raises issues about human rights and moral leadership as well as about military effectiveness. The Powell Doctrine has widespread support. Still, most Americans believe it would be a mistake to forsake our unique leadership position and abandon responsibilities to encourage peace and human rights at this time of incredible global change.[43]

THE ALL-VOLUNTEER FORCE   The Constitution authorizes Congress to do what is "necessary and proper" in order to "raise and support Armies," "to provide and maintain a Navy," and "to provide for calling forth the Militia." The problem is that the role of the United States in the world has changed dramatically since 1789, as have the nation's military needs. Although our boundaries once defined our major national interest, U.S. interests now reach around the globe.

Military conscription (the draft) was first instituted in 1862, during the Civil War. It was used during World War I, when Congress passed the Selective Service Act. This act called for a draft of males between the ages of 21 and 30, with exemptions for certain public officials and for clergy. In both instances, conscription ended when the conflicts ended. The first peacetime draft began in 1940, with the Selective Service and Training Act. By the time of Pearl Harbor, in late 1941, men between the ages of 18 and 35 were eligible for the draft. When World War II ended, however, the draft continued, in various

PEOPLE IN POLITICS
COLIN L. POWELL

Few Americans benefited more from President Harry S Truman's 1948 executive order to integrate the military than future Secretary of State Colin Powell. Born in 1937, Powell entered the Army after finishing college at the City College of New York. Entering as a second lieutenant in 1958, Powell rose quickly through the ranks. He served two tours of duty in Vietnam, commanded the 2nd Brigade, 101st Airborne division, and the U.S. V Corps in Europe, paying the dues that would eventually lead to his appointment as the first African American chair of the Joint Chiefs of Staff, the highest military position in the U.S. armed forces, and as the nation's first black secretary of state.

Throughout his steady climb, Powell benefited from equality of opportunity but not racial preferences. As he argues in his autobiography, the difference was critical for his success:

> I benefited from equal opportunity and affirmative action in the Army, but I was not shown preference. The Army, as a matter of fairness, made sure that performance would be the only measure of advancement. When equal performance does not result in equal advancement, then something is wrong with the system, and our leaders have an obligation to fix it. If a history of discrimination has made it difficult for certain Americans to meet standards, it is only fair to provide temporary means to help them catch up and compete on equal terms. Affirmative action in the best sense promotes equal consideration, not reverse discrimination. Discrimination "for" one group means, inevitably, discrimination "against" another; and all discrimination is offensive.*

Powell confronted and stood up to racism inside the military, whether on the battlefields of Vietnam or in the corridors of the Pentagon. He also confronted concerns among civil rights advocates that the all-voluntary army of the 1980s and 1990s put too many African Americans in harm's way. Powell had sent his share of young men and women into danger zones during his career, both as a commander in Vietnam and as Ronald Reagan's national security adviser.

As chair of the Joint Chiefs in 1990, he was in charge of more than 750,000 soldiers about to go to war in the Persian Gulf, of whom one quarter were African Americans. His answer to those who worried that blacks would bear more than their fair share of casualties was simple: "The military had given blacks more equal opportunity than any other institution in American society. . . . There was only one way to reduce the proportion of blacks in the military: let the rest of American society open its doors to blacks and give them the opportunities they now enjoyed in the armed forces."†

Having left the military in 1993, Powell continued to act as an agent of change. As one of the most admired Americans, Powell debated hard and long about running for the Republican presidential nomination in 1996. With a best-selling autobiography, *My American Story,* a hero's résumé, and a moderate policy agenda, he would have been a formidable candidate. After months of soul-searching, he decided not to run, in part because of concerns about the amount of time and scrutiny that would come with a presidential campaign, choosing instead to run a national campaign for volunteerism called America's Promise.

To this day, however, he retains his mystique as one of the nation's most popular politicians. As of May 2002, for example, 85 percent of Americans had a favorable opinion of Powell, an approval rating 10 percentage points higher than that of the president. He also continues to attract fire for his moderate Republican positions. Early in the 2000 campaign, Vice President Gore's campaign manager, Donna Brazile, herself the first black to hold a top campaign job, criticized Republicans on race. "Al Gore and Bill Clinton have worked hard for the last seven years to improve the lives of African Americans and Hispanics," she said. "On the other hand, the Republicans bring out Colin Powell and [Rep.] J. C. Watts [R.-Okla.] because they have no program, no policy. They play that game because they have no other game. They have no love and no joy. They'd rather take pictures with black children than feed them."‡

Despite Powell's efforts to create a barrier-free armed services, there is still significant work to be done to eliminate racism in the armed services. According to a 1999 survey of 40,000 members of the armed services, African and Hispanic Americans continue to report high levels of racially offensive remarks and incidents, and women have yet to gain the full respect of their colleagues.

Moreover, even though roughly half of all the respondents reported that race relations are better in the military than in the nation as a whole, minorities appear to still have trouble rising to the top. On the one hand, women and minorities have made significant gains as a proportion of the officer corps, more than doubling their share of total appointments over the past two decades. On the other hand, women and minorities tend to be concentrated in administrative and supply areas of the armed services and underrepresented in tactical, war-fighting operations.

*Colin L. Powell with Joseph Persico, *My American Journey: An Autobiography* (Random House, 1995).

†Ibid.

‡"Race and Gender in the Military," *New York Times,* November 25, 1999, p. A36.

The "Don't Ask, Don't Tell" Controversy

Controversy persists over whether the military has the right to expel homosexuals because of their sexual orientation. In the mid-1990s, the U.S. military expelled about 1,000 men and women every year because of sexual preference. The Pentagon defended the ban by saying that homosexuals in a military setting create difficulty because there is no privacy and no choice of association or living quarters.

Many leaders in Congress and elsewhere criticized the ban, calling it the final bastion of discrimination in the military and saying it reminded them of the Army's former official opposition to African Americans in uniform. Bill Clinton called for a complete end to the ban when he campaigned for his first term as president. Once in office, however, he had to settle for a compromise that merely modified the ban. Under the "Don't Ask, Don't Tell" policy, military officials are not permitted to question recruits about their sexual orientation, and gays and lesbians are required to refrain from sexual activities while on duty or on assignment. Those who commit homosexual acts are still subject to discharge.

The "Don't Ask, Don't Tell" plan was intended to provide more humane treatment for gays by permitting them to serve in the military if they did not disclose their sexual orientation or engage in homosexual practices. "It has, instead, forced gays to lie, and has resulted in more harassment and a near doubling in the number of people being discharged annually on the basis of homosexuality."* Critics say the policy may well be worse than the policy it replaced, which forced gays to resign.

Gay rights groups have turned to the courts to try to get the regulations overruled as unconstitutional. Some U.S. district courts have ruled that the military may not discharge a person simply because of declared sexual orientation. Various federal court rulings have upheld the regulations set by the Clinton White House, saying they were properly based on a law enacted by Congress and that courts are traditionally obligated to defer to the other branches of government, especially when the matter involves military policy.†

The U.S. Supreme Court has never ruled definitely on the "Don't Ask, Don't Tell" policy. But several federal appeals courts have upheld the policy, and the Supreme Court has on several occasions rejected a challenge to the policy.‡

Americans are divided over this issue. Many conservatives would like an unambiguous rejection of gays in the military. They claim it discourages both military enlistment efforts and unit cohesion. However, as former Republican presidential candidate Barry Goldwater said, "You don't need to be straight to fight and die for your country. You just need to shoot straight."§

"The one's for not asking and this one's for not telling."

*"The Pentagon's Anti-Gay Policies," editorial, *New York Times*, July 27, 2000, p. A26.

†See Neil A. Lewis, "Court Upholds Clinton Policy on Gay Troops," *New York Times*, April 6, 1996, pp. 1, 7.

‡Richard Carelli, "'Don't Ask, Don't Tell' Survives First Test in Supreme Court," *USA Today*, October 20, 1998, p. A4.

§Barry M. Goldwater, "The Gay Ban: Just Plain Un-American," *Washington Post National Weekly Edition*, June 21, 1993, p. 28.

forms, for almost three decades. Shortly before the Vietnam War ended, Congress established the *all-volunteer force* (AVF). This force is charged with providing for our peacetime military personnel needs; in time of war, a draft could be reinstituted.

The all-volunteer force continues to raise questions 30 years after its establishment. Some experts contend that the AVF has worked, that the quality and quantity of recruits are as good as or better than under the draft, and that the social costs are much lower. Other experts say that quality has dropped and that the AVF is inadequate to defend our vital interests abroad.

The military has had problems attracting the desired number of recruits. The services reported serious shortfalls, and active reserves have fewer members than in earlier decades. The number of total full-time, active personnel in all services is 1.4 million, down from a cold war high of 2.2 million in the late 1980s. Minorities are overrepresented in the armed services, notably in the Army, where African Americans constitute more than 30 percent of the enlisted ranks. Women are underrepresented, although the proportion of women to men in the armed forces has grown.

Preparedness may be judged in part by the educational level of new recruits. About 80 percent of all new enlisted troops have graduated from high school, a higher level than the eligible pool. But maintaining this level requires extensive recruiting and higher pay and fringe benefits, which the Bush administration has advocated.

The all-volunteer force was set up as a peacetime measure. If major emergencies came, so, presumably, would the draft. However, President Jimmy Carter asked for and won congressional approval for the resumption of draft registration. Carter's initial plan called for the registration of men and women within 30 days of their eighteenth birthday. Congress refused to appropriate funds for the registration of women. Later the Supreme Court upheld the men-only registration. This is the practice today. All males, by law, must report at age 18. (College-age males 18 and over who have failed to do so are ineligible for federal financial aid.)

Some Americans at the time opposed the draft registration because they believed it would inevitably lead to a draft. They also believed that Carter was playing politics with the process and that it was entirely unnecessary during peacetime. The Selective Service said registration would save less than two weeks in the event of a mobilization.

Women now make up approximately 14 percent of the total enlistment in the U.S. armed forces.

WOMEN IN THE MILITARY AND IN COMBAT   Women constitute 14 percent of the total enlistment in the armed forces; 6 percent of our forces in the Persian Gulf War were female, and 10 percent of the U.S. troops serving in the NATO mission to implement the peace accords in Bosnia were women.[44] The women in Operation Desert Storm piloted troop transport and supply aircraft, helped operate Patriot antimissile systems, and worked as tank mechanics and military police guarding Iraqi prisoners of war.

Congress has lifted any legal restrictions on Air Force and Navy women becoming combat pilots, and the Pentagon has now opened thousands of combat-related positions in the military services to women. The military is redesigning its assignments to ensure that equal opportunity exists within its ranks but has yet to assign women to specific combat roles.

A majority of Americans think that women should be assigned to ground combat units, but others are still concerned about women in combat situations. Many women in the military have said that while they would like to have the right to serve in combat positions, most of them would not opt for those roles. The difficulty in deciding whether women should participate in combat often comes in defining what combat is.

Despite their accomplishments, women in the armed forces have faced countless problems, including sexual harassment, and women officers have complained of men refusing to take orders from them and of being given inappropriate assignments. Female Navy combat pilots complain about the "silent treatment" and gender prejudice.[45] Still, women are generally winning acceptance in the military at all levels and will continue to play significant roles in virtually all aspects of the armed forces.

The Politics of Defense Spending

The U.S. defense budget reached $365 billion in 2003. About half the people employed by the national government work in the Defense Department. About three-quarters of federal purchases of goods and services originate in the defense budget; several thousand defense installations are scattered across the country. Contracts in excess of $100 billion result in defense-related civilian employment of nearly 2 million workers. More than 1.5 million retired Defense Department personnel draw pensions and other fringe benefits. The defense budget also includes more than $12 billion dedicated to nuclear weapons research and maintenance and environmental cleanup projects that are actually run by the Department of Energy.[46]

Reflecting the end of the cold war, the demise of the Soviet Union, and the lack of support for maintaining defense spending at 1980s levels, defense spending decreased during most of the 1990s. Weapons systems were canceled or postponed, bases closed, ships retired, and large numbers of troops brought home from Germany, the Philippines, and elsewhere. A number of major weapons systems whose primary justification was to fight the former Soviet Union were canceled or had their production greatly curtailed. All the services lost personnel. The Army was cut over 30 percent, and the National Guard and the military reserve have been cut back about 25 percent. As a result, defense spending has also fallen, dropping from 25 percent at the height of the cold war in the mid-1980s to 16 percent by 2001.[47]

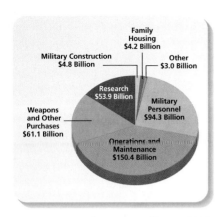

FIGURE 21–2   Defense Expenditures, 2003.

SOURCE: Michael O'Hanlon, "Protecting the American Homeland," *Brookings Review,* 20 (Summer, 2002), p. 15.

The defense budget is going to increase dramatically in coming years, but not just because of the war on terrorism. Both presidential candidates promised a major increase in defense spending in the 2000 campaign, in part because military pay was lagging far behind comparable private sector salaries, greater health care costs for military personnel, and long-planned purchases of new fighter jets, ships, and the proposed missile shield.

As Figure 21-2 shows, more than half of all defense spending goes to people, actual operations such as the war in Afghanistan, and maintenance. It is important to note that only 8 percent of the defense budget for 2003 involved costs associated with the war in Afghanistan and other military operations associated with strengthening homeland security. Those figures would obviously change if the United States went to war with Iraq, for example.

BUILDING A MODERN DEFENSE   Despite the newfound enthusiasm for increased defense spending, some experts argue that the nation needs a much lighter, highly mobile force to combat terrorism and that further spending on "cold war legacy" systems such as nuclear attack submarines and heavy tanks is wasteful.[48] They argue that the United States cannot have it all—meaning old cold war systems, high-tech space defenses, decent military pay, and the kind of expensive precision weaponry used in Afghanistan. Nor do they believe that the United States should continue spending money on weapons systems, such as the Comanche helicopter or V-22 tilt-rotor aircraft, that do not work.

Despite the logic, Congress can rarely muster the will to kill a weapons system. Cutting defense spending means cutting jobs, and cutting jobs, especially those in the home districts of powerful members of Congress, is politically painful.[49] The B-52 Stealth bomber is often pointed to as notable case. The Pentagon has not asked for more of these billion-dollar planes, yet Congress often approves funds for them because cuts in weapons systems and plant closings mean not only that people in the Defense Department and on bases lose their jobs but also that local shopkeepers, bankers, lawyers, doctors, contractors, housekeepers, baby-sitters—the list goes on and on—are put out of work.

Weapons are, in fact, a major American industry, an industry that members of Congress work hard to promote and protect. The agreement that operates in other pork-barrel areas works here as well: "You help me in my district, and I'll help you in yours." Even the most ardent balance-the-budget conservatives change their tune when a contract termination hits close to their district.

This is not to say that members of Congress cast their votes on military spending solely on whether their district would profit from the decisions. An analysis of the relationships between campaign contributors and votes on weapons systems concludes that issues of defense strategy, cost, and a legislator's political philosophy are equally important.[50]

Nor is this to say that the Defense Department never cancels a weapons system. In spring 2002, for example, Secretary of Defense Donald Rumsfeld canceled the Army's $11 billion Crusader mobile cannon. As Deputy Secretary of Defense Paul Wolfowitz explained, "This decision is not about killing a bad system. This decision is about canceling a system originally designed for a different strategic context, to make room for more promising technologies that offer greater payoffs."[51] Ironically, the Crusader is one of a handful of weapons systems that actually came in on time and on budget.

Nevertheless, as former World War II hero Dwight Eisenhower noted in his presidential Farewell Address in 1960, there is a *military-industrial complex* in the United States that supports increased defense spending as a way to protect jobs. One tactic for defeating this alliance is to force members of Congress to consider cuts in a single yes-or-no vote that imposes equal shares of pain on all states.

That is how the Defense Department was able to close obsolete, unneeded military bases in the wake of the cold war. In an effort to thwart its own self-interest in keeping those bases open, Congress established a blue-ribbon commission in 1988 to generate a single list of bases that were submitted for a yes-or-no vote. At least three additional commissions have been appointed in subsequent years. These commissions are appointed by Congress and the president, but they work independently of both branches. They review the base-closing suggestions made by the Pentagon and make recommendations, which have to be accepted in toto or else be rejected by the president. If the president accepts the closings, the package then goes to Congress, where each chamber is allowed 45 days to consider the entire package. Congress also has to accept the entire package or else no closings take place.[52] More than 200 bases have been closed under the process, and the savings will run to the billions of dollars. Despite grumbling from the big losers, some lawsuits, and attempts by members of Congress to delay closings, the federal courts have upheld these procedures, and bases continue to be closed.

Prospects for the Future

Although some experts have likened the war on terrorism to the cold war, it is not yet clear whether the war on terrorism will become the defining theme for U.S. foreign and defense policy over the coming decades. There is no doubt that the United States will pursue the war with great intensity, nor is there any question that Democrats and Republicans alike will support increased defense spending for the effort. Americans want to feel safe again and will not rest until Osama bin Laden has been caught and his terror network laid to rest.

The war on terrorism is unlike any war the nation has fought, however. The targets are hard to find and equally hard to destroy. Individual terrorists can disappear for years as "sleepers" in their communities before springing to action when the moment is right. Because they are trained to strike when and where least expected, the United States must try to prepare for every possible contingency to restore at least some sense of security.

The weapons of war are also different. The heavy weaponry of the cold war is almost useless against such a highly mobile, zealous enemy. The world has rarely confronted enemies so completely willing to sacrifice their own lives for what they perceive as the greater cause.

Daunting though it is, the war on terrorism is only one of many issues that the United States will face in the coming years. The world is getting hotter in both military and environmental terms as weapons of mass destruction proliferate and global warming increases. It is also getting more demanding as the Internet spreads democratic and capitalistic ideas to once isolated corners of the world. Successful foreign and defense policy involves a balancing act among competing priorities. The United States cannot become so focused on the war on terrorism that it loses sight of what the world will be like once that war is over.

Although Secretary of Defense Donald Rumsfeld asked Congress to cancel the Crusader mobile cannon in the spring of 2002, members of Congress were able to salvage funding for continued development.

"How else are we going to pay for the war?"

PoliSim

THE IMPACT OF FOREIGN AID

U.S. policy makers have at least three choices to make in giving foreign aid to a country. First, they must decide whether to give any funding at all. The decision depends in part on the strategic value of the recipient nation to U.S. foreign policy goals such as fighting the war on terrorism or reducing the flow of illegal drugs. Second, they must decide what kind of aid to give. Third, they must decide how much to give. Because the foreign aid budget is limited, these decisions determine which nations will be helped or hurt, which in turn determines whether the United States is able to achieve its policy goals. This simulation challenges readers to make the key decisions in distributing a fixed foreign aid budget. Where should the money go, and in what form?

Go to PoliSim "The Impact of Foreign Aid."

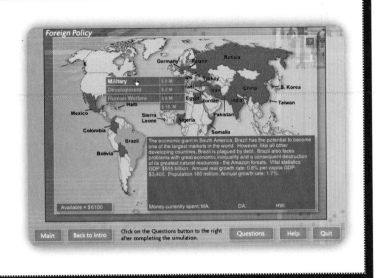

Summary

1. The nation's top foreign policy challenges today are the war on terrorism; control of nuclear, chemical, and biological arms; finding peace in the Middle East; promoting U.S. trade; and strengthening democracy in the former Soviet Union. The war on terrorism is clearly the top priority and has reframed U.S. relations with former friends and adversaries.

2. The president has the primary responsibility to shape foreign and defense policy. The principal foreign policy adviser is the secretary of state, although other cabinet secretaries, including the secretary of defense, are also influential. The National Security Council and the intelligence agencies also play key roles. Public opinion, interest groups, foreign countries, political parties, and Congress also affect the making of foreign policy.

3. Presidents, Congress, and the American people all become involved in defining our vital national security interests, but they often have contradictory views. Presidents must sometimes act swiftly and decisively. Plainly, the role of the president in foreign affairs was strengthened during the cold war years as the United States developed an enormous standing military capability and an extensive intelligence network. Presidents are often in a good position to see the nation's long-term interests above the tugging of bureaucratic and special interests. But in our constitutional democracy, presidents and their advisers must consult with Congress and inform the American people. The media and special interests also play a role.

4. U.S. foreign policy interests are advanced by one or a combination of the following strategies: diplomacy, foreign aid, economic sanctions, political coercion (including the breaking off of diplomatic relations), covert action, and military intervention. Traditional diplomacy is often augmented by the U.S. role in the United Nations.

5. The U.S. military is an all-volunteer force. Although the military does provide enormous opportunities for women and minorities, women have yet to play a significant role in combat.

6. Although the past decade witnessed major reductions in the size of the military and major cuts in military spending, some critics say the defense budget can be cut much further. Critics on the right, however, claim that we have weakened our defense preparedness. The nature of warfare and the preventing of wars are changing in ways that are hard to predict.

Key Terms

permanent normal trade
   relations (PNTR) status

bipartisanship

economic sanctions

Further Reading

GEORGE H. W. BUSH and BRENT SCOWCROFT, *A World Transformed* (Knopf, 1998).

WARREN CRISTOPHER, *In the Stream of History: Shaping Foreign Policy for a New Era* (Stanford University Press, 1998).

IVO H. DAALDER and MICHAEL E. O'HANLON, *Winning Ugly: NATO's War to Save Kosovo* (Brookings Institution, 2000).

JOSEPH G. DAWSON III, ED., *Commanders-in-Chief: Presidential Leadership in Modern Wars* (University Press of Kansas, 1993).

LOUIS FISHER, *Presidential War Power* (University Press of Kansas, 1995).

JOHN LEWIS GADDIS, *The United States and the End of the Cold War* (Oxford University Press, 1992).

RICHARD N. HAASS, *The Reluctant Sheriff: The United States After the Cold War* (Council on Foreign Relations, 1997).

RICHARD N. HAASS and MEGHAN L. O'SULLIVAN, EDS., *Honey and Vinegar: Incentives, Sanctions, and Foreign Policy* (Brookings Institution, 2000).

OLE HOLSTI, *Public Opinion and American Foreign Policy* (University of Michigan Press, 1996).

SAMUEL HUNTINGTON, *The Clash of Civilization and the Remaking of World Order* (Simon & Schuster, 1996).

LOCH K. JOHNSON, *Secret Agencies: U.S. Intelligence in a Hostile World* (Yale University Press, 1996).

HAROLD HONGJU KOH, *The National Security Constitution: Sharing Power After the Iran-Contra Affair* (Yale University Press, 1990).

STEVEN KULL AND I. M. DESTLER, *Misreading the Public: The Myth of a New Isolationism* (Brookings Institution, 1999).

THOMAS W. LIPPMAN, *Madeleine Albright and the New American Diplomacy* (Westview Press, 2000).

ROBERT LITAN, *Globalphobia* (Brookings Institution, 2002).

ROBERT S. LITWAK, *Rogue States and U.S. Foreign Policy: Containment After the Cold War* (Johns Hopkins University Press, 2000).

MICHAEL E. O'HANLON, *How to Be a Cheap Defense Hawk* (Brookings Institution, 2002).

WILLIAM PERRY, *Preventive Defense: A New Security Strategy for America* (Brookings Institution, 1999).

JOHN PRADOS, *Keepers of the Keys: A History of the National Security Council from Truman to Bush* (Morrow, 1991).

ROSEMARY RIGHTER, *Utopia Lost: The United Nations and World Order* (Twentieth Century Fund, 1995).

JOSEPH ROMM, *Defining National Security: The Nonmilitary Aspect* (Council on Foreign Relations, 1993).

GEORGE SHULTZ, *Turmoil and Triumph: My Years as Secretary of State* (Scribner, 1993).

RONALD STEEL, *Temptations of a Superpower* (Harvard University Press, 1995).

STEPHEN R. WEISSMAN, *A Culture of Deference: Congress's Failure of Leadership in Foreign Affairs* (Basic Books, 1995).

GEORGE C. WILSON, *This War Really Matters: Inside the Fight for Defense Dollars* (CQ Press, 2000).

22 CHAPTER

STATE AND LOCAL POLITICS
Who Governs?

HO PAVES OUR ROADS, RUNS OUR SCHOOLS, SHAPES WELFARE POLICY, DECIDES WHO GOES TO PRISON OR GETS probation, and levies property and sales taxes? Most of these policies are determined by elected and appointed officials in our states and localities. Many of the most critical domestic and economic issues facing the United States today are decided by our state and local officials. Such challenging responsibilities as overseeing the transition from welfare to work, maintaining prisons and jails (over 90 percent of the people incarcerated in America are in state and local facilities, not federal prisons), and bringing the residents of the inner cities in our large metropolitan areas into the economic mainstream require imaginative leadership and thoughtful public policy making at the state and local levels of government as well as in Washington, D.C.

Most state and local governments currently face big deficits. In 2003, New Jersey had a deficit of $5.3 billion, and New York a shortfall of $5.1 billion; New York City's was $4.7 billion. Each responds differently, based on its own set of problems (especially those stemming from the September 11, 2001, terorist attacks), history, and the leadership of elected officials. New Jersey's governor, James E. McGreevey, cut funding for state agencies and building construction, whereas New York's governor, George E. Pataki, is drawing on hundreds of millions of dollars that the state squirreled away during the economic boom of the 1990s and reserved "for a rainy day," which Pataki said has turned out to be more like a "monsoon."[1]

State and local governments flourished long before there was a national government. Indeed, the framers of our Constitution shaped the national government largely according to their practical experience with colonial and state governments. What happens today in state and local governments continues to influence the policies of the national government. The reverse, of course, is also true: The national government and its policies have an important impact on local and state government. The national government's activities—such as the war against international terrorism, diplomatic maneuvers in the Middle East, key Supreme Court decisions, and major congressional debates and investigations—receive such great publicity that we often overlook the countless ways governments closer to home affect our lives.

Studying state and local governments to find out how they operate and who governs them is a challenge. It is one thing to study our national system, vast and complex as it is; it is something else to study 50 separate state governments, each with its own legislature, executive, and judiciary and each with its own intricate politics and political traditions. Moreover, state and local governments are only part of a much larger picture. To discuss the government of the state of Mississippi or of the city of Detroit without mentioning race, the government of New York City or of Los Angeles without noting the politics of ethnic groups, or the government of Texas without referring to the cattle and oil industries would be to ignore the real dynamics of the political process. State and local governments, like the national government, are more than organizational charts. They are systems of politics and people with their own unique histories. The great variations among the states and localities—in population, economic resources, and environment—make comparisons and generalizations difficult.

Still, every government system is part of a larger social system. A government is a structure and a process that resolves, or at least manages, conflicts. It regulates, distributes, and sometimes redistributes property and wealth. It is also a means for achieving certain goals and performing services desired both by those who govern and by the governed. It operates in the context of an economic system, class structure, and lifestyle that are often more important than the structure of the government itself or even the nature of its political processes. The interrelations among the economic, social, and political systems are complex and hard to unscramble, and it is difficult to decide which is cause and which is effect.[2]

This already complex picture is complicated further by the fact that more than 87,500 cities, counties, towns, villages, school districts, water control districts, and other governmental units are piled one on top of another within the states. If all states or cities or towns were alike, the task might be manageable. But of course they are not. Each city, like each state, has distinct characteristics.[3]

Who Has the Power?

How can we grasp the operations and problems of state and local government without becoming bogged down in endless detail? We can do so by focusing on the core components of democratic governance: citizen participation, liberty, constitutional checks and balances, representation, and responsible leadership. Further, we can address several questions that throw light on all these problems: Who governs? How much influence or control is in the hands of the business community? Does political power tend to gravitate toward a relatively small number of people? If so, who are these people? Do they work closely together, or do they oppose each other? Do the same people or factions shape the agenda for public debate and dominate all decision making? Or do some sets of leaders decide certain questions and leave other questions to other leaders or simply to chance?

In 1924, two sociologists from Columbia University, Robert and Helen Lynd, decided to study a typical American city as though they were anthropologists investigating a tribe in Africa or Indonesia. For two years, they lived in Muncie, Indiana—at that time a city of 38,000 residents—asking questions and watching how people made their living, raised their children, used their leisure time, and joined in civic and social associations. The Lynds reported that despite the appearance of democratic rule, a social and economic elite actually ran things.[4] Their work stimulated studies in all kinds of communities to find out whether power is concentrated in the hands of the few, is dispersed among the many, or operates in some other way.

Relying on a mix of research methods, social scientists since the Lynds' time have studied patterns of power in communities and arrived at a variety of findings. Floyd Hunter, a sociologist who analyzed Atlanta in the 1950s, found a relatively small and stable group of top policy makers drawn largely from the business class. This elite operated through secondary leaders who sometimes modified policy, but the power of the elite was almost always important.[5] In contrast, Robert Dahl and his graduate students at Yale studied New Haven at the same time and concluded that although some people had a great deal of influence, there was no permanent elite. Instead, there were shifting coalitions of leaders who sometimes disagreed among themselves but who always had to keep in mind what the public would accept when making decisions.[6]

Rule by a Few or Rule by the Many?

One group of investigators, chiefly sociologists such as Hunter, have been concerned with **social stratification** in the political system—how politics is affected by divisions among socioeconomic groups or classes in a community. These social scientists assume that political influence is a function of social stratification. They try to find out who governs particular communities by asking various citizens to identify the people who are most influential. Then they study those influential people to determine their social characteristics, their roles in decision making, and the interrelations among them and between them and the rest of the citizens. Using this technique, they find that the upper socioeconomic groups make up the *power elite,* that elected political leaders are subordinate to that elite, and that the major conflicts within the community are between the upper and the lower socioeconomic classes.

Other investigators question these findings and raise objections to the research techniques used. They contend that the evidence in social stratification studies does not support the conclusion that communities are run by a power elite. Rather, the notion of a power elite is merely a reflection of the techniques used and the assumptions made by stratification theorists. Instead of studying the activities of those who are thought to have "clout," these researchers insist, one should study how decisions are actually made.

Researchers who conduct *community power* studies analyzing the making of decisions usually find a relatively open, pluralistic power structure. Some people do have more influence than others, but that influence is shared among many people and tends to be limited to particular issues and areas. For example, those who decide how the public schools are run may have little influence over other economic policies. In many communities and for many issues, there is no identifiable group of influential people. Policies emerge not from the actions of a small group but rather from the unplanned and unanticipated consequences of the behavior of a relatively large number of people, especially from the countless contending groups that form and win access to those who make the important decisions. According to community power theorists, the social structure of the community is certainly one factor, but not the determining factor in how goods and services are distributed.

Comparing power elite and community power studies highlights the fact that how we ask questions often influences the answers we get. If we ask highly visible and actively involved citizens for their opinions of who is powerful, we find that they name a relatively small number of people as the real holders of power. But if we study dozens of local events and decisions, we find that a variety of people are involved—different people in different policy areas.

Other studies of local politics suggest that local values, traditions, and the structure of governmental organizations also determine which issues get on the local agenda.[7] Thus tobacco, mining, or steel interests may be so dominant in some areas that tax, regulation, or job safety policies are kept off the local policy agenda for fear of offending the "powers that be." Those "powers" may indeed go to great lengths to prevent what they deem to be adverse policies. This type of research alerts us to weigh carefully the possibility that defenders of the status quo can mobilize power resources in such a way that nondecisions may be more important than decisions. In effect, these researchers tell us not only to study who

Local communities often give special status and recognition to prominent local business people and other community leaders. Here, Limestone County Commission Chairman Stanley Meneffe, Dura Coat Founder Mike Hoag, Huntsville Mayor Loretta Spencer, and Huntsville-Madison County Chamber of Commerce Chairman Clay Vandiver break ground in Greenbrier, Alabama for a building that will employee 150 people.

social stratification
Divisions in a community among socioeconomic groups or classes.

governs but also to study the procedures and rules of the game. They urge us to determine which groups or interests would gain and which would lose by political decisions.[8]

On many economic policy matters, local corporations and business elites are involved. Studies of cities in Michigan and of Atlanta employing refined and contextual analysis of political decision making concluded that business elites are indeed important, but they are not necessarily the controlling factor in city governance:

> There is, then, no controlling hand in community politics. No conspiracy of business and government exists. Business interests do not invariably dominate government policy even where a single industry dominates the community. However, the giant industrial companies do provide the backdrop against which the public policy process operates in the industrial city. They are always there, seldom intervening in specific policy matters but never far from the calculations of policy makers.[9]

Studies of states and communities have now produced enough findings that we can see how formal government institutions, social structure, economic factors, and other variables interact in a working political system.

The Stakes in the Political Struggle

The national government has become the driving force behind the nation's economic strength and security. It assumes major responsibility for protecting civil rights, fighting inflation and unemployment, regulating sectors with great economic power, and subsidizing weaker sectors of the economy—not to mention matters of war and peace. State and local governments cannot claim so central a role. Yet the role of states and localities is increasing over a range of domestic policies, even though they diverge in their priorities and policies as a result of the maze of interests in each state. In response to health concerns and budget deficits, for example, seven states charge more than $1 per pack of cigarettes in taxes, while about half charge just 33 cents or less, with Virginia the lowest at 2.5 cents (see Figure 22-1).

Tax per pack
- ☐ 0¢ to 33¢
- 34¢ to 66¢
- 67¢ to 99¢
- $1 and over

FIGURE 22–1 **State Taxes on Tobacco Products.**

SOURCE: "Sinful Tax?" *New York Times,* March 17, 2002, p. WK5.

Since World War II, state and local government activities have increased much faster than the nondefense activities of the federal government. In the past decade, the federal government has been downsizing while state and local governments have been growing. Six times as many people work for state and local governments—18 million—than work for the Federal government, which has fewer than 3 million civilian employees.[10] States have had to assume greater responsibilities for raising taxes, setting economic and social priorities, and administering most welfare and job creation programs as a result of cutbacks in federal funds and devolution of responsibilities to the states.

State and local governments deal more directly with the average person than the national government does, because neighborhood, school, and housing problems are closely regulated at the state and local levels. The points at which people come into contact with government services and officials most often concern schools, streets and highways, parks and playgrounds, police and fire protection, zoning, and health care. But even in these areas, the mix of national, state, and local programs and responsibilities is such that it is often hard to isolate which level of government does what to or for whom. Also, there are some national-to-individual relationships that bypass state and local governments altogether, such as the Internal Revenue Service, the U.S. Postal Service, and Social Security.

Government reaches into many trivial aspects of our lives, such as restrictions on our pets.

The Maze of Interests

Special-interest groups can be found in varying forms in every state and locality. For example, industrial Rhode Island has farm organizations, and rural Wyoming has trade unions. Influential economic pressure groups and political action committees, organized to raise and disburse campaign funds to candidates for public office, operate in the states much as they do nationally. They try to build up the membership of their organizations, they lobby the state capitals and city halls, they educate and organize the voters, and they support their political friends in office and oppose their enemies. They also face the same internal problems all groups face: maintaining unity, dealing with subgroups that break off in response to special needs, and balancing democracy with discipline.

One great difference, however, is that group interests can be concentrated in states and localities, whereas their strength tends to be diluted in the national government. Big business does not really run things in Washington, D.C., any more than Wall Street, the Catholic Church, or the American Legion does. But in some states and localities, certain interests do clearly dominate because they represent the social and economic majorities of the area. Few politicians in Wisconsin will attack dairy farmers, few candidates for office in Florida will oppose benefits for senior citizens, and few officeholders in Idaho will support gun control. In other areas, industries such as timber or energy are influential because of their role in the local economy.

It is the range and variety of these local groups that give American politics its special flavor, excitement, and challenge: auto unions and manufacturers in Michigan, corn and hog farmers in Iowa, gas and oil dealers in Texas, gun owners in New Hampshire and Idaho, tobacco farmers in North Carolina and Virginia, poultry growers in Arkansas, Boeing and Microsoft in the Seattle area, coal miners in West Virginia, and sheep ranchers in Utah. However, the power of these groups should not be exaggerated.

We have to be cautious about lumping all workers, all business people, all teachers, all Hispanics, or all African Americans together. The union movement is sometimes sharply divided among the truckers, building trades, machinists, auto workers, and so on. The business community is often divided between big industrial, banking, and commercial firms on the one hand and small merchants on the other. In New England, Irish and Italian fraternal societies express the opinions of their respective groups on public issues; other organizations speak for people of French Canadian or Polish descent. New England politicians fear the power of ethnic groups to influence elections, especially primaries, yet there are plenty of examples of "Yankees" winning in heavily ethnic areas. Similarly, Asian American, Latino, and African American communities are playing an increasingly important role in elections in states such as California, Florida, and Texas.

Pet Peeves

Some areas of life might seem far removed from any government—having a dog or a cat as a pet, for example. But a dog needs a license and a collar, it must be confined, and it must be inoculated. And if anyone thinks that cats are beyond the reach of the law, they should remember Adlai E. Stevenson's famous veto of the "cat bill" when he was governor of Illinois. The bill would have imposed fines on cat owners who let their pets run off their premises, and it would have allowed cat haters to trap them. Stevenson said:

> I cannot agree that it should be declared public policy of Illinois that a cat visiting a neighbor's yard or crossing the highway is a public nuisance. It is in the nature of cats to do a certain amount of unescorted roaming. . . . I am afraid this bill could only create discord, recrimination, and enmity. . . . We are all interested in protecting certain varieties of birds. . . . The problem of cat versus bird is as old as time. If we attempt to resolve it by legislation, who knows but what we may be called upon to take sides as well in the age-old problem of dog versus cat, bird versus bird, or even bird versus worm.*

So the governor sided with cat supporters over bird lovers while staying neutral between bird lovers and worm diggers. Such incidents illustrate how the complex workings of modern society can lead to government intervention in or overregulation of our lives.

*Governor Adlai Stevenson, veto message to members of the State Assembly, Springfield, Illinois, 1949.

Compared to the other considerations affecting voters' choices, the ethnic factor may be small. Still, even a small percentage of the populace voting according to their ethnic interests can have a decisive effect on an election. Much depends on the character of the candidates and their personal appeal. Any group, no matter how strong, must cope with a variety of cross pressures, including a general sense that the voter does not vote for "one of our own" on that ground alone.

Other interests that are more specialized may also have a close relationship with local government. Many businesspeople sell products to the state or perform services for it: milk dealers, printers, contractors, parking meter manufacturers, computer and communications technology firms, makers of playground equipment, textbook publishers, and so on. They often organize formally or informally to improve their relations with purchasing officials. At the local level, developers and home builders and their lawyers press for zoning and planning commission action. Millions of dollars are often at stake, and the resulting action or inaction frequently shapes both the economic growth and the environmental quality of a community.

Business interests are inevitably involved in city and county politics and policy making. As one study of Atlanta found, the business elite is rarely a passive or reluctant partner in setting local priorities. "Atlanta's postwar political experience is a story of active business-elite efforts to make the most of their economic and organizational resources in setting the terms on which civic cooperation occurs."[11] Businesses everywhere depend on local governments for parking, good roads and transportation, safety, urban renovations, and much more. Business elites get involved in long-range community planning, are keenly interested in who gets elected, and are ever watchful of changes in taxation structures.

Another type of interest group intimately concerned with public policy is the professional association. States license barbers, beauticians, architects, lawyers, doctors, teachers, accountants, dentists, and many other occupational groups. You will find representatives from the Beauticians Aid Association, the Funeral Directors and Embalmers Association, the Institute of Dry Cleaning, and the Association of Private Driver-Training Schools lobbying at the statehouse. Associations representing such groups are concerned with the nature of the regulatory laws and the makeup of the boards that do the regulating. They are especially concerned about the rules for admission to their profession or trade and about the way

in which professional misconduct is defined and punished. Stiffening licensing requirements for physicians will decrease the supply of new doctors, for example, and thereby raise
the incomes of those in practice. Bar associations, for the same reason, closely monitor licensing standards for the legal profession and the appointment of judges.

Today, other groups of citizens are also likely to organize to influence decisions in
the state capital: those who are pro-life and those who are pro-choice, those who want
stiffer sentences for drunken driving, and those who favor three-strikes-and-you're-out
legislation to send repeat criminals to jail for life. Right to Life groups, Planned Parenthood, antismoking groups, animal rights activists, and prison guards are also well organized. Increasingly significant are environmental groups such as the Sierra Club, both
in forging public policies and as forces in election contests.

Lobbyists at the Statehouse

Many businesses, especially larger corporations, employ lobbyists, public relations specialists, political consultants, or law firms to represent them.[12] One of the growth businesses
in state politics is consulting, usually by specialized lawyers or former state legislators.
For a fee, lobbyists push desired bills through the legislature or block unwanted ones.
This kind of activity again raises the question of who has clout or who governs. Clearly,
those who can hire skilled lobbyists and other experts to shape the public agenda often
wield more influence than unorganized citizens, who rarely even follow state and regional
governmental decision making.

Lobbyists are present in every state capital, and they are there to guide through the
legislature a small handful of bills their organization wants passed or to stop those their
organization wants defeated.[13] Legislators process hundreds or even thousands of bills
each year, in addition to doing casework on behalf of constituents and worrying about
reelections. Shrewd lobbyists usually get a chance—sometimes several chances—to influence the fate of their few bills.

There is a widespread impression that lobbyists have freer rein in state legislatures
than they do in the U.S. Congress and, what is more, that bribes or informal payoffs by
lobbyists are cruder and more obvious in state legislatures. Certainly lobbying restrictions
in the states are more relaxed than at the federal level, although in some of the larger

*Professions and occupations of various types are regulated by the government through licensing
and standards.*

states they may be even more stringent. There is less media coverage of state politics in many states than is focused on national politics in Washington, D.C.

Corruption of legislators and state officials is usually hard to prove. Exposure of scandals in several states pushed many legislatures to curb election abuses and pass ethics codes with stringent conflict-of-interest provisions.[14] Several legislatures have enacted comprehensive financial disclosure laws, and today most state governments are more open, professional, and accountable than in the past.[15] Former President Jimmy Carter, who served in the Georgia Senate and then became governor, recalled that only a "tiny portion" of the 259 members of the Georgia legislature were not good or honest people. But Carter found that "it is difficult for the common good to prevail against the intense concentration of those who have a special interest, especially if the decisions are made behind locked doors."[16]

In a few states, one corporation or organization may exercise considerable influence; in others, a "big three" or "big four" dominate politics. But in most states, there is competition among organizations; no single group or coalition of groups stands out. In no state does only one organization control legislative politics, although the powerful Anaconda Company once came close in Montana. For example, some 400 lobbyists are registered in Arkansas. Of these, 125 represent utilities; more than 200 represent individual businesses, industry, or professions; nine represent labor interests; eight work on behalf of senior citizens; and three lobby for environmental interests. The Arkansas Power and Light Company, the railroads, the poultry and trucking industries, the teachers, and the state Chamber of Commerce are the most effective lobbyists. "It is still true that ordinarily those with greater economic resources, greater numbers, and higher status have far more impact than those who lack these attributes," writes political scientist Diane Blair. "Nevertheless, an increasingly complex economy has produced many more actors in the political system, and especially when there is division among the economic elite, some of the lesser voices can be heard."[17]

In Michigan, about 1,250 lobbyists are registered with the state, including representatives of the "big three" automakers, the United Auto Workers, the AFL-CIO, the Michigan Education Association, the Michigan Manufacturers Association, the city of Detroit, the Michigan Chamber of Commerce, certain conservation and environmental groups, and various antitax groups.[18]

Not to be overlooked are the growing number of groups and media outlets that view themselves as "watchdogs" of the public policy process. Groups such as the League of Women Voters, Common Cause, and various citizens' groups regularly monitor state politics for questionable fund-raising or lobbying practices. Their "watchdog" efforts are sometimes aided by reporters who cover state capitals.

Participation Patterns in Small and Medium-Sized Cities

Although it is widely believed that citizens feel "closer" to city and county governments than they do to the more remote national government in Washington, D.C., citizens generally take less interest in, vote less often in, and are less informed about their local governments than they are about the national government. There are understandable reasons for the lower involvement in local government. Although issues about where to locate a garbage dump or a prison or how to deal with police brutality can arouse considerable heat, most of the time local governments are preoccupied with relatively noncontroversial routine matters, such as keeping the roads in shape, providing fire and police service, attracting businesses that can create more jobs, or applying for state and federal financial assistance.

Local communities want to keep their tax rates down and promote their cities as "nice places" in which to live, work, and raise families. Mayors and city officials generally try to avoid controversy and the kind of criticism that will divide a community. Although they do not always succeed, they go to considerable lengths to be reasonable and work for the good of the community. Few aggressively seek to alter the status quo. They do not, as a rule, try to promote equality by redistributing various resources to needier citizens. **Redistributive policies** are programs to shift wealth or benefits from one segment of the population to another, usually from the rich to the poor. Local officials tend to believe that this is the task of the national or state authorities—if they think it should be done at all. Typically, they say their communities do not have the funds for such programs. They might add, "Go see the governor" or "Go talk to your member of Congress." This may be good advice, because various programs (educational loans, unemployment compensation, disability assistance, and so on) explicitly designed to help the less fortunate are administered at the state or federal level.

Neighborhood groups sometimes become involved in protecting their neighborhoods and petitioning for improvements. One concern that often activates neighborhood groups is the possibility that "undesirable" facilities might be located in their neighborhood, such as drug rehabilitation clinics, prisons, dumps, or homeless shelters. Although attendance at local government meetings is usually low, the announcement of a land-fill area or a prison construction project often stimulates the reaction that local officials call NIMBY, an acronym for "Not In My Back Yard!"

Don Wright/Don Wright, Inc.

The Role of Local Media

Most communities have only one newspaper, and in small communities it is often a weekly. Some newspapers and local radio and television stations do a good job of covering city and county politics, but this is the exception rather than the rule. Reporters assigned to cover local politics are often inexperienced beginners, yet they provide the only news that citizens get about their city council or zoning board. Even the best of them have difficulty conveying the full complexities of what is going on in a column or two of newsprint.

Some local newspapers enjoy a cozy relationship with elected local officials. Sometimes the owners or editors are social friends or golfing buddies of local officials. Friendships and mutual interests develop, and close scrutiny of what goes on in city hall takes a back seat to city boosterism. In effect, "newspapers boost their hometown, knowing that its prosperity and expansion aid their own. Harping on local faults, investigating dirty politics, revealing unsavory scandals, and stressing governmental inefficiencies only provide readily available documentary material to competing cities."[19]

Editors and station managers recognize that their readers or listeners are more interested in state or national news, and especially in sports, than in what is going on at municipal planning meetings or county commission sessions. Much of what takes place in local government is rather dull. It may be important to some people, yet it strikes the average person as decidedly less exciting than what goes on at the White House or whether Congress has finally solved the Social Security problem or whether their stocks have gone up or down or whether the New York Jets or the Los Angeles Lakers won last night. We have dozens of ways to find out about Congress and the White House, but we usually have only one source for stories about the mayor or sheriff or school board. Of course, we could attend board meetings or even talk with our mayor, but that is not what most people are likely to do.

Apathy in Grassroots America

Voter apathy in local elections is summed up in the bumper sticker "DON'T VOTE. IT ONLY ENCOURAGES THEM." Many important political and economic transactions in communities are ignored by the press and citizens. Charter revision and taxation often galvanize only those directly affected by the new taxes or regulations. Even New England town meetings have difficulty getting people to participate—despite the fact that decisions made at these meetings have major consequences for local tax rates and the quality of the schools, the police force, and the parks and recreational areas. Thomas Jefferson once proclaimed the town meeting to be the noblest, wisest instrument yet devised for the

redistributive policies
Governmental tax and social programs that shift wealth or benefits from one segment of the population to another, often from the rich to the poor.

WE THE PEOPLE

What One Person Can Accomplish

Urban League leader T. Willard Fair is a committed problem solver for his Liberty City community in Miami. He is recognized as a one-man force trying to rid Liberty City of drug dealers. In the late 1980s, Fair started a private-public collaboration to improve the quality of life in this inner-city community. Among many other results, his efforts led to 3,500 arrests, the breakup of 27 crack houses, the towing of many abandoned vehicles, and the trimming of trees to expose shaded areas where drug deals were made. But above all, Fair was able to get his neighbors in Liberty City to band together and have faith that their neighborhood could be rid of its pushers.

T. Willard Fair.

Fair started the program after reading about a young woman who had been shot. Residents were too fearful of drug dealers to cooperate with police. Fair became a catalyst for change, enlisting the help of government and school officials, police and fire officers, churches, residents, and local businesses. He also persuaded the national drug program to share some funds, and he raised other funds by whatever means he could. By the early 1990s, he could declare, along with the Liberty City residents, that their 70-square-block, drug-free zone was "off limits" to what he calls "the drug boys."

Fair has received over 100 awards, including Florida's Outstanding Citizen Award, for his dedication and efforts in community building, combating crime, and promoting education among inner-city children. He remains the president of the Urban League of Greater Miami.

SOURCE: Catherine Foster, "One Man Rallies a Neighborhood Against Pushers," *Christian Science Monitor,* June 11, 1992, p.7.

---

conduct of public affairs, but today most towns find that only about 2 or 3 percent of the population cares enough to come.[20]

The major reason for grassroots apathy is that local politics simply does not interest the average person. Most people are content to leave politics and political responsibilities to a relatively small number of activists while they pursue their own private concerns—their bowling leagues, their children's Little League or soccer games, golf, or fishing. In a healthy democracy, we can expect that most people will be involved with their families and jobs; other than voting occasionally, they tend to leave civic responsibilities to a relatively small number of their fellow citizens. This is probably a reasonable choice. It may also be an indication of satisfaction with the state of the community.

Cynicism about the effectiveness and fairness of local political processes is sometimes reflected in the politics of protest—mass demonstrations, economic boycotts, even civil disorders—to make demands on government. When certain issues become intense, people become politically active. African Americans, Hispanics, gays, and others form political organizations to present their grievances and marshal votes. Neighborhood organizations work for better housing and enforcement of inspection ordinances and to prevent crime and drug dealing.

Civic Initiatives in Local Governments

Just as there will always be indifference toward politics and apathy about government, so too will there always be creative, entrepreneurial people who are willing to step forward

School board meetings in Austin, Texas do not usually draw a crowd, but when the topic of sex education was discussed, a vocal and concerned crowd turned out.

and find new ways of solving problems. States such as Oregon and Minnesota seem to encourage a climate of innovation and civic enterprise, and a wider look at the United States finds buoyant, optimistic, creative problem solvers in nearly every corner of the nation.

Enterprising local activists have advocated and implemented cost-saving energy programs, environmental cleanup campaigns, recycling and solar energy initiatives, job training centers, AIDS prevention efforts, housing for the elderly, tutoring for the illiterate, housing for the poor, and hundreds of other problem-solving and opportunity-enhancing community efforts.[21] In almost every case, they create partnerships with elected officials at city hall, sometimes with the Urban League or Chamber of Commerce, and often with local foundations and business corporations.

Sometimes it takes a tragedy to get community groups mobilized. Such a tragic event happened in Boston when gang members burst into the funeral of a young man. "In the presence of the mourners, the gang killed one of those in attendance," writes the Reverend Eugene Rivers of the Azusa Christian Community.

> That brazen act told us we had to do more. Now. That young man's death galvanized us, and soon the Ten Point Coalition was reaching out to at-risk youth. Our mission was to pair the holy and the secular, to do whatever it took to save our kids. The black churches worked hand-in-hand with the schools, courts, police, and social service agencies. We called on anyone and everyone who had the means to help our children. We formed programs for teens, neighborhood watches, and patrols. . . . We established ourselves in the neighborhood, standing on the same street corner where the drug dealers once stood. We tracked down the thieves, dealers, and gangs. We tried to give people a chance, but if they wouldn't take it, we staked our claim and ran them out of our neighborhood.[22]

There are persistent debates about how to solve social, economic, and racial problems in our large metropolitan areas. Some people contend that government can't undertake this task and that private initiatives can be more effective. Others insist that state and local governments are best suited to deal with these challenges. Still others contend that imaginative public-private collaboration is needed to fashion the strategies and mobilize the resources to revive our cities and bring about greater opportunity. Whatever the merits of such contending interpretations, it is clear that neighborhood organizations and spirited civic renewal are critical to the vitality of local government.[23]

Not all citizens are apathetic. These young people are spending their free time rehabilitating a community center.

Challenges for State and Local Governments

Most states and communities are confronting testing times. Virtually all of the states and major cities face serious budget problems and increasing demands for services. People don't like tax increases, but they also want better schools, a clean environment, and safe roads.[24] About one-third of our inner-city governments and school systems are in financial distress. The cycle of poverty in the inner cities remains one of the greatest threats to the economic health of the country. Cities, though, often cannot raise enough funds through local taxes to create jobs and housing. Federal and state initiatives have attempted to create economic opportunities for inner-city residents. Community development banks, "empowerment zones," Head Start, charter schools, and national service (Americorp) programs have all been tried in an attempt to bring residents of depressed inner cities into the economic mainstream. But these efforts have been inadequate and must compete with other demands on financially pressed states and localities.

The following central issues in the states and local communities command the attention of the country. They vary depending on location, of course, yet these urgent challenges are part of the unfinished business of a government by the people:

• *People want more services* yet at the same time would like to see their taxes cut. City and state officials are constantly trying to do more with less and introduce

Local residents often form groups to handle and discuss issues that are important to their neighborhood, as illustrated by this gathering of Neighborhood Watch volunteers.

efficiencies into city and state operations. Voters in many communities have enacted spending limits that constrain growth in public budgets.

- *Racism still exists in many communities.* As our nation has become more diverse, most Americans have learned to appreciate the strength that comes from multiple cultures and races. Yet the Ku Klux Klan and other racist groups still thrive in many areas, and bigotry and discrimination persist.

- *Drugs, gangs, and drug-related crime impose tough policy challenges.* The costs of corrections and prisons have skyrocketed in recent years, yet gangs, drugs, and crime are still a menace in our urban areas. Most state and local "wars on drugs" have failed, and the ravages of drug abuse are enormously costly to the nation. Drug abusers lose their jobs; they make our streets, schools, and neighborhoods unsafe; they add to our welfare rolls; they make it necessary for states to build more prisons; and in numerous ways they undermine the vitality of a great many cities and towns.

- *Poverty in the inner cities persists.* We have extremes of rich and poor within metropolitan regions, and often the wealthier suburbs turn their backs on the problems and poverty of the older cities. Indifference to these inequalities and lack of opportunities may undermine a sense of community and fairness in America.

- *We need to guarantee the best possible education for all our young people.* Parents are demanding better education and more parental involvement. Many communities are experimenting with educational choice and competition, school vouchers, and charter schools. Improving the public schools is necessary, but their resources and the salaries of teachers are often too low to attract and retain the best-qualified teachers. State and local governments have the responsibility to pay for public education, so educational reform and the search for excellent teachers and learning processes will remain a top state and local priority.

- *Environmental regulation, land use, and recycling are also major challenges at the local level.* Every city and state wants economic growth and economic opportunities for its workers and businesses, but many forms of economic development impose costs in terms of the quality of air, water, landscapes, and health. Local officials face tough decisions about the need to balance economic and environmental concerns.

- *Health care costs and delivery are challenges to all levels of government.* Health care reform has been an important policy issue for many years. Some states have experimented with universal health care; others have worked to control costs. Many of the uninsured end up obtaining health care in emergency rooms in local public hospitals, which in turn seek funding from the local and state governments.

For more information on these and other issues confronting state and local governments go to our home page at www.prenhall.com/burns, or to the Web site of the Council of State Governments at www.csg.org, or that of the National Conference of State Legislatures at www.ncsl.org.

Summary

1. Many of the most critical domestic and economic issues facing the United States today are decided at the state and local levels of government.

2. Studies of states and communities have investigated how formal government institutions, social structure, economic factors, and local traditions interact to create a working political system. Some studies find that a power elite dominates, whereas community power studies find pluralism and diverse interest groups competing for influence over a range of policy areas. Special-interest groups operate in every state and locality, but their influence varies.

3. Although it is widely believed that local governments are "closer to the people" than the national government, voting and other forms of participation at the local level are low.

4. Innovative programs at the local level address problems in education, the environment, crime and violence, and ways to improve community life. Local civil action is one of the most important forms of citizen participation in politics.

Key Terms

social stratification   redistributive policies

Further Reading

THAD L. BEYLE, ED., *State Government: CQ's Guide to Current Issues and Activities, 2001–2002* (CQ Press, 2001).

BUZZ BISSINGER, *A Prayer for the City* (Random House, 1997).

PAUL BRACE, *State Government and Economic Performance* (Johns Hopkins University Press, 1993).

ALLAN CIGLER AND BURDETT LOOMIS, EDS., *Interest Group Politics,* 5th ed. (CQ Press, 1998).

FRANK J. COPPA, *County Government* (Praeger, 2000).

THOMAS E. CRONIN AND ROBERT D. LOEVY, *Colorado Politics and Government: Governing the Centennial State* (University of Nebraska Press, 1993).

E. J. DIONNE JR., ED. *Community Works: The Revival of Civil Society in America* (Brookings Institution, 1998).

THOMAS D. DYE, *Politics in States and Communities,* 10th ed. (Prentice Hall, 2000).

ROBERT S. ERIKSON, GERALD C. WRIGHT, AND JOHN P. McIVER, *Statehouse Democracy: Public Opinion and Policy in the American States* (Cambridge University Press, 1993).

JOEL GARREAU, *Edge City: Life on the New Frontier* (Doubleday, 1991).

STEPHEN GOLDSMITH, *The Twenty-First Century City* (Regnery, 1997).

VIRGINIA GRAY, RUSSELL HANSON, AND HERBERT JACOB, EDS., *Politics in the American States,* 7th ed. (CQ Press, 1999).

JONATHAN HARRIS, *A Civil Action* (Vintage, 1996).

DENNIS R. JUDD AND PAUL KANTOR, EDS., *Politics of Urban American: A Reader* (Addison-Wesley, 1997).

DANIEL KEMMIS, *The Good City and the Good Life* (Houghton Mifflin, 1995).

DAVID L. KIRP, JOHN P. DWYER, AND LARRY A. ROSENTHAL, *Our Town: Race, Housing, and the Soul of Suburbia* (Rutgers University Press, 1997).

MADELEINE KUNIN, *Living a Political Life* (Vintage, 1995).

TOM LOFTUS, *The Art of Legislative Politics* (CQ Press, 1994).

JOHN O. NORQUIST, *The Wealth of Cities* (Addison-Wesley, 1998).

ALAN ROSENTHAL, *The Third House: Lobbyists and Lobbying in the States,* 2d ed. (CQ Press, 2001).

TODD SWANSTROM AND DENNIS R. JUDD, EDS., *City Politics: Private Power and Public Policy,* 3d ed. (Addison-Wesley, 2002).

JOSEPH F. ZIMMERMAN, *The New England Town Meeting: Democracy in Action* (Praeger, 1999).

See also the *State Politics and Policy Quarterly* and the Web site of the Council of State Governments at www.csg.org.

23
CHAPTER

STATE CONSTITUTIONS
Charters or Straitjackets?

The state of New York has had four constitutions since 1777. By constitutional mandate, every 20 years the people of New York are asked on a general election ballot if they would like to convene a constitutional convention to propose a new constitution. In addition, the legislature—with the concurrence of the governor—put the question before the voters in 1965, the voters approved, and a convention was held in 1967, but its work was rejected. When voters were asked in 1977 if they wanted to convene another convention, they said no. The question came before them again in 1997, as it will in 2017.

In preparation for the 1997 vote, the Temporary Commission on Constitutional Revision was set up to identify issues and to inform voters about the need for a new constitution. The commission called for a convention of ordinary citizens and suggested that New Yorkers take advantage of new technology such as cable television and electronic town meetings to observe convention proceedings. The commission targeted the budget process, state-local relations, education, and public safety as being of special importance.[1] A constitutional convention, commission members argued, could then write a new constitution in clear English, simplify voter registration, improve voting rules and ballot access, regulate campaign finance and lobbying, reform the legislative process, restore confidence in the courts, rethink the tax structure, improve government, and protect the environment.[2]

Opposing the calling of a constitutional convention were the AFL-CIO, the Conservative party, the Sierra Club, the National Abortion Rights Action League, some anti-tax groups, and some legislative leaders from both parties. Labor unions saw a convention as a threat to their right to organize, trial lawyers worried about limits on lawsuits, environmentalists feared that a convention might jeopardize provisions protecting open spaces, some women's groups were fearful that the convention might restrict abortion rights, and some conservatives feared that liberal interests would control the convention.

There was little interest in the campaign for a constitutional convention. Two weeks before the election, polls indicated that voters, upset by the apparent inability of the state government to get anything done, were overwhelmingly in favor of calling for a constitutional convention to make government work better. Then opponents of constitutional revision got busy. Unions and other anticonvention groups launched television advertisements, direct-mail operations, and phone banks, arguing that the convention was a waste of money and would open the door to dangerous changes. On November 5, 1997, 62 percent of New York voters rejected the call for the convention.[3]

New York's experience is not unusual. In recent years, voters in several states have rejected calls for a constitutional convention. For example, in Michigan in November 1994, voters rejected the call for a convention by almost 3 to 1 in all 183 counties; Arkansas voters in December 1995 rejected the call by 4 to 1 in all 75 counties.[4] We have not had any constitutional conventions since Rhode Island had one in 1986, and it won approval of the voters for only eight of 14 proposed revisions.

You might give some thought now to your own state constitution. Like the U.S. Constitution, state constitutions are both instruments of government and limitations on government. However, unlike the federal one, state constitutions are not popular symbols. On a trip to your state capitol, you are unlikely to find the state constitution "displayed [like] the federal Constitution, in a setting similar to a Shinto shrine."[5]

In this chapter, we examine the roots of state constitutions and some of the ways we work around constitutional rigidity. Then we look at methods of amending state constitutions, ending with a few case studies of states that have tried, for the most part unsuccessfully, to adopt new constitutions.

The Roots of State Constitutions

The first state constitutions were outgrowths of colonial charters. Massachusetts and New Hampshire can boast of charters still in effect that are older than the federal Constitution. Virginia added a bill of rights to its constitution in 1776—13 years before the national one was proposed by Congress. In 1787, the framers of the U.S. Constitution drew heavily on their experience with these state charters. "What is the Constitution of the United States but that of Massachusetts, New York, and Maryland!" remarked John Adams. "There is not a feature in it," he said, "which cannot be found in one or the other."[6]

Subject only to the broad limitations of the U.S. Constitution, the people of each state are free to create whatever kind of republican government they wish. All state constitutions are similar in general outline (see Figure 23-1). A state constitution typically consists of a preamble, a bill of rights, articles providing for the separation of powers (although the supreme court of Rhode Island recently ruled that there is no separation of powers in that state, leading for calls by the governor and the *Providence Journal* for a constitutional convention to overrule the decision),[7] a two-house legislature, an executive department (usually consisting of a governor, a lieutenant governor, and a half-dozen or more statewide elected officials), an independent judiciary with the power of judicial review, a description of the form and powers of local units of government, an article on how to amend the constitution, and miscellaneous provisions dealing with election procedures, corporations, railroads, finances, education, and other specific topics.

The bills of rights in state constitutions are, in general, similar to the federal Bill of Rights, although they sometimes use different language and cover different rights. For example, "Twenty-seven states have speech and press guarantees quite different from the First Amendment's, thirty-eight have equality guarantees dissimilar to the equal protection clause, and thirty-nine have guarantees of a separation of church and state that differ from the federal establishment clause."[8] Fourteen states adopted the Equal Rights Amendment even though it was never ratified to become part of the U.S. Constitution.

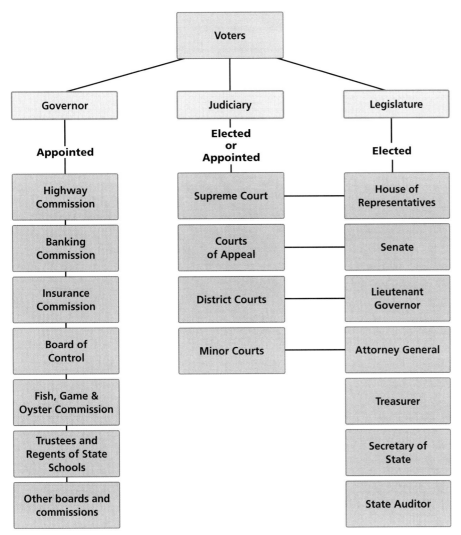

FIGURE 23–1   Government Under a Typical State Constitution.

Constitutional Rigidity and Evasion

State constitutions contain more details than the U.S. Constitution does. They are longer and less flexible, and they require more frequent amendment[9] (see Figure 23-2). Louisiana has had 11 constitutions; Georgia has had ten; South Carolina, seven; and Alabama, Florida, and Virginia, six.[10] State constitutions vary in length—from the 8,295 words of Vermont's (the only state constitution shorter than the Constitution of the United States as amended) to the 310,296 words of Alabama's. The U.S. Constitution has only 7,400 words; most state constitutions have around 26,000.[11]

Although most state constitutional provisions deal with matters of significance, some also deal with trivial subjects. California's much-amended constitution (500 amendments since it was adopted in 1879) goes into great detail about the taxation of fish and the internal organization of various departments. The Oklahoma constitution proclaims, "Until changed by the Legislature, the flash test for all kerosene oil for illuminating purposes shall be 115 degrees Fahrenheit; and the specific gravity test for all such oil shall be 40 degrees."[12] The South Dakota constitution declares that providing hail insurance is a public purpose and authorizes the legislature to levy a tax to provide for it.[13] The Alabama constitution authorizes the legislature to indemnify peanut farmers for losses incurred as a result of *Aspergillus flavus* (a fungus) and freeze damage in peanuts.[14]

In addition to the inclusion of these statutelike details, state constitutions and their more frequently adopted amendments tend to be longer than the national one because their bills of

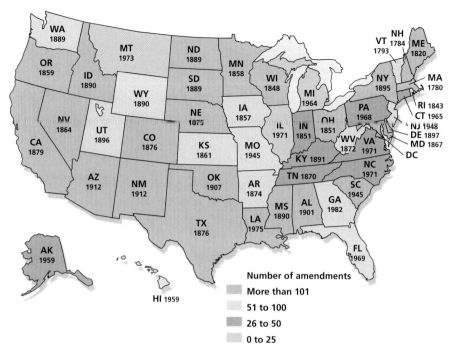

FIGURE 23–2   Amending State Constitutions.

SOURCE: *The Book of the States, 2002–2003* (Council of State Governments, 2002), p. 14.

rights cover, in addition to the traditional rights, more recently emerging protections, such as the rights of victims of crimes. Finally, state constitutions have to deal with a much wider range of functions, educational provisons, and criminal codes than the U.S. Constitution, which created a national government of intentionally limited powers to deal with a limited range of functions.[15] It has long been asserted that the length and detail of state constitutions account for the fact that many of them have not had the longevity of the national Constitution. However, a careful empirical study shows that short state constitutions that avoid detail last no longer than those that are lengthy and more statutory in content. In fact, "longer and more detailed design of state constitutions actually enhances rather than reduces their longevity."[16]

Constitutions as Roadblocks

The earliest state constitutions granted authority to the legislatures without much restriction on how their powers should be exercised. But after many legislatures gave special privileges to railroads, canal builders, and other interests, constitutional amendments were adopted to prevent such abuses. Distrusting the legislatures, reform groups began to insist that certain controls be incorporated into state constitutions. In time, state constitutions became encrusted in layer upon layer of procedural detail.

What does this mean for democratic government? Most simply, it means that state constitutions—intended as charters of self-government—are often like straitjackets imposed on the present by the past. Some outdated provisions do no harm, but more often they are roadblocks to effective government. For example, fixed salaries do not reflect changing economic conditions, and a rigidly organized administrative structure is incapable of adjusting to new needs. When a constitution allocates revenues, elected officials are deprived of discretion to deal with budget difficulties as they arise. Under such conditions, the legislature cannot act, and voters then turn to constitutional amendments.

Getting Around the Constitution

Can state constitutions forever prevent the wishes of the people from being carried out? Not necessarily. The constitutional system of the states, like that of the national government, includes more than the formal written document. Unwritten rules, practices, political parties,

Comparing State Constitutions

As an experiment, compare two or three provisions of your own state constitution with those of two or three states from other regions and political cultures. State constitutions can be found by following the links at www.findlaw.com/11state gov/indexconst.html.

and interest groups also shape events. When people see a need for change, they usually find ways to overcome formal barriers.

One device for constitutional change is **judicial interpretation**, whereby judges modify a constitutional provision by a new interpretation of its meaning. The more complex and detailed the constitution, the easier it is for judges to redefine meanings. Actually, one reason for the growing length of some constitutions is that amendments are often required to reverse judicial interpretations. In addition, some sections of state constitutions have been invalidated by federal action, especially in the area of civil rights and suffrage.

The New Judicial Federalism

In what is called **new judicial federalism**, state constitutions have taken on greater importance. For decades, state judges tended to look only to the U.S. Constitution and how it had been interpreted by the U.S. Supreme Court. But since the 1970s, as the Supreme Court has become more conservative, some states have begun applying their own state constitutions and state bills of rights to review the actions of state and local officials.

This trend takes its inspiration from the U.S. Supreme Court, which sent clear messages to state supreme court judges that they are free to interpret their own state constitutions to impose greater restraints than the U.S. Constitution does. The U.S. Supreme Court and the U.S. Constitution set the floor, not the ceiling, for the protection of rights.[17] As a result, some state judges are now using their constitutions to require state legislatures to provide better schools for children living in poor neighborhoods, build low-income housing, provide public financing of abortions for poor women, and regulate business enterprises to protect the environment.[18]

When state judges rely on their own state constitutions to protect rights beyond those required by the U.S. Constitution, they do so at some political peril, since most judges are dependent on voter approval to keep their office. This risk has increased now that the Supreme Court requires state judges who wish to escape a review of their decisions by the Supreme Court to make it clear they have decided a case on adequate and independent state constitutional grounds.[19]

The Web site of the Center for State Constitutional Studies of Rutgers University (www.camlaw.rutgers.edu/statecon/overview) provides links that review a conference titled "The State of State Constitutions" held in Philadelphia May 4–6, 2000. This conference brought together experts to discuss "the strengths and weaknesses of contemporary state constitutions and directions for state constitutional reform." The Web site provides the keynote address by G. Alan Tarr, director of the center, and summarizes the workshops on all aspects of state constitutions.

Amending State Constitutions

Amendments may be proposed by the state legislature, citizen-initiated ballot petitions, or constitutional conventions. After an amendment has been proposed, it must be ratified. In all states except Delaware, where the legislature can ratify as well as propose amendments, ratification is by the voters. In most states, an amendment becomes part of the constitution when approved by a majority of those voting on the amendment. In some states—for example, Minnesota—approval by a majority of all those voting in the election is required. This provision makes ratification difficult, because some people who vote for candidates do not vote on amendments. Slightly more than three-quarters of all constitutional amendments proposed by legislatures have been adopted in recent years.[20]

Legislative Proposals

All states permit their legislature to propose amendments; in fact, this is the most commonly used method. Although provisions vary, the general practice is to require the approval by two-thirds of each chamber of the legislature. Some states, however, permit proposal of an amendment by a simple majority in two successive legislatures.

judicial interpretation
A method by which judges modify the force of a constitutional provision by reinterpreting its meaning.

new judicial federalism
The practice of some state courts using the bill of rights in their state constitutions to provide more protection for some rights than is provided by the Supreme Court's interpretation of the Bill of Rights in the U.S. Constitution.

The California Revision Commission

In 1992, after the California senate rejected a proposal asking voters if they wanted a constitutional convention (the first such convention in 113 years) to change the way the state does business, California turned to a revision commission to overcome its budgetary gridlock. Over the last several decades, the people of California had amended their state constitution so frequently that amendments and federal mandates allocated 85 percent of the state's annual revenues before the governor and state legislature even started to work on the budget! For example, Proposition 13 set limits on property taxes, and Proposition 98 allocated 40 percent of the state budget to the public schools. Eventually, *all* state revenues could be allocated constitutionally if the trend continued, and there would be no state funds available for programs such as higher education and health care.

A 23-member revision commission, consisting of members appointed by the governor, the speaker, the senate Rules Committee, and some *ex officio* officers like the chief justice, was created in 1993 to examine the budget process and the configuration of state and local government duties. Two years later, in its report to the legislature, the commission recommended that California

- Reduce the number of statewide elective offices by making the state treasurer, the superintendent of public instruction, and the insurance commissioner appointive rather than elected
- Change the initiative process to allow the legislature to amend statutory initiatives after six years
- Require two-year state budgets
- Allow the legislature to approve budgets by a simple majority instead of the current two-thirds
- Allow school districts to raise additional revenue
- Require the governor to submit to the legislature a state and local reassignment plan
- Strengthen the home-rule powers of local governments

The California legislature failed to act on any of the commission's recommendations, perhaps in part because they were proposed in an election year. Also, because the state senate was Democratic and the state assembly Republican, it was hard to work out any compromises.

A legislature may appoint a **revision commission** to make recommendations for constitutional change that, except in Florida, have no force until acted on by the legislature and approved by the voters. The legislature creates a commission of a relatively small number of people—some selected by the governor and some by the legislature—and charges it with presenting proposals for constitutional revision. A commission is less expensive than a full-blown constitutional convention, does not require initial voter approval, and gives the legislature final control of what is presented to the electorate.

Constitutional commissions have been used frequently. Florida, Virginia, and Louisiana have used the commission procedure to bring about significant constitutional change. Mississippi has tried, so far unsuccessfully, to use it for changing its 1890 constitution, which was designed to keep African Americans out of the political process.[21] The Utah Constitutional Revision Commission is a permanent body, required by law to submit recommendations for constitutional revision to the legislature 60 days before each regular session.[22] It has initiated revisions relating to the rights of crime victims as well as to changes in revenue and taxation.[23] Florida has a Taxation and Budget Reform Commission that is called into session every ten years. Unlike other such commissions, in addition to making recommendations to the legislature, it may propose constitutional amendments directly to the voters.[24] In 1998, the commission recommended nine amendments; Florida voters approved eight of them.

The recommendations of revision commissions are seldom implemented quickly, perhaps because the commissioners have not been responsive to political currents or are not representative of broad enough interests. Still, a commission may provide less partisan consideration of amendments and be more resistant to single-interest groups than either the legislature or a convention.

Initiative Petitions

At the end of the nineteenth century, revelations of corruption pushed the prestige of state governments, especially state legislatures, to a new low. Out of this disillusionment came a variety of reforms as part of the Progressive movement. Among them was the **constitutional initiative petition**, a device that permits voters to place specific constitutional amendments on the ballot by petition. Eighteen states allow amendments to their constitutions to be proposed by initiative petitions.

revision commission
A state commission that recommends changes in the state constitution for action by the legislature and vote by the voters.

constitutional initiative petition
A device that permits voters to place specific amendments to a state constitution on the ballot by petition.

The number of signatures required on petitions varies from 4 to 15 percent of either the total electorate or the number of voters who voted in the last election.[25] Although it takes more signatures to propose a constitutional amendment than to place other kinds of initiatives on the ballot, "the higher threshold is no longer a significant impediment to well-financed special-interest groups."[26]

Once the appropriate state official (attorney general or secretary of state) approves the precise wording of a petition, the amendment is placed on the ballot at the next general election. (California allows initiatives to appear on primary election ballots.) The number of votes required to approve a constitutional amendment is typically a majority vote, although a few states have a more demanding requirement. Illinois requires a majority of those voting in the election or three-fifths of those voting on the amendment, and Nevada requires a majority vote on the same measure in two successive elections.

In some states, initiative proposals are limited to *amending* the state constitution, not to *revising* it. The distinction between revision and amendment is that revision refers to a comprehensive change to the basic governmental plan, a substantial alteration in the basic governmental framework,[27] or a substantial alteration of the entire constitution, rather than to a less extensive change in one or more of its provisions.[28] Some states exclude certain subjects from amendment by initiative. Massachusetts, for example, does not allow amendments by popular initiative that concern religion, the judiciary, or judicial decisions; that are restricted to a particular town, city, or political division; that appropriate money from the state treasury; or that restrict rights such as freedom of speech.[29]

In recent years, voters have approved about 50 percent of amendments proposed by initiative petitions. This figure compares with a slightly more than 75 percent approval rate for amendments proposed by state legislatures.[30] A variety of factors may account for the lower adoption rate of initiative measures. Initiatives tend to be used for controversial issues that have already been rejected by the legislature and engender an organized opposition. Initiatives are also often proposed by narrow-based groups or by reform-minded elites who

Initiative petitions deal with a great variety of reforms.

You Decide · Thinking It Through

WHO SHOULD PROPOSE CONSTITUTIONAL AMENDMENTS?

You Decide... Of the 24 states that have the popular initiative, only 18 permit constitutional amendments by initiative. Are states well served by having citizens propose amendments, or is it a bad idea? Should all states be required to permit constitutional alteration by the initiative process? What do you think?

Thinking It Through... Critics charge that when several complex initiatives are on the ballot, voters are asked to make decisions for which they are not well prepared. Others contend that the use of the initiative petition prevents elected representatives from exercising their proper authority. Still others hold that the initiative process encourages detailed and frequent amendment of a constitution, which should be a blueprint of enduring principles and not be too specific about how government operates on a day-to-day basis. Critics also charge that the initiative process has recently become the tool of well-organized single-interest groups that present voters with simplistic choices of yes or no on complex matters.

Defenders of the constitutional initiative petition contend that it is a valuable safety valve against an unresponsive legislature. When a legislature is tied so closely to special interests that it refuses even to acknowledge the real needs of a majority of citizens, the initiative process can be a corrective. Defenders also contend that voters are much smarter than critics think they are and that they have in fact acted rather prudently when asked to decide most constitutional questions.

A Challenging Ballot

California voters are regularly given ballots that, in addition to a long list of candidates for national, state, and local offices, contain constitutional amendments proposed by the legislature, a dozen or so highly technical amendments submitted by citizens by the initiative process, and numerous bond issues. In the larger California cities, voters are routinely asked in general elections to decide 40 to 50 separate state, local, and special-district ballot questions. Shown here are some of the decisions faced by California voters in the November 2002 election.

MEASURES SUBMITTED TO THE VOTERS

STATE

46 HOUSING AND EMERGENCY SHELTER TRUST FUND ACT OF 2002. This act provides for the Housing and Emergency Shelter Trust Fund Act of 2002. For the purpose of providing shelters for battered women, clean and safe housing for low-income senior citizens, emergency shelters for homeless families with children, housing with social services for the homeless and mentally ill, repairs and accessibility improvements to apartments for families and handicapped citizens, homeownership assistance for military veterans, and security improvements and repairs to existing emergency shelters, shall the state create a housing trust fund by issuing bonds totaling two billion one hundred million dollars ($2,100,000,000), paid from existing state funds at an average annual cost of one hundred fifty seven million dollars ($157,000,000) per year over the 30-year life of the bonds, with the requirement that every city and county is eligible to receive funds as specified in the measure and with all expenditures subject to an independent audit?
Yes +
No +

47 KINDERGARTEN-UNIVERSITY PUBLIC EDUCATION FACILITIES BOND ACT OF 2002. This thirteen billion fifty million dollar ($13,050,000,000) bond issue will provide funding for necessary education facilities to relieve overcrowding and to repair older schools. Funds will be targeted to areas of the greatest need and must be spent according to strict accountability measures. Funds will also be used to upgrade and build new classrooms in the California Community Colleges, the California State University, and the University of California, to provide adequate higher education facilities to accommodate the growing student enrollment. These bonds may be used only for eligible projects. Fiscal Impact: State cost of about $26.2 billion over 30 years to pay off both the principal ($13.05 billion) and interest ($13.15 billion) costs on the bonds. Payments of about $873 million per year.
Yes +
No +

48 COURT CONSOLIDATION. LEGISLATIVE CONSTITUTIONAL AMENDMENT. Amends Constitution to delete references to the municipal courts, which references are now obsolete due to the consolidation of superior and municipal trial courts into unified superior courts. Fiscal Impact: No additional cost to state or local government.
Yes +
No +

STATE

49 BEFORE AND AFTER SCHOOL PROGRAMS. STATE GRANTS. INITIATIVE STATUTE. Increases state grant funds available for before/after school programs, providing tutoring, homework assistance, and educational enrichment. Requires that, beginning 2004-05, new grants will not be taken from education funds guaranteed by Proposition 98. Fiscal Impact: Additional annual state costs for before and after school programs of up to $455 million, beginning in 2004-05.
Yes +
No +

50 WATER QUALITY, SUPPLY AND SAFE DRINKING WATER PROJECTS. COASTAL WETLANDS PURCHASE AND PROTECTION. BONDS. INITIATIVE STATUTE. Authorizes $3,440,000,000 general obligation bonds to fund a variety of specified water and wetlands projects. Fiscal Impact: State cost of up to $6.9 billion over 30 years to repay bonds. Reduction in local property tax revenues, up to roughly $10 million annually; partially offset by state funds. Unknown state and local operation and maintenance costs.
Yes +
No +

51 TRANSPORTATION. DISTRIBUTION OF EXISTING MOTOR VEHICLE SALES AND USE TAX. INITIATIVE STATUTE. Redistributes portion of existing state motor vehicle sales/lease revenues from General Fund to Trust Fund for transportation, environmental, and highway and school bus safety programs. Fiscal Impact: Redirects specified General Fund revenues to transportation-related purposes, totaling about $420 million in 2002-03, $910 million in 2003-04, and increasing amounts annually thereafter, depending on increases in motor vehicle sales and leasing.
Yes +
No +

52 ELECTION DAY VOTER REGISTRATION. VOTER FRAUD PENALTIES. INITIATIVE STATUTE. Allows legally eligible persons to register to vote on election day. Increases criminal penalties for voter and voter registration fraud. Criminalizes conspiracy to commit voter fraud. Fiscal Impact: Annual state costs of about $6 million to fund counties for election day voter registration activities. No anticipated net county costs. Minor state administrative costs and unknown, but probably minor, state costs to enforce new election fraud offense.
Yes +
No +

lack broad support for their views. Sometimes initiatives are proposed to launch educational campaigns rather than to win adoption.

People anxious to limit the power of state and local governments are using the initiative process in more states. Since California adopted Proposition 13, which limited the state government's right to raise property taxes, in 1978, other states have followed suit. In addition, these "new reformers" have produced "a series of state constitutional amendments that, taken together, fundamentally altered the character and powers of state governments by limiting the tenure of governmental officials, reducing their powers, and transferring policy making responsibilities to the people."[31] In addition, "the focus of constitutional initiatives . . . has shifted from questions of governmental structure . . . to questions of substantive policy," such as initiatives on tort liability, rights of gays, affirmative action, and the rights of immigrants.[32]

Constitutional Conventions

Americans love constitutional conventions (or at least we used to); we have had 233 of them—144 in the nineteenth century but only 63 in the twentieth century.[33] One scholar noted that calling conventions of the people is a uniquely American idea, emphasizing that legislators cannot be trusted and that the supreme power belongs to the people.[34]

Forty-one state constitutions authorize their legislature to submit the calling of a convention to the voters; the other states assume that the legislature has the power to do so. Fourteen state constitutions require the legislature to question voters about a convention at fixed intervals, varying from every 9 to every 20 years. For example, Missouri is required to submit the question to the voters every 20 years; Hawaii raises the issue every 9 years; Michigan, every 16 years.

If the voters approve, the next step is to elect delegates to a convention. Some state constitutions contain elaborate procedures governing the number of delegates, the method of election, and the time and place of the convention. Others leave the details to the legislature. The way convention delegates are selected seems to affect the kind of document the convention proposes. Selection by nonpartisan, multimember districts is more likely to result in a reform convention that makes major changes than one in which political parties play a major role.[35]

After delegates have been chosen, they usually assemble at the state capital. When the convention has prepared a draft of the new constitution, the document is submitted to the voters. But first the convention delegates have to make a difficult choice: Should the voters be asked to accept or reject the new constitution as a whole? Or should they vote on each section separately?

The advantage of the first method is that each provision of a constitution ties in with another, and to secure all the advantages of revision, the entire constitution should be adopted. The disadvantage is that those who oppose a particular provision may vote against the entire constitution. When convention delegates know that a particular provision is controversial, they may decide to submit that provision separately. Whichever method they choose, the supporters of change must rally their forces to gain voter approval of their work.

The Politics of Constitutional Revision

Constitutions are not a neutral set of rules perched above the world of everyday politics. Rather, they significantly affect who gets what from government. Therefore, how a constitution is changed can help or hinder various groups.

Although there are campaigns for constitutional reform under way in Alabama, Oklahoma, and Texas, most people simply do not care.[36] It is difficult to work up enthusiasm for revising a state constitution except among people with special interests, and they are more likely to oppose than to favor adoption. Supporters of the status quo thus have a built-in advantage, which, combined with obstacles to the amending process in the constitution, helps explain the lack of action. "Revision is time-consuming, requiring sophisticated legal and drafting skills of the highest order, and involves negotiation and compromise. To be successful, revision requires gubernatorial as well as legislative leadership. . . . An effective political campaign is essential. . . . Success at the polls is not assured. Constitutional revision can be a high-risk endeavor and will continue to be."[37] Following are some case studies that illustrate the risky nature of constitutional revision.

Rhode Island Amends Its Constitution

Rhode Island's constitutional convention produced 14 separate propositions for amending its 1843 constitution. On November 4, 1986, voters approved eight of the 14 provisions, rejecting attempts to increase compensation of state legislators, to provide for merit selection of judges, and to create a "paramount right to life without regard to age, health, function, or condition of dependency," which would have banned abortions or public funding of them. The voters approved provisions strengthening free speech, due process, and equal protection rights and expanding fishing rights and access to the shore, as well as a statement that the rights protected by the Rhode Island constitution "stand independent of the U.S. Constitution."

The Rhode Island constitution calls for voters to be asked every ten years if they want to convene a constitutional convention. In November 1994, the voters rejected a convention by a vote of 173,693 to 118,545.[38] At the moment, there is considerable public pressure in the form of a 2-to-1 vote in November 2001 in favor of a nonbinding ballot question for a constitutional convention focused on separation of powers issues in order to reverse a decision of the Rhode Island supreme court to the effect that the Rhode Island constitution allows the state legislature to both make and execute state laws. So far the legislature has failed to act.[39]

Louisiana Revises Its Constitution

The Louisiana Constitutional Revision Commission set out during 1973 and 1974 to write a streamlined "people's constitution"—one the average person could understand.[40] The AFL-CIO, National Association for the Advancement of Colored People, League of Women Voters, Committee for a Better Louisiana, National Municipal League, and many other lobbying groups became involved in shaping the new constitution. It took well over a year to write, and it cost the taxpayers approximately $4 million. In the end, a readable 26,000-word document replaced the existing 265,000-word document that contained some 536 amendments. In April 1974, Louisiana voters approved the new charter by a large margin.

The Louisiana constitution can no longer be cited as the prime example of an unworkable state constitution, although 107 amendments have been added since 1974 and the length has inched back up to 54,112 words. "Indeed," according to one commentator, constitutional amendment in Louisiana is "sufficiently continuous to justify including it with Mardi Gras, football, and corruption as one of the premier components of state culture."[41]

Changing the Hawaii Constitution

More than 800 proposals for constitutional changes were submitted to the Hawaii state constitutional convention of 1978. The League of Women Voters and other groups conducted extensive information and discussion meetings, and the convention held many public hearings on key issues. The 102 delegates to the convention met for nearly three months during the summer of 1978. After extensive debate, the convention narrowed the proposals to 34 questions to be placed on the fall ballot. Convention delegates rejected proposals for the initiative, referendum, and recall; for a unicameral legislature; and for an elected (instead of an appointed) attorney general.

The delegates were not opposed to all government reforms, however, for they endorsed a two-term limit for governor and lieutenant governor, moved to make Hawaii party primaries more open by allowing voters to cast ballots without declaring party preference, and authorized the state legislature to provide partial public funding for election campaigns and establish spending limits. The convention reflected concern over government spending by setting tougher overall debt and spending limits for the state. It also strengthened environmental safeguards and gave further constitutional and financial protection to the special status of native Hawaiians.

On November 7, 1978, 74 percent of the voters went to the polls; all 34 amendments were adopted; 20 percent of the voters had accepted the amendments as a package.

In 1986, Hawaiians rejected the periodic question of whether to call a convention by a vote of 173,977 to 139,236. Again in 1996, the question of calling a convention was put to the voters, and the vote was 163,869 in favor and 160,153 against, but 45,245 people left the question unanswered. Blank ballots were tallied as a no, in response to a decision of the state supreme court that the Hawaii constitution required approval by a majority of all ballots cast. The Ninth U.S. Circuit Court of Appeals, which refused to order a new election, sustained this decision.

Proposals for a convention had been backed by several interests, including those who wanted to overturn a decision of the Hawaii supreme court favoring the legalization of same-sex marriages, by those who wanted to impose term limits, and by those who wanted to limit the power of state courts to restrict police searches.[42]

Hawaii's experiences with the revision process are reminders that constitution making is not just an exercise in abstract argument or logical reasoning but flows directly from a state's political life.

Texas Keeps Its Old Constitution

Texas has a lengthy constitution. Adopted in 1876, it has been amended more than 370 times. The most recent effort to thoroughly revise it was in 1972, after political scandals brought in a new governor, Dolph Briscoe, and a reform-oriented state legislature. After pushing through a variety of reforms dealing with the ethics of officeholders, campaign practices, and registration of lobbyists, the legislature did an unconventional thing by calling into being a constitutional convention consisting of members of the legislature rather than a specially elected body.

After working for 17 months, the legislator-delegates came up with a much revised and shortened document intended to modernize many obsolete governmental practices. The convention deadlocked, however, over whether to give constitutional status to the state's right-to-work law, which prohibits labor contracts that require union membership as a condition of employment, so this issue was referred to the voters. In the end, neither the AFL-CIO nor Governor Briscoe supported all of the convention's recommendations. The governor was especially opposed to the proposal that legislative sessions be held annually, rather than every two years, which he argued would cause higher taxes. Advocates of the revised constitution tried to salvage their work by offering substantial parts of the new charter to the voters as amendments to the existing constitution.

Conservatives praised the old constitution, claiming it had served Texas well for 100 years. Progressives complained that the old constitution was elitist, permitted only the narrowest governmental objectives, and made real change nearly impossible. In November 1975, amid charges and countercharges, Texas voters rejected the amendments by a 2-to-1 margin.[43] Since then, Texans have approved 143 amendments and rejected 33 but have not held another convention.

The Arkansas Constitution

Arkansas's eighth constitutional convention was a protracted affair. The 100 delegates who were elected in 1978 held their organizational session in the winter of that year but did not get down to work until the spring of 1979. Having reconvened in June 1980 to revise the final draft, they submitted the proposed constitution to the voters in November 1980.

Opposition developed to a provision in the new constitution allowing the legislature, by a two-thirds vote, to set interest rates rather than limit them, as in the current constitution. Other groups opposed a provision enlarging the taxing powers of local governments. Even though then Governor Bill Clinton, the Democratic party, and the Arkansas Education Association endorsed the new constitution, the voters rejected it, 2 to 1.

As noted, the question of a constitutional convention was again put to Arkansas voters in December 1995. Those planning the 1995 convention structured the convention call in such a way that the convention would avoid addressing "issues which were not critical to state government but which would inflame folks" and would concentrate on "issues of pure governance."[44] Nonetheless, the call for the convention was decisively rejected.

Alabama Considers a New Constitution

Alabama has had six constitutions. The most recent, written in 1901 and adopted in 1902, was "a document of the Old South,"[45] unashamedly and openly designed to keep African

After three years of preparations and deliberation, the proposed Texas constitution of 1974 failed by three votes in the final hectic session of the constitutional convention.

Americans from voting or otherwise participating in governmental matters.[46] It has been amended more than 700 times and there have been many unsuccessful attempts to modernize and replace it.

The issue of constitutional reform is again now on Alabama's agenda. Governor Bob Riley, a Republican, and his Democratic opponent in the 2002 election, then Governor Donald Siegelman, as well as most of the state's newspapers, are calling for the legislature to put the question of a constitutional convention on a statewide ballot. One poll shows that 61 percent of Alabama residents favor constitutional reform.[47] A 21-member commission called the Alabama Citizens for Constitutional Reform has been incorporated to push the idea. Secretary of State Jim Bennett chairs this commission. It proposes that the legislature put the issue before the voters and if the voters approve of holding a constitutional convention, the voters would elect a delegate from each of the 105 House districts, all of whom would convene on August 5, 2003.[48] After the convention completes its work, the proposed constitution would be presented to the people for approval or rejection.[49]

Others in Alabama are seeking to rewrite the 1901 constitution article-by-article, rather than via a constitutional convention.[50] Some conservatives, including The Association for Judeo-Christian Values, which contends that a new constitutional convention will "bring new taxes in and throw God out" are opposing constitutional revision.[51] The convention is also being opposed by James Blast, a businessman and son of former Governor Fob James, as well as a frequent candidate for governor.[52]

Summary

1. State constitutions attempt to spell out the fundamental laws of the states. Although they vary considerably in detail, each outlines the organizational framework of the state, vesting powers in the legislature and other departments. Each includes a bill of rights, sets procedures for holding elections, provides for local governments, and contains a variety of provisions dealing with finances, education, and other state issues.

2. Most state constitutions are cumbersome documents containing more detail than the U.S. Constitution. Although reformers may have introduced such detail to prevent abuse, most constitutional scholars believe such matters are better left to statutory law.

3. In the past 20 years, there has been a flurry of renewed interest in state constitutions as they have been discovered to be additional instruments for protecting and expanding rights in what is known as the new judicial federalism.

4. State constitutions can be amended by ratification by the voters of proposals submitted by the legislature, by popular initiative petitions, or by constitutional conventions. Conventions tend to revise the entire constitution rather than just amend portions of it.

5. In recent decades, there has been an expanded use of the initiative process in several states to bring about narrowly targeted constitutional change.

6. Despite the considerable constitutional change brought about during the last half-century through amendments, voters have often been resistant to sweeping constitutional revision.

Key Terms

judicial interpretation   new judicial federalism   revision commission   constitutional initiative petition

Further Reading

The Greenwood Publishing Group has commissioned reference guides for the constitution of each state, written by an expert on the state. As of 2002, guides for Alabama, Arizona, Arkansas, Alaska, California, Colorado, Hawaii, Indiana, Iowa, Kansas, Kentucky, Louisiana, Michigan, Maine, Montana, Nebraska, New Mexico, New York, Oklahoma, Tennessee, Texas, Utah, Wisconsin, and West Virginia were available.
BURTON C. AGATA AND ERIC LANE, EDS., *State Constitutions: Competing Perspectives*

(Hofstra Law and Policy Symposium, 1996), vol. 1.

BRUCE E. CAIN AND ROGER G. NOLL, EDS., *Constitutional Reform in California* (Institute of Governmental Studies Press, 1995).

CONGRESSIONAL INFORMATION SERVICE, *State Constitutional Conventions, Commissions and Amendments, 1979–1988: An Annotated Bibliography* (U.S. Congressional Information Service, 1989).

ELMER E. CORNWELL JR., JAY S. GOODMAN, AND WAYNE R. SWANSON, *State Constitutional Conventions: The Politics of the Revision Process in Seven States* (Praeger, 1975).

PAUL FINKELMAN AND STEPHEN E. GOTTLIEB, EDS., *Toward a Usable Past: Liberty Under State Constitutions* (University of Georgia Press, 1991).

JOHN KINCAID, ED., "State Constitutions in the Federal System," *Annals of the American Academy of Political and Social Science* 496 (March 1988).

SANFORD LEVINSON, ED., *Responding to Imperfection: The Theory and Practice of Constitutional Amendment* (Princeton University Press, 1995).

BERNARD D. REAMS JR. AND STUART D. YOAK, *The Constitutions of the States: A State-by-State Guide and Bibliography to Current Scholarly Research* (Oceana Publications, 1988).

G. ALAN TARR, *Constitutional Politics in the States: Contemporary Controversies and Historical Patterns* (Greenwood Press, 1996).

G. ALAN TARR, *Understanding State Constitutions* (Princeton University Press, 1998).

ROBERT F. WILLIAMS, *State Constitutional Law: Cases and Materials* (Michie, 1993).

See also the quarterly review *State Constitutional Commentaries and Notes,* published by the Edward McNail Burns Center for State Constitutional Studies at Rutgers University.

PARTIES
AND ELECTIONS
IN THE STATES

MOST CITIZENS OF THE UNITED STATES TAKE FOR GRANTED THAT ELECTIONS WILL BE FAIRLY ADMINISTERED AND THAT POWER will be peacefully transferred to the election's winner. In stark contrast to these fundamentals of our electoral democracy is what happened in the 2000 presidential election in Yugoslavia. Incumbent President Slobodan Milosevic, indicted for war crimes for his actions in Bosnia, was defeated by challenger Vojislav Kostunica by at least 10 percentage points. Neutral observers estimated that Kostunica had received 51 percent of the vote.[1] Milosevic, in a desperate attempt to retain power, claimed that Kostunica fell short of the 50 percent needed to win the election and called for a runoff election. Kostunica refused to participate in the runoff, claiming he had won a majority in the first election. He cited instances of election fraud, including 350 "phantom" polling stations and an extra 150,000 votes for Milosevic in Kosovo.[2]

The citizens of Yugoslavia took matters into their own hands through protest demonstrations, civil disobedience, and widespread strikes. Schools and businesses closed, and some shopkeepers hung signs in their windows that read CLOSED BECAUSE OF ROBBERY—a reference to Milosevic's election theft. Blackouts started throughout the country when an estimated 10,000 coal miners went on strike.

Hundreds of thousands of protesters took to the streets of Belgrade and stormed the parliament building, setting parts of it on fire. They also took control of the state-owned television stations. Coal miners, protesters, and opposition party leaders risked their lives by standing up to the government. There was no guarantee that their efforts would be successful. The military and police did not take any serious action against the protesters, and some even joined in the throng. Milosevic fled the capital to the countryside, and Kostunica claimed leadership. Within days, he was recognized as the legitimate president by the international community, including Russia.[3] Clearly, it was not the election of Kostunica alone that produced these dramatic events; the opportunity to express popular discontent against a despot and an illegitimate government contributed as well.

The Yugoslav election demonstrates that honest election procedures and accurate vote counting are not universal. Nor is it always the case that the winner of an election will take office. Election fraud in other countries helps us appreciate our own democracy. We find it unthinkable that an American mayor, governor, or president would annul an election when his or her party did not win. But if election violations do occur, people in the United States have recourse to the courts and even to the police to redress them. We expect the losing candidate to exit the office peacefully so that the winning candidate can assume power. Yet as we Americans learned in the aftermath of the 2000 presidential and 2002 midterm elections, our own ballots and election procedures are flawed, and not just in Florida. However, modernizing how we vote may involve complex legislation and even constitutional amendments since U.S. elections are largely governed by state law and administered at the county level. In 2002, Congress passed legislation creating minimum federal standards for all U.S. elections, including keeping computerized statewide lists of voters to combat election fraud.

The 2002 elections saw no repeats of the troubled recounts in Florida in 2000. There was, however, some controversy in South Dakota about the registration drives among Native Americans. Charges of fraud in Native American voter registration surfaced before the election but were dismissed by the South Dakota attorney general. In other states, like Arkansas, there was some evidence of efforts to discourage African American voters from casting early ballots. In neither South Dakota nor Arkansas, however, did the contested ballots appear to alter the outcome of the election.

Electoral Politics in the States and Localities

The U.S. Constitution provides only the most general guidelines to the states concerning the regulation of elections for members of the U.S. Congress. Article I, Section 4, says, "The Times, Places and Manner of holding Elections for Senators and Representatives shall be prescribed in each State by the Legislature thereof; but the Congress may at any time by Law make or alter such Regulations, except as to the Places of choosing Senators." The constitutional language regarding presidential elections also defers to state law: "Each State shall

When presidential candidate Slobodan Milosevic refused to accept defeat in the election in Yugoslavia, the citizens of Belgrade took to the streets night after night, and some set fire to the Parliament building. Finally, Milosevic capitulated, and Vojislav Kostunica took over as president.

appoint, in such Manner as the Legislature thereof may direct, a Number of Electors." The role of the state legislature in naming electors became part of the drama of the 2000 presidential election as the Florida legislature went into special session, prepared, if necessary, to name an alternate slate of electors, in part because of uncertainty surrounding the various state and federal court rulings regarding the counting and recounting of ballots.

Amendments to the U.S. Constitution relating to elections do not alter the central role of state constitutions and state law regarding voting rights. Rather, these amendments expressly forbid the states to restrict the right to vote in any election, for state and local as well as for national offices, to certain kinds of people. States cannot deny the franchise on the basis of "race, color, or previous condition of servitude" (Fifteenth Amendment), gender (Nineteenth Amendment), failure to pay a poll tax (Twenty-Fourth Amendment), or age for persons over age 18 (Twenty-Sixth Amendment).

Federalism and Elections

Political federalism in this country is noteworthy. State identities are important to both politicians and voters. We tend to think of ourselves not only as citizens of the United States but also as citizens of a particular state. Each state has a distinctive political tradition and political culture. It should not be surprising, then, that state parties are in many ways more important than national parties. Indeed, national parties, aside from their congressional campaign committees, are largely federations of state parties. And since our national parties as electoral organizations have never been strong, the activities they undertake usually end up being carried out by the state parties. The independence of state parties also helps explain why, for instance, Democratic voters in one state can be so different from those in another and why Republicans from different states can come down on opposite sides of some major issues.

The electoral process in the United States is *decentralized* in its rules and administration. All elections in the United States are administered by state and local governments, not by the national government. The president is chosen in state elections conducted according to state rules. Because of the electoral college and the winner-take-all system, presidential politics focuses not on getting the most popular votes but instead on getting a plurality of votes in as many states as possible. State elections also determine who will serve as members of Congress, as governor, and as other statewide officials like attorney general, as well as the outcome of many ballot measures.

Most states prescribe the organization of the state parties, the means by which their officers are elected, and the nomination process for president and other offices.[4] In states that have some form of public financing of elections or parties, such as Maine and Arizona, the state also regulates the distribution of public funds to the parties and the reporting of how those funds are spent.

States differ in the hours the polls are open, how close to the voting place campaigning may be conducted, and whether they require voter registration. Largely because of overriding federal legislation, differences between the states in how long you must have lived in the state before voting and how you may register to vote have diminished in recent years.

And as we learned in the 2000 presidential election in Florida, there is great variation in how people vote, even from county to county. Some Florida counties used ballots read by optical scanners, and others used punch-card ballots. Other states use these same types of ballots as well as paper ballots, voting machines, and even the Internet. Following the 2000 election, Florida mandated that voting in statewide elections be by computerized touch screens or ballots read by optical scanning machines.[5] Some of these devices malfunctioned in the 2002 Florida primary election.

Along with the variation in ballots, we have many types of elections, including *general elections* to determine who holds office and *primary elections* to determine who will run in the general elections. Most statewide elections are partisan, whereas most local elections for school boards, water districts, and city governments are nonpartisan. State

WE THE PEOPLE

A Demographic Profile of Local Government Officials

Number of local elected officials	**494,093**
Gender	
Male	76.3%
Female	23.7
Race	
White	96.7
Black	2.8
American Indian or Alaskan Native	0.4
Asian or Pacific Islander	0.1
Hispanic	1.4

SOURCE: U.S. Bureau of the Census, "Popularly Elected Officials in 1992," *1992 Census of Governments* (U.S. Government Printing Office, 1992).

legislative elections are partisan except in Nebraska, where the legislature is nonpartisan. Many city elections are nonpartisan. Voters in all states but Delaware must ratify changes to the state constitution in a referendum. Roughly half of the states allow votes on initiatives and referendums put on the ballot by petition. The initiative and referendum are also found in many local governments.

The Role of Political Parties

Although political parties are not mentioned in the U.S. Constitution, they are vital not only to our national government but also to the functioning of the electoral system within the states. Parties organize the competition by recruiting and nominating candidates, function as the loyal opposition when out of power, unify and organize the electorate, and provide a link between the people and their government. The existence of political parties is acknowledged in many state constitutions.

Election rules in general favor the two major parties over minor parties. The Republican and Democratic parties have a "preferred position"—that is, their candidates will definitely be placed on the ballot. Ballot access for minor party and independent candidates is less certain. State laws typically require minor parties to garner a minimum number of votes in the previous election or submit a prescribed number of signatures of registered voters in order to appear on the ballot. States vary in the difficulty of ballot access for minor parties, depending on three factors: the number of signatures required, the time allowed to collect them, and whether signatures must be distributed across several counties.

State election ballots are of two kinds. The **party column ballot** (also known as the *Indiana ballot*), which encourages party-line voting, is organized by parties, with the party name and symbol at the top of a column that lists all the party's candidates running for offices in that election (see Figure 24-1). Typically, there is a spot at the top of the column to make a single mark or pull a single lever on the voting machine to cast votes for all candidates of that party. When voters make such a mark or pull the party lever, they cast a **straight ticket** vote. Voters may also have to work their way through state constitutional amendments, referendums, and initiatives on the ballot.

Partly to discourage straight ticket voting, some states use the **office block ballot** (also known as the *Massachusetts ballot*), which lists all the candidates running for an office together in one block, all those running for another office in another block, and

party column ballot
Type of ballot that encourages party-line voting by listing all of a party's candidates in a column under the party name.

straight ticket
A vote for all of one party's candidates.

office block ballot
Ballot on which all candidates are listed under the office for which they are running.

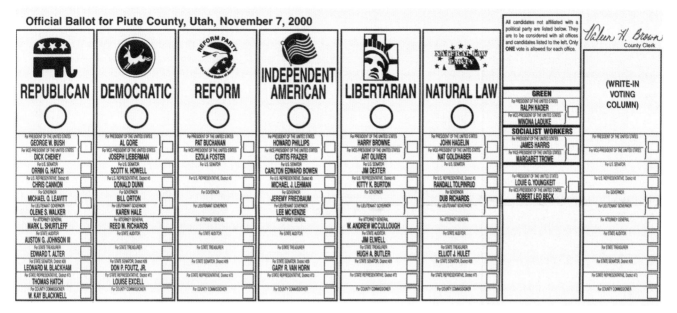

FIGURE 24–1   A Sample Party Column Ballot.

so on (see Figure 24-2). If voters want to cast a straight ticket vote, they have to hunt through each column for their preferred candidate. Office block ballots encourage **split ticket** voting, or voting for candidates from more than one party. One consequence of computerized ballots will be a shift to office block formats.

Party Organization and Officers

Although state party organizations are not all alike, most organize themselves along the same lines as the national parties. In all states, there is a *party chair* who is elected by the party's central committee or delegates to a party convention. Other statewide party officers include the *vice chair,* who by state law or party bylaws often must be of the opposite gender from the party chair,[6] plus officers like treasurer and secretary. Party leaders

split ticket
A vote for some of one party's candidates and some of another party's.

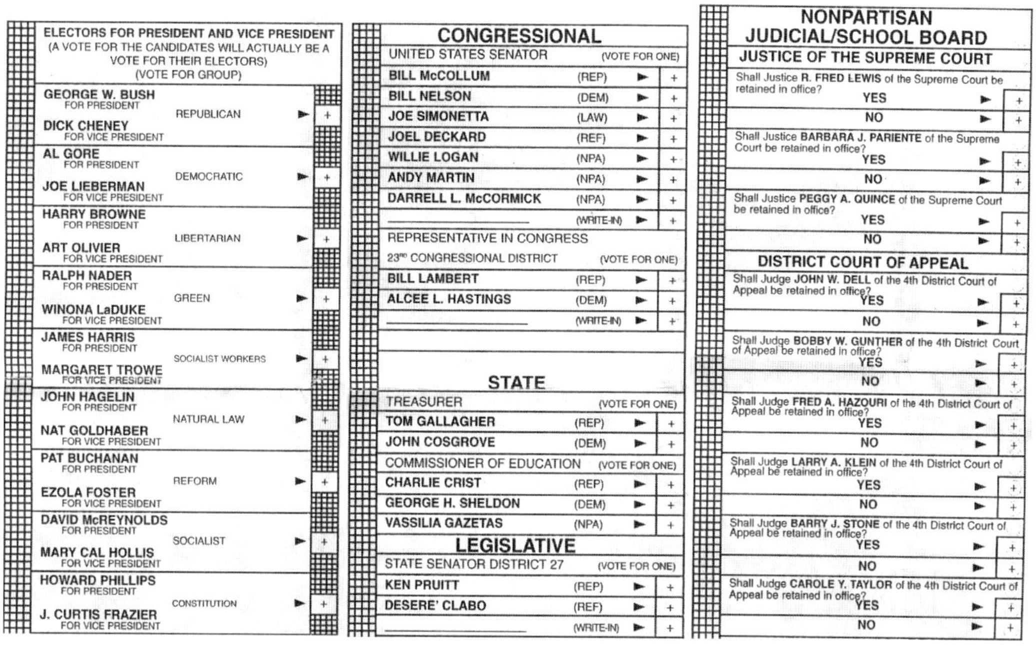

FIGURE 24–2   A Sample Office Block Ballot.

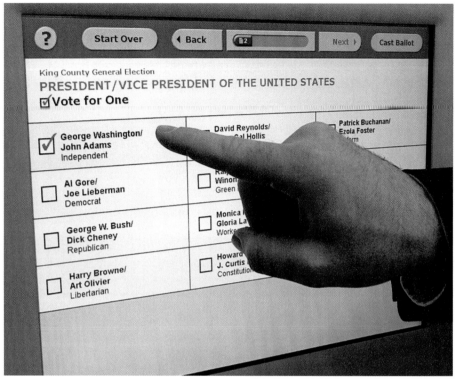

Modern voting machines, such as the touch-screen model shown here, tend to favor the office block ballot over the party column ballot.

Machines and Bosses

In the nineteenth century, political *machines* became established in a number of American cities. Typically, these were organizations in which one political party dominated the political life of the city, often by recruiting new immigrants as supporters and voters by offering them patronage jobs and social welfare benefits. For many years, the epitome of a political machine in the United States was Tammany Hall, the building where the Tammany Society (named after a Delaware Indian chief) met and ran New York City politics. Tammany Hall was closely identified with Democrats and was ruled by William Tweed, the boss of New York City politics.

A *boss* is a party leader who uses patronage, government contracts, and access to power to dictate policy. Some bosses, like Tweed, were never elected to office but were powers behind the scene who told the mayor and other city officials what to do. Party bosses were common after the Civil War and well into the twentieth century. Other cities with powerful political machines were Chicago, Los Angeles, Boston, Pittsburgh, Cincinnati, Philadelphia, Indianapolis, San Francisco, and Baltimore.

The principal objective of the urban reform movement in the early twentieth century was to overthrow the bosses and the political machines. Reformers advocated nonpartisan local elections, competitive bids for projects, and civil service in place of patronage. They achieved most of their goals, although it is not clear whether the power of political machines was reduced by these reforms or by other social and economic forces.

generally answer to a *central committee*, which consists of 20 or more persons who are elected or otherwise chosen for specified terms.

The state party chair is the spokesperson for the party, especially when the party does not control the governorship. He or she raises money for the party and its candidates. When the party controls the governorship, the central committee defers to the governor in the selection of the chair. Because overt expressions of partisanship are thought to be unbecoming of elected officials, it is often the party chair who defends the party and, when necessary, goes on the offensive against the opposition party.

The day-to-day operations of the party are usually carried out by the party's *executive director*, a full-time employee who oversees the staff, assists the chair, and coordinates the work of the central committee and other party officials. The executive director schedules functions and serves as a liaison with the national organizations.

At the local level, political parties generally have a structure patterned after the state party organization. In some counties, party organizations are fully staffed and functioning, but in most counties, they are run by volunteers and are mostly inactive until just before an election. Local parties provide opportunities for ordinary citizens to become involved in politics, a first step that can eventually lead to running for office. Some states, like Minnesota, have congressional district parties as well.[7]

Although party bosses and strong party machines are a thing of the past, local politics is still organized on a partisan basis in many of our largest cities. However, local politics is more often characterized by nonpartisanship. Three-fourths of U.S. cities have nonpartisan elections.[8]

Party Activities in Elections

American politics is candidate-centered. Candidates create their own campaign organizations. Yet parties serve important secondary roles in elections. They provide the structure for elections; in some places, they recruit candidates, register voters, mobilize voters on election day, and supply resources and campaign help to their candidates.

STRUCTURE FOR ELECTIONS   Our election system would function in a dramatically different way if we had no political parties to organize the competition. Parties narrow the field of candidates through a primary election or convention process, providing voters with relatively few choices in the general election. Candidates, to one degree or another, must secure the support of fellow partisans to win a place on the ballot as the party's nominees for the offices they are seeking.

CANDIDATE RECRUITMENT   Party officials often seek out candidates to run for office, help train them in how to run, and occasionally provide modest financial support.

A sign of the weakness of our parties is the fact that many offices go uncontested, including some members of Congress. The number of unopposed candidates increases as you go down the ballot. To be sure, some incumbents have done such a good job that to oppose them would be an exercise in futility. Yet lack of competition in elections violates American assumptions about democracy and is reminiscent of politics in the former communist states, where party officers ran unopposed. One important characteristic of American parties at all levels is that they are extremely open to would-be candidates. Virtually anybody can run for the state legislature. Generally speaking, the greater the likelihood that a party nomination will help with winning the general election, the more competition there is for that nomination.

VOTER REGISTRATION   All states except North Dakota require citizens to register before permitting them to vote. In California, you can register online, at www.ss.ca.gov/elections/elections.htm, and some states, like Wisconsin, allow registration at the polls on election day. Voter registration became easier when Congress passed the National Voter Registration, or Motor Voter, Act in 1993. People are now able to register to vote when they apply for or renew their driver's license or visit certain public agencies. The half-dozen states that permit election day registration or do not require voter registration are exempt from the law. The idea behind Motor Voter is to ease the registration process thereby increasing the number of registered voters and turnout.

What difference has Motor Voter made? Since January 1995, when the law went into effect, almost 12.5 million people have been added to the voter registration rolls, or just over one-third of all new registrants.[9] Many of the new Motor Voter registrants are registering as Independents. In terms of party balance, Motor Voter appears not to have made much difference, contrary to expectations that it would result in a bias in favor of Democrats.[10]

At the time of registration, some states ask voters to register with a political party; in other states, party registration is optional. Most states do not register voters by party. To see what your state requires, visit the voter registration section of the Federal Election Commission Web site at www.fec.gov. Even in states that require party registration, voters have the option to decline to state their party at the time of registration. For example, in California in 2002, 15 percent of the registered voters declined to state their party preference.[11] Opting out of party registration often means voters may not vote in a party primary, which in some states may be the election that effectively decides the officeholder. An excellent data bank on voter registration and turnout is maintained by the National Conference of State Legislatures at www.ncsl.org.

Helping register sympathetic voters is important to candidates, parties, and interest groups. These efforts are typically aimed at citizens they anticipate will vote for their party's candidate. Voter registration drives targeted at African Americans helped Democrats in key states and congressional districts. Both parties worked to register Hispanic voters in 2002. Interest groups with active voter registration efforts include organized labor, business groups, and groups concerned about the environment and abortion.

Political parties favor laws requiring voters to disclose their party preference at the time they register. First, this requirement permits parties to limit participation in their primaries to registered party members in states that have a closed primary system. Second, party registration creates voter registration lists, which parties find extremely useful for

Party volunteers keep the phone lines humming as they urge potential voters to come out on election day and support their candidate.

State and Local Campaign Financing

- 35 states limit the size of individual contributions.

- 21 states prohibit corporate contributions, and 14 states prohibit labor union contributions.

- 35 states limit contributions from PACs.

- Minnesota places much lower contribution limits during nonelection years.

- 25 states offer limited public financing from the government to statewide candidates or political parties. Hawaii, Wisconsin, and Minnesota also give funding directly to state legislative candidates.

- Five states offer partial or total tax credits to encourage small contributions.

- 13 states raise campaign money through their income tax system.

SOURCE: James A. Palmer and Edward D. Feigenbaum, *Campaign Finance Law, 2000* (Federal Election Commission, 2000), charts 2A and 4.

campaigning and fund raising. In addition, *list vending*—selling voter lists with addresses, phone numbers, and party preferences—is a multimillion-dollar industry. Third, voter registration helps the parties in the redistricting process because state legislators, using party registration, voting, and other data, can draw new congressional and state legislative district boundaries in ways that give their party an advantage. Examples of states where partisanship was a major factor in the 2001–2002 redistricting are Georgia for the Democrats and Utah for the Republicans.[12]

VOTER MOBILIZATION   Only 76 percent of eligible voters are registered, and of that number, only about 67 percent vote in presidential elections, meaning that *only half the voting-age population bothers to vote* in a presidential election and fewer still in a midterm election.[13] Get-out-the-vote drives are therefore a major activity of candidates and parties. Elections are often decided by which party does better at turning out its supporters. Party workers, through telephone or door-to-door canvassing, identify registered voters who are likely to support their party and then contact those voters personally on election day, perhaps more than once, to encourage them to go to the polls. Where resources permit, the parties may even provide transportation to the polls or baby-sitting services.[14]

In states that permit registration by mail or by roving registrars, volunteers register voters at the same time they find voters who will support their party's candidates in the election. When absentee or mail ballots are options, voter mobilization efforts help voters fill out the form requesting an absentee ballot and then mail the form for them. A few weeks later, a party volunteer checks to make sure a ballot has arrived and has been filled out and returned. Because most voters prefer one party over another, it makes sense for candidates from the same party to consolidate their efforts.

CAMPAIGN RESOURCES   American political parties, with some notable exceptions, are organizationally weak. In better-organized states, parties often provide campaign funds and campaign help. They raise funds for their party organization and finance voter registration and mobilization efforts, often with the help of national parties. As at the national level, control of the governorship helps in fund raising because interest groups are much more likely to contribute to the governor's party. Texas Governor George W. Bush not only tapped into his base of affluent Texans but also won the support of other governors to finance much of his 2000 presidential campaign.

In states with well-organized parties, the parties train the candidates they have recruited. Wisconsin and New York have strong state legislative campaign committees that distribute resources to candidates, as the national party committee does to congressional candidates.[15] Sometimes the state parties provide polling data to state and local candidates, help establish campaign themes, or prepare generic advertising that can be used in several state legislative districts.

Until 2004, parties also channeled money from the national congressional and senatorial campaign committees to local candidates for U.S. Senate or U.S. House involved in competitive races. This **soft money**, which could come in disclosed but unlimited amounts, was banned at the national level in 2002.[16] State parties operate under their own rules, and all but Connecticut permit soft money for state and local candidates. Moreover, the 2002 reforms permit limited amounts of soft money, $10,000, to go to state and local parties for voter registration and mobilization. This provision could make up for the soft money spent by parties in the past and may become even more frequently used in the future.[17] Between 1996 and 2002, Republican and Democratic national party committees, including the congressional and senatorial campaign committees, raised and distributed large amounts of soft money. Because state parties largely spend the soft money for the national parties, this expenditure has not generally made state parties stronger.

One of the reasons parties raised soft money was to respond to **issue advocacy**, in which an interest group attacks some political candidates or supports others but carefully avoids specifically telling voters to vote for or against that individual. Though much of the soft money and issue advocacy advertising focuses on presidential and congressional elections, both parties have also devoted these resources to gubernatorial and state legislative races, especially in anticipation of the redistricting after the 2000 census.

Issue advocacy, which aims to defeat or elect a particular candidate, was again significant in 2002. One notable example was again the pharmaceutical industry, which in 2000 provided substantial funding for a group named Citizens for Better Medicare. In 2002, their money was directed to another group—United Seniors. In both instances, the issue advocacy was important in reshaping the debate on the prescription drug issue for senior citizens. A wide range of interest groups engage in issue advocacy.

Voting Choices

Voters generally base their election decisions on three factors, listed in decreasing order of importance: political party identification, candidate appeal, and issues. But in many local elections, since party labels are absent from the ballot, voters rely more on candidate appeal, issues, and factors like incumbency, media endorsements, and name recognition.

PARTY IDENTIFICATION   Party identification is the most important predictor of voting behavior. Parties provide a party label that guides voters in making their decisions. Party labels are especially important in elections where voters have little information about candidates, as in contests for attorney general, state senator, state representative, or county commissioner. The simplifying device of party labels helps voters sort through the many candidate choices they encounter on election day.

People who identify themselves as strong Democrats and strong Republicans are remarkably loyal to their party when voting for governor and other state and local offices. Independent-leaners have clear partisan preferences in the direction of one party or the other. Pure Independents have no party preference and are most inclined to vote for one party and then another with changing circumstances, but there are few Pure Independents in the total electorate.[18]

CANDIDATE APPEAL   Although party identification is important, it is not decisive. Candidate appeal can be crucial. For example, in the 1998 Minnesota gubernatorial election, Reform party candidate Jesse Ventura was elected largely because his style and approach generated interest among voters, and a plurality preferred him over the established candidates in the major parties. Minnesota's system of public financing helped Ventura become visible, and he worked hard to become credible. In the end, he won in a stunning upset. As governor, he remained unconventional, abandoned the Reform Party for the Independent party, found working with the state legislature difficult, and took exception to media scrutiny of his family.[19] He decided not to run for reelection in 2002.

In state and local elections, name identification and the advantages of incumbency are important. Incumbents generally have an advantage in candidate appeal because of greater name recognition and access to campaign resources. Candidates sometimes use creative means to generate positive name recognition. For example, when Bob Graham was governor of Florida, he often worked one day a week in different jobs around the state to demonstrate his desire to relate to his constituents.

ISSUE VOTING   Issues can be very important to the outcome of elections. Economic conditions are an important factor in state and local elections, as they are in national ones. William Weld, a Republican, was able to win his first Massachusetts gubernatorial election in 1990, despite the fact that Massachusetts is a very strong Democratic state, because the economy was so bad. Former New Jersey Governor Christine Todd Whitman won election in part because her incumbent opponent had raised state taxes and she promised a 30 percent tax cut. Mitt Romney campaigned successfully in 2002 for governor of Massachusetts on the theme of an outsider being able to restore economic growth and fiscal discipline. His

soft money
Unlimited contributions to political parties for party-building purposes.

issue advocacy
Promoting a particular position on an issue, often funded by interest groups and designed to influence voters' choices on election day.

Partisanship in Judicial Elections

Judicial elections in some states are partisan and resemble campaigns for other offices in intensity. In 2000, the Michigan Democratic party ran ads attacking incumbent candidates for the Michigan supreme court who had been appointed by a former Republican governor. One of the ads showed an insurance executive sitting at his desk searching through papers and asking the secretary, "Where are my judges?" She replies, "Just where they've always been, right in your pocket." The executive looks in his suit coat pocket to see three justices frolicking in handfuls of money. Three pictures appear on the screen and a voice says, "Justices Markman, Taylor, and Young have accepted hundreds of thousands from insurance and big business. Justice should not be for sale."

Ads attacking judicial candidates like this were not unique to Michigan in 2000. Ohio, Illinois, Alabama, and Idaho had races in which similar ads were used by political parties or interest groups. Substantial levels of campaign spending by political parties and interest groups in judicial elections has prompted criticism by good-government groups and led the American Bar Association to form a task force on this topic.

SOURCE: William Glaberson, "Fierce Campaigns Signal a New Era for State Courts," *New York Times,* June 5, 2000, p. A1.

party caucus
A meeting of the members of a party in a legislative chamber to select party leaders and develop party policy. Called a *conference* by the Republicans.

redistricting
The redrawing of congressional and other legislative district lines following the census, to accommodate population shifts and keep districts as equal as possible in population.

success as a businessman and as head of the 2002 Salt Lake City Winter Olympics reinforced this message. Although issues are important in state and local elections, it is fair to say that they are probably less important than at the national level.[20]

NONPARTISAN LOCAL ELECTIONS   Nonpartisan elections were intended to weaken political parties in local elections, and they have been successful. Arguing that political parties had little to contribute to the administration of local government, reformers during the first half of the twentieth century introduced nonpartisan elections. The two parties were, in effect, blocked from exerting an open influence on local politics.

Some observers contend that nonpartisan local elections make it more difficult for poor persons, minorities, and the less educated to participate effectively. For such people, the party label serves to identify politicians who share their values and perspectives on government. Well-educated and wealthy voters know more about who is running and what they stand for, even without party labels. Nonpartisan elections sometimes help Republican candidates, especially in cities with populations of more than 50,000, because Republican voters tend to vote more in low-turnout elections and are more likely to know which candidates are Republicans.[21]

Parties in State Government

PARTIES IN THE EXECUTIVE BRANCH   Just as winning the presidency is the big prize at the national level, so is winning the governorship at the state level. The party that controls the governorship has the power to appoint executive department officials and some state judges. Governors are usually perceived as the leaders of their party, and they establish the political agenda and help define the party for their state. They customarily win office with the help of fellow partisans, and they know from the day they take office that the other party is planning ways to defeat them and their party in the next election.

Governors often assist in recruiting candidates for the state legislature; they sometimes campaign on behalf of their party, even when they are not on the ballot for reelection. Presidential candidates often seek the help of governors. Governors raise money for campaigns as well as for the state party. They have wide latitude in appointing boards, commissions, judges, and state administrators, and they almost always take party affiliation and activity into account when making appointments.

PARTIES IN THE LEGISLATURE   Like Congress, state legislatures (excluding Nebraska, which is nonpartisan) are organized largely along party lines. The *speaker of the house or assembly* and the *president of the senate* are elected by the majority party in most states. They preside over floor proceedings and make key assignments to standing committees and study committees. Most state legislatures have floor leaders, called *majority leaders* and *minority leaders* and majority and minority *whips.*

In most states, parties sit on different sides of the aisle in the legislative chambers and are separated in committee meetings as well. Committee chairs in most state legislatures go to members from the majority party in that chamber, with the leaders of the majority party wielding great power in the final decision. The **party caucus** is often important in state legislatures. The caucus is a meeting of party leaders and legislators to discuss party policy. Because some state legislatures meet for only a few months a year, the party caucus can help hammer out agreements rapidly.

One area on which legislatures are predictably partisan is **redistricting**. Each decade, following the national census, state legislatures are constitutionally required to realign congressional and state legislative district boundaries to make them equal in population and reflect population changes. The 2001–2002 redistricting was especially important because the two parties were so evenly divided in numbers of legislative chambers controlled. Going into the 2002 elections, the Democrats controlled 49 chambers, the Republicans 47, and two were tied.

How district lines are drawn can help or hurt a party. Where one party controls both houses and the governorship or has a veto-proof majority in the legislature, the majority party can do pretty much what it wants with district boundaries, so long as it keeps the districts equal in population and respects the rights of racial minorities. Where power is divided between the parties, the result is often a redistricting that protects incumbents. Initial assessments of the product of legislative redistricting in 2002 suggest that protecting incumbents was the prevailing pattern. In states where commissions did the redistricting, this was less the case.[22]

Parties in Local Government

Political parties are still important in the politics of many cities, especially the larger ones, although they are in a much weaker position now than they were 25 or 50 years ago. Mayors often lead city party organizations and play a role in the campaigns of presidents, senators, and governors. The mayor's office is sometimes a stepping-stone to other offices. Former Governor Jesse Ventura began his political career as mayor of Brooklyn Park, Minnesota; U.S. Senator Richard Lugar was once mayor of Indianapolis; George Voinovich was mayor of Cleveland and became governor of Ohio before going on to the U.S. Senate; and U.S. Senator Dianne Feinstein was mayor of San Francisco. In 2002, former St. Paul mayor Norm Coleman was elected to the U.S. Senate from Minnesota, defeating former vice-president Walter Mondale, who was running in place of deceased Senator Paul Wellstone.

Parties rarely get involved in initiative and referendum elections at the local or state levels, but some nonpartisan local elections have partisan overtones as candidates may be identified with the parties, or the parties may want to advance the career of a local nonpartisan candidate.

Party Balance and Imbalance

State politics may be classified according to how the parties share public offices. In a **two-party state**, the Republican and Democratic parties regularly assemble winning majorities. Two-party states include Indiana, Illinois, and Missouri. In a **one-party state**, one party wins all or nearly all the offices, and the second party usually receives only one-third or less of the popular vote. One-party Republican states currently include Utah, Idaho, and Kansas. Massachusetts is an example of a Democratic one-party state. Democrats occasionally win in Utah, and the same is true for Republicans in Massachusetts, but the more predictable tendency is to support the predominant party.

Since the end of World War II, there has been an accelerating trend toward two-party politics. The Democratic party lost its previously solid support in the South as more and more white southerners moved over to the Republican party. At first, Republican resurgence in the South was mainly evident in presidential and congressional elections, but in recent years, Republicans have regularly been elected to southern state legislatures. Since the mid-1970s, the number of Republicans in southern state legislatures has increased from about 12 percent to around 46 percent, climbing 4 percent in 2002.[23]

Republican gains have also been evident in contests for governor. Since 1966, all southern states have at least once elected Republican governors, and in 2003, five southern states were led by Republican governors. In terms of the popular vote for president, the South has voted more Republican than the country as a whole in nine of the last 11 presidential elections.[24] Even with a southerner like Al Gore on the ballot, the Democrats carried no southern state in 2000.

Outside the South, there has also been a gradual spread of two-party politics, with the rise of Democratic strength in the formerly solid Republican states of Iowa, Maine, and New Hampshire. Democrats have lost strength in parts of the Rocky Mountain area; however, the Democratic party has been gaining loyalists in the Midwest, Northeast, and Pacific Coast states.

What are the consequences of party balance? When parties and their candidates compete on an equal basis, they are more likely to be sensitive to public opinion, for the loss of even a fraction of the voters can tip the scales to the other side in the next election.

two-party state
A state in which the two major parties alternate in winning majorities.

one-party state
A state in which one party wins all or nearly all the offices and the other party receives only a small proportion of the popular vote.

Incumbent Protection and the 2002 Redistricting

Typically, after the decennial census is taken and redistricting occurs, several U.S. House incumbents retire rather than face the uncertainty of an election in a newly drawn district or the prospect of running against another incumbent. This was less the case in 2002 because to a very large extent, state legislatures drew district boundaries to protect incumbents.

Two notable exceptions to this are the partisan gerrymandering engaged in by Utah Republicans and Georgia Democrats. In both cases, the parties controlled the process and sought to create districts more favorable to their party, even if it gave incumbents from their party districts that were less safely partisan.

In five states, commissions rather than the legislature do the redistricting. One of the objectives of commissions like the one in Arizona is to foster electoral competition. Arizona's new congressional district, the First District, had nearly equal numbers of registered Democrats and Republicans and was seen as a toss-up by political prognosticators.

Many of these same tendencies also existed in state legislative redistricting in 2002. Incumbents often drew districts favorable to themselves while seeking to hurt the other party if it was not strong enough to defend itself. Commissions tended to be more neutral and often created more competitive districts.

SOURCE: Gregory L. Giroux, "Remaps' Clear Trend: Incumbent Protection," *Congressional Quarterly Weekly,* November 3, 2001, p. 2627; David E. Rosenbaum, "As Redistricting Unfolds, Power Is Used to Get More of It," *New York Times,* August 13, 2001, p. A14.

Party competition tends to push leaders within each party to work together, at least as elections draw near. Any defection may throw a race to the opponents, so competition generally produces more teamwork and efficiency in government. It may also generate more service to constituents by legislators.

In a one-party state, party imbalance may have a serious effect on the accountability that is part of electoral competition. Competition that otherwise would occur *between* the major parties occurs *within* the majority party. The most important contests in some states like Massachusetts are not between Democrats and Republicans but among Democrats in the primary; the same is true for Republicans in Utah. In these intraparty fights, personalities dominate the campaign. Voters do not participate as much as they do in two-party contests.

If party imbalance disorganizes the dominant party, it pulverizes the minority party. With faint hope of winning, minority party leaders do not put up much of a fight. They find it difficult to raise money for campaigns and to persuade people to become candidates. They have no state or local patronage to give out. Volunteers are slow to come forward. Young people wishing to succeed in politics drift into the dominant party. The second party is likely to be concerned only with national politics, where it may win an election, and the patronage that could come its way if its candidate wins the White House.

Party imbalance can be found in more extreme forms in cities and towns than at the state level. Republicans hardly ever carry Chicago, Boston, Washington, Baltimore, Albany, Hartford, Pittsburgh, and many other cities throughout the industrial North. But party balance is not always a determining factor. In heavily Democratic New York City, for example, voters elected a Republican, Michael Bloomberg, as mayor. Bloomberg had been a Democrat but ran for mayor as a Republican with the strong endorsement of outgoing Republican mayor Rudolph Giuliani.

Elections at the State and Local Levels

Each year, there are thousands of state and local elections. Europeans, who are used to voting for one or two candidates at the national and local levels and voting only once every two or three years, are flabbergasted to learn that we engage in elections almost continuously. Selection of town and local officials in the late winter may be followed in the spring by primaries to choose delegates to conventions, then primaries to choose party candidates, then general elections in the fall in which the actual officeholders are chosen—all interspersed with special elections, special town or state referendums, and even, in some states, recall elections to throw officials out of office.

Even more bewildering to some Europeans is the number of offices we vote on, from president to probate judge, from senator to sheriff, from governor to library board member. This is the *long ballot.* Europeans are more accustomed to electing a handful of key officials, who in turn appoint career officials. Given this volume of election activity, it is fair to conclude that Americans like elections, even though most of them choose not to vote in most of those elections.

Differences in Who May Vote

Subject to constitutional constraint, states can regulate who may vote. Most, for example, do not permit prison inmates to vote. If a state wanted to permit 16-year-olds to vote, it could do so. Voter registration rules can discourage people from participating in elections. States differ in the length of their residency requirement, as well as in whether they permit roving registrars, postcard registration, online registration, or election day registration. Most states require a periodic purge of the voter registration list to remove people who have moved or died.

A common reason why people do not register is that they have moved and have not registered at their new address. Fifteen percent of Americans change their residence every year.[25] After moving, they may not realize that they need to register at their new address until only a few days before the election, and then it is too late. Maryland, North Carolina, and the District of Columbia allow college students who have moved within a city or

How We Vote

Although millions of Americans carry cell phones, own computers, and shop on the Internet, as a nation we still vote in an antiquated way. One of the surprises of the 2000 Florida presidential election was the extent to which we are still using 1970s technology. Nearly one in five counties in the United States use punch-card ballots, which are subject to problems like dangling or dimpled chads that do not clearly indicate the voter's intent. Another two in five communities use optically scanable ballots on which the voter uses a pencil to mark the ballot and a scanner records the vote. Although much more reliable than punch cards, scanned ballots are also subject to problems if voters mark outside the box or do not use a pencil.

Voting machines with levers are used in 15 percent of counties, and paper ballots are used in 12 percent. Unlike punch cards, optical scanners, and paper ballots, voting machines do not permit an audit of the vote.

Surprisingly, fewer than 10 percent of counties use electronic or computer voting systems. When Congress considers election reform, there may be a move to computerized voting. Such voting could be facilitated by the fact that many high school computer labs are connected to the Internet. The costs for these types of reforms are estimated to be around $3.5 billion over five years.* One concern will be the secrecy of voting by computer, and another will be how to do a recount. Despite these concerns, significant changes in how we vote are certain to occur.

SOURCE: Data from Election Data Service. Map courtesy of *The New York Times*.

*"Vote for Voting Reforms," *New York Times*, March 1, 2002, p. A22.

Voting machines in the United States vary from simple boxes to state-of-the-art computer screens.

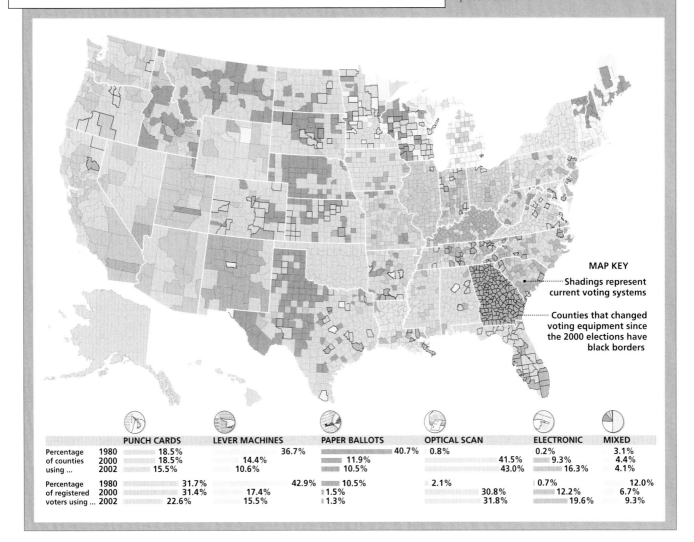

MAP KEY

········ Shadings represent current voting systems

──── Counties that changed voting equipment since the 2000 elections have black borders

		PUNCH CARDS	LEVER MACHINES	PAPER BALLOTS	OPTICAL SCAN	ELECTRONIC	MIXED
Percentage	1980	18.5%	36.7%	40.7%	0.8%	0.2%	3.1%
of counties	2000	18.5%	14.4%	11.9%	41.5%	9.3%	4.4%
using ...	2002	15.5%	10.6%	10.5%	43.0%	16.3%	4.1%
Percentage	1980	31.7%	42.9%	10.5%	2.1%	0.7%	12.0%
of registered	2000	31.4%	17.4%	1.5%	30.8%	12.2%	6.7%
voters using ...	2002	22.6%	15.5%	1.3%	31.8%	19.6%	9.3%

county to vote without registering if they notify election officials of their move. All told, a state's registration rules can lower turnout by as much as 9 percent.[26]

Voting by Mail and by Absentee Ballot

Modern technology makes it possible to vote by other means than appearing in person at a voting place on election day. Cities like San Diego, Berkeley, and Vancouver first experimented with holding *elections by mail*. Voters are mailed a pamphlet that describes the questions to be decided in the election and gives instructions on how to complete the ballot and return it by mail. Voters sign the return envelope, and their signature is compared against their signature on the voter registration form. There have been no major problems in administering these local mail ballot elections, and the response has been considerably higher than the norm for in-person special elections.[27]

In January 1996, Oregon voters elected a U.S. senator in a special election through the mail rather than in person. Oregonians had 20 days from the date the ballots were mailed to return them to county clerks, and two-thirds of those who received ballots returned them. Now all Oregon elections are conducted through the mail, including the 2000 and 2002 general elections. There appear to have been few instances of fraud, and the Oregon election officials are strong advocates of vote-by-mail elections in the future.

Opponents of the vote-by-mail system worry about fraud and that voters might be pressured to vote a certain way. For example, supporters of a candidate might visit voters at home soon after the ballots are delivered and pressure people to vote on the spot, perhaps offering to mail the ballot. Supporters point to the higher turnout and lower costs in administering vote-by-mail elections. They also point to the absence of fraud or abuse in the Oregon vote-by-mail elections.

A less dramatic reform of election laws is the *absentee ballot*. In most of the country, voters may request a ballot by mail, often without having to state a reason for doing so.[28] Absentee balloting is especially useful for initiative measures. In states like California or Washington, where voters may face 20 or more complicated ballot questions, those who vote by absentee ballot can take their time researching and pondering how they are going to vote and do not have to decide within the few minutes they would have in a voting booth.

Ease of obtaining ballots has significantly expanded the rate of absentee voting in California. It has been used especially by Republicans to activate retirees and other voters who find it difficult to get from their homes to the polling places. Absentee ballots made up nearly half of all ballots in Washington in 1998.[29] Other states have also liberalized their absentee voting provisions. Oklahoma and Texas, for instance, have *early voting*, whereby voters may vote for several days before an election at several locations in each county.

Absentee ballots also figured in the controversy in the Florida 2000 presidential voting. In two counties, absentee ballot request forms had incorrect voter identification numbers, but the county clerk permitted the Republican party to correct the mistake after the forms were returned to the county. In other Florida counties, some absentee ballots from military personnel did not have postmark dates or were otherwise technically not in compliance with the law. Initially, some counties did not count these ballots, but eventually, most military ballots were counted.

Differences in Nomination Processes

State law establishes the process by which party nominees are selected. Most states use a *primary election*, but some permit the parties to nominate their candidates through a *caucus* or *convention*. In the caucus system, party delegates who are elected in local voting district meetings decide on the party nominee. In some states, a convention narrows the field to two candidates if no candidate gets a set percentage of delegate votes at the party convention.

The dynamics of winning a nomination in states with a caucus system are different from those in states with a primary. In a caucus system, having a grassroots organization that can mobilize voters to attend a neighborhood meeting is essential for candidates. The state best known for the caucus system is Iowa, whose party caucuses yield the first deci-

Alternative Voting

State governments in several states have liberalized the rules regarding absentee voting, making it easier to use alternative forms of voting. Now, in many states, practically anyone can vote by using an absentee ballot, even if they are able to go to the polls on election day. In Oregon, all registered voters receive a mail ballot, another alternative mode of voting. Nontraditional forms of voting, such as absentee ballots, mail ballots, and early ballots, were increasingly popular in the 2000 election. Requests for absentee ballots tripled in Denver, Colorado, and absentee or early voting was popular in California, New Mexico, North Carolina, Washington, and Texas. Absentee and early voting are convenient for voters. With few exceptions, however, voter turnout has not risen because of the increase in alternative voting forms.

Opponents of greater use of absentee, early, and mail ballots argue that fraud will be easier because ballots could be sold or voters could be more easily pressured. They point out that election day voting occurs with election judges watching the process and with rules limiting electioneering near the voting booth. Furthermore, they say that campaigns will be more costly because voting is stretched out over a number of days or weeks, and candidates must accommodate this factor. Absentee ballots can also make it more difficult to count the ballots. In Washington State, it took more than a week to tally the ballots after the 2000 election. For many people, it comes down to convenience for the voter at the cost of the system's security and efficiency.

SOURCE: Leslie Wayne, "The 2000 Campaign: Alternative Voting; Popularity Is Increasing for Balloting Outside the Box," *New York Times,* November 4, 2000, p. A13.

These vote-by-mail ballots will be sent to voters in Oregon as an alternative to the conventional practice of going to the polls to vote.

sion in our presidential election system and are covered extensively by the media. Some form of the caucus or convention system is used in about a dozen states.

There are two kinds of party primaries, closed and open. In a **closed primary**, only voters registered in a party may vote in that party's primary. Such a primary discourages **crossover voting**—allowing voters from outside the party to help determine the party's nominee—which is why partisans prefer closed primaries. In an **open primary**, any voter can participate in any party's primary. Wisconsin has long had open primaries.

Some states, like Washington and California, allowed voters to vote for more than one party in the same primary election; this is called a **blanket primary**. Thus a voter could choose a Democratic nominee for governor and Republican nominees for U.S. senator and attorney general. The blanket primary, according to those who advocated it, encouraged voters to select the best nominees regardless of party and was thought to help moderate candidates. Opponents said it further weakened parties, made our system even more candidate-driven, and gave voters from one party the opportunity to choose the weakest candidate from the opposing party. However, research shows that less than 5 percent of voters actually vote for the weakest candidate from the opposing party.[30] In July 2000, the Supreme Court ruled that blanket primaries are unconstitutional because they violate the right to political association under the First Amendment.[31]

In a primary election, when all the candidates are from the same party, voters make their choices based on candidate appeal and issues. They may also vote for the candidate they perceive has the best chance of winning the general election.[32]

Louisiana has a unique system. All candidates, regardless of party, run in a single election. If no candidate gets a majority of the votes, there is a runoff election to determine the winner. It is not uncommon for both candidates in a runoff to be from the same party.

closed primary
Primary election in which only persons registered in the party holding the primary may vote.

crossover voting
Voting in another party's primary.

open primary
Primary election in which any voter, regardless of party, may vote.

blanket primary
Primary election open to all voters, who may vote for a candidate from any party for each office.

To encourage voter participation, election signs and ballots are often printed in several languages.

Differences in Timing and Frequency of Elections

Federal law sets the date of the presidential election as "the Tuesday next after the first Monday in November, in every fourth year," with similar language applying to elections for the House and Senate. States are free to determine the dates of all other elections, but for ease of administration, they usually consolidate gubernatorial and state general elections on the first Tuesday after the first Monday in November. Two states elect their governor every two years. Five states conduct their elections (primary and general) for governor, other state officials, and the state legislature in odd-numbered years, leaving the even-numbered years for federal elections. Two-thirds of the states (including the two-year states) elect governors in presidential midterm years, halfway between presidential elections.

Separating state elections from presidential or federal elections permits voters to focus more closely on state issues than if they had to vote for state and federal candidates at the same time. Separating elections also means that state and local officials are not as likely to be hurt by an unpopular presidential candidate at the top of the ticket. The passage of campaign finance reform at the federal level may prompt some states to consider off-year state elections. Having state elections in a different year from federal elections may reduce federal oversight and encourage soft money donors to contribute more to state parties.

Some states hold their primaries in late spring, others in mid-September. Primary elections are under the control of state law. Some states have two primaries in presidential years, one for the presidency in the spring and one for other contests in the fall.

State law establishes the rules for local elections but often allows cities and towns some discretion in setting the dates of elections. Many municipal elections are held in the spring of odd-numbered years, again to avoid any positive or negative carryover from candidates running for federal or statewide office. Counties usually conduct their elections at the same time state officials are elected.

State governments can also hold *special elections* to vote on a ballot initiative, a statewide constitutional change, or even a whole new constitution or to replace a U.S. senator who has died or resigned. Participation in special elections varies greatly, depending on what is being decided, but turnout is generally lower than in midterm general elections. Before states hold special elections to fill a vacated U.S. Senate seat, they often have a special primary election to determine the party nominees for that election. In these primaries, turnout is even lower than in the special general election.

The frequency of our elections and the range of choices sometimes make it hard for voters to pay enough attention to cast informed votes. For this reason, some reformers have proposed consolidating elections to once or twice every couple of years.

Participation

What are the consequences of holding so many elections at so many different times? One is that Americans pick and choose which elections, if any, they participate in. States vary significantly in their rate of **turnout**, the proportion of the voting-age public that votes. Note that political scientists do not calculate turnout on the basis of voter registration because there is such variability in state registration rules that it is unfair to compare the turnout in a state with difficult registration laws with the turnout in a state whose laws make voting registration much more accessible. Rather turnout is calculated on the Census Bureau's estimate of the voting-age population in each state.

Primaries usually draw fewer voters than general elections, and sometimes the turnout is quite low. Low turnout raises concerns about whether voters in primary elections reflect the general public. Primary voters are generally better educated, earn more money, and are more likely to be white than voters in general elections, who themselves are not representative of the voting-age population.[33] Primary election turnout is also related to strength of partisan identification, ease of voter registration, and the issues in the campaign.

Campaign Finance

In the early 1970s, many states enacted campaign finance disclosure laws, a few instituted partial public financing of elections, and others provided partial underwriting of the

turnout
The proportion of the voting-age public that votes.

You Decide — Thinking It Through

WHY NOT VOTE ON THE INTERNET?

You Decide... The 2000 ballot-counting controversies in Florida illustrate how outdated our modes of voting are. Punch cards were the state of the art in the 1960s and 1970s, before the advent of computer terminals and personal computers. The fact that many states still employ this form of voting tells us that funding election reform is a low priority. With more and more Americans having access to the Internet, why not vote via the Internet?

Thinking It Through... One reason is that not all Americans have access to computers or the Internet. Less educated and poorer Americans, some of the groups who already turn out to vote less than others, could be further discouraged from participation in elections if this became the means of voting. Conversely, younger people, who tend to vote least often, are the most interested in the Internet, and this may be a means to reach and involve them.

A second reason for not switching to Internet voting is ballot security. How would election officials know if a voter was actually casting someone else's ballot? The obvious answer is a personal identification number, or PIN, much like what you use for banking purposes. Although such processes are technically possible, they would impose costs on election officials to maintain lists of PINs, to be able to remind voters who forget their PIN, and to create software that handles electronic ballot submissions.

Despite all this, many groups still advocate Internet voting. One such organization is the Internet Voting Technology Alliance (www.ivta.org). Another source of interesting information on this topic is www.securepoll.com. Some Web sites also offer sample Internet voting systems and plans for implementing the process. Some of these sites are www.internetvoting.com, www.safevote.com, and www.election.com. Some groups, like People for Internet Responsibility, maintain that states like Arizona, which have experimented with Internet voting, were too hasty, especially in light of large-scale releases of credit card numbers retrieved from major Internet vendors. To see their statement on Internet voting, go to www.pfir.org.

---

costs of parties. **Disclosure** is a common element of campaign finance legislation at the state and local levels. Candidates are typically asked to file disclosure statements specifying where the money came from to finance their campaign. Interest groups are often required to file reports on how they distribute their campaign contributions. Once elected, most state and local officials are required to file a different kind of disclosure form, one that indicates their personal wealth, investments, and other financial matters that may reveal conflicts of interest.

Roughly three-fourths of the states have enacted campaign finance reforms that limit individual contributions, and several states provide some form of public financing. State laws are often patterned after federal law, but states have experimented with lower contribution limits than those allowed in federal elections.[34] Other states have experimented with tax credits to encourage small contributions. In 1996, Maine voters passed a ballot initiative that provided what supporters call a "clean money" option of public financing.[35] Under this system, candidates who agree to raise a limited amount of private money and accept spending limits receive public funds for their campaigns.

Voting on Ballot Questions

Voting on ballot questions is heavily influenced by campaign spending. Presumably, greater expenditures make the most difference when there is a low level of information, as is the case with many ballot propositions. And opinions on ballot propositions are more volatile because voters' views on such matters are not deeply rooted in party affiliation, feelings toward an incumbent, or party appeal.[36]

disclosure
A requirement that candidates specify where the money came from to finance their campaign.

Because many initiatives are supported by well-funded interests and because a vote in one state can start a national movement on an issue, initiative campaigns can attract large sums of money. Some examples of heavy spending include a 1988 election in Maryland in which the National Rifle Association and other groups spent a record $6.8 million in an unsuccessful attempt to defeat a handgun registration referendum. The tobacco industry spent more than $21 million in California in 1988 to defeat an initiative raising the cigarette tax. More than $101 million was spent in California in that year on five initiatives that dealt with automobile insurance reform. A decade later, in what remains one of the most expensive initiative battles in U.S. history, over $92 million was spent for and against a successful initiative to permit casinos on Native American lands in California.[37]

Voting on ballot questions is different from voting for candidates because voters do not have such simplifying factors as party identification and candidate appeal to rely on. More people vote for candidates than vote on ballot questions. Voters who are confused tend to vote no. "Ballot fatigue," tiring from too many contests and questions on the ballot, also makes people more likely to vote no.[38]

The Future of Grassroots Democracy

Political parties are vital to the operation of our democracy. Many political scientists believe that our system would be strengthened if we had stronger political parties. The first step in the renewal of the parties would be to change their negative image and persuade citizens that political activity is essential to a healthy constitutional democracy. The next would be to give people who support parties a greater say in choosing the candidates who run under their party's label. Although our candidate-centered tradition will certainly remain, it is important to moderate it with strengthened parties that can discipline candidates, at least by withholding resources that candidates cannot easily acquire elsewhere. We would do well to make ballots and elections more voter-friendly. The proliferation of elections, including special elections, turns off even the most committed citizens. Why not, many reformers argue, consolidate elections so that voters might exercise their vote only once or twice, rather than three or four times, a year?

Getting qualified people to run for office is another challenge. The spiraling cost of campaigns and the advantages enjoyed by incumbents have deterred many good potential candidates. Others are repelled by the nasty and negative tone of recent elections. But unless a democracy produces able citizens who are willing to run for office, it loses its ability to hold incumbents accountable.

One of the advantages of 50 states and thousands of communities is that they afford citizens a multitude of opportunities for participation, making involvement less intimidating. The fact that our states do not all have the same approach to elections, parties, or voting also provides valuable data for states considering changing their process. One disadvantage of so many governmental units and so many different elected officials is that they make politics seem more complicated. Citizens willing to become involved, however, often find they can have more influence than they expected.

Summary

1. In the United States, there are no national elections, only state elections. Even the presidential election is really a set of 51 different elections to choose electors who will in turn cast their ballots for president. Elections for U.S. senators and representatives are conducted largely under state law.

2. Political parties are essential to the functioning of democracy at all levels, but they are principally organized at the state, congressional district, or county levels. This arrangement makes state parties vitally important. Routinely, they are patterned after the national party organization and in-

clude a chair, a vice chair, and a central committee. State parties are often run by full-time party administrators called executive directors.

3. Political parties play important roles in candidate recruitment, voter registration, voter mobilization, and fund raising, and they pro-

vide a link between people and government. Parties are also important to the operation of most state legislatures. The governor is the head of his or her party. Governors consider party loyalty when appointing people to executive and judicial openings.

4. Voters usually vote along party lines in state and local elections, although candidate appeal and issues can also influence them.

5. Political parties were once strong and well organized at the local level; in some cities, these organizations were called machines and were led by party bosses. Reaction to the abuses of these machines led to reform efforts. One of these reforms was to make most local politics officially nonpartisan.

6. States vary in whether the two parties are competitive. In one-party states, elections are always won by one party, while in two-party states, the parties alternate in holding power.

7. State election law is important in defining who may vote, when elections will be held, how party nominees are chosen, and which candidates will appear on the ballot. State election law also establishes a framework for ensuring fair elections.

8. State registration laws make voting more or less difficult, depending on their requirements. States may require persons to register by party to vote in primary elections; when voting is thus limited, the primaries are called closed primaries. Over the course of U.S. history, states have gradually eased registration requirements.

9. Turnout varies by type of election; it is higher in general than primary elections and higher in presidential than midterm elections. Turnout is higher in state than local elections, and regularly scheduled elections typically have higher turnout than special elections. Turnout in vote-by-mail elections is also higher than in in-person elections in most cases. More people vote for major candidate races than vote on ballot questions.

Key Terms

party column ballot	soft money	two-party state	open primary
straight ticket	issue advocacy	one-party state	blanket primary
office block ballot	party caucus	closed primary	turnout
split ticket	redistricting	crossover voting	disclosure

Further Reading

BRUCE E. CAIN AND ELISABETH R. GERBER, EDS., *Voting at the Political Fault Line: California's Experiment with the Blanket Primary* (University of California Press, 2002).

THOMAS M. CARSEY, *Campaign Dynamics: The Race for Governor* (University of Michigan Press, 2000).

THOMAS E. CRONIN, *Direct Democracy: The Politics of Initiative, Referendum, and Recall* (Replica Books, 2000).

PAUL S. HERRNSON, *Party Campaigning in the 1980s* (Harvard University Press, 1988).

MALCOLM E. JEWELL AND SARAH M. MOREHOUSE, *Political Parties and Elections in American States,* 4th ed. (CQ Press, 2001).

V. O. KEY JR., *American State Politics: An Introduction* (Knopf, 1956).

NORMAN R. LUTTBEG, *The Grassroots of Democracy* (Lexington Books, 1999).

DAVID B. MAGLEBY, *Direct Legislation: Voting on Ballot Propositions in the United States* (Johns Hopkins University Press, 1984).

L. SANDY MAISEL, *Parties and Elections in America: The Electoral Process,* 3d ed. (Rowman & Littlefield, 2001).

A. JAMES REICHLEY, ED., *Elections American Style* (Brookings Institution, 1987).

ALAN ROSENTHAL, *Governors and Legislators: Contending Powers* (CQ Press, 1990).

ALAN ROSENTHAL, *Legislative Life: People, Process, and Performance in the States* (Harper & Row, 1981).

LINDA WITT, KAREN M. PAGET, AND GLENNA MATTHEWS, *Running as a Woman: Gender and Politics in American Politics* (Free Press, 1994).

JOSEPH FRANCIS ZIMMERMAN, *The Initiative: Citizen Lawmaking* (Greenwood Press, 1999).

25
CHAPTER

STATE
LEGISLATURES

STATE LEGISLATURES ARE READY TARGETS FOR HUMOR, CRITICISM, AND "CHEAP SHOTS," SUCH AS THE ONCE POPULAR ADAGE "NO PERSON'S life, liberty, or property is safe so long as the legislature is in session." Some criticism is deserved. Yet even though state legislatures have improved greatly in recent decades, the criticism continues. Some of the negative image is due to legislators themselves, as Pennsylvania state senator Robert Jubelirer explains: "A lot of this has been done by us to us. So many campaigns are nothing but 30-second spots making the opponent out to be less than slime."[1] Yet some of it is due to stories that circulate in nearly every state about the questionable deals that are made between legislators and lobbyists, a few of which lead to corrupt proceedings but most of which become part of how things get done in a state.[2]

The legislative process is not easy to understand. Only those directly involved can fully comprehend its slow pace and elaborate procedures, which are informal as well as formal, consensual as well as conflictual, behind-the-scenes as well as open, combative as well as collegial, and often just plain messy.[3]

State legislatures are the oldest part of our government. They were around long before the adoption of the U.S. Constitution. Legislatures were the most powerful governing institutions in the country during the Revolutionary period. Indeed, the creation of the Constitution was in part a reaction against the excessive power of the state legislatures. The framers of the Constitution imposed limits on the powers of the state legislatures (see especially Article I, Section 9).

The Tenth Amendment to the U.S. Constitution makes it clear that any power not given to the national government or denied to the states lies with the states or with the people. State constitutions, in turn, give some of this reserved power exclusively to non-legislative agencies and specifically deny some to the legislature. What is left is inherited by the state legislatures.

Although state legislatures today do not dominate state policy making the way they did in 1787, they do play a vital role in state politics and policy. State legislators strive to solve problems and provide services—and do so, whenever possible, without raising taxes or creating larger bureaucracies. Legislators these days seek to make the legislature a counterbalance to powerful governors and powerful state bureaucracies.

In recent years, legislatures have been involved in a remarkable variety of activities:

- Colorado's legislature adopted stronger gun control legislation.
- New Hampshire legislators voted to prevent the use of death penalty sentencing.
- Vermont voted to recognize "civil unions" between same-sex couples, granting them virtually all the benefits, protections, and responsibilities given to married couples.
- Mississippi legislators overrode their governor's veto of a major Medicaid program.
- South Carolina legislators voted, by a narrow margin, to remove the Confederate flag over their statehouse dome but allowed it to fly over a monument on the capitol grounds.
- Hawaii's legislature approved the medical use of marijuana.
- The Tennessee legislature overrode the governor's veto and enacted an $18.3 billion budget without a state income tax their governor had demanded.
- The Minnesota legislature, at the request of Governor Jesse Ventura, considered a constitutional amendment to convert to a unicameral legislature similar to that in Nebraska, but the proposal never got out of committee.
- New York adopted legislation banning cell phone use while driving.
- By enacting large penalties for "excessive prices," Maine has attempted to force down drug prices.
- Many states have adopted some form of election reform, including new ballots, a ban on punch cards, and new computer voting systems.
- In the wake of the terrorist attacks of September 11, 2001, many states have created a homeland security office similar to that of the national government.

In short, legislatures everywhere make or modify policies on all kinds of issues. Although there are influential and even occasionally charismatic state legislators, strong governors generally overshadow the legislative body and its leaders. By its very nature, a legislature made up of many individuals from different parties, speaking with many voices, cannot provide unified, swift policy leadership. Even in states with well-paid and well-staffed legislative bodies, the legislature is seldom the dominant policy-making branch. Rarely can legislators compete with governors for the public's attention.

State legislatures help balance conflicting political pressures and facilitate compromises between political factions or different parts of the state. They also make laws and modify and approve budgets. Legislatures perform countless constituency services and, along with the governor and the courts, help keep state agencies accountable to both the laws and the citizens. Legislators must constantly reconcile pressures among competing interest groups. Representing local views at the state level, they dramatize issues and bring them into the open. A state legislature serves as a lightning rod to which most of the conflicting pressures of American society are drawn.

You may know someone who has run for state legislator—about 11,000 people seek this job every two years. Sometimes there is no real contest; able and entrenched incumbents often run unopposed. About one-third of state legislative elections are uncontested; this is especially true in smaller, one-party states and in the South.[4] Moreover, about 75 percent of incumbents who are eligible run for reelection, and they have at least a 90 percent chance of winning renomination and reelection. An incumbent seeking reelection has many advantages over a challenger: name recognition, better access to campaign funds, experience in running campaigns, and a record of helping with constituent problems. Still, few legislators feel politically secure, even when they have not been opposed in the last election.

In an incumbent's mind, there is seldom such a thing as a "safe district" and a sure reelection. "Whatever their margins of victory in prior elections, however 'safe' their district may appear to the analyst, incumbents know that lightning can strike. . . . They have seen colleagues relax their efforts and subsequently lose their seats. They live in perpetual danger of casting a roll-call vote that upsets their constituency or mobilizes a key interest group to seek their defeat."[5] Incumbents also worry about scandals in their party or having to run with an unpopular candidate at or near the top of their party ticket.

Why do people seek this office? For many reasons: excitement, an opportunity to serve their fellow citizens, personal gain, a chance to advertise themselves, the desire to make better laws, a sense of loyalty to their political party, and as a stepping-stone to higher elective office. Often the reason is a mixture of these factors as well as a desire to be where the action is.

The Legislative Branch

All states except Nebraska have a two-house **bicameral legislature**. Nebraska has a one-house **unicameral legislature**.[6] The larger chamber is generally called the house of representatives. (In a few states, it is called the assembly or house of delegates.) It contains from as few as 40 members (in Alaska) to as many as 400 members (in New Hampshire); the typical number is around 100. In all but five states, representatives serve two-year terms; in Alabama, Louisiana, Maryland, Mississippi, and North Dakota, representatives serve for four years. The smaller chamber, known as the senate, is typically composed of about 40 members. State senators serve four-year terms in most states.

Legislative professionalism sometimes, but not always, correlates with district size. The professional nature of state legislatures is in part a product of population but also a product of how many representatives the state has chosen to have. Certain states, such as New Hampshire and Wyoming, have part-time "citizen legislatures," whereas New York and California are sometimes characterized as full-time "professional legislatures." In the New Hampshire House of Representatives, legislators are essentially volunteers. These "citizen-legislators" represent districts of about 3,000 people. They earn $200 for the year and meet for no more than 45 days a year. In contrast, the California Assembly has 80 members, each representing a district of about 450,000 people. California legislators earn $99,000 a year in addition to expense allowances, meet nearly all year long, and consider their legislative work a full-time occupation (see Table 25-1).

Forty-three state legislatures meet every year from January through May or June. Legislatures in seven states, including Arkansas, Montana, Nevada, and Texas, meet only every other year. Some state constitutions limit their legislatures to regular sessions of a fixed number of days, usually 60 or 90. Such restrictions reflect distrust of government and the feeling that "the faster we get it over with, the better." *Special sessions* have been developed to get around these limitations. The governor has the power to call the legislature into special session and in some states to determine the issues that may be discussed in the special session—a power governors frequently use.

The organization and procedures of state legislatures are similar to those of the United States Congress. A *Speaker,* usually chosen by the majority party, presides over the lower house. In many states, Speakers have more power to control proceedings than their national counterpart has. For example, most state Speakers have the right to appoint committees and thus play a key role in determining policy. But the power of Speakers varies a lot: Speakers have great powers in West Virginia, New Hampshire, and Arizona but minimal powers in Alaska, Mississippi, Hawaii, and Wyoming.[7] In 26 states, lieutenant governors preside over the senate, though they are usually mere figureheads; in other states, the presiding officer is chosen by the majority party in the senate.[8]

As in the U.S. Congress, the committee system prevails. In several states, such as Maine and Massachusetts, *joint committees* are used to speed up legislative action. However, state legislative committees usually do not have the same power over bills as their na-

bicameral legislature
A two-house legislature.

unicameral legislature
A one-house legislature.

The Roles of State Legislators

- Studying the problems of their districts and states
- Helping enact legislative programs
- Developing support for priority programs
- Keeping informed on all bills and amendments
- Attending sessions, taking part in debate, and voting on business before the legislative chambers
- Attending committee meetings and hearings
- Responding to calls and letters from constituents
- Exercising legislative oversight over the administration's and the state's budgets through hearings, personal visits, and inspections
- Participating in the confirmation and impeachment processes involving various state officials
- Serving as connecting links between local officials and state officials and between state officials and national officials
- Maintaining their own campaign organizations and perhaps playing active roles in their county and state political party organizations
- Taking part in ceremonial functions
- Voting on proposed amendments to U.S. Constitution and on various interstate compacts

TABLE 25–1   The Diversity of State Legislatures

State legislatures across the country vary greatly in many respects. The National Conference of State Legislatures grouped them into three types based on their length of session.

Type 1: Full-Time, High-Pay, Large-Staff "Professional Legislatures"

California	New York
Florida	Ohio
Illinois	Pennsylvania
Massachusetts	Wisconsin
Michigan	
New Jersey	

Type 2: In-Between Hybrid

Alabama	Minnesota
Alaska	Missouri
Arizona	Nebraska
Colorado	North Carolina
Connecticut	Oklahoma
Delaware	Oregon
Hawaii	South Carolina
Iowa	Tennessee
Kansas	Texas
Kentucky	Virginia
Louisiana	Washington
Maryland	

Type 3: Part-Time, Low-Pay, Small-Staff "Citizen Legislatures"

Arkansas	New Mexico
Georgia	North Dakota
Idaho	Rhode Island
Indiana	South Dakota
Maine	Utah
Mississippi	Vermont
Montana	West Virginia
Nevada	Wyoming
New Hampshire	

SOURCE: National Conference of State Legislatures, cited in Charles Mahtesian, "The Sick Legislature Syndrome," *Governing,* February 1997, p. 20.

tional counterparts: Some still lack adequate professional assistance, the seniority system is not as closely followed as in Congress, and membership turnover is somewhat higher, especially where term limits have taken effect.

Every legislature has committees on education, transportation, agriculture, and energy or natural resources. Most also have important committees on rules, appropriations, and taxes (sometimes called the Ways and Means Committee). Legislators generally specialize and become experts on one or two substantive matters, such as education, crime, taxation, or the budget process. As in any organization or large assembly, an individual earns respect and influence primarily by developing specialized knowledge about either policy or procedural matters.

Striking differences exist among state legislatures. Some have excellent staff and splendid information technology and are well-run professional organizations. Others are no more professional than they were a generation or two ago.[9] These differences sometimes stem from historical or ethnic traditions. They can also arise from urban-rural or east-west factional splits and sometimes from regional differences, as is the case with the "Hill people" versus the "Delta people" in Mississippi. Here is how one expert on state politics viewed some of the more distinctive characteristics shaping state politics in the United States:

In New York professional politics, political wheeling and dealing and frantic activity are characteristic. In Virginia, one gets a sense of tradition, conservatism, and gentility. . . . Louisiana's politics are wild and flamboyant. By contrast, moderation and caution are features of Iowa. A strong disposition of compromise pervades Oregon, with politicians disposed to act as brokers and deal pragmatically rather than dogmatically. In Kansas, hard work, respect for authority, fiscal prudence, and a general conservatism and resistance to rapid social change are pervasive features of the state environment. Indiana is intensely partisan. Wyoming is mainly individualistic, and Ohio is fundamentally conservative. In Hawaii, the relatively recent political dominance of Japanese and the secondary status of Chinese, native Hawaiians, and Haoles (whites) makes for tough ethnic politics. Yankee Republicans used to run Massachusetts, but now the Irish dominate. Their personalized style, which blends gregariousness and political loyalty, results in a politics of the clan. Mormonism of course dominates Utah.[10]

What Do State Legislators Do?

What do the nation's 7,387 state legislators do? Among other things, they enact laws that create state parks; specify salaries for state officials; draw up rules governing state elections; fix state tax rates; set workers' compensation policies; determine the quantity and quality of state

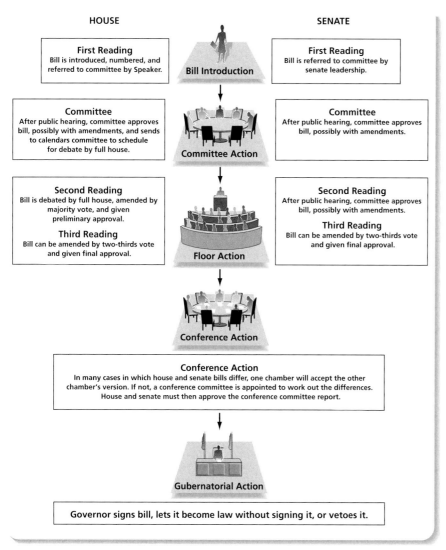

HOUSE

First Reading
Bill is introduced, numbered, and referred to committee by Speaker.

Committee
After public hearing, committee approves bill, possibly with amendments, and sends to calendars committee to schedule for debate by full house.

Second Reading
Bill is debated by full house, amended by majority vote, and given preliminary approval.

Third Reading
Bill can be amended by two-thirds vote and given final approval.

Bill Introduction

Committee Action

Floor Action

Conference Action

SENATE

First Reading
Bill is referred to committee by senate leadership.

Committee
After public hearing, committee approves bill, possibly with amendments.

Second Reading
After public hearing, committee approves bill, possibly with amendments.

Third Reading
Bill can be amended by two-thirds vote and given final approval.

Conference Action
In many cases in which house and senate bills differ, one chamber will accept the other chamber's version. If not, a conference committee is appointed to work out the differences. House and senate must then approve the conference committee report.

Gubernatorial Action

Governor signs bill, lets it become law without signing it, or vetoes it.

FIGURE 25–1   How a Bill Becomes a State Law.

Members of the Texas House of Representatives gather around the Speaker's podium to iron out a disputed point.

correctional, mental health, and educational institutions; and oversee welfare programs. State legislators approve all appropriations and thereby confirm or modify a governor's proposed budget. Legislators in most states are also responsible for overseeing the administration of public policy. Although they do not administer programs directly, legislators can and do determine whether programs are being carried out according to legislative intentions through hearings, investigations, audits, and the budgetary process. Bill passage rate varies greatly from state to state, depending on a variety of factors, including procedural necessities, constitutional requirements, and local culture. Figure 25-1 (see page 615) outlines the steps involved in passing state laws.

State legislatures perform various functions within the larger federal system, such as ratifying proposed amendments to the U.S. Constitution, exercising the right to petition Congress to call for a constitutional convention to propose an amendment to the U.S. Constitution, and approving interstate compacts on matters affecting state policies and their implementation. The national government has recently turned back many health and welfare responsibilities to the states.

Each state's constitution prescribes the procedures its legislatures must follow and sets limits on the rate of taxation, the kinds of taxes, the subjects that may be taxed, and the purposes of taxation. State legislatures participate in amending their states' constitutions by proposing amendments for voter ratification. Legislatures also have authority to impeach and try state officials, and they are involved in the appointive process.

State legislators help translate public wants and aspirations into laws and regulations. In addition to their lawmaking functions, they also try to be ombudsmen—to listen, learn, and find solutions to problems. Invariably, state legislators wind up doing a lot of favors: getting a merchant a license to sell lottery tickets, persuading some state agency to look into safety standards at the local hospital, pushing for funds to repair county roads, arranging for a campaign supporter to be appointed to the state labor commission, and so on. State legislators are accessible. Citizens and students can nearly always contact their legislators directly and communicate with them in person, by telephone, or via e-mail. In addition, nearly every department in every state has its own page posted on the World Wide Web. Citizens in Hawaii are encouraged to send ideas and opinions about proposed legislation to a specific e-mail address.

With the growth of state functions, legislators are spending increasing amounts of time on casework or constituency services. Constituent relations are often the most time-consuming aspect of a legislator's job. Local city and school officials always need the help of legislators, and interest groups back home are always pressing their views. Legislators usually try hard to perform constituent casework because they recognize its political value. The more help they give to home-district citizens and businesses, they reason, the more they will earn respect, win reelection, or perhaps gather support for election to higher office.

Who Are the State Legislators?

The typical American state legislator is a 48-year-old white male, well educated and well off, often a businessman or lawyer of Anglo-Saxon origin who has had some type of previous political experience—not always elective—at the city or county level. Some have worked as a staff member in the legislature or in state government.[11] Most state legislators have held some type of local party position and have been active in political campaigns. Surprisingly, about one-third were born in some other state, a reflection of our increasingly mobile population.

As of the 2002 eleccctions, slightly more of the nation's state legislators are Republicans; most of the rest call themselves Democrats. About 20 of the 7,387 legislators consider themselves Independents or are affiliated with a third party. All 49 members of Nebraska's unicameral legislature are nonpartisan.[12] Not long ago, Democrats dominated state legislatures in most urban and southern states, but no

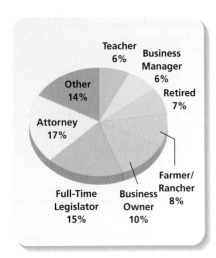

FIGURE 25–2   A Profile of State Legislators.

SOURCE: National Conference of State Legislatures.

Women in the Statehouse

In the late 1960s, state legislatures were dominated by men and often had the look of a "good old boys' club." This has changed in recent years as more women have been elected, bringing the national average up from just 4.5 percent in 1971 to almost 23 percent today. In the Washington State legislature, 39 percent of the seats are held by women; in Nevada, 35 percent; in Arizona, 35.6 percent; in Colorado, 34 percent; and in Kansas, 32 percent. In Alabama, by contrast, only 8 percent of the lawmakers are women.

As women have won election to state legislatures across the country, their influence has grown, and more women win election to key legislative posts. About half the states now have women's caucuses within state legislatures, which can serve as a counterpoint to the traditional caucuses. For example, all women legislators in Maryland meet once a week during legislative sessions and from time to time when not in session. These Maryland legislators even hold an annual October retreat to discuss legislative priorities for their upcoming session. California's women lawmakers meet monthly. Illinois's Council of Women Legislators meets monthly on an issue-by-issue basis and has three volunteer staff members.*

Does the election of women to state legislatures make a significant difference in how women are represented? Some analysts believe female legislators are more likely to offer leadership on women, family, and children's policy issues.† Yet another study of legislators of the Arizona and California state legislatures found

Women members of the Washington legislature constitute the highest percentage of women in any legislature in the nation's history.

there was often little or no difference in how men and women dealt with gender policy issues.‡

SOURCE: Sam Howe Verhovek, "Record for Women in Washington Legislature," *New York Times,* February 4, 1999, p. A14.

*Rita Thaemert, "Twenty Percent and Climbing," *State Legislatures,* January 1994, pp. 24–27.

†Sue Thomas, *How Women Legislate* (Oxford University Press, 1996). See also Kathleen Bratton and Kerry L. Haynie, "Agenda Setting and Legislative Success in State Legislatures: The Effects of Gender and Race," *Journal of Politics* 61 (August 1999), pp. 658–679.

‡Beth Reingold, *Representing Women: Sex, Gender, and Legislative Behavior in Arizona and California* (University of North Carolina Press, 2000).

2003: 1,680 women; 22.8% of legislators

Current Percentage of Women in State Legislatures.

SOURCE: Center for the American Women and Politics; reprinted from *New York Times,* January 4, 1999, p. A18. Updated by the authors.

longer. Republicans made significant gains in the past decade, and the two parties today are often separated by only a few seats for control of one of the chambers of their statehouse.

Lawyers continue to be the largest occupational group in most state legislatures, yet the percentage of attorneys has leveled off; today attorneys constitute only about 17 percent of state legislators nationwide. There has been an increase in those who consider themselves full-time legislators, and there has been a slight increase as well of teachers, homemakers, retirees, and students.[13] Real estate and insurance dealers and sales representatives are also commonly found in legislatures (see Figure 25-2 on page 616). The

Potential Influences on Legislators' Voting Patterns

- Personal political philosophies
- Legislative colleagues
- Legislative staff specialists
- Committee recommendations
- Interest group lobbyists
- The governor
- Cabinet and agency heads
- Legislative party leaders
- Party leaders
- Local elected officials
- Local and state media
- Constituent mail and opinion
- Urban and rural splits in the state
- Regional blocs within the state
- National trends
- Programs that have worked in other states
- Family and friends

number of farmers continues to fall as redistricting continues to shift power away from rural areas and as the number of farms declines. Moreover, longer sessions of the legislatures make it less possible to be both a farmer and a legislator. When legislatures used to meet for just a few months in winter, farmers were able to fit their schedules to the legislative cycle.

More women and African Americans are winning election to state legislatures, yet both groups are still notably in the minority. Of the 7,387 state legislators, about 23 percent are women, about 600 are African American, and about 190 are Latinos. Approximately 60 Asian Americans and more than 45 Native Americans served as state legislators in 2003.[14]

Because legislators must have flexible schedules, the job often attracts retired people and those whose businesses or professional practices have been so successful that they can afford to take time off. Legislators used to identify themselves by their occupations outside the legislature, but this is less the case now; many refer to their occupation as legislator.

The trend in many states has been to somewhat longer annual legislative sessions and higher salaries. California legislators earn $99,000 a year plus $121 a day for expenses. New York legislators earn $79,500 a year plus $89 per day for expenses. Pennsylvania pays its legislators $59,245 annually plus $115 per day for expenses. A few other states pay at least $40,000. Other states, such as Maryland and Oklahoma, provide "living wages." But in most states, legislators receive modest salaries: Florida pays $26,388, Texas pays $7,200, and Georgia, Indiana, and Nebraska pay about $12,000 a year.[15] In some states, legislators go to the capital for only a few months a year, and they are paid so little that many are able to serve only if they are independently wealthy, are supported by a spouse, or have other jobs that can be readily combined with legislative service.[16]

Legislative salaries are most often set by the legislature. Most legislators are reluctant to increase their salaries, and as a result, lawmakers' salaries lag well behind the rate of inflation and increases in the cost of living. Most people run for the legislature for reasons other than compensation. "No one goes into politics to get rich," notes Massachusetts state Senator Tom Birmingham. "But you can't have a system where only the rich get into politics."[17]

State legislators are better educated than the average person. They also come from middle- and upper-income groups. They are usually hardworking, public-spirited citizens who believe being in the legislature is a good opportunity for service. Yet state legislators enjoy less prestige than members of Congress, especially in states that have large legislatures. Discouraged by modest salaries and long hours, many serve a few terms and then either retire voluntarily or run for higher office. Some leave after just a couple of terms because they get bored listening to matters that do not interest them. As one one-termer explained, "A great deal in the political process does not—repeat, does not—involve the glamorous policy issues. Most of the work is sheer routine and hardly awe-inspiring."[18] And of course, some are now leaving because of term limits in their states that prevent more than two or three terms.

What Do Legislative Committees Do?

A legislative committee is where bills get drafted, hearings are held, and the general policy making and preliminary lawmaking takes place. Committees vary in power and influence from state to state. In general, however, the influence of committees has increased in recent decades. They used to be pale shadows of their counterparts in the U.S. Congress, and they often still are in the less populous states because of short sessions, limited staffing, and turnover of both staff and legislators. Still, legislative committees process and shape hundreds or even thousands of bills and resolutions every year.[19]

Committees do the legislature's work. They consider and amend legislation, oversee the implementation of the laws, interview judges, and serve as the major access point for citizens, interest groups, and lobbyists. The functions of a legislative committee are advisory; all of its proposals are subject to review, approval, or rejection by the legislative body of which it is a part.

Some of the functions of standing committees or interim committees include:

- Studying pending legislation
- Conducting public hearings on proposed bills and resolutions
- Debating and modifying initial proposals
- Grading legislation in terms of desirability
- Screening, eliminating, or burying undesirable legislation
- Confirming key administrative personnel
- Monitoring or overseeing administrative practices and regulations

The committee system allows members to concentrate their energies on specific areas of governmental operations. Over time, legislative committees and their members develop extensive knowledge about particular activities and provide greatly valued information about the content and desirability of proposed bills to their colleagues. Since it is impossible for everybody to be an expert on all aspects of state government, properly staffed and run committees can evaluate the merits and faults of a proposed law more effectively than any individual legislator can.

State representatives often meet with local constituents to discuss local concerns.

What Influences State Legislators?

POLITICAL PARTIES   Candidates for state legislatures are nominated by political parties in primaries or by party conventions and caucuses, and they are elected *as party members.* Although the official party organization is sometimes not a dominant influence in recruiting state legislative candidates, a candidate nonetheless has to go through the party to gain the nomination. Figure 25-3 shows the current party control of the state legislatures.

The role of political parties in the governance of legislatures and in policy making varies widely from state to state. In nearly half the states—especially in the urban,

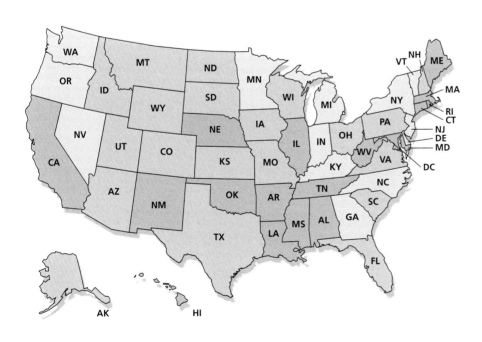

Democratic Control (16)   Republican Control (21)   Split Control (12)   Nonpartisan (1)

FIGURE 25–3   Party Control of State Legislatures, 2003.

Interest Groups Perceived to Have the Most Influence

1. General business organizations
2. School teachers' organizations
3. Utility companies
4. Lawyers
5. Hospital and health care organizations
6. Insurance associations
7. General local government groups
8. Manufacturing groups
9. General farm organizations
10. Physicians/state medical organizations
11. Labor organizations
12. Bankers' associations

SOURCE: Clive S. Thomas and Ronald Hrebenver, "Interest Groups in the States," in *Politics in the American States*, 7th ed., eds. Virginia Gray, Russell Hanson, and Herbert Jacob (CQ Press, 1999), p. 134.

party caucus
A meeting of the members of a party in a legislative chamber to select party leaders and develop party policy.

lobbying
Engaging in activities aimed at influencing public officials, especially legislators, and the policies they enact.

lobbyist
A person who is employed by and acts for an organized interest group or corporation to influence policy decisions and positions in the executive and legislative branches.

industrialized states and in the Northeast—the political party is a key factor in decision making. In other states—in the Southwest, for example—parties appear less significant. Coalitions there tend to form along rural-urban, conservative-liberal, or regional lines.

Parties in most states are less influential than they used to be. Candidates welcome what help they can get from the parties, but that is often not much. However, in some states, party leaders in the legislature raise and allocate campaign contributions that prove helpful to those running for the first or second time, particularly in competitive races. Party organizations and political action committees are major sources of money for many legislative candidates. Still, legislative candidates almost always have to form their own personal organization, separate from the local party apparatus, to wage a winning campaign.

In nearly every state where there are two active parties, the political party selects legislative leaders and assigns members to committees. Party leaders in many state legislatures distribute sought-after perks, ranging from committee assignments to parking spaces. **Party caucuses**—meetings of all the members of one party in the chamber—also distribute campaign funds to their members and to specifically targeted districts.

Party unity on policy matters is typically found in states with a highly competitive two-party system. In those states, party caucuses develop party positions, and party members are expected to support them in the legislative chambers. In a few states, binding votes in party caucuses virtually (although not legally) force party members to vote as a unified bloc on the floor of their chamber. Binding caucus votes are taken on relatively few issues, however. Voting regularly with the party and being a member of the majority party can help legislators win discretionary grants or other favors for their districts.

The party caucus is a principal instrument for legislative decision making in about half the states, including Colorado, Delaware, Idaho, Montana, California, and Utah. In states where a party holds a slim majority of the seats in a legislative chamber, representatives are more likely to feel pressure to "toe the party line" than where a party commands a large majority.[20] Similarly, legislators are more likely to vote with their party in states where the political party plays an important role in recruiting and nominating candidates.

In legislatures in which a single party has had long-standing dominance or control, as used to be in some southern states, parties are less important in conducting and shaping legislative business. Because of the recent rise of the Republican party in the South and Southwest, however, parties and partisanship are gradually increasing in strength in such states as Florida, Texas, and North Carolina. A rebirth of partisanship and growing attention to elections of legislators are apparently making the parties more important than they have been in the past.

LOBBYISTS AND INTEREST GROUPS   **Lobbying** is attempting to influence the decisions of public officials, especially legislators. The right to lobby is secured by the First and Fourteenth Amendments to the Constitution, which protect the right of the people to petition the government for redress of grievances. State constitutions provide similar protections.

Anyone can try to influence how a state legislator votes. States usually define a professional **lobbyist** as someone who is paid to influence legislators on behalf of a client or clients. States now require lobbyists to register annually, either with the secretary of state's office or with an elections or lobbyist commission. In most states, lobbyists must pay a fee for lobbying. In Texas, for example, professional lobbyists pay a $300 fee, although lobbyists for tax-exempt public interest groups pay only $100.

Hundreds of lobbyists openly ply their trade in the committee rooms and corridors of the state capitols. The more populated states register thousands of lobbyists. In one recent year, Texas and New York each registered as many as 1,800 professional lobbyists. At least 1,200 lobbyists work the state capitol in California. Even less populated Vermont had more than 600 lobbyists registered with the secretary of state.

Most lobbyists are regular employees of corporations, unions, or trade associations. Many are members of law firms; others are former state employees. Effective lobbyists are specialists in both subject matter and legislative procedure. Lobbyists for organized interests know the schedule of general hearings, committee meetings, floor debates, and social events. They also know as much as possible about the legislators, their electoral support, their values, their hobbies, and who has their "ear." They are present and prepared when their interests are affected. Veteran lobbyists know how to influence legislators. Lobbyists live by two important rules: First, it's a lot easier to kill a bill than to pass it. And second, work in such a way that you have no permanent allies and no permanent enemies. Today's opponent may be your supporter on the next issue for which you are lobbying.[21]

For obvious reasons, some of the most effective lobbyists are retired state legislators. Five of the ten highest-paid lobbyists in Colorado in one recent year were former state legislators. They all have good contacts with their former colleagues, and they can be pretty effective in killing bills, which sometimes can be done in a senate or house committee with just a handful of legislators. "If you happen to know the four people on a certain senate committee," said one Colorado legislator, "it's pretty damn easy to kill a bill."[22]

Super Bowl tickets as well as tickets to other major sports events are sometimes used as bribes by individuals who want to influence specific state or federal representatives.

Information is usually the key ingredient in gaining or losing a vote. Lobbyists are useful providers of such information to anyone who can influence state policy making. "Lobbyists are strategists, tacticians, builders of coalitions among groups, experts and communicators. They testify in committees, buttonhole lawmakers one-on-one, organize meetings between their members and legislators, stage rallies and demonstrations, and try to put a favorable 'spin' on media coverage of their issues."[23] Plainly, however, lobbyists recognize that information and statistics are malleable and can be used to either support or oppose a bill.

Groups that may be affected by legislative decisions seek to bend those decisions to their advantage. Bankers, insurance companies, road builders, developers, and large landholders have, on occasion, sought contracts or special rulings by illegal means. This problem challenges the integrity of representative government in the United States, especially since legislators often get the money with which they run for office from the people who have the greatest stake in pending legislation. There is sometimes a hazy line between a campaign contribution and a bribe.

Illegal use of lobbying techniques, primarily bribery, has been found in some states. Scandals have been exposed in Arkansas, Arizona, Kentucky, Massachusetts, New Mexico, and South Carolina, among others, in recent years. For example, F. William Sawyer, a highly regarded veteran lobbyist who worked for the John Hancock Mutual Life Insurance Company on issues before the Massachusetts legislature, was convicted in federal court in 1995 of illegally giving gifts to a number of Massachusetts lawmakers. Most of his gifts were meals and golf outings; one was picking up the $3,200 tab for flying a legislator and his wife to a Super Bowl game in New Orleans.[24]

Still, bribery is not a widespread problem in most states. Writing about his own experiences in the Vermont Senate, Frank Smallwood observed that as a general rule, most of the lobbyists

> were articulate, hard-working, and extremely well informed in their particular areas of expertise. This last attribute—information—represented their chief weapon and gave them real clout. As far as I could find out, the lobbyists didn't offer legislators any money or other direct inducements, at least, they never offered me anything, not even a sociable drink. Instead they relied on information.[25]

What Makes a Good Legislator?

There are many ways to be an effective legislator. Some legislators specialize in issues, others focus on procedures or helping their districts through casework, and still others become chamber or party leaders. Nearly everyone learns that there is more to the job than making speeches and trying to get bills passed.

Legislators themselves say they admire colleagues who are confident but not arrogant, cooperative but not spineless, principled but flexible, and humorous but not silly. Retired lawmakers suggest these rules:

- Keep your word.
- Be patient.
- Be honest.
- Don't promise too soon.
- Make friends with the staff.
- Never surprise a politician.
- Learn how to build alliances.
- Learn the procedures.
- Think beyond party labels.
- Know how to count votes.
- Know that timing is often the key.
- Don't hog the credit.

trustee

An official who is expected to vote independently, based on his or her judgment of the circumstances; one interpretation of the role of a legislator.

delegate

An official who is expected to represent the views of his or her constituents even when personally holding divergent views; one interpretation of the role of a legislator.

How important are interest groups and state political action committees as a source of influence on state legislatures? Teacher organizations, trade associations, labor groups, trial attorneys, taxpayer associations, insurance, mining, real estate, road builders, and banking interests are often the most visible single-interest groups. In states with an obvious major economic interest, legislators pay close attention to the needs of that interest, regardless of whether the group employs lobbyists. The legislatures in these states seldom pass legislation hostile to their own state's principal economic interests.

Interest groups are usually the major financial backers of incumbent legislators, and in return the lobbyists for those groups get unusual access. As the costs of state legislative races climb, so does the dependence of legislators, legislative leaders, and political parties on organized interests.[26]

In recent years, states have sought to regulate lobbying activities, conflicts of interest, and the financing of political campaigns. Wisconsin and Minnesota ban such favors as buying meals for a legislator. In the wake of a 1992 Federal Bureau of Investigation sting, lawmakers in Kentucky are now barred from taking anything from a lobbyist except $100 per year in meals and drinks. State senators in New York voluntarily declined the meals and gifts worth more than $25 that interest groups had routinely lavished on them.[27]

Not all these reforms have been easy to implement, nor have they all worked according to the original intentions. Laws that control lobbying and regulate how much individuals may spend to influence either elections or the legislative process are difficult to enforce. It is sometimes unclear, too, whether they infringe on the constitutional right of persons to petition their government and to spend their own money for political purposes. In some cases, states have probably overcompensated in their efforts to avoid even the appearance of having legislators' integrity compromised.[28]

OTHER INFLUENCES ON STATE LEGISLATORS   A legislator's personality, leadership style, and conception of responsibilities influence how he or she will vote and perform constituent service.

Many legislators believe they have a responsibility to rail against wasteful government spending yet at the same time fight to see that their own district gets a fair share of state government construction projects and subsidies. Voting for one's home district makes sense to many legislators. Former state legislator John E. Brandl writes that state legislators understand that on election day, their constituents who are grateful for favors received "are more apt to express positive sentiments on the ballot than those not receiving benefits from the capitol. . . . A former colleague of mine in the Minnesota House of Representatives seemed bewildered when he heard the suggestion that his first responsibility as a legislator might not be to look out for his district but rather to be concerned for the good of the whole state. 'Nobody who thinks like that could ever get elected from my district,' he maintained."[29]

But if state legislators are elected to represent the people and their views at the statehouse, few lawmakers think they should merely mirror or "re-present" the views of their district's constituents. Most legislators like to consider themselves **trustees** of their constituents, claiming to rely on their own conscience or on their considered judgments in making decisions. Legislators who view themselves as **delegates**, by contrast, adhere more closely to instructions from their constituents. Not surprisingly, the trustee role is not only more popular but also easier and more realistic to practice. Given the complexity of government and the difficulty of finding out where citizens stand on a wide variety of issues, the trustee role is a more workable one in the day-to-day decision making of a legislator during legislative sessions.

Views of constituents back home are influential on matters such as taxes and major construction on highway projects, yet on most issues, the people back home have little direct influence on lawmaking. On issues that are of keen local interest, legislators certainly do take their constituents into account when they vote. In other words, state lawmakers act as trustees on some issues and delegates on others. Yet conscience and personal philosophy are seldom the only, or even the most important, guide. Colleagues, committee recommendations, party leadership, staff counsel, and lobbying by the affected interests are also influential.

Newly elected legislators soon learn it makes sense to depend on friendly colleagues to inform them about issues. According to a Pennsylvania legislator, "Very early in the session, you try to find other representatives who sit on other committees and who are similar to you in their outlook politically. When a bill comes to the floor for a vote, you have to look to that person, you have to trust him."[30]

Another aspect of state politics that often fuels legislation is action taken by other states. Legislators frequently ask their staffs, "What is California, Minnesota, or Oregon doing on this problem?" Legislators are always on the lookout for innovative tax, educational, or welfare policies implemented elsewhere. Legislators are keenly interested in how their state compares to others in certain areas—on sales taxes, for example, high school dropouts, clean air, or federal moneys coming to the state. The press often uses such rankings in headlines and editorials.

The National Conference of State Legislatures, a nonpartisan professional organization funded by all 50 state legislatures, acts as an effective clearinghouse for new ideas (www.ncsl.org). With about 180 staff members located mainly in Denver, Colorado, it distributes studies to legislators across the country. A rival yet smaller and more conservative group, the American Legislative Exchange Council, has developed in recent years (www.alec.org). The Council of State Governments (www.csg.org) and the State Legislative Leaders Foundation (sllf.org) are two groups that also help serve state legislative leaders.

Actions taken by the federal government also influence state laws and regulations. Over the past 30 years, state legislatures have been burdened by **federal mandates**, which require states to allocate state funds to match federally stipulated programs such as Medicare. Funding for federal mandates was often the fastest-growing part of a state's budget, a sore point with state legislators. In the 1990s, Congress began to place some mild restraints on the growth of federal mandates.

Legislatures today face new pressures: Lobbying is more intense than ever, campaign costs have increased, and fewer members follow the old folkways that used to make for an almost clubhouse collegiality in most legislatures. The greater participation of women, minorities, and more independent-minded legislators has meant a broader mix of agendas and ideas. The influence of legislative leaders has decreased, and that of the media and staff has grown.[31] According to state legislative scholar Alan Rosenthal, "Earlier, leaders were truly in command, and power was tightly held. Partly as a consequence of modernization and reform, legislatures have been democratized. Resources are more broadly distributed, and the gap between leaders and other legislators is narrower."[32]

Modernization and Reform

State legislatures in the past were criticized as inefficient, ineffective, poorly staffed, boss-ridden, secretive, sexist, unrepresentative, and often dominated by rural interests. Most legislatures had little or no staff and high rates of turnover among members. Legislators had to rely primarily on information that came to them from lobbyists or the governor's office. Legislatures were often run by factions that could not be held accountable, and parliamentary procedures and inadequate committee systems either prevented action or served narrow or specially favored interests.

> Given the goals of members, the demands of groups, and the heavy workload, deliberation gives way to expediency. Members frequently are unwilling to say no to their colleagues, lest their colleagues say no to them. They also are averse to saying no to constituents, lest their constituents withdraw support. The process has become porous; much seeps through that probably should not. Standing committees do not screen the wheat from the chaff as diligently as they might.[33]

federal mandate
A requirement imposed by the federal government as a condition for the receipt of federal funds.

To remedy these perceived shortcomings and to strengthen the policy-making role of legislators in state governments, legislatures have adopted some internal reforms. Thus most legislatures now have longer annual sessions, expanded and more competent staffs, more effective committee systems, streamlined procedures such as automated bill status and statute retrieval systems, higher salaries, and modern information systems.[34] Every legislature now has a colorful Web site with detailed information about the workings of the lawmaking body. Hawaii has a fully equipped and staffed "public access room," making it easy for citizens to lobby their state legislators.[35] Virginia is considered a leader in e-government technology for its commitment to citizen-legislator communication through e-mail.[36] And most important, prodded by federal court rulings, legislative districts are now approximately equal in population and thus more representative of the people.

In short, the largely amateur, part-time state legislatures are a thing of the past in most states. The new professionalism reflects a determination on the part of most legislators—especially the leaders—to take charge of their own branch as major players in shaping state public policy.

The movement to encourage full-time professional legislatures with substantial staffs, however, has not been universally praised. In fact, in recent years, some political scientists and some citizens have contended that we were better off when we had part-time citizen-legislators. The groundswell in the early 1990s to enact term limits was in many ways a voters' protest against professionalized legislators who appeared to be making their job of representation into a career.

Legislative Term Limits: Problem or Solution?

Although the complexity of state problems may well require professional legislators who devote full-time attention to legislative issues, this professionalism "runs counter to the traditional theory of American politics in which citizens come together, conduct the public's business and return to their other occupations."[37] In the 33 states where there are no term limits, many legislators are now viewed as career politicians—and hence less like the people they represent.

Term limits were the most talked-about legislative "reform" in the 1990s. It began in 1990 when voters in California, Colorado, and Oklahoma approved the first term-limit restrictions through citizen-instigated ballot initiatives. Two years later, another 11 states enacted voter initiatives along the same lines. Several more approved term-limit provisions of some type for their constitutions, while voters in three states rejected them. In addition, state legislators in Utah and Louisiana voted to impose term limits on themselves; in Louisiana, it was then passed on to the voters for their approval. State supreme courts in four states—Massachusetts, Nebraska, Oregon, and Washington—have struck down term limits as unconstitutional. Note, however, that Nebraska voters in 2000, four years after their court nullified voter-approved limits, voted to reinstate them.

In 2002, Idaho legislators voted to repeal term-limit provisions that had been approved on several occasions by Idaho voters. Term-limit supporters complained that this legislative repeal constituted "a slap in the face to all Idaho voters. The arrogance of the Legislature to repeal an issue that has been supported by four separate votes is unconscionable."[38] But Idaho legislative leader Bruce Newcomb responded that term limits won approval only because out-of-state money influenced the votes: "We were a cheap state to buy; it was not in the public interest. . . . There was never a real debate. . . . They had no opposition."[39] Is this Idaho repeal likely to begin a trend? It is too early to tell. But term-limit "reform" movement has very likely run its course.

Term-limit provisions exist in 17 states (see Table 25-2). These provisions limit state legislators to legislative service of six to 12 years. In some states, lawmakers are barred from serving in the same office beyond a set number of years. In 11 other states, they must skip one term (more in some states) before running for the same office.

"Yes, I think some officials should be limited to one or two terms, and others to none."

Dunagin's People by Ralph Dunagin. © Tribune Media Services, Inc.

TABLE 25–2   Term Limits in the States

State	House			Senate		
	Year Enacted	Limit (years)	Year of Impact	Limit (years)	Year of Impact	Popular Vote in Favor
Maine	1993	8	1996	8	1996	67.6%
California	1990	6	1996	8	1998	52.2
Colorado	1990	8	1998	8	1998	71.0
Arkansas	1992	6	1998	8	2000	59.9
Michigan	1992	6	1998	8	2002	58.8
Florida	1992	8	2000	8	2000	76.8
Missouri*	1992	8	2002	8	2002	75.0
Ohio	1992	8	2000	8	2000	68.4
South Dakota	1992	8	2000	8	2000	63.5
Montana	1992	8	2000	8	2000	67.0
Arizona	1992	8	2000	8	2000	74.2
Oklahoma	1990	12	2004	12	2004	67.3
Nevada	1996	12	2008	12	2008	70.4
Utah	1994	12	2006	12	2006	—†
Wyoming	1992	12	2006	12	2006	77.2
Louisiana	1995	12	2007	12	2007	76.0
Nebraska‡	2000	8	2008	—	—	55.8

SOURCE: National Conference of State Legislatures; *Wall Street Journal,* "Term Limits Have Unexpected Outcomes," March 4, 2002, p. A16.

*Because of special elections, term limits became effective in 2000 for eight current members of the house and one senator in 1998.

†Passed by the legislature.

‡Nebraska has a unicameral legislature.

Voters in California went even further and enacted a measure that slashed legislative staffs and curbed legislative pension benefits as well as limited the number of terms legislators could serve. This citizen-sponsored and citizen-enacted law also prohibited legislators from ever running again for the legislature.

Voters can, of course, dispatch legislators from office by voting for challengers. But voters seem to want the added constitutional device of doing for them what most voters do not do themselves—throw the rascals out! All the hoopla about term limits diverts attention from other serious problems, including weak parties, too many safe-seat districts where one party virtually always wins, and neglect of educational investment and economic development in the states.

What have been the consequences of term limits? In California, novice lawmakers now chair committees and hold leadership positions, and there are signs in California and elsewhere that term limits discourage legislative cooperation, decrease institutional expertise, and generally weaken legislatures relative to governors, bureaucrats, and lobbyists. Term limits thus far have not brought a different type of person to the legislatures.[40] Indeed, opponents contend correctly, it takes several years for new legislators to become acquainted with rules, procedures, and regulations; therefore, to jettison politicians just as they begin to feel comfortable, confident, and knowledgeable is to lose a wealth of accumulated experience.

The Politics of Drawing Legislative District Lines

State legislatures are required by their state constitutions, by federal laws, and by court rulings to draw district boundaries for both their state legislature and U.S. House of Representative seats after each population census. The 2000 census once again triggered redistricting of congressional and state legislative lines.

You Decide   Thinking It Through

SHOULD TERM LIMITS BE IMPOSED ON STATE LEGISLATORS?

You Decide... Proponents of term limits contend that the principle of rotation is an old and cherished one in the United States and that we should encourage citizen-legislators and discourage career politicians. Supporters also say incumbents have voted too many perks and advantages for themselves and that term limits may be the only way to restore real competition to legislative races. They argue that *permanent incumbency*—legislators and state officials staying on for multiple terms spanning decades— is creating a kind of professional ruling class that is out of touch with ordinary citizens. The term-limit movement is a manifestation of public frustration with what is viewed as a failure of government. Would placing limits on how long legislators can serve solve the problem?

Thinking It Through... Support for term limits comes from both Republicans and Democrats, yet organized support and financial aid have generally come from conservative antitax and antigovernment groups. The *Wall Street Journal* has frequently editorialized in support of term limits. Consumer activist and Green party presidential candidate Ralph Nader has also been among their most vocal supporters. He and like-minded populists on the left believe that only the bludgeon of term limits will motivate legislators to give reforms like public funding of political campaigns a serious chance. Many term limits were aimed at the U.S. Congress as the primary target, but that restriction was struck down by the U.S. Supreme Court.

Legislators and most political scientists have opposed this reform. They contend that term limits are a solution in search of a problem that does not exist. Most state legislators, they note, stay in the legislature for only three or four terms anyway. Indeed, most states have more of a problem nurturing and retaining experienced leaders than they have bringing in new blood. The expertise and institutional memory once available from veteran members and longtime leaders, critics say, will be diminished by term limits.*

Critics of term limits think this reform will have the unintended consequence of increasing the power of various unelected officials, such as lobbyists, legislative staffers, and bureaucrats. Power resides somewhere, critics say, and you don't get rid of it so much as shift it. "I calculate that term limits is costing the legislature 694 years of collective experience," complained Ohio state legislator Jo Ann Davidson. "Now the institutional memory vote will be in the hands of the lobbyists and the legislative staff when it should rest with the elected policy makers."†

*See David S. Broder, Democracy Derailed: Initiative Campaigns and the Power of Money (Harcourt, 2000), p. 223.

†Jo Ann Davidson, quoted in Francis X. Clines, "Term Limits Bring Wholesale Change into Legislatures," New York Times, February 14, 2000, p. A19. See also the criticism in Peter Schrag, Paradise Lost: California's Experience, America's Future (New Press, 1998), p. 3. See also John M. Carey, Richard G. Niemi, and Lynda W. Powell, Term Limits in the State Legislatures (University of Michigan Press, 2000).

Redistricting is the action of a state legislature or other body in redrawing legislative electoral district lines. About a dozen states delegate these responsibilities to independent redistricting or reapportionment commissions. In Alaska, the governor's office draws the legislative districts. Most legislatures, however, consider these once-a-decade responsibilities so important that they are unwilling to turn control of this task over to anybody else.

The drawing of legislative district boundaries has always been controversial, in large part because redistricting decisions are made by partisan majorities in legislatures. The highly political nature of the undertaking is usually reflected in the results. "Redistricting is the political equivalent," says one observer, "of moving the left field fence for a right-handed pull hitter. By changing the boundaries, redistricting helps some, hurts others—and leaves just about everyone else scrambling."[41]

The politics and debate about redistricting are most intense in the years immediately after a census is taken. Drawing district boundaries to benefit a party, group, or incumbent

redistricting
The redrawing of congressional and other legislative district lines following the census, to accommodate population shifts and keep districts as equal as possible in population.

is called **gerrymandering**. The term was first used in 1811 to describe a strange, salamander-shaped legislative district drawn in northeastern Massachusetts when Elbridge Gerry was governor. A district does not need to be odd in shape, however, to be gerrymandered.

As a result of huge differences in population among the districts, state legislative districts used to face problems of **malapportionment**. State legislatures for decades had given rural and small-town voters more votes in the legislature than they were entitled to on the basis of their declining share of the population. In Georgia, for instance, the 1960 reapportionment gave the largest county, with 556,326 inhabitants, no more representation than the three smallest counties, whose combined population was 6,980.[42] City officials complained bitterly that small-town and farm-dominated legislators were unsympathetic to their problems and had different legislative priorities.

But no matter how much they protested, people who were underrepresented in the state legislatures made little progress. Legislators from small towns and farm areas naturally did not wish to reapportion themselves out of jobs, and their constituents did not wish to lose their influence. Even though the failure of state legislatures to reapportion often violated express provisions of state constitutions and raised serious questions under the U.S. Constitution, state and federal judges took the position that issues having to do with legislative districting were "political questions" and outside the scope of judicial authority.

Finally, the U.S. Supreme Court stepped in. In 1962, in *Baker* v. *Carr,* the Court held that voters do have standing to challenge legislative apportionment and that such questions should be considered by the federal courts. Arbitrary and capriciously drawn districts deprive people of their constitutional rights of representation, and federal judges may take jurisdiction over such cases.[43] *Baker* v. *Carr* started a small tidal wave.

One Person, One Vote

In *Wesberry* v. *Sanders* (1964), the U.S. Supreme Court announced that as far as congressional representation is concerned, "as nearly as practicable one man's vote in a congressional election is to be worth as much as another's."[44] The Court extended this principle to representation in the state legislatures, although it subsequently modified this decision allowing for somewhat more population discrepancies among state legislative districts than for congressional districts.

In *Reynolds* v. *Sims* (1964), the Court held that "the fundamental principle of representative government in this country is one of equal representation for equal numbers of people, without regard to race, sex, economic status, or place of residence within a state." In the Court's view, this principle applied not only to the more numerous house of the state legislature, which was usually based on population, but also to the state senate, where representation was often based on area, such as the county or some other governmental unit. Defenders of this pattern had argued that as long as the more numerous chamber represented population, the senate could represent geographical units. Look at the federal system embodied in the U.S. Constitution, they said. Isn't representation in the U.S. Senate based on area? Although many thought this a compelling argument, a majority of the Court did not. Chief Justice Earl Warren explained: "Legislators represent people, not trees or acres. Legislators are elected by voters, not farms or cities or economic interests. . . . The right to elect legislators in a free unimpaired fashion is a bedrock of our political system."[45] The U.S. Senate analogy, in short, did not hold.

The Supreme Court has been especially strict about how states draw districts for the U.S. House of Representatives. A state legislature must justify any variance from mathematical equality by showing it made a good-faith effort to come as close as possible to the standard. The Supreme Court is, however, less insistent on absolute equality for state legislative districts. Thus the Court in 1983 upheld a Wyoming plan that allocated at least one state legislative seat per county, saying that Wyoming's policy was rational and appropriate to the special needs of that sparsely populated state.[46] This ruling was a rare exception to the general principle of allowing at most a 10 percent deviation between state legislative districts. The requirement that the districts be established in accordance with the one-person, one-vote principle still remains.

gerrymandering
The drawing of legislative district boundaries to benefit a party, group, or incumbent.

malapportionment
Having legislative districts with unequal populations.

New Rules for Redrawing the Districts

Even though the one-person, one-vote principle is firmly established, many issues affecting the nature of legislative representation continue to be hotly debated. In northern metropolitan areas, for instance, the general pattern has been for the center city to be Democratic and the outlying suburbs Republican. If legislative district lines in these areas are drawn like spokes from the center city to the suburbs, fewer Republicans will probably be elected than if the district lines are drawn in concentric circles.

In recent decades, African Americans and Hispanics have begun to charge that state legislatures have an obligation under the Voting Rights Act of 1965 to redraw legislative districts to avoid dilution of the influence of minorities at the ballot box. They have gone to court to force legislators to create **majority-minority districts**. The U.S. Supreme Court, however, has put restraints on implementation of the act. The Court has held that although legislatures may take race into account in drawing state and federal legislative district lines and must act to avoid diluting the voting strength of minorities, a legislature violates the constitutional rights of white voters if race becomes the overriding motive.[47]

Controversy continues to surround reapportionment, no matter what processes are used. No one ever doubts the ability of incumbents in the majority to rig elections through reapportionment. In the words of the old-time politicians, "You tell me the results you want, and I'll draw the district map to do it." Today, computers are shaping the districts, and the people who control the computers, their programming, and their data can influence the outcome.

Neither the courts nor the two major parties have adequately addressed the competitive integrity of the electoral process as a constitutional issue. But a case can be made that the vast majority of state legislative elections offer little meaningful competition. Whether designed by legislative party leaders or redistricting commissioners, those who carve up legislative districts every ten years do so primarily with the intent to protect incumbents or create districts that at least leave their party no worse off than it was before.

"Real competition, where a challenger to an incumbent might have some actual chance of winning, is evident in elections that are won by margins of less than 10 percent of the vote," writes Columbia University law professor Samuel Issacharoff.[48] But this is rarely the case in state after state. The wonder is "that anyone bothers to participate at all in such hollow elections."[49] And this was, in part, the reason that the term-limit crusade gained support in the first place.

Direct Legislation: Policy Making by the People?

Does "We the People" in our Constitution mean that the people themselves should govern directly? Around the start of the twentieth century, Populist and Progressive reform movements fought to "return the government to the people" through the initiative, referendum, and recall. Give the voters the power to make or veto laws and to recall officials, they said, and the political machines will be destroyed and the special interests beaten.

Populists and Progressives had good reason between 1890 and 1912 to want to bypass their legislatures, for the legislatures in several states were either incompetent or under the domination of the political machines. For example, the Southern Pacific Railroad's political machine in California had dominated the selection of state legislators, governors, and U.S. senators for years.[50] The Progressives placed enormous trust in the wisdom of the people, assuming that voters would inform themselves about issues and make responsible decisions on a variety of policy questions put before them.

Initiative

The **initiative** permits a designated minimum number of voters to propose a law or constitutional amendment by petition. It becomes law if approved by a majority of the voters at a subsequent election. Twenty-four states, mostly in the West, authorize the making

majority-minority district
A legislative district created to include a majority of minority voters; ruled constitutional so long as race is not the main factor in redistricting.

initiative
Procedure whereby a certain number of voters may, by petition, propose a law or constitutional amendment and have it submitted to the voters.

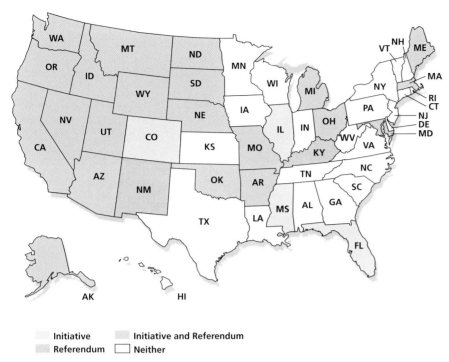

Initiative   Initiative and Referendum
Referendum   Neither

FIGURE 25–4 Citizen-Initiated Initiative and Referendum at the State Level.

of laws by means of the initiative petition (see Figure 25-4). In California, Oregon, Washington, North Dakota, Arizona, Colorado, Michigan, and Massachusetts, the initiative has become an important feature of state political life.

In some states, the *direct initiative* applies to constitutional amendments and to legislation; in others, it can be used only for one or the other. Thus in Florida, the direct initiative can be used only to change the state constitution, while in Idaho, direct initiative can be used only for statutory lawmaking. In a state that permits the direct initiative, any individual or interest group may draft a proposed law and file it with a designated state official, usually the secretary of state. Supporters have only to secure a certain number of signatures (between 2 and 15 percent of the vote in the last election) to place the measure on the next general election ballot. Only California permits initiatives on primary election ballots.

The *indirect initiative* is used in a few states, including Alaska, Maine, and Massachusetts. After a certain number of petition signatures have been collected, the state legislature is given an opportunity to act on the measure without alteration; if approved, the law simply goes into effect. If not approved, the proposed legislation is then placed on the ballot, although in some states, additional signatures are required before the proposal can be placed before the voters.

Referendum

A **referendum** permits voters to vote on, and possibly overturn, recently passed laws or legislatively proposed amendments to a state's constitution. A majority vote is required to overturn legislatively approved laws. The referendum, it should be noted, is required in every state except Delaware for the ratification of constitutional amendments.

Legislation may be subject to mandatory or optional referendums. The *mandatory referendum* calls for a waiting period, usually 60 to 90 days, before legislation goes into effect. If during this period a prescribed number of voters sign a referendum petition requesting that the act be referred to the voters, the law does not go into effect unless a majority of the voters give their approval at the next election. The *optional referendum* permits the legislature, at its discretion, to provide that a measure shall not become law until it has been approved by the voters at an election. This second kind is the more common.

Although statewide initiatives and referendums get the most attention, the same processes also flourish at the local level in many states. The annual volume of measures

referendum
Procedure for submitting to popular vote measures passed by the legislature or proposed amendments to a state constitution.

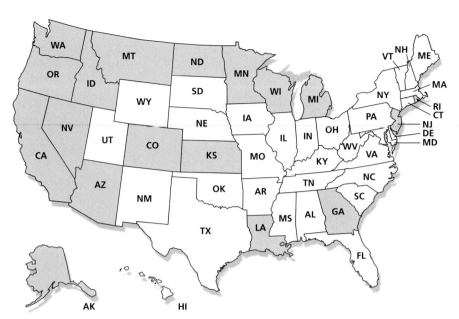

FIGURE 25–5 States That Provide for Citizen-Initiated Recall of Elected State Officials.

presented to voters in school districts, cities, and counties runs to several thousand, and many are on topics of considerable importance and controversy: bonds for school buildings, fluoridation of water, banning of glass bottles, restrictions on nuclear power facilities, and approval or rejection of convention facilities or sport stadiums.

Recall

Recall is the means by which voters may remove elected public officials before the end of their term. Eighteen states, mostly in the West, provide for the recall of state officers, but many others permit the recall of local officials (see Figure 25-5). Recall also requires a petition, but it needs more signatures (typically 25 percent of voters in the last election for the position in question) than the initiative or referendum. There are various kinds of recall elections. In some, the official must run and try to win reelection in a yes-or-no vote of confidence election; in others, candidates are permitted to file and run against the incumbent, making it, in effect, a new election. If in the former case an incumbent is voted out of office, a new election is required.

Recall is akin to impeachment by the public. But unlike impeachment, formal charges of wrongdoing against the incumbent are not required. Rather, recall permits throwing people out of office merely because of policy differences. For recall, voters need only circulate petitions and obtain the required number of signatures. Recall is seldom used at the state level, although one governor and several state legislators have been recalled. In 2000, a recall effort was mounted in California against Insurance Commissioner Chuck Quackenbush. His critics faulted him for being too generous to donors he was supposed to be regulating. The recall drive was doubtless a contributing factor in Quackenbush's decision to resign. Although the recall is rarely used successfully in the 18 states that now permit it, even the threat of a recall serves to remind legislators and other state officials of their obligations to the voters.[51]

A few years ago, New Jersey voters were asked to approve the right to recall local, state, and federal elected officials. Taxpayer and antipolitician groups argued passionately in favor of passage. The *New York Times* vigorously opposed the recall, saying it would discourage public officials from making unpopular decisions that nevertheless bring about long-term public benefits. The *Times* also editorialized that the recall authority was unnecessary: "If voters are unhappy with someone they have elected, they can vote that person out the next time! If an official breaks the law, prosecutors can deal with it."[52] But over 70 percent of New Jersey voters voted in favor of adopting the recall.

recall
Procedure for submitting to popular vote the removal of public officials from office before the end of their term.

The Debate over Direct Democracy

Hundreds of issues have been placed on state election ballots by citizen initiative in recent years. Citizens have turned to the initiative process to try to regulate handguns in California, to protect the moose in Maine, to encourage the death penalty in Massachusetts, to approve the sale of wine in grocery stores in Colorado, to abolish daylight savings time in North Dakota, and in several states to allow marijuana to be used for specific medicinal purposes. Voters in Oregon approved the so-called Death with Dignity law that allows legally assisted suicide, and voters in Washington State approved a measure mandating that criminals convicted of three felonies be sentenced to life in prison without parole. Voters in California and Washington voted to overturn affirmative action programs in state hiring and college admissions programs.

In Oregon's November 2000 election, voters had to vote on 26 ballot measures, most of which were placed there by citizen initiatives. The voters had to decide on initiatives proposing huge tax cuts, repealing the death penalty, banning animal trapping, requiring background checks to buy firearms at gun shows, limiting the amount of money spent on political campaigns, and forbidding public school teachers to speak favorably of homosexuality.

A total of 202 ballot measures were voted on in 42 states in November 2002. Forty-nine of the 202 measures were citizen-initiated; 22 were approved. Most of the remainder were referred by the legislatures and 66 percent of these passed.[53]

Political scientists, law professors, and lawmakers are often critical of direct legislation.[54] Early opponents had argued that such measures would undermine the legitimacy of representative government and open the way for radical or special-interest legislation. Critics of the initiative and the referendum believe that the Progressives who advocated direct legislation were naively idealistic and that these mechanisms are more likely to be used by special interests. Only well-organized interests can gather the appropriate number of signatures and mount the required media campaigns to gain victory. Critics of direct democracy say that this is indeed what has happened in California, Oregon, and elsewhere.[55]

In addition to giving advantages to well-organized interests, direct legislation often introduces confusion because some petitions are worded not so much for clarity but to win votes. Moreover, the 30-second ads that support or oppose many initiatives also tend to confuse rather than clarify.

What have been the results of these populist devices? Historically, direct legislation by initiative has resulted in progressive victories on many consumer and economic issues and conservative victories on social issues. Direct democracy has not weakened our legislatures; seats in state legislatures are still valued, sought after, and competed for by able citizens. Nor, with some exceptions, has unwise legislation generally been enacted. The overall record suggests that voters reject most unsound ideas that get on the ballot. However, voters in California, Colorado, Oregon, and Washington have adopted budget and tax measures in recent years that have had a considerable impact on state taxes and spending. These measures have pleased many conservatives, upset liberals, and made life difficult for governors and state legislators.

A problem in a few states is the number of issues on the ballot. California and Oregon voters often have had to decide on a dozen or more ballot issues, some initiated by interest groups and the rest placed on the ballot by the legislature. States are now seeing multiple initiatives on a single topic, with counterinitiatives sponsored by people who actually oppose one of the measures but have decided that the best way to defeat the undesirable initiative is by sponsoring a competing version of their own.

Another serious problem has arisen in western states. Political consulting firms, for a price, will gather signatures and put nearly anything you want on the ballot. Deceptive pitches are sometimes made to get people to sign petitions. It takes a small fortune to do this, and only well-organized, well-financed, single-interest groups can afford it.[56]

Still another problem with the initiative process is that it can be used to target minorities, as California's limitations on illegal immigrants in 1994 and affirmative action in 1996 did. Similarly, Colorado's controversial Measure 2 in 1992 targeted gays and lesbians. How far can the majority go in using the initiative process against minorities? The courts have generally reversed part or all of discriminatory initiatives that were successful at the polls, yet such reversals put the courts in the awkward position of opposing a vote of the people.

The initiative process has become a powerful tool used by interest groups, politicians, and ideologues. "A vote on an issue in a single state can propel an issue onto the national agenda because of the widespread media attention given to some controversial initiatives."[57] Interest groups have set state policy by means of the initiative and have used it to reduce local government options in taxing, zoning and planning, and related matters. "One reason for this tendency to take on matters that were previously local and decide them at the statewide level is interest group efficiency. It is easier to restrict local taxing powers, strike local rent control laws, and eliminate ordinances protecting gays and lesbians by mobilizing a single statewide vote" rather than by campaigning to reverse or defeat local initiatives.[58]

Viewed from another perspective, most of the perceived flaws of the populist processes of direct democracy are also the flaws of democracy. When we vote in an election, we often wish we had more information about issues and candidates. Delegates at constitutional conventions or national party conventions frequently have similar misgivings when they are forced to render yes-or-no votes on complicated issues. So, too, members of state legislatures—especially in those frantic days near the end of their sessions—yearn for more information, more clarity about consequences, and more discussion and compromise than time will permit.

Critics lament the rise in what they call "public policy making by bumper sticker." Opponents of direct legislation fear that the very fabric of legislative processes and representative government is at stake. To be sure, lack of faith in legislative bodies has sometimes prompted the use of direct legislation devices, but the best way to restore faith in the legislature is not to bypass it but to elect better people to it.

Supporters of populist democracy say they have not given up on the legislative process. Rather, they wish to use direct legislation primarily when legislatures prove unresponsive. If our legislature will not act, they say, give us the opportunity to debate our proposals in the open arena of election politics. Supporters further contend that the people are capable of making decisions on complex matters.

Voters throughout the country say that citizens ought to have the right, at least occasionally, to vote directly on policy issues. Surveys find that both voters and nonvoters say they would be more likely to become interested in politics and vote if some issues appeared along with candidates on their ballots.[59] Moreover, Californians, who have had to deal with more ballot issues than voters in any other state, continue to say statewide ballot propositions elections are overall "a good thing for California" (74 percent), even as they acknowledge limits to their own grasp of the process.[60]

The legislative process is never perfect. Even with larger professional staffs, hearings, new technologies, bicameralism, and other distinctive features of constitutional democracy, mistakes are made and defective bills are enacted into law in our legislatures. The Supreme Court has overturned hundreds of laws passed by state legislatures as unconstitutional, and state legislatures often spend much of their time amending or otherwise improving measures they passed in previous years. As a practical matter, however, Americans should be at least as skeptical and questioning of the initiative and referendum process as they already are of their state legislators.

Summary

1. Although Americans value the state legislature as a vital institution in our constitutional form of government, we are quick to criticize its imperfections. Perhaps we overestimate the possibilities for responsive and representative legislatures. Yet today, state legislatures are stronger than they were 40 years ago, and they play a vital role in state politics and state policy making.

2. The nation's 7,387 state legislators are called on to represent diverse views, help formulate state public policy, oversee the administration of state laws, and mediate political conflicts that arise in the state.

3. The main influences on a state legislator's voting decisions are political parties, lobbyists and interest groups, district considerations, constituent views, colleagues, committee rec-

ommendations, the party leaders, the media, and actions taken by other states and the federal government.

4. State legislators are constantly subjected to intense lobbying by organized interests. Lobbyists and interest group representatives are important sources of information.

5. As a result of legislative reform efforts, most states now have longer annual sessions, larger and more competent staffs, open-meeting laws, and a variety of electronic-age information systems.

6. Seventeen states have limited the number of terms legislators can serve. Most state legislators and political scientists oppose term limits for a variety of reasons, yet voters in many states have viewed them as a way of keeping their representatives accountable and encouraging the notion of citizen representation.

7. The politics of redistricting, or redrawing legislative boundaries, heats up every ten years after the census is taken. Redistricting is never easy; political careers can be ruined by redrawn boundaries. Major controversies have arisen over partisan and racially motivated drawing of legislative district lines, and the federal courts are increasingly asked to establish guidelines that will limit such outcomes.

8. Direct legislative procedures, especially the initiative petition, are a prominent part of the legislative process, particularly in the West. Other direct mechanisms, such as the referendum and the recall, are also available to voters in many states.

Key Terms

bicameral legislature	lobbyist	redistricting	initiative
unicameral legislature	trustee	gerrymandering	referendum
party caucus	delegate	malapportionment	recall
lobbying	federal mandate	majority-minority district	

Further Reading

SHAWN BOWLER AND TODD DONOVAN, *Demanding Choices: Opinions, Voting, and Direct Democracy* (University of Michigan Press, 1998).

SHAWN BOWLER, TODD DONOVAN, AND CAROLINE J. TOLBERT, EDS., *Citizens as Legislators: Direct Democracy in the United States* (Ohio State University Press, 1998).

DAVID S. BRODER, *Democracy Derailed: Initiative Campaigns and the Power of Money* (Harcourt, 2000).

WILLIAM M. BULGER, *While the Music Lasts: My Life in Politics* (Houghton Mifflin, 1996).

BRUCE E. CAIN, *The Reapportionment Puzzle* (University of California Press, 1984).

JOHN M. CAREY, RICHARD G. NIEMI, AND LYNDA W. POWELL, *Term Limits in the State Legislatures* (University of Michigan Press, 2000).

THOMAS E. CRONIN, *Direct Democracy: The Politics of the Initiative, Referendum, and Recall* (Harvard University Press, 1989).

RICHARD J. ELLIS, *Democratic Delusions: The Initiative Process in America* (University Press of Kansas, 2002).

VIRGINIA GRAY, RUSSELL HANSON, AND HERBERT JACOB, EDS., *Politics in the American States,* 7th ed. (CQ Press, 1999).

JOHN J. KENNEDY, *The Contemporary Pennsylvania Legislature* (University Press of America, 1999).

TOM LOFTUS, *The Art of Legislative Politics* (CQ Press, 1994).

BURDETT A. LOOMIS, *A Legislative Year: Time, Politics, and Policies* (University Press of Kansas, 1994).

DAVID B. MAGLEBY, *Direct Legislation: Voting on Ballot Propositions in the United States* (Johns Hopkins University Press, 1984).

JAY MICHAEL AND DAN WALTERS, *The Third House: Lobbyists, Money, and Power in Sacramento* (Berkeley Public Policy Press, 2002).

GARY MONCRIEF, PEVERILL SQUIRE, AND MALCOLM E. JEWELL, *Who Runs for the Legislature?* (Prentice Hall, 2001).

NATIONAL CONFERENCE OF STATE LEGISLATURES AND AMERICAN SOCIETY OF LEGISLATIVE CLERKS AND SECRETARIES, *Inside the Legislative Process* (National Council of State Legislatures, 1998).

ALBERT J. NELSON, *Emerging Influentials in State Legislatures: Women, Blacks, and Hispanics* (Praeger, 1991).

BETH REINGOLD, *Representing Women: Sex, Gender, and Legislative Behavior in Arizona and California* (University of California Press, 2000).

JAMES RICHARDSON, *Willie Brown: A Biography* (University of California Press, 1996).

ALAN ROSENTHAL, *The Decline of Representative Democracy* (CQ Press, 1998).

ALAN ROSENTHAL, *Drawing the Line: Legislative Ethics in the States* (University of Nebraska Press, 1996).

PETER SCHRAG, *Paradise Lost: California's Experience, America's Future* (New Press, 1998).

FRANK SMALLWOOD, *Free and Independent: The Initiation of a College Professor into State Politics* (Stephen Greene Press, 1976).

JOHN A. STRAAYER, *The Colorado General Assembly,* 2d ed. (University Press of Colorado, 2000).

SUE THOMAS, *How Women Legislate* (Oxford University Press, 1994).

SUE THOMAS AND CLYDE WILCOX, EDS., *Women and Elective Office* (Oxford University Press, 1998).

JOEL A. THOMPSON AND GARY F. MONCRIEF, EDS., *Campaign Finance and State Legislative Elections* (CQ Press, 1998).

See *State Legislatures,* published ten times a year by the National Conference of State Legislatures. *Legislative Studies Quarterly* often has articles on state legislatures; it is published by the Legislative Studies Section of the American Political Science Association. *Governing,* published monthly by Congressional Quarterly, Inc., regularly covers state politics and state legislative issues. *Spectrum: The Journal of State Government* is a useful quarterly published by the Council of State Governments.

26
CHAPTER

STATE
GOVERNORS

T HE JOB OF GOVERNOR IS ONE OF THE MOST IMPORTANT AND EXACTING IN AMERICAN POLITICAL LIFE. OVER THE PAST two decades, Congress and the White House have decentralized many activities to the states that were for a time considered national responsibilities, such as welfare assistance. This transfer has meant governors now have to be even more effective managers. They have to ask the right questions and consider the long-term implications and side effects of their policies more carefully than ever.

In good economic times, governors, with the concurrence of the state legislatures, get to spend vast sums of new money on state priorities such as education, economic development, transportation, health, and environmental protection. Such was the case during the boom times of the 1990s. Then came the recession of the early 2000s, which brought dramatic revenue shortfalls in more than 40 states. This put governors in a difficult position. To balance state budgets, they had to recommend cuts in services, project delays, state employee layoffs, pay raise postponements, and in some cases, higher taxes. In good economic times and bad, governors are invariably at the center of public policy developments.

Governors are also frequently involved in national politics and often viewed as national leaders. Seventeen governors have gone on to serve as U.S. presidents, and at least 17 members of the current U.S. Senate served earlier as governors in their states. Two or three former governors are typically in the president's cabinet, as is the case in George W. Bush's cabinet (Tom Ridge of Pennsylvania, Tommy Thompson of Wisconsin, and Christy Whitman of New Jersey).

In this chapter, we look at how governors come into and keep office, a typical governor's power and influence, efforts to bring modern management techniques to the governor's office, ways that governors interact with other elected state officials, and the rewards of being governor. But first, we examine the rising expectations we have for governors.

Governor: Impeached, Convicted, and Removed

In 1988, the Arizona state legislature impeached and convicted Governor Evan Mecham after 15 months of stormy politics, the first ouster of a governor by a legislature since 1917. Mecham was impeached by the Arizona House and removed from office when the Arizona Senate convicted him of misusing money from a state protocol fund and trying to thwart the investigation of a death threat. Had he not been removed by the legislature, he would probably have been recalled by Arizona voters, who had collected at least 390,000 signatures to force a special election scheduled for May 1988.

Mecham's opponents faulted him for insensitive remarks about women and ethnic minorities, arrogance, inept leadership, and questionable integrity. A conservative Republican, Mecham blasted the press and leftist groups and vowed a comeback, but it was a Republican-dominated state legislature that impeached him. Five other governors have been impeached and removed since 1900, including Alabama Governor Guy Hunt in 1993.

Governor Gary Locke, the first Chinese American governor in U.S. history, came to the office after years of public service. He was elected to the Washington State House of Representatives in 1982, served on both the House Judiciary and Appropriations Committees, and in his last five years was chairman of the House Appropriations Committee. In 1993 he became the chief executive of King County.

Rising Expectations for Governors

How do we evaluate governors? Although the constitutional powers of governors vary from state to state, we assess and rate governors pretty much as we do presidents.[1] Governors in the large and even medium-sized states are responsible for running complex enterprises that are at least as complicated as *Fortune* 500 corporations. Lamar Alexander, former governor of Tennessee, said that a governor needs to "see the state's few most urgent needs, develop strategies to address them, and persuade at least half the people that he or she is right."[2] An effective governor also has to perform countless symbolic and ceremonial functions and win the respect of the people and the legislature in order to exercise fully the executive functions of the office.

Today, a governor is expected to be, among other things, the state's chief policy maker, shaper of the state budget, a savvy political party leader, chief recruiter of the best available advisers and administrators, and an inspiring renewer of confidence in state programs. The governor must also champion the state's interests against the encroachments of federal or local governments and be the state's chief booster to attract business and tourism. In order to be effective, governors are expected to take trips abroad to encourage foreign investment in their states and promote their local products.[3] Thirty-eight states even operate some form of overseas office, including trade mission posts in Harare and Kuala Lumpur.[4] Governors also work with their legislatures to raise revenues for such programs as welfare, education, and economic development. Governors act as crucial links among the states and between the local and the national governments.

Becoming and Remaining Governor

Each state's constitution and laws spell out the rules of eligibility, tenure, and salary for its governor. In most states, to run for the office, a person must be at least 30 years of age and a state resident for at least five years immediately preceding the election. You are constitutionally eligible to be governor in California, Ohio, South Dakota, Washington, and Wisconsin when you become 18, although your chances of being elected at such an age are not very good. In theory, any qualified voter of the state who meets a state's age qualification is eligible for the office of governor; in practice, however, there are well-traveled career paths to the governor's office.

Most governors are white male attorneys about 40 to 55 years old. Only about sixteen women have served as governors in the past generation. Most governors were state legislators or held statewide elective office, and some have had law enforcement experience. For example, New York's George Pataki, Georgia's Roy Barnes, and Colorado's Bill Owens all served earlier in their state legislatures. In one recent year, 31 governors were attorneys, two were farmers, one was a dentist, and most of the rest were businesspeople.

A common path is election to the state legislature, followed by election to a statewide office such as lieutenant governor, secretary of state, or attorney general. Illinois Governor George Ryan spent nearly 30 years in state politics, first as a state legislator, then as Speaker of the state house, then as a two-term lieutenant governor, and then as a two-term secretary of state before becoming governor. Mayors often run for governor; the mayors of Albuquerque, Phoenix, Indianapolis, Lincoln, and Las Vegas have all run for governor in their states in recent years. Recent Minnesota Governor Jesse Ventura, who many people recall mainly as a professional wrestler, had also served four years as mayor of a suburban community.

Occasionally a person who has not held any elective office will win a governorship, although such individuals typically have been active in other ways in political life. Former Texas Governor George W. Bush was a businessman who enjoyed widespread name recognition as the son of a former president, as did his younger brother, Jeb Bush, who also went from a business career to the Florida governorship.

Two hundred years ago, most states had one- or two-year terms for their governors. Today, all states except New Hampshire and Vermont have four-year terms, and all states except Virginia allow governors to run for more than one term. Some governors, such as Jim Thompson in Illinois, Roy Romer in Colorado, Cecil Andrus in Idaho, Mario

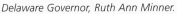

WE THE PEOPLE

Women Governors

Delaware Governor, Ruth Ann Minner.

Montana Governor, Judy Martz.

Kansas Governor, Kathleen Sebelius.

Governor	State	Term of Office	Governor	State	Term of Office
Nellie Taylor Ross	Wyoming	1925–1927	Barbara Roberts	Oregon	1991–1995
"Ma" Ferguson	Texas	1925–1927, 1933–1935	Christine Todd Whitman	New Jersey	1994–2001
Lurleen Wallace	Alabama	1967–1968	Jeanne Shaheen	New Hampshire	1997–2002
Ella Grasso	Connecticut	1975–1980	Jane Dee Hull	Arizona	1998–2002
Dixie Lee Ray	Washington	1977–1981	Judy Martz	Montana	2001–
Martha L. Collins	Kentucky	1983–1987	Ruth Ann Minner	Delaware	2001–
Madeleine Kunin	Vermont	1985–1991	Jane Swift	Massachusetts	2001–2002
Kay Orr	Nebraska	1987–1991	Janet Napolitano	Arizona	2003–
Rose Mofford	Arizona	1988–1991	Linda Lingle	Hawaii	2003–
Joan Finney	Kansas	1991–1995	Kathleen Sebelius	Kansas	2003–
Ann Richards	Texas	1991–1995			

Cuomo in New York, Jim Hunt in North Carolina, and Tommy Thompson in Wisconsin, were elected to three or four terms as governors, but 37 states now have a two-term limit on governors, and Utah has a three-term limit.

Governors on the Spot

Once elected, governors enjoy high visibility in their states. Governors earn more than $100,000 in most states; salaries range from $179,000 in New York to $65,000 in Nebraska.[5] In addition, governors receive an expense allowance; all but four are provided an executive mansion; 42 of them have regular access to a state plane or helicopter or both.

But just as governors have become increasingly important in recent decades, they have also had to deal with the twin problems of rising aspirations and scarcity of resources. People want better schools, highways that do not spoil the environment, adequate welfare programs, protections for civil rights, safe streets, and clean air and streams. But citizens seldom, if ever, want higher taxes.

Former New York Governor Mario Cuomo (who served from 1983 until 1995) used to say he was always running into people who wanted him to expand programs. He would look them in the eye and say, "Now what are you going to give me so that I can pay for it? Do you want to wait longer in line at the Motor Vehicle office to get your license renewed? Do we stop paving the road in front of your home? Do you mind if we plow the snow less often?" Typically, of course, he heard that the people requesting additional spending did not want to forgo any of those things, which prompted him to say, "Well, then, I don't understand. Where do I get what I need to do what you want?" His point is simple. Given limited resources, choices must be made. Elected officials cannot afford to do everything people would like. Politicians are elected to negotiate trade-offs. You must "give to get."[6]

Governors and state legislators face the challenge of administering federally mandated welfare programs with fewer federal dollars. They have campaigned for the federal government to give more dollars to the states—without strings. The Republican-controlled U.S. Congress in the late 1990s responded by terminating some underfunded federally mandated programs and shifting a few other federal programs to the states. Governors and state legislators now face the challenge of reworking old federal welfare programs as state welfare programs with cutbacks in federal grants.

Reelection and Raising Taxes

About 75 percent of incumbent governors who run for reelection are reelected.[7] Nearly three-quarters of elections for governor are scheduled for nonpresidential or midterm election years (for example, 2006); Kentucky, Louisiana, Mississippi, New Jersey, and Virginia elect governors in odd-numbered years. Reformers have successfully argued that presidential and gubernatorial elections should be separated so that governors are not subject to the tides of national politics.

Why are some governors not reelected? Incumbency is not always an advantage. Governors have to make tough decisions, which can antagonize major interests and arouse public criticism. Governors in Arizona, Alabama, Arkansas, and Oklahoma left office in recent years because of personal scandals. Governors in Oregon and Kansas left because they had such low approval ratings in the polls that they chose not to run again. Incumbents sometimes lose because of a depressed state economy or because they increased state taxes and became unpopular. In 1993, for example, New Jersey Governor James Florio was narrowly defeated by Christine Todd Whitman due in part to a recession but mostly because Florio had recommended, and the legislature had enacted, a major tax increase. That tax increase came back to haunt Florio when he ran for U.S. senator in the New Jersey Democratic primary in 2000. His opponent, Jon Corzine, ran ads stressing Florio's role as a big spender and won the primary.

Circumstances often dictate what a governor can or cannot do. The health of the state's economy and the public's attitude toward proposed programs are critical factors. The good economic times in the late 1990s plainly helped most governors who ran for reelection. Thus in 1998, all but two of the 25 incumbents who ran for reelection were victorious; in 2000, all but one of the six who ran for reelection won another term. In November 2002, 12 incumbent governors won reelection, yet 4 incumbents were defeated.

Some candidates for governor effectively campaign on promises to cut taxes. Republican James Gilmore in Virginia won a landslide victory in his race for governor by repeatedly saying "No Car Tax"—a reference to a highly unpopular personal property tax on cars, trucks, and motorcycles. George Pataki became governor in New York by pledging a property tax reduction.[8]

Because voters reward frugality and sometimes punish elected officials for tax increases, most governors go to considerable lengths to avoid having to raise taxes, especially with an election approaching. Indeed, many politicians believe that a governor who proposes new taxes will face defeat in the next election, although some studies cast doubt on this fear.[9] Voters and legislatures often go along with governors who can make a compelling case for new revenues and new investments. When governors request a tax increase targeted for a specific worthy cause (for example, improving the schools), voters often support them. This is especially true if "political leaders are candid about why they need the money, sensible and fair in how they intend to spend it and courageous enough to lead the fight themselves. Americans are neither selfish nor short-sighted on taxes—they just want assurance that their money will be spent wisely."[10] Several governors around the country have proposed and campaigned for *investment taxes* (that is, taxes that could be invested in building better highways or increasing teachers' salaries) and became popular because of their targeted efforts to improve their state.

A Governor's Formal Powers

Before the American Revolution, royal governors, appointed by and responsible to the British crown, had broad powers, including extensive veto power over the voter-elected colonial legislatures. As anti-British sentiment increased, royal governors became more and more unpopular. The position of state governor in the new Republic was born in this atmosphere of distrust. In the 1770s and 1780s, state legislatures elected state governors, a method that ensured that governors would remain under the control of the people's representatives. The early state constitutions also limited governors to few powers and terms of just a year or two.

Gradually, however, the office of governor grew in importance. In New York, the position of chief executive was sufficiently developed and effective by 1787 that it became one of the main models for the proposed American presidency. If we compare the formal sources of authority in the U.S. Constitution and in a typical state constitution, we see significant differences. "The executive Power," says the Constitution, "shall be vested in a President of the United States of America." Compare this statement with its counterpart in a typical state constitution: "The executive department shall consist of a Governor, Lieutenant Governor, Secretary of State, Treasurer, Attorney General," and perhaps other officials. Unlike the president, the governor *shares* executive power with other elected officials. Most state constitutions go on to say, however, that "the supreme executive power shall be vested in the Governor, who shall take care that the laws be faithfully executed." Thus the public looks to the governor for law enforcement and the management of bureaucracies. In some states, the governor has been given authority to supervise the activities of local prosecutors.

Twenty-four states have strengthened the governorship by making the lieutenant governor run with the governor as a team so that the chief executive is less likely to be paired with a hostile lieutenant governor. In 39 states, the lieutenant governor, like the U.S. vice president, takes over executive office responsibilities if for any reason the governor cannot fulfill the duties of the office. Most important, in almost all states, the governor presents the state budget to the legislature and controls spending after the budget has been approved. Thus state officials must look to the governor as well as the legislature for funds.

The constitutional powers of governor vary from state to state (see Table 26-1). Yet regardless of a governor's formal constitutional authority, a governor's actual power and influence depend on his or her ability to persuade.[11] This power, in turn, usually depends on the governor's reputation, popularity, knowledge of what should be done, and, of course, ability to communicate. Governors must have political skills as well as constitutional authority if they are to provide leadership.

To supplement their formal constitutional powers, governors may hold town meetings around the state, appear on radio and television talk shows, or invite legislators and other influential party and policy leaders to the executive mansion for lobbying and consultation sessions. Remember, however, that not all states vest great constitutional power in the governor. Whether the state constitution defines a strong role is just one of the factors in determining the effectiveness of a governor.

Most governors have the following constitutional authority:

- To make appointments
- To prepare the state budget
- To veto legislation and to exercise an item veto over appropriations measures
- To issue executive orders
- To command the state National Guard
- To pardon or grant clemency
- To help establish the legislature's agenda

California Governor Gray Davis. Davis enjoyed serving as governor during the boom times of the late 1990s but faced staggering state deficits after his reelection in 2002.

TABLE 26–1 Rankings of States According to the Formal Powers of the Governor	
Strong	
Maryland	Ohio
New Jersey	Pennsylvania
New York	Utah
Moderately Strong	
Alaska	Nebraska
Colorado	North Dakota
Connecticut	South Dakota
Iowa	Tennessee
Kansas	West Virginia
Michigan	Wisconsin
Minnesota	Wyoming
Montana	
Moderate	
Arizona	Louisiana
California	Maine
Delaware	Massachusetts
Florida	Missouri
Hawaii	Nevada
Idaho	New Mexico
Illinois	Oregon
Indiana	Texas
Kentucky	Virginia
Weak	
Alabama	Oklahoma
Arkansas	Rhode Island
Georgia	South Carolina
Mississippi	Vermont
North Carolina	Washington
New Hampshire	

SOURCE: Adapted from Thad L. Beyle, "The Governors," in *Politics in the American States: A Comparative Analysis,* 7th ed., eds. Virginia Gray, Russell Hanson, and Herbert Jacob (CQ Press, 1999), pp. 210–211.

Note: Rankings are based on budget powers, appointive and organizational powers, tenure potential, veto powers, and party control.

Appointive Power

Perhaps a governor's most important job is to recruit talented leaders and managers to head the state's departments, commissions, and agencies.[12] Through recruitment of effective people and prudent delegation of responsibilities to them, a governor can provide direction for the state government.

In most states, the governor is one executive among many, with only limited authority over elected officials, whom the governor can neither appoint nor dismiss. And if these officials are from a different political party than the governor, they are likely to oppose the governor's recommendations. Governors have greater, yet still limited, power over officials they appoint. Some governors appoint hundreds of key officials; others, such as those in Mississippi, South Carolina, and Texas, have severe restrictions on their appointive power. Moreover, in most states, governors must share their appointive power with the state senate and may remove people only when they have violated the law or failed in their legal duties. State administrators whose programs are supported by federal funds also have a measure of independence from the governor.

But along with the appointive power comes a host of challenges. First, salaries for cabinet and agency administrators are modest in many states, especially in the smaller ones, and it is often hard to get people to leave better-paying jobs in private industry. The situation is even worse when the state capital is in a remote or rural section of the state. Second, powerful politicians may demand that their friends be appointed to certain top posts, and they may threaten to be uncooperative if the governor does not go along with their "suggestions." Finally, relatively high turnover in many state positions often hampers a governor's efforts to carry out programs.

Fiscal and Budgetary Power

A governor's financial planning and budgetary powers are key weapons in getting programs passed. Purchasing, budgeting, and personnel matters are centralized under the governor. When implemented by a strong staff and backed by a strong political base, a governor's fiscal powers are extremely important.

In almost all states, the governor has responsibility for preparing the budget and presenting it to the state legislature. This takes place every year in 30 states and every second year in 20 states. The art of budget making involves assessing requests from various departments and agencies and balancing them against available resources. Governors and their staffs have to calculate the costs of existing and newly proposed programs and weigh those costs against estimated revenues for the state.

This is how the budget process works in most states. In May and June, the governor's budget office, which may be called Office of Management and Budget or Department of Administration, sends request forms to the various executive agencies. From July to October, the agencies complete their detailed requests and send them back for consideration. Their requests are invariably 10 to 15 percent higher than what is available and also much higher than the governor's proposed guidelines. The governor's budget chief evaluates all requests, sometimes holds internal administrative hearings, and then makes recommendations to the governor. Finally, the governor presents the recommendations to the legislature at the beginning of the new year.

Although the governor and chief budget officials may appear to control the budgetary process, considerable budgeting influence remains in the hands of the executive branch agencies. Further, a governor's budget reflects to a very high degree budgetary decisions made over the years (costs such as prisons or state universities that will not be shut down), so what governors end up doing in practice is tinkering or adjusting at the edges of the overall budget.

The final budget document is presented to the legislature for adoption as an *appropriations measure.* State moneys cannot be spent without legislative appropriations. Legislators can, and usually do, make a number of alterations in a governor's budget. In theory, a legislature controls all state activities through the budget process because it has the final say in approving the budget. In practice, however, most legislatures do not review every budgetary item; they merely trim or make additions at the margins. Hence budgets reflect the policy views of those responsible for their preparation—namely, the governor and the governor's budget office. A governor who has control over the budget and uses this power effectively has an important asset.

Most states spend at least 40 percent of their state's budget on education. Welfare assistance, highways, prisons and criminal justice programs, health and rehabilitation efforts, and state parks and recreation consume other large portions of the budget. Fifty percent of a state's revenue usually comes from taxes; another 20 percent comes from federal sources. When state revenues do not match expenses, governors have to cut or delay programs, since state constitutions as a rule require a balanced budget, and states cannot print money as the federal government can.

"Nobody Listens to Me!"

Governor Samuel W. Pennypacker, Pennsylvania's chief executive from 1903 to 1907, once told how he had come to office eager to take care that the laws of the state were faithfully executed. Looking around to see what tools he had to carry out this responsibility, he discovered that the only people to whom he could look for help were his secretary, the janitor, and his chauffeur. The prosecutors and police, locally elected and locally controlled, were subject to little or no gubernatorial supervision. The attorney general was elected independently by the voters and was not responsible to the governor. Of course, the governor could call out the National Guard, but this was a clumsy way to enforce the law. So Governor Pennypacker created the state police. Today all states have a police organization.

veto

Rejection by a president or governor of legislation passed by a legislature.

item veto

Right of an executive to veto parts of a bill approved by a legislature without having to veto the entire bill.

reduction veto

The power of governors in a few states to reduce a particular appropriation.

amendatory veto

The power of governors in a few states to return a bill to the legislature with suggested language changes, conditions, or amendments. Legislators then decide either to accept the governor's recommendations or to pass the bill in its original form over the veto.

executive order

Directive issued by a president or governor that has the force of law.

Veto Power

Among the most useful gubernatorial powers is the **veto**, the power to conditionally reject legislative bills, especially appropriations measures. For example, Governor Jeanne Shaheen in New Hampshire vetoed a bill in 2000 that would have repealed the death penalty in her state, and in 1997, New Mexico's governor, Gary Johnson, vetoed legislation that would have allowed the early release of some nonviolent criminals.[13]

In all but eight states, governors have the **item veto**, which permits them to veto individual items in an appropriations bill while signing the remainder of the bill into law. Thus they can influence the flow of funds to the executive departments and thereby attempt to control their activities.

In several states, a governor can reduce particular appropriations; this power is called the **reduction veto**. In 19 states, governors can exercise what is called an **amendatory veto**, which allows the governor to return a bill to the state legislature with suggested language changes, conditions, or amendments. In this last case, legislators must decide to accept the governor's recommendations or approve the bill in its original form, which in some cases requires a majority vote and in other cases a three-fifths or supermajority vote.

State legislatures can override a governor's veto; in most states, it takes a two-thirds majority of both legislative chambers. Some governors, like Wisconsin's Tommy Thompson, vetoed thousands of legislative measures. New York Governor George Pataki vetoed 1,379 provisions the legislature sent him in 1998.[14] Governors on average veto about 4 percent of the bills sent to them, but only about 2 percent of gubernatorial vetoes are overridden by legislatures.[15] Most governors believe the veto power should be used sparingly. Indeed, some observers think too frequent use of the veto is a sign of gubernatorial weakness because an effective governor usually wins battles through negotiations rather than by confronting state legislators.[16]

Legislators in several states have established a *veto session*—a short session following adjournment—so they can reconsider any measures vetoed by their governor. This is clearly an effort to reassert the legislature's check-and-balance authority in relation to the governor. Most states using veto sessions have legislatures that meet for a limited time; in full-time legislatures, a veto session would be unnecessary.

Executive Orders

One long-standing power of governors is their authority to issue **executive orders** that have the force of law. Even though executive orders differ from statutes or formal acts passed by the legislature, they have almost the same binding effect. Depending on the state, governors get their authority to issue executive orders from implied powers as chief executive, from specific constitutional grants, or from delegations of authority by their state legislatures. Executive orders supplementing a law are both more detailed and more important than the general guidelines contained in legislation. Governors have issued executive orders during such emergencies as natural disasters and energy crises, in compliance with federal rules and regulations, and to create advisory commissions. State legislators are sometimes angered by sweeping executive orders. They insist that they, not the governors or the courts, should be the primary lawmakers in a state.

In 1996, Governor Kirk Fordice of Mississippi issued an executive order banning same-sex marriages in his state. The intended effect of Fordice's executive order was to prevent county clerks from issuing marriage licenses for gays or lesbians after a similar measure had failed to win passage in the state's legislature.[17] Gay rights activists, joined by the Mississippi American Civil Liberties Union, criticized the governor, saying he was trying to circumvent the state legislature, adding that the state's constitution makes it plain that it is the legislature, not the governor, who defines the authority and duty of county clerks. In this instance, this governor's executive order brought about what the state legislature had not been able to approve.

Commander in Chief of the National Guard

Emergencies enhance the authority of an executive because they call for decisive action. As commander in chief of the state's National Guard when it is not in federal service, a governor may use this force when local authorities are inadequate—in case of riots, floods, and other catastrophes. The National Guard has played a role in the aftermath of floods in midwestern states, riots and earthquakes in California, fires in Florida, and hurricanes throughout the southeastern states. In most states, the state police are also available for emergencies.

Congress provides most of the money to operate the National Guard. This fact, along with the supremacy clause of the U.S. Constitution, gives Congress and the president the power to take charge of a state's National Guard even against the wishes of a governor. In 1990, the Supreme Court ruled unanimously that Congress can authorize the president to call National Guard units to active duty and send them outside the United States despite the objections of the governors, several of whom had tried to keep President Ronald Reagan from calling their respective National Guards to training exercises in Honduras.[18] States could if they wish provide and maintain from their own funds a defense force exempt from being drafted into the armed forces of the United States, but none has done so.

As commander in chief of the state's National Guard when it is not in federal service, a governor may use this force to handle state emergencies such as fires, floods, earthquakes, and other disasters. Here Oregon Governor John Kitzhaber visits with National Guard troops at the Quartz Fire in southern Oregon.

Pardon Power

In half the states, governors may pardon violators of state law; in the other states, they share this duty with a pardoning board. Except in cases of impeachment or certain specified crimes, the governor may pardon the offender, commute a sentence by reducing it, or grant a reprieve by delaying the punishment. The governor is normally assisted by pardon attorneys or pardon boards that hold hearings and determine whether there are sufficient reasons for a pardon.

A Tennessee governor, Ray Blanton (1975–1979), caused considerable controversy and sparked a federal investigation when he pardoned or paroled several dozen convicts just before leaving office in 1979. Critics charged that some of these convicts allegedly "purchased" their releases. Blanton's misuse of his pardon powers created such a ruckus that his elected successor, Lamar Alexander, was sworn in early and the locks to the governor's office were quickly changed so Blanton was not able to enter the office, let alone grant any additional pardons. Seldom, however, is the pardon power the subject of such controversy, because it is generally administered with appropriate care.

Similar to the governor's pardon power is the authority for a governor to grant a stay of execution in death penalty cases. This is one of the most controversial aspects of executive power in states that provide for the death penalty.[19] While he was governor of Texas, George W. Bush came under attack from many people because more than 130 Texas inmates had been executed; yet he insisted all were guilty as charged. Former Illinois Governor George Ryan, also a Republican, won national attention in 2000 for imposing a moratorium on executions in his state. Ryan had long been a death penalty supporter, but he became persuaded that too many mistakes had been made by the courts in sentencing innocent people to death row. Indeed, 13 Illinois inmates in the past generation had been exonerated. "A series in *The Chicago Tribune* found that of 266 capital cases that had been appealed, fully half have been reversed for a new trial or sentencing hearing. In more than 30 cases, lawyers representing death row inmates were disbarred or suspended."[20] During the moratorium, Ryan established a special committee to make recommendations regarding Illinois death penalty procedures. The Ryan Commission report recommended a series of reforms aimed at creating a more just system of capital punishment.[21] Before leaving office in early 2003, Ryan commuted all Illinois death sentences to prison terms of life or less.

Policy-Making Influence

How much policy-making influence do governors have? Obviously, they can send detailed policy and program messages to their legislature and argue for their programs. In some states, they can trade appointive jobs for legislative support, and they can also use their veto power to trade for votes. They can attract more public attention to their views

Former Illinois Governor George Ryan. A conventional politician in most ways, Ryan was plagued by various scandal accusations. Yet he will be remembered mostly for his bold and controversial review of death penalty practices in Illinois and for his criticism of state-sponsored executions. He commuted the death sentences of 163 men and 4 women to prison sentences of life or less.

than any single legislator can. Much depends on a governor's ability, political base, and personal popularity, as well as on the political situation in which he or she operates.

Some states have a long tradition of strong executive leadership. When governors have the support of powerful political organizations, as well as ample constitutional authority, the chances for their success increase. The governors of Pennsylvania and New York, for example, have strong constitutional powers, and they usually have strong party organizations behind them, which enhance close ties with followers in their respective legislatures.[22] Figure 26-1 shows the current political party control of governorships.

The governor of Nevada has much less formal power than the governor of New York and carries less weight on the national political scene, yet within Nevada, control over jobs, contracts, and patronage enhance the governor's prestige. Governors of rural and smaller states generally have few other competing institutions or interests when exercising policy leadership.[23] "Powerful governors in large urbanized states have many others with whom they must compete—heads of major industries, media personalities, mayors of large cities, and even presidents of prestigious universities," comments political scientist Thad Beyle. "There are lots of big fish in a larger pond, which can mean that a governor may not be as powerful as it might first appear."[24]

Consider these two contrasting evaluations of the governorships in New York and Mississippi:

> The office of governor of the Empire State is surely not small. On the contrary, because of substantial grants of formal power in the state constitution, the historical exercise of such power by formidable incumbents, and widespread expectations that the governor provide leadership, the New York governor is one of the strongest in the nation.[25]

> Mississippi's governor remained less powerful than the state legislature. The large number of independent boards and commissions and independently elected executive officials limits his ability to effectively manage the executive branch. It is easy for agency heads to "go native" and reflect the views of their co-workers and clients rather than those of the chief executive. . . . The office of governor in Mississippi has nevertheless become more influential in recent years.[26]

Balanced against a governor's formal powers are great obstacles, which may include a hostile legislature, cutbacks in federal funding, a depressed state economy, corrupt party or administrative officials, regional tensions in the state (downstate versus upstate, east

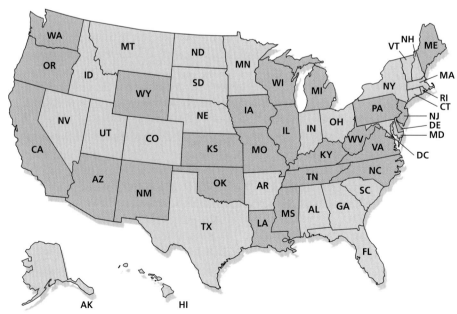

FIGURE 26–1 **Party Control of the Governor's Office, 2003.**

versus west, urban versus rural), special interests and lobbyists, a cynical press, an indifferent or apathetic public, the sheer inertia of a vast bureaucracy, antiquated civil service systems, and the reluctance of most citizens to get involved.[27]

Some western governors complain that many of their states' problems are caused by absentee landlords or the national government, which together control much land in the West. The federal government owns 83 percent of Nevada, 68 percent of Alaska, 65 percent of Utah, and 53 percent of Oregon. This land is managed, regulated, and overseen by a score of federal agencies, such as the National Park Service, the Forest Service, the Bureau of Land Management, the Fish and Wildlife Service, and the Department of Defense. Governors of western states find they must constantly negotiate with these many federal agencies. In contrast, states east of the Rockies have only small amounts of land owned by the federal government. In Kansas and Maine, for example, less than 1 percent of the land is owned by the federal government.[28]

Governors also find they must become preoccupied with daily housekeeping tasks, and this focus often collides with their efforts to define long-range priorities. Former Vermont Governor Madeleine Kunin recalls she had to fix problems as they happened and yet simultaneously had to define her policy vision for the future. "Finding the time, energy, and perspective to carry out a dual strategy was to be the physical and mental challenge of governing."[29] Even though management duties occupy a fair amount of time, many governors consider these the least glamorous of their responsibilities (see Table 26-2).

Although governors come to office hoping to introduce new programs and reforms, they often spend most of their time raising money just to keep things going; hence some governors are viewed as merely budget balancers rather than leaders or shapers of a state's future. The governor's role as leader of his or her political party also has an important impact on policy. The coalitions that governors form within their political parties help them put into effect the policies they desire. A governor's power increases in a state that has a competitive two-party system. In such a state, legislators of the governor's party are likely to work more closely with the governor to produce a successful legislative record.

Recent years have witnessed the election of a new breed of well-educated and able governors who have been effective in enlarging their policy-making roles: Tom Ridge in Pennsylvania, Gary Locke in Washington, Bob Taft in Ohio, John Kitzhaber in Oregon, and Tommy Thompson in Wisconsin. Because many contemporary governors come to office with impressive legislative and administrative experience, they are more likely to be real executive heads of government, not mere figureheads. Some have initiated experimental welfare and job-training programs that have become models for others to emulate. Because states are now playing a larger role in planning and administering a wide range of social and economic programs, the managerial and planning ability of a governor is clearly important.

Governors and Media Relations

A significant source of influence comes to governors who are effective in dealing with the media. Because the media can distribute ideas and help shape public opinion, most modern governors attempt to use newspapers and television to their advantage. Many effectively worked with media during their gubernatorial campaign and therefore understand their potential. Once in office, however, governors are thrust into a defensive rather than an offensive role as they were during the election. Instead of running aggressive advertisements for their campaign, they are now under the media's magnifying glass, subject to scrutiny and dirt digging by reporters. They are quickly evaluated in light of campaign promises and in comparison to previous governors.[30]

Past governors have been very aware of the media, with a handful having professional backgrounds in reporting or public relations. For example, Oregon Governor Tom McCall and Governor Thomas Kean of New Jersey both had prior experience in public

TABLE 26–2   How Governors Say They Spend Their Time

Activity:	Percentage of Time Spent*
Managing state government	29%
Working with the legislature	16
Meeting the general public	14
Performing ceremonial functions	14
Working with press and media	9
Working with federal government	7
Working with local governments	7
Carrying out political activities	6†
Recruiting and appointing	6
Doing miscellaneous activities (staff, interstate, reading, phoning)	16

SOURCE: Thad L. Beyle, "The Governor as Chief Legislator," *State Government,* Winter 1978, p. 3.

*Totals do not add to 100 percent but are averages of the governors' estimates of the time they devoted to the particular activities. Percentages based on responses from those scheduling gubernatorial time in 40 states.

†Plainly, some governors understate time spent campaigning for reelection.

New York Governor George Pataki was a constant positive presence after September 11, 2001. On January 17, 2002 he attended a rally in support of World Trade Center survivors. He is shown here at that rally comforting the sister of a state employee who died in the attacks. He easily won reelection in November 2002.

relations positions—McCall as a journalist and radio announcer and Kean as a state campaign chair for President Ford and a television reporter during the Reagan campaign. Governor Kean notes the importance of communication with the media: "The most important power the governor has is the power of communicating. If that isn't done properly, you lose your power very fast."[31] But not all governors are effective in dealing with the media, nor do they necessarily enjoy it. Minnesota's former Governor Jesse Ventura speaks out about the media: "The American media are suffering from very serious problems, and now I've seen them first-hand. They have the most twisted set of biases I've ever seen. As their whipping-boy-of-choice, I've been in a unique position to see what the media have become. There are a few honorable exceptions, but for the most part, they're corrupt, shameless, and irresponsible as hell."[32]

Each governor tends to have a personal style in dealing with the media. Some are very vocal, preferring to host daily radio or television talk shows, while others prefer to avoid the spotlight unless necessary. To capitalize on the media's ability to disseminate information, governors have been known to request special time on television attempting to explain and make an argument for policy changes, especially tax increases. Others become visible by attending community functions such as building dedications or opening ceremonies or even crowning beauty queens. It is especially important for governors to be publicly active as a calming influence during an emergency situation. During a disaster, such as an earthquake, hurricane, or terrorist action, governors have the ability to call out the National Guard and organize official aid groups. To visit, show concern for, and help ameliorate the suffering of involved families can do wonders for a governor's public opinion ratings. Governors must face public scrutiny yet they can use the media to set and gain support for the state's agenda.[33]

Managing the State

Governors and their senior staffs perform a variety of functions:

- Provide strategic planning and vision
- Restructure ineffective programs and agencies
- Initiate policy
- Maintain a policy or position under pressure
- Settle disputes among different agencies
- Promote the state (attracting tourism, exports, investment)
- Recruit top state administrative and judicial officials
- Propose budget priorities and new revenue strategies
- Improve the quality of services rendered to the taxpayers
- Negotiate disputes with the federal government and with nearby states

Much recent federal legislation turning programs over to the states specifically designates the governor as the chief planning and administrative officer. This role has given governors both more flexibility and more headaches. On one hand, governors can now dispense federal funds as a form of patronage, supporting services and programs for influential professional and local communities. On the other hand, this new intergovernmental relations role requires more time, more staff, and constant negotiations both with the "feds" and with local interest group leaders vying for the money or services involved.

Who Runs the State?

Although most state civil servants are part of the executive branch, they are also subject to pressure from legislators. Indeed, state legislators are often viewed by state employees as having more of an impact on key policy and budget decisions than governors have[34] (see Table 26-3). But as a general rule, governors enjoy a lot of influence. Some agencies are not as cooperative with their governors as governors would like. State agencies operate in a highly political culture, and sometimes bureaucrats are more responsive to interest groups, the legislature, or their own definitions of the public interest.

Some reformers have suggested that all state agencies should be accountable to the governor all the time, but others believe politics should be kept out of the day-to-day operations of a state agency. For example, how much influence should a governor have over the running of the department of corrections in a state? Should public agencies respond to fluctuations in public opinion or to a governor's political mood? Which policy decisions should be made by professionals and experts, and which should be controlled by elected officials or by partisan appointees?

Modernizing State Government

Governors in recent years have had more managerial control over their states as a result of the use of modern management techniques: strategic planning, systems analysis, and sophisticated information technology and budgeting systems. In fact, a modern system of professional management has gradually replaced the old "buddy system" in which governors relied on political pals to get things done.

In urban states with competitive party systems, such as New York, Illinois, New Jersey, Pennsylvania, Washington, and California, governors have considerable formal constitutional authority to organize their administrations as they see fit. Even in more rural states, such as South Dakota, scores of agencies have been consolidated into a few comprehensive units as the result of executive orders from the governors.

A few years ago, in the wake of highly publicized scandals, the South Carolina legislature agreed to abolish 75 state boards, folding them into 17 larger executive agencies. This restructuring also gave the governor the authority to hire and fire the directors of most of these agencies.[35]

During the past several decades, various reformers have urged that the governor be made the true manager of the executive branch. The following principles of reorganization are often suggested:

- Agencies should be consolidated and integrated into as few departments as possible so that similar functions will be grouped together and the governor will be able to exercise real control.
- Lines of responsibility should be fixed and definite.
- Single executives are preferable to boards and commissions.
- The governor should have power to appoint and remove subordinates, including officers now elected, with the possible exception of the auditor.

TABLE 26–3 Gubernatorial Versus Legislative Influence over State Administrative Agencies

		Governor	Legislature	Equal
Who exercises greater degree of control?	1984	42%	35%	23%
	1998	49	27	24
Who exercises more detailed review of agency budget requests?	1984	37	30	33
	1998	35	26	39
Who has a greater tendency to reduce your budget?	1984	36	44	20
	1998	49	27	24

SOURCE: Deil S. Wright, from the 1998 data files of the American State Administrators Project, Institute for Research in Social Science, University of North Carolina.

Note: Questions were asked of top state administrators in all 50 states.

• The governor should have control over budgeting, accounting, reporting, purchasing, personnel, and planning and should have the staff necessary to do these jobs.

However, attempts to reorganize state governments have not received universal praise. In some states, reorganization commissions have submitted reports that were filed away and forgotten. Groups that profit from the existing structure can be counted on to resist change. So, too, can officials who fear loss of job or prestige. Also, legislators are sometimes reluctant to approve recommendations that might make a governor too powerful.

Many critics oppose not so much the idea of reorganization as the basic principle of strengthening executive power and responsibility, which has dominated the reorganization movement. Often, they say, there is little evidence to support the adoption of these reforms, and there is a real danger that reorganizers are overlooking basic values in their concern with saving money. Intent on efficiency and economy, reformers often fail to foresee the risks involved in creating a powerful chief executive where no effective party or legislative opposition exists to keep a strong governor in check.

Reorganizers agree it is wrong to make changes without regard to local conditions and problems. However, they maintain that the basic ideas—integrated authority, centralized direction, simplified structure, clear responsibility—are sound. In fact, it is more likely that narrow special interests not responsible to the voters will take over government when the administrative structure is cumbersome, confusing, and too spread out.

You Decide   Thinking It Through

SHOULD GOVERNORS BE INVOLVED IN POLICY DECISIONS AT A UNIVERSITY?

You Decide... Governors generally leave the running of state universities to boards of trustees, but there have been instances when governors have intervened to impose policies that clashed with the judgment of education professionals. State colleges and universities are dependent on funds appropriated by state legislatures, following recommendations by the governor. Universities and colleges are generally governed by appointed or elected boards of trustees that serve to buffer and protect them from political parties and interest groups. With advice from search committees consisting of representatives of the faculty, staff, alumni, and students, these boards appoint professional university presidents and delegate to them the responsibility for recommending and carrying out university policies.

Governor Pete Wilson persuaded the California Board of Regents to reject the recommendations of the university president, the chancellors, and the academic senate to continue affirmative action policies. The governor wanted the board to remove gender and race as factors that might be considered in recruitment and admission policies. The board followed his recommendation.

Was he right or wrong to intervene?

Thinking It Through... Clearly, any state agency such as a university that uses state tax revenues and provides services to citizens needs a certain amount of regulation and supervision by the people's representatives. The question is how much influence should a governor have? How much influence should a state agency have?

In the final analysis, the governor is accountable to the voters. A governor can be voted out of office, is subject to a recall (in several states), and can be impeached by the legislature. Agency heads can be removed by either the governor or the boards that supervise them. Ultimately, all who exercise public power are, in our complicated political system, held accountable for the way they exercise the power temporarily granted to them. It is often a seemingly messy rather than a tidy way of organizing leadership and accountability, yet generally it works.

The legislature can more effectively supervise an administration integrated under the governor's control than one in which responsibility is split.

Effects of Reorganization

Although large savings have been realized through centralized purchasing and the adoption of modern money management practices, it is difficult to measure the results of consolidating departments, strengthening the governor's control over the executive branch, or establishing an ombudsman office to handle citizen complaints. However, the best-governed states do seem to be those in which the administrative structure has been closely integrated under the governor.

Overall formal reorganization is not the only way states modify and modernize their governmental structures. Often they change in stages, copying innovations from other states. Certain states, in fact, serve as exporters of innovations. So does the federal government. When the federal government creates, say, the Department of Housing and Urban Development, states often respond by creating similar departments; when the federal government establishes the Department of Transportation, so do several of the states; and when the federal government creates a special White House–level office for trade, many governors set up their own offices for trade and export responsibilities.

Although governors are more powerful today than they have ever been, vigorous gubernatorial direction of a state's bureaucracy is still more the exception than the rule. Some governors fail to exploit their powers of appointment or budget setting. "Governors also have other tasks than functioning as chief bureaucrat. . . . Bureaucratic complexity also discourages involvement. Given these realities, involvement with state bureaucracies is very much a matter of governors picking their spots."[36]

Several former governors, including Mario Cuomo of New York and Pete Wilson of California, experimented with private sector reforms such as total quality management (TQM) and performance-based pay initiatives, but these reforms were opposed by public employee labor unions. Such proposals have also been viewed as impractical: "From TQM to vision statements to performance measurements to virtual organizations, the management theories and trends come thick and fast—faster than a lot of government employees can keep up with them."[37] Moreover, management reform often gets cast aside when one governor takes over from another, as when Republican Governor George Pataki replaced Democratic Governor Mario Cuomo in New York.

"Although the analogy between a governor and a private sector chief executive is apt," writes political scientist Thad Beyle, "governors have a distance to go before possessing comparable power of appointment and removal."[38] Many governors don't have the flexibility in hiring and firing personnel that business executives have, and they must share control with various boards, commissions, and elected officials.

In sum, governors can be influential in leading certain reforms and introducing management improvements, but they are rarely as influential and as effective as most citizens assume is the case. All kinds of constitutional, legal, and political restraints put brakes on their attempts to bring about fundamental change. Still, in good economic times, governors are generally able to begin new programs and improve the performance of existing state operations.

Other Statewide Elected Officials

Other executive officials elected by the people in most states include the lieutenant governor, secretary of state, attorney general, treasurer, and auditor (see Table 26-4).

Lieutenant Governor

Forty-two states have a lieutenant governor, a post similar to vice president at the national level. In nearly half the states, the lieutenant governor is elected on the same ticket as the governor, and in those states, the job is indeed like that of the vice president—the

---

TABLE 26–4 States with Elected Officials

Governor	50
Attorney general	44
Lieutenant governor	42*
State treasurer	40
Secretary of state	36
Superintendent of education	14
Agriculture commissioner	13
Comptroller	13
Insurance commissioner	11

SOURCE: *The Book of the States, 2000–2001* (Council of State Governments, 2000), p. 33. Copyright by the Council of State Governments. Reprinted with permission.

In Alaska, Hawaii, and Utah, one elected official serves as both lieutenant governor and secretary of state. In Tennessee, there is no lieutenant governor, but the Speaker of the state senate has the additional statutory title of lieutenant governor.

job and its influence depend very much on the mood of the governor. In 26 states, the lieutenant governor presides over the state senate. In 39 states, the lieutenant governor becomes governor or acting governor in case of the death, disability, or absence of the governor from the state. Doubtless for this reason, more governors have sprung from this office than from other statewide elective offices. For example, in 2000, two lieutenant governors were elected governor: Judy Martz of Montana and Ruth Ann Minner of Delaware. And the lieutenant governor in Texas, Rick Perry, became governor there when George W. Bush moved to the White House. Perry won his own election in 2002.

In states where the governor and lieutenant governor are elected on the same ticket, the lieutenant governor is likely to be given some significant responsibilities. Still, many lieutenant governors have no statutory duties, and in some smaller states, being lieutenant governor is really a part-time job. In the states where the lieutenant governor is elected independently of the governor, the lieutenant governor can sometimes be a member of the opposition party, and he or she can become a thorn in the side of the chief executive. In states like Texas, where the lieutenant governor is elected separately, the lieutenant governor is sometimes as politically powerful as the governor.[39]

Are lieutenant governors really necessary? Eight states, including Arizona, Georgia, and New Jersey, are doing without one. If the job they perform best is assuming the governor's job in case of death, resignation, or impeachment, the replacement function could be performed by a state's attorney general, secretary of state, or the ranking member of the governor's party in the legislature.

Although the position of lieutenant governor has worked well in some states, the view persists that lieutenant governors are often in search of job assignments that make them look important. The staffs and cabinets that are currently growing up around governors make the governor's chief of staff more of a deputy governor than most lieutenant governors. Moreover, many candidates for lieutenant governor appear to seek the post primarily for the name recognition and statewide experience to advance their political careers. In sum, the value to the state of the often obscure office of lieutenant governor is debatable.[40]

Attorney General

The attorney general—the state's chief lawyer—gives advice to state officials, represents the state before the courts, and in some states supervises local prosecutors. Some state attorneys general have real authority over local prosecutors and may prosecute cases on their own initiative, although in most states, criminal prosecution remains under the control of the local county prosecutor. In many states, attorneys general have taken the lead as champions of the consumer and protectors of the environment. They have launched major investigations into the insurance industry and into business practices. They have also led the fight against the tobacco companies and have waged antitrust investigations against corporations such as Microsoft.[41]

An additional power of the attorney general is to make sure the state's laws are implemented properly. Attorneys general work in narcotics enforcement, investigate illegal activities, and often concentrate on laws that affect public safety. For example, Florida's attorney general, Bob Butterworth, recently set up a hot line to help eliminate Medicaid fraud.[42] In California, due to power companies' recent noncompliance with laws and allegations of gouging of California citizens, Attorney General Bill Lockyer has filed complaints against four major power companies.[43]

Disputes between attorneys general and governors can be partisan if they belong to different parties or have conflicting ambitions, but disputes can also be issue-oriented. Thus governors in many states have their own staff lawyers to represent them in contests with attorneys general. The office is sometimes a stepping-stone to the governorship.

Secretary of State

The secretary of state publishes the laws, supervises elections, and issues certificates of incorporation. In some states, the secretary issues automobile licenses and registers corporate securities. Voters in 36 states elect secretaries of state. In eight states, governors appoint people to this position. In three states, secretaries of state are elected by the legislature. And three states don't have this position at all.

This office is sometimes the dumping ground for jobs that do not seem to belong to any other office and are not important enough to justify setting up a new agency. Yet several secretaries of state in recent years have modernized voter registration procedures or sponsored campaign finance and disclosure reforms. For example, former Illinois Secretary of State Jim Edgar, whose office regulated motor vehicles, used a campaign against drunk driving to help propel himself into the governor's office.

Treasurer and Auditor

The treasurer is the guardian of the state's money. Although in some states the job is largely ministerial, state treasurers generally have the responsibility of ensuring that cash is available to meet the obligations of the state and that all available funds are invested to maximize interest return. Texas recently abolished the position.

The auditor in most states has two major jobs: to authorize payments from the state treasury and to make periodic audits of officials who handle state money. In Montana, the state auditor serves as insurance commissioner. Before money can be spent, the auditor must sign a *warrant* certifying that the expenditure is authorized by law and that the money is available in the treasury. This job is more accurately called the *preaudit* and is increasingly being assigned to a comptroller appointed by and responsible to the governor. Auditing *after* money has been spent, however, is a job most observers believe should be given to an officer responsible to the legislature. Even advocates of much more centralized administration believe that the auditor should not be responsible to the governor.

Other Officials

Such positions as superintendent of public education, agriculture commissioner, public utilities commissioner, comptroller, and insurance commissioner are less likely to be elected than treasurers or auditors. Putting positions like these on the ballot results in a longer ballot and voter fatigue; in one election, fully half the people who went to the polls failed to vote for superintendent of public instruction. Proliferation of elected officials also makes it more difficult for governors to manage and lead state government. Think of the kinds of challenges a president of the United States would face if the secretary of defense and the head of the Environmental Protection Agency were elected rather than appointed!

As part of the trend toward integrated administration, the duties of elected state officials have generally been limited to those specified in the state constitution. Some important functions have been given to officials appointed by the governor. In many states, the budget director appointed by the governor has a more important role than the elected treasurer or secretary of state. Yet elected officers can often control patronage, attract a following, and thus develop a political base from which to attack the governor's program and administration.

Sometimes progressive and controversial initiatives in state governments come from elected officials. An attorney general in Texas helped design and pass the Texas Open Records Act, one of the broadest and most strictly enforced freedom-of-information statutes in the country. A secretary of state in Massachusetts modernized election laws, helped enact campaign finance laws, and championed conflict-of-interest reforms. A state treasurer in Colorado battled to transfer some of his state's revenue deposits from a few large Denver banks to smaller banks around the state and devised incentives for these banks to loan money to students and small businesses and to support low-income housing and family farms.

The Rewards of Being a Governor

No one thinks governors have an easy job. Most governors earn praise for their leadership, and most governors enjoy solid public approval ratings.[44] Recent governors—Zell Miller of Georgia, Marc Racicot of Montana, Thomas J. Vilsack of Iowa, Gary Locke of Washington, Frank O'Bannon of Indiana, Mike Foster Jr. of Louisiana—became popular despite the political "heat" and the need to make tough decisions. "A governor achieves his personal best by being honest and by staying in touch with the people who elected him to serve them," says former Governor Lamar Alexander of Tennessee.[45] Former Governor Tom Kean of New Jersey echoed similar thoughts: "I have tried to show during my political career, and especially my years as governor, that responsible government can meet people's needs and bring them together, that government can make a difference in the way we live."[46]

Who are the best governors? A popular former governor of Utah, the late Scott Matheson, wrote that they have been the men and women who have the right combination of values "for quality service, the courage to stick to their convictions, even when in the minority, integrity by instinct, compassion by nature, leadership by perception, and the character to admit wrong, and when necessary, to accept defeat."[47]

GOVERNOR OF TEXAS AND THE VETO

Constitutional restrictions make the Texas governor one of the weakest in the nation. The Texas Constitution sets up a plural executive system, in which the executive officeholders are elected independently of the governor and this fragments authority. The governor has no appointed cabinet and the heads of some of the most important state agencies are independently elected. Such discord makes the coordination of policy difficult and severely limits gubernatorial power. However, the Texas governor has one of the strongest veto powers in the nation. He/she has ten days after passage to sign, veto, or allow legislation to become law without his/her signature.

Go to PoliSim "Governor of Texas and the Veto."

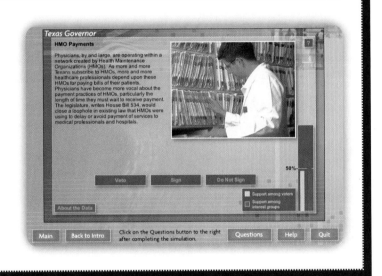

Summary

1. The job of governor is one of the most important and exacting in American political life. Governors are usually white male lawyers in their forties or fifties. At least three out of four governors who run again win reelection.

2. Today, a governor is expected to be the state's chief policy maker, the architect of the state budget, the chief manager of the state administration, and the political and symbolic leader of the state. The governor also plays an increasingly complex role as the crucial link between the national and local governments.

3. Governors have many formal powers. The most important are their appointive and budgetary powers. Governors also have veto and pardon powers and the power to issue executive orders. They are commanders in chief of the National Guard. But a governor's formal powers mean little if he or she is not a persuasive communicator with good judgment and the capacity to focus simultaneously on daily tasks and long-range priorities. Governors who are effective with the media find this an additional source of informal power. Governors help set the policy agenda and frame the debate on important public issues. Yet governors, as a general rule, have more responsibility than power.

4. Over the past generation, reforms in management and organization have strengthened most governorships. Most governors have gained powers that enable them to achieve more of their goals. But constitutional, legal, and political restraints continue to limit their efforts. Thus few governors have an easy tenure, and it is generally agreed that public demands and expectations on governors today are higher than ever.

5. In addition to a governor, the voters in most states also elect other statewide officials such as a lieutenant governor, secretary of state, attorney general, and state treasurer. In about half of the states, the governor and lieutenant governor run as a team ticket, but elsewhere this is not the case, and all other statewide elected officials run separately. Many of the officials play important political and policy roles in their states, and many current governors previously served in some other statewide elected capacity.

Key Terms

veto   reduction veto   executive order
item veto   amendatory veto

Further Reading

LAMAR ALEXANDER, *Steps Along the Way: A Governor's Scrapbook* (Nelson, 1986).

CECIL ANDRUS AND JOEL CONNELLY, *Cecil Andrus: Politics Western Style* (Sasquatch Books, 1998).

THAD L. BEYLE, ED., *Governors and Hard Times* (CQ Press, 1992).

THOMAS M. CARSEY, *Campaign Dynamics: The Race for Governor* (University of Michigan Press, 2000).

THOMAS E. CRONIN AND ROBERT D. LOEVY, *Colorado Politics and Government* (University of Nebraska Press, 1993).

ROBERT S. ERIKSON ET AL., *Statehouse Democracy: Public Opinion and Policy in the American States* (Cambridge University Press, 1993).

EARL H. FRY, *The Expanding Role of State and Local Governments in U.S. Foreign Affairs* (Council on Foreign Relations Press, 1998).

VIRGINIA GRAY, RUSSELL HANSON, AND HERBERT JACOB, EDS., *Politics in the American States: A Comparative Analysis*, 7th ed. (CQ Press, 1999).

MADELEINE M. KUNIN, *Living a Political Life* (Vintage, 1995).

GERALD C. LUBENOW AND BRUCE E. CAIN, EDS., *Governing California* (Institute of Governmental Studies Press, 1997).

SARAH M. MOREHOUSE, *The Governor as Party Leader* (University of Michigan Press, 1998).

DAVID OSBORNE, *Laboratories of Democracy: A New Breed of Governor Creates Models for National Growth* (Harvard Business School Press, 1988).

GEORGE PATAKI WITH DANIEL PAISNER, *Pataki: An Autobiography* (Viking, 1998).

ALAN ROSENTHAL, *Governors and Legislatures: Contending Powers* (CQ Press, 1990).

SUE THOMAS AND CLYDE WILCOX, *Women and Elective Office* (Oxford University Press, 1998).

TOMMY G. THOMPSON, *Power to the People: An American State at Work* (HarperCollins, 1996).

JESSE VENTURA, *Do I Stand Alone?* (Pocket Books, 2000).

JESSE VENTURA, *I Ain't Got Time to Bleed* (Signet, 2000).

See also the quarterly *Spectrum: The Journal of State Government; Governing; State Policy Reports;* and *State Government News;* see also the valuable University of Nebraska Press series on state politics in the individual states, each of which has a chapter on governors.

The National Governors' Association publishes a variety of surveys, reports, and studies, including the weekly *Governors' Bulletin* and the *Proceedings of the National Governors' Association* annual meetings. These and related documents can be purchased by writing to the National Governors' Association, 444 N. Capitol Street NW, Washington, DC 20001.

JUDGES
AND JUSTICE
IN THE STATES

YOU PROBABLY DO NOT KNOW THE NAME OF THE CHIEF JUSTICE OF YOUR STATE SUPREME COURT. YOU ARE NOT ALONE—ABOUT 99 percent of your fellow citizens don't either! Although we hear more about federal judges than about their state counterparts, most of the nation's judicial business is conducted by the 28,000 state and municipal judges. Most of these judges are white males, but this imbalance is changing rapidly. Nationwide there are about 5,000 women state court judges, about one in five, and they are now represented on all but one state supreme court.[1] State judges preside over most criminal trials, settle most lawsuits between individuals, and administer most estates. They also interpret state laws and play a vital role in determining who gets what, where, when, and how. Thus they have a crucial role in making public policy.

State judges have the final say—most of the time. Through **writs of habeas corpus**—petitions to federal courts alleging that petitioners are being held by a state as the result of a proceeding that denies them due process of law in violation of the U.S. Constitution—criminal defendants may occasionally get federal district judges to review the actions of state courts. Or if state judges have to interpret the meaning of the U.S. Constitution, a national law, or a national treaty—that is, if the case raises a *federal question*—the losing party may request that the U.S. Supreme Court review the decision of the highest state court to which it may be taken under state law. Of the hundreds of thousands of decisions by state judges each year, very few are reviewed by the U.S. Supreme Court.

In recent decades, state courts have become more prominent in the political life of their state. In many states, a **new judicial federalism** has emerged, with judges interpreting the bill of rights in their state constitutions more broadly than the U.S. Supreme Court has in applying the national Bill of Rights, in such areas as the right of privacy, public school financing, and equal protection of the law.[2] There has also been a revolution in **tort law**—law relating to compensation for injuries to person, reputation, or property.

Family court judges deal with the legal issues of minors—children under the age of 18.

writ of habeas corpus
Court order requiring explanation to a judge why a prisoner is being held.

new judicial federalism
The practice of some state courts using the bill of rights in their state constitutions to provide more protection for some rights than is provided by the Supreme Court's interpretation of the Bill of Rights in the U.S. Constitution.

tort law
Law relating to injuries to person, reputation, or property.

misdemeanor
A minor crime; the penalty is a fine or imprisonment for a short time, usually less than a year, in a local jail.

felony
A serious crime, the penalty for which can range from death to imprisonment in a penitentiary for more than a year.

This "tort revolution" has flooded state courts as more people sue more often about more disputes. For example, *product liability suits* are brought by people who believe they have been injured as the result of faulty products, and *malpractice suits* are brought by people who believe they have been injured as the result of mistakes by doctors, hospitals, lawyers, and other professionals. And there have been notable increases in cases relating to property rights and breaches of contract. However, this has triggered a backlash against the explosion of tort filings, and many states have instituted legislative tort reforms making it more difficult to bring lawsuits.

There has also been a significant increase in criminal cases as people press for tougher action against criminals. Many states have passed so-called three-strikes-and-you're-out laws, which prescribe a mandatory life sentence after three felony convictions. These felony cases are threatening to overwhelm our courts and our prisons.

As state courts have become more active in our political life, state judges have become embroiled in controversial issues. And as the public has grown more sophisticated about the importance of judges as policy makers, judicial politics in the states is becoming a significant feature of the political landscape.

The Structure of State Courts

Each state has its own court system. Because the 50 systems vary, it is difficult to generalize about them. For convenience, we categorize and discuss state courts as (1) minor courts of limited jurisdiction, (2) trial courts of general jurisdiction, and (3) appellate courts (see Figure 27-1).

Minor Courts

In most states, minor courts handle **misdemeanors**—relatively minor violations of state and local laws—as well as traffic cases and civil suits involving small amounts of money. In some places, they also hold preliminary hearings and set bail for more serious charges. **Felonies** are serious crimes, the penalty for which can range from imprisonment in a penitentiary for more than a year to death. They are tried in trial courts. Decisions of the minor courts may be appealed and in most instances tried *de novo*—that is, tried all over again without reference to what happened in the minor courts. In most places, these courts are financed and administered by the local unit of government—the township, city, or county. In cities, these minor courts are known as *municipal courts* and are often divided into traffic courts, family courts, small claims courts, and police courts. Paid *magistrates* trained in the law preside over most of these courts.

Although traditional justice of peace courts are being phased out, the *justice of the peace* system survives in some states (Arizona, Arkansas, Delaware, Louisiana, Montana, Texas, and Wyoming) and in rural areas; in New York, these civil authorities are called *town justices*. Justices of the peace are elected for short terms, usually two to six years. They need not be trained in the law, and their authority is limited to performing marriages, notarizing papers, handling traffic violations, and hearing misdemeanors, usually those involving fines of less than $200. They also hear minor civil disputes. Because plaintiffs can often choose among several justices of the peace in a county, they may pick the one most likely to decide in their favor. Thus it has been said that the initials for *justice of the peace,* JP, stand for "judgment for the plaintiff."

Courts handling minor crimes are often so crowded that cases are "processed" with little time for individual attention. While many critics of the legal system contend that judges are too lenient and criminals are back on the streets too quickly, others charge that poor and ignorant defendants often spend days in jail waiting for their cases to go to trial. A new and apparently effective reform is the establishment of *court-watching groups.* In some cities, these groups are sponsored by organizations concerned with seeing that the courts treat those charged with crimes fairly. In other cities, groups are sponsored by organizations concerned that judges are too easy on defendants. Prosecutors, public de-

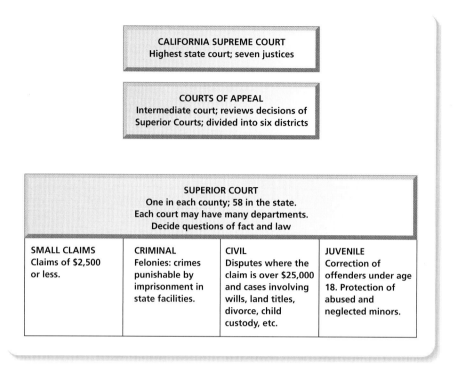

FIGURE 27–1   The California State Courts.

Source: Guide to California Courts, at www.courtinfo.ca.gov/reference/guide.

fenders, and judges, it is alleged, become a comfortable work group, with little or no public scrutiny. Court watchers make these professionals more sensitive to the views of the general public.

Trial Courts of General Jurisdiction

Trial courts where cases first appear (**original jurisdiction**) are called county courts, circuit courts, superior courts, district courts, and common pleas courts. They administer common, criminal, equity, and statutory law. Some states maintain separate courts for criminal and civil matters. States generally also have special *probate courts* to administer estates and handle related matters. These courts are all *courts of record* in which trials take place, witnesses are heard, and juries render verdicts, although most cases are heard and decided by a judge. *Appellate courts* may review decisions of trial courts; however, most decisions of trial judges are not reviewed and are final. There is a growing recognition that these courts do more than apply the law; they also participate in the never-ending process of shaping the law and public policy.[3]

Appellate Courts

In a few states—Delaware, Montana, New Hampshire, Nevada, North Dakota, Rhode Island, West Virginia, and Vermont—trial court decisions are appealed directly to the state supreme court. (In North Dakota, the supreme court can assign cases to a court of appeals composed of three judges chosen from among the trial judges.) Most states, however, have intermediate appeals courts that fit into the system in much the same way that the United States courts of appeals fit into the federal structure.

All states have a *court of last resort,* usually called the supreme court. In Maine and Massachusetts, the court of last resort is called the supreme judicial court; in Maryland and New York, this court is called the court of appeals; in West Virginia, it is the supreme court of appeals. And if that is not confusing enough, in New York, the trial courts are called supreme courts. Texas and Oklahoma have two courts of last resort—a supreme court that handles civil matters and a court of criminal appeals.

original jurisdiction
The authority of a court to hear a case "in the first instance."

"Due to an overcrowded prison system, I'm sentencing you to stand in that corner for the next six months."

The Wall Street Journal.

Unless a federal question is involved, state supreme courts are the highest tribunal to which a case may be appealed. State courts of last resort have five to nine judges; most have seven. Each state court has developed its own method of operating, with the pattern and practices varying widely among the states. Of the more than 60,000 decisions by state supreme courts, only 2 percent are appealed to the U.S. Supreme Court, which reviews even fewer of them.[4]

All state judges of all state courts take an oath to uphold the supremacy of the U.S. Constitution, and all state judges have the power of **judicial review**. That is, they may refuse to enforce, and may restrain state and local officials from enforcing, state laws or regulations or actions if they conclude that these conflict with the state constitution or the U.S. Constitution. State judges may also declare actions of federal officials or federal laws or regulations to be in conflict with the U.S. Constitution, subject to final review by the U.S. Supreme Court.

State supreme courts have also led the way in making judicial decisions available on the Internet. All have Web sites, and about 98 percent provide access to written opinions and decisions, along with other information, and 10 percent make oral arguments available.[5] The Web site of the National Center for State Courts (www.ncsconline.org) provides links to state court Web sites.

State Courts and State Politics

Judges are a much more prominent part of the American political scene, at both the national and state levels, than in other countries. But state courts differ from federal courts in a number of ways:

1. State judges are more likely to decide cases involving their legislative and executive branches than the U.S. Supreme Court is with respect to congressional and presidential matters.[6] State judges are likely to be part of the state's legal culture, since most of them have been educated in the state's law schools.[7]

2. State judges are unconstrained by the doctrine of federalism in dealing with local units of government.

3. State judges are much less constrained than federal courts from hearing cases brought by taxpayers. In federal courts, persons lack *standing to sue*—the legal right to sue—unless they show some immediate personal injury. In fact, in nine states, the state supreme court can give advisory opinions at the request of the governor or state legislature. An **advisory opinion** is an opinion unrelated to a particular case that gives a court's view about a constitutional or legal issue.

4. Unlike federal judges, most state judges serve for limited terms and stand for election, so they can claim to be representatives of the people. "As elected representatives, like legislators, they feel less hesitant to offer their policy views than do appointed judges."[8] In addition, if there is dissatisfaction with a decision of a state supreme court, it can be more readily set aside than a decision of the U.S. Supreme Court can.[9]

How Judges Are Chosen

Judges are selected in four different ways (see Figure 27-2): appointment by the governor, election by the legislature, popular election, or a modified appointment plan known as the Missouri Plan.

Appointment by the Governor and Election by the Legislature

In Delaware, Hawaii, Maine, New Jersey, New York, and Vermont, judges are appointed by the governor and confirmed by the state senate. In Delaware and Massachusetts, governors select appointees from names submitted by judicial nominating commissions.

judicial review
The power of a court to refuse to enforce a law or a government regulation that in the opinion of the judges conflicts with the U.S. Constitution or, in a state court, the state constitution.

advisory opinion
An opinion unrelated to a particular case that gives a court's view about a constitutional or legal issue.

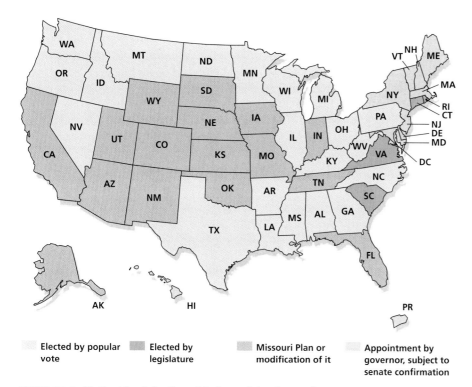

FIGURE 27–2 **Method for Selection of Judges of the Court of Last Resort.**

SOURCE: *The Book of the States, 2000–2001* (Council of State Governments, 2002), p. 53.

Election by the legislature is the constitutional practice in Connecticut, Rhode Island, South Carolina, and Virginia. However, we need to look beyond the formal election procedures. "A majority of the judges serving in states utilizing an elective judiciary . . . are in fact initially appointed by the governor to fill mid-term vacancies, usually occasioned by the retirement or death of sitting judges . . . and these appointed judges are overwhelmingly favored in their first electoral bids following appointment."[10]

In addition to the formal process of nomination and selection, there are several informal processes. Lawyers interested in becoming judges may make their interest known either directly or indirectly to party officials; leaders of the local bar associations may promote favored members; various members of the bar may seek out candidates and recruit them. Political leaders and interest groups also participate. Following such suggestions, the names go through the formal appointment process.[11]

Popular Election

In nearly half the states, judges are chosen in elections. Some states, mostly in the West and upper Midwest, hold *nonpartisan* primaries for nominating judicial candidates and elect them on nonpartisan ballots. But nonpartisan judicial elections do not necessarily mean that political parties are not involved. In at least half of the states with nonpartisan judicial elections, parties actively campaign on behalf of candidates. Some states try to isolate judicial elections from partisanship by holding them separately from other elections. However, more than 80 percent of state judges face elections, which are becoming increasingly contentious.[12]

In 1986, California amended its constitution to forbid political parties from endorsing candidates for judicial office. However, federal courts declared the proposition unconstitutional, and California political parties are once again endorsing judicial candidates. Apparently the prevailing view, as Justice Thurgood Marshall observed, is that "the prospect that voters might be persuaded by party endorsements is not a *corruption* of the democratic political process; it *is* the democratic political process."[13]

In states with elected judges, campaigns can become very competitive.

In recent years, most states have adopted provisions similar to the American Bar Association's code of judicial conduct that bar judicial candidates from telling the electorate anything about their views on legal and political matters—whether they are in favor, for example, of punishing criminals harshly or of expanding privacy rights. In 2000, a "chief justices' summit" was convined by the chief justice of the 17 most populous states with judicial elections and recommended reforms, including public funding for judicial elections and closer monitoring of judicial campaigns. Some states have gone further; the Minnesota Supreme Court, for instance, prohibited judicial candidates from soliciting campaign contributions, declaring their party affiliation, or publicly voicing their positions on controversial issues. But in 2002, the U.S. Supreme Court struck down Minnesota's ban on judicial candidates' announcing their position on controversial legal and political matters as a violation of the First Amendment guarantee of free speech.[14] State and federal courts in Alabama, Georgia, Michigan, Ohio, and other states have also handed down decisions that are "a roadblock for efforts to curb the increasingly raucous nature of judicial politics."[15]

Until recently, there was little interest in judicial elections, and voter turnout tended to be low. But judicial elections are becoming increasingly costly and spirited.[16] In the 2000 elections, candidates for state supreme courts raised an unprecedented $45 million, and interest groups in five states with the most hotly contested judicial races raised an additional $16 million.[17] Special-interest groups focus attention on judges whose decisions they find objectionable. The issues vary from election to election and from state to state. In some states, the issue has been the death penalty. In Texas and California, efforts to limit liability lawsuits and damage awards have led to campaign clashes over judicial candidates, with trial lawyers, consumers, and union groups on one side and business interests on the other. In Idaho, one candidate for the supreme court campaigned on a platform that the theory of evolution could not be true—and won. In Wisconsin, the chief justice won reelection, although she had to fight for her seat and felt compelled to explain why she had once allowed an aerobics class in the court's hearing room. An Illinois judge was unseated because of his decisions in abortion cases. Judges now have to act like politicians and "feel they are under increasing pressure to be accountable to public opinion."[18] The image of impartial courts may well become a casualty of the increasingly heated politics of judicial campaigns and elections.

The costs of judicial elections are escalating. Critics charge that the need to raise large sums for their campaigns compromises judges and judicial candidates. Judicial campaigns have been especially expensive in Alabama, Illinios, Michigan, Mississippi, and Ohio, in which almost $35 million was spent on state supreme court candidates in those five states alone.[19] Nevada has featured attack ads and increasingly expensive campaigns, with judicial candidates turning to the gambling casinos for campaign contributions.[20] In many states that elect judges, it is increasingly clear that judicial candidates are dependent on a small number of law firms or special interests for their campaign funds.

Since the passage of the Voting Rights Act of 1965, minorities have had greater opportunities to be elected judges.

MINORITY REPRESENTATION   The one-person, one-vote rule that applies to legislative elections does not apply to judicial elections.[21] States may create judicial districts so that one judge "represents" many more voters than another judge. However, although there is no requirement that states elect judges, if they choose to do so, the federal Voting Rights Act of 1965 applies to these judicial elections.[22]

Because the Voting Rights Act of 1965 forbids any practice or procedure that dilutes the voting power of minorities, it raises a question about the constitutionality of at-large judicial elections. When judges are elected at large for a city or a state, African American and Hispanic candidates sometimes find it difficult to get elected. African American and Hispanic voters tend to be concentrated in the inner cities or in certain geographical areas; thus their impact is diluted in citywide or statewide elections. For example, in a state in which the population consists of 20 percent African American voters, 20 percent Hispanic voters, and 60 percent Anglo voters, with five judges to be elected on a statewide basis, few if any African American judges or Hispanic judges will be

Female and Minority State Supreme Court Justices

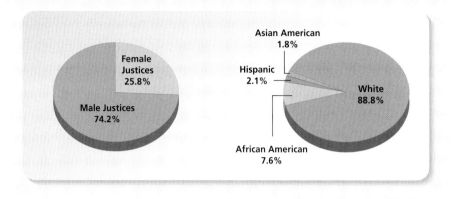

Female Justices 25.8%

Male Justices 74.2%

Asian American 1.8%

Hispanic 2.1%

White 88.8%

African American 7.6%

SOURCE: Chris W. Bonneau, "The Composition of State Supreme Courts," *Judicature* 85 (July–August, 2001), pp. 26–31.

elected. Some Hispanics and African Americans argue that the solution is to divide such a state into five districts, with one judge elected in each district, and draw district lines in such a way that African Americans and Hispanics make up a majority of voters in as many districts as possible, giving them a chance to elect at least one of their own.

Merit Selection: The Missouri Plan

Many lawyers and political scientists have argued in favor of some kind of selection procedure in which there is a screening process before judges are appointed or elected to ensure that only candidates of merit will be considered. One such merit plan is the Missouri Plan.[23] The **Missouri Plan**, as used in most states, provides that when a judicial vacancy occurs, a special *nominating commission* (usually composed of three lawyers elected by the bar, three citizens appointed by the governor, and the chief justice) nominates three candidates.[24] The governor selects one, who then serves as a judge for at least a year. At the next general election, the voters are asked, "Shall Judge X be retained in office?" If a majority of the voters agree, the judge serves a new full term (typically six to 12 years); if not, another person is selected by the same procedure. At the end of his or her term, the judge may ask to have his or her name placed on the ballot, and the voters are again asked whether they want to retain that judge in office.[25] These uncontested elections, in which judges run against their own record, are called *retention elections,* and some require a supermajority vote.

In California, the governor appoints judges to the supreme court and the appellate court for 12-year terms, with the approval of the Commission on Judicial Appointments. The commission consists of the attorney general, chief justice, and senior appellate presiding justice for supreme court appointments or the senior presiding justice in the appellate district for appellate court appointments. In the next statewide election, the judge runs against his or her own record. The governor appoints trial judges to six-year terms; they may be challenged when seeking reelection, but their names do not appear on the ballot if they are running unopposed.

Even more of a hybrid is the system used in New Mexico, where a judicial nominating commission sends names to the governor, who selects a judge. At the next general election, an opponent nominated in the other party's primary may challenge the judge

Missouri Plan
A system for selecting judges that combines features of the appointive and elective methods. The governor selects judges from lists presented by panels of lawyers and laypersons, and at the end of their term, the judges may run against their own record in retention elections.

Standards of Conduct for Judicial Candidates

Citizens for Independent Courts (a program of the Constitution Project) has developed standards that will encourage judicial candidates to seek the "higher ground" in their campaigns. The Higher Ground Standards create a yardstick against which all candidates can be judged. The standards were developed with the assistance of former judges, legal scholars, and good government groups. Almost all of them can be found in judicial canons that govern the behavior of judges. However, the Higher Ground Standards distill volumes of "legalese" into a few concise and easy-to-understand principles.

Judges Are Not Politicians

Judicial candidates should not be political candidates in the traditional sense. Political candidates are expected to represent the interests of a geographically defined group of people. They are expected to be partisan and favor a political party and certain interest groups. As a qualification for election, voters expect them to declare their positions on controversial public policy issues in advance. As surprising as it may sound to some, judges do not, or at least should not, do any of these things.

Judges do not represent constituents. They represent the law. Their decisions must be based on an informed and good faith interpretation of the law and the Constitution, not popular opinion or special interests. Judicial candidates should not support any political or ideological agenda. They should not declare in advance how they would decide a case, since the facts are different in each case. Such a declaration would be the equivalent of an umpire calling a pitch before it's thrown.

The Right to Impartial Justice

If you enter a courtroom as a litigant, you have a right to expect three things:

- That the judge is impartial
- That the judge is fair
- That the judge is knowledgeable about the law

Wouldn't it be distressing if you had a case before a judge who had expressed an opposing position on cases such as yours during his or her campaign? Wouldn't it be equally disconcerting to know that your opponent in the case was a major campaign contributor to the judge? Of course it would. Justice that is absolutely impartial is a cornerstone of democracy. And yet these scenarios are played out in many courtrooms daily. If justice is to remain impartial, the rulings of judges must be independent of popular opinion and political pressure.

Higher Ground Standards for Judicial Candidates

Courts are often the last and best hope for the redress of grievances and the realization of justice. They protect the general welfare from those seeking privileged advantage and preserve individual rights from the heavy hand of government. Our courts can decide cases fairly only when judges are free to make decisions according to the law and constitutional principles, without regard to political or public pressure.

Because of the unique role of judges in our democratic system, candidates for judicial offices must be held to higher standards than candidates for other elected offices. Thus not only must judicial candidates be unbiased and impartial, but they must also avoid any appearance of bias or impropriety. Therefore:

- Candidates should refrain from making promises about how they will decide issues that may come before them as judges, since it would be improper for them to prejudge a case.

- Candidates should solicit or accept campaign funds only through an official campaign committee.

- Candidates should disclose publicly each contributor's name, occupation, and the amount of any contribution of $100 or more (or the amount specified by state law if it is lower) within five days of the donation.

- Candidates should take responsibility for all advertising, statements, and other campaigning done on their behalf by staff and supporters and should condemn all campaigning on their behalf that is misleading or unfair.

- Candidates should not make misleading or unfair references to opponents or misrepresent their records.

- Candidates should conduct themselves in a manner that promotes public confidence in the integrity, independence, and impartiality of the judiciary.

A judge's position is one of great and sacred trust. Judicial candidates should adhere to these and all principles that uphold the dignity of the courts, promote judicial independence, and avoid even the appearance of partiality.

For more information, contact the Constitution Project, 50 F Street NW, Suite 1070, Washington, DC 20001 (www.constitutionproject.org).

in a partisan election. If no opponent is nominated, the incumbent gets a "free ride." Whoever wins that election then serves one term and thereafter runs against his or her own record in a retention election.

Until recently, retention elections generated little interest and low voter turnout.[26] In all, of the almost 4,600 judicial retention elections since 1960, fewer than 60 judges have been removed by voters, although a few judges have decided not to run when they realized they might fail to be retained.[27] Recently, some state supreme court justices have been vigorously challenged in retention elections, especially when their decisions differed appreciably from the mainstream of public opinion and aroused the hostility of significant special interests. Frequently, the charge was that the judge was "soft on crime." A Republican group, the Emergency Florida State Supreme Court Project, raised funds to oppose three Florida Supreme Court justices in their 2002 retention election because they had ruled in favor of Al Gore's request for a hand recount of some ballots in the 2000 presidential elections. Florida limits what justices can say in public and how they may campaign for retention.[28] Interest groups have learned that it is relatively easy to target incumbents, but because of constraints on the way judicial candidates are expected to campaign, it is "difficult for targeted judges to defend themselves."[29]

Most voters know little about judges, and what information they get comes from interested parties and persons, especially those who dislike what the judges have done. To provide a more balanced picture, a few states—Alaska, Utah, Colorado, Arizona, Tennessee—have tried to supply more neutral information about judicial performance. In Colorado, an *evaluation committee* in each judicial district—jointly appointed by the chief justice, governor, president of the senate, and speaker of the house—disseminates information through newspaper supplements, including a final recommendation of "retain" or "do not retain."[30] In Alaska, a judicial council composed of three lawyers, three nonlawyers, and the chief justice provides evaluations that are widely publicized.[31] In Utah, the Judicial Council—consisting of the chief justice, another justice, an appellate court judge, five district court judges, two juvenile court judges, three other lower court judges, a state bar representative, and the state court administration—certifies incumbents, and this certification, or lack of it, is indicated on the ballot.

Even though contested retention elections are the exception, sitting judges are aware that if they make decisions that offend organized interest groups, they may face opposition the next time their names are placed on the ballot. Whether these pressures threaten the independence of the courts or are necessary to ensuring judicial accountability within our political system in which judges play such an important role remains a matter of the political debate.[32]

The Appointive Versus the Elective System

For more than 200 years, people have debated the merits of an appointive versus an elective system for the selection of judges. Those who favor the appointive method contend that voters are generally uninformed about candidates and are not competent to assess legal learning and judicial abilities. Popular election, they claim, puts a premium on personality, requires judges to enter the political arena, and discourages many able lawyers from running for office. They also contend that the elective process conceals what is really going on. Absent name recognition, voters go for party labels, which are increasingly less significant as indicators of ideology.[33] In addition, because retirement and death create many vacancies, it is often the governor who selects the judges. The governor makes an interim appointment until the next election, and the temporary appointee usually wins the election.

Those who favor judicial elections counter that judges should be directly accountable to the people. When judges are appointed, they may lose touch with the general currents of opinion of the electorate. Moreover, the appointive process gives governors too much power over judges. And even if judicial elections do not result in the defeat of many sitting judges, elections serve to foster accountability because judges do not want to be defeated and will try to maintain popular support. In general, bar associations, corporate law firms, and judges themselves tend to favor some kind of merit selection system; plaintiffs, attorneys, women's associations, minority associations, and labor groups are skeptical or opposed.

How Judges Are Judged

Unlike federal judges who hold office during "good behavior"—essentially for life—most state judges are selected for fixed terms, typically six to 12 years. In Massachusetts, New Hampshire, and Puerto Rico, judges serve to age 70; in Rhode Island, they serve for life. Thirty-seven states and the District of Columbia mandate the retirement of judges at a certain age, usually 70.[34]

The states, rather than the national government, have taken the lead in establishing procedures to judge judges. Because impeachment has proved to be an ineffective means to remove judges, today each of the 50 states has a board, commission, or court to handle allegations of judicial misbehavior. Despite the objections of many judges, these

SHOULD JUDGES BE ELECTED OR APPOINTED?

You Decide... Which method produces better judges? The first problem is to define a "good judge." Most people define a good judge as one who makes decisions they like. Even if the desirable features are defined more precisely—ability to maintain neutrality between parties, knowledge of the law, writing ability, personal integrity, physical and mental health, and ability to handle judicial power sensibly—these are still factors that are hard to measure.

Are judges selected by appointment more likely to make decisions of a certain kind than judges chosen by election? Are judges of greater legal knowledge and probity more likely to be selected by one method rather than by another?

Thinking It Through... Some studies point to judicial elections as working against women and minorities. One study found that judicial elections "have a built-in bias for men. . . . Few women, blacks, Hispanics, or Asians have the political connections, financial resources, and campaign sophistication to overcome the stereotype that has the blindfolded woman holding the scales of justice, but a white man sitting at the bench dispensing it."[*] Other studies show that more women are chosen by gubernatorial appointment and merit methods but that African Americans fare as well in judicial elections and nearly as well in legislative ones. Another study found that merit systems tend to produce higher proportions of Protestant judges, in contrast to Catholic and Jewish judges.

There is some evidence that elected judges are more likely to impose the death sentence than either appointed judges or juries.[†] Democratic judges tend to make more liberal decisions than their Republican colleagues do.[‡] And courts to which judges are nominated and elected on a nonpartisan ballot show less partisan division than those whose judges are nominated by party conventions and elected in partisan elections.

[*]John H. Culver, "Politics and the California Plan for Choosing Appellate Judges," Judicature 66 (September–October 1982), p. 158.

[†]Stuart Taylor Jr., "Taking Politics for a Fatal Ride," Recorder, October 30, 1995, p. 6. See also Justice John Paul Stevens, dissenting in Harris v. Alabama, 513 U.S. 504 (1995).

[‡]Sheldon Goldman, "Voting Behavior on the U.S. Courts of Appeals Revised," American Political Science Review 69 (June 1975), pp. 491–506.

commissions are most often composed of both nonlawyers and lawyers. They investigate complaints and hold hearings for judges who have been charged with improper performance of their duties or unethical or unfair conduct. Establishment of these commissions appears to have helped restore public confidence in the state judicial systems.[35] For developments in the states and efforts to establish standards of conduct for judicial candidates, go to www.constitutionproject.org, the Web site of a nonpartisan group dedicated to protecting the independence of courts from partisan political attacks. See also the site of the Brennan Center's Project on Judicial Independence at the New York University Law School, www.brennancenter.org. You can also subscribe to its biweekly e-mail list to get summaries of news stories relating to judicial independence, judicial elections, and judicial appointments. Another valuable site for information about courts is that of the American Judicature Society, www.ajs.org.

The Judicial Reform Movement

Many reforms—court unification, centralized management, state financing, and merit selection—have been adopted, but waste and delay continue to plague our courts. We are, many charge, a "litigious society." Dockets are crowded, relief is costly, and inordinate delays are common.[36]

Proposed reforms for improving the administration of justice include the following:

- Judges should be selected by some kind of merit system that screens candidates in terms of their qualifications.
- Judges should be paid adequately so that they have the financial independence to concentrate on their work and so that successful lawyers will be willing to serve on the bench. In most states, judges' salaries are considerably less than the average incomes of practicing attorneys of the same age and experience. Judges are unable to earn anything beyond their salaries, and they must be cautious about investments in order to avoid conflicts of interest.
- Judges should serve for long terms so that they can make decisions without fear of losing their jobs.
- Rule-making powers should be given to the state supreme court or its chief justice. States are permitting judges to adopt procedural rules and codes of professional conduct. Most require lawyers to continue their education by taking refresher courses.
- Although no person should be appointed or elected to a court solely because of race, sex, or ethnic background, our courts need to become more representative of the communities they serve.[37]
- States should provide for alternative dispute resolution.

Alternative dispute resolution (ADR) refers to procedures that serve as alternatives to formal trials. These procedures include mediation, arbitration, conciliation, private judging, and advisory settlement conferences. From time to time, Congress has made grants to encourage states and localities to develop alternative dispute resolution mechanisms, especially for domestic relations issues. ADRs can be part of the established court system or separate from it in neighborhood justice centers or arbitration and mediation forums. Half the states operate arbitration programs as part of their court system.

Despite the trendy nickname "rent-a-judge," the rather old practice of hiring private decision makers has been revived. These decision makers, often retired judges and lawyers, are paid by the parties to the dispute, who agree in advance to abide by the outcome. In some states, appeals courts can review these decisions. There is some concern that these alternative practices are drawing the best lawyers into the private system, resulting perhaps in one system for the rich, a private one, and one for the poor, a public one.

The judicial reform movement has been successful, but like most reform movements, it has its critics and skeptics. Some observers maintain that court delay is not as serious a problem as has been charged and that the remedies may undercut our system of checks and balances. Delay, for example, often works to the advantage of defendants and their attorneys, who wish to postpone trials. At other times, prosecutors want delays in order to put pressure on defendants to accept guilty pleas. Lawyers may seek delays so that they can accept more clients.

No matter how "modernized" the management of court business, the flow of legal business grows continuously. Some people have proposed that traffic violations, automobile injury cases, and so-called victimless crimes be handled by some procedure other than a court trial. New York has led the way in removing from the courts minor traffic offenses that do not involve serious moving violations; other states are following its lead. No-fault insurance programs could reduce the large number of cases stemming from automobile accidents. Because half the people in prison, as well as half the trials that are held, involve victimless crimes such as using marijuana, *decriminalization* could substantially reduce the load on the courts. Six states, for example, have already repealed statutes on public drunkenness and now consider alcoholism a disease rather than a crime.

The reform of state judicial systems is enmeshed in partisan, ideological, and issue politics. Judges are but one part of the total justice system, and their operations are best studied in the context of the entire justice system.

Is Judicial Independence in Danger?

The role of judges in making decisions that affect the lives of so many people makes it inevitable that they will be subject to criticism. Attacks on judges have always been part of the American political scene. In recent years, however, judges and bar groups are concerned that the intensity and nature of the criticism may be undermining judicial independence. They point to threats to impeach judges because of unpopular rulings, negative campaigns against state court judges that distort their records, and legislative threats to cut judicial budgets. The attack on state courts is perhaps of greater concern because most state judges lack lifetime tenure and are thus much more subject to public criticism, by constitutional design.

The American Bar Association, the American Judicature Society, the Century Foundation, and other groups have started projects to increase public understanding of the role of judges and to build bipartisan support for protecting the independence of judges, both state and federal. For information on judicial independence, go to www.abnet.org, www.ajs.org, www.brennancenter.org, and www.constitutionproject.org.

SOURCE: Linda Greenhouse, "Judges Seek Aid in Effort to Retain Independence," *New York Times,* December 10, 1998, p. A16.

The Justice System

Justice is handled in the United States by a series of institutions that are only loosely connected to each other. In addition to judges, there are juries, prosecutors, defense counsels, public defenders, victims, and defendants. Parole, probation, and prison officials are also part of the justice system.

The Jury

Although most of us will never be judges or serve as professionals in the administration of justice, all adult citizens have an opportunity—even an obligation—to be jurors. Trial by jury in civil disputes is used less often these days; people make settlements prior to trial, elect to have their cases decided by a judge alone, or have their cases referred to a mediator or arbitrator. Furthermore, only a small fraction of criminal cases are actually disposed of by a trial before a jury. Still, jury trials, or the threat of them, remain a key feature of our justice system.

We have moved from a jury system in which service was restricted to white male property owners to one in which jury duty is the responsibility of *all* adult citizens. Today more time and energy are spent in trying to persuade (or coerce) people to serve on juries than in trying to exclude them. Because jury service may be time-consuming and burdensome, many busy people do their best to avoid serving. In the past, judges were often willing to excuse doctors, nurses, teachers, executives, and other highly skilled persons who pleaded that their services were essential outside the jury room. As a result, juries were often selected from panels consisting in large part of older people, those who were unemployed or employed in relatively low-paying jobs, single people, and others who were unable to be excused from jury service. Most states have reacted to these problems by making it more difficult to be excused. In addition, many states have adopted a "one-day, one-trial" policy, which makes jury service less frequent and less onerous. Because jury trials take more time than bench trials (trials before judges) and cost more, some states use juries of fewer than 12 people for some criminal trials. A few states also permit verdicts by less than a unanimous vote. The U.S. Supreme Court has approved these practices, provided the juries consist of at least six persons.[38]

Only a handful of those accused of committing a crime actually stand trial, and only 10 to 15 percent of those who are convicted are declared guilty as the result of a formal trial before either a judge or a jury. Most people who go to prison or who have to pay a criminal fine do so because they plead guilty.

All citizens have an obligation to serve on juries, and lawyers develop skills in selecting people they think may be sympathetic to their client.

The Prosecutor

The prosecutor is largely an American invention, one of the few governmental positions we did not inherit from England. The 18,000 prosecutors in the United States are usually county officials; most are locally elected and subject to little supervision by state authorities. In Connecticut, however, they are appointed by judges, in the Virgin Islands by the attorney general, and in New Jersey by the governor with the consent of the state senate. A prosecutor has "more control over life, liberty, and reputation than any other person in America."[39]

When presented with a case by the police, the prosecutor must decide first whether to file formal charges. He or she may (1) divert the matter out of the criminal justice system and turn it over to a social welfare agency; (2) dismiss the charges; (3) take the matter before a grand jury, which almost always follows the prosecutor's recommendation; or (4) in most jurisdictions, file an **information affidavit**, which serves the same function as a grand jury **indictment**.

A prosecutor who decides not to charge a person accused of some notorious crime is often subject to political pressure and public criticism. But for routine crimes, the prosecutor is politically in a better position to dismiss a charge than the police are. Police are supposed to enforce every law all the time. Of course, it is impossible for them to do so, and they must exercise discretion.[40] But officers who fail to arrest a person alleged to have committed a crime could well be charged with failing in their duty. The prosecutor, however, has more leeway. In fact, the prosecutor is less likely to be criticized for dropping a case because of insufficient evidence than for filing a charge and failing to get a conviction.

Defense Counsel, Public Defenders, and Others

Many defendants cannot afford the legal counsel to which they are constitutionally entitled. The **assigned counsel system** is the oldest system to provide such defendants with an attorney, and it continues to be used, especially in rural areas. Judges appoint attorneys to represent defendants who cannot afford them. Most such attorneys are paid from the public treasury, but sometimes they are expected to do the work *pro bono*—for the public good. Seldom are they given funds to do any investigatory work on behalf of their

information affidavit
Certification by a public prosecutor that there is evidence to justify bringing named individuals to trial.

indictment
A formal written statement from a grand jury charging an individual with an offense; also called a *true bill*.

assigned council system
Arrangement whereby attorneys are provided for persons accused of crimes who are unable to hire their own attorneys. The judge assigns a member of the bar to provide counsel to a particular defendant.

pro bono
To serve the public good; term used to describe work that lawyers (or other professionals) do for which they receive no fees.

A disproportionate number of prisoners tend to be young, poorly educated, black males.

clients. Often judges pick young lawyers just beginning their careers or old ones about to retire. Some less scrupulous lawyers make their living as assigned counsel; because it is often to their financial advantage to do so, they are quick to plead their clients guilty. They are known contemptuously as members of the "cop-out bar."[41]

Dissatisfaction with the assigned counsel system led to the creation of the **public defender system**, first started in Los Angeles in 1914 and now used in most big cities. Under this system, the government provides a staff of lawyers whose full-time job is to defend individuals who cannot pay. This system provides experienced counsel and relieves the bar of an onerous duty. Critics—including some defendants—protest that because public defenders are paid employees of the state, they are not likely to work as diligently on behalf of their clients as they would if they were specifically assigned to those clients. But most observers consider the defender system superior to the assigned counsel system. Steps are being taken to increase the pay of public defenders, protect their independence, and see that they win the confidence of the defendants they represent.

Victims and Defendants

When we talk about our criminal justice system, we sometimes forget the two most important parties in any criminal case—the victim of the crime and the person accused of it.

> The rights of victims or potential victims are not of the same order as the rights of the accused; the rights of the accused are constitutional rights spelled out in amendments, but nowhere in the Constitution is there any mention of the rights of victims or the public. The framers of the Constitution apparently were much more worried about protecting citizens against the government than about protecting citizens from each other.[42]

In general terms, defendants are likely to be "younger, predominantly male, disproportionately black, less educated, seldom fully employed, and typically unmarried. By the time the sorting process has ended, those sent to prison will consist of an even higher proportion of young, illiterate, black males."[43] Victims, too—compared to the rest of the population—tend to be young, black or another minority, and uneducated. A substantial number of victims—either because of lack of knowledge of what to do or fear of doing it, or because, as in the case of rape victims, they believe they have little chance of proving their attackers to be guilty—never report crimes to police and prosecutors.

Our system puts the responsibility for prosecuting criminals on the government. In most instances, victims have no role other than as witnesses. They are not consulted about what the charge should be or asked what they think might be an appropriate penalty. The matter is strictly between the state, represented by the prosecutor, and the accused, represented by an attorney.

Plea Bargaining

Although a large percentage of all criminal cases end with a guilty plea, a common practice is for the prosecution to offer to reduce the seriousness of the charge and sentence if a defendant will enter a plea of guilty to a lesser crime. This practice is called a **plea bargain**. At one time, this practice was universally condemned. Many people still consider there is something improper about it, like bartering away justice.

Critics say that plea bargaining forces people to give up their rights; moreover, defendants often do not get off much more leniently by pleading guilty to lesser offenses than if they stood trial.[44] Defenders of plea bargaining contend it works, producing "a result approximating closely, but informally and more swiftly, the results which ought to ensue from a trial, while avoiding most of the undesirable aspects of that ordeal."[45] Many experts and investigators who have looked into the matter have endorsed plea bargaining.

Plea bargaining offers something to all involved. Prosecutors are able to dispose of cases quickly, avoid long and drawn-out trials, eliminate the risk of losing cases, and build up better "election-worthy" conviction records. The accused avoid the danger of being sentenced for more serious charges by pleading guilty to lesser offenses. Defense attorneys

public defender system
Arrangement whereby public officials are hired to provide legal assistance to those persons accused of crimes who are unable to hire their own attorneys.

plea bargain
Agreement between a prosecutor and a defendant that the defendant will plead guilty to a lesser offense to avoid having to stand trial for a more serious offense.

Victims' Rights

The victims' rights movement, initiated originally by liberals (chiefly feminists concerned about the difficulty of winning prosecutions for rape and about the harsh treatment of women witnesses), gained the support of conservatives who considered the judicial system unfair to victims. In the 1984 Victims of Crime Act, Congress authorized federal funds, which are distributed by the Office of Crime Victims in the Department of Justice, to support state programs compensating victims and to provide funds to some victims of federal crimes as well.

More than 30 states and Congress have adopted so-called Son of Sam laws. They are named after multiple murderer David Berkowitz, who referred to himself as the Son of Sam. Such laws seek to take from convicted criminals any financial gain they might earn from selling the rights to their stories and make these funds available to compensate their victims.

About 30 states have amended their constitutions to provide for a "victims' bill of rights," which makes it easier for victims to recover their stolen property held in police custody. It also gives victims a chance to be heard when prosecutors file formal charges, when judges set bail and impose sentences, and when parole boards consider releasing prisoners.[*] These victims' bills of rights are not without constitutional problems. The U.S. Supreme Court, after first holding to the contrary, has upheld the right of a prosecutor to make statements to a jury in a murder trial about the personal qualities of the victim and to allow such a jury to consider evidence relating to the personal characteristics of the murder victim and the emotional impact of the crime on the victim's family.[†]

Congress has considered passing a victims' rights amendment to the U.S. Constitution. It would give victims the right to be informed of and be present at every proceeding, to be heard at any proceeding involving sentencing, to be informed of any release or escape, and to receive full restitution from the convicted offender.

Under the stimulus of federal matching funds, most states now provide a victims' compensation program. Almost all states now compensate victims or permit victims and their families to sue for civil damages. Yet even if victims win the right to collect damages from the defendants, defendants seldom have the resources to pay the damage awards.

[*]Naftali Bendavid, "Victims Strike Back," *Recorder,* July 3, 1996, p. 14.

[†]*Payne* v. *Tennessee,* 501 U.S. 808 (1991), overruling *Booth* v. *Maryland,* 482 U.S. 496 (1987) and *South Carolina* v. *Gathers,* 490 U.S. 805 (1989).

avoid "the dilemma of either incurring the expense of going to trial with a losing case or appearing to provide no service whatever to their clients."[46] By being able to handle more clients, they can also make more money. Judges are able to dispose of cases on their dockets more rapidly. In fact, were every case tried, it would overwhelm the judicial system.

Once the bargain between the prosecutor and the defendant's attorney has been accepted, the matter is taken before a judge. The judge goes through a series of questions to the defendant: "Are you pleading guilty because you are guilty? Are you aware of the maximum sentence for the crime to which you are entering a guilty plea? Were you coerced into pleading guilty or offered anything in return for it? Are you satisfied with the representation afforded by your attorney?" Following appropriate responses, the plea is accepted.[47] As long as defendants know what they are doing and enter into the bargain intelligently, they waive their constitutional rights to trial by pleading guilty and may not subsequently back out of the arrangement. Prosecutors must also live up to their side of the bargain.[48]

Sentencing

Due process must be observed in sentencing, which takes place in open court. The prisoner must be present and represented by counsel. In many places, social workers are assigned to help the judge determine the proper sentence. The judge also receives recommendations from the prosecution (and in some jurisdictions from the victim as well), hears the arguments of the defense, and then sets the sentence within the limits prescribed by the state.

The judge sets the sentence, but concerns about sentencing permeate the judicial system. One writer has put it this way:

Because police and prosecutors screen out a large proportion of the doubtful cases, most left to be dealt with by the courts are those in which there is no serious dispute over the guilt or innocence of the defendant. . . . This fact sets the tone for the process. . . . Everyone concerned—the defense lawyers, the prosecutor, the judge, the probation officer—becomes aware of the fact that he or she is involved in a process where the primary focus is on deciding what to do with the people who are in fact guilty.[49]

Early in our national history, retribution, deterrence, and protection of society were the primary purposes of sentencing. Then rehabilitation became the major goal, and many people thought it was a more humane approach. The indefinite sentence became popular, motivated by the idea that each prisoner should be considered an individual suffering from an "illness." Each prisoner should be diagnosed, a course of treatment should be prescribed, and if and when such experts as psychologists and social workers could certify a "cure," the prisoner should be released.

Most political leaders and many scholars have become disillusioned about our ability to bring about "cures."[50] Others are disillusioned about the deterrent effect of imprisonment. A comprehensive study of rehabilitative efforts inside prisons, although rejecting the conclusion that "nothing works," nonetheless stated: "We do not know of any program or method of rehabilitation that could be guaranteed to reduce the criminal activity of released offenders."[51]

Moreover, judges may enjoy considerable discretion in sentencing, and they frequently give different sentences to defendants convicted of the same crime.[52] To reduce such disparities in sentencing, several reforms have been suggested, including establishing more precise legislative standards, creating advisory sentencing councils, and adopting the British practice of allowing appellate courts to modify sentences.

Disillusionment with rehabilitation and disparate sentencing by judges, combined with growing concerns about crime in the streets and mounting criticism about alleged judicial leniency, has fueled legislative action for mandatory minimum sentencing requirement and for narrowing judicial discretion.[53] State after state has adopted mandatory prison terms—also known as *determinate sentencing*—for more and more crimes. As noted earlier, a three-strikes-and-you're-out requirement is being adopted by many states.

Probation and Prisons

Prison populations in the United States are skyrocketing. Including juvenile facilities, the United States has over 2 million people behind bars, over 1.3 million in state and federal prisons, 621,000 in local jails, and more than 100,000 in juvenile facilities[54] (see Table 27-1). (*Prisons* are for committed criminals serving long sentences; *jails* are for short-term stays for persons awaiting trial and those with sentences of a year or less.) More people are imprisoned in the United States than in any other country. "The American in-

---

TABLE 27–1 Prisoners Under the Jurisdiction of State and Federal Correctional Authorities

State and federal prisons	1,312,354
Local jails	621,149
Juvenile facilities	108,965
Territorial prisons	16,130
Immigration and Naturalization Service facilities	8,894
Military facilities	2,420
Indian country jails	1,775

SOURCE: U.S. Department of Justice, Bureau of Justice Statistics, "Nation's State Prison Population Falls in Second Half of 2000—First Such Decline Since 1972," press release, August 12, 2001.

mate population has grown so large that it is difficult to fathom: imagine the combined population of Atlanta, St. Louis, Pittsburgh, Des Moines, and Miami behind bars."[55]

In addition to those in prison or jails, there are almost 4.5 million adult men and women on probation or parole. (*Probationers* are offenders courts have placed in community supervision rather than putting them in prison; *parolees* are people released after serving a prison term who are under supervision and are subject to being returned to prison for rule violations or other offenses.)

State and federal prison populations in the United States actually declined during the 1960s, but public demands for tougher sentences caused them to climb after 1969. The prison population has more than tripled since 1980 (see Figure 27-3), though declining slightly for the first time in 30 years in 2001.

The increase in prison population has resulted in serious overcrowding. In some states, conditions are so bad that in recent years federal judges have issued orders calling for either immediate improvement or the release of persons being held in conditions that violate the Eighth Amendment prohibition against cruel and unusual punishment. Most states are responding to judicial intervention by spending millions to build new prisons and renovate old ones. It costs at least $60,000 to build each cell, and an average of $20,000 a year must be spent to guard and feed each prisoner.[56]

Relatively few people commit most violent crimes. One out of every three persons let out of prison returns in three years. If we could identify these "career criminals" (**recidivists**) and keep them in prison, while at the same time releasing offenders who are not likely to commit other crimes, we might be able to cut down on the overcrowding in the prisons and better protect the public. The trouble with this idea is that it is not easy to determine in advance who is a career criminal and who is not. For this reason, some people argue that requiring every criminal convicted of a second offense to stay in prison for five years would cut the crime rate significantly.

Some cities and counties have even resorted to **privatization**, turning over the responsibility for operating jails to private firms on a contractual basis. Prison facilities have been privatized in New Jersey, Wisconsin, and the District of Columbia, as well as in many southern and western states, with Texas and California having the largest number. Correctional peace officers strongly oppose privatization and have become a potent interest group making major contributions to gubernatorial elections.

The high cost of corrections is leading some states to rethink the wisdom of mandatory sentencing and to reconsider the need to create such alternatives for nonviolent offenders as halfway houses, intensive probation, work release programs, and other community corrections facilities, even home confinement, first pioneered in New Mexico in 1983, whereby prisoners are observed by a variety of monitoring devices.[57] The problem is that these alternative solutions are subject to political attack for being "soft on criminals." Even so, pressure to find places to hold prisoners is so great that correction officials believe that these alternatives, including home confinement, will become an increasingly important part of the criminal justice system.[58]

Courts in Crisis

Crime is a national issue confronting everyone involved in the criminal justice system in America. The public's attention has been focused on terrorist attacks, drive-by shootings, random killings—especially in schools—and other forms of violence. Yet courts are already overwhelmed by a huge volume of cases. As the American Bar Association observed, "Justice in the United States takes too long, costs too much and is virtually inaccessible and unaffordable for too many Americans. . . . Our courts are grossly overburdened . . . and woefully underfunded. . . . The justice system is no longer a 'court of last resort' . . . but is becoming an emergency room for every social trauma."[59]

There is widespread agreement that our justice system, on both the civil and the criminal side, is in recurring crisis. There is less agreement on what to do about it. The

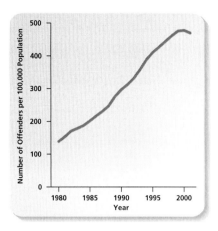

FIGURE 27–3 Incarceration Rates in Federal and State Jurisdictions, 1980–2001.

Source: U.S. Department of Justice, Bureau of Justice Statistics, "The Incarceration Rate Has More than Tripled Since 1980," at www.ojp.usdoj.gov/bjs/glance/incrt.htm.

recidivist
A repeat offender.

privatization
Contracting public services to private organizations.

problems are complex, and the issues are political in the best sense of the word: each suggested reform—alternative dispute resolution, mandatory sentencing, or decriminalization, for instance—has costs and benefits. Change and reform are likely to come slowly, and perhaps this is as it should be, for our justice system has been created over the centuries, built on the accumulated wisdom of the past. How best to administer justice is likely to remain high on our political agenda.

Summary

1. State and local courts are important forums for the making and carrying out of public policy. As they have become more active in political life, state judges have become embroiled in controversial issues, and the public has recognized their importance as policy makers. A new judicial federalism has emerged with state courts interpreting their state bills of rights more broadly than the U.S. Supreme Court applies the national Bill of Rights.

2. Each state has its own court system. Although the systems vary, they generally include minor courts of limited jurisdiction, trial courts of general jurisdiction, and appellate courts.

3. Judges are selected in four different ways: through appointment by the governor, election by the legislatures, popular election, or a modified appointment plan known as the Missouri Plan. Most legal reformers and political scientists appear to favor either the Missouri Plan or some merit selection system over judicial elections.

4. Judicial reforms are aimed at eliminating the waste and delay that plague courts. Among those suggested are alternative dispute resolution mechanisms, mandatory sentencing, and the decriminalization of some nonviolent crimes. Other reforms include merit systems that screen candidates for judgeships, higher pay and longer terms for judges to increase their judicial independence, rule-making powers for state supreme courts, and the appointment of judges more representative of the communities they serve.

5. Judges, together with jurors, prosecutors, defense counsel, public defenders, and correction officials, make up a loosely interrelated justice system. Many observers believe that this system is not properly dispensing justice to individual defendants or protecting the public from career criminals.

6. In recent years, more attention has been paid to the rights of victims at both the national and state levels, including amendments to state constitutions giving victims and their families the right to participate in the trial and providing for compensation to victims and their families.

7. There are over 2 million persons in our prisons. Prisons are overcrowded. Imprisonment has been justified as retribution, deterrence, protection of society, and rehabilitation. Disillusionment with rehabilitation and the disparate sentencing by judges has led to the enactment of mandatory minimum sentencing requirements, including three-strikes-and-you're-out legislation.

Key Terms

writ of habeas corpus
new judicial federalism
tort law
misdemeanor
felony

original jurisdiction
judicial review
advisory opinion
Missouri Plan
information affidavit

indictment
assigned council system
pro bono
public defender system
plea bargain

recidivist
privatization

Further Reading

STEPHEN J. ADLER, *The Jury: Trial and Error in the American Courtroom* (Times Books, 1994).

LAURENCE BAUM, *American Courts: Process and Policy,* 4th ed. (Houghton Mifflin, 1998).

MATTHEW BOSWORTH, *Courts as Catalysts: State Supreme Courts and Public School Finance Equity* (State University of New York Press, 2001).

ANTHONY CHAMPAGNE AND JUDITH HAYDEL, EDS., *Judicial Reform in the States* (University Press of America, 1993).

DAVID COLE, *No Equal Justice: Race and Class in the American Criminal Justice System* (New Press, 1999).

GEORGE F. COLE, *Criminal Justice in America* (Brooks/Cole, 1996).

NORMAN J. FINKEL, *Commonsense Justice: Jurors' Notions of the Law* (Harvard University Press, 1995).

SUSAN P. FINO, *The Role of State Supreme Courts in the New Judicial Federalism* (Greenwood Press, 1987).

JULIA FIONDA, *Public Prosecutors and Discretion* (Oxford University Press, 1995).

John B. Gates and Charles A. Johnson, *The American Courts: A Critical Assessment* (CQ Press, 1991).

Joseph R. Grodin, *In Pursuit of Justice: Reflections of a State Supreme Court Justice* (University of California Press, 1989).

David Heilbrone, *Rough Justice: Days and Nights of a Young D.A.* (Pantheon Books, 1990).

Laura Langer, *Judicial Review in State Supreme Courts: A Comparative Study* (State University of New York Press, 2002).

James P. Levine, *Juries and Politics* (Brooks/Cole, 1992).

Charles Lopeman, *The Activist Advocate: Policymaking in State Supreme Courts* (Praeger, 1999).

Marilyn D. McShane and Frank P. Williams III, eds., *Encyclopedia of American Prisons* (Garland Press, 1996).

David W. Neubauer, *America's Courts and Criminal Justice System,* 7th ed. (Wadsworth, 2001).

Elliot E. Slotnick, ed., *Judicial Politics: Readings from Judicature,* 2d ed. (American Judicature Society, 1999).

Michael Solimine and James Walker, *Respecting State Courts: The Inevitability of Judicial Federalism* (Greenwood Press, 2000).

Harry P. Stumpf and John H. Culver, *The Politics of State Courts* (Longman, 1992).

G. Alan Tarr and Mary Cornelia Aldis Porter, *State Supreme Courts in State and Nation* (Yale University Press, 1988).

Paul B. Wice, *Court Reform and Judicial Leadership* (Praeger, 1995).

See also *Judicature, The Journal of the American Judicature Society,* published bimonthly, and its Web site at www.ajs.org. The National Center for State Courts does not publish a regular journal but is an independent, nonprofit organization dedicated to the improvement of justice. Its materials can be obtained from its headquarters at 300 Newport Avenue, Williamsburg, VA 23185; its home page is www.ncsconline.org.

28
CHAPTER

LOCAL GOVERNMENTS AND METROPOLITICS

L OCAL GOVERNMENT IS BIG, COSTLY, AND OVERLAPPING, AND IT AFFECTS EVERY ONE OF US EVERY DAY. COUNTIES, CITIES, SUBURBAN communities, school districts, townships, metropolitan planning agencies, water control districts—all are crowded together and piled on top of one another. We typically live under several layers of government, pay taxes to nearly all of them, and also elect most of their leaders.

Local governments in the United States employ about 12 million people in over 87,500 different jurisdictions (see Table 28-1). North Carolina, for example, has 953 units of local government, including 100 counties, 518 municipalities, 335 special districts, and 192 school districts of one type or another.[1] Illinois has 6,800 units of local government, made up of 102 counties, 1,288 municipalities, 1,433 townships, 3,068 special districts, and 944 school districts. The Chicago metropolitan area alone has another 1,200 different jurisdictions

Why do we have such a labyrinth of government in this country? The basic pattern was imported from England, as were many of our governmental forms. Over time, new governments were created to take on new jobs when existing units proved either too small or unequal to the task. Also, people kept moving into, or at least near, the large cities. The past two generations have seen millions of Americans moving from the cities to the suburbs, and a steady migration to urban and suburban areas continues from rural areas as well. Decades of compromise and struggle among conflicting groups have given us our present system. It creaks and groans. It costs a lot of money. People claim it is inefficient. But these local governments are democratically accountable and encourage experimentation in making public policy.

TABLE 28–1 Growth of Governments in the United States				
Type of Government	1972	1982	1992	1997
U.S. government	1	1	1	1
State governments	50	50	50	50
Local governments	78,218	81,780	84,955	87,453
County	3,044	3,041	3,043	3,043
Municipal	18,517	19,076	19,297	19,372
Township	16,991	16,734	16,656	16,629
School district	15,781	14,851	14,422	13,726
Special district	23,885	25,078	33,555	34,683
Total	78,269	81,831	85,006	87,504

SOURCE: U.S. Bureau of the Census, at www.census.gov.

The Nature of State and Local Relations

Local governments vary in structure, size, power, and relation to one another. But in a *constitutional* sense, they all rely on power "borrowed" from the state. Most state constitutions create a **unitary system** in which power is vested in the *state* government, and local units exist only as agents of the state. Local government is not mentioned in the U.S. Constitution. Local units exercise only those powers expressly given to them by their respective state governments. Most local units of government, unlike states, do not have constitutional status. State-local relations are generally unitary in nature, in contrast to the federal nature of nation-state relations.

Because local governments are typically created by the state legislatures and usually have no constitutional authority in their own right, there are fewer obstacles to state

Layers of Governance in a Typical Small Town

1. Borough of Whitehall
2. Baldwin-Whitehall School District
3. Baldwin-Whitehall Schools Authority
4. Pleasant Hills Sanitary Authority
5. South Hills Regional Planning Commission
6. South Hills Area Council of Governments
7. City of Pittsburgh
8. Allegheny County Sanitary Authority
9. Allegheny County Soil and Water Conservation District
10. Allegheny County Criminal Justice Commission
11. Allegheny County Port Authority
12. Allegheny County
13. Western Pennsylvania Water Company
14. Southwestern Pennsylvania Regional Planning Commission
15. Air Quality Control Region
16. Commonwealth of Pennsylvania
17. United States of America

unitary system
Constitutional arrangement in which power is concentrated in a central government.

interference in local matters than there are to national interference in state matters. State officers participate in local government to a much greater extent than federal officers do in state politics. When doubts arise about the authority of local governments, courts generally decide against them.

In the beginning, state legislatures were given almost unlimited constitutional authority over their local governments and ran them pretty much at will. They granted, amended, and repealed city charters, established counties, determined city and county structure, set debt limits, and passed laws for the local units.

But by the end of the nineteenth century, voters were adopting state constitutions that curtailed the power of state legislatures. Many state constitutions forbade state legislatures from passing laws dealing with local governments, and constitutional provisions determined the structure, and in some cases even the process, of local governments.

Constitutional home rule granted constitutional independence to some local units, primarily larger cities, giving them constitutional authority over their form of government and a whole range of other matters. With the protection of constitutional home rule, state legislatures no longer determined the structure and powers of local units.

The extent of state control over local units today varies from state to state and also among the different kinds of local government within each state. At one extreme, local officials merely have to file reports with specified state officials. At the other extreme, state officials have the authority to appoint and remove some local officials, thus exerting considerable control over local affairs. When local governments prove ineffective, state officials may offer local governments financial assistance with certain strings attached or may even take over responsibilities previously handled by local people. In an unusual move in 2002, for instance, a Pennsylvania school reform commission, created to improve Philadelphia's public school system, decided take over from the city and privatize 42 of the city's failing schools, the largest experiment yet in the privatization of public schools.[2] By contrast, governments took over from private companies responsibility for screening airline passengers after the September 11, 2001, terrorist attacks.

State officials are genuinely conscious of local problems. That is in part because problems once thought to be local have come to be viewed as involving the entire state, especially problems relating to law enforcement, the environment, finance, and welfare. This heightened concern is acknowledged by mayors and city managers, who regularly work with both state and federal officials. In recent years, the direct ties between national and local officials, especially in the larger urban areas—ties that used to ally them against state officials—have weakened as federal assistance has been cut back.

After the terrorist attacks of September 11, 2001, New Jersey National Guard soldiers were deployed to Newark International Airport in Newark, New Jersey.

New York and New Jersey Tighten Airport Security

In response to the devastating terrorist attacks on the World Trade Center in New York City and the Pentagon in Virginia in September 2001, Congress enacted the Aviation and Transportation Security Act of 2001, which transferred authority for screening passengers from private companies to government and requires background checks for security guards and baggage handlers but not for other workers at airports.

New York and New Jersey subsequently adopted even tougher security plans for their three major international airports. Governors George E. Pataki and James E. McGreevey agreed to a joint plan that goes beyond the federal requirements in requiring criminal background checks for workers at airport stores as well as requiring counterterrorism training for state and local police at airport security checkpoints. Ground-based radar, closed-circuit cameras, and motion detectors will also be installed in order to improve surveillance of the airports. As a result, their airports will be at the forefront of airport security.

SOURCE: James C. McKinley, "Tighter Security Planned for New York Airports," *New York Times,* April 12, 2002.

constitutional home rule
State constitutional authorization for local governments to conduct their own affairs.

TABLE 28–2   The 15 Largest U.S. Counties by Population

1. Los Angeles Co., Calif.
2. Cook Co., Ill.
3. Harris Co., Tex.
4. Maricopa Co., Ariz.
5. Orange Co., Calif.
6. San Diego Co., Calif.
7. Kings Co., N.Y.
8. Miami-Dade Co., Fla.
9. Queens Co., N.Y.
10. Dallas Co., Tex.
11. Wayne Co., Mich.
12. King Co., Wash.
13. San Bernardino Co., Calif.
14. Santa Clara Co., Calif.
15. Broward Co., Fla.

SOURCE: U.S. Bureau of the Census, *Statistical Abstract of the United States, 2001* (U.S. Government Printing Office, 2001).

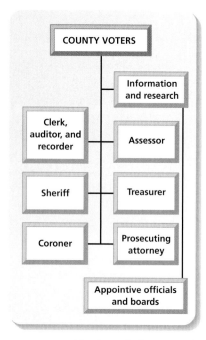

FIGURE 28–1   The Commission Form of County Government.

Counties in the United States

Counties are the largest jurisdiction within a state. Yet they get a lot less attention from citizens and the media than cities or school districts do. There are two major types of counties: large urban ones and rural ones. Urban counties have many of the same structures as their rural counterparts, but they are more intertwined with their urban centers. A few counties are better known than the cities or local municipalities within them: for example, Westchester County, New York; Montgomery County, Maryland; Marin and Orange Counties, California; and Cook County, Illinois (which includes Chicago). Some cities, such as Boston, New York, Denver, Baltimore, Philadelphia, San Francisco, and Honolulu, are simultaneously cities and counties.

States are divided into counties (in Louisiana they are called *parishes,* and in Alaska they are known as *boroughs*). With a few exceptions (such as Connecticut and Rhode Island, where counties have lost their governmental function), county governments exist everywhere in the United States. There are 3,043 of them, and they vary in size, population, and functions. Loving County, Texas, for example, has fewer than 150 inhabitants; Los Angeles County, California, has nearly 10 million. (Table 28-2 lists the 15 largest counties.)

Counties were originally organized on the idea that a county seat would be no more than a day's journey for everyone within the county's borders. Farm families could pile into their wagons and head for the county seat, and while farmers were attending to business, their families could shop and pick up the local gossip. Then they could all get home in time to do the evening chores. Today, of course, a farmer can drive across a whole state or several states in a day.

The traditional functions of counties are law enforcement, highway construction and maintenance, tax collection and property assessment, recording of legal papers, and welfare. Until recently, counties were convenient subdivisions; they spent most of their time merely carrying out policies established elsewhere. Over the past generation, however, counties have taken on more tasks than they have lost. Counties in a few states have given up some of their responsibilities, but in most other states, especially in the South, they are taking over from the states such urban functions as transportation, water and sewer operation, and land use planning.[3] Elsewhere, cities are contracting with counties to provide such joint services as personnel training, law enforcement, and correctional facilities. County governments are least active in the New England states, where the county is little more than a judicial and law enforcement district; county officials do some road building but not much else.

County Government

Most counties have little legislative power. The typical county has a central governing body, variously titled but most frequently called the *county commission* or *board of supervisors.* Most boards have from three to seven members, with a median size of six. They administer state laws, levy taxes, appropriate money, issue bonds, sign contracts on behalf of the county, and handle whatever jobs the state laws and constitution assign to them (see Figure 28-1).

County boards are of two types. The larger boards are usually composed of township supervisors or other township officials; the smaller boards are usually, though not always, elected in at-large elections. At-large elections make it difficult for minorities to be elected to office, especially when they are concentrated in a few areas. Minorities usually win more seats in a district election than in an at-large system.

The county board shares its powers with a number of other officials, most commonly the sheriff, the county prosecutor or district attorney, the county clerk, the coroner, and the auditor, who are generally elected rather than appointed. Sometimes county treasurers, health officers, and surveyors are also found on the ballot.

In general, counties are administered by an unwieldy collection of relatively independent agencies, and until recently, there was seldom a single executive responsible for coordinating such activities. However, today about 800 counties appoint a chief administrative officer who serves at the pleasure of the county commissioners. Approximately 400 counties now elect a *county executive* who is responsible for most administrative functions (see Figure 28-2).

County Performance

How well do counties do their job? The picture is mixed. The existence of counties adds to the fragmentation of authority and responsibility among a variety of elected officials, often producing needless jurisdictional conflicts, inefficiencies in purchasing, duplication of costs, and resistance to developing modern purchasing and personnel systems.

Although counties have often been the forgotten government within the states, this is changing. Their jurisdictional boundaries give them great potential for solving complex problems that are difficult to solve at the city level or have been decentralized to local levels of government by the states. The growing professionalization of county work forces and the trend of electing or appointing professional county executives are improving efficiency. "City-county functional consolidation in areas such as emergency medical services and natural-disaster planning is growing throughout the United States. . . . Increasing cooperation is likely to occur in the future as cities and counties struggle to provide more services to a tax-resistant public."[4]

Towns, Cities, Suburbs

Since the 1940s, the areas around the cities have been the fastest-growing places in the United States (see Figure 28-3). At least 50 percent of Americans now live in suburban communities. Suburbs grew at the expense of cities for a variety of reasons: inexpensive land, lower taxes, cleaner air, more open space for recreational purposes, less crime, better highways, and the changing character of the inner cities. There is no one explanation for the exodus to the suburbs. In part it was because people wanted to escape the deteriorating central cities. Resistance to mandatory busing to achieve integrated schools in the 1960s and 1970s also contributed to so-called white flight. But it was just as much a matter of class as of race, with middle- and upper-middle-income-level whites, Asians, and African Americans fleeing to the suburbs to escape urban crime and to seek more attractive environments in terms of class, religion, race, and lifestyle.[5]

FIGURE 28–2 The Council with Elected Executive Form of County Government.

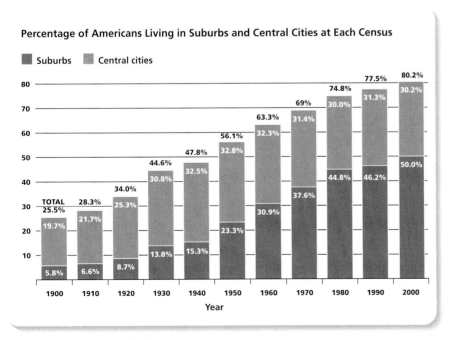

FIGURE 28–3 Moving to the Suburbs.

Sixty miles outside Los Angeles, California, the town of Palmdale is in the midst of a housing construction boom as more people want to live near, but not in, the vast metropolis of L.A.

Young families who could afford it left the crowded and blighted cities in search of a house with a lawn and a back yard. Parents wanted good school systems with modern facilities. Industries moved from the central cities in search of cheaper land, lower taxes, and less restrictive building and health codes. Businesses followed the people and the industries, and a myriad of shopping centers grew in outlying communities. Much of this exodus was accelerated by federal policies, such as new interstate highways, mortgages insured by the Federal Housing Administration, and the construction of public housing. Most of the new jobs created in the United States continue to be located in the suburbs or newer cities on the fringes of the central cities.

The major tasks of suburban government are often bound together with those of the metropolis.[6] Larger cities usually maintain an elaborate police department with detective bureaus, crime detection laboratories, and communications networks, but its jurisdiction stops at the city line. Criminals, however, seldom stop at the city line. Suburbs have fewer police, and they are often untrained in criminology, so they call on urban police expertise. Cities and suburbs are also tied together by highways, all of which have local access roads. In matters of health, too, there are often wide differences in services between city and suburb, but germs, pollution, and smog do not notice city signposts.

Older suburbs from Long Island to the San Francisco Bay Area are now experiencing some of the problems long associated with disinvestment and population decline. Some suburbs, too, are challenged by sprawling growth that creates crowded schools, traffic congestion, loss of open spaces, and a lack of affordable housing. Many people believe there is a need for collaborative city-suburb strategies to address sprawl and the structural challenges facing older suburbs and inner cities. We'll return to this topic later in this chapter.

The Rise of "Edge Cities"

In recent decades, cities have been built on the edges of cities. Writer Joel Garreau calls these "edge cities" and suggests that virtually every expanding American city grows in the fashion of Los Angeles, with multiple urban cores.[7] Thus we have Tysons Corner, Virginia, outside Washington, D.C.; the Perimeter Center at the northern tip of Atlanta's Beltway; the Galleria area west of downtown Houston; and the Schaumburg area outside of downtown Chicago.

Edge cities are defined as places with 5 million or more square feet of office space, 600,000 or more square feet of retail space, and more jobs than bedrooms. More often than not, these edge cities were empty spaces or farmland just 30 years ago. New freeways appeared first, then a shopping mall or two, and then industrial parks.

Some of the problems of the inner city have caught up with edge cities, just as they have with suburbs: traffic congestion, parking problems, crime, pollution, and urban blight. Political problems have cropped up as well. Most edge cities are in unincorporated areas of counties and are subject in varying degrees to control by county governments. These edge cities are sometimes run by "shadow governments"—private owners who set the fees for policing, transportation, and various other services that are normally financed by taxes. There is not much room for government by the people in a community that is essentially a business.

City Government Today

What does the word "city" call to mind? Bright lights and crowded streets? A city is not merely improved real estate; it is also people—men and women living and working together. Aristotle observed that people came together in the cities for security, but they stayed there for the good life.

The "good life" is defined differently by different people, yet it often includes these attractions:

- Employment opportunities
- Cultural centers, museums, performing arts centers, theaters
- Diverse educational institutions
- Entertainment and night life
- Professional sports teams
- Wide variety of stores and specialty shops
- Good restaurants
- Diversity of people, architecture, and lifestyles

Although a few cities existed when the U.S. Constitution was written, the nation was overwhelmingly rural in 1787, and seven out of ten people worked on farms. People clustered mainly in the villages and small towns scattered throughout the 13 states and adjacent territories. The villages and cities were the indispensable workshops of democracy, the places where democratic skills were developed, where grand issues were debated, and above all, where the people resolved to fight the British to secure their fundamental rights.

The United States is now a nation of about 19,300 cities, and although some cities have just a few hundred people, others have millions. Three American supercities and their suburbs (New York, Los Angeles, and Chicago) have populations larger than the total population of the Republic in the 1780s (see Table 28-3).

Every municipality has two major purposes. One is to provide government within its boundaries: to maintain law and order, keep streets clean, educate children, purify water, create and maintain parks, and make the area a good place in which to live.[8] As an instrument of the state, the city has a second major purpose: to carry out state functions.

A **charter** is to a city what a constitution is to a national or state government. It outlines the structure of the government, defines the authority of the various officials, and provides for their selection. Although charters are good sources of information on how the people in our cities are governed, they can be misleading. Different structures are not neutral in their impact, for different forms encourage different kinds of participation and responsiveness. In short, power and clout and who gets what, where, and how can definitely be shaped by a city's structural arrangements.

TABLE 28–3 The 15 Largest U.S. Cities by Population

1. New York, N.Y.
2. Los Angeles, Calif.
3. Chicago, Ill.
4. Houston, Tex.
5. Philadelphia, Pa.
6. Phoenix, Ariz.
7. San Diego, Calif.
8. Dallas, Tex.
9. San Antonio, Tex.
10. Detroit, Mich.
11. San Jose, Calif.
12. Indianapolis, Ind.
13. San Francisco, Calif.
14. Jacksonville, Fla.
15. Columbus, Ohio

SOURCE: U.S. Bureau of the Census, *Statistical Abstract of the United States, 2001* (U.S. Government Printing Office, 2001).

charter
City "constitution" that outlines the structure of city government, defines the authority of the various officials, and provides for their selection.

The New England Town Meeting

The New England town meeting has long been a celebrated institution. The traditional picture of sturdy, independent citizens coming together to settle public affairs and speak their minds is a stirring one. The New England town is sometimes pointed to as the one place in the United States where there is no elite and where participatory democracy really exists. The town meeting is our most obvious example of *direct democracy;* voters participate directly in making rules, passing new laws, levying taxes, and appropriating money. Despite this idealized picture, it is generally a veteran group of activists that provides political and policy-making leadership.

At least 1,000 New England towns (especially those with populations under 20,000) still hold annual town meetings open to all voters. Maine has nearly 400 towns that use the town meeting system of democracy; Vermont has about 200.

The assemblies at town meetings usually choose a board of executive officers, historically called *selectmen.* These boards, which generally have three to five members, carry on the business of the town between meetings. The selectmen are in charge of town property; they also grant licenses, supervise other town officials, and call special town meetings. A town treasurer, assessor, constable, and the school board, as well as others, are elected by the voters or appointed by the selectmen. A town administrator often functions as a city manager and reports to the board of selectmen.

Some state and local officials in New England say the town meeting is on the decline. Derry, New Hampshire, for example, held its last town meeting in 1985; then it switched to a mayor-council system. The town meeting had served Derry well for most of its 158-year history, but it proved unable to deal with rapid growth and an influx of people who commute long distances to work. In 1996, nearly 60 communities or school districts in New Hampshire modified their town meeting process so that meetings are for discussion purposes only, with final decisions on proposed laws made by the voters at the polls one week later. In Rhode Island, 13 towns abandoned the town meeting, and 18 towns use the meeting only to adopt the town budget.

Many larger communities in New England with populations of more than 25,000 have modified the town meeting by moving to a *representative* town meeting. At representative town meetings, between 50 and 300 local residents from various town precincts are elected to serve three-year terms representing their neighborhoods at their annual town meetings. This is a popular format in many suburbs of Boston with 25,000 to 50,000 residents.

The New England town meetings are tenacious institutions that continue to work well. Crucial to their success is a committee system. "Committee members become subject matter experts and provide advice to the town meeting which is followed most of the time."* Thus the open town meeting, at least in small towns in New England, still proves to be a vital way for people to participate in the policy making of their communities.

*Joseph F. Zimmerman, "The New England Town Meeting: A De Facto Representative Assembly," paper presented at the annual meeting of the American Political Science Association, Boston, September 5, 1998, p. 25.

The New England town meeting, like this one in Sandwich, New Hampshire, has long been a celebrated American institution.

The Mayor-Council Charter

The **mayor-council charter** is the oldest and most popular charter (see Figure 28-4). Under this type of charter, the city council is usually a single chamber. The size of the council varies from as few as two members to as many as 50, though seven is the median size in cities with more than 5,000 people.

Many methods are used to select council members: nonpartisan and partisan elections, elections by large and small wards, or elections from the city at large. Large cities that elect members affiliated with political parties generally choose them by small districts or wards rather than at large. This arrangement tends to support strong party organizations. Nonpartisan at-large elections make party influence difficult. The larger the election districts, the more likely citywide considerations will affect the selection of council members, and the greater the influence of citywide institutions such as local newspapers.

The difference between at-large citywide elections and elections based on small, single-member districts within a city can be significant for racial and ethnic representation on the city council. The at-large system tends to produce councils made up of the city's elite and middle classes. The small district gives minorities and the less advantaged a somewhat better chance for representation where neighborhoods may have high concentrations of one minority.

mayor-council charter
The oldest and most common form of city government, consisting of either a weak mayor and a city council or a strong mayor and council.

The Voting Rights Act of 1965 forbids cities with a past history of discrimination against minority voters from adopting the at-large system for electing council members if the effect would be to dilute the voting strength of these minorities. In fact, no local government in regions spelled out in this act can make a change in its voting system without the approval of the U.S. attorney general. But what of cities or counties that have long had at-large elections? Can they be forced to give them up because at-large elections virtually ensure that minorities will never be elected? The mere fact that no African American is elected under a certain system does not by itself constitute a violation of the Fourteenth or Fifteenth Amendment. The Constitution forbids only practices adopted or maintained *with the intent to discriminate.*

When Congress debated the extension of the Voting Rights Act in 1982, civil rights advocates urged it to outlaw at-large systems. They contended that city officials are not so foolish as to admit that they want to keep minorities from being elected. Others argued that cities should be free to adopt whatever election system they wished; after all, the Constitution guarantees that no person will be denied the right to vote because of race, not that candidates of the voter's own race will win an election.

The Voting Rights Act as interpreted by the Supreme Court has made it easier to prove that at-large systems violate civil rights. Discriminatory intent need not be proved by direct evidence; it may be inferred if a city or county has a past history of discrimination designed to keep minorities from voting, minorities make up a large majority of the population, and no member of a minority has ever been elected to office under an at-large system.[9]

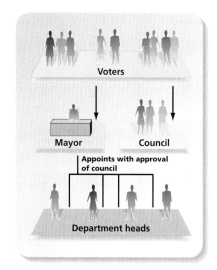

FIGURE 28–4 The Mayor-Council Form of City Government.

Weak Mayor Councils and Strong Mayor Councils

The powers of the mayor-council form of government vary from charter to charter and even more widely from city to city and mayor to mayor. There are, however, two basic variations of the mayor-council form: the weak mayor council and the strong mayor council.

In cities with the **weak mayor-council form**, mayors are often chosen from members of the elected city council rather than elected directly by the people. The mayor's appointive powers are usually restricted, and the city council as a whole generally possesses both legislative and executive authority. The mayor must usually obtain the council's consent for all major administrative decisions. Often weak mayor-council cities permit direct election by the voters of a number of department heads, such as police chief or controller. In weak mayor-council cities, there is no single administrative head for the city, and power is fragmented. The weak mayor-council plan was designed for an earlier era, when cities were smaller and government was simpler. It is ill-suited to large cities, where political and administrative leadership is vital.

Under the **strong mayor-council form**, the mayor is elected directly by the people and given fairly broad appointment powers. The mayor, often with the help of his or her staff, prepares and administers the budget, enjoys almost total administrative authority, and has the power to appoint and dismiss department heads. This system obviously calls for a mayor to be both a good political leader and an effective administrator—qualities not always found in the same person.

Many people believe the strong mayor-council system is the best form of government for large cities because it gives the cities strong political leaders and makes responsive administration possible. Further, by centering authority in the hands of a few individuals, it makes less likely the growth of "invisible government" by people who have power but are not publicly accountable for its use.

The Council-Manager Charter

Reformers in the early 1900s acclaimed the **council-manager plan** (also known as the *city-manager plan*), in which the city council hires a professional administrator to manage city affairs. It was indeed a significant governmental innovation. In 1908, the small city of Staunton, Virginia, appointed a general manager to direct the city's work. Little note was taken of the step, but the council-manager plan soon became the darling of

weak mayor-council form
Form of local government in which the members of the city council select the mayor, who then shares power with other elected or appointed boards and commissions.

strong mayor-council form
Form of local government in which the voters directly elect the city council and the mayor, who enjoys almost total administrative authority and appoints the department heads.

council-manager plan
Form of local government in which the city council hires a professional administrator to manage city affairs; also known as the *city-manager plan.*

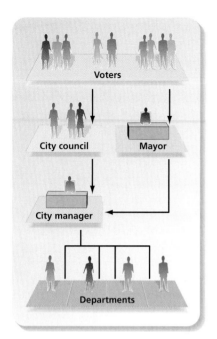

FIGURE 28–5 The Council-Manager Form of City Government.

both reformers and the business elite. They liked the idea that the council would serve as a sort of "board of directors" in the business sense of setting broad policies, while a professional executive would see that these policies were carried out with businesslike efficiency (see Figure 28-5).

Under the council-manager charter, the council is usually elected in nonpartisan primaries and elections, either on a citywide basis or by election districts much larger than the wards in mayor-council cities. The council appoints a city manager and supervises the manager's activities. The council still makes the laws and approves the budget, and although it is not supposed to interfere in administration, the council often supervises city government through the manager. The mayor is expected to preside over the council and represent the city on ceremonial occasions, but many mayors in fact do a good deal more than this. Contrary to what some textbooks imply, the mayor in council-manager cities can sometimes be a strong policy and political leader as well as a dominant influence in exercising political power.[10] This has surely been the case in cities as different as Cambridge, Massachusetts; San Antonio, Texas; and Colorado Springs, Colorado.

The city manager advises the council on policy and supervises the administration of city business. Because council-manager cities try to attract the best available persons, few of their charters require the councils to select managers from among local citizens, nor do they prescribe detailed qualifications. Although city-manager charters seem to call for a nonpolitical city manager who merely carries out policies adopted by the council and for council members who refrain from interfering with the administration of city affairs, it is often difficult to distinguish clearly between making and applying policy.

Today more than 2,700 cities, located in virtually every state, operate under a council-manager charter. It has, in fact, become the most popular form of local government in medium-sized cities of more than 10,000 citizens. It is especially popular in California, where about 98 percent of the cities now use it, as well as in other western and Sun Belt cities. The largest cities operating under a city manager are Dallas, San Antonio, San Diego, Phoenix, Kansas City, Cincinnati, Oakland, and Fort Worth.

How has the city-manager plan worked? In cities characterized by low social diversity and high consensus about community goals, the council-manager form has met with success. Such cities have generally enjoyed improved standards of public employment, reduced costs, and better services. But some observers say this plan has also weakened political leadership in these cities and has confused citizens as to who really provides policy leadership.

In an effort to become more responsive, some council-manager cities have expanded the size of their councils and have abandoned at-large elections for district elections. More than 60 percent of the city-manager cities now also directly elect their mayors in an effort to provide greater political accountability and leadership.[11]

Special Districts

The sheer complexity and fragmentation of government administrations in suburbia often create confusion and frustration. With few exceptions, each suburb has its own government, fire and police departments, school system, street-cleaning equipment, and building and health codes. *Special districts* piled one on top of the other further complicate the situation.

Special districts are units of government typically established to provide one or more specific services, such as sewage disposal, fire protection, water supply, or pollution control for a local or regional area. They are often created to enable an existing unit of government to evade established tax and debt limits and to spread the tax burden over an area wider than individual municipalities or counties. Many smaller special districts are formed in suburban areas to obtain urban services without having to create a city government or be annexed by one.

Special districts usually have governing boards appointed by officials of other governments or elected by the general public. Special districts are useful for dealing with urgent problems that overlap boundaries of existing units of government. Many urban and regional problems defy city and county boundaries, and special districts offer economies of scale that make sense.

Some critics say that the rapid increase in special districts in the past 30 years has prevented comprehensive planning. Critics also lament that few citizens know who runs these special districts, and even fewer know how these officials make decisions.

PEOPLE IN POLITICS
NEW YORK CITY MAYOR MICHAEL BLOOMBERG

Michael Bloomberg was elected mayor of New York in 2001 in what was called the biggest-ever political upset. A longtime Democrat, he switched to the Republican party shortly before running for the office. A billionaire and head of a business and media enterprise, Bloomberg spent $55 million of his own money on the election.

Mayor Bloomberg faces tough challenges in governing the city. He has never held an elected office before. And he succeeded the highly popular Republican Mayor Rudolph W. Giuliani. Intially, Giuliani was criticized for his bluntness and hard-hitting crackdown on crime. But during his two terms as mayor, he reduced crime by 60 percent, attracted businesses and tourists, and made possible a cultural renaissance. In the aftermath of the World Trade Center disaster, Giuliani demonstrated compassion and leadership that endeared him to New Yorkers.

New York's economy, like that of other cities, was already declining before the September 11 attacks. But the destruction of the Twin Towers made matters much worse and hurt the city's tourism industry. New York confronts a huge billion-dollar deficit. Even with federal aid for rebuilding, Mayor Bloomberg faces the prospect of raising taxes and making spending cuts while also rebuilding public confidence in the security of the city and once again attracting businesses and tourists in reviving the economy of the city.

The Role of the Mayor

Two hundred years ago, the notion of a strong mayor providing vigorous leadership was nonexistent. The need for strong mayoral leadership developed in the late nineteenth century. It was seen as a means to deal with the social revolution brought on by urbanization, massive waves of immigration, and mounting economic problems of growing cities. In the larger cities, gradually and often grudgingly, the office of mayor became a key position for political leadership.

The typical mayor is a college graduate, an experienced grassroots politician, a business or legal professional, and between 40 and 50 years old. Mayors in the largest cities earn $90,000 to $170,000 and in middle-sized cities between $40,000 and $80,000. City managers, chief city administrators, and top appointees sometimes make more than the mayors.

Although most mayors are male, several of the nation's largest cities have had women mayors, including Pittsburgh, Houston, Dallas, San Diego, San Antonio, and Portland. In fact, about 20 percent of municipal governments in the United States with a population of 30,000 or more are headed by women, and the number is growing. Many of them worked their way up through service on school boards and city councils and in the League of Women Voters. An increasing number of African Americans also serve as mayors. Currently, more than 300 cities have African American mayors, including Atlanta, Philadelphia, Denver, Detroit, Houston, San Francisco, Newark, Richmond, and Washington, D.C.

The main job of the mayor is administrative in the broadest sense of the term. Mayors supervise the line agencies—police, fire, public safety, traffic, health, sanitation—as well as a host of special agencies, such as the board of elections, the city planning agency, and commissions that regulate particular occupations and professions. Big-city mayors usually have staffs that carry out typical executive office functions such as personnel, management, budgeting, scheduling, and public relations. In this respect, mayors face the same tasks as corporate executives: coordinating a variety of activities, assigning responsibilities, checking that projects are carried out, finding the ablest people to take charge, and allocating money through control of the budget.

Mayors' Responses to the "Post–September 11" Challenges of Governing

The mayors of major cities have been responding to the September 11, 2001, terrorist attacks in a variety of ways. To find out more, go to the Web site of the U.S. Conference of Mayors at www.usmayors.org/uscm/home.asp. In short video clips, 54 mayors discuss the challenges and opportunities for their cities in responding to the need for increased security and greater cooperation with state and federal law enforcement agencies, at www.usmayors.org/uscm/meet_mayors/monitor4.asp.

Mayor-elect Michael Bloomberg with New York City Mayor Rudolph Giuliani and New York Governor George Pataki, after Bloomberg's victory over Democratic candidate Mark Green on November 7, 2001.

Usually mayors become involved with the private sector in an effort to promote economic opportunities. They try to secure additional jobs, increase the tax base, make the city more attractive to certain kinds of businesses, and coordinate public service expansion with private sector requirements. The private sector becomes involved in economic development because its success depends on having an educated labor base with appropriate skills, a constant consumer population, stable communities, and increasing property values.

Many mayors, such as those in New York, San Francisco, Seattle, Atlanta, Chicago, and Miami, have their own "foreign policies." That is, they play host to foreign dignitaries and business delegations and travel abroad seeking foreign investments as they sing the praises of local exportable goods.[12]

Sometimes a mayor must depend on the party organization to ensure support in the council, as in Chicago, where the huge city council consists of 50 members. Other mayors may have to deal with smaller councils, but they are likely to be weak unless they have enough political support to win cooperation.

Although partisan politics is waning as a feature of city government, mayors as party leaders still often dominate the party's city organizations. Mayors help recruit candidates for office, deal with revolts and opposition within their parties, and represent their parties in Washington or the state capitals. As chief legislator, mayors draw up proposed legislation and also make many specific policies. As chief fund-raisers, mayors bargain for more money for their cities before state and national legislatures. Mayors often climb the political ladder to run for governor or sometimes even president. For example, Ohio's former governor and now U.S. senator, George Voinovich, had previously been mayor of Cleveland, and former California governor Pete Wilson had been mayor of San Diego. U.S. Senator Richard Lugar of Indiana had been mayor of Indianapolis.

Mayors are expected to help revitalize the economy and attract investors, sports teams, tourists, and conventions. It takes courage and missionary zeal to overcome the pessimism and decay that beset most inner cities. But several recent mayors—including Rudolph Giuliani in New York City and both Richard J. Daley and his son Richard M. Daley in Chicago—succeeded in reducing crime, increasing economic opportunities, and revitalizing downtown businesses and residential areas.

In recent decades, mayors, like presidents and governors, have grown in power and importance. Most cities have altered their charters to give their mayors power to appoint and remove heads of departments, investigate departmental activities, send legislative messages to the city councils, prepare budgets, and veto council ordinances. In other words, mayors have been given a share in policy making, and city administration has been centralized under the mayor's direction.

Who Influences Local Policy Making?

Most Americans, most of the time, leave the responsibility of running the cities and counties to local officials and people willing to serve on boards and in local civic organizations. This does not mean that Americans rave about the quality of services received from local governments. Although they generally respond favorably to the services they get from city government and local public transportation agencies, they often rate them less favorably than they do the services provided by commercial organizations.

But if most people do not choose to be leaders in their communities, that does not mean they do not care about tax rates, the quality of schools in the community, and the availability of services. Hundreds of local people can be mobilized quickly if city hall mishandles local affairs or makes unpopular decisions. Indeed, activism has increased in recent years. It is now common for people to form groups to protect their communities from landfills, toxic dumps, shopping malls, and highways. With dogged perseverance and shoestring budgets, grassroots protest groups have often successfully taken on city hall or won victories for their neighborhoods in the courts.

A sure way to involve people in city government is to propose a policy that threatens the value or safety of the homes of middle- or upper-middle-class taxpayers. The slightest hint that a correctional facility, a freeway, a garbage dump, or a toxic disposal site is coming to their neighborhood will swiftly mobilize citizens who are otherwise happy to be passive spectators in local government. Similarly, the firing of a popular school principal, the closing of a neighborhood school, or a major increase in the property tax will produce a volley of citizen protests that can change the policy-making process at city hall.

Elected and appointed officials try to sense the mood of the local citizenry. They want to avert marches on city hall, recall elections, and citizen dissatisfaction. Their desire to be reelected and respected keeps them reasonably accountable.[13]

Interest Groups in Cities

The stakes and prizes in city politics are considerable: city jobs and commissioner posts, tax breaks, city contracts, regulations, licenses, and much more. Local politicians must deal with the kinds of interest groups found in any industrial society: organized workers, business leaders, neighborhood associations, professional associations, good government associations, home builders and developers, consumers, taxpayers, environmentalists, and various racial and ethnic groups.

The most powerful groups in most cities are typically business groups. Employers provide the economic base for taxes and for jobs, and mayors know they will win or lose the next election in large part on how well they promote the local economy.

Investors and businesses are free to locate wherever they please. Thus they may move from a central city to a nearby suburb or from one city to another. City policy makers, therefore, must follow an "economic logic" that requires them to adopt policies that persuade businesses and investors to remain as participants in the local economy, either by keeping tax rates relatively low or by increasing the quality of service and amenities. If successful, this kind of growth politics enhances the prospects of city officials for reelection because economic growth, especially business investment, boosts the tax base and increases economic opportunities.[14]

TABLE 28–4 The Five Fastest-Growing Metropolitan Areas

1. Las Vegas, Nev.
2. Naples, Fla.
3. Yuma, Ariz.
4. McAllen-Edinburg-Mission, Tex.
5. Austin–San Marcos, Tex.

SOURCE: U.S. Bureua of the Census, *Statistical Abstract of the United States, 2000* (U.S. Government Printing Office, 2000).

But business groups have to share political power and influence with unions, environmentalists, ethnic groups, and many others. Most business officials learn that they can influence city political decision making by cultivating allies.[15] City politics generally involves informal alliances of public officials working together with private sector individuals and institutions.[16]

Police, firefighters, street cleaners, teachers, and other public employees have organized into unions, many of which are affiliated with national unions. Such unions are often a major influence in larger cities. They fight for improved pay, working conditions, and job security. Although strikes by city employees providing vital services are prohibited by law in most states, enforcement is difficult. Teachers and municipal workers use the strike, or the threat of a strike, to force cities to increase wages and provide better benefits. Mayors complain that public employee unions are sometimes so powerful that they make the old-fashioned political machine look tame.

In addition, nonprofit groups such as the League of Women Voters, cultural foundations, local nonpartisan civic city clubs, independent local planning groups, and arts leagues exist in most urban areas, and they, too, want to be heard in the policy-making discussions of their cities.

Americans would like to believe that every citizen has a say in local government. We know, however, that prominent families and local business leaders have more influence than the rest of us. Nursing home residents, the unemployed, migratory workers, young drifters, and the homeless are unlikely to have much influence. Participation in community affairs is often a middle-class and upper-middle-class practice. Low-income residents and the homeless are often ignored when mayors and business elites pursue aggressive economic development policies. "For renters and low-income residents, . . . a booming economy with rising land values may put affordable housing out of reach."[17] This is true in New York City as well as in places like Aspen, Colorado. There are costs as well as benefits to urban growth. Economic development can destroy neighborhoods and drive cities into debt.

The Central City and Its Politics

Today most Americans live in *metropolitan areas*, which include large cities and their suburbs, rather than on the farms or in the small towns so beloved in American fact and fiction. A metropolitan area is, in the minds of most people, a big city and its suburbs. But the Census Bureau, which counts 280 metro areas, down from 284 in 1990, uses a more formal definition:

> A metro area is built around one or more central counties containing an urban area of at least 50,000 people. It also includes outlying counties with close ties—economic and social—to the central counties. To be considered part of the metro area, the outlying counties must meet certain criteria, including numbers of commuters, population density and growth, and urban population.[18]

About 80 percent of Americans (226 million) live in metropolitan areas, 55 percent live within 60 miles of a coastal shoreline (Atlantic, Pacific, Gulf of Mexico, Great Lakes, or St. Lawrence River), and 30 percent live in central cities. The fastest-growing metropolitan areas are in the South and the West (see Table 28-4).

In the nineteenth century, masses of new immigrants arrived in the cities from Europe; in the twentieth century, migrants came from the rural areas, especially from the South; and more recently, this country experienced waves of newcomers from Cuba, Korea, Vietnam, the Philippines, Nicaragua, Haiti, Mexico, and other Latin American countries. The majority of newcomers settled first in the inner cities—usually in the poorest and most decayed sections—which inevitably put great stress on the schools and sometimes on community safety as well. Overcrowding and substandard housing in these areas increased health and fire hazards.

Any picture of central cities as composed exclusively of huddled, starving, homeless youth gangs and unemployed masses, however, is misleading. Nor is it fair to say simply that central cities have all the problems and suburbs have all the resources. Central cities do have more "high-cost citizens" (truly needy, handicapped, and senior citizens), and most aging cities are losing population. They are losing businesses, too, because land, rents, utilities, and taxes are often less expensive in the outer suburbs, and businesses move to lower their operating costs. But their departure means that cities have smaller tax bases. Higher operating costs in the cities also result from aging public works.

As the income gap between city and suburban residents widens, central cities find it hard to raise new revenues or to force suburbanites to pay a larger share of the bill for the city services they use. This is the economic problem. The legal problem is that most of the states have not permitted their cities to raise funds in any meaningful way with a local income tax.[19]

In an effort to recapture part of the tax base that escapes to the suburbs in the evenings, some cities have imposed local payroll or other types of *commuter taxes* to obtain revenue from people who work in the central cities and make frequent use of city facilities yet live in the suburbs. Some city officials say the payroll or commuter tax is an effective way to shift some of the burden to those who benefit from the city but live beyond its borders. But others say it is unlikely to provide significant long-term revenue growth, and they think it encourages even more businesses to leave the city.

Today, however, many of the once down-and-out central cities are showing signs of rejuvenation and gentrification. Cities such as Boston, Cleveland, Newark, and Washington, D.C., that were losing population a decade or two ago are now gaining new residents. Gentrification and "yuppie" development have attracted some suburbanites to come back to central cities. The reasons for the rebound of many central cities varies from city to city, yet analysts believe that the sustained economic boom of the 1990s grew local tax revenues, which were then invested heavily in local infrastructure to make cities more appealing. The boom and investment in cities also helped create more jobs.[20]

In recent years, though, there has also been a growing sentiment against trying to strengthen metropolitan structures and instead to move in the opposite direction. Perhaps the strongest movement in that direction is in Los Angeles, where there are serious attempts to have the San Fernando Valley withdraw from Los Angeles and create its own city. The issue is extremely controversial, especially among the large Hispanic populations in the area and, even though the vote on succession failed in 2002, the matter will continue to be debated.

Urban renewal in many communities is replacing large apartment houses with smaller individual homes.

Meeting the Challenges of Growth and Economic Development

Until recently, almost everybody wanted to see his or her city grow. Everybody was a city booster. The local newspaper, the television stations, the radio stations, the Chamber of Commerce, the union leaders, the business community, the developers, the teachers, and proud citizens worked together to attract new industries. Such industries would bring, they hoped, new jobs, more amenities, increased land values, and more opportunities for the young. The consensus was that a city with a growing population was a healthy one; one with a decreasing population was a sick one.

Local politicians found it risky to oppose economic development and economic growth; those who did feared that they would not be reelected. However, beginning two decades ago, an *antigrowth* movement developed in many cities. There had always been restraints in the wealthy suburbs outside of the central cities; in fact, many suburbs were created to escape the growth taking place in central cities. These suburbs adopted building and zoning codes and land use regulations to make it difficult, if not impossible, for industries to be located there and to keep out people who could not afford large houses on large lots. New suburbs were carefully planned to ensure that they would not become too crowded. These zoning regulations were attacked in the courts as strategies to keep the poor and minorities out, but as long as they were racially neutral on their face, the courts left them undisturbed.

In the last two decades, environmental awareness spread, and coalitions formed to fight unregulated growth. Disturbed by noise, pollution, and traffic jams and fearful that developers would build too many houses too close together and overload the infrastructure of roads, sewage disposal, and schools in the community, opponents of growth joined together.

Strategies to Govern Metro Regions

Divided executive authority, fragmented legislative power, splintered and noncompetitive political parties, the absence of strong central governments, and the necessity to bargain with national, state, and local officials—all these factors suggest that metro regions, where about 80 percent of Americans now live, are shapeless giants with nobody in charge.

People Helping People

Countless people are coming together in their own neighborhood to tackle common problems or to form neighborhood cooperatives. Some of these self-help groups simply handle baby-sitting arrangements or organize charity events or golf tournaments; others are involved in neighborhood crime watches or Little League field construction. Local nonprofit groups in New York have built award-winning apartment complexes amid burned-out inner-city tenements. Other groups have mobilized to bring about storefront revitalization, street improvement, and area beautification programs by initiating farmers' markets, miniparks, and gardens.*

The contemporary self-help movement is rooted in an American past that has long been marked by volunteerism and local associations. In former times, the whole community often rallied when a neighbor's barn burned down; volunteer fire departments emerged out of this tradition. But as the nation has become more mobile and impersonal, we have drifted away from these traditions. Today, most Americans shop at shopping malls rather than on Main Street or in the old downtown area. At the same time, they resent the fact that public institutions have become remote and overly professionalized.

Thus people across the country are joining together to do in an informal and decentralized way what extended families or small villages of the past used to do. Simply, they come together to lend a hand.

Many local groups seeking help from city hall or from county officialdom give up after running into a maze of building codes, zoning rules, and countless regulations that inhibit innovation in local government. The alternative to despair is to do it yourself. And this is exactly what is happening at the grassroots level right now. The more successful experiments are watched carefully by the professionals at city hall, and some of the innovations are copied by those in office.

Sometimes progress or justice comes about because some activists take issues to court. Such was the case in bringing in alternative housing for lower-income residents in Mount Laurel, New Jersey. And it was also the case in addressing the fatal effects of toxic dumping by businesses in Woburn, Massachusetts.†

*See E. J. Dionne Jr., ed., *Community Works: The Revival of Civil Society in America* (Brookings Institution, 1998).

†See David L. Kirp et al., *Our Town: Race, Housing, and the Soul of Suburbia* (Rutgers University Press, 1997), and Jonathan Harr, *A Civil Action* (Vintage, 1996).

Metro regions, of course, typically encompass many cities, counties, towns, and suburbs, so they too are complicated and often splintered.

At the turn of the twentieth century, reformers were afraid of domination by political bosses. But in the modern metropolis, political machines do not run the central city. Urban bureaucracies may wield a lot of power, but they do not offer metropolitan leadership. Special interests seldom really control the metropolis, nor does a business elite. Who, then, governs the metropolis? It's typically a "nobody's in charge" arrangement.

Growing fragmentation of government in large metropolitan areas has brought about a variety of reform movements and structural innovations aimed at improving efficiency, effectiveness, and performance. Political scientists and public administration specialists have never been bashful about proposing remedies. Here are the better-known ideas, all of which have been tried somewhere, yet none of which has been adopted nationwide.

ANNEXATION   In the South, West, and Southwest, large central cities have absorbed adjacent territories. Oklahoma City, for example, added almost 600 square miles. Houston, Phoenix, San Antonio, El Paso, Colorado Springs, and Kansas City, Missouri, also expanded their boundaries. The now-extended cities serve almost as regional governments.[21]

But annexation has not proved helpful to cities in the Northeast and Midwest because these cities are ringed by entrenched suburban communities that seldom want to be annexed, and state laws make it difficult for the central city to do so against the wishes of the suburbs. Even in such places as the Houston metropolitan area, the annexation option is plagued by legal obstacles and political jealousies.

AGREEMENTS TO FURNISH SERVICES   The most common solution to the problems of overlapping and duplicating jurisdictions is for the units of government to contract for services. This reform is applauded by many economists, who say it comes close to providing a market that operates according to laws of supply and demand. Most of these agreements involve a few cities sharing a single activity. For example, a city may provide hospital services to its neighbors or contract with the county for law enforcement. Especially popular in the Los Angeles area, the contract system is used with increasing success in many parts of the country.

REGIONAL COORDINATING AND PLANNING COUNCILS   Just about all metro regions have some kind of *council of government* (COG). COGs began in the 1950s and were encouraged by the national government. Congress, in fact, mandated that certain federal

Public Authorities

Public authorities such as the Port Authority in the New York City area or the Tennessee Valley Authority in the South have been set up to undertake specialized functions in their regions. They have a legal mandate granted to them by the state (or states) to raise money, hire experts, and take over some city services, such as transportation, water, and housing. The Port Authority of New York built the Twin Towers of the World Trade Center, which were destroyed by the terrorist attacks. It is responsible for the rebuilding of the center and for overseeing the operation and security of the bridges and tunnels connecting New York and New Jersey. For more information, go to the Web site at www.panynj.gov.

Why public authorities? In part because state legislatures are sometimes hostile to mayors and prefer to place important functions outside the reach of mayors and political machines and in part because such authorities have financial flexibility (for example, they

might be able to incur debt outside the limits imposed on the city by the state). But most important, many problems are simply too big or cover too wide a geographical area to be handled properly by a city or a group of cities.

Public authorities pose a special problem for mayors. Not only are many of the vital functions of metropolitan government removed from the mayors' direct control, but even worse, special authorities and special districts constantly come into conflict with local agencies dealing with the same problems in the city.

But if public authorities are a problem for mayors, they are also a temptation. By sponsoring these independent agencies, mayors can sometimes cut down on their administrative load. They can tap other sources of funds and keep city tax rates lower than they would otherwise be. If things go wrong, mayors can say they did not have authority over a certain function and hence cannot be held responsible.

After September 11, 2001, the New York Port Authority and the Lower Manhattan Development Corporation began to search for appropriate ways to rebuild the World Trade Center site. On July 16, 2002 John H. Beyer, a founding partner of Beyer Blinder Belle architects, explained various facets of the first six designs to be considered. Whatever plan is accepted, it is generally believed that it will include not only housing and office space but a memorial as well.

grants be reviewed by regional planning groups. In essence, these councils bring locally elected officials together. They devote most of their time and resources to physical planning; rarely do they tackle problems of race, poverty, and financial inequities in metro regions. Councils are set up, moreover, in such a way as to give suburbs a veto over virtually any project that would threaten their autonomy. In a few regions, the councils assume operating responsibilities over such regional activities as garbage collection, transportation, and water supply. Critics say these councils rarely provide for creative areawide governance, yet they serve as an important common ground for elected officials to talk about mutual problems, and they help solve some problems in many of the regions.

CITY-COUNTY CONSOLIDATIONS   One traditional means of overcoming the fragmentation of metro regions is to merge the city with the county. This is a pet reform of business elites, the League of Women Voters, and Chambers of Commerce. It is viewed as a rational, efficient way to simplify administration, cut costs for taxpayers, and eliminate duplication.

About 30 city-county mergers have taken place. Occasionally, one city joins with another, as Sacramento and North Sacramento did in the 1960s. Such mergers can usually be brought about only by a referendum approved by the citizens of the region. Although efforts have been made to consolidate cities with counties, few have been successful in recent decades. Other than St. Louis, Nashville, Jacksonville, and Indianapolis, consolidations have occurred in only a handful of smaller urban areas.

What happened in Indianapolis is typical of these consolidations, most of which are in the South and West. In 1970, Indianapolis combined with Marion County to create UNIGOV. This merger required special permission by the legislature. UNIGOV provides many services, but the school systems remain separate, as do the police and sheriff departments.

The era of city-county consolidation appears over. Only about ten consolidations have taken place since 1970, and only one—Athens and Clark Counties in Nevada—occurred in the 1990s. Proposed mergers are usually defeated by county voters. But it is no longer unusual to find counties running what used to be city jails, zoos, libraries, and similar services. Formal and informal agreements abound as cities and counties remedy overlap and fragmentation by shifting responsibilities for providing specific services among themselves.

FEDERATED GOVERNMENT   This strategy attempts to take political realities into account by building on existing governments but assigning some crucial functions to an areawide metro government.[22] One of the few attempts—and there have been only a few—to create a federated government is the Twin Cities Metropolitan Council for the Minneapolis–St. Paul region. This regional organization, established by the legislature in 1967, consists of a 17-member council. Sixteen members are appointed by the governor to represent equal-population districts, and the seventeenth is a full-time executive who serves at the pleasure of the governor.

Today the Metropolitan Council, in essence a new layer of government superimposed on top of existing units, serves as a metropolitan planning and policy-making as well as policy-coordinating agency. It reviews applications for federal funds from the region. It guides regional planning and development and opposes local actions that would endanger the overall welfare of the region. It also has taxing authority for the region. The Twin Cities model appears to be a ready candidate for transfer elsewhere, yet this has happened only in Portland, Oregon.

Portland adopted a bold new charter for the Portland Metropolitan Services District, created by the state legislature several years earlier. It is a directly elected regional government serving three counties and 24 cities. Its nonpartisan commission members and elected executive officer have an impressive budget and more than 1,200 employees. They oversee waste collection, a zoo, recycling, waste disposal, transportation planning, and regional air and water quality programs, and they constructed Oregon's new Convention Center. They have also created a greenbelt around the metro area that preserves extensive open areas.

The Politics of Metropolitan Reorganization

In most metropolitan regions, to combine city and suburbs would be to shift political power to the suburbs. In most northern centers, this would give suburban Republicans more control of city affairs. In other cases, it would enable Democrats to threaten the one-party Republican systems in the suburbs. Under these circumstances, neither Democratic leaders in the central cities nor Republicans in the suburbs show much enthusiasm for metropolitan schemes. African Americans and Hispanics often oppose area consolidation or similar reform proposals that would invariably dilute their political power, often severely.

The Times Square area of New York City has undergone major redevelopment, with new theatres and hotels replacing porno movie houses and rundown buildings.

Some people believe that solutions to metropolitan problems are beyond the capacity of the metropolis itself. They favor a strengthened role for the national government, with special emphasis on ensuring "equity" or on relating services directly to needs. Some advocate reviving federal revenue sharing. Others believe that the job must be done by the states, which hold the fundamental constitutional power. Still others put forward bold proposals to establish regional planning and governance arrangements that would embrace "citistate" areas that include two or more metropolitan clusters, like Baltimore and Washington, D.C.[23]

Today's aging central cities unquestionably face problems: congestion, slums, smog, tension, loss of community, drugs, unsafe streets, neglected children, and visual pollution. They live with racial and ethnic tensions, not just white-black rivalry but rivalry among Latinos, Koreans, and a host of other racial and ethnic groups. Gangs, poverty, broken families, drive-by shootings, and drug-related crimes make life miserable for many who live in the inner cities. Yet is this new? Writers and critics since Thomas Jefferson have projected an unflattering image of the city as a cold, impersonal, and often brutal environment in which crime flourishes and people lose their dignity.

Supporters contend, however, that the big city is not just a place of smog and sprawl; it is the center of innovation, excitement, and vitality. In the last couple of decades, many major cities, including New York and Boston, have promoted the gentrification of run down areas. The city offers social diversity and puts less community pressure on the individual to conform. The large community is a meeting place for talent from all over the nation and the world: dancers, musicians, writers, scholars, actors, and business leaders.

Some observers dismiss the notion of an "urban crisis." They contend that most city dwellers live more comfortably than ever before, with more and better housing, schools, and transportation. By any conceivable measure of material welfare, the present generation of urban Americans is better off than other large groups of people anywhere at any time. Most cities, especially in the West and South, are thriving, and older cities such as Boston, Pittsburgh, and Indianapolis are generally viewed as revived and vital, not decaying.

Throughout history, cities have been threatened by political, social, and environmental catastrophes. Urban decay, in one form or another, has always been with us.[24] Cities thrive because over time they respond to crises and because they are an economic necessity. The economy, transportation systems, past investments, and cultural contributions all make cities inevitable. How well cities survive, and with what mix of people, will depend on the tides of the national economy, the way our regions are organized, the way our social and economic policies are designed, the vision and leadership individual cities muster to build their future, and the degree to which our national leaders promote policies that can help our central cities.[25]

Summary

1. Local government is big, costly, and over-lapping. Local governments in the United States come in a variety of shapes and structures and perform various functions. However, since constitutional power is vested in the states, most counties, cities, towns, and special districts are agents of the state.

2. The most common governmental form at the county level is a board of county commissioners, although larger urban counties are moving to council-administrator or council–elected executive plans.

3. There is no typical suburb. Although many suburbs are homogeneous, the suburban United States is highly heterogeneous. Suburbs are confronting the same problems as the urban areas they surround. In fact, big cities and their suburbs are now referred to as metropolitan areas and are growing fastest in the South and West.

4. The most common governmental forms at the city level are the mayor-council and the council-manager (city-manager) plans. Mayor-council governments generally have a strong mayor elected by voters, though some plans have a weak mayor elected by the council. Council-manager plans appoint a professional administrator. In general, council-manager plans are found in medium-sized to large cities and in cities in the West, especially in the Sun Belt. Mayors and managers are key political leaders.

5. Although local governments are run by officials, business interests and interest group activism also influence policy.

6. The standard of living in the central cities of the United States may be much better than it was 50 years ago, but the inequalities between many central cities and their middle and outer rings of affluent suburbs are increasing. Central cities often

face economic hardships, intense racism, and drug-related gangs and criminals. Fragmentation and dispersal of political authority in the metropolitan areas and even in many of the central cities themselves often make it difficult not only to govern the big cities but also to respond with adequate policies and funds to treat the problems of the metropolis.

7. Cities, suburbs, and metro areas all face problems related to growth, uneven tax bases, environmental concerns, and fragmented authority. A variety of strategies have been used in an effort to solve these problems—annexation, agreements to furnish services, regional coordinating and planning councils, city-county consolidations, federated government, and multipurpose special districts. Almost all proposals for metropolitan reorganization involve shifts in political power.

Key Terms

unitary system
constitutional home rule
charter
mayor-council charter
weak mayor-council form
strong mayor-council form
council-manager plan

Further Reading

BARBARA ACKERMANN, *"You the Mayor?" The Education of a City Politician* (Auburn House, 1989).

ROGER BILES, *Richard J. Daley: Politics, Race, and the Governing of Chicago* (Northern Illinois University Press, 1996).

BUZZ BISSINGER, *A Prayer for the City* (Random House, 1997).

MICHAEL BRIAND, *Practiced Politics: Five Principles for a Community That Works* (University of Illinois Press, 1999).

ALAN EHRENHALT, *The Lost City: Discovering the Forgotten Virtues of Community in the Chicago of the 1950s* (Basic Books, 1995).

JOEL GARREAU, *Edge City* (Doubleday, 1991).

STEPHEN GOLDSMITH, *The Twenty-First Century City: Resurrecting Urban America* (University Press of America, 1999).

JOHN J. HARRIGAN, ROGER VOGEL, AND JOHN A. HARRIGAN, *Political Change in the Metropolis,* 6th ed. (HarperCollins, 1999).

DENNIS R. JUDD AND TODD SWANSTROM, *City Politics: Private Power and Public Policy,* 2d ed. (Longman, 1998).

DANIEL KEMMIS, *The Good City and the Good Life* (Houghton Mifflin, 1995).

DAVID L. KIRP ET AL., *Our Town: Race, Housing, and the Soul of Suburbia* (Rutgers University Press, 1997).

PAUL G. LEWIS, *Shaping Suburbia: How Political Institutions Organize Urban Development* (University of Pittsburgh Press, 1996).

DONALD C. MENZEL, ED., *The American County: Frontiers of Knowledge* (University of Alabama Press, 1996).

JOHN O. NORQUEST, *The Wealth of Cities: Revitalizing the Centers of American Life* (Addison-Wesley, 1998).

MYRON ORFIELD, *Metropolitics: A Regional Agenda for Community and Stability* (Brookings Institution, 1997).

DONALD N. ROTHBLATT AND ANDREW SANCTON, EDS., *Metropolitan Governance: American-Canadian Intergovernmental Perspectives* (Institute of Governmental Studies, 1993).

DAVID RUSK, *Cities Without Suburbs,* 2d ed. (Woodrow Wilson Center Press/Johns Hopkins University Press, 1995).

MICHAEL H. SHUMAN, *Going Local: Creating Self-Reliant Communities in a Gobal Age* (Routledge, 2000).

CLARENCE N. STONE, *Regime Politics: Governing Atlanta, 1946–1988* (University Press of Kansas, 1989).

JON C. TEAFORD, *Post-Suburbia: Government and Politics in the Edge Cities* (Johns Hopkins University Press, 1996).

HEATHER ANN THOMPSON, *Whose Detroit? Politics, Labor, and Race in a Modern American City* (Cornell University Press, 2002).

ROBERT J. WASTE, *Independent Cities: Rethinking U.S. Urban Policy* (Oxford University Press, 1998).

WILLIAM JULIUS WILSON, *When Work Disappears: The World of the New Urban Poor* (Harvard University Press, 1996).

JOSEPH F. ZIMMERMAN, *State-Local Relations: A Partnership Approach* (Praeger, 1995).

See also *Governing: The Magazine of States and Localities,* published monthly by Congressional Quarterly, Inc.; *The National Civic Review,* published by the National Civic League; *The Municipal Yearbook,* published annually by the International City Management Association; and the Web site of the U.S. Conference of Mayors at www.usmayorsorg/uscm/home.asp.

29
CHAPTER

MAKING STATE
AND LOCAL
POLICY

STATE AND LOCAL OFFICIALS CONSTANTLY WRESTLE WITH CHALLENGING POLICY DILEMMAS. WHAT IS THE BEST WAY TO ATTRACT business and increase the number of jobs yet encourage environmental quality? How should our state deal with the soaring costs of providing Medicaid? What can be done about frustrating and costly peak-hour gridlock on our highways? Should a community close one of its hospitals? Will voters approve a bond issue to construct a needed new high school? State and local authorities are also puzzled by how much they can do about homeland security—an obvious concern in the aftermath of the September 2001 terrorist attacks.

Mayors, governors, state legislators, county commissioners, judges, union officials, developers, Chambers of Commerce, political party leaders, and many others strive to come up with public policy compromises to questions such as these. The decisions of these policy makers don't receive much media attention compared to the attention paid to decisions made in Washington, D.C., yet the effect of these decisions on our day-to-day lives is often equally or perhaps even more important.

This chapter will examine some of the policy areas that consume a lot of the attention of state and local officials and the budgets of state and local governments. State and local governments spend most of their budgets on educating people, on welfare and health-related matters, on highway and transportation systems, and on safety and law enforcement issues. We will discuss them as well as the issues of planning and regulation.

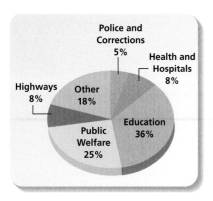

FIGURE 29–1   Typical State Government Expenditures.

SOURCE: *The Book of the States, 2002* (Council of State Governments, 2002), p. 282.

Public Education

In ancient Greece, Plato and Aristotle saw education as a vital task of government. Thomas Jefferson, too, was convinced that an educated citizenry was essential to democratic government. But only in the twentieth century did the idea that government should provide tax-supported education for everyone become generally accepted.

For a long time, many people opposed "free" education. They feared it would lead to social unrest, undermine the family, give government control over the minds of the young, require huge bureaucracies, and result in a fatal mixture of education and politics. And was it fair, they asked, to make people who could afford to educate their own children in private schools pay taxes to educate other people's children? Despite these objections, today free public education for grades 1 through 12 is an established practice in the United States.

Education is now the number one policy priority for most states. State and local governments have the primary responsibility for education and put up most of the funds. In recent years, there has been a decline in the federal contribution to education; however, this has not deterred the federal government from pushing federal goals for education. An excellent example of this was the George W. Bush–sponsored and congressionally approved No Child Left Behind Act of 2001, a reauthorization of an earlier law that required greater school district accountability, more testing, and increased emphasis on reading, especially for younger children.[1]

Approximately one-third of all state and local government expenditures are for education—more than for any other function of government[2] (see Figure 29-1). The federal government's contribution to education is fairly constant across states, but since 1979, overall state funding has surpassed that of local governments, with the exception of a few states in which revenues for education continue to come primarily from local government.[3] The state role in financing education has increased over the last generation as a result, at least in part, of pressure from the courts to equalize expenditures on education across local school districts. There is also wide variation between states in the total amount of state and local spending per student, from a high of almost $10,000 in New Jersey to a low of under $4,000 in Utah, with an average of roughly $6,360.[4]

Administration

Unlike most other democracies, which administer and fund education at the national level, the basic unit responsible for public elementary and secondary education in the United States is the local school district, of which there are nearly 15,000.[5] In almost all districts, voters elect a board of education that sets the school tax rate, appoints a superintendent of schools and other personnel, hires teachers, and runs the schools from kindergarten or grade 1 through grade 12. Each state has a state superintendent of public instruction or commissioner of education. In about a third of the states, this official is popularly elected; in almost all states, he or she shares authority with a state board of education.

Although actual operation of the public schools is the responsibility of the local community, state officers have important supervisory powers and distribute financial assistance to the communities. State money is distributed according to many formulas, but as noted, the trend is toward giving more money to poorer communities to equalize education spending. Many policies are established at the state level, and it is up to local authorities to enforce them. Local authorities must ensure that new school buildings meet the minimum specifications set by the state. In some states, officials have the authority to set the course of study in schools—that is, to determine what must be taught and what may not be taught. In several states, especially in the South and Southwest, state authorities determine which textbooks will be used as well.

The Role of the National Government

After the former Soviet Union's successful launch of *Sputnik,* the first satellite put into orbit, in 1957, Congress responded by increasing federal funding for education to strengthen math and science education. The national government's share in financing local edu-

Violence in Public Schools

Violence in public schools has increased in recent years. In a survey of school administrators, 97 percent indicated that they believed school violence had increased, and more than 25 percent of middle school principals reported an increasing number of acts of violence. As many as 35 percent of male students in some urban areas carry guns, and 45 percent of all students claim to have been threatened with a gun or shot coming from or going to school. Some students even bring semiautomatic rifles to school. In several incidents, students were killed or wounded before their attackers were subdued.

In response, federal, state, and local governments increased spending on student and teacher protection. School districts increased surveillance to identify students bringing weapons to school. Many schools installed metal detectors and surveillance cameras to discourage students from bringing guns and knives into the classroom. There are also more closed campuses, more police officers patrolling hallways, and more undercover police working in schools to address problems of violence and drugs. Some schools have adopted a "zero tolerance" policy (automatic expulsion on the first offense) for students who bring a weapon to school or are found to be in possession of drugs.

Efforts to combat school violence appear to be slowly paying off. According to the Department of Education, the number of student expulsions for weapons violations was declining by the end of the 1990s.

Under the guidance of local police, students at Colorado's Columbine High School escaped the terror inside their school when two fellow students went on a killing and bombing spree.

cation rose from about 2 percent in 1940 to about 9 percent in 1980. Since then, however, the trend has reversed, and the federal share of spending on local education declined and has stabilized at 6 percent.

Through the national Department of Education (created in 1979) and other agencies, the federal government makes grants to the states for facilities, equipment, scholarships, loans, research, model programs, and general aid at the elementary, secondary, and higher education levels. But federal control over how the money may be spent comes with these federal dollars. Today federal regulations cover school lunch programs, employment practices, admissions, record keeping, care of experimental animals, and many other matters. Indeed, school authorities complain that there are more regulations than dollars.

Educational Issues

What shall be taught and who shall teach it are hotly contested matters. Schools are favorite targets for groups eager to have children taught the "right" things. Religious groups want family values and morality emphasized, and some want constraints imposed on the teaching of evolution. Others want the schools to teach facts only, without regard for values, especially in areas like sex education. Labor leaders want students to get the right impression about labor and its role in society. Business leaders are eager for children to see the capitalism and free enterprise system in a favorable light. Minorities and women's groups want textbooks to present diversity issues from the perspective they consider correct. Professional educators and civil libertarians try to isolate schools from the pressures of all outside groups—or at least the ones with which they disagree. They say decisions regarding what textbooks should be assigned, what books should be placed in school libraries, and how curricula should be designed are best left to professionals.

It has long been an American tradition that education should be kept free from partisan political influences. The separation of schools from politics is strongly supported. Most local school boards are nonpartisan and are often elected when no partisan races are on the ballot. Elaborate attempts have been made to isolate educational agencies from the rest of government. This separation is strongly supported by parent-teacher associations, the National Education Association, the American Federation of Teachers, and other educational groups. Most citizens also believe education should be kept out of the hands of mayors and city councils. However, education is of such concern to so many people, and there are so many different ideas about how schools should be run, that it cannot be divorced from politics.

PUBLIC SCHOOL INTEGRATION   During the 1970s and 1980s, battles were fought in many cities over how to overcome racial segregation in the public schools. One method, which became contentious, was to bus students from one neighborhood to another to achieve racial balance in the schools and overcome the effects of past segregation. By the 1990s, battles over school busing were ending, but despite the efforts of the federal courts, racial segregation is still the pattern for the inner-city schools of most large cities in parts of the North, South, and West.[6]

EDUCATIONAL REFORM   Over the past two decades, a series of reports on education helped focus national attention on educational reform.[7] A 1990 meeting between President George H. W. Bush and many of the nation's governors laid the foundation for the Goals 2000: Educate America Act, which sought to achieve many of the goals identified as important since the 1960s. With the aid of federal money, states were encouraged to set educational standards in order to achieve a number of goals, including these:

- All children will start school ready to learn.
- The high school graduation rate will be at least 90 percent.
- Students will have mastered a challenging curriculum by grades 4, 8, and 12.
- Teachers will have access to professional development opportunities.
- U.S. students will rank first in the world in science and math achievement.
- All adults will be literate.
- Schools will be free of drugs, violence, and firearms.
- Every school will promote parental involvement in education.[8]

Several states initially objected to Washington's setting goals and standards for public education, which had traditionally been a local function. Further, some observers thought it unfair to "hold students to nationwide standards if they have not had the equal opportunity to learn" due to unequal resources among communities.[9] These concerns, however, did not deter states from setting goals and standards. The autonomy of local and state authorities is also protected, with the federal government's role defined in terms of general goals.

Education was a key theme in the 2000 elections at all levels, with candidates from both major parties and all ideologies insisting that we must improve the quality of public education. However, there was little agreement on how that should be done. Proposed reforms debated revolved around vouchers, charter schools, national student testing, and more emphasis on reading. Some of these found their way into the Elementary and Secondary Education Act of 2001.

VOUCHERS   Some reformers contend we will not see real progress in public education until we inject competition into the system by permitting parents to shop for schools the way they shop for goods and services in the economy. One way to do this would be to provide parents with a set amount of money—**vouchers**—that they could use to pay for part or all of their children's education in a public or private school of their choice. This reform has been labeled "choice in education" because it would give parents the freedom to choose where to send their children to school.[10]

Voucher programs have been tried since the mid-1980s in New York, Indianapolis, San Antonio, and Milwaukee. Some programs were directed at low-income students, a plan that, according to one observer, meant some poor families formed political alliances with conservative Republicans, not their more natural liberal Democratic allies. Political scientist and voucher advocate Terry Moe argues:

vouchers
Money provided by the government to parents for payment of their children's tuition in a public or private school of their choice.

In the new politics of education, the conservatives have become the progressives, pushing for major change, promoting the causes of the disadvantaged, and allying themselves with the poor. The progressives of yesteryear, meantime, have become the conservatives of today, resisting change, defending the status quo against threats from without, and opposing the poor constituents they claim to represent.[11]

Among the most vigorous opponents of vouchers are teachers' unions, including the National Education Association (NEA) and the American Federation of Teachers (AFT), which, understandably, see vouchers as a threat to their jobs and benefits because the use of vouchers could drain off financial support from the public schools.

Some proponents have proposed that voucher programs should include religious schools. Well over 80 percent of the students receiving vouchers in places like Milwaukee and San Antonio attend religious schools, with most of them Catholic schools.[12] Opponents of vouchers for religious schools argue that such an arrangement violates the constitutional separation of church and state. They fear too that in some parts of the country, vouchers would be used for schools that practice racial segregation.

Other people oppose the voucher system, even for public schools, on the grounds that such a system would have a negative impact on efforts to reform the public schools. Some argue that it would promote "skimming," meaning that the higher-achieving students would opt out of public schools, leaving behind the underachievers and the discipline problems and creating an increasingly negative atmosphere in public schools. In rural areas, where few private schools exist, some people fear that vouchers might encourage parents to keep the money under the guise of providing "private" home schooling.

Proposals for school vouchers that have been put before the voters have been defeated in Oregon, Colorado, and Washington. In recent years, California and Michigan voters have turned down initiatives that would have established vouchers, in spite of well-financed campaigns supporting their adoption. The political movement pushing vouchers lost some of its steam because of these defeats, the opposition of the teachers' unions, and court rulings that said poor families do not have the right to demand vouchers from state and local governments to allow their children to attend better schools.

In 2002, a divided U.S. Supreme Court ruled that poor children could be granted public money (vouchers) to attend religious schools without violating the separation of church and state provisions in the Bill of Rights. Chief Justice William Rehnquist wrote that his majority opinion was "not an endorsement of religious schooling" but merely a means "to assist poor children in failed schools."[13]

CHARTER SCHOOLS   One educational reform that does not go as far as vouchers but still provides publicly funded alternatives to standard public schools is the **charter school**. Some states now grant charters to individuals or groups to start schools and receive public funds if they can meet standards specified by law. Unlike vouchers, which provide funds to the parents, charter schools deal directly with the local school boards. There are over 2,000 charter schools, with more than half a million students. "The vast majority of the schools are operated by local nonprofit organizations, and the educational theories that guide them are as various as the communities they serve."[14]

An Arizona law that permits any person or organization to found a charter school has not led to the founding of a wide variety of schools with different emphases. Most of Arizona's charter schools have been for secondary education, with several targeting at-risk students. An early study in the state found that 67 percent of students attending charter schools had previously attended public schools. Charter schools did not cause a brain drain from the public schools; in fact, the average test scores of students entering were lower than the state and national averages. The ethnic mix and socioeconomic status of the families of charter school students were not very different from those of Arizona public school students.[15]

As with privatization in other government services, charter schools are intended to interject the competition of the marketplace into elementary and secondary education.

charter school
A publicly funded alternative to standard public schools in some states, initiated when individuals or groups receive charters; charter schools must meet state standards.

Charter Schools

In East Los Angeles sits Vaughn Street School, California's first charter school, established in 1992. Most of the children at this elementary school speak English as their second language and live in dangerous neighborhoods. Once the children had to step around a dead body as they approached the school's entryway. It was not a healthy learning environment.

In 1992, Vaughn Street's pupils ranked in the 9th percentile in reading (91 percent of public school students in America could read better than they) and the 14th percentile in math. Now their reading and math scores rank in the 47th and 59th percentile, respectively. Today these students experience hands-on learning about computers in the $1.6 million learning center, and parents from more wealthy neighborhoods want to send their kids to Vaughn. Principal Yvonne Chan attributes these changes to freedom from bureaucracy.

During the past decade, the number of charter schools has grown steadily because of concerns about students' poor academ-ic performance and high dropout rate. About a fifth of all high school students do not graduate. For more state-by-state information, visit the Web site of the Center for Education at www.edreform.com/pubs/chglance.htm.

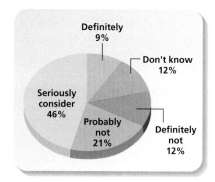

Would Parents Choose Charter Schools?

SOURCE: Public Agenda, reported in "Issues 2000: Education," *The Economist,* September 30, 2000, p. 20.

Charter schools generally have more flexibility to hire and fire teachers and are not subject to the collective bargaining arrangements that prevail in many public school systems. Proponents of charter schools want to remove these schools from state and local regulation as much as possible. Some of their teachers may not have training in education, but proponents of charter schools maintain that classroom performance is more important than the undergraduate major of the teacher.

In many poorer communities, classes are conducted in overcrowded, poorly equipped buildings.

The biggest opponents of charter schools are teachers' unions, which stand to lose their collective bargaining position with school boards if charter schools multiply. Other opponents contend that in school systems already strapped for money, it does not make sense to divert funds to such untested experiments. Concerns about what will be taught in charter schools and the level of teacher competence are often expressed. Also at issue is whether religious schools should qualify for public funds as charter schools.

Spending on charter schools remains small compared to the billions spent on public education, but it has been growing in recent years. As charter schools become more visible, they are likely to become more controversial. Yet individuals and groups appear to be willing to give the idea of charter schools a try, and even the National Education Association has indicated that it plans to set up some charter schools itself, although with less autonomy from school boards than many charter school supporters favor.

NATIONAL STUDENT TESTING   Standardized testing is not new or controversial. What is new and controversial is *statewide* standardized testing. In 1990, only 14 states had standards for their core curriculum, but 49 states have now adopted standards. After adopting standardized testing for students, Oregon rejected a ballot initiative that would have amended the state constitution to require annual testing of math and verbal skills of public school students in grades 4 through 12.

Even more controversial are *national* tests and *national* norms or goals. Such tests would be administered to students periodically to permit parents, administrators, and legislators to assess how individual students, classes, schools, school districts, and states compare with one another. Moreover, once such testing is established, it could be expanded to include year-to-year measurement of individual students as they progress through the public schools.

Some critics of standardized national tests contend it is unfair and misleading to use such tests to measure learning. Minority students and students in districts in impoverished areas may not do well on these tests, and their low scores will reinforce cultural bias. Other critics worry that the use of such tests will force teachers to "teach the test." Sensitive to the fact that their students will be compared with students in other classes, teachers will attempt to "beat the test" by emphasizing certain topics and ignoring others. This strategy might work for some students but would limit the learning of others. The main contention of the opponents of national testing, however, is that such measurement will not produce positive changes in education.

This charter school in Jersey City, New Jersey, provides a computer lab for its science classes.

Higher Education

Until the 1950s, most local school districts provided only elementary and secondary education, although some larger cities also supported junior colleges and universities. Since the end of World War II, however, there has been a major expansion of *community colleges.* Now students may attend the first two years of college or receive a technical education right in their own communities. The trend is to create separate college districts to operate and raise funds for these local colleges.

Administration

States support many kinds of universities and colleges, including land-grant universities such as Michigan State University, created by the Morrill Act of 1862. State colleges and universities are governed by boards appointed by the governor in some states and elected by the voters in others. These boards are designed to give public institutions of higher education some independence, even though they greatly depend on the state legislature and governor for funding. A few states have gone so far as to protect the independence of their universities in the state constitution.

With about 80 percent of our more than 15 million college students now attending publicly supported institutions, the control and support of higher education have

HOPE Scholarships

During the past decade, a number of states have established HOPE scholarships, modeled after Georgia's Helping Outstanding Pupils Educationally (HOPE) program. Under the leadership of former Governor Zell Miller, in 1993 Georgia instituted HOPE scholarships providing any high school graduate with a B average or better full tuition, all mandatory fees, plus a book allowance of $100 a quarter or $150 a semester if he or she attends a state public college, university, or technical institute. The program was later expanded to provide up to $3,000 per year for students meeting the same standards who attend a private Georgia university. Students can keep their scholarship so long as they maintain their B average.

Thirteen states currently have versions of HOPE scholarship programs.

For more state-by-state information, go to the Web site of the Education Commission of the States at www.ecs.org.

become significant political issues. States have created boards with varying degrees of control over operations and budgets. In addition, governors have tried to impose controls on universities and colleges that many university administrators insist are inappropriate. Yet institutions of higher education have greater independence from political oversight than other tax-supported institutions. Publicly funded colleges and universities usually can control teaching loads, internal procedures, areas of teaching emphasis, hiring and promotion, and the allocation of funds among internal units.

Funding Higher Education

In the twenty-first century, we face questions of access and funding for our colleges and universities due to increasing enrollments. Who should go? Only those who can afford it? What about minorities who are underrepresented in our colleges and universities? Access to colleges and universities for all students who wish to go has long been the declared goal in many states, but is this goal realistic? Should students be required to pay higher tuition to cover the cost of their education?

Tuition at state universities has gone up, often at two or three times the rate of inflation. Professors' salaries have not kept pace with tuition increases and have grown only slightly more than the rate of inflation (see Table 29-1). Although many people agree we need an infusion of new money to update college laboratories, improve libraries, and recruit and keep first-rate college professors, there is little consensus about who should pay for these efforts. The federal government is the chief supplier of student financial aid, and many states are now making major efforts to expand their programs of student aid. Many states, such as Georgia, California, Washington, and Alaska, are investing in programs aimed at keeping top students in their states at state-run or independent colleges.

Most institutions of higher education—both independent and state-run—receive some kind of government subsidy, through a variety of devices, so that students do not pay the full cost of their education. The national government and most states provide need-based financial assistance in the form of loans and grants, with students in the greatest financial need at the higher-cost institutions eligible for the most aid. Thus higher education has what is in effect a voucher system; students receive funds and can choose the kind of college or university that best serves their needs. It also means that in the United States, we have avoided a *two-track system*—one set of colleges and universities for the poor and another for the rich. Poor students can be found in most high-cost independent colleges and universities along with students from higher-income families. Funding for the public universities must compete with the rising costs of other state services, notably Medicaid, transportation, the criminal justice system, and prisons.

TABLE 29–1   Tuition and Professors' Salary Increases, 1985–2000

	Tuition or Required Fees*		Professors' Salaries†	
	Public	**Private**	**Public**	**Private‡**
1985	$1,386	$6,843	$46,539	$49,224
1990	2,035	10,348	51,453	55,383
1995	2,977	14,537	51,710	58,344
2000	3,774	19,312	57,700	66,300

SOURCE: U.S. Bureau of the Census, *Statistical Abstract of the United States, 2001* (U.S. Government Printing Office, 2001), p. 173.

*Annual average in-state tuition for a four-year degree. In-state tuition is assumed for public universities.

†Annual average salary and benefits for full-time professors of all ranks in four-year institutions.

‡Excludes church-related colleges and universities.

Social Services

What role should state and local governments play in making sure all citizens have basic housing, health, and nutritional needs met? How important are these social services compared to government's obligation to provide police and fire protection, education, parks and recreation, and other services? For much of our history, human service needs were left to private charities that ran orphanages, old-age homes, hospitals, and other institutions. Philosophically, this reliance on private charity fit well with the American notions of limited government and self-reliance. That view changed dramatically during the Great Depression of the 1930s, when poverty, unemployment, and homelessness affected such large numbers of people that the government could no longer act as if these were private matters. Then in the mid-1960s, with President Lyndon Johnson's Great Society agenda, the nation embarked on a second major wave of social service programs, which Johnson called the War on Poverty. Today we continue to debate whether such programs accomplish their goals and whether alternatives would prove more successful.

Welfare

Pressure to reform the welfare system increased among both Democrats and Republicans in the last decades of the twentieth century. The number of Americans on welfare soared from about 2 million households in 1950 to close to 6 million in the early 1990s[16] (see Figure 29-2). Why such growth? Some said that this country had finally recognized its obligation to care for the truly poor. Others charged that "government handouts"

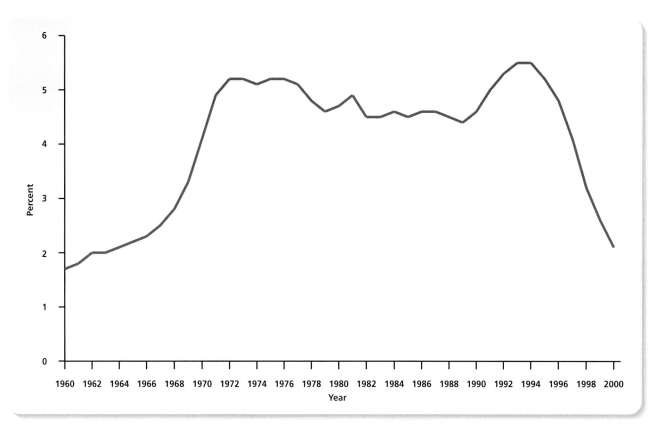

FIGURE 29–2 Percentage of the U.S. Population on Welfare Since 1960.

SOURCE: U.S. Department of Health and Human Services, at www.acf.dhhs.gov/news/stats/6097rf.htm.

Note: For more information on welfare and Temporary Assistance for Needy Families statistics, go to www.acf.dhhs.gov/news/stats/6090 ch2.htm.

This welfare-to-work trainee is learning skills that will enable her to find employment at a steady, well-paid job.

robbed recipients of the self-confidence they need to go to work and succeed; in this sense, dependence on welfare becomes a curse.

Welfare policy has been a complex web of federal, state, and local programs that shared or matched financial responsibilities. Until recently, the federal government picked up the lion's share of welfare costs. Most of the administrative burden, however, fell on state and local governments. Every state had a department of human services or welfare that either administered welfare programs directly or supervised local officials who administered these programs. County welfare departments determined who was entitled to assistance and dealt directly with recipients.

In 1996, fundamental changes were made in the role of the federal government in providing welfare. Most of the responsibility for welfare was shifted to the states, with national guidelines for administration. The landmark legislation that ended the Aid to Families with Dependent Children (AFDC) program was named Temporary Assistance for Needy Families (TANF).[17] States now receive federal block grants that require state matching funds. Each state files a plan with the secretary of health and human services every two years that (1) explains how it will ensure that recipients engage in work activities within two months of receiving benefits, (2) establishes goals to prevent and reduce out-of-wedlock pregnancies, (3) describes treatment of families moving into the state, and (4) explains whether it intends to provide aid to noncitizens. Money is distributed to states based on the highest amount of federal funding they received in the previous three fiscal years. To continue receiving federal funds, states must spend at least 75 percent of the amount they spent in 1994. Federal money is disbursed through the state legislatures, not controlled by the governors. Additional federal funds are available to states as incentives for high performance and as loans in times of financial hardship for the state.

States are encouraged to experiment with welfare programs. Their experiments are evaluated by the federal government in order to ensure that they meet policy goals. Some states had previously started to cut back on welfare payments. For example, Wisconsin's governor, Tommy Thompson (now President George W. Bush's secretary of health and human services), proposed capping welfare payments for unwed teenage mothers, regardless of the number of children they have. Larger grants were paid to those who were married.[18] This provision is now included in national law. Previously, federal laws had unintentionally encouraged fathers to leave the family by making it easier for single-parent families to receive benefits. Current law seeks to overcome this disincentive by offering higher benefits to two-parent families.

Other states have developed **responsibility contracts**, requiring recipients to sign a written agreement specifying their responsibilities and outlining a plan for them to obtain work and achieve self-sufficiency. Some states provide child care and Medicaid benefits beyond the federal one-year extension for families who lose benefits due to unemployment.

About half of the states, including Massachusetts, New York, Wisconsin, and California, have experimented with **workfare** programs designed to help welfare recipients develop the self-confidence, skills, and habits necessary for regular employment. Workfare gives able-bodied adults who do not have preschool-aged children the opportunity to learn job skills that can lead to employment. Another government program creates **enterprise zones** in large cities that give tax incentives to companies that provide job training for the unemployed in depressed neighborhoods.[19]

As a result of the 1996 welfare reform, the percentage of people on welfare was reduced by more than half—from close to 6 million families in the early 1990s to about 2.3 million in 2000. Initially, federal and state welfare expenditures declined significantly, though the booming economy of the late 1990s may have helped create a lot of jobs and thus contributed to this decline. A number of states—including Hawaii, New York, Kentucky, and West Virginia—set aside unspent TANF funds as "rainy day" reserves to invest in benefits and services to help needy families overcome transportation and child care barriers to staying employed.[20]

At first glance, the 1996 welfare reform seemed a successful policy; however, the program has had its shortcomings. One critic who worked closely with the bill, George-

responsibility contract
A welfare strategy adopted by some states in which recipients sign a written agreement specifying their responsibilities and outlining a plan for obtaining work and achieving self-sufficiency.

workfare
A welfare strategy adopted by some states that gives able-bodied adults who do not have preschool-aged children the opportunity to learn job skills that can lead to employment.

enterprise zone
Inner-city area designated as offering tax incentives to companies that invest in plants there and provide job training for the unemployed.

town University Law Center's Peter Edelman, says: "The main lesson of the 1996 law is that having a job and earning a livable income are two different things."[21] It is true that many of the recipients who found jobs through the 1996 law found low-income or part-time jobs. While these jobs technically removed names from the poverty list, they did not decrease the very real difficulty of finding grocery money each week. Now the Bush administration is faced with designing a new welfare bill. Instead of learning from the shortcomings of the 1996 bill, many contend that the Bush administration's plan continues to push the marginal group toward poverty by drawing hard eligibility lines. A survey conducted by the National Governors' Association found that most governors feel the plan requires more contrived community service jobs and costs far more money than allotted. Governor Howard Dean of Vermont summed up the sentiments of many governors: "A majority of states see the president's proposal, especially the 40-hour workweek, as unworkable. That's a bipartisan view."[22] In times of recession, and because many of those left on welfare after the 1996 law are the hard cases—people with little education, no work experience, and tenuous personal backgrounds—creating even more stringent work requirements does not even begin to address the individual needs of those on welfare.

States are now the prime laboratories for making and implementing social policy. The federal government originally became involved in welfare programs because states had been unwilling or unable to tackle these problems on their own. When confronted with competing demands in other policy areas, will states give the needs of poor people a lower priority? And what happens when good economic times turn bad? How will the states cope with larger numbers of needy people?

Health

During the hot summer of 1794, a yellow fever epidemic ravaged Philadelphia. The streets were deserted. All who could afford to do so had fled with their families to the country. Every night, the sounds of the death cart echoed through the nearly empty city. Most families that remained behind lost a child, a father, or a mother. Only when cool weather returned did the city resume normal activity.

Yellow fever, dysentery, malaria, and other diseases periodically swept American cities in the eighteenth and nineteenth centuries. As late as 1879, yellow fever struck hard in the South. Memphis was nearly depopulated. Following the lead of Louisiana and Massachusetts, state after state established a board of health to deal with such epidemics. Spurred by the medical discoveries of Louis Pasteur and other scientists, authorities undertook additional efforts to protect public health. Open sewers were covered, and hygienic measures were instituted.

Prevention and disease control are still major public health activities today. Doctors are required to report cases of communicable disease. Health department officials then investigate to discover the source of the infection, isolate the afflicted, and take whatever action is called for. Most state health departments give doctors free vaccine and serum, and many local departments give free vaccinations to those who cannot afford private physicians. Mobile units take free x-rays of schoolchildren, teachers, and the general public; county health departments provide free or low-cost inoculations, vision tests, and hearing tests. Public health officials try to protect water supplies and ensure the safe disposal of waste and sewage. They protect the community's food supply by inspecting hotels, restaurants, and food markets.

Today the overwhelming public health issues are pollution, AIDS, smoking, and drug abuse. Like the contagious and infectious disease issues of prior times, they require concerted efforts and public health policies. Thousands of local governments—counties, cities, townships, and special health districts—have some kind of public health program. Every state has an agency, usually called a department of health, that administers the state program and supervises local health officials. At the national level, the U.S. Public Health Service conducts research, assists state and local authorities, and administers federal grants to encourage local agencies to expand their programs. Every state also administers

Going Up in Smoke

One cause of rising health care costs has been treating illnesses related to the use of tobacco. The battle to recover some of the costs incurred by government has gone on for years, but in 1998, the state attorneys general worked out a $206 billion settlement of the Medicare lawsuit against tobacco companies, the money to be used to offset the costs incurred by the states for treating sick smokers. A part of the money may also go to Medicaid. Smoking prevention programs and a ban on billboard advertising were also included in the deal. Under the terms of the settlement, states may pass additional legislation further taxing the tobacco industry at the state level.

In 1998, California voters narrowly approved Proposition 10, which provided for a 50-cent-per-pack increase in the tax on cigarettes and a $1.00 increase per pack on other forms of tobacco. The money generated by this tax will be used to establish a new county commission to create and oversee early childhood smoking prevention programs.*

*Alan K. Ota, "Multi-State Agreement Renews Democrats' Interest in Pushing Tobacco Legislation," *Congressional Quarterly Weekly*, November 21, 1998, p. 3178.

police powers
Inherent powers of state governments to pass laws to protect public health, safety, and welfare; the national government has no directly granted police powers but accomplishes the same goals through other delegated powers.

Public health clinics provide free vaccinations and other health services to children whose families cannot afford medical insurance.

various federally funded medical benefit programs for the needy, such as Medicaid, not to be confused with Medicare, the Social Security health care program for people over 65.

The current health care crisis in the United States involves access. Wealthy people can afford the costs and gain access; poor people on welfare usually have access to health care, although the quality of their care may be lower. It is the people in the middle who are often worried about whether their personal insurance will be adequate to cover their health care needs. Programs such as Medicaid seek to fill the health insurance gaps for low-income persons. The larger goal of Medicaid is to improve the health of those who might otherwise go without health care.

Medicaid has recently resurfaced as a major issue of concern for state governments nationwide. The increasing number of Medicaid-eligible citizens, coupled with the skyrocketing costs of prescription drugs, long-term health care, and HMOs—all far beyond the rate of inflation—add up to a Medicaid program in need of help. Further, the program was expanded during strong financial times, often to include low-income children as well as parents, but now that state fiscal conditions are less than perfect, Medicaid is in danger. "That's the irony of Medicaid: The program has a difficult time doing its job when its services are most needed. A sour economy increases demand for coverage and spending, at the same time revenues are eroding and putting heavy pressure on state budgets," notes Trinity Tomsie, who covers Medicaid issues for the National Conference on State Legislator's Fiscal Affairs Program.[23]

State policy makers now face tough questions about whether or not to maintain coverage and if so, how: Should reforms limiting the number of people eligible be implemented to cut costs? Can drug manufacturers be leaned on for rebates? Should a preferred-drug list, based on cost and efficacy, be established? The program is enormous, covering the health care needs for nearly 40 million Americans and taking an average of about 13 percent of annual state funds. Perhaps this is why Professor Sara Rosenbaum called Medicaid "one of the pillars that holds up the American health care system" and also why state governments are scrambling to continue the program.[24]

Governors around the country pressed President George W. Bush and Congress to increase the federal share of Medicaid's costs, to no avail. Many were frustrated when the president advocated a large farm bill appropriating money for farm subsidies, seemingly ignoring what many think a more pressing financial issue, Medicaid funding. State officials acknowledge nowadays that soaring Medicaid spending threatens recent state goals such as reducing public school class size, increasing public transportation infrastructure, and funding innovative environmental programs. Many states "have reached into the funds received in settling their suits with tobacco companies, or tapped public employee pension funds, or drained their rainy day reserves in order to meet the requirement in state constitutions that they balance their budgets."[25] The Washington state government, led by Governor Gary Locke, has proposed imposing premiums, copayments, and enrollment caps on Medicaid clients as a way to cut costs and raise revenues.[26] No relief from health and Medicaid costs is in sight.

Law Enforcement

Many state and local government powers stem from their **police powers**, the inherent power of states to use physical force if necessary to protect the health, safety, and welfare of their citizens. This power is among those not delegated to the federal government by the Constitution and reserved to the states. It is on this basis that mayors or governors impose curfews, as they have in some urban riots. But the police power extends to other activities of government, such as regulating public health, safety, and morals.

The State Police

In 1835, the famous Texas Rangers were organized as a small border patrol. In 1865, Massachusetts appointed a few state constables to suppress gambling, a job the local police had proved unable or, more probably, unwilling to do. But not until 1905, with the

Racial Profiling

Racial profiling—state police stopping and arresting minorities—made news in New Jersey but was also found to occur in other states as well. An extensive review based on interviews with troopers, state officials, and victims revealed a pattern of selective enforcement that had gone on for more than a decade.

The story begins in the mid-1980s, when the federal Drug Enforcement Administration (DEA) responded to the street violence of the crack epidemic by enlisting local police forces to catch smugglers who were importing drugs from Latin America, often to Florida, and moving them to major American cities by car.

By 1989, the New Jersey State Police had become such a successful part of "Operation Pipeline" that DEA officials hailed the troopers as exemplary models for most other states.

But on New Jersey roadways, black and Hispanic drivers were subjected to such frequent and unjustified traffic stops and searches that they complained of a new violation in the state's traffic code: "DWB—driving while black." In state police barracks, some black and Hispanic troopers bitterly acknowledged that even though the state officially prohibited racial profiling, senior troopers trained them to single out drivers on the basis of their ethnicity or race.

On April 22, 1998, troopers shot and wounded three unarmed black and Hispanic men during a traffic stop on the New Jersey Turnpike, propelling the controversy to the center of the state's political stage. State officials, including Governor Christine Todd Whitman, at first clung to their insistence that there was no pattern of profiling. But under pressure from civil rights leaders and the federal Justice Department's Civil Rights Division, the Whitman administration ultimately acknowledged racial profiling, revamped its narcotics strategy, and agreed to let a federal judge monitor the force.

A 2001 court decision wiped out most of these arrests and paid compensation to the victims.

SOURCE: Adapted from David Kocieniewski and Robert Hanley, "An Inside Story of Racial Bias and Denial," *New York Times*, December 3, 2000, pp. 53, 56.

State police in New Jersey and other states have been stopping and arresting minority drivers because they fit a profile of potential drug dealers.

organization of the Pennsylvania State Constabulary, did a state police system come into being. It was so successful that other states soon followed.

The establishment of the Pennsylvania State Constabulary marked a sharp break with traditional police methods. This was a mounted and uniformed body organized on a military basis; centralized control was given to a superintendent directly responsible to the governor. The Pennsylvania pattern was followed by other states.

State police became a part of our law enforcement system for a variety of reasons. The growth of urban and metropolitan areas, the coming of the automobile (and the resulting demand for greater protection on the highways and the creation of a mobile force for catching fleeing criminals), and the need for a trained force to maintain order during strikes, fires, floods, and other emergencies all promoted the creation of state police.

Other Police Forces

State police are not the only law enforcement agencies maintained by state governments. There are liquor law enforcement officials, fish and game wardens, fire wardens, detective bureaus, and special motor vehicle police. This dispersion of functions has been criticized, yet each department insists it needs its own law enforcement agency to handle its special problems.

At the local level, almost every municipality maintains its own police force; the county has a sheriff and deputies, and some townships have their own police officers. In fact, there are more than 40,000 separate law enforcement agencies in the United States, employing more than 600,000 men and women.

With crime continuing to be an important issue to many voters, crime control is always on the minds of elected officials. State and local governments spend more than $35 billion on police protection. Local governments pay for over 70 percent of all law enforcement costs, including such routine activities as controlling traffic and patrolling neighborhoods but also maintaining court security and preventing juvenile crime. The number of police officers increased by 10 percent during the 1990s and may increase even more with recent state and federal legislation.[27] The federal government in the 1990s provided grants for recruiting and temporarily paying for nearly 100,000 new local police officers throughout the country. But when these grants later expired, many local governments experienced fiscal budget shortfalls. Now local governments are struggling to pay for these recently added police officers.[28]

Federal-State Action

The national government has gradually moved into law enforcement, a field traditionally reserved for state and local governments, although the main cost of local law enforcement is still borne by local governments. Today, for example, it is a federal offense to transport kidnapped individuals or stolen goods across state lines. Taking firearms, explosives, or even information across state lines for illegal purposes is also a federal offense. Federal law enforcement agencies include the Federal Bureau of Investigation (FBI), the Bureau of Alcohol, Tobacco and Firearms (ATF), and the Drug Enforcement Administration (DEA).

Crime rates have been declining. Despite positive trends, politicians in both parties continue to press for government to do more about crime. Some advocate stricter laws regulating guns, while others favor more police on the street or more prisons. Because politicians fear appearing "soft on crime," taking action on crime is almost always a high priority at all levels of government.

Since the September 11, 2001 terrorist attacks on New York City and the Pentagon, every state has designated a homeland security coordinator. These state officials are working with the national homeland security office to beef up preparedness and training efforts aimed at preventing and dealing with future terrorist attacks. The national government approved federal funds for the fall of 2002 that were to be used to train and equip "so-called first responders, along with grants to prevent bioterrorism, which have increasingly become the focus of many state officers."[29] While there is a clear need for new and expanded homeland security efforts, few states have the resources to do so. As South Carolina's homeland security director, Steve Siegfried, put it, "All of us homeland security advisers talk to each other and all of us are strapped."[30]

Planning the Urban Community

Are our cities good places in which to live and work? Crime, pollution, garbage, crowded shopping areas, dented fenders, slums and blighted areas, inadequate parks, impossible traffic patterns, and shattered nerves—are these the inevitable costs of urban life?

For at least the first century of the United States' existence, American cities were allowed to grow unchecked. Industrialists were permitted to erect factories wherever they wished; developers were allowed to construct towering buildings that prevented sunlight from reaching the streets below; commuters, bicyclists, and pedestrians ended up with transportation systems that rarely met their needs.

Zoning Laws

The most common method of ensuring orderly growth is *zoning*—creating specific areas and limiting property usage in each area. A community may be divided into designated areas for single-family, two-family, or multifamily dwellings; for commercial purposes; and for light or heavy industry. Regulations restrict the height of buildings or require that buildings be located a certain distance apart or a certain distance from the boundaries of the lot.

Zoning regulations attempt to enable the city or county government to coordinate services with land use and to stabilize property values by preventing, for example, garbage dumps from being located next to residential areas. Day-to-day enforcement is usually the responsibility of a building inspector, who ensures that a projected construction project is consistent with building, zoning, fire, and sanitary regulations before granting a building permit. A zoning ordinance, however, is no better than its enforcement. In most cases, a zoning or planning commission or the city council can amend ordinances and make exceptions to regulations, and these officials are often under tremendous pressure to grant exceptions. But if they go too far in permitting special cases, the whole purpose of zoning is defeated.

Zoning is only one kind of community planning. Until recently, city planners were primarily concerned with streets and buildings. Today most are also concerned with the quality of life. Consequently, planning covers a broad range of activities, including methods to avoid air pollution, improve water quality, and provide for better parks. Planners collect all the information they can about a city and then prepare long-range plans. Can smaller-scale communities be devised within urban centers? Can downtown areas be revitalized, and if so, how? Where should main highways or mass-transit facilities be constructed to meet future needs? Will the water supply be adequate for the population 10, 20, or 50 years from now? Are hospitals and parks accessible to all? Does the design of public buildings encourage crime or energy waste?

Repair of deteriorating infrastructure, although a nuisance to residents, is necessary to maintain the quality of life in cities and also attract businesses and consumers.

Controlling Growth

Critics of urban and state planning are skeptical whether governors, mayors, or state and local legislators can prevent what they sometimes call the "Los Angelization" of the United States, by which they mean urban growth without much planning for transportation, environmental protection, or management of water and other resources. Unregulated market forces can cause severe harm to residents, and "politics as usual" does not ensure sensible growth patterns or protect the air, water, and beauty of most states and communities.

Seattle and San Francisco residents voted to limit the height and bulk of downtown buildings in an effort to protect these cities from excessive growth. Maryland and many other states have passed "smart growth" laws aimed at preserving large blocks of contiguous land and ensuring that the necessary roads, sewers, and schools are in place before development proceeds. This legislation is implemented in two ways. The state gives priority funding to development in areas designated by counties as having the proper infrastructure and meeting other guidelines; state funds are also allocated to local governments and private land trusts to purchase the development rights to land "rich in agricultural, forestry, natural, and cultural resources."[31]

The population of the United States will soar by 50 to 60 million by 2025. A few urban planners recommend looking at European cities such as Paris, where choice neighborhoods in the heart of the city combine elegant six- and seven-story apartment buildings above neighborhood retail stores. Most Americans would reject this dense, crowded lifestyle devoid of driveways, grassy front lawns, and backyard pools. But a closer look at European cities often finds a great number of interior gardens within apartments and meticulously groomed neighborhood parks. Columnist Neal Peirce writes that "density and mixed use aren't bad; they're just different—and sometimes better" and notes the discussion and advocacy of a U.S. version of Parisian greenery in a group called Community Greens: Shared Parks in Urban Blocks (www.communitygreens.org).[32]

Obviously, planning and sensible growth depend on public support. They also depend on market forces. No plan will be effective, however, unless it reflects the interests and values of major groups within the community. Planning is clearly a political activity. Different groups view the ends and means of planning differently, and agreements on tough policy options are often hard to reach. Moreover, one of the barriers to successful planning is the general fear of government power. Effective planning therefore requires imaginative collaboration among planners, community leaders, and the popularly elected officials who must bear the responsibility for implementing the plans.[33]

Environmental Regulation

State and local governments have long been concerned about managing land use and protecting the environment. In such heavily polluted places as Pittsburgh, smoke abatement ordinances were enacted as early as 1860, but aggressive action on air pollution did not come until after World War II.[34] By the 1950s, states had established agencies to deal with resource management issues, but it was the federal legislation of the early 1970s that pushed environmental protection onto their agendas.[35] One important reason for the expanded federal role is the reality that pollution does not recognize state boundaries. Air and water pollution are particular examples of the interstate nature of environmental problems.

In the 1950s and 1960s, the federal government provided grants to state and local governments for research and assistance in developing and implementing their own environmental standards. The key piece of legislation in the transition to a greater role for the federal government was the Federal Environmental Protection Act, passed in 1970, which created the Environmental Protection Agency (EPA). Other acts dealing with specific environmental problems followed: the Clean Air Act of 1970, the Clean Water Act of 1972, the Safe Drinking Water Act of 1974, the Toxic Substances Control Act of 1976, and Superfund (the federal Comprehensive Environmental Response, Compensation and Liability Act) of 1980. Most of these acts have been amended one or more times. Subsequent to the passage of the Superfund Act in 1980, which was created in response to public outcry regarding the most contaminated toxic dump sites across the United States, several state and local policies have been established to cover the toxic sites that do not qualify as Superfund sites but still warrant cleanup action.[36]

As states became more involved in toxic waste regulation and air pollution in the 1960s and early 1970s, pressure on the national government to develop national environmental standards increased. Part of the pressure for federal legislation was due to the inconsistent state policies being considered and enacted. Not surprisingly, states tend to have different environmental concerns. For example, swine and poultry regulations are more important in the Midwest and Plains states, whereas nuclear cleanup is important in the West and Southwest and timber regulation is of concern to the Pacific Northwest.[37] Not only did environmental activists want a single national approach to the overarching problems of air and water pollution, but so did many of those who were being regulated. Automobile manufacturers, for instance, preferred one national standard for automobile emissions rather than dozens of differing state standards. Businesses operating in several states also pressed for uniform federal environmental standards.[38]

The basic model of environmental regulation has been for the federal government to set national standards for water and air quality. State and local governments have since been put in charge of both implementing standards and monitoring compliance. As a result, states have long argued that these unfunded mandates impose a heavy financial burden on them. Water and sewage services, for example, make up the largest local government expenditure. Environmental lobby groups have since begun to focus on state and local government, advocating change for more specific toxic waste cleanup or a specific area of contaminated groundwater, for example.[39]

Another area in which states are increasingly responsible for environmental policy is waste management. Not unexpectedly, states where the economy is growing have regulated waste management more aggressively than states where this is not the case. Economically hard-pressed states fear driving industries away.[40] Fears about nuclear waste, acid rain, and hazardous wastes have sparked extensive efforts at regulation within states, as well as court battles with nearby states over the export of unwanted byproducts of energy development.

Although the EPA gets lots of headlines, state and local governments have more people working to control pollution. States can and do experiment with ways to improve air quality. California, for instance, has been a leader in testing automobile emissions. One innovation being considered is *remote sensing,* which uses roadside devices that shoot an infrared beam across a road to detect the emissions of passing cars. This device also has a video camera that records the license plates of vehicles in violation of emission standards. Such a system could replace the periodic state inspections now required for all vehicles.

In addition to simply managing past contamination, recently states have been taking a proactive approach in the area of energy. Many states have been using alternative renewable energy both to cut down on energy costs and to rejuvenate dwindling rural economies. Large-scale wind-energy projects, for example, have been started in New

These wind turbines near Palm Springs, California, constitute an alternative source of energy.

York, Pennsylvania, Colorado, Iowa, Kansas, Texas, and Washington, among other states. Most of these were begun after 1990. As fossil fuel costs became increasingly unpredictable, states started to diversify their approach by investing in biomass, wind, hydroelectric, solar, and geothermal projects. Some states have even implemented innovative tax incentives and "net metering" programs (a practice allowing customers who have solar panels or other personal energy-generating capital to sell their energy back to the overall grid) in order to encourage more individual responsibility. Although none of these tactics have yet become widely accepted, nor is renewable energy expected to soon replace traditional energy sources, they are evidence of active state and local environmental efforts[41] (see Figure 29-3).

Environmental interest groups continue to press for stronger state and local environmental regulation, cars that go more miles on a gallon of gas, and "smart" hybrid cars and continue to demand that stiff penalties be imposed for violations of environmental laws. Further, some of the effort has shifted to individual action—recycling, conservation, saving and planting trees, and using public transportation. As the need for environmental regulation becomes more and more pressing, many state and local governments continue to react by expanding existing legislation and appropriating money for research and regulatory agency staff.

Transportation

Before the automobile, long-distance commercial travel was mainly by canal and railroad. Local roads were built and repaired under the direction of city, township, and county officials. Able-bodied male citizens were required either to put in a certain number of days working on the public roads or to pay taxes for that purpose. By the 1890s, bicycle clubs began to urge the building of hard-surfaced roads, but it was not until the early 1900s and the growing popularity of the automobile that road building became a major industry. This function was gradually transferred from the township to larger units of government, but counties and townships still have important building and maintenance functions.

Although much of the money comes from the federal government, it is the state and local governments that build the highways, public buildings, airports, parks, and recreational facilities. State and local governments, in fact, spend more money on transportation than on anything else except education and welfare. Because highways and bridges around the nation are aging, a federal tax on gasoline was levied to help rebuild these public facilities.

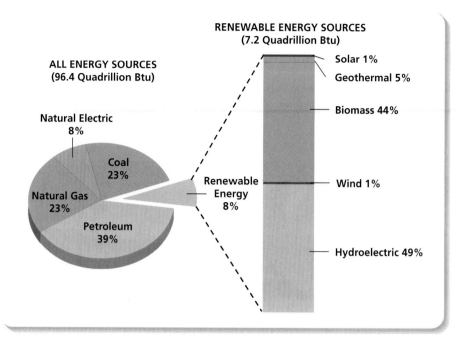

FIGURE 29–3   U.S. Energy Consumption by Source, 1999.

From 1998 to 1999, electricity generated from wind power increased 50 percent and geothermal use increased 14 percent.

SOURCE: Energy Information Administration.

To encourage residents to purchase vehicles that use clean-burning fuel, Utah has issued these special license plates that allow people to drive in the carpool lane of I-15 without a passenger. Those with energy-efficient vehicles are also eligible to receive tax credits.

The national government has supported state highway construction since 1916, and through various federal highway laws passed since then, federal aid has increased. States do the planning, estimate the costs, and arrange for the construction work, even when they receive federal assistance. In order to receive support, however, states must submit their plans to, and have their work inspected by, the U.S. Department of Transportation (DOT). All federally funded highways must meet DOT standards governing the engineering of the roadbed, employment conditions for construction workers, and weight and load conditions for trucks.

Under the Federal Highway Act of 1956, states planned and built the National System of Interstate and Defense Highways. The interstate system consists of 43,000 miles of superhighways linking almost all cities with a population of 50,000 or more. The federal government paid 90 percent of the cost of this system, with most of the money coming from taxes on gasoline, tires, and trucks that are placed in a trust fund designated for that purpose.

In 1998, Congress passed a $216 billion, six-year surface transportation bill that included $173 billion in funding for highways as well as $2 billion for highway safety. The bill funds repairing cracked asphalt, increasing safety reinforcements on bridges, and expanding the network of highways. One billion dollars is dedicated to state programs to increase the percentage of drivers who use safety belts and to prevent drunk driving. The legislation also provides $41 billion for mass transit.[42] This massive federal investment is funded by continuing the 18.3 cents-per-gallon tax on gas.

Traffic has become a major problem in recent years—especially in older cities such as Boston, Denver, Los Angeles, Seattle, San Francisco, Washington, D.C., and New York. In addition to a growing population and an increasing number of car owners, drivers are driving more each year. As a result, traffic and congestion have become pressing issues for state governments. Increasing road space, building public transportation systems, or establishing staggered work hours should help; however, transportation policy makers have

You Decide · Thinking It Through

ARE GASOLINE TAXES AND USER FEES FAIR?

You Decide... Few aspects of government are more enmeshed in politics than highway building and maintenance. Groups such as the American Automobile Association (AAA) support highway development. Automobile and tire manufacturers, oil companies, motel and restaurant associations, automobile and tourist clubs, trucking associations, and others join hands to advance their common cause. In most states, they have been strong enough to persuade legislatures to allocate gasoline taxes, drivers' license fees, trucking fees, and other user taxes for building and improving roads and highways. But there is always conflict over where the money should be spent. Farmers want secondary roads developed, truckers and tourists favor the improvement of main highways, and merchants prefer that roads come through their towns. Do you favor increased gasoline taxes to provide better roads?

Thinking It Through... With only one exception, federal and state taxes on motor fuels (gasoline and diesel) go directly to pay for highway construction. The exception is a gasoline tax that was part of President Bill Clinton's 1993 deficit reduction package. The trucking industry and others strongly objected to the tax because it broke with the tradition of gasoline taxes paying for highway construction and maintenance. Republican congressional leaders vowed to repeal the tax, which was done in 1998.*

Not everyone is pleased by the heavy commitment of public funds to highways. These roads, some say, are a massive subsidy for automobile users and makers; without highways, autos would not be so popular or so widely used, and mass transit would be used more. Some people use the highways far more than others, yet everyone must contribute to the taxes that pay for highway construction. Why not tax people in proportion to their actual use of the highways? Some people advocate installing a meter in every vehicle at a cost of less than $20 to measure usage of roadways in order to extract adequate federal user fees. Others favor incentives or restrictions on employers to foster mass transit and car pools, such as limiting parking space as part of a building permit for a new business.

*Alissa J. Rubin and Andrew Taylor, "GOP Goes for a Gas Tax Repeal," Congressional Quarterly Weekly, May 11, 1996, p. 1276.

---

not found it that simple. Adding roads or lanes often leads more people to use them and may ultimately result in new traffic patterns that are no better than the old ones. Public transportation is an option, but Americans like their vehicles, evidenced by the fact that cities with public transportation often have more traffic problems than those without. Staggering work hours is also difficult because businesses work most effectively through collaboration—both with other businesses and within a firm—and so, it is most efficient for workers to be on the job at the same time each day. Consequently, as population and car ownership continue to rise and the traffic solution remains elusive, automobile congestion will continue to be a pressing state public policy issue.

Economic Development

A primary concern of governors and mayors, as well as other state and local officials, is providing jobs for their citizens. It is not uncommon for governors to spend a significant amount of time encouraging companies to relocate within their borders, courting corporate officials, going on trade missions to other countries to promote their state's products, and negotiating favorable tax and other incentives with new businesses. This interest is not new. What is new is the international scope of these activities. Former Utah Governor Norman Bangerter was fond of saying, "The one thing you will always see on an economic development trip to Tokyo is another governor."

States compete with one another because economic development is the key to increasing the tax base that funds government services. But states face a dilemma, because

The San Francisco-bound Oakland–San Francisco Bay Bridge. The Texas Transportation Institute's annual study of 75 urban areas found that rush hours are more common and their delays are more extensive than in the past. In 2000 the average urban motorist spent 62 hours a year sitting in traffic.

satisfying the demands of new businesses can be expensive, and tax incentives can reduce the tax return the new companies will generate. Competition among states has intensified to the point that localities are worried about keeping the jobs they have, not just persuading new companies to move to their area. New York City has offered billions of dollars in incentives to influence several companies not to leave. Critics of these "bidding wars" believe that states should spend tax money on rebuilding infrastructure and strengthening education rather than offering public funds to selected large private companies.

Regulation

States and local communities adopt safety regulations on the assumption (sometimes mistaken) that the benefits to the general public will outweigh the costs to the individuals and groups being regulated. Thus laws requiring drivers' licenses, compelling motorists to stop at red lights, mandating seat-belt use, or imposing severe penalties on people caught driving under the influence of alcohol or drugs are intended to protect the safety and freedom of innocent pedestrians or occupants of other motor vehicles. Most such laws are accepted as both necessary and legitimate. States have raised the drinking age and stiffened the punishments for drunk driving, in most cases because the federal government tied federal funds to the passage of such legislation. An interest group, Mothers Against Drunk Driving (MADD), also lobbied effectively to force the issue.

Public Utilities

Corporations receive their charters from the states. Banks, insurance companies, securities dealers, doctors, lawyers, teachers, barbers, and various other businesses and professions are licensed by the states, and their activities are supervised by state officials. Farmers and industrial and service workers are also regulated. But of all businesses, public utilities are the most closely monitored.

It is easier to list than to define public utilities. They include water plants, electric power companies, telephone companies, railroads, and buse lines. Public utilities are distinguished from other businesses because government gives them special privileges, such as the power of **eminent domain** (the right to take private property for public use), the right to use public streets, and protection from competition (monopoly). In return, utilities are required to give the public adequate service at reasonable rates.

Public utilities supply essential services in fields in which market competition may be counterproductive. In the United States, private enterprise—subject to public regulation rather than public ownership—has been the usual method of providing essential services. Nevertheless, more than two-thirds of our cities own their own waterworks, about 100 operate their own gas utilities, and many are taking over the operation of their transit systems. But other services—intercity transportation, airlines, telephone, and the supply of natural gas—are almost everywhere provided by private enterprises subject to government regulation.

Every state has a utilities commission (usually called the Public Utilities Commission, or PUC) to ensure that utilities operate in the interest of the public. In 31 states, utility commissioners are appointed by the governor with the consent of the state senate. In Virginia, they are chosen by the legislature, and in about a dozen other states, they are elected by the voters.[43]

PUCs must strike a balance between fair rates for consumers and adequate profits for the utility companies. "The tremendous work load on these commissions," writes one observer, "finds commissioners constantly walking a tightrope between helping a regulated industry get a decent return on investment, and making sure consumers get good service at a fair price."[44] Utility commissioners raise or lower utility rates—perhaps the most visible part of their job—but they are also involved in toxic waste disposal, nuclear power, and truck regulation, as well as telephone, cable television, and other energy-related disputes. The average tenure for commissioners is only about three and a half years, a statistic that suggests the burnout and fatigue involved in the job.

eminent domain
Power of a government to take private property for public use; the U.S. Constitution gives national and state governments this power and requires them to provide just compensation for property so taken.

Utility commissioners operate under the assumption that their decisions are not political, yet nearly every decision they make comes under political attack or stirs political reaction. Several states have enacted laws prohibiting conflicts of interest, limiting commissioners' affiliations with the utilities they regulate and, for at least a year after they resign from the PUC, prohibiting them from accepting employment with any company that was under their regulation. Other states have established a separate office of consumer advocate to encourage even greater responsiveness to consumer needs.

Technology and innovation are driving the deregulation of utilities across the nation. The deregulation of utilities is a controversial topic in virtually every state legislature, as telephone and power companies seek to influence the new rules for competition. Telephone communication is no longer limited to transmissions over telephone lines but now includes cellular and satellite communications. Gas turbines now make it possible for some consumers to generate their own electricity rather than depend on power from public utility companies. Much of the political pressure for deregulation of utilities comes from consumers.

State legislatures and utility regulators are adopting a marketplace model in which competition between providers is encouraged rather than restricted. In the past, state utility regulators structured rate systems to provide a subsidy to rural and low-income consumers of telephone and electricity services. It is likely that these subsidies will continue, but it is more difficult to identify who pays the subsidy with so many firms now providing telephone and electricity services.

The politics of regulation, especially regulation of public utilities, is of growing interest to citizens and consumers. In many areas, citizens' groups make presentations to the PUC and regularly monitor PUC operations. There has been an increasing interest in PUC activity all across the country, especially in regulating nuclear power and monitoring the cost of energy. For example, after many years of citizen concern over the environmental impact of the San Onofre Nuclear Generating Station, the California Coastal Commission adopted a plan that would mitigate, but not prevent, the destruction of fish and kelp.[45] In Virginia, the water in Chesapeake Bay was found to contain high levels of pollutants that cause an increased risk of cancer, and that discovery led the public utilities director to impose a strict monitoring program and stiff fines for violations.

The San Onofre nuclear plant at San Onofre Beach, approximately 60 miles south of Los Angeles, California.

Employers and Employees

Despite the expanded regulations of the national government, state and local governments still have much to say about working conditions.

- *Health and safety legislation:* States require proper heating, lighting, ventilation, fire escapes, and sanitary facilities in work areas. Machinery must be equipped with safety guards. Some standards have also been established to reduce occupation-related diseases. Health, building, and labor inspectors tour industrial plants to ensure compliance with the laws.

- *Workers' compensation:* Today all states have workers' compensation programs based on the belief that employees should not have to bear the cost of accidents or illnesses incurred because of their jobs. The costs of accidents and occupational diseases are borne by employers and passed on to consumers in the form of higher prices. In the past, employees had to prove that their employers were at fault if they suffered an accident on the job. Today if people are injured or contract a disease in the ordinary course of employment, they are entitled to compensation set by a prearranged schedule. Workers' compensation is a controversial issue, with employers arguing that employee claims of workplace stress are excessive and will make American firms uncompetitive.

- *Child labor:* All states forbid child labor, yet state laws vary widely in their coverage and in their definition of child labor. Many states set the minimum age for employment at 14. Higher age requirements are normal for employment in hazardous occupations and during school hours. Many of these regulations have been superseded by stricter federal laws.

• *Consumer protection:* This movement, which became prominent in the 1960s, maintains that consumers should be provided with adequate safety information and should have their complaints heard. Most states have offices to hear consumer complaints, including lawyers working in the offices of the state attorney general. State governments often establish professional standards and handle complaints about legal and medical services or insurance practices.

Recent state activity to protect consumers has focused on fraud, especially "guaranteed prize schemes," which are mailed to more than 50 million Americans and to which millions respond. When the prize is not exactly what was promised or the method for selecting winners is deceptive, people often complain to their state government. Other areas in which state governments have been active in attempting to protect consumers include charitable solicitations by telephone, long-distance phone service promotions, credit card promotions, and guaranteed loan scams.

The Importance of State and Local Policy

All 50 state governments and more than 86,000 local governments are on the front lines of trying to solve community and regional social problems. They must often work closely with one another and the national government, and this is a frequent source of frustration.

Divided government in Washington in recent years has meant neither political party could have its way with domestic policy. Bill Clinton and George W. Bush had different priorities, and the almost evenly divided U.S. Senate in recent years has usually taken a cautious approach on such issues as health care and environmental regulation.

State officials continue to be frustrated with national legislation such as the 2001 reauthorization of the Elementary and Secondary Education Act, which mandated extensive federal requirements into core areas of state and local policy responsibilities yet provides inadequate federal funds to assist in the achievement of these goals.

Innovative governors and state legislators have sponsored important changes in welfare reform, educational testing, transportation, and urban planning. But the challenges facing state and local officials never let up.

Summary

1. We ask our state and local governments to do many things for us, and what we request in the areas of education, public welfare, health and hospitals, public safety, and transportation are the most costly, accounting for most state and local expenditures.

2. In addition, we ask states and communities to keep our streets safe, protect our natural resources, provide parks and recreation, encourage job opportunities, and protect consumers. There are, of course, great differences in how states and communities set their priorities in these areas. Some communities are so concerned about environmental quality that they are settling for selective growth at the expense of job opportunities. Other communities favor attracting jobs and industry despite environmental costs.

3. Education has been a major area of state and local government activity and concern. It moved to center stage because of a growing concern that our system was not keeping pace with our needs or our global competitors. Several reform efforts originating at the state and local levels have sought to improve our system.

4. Concern about the U.S. system of higher education has also grown as states attempt to balance budgets and meet pressing demands in corrections, health, welfare, and other areas. Few people question the need for a major investment in laboratories, computer instruction, and libraries at colleges and universities, but the federal government has not offered to pay for these things, and most states do not have the resources to do more than stay afloat in this policy area.

5. The huge national welfare overhaul legislation in 1996 eliminated any federal implementation of programs, transferring all responsibility to the states, supported with block grants of federal money. It was prompted by a desire to trim the federal budget and to eliminate disincentives for self-sufficiency and responsibility that the former welfare system seemed to create. Before the national legislation was passed, many states had experimented with limiting their caseload, placing time limits on welfare, implementing a work requirement, and placing special requirements on teenage mothers. Most of these ideas were then included in the 1996 federal law.

6. States play an important role in setting policies relating to public health. States have long sought to eradicate disease and foster prac-

tices conducive to a healthy population. The challenges for states today include the administration of federal outlay programs such as Medicaid, reforming health care services, and controlling the AIDS epidemic. Recent years' soaring Medicaid costs have posed an additional challenge to state governments.

7. Law enforcement is a traditional responsibility of state and local governments. After several decades of rising crime rates, that trend has recently been reversed, in part because of increased national and state expenditures.

8. Some state and local governments have taken the lead in protecting the environment, but more generally it has been the federal government that sets the policy standard in environmental matters.

Businesses operating in several states are often most involved in pressing for national standards of air and water quality and policies on toxic wastes. The federal government typically sets environmental standards; the states enforce them.

9. Transportation is a major area of state and local government activity. Although the federal government provides some financial assistance with the construction of roads and highways as well as urban mass transit, the responsibility of planning, building, and maintaining these transportation systems lies with the states. Federal and local fuel taxes have been used to help pay for transportation.

10. States openly compete with one another in the area of economic development by

offering tax incentives, waiving environmental regulations, and giving other enticements to businesses to locate or stay within their boundaries.

11. The primary purpose of regulation is to protect the health and safety of individuals and to promote fairness in the marketplace. Among the most regulated industries are public utilities because they enjoy a monopoly. Government usually gives these companies special privileges, specifically eminent domain—the power to take private property for public use. Public utilities, like other industries, are being deregulated as state and federal governments permit competition in these areas. States regulate other economic activities by conducting inspections, granting licenses, and limiting land uses.

Key Terms

vouchers
charter school

responsibility contract
workfare

enterprise zone
police powers

eminent domain

Further Reading

BURT S. BARNOW, THOMAS KAPLAN, AND ROBERT A. MOFFITT, EDS., *Evaluating Comprehensive State Welfare Reforms* (Brookings Institution, 2000).

JOHN D. DONAHUE, *Disunited States* (Basic Books, 1997).

DENNIS DRESANG AND JAMES GOSLING, *Politics and Policy in American States and Communities,* 2d ed. (Prentice Hall, 1998).

THOMAS DYE, *Politics in States and Communities,* 10th ed. (Prentice Hall, 2000).

CHESTER E. FINN, BRUNO V. MANNO, AND GREGG VANOUREK, *Charter Schools in Action: Renewing Public Education* (Princeton University Press, 2000).

R. KENNETH GODWIN AND FRANK KEMERER, *School Choice and Tradeoffs: Liberty, Equity, and Diversity* (University of Texas Press, 2002).

VIRGINIA GRAY, RUSSELL HANSON, AND HERBERT JACOB, EDS., *Politics in the American States: A Comparative Analysis,* 7th ed. (CQ Press, 1999).

JOHN J. HARRIGAN, *Politics and Policy in States and Communities,* 6th ed. (HarperCollins, 1997).

NORMAN R. LUTTBEG, *The Grassroots of Democracy: A Comparative Study of Competition and Its Impact in American Cities in the 1990s* (Lexington Books, 1999).

DAVID C. NICE, *Policy Innovation in State Government* (Iowa State University Press, 1994).

MICHAEL A. PAGANO AND ANN O. M. BOWMAN, *Cityscape and Capital: The Politics of Urban Development* (Johns Hopkins University Press, 1997).

MARK SCHNEIDER, PAUL TESKE, AND MELISSA MARSHALL, *Choosing Schools: Consumer*

Choice and the Quality of American Schools (Princeton University Press, 2002).

C. EUGENE STEUERLE, VAN DOORN OOMS, GEORGE PETERSON, AND ROBERT D. REISCHAUER, EDS., *Vouchers and the Provision of Public Services* (Brookings Institution, 2000).

R. KENT WEAVER, *Ending Welfare As We Know It* (Brookings Institution, 2000).

JOHN F. WITTE, *The Market Approach to Education: An Analysis of America's First Voucher Program* (Princeton University Press, 1999).

See also *Governing: The Magazine of State and Localities,* published monthly by Congressional Quarterly, Inc., and the series of excellent books on state political cultures and public policy making published by the University of Nebraska Press under the editorship of Daniel Elazar and John Kincaid.

30
CHAPTER

STAFFING
AND FINANCING
STATE AND LOCAL
GOVERNMENTS

D

EVASTATING WILDFIRES BURNED 6.7 MILLION ACRES ACROSS 11 WESTERN STATES DURING THE SUMMER OF 2000. IDAHO was hardest hit, with 1.2 million acres burned. Some 852 buildings were destroyed by the fires, which cost $878 million to put out. Governments at all levels assisted in fighting the fires and in providing disaster relief. Democratic and Republican governors forged a bipartisan partnership to persuade Congress and the White House to increase federal funding for firefighting and to revise fire prevention policies.[1]

Emergencies like this one remind us how much we rely on government for basic services. When an earthquake hits, a tornado strikes, or a forest fire forces large-scale evacuations, we expect governments to come to the rescue. Things as simple as working traffic lights, accessible roads and highways, and safe drinking water all come under the purview of state and local governments.

Public Employees: Essential to Government

Government involves many intangibles—legal authority, popular consent, shared values—but it is also very much a matter of people and money. People must be elected and hired, salaries must be negotiated and paid, and materials must be purchased. Some 18 million people work in our state and local governments.[2] They include doctors, lawyers, teachers, accountants, engineers, construction workers, secretaries, administrators, and persons with training in many different areas. The cost and quality of government depend partly on the ability and performance of these public employees and partly on the adequacy of the resources they use.

Merit Systems

More than one-third of the cost of state and local government is for people. How are these people chosen? A few of them are elected. The rest are generally hired through some kind of **merit system** in which selection and promotion depend on demonstrated performance (merit) rather than on political patronage. Although in many jurisdictions it still helps to know the right people and belong to the right party, patronage is not as prevalent as it once was. Affirmative action requirements call for recruitment through open procedures. The fact that many public employees now belong to unions has also reduced patronage.

Throughout much of the nineteenth century, governments at all levels were dominated by political patronage, a political **spoils system** in which employment was a reward for partisan loyalty and active political support in campaigns and elections. However, in 1939, Democratic Senator Carl Hatch of Arizona pushed through Congress the first Hatch Act, which promoted the merit principle and limited the political activities of federal, state, and local employees whose salaries were supported with federal funds. Subsequently, state and local governments enacted "little Hatch Acts" that enforced merit principles and restricted the political activities of their employees. Merit testing is now used in 30 states for hiring or promoting employees.[3] Moreover, in 1976, the Supreme Court declared it unconstitutional for all but a few top policy-making public employees to be dismissed for political reasons.[4]

Merit systems are generally administered by an office of state personnel, which prepares and administers examinations, provides lists of job openings, establishes job classifications, and determines salary schedules. It also serves as a board of appeal for employees who are discharged. State personnel offices are concerned with training the already employed, bargaining with labor unions, administering affirmative action programs, and filling top-level executive positions.

How well do state personnel offices do their job? Critics complain that they are too slow because they are hampered by red tape and clumsy rules; since job lists are not kept up-to-date, it often takes weeks to fill vacancies. A more serious charge is that their hiring and firing rules deprive responsible officials of authority over their subordinates. It is argued that there is so much emphasis on insulating public employees from political coercion that employees enjoy too much job security. Administrators cannot get rid of incompetents; sometimes it takes months and several elaborate hearings to dismiss public employees unwilling or unable to do their jobs. Although merit systems are supposed to emphasize ability and minimize political favoritism, they sometimes discourage able people from seeking public sector jobs.

Public Employee Unions

Public employee unions grew rapidly over the past generation as government workers organized to demand better wages, hours, working conditions, and pensions. These unions now wield considerable political clout in most states and cities. In places such as New York City, they are viewed as one of the most powerful forces in political life. In dealing with unions, state and local governments participate in **collective bargaining**—negotiating disputes between unions and management—and **binding arbitration**—settling disputes by agreeing to adhere to the decision of an arbitrator.

More than half of all state and local public employees are unionized. The American Federation of State, County, and Municipal Employees (AFSCME), representing over 1.3 million members, has been one of the fastest-growing unions in the country in recent decades.[5] Among other large public employee unions are the American Postal Workers Union, with approximately 350,000 members;[6] the Service Employees International Union (SEIU), with more than 600,000 of its 1.4 million members working in the public sector;[7] and the American Federation of Teachers (AFT), which represents 1 million teachers, and the National Education Association (NEA), which represents 2.5 million teachers.[8]

merit system
A system of public employment in which selection and promotion depend on demonstrated performance rather than on political patronage.

spoils system
A system of public employment based on rewarding party loyalists and friends.

collective bargaining
Method whereby representatives of the union and the employer determine wages, hours, and conditions of employment through direct negotiation.

binding arbitration
A collective bargaining agreement in which both parties agree, in case of dispute over the terms of the union contract, to adhere to the decision of an arbitrator.

You Decide   Thinking It Through

SHOULD PEOPLE ON THE PUBLIC PAYROLL
BE ENTITLED TO STRIKE?

You Decide... Deeply embedded in our civic ethic is the idea that civil servants should not strike, especially those (like police and firefighters) on whom the public depends for vital services. Many state and local elected officials, and certainly many ordinary citizens, believe it is wrong and dangerous for police, firefighters, and hospital workers to strike. In 1919, Massachusetts Governor Calvin Coolidge became famous for opposing the Boston police strike with these words: "There is no right to strike against the public safety by anybody, anywhere, anytime."

At the national level, Ronald Reagan's decision to fire all 11,000 air traffic controllers who engaged in an illegal strike in 1981 was supported by most of the public. When serious problems arise, like the summer wildfires in the West, residents don't want their local firefighters to be in the middle of a public employee strike.

Should public employees be allowed to strike? If you would limit the right of public employees to strike, would you limit all public employees? Would you feel differently if you were a public employee yourself?

Thinking It Through... Strikes by all public unions are illegal in most states, and even states that permit them prohibit strikes by those who provide "vital and essential services." Nevertheless, such strikes do occur, and in most instances, local and state officials are more concerned with getting people back to work than with sending them to jail for violating the law. Thus amnesty for the strikers has usually been the rule. Union organizers, for their part, refuse to consider such strikes as defying the law; instead, they believe the strike is a legitimate and useful weapon in a labor dispute. Still, the strike is generally viewed as a weapon of last resort, to be used only under intolerable conditions.

Moreover, striking has political risks for the public employee unions. Adverse public reaction may strengthen the hand of governors, mayors, or other politicians who oppose the unions. Many union leaders now favor compulsory arbitration over the strike, and more than 20 states have enacted laws providing for some form of arbitration. In binding arbitration, a neutral third party or mediating board hears the arguments of both sides in the dispute and devises what it considers to be a fair settlement. The arbitrator's verdict is final. Union leaders who favor arbitration hope that it will gain them something they might not get at the bargaining table, but without arousing the public backlash that usually accompanies strikes. Binding arbitration is used in several states, mostly in such public safety areas as police and fire protection.

Although binding arbitration does not guarantee there will be no public employee strikes, the number of such strikes has been reduced in states where it is practiced. However, the settlements that result from binding arbitration are often expensive. Each decision in a binding arbitration case has a ripple effect on the rest of a city or state administration. A pay raise for one group sets the standard for other public workers.

The firefighters' union, often considered one of the most effective political organizations among public employee unions, sometimes engages in door-to-door and telephone campaigning to elect city officials. Unions often raise funds for candidates and sponsor letter-writing campaigns to influence local and national elections. Union pressure in the 1970s and 1980s was a major reason the average pay of public employees, including benefits, rose faster than that of workers in private industry. However, since 1995, employees in private businesses have done better than public employees.[9]

The failure of the merit system to meet many of the needs of public employees encouraged the growth of public sector unions. Growth was also spurred by the example of the success of collective bargaining in the private sector (see Table 30-1). But much of the success of public employee unions has come about because government workers learned how to become a political force in government. Most public employees are

TABLE 30–1   Comparison of Merit and Collective Bargaining Systems

	Merit System	Collective Bargaining
Management rights	Extensive	Minimal
Employee participation and rights	Union membership not required	Union membership required
Recruitment and selection	Open competitive exam; open at any level	Union membership and/or occupational license
Promotion	Competitive on basis of merit (often including seniority)	On basis of seniority
Classification of position	Based on objective analysis	Classification negotiable
Pay	Based on balanced pay plan or subject to prevailing rates	Negotiable and subject to bargaining power of union
Hours, leave, conditions of work	Based on public interest as determined by legislature and management	Negotiable
Grievances	Appeal through management with recourse to civil service agency	Appeal by union representation to impartial arbitrators

SOURCE: From *Democracy and the Public Service,* Second Edition by Frederick C. Mosher, © 1982. Used by permission of Oxford University Press, Inc.

educated, intelligent people who can deliver two of the most valuable components of campaigns: money and labor (not to mention the votes of their members, members' families, and friends).

Many people think that public workers have more job security and better wages and fringe benefits than people working in the private sector. Critics point out that public employees seem to have the best of both worlds: job protection coupled with the bargaining power of a labor union. Although collective bargaining and unionization have been generally accepted in the private sector, these rights were not as widely accepted in the public sector.

Because the public sector provides services almost everyone wants and perceives as necessities, demand is relatively constant. Also, public employee unions are an effective political force, so they can influence crucial decisions that affect taxation and the allocation of revenue. Some analysts believe these two factors may result in policies that favor public employees. Awareness of this political clout of the unions has stiffened the spines of some city and state officials. Today it is not uncommon for mayors in large cities to fight the unions and win support from taxpayers and business groups who think the unions have overstepped their bounds.

Mayors as Collective Bargainers

In dealing with labor unions, mayors differ from presidents of private corporations in several ways. First, they have a responsibility to the voters. Second, union members' votes helped put them in their job, so in a sense, mayors are employees of their own employees.

Public services are primarily monopolistic in character. Usually no one else supplies the services governments provide, and many are so vital to public health and survival that a stoppage would be catastrophic. These factors place great pressure on the bargainer. Then, too, because of the public nature of government operations, bargaining often takes place in a goldfish bowl of publicity. Mayors are also more restricted than executives in private industry in dealing with labor unions because the results must be accepted by their legislative bodies. This is particularly true wherever a strong city council can exert a check on executive power.

Should Public Services Make a Profit?

privatization
Contracting public services to private organizations.

To make government more efficient and curb the growing influence of public employee unions, many communities have "contracted out" certain public services to the private sector. This practice, called **privatization**, can mean that governments save money while the private sector providers still make a profit.[10] Today virtually every community service is contracted out somewhere in the United States, and this trend is expected to continue.[11] Although states and localities vary widely in the extent to which they privatize, public-private partnerships have grown during the past two decades in order to reduce the costs of government services and to improve economic development. One frequently cited example of privatization is Indianapolis; under the leadership of former Mayor Stephen Goldsmith, the city claimed to have saved $230 million over a decade through privatization.[12]

As cities and states have become pressed for cash, efforts to encourage entrepreneurs to provide public services at a profit have increased. Delegation of emergency and police powers to profit-making corporations, however, raises questions of liability and protection of individual rights. It also raises fears that private contractors will hire transient help at less pay, undermining merit systems and public employee morale.

For successful privatization to occur, the contract between the government and the private company providing the service must define that service to the satisfaction of both parties. On one hand, because of the wide range of services provided by local police departments or health departments, it may be difficult to word such a contract. On the other hand, garbage collection and snow removal can easily be defined and specified in a contract, making these services attractive for privatization, so the trend toward outsourcing municipal services like these will continue.[13]

Paying for State and Local Government

State and local governments get most of their money from taxes.[14] Yet unlike the federal government, they are more likely to share control of the process of raising taxes with the voters through referendums, which are sometimes required before they can levy new or higher taxes. In addition, state and local governments frequently have to meet responsibilities mandated by higher levels of government, which do not always provide the funding for those mandates.

The politics of reducing the federal budget deficit and the antitax mood of the public in recent decades have meant that Congress and the president often enacted policies and expected state and local governments to pick up the tab. At the same time, citizens had high expectations for services provided by their state and local governments—and wanted even more services. This combination of increasing demand and decreasing federal funding

California Governor Gray Davis explains the projected state revenue shortfall at a news conference in Sacramento. To compensate for an estimated $35 billion budget gap, Governor Davis suggests severe spending cuts and increased taxes.

made state and local governments the fiscal "stress joints" of American government. When the economy is thriving, states often have surplus revenue and enact tax cuts; but when times are not as good, they have to raise taxes and cut spending. Because most states are constitutionally forbidden to use deficit spending for general government programs, they have to balance their budgets and respond to shortfalls by strengthening and diversifying their revenue bases.[15]

The overlapping layers of government in the United States complicate the tax picture. Tax policies at different levels of government often conflict. While the federal government is reducing taxes, states may be raising them. Indeed, when the federal government cuts both taxes and federal grants, state and local governments have little choice but to raise taxes or cut spending. This is precisely what happened in the late 1970s, early 1980s, and in the economic slow-down of 2002.[16] But the ability of states to respond to changing economic circumstances is hampered by the tax revolt of the late 1970s, which lowered taxes and brought forth constitutional amendments that make it harder to raise them. Many states also enacted spending limits, which reduced the discretion of state and local elected officials.

The ability of different levels and units of government to make their own tax policy has made tax collection more complicated and expensive. For example, national officials, state officials, and some local officials collect taxes on gasoline, and each level of government maintains its own tax-collecting office. Taxpayers are allowed to deduct certain business expenses and state income taxes from their federal income tax. Texas, Florida, South Dakota, New Hampshire, Nevada, Washington, and Wyoming have no personal income tax and rely primarily on sales taxes. In those states, taxpayers lose the deduction for state income taxes on their federal tax returns. By contrast, in Alabama, Iowa, Louisiana, Missouri, Montana, North Dakota, Oklahoma, Oregon, and Utah, taxpayers may deduct their federal income tax from their state taxes.[17] Thus changes in state laws can affect the amount of federal and state taxes a person must pay. Although there is little coordination in setting tax policy, there is cooperation between state and federal tax administrators.

No matter who collects the taxes, all the money comes out of a single economy. Although each level of government has a different tax base and each tax hits some groups rather than others, all taxes ultimately depend on the productivity of the American people. And that productivity is affected by many of the activities of government.

Who Pays the Taxes?

Who bears the cost of state and local services is decided in the United States by politics. State and local governments are free to extract whatever taxes they wish from whomever they wish, as long as their taxing practices meet the stipulations of the U.S. Constitution and in most cases unless the tax is in conflict with federal laws. The Constitution has been interpreted to prohibit states from taking the following actions:

1. Taxing exports or imports or levying tonnage duties without the consent of Congress
2. Using their taxing power to interfere with federal operations
3. Discriminating against interstate commerce, unduly burdening it, or taxing it directly
4. Using their taxing power to deprive persons of equal protection of the law
5. Depriving individuals of their property without due process

Constitutional lawyers and judges spend much of their time applying these principles to concrete situations. Out of hundreds of disputes, courts have decided that states may collect sales taxes from interstate sales and income taxes from persons and corporations within the states, even if the income was earned from interstate business. However, states may not tax the privilege of engaging in interstate commerce or the profits made through interstate transactions that cannot be apportioned to a single state. Congress has placed a moratorium on state sales taxes on Internet sales, to the anguish of most state officials and traditional firms competing with Internet commerce.

State constitutions also restrict state legislatures' taxing power. Certain kinds of property, such as that used for educational, charitable, and religious purposes, are exempt from taxation. State constitutions frequently list the kinds of taxes that may be collected and stipulate the amount of tax that may be collected from various sources.

General Property Tax

Widely criticized as "one of the worst taxes known to the civilized world," the **general property tax** is a chief revenue source for local governments. The property tax is difficult to administer, leads to favoritism and inequities, and takes little account of ability to pay.[18] Forty years ago, it provided 45 percent of the revenues for state governments and an even higher percentage of the revenues for local governments. But during the past two decades, reliance on property taxes has declined. Today they provide less than one-third of total state and local government revenues. But some states remain acutely dependent on property taxes. New Hampshire, for instance, raises nearly two-thirds of its state and local revenues from the property tax. At the other end of the scale, Alabama and New Mexico raise only about one-tenth of their state and local tax dollars from the property tax.[19]

ADMINISTRATION OF THE PROPERTY TAX   A hundred years ago, wealth was primarily *real property*—land and buildings—that was relatively easy to value. Assessors could guess the value of the property a person owned, and that assessment was a good indicator of his or her ability to pay taxes. Today wealth takes many forms. People own varying amounts of personal property—both *tangible* (furniture, jewels, washing machines, rugs, paintings) and *intangible* (stocks, bonds, money in the bank). It is possible to concentrate a large amount of wealth in a small rented apartment. The nature of real property has also changed. It no longer consists mainly of barns, houses, and land but rather of large industrial plants, huge retail stores, and office buildings whose values are hard to measure. In addition, property ownership is less likely these days to reflect ability to pay taxes. An elderly couple with a large house valued at $300,000 may be living on Social Security payments and a small allowance provided by their children. But they have to pay higher property taxes than a young couple with two healthy incomes who live in a rented apartment.

Although many communities stipulate that the general property tax be imposed on all property, this is not what actually happens. Significant amounts of real property are exempted from property taxes because they are owned by tax-exempt groups, such as churches and charitable organizations. Local governments often waive the tax as an economic development inducement or for other reasons. As a result, two taxpayers may own similar property, but one is assessed at a higher rate, and the principle of horizontal equity is violated. Intangible personal property is also seldom taxed. Some communities deliberately impose a lower rate on intangible property to induce owners to declare ownership. In addition, tangible personal property such as watches, rings, and other jewelry often escapes taxation or is grossly undervalued.

The general property tax is hard to adjust to changing circumstances. This tax is typically administered by an assessor, who attempts to place a value on property—an **assessment**. The assessment may or may not reflect the real market value of the property. In some states, the assessment is legally required to be a percentage of market value— say, 25 percent. The property tax rate is usually a tax per $100 or $1,000 of assessed valuation or some other such measure. Local and state governments can do very little to change the assessment, but they can raise or lower the tax rates.

During times of rising prices, assessed values increase much more slowly than the general price level does. So when governments need more money, the lagging tax bases fail to provide it. When prices fall, valuations do not drop at the same rate. When people cannot pay taxes, property may be sold on the market to cover tax delinquency, but such occurrences are rare. In some areas, property taxes are already so high that to increase them may discourage businesses and lower-income families from moving into the locality.

general property tax
Tax levied by local and some state governments on real property or personal, tangible property, the major portion of which is on the estimated value of one's home and land.

assessment
The valuation a government places on property for the purposes of taxation.

Third grade students at Green Bay Elementary School in North Chicago, Illinois, which has the highest poverty level in its district. There is a continuing debate as to whether funding for such schools should come primarily from local property taxes.

A property tax bill typically includes fees or taxes charged by three, four, or more governmental units, such as the city, county, school board, water utility, and other special districts. The lump-sum payment aspect of the property tax is one reason for its widespread unpopularity and has prompted some places to permit taxpayers to pay their taxes in installments, often collected with their mortgage payments.

PROPERTY TAXES AND PUBLIC EDUCATION   In recent years, controversy has been stirred up by reliance on the local property tax to support public schools. The amount of money available to finance education varies tremendously from area to area; rich suburban areas with a high property valuation per pupil are able to spend much more than poor areas like the central cities, which need the money most. Reformers have urged the states to take over the financing of public education, or at least to assume a greater share of the burden, in order to equalize differences from community to community. Although this is not a popular idea, most states do distribute funds to local districts in an attempt to ensure more equitable expenditures.

Those hoping for greater state support for the public schools have often turned to the courts. Several state courts have ruled that wide differences between school districts in per-pupil expenditures are inconsistent with the equal protection clause of the Fourteenth Amendment.[20] The California Supreme Court, for example, saw such differences as violating the California constitution.[21] However, in 1973, the U.S. Supreme Court held that there is no federal constitutional requirement that the amount spent per pupil in each school district must be the same.[22] The Court's 1973 decision temporarily slowed the push toward equalization of school expenditures, but the controversy and the issues remain. Several state courts have now handed down rulings similar to that of the California Supreme Court. Kentucky, New Hampshire, New Jersey, New York, Ohio, Texas, and Wyoming courts, for example, have held that their state constitutions require that education be financed in a way that avoids differences in funding due to differences in wealth among local school districts.[23]

Despite its weaknesses, the general property tax remains an important source of revenue for local government. Supporters of the tax say it is a practical and suitable tax because real rather than personal property is the chief beneficiary of many local services, such as fire protection. Alternatives are few, and each has disadvantages. Moreover, some of the bad features of the general property tax can be corrected by improving assessment and administration methods.

One effort to reform the general property tax is the *circuit-breaker exemption* (sometimes called a *negative income tax*) by which most states and certain cities give a form of tax relief to lower-income families and the elderly. The idea is to protect family income from property tax overload in the same way an electrical circuit breaker protects a family home from an electrical current overload: "When the property tax burden of an individual exceeds a predetermined percentage of personal income, the circuit breaker goes into effect to relieve the excess financial pressure."[24] The circuit-breaker property tax exemption seems to be most popular in the Great Lakes and Plains states and least popular in the Southeast, where property tax burdens are low.

TAX REFORM AND REVOLT   Hostility to the property tax spawned the tax revolts of the last three decades of the twentieth century. The watershed event in the politics of tax cutting was the passage in 1978 of California's Proposition 13, which limits increases in property taxes to a maximum 2 percent each year. Throughout the 1970s, California property taxes had risen dramatically, spurring voters to pass this initiative to cut them. Such direct citizen involvement in making fiscal policy is not uncommon in the United States, and there has been a resurgence of initiative and referendum activity in recent decades.[25] Passage of Proposition 13 made tax reduction an important issue nationwide. Heralded as the start of a modern tax revolt, it triggered taxing and spending limits in more than a dozen states and helped launch movements for constitutional amendments setting federal spending limits, requiring a balanced federal budget, and **indexing** income tax brackets (automatically adjusting income tax rates to rise with inflation so that in effect, they remain constant). Tax reduction was not limited to ballot initiatives but spread to state legislatures, most of which reduced income, sales, or property taxes.

The importance of California's example grew as Proposition 13 received national attention. Political commentators frequently observed that its passage signified a new move toward conservatism, the resurgence of the middle class, a general tendency toward tax cutting, and a strong message to government. Indeed, one of the most important consequences of Proposition 13 was that it gave rise to a new conventional wisdom that the public had become more conservative and desired less government. Proposition 13 prompted leaders in both parties to speak in more fiscally conservative tones.[26]

Cutting taxes, at either the state or the local level, is one way of attempting to limit government spending. Loss of revenue from taxes, however, can be made up temporarily by taking money from some other source or drawing on budget surpluses if available. More permanent solutions may involve creating new revenue sources. Thus tax cuts do not necessarily achieve the end of reducing or limiting government spending. Recognition of this fact has fostered a wide variety of more direct limitations on government spending. In their simplest form, such limitations restrict future spending to current levels; more typically, they provide for an annual increase in spending that is either limited to a fixed percentage or tied to increases in personal income or inflation. Spending limitations can be enacted without tax cuts and, unlike tax cuts, can incur few political costs since no services are being reduced in the short run. New Jersey was the first state to enact spending limits that applied to both state and local governments. Passed in 1976, the New Jersey law limited the growth in state expenditures to the annual percentage increase in per capita personal income and restricted localities to increases of no more than 5 percent without voter approval. Nearly half of the states have followed New Jersey's example and imposed limits on state expenditures.[27]

Citizen rebellions against the large tax bite of local taxes have been occurring in states all over the country.

indexing
Providing automatic increases to compensate for inflation.

FIGURE 30–1   State Revenues by Type of Tax.

SOURCE: U.S. Bureau of the Census, "State Government Tax Collections," reported in *The New York Times Almanac, 2000* (Penguin, 1999), p. 217.

One consequence of the tax revolt is that the property tax has become a less significant part of the tax base of local governments. As a result, local governments have had to develop other sources of funding (see Table 30-2).

Other Taxes

State and local governments employ a wide range of other taxes that have become increasingly popular since the property tax revolts of the 1970s and 1980s (see Figure 30-1). States and localities seek to diversify their taxes to "spread the pain" of taxes as much as possible.

SALES TAXES   Born during the Great Depression, the **sales tax** is now the most important source of revenue for states, which annually collect over $252 billion.[28] Almost all states impose some kind of general sales tax, normally on retail sales. Local sales taxes were uncommon until after World War II, but now 34 states also allow cities to impose sales taxes. Sales taxes are unpopular with local merchants, who fear they drive business away. In most cases, this is a minor issue that arises only along state borders where consumers can drive into another state with a lower sales tax to make purchases. Most consumers do not pay that much attention to the sales tax on most items.

Sales taxes are easy to administer and produce large amounts of revenue. Many consumers consider sales taxes relatively painless because paying a small amount every day avoids having to pay a large tax bill all at one time. But labor groups and low-income con-

TABLE 30–2   State and Local Revenues and Expenditures

	Share of Total Revenues
Taxes	
Property	0.9%
Individual income	13.9
Corporate income	2.9
Vehicle licenses	1.2
Motor fuels	2.6
Other	20.9
Intergovernmental revenue	
From federal government*	$215,421,000,000
Education	15.6%
Public welfare	57.1
Highways	8.9
Other	12.8
From local government	1.4
Utilities and liquor stores	0.7
Insurance trust revenue	20.9
Charges and miscellaneous	13.5
Total Revenues	**$1,039,422,000,000**

	Share of Total Expenditures
Education	29.4%
Public welfare	21.7
Hospitals and health programs	6.7
Highways	6.4
Police protection	0.8
Correction (prisons)	3.1
Utilities and liquor stores	1.2
Insurance trust expenditures	10.1
Debt redemption	4.4
Other	15.9
Total Expenditures	**$935,208,000,000**

SOURCE: U.S. Bureau of the Census, *Statistical Abstract of the United States, 2000* (U.S. Government Printing Office, 2000), p. 324. See also www.census.gov/ftp/pub/govs/www/state.html.

Percentages are based on state revenues from the federal government and not on state revenues as a whole.

sales tax
General tax on sales transactions, sometimes exempting food and drugs.

sumers remain opposed to sales taxes, favoring wider use of the income tax instead. They argue that people with small incomes spend a larger percentage of their budgets on food and clothing than the wealthy do, so sales taxes fall heaviest on those least able to pay. That is why many states exempt necessities—primarily food and drugs—from the sales tax.

States continue to search for ways to tax services, both because the states are under acute pressure to find new revenues and because the service sector of the economy continues to expand. All states tax some services, but none has a broad-based tax on services. Among the kinds of services taxed are cable television, landscaping, income tax preparation, pest control, videotape rental, laundry and dry cleaning, and photocopying.

State and local officials listen with concern to talk about the federal government's imposing a **value-added tax (VAT)** like that used in many western European countries. This tax is imposed on the value added to a product at *each stage* of production and distribution. Should the federal government impose such a tax, state and local officials fear that their ability to use the sales tax will be reduced.

There is a running battle about whether states can tax mail-order catalog and Internet sales. Opponents contend that taxing such sales violates the constitutional provisions governing interstate commerce. The Supreme Court, in general, has left the issue to be decided by Congress. The stakes are high. Online retail sales are estimated to reach $130 billion by 2006.[29] It is expected that by 2005, 10 to 12 percent of apparel, accessory, and toy sales and 20 to 25 percent of book, music, software, video, and consumer electronics sales could be by Internet.[30] Billions in revenues could go to states and localities if they taxed these purchases at the same rate they tax merchants operating within their states.

But there is a question of fairness. Local merchants who have to collect sales taxes are at a disadvantage if mail-order and Internet firms can escape these taxes. Mail-order merchants and their lobbyists claim it would be an administrative nightmare to collect and reimburse all the sales taxes, and they argue that they should not be obligated to collect taxes for a state in which they do not have a physical presence. But this position does not reduce complexity. It means if there is an Eddie Bauer store in your state and you buy a shirt from the Eddie Bauer catalog, you are charged sales tax, while a similar shirt from a Lands' End catalog would escape the tax in every state where it has no stores.

The large volume of commerce now conducted electronically suggests that some more sensible and consistent policy will have to be developed. Congress enacted the Internet Tax Freedom Act of 1998, creating the Advisory Commission on Electronic Commerce to study the matter. In the meantime, the federal government imposed a moratorium on state and local taxes on e-commerce. State and local governments contend that the moratorium unfairly preempts their authority and will erode the tax base of many governments. The issue of taxation of e-commerce is becoming more controversial and significant as the size of e-commerce grows. On one hand, how can retailers avoid multiple taxation, overregulation, and conflicting state regulations? On the other hand, is it fair to require bricks-and-mortar firms to collect sales taxes but not their electronic competitors? And as e-commerce grows and is exempted from state taxes, state sales tax revenues will decline, and schools and other institutions supported by such taxes will suffer, or other taxes will have to be increased.

INCOME TAXES The state income tax has been one of the fastest-growing revenue sources for most states. Several states impose a tax on personal income, and income tax revenue is higher than general sales tax revenue in more than 20 states. Personal income taxes are generally mildly **progressive taxes**; that is, the rate goes up with the size of the income. State income tax rates, however, do not rise as sharply as the federal income tax and seldom go above 8 percent of taxable income. Corporation incomes are frequently taxed by states at a flat rate. In some states, exemptions are generous.

States generally do not allow local governments to levy income taxes. However, some cities—following the lead of Philadelphia and Toledo—now collect a *wage tax*, and most cities in Ohio and cities, towns, and school districts in Pennsylvania levy a similar *payroll tax* on all

value-added tax (VAT)
A tax on increased value of a product at each stage of production and distribution rather than just at the point of sale.

progressive tax
A tax graduated so that people with higher incomes pay a larger fraction of their income than people with lower incomes.

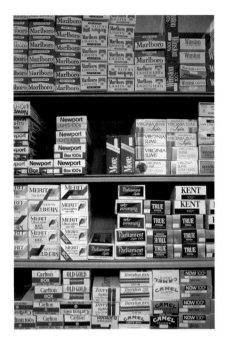

Governments impose an excise tax on cigarettes to generate revenue but also to discourage smoking and to fund the cost of treating smokers.

persons. For instance, visiting professional athletes who compete in Philadelphia are subject to the city's earned-income tax. The Toledo tax also applies to corporate profits. A municipal income tax enables hard-pressed cities to collect money from citizens who use city facilities but live in the suburbs. Similar taxes are collected by New York City, Detroit, and Louisville.

EXCISE TAXES   Almost all states tax gasoline, alcohol, and cigarettes; taxes on specific items are known as **excise taxes**. Because many cities also tax these items, the combined local, state, and federal levies often double the cost of these "luxury" items to the consumer. Gasoline taxes are sometimes combined with the funds collected for automobile and driver's licenses and are earmarked for highway construction and maintenance. Liquor taxes often consist of both license fees to manufacture or sell alcoholic beverages and levies on their sale or consumption; they are often used for general government spending.

Some states own liquor stores, with the profits going to the state treasury. High taxation of liquor is justified on the grounds that it reduces the amount of alcohol consumed, falls on an item that is not a necessity of life, and eases the task of law enforcement. Some states, like North Carolina, set aside part of their alcohol taxes for mental health programs and the rehabilitation of alcoholics. If the tax is raised too high, however, liquor purchases tend to be diverted into illegal channels, and tax revenues fall off.

The rationale for taxing cigarettes is similar. High tobacco taxes in states like Alaska, New Jersey, and Hawaii, which do not grow tobacco, and low tobacco taxes in tobacco-growing states like Virginia and the Carolinas, have led to interstate smuggling. Some states levy a general sales tax on top of the excise tax, especially on tobacco products.

SEVERANCE TAXES   In several states, **severance taxes** have been a key source of revenue. These are taxes on the privilege of "severing" or removing such natural resources as coal, oil, timber, and gas from the land. In recent years, severance taxes accounted for more than 20 percent of tax collections in eight states: Alaska, Louisiana, Montana, New Mexico, North Dakota, Oklahoma, Texas, and Wyoming. Although more than 30 states rely on some type of severance tax, significant revenues from this tax are not available to most states. Tax revenues from severance taxes go up and down with the price of oil, gas, and coal.

The state and local taxes described here do not begin to exhaust the kinds of taxes collected by state and local governments. Admission taxes, stock transfer taxes, inheritance taxes, parimutuel taxes, corporate franchise taxes, and taxes on utilities and insurance are common.

Nontax Revenues

In addition to taxation, states derive revenue from fees and special service charges. At least 10 percent of the money collected by state and local governments comes from inspecting buildings, recording titles, operating courts, licensing professions, disposing of garbage, and other services. Parking meters have become an important revenue source for some cities. Municipal governments frequently operate water supply and local transit systems. City-operated liquor stores are administered by, and turn a profit in, certain cities in Alaska, Minnesota, North Carolina, and South Dakota. The city of Dallas owns and operates an FM radio station (WRR), which plays classical music. Some states and cities run other business enterprises, such as cable television services, from which they make money (and sometimes lose it, too). North Dakota, for example, operates a state-owned bank. Municipally owned gas and power companies often contribute to city treasuries. In some cases, utility profits are large enough to make other city taxes unnecessary.

LEGALIZED GAMBLING   Recent years have seen a dramatic increase in legalized gambling in the United States. Only Hawaii and Utah do not permit some form of legalized gambling. For many years, only Nevada permitted legalized casino gambling, but now 37 states, the District of Columbia, and Puerto Rico have legalized gambling, including lotteries, and 20 states allow casinos. This increase occurred because American Indian tribes asserted their right to self-rule on reservations and brought casinos to states like California, Michigan, Connecticut, and South Dakota. In addition, gambling companies as-

excise tax
Consumer tax on a specific kind of merchandise, such as tobacco.

severance tax
A tax on the privilege of "severing" such natural resources as coal, oil, timber, and gas from the land.

serted that prohibitions against land-based casinos did not apply to floating ones, and they promoted gambling on riverboats and dockside casinos. A casino is estimated to be within a four-hour drive for 95 percent of all Americans. "The Bible Belt might as well be renamed the Blackjack Belt, with floating and land-based casinos."[31]

As more states permit legalized casinos, neighboring states rush to follow their lead to avoid losing tax revenues. Opponents of gambling assert that lotteries and legalized gambling have not produced as much revenue as promised and see negative social consequences flowing from expanded gambling opportunities.[32]

USER FEES OR CHARGES   State and local collection of **user fees**—fees paid directly by individuals to use public services such as parks and municipal golf courses—has grown rapidly in recent years. In some cities, these fees account for more than one-third of total local

---

Selling Hope: Lotteries as a Source of Revenue

Lotteries are state-sponsored and state-administered gambling used to raise money for public purposes. Along with the District of Columbia and Puerto Rico, 37 states operate lotteries to generate revenue without raising taxes. Lotteries are not entirely new; the Continental Congress ran a lottery to help finance the Revolutionary War. Indeed, all 13 original states used lotteries as a form of voluntary taxation in the 1780s. Lotteries also helped establish some of the nation's earliest colleges, notably Princeton, Harvard, and Yale. In 1964, New Hampshire was the first state to revive the practice in modern times to help balance its budget.

In recent decades, state lotteries have increased in popularity, and gross receipts have generally grown over time. State-run lotteries provide less than 3 percent of all state tax revenues, but few states that have lotteries would want to increase other taxes to make up for lottery income. States pay out between 50 and 70 percent of their gross receipts from lotteries in prizes and roughly 6 percent to cover administration costs. The remaining revenues are used for public purposes.

Elected officials like lotteries because they raise revenue without raising taxes. Critics contend that lotteries take advantage of poor people: "You're seven times more likely to be killed by lightning than to win a million in the state lottery."* Despite these economic arguments, Americans are hooked on gambling. They gamble an average of $300 per year per family. "Washington, D.C., is the lottery capital of the nation, with spending of about $1,000 per household."†

Revenues from lotteries are used for a variety of purposes. About half of the states with lotteries earmark most or all of their proceeds for education; a significant number of the remaining states commit

their proceeds to the state general fund. Some states, like Kansas and Oregon, designate lottery profits for economic development; Minnesota commits part of what it makes through the lottery to the environment; Pennsylvania and West Virginia designate senior citizens programs to receive lottery profits.

Proponents of lotteries identify a popular cause like education, the environment, or senior citizens as the beneficiaries of lottery profits in hopes of getting popular support for passage of the lottery. Opposition to the lottery often comes from church groups, which contend that state lotteries are immoral because they are a form of legalized gambling. Proponents counter that churches often raise funds through raffles, bingo, and other games of chance. Opponents also argue that lotteries are a bad investment because they yield a poor rate of return. Proponents respond that tickets are purchased more for their entertainment value than as an investment.

To find out more about lotteries go on the Web site of the Multi-State Lottery Association at www.musl.com or the North American Association of State and Provincial Lotteries at www.naspl.org. You may find more about the history of lotteries at www.scigames.com.

SOURCE: Peter Passell, "Maybe the Lottery Raises a Lot of Revenue, but as an Investment, It's Chancier than You Might Think," *New York Times,* August 6, 1998, p. D2.

*Susannah Calkins, "State Lotteries: Has a Growth Industry Faltered?" *Tax Notes,* March 23, 1992, p. 1563.

†James K. Glassman, "Lottery Madness," *Washington Post,* July 28, 1998, p. A15.

A Texas lottery winner collects over $21 million dollars.

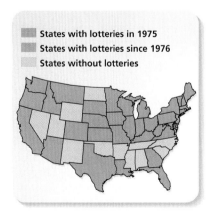

SOURCE: Roper Center for Public Opinion Research.

Betting on the Internet

States have become some of the largest sponsors of gambling, most notably through state lotteries, which are used in states as well as Canadian provinces and generate net profits in excess of $37.8 billion. Many of the state lotteries were adopted as a result of statewide referendums, which sometimes promised to provide funding for education or other important state services. New York State provides an explanation of how the lottery benefits public education at www.nylottery.org. Not surprisingly, there is now a North American Association of State and Provincial Lotteries, and its Web site (www.naspl.org) provides a broad range of information on gambling in the United States.

More recently, video poker and other forms of gambling have been spreading to more states. As improvements have been made in data encryption, it is now technologically possible for people to engage in virtual gambling in the privacy of their homes. What does this technology do to state laws limiting or banning gambling? The possibility of betting online also raises the issue of whether those who take bets can be prosecuted for permitting underage gambling.

The federal government has tried to play a role in restricting gambling in various forms, such as betting on college or high school sports and underage gambling. Many coaches of college sports have requested that limitations be placed on betting on their games. The American Gaming Association (www.americangaming.org) provides media updates on government efforts to restrict gambling. Or you can refer to the links and resources provided by the North American Gaming Regulators Association at www.nagra.org.

tax revenue.[33] Examples of services for which users pay fees are toll roads, higher education, hospitals, airports, parks, sewerage, and solid waste management. It is harder to impose fees on other kinds of services because such charges would raise questions of fairness and access. The cost of libraries could be paid entirely by library users, for instance, but most localities seek to encourage library use by the disadvantaged through heavy subsidies.

It is not always easy to distinguish between individual and community benefits. Public schools obviously benefit the families who use them more than the families who do not. Yet education is generally thought to yield considerable benefits for the community at large, so it is financed by taxes rather than user fees. Similarly, it would not be fair to support fire departments by charging people whose homes or businesses experienced fires in a given year.

GRANTS   Grants from states to local governments have become increasingly important during the past several decades. The national government once allocated large sums to cities, but that stopped in the 1980s. Local governments now go to the states to get more than $275 billion in assistance. State officials return revenues collected from certain taxes to local governments, often without specifying the purposes for which the money should be used. Local governments receive state and federal grants in a wide range of areas, including education, transportation, corrections, law enforcement, housing, welfare, community development, and health care. One reason local governments receive so much money in the form of grants is that they are the unit of government closest to the people and most experienced at providing services.

Local governments often see state and federal grants as enhancing the services they provide. In return for a modest investment of local tax revenue, local governments can get grant money from state or federal governments. But grant money may not be available for some pressing local priorities, or the strings attached to the money may permit state and federal governments to set local priorities. In such cases, are local governments wise to pursue the grants, or should they put their money into their most pressing priorities? Local governments also worry about depending on grant money if state or federal money should dry up in the future.

Borrowing Money

State and local governments collect large sums of money to pay for current operating expenses—garbage collection, police protection, and social services. To fund long-term

user fees
Fees charged directly to individuals who use certain public services on the basis of service consumed; also called a *user charge*.

projects—so-called *capital expenditures*—cities and states often have to borrow money. This long-term borrowing is necessary for building schools, constructing roads, and clearing slums—projects whose costs are so large that it is not feasible to pay for them out of current revenue. Moreover, because these improvements have long lives and add to the wealth of the community, it is reasonable to pay for them over time. For this purpose, governments issue bonds, most often with voter approval.

During the early years of the nineteenth century, states and cities subsidized railroad and canal builders. The money for these and other public improvements came from bonds issued by the cities or states and purchased by investors. Provision for payment of these debts was inadequate, and citizens were burdened with debts long after the improvements had lost their value. As a result, default on obligations was frequent. Aroused by the legislatures' abuse of their authority, voters insisted on constitutional amendments restricting legislative discretion to borrow money. The power to borrow money for the long term now routinely requires voter approval.

Increasingly important since the passage of the National Tax Reform Act are special-purpose governments or special districts: airport authorities, bridge and highway authorities, water and wastewater districts, public transit authorities, and community college districts. Their creation has resulted in turning more and more to *revenue bonds* to help finance their operations. The repayment and dividends due investors come from tolls and fees charged by the facility. In most cases, revenue bonds do not require voter approval, making it much easier to issue this kind of debt and also to spend more on services like public transportation.[34]

State and local bonds are attractive to investors because the interest is exempt from federal income tax. State and local governments can borrow money at a lower interest rate than private businesses can, and although credit ratings differ sharply according to economic health, the credit of most cities and states is good. Hence they can easily find buyers for their bonds. Because governments are often permitted to issue bonds beyond the limitations on their general indebtedness, they use them whenever possible. However, as New York City learned in the 1970s, excessive reliance on bonds can be detrimental to the fiscal health of a state or city.

User fees, like the tolls collected at this tunnel entrance in New York City, contribute to the maintenance of such facilities.

Doing More with Less

John Shannon, an authority in the field of public finance, has written that there were three "R's" that shocked state and local governments in the recent past. The first "R" was the *revolt* of the taxpayers, which started with California's Proposition 13 and quickly became a national phenomenon. The second "R" was the *recession* of the late 1980s and early 1990s, which placed demands on state and local governments to care for the unemployed and needy. And the third "R" was the *reduction* in federal grants, which meant state and local governments were on their own.[35] States had to search for ways to make ends meet and to live within their revenue projections.

As discussed in Chapter 29, welfare reform in the mid-1990s encouraged states to experiment and modify welfare funding within broad parameters. The federal government would still pay for most of welfare, but with far fewer strings attached. Whether this division of responsibility between the national and state governments will become a model for other areas of public policy is not yet clear.

Another area where policy is in flux is telecommunications. The Telecommunications Act of 1996 opened local telephone markets to competition, set conditions for the powerful telephone companies to enter new markets, and regulated competition between telephone and cable companies. States were allowed to continue regulating telephone company profits. The act stresses that there shall be no barriers to entry and assigns the Federal Communications Commission regulatory power over that of the states. Many cellular and satellite services are provided by out-of-state companies that traditionally have not been taxed by the states. Property taxes may need to be adjusted in several states as utilities contest their tax assessments.

Intergovernmental Competition

State and local governments exist in a competitive environment in which they seek to enhance their own economy and overall reputation. They have become more competitive in courting business and economic growth because of the increasing mobility of business and the stagnant growth in some sectors of the economy and in some regions of the country. One way governments compete in this marketplace is through the use of *tax incentives* that offer reduced tax rates to promote business investment in the local community. Government officials assume that a progrowth policy is good politics because voter confidence increases when new jobs and businesses move into a community or state.

Local governments that are successful in luring businesses to locate within their boundaries also assume that in the long run these new businesses will add to the tax base by stimulating sales taxes and property taxes. In the case of large shopping malls that attract shoppers from surrounding communities, the revenues from the sales tax may actually lower the tax burden for residents of the city because of sales taxes paid by nonresidents.

Developers of shopping malls or office complexes who are thinking about relocating often play one local government against another in an effort to drive down their tax burden. Established businesses in the community then cry foul about the tax incentives offered to attract new businesses or keep those who threaten to leave. Economists are skeptical about how important these incentives really are. Some believe that such factors as space availability, cost of land, cost of labor, and quality of life are at least as important in decisions about where businesses locate.[36]

Another example of intergovernmental competition for tax incentives and subsidies concerns sports teams and stadiums or arenas. In recent years, competition between cities, especially larger cities, has drawn them into funding the construction of major sports facilities for professional football, basketball, hockey, or baseball teams. Because the teams are identified with the city or state and are perceived to enhance the community's reputation, local and state governments have been responsive to the demands of team owners. Some cities have offered team owners "sweetheart deals" to keep the team or build them a new stadium.[37] The New York Yankees threatened to leave their historic location in the Bronx for New Jersey's Meadowlands but agreed to stay put after getting concessions from local government. Often the building of new facilities requires a referendum, but other arrangements, such as the proceeds from parking and vendors, are open to negotiations between the owners and government officials.[38]

Safeco Field in Seattle, Washington, home to the Seattle Mariners, is one of the country's new sports stadiums built with a combination of state, local, and private funding.

Summary

1. Wages for public employees constitute more than one-third the cost of state and local government. These public employees are hired through merit systems.

2. One of the most controversial aspects of state and local government in recent years has been the unionization of over 50 percent of public employees at the state and local levels. Public employee unions have been increasingly successful in recruiting new members and bargaining for better wages, hours, working conditions, and pensions. Their success has caused some public backlash.

3. One response to growing costs has been outsourcing of public services to the private sector. Garbage collection, recreation, and even emergency services are now contracted out in some cities. Arguments in favor of privatization include lower cost and better services. But others argue that this movement reduces government accounta-

bility and may lead to corruption in the awarding of contracts.

4. State and local governments get most of their money from taxes. Decreasing federal funding has made state and local governments the "stress joints" of American government.

5. The general property tax, despite its unpopularity, remains the most important source of revenue for many local governments. Property is generally thought of as real estate but can include other personal property like automobiles or boats. Administration of the tax is generally handled at the local level, but several states provide oversight. The property tax is a major revenue source for public schools.

6. Tax revolts in the 1970s and 1980s resulted in limits on property taxes in several states and often made it more difficult to raise property taxes. The property tax is now a less significant part of the tax base of local governments.

7. State and local governments have traditionally received revenues primarily from property taxes but also from sales taxes, income taxes, excise taxes, and severance taxes. Recently, they have diversified their revenue sources by turning to such devices as lotteries, legalized gambling, user fees, other fees and special service charges, and taxes not previously used at the state and local levels. This diversification was made necessary by economic downturns and by cutbacks in federal support. Intergovernmental grants from states to cities and school districts have increased in importance as local governments have had to deal with rising costs and expectations but limited revenues. In addition, the growth in special-district governments has led to greater reliance on revenue bonds to finance local services.

8. States and local governments have also become more competitive in courting business and economic growth, especially through tax incentives and subsidies.

Key Terms

merit system
spoils system
collective bargaining
binding arbitration

privatization
general property tax
assessment
indexing

sales tax
value-added tax (VAT)
progressive tax
excise tax

severance tax
user fees

Further Reading

J. RICHARD ARONSON, ELI SCHWARTZ, AND DAVID S. ARNOLD, *Management Policies in Local Government Finance,* 4th ed. (International City/County Management Association, 1996).

DAVID BRUNORI, ED., *The Future of State Taxation* (University Press of America, 1998).

TERRY N. CLARK AND LORNA C. FERGUSON, *City Money: Political Processes, Fiscal Strain, and Retrenchment* (Columbia University Press, 1983).

RONALD C. FISHER, *Intergovernmental Fiscal Relations* (Kluwer, 1997).

KATHRYN A. FOSTER, *The Political Economy of Special-Purpose Government* (Georgetown University Press, 1997).

M. DAVID GELFAND, ED., *State and Local Taxation and Finance in a Nutshell,* 2d ed. (West, 2000).

STEVEN D. GOLD, ED., *The Fiscal Crisis of the States: Lessons for the Future* (Georgetown University Press, 1995).

CHARLES T. GOODSELL, *The Case for Bureaucracy,* 3d ed. (Chatham House, 1994).

ROY T. MEYERS, ED., *Handbook of Government Budgeting* (Jossey-Bass, 1999).

NATIONAL CONFERENCE OF STATE LEGISLATURES, *Legislative Budget Procedures in the 50 States* (National Conference of State Legislatures, 1998).

DAVID ALAN NIBERT, *Hitting the Lottery Jackpot: State Governments and the Taxing of Dreams* (Monthly Review Press, 2000).

MICHAEL PAGANO AND RICHARD MOORE, *Cities and Fiscal Choices* (Duke University Press, 1985).

B. GUY PETERS, *The Politics of Taxation: A Comparative Perspective* (Blackwell, 1991).

JOHN E. PETERSEN AND DENNIS R. STRACHOTA, EDS., *Local Government Finance: Concepts and Practices* (Government Finance Officers Association, 1991).

HENRY J. RAIMONDO, *Economics of State and Local Government* (Praeger, 1992).

HARVEY S. ROSEN, *Public Finance,* 6th ed. (McGraw-Hill, 2002).

E. S. SAVAS, *Privatization: The Key to Better Government,* 2d ed. (Chatham House, 1998).

RONALD SNELL, ED., *Financing State Government in the 1990s* (National Conference of State Legislatures and National Governors' Association, 1993).

THOMAS R. SWARTZ AND JOHN E. PECK, EDS., *The Changing Face of Fiscal Federalism* (Sharpe, 1990).

Also, the U.S. Bureau of the Census regularly publishes reports on state and municipal finances.

31
CHAPTER

SUSTAINING CONSTITUTIONAL DEMOCRACY

AMERICA'S FOUNDING GENERATION FOUGHT AN EIGHT-YEAR REVOLUTION TO SECURE ITS RIGHTS AND LIBERTY. FIRST AT THE Constitutional Convention in 1787 and later in the first Congress, they faced the challenges of creating a government, writing a Constitution, and drafting a Bill of Rights that would protect the rights to life, liberty, and self-government for themselves and all who would come later. But they knew, as we also know, that passive allegiance to ideals and rights is never enough. Every generation must see itself as having a duty to nurture these ideals by actively renewing the community and nation of which it is a part.

The framers knew about the rise and decline of ancient Athens. They were familiar with Pericles and his famed funeral oration in which he said that the person who takes no part in public affairs is a useless person, a good-for-nothing.[1] The city's business, as Pericles and many Athenians saw it, was everyone's business. Athens had flourished as an example of what a civilized city might be, but it collapsed when greed, self-centeredness, and complacency set in. As time went on, the Athenians wanted security more than they wanted liberty; they wanted comfort more than they wanted freedom. In the end they lost it all—security, comfort, and freedom. "Responsibility was the price every man must pay for freedom. It was to be had on no other terms."[2]

If we are to be responsible citizens of the United States in the truest meaning of the term, our dreams must transcend personal ambition and the accumulation of material goods. Our country needs citizens who understand that our well-being is tied to the well-being of our neighbors, community, and country. This spirit was evident in the days and weeks following the terrorist attacks on New York City and Washington, D.C., on September 11, 2001. All across the country, people contributed to relief efforts. In an address to the nation in the evening of the day of the attacks, President Bush said, "Terrorist attacks can shake the foundations of our biggest buildings, but they cannot touch the foundation of America. These acts shatter steel, but they cannot dent the steel of American resolve."[3] As the war on terrorism was waged, what also became clear was the tremendous contrast between the freedom of citizens in the United States and the repression of the Taliban regime in Afghanistan.

More people today live under conditions of political freedom than under authoritarian governments than at any previous time. Throughout history, most people have lived in societies in which a small group at the top imposed its will on others. Authoritarian governments justify their actions by saying that people are too weak to govern themselves; they need to be ruled. Thus neither in Castro's Cuba nor in the military regime of North Korea, neither in the People's Republic of China nor in Saudi Arabia, do ordinary people have a voice in the type of decisions we Americans routinely make: Who should be admitted into college or serve in the military? Who should be allowed to immigrate into the country? How much money should be spent for schools, economic development initiatives, health care, or environmental protection? In America, we take the freedom to make such decisions for granted, but the events of September 2001 have reminded us that we should not.

The theme in this last chapter is simple: Elected leadership and constitutional structures and protections are important, but an active, committed citizenry is equally important. Freedom and obligation go together. Liberty and duty go together. The answer to a nation's problems lies not in producing a perfect constitution or a few larger-than-life leaders. The answer lies in encouraging a nation of attentive and active citizens who will, above and beyond their professional and private ambitions, care about the common concerns of the Republic and strive to make democracy work.

The Case for Government by the People

The essence of our Constitution is that it both grants power to government and withholds power from it. Fearing a weak national government and popular disorder, the framers wanted to strengthen the powers of the national government so that it could carry out its

Voices on the Democratic Faith

I dream of a republic that is independent, free, and democratic; a republic with economic prosperity yet social justice; a humane republic that serves the individual and therefore hopes that the individual will serve it in turn; a republic of well-rounded people, because without such people, it is impossible to solve any of our problems.

Vaclav Havel, New Year's Day Speech, January 1, 1990

We have awakened the people
We have seeded democracy
We will win
Our next generation will continue.
It doesn't matter
If we don't succeed.

Anonymous democracy demonstrator,
Tiananmen Square, Beijing, Spring 1989

During my lifetime I have dedicated myself to this struggle of the African people. I have fought against white domination, and I have fought against black domination. I have cherished the ideal of a democratic and free society in which all persons live together in harmony and with equal opportunities. It is an ideal I hope to live for and to achieve. But if needs be, it is an ideal for which I am prepared to die.

Nelson Mandela, Statement at the Rivonia Trial, 1964

responsibilities, such as ensuring domestic order and maintaining national defense. They also wanted to limit state governments in order to keep them from interfering with interstate commerce and property rights. Valuing above all the principle of individual liberty, the framers wanted to protect the people from too much government. They wanted a limited government—yet one that would work. The solution was to divide up the power of the national government, to make it ultimately responsive, if only indirectly, to the voters.

Most Americans want a government that is efficient and effective but that also promotes social justice. We want to maintain our commitment to liberty and freedom. We want a government that acts for the majority yet also protects minorities. We want to safeguard our nation and our streets in a world full of change and violence. We want to protect the rights of the poor, the elderly, and minorities. Do we expect too much from our elected officials and public servants? Of course we do!

Constitutional democracy is a system of checks and balances. It balances values against competing values. Government must balance individual liberties against the collective security and needs of society. The question always is, which rights of which people are to be protected by what means and at what price to individuals and to the whole society? These questions arose again and again in the wake of the terrorist attacks of September 2001 and thereafter.

This participant in a Black Voter Awareness Rally urges citizens to accept responsibility for perpetuating democracy.

Participation and Representation

No political problem is more complicated than working out the proper relationship between voters and elected officials. It is not just a simple issue of being sure that elected officials do what the voters want them to do. Every individual has a host of conflicting desires, fears, hopes, and expectations, and no government can represent them all. But even if millions of voters could be represented in their many interests, the question of how they would be represented would remain. Through direct representation, such as a traditional New England town meeting or ballot initiatives and referendums? Through economic or professional associations, such as labor unions or political action committees? Through a coalition of minority groups? All of these and other alternatives can be defended as proper forms of representation in a constitutional democracy. Yet all also have limitations.

Some propose to bypass this thorny problem of representation by vastly increasing the role of direct popular participation in decision making.[4] What many people regard as the most perfect form of democracy would exist when every person has a full and equal opportunity to participate in all decisions and in all processes of influence, persuasion, and discussion that bear on those decisions. Direct participation in decision making, its advocates contend, will serve two major purposes. It will enhance the dignity, self-respect, and understanding of individuals by giving them responsibility for the decisions that shape their lives. And it will act as a safeguard against undemocratic and antidemocratic forms of government and prevent the replacement of democracy by dictatorship or tyranny. This idea rests on a theory of self-protection that says interests can be represented, furthered, and defended best by the people they concern directly.

New technologies as well as new uses of old technologies present ways in which governments can appeal directly to voters and voters can speak directly to public officials. We now have voting by mail in Oregon and other places, and some people advocate voting on the Internet. Digital town halls may be next. Some applaud these developments; others are appalled by them.

But we still need institutions such as elected legislatures, which can take the time to digest complicated information and conduct impartial hearings to air competing points of view. The average citizen rarely has the time or experience to evaluate all the available information. Experience with many forms of participatory democracy also suggests its limitations as a form of decision making. In an age of rapidly growing population, increasingly complex economic and social systems, and enormously wide-ranging decision-making units of government, direct participation can work only in small communities or at the neighborhood level. As a practical matter, people simply cannot put in endless hours taking part in every decision that affects their lives.

Participatory democracy can still play an important role in smaller units—in neighborhood associations, local party committees, and the like. And perhaps the idea of participation could be greatly extended, for example, to greater influence of workers in the running of factories and corporations. But we must distinguish between democracy as direct participation and as citizen participation. One course of action would be to enlarge the role of participation in representation—that is, to broaden the power of all people to take part in choosing their representatives in larger units of government. This brings us back to the hard questions of indirect representation.

If we must have representatives, who shall represent whom? By electing representatives in a multitude of districts, it is possible to build into representative institutions—the U.S. Congress, for example—most minority interests and attitudes. In the United States, we generally have election processes in which only the candidate with the most votes wins. But there are other ways. For example, one way widely used in European nations is proportional representation—a system in which each party running receives the proportion of legislative seats corresponding to its proportion of votes.

Representation can also be influenced by whether there is only one party, two, or several. Ours is a generally strong two-party system that knits local constituencies into coalitions that can elect and sustain national majorities. A major factor in maintaining our two-party system is that single-member legislative districts such as those for the U.S. Congress and state legislatures tend to lead to two-party systems. This regularity, called *Duverger's law,* is generally seen as helping moderate our politics.[5] In contrast, when countries adopt proportional representation, more minor parties come to the fore.

Which is better, elected officials who represent coalitions of minorities or officials who represent a relatively clear-cut majority and have little or no obligation to the minority? The answer depends on what you expect from government. A system that represents coalitions of minorities usually reflects the trading, competition, and compromising that must take place in order to reach agreement among the various groups. Such a government has been called *broker rule:* Elected officials act essentially as a go-between or mediator among organized groups that have definite policy goals. Under broker rule, leaders cannot get too far ahead of the groups; they must talk back and forth, shifting in response to changing group pressures. Instead of acting for a united popular majority with a fair-

To Protect the Dissenter

We have devised a variety of ways to protect the dissenter. Our civil liberties are a part of that system, and so are Robert's Rules of Order, and grievance procedures, and the commonly held view that we should hear both sides of an argument. In short, we have a tradition, a set of attitudes and specific social arrangements designed to ensure that points of view at odds with prevailing doctrine will not be rejected out of hand.

But why be so considerate of dissent and criticism? To answer this question is to state one of the strongest tenets of our political philosophy. We do not expect organizations or societies to be above criticism, nor do we trust the men who run them to be adequately self-critical. We believe that even those aspects of society that are healthy today may deteriorate tomorrow. We believe that power wielded justly today may be wielded corruptly tomorrow. We know that from the ranks of the critics come cranks and troublemakers, but from the same ranks come the saviors and innovators. And since the spirit that welcomes nonconformity is a fragile thing, we have not depended on that spirit alone. We have devised explicit legal and constitutional arrangements to protect the dissenter.

SOURCE: John W. Gardner, *Self-Renewal,* rev. ed. (Norton, 1981), pp. 71–72.

ly definite program, either liberal or conservative, the government tries to satisfy all major interests by giving them a voice in decisions and sometimes a veto over actions. In the pushing and hauling of political groups, the government is continually involved in delicate balancing acts, and no one wins all the time.

Some critics argue that fair representation has not been achieved in the American system. In the U.S. Congress and many state legislatures, for example, we still have relatively few women and minorities. Critics also point to the extent of nonvoting and other forms of nonparticipation in politics; the fact that low-income persons are less well organized than upper-income persons; the bias of strong organized groups toward the status quo; the domination of television and the press by a few corporations; and the virtual monopoly of party politics by the two major parties, which do not always offer the voters meaningful alternatives. Critics are concerned that our system of government builds in procedures designed to curtail legislative majorities—for example, the filibuster in the Senate or the power of the Supreme Court to declare laws unconstitutional. Critics also point to the many mistakes made by voters and election machines in the 2000 elections in Florida as yet another weakness of our democratic system.

Such charges may be exaggerated, but they cannot be denied. Those who believe that governments should be more directly responsive to political majorities can point to steady improvement in recent years. Election laws have been changed to simplify voter registration, expand and improve voting procedures, and enforce one-person, one-vote standards. Pressure has been building to limit the ability of rich people and well-financed interests to influence elections. Pressure has also been building to streamline voting systems and pass campaign reform measures.

Over the course of U.S. history, there has been a shift toward greater direct democracy, and this trend is likely to continue. The founders designed a system with direct representation limited to the House of Representatives. Today both the House and Senate are directly elected. Moreover, with the advent of direct primaries, voters decide the nominees for federal office. The initiative and referendum process provides an even more direct way for citizens to enact or overturn laws. Who may vote in our elections has also been dramatically expanded from white male property owners to all citizens over 18 years of age. In the age of the Internet, pressures to expand the role of citizens in making laws and voting on candidates or recalling officeholders via petition are examples of how direct democracy may be further expanded.

By this point, you undoubtedly appreciate that democracy has to mean much more than popular government and unchecked majority rule. A democracy needs competing politicians with differing views about the public interest. A vital democracy, living and growing, places its faith in the participation of citizens as voters, faith that they will elect not just people who will mirror their views but leaders who will exercise their best judgment—"faith that the people will not condemn those whose devotion to principle leads them to unpopular courses, but will reward courage, respect honor, and ultimately recognize right."[6]

The Role of the Politician

Americans today have decidedly mixed views about elected officials. They realize that at their best, politicians are skillful at compromising, mediating, negotiating, and brokering—and that governing often requires these qualities. But they also suspect politicians of being ambitious, conniving, unprincipled, opportunistic, and corrupt. Americans hold politicians in low esteem compared with people in other professions.

Still, we often find that individual officeholders are bright, hardworking, and friendly (even though we may suspect they are simply trying to win our vote). And our liking sometimes turns into reverence after these same politicians die. George Washington, Abraham Lincoln, Dwight D. Eisenhower, and John F. Kennedy are acclaimed today. Harry Truman liked to joke that a statesman is merely a politician who has been dead for about ten years.

Of course, we must put the problem in perspective. In all democracies, the public probably expects too much from politicians. Further, people naturally distrust those who wield power. Public officeholders, after all, tax us, regulate us, and conscript us. We dislike political compromisers and ambitious opportunists—even though we may need such people to get things done.[7]

Yet as we have demonstrated with numerous examples in this book, individuals can and do make a difference in public life. Individuals can make a difference in shaping policy on the local, state, national, and international levels, whether the policy be drunk driving, early childhood medical care, land mines, or using the courts to influence a policy agenda.

Politics is a necessity. Politics is a vital and at times a noble leadership activity. Politicians are essential for running the American Republic, whose fragmented powers require them to mediate among factions, build coalitions, and compromise among and within branches of government to produce policy and action.

Leadership in a Constitutional Democracy

Even though one of the most universal cravings of our time is a hunger for creative and compelling leadership, defining leadership is a challenge in itself. Leadership can be understood only in the context of both leaders and followers. A leader without followers is a contradiction in terms. Leadership is also situational and contextual; a person is often effective in only one kind of situation. Leadership is not necessarily transferable. James Madison, for example, was a brilliant political and constitutional theorist; he was also a superb politician. Yet he was not a brilliant president.[8] The leadership required to lead a marine platoon up a hill in battle is different from the leadership needed to change racist or sexist attitudes in city governments. The leadership required of a campaign manager differs from that required of a candidate.

Although leaders are often skilled managers, they need more than just managerial skills. Managers are concerned with doing things the right way; leaders are concerned with doing the right thing. Managers are concerned with efficiency and process, especially routines and standard operating procedures. Leaders, by contrast, concentrate on goals, purposes, and a vision of the future. Some leaders have indispensable qualities of contagious self-confidence, unwarranted optimism, and dogged idealism that attract and mobilize others to undertake tasks they never dreamed they could accomplish. In short, they empower others and enable many of their followers to become leaders in their own right. Most of the significant breakthroughs in our nation, as well as in our communities, have been made or shaped by people who, while seeing all the complexities and obstacles ahead of them, believed in themselves and in their purposes so much that they refused

---

 Proud to Be a Politician

Must a politician gain public office by denouncing the profession? From the tone of many recent congressional races, it would appear that this is a growing trend. Journalist Charles McDowell of the *Richmond Times-Dispatch* noted this trend on the PBS series *The Lawmakers* and suggested that such a tactic "demeans an honorable and essential profession—that of the politician." McDowell proposed that every member of Congress be required to take the following oath:

I affirm that I am a politician. That I am willing to associate with other known politicians. That I have no moral reservations about committing acts of politics. Under the Constitution, I insist that politicians have as much right to indulge in politics as preachers, single-issue zealots, generals, bird-watchers, labor leaders, big business lobbyists, and all other truth-givers.

I confess that, as a politician, I participate in negotiation, compromise, and trade-offs in order to achieve something that seems reasonable to a majority. And although I try to be guided by principle, I confess that I often find people of principle on the other side, too.

So help me God.

to be overwhelmed and paralyzed by self-doubts. They were willing to gamble, to take risks, to look at things in a fresh way, and often to invent new rules.[9]

Leaders recognize the fundamental—unexpressed as well as expressed—wants and needs of potential followers. By bringing followers to a fuller consciousness of their needs, they help convert their hopes and aspirations into practical demands on other leaders, especially leaders in government. A leader in a democracy consults and listens while educating followers and attempting to renew the goals of an organization.

Reconciling Democracy and Leadership

Americans are fond of saying, "It is all politics, you know." This greatly oversimplified insight is offered as profound. More important, it is intended as a negative judgment, as if things somehow would be improved if we did not have politics and politicians.

But politics is the lifeblood of democracy, and without politics, there is no freedom. To conclude that politicians are interested in winning elections is about as profound as to conclude that businesspeople are interested in profits. Of course they are! We do not expect our economy to operate because the shoe store owner is motivated only by a desire to see that people have dry, warm feet. Rather, we harness the store owner's desire to make a living as a way to see to it that the largest number of people get the shoes they want at the lowest possible price. Similarly, we harness the elected official's desire for reelection as the way to ensure that elected officials do what most of the voters want them to do. It is the politician's need to serve and please the voters that is the indispensable link in making democracy work.[10]

One of our major political challenges is to reconcile democracy and leadership. In the past, we often have held a view of leaders as all-powerful. Yet a nation of subservient followers can never be a democratic one. A democratic nation requires educated, skeptical, caring, engaged, and conscientious citizens. It also requires citizens who will recognize when change is needed and have the courage to bring about necessary reforms and progress.[11] Such citizens provide the leaders that enable constitutional democracy to survive and thrive. Constitutional democracy requires citizens who are willing to run for office and then serve with integrity. It is understandable that good people shy away from seeking office, with the ensuing loss of privacy and other burdens of public office. But no matter how brilliant our Constitution or strong our economy, ultimately our system depends on individuals willing to compete for office.

Why People Run for Office

- To solve problems and promote the American dream
- To advance fresh ideas and approaches
- To "throw some rascal out" whose views they dislike
- To gain a voice in policy making
- To serve as a spokesperson
- To acquire political influence and a platform from which to influence public opinion
- To gain prominence and power
- To satisfy ego needs
- To gain opportunities to learn, grow, travel, and meet all kinds of people
- To be "where the action is"—involved in the thick of government and political life—campaigning, debating, drafting laws, reconciling diverse views, and making the system responsive

Why People Are Reluctant to Run for Office

- Loss of privacy
- Less time for family or favorite pastimes
- Less income than in many business or professional occupations
- Exposure to partisan and media criticism
- Involvement in many things most people would rather not do—such as marching in parades, attending county fairs, and going to political dinners, banquets, and meetings
- Fear of compromising principles because of the complexity of our adversarial system
- Expense of campaigning
- Aversion to conflict, divisiveness, and ambition
- Concern that the constitutional structure and party system make it nearly impossible to exercise meaningful leadership

Experience teaches that power wielded justly today may be wielded corruptly tomorrow. It is right and necessary to protest when a policy is wrong or when the rights of other citizens are diminished. Democracy rests solidly on a realistic view of human nature. Criticism of official error is not unpatriotic. Our capacity for justice, as theologian and philosopher Reinhold Niebuhr observed, makes democracy possible. But our "inclination to injustice makes democracy necessary."[12] Democratic politics is the forum where, by acting together, citizens become and remain free.[13]

Leadership thought of as an engagement among equals can empower people and enlarge their opinions, choices, and freedoms. The answer for our republic lies not in producing a handful of great, charismatic, Mount Rushmore–type leaders but in educating a citizenry who can boast that we are no longer in need of superheroes because we have become a nation of citizens who believe that each of us can make a difference and that all of us should regularly try to do so.[14]

Leaders will always be needed. However, our system of government is, in many ways, designed to prevent strong and decisive action, lest too much political power be placed in the hands of too few people. Thus, although we have emphasized the role of leadership in constitutional democracies in these last few pages, the potential for abuse is checked not only by an involved citizenry but also by the very structure of our constitutional system—separation of powers, checks and balances, federalism, bicameral legislatures, and the rule of law.

The ultimate test of a democratic system is the legal existence of an officially recognized opposition. A cardinal characteristic of a constitutional democracy is that it not only recognizes the need for the free organization of opposing views but also positively encourages this organization. Freedom for political expression and dissent is basic—even freedom for nonsense to be spoken so that good sense not yet recognized gets a chance to be heard.[15]

The Democratic Faith

Crucial to the democratic faith is the belief that a constitutional democracy cherishes the free play of ideas. Only where the safety valve of public discussion is available and where almost any policy is subject to perpetual questioning and challenge can there be the assurance that both minority and majority rights will be served. To be afraid of public debate is to be afraid of self-government. "Rulers always have and always will find it dangerous to their security to permit people to think, believe, talk, write, assemble, and particularly to criticize the government as they please," said former Supreme Court Justice William J. Brennan, "but the language of the First Amendment indicates the framers weighed the risk involved in such freedoms and deliberately chose to stake this government's security and life upon preserving liberty to discuss public affairs intact and untouched by government."[16]

Your authors hold with Thomas Jefferson that there is nothing in the country so radically wrong that it cannot be cured by good newspapers, sound schoolmasters, and a critical reading of history. Inform and educate the citizenry, and a major hurdle is overcome. Jefferson had boundless faith in education. He believed that people are rationally endowed by nature with an innate sense of justice; the average person has only to be informed to act wisely. In the long run, said Jefferson, only an educated and enlightened democracy can hope to endure.

Education is one of the best predictors of voting, participation in politics, and knowledge of public affairs. People may not be equally involved or equally willing to invest in democracy, but the attentive public—frequently people like yourself who have gone to college—has the willingness and self-confidence to see government and politics as necessary and important. An educated public has an understanding of how government works, how individuals can influence decision makers, and how to elect like-minded people.

As college students who are studying American government, you have knowledge of ways to influence public policy and the political process. You have gained an appreciation for the ways individuals and groups can both push and block an agenda. You

Mississippi Governor Ronnie Musgrove at his inauguration on January 11, 2000. The peaceful transfer of power is a sign of a mature and successful democracy.

also know that many people choose not to participate in elections or politics, enhancing the power of those who do. Finally, you should also have an appreciation that when knowledge is combined with political activity, the influence of the individual participant is expanded.

Does political participation by committed individuals bring about constructive change? It is important to recall that in the last half-century, restaurants, motels, and landlords once openly discriminated against individuals on the basis of race. Racial segregation in education was commonplace in several states; segregated neighborhoods were a fact of life in others and in some places remains so. Finally, in some sections of the country, discriminatory practices denied blacks and poor whites access to voting. Women were discriminated against in the workplace and in government. The significant changes toward more freedom and equality that have resulted from civil rights legislation and court cases are remarkable. This is not to say that we have erased the legacies of racism and other kinds of discrimination from our national life. But as historian Arthur M. Schlesinger Jr. writes, "The genius of America lies in its capacity to forge a single nation from peoples of remarkably diverse racial, religious, and ethnic origins." Schlesinger acknowledges that our government and society have been more open to some than to others, "but it is more open to all today than it was yesterday and it is likely to be even more open tomorrow than today."[17]

We are a restless, dissatisfied, and searching people. We are often our own toughest critics. Our political system is far from perfect, but it still is an open system and one that has become more and more democratic over time. People *can* fight city hall. People who disagree with policies in the nation can band together and be heard. We know only too well that the American dream is never fully attained. It must always be pursued.

Millions of Americans visit the great monuments in our nation's capital each year. They are always impressed by the memorials to Washington, Jefferson, Lincoln, Franklin D. Roosevelt, and the Vietnam and Korean War veterans; they are awed by the beauty of the Capitol, the Supreme Court, and the White House. The strength of the nation, however, resides not in these official buildings and monuments but in the hearts, minds, and behavior of citizens. If we lose faith, stop caring, stop participating, and stop believing in the possibilities of self-government, the monuments "will be meaningless piles of stone, and the venture that began with the Declaration of Independence, the venture familiarly known as America will be as lifeless as the stone."[18]

The future of democracy in America will be shaped by citizens who care about preserving and extending our political rights and freedoms. Our individual liberties will never be assured unless there are people willing to take responsibility for the progress of the whole community, people willing to exercise their determination and democratic faith. Carved in granite on one of the long corridors in a building on the Harvard University campus are these words of American poet Archibald MacLeish: "How shall freedom be defended? By arms when it is attacked by arms, by truth when it is attacked by lies, by democratic faith when it is attacked by authoritarian dogma. Always, in the final act, by determination and faith."

Education fosters self-confidence in dealing with bureaucracy, is a strong predictor of voting, and provides a knowledge base important to political influence.

Further Reading

DEREK BOK, *The Trouble with Government* (Harvard University Press, 2001).

RICHARD D. BROWN, *The Strength of a People: The Idea of an Informed Citizenry in America, 1650–1870* (University of North Carolina Press, 1996).

JAMES MACGREGOR BURNS, *Leadership* (Harper & Row, 1978).

ROBERT COLES, *Lives of Moral Leadership: Men and Women Who Have Made a Difference* (Random House, 2000).

AMY GUTMANN AND DENNIS THOMSON, *Democracy and Discontent: Why Moral Conflict Cannot Be Avoided in Politics, and What Should Be Done About It* (Belknap Press, 1996).

APPENDIX

The Declaration of Independence

Drafted mainly by Thomas Jefferson, this document adopted by the Second Continental Congress, and signed by John Hancock and fifty-five others, outlined the rights of man and the rights to rebellion and self-government. It declared the independence of the colonies from Great Britain, justified rebellion, and listed the grievances against George the III and his government. What is memorable about this famous document is not only that it declared the birth of a new nation, but that it set forth, with eloquence, our basic philosophy of liberty and representative democracy.

IN CONGRESS, JULY 4, 1776
(The unanimous Declaration of the Thirteen United States of America)

PREAMBLE
When, in the course of human events, it becomes necessary for one people to dissolve the political bands which have connected them with another, and to assume, among the powers of the earth, the separate and equal station to which the laws of nature and of nature's God entitle them, a decent respect to the opinions of mankind requires that they should declare the causes which impel them to the separation.

New Principles of Government
We hold these truths to be self-evident; that all men are created equal, that they are endowed by their Creator with certain unalienable rights, that among these are life, liberty, and the pursuit of happiness.

That, to secure these rights, governments are instituted among men, deriving their just powers from the consent of the governed.

That whenever any form of government becomes destructive of these ends, it is the right of the people to alter or to abolish it, and to institute new government, laying its foundation on such principles, and organizing its powers in such form, as to them shall seem most likely to effect their safety and happiness. Prudence, indeed will dictate that governments long established should not be changed for light and transient causes; and accordingly all experience hath shown that mankind are more disposed to suffer while evils are sufferable, than to right themselves by abolishing the forms to which they are accustomed. But when a long train of abuses and usurpations, pursuing invariably the same object, evinces a design to reduce them under absolute despotism, it is their right, it is their duty, to throw off such government, and to provide new guards for their future security.

Reasons for Separation

Such has been the patient sufferance of these colonies; and such is now the necessity which constrains them to alter their former systems of government. The history of the present king of Great Britain is a history of repeated injuries and usurpations, all having in direct object the establishment of an absolute tyranny over these states. To prove this, let facts be submitted to a candid world.

He has refused his assent to laws, the most wholesome and necessary for the public good.

He has forbidden his governors to pass laws of immediate and pressing importance unless suspended in their operation till his assent should be obtained; and when so suspended, he has utterly neglected to attend to them.

He has refused to pass other laws for the accommodation of large districts of people, unless those people would relinquish the right of representation in the legislature, a right inestimable to them, and formidable to tyrants only.

He has called together legislative bodies at places unusual, uncomfortable, and distant for the depository of their public records, for the sole purpose of fatiguing them into compliance with his measures.

He has dissolved representative houses repeatedly, for opposing, with manly firmness, his invasions on the rights of people.

He has refused, for a long time after such dissolutions, to cause others to be elected; whereby the legislative powers incapable of annihilation, have returned to the people at large for their exercise; the state remaining, in the meantime, exposed to all the dangers of invasion from without and convulsions within.

He has endeavored to prevent the population of these states; for that purpose obstructing the laws of naturalization of foreigners, refusing to pass others to encourage their migration hither, and raising the conditions of new appropriations of lands.

He has obstructed the administration of justice, by refusing his assent to laws for establishing judiciary powers.

He has made judges dependent on his will alone for the tenure of their offices, and the amount and payment of their salaries.

He has erected a multitude of new offices, and sent hither swarms of officers to harass our people and eat out their substance.

He has kept among us, in times of peace, standing armies, without the consent of our legislature.

He has affected to render the military independent of, and superior to, the civil power.

He has combined with others to subject us to jurisdiction foreign to our constitution and unacknowledged by our laws, giving his assent to their acts of pretended legislation:

For quartering large bodies of armed troops among us;

For protecting them, by a mock trial, from punishment for any murders which they should commit on the inhabitants of these states;

For cutting off our trade with all parts of the world;

For imposing taxes on us without our consent;

For depriving us, in many cases, of the benefits of trial by jury;

For transporting us beyond seas, to be tried for pretended offenses;

For abolishing the free system of English laws in a neighboring province, establishing therein an arbitrary government, and enlarging its boundaries, so as to render it at once an example and fit instrument for introducing the same absolute rule into these colonies;

For taking away our charters, abolishing our most valuable laws, and altering, fundamentally, the forms of our governments;

For suspending our own legislatures, and declaring themselves invented with power to legislate for us in all cases whatsoever.

He has abdicated government here, by declaring us out of his protection and waging war against us.

He has plundered our seas, ravaged our coasts, burned our towns, and destroyed the lives of our people.

He is at this time transporting large armies of foreign mercenaries to complete the works of death, desolation, and tyranny already begun with circumstances of cruelty and perfidy scarcely paralleled in the most barbarous ages and totally unworthy of the head of a civilized nation.

He has constrained our fellow-citizens, taken captive on the high seas, to bear arms against their country, to become the executioners of their friends and brethren, or to fall themselves by their hands.

He has excited domestic insurrections among us, and has endeavored to bring on the inhabitants of our frontiers the merciless Indian savages, whose known rule of warfare is an undistinguished destruction of all ages, sexes, and conditions.

In every stage of these oppressions we have petitioned for redress in the most humble terms; our repeated petitions have been answered only by repeated injury. A prince whose character is thus marked by every act which may define a tyrant is unfit to be the ruler of a free people.

Nor have we been wanting in attention to our British brethren. We have warned them, from time to time, of attempts by their legislature to extend an unwarrantable jurisdiction over us. We have reminded them of the circumstances of our emigration and settlement here. We have appealed to their native justice and magnanimity; and we have conjured them, by the ties of our common kindred, to disavow these usurpations, which would inevitably interrupt our connections and correspondence. They, too, have been deaf to the voice of justice and of consanguinity. We must, therefore, acquiesce in the necessity which denounces our separation, and hold them, as we hold the rest of mankind, enemies in war, in peace, friends.

We, therefore, the representatives of the United States of America, in General Congress assembled, appealing to the Supreme Judge of the world for the rectitude of our intentions, do, in the name and by authority of the good people of these colonies, solemnly publish and declare, that these united colonies are, and of right ought to be, free and independent states; that they are absolved from all allegiance to the British crown, and that all political connection between them and the state of Great Britain is, and ought to be, totally dissolved; and that, as free and independent states, they have full power to levy war, conclude peace, contract alliances, establish commerce, and do all other acts and things which independent states may of a right do. And, for the support of this declaration, with a firm reliance on the protection of Divine Providence, we mutually pledge to each other our lives, our fortunes, and our sacred honor.

The Federalist, No. 10, James Madison

The Federalist, No. 10, written by James Madison soon after the Constitutional Convention, was prepared as one of several dozen newspaper essays aimed at persuading New Yorkers to ratify the proposed constitution. One of the most important basic documents in American political history, it outlines the need for and the general principles of a democratic republic. It also provides a political and economic analysis of the realities of interest group or faction politics.

To the People of the State of New York: Among the numerous advantages promised by a well-constructed union, none deserves to be more accurately developed than its tendency to break and control the violence of faction. The friend of popular governments, never finds himself so much alarmed for their character and fate, as when he contemplates their propensity of this dangerous vice. He will not fail, therefore, to set a due value on any plan which, without violating the principles to which he is attached, provides a proper cure for it. The instability, injustice, and confusion introduced into the public councils, have, in truth, been the mortal diseases under which popular governments have everywhere perished; as they continue to be the favorite and fruitful topics from which the adversaries to liberty derive their most specious declamations. The valuable improvements made by the American constitutions on the popular models, both ancient and modern, cannot certainly be too much admired; but it would be an unwarrantable partiality, to contend that they have as effectually obviated the danger on this side, as was wished and expected. Complaints are everywhere heard from our most considerate and virtuous citizens, equally the friends of public and private faith, and of public and personal liberty, that our governments are too unstable; that the public good is disregarded in the conflicts of rival parties; and that measures are too often decided, not according to the rules of justice, and the rights of the minor party, but by the superior force of an interested and overbearing majority. However anxiously we may wish that these complaints had no foundation, the evidence of known facts will not permit us to deny that they are in some degree true. It will be found, indeed, on a candid review of our situation, that some of the distresses under which we labor have been erroneously charged on the operations of our governments; but it will be found, at the same time, that other causes will not alone account for many of our heaviest misfortunes; and, particularly, for that prevailing and increasing distrust of public engagements, and alarm for private rights, which are echoed from one end of the continent to the other. These must be chiefly, if not wholly, effects of the unsteadiness and injustice, with which a factious spirit has tainted our public administrations.

By a faction, I understand a number of citizens, whether amounting to a majority of the whole, who are united and actuated by some common impulse of passion, or of interest, adverse to the rights of other citizens, or to the permanent and aggregate interests of the community.

There are two methods of curing the mischiefs of faction: the one, by removing its causes; the other, by controlling its effects.

There are again two methods of removing the causes of faction: the one, by destroying the liberty which is essential to its existence; the other, by giving to every citizen the same opinions, the same passions, and the same interests.

It could never be more truly said, than of the first remedy, that it was worse than the disease. Liberty is to faction what air is to fire, an aliment without which it instantly expires. But it could not be a less folly to abolish liberty, which is essential to political life, because it nourishes faction, than it would be to wish the annihilation of air, which is essential to animal life, because it imparts to fire its destructive agency.

The second expedient is as impracticable, as the first would be unwise. As long as the reason of man continues fallible, and he is at liberty to exercise it, different opinions will be formed. As long as the connection subsists between his reason and his self-love, his opinions and his passions will have a reciprocal influence on each other; and the former will be objects to which the latter will attach themselves. The diversity in the faculties of men, from which the rights of property originate, is not less an insuperable obstacle to an uniformity of interests. The protection of these faculties is the first object of government. From the protection of different and unequal faculties of acquiring property, the possession of different degrees and kinds of property immediately results; and from the influence of these on the sentiments and views of the respective proprietors, ensues a division of the society into different interests and parties.

The latent causes of faction are thus sown in the nature of man; and we see them everywhere brought into different degrees of activity, according to the different circumstances of civil society. A zeal for different opinions concerning religion, concerning government, and many other points, as well of speculation as of practice; an attachment to different leaders ambitiously contending for preeminence and power; or to persons of other descriptions whose fortunes have been interesting to the human passions, have, in turn, divided mankind into parties, inflamed them with mutual animosity, and rendered them much more disposed to vex and oppress each other, than to cooperate for their common good. So strong is this propensity of mankind, to fall into mutual animosities, that where no substantial occasion presents itself, the most frivolous and fanciful distinctions have been sufficient to kindle their unfriendly passions and excite their most violent conflicts. But the most common and durable source of factions, has been the various and unequal distribution of property. Those who hold, and those who are without property, have ever formed distinct interests in society. Those who are creditors, and those who are debtors, fall under a like discrimination. A landed interest, a manufacturing interest, a mercantile interest, a moneyed interest, with many lesser interests, grow up of necessity in civilized nations, and divide them into different classes, actuated by different sentiments and views. The regulation of these various and interfering interests forms the principal task of modern legislation, and involves the spirit of the party and faction in the necessary and ordinary operations of the government.

No man is allowed to be a judge in his own cause; because his interest will certainly bias his judgment, and, not improbably, corrupt his integrity. With equal, nay, with greater reason, a body of men are unfit to be both judges and parties at the same time; yet what are many of the most important acts of legislation, but so many judicial determinations, not indeed concerning the right of single persons, but concerning the rights of large bodies of citizens? And what are the different classes of legislators, but advocates and parties to the causes which they determine? Is a law proposed concerning private debts? It is a questions to which the creditors are parties on one side, and the debtors on the other. Justice ought to hold the balance between them. Yet the parties are, and must be, themselves the judges; and the most numerous party, or, in other words, the most powerful faction, must be expected to prevail. Shall domestic manufacturers be encouraged, and in what degree, by restrictions on foreign manufacturers? Are questions which would be differently decided by the landed and the manufacturing classes; and probably by neither with a sole regard to justice and the public good. The apportionment of taxes, on the various descriptions of property, is an act which seems to require the most exact impartiality; yet there is, perhaps, no legislative act, in which greater opportunity and temptation are given to a predominant party to trample on the rules of justice. Every shilling, with which they overburden the inferior number, is a shilling saved to their own pockets.

It is in vain to say, that enlightened statesmen will be able to adjust these clashing interests, and render them all subservient to the public good. Enlightened statesmen will not always be at the helm, nor, in many cases, can such an adjustment be made at all, without taking into view indirect and remote considerations, which will rarely prevail over the immediate interest which one party may find in disregarding the rights of another, or the good of the whole.

The inference to which we are brought is, that the causes of faction cannot be removed; and that relief is only to be sought in the means of controlling its effects.

If a faction consists of less than a majority, relief is supplied by the republican principle, which enables the majority to defeat its sinister views, by regular vote. It may clog the administration, it may convulse the society; but it will be unable to execute and mask its violence under the forms of the Constitution. When a majority is included in a faction, the form of popular government, on the other hand, enables it to sacrifice to its ruling passion or interest, both the public good and the rights of other citizens. To secure the public good, and private rights, against the danger of such a faction, and at the same time to preserve the spirit and the form of popular government, is then the great object to which our inquiries are directed. Let me add, that it is the great desideratum, by which alone this form of government can be rescued from the opprobrium under which it has so long laboured, and be recommended to the esteem and adoption of mankind.

By what means is this object attainable? Evidently by one of two only. Either the existence of the same passion or interest in a majority, at the same time, must be prevented; or the majority, having such coexistent passion or interest, must be rendered, by their number and local situation, unable to concert and carry into effect schemes of oppression. If the impulse and the opportunity be suffered to coincide, we well know that neither moral nor religious motives can be relied on as an adequate control. They are not found to be such on the injustice and violence of individuals, and lose their efficacy in proportion to the number combined together; that is, in proportion as their efficacy becomes needful.

From this view of the subject, it may be concluded, that a pure democracy, by which I mean a society consisting of a small number of citizens, who assemble and administer the government in person, can admit of no cure for the mischiefs of faction. A common passion or interest will, in almost every case, be felt by a majority of the whole; a communication and concert, results from the form of government itself; and there is nothing to check the inducements to sacrifice the weaker party, or an obnoxious individual. Hence, it is, that such democracies have ever been spectacles of turbulence and contention; have ever been found incompatible with personal security, or the rights of property; and have in general been as short in their lives, as they have been violent in their deaths. Theoretic politicians, who have patronized this species of government, have erroneously supposed, that by reducing mankind to a perfect equality in their political rights, they would, at the same time be perfectly equalized and assimilated in their possessions, their opinions, and their passions.

A republic, by which I mean a government in which the scheme of representation takes place, opens a different prospect, and promises the cure for which we are seeking. Let us examine the points in which it varies from pure democracy, and we shall comprehend both the nature of the cure and the efficacy which it must derive from the union.

The two great points of difference, between a democracy and a republic, are, first, the delegation of the government, in the latter, to a small number of citizens, elected by the rest; secondly, the greater number of citizens, and greater sphere of country, over which the latter may be extended.

The effect of the first difference is, on the one hand, to refine and enlarge the public views, by passing them through the medium of a chosen body of citizens, whose wisdom may best discern the true interest of their country, and whose patriotism and love of justice, will be least likely to sacrifice it to temporary or partial considerations. Under such a regulation, it may well happen, that the public voice, pronounced by the representatives of the people, will be more consonant to the public good, than if pronounced by the people themselves, convened for the purpose. On the other hand the effect may be inverted. Men of factious tempers, of local prejudices, or of sinister designs, may by intrigue, by corruption, or by other means, first obtain the suffrages, and then betray the interest of the people. The question resulting is, whether small or extensive republics are most favourable to the election of proper guardians of the public weal; and it is clearly decided in favour of the latter by two obvious considerations.

In the first place, it is to be remarked that, however small the republic may be, the representatives must be raised to a certain number, in order to guard against the cabals of a few; and that however large it may be, they must be limited to a certain number, in order to guard against the confusion of a multitude. Hence, the number of representatives in the two cases not being in proportion to that of the constituents, and being proportionally greatest in the small republic, it follows, that if the proportion of fit characters be not less in the large than in the small republic, the former will present a greater option, and consequently a greater probability of a fit choice.

In the next place, as each representative will be chosen by a greater number of citizens in the large than in the small republic, it will be more difficult for unworthy candidates to practice with success the vicious arts, by which elections are too often carried; and the suffrages of the people being more free, will be more likely to centre in men who possess the most attractive merit, and the most diffusive and established characters.

It must be confessed, that in this, as in most other cases, there is a mean, on both sides of which inconveniences will be found to lie. By enlarging too much the number of electors, you render the representatives too little acquainted with all their local circumstances and lesser interests; as by reducing it too much, you render him unduly attached to these, and too little fit to comprehend and pursue great and national objects. The federal constitution forms a happy combination in this respect; the great and aggregate interests being referred to the national, the local and particular to the state legislatures.

The other point of difference is, the greater number of citizens, and extent of territory, which may be brought within the compass of republican, than of democratic government; and it is this circumstance principally which renders factious combinations less to be dreaded in the former, than in the latter. The smaller the society, the fewer probably will be the distinct parties and interests composing it; the fewer the distinct parties and interests, the more frequently will a majority be found of the same party; and the smaller the number of individuals composing a majority, and the smaller the compass within which they are placed, the more easily will they concert and execute their plans of oppression. Extend the sphere, and you take in a greater variety of parties and interests; you make it less probable that a majority of the whole will have a common motive to invade the rights of other citizens; or if such a common motive exists, it will be more difficult for all who feel it to discover their own strength, and to act in unison with each other. Besides other impediments, it may be remarked, that where there is a consciousness of unjust or dishonourable purposes, communication is always checked by distrust, in proportion to the number whose concurrence is necessary.

Hence, it clearly appears, that the same advantage, which a republic has over a democracy, in controlling the effects of faction, is enjoyed by a large over a small republic—is enjoyed by the union over the states composing it. Does this advantage consist in the substitution of representatives, whose enlightened views and virtuous sentiments render them superior to local prejudices, and to schemes of injustice? It will not be denied that the representation of the union will be most likely to possess these requisite endowments. Does it consist in the greater security afforded by a greater variety of parties, against the event of any one party being able to outnumber and oppress the rest? In an equal degree does the increased variety of parties, comprised within the union, increase the security? Does it, in fine, consist in the greater obstacles opposed to the concert and accomplishment of the secret wishes of an unjust and interested majority? Here, again, the extent of the union gives it the most palpable advantage.

The influence of factious leaders may kindle a flame within their particular states, but will be unable to spread a general conflagration through the other states; a religious sect may degenerate into a political faction in a part of the confederacy; but the variety of sects dispersed over the entire face of it, must secure the national councils against any danger from that source: a rage for paper money, for an abolition of debts, for an equal division of property, or for any other improper or wicked project, will be less apt to pervade the whole body of the union than a particular member of it; in the same proportion as such a malady is more likely to taint a particular county or district, than an entire state.

In the extent and proper structure of the union, therefore, we behold a republican remedy for the diseases most incident to republican government. And according to the degree of pleasure and pride we feel in being republicans, ought to be our zeal in cherishing the spirit, and supporting the character of federalists.

The Federalist, No. 51, James Madison

The Federalist, *No. 51, also written by Madison, is a classic statement in defense of separation of powers and republican processes. Its fourth paragraph is especially famous and is frequently quoted by students of government.*

To what expedient, then, shall we finally resort, for maintaining in practice the necessary partition of power among the several departments as laid down in the Constitution? The only answer that can be given is that as all these exterior provisions are found to be inadequate the defect must be supplied, by so contriving the interior structure of the government as that its several constituent parts may, by their mutual relations, be the means of keeping each other in their proper places. Without presuming to undertake a full development of this important idea I will hazard a few general observations which may perhaps place it in a clearer light, and enable us to form a more correct judgment of the principles and structure of the government planned by the convention.

In order to lay a due foundation for that separate and distinct exercise of the different powers of government, which to a certain extent is admitted on all hands to be essential to the preservation of liberty, it is evident that each department should have a will of its own; and consequently should be so constituted that the members of each should have as little agency as possible in the appointment of the members of the others. Were this principle rigorously adhered to, it would require that all the appointments for the supreme executive, legislative, and judiciary magistracies should be drawn from the same fountain of authority, the people, through channels having no communication whatever with one another. Perhaps such a plan of constructing the several departments would be less difficult in practice than it may in contemplation appear. Some difficulties, however, and some additional expense would attend the execution of it. Some deviations, therefore, from the principle must be admitted. In the constitution of the judiciary department in particular, it might be inexpedient to insist rigorously on the principle: first, because peculiar qualifications being essential in the members, the primary consideration ought to be to select that mode of choice which best secures these qualifications; second, because the permanent tenure by which the appointments are held in that department must soon destroy all sense of dependence on the authority conferring them.

It is equally evident that the members of each department should be as little dependent as possible on those of the others for the emoluments annexed to their offices. Were the executive magistrate, or the judges, not independent of the legislature in this particular, their independence in every other would be merely nominal.

But the great security against a gradual concentration of the several powers in the same department consists in giving to those who administer each department the necessary constitutional means and personal motives to resist encroachments of the others. The provision for defense must in this, as in all other cases, be made commensurate to the danger of attack. Ambition must be made to counteract ambition. The interest of the man must be connected with the constitutional rights of the place. It may be a reflection on human nature that such devices should be necessary to control the abuses of government. But what is government itself but the greatest of all reflections on human nature? If men were angels, no government would be necessary. If angels were to govern men, neither external nor internal controls on government would be necessary. In framing a government which is to be administered by men over men, the great difficulty lies in this: you must first enable the government to control the governed; and in the next place oblige it to control itself. A dependence on the people is, no doubt, the primary control on the government; but experience has taught mankind the necessity of auxiliary precautions.

This policy of supplying, by opposite and rival interests, the defect of better motives, might be traced through the whole system of human affairs, private as well as public. We see it particularly displayed in all the subordinate distributions of power, where the constant aim is to divide and arrange the several offices in such a manner as that each may be a check on the other—that the private interest of every individual may be a sentinel over the public rights. These inventions of prudence cannot be less requisite in the distribution of the supreme powers of the State.

But it is not possible to give to each department an equal power of self-defense. In republican government, the legislative authority necessarily predominates. The remedy for this inconveniency is to divide the legislature into different branches; and to render them, by modes of election and different principles of action, as little connected with each other as the nature of their common functions and their common dependence on the society will admit. It may even be necessary to guard against dangerous encroachments by still further precautions. As the weight of the legislative authority requires that it should be thus divided, the weakness of the executive may require, on the other hand, that it should be fortified. An absolute negative on the legislature appears, at first view, to be the natural defense with which the executive magistrate should be armed. But perhaps it would be neither altogether safe nor alone sufficient. On ordinary occasions it might not be exerted with the requisite firmness, and on extraordinary occasions it might be perfidiously abused. May not this defect of an absolute negative be supplied by some qualified connection between this weaker department and the weaker branch of the stronger department, by which the latter may be led to support the constitutional rights of the former, without being too much detached from the rights of its own department?

If the principles on which these observations are founded be just, as I persuade myself they are, and they be applied as a criterion to the several State constitutions, and to the federal Constitution, it will be found that if the latter does not perfectly correspond with them, the former are infinitely less able to bear such a test.

There are, moreover, two considerations particularly applicable to the federal system of America, which place that system in a very interesting point of view.

First. In a single republic, all the power surrendered by the people is submitted to the administration of a single government; and the usurpations are guarded against by a division of the government into distinct and separate departments. In the compound republic of America, the power surrendered by the people is first divided between two distinct governments, and then the portion allotted to each subdivided among distinct and separate departments. Hence a double security arises to the rights of the people. The different governments will control each other, at the same time that each will be controlled by itself.

Second. It is of great importance in a republic not only to guard the society against the oppression of its rulers, but to guard one part of the society against the injustice of the other part. Different interests necessarily exist in different classes of citizens. If a majority be united by a common interest, the rights of the minority will be insecure. There are but two methods of providing against this evil: the one by creating a will in the community independent of the majority—that is, of the society itself; the other, by comprehending in the society so many separate descriptions of citizens as will render an unjust combination of a majority of the whole very improbable, if not impracticable. The first method prevails in all governments possessing an hereditary or self-appointed authority. This, at best, is but a precarious security; because a power independent of the society may as well espouse the unjust views of the major as the rightful interests of the minor party, and may possibly be turned against both parties. The second method will be exemplified in the federal republic of the United States. Whilst all authority in it will be derived from and dependent on the society, the society itself will be broken into so many parts, interests and classes of citizens, that the rights of individuals, or of the minority, will be in little danger from interested combinations of the majority. In a free government the security for civil rights must be the same as that for religious rights. It consists in the one case in the multiplicity of interests, and in the other in the multiplicity of sects. The degree of security in both cases will depend on the number of interests and sects; and this may be presumed to depend on the extent of country and number of people comprehended under the same government. This view of the subject must particularly recommend a proper federal system to all the sincere and considerate friends of republican government, since it shows that in exact proportion as the territory of the Union may be formed into more circumscribed Confederacies, or States, oppressive combinations of a majority will be facilitated; the best security, under the republican forms, for the rights of every class of citizen, will be diminished; and consequently the stability and independence of some member of the government, the only other security, must be proportionally increased. Justice is the end of government. It is the end of civil society. It ever has been and ever will be pursued until it be obtained, or until liberty be lost in the pursuit. In a society under the forms of which the stronger faction can readily unite and oppress the weaker, anarchy may as truly be said to reign as in a state of nature, where the weaker individual is not secured against the violence of the stronger; and as, in the latter state, even the stronger individuals are prompted, by the uncertainty of their condition, to submit to a government which may protect the weak as well as themselves; so, in the former state, will the more powerful factions or parties be gradually induced, by a like motive, to wish for a government which will protect all parties, the weaker as well as the more powerful. It can be little doubted that if the State of Rhode Island was separated from the Confederacy and left to itself, the insecurity of rights under the popular form of government within such narrow limits would be displayed by such reiterated oppressions of factious majorities that some power altogether independent of the people would soon be called for by the voice of the very factions whose misrule had proved the necessity to it. In the extended republic of the United States, and among the great variety of interests, parties, and sects which it embraces, a coalition of a majority of the whole society could seldom take place on any other principles than those of justice and the general good; whilst there being thus less danger to a minor from the will of a major party, there must be less pretext, also, to provide for the security of the former, by introducing into the government a will not dependent on the latter, or, in other words, a will independent of the society itself. It is no less certain that it is important, notwithstanding the contrary opinions which have been entertained that the larger the society, provided it lie within a practicable sphere, the more duly capable it will be of self-government. And happily for the *republican cause,* the practicable sphere may be carried to a very great extent by a judicious modification and mixture of the *federal principle.*

The *Federalist,* No. 78, Alexander Hamilton

The Federalist, *No. 78, written by Alexander Hamilton, explains and praises the provisions for the judiciary in the newly drafted Constitution. Notice especially how Hamilton asserts that the courts have a key responsibility in determining the meaning of the Constitution as fundamental law. Hamilton is outlining here the doctrine of judicial review as we now know it.*

We proceed now to an examination of the judiciary department of the proposed government.

In unfolding the defects of the existing Confederation, the utility and necessity of a federal judicature have been clearly pointed out. It is the less necessary to recapitulate the considerations there urged as the propriety of the institution in the abstract is not disputed; the only questions which have been raised being relative to the manner of constituting it, and to its extent. To these points, therefore, our observations shall be confined.

The manner of constituting it seems to embrace these several objects: 1st. The mode of appointing the judges. 2nd. The tenure by which they are to hold their places. 3rd. The partition of the judiciary authority between different courts and their relations to each other.

First. As to the mode of appointing the judges: this is the same with that of appointing the officers of the Union in general and has been so fully discussed in the two last numbers that nothing can be said here which would not be useless repetition.

Second. As to the tenure by which the judges are to hold their places: this chiefly concerns their duration in office, the provisions for their support, the precautions for their responsibility.

According to the plan of the convention, all judges who may be appointed by the United States are to hold their offices *during good behavior;* which is conformable to the most approved of the State constitutions, and among the rest, to that of this State. Its propriety having been drawn into question by the adversaries of that plan is no light symptom of the rage for objection which disorders their imaginations and judgments. The standard of good behavior for the continuance in office of the judicial magistracy is certainly one of the most valuable of the modern improvements in the practice of government. In a monarchy it is an excellent barrier to the despotism of the prince; in a republic it is a no less excellent barrier to the encroachments and oppressions of the representative body. And it is the best expedient which can be devised in any government to secure a steady, upright, and impartial administration of the laws.

Whoever attentively considers the different departments of power must perceive that, in a government in which they are separated from each other, the judiciary, from the nature of its functions, will always be the least dangerous to the political rights of the Constitution; because it will be least in a capacity to annoy or injure them. The executive not only dispenses the honors but holds the sword of the community. The legislature not only commands the purse but prescribes the rules by which the duties and rights of every citizen are to be regulated. The judiciary, on the contrary, has no influence over either the sword or the purse; no direction either of the strength or of the wealth of the society, and can take no active resolution whatever. It may truly be said to have neither FORCE NOR WILL but merely judgment; and must ultimately depend upon the aid of the executive arm even for the efficacy of its judgments.

This simple view of the matter suggests several important consequences. It proves incontestably that the judiciary is beyond comparison the weakest of the three departments of power; that it can never attack with success either of the other two; and that all possible care is requisite to enable it to defend itself against their attacks. It equally proves that though individual oppression may now and then proceed from the courts of justice, the general liberty of the people can never be endangered from that quarter; I mean so long as the judiciary remains truly distinct from both the legislature and the executive. For I agree that "there is no liberty if the power of judging be not separated from the legislative and executive powers." And it proves, in the last place, that as liberty can have nothing to fear from the judiciary alone, but would have everything to fear from its union with either of the other departments, that as all the effects of such a union must ensue from a dependence of the former on the latter, notwithstanding a nominal and apparent separation; that as, from the natural feebleness of the judiciary, it is in continual jeopardy of being overpowered, awed, or influenced by its co-ordinate branches; and that as nothing can contribute so much to its firmness and independence as permanency in office, this quality may therefore be justly regarded as an indispensable ingredient in its constitution, and, in a great measure, as the citadel for the public justice and the public security.

The complete independence of the courts of justice is peculiarly essential in a limited Constitution. By a limited Constitution, I understand one which contains certain specified exceptions to the legislative authority; such, for instance, as that it shall pass no bills of attainder, no *ex post facto laws,* and the like. Limitations of this kind can be preserved in practice no other way than through the medium of courts of justice, whose duty it must be to declare all acts contrary to the manifest tenor of the Constitution void. Without this, all the reservations of particular rights or privileges would amount to nothing.

Some perplexity respecting the rights of the courts to pronounce legislative acts void, because contrary to the Constitution, has arisen from an imagination that the doctrine would imply a superiority to the judiciary to the legislative power. It is urged that the authority which can declare the acts of another void must necessarily be superior to the one whose acts may be declared void. As this doctrine is of great importance in all the American constitutions, a brief discussion of the grounds on which it rests cannot be unacceptable.

There is no position which depends on clearer principles than that every act of a delegated authority, contrary to the tenor of the commission under which it is exercised, is void. No legislative act, therefore, contrary to the Constitution, can be valid. To deny this would be to affirm that the deputy is greater than his principal; that the servant is above his master; that the representatives of the people are superior to the people themselves; that men acting by virtue of powers do not authorize, but what they forbid.

If it be said that the legislative body are themselves the constitutional judges of their own powers and that the construction they put upon them is conclusive upon the other departments it may be answered that this cannot be the natural presumption where it is not to be collected from any particular provisions in the Constitution. It is not otherwise to be supposed that the Constitution could intend to enable the representatives of the people to substitute their *will* to that of their constituents. It is far more rational to suppose that the courts were designed to be an intermediate body between the people and the legislature in order, among other things, to keep the latter within the limits assigned to their authority. The interpretation of the laws is the proper and peculiar province of the courts. A constitution is, in fact, and must be regarded by the judges as, a fundamental law. It therefore belongs to them to ascertain its meaning as well as the meaning of any particular act proceeding from the legislative body. If there should happen to be an irreconcilable variance between the two, that which has the superior obligation and validity ought, of course, to be preferred; or, in other words, the Constitution ought to be preferred to the statute, the intention of the people to the intention of their agents.

Nor does this conclusion by any means suppose a superiority of the judicial to the legislative power. It only supposes that the power of the people is superior to both, and that where the will of the legislature, declared in its statutes, stands in opposition to that of the people, declared in the Constitution, the judges ought to be governed by the latter rather than the former. They ought to regulate their decisions by the fundamental laws rather than by those which are not fundamental.

This exercise of judicial discretion in determining between two contradictory laws is exemplified in a familiar instance. It not uncommonly happens that there are two statutes existing at one time, clashing in whole or in part with each other and neither of them containing any repealing clause or expression. In such a case, it is the province of the courts to liquidate and fix their meaning and operation. So far as they can, by any fair construction, be reconciled to each other, reason and law conspire to dictate that this should be done; where this is impracticable, it becomes a matter of necessity to give effect to one in exclusion of the other. The rule which has obtained in the courts for determining their relative validity is that the last in order of time shall be preferred to the first. But this is a mere rule of construction, not derived from any positive law but from the nature and reason of the thing. It is a rule not enjoined upon the courts by legislative provision but adopted by themselves, as consonant to truth and propriety, for the direction of their conduct as interpreters of the law. They thought it reasonable that between the interfering acts of an equal authority that which was the last indication of its will should have the preference.

But in regard to the interfering acts of a superior and subordinate authority of an original and derivative power, the nature and reason of the thing indicates the converse of that rule as proper to be followed. They teach us that the prior act of a superior ought to be preferred to the subsequent act of an inferior and subordinate authority; and that accordingly, whenever a particular statute contravenes the Constitution, it will be the duty of the judicial tribunals to adhere to the latter and disregard the former.

It can be of no weight to say that the courts, on the pretense of a repugnancy, may substitute their own pleasure to the constitutional intentions of the legislature. This might as well happen in the case of two contradictory statutes; or it might as well happen in every adjudication upon any single statute. The courts must declare the sense of the law; and if they should be disposed to exercise WILL instead of JUDGMENT, the consequence would equally be the substitution of their pleasure to that of the legislative body. The observation, if it prove anything, would prove that there ought to be no judges distinct from that body.

If, then, the courts of justice are to be considered as the bulwarks of a limited Constitution against legislative encroachments, this consideration will afford a strong argument for the permanent tenure of judicial offices, since nothing will contribute so much as this to that independent spirit in the judges which must be essential to the faithful performance of so arduous a duty.

This independence of the judges is equally requisite to guard the Constitution and the rights of individuals from the effects of those ill humors which the arts of designing men, or the influence of particular conjunctures, sometimes disseminate among the people themselves, and which, though they speedily give place to better information, and more deliberate reflection, have a tendency, in the meantime, to occasion dangerous innovations in the government, and serious oppressions of the minor party in the community. Though I trust the friends of the proposed Constitution will never concur with its enemies in questioning that fundamental principal of Republican government which admits the right of the people to alter or abolish the established Constitution whenever they find it inconsistent with their happiness; yet it is not to be inferred from this principle that the representatives of the people, whenever a momentary inclination happens to lay hold of a majority of their constituents incompatible with the provisions in the existing Constitution would, on that account, be justifiable in a violation of those provisions; or that the courts would be under a greater obligation to connive at infractions in this shape than when they had proceeded wholly from the cabals of the representative body. Until the people have, by some solemn and authoritative act, annulled or changed the established form, it is binding upon themselves collectively, as well as individually; and no presumption, or even knowledge of their sentiments, can warrant their representatives in a departure from it prior to such an act. But it is easy to see that it would require an uncommon portion of fortitude in the judges to do their duty as faithful guardians of the Constitution, where legislative invasions of it had been instigated by the major voice of the community.

But it is not with a view to infractions of the Constitution only that the independence of the judges may be an essential safeguard against the effects of occasional ill humors in the society. These sometimes extend no farther than to the injury of the private rights of particular classes of citizens, by unjust and partial laws. Here also the firmness of the judicial magistracy is of vast importance in mitigating the severity and confining the operation of such laws. It not only serves to moderate the immediate mischiefs of those which may have been passed but it operates as a check upon the legislative body in passing them; who, perceiving that obstacles to the success of iniquitous intention are to be expected from the scruples of the courts, are in a manner compelled, by the very motives of the injustice they mediate, to qualify their attempts. This is a circumstance calculated to have more influence upon the character of our governments than but a few may be aware of. The benefits of the integrity and moderation of the judiciary have already been felt in more States than one; and though they may have displeased those whose sinister expectations they may have disappointed, they must have commanded the esteem and applause of all the virtuous and disinterested. Considerate men of every description ought to prize whatever will tend to beget or fortify that temper in

the courts; as no man can be sure that he may not be tomorrow the victim of a spirit of injustice, by which he may be a gainer today. And every man must now feel that the inevitable tendency of such a spirit is to sap the foundations of public and private confidence and to introduce in its stead universal distrust and distress.

That inflexible and uniform adherence to the rights of the Constitution, and of individuals, which we perceive to be indispensable in the courts of justice, can certainly not be expected from judges who hold their offices by a temporary commission. Periodical appointments, however regulated, or by whomsoever made, would, in some way or other, be fatal to their necessary independence. If the power of making them was committed either to the executive or legislature there would be danger of an improper complaisance to the branch which possessed it; if to both, there would be an unwillingness to hazard the displeasure of either; if to the people, or to persons chosen by them for the special purpose, there would be too great a disposition to consult popularity to justify a reliance that nothing would be consulted by the Constitution and the laws.

There is yet a further and a weighty reason for the permanency of the judicial offices which is deducible from the nature of the qualifications they require. It has been frequently remarked with great propriety that a voluminous code of laws is one of the inconveniences necessarily connected with the advantages of a free government. To avoid an arbitrary discretion in the courts, it is indispensable that they should be bound down by strict rules and precedents which serve to define and point out their duty in every particular case that comes before them; and it will readily be conceived from the variety of

controversies which grow out of the folly and wickedness of mankind that the records of those precedents must unavoidably swell to a very considerable bulk and must demand long and laborious study to acquire a competent knowledge of them. Hence it is that there can be but few men in the society who will have sufficient skill in the laws to qualify them for the stations of judges. And making the proper deductions for the ordinary depravity of human nature, the number must be still smaller of those who unite the requisite integrity with the requisite knowledge. These considerations apprise us that the government can have no great option between fit characters; and that a temporary duration in office which would naturally discourage such characters from quitting a lucrative line of practice to accept a seat on the bench would have a tendency to throw the administration of justice into hands less able and less well qualified to conduct it with utility and dignity. In the present circumstances of this country and in those in which it is likely to be for a long time to come, the disadvantages on this score would be greater than they may at first sight appear; but it must be confessed that they are far inferior to those which present themselves under the other aspects of the subject.

Upon the whole, there can be no room to doubt that the convention acted wisely in copying from the models of those constitutions which have established *good behavior* as the tenure of their judicial offices in point of duration, and that so far from being blamable on this account, their plan would have been inexcusably defective if it had wanted this important feature of good government. The experience of Great Britain affords an illustrious comment on the excellence of the institution.

Presidential Election Results 1789–2000

Year	Candidates	Party	Popular Vote	Electoral Vote
1789	George Washington			69
	John Adams			34
	Others			35
1793	George Washington			132
	John Adams			77
	George Clinton			50
	Others			5
1796	John Adams	Federalist		71
	Thomas Jefferson	Democratic-Republican		68
	Thomas Pinckney	Federalist		59
	Aaron Burr	Democratic-Republican		30
	Others			48
1800	Thomas Jefferson	Democratic-Republican		73
	Aaron Burr	Democratic-Republican		73
	John Adams	Federalist		65
	Charles C. Pinckney	Federalist		64
1804	Thomas Jefferson	Democratic-Republican		162
	Charles C. Pinckney	Federalist		14
1808	James Madison	Democratic-Republican		122
	Charles C. Pinckney	Federalist		47
	George Clinton	Independent-Republican		6
1812	James Madison	Democratic-Republican		128
	DeWitt Clinton	Federalist		89
1816	James Monroe	Democratic-Republican		183
	Rufus King	Federalist		34
1820	James Monroe	Democratic-Republican		231
	John Quincy Adams	Independent-Republican		1
1824	John Quincy Adams	Democratic-Republican	108,740(30.5%)	84
	Andrew Jackson	Democratic-Republican	153,544(43.1%)	99
	Henry Clay	Democratic-Republican	47,136(13.2%)	37
	William H. Crawford	Democratic-Republican	46,618(13.1%)	41
1828	Andrew Jackson	Democratic	647,231(56.0%)	178
	John Quincy Adams	National Republican	509,097(44.0%)	83
1832	Andrew Jackson	Democratic	687,502(55.0%)	219
	Henry Clay	National Republican	530,189(42.4%)	49
	William Wirt	Anti-Masonic		7
	John Floyd	National Republican	33,108(2.6%)	11
1836	Martin Van Buren	Democratic	761,549(50.9%)	170
	William H. Harrison	Whig	549,567(36.7%)	73
	Hugh L. White	Whig	145,396(9.7%)	26
	Daniel Webster	Whig	41,287(2.7%)	14
1840	William H. Harrison	Whig	1,275,017(53.1%)	234
	Martin Van Buren	Democratic	1,128,702(46.9%)	60
1844	James K. Polk	Democratic	1,337,243(49.6%)	170
	Henry Clay	Whig	1,299,068(48.1%)	105
	James G. Birney	Liberty	63,300(2.3%)	
1848	Zachary Taylor	Whig	1,360,101(47.4%)	163
	Lewis Cass	Democratic	1,220,544(42.5%)	127
	Martin Van Buren	Free Soil	291,163(10.1%)	
1852	Franklin Pierce	Democratic	1,601,474(50.9%)	254
	Winfield Scott	Whig	1,386,578(44.1%)	42
1856	James Buchanan	Democratic	1,838,169(45.4%)	174
	John C. Fremont	Republican	1,335,264(33.0%)	114
	Millard Fillmore	American	874,534(21.6%)	8
1860	Abraham Lincoln	Republican	1,865,593(39.8%)	180
	Stephen A. Douglas	Democratic	1,381,713(29.5%)	12
	John C. Breckinridge	Democratic	848,356(18.1%)	72
	John Bell	Constitutional Union	592,906(12.6%)	79
1864	Abraham Lincoln	Republican	2,206,938(55.0%)	212
	George B. McClellan	Democratic	1,803,787(45.0%)	21
1868	Ulysses S. Grant	Republican	3,013,421(52.7%)	214
	Horatio Seymour	Democratic	2,706,829(47.3%)	80
1872	Ulysses S. Grant	Republican	3,596,745(55.6%)	286
	Horace Greeley	Democratic	2,843,446(43.9%)	66
1876	Rutherford B. Hayes	Republican	4,036,571(48.0%)	185
	Samuel J. Tilden	Democratic	4,284,020(51.0%)	184
1880	James A. Garfield	Republican	4,449,053(48.3%)	214
	Winfield S. Hancock	Democratic	4,442,035(48.2%)	155
	James B. Weaver	Greenback-Labor	308,578(3.4%)	
1884	Grover Cleveland	Democratic	4,874,986(48.5%)	219
	James G. Blaine	Republican	4,851,931(48.2%)	182
	Benjamin F. Butler	Greenback-Labor	175,370(1.8%)	
1888	Benjamin Harrison	Republican	5,444,337(47.8%)	233
	Grover Cleveland	Democratic	5,540,050(48.6%)	168

Presidential Election Results 1789–2004

Year	Candidates	Party	Popular Vote	Electoral Vote
1892	Grover Cleveland	Democratic	5,554,414(46.0%)	277
	Benjamin Harrison	Republican	5,190,802(43.0%)	145
	James B. Weaver	Peoples	1,027,329(8.5%)	22
1896	William McKinley	Republican	7,035,638(50.8%)	271
	William J. Bryan	Democratic; Populist	6,467,946(46.7%)	176
1900	William McKinley	Republican	7,219,530(51.7%)	292
	William J. Bryan	Democratic; Populist	6,356,734(45.5%)	155
1904	Theodore Roosevelt	Republican	7,628,834(56.4%)	336
	Alton B. Parker	Democrat	5,084,401(37.6%)	140
	Eugene V. Debs	Socialist	402,460(3.0%)	0
1908	William H. Taft	Republican	7,679,006(51.6%)	321
	William J. Bryan	Democratic	6,409,106(43.1%)	162
	Eugene V. Debs	Socialist	420,820(2.8%)	0
1912	Woodrow Wilson	Democratic	6,286,820(41.8%)	435
	Theodore Roosevelt	Progressive	4,126,020(27.4%)	88
	William H. Taft	Republican	3,483,922(23.2%)	8
	Eugene V. Debs	Socialist	897,011(6.0%)	0
1916	Woodrow Wilson	Democratic	9,129,606(49.3%)	277
	Charles E. Hughes	Republican	8,538,211(46.1%)	254
1920	Warren G. Harding	Republican	16,152,200(61.0%)	404
	James M. Cox	Democratic	9,147,353(34.6%)	127
	Eugene V. Debs	Socialist	919,799(3.5%)	0
1924	Calvin Coolidge	Republican	15,725,016(54.1%)	382
	John W. Davis	Democratic	8,385,586(28.8%)	136
	Robert M. La Follette	Progressive	4,822,856(16.6%)	13
1928	Herbert C. Hoover	Republican	21,392,190(58.2%)	444
	Alfred E. Smith	Democratic	15,016,443(40.8%)	87
1932	Franklin D. Roosevelt	Democratic	22,809,638(57.3%)	472
	Herbert C. Hoover	Republican	15,758,901(39.6%)	59
	Norman Thomas	Socialist	881,951(2.2%)	0
1936	Franklin D. Roosevelt	Democratic	27,751,612(60.7%)	523
	Alfred M. Landon	Republican	16,681,913(36.4%)	8
	William Lemke	Union	891,858(1.9%)	0
1940	Franklin D. Roosevelt	Democratic	27,243,466(54.7%)	449
	Wendell L. Wilkie	Republican	22,304,755(44.8%)	82
1944	Franklin D. Roosevelt	Democratic	25,602,505(52.8%)	432
	Thomas E. Dewey	Republican	22,006,278(44.5%)	99
1948	Harry S. Truman	Democratic	24,105,812(49.5%)	303
	Thomas E. Dewey	Republican	21,970,065(45.1%)	189
	J. Strom Thurmond	States' Rights	1,169,063(2.4%)	39
	Henry A. Wallace	Progressive	1,157,172(2.4%)	0
1952	Dwight D. Eisenhower	Republican	33,936,234(55.2%)	442
	Adlai E. Stevenson	Democratic	27,314,992(44.5%)	89
1956	Dwight D. Eisenhower	Republican	35,590,472(57.4%)	457
	Adlai E. Stevenson	Democratic	26,022,752(42.0%)	73
1960	John F. Kennedy	Democratic	34,227,096(49.9%)	303
	Richard M. Nixon	Republican	34,108,546(49.6%)	219
1964	Lyndon B Johnson	Democratic	43,126,233(61.1%)	486
	Barry Goldwater	Republican	27,174,989(38.5%)	52
1968	Richard M. Nixon	Republican	31,783,783(43.4%)	301
	Hubert H. Humphrey	Democratic	31,271,839(42.7%)	191
	George C. Wallace	American Independent	9,899,557(13.5%)	46
1972	Richard M. Nixon	Republican	46,632,189(61.3%)	520
	George McGovern	Democratic	28,422,015(37.3%)	17
1976	Jimmy Carter	Democratic	40,828,587(50.1%)	297
	Gerald R. Ford	Republican	39,147,613(48.0%)	240
1980	Ronald Reagan	Republican	42,941,145(51.0%)	489
	Jimmy Carter	Democratic	34,663,037(41.0%)	49
	John B. Anderson	Independent	5,551,551(6.6%)	0
1984	Ronald Reagan	Republican	53,428,357(59%)	525
	Walter F. Mondale	Democratic	36,930,923(41%)	13
1988	George Bush	Republican	48,881,011(53%)	426
	Michael Dukakis	Democratic	41,828,350(46%)	111
1992	Bill Clinton	Democratic	38,394,210(43%)	370
	George Bush	Republican	33,974,386(38%)	168
	H. Ross Perot	Independent	16,573,465(19%)	0
1996	Bill Clinton	Democratic	45,628,667(49%)	379
	Bob Dole	Republican	37,869,435(41%)	159
	H. Ross Perot	Reform	7,874,283(8%)	0
2000	George W. Bush	Republican	50,456,169(48%)	271
	Al Gore	Democrat	50,996,116(48%)	266
	Ralph Nader	Green	2,767,176(3%)	0
2004	George W. Bush	Republican	59,459,765(51%)	286
	John Kerry	Democrat	55,949,407(48%)	252
	Ralph Nader	Independent	400,706(1%)	0

Presidents and Vice Presidents

1. George Washington (1789)
   John Adams (1789)

2. John Adams (1797)
   Thomas Jefferson (1797)

3. Thomas Jefferson (1801)
   Aaron Burr (1801)
   George Clinton (1805)

4. James Madison (1809)
   George Clinton (1809)
   Elbridge Gerry (1813)

5. James Monroe (1817)
   Daniel D. Tompkins (1817)

6. John Quincy Adams (1825)
   John C. Calhoun (1825)

7. Andrew Jackson (1829)
   John C. Calhoun (1829)
   Martin Van Buren (1833)

8. Martin Van Buren (1837)
   Richard M. Johnson (1837)

9. William H. Harrison (1841)
   John Tyler (1841)

10. John Tyler (1841)

11. James K. Polk (1845)
    George M. Dallas (1845)

12. Zachary Taylor (1849)
    Millard Fillmore (1849)

13. Millard Fillmore (1850)

14. Franklin Pierce (1853)
    William R. King (1853)

15. James Buchanan (1857)
    John C. Breckinridge (1857)

16. Abraham Lincoln (1861)
    Hannibal Hamlin (1861)
    Andrew Johnson (1865)

17. Andrew Johnson (1865)

18. Ulysses S. Grant (1869)
    Schuyler Colfax (1869)
    Henry Wilson (1873)

19. Rutherford B. Hayes (1877)
    William A. Wheeler (1877)

20. James A. Garfield (1881)
    Chester A. Arthur (1881)

21. Chester A. Arthur (1881)

22. Grover Cleveland (1885)
    T. A. Hendricks (1885)

23. Benjamin Harrison (1889)
    Levi P. Morton (1889)

24. Grover Cleveland (1893)
    Adlai E. Stevenson (1893)

25. William McKinley (1897)
    Garret A. Hobart (1897)
    Theodore Roosevelt (1901)

26. Theodore Roosevelt (1901)
    Charles Fairbanks (1905)

27. William H. Taft (1909)
    James S. Sherman (1909)

28. Woodrow Wilson (1913)
    Thomas R. Marshall (1913)

29. Warren G. Harding (1921)
    Calvin Coolidge (1921)

30. Calvin Coolidge (1923)
    Charles G. Dawes (1925)

31. Herbert C. Hoover (1929)
    Charles Curtis (1929)

32. Franklin D. Roosevelt (1933)
    John Nance Garner (1933)
    Henry A. Wallace (1941)
    Harry S Truman (1945)

33. Harry S Truman (1945)
    Alben W. Barkley (1949)

34. Dwight D. Eisenhower (1953)
    Richard M. Nixon (1953)

35. John F. Kennedy (1961)
    Lyndon B. Johnson (1961)

36. Lyndon B. Johnson (1963)
    Hubert H. Humphrey (1965)

37. Richard M. Nixon (1969)
    Spiro T. Agnew (1969)
    Gerald R. Ford (1973)

38. Gerald R. Ford (1974)
    Nelson A. Rockefeller (1974)

39. James E. Carter Jr. (1977)
    Walter F. Mondale (1977)

40. Ronald W. Reagan (1981)
    George H. W. Bush (1981)

41. George H. W. Bush (1989)
    James D. Quayle III (1989)

42. William J. B. Clinton (1993)
    Albert Gore (1993)

43. George W. Bush (2001)
    Richard Cheney (2001)

GLOSSARY

administrative discretion Authority given by Congress to the federal bureaucracy to use reasonable judgment in implementing the laws.

adversary system A judicial system in which the court of law is a neutral arena where two parties argue their differences.

advisory opinion An opinion unrelated to a particular case that gives a court's view about a constitutional or legal issue.

affirmative action Remedial action designed to overcome the effects of past discrimination against minorities and women.

amendatory veto The power of governors in a few states to return a bill to the legislature with suggested language changes, conditions, or amendments. Legislators then decide either to accept the governor's recommendations or to pass the bill in its original form over the veto.

American dream The widespread belief that the United States is a land of opportunity and that individual initiative and hard work can bring economic success.

amicus curiae brief Literally, a "friend of the court" brief, filed by an individual or organization to present arguments in addition to those presented by the immediate parties to a case.

Annapolis Convention A convention held in September 1786 to consider problems of trade and navigation, attended by five states and important because it issued the call to Congress and the states for what became the Constitutional Convention.

Antifederalists Opponents of ratification of the Constitution and of a strong central government generally.

antitrust legislation Federal laws (starting with the Sherman Act of 1890) that try to prevent a monopoly from dominating an industry and restraining trade.

appellate jurisdiction The authority of a court to review decisions made by lower courts.

Articles of Confederation The first governing document of the confederate states, drafted in 1777, ratified in 1781, and replaced by the present Constitution in 1789.

assessment The valuation a government places on property for the purposes of taxation.

assigned council system Arrangement whereby attorneys are provided for persons accused of crimes who are unable to hire their own attorneys. The judge assigns a member of the bar to provide counsel to a particular defendant.

attentive public Those citizens who follow public affairs carefully.

Australian ballot A secret ballot printed by the state.

bad tendency test Interpretation of the First Amendment that would permit legislatures to forbid speech encouraging people to engage in illegal action.

bicameral legislature A two-house legislature.

bicameralism The principle of a two-house legislature.

bill of attainder Legislative act inflicting punishment, including deprivation of property, without a trial, on named individuals or members of a specific group.

binding arbitration A collective bargaining agreement in which both parties agree, in case of dispute over the terms of the union contract, to adhere to the decision of an arbitrator.

bipartisanship A policy that emphasizes a united front and cooperation between the major political parties, especially on sensitive foreign policy issues.

blanket primary Primary election open to all voters, who may vote for a candidate from any party for each office.

bundling A tactic of political action committees whereby they collect contributions from like-minded individuals (each limited to $2,000) and present them to a candidate or political party as a "bundle," thus increasing their influence.

bureaucracy A professional corps of officials organized in a pyramidal hierarchy and functioning under impersonal, uniform rules and procedures.

bureaucrat A career government employee.

cabinet Advisory council for the president, consisting of the heads of the executive departments, the vice president, and a few other officials selected by the president.

candidate appeal How voters feel about a candidate's background, personality, leadership ability, and other personal qualities.

capitalism An economic system characterized by private property, competitive markets, economic incentives, and limited government involvement in the production and pricing of goods and services.

caucus A meeting of local party members to choose party officials or candidates for public office and to decide the platform.

central clearance Review of all executive branch testimony, reports, and draft legislation by the Office of Management and Budget to assure that each communication to Congress is in accordance with the president's program.

centralists People who favor national action over action at the state and local levels.

charter school A publicly funded alternative to standard public schools in some states, initiated when individuals or groups receive charters; charter schools must meet state standards.

charter City "constitution" that outlines the structure of city government, defines the authority of the various officials, and provides for their selection.

checks and balances Constitutional grant of powers that enables each of the three branches of government to check some acts of the others and therefore ensure that no branch can dominate.

chief of staff The head of the White House staff.

civil disobedience Deliberate refusal to obey a law or comply with the orders of public officials as a means of expressing opposition.

class action suit Lawsuit brought by an individual or a group of people on behalf of all those similarly situated.

clear and present danger test Interpretation of the First Amendment that holds that the government cannot interfere with speech unless the speech presents a clear and present danger that it will lead to evil or illegal acts. To shout "Fire!" falsely in a crowded theater is Justice Oliver Wendell Holmes's famous example.

closed primary Primary election in which only persons registered in the party holding the primary may vote.

closed rule A procedural rule in the House of Representatives that prohibits any amendments to bills or provides that only members of the committee reporting the bill may offer amendments.

closed shop A company with a labor agreement under which union membership is a condition of employment.

cloture A procedure for terminating debate, especially filibusters, in the Senate.

coattail effect The boost that candidates may get in an election because of the popularity of candidates above them on the ballot, especially the president.

collective bargaining Method whereby representatives of the union and the employer determine wages, hours, and conditions of employment through direct negotiation.

commerce clause The clause of the Constitution (Article I, Section 8, Clause 3) that gives Congress the power to regulate all business activities that cross state lines or affect more than one state or other nations.

commercial speech Advertisements and commercials for products and services; they receive less First Amendment protection, primarily to discourage false and misleading ads.

community policing Assigning police to neighborhoods where they walk the beat and work with churches and other community groups to reduce crime and improve relations with minorities.

concurrent powers Powers that the Constitution gives to both the national and state governments, such as the power to levy taxes.

concurring opinion An opinion that agrees with the majority in a Supreme Court ruling but differs on the reasoning.

confederation Constitutional arrangement in which sovereign nations or states, by compact, create a central government but carefully limit its power and do not give it direct authority over individuals.

conference committee Committee appointed by the presiding officers of each chamber to adjust differences on a particular bill passed by each in different form.

Congressional Budget Office (CBO) An agency of Congress that analyzes presidential budget recommendations and estimates the costs of proposed legislation.

Connecticut Compromise Compromise agreement by states at the Constitutional Convention for a bicameral legislature with a lower house in which representation would be based on population and an upper house in which each state would have two senators.

conservatism A belief that limited government ensures order, competitive markets, and personal opportunity.

Constitutional Convention The convention in Philadelphia, May 25 to September 17, 1787, that framed the Constitution of the United States.

constitutional democracy A government that enforces recognized limits on those who govern and allows the voice of the people to be heard through free, fair, and relatively frequent elections.

constitutional home rule State constitutional authorization for local governments to conduct their own affairs.

constitutional initiative petition   A device that permits voters to place specific amendments to a state constitution on the ballot by petition.

constitutionalism   The set of arrangements, including checks and balances, federalism, separation of powers, rule of law, due process, and a bill of rights, that requires leaders to listen, think, bargain, and explain before they act or make laws. We then hold them politically and legally accountable for how they exercise their powers.

contract clause   Clause of the Constitution (Article I, Section 10) originally intended to prohibit state governments from modifying contracts made between individuals; for a while interpreted as prohibiting state governments from taking actions that adversely affect property rights; no longer interpreted so broadly and no longer constrains state governments from exercising their police powers.

council-manager plan   Form of local government in which the city council hires a professional administrator to manage city affairs; also known as the *city-manager plan.*

court of appeals   A court with appellate jurisdiction that hears appeals from the decisions of lower courts.

cross-cutting cleavages   Divisions within society that cut across demographic categories to produce groups that are more heterogeneous or different.

crossover voting   Voting by a member of one party for a candidate of another party.

de facto segregation   Segregation resulting from economic or social conditions or personal choice.

de jure segregation   Segregation imposed by law.

dealignment   Weakening of partisan preferences that points to a rejection of both major parties and a rise in the number of Independents.

debt   The accumulated total of federal deficits, minus surpluses, over the years.

decentralists   People who favor state or local action rather than national action.

defendant   In a criminal action, the person or party accused of an offense.

deficit   The difference between the revenues raised annually from sources of income other than borrowing and the expenditures of government, including paying the interest on past borrowing.

delegate   An official who is expected to represent the views of his or her constituents even when personally holding divergent views; one interpretation of the role of a legislator.

democracy   Government by the people, either directly or indirectly, with free and frequent elections.

democratic consensus   Widespread agreement on fundamental principles of democratic governance and the values that undergird them.

demographics   The study of the characteristics of populations.

department   Usually the largest organization in government; also the highest rank in federal hierarchy.

deregulation   A policy promoting cutbacks in the amount of federal regulation in specific areas of economic activity.

devolution revolution   The effort to slow the growth of the federal government by returning many functions to the states.

direct democracy   Government in which citizens vote on laws and select officials more directly.

direct primary   Election in which voters choose party nominees.

discharge petition   Petition that, if signed by a majority of the members of the House of Representatives, will pry a bill from committee and bring it to the floor for consideration.

disclosure   A requirement that candidates specify where the money came from to finance their campaign.

dissenting opinion   An opinion disagreeing with the majority in a Supreme Court ruling.

divided government   Governance divided between the parties, especially when one holds the presidency and the other controls one or both houses of Congress.

double jeopardy   Trial or punishment for the same crime by the same government; forbidden by the Constitution.

dual citizenship   Citizenship in more than one nation.

due process clause   Clause in the Fifth Amendment limiting the power of the national government; similar clause in the Fourteenth Amendment prohibiting state governments from depriving any person of life, liberty, or property without due process of law.

due process   Established rules and regulations that restrain people in government who exercise power.

economic sanctions   Denial of export, import, or financial relations with a target country in an effort to change that nation's policies.

electoral college   The electoral system used in electing the president and vice president, in which voters vote for electors pledged to cast their ballots for a particular party's candidates.

eminent domain   Power of a government to take private property for public use; the U.S. Constitution gives national and state governments this power and requires them to provide just compensation for property so taken.

enterprise zone   Inner-city area designated as offering tax incentives to companies that invest in plants there and provide job training for the unemployed.

entitlements   Programs such as unemployment insurance, disaster relief, or disability payments, that provide benefits to all eligible citizens.

enumerated powers   The powers explicitly given to Congress in the Constitution.

environmental impact statement   A statement required by federal law from all agencies for any project using federal funds to assess the potential effect of the new construction or development on the environment.

environmentalism   An ideology that is dominated by concern for the environment but also promotes grassroots democracy, social justice, equal opportunity, nonviolence, respect for diversity, and feminism.

equal protection clause   Clause in the Fourteenth Amendment that forbids any state to deny to any person within its jurisdiction the equal protection of the laws. By interpretation, the Fifth Amendment imposes the same limitation on the national government. This clause is the major constitutional restraint on the power of governments to discriminate against persons because of race, national origin, or sex.

establishment clause   Clause in the First Amendment that states that Congress shall make no law respecting an establishment of religion. It has been interpreted by the Supreme Court as forbidding governmental support to any or all religions.

ethnicity   A social division based on national origin, religion, language, and often race.

ethnocentrism   Belief in the superiority of one's nation or ethnic group.

ex post facto law   Retroactive criminal law that works to the disadvantage of an individual; forbidden in the Constitution.

excise tax   Consumer tax on a specific kind of merchandise, such as tobacco.

exclusionary rule   Requirement that evidence unconstitutionally or illegally obtained be excluded from a criminal trial.

executive agreements   Agreements between the U.S. president and the leaders of other nations that do not require Senate approval.

Executive Office of the President   The cluster of presidential staff agencies that help the president carry out his responsibilities. Currently the office includes the Office of Management and Budget, the Council of Economic Advisers, and several other units.

executive order   Directive issued by a president or governor that has the force of law.

executive privilege   The right to keep executive communications confidential, especially if they relate to national security.

express powers   Powers specifically granted to one of the branches of the national government by the Constitution.

extradition   Legal process whereby an alleged criminal offender is surrendered by the officials of one state to officials of the state in which the crime is alleged to have been committed.

faction   A term used by the founders of this country to refer to political parties and special interests or interest groups.

fairness doctrine   Federal Communications Commission policy that required holders of radio and television licenses to ensure that different viewpoints were presented about controversial issues or persons; repealed in 1987.

federal mandate   A requirement imposed by the federal government as a condition for the receipt of federal funds.

Federal Register   Official document, published every weekday, that lists the new and proposed regulations of executive departments and regulatory agencies.

Federal Reserve System   The system created by Congress in 1913 to establish banking practices and regulate currency in circulation and the amount of credit available. It consists of 12 regional banks supervised by the Board of Governors. Often called simply *the Fed.*

federalism   Constitutional arrangement whereby power is distributed between a central government and subdivisional governments, called states in the United States. The national and the subdivisional governments both exercise direct authority over individuals.

Federalists   Supporters of ratification of the Constitution whose position promoting a strong central government was later voiced in the Federalist party.

felony   A serious crime, the penalty for which can range from death to imprisonment in a penitentiary for more than a year.

fighting words   Words that by their very nature inflict injury on those to whom they are addressed or incite them to acts of violence.

filibuster   A procedural practice in the Senate whereby a senator refuses to relinquish the floor and thereby delays proceedings and prevents a vote on a controversial issue.

fiscal policy   Government policy that attempts to manage the economy by controlling taxing and spending.

free exercise clause   Clause in the First Amendment that states that Congress shall make no law prohibiting the free exercise of religion.

free rider An individual who does not join a group representing his or her interests yet receives the benefit of the influence the group achieves.

full faith and credit clause Clause in the Constitution (Article IV, Section 1) requiring each state to recognize the civil judgments rendered by the courts of the other states and to accept their public records and acts as valid.

gender gap The difference between the political opinions or political behavior of men and of women.

General Agreement on Tariffs and Trade (GATT) An international trade organization with more than 130 members, including the United States and the People's Republic of China, that seeks to encourage free trade by lowering tariffs and other trade restrictions.

general property tax Tax levied by local and some state governments on real property or personal, tangible property, the major portion of which is on the estimated value of one's home and land.

gerrymandering The drawing of legislative district boundaries to benefit a party, group, or incumbent.

government corporation A government agency that operates like a business corporation, created to secure greater freedom of action and flexibility for a particular program.

grand jury A jury of 12 to 23 persons who, in private, hear evidence presented by the government to determine whether persons shall be required to stand trial. If the jury believes there is sufficient evidence that a crime was committed, it issues an indictment.

gross domestic product (GDP) The total output of all economic activity in the nation, including goods and services.

Hatch Act Federal statute barring federal employees from active participation in certain kinds of politics and protecting them from being fired on partisan grounds.

health maintenance organization (HMO) Alternative means of health care in which people or their employers are charged a set amount and the HMO provides health care and covers hospital costs.

hold A procedural practice in the Senate whereby a senator temporarily blocks the consideration of a bill or nomination.

honeymoon Period at the beginning of a new president's term during which the president enjoys generally positive relations with the press and Congress, usually lasting about six months.

horse race A close contest; by extension, any contest in which the focus is on who is ahead and by how much rather than on substantive differences between the candidates.

ideology A consistent pattern of beliefs about political values and the role of government.

immunity Exemption from prosecution for a particular crime in return for testimony pertaining to the case.

impeachment Formal accusation against a public official, the first step in removal from office.

implementation The process of putting a law into practice through bureaucratic rules or spending.

implied powers Powers inferred from the express powers that allow Congress to carry out its functions.

impoundment Presidential refusal to allow an agency to spend funds authorized and approved by Congress.

incumbent The current holder of an office.

independent agency A government entity that is independent of the legislative, executive, and judicial branches.

independent expenditures Money spent by individuals or groups not associated with candidates to elect or defeat candidates for office.

independent regulatory commission A government agency or commission with regulatory power whose independence is protected by Congress.

indexing Providing automatic increases to compensate for inflation.

indictment A formal written statement from a grand jury charging an individual with an offense; also called a *true bill.*

inflation A rise in the general price level (and decrease in dollar value) owing to an increase in the volume of money and credit in relation to available goods.

information affidavit Certification by a public prosecutor that there is evidence to justify bringing named individuals to trial.

inherent powers The powers of the national government in the field of foreign affairs that the Supreme Court has declared do not depend on constitutional grants but rather grow out of the very existence of the national government.

initiative Procedure whereby a certain number of voters may, by petition, propose a law or constitutional amendment and have it submitted to the voters.

interest group A collection of people who share some common interest or attitude and seek to influence government for specific ends. Interest groups usually work within the framework of government and employ tactics such as lobbying to achieve their goals.

interested money Financial contributions by individuals or groups in the hope of influencing the outcome of an election and subsequently influencing policy.

interstate compact An agreement among two or more states. The Constitution requires that most such agreements be approved by Congress.

iron triangle A mutually supporting relationship among interest groups, congressional committees and subcommittees, and government agencies that share a common policy concern.

issue advertising Commercial advertising on radio and television advocating a particular position on an issue, paid for by interest groups and often designed to influence voters' choices on election day.

issue advocacy Promoting a particular position on an issue, paid for by interest groups or individuals but not candidates. Much issue advocacy is often electioneering for or against a candidate, and until 2004, had not been subject to any regulation.

item veto Right of an executive to veto parts of a bill approved by a legislature without having to veto the entire bill.

Jim Crow laws State laws formerly pervasive throughout the South requiring public facilities and accommodations to be segregated by race; ruled unconstitutional.

joint committee A committee composed of members of both the House of Representatives and the Senate; such committees oversee the Library of Congress and conduct investigations.

judicial activism Philosophy proposing that judges should interpret the Constitution to reflect current conditions and values.

judicial interpretation A method by which judges modify the force of a constitutional provision by reinterpreting its meaning.

judicial review The power of a court to refuse to enforce a law or government regulation that in the opinion of the judges conflicts with the U.S. Constitution or, in a state court, the state constitution.

judicial self-restraint Philosophy proposing that judges should interpret the Constitution to reflect what the framers intended and what its words literally say.

justiciable dispute A dispute growing out of an actual case or controversy and that is capable of settlement by legal methods.

Keynesian economics Theory based on the principles of John Maynard Keynes, stating that government spending should increase during business slumps and be curbed during booms.

labor injunction A court order forbidding specific individuals or groups from performing certain acts (such as striking) that the court considers harmful to the rights and property of an employer or a community.

laissez-faire economics Theory that opposes governmental interference in economic affairs beyond what is necessary to protect life and property.

libel Written defamation of another person. Especially in the case of public officials and public figures, the constitutional tests designed to restrict libel actions are very rigid.

liberalism A belief in the positive uses of government to bring about justice and equality of opportunity.

libertarianism An ideology that cherishes individual liberty and insists on a sharply limited government, promoting a free market economy, a noninterventionist foreign policy, and an absence of regulation in the moral and social spheres.

line item veto Right of an executive to veto parts of a bill approved by a legislature without having to veto the entire bill.

literacy test Literacy requirement imposed by some states as a condition of voting, generally used to disqualify blacks from voting in the South; now illegal.

lobbying Engaging in activities aimed at influencing public officials, especially legislators, and the policies they enact.

lobbyist A person who is employed by and acts for an organized interest group or corporation to try to influence policy decisions and positions in the executive and legislative branches.

logrolling Mutual aid and vote trading among legislators.

magistrate judge An official who performs a variety of limited judicial duties.

majority The candidate or party that wins more than half the votes cast in an election.

majority leader The legislative leader selected by the majority party who helps plan party strategy, confers with other party leaders, and tries to keep members of the party in line.

majority rule Governance according to the expressed preferences of the majority.

majority-minority district A congressional district created to include a majority of minority voters; ruled constitutional so long as race is not the main factor in redistricting.

malapportionment Having legislative districts with unequal populations.

mandate The perceived level of support for a president's policy priorities.

manifest destiny A notion held by nineteenth-century Americans that the United States was destined to rule the continent, from the Atlantic to the Pacific.

mass media   Means of communication that reach the mass public, including newspapers and magazines, radio, television (broadcast, cable, and satellite), films, recordings, books, and electronic communication.

mayor-council charter   The oldest and most common form of city government, consisting of either a weak mayor and a city council or a strong mayor and council.

means-tested entitlements   Programs such as Medicaid and welfare under which applicants must meet eligibility requirements based on need.

Medicaid   Federal program that provides medical benefits for low-income persons.

medical savings account   Alternative means of health care in which individuals make tax-deductible contributions to a special account that can be used to pay medical expenses.

Medicare   National health insurance program for the elderly and disabled.

merit system   A system of public employment in which selection and promotion depend on demonstrated performance rather than political patronage.

minor party   A small political party that rises and falls with a charismatic candidate or, if composed of ideologies on the right or left, usually persists over time; also called a *third party.*

minority leader   The legislative leader selected by the minority party as spokesperson for the opposition.

misdemeanor   A minor crime; the penalty is a fine or imprisonment for a short time, usually less than a year, in a local jail.

Missouri Plan   A system for selecting judges that combines features of the appointive and elective methods. The governor selects judges from lists presented by panels of lawyers and laypersons, and at the end of their term, the judges may run against their own record in retention elections.

monetarism   A theory that government should control the money supply to encourage economic growth and restrain inflation.

monetary policy   Government policy that attempts to manage the economy by controlling the money supply and thus interest rates.

monopoly   Domination of an industry by a single company by fixing prices and discouraging competition; also the company that dominates the industry.

movement   A large body of people interested in a common issue, idea, or concern that is of continuing significance and who are willing to take action. Movements seek to change attitudes or institutions, not just policies.

national party convention   A national meeting of delegates elected in primaries, caucuses, or state conventions who assemble once every four years to nominate candidates for president and vice president, ratify the party platform, elect officers, and adopt rules.

national supremacy   Constitutional doctrine that whenever conflict occurs between the constitutionally authorized actions of the national government and those of a state or local government, the actions of the federal government prevail.

natural law   God's or nature's law that defines right from wrong and is higher than human law.

natural rights   The rights of all people to dignity and worth; also called *human rights.*

naturalization   A legal action conferring citizenship upon an alien.

necessary and proper clause   Clause of the Constitution (Article I, Section 8, Clause 18) setting forth the implied powers of Congress. It states that Congress, in addition to its express powers, has the right to make all laws necessary and proper for carrying out all powers vested by the Constitution in the national government.

New Jersey Plan   Proposal at the Constitutional Convention made by William Paterson of New Jersey for a central government with a single-house legislature in which each state would be represented equally.

new judicial federalism   The practice of some state courts of using the bill of rights in their state constitutions to provide more protection for some rights than is provided by the Supreme Court's interpretation of the Bill of Rights in the U.S. Constitution.

news media   Media that emphasizes the news.

nonpartisan election   A local or judicial election in which candidates are not selected or endorsed by political parties and party affiliation is not listed on ballots.

nonprotected speech   Libel, obscenity, fighting words, and commercial speech, which are not entitled to constitutional protection in all circumstances.

North American Free Trade Agreement (NAFTA)   Agreement signed by the United States, Canada, and Mexico in 1992 to form the largest free trade zone in the world.

obscenity   Quality or state of a work that taken as a whole appeals to a prurient interest in sex by depicting sexual conduct in a patently offensive way and that lacks serious literary, artistic, political, or scientific value.

office block ballot   Ballot on which all candidates are listed under the office for which they are running, making split-ticket voting easier.

Office of Management and Budget (OMB)   Presidential staff agency that serves as a clearinghouse for budgetary requests and management improvements for government agencies.

Office of Personnel Management (OPM)   Agency that administers civil service laws, rules, and regulations.

one-party state   A state in which one party wins all or nearly all the offices and the other party receives only a small proportion of the popular vote.

open primary   Primary election in which any voter, regardless of party, may vote.

open rule   A procedural rule in the House of Representatives that permits floor amendments within the overall time allocated to the bill.

open shop   A company with a labor agreement under which union membership cannot be required as a condition of employment.

opinion of the court   An explanation of a decision of the Supreme Court or any other appellate court.

original jurisdiction   The authority of a court to hear a case "in the first instance."

override   An action taken by Congress to reverse a presidential veto that requires a two-thirds majority in each chamber.

oversight   Legislative or executive review of a particular government program or organization. Can be in response to a crisis of some kind or part of routine review.

parliamentary system   A system of government in which the legislature selects the prime minister or president.

party caucus   A meeting of the members of a party in a legislative chamber to select party leaders and to develop party policy. Called a *conference* by the Republicans.

party column ballot   Type of ballot that encourages party-line voting by listing all of a party's candidates in a column under the party name.

party convention   A meeting of party delegates to vote on matters of policy and in some cases to select party candidates for public office.

party identification   An informal and subjective affiliation with a political party that most people acquire in childhood.

party registration   The act of declaring party affiliation; required by some states when one registers to vote.

patronage   The dispensing of government jobs to persons who belong to the winning political party.

permanent normal trade relations (PNTR) status   Trade status granted as part of an international trade policy that gives a nation the same favorable trade concessions and tariffs that the best trading partners receive.

petit jury   A jury of 6 to 12 persons who determine guilt or innocence in a civil or criminal action.

plea bargain   Agreement between a prosecutor and a defendant that the defendant will plead guilty to a lesser offense to avoid having to stand trial for a more serious offense.

plurality   Candidate or party with the most votes cast in an election, not necessarily more than half.

pocket veto   A veto exercised by the president after Congress has adjourned; if the president takes no action for ten days, the bill does not become law and is not returned to Congress for a possible override.

police powers   Inherent powers of state governments to pass laws to protect the public health, safety, and welfare; the national government has no directly granted police powers but accomplishes the same goals through other delegated powers.

political action committee (PAC)   The political arm of an interest group that is legally entitled to raise funds on a voluntary basis from members, stockholders, or employees in order to contribute funds to favored candidates or political parties.

political culture   The widely shared beliefs, values, and norms concerning the relationship of citizens to government and to one another.

political ideology   A consistent pattern of beliefs about political values and the role of government.

political party   An organization that seeks political power by electing people to office so that its positions and philosophy become public policy.

political predisposition   A characteristic of individuals that is predictive of political behavior.

political question   A dispute that requires knowledge of a nonlegal character or the use of techniques not suitable for a court or explicitly assigned by the Constitution to Congress or the president; judges refuse to answer constitutional questions that they declare are political.

political socialization   The process, most notably in families and schools, by which we develop our political attitudes, values, and beliefs.

poll tax   Payment required as a condition for voting; prohibited for national elections by the Twenty-Fourth Amendment (1964) and ruled unconstitutional for all elections in *Harper v. Virginia Board of Elections* (1966).

popular consent   The idea that a just government must derive its powers from the consent of the people it governs.

popular sovereignty   A belief that ultimate power resides in the people.

preemption   The right of a federal law or regulation to preclude enforcement of a state or local law or regulation.

preferred position doctrine Interpretation of the First Amendment that holds that freedom of expression is so essential to democracy that governments should not punish persons for what they say, only for what they do.

president pro tempore Officer of the Senate selected by the majority party to act as chair in the absence of the vice president.

presidential ticket The joint listing of the presidential and vice presidential candidates on the same ballot as required by the Twelfth Amendment.

prior restraint Censorship imposed before a speech is made or a newspaper is published; usually presumed to be unconstitutional.

privatization Contracting public services to private organizations.

pro bono To serve the public good; term used to describe work that lawyers (or other professionals) do for which they receive no fees.

procedural due process Constitutional requirement that governments proceed by proper methods; places limits on how governmental power may be exercised.

progressive tax A tax graduated so that people with higher incomes pay a larger fraction of their income than people with lower incomes.

property rights The rights of an individual to own, use, rent, invest in, buy, and sell property.

proportional representation An election system in which each party running receives the proportion of legislative seats corresponding to its proportion of the vote.

protectionism Policy of erecting trade barriers to protect domestic industry.

public assistance Aid to the poor; "welfare."

public defender system Arrangement whereby public officials are hired to provide legal assistance to people accused of crimes who are unable to hire their own attorneys.

public opinion The distribution of individual preferences for or evaluations of a given issue, candidate, or institution within a specific population.

quid pro guo Something given with the expectation of receiving something in return.

race A grouping of human beings with distinctive characteristics determined by genetic inheritance.

racial gerrymandering The drawing of election districts so as to ensure that members of a certain race are a minority in the district; ruled unconstitutional in *Gomillion* v. *Lightfoot* (1960).

racial profiling Police targeting of racial minorities as potential suspects of criminal activities.

rally point A rise in public approval of the president that follows a crisis as Americans "rally 'round the flag" and the chief executive.

realigning election An election during periods of expanded suffrage and change in the economy and society that proves to be a turning point, redefining the agenda of politics and the alignment of voters within parties.

reapportionment The assigning by Congress of congressional seats after each census. State legislatures reapportion state legislative districts.

recall Procedure for submitting to popular vote the removal of public officials from office before the end of their term.

recidivist A repeat offender.

redistributive policies Governmental tax and social programs that shift wealth or benefits from one segment of the population to another, often from the rich to the poor.

redistricting The redrawing of congressional and other legislative district lines following the census, to accommodate population shifts and keep districts as equal as possible in population.

reduction veto The power of governors in a few states to reduce a particular appropriation.

referendum Procedure for submitting to popular vote measures passed by the legislature or proposed amendments to a state constitution.

regressive tax A tax whereby people with lower incomes pay a higher fraction of their income than people with higher incomes.

regulation The attempt by government to control the behavior of corporations, other governments, or citizens through altering the natural workings of the open market to achieve some desired goal.

regulations The formal instructions that government issues for implementing laws.

regulatory taking Government regulation of property so extensive that government is deemed to have taken the property by the power of eminent domain, for which it must compensate the property owners.

reinforcing cleavages Divisions within society that reinforce one another, making groups more homogeneous or similar.

representative democracy Government that derives its powers indirectly from the people, who elect those who will govern; also called a *republic.*

responsibility contract A welfare strategy adopted by some states in which recipients sign a written agreement specifying their responsibilities and outlining a plan for obtaining work and achieving self-sufficiency.

restrictive covenant A provision in a deed to real property prohibiting its sale to a person of a particular race or religion. Judicial enforcement of such deeds is unconstitutional.

revision commission A state commission that recommends changes in the state constitution for action by the legislature and vote by the voters.

revolving door Employment cycle in which individuals who work for governmental agencies regulating interests eventually end up working for interest groups or businesses with the same policy concern.

rider A provision attached to a bill—to which it may or may not be related—in order to secure its passage.

right of expatriation The right to renounce one's citizenship.

rule-making process The formal process for making regulations.

safe seat An elected office that is predictably won by one party or the other, so the success of that party's candidate is almost taken for granted.

sales tax General tax on sales transactions, sometimes exempting food and drugs.

search warrant A writ issued by a magistrate that authorizes the police to search a particular place or person, specifying the place to be searched and the objects to be seized.

sedition Attempting to overthrow the government by force or to interrupt its activities by violence.

select or special committee A congressional committee created for a specific purpose, sometimes to conduct an investigation.

selective exposure The process by which individuals screen out messages that do not conform to their own biases.

selective incorporation The process by which provisions of the Bill of Rights are brought within the scope of the Fourteenth Amendment and so applied to state and local governments.

selective perception The process by which individuals perceive what they want to in media messages.

senatorial courtesy Presidential custom of submitting the names of prospective appointees for approval to senators from the states in which the appointees are to work.

Senior Executive Service Established by Congress in 1978 as a flexible, mobile corps of senior career executives who work closely with presidential appointees to manage government.

seniority rule A legislative practice that assigns the chair of a committee or subcommittee to the member of the majority party with the longest continuous service on the committee.

separation of powers Constitutional division of powers among the legislative, executive, and judicial branches, with the legislative branch making law, the executive applying and enforcing the law, and the judiciary interpreting the law.

severance tax A tax on the privilege of "severing" such natural resources as coal, oil, timber, and gas from the land.

Shays' Rebellion Rebellion by farmers in western Massachusetts in 1786-1787, protesting mortgage foreclosures; led by Daniel Shays and important because it highlighted the need for a strong national government just as the call for the Constitutional Convention went out.

single-member district An electoral district in which voters choose one representative or official.

social capital Participation in voluntary associations that reinforce democratic and civic habits of discussion, compromise, and respect for differences.

social insurance Programs in which eligibility is based on prior contributions to government, usually in the form of payroll taxes.

Social Security A combination of entitlement programs, paid for by employer and employee taxes, that includes retirement benefits, health insurance, and support for disabled workers and the children of deceased or disabled workers.

social stratification Divisions in a community among socioeconomic groups or classes.

socialism An economic and governmental system based on public ownership of the means of production and exchange.

socioeconomic status (SES) A division of population based on occupation, income, and education.

soft money Money raised in unlimited amounts by political parties for party-building purposes. Now largely illegal except for limited contribution to state and local parties for voter registration and get-out-the-vote efforts.

Speaker The presiding officer in the House of Representatives, formally elected by the House but actually selected by the majority party.

split ticket A vote for some of one party's candidates and some of another party's.

spoils system A system of public employment based on rewarding party loyalists and friends.

standing committee A permanent committee established in a legislature, usually focusing on a policy area.

stare decisis The rule of precedent, whereby a rule or law contained in a judicial decision is commonly viewed as binding on judges whenever the same question is presented.

State of the Union Address   The president's annual statement to Congress and the nation.

states' rights   Powers expressly or implicitly reserved to the states and emphasized by decentralists.

statism   The idea that the rights of the nation are supreme over the rights of the individuals residing in that nation.

straight ticket   A vote for all of one party's candidates.

strong mayor-council form   Form of local government in which the voters directly elect the city council and the mayor, who enjoys almost total administrative authority and appoints the department heads.

substantive due process   Constitutional requirement that governments act reasonably and that the substance of the laws themselves be fair and reasonable; places limits on what a government may do.

take care clause   The constitutional requirement (in Article II, Section 3) that presidents take care that the laws are faithfully executed, even if they disagree with the purpose of those laws.

tariff   Tax levied on imports to help protect a nation's industries, labor, or farmers from foreign competition. It can also be used to raise additional revenue.

tax expenditure   Loss of tax revenue due to federal laws that provide special tax incentives or benefits to individuals or businesses.

The Federalist   Series of essays promoting ratification of the Constitution, published anonymously by Alexander Hamilton, John Jay, and James Madison in 1787 and 1788.

theocracy   Government by religious leaders, who claim divine guidance.

three-fifths compromise   Compromise agreement between northern and southern states at the Constitutional Convention that three-fifths of the slave population would be counted for determining direct taxation and representation in the House of Representatives.

tort law   Law relating to injuries to person, reputation, or property.

trade deficit   An imbalance in international trade in which the value of imports exceeds the value of exports.

trust   A monopoly that controls goods and services, often in combinations that reduce competition.

trustee   An official who is expected to vote independently, based on his or her judgment of the circumstances; one interpretation of the role of a legislator.

turnout   The proportion of the voting-age public that votes, sometimes defined as the number of registered voters that vote.

two-party state   A state in which the two major parties alternate in winning majorities.

uncontrollable spending   The portion of the federal budget that is spent on programs, such as Social Security, that the president and Congress are unwilling to cut.

unicameral legislature   A one-house legislature.

union shop   A company in which new employees must join a union within a stated time period.

unitary system   Constitutional arrangement in which power is concentrated in a central government.

user fees   Fees charged directly to individuals who use certain public services on the basis of service consumed; also called a *user charge*.

value-added tax (VAT)   A tax on increased value of a product at each stage of production and distribution rather than just at the point of sale.

veto   Rejection by a president or governor of legislation passed by a legislature.

Virginia Plan   Initial proposal at the Constitutional Convention made by the Virginia delegation for a strong central government with a bicameral legislature, the lower house to be elected by the voters and the upper chosen by the lower.

voter registration   System designed to reduce voter fraud by limiting voting to those who have established eligibility by submitting the proper form.

vouchers   Money provided by the government to parents for payment of their children's tuition in a public or private school of their choice.

weak mayor-council form   Form of local government in which the members of the city council select the mayor, who then shares power with other elected or appointed boards and commissions.

whip   Party leader who is the liaison between the leadership and the rank-and-file in the legislature.

white primary   Primary operated by the Democratic party in southern states that, before Republicans gained strength in the "one-party South," essentially constituted an election; ruled unconstitutional in *Smith* v. *Allwright* (1944).

winner-take-all system   An election system in which the candidate with the most votes wins.

women's suffrage   The right of women to vote.

workfare   A welfare strategy adopted by some states that gives able-bodied adults who do not have preschool-aged children the opportunity to learn job skills that can lead to employment.

World Trade Organization (WTO)   International organization derived from the General Agreement on Tariffs and Trade (GATT) that promotes free trade around the world.

writ of certiorari   A formal writ used to bring a case before the Supreme Court.

Writ of habeas corpus   Court order requiring explanation to a judge why a prisoner is being held in custody.

writ of mandamus   Court order directing an official to perform an official duty.

yellow-dog contract   Contract by an anti-union employer that forces new workers to promise they will not join a union as a condition of employment.

NOTES

Chapter 1

1. "2001 Was Two Years in One: Pre–Sept. 11 and After," *Houston Chronicle*, January 1, 2002, p. A34.
2. "Economic Costs of Attacks Less Than Bin Laden's Estimates," *ABC News*, December 28, 2001.
3. "Sharp Disagreements on Campaign Tactics and Rebuilding," *New York Times*, October 8, 2001, p. F5.
4. www.bartleby.com/124/pres61.html.
5. *Bush* v. *Gore*, 531 U.S. 98 (2000).
6. www.cnn.com/ELECTION/2000/transcripts/121300/bush.html.
7. Frank Newport, "What Has Changed, and What Hasn't," *Gallup Poll*, October 29, 2001, at www.gallup.com/poll/fromtheed/ed0110.asp.
8. David W. Moore, "High Approval for Most People/Institutions Handling War on Terrorism," *Gallup Poll*, November 16, 2001, at www.gallup.com/poll/releases/pr011116.asp.
9. thomas.loc.gov/home/terrorleg.htm.
10. Darren Irby, "American Red Cross Reports Record Distribution of Contributions from Liberty Fund to September 11 Families," *Press Room*, November 6, 2001, at www.redcross.org/press/disaster/ds_pr/011106record.html.
11. Robert A. Dahl, *On Democracy* (Yale University Press, 1998), p. 145.
12. Harold Stanley and Richard Niemi, *Vital Statistics on American Politics, 2001–2002* (CQ Press, 2001), pp. 25–29.
13. For a major theoretical work on the principle of majority rule, see Robert A. Dahl, *Democracy and Its Critics* (Yale University Press, 1989).
14. Seymour Martin Lipset, "The Social Requisites of Democracy Revisited," *American Sociological Review* 59 (1994), pp. 1–22.
15. For a discussion of the importance for democracy of such overlapping group memberships, see David Truman's seminal work, *The Governmental Process*, 2d ed. (Knopf, 1971).
16. See Robert D. Putnam, *Bowling Alone: The Collapse and Revival of American Community* (Simon & Schuster, 2000), p. 19. See also Pippa Norris, ed., *Critical Citizens: Global Support for Democratic Governance* (Oxford University Press, 1999), and for a somewhat different point of view, Everett Carl Ladd, *The Ladd Report* (Free Press, 1999).
17. Michael Schudson, *The Good Citizen: A History of American Civic Life* (Harvard University Press, 1998), p. 296.
18. Quoted in D. W. Miller, "Perhaps We Are Bowling Alone, But Does It Really Matter?" *Chronicle of Higher Education*, July 16, 1999, p. A17.
19. Joyce Appleby, "The American Heritage: The Heirs and the Disinherited," *Journal of American History* 74 (December 1987), p. 808.
20. Kevin Butterfield, "What You Should Know About the Declaration of Independence," *St. Louis Post-Dispatch*, July 4, 2000, p. F1.
21. Richard L. Hillard, "Liberalism, Civic Humanism and the American Revolutionary Bill of Rights, 1775–1790," paper presented at the annual meeting of the Organization of American Historians, Reno, Nevada, March 26, 1988.
22. Quoted in Charles L. Mee Jr., *The Genius of the People* (Harper & Row, 1987), p. 51.
23. Seymour Martin Lipset, "George Washington and the Founding of Democracy," *Journal of Democracy* 9 (October 1998), p. 31.
24. See the essays in Thomas E. Cronin, ed., *Inventing the American Presidency* (University Press of Kansas, 1989). See also Richard J. Ellis, ed., *Founding the American Presidency* (Rowman & Littlefield, 1999).
25. Charles A. Beard and Mary R. Beard, *A Basic History of the United States* (New Home Library, 1944), p. 136.
26. See Herbert J. Storing, ed., abridgment by Murray Dry, *The Anti-Federalist: Writings by the Opponents of the Constitution* (University of Chicago Press, 1985).
27. On the role of the promised bill of rights amendments in the ratification of the Constitution, see Leonard W. Levy, *Constitutional Opinions* (Oxford University Press, 1986), chap. 6.

Chapter 2

1. Max Lerner, *Ideas for the Ice Age* (Viking, 1941), pp. 241–242.
2. Sanford Levinson, *Constitutional Faith* (Princeton University Press, 1988), pp. 9–52.
3. Richard Morin, "We Love It—What We Know of It," *Washington Post National Weekly Edition*, September 22, 1997, p. 35.
4. Thomas Jefferson, quoted in Alpheus T. Mason, *The Supreme Court: Palladium of Freedom* (University of Michigan Press, 1962), p. 10.
5. Alexander Hamilton, James Madison, and John Jay, *The Federalist Papers*, ed. Clinton Rossiter (New American Library), p. 301.
6. Justice Brandeis dissenting in *Myers* v. *United States*, 272 U.S. 52 (1926).
7. James L. Sundquist, "Needed: A Political Theory for the New Era of Coalition Government in the United States," *Political Science Quarterly* 103 (1988), pp. 613–635; Robert A. Godwin and Art Kaufman, eds., *Separation of Powers: Does It Still Work?* (AEI Press, 1986).
8. Charles O. Jones, "The Separate Presidency," in Anthony King, ed., *The New American Political System*, 2d ed. (AEI Press, 1990), p. 3.
9. Morris P. Fiorina, "An Era of Divided Government," *Political Science Quarterly* 107 (1992), p. 407.
10. David R. Mayhew, *Divided We Govern: Party Control, Lawmaking, and Investigations, 1946–1990* (Yale University Press, 1991), p. 4. See also James A. Thurber, ed., *Divided Democracy: Presidents and Congress in Cooperation and Conflict* (CQ Press, 1991).
11. Charles O. Jones, *Separate but Equal Branches: Congress and the Presidency* (Chatham House, 1995).
12. Judith A. Best, *The Choice of the People? Debating the Electoral College* (Rowman & Littlefield, 1996).
13. See Alec Stone Sweet, Wayne Sandholtz, and Neil Fligstein, *The Institutionalization of Europe* (Oxford University Press, 2001); Alec Stone Sweet, *Governing with Judges: Constitutional Politics in Europe* (Oxford University Press, 2000); and Anne-Marie Slaughter, Alec Stone Sweet, and J. H. H. Weiler, *The European Court and National Courts—Doctrine, Jurisprudence: Legal Change in Its Social Context* (Hart, 1998).
14. *Marbury* v. *Madison*, 1 Cranch 137 (1803).
15. Dumas Malone, *Jefferson the President: First Term, 1801–1805* (Little, Brown, 1970), p. 145.
16. J. W. Peltason, *Federal Courts in the Political Process* (Random House, 1955).
17. See Eleanore Bushnell, *Crimes, Follies, and Misfortunes: The Federal Impeachment Trials* (University of Illinois Press, 1992), and Michael J. Gerhardt, *The Federal Impeachment Process: A Constitutional and Historical Analysis* (Princeton University Press, 1996).
18. Richard E. Neustadt, *Presidential Power* (Free Press, 1990), pp. 180–181.
19. Ronald L. Goldfarb, "The 11,000th Amendment: There's a Rush to Amend the Constitution, and It Shows No Signs of Letting Up," *Washington Post National Weekly Edition*, November 25, 1996, p. 22.
20. See Committee on the Constitutional System, *A Bicentennial Analysis of the American Political Structure: Report and Recommendations of the Committee on the Constitutional System* (1987), for recommendations of a committee cochaired by Nancy L. Kassebaum, C. Douglas Dillon, and Lloyd Cutler. For critical comments, see Mark P. Petracca, "To Right What the Constitution Has Wrought or to Wrong What Is Right," paper presented at the annual meeting of the American Political Science Association, Washington, D.C., August 1988.

21. Ann Stuart Diamond, "A Convention for Proposing Amendments: The Constitution's Other Method," *Publius* 11 (Summer 1981), pp. 113–146; Wilbur Edel, "Amending the Constitution by Convention: Myths and Realities," *State Government* 55 (1982), pp. 51–56.

22. Russell L. Caplan, *Constitutional Brinksmanship: Amending the Constitution by National Convention* (Oxford University Press, 1988), p. x. See also David E. Kyvig, *Explicit and Authentic Acts: Amending the U.S. Constitution, 1776–1995* (University Press of Kansas, 1996), p. 440.

23. Samuel S. Freedman and Pamela J. Naughton, *ERA: May a State Change Its Vote?* (Wayne State University Press, 1979).

24. Kyvig, *Explicit and Authentic Acts,* p. 286; *Dillon v. Gloss,* 256 U.S. 368 (1921).

25. Gregory A. Caldeira, "Constitutional Change in America: Dynamics of Ratification Under Article V," *Publius* 15 (Fall 1985), p. 29.

26. Mark R. Daniels, Robert Darcy, and Joseph W. Westphal, "The ERA Won—at Least in the Opinion Polls," *P.S.: Political Science and Politics* (Fall 1982), p. 583.

27. Ibid.

28. Janet K. Boles, *The Politics of the Equal Rights Amendment: Conflict and Decision-Making Powers* (Longman, 1979), p. 4.

29. Gilbert Y. Steiner, *Constitutional Inequality: The Political Fortunes of the Equal Rights Amendment* (Brookings Institution, 1985), p. 64. See also Mary Frances Berry, *Why the ERA Failed: Politics, Women's Rights, and the Amending Process of the Constitution* (Indiana University Press, 1986).

Chapter 3

1. For background, see Samuel H. Beer, *To Make a Nation: The Rediscovery of American Federalism* (Harvard University Press, 1993).

2. The term "devolution revolution" was coined by Richard P. Nathan in testimony before the Senate Finance Committee; quoted in Daniel Patrick Moynihan, "The Devolution Revolution," *New York Times,* August 6, 1995, p. B15.

3. See Michael Burgess, *Federalism and the European Union: The Building of Europe, 1950–2000* (Routledge, 2000), and Kalypso Nicolaidis and Robert Howse, eds., *The Federal Vision: Legitimacy and Levels of Governance in the United States and the European Union* (Oxford University Press, 2001).

4. *United States v. Lopez,* 514 U.S. 549 (1995).

5. *Alden v. Maine,* 527 U.S. 706 (1999); *Kimel v. Florida Board of Regents,* 528 U.S. 62 (2000); *Vermont Agency of Natural Resources v. United States ex rel. Stevens,* 529 U.S. 765 (2000).

6. *Saenz v. Roe,* 526 U.S. 489 (1999). See also Roderick M. Hills Jr., "Poverty, Residency, and Federalism: States' Duty of Impartiality Toward Newcomers," in Dennis J. Hutchinson, David A. Strauss, and Geoffrey R. Stone, eds., *The Supreme Court Review, 1999* (University of Chicago Press, 2000), pp. 277–336.

7. *Reno v. Condon,* 528 U.S. 141 (2000).

8. Martha Derthick, "American Federalism: Half-Full or Half-Empty?" *Brookings Review* (Winter 2000), pp. 24–27.

9. William H. Stewart, *Concepts of Federalism* (Center for the Study of Federalism/University Press of America, 1984). See also Preston King, *Federalism and Federation,* 2d ed. (Cass, 2001).

10. Morton Grodzins, "The Federal System," in *Goals for Americans: The Report of the President's Commission on National Goals* (Columbia University Press, 1960).

11. Thomas R. Dye, *American Federalism: Competition Among Governments* (Lexington Books, 1990), pp. 13–17.

12. Michael D. Reagan and John G. Sanzone, *The New Federalism* (Oxford University Press, 1981), p. 175.

13. Gregory S. Mahler, *Comparative Politics: An Institutional and Cross-National Approach* (Prentice Hall, 2000), p. 31.

14. Frederick K. Lister, *The European Union, the United Nations, and the Revival of Confederal Governance* (Greenwood Press, 1996); Daniel J. Elazar, "The United States and the European Union: Models for their Epochs," in Nicolaidis and Howse, *The Federal Vision,* pp. 31–52.

15. William H. Riker, *The Development of American Federalism* (Academic, 1987), pp. 14–15. Riker contends not only that federalism does not guarantee freedom but also that the framers of our federal system, as well as those of other nations, were animated not by considerations of safeguarding freedom but by practical considerations of preserving unity.

16. The Court, however, ruled in several recent cases that Congress exceeded its power to regulate interstate commerce. See *Printz v. United States,* 521 U.S. 898 (1997); *United States v. Lopez,* 514 U.S. 549 (1995); *New York v. United States,* 505 U.S. 144 (1992); and *United States v. Morrison,* 529 U.S. 598 (2000).

17. *Gibbons v. Ogden,* 9 Wheaton (22 U.S.) 1 (1824).

18. *Champion v. Ames,* 188 U.S. 321 (1907).

19. *Caminetti v. United States,* 242 U.S. 470 (1917).

20. *Federal Radio Commission v. Nelson Brothers,* 289 U.S. 266 (1933).

21. *Heart of Atlanta Motel v. United States,* 379 U.S. 241 (1964).

22. See *United States v. Morrison,* 529 U.S. 598 (2000), striking down the Violence Against Women Act, discussed later in this chapter.

23. See *New York v. United States,* 505 U.S. 144 (1992), and *Printz v. United States,* 521 U.S. 898 (1997).

24. Ibid.

25. *Seminole Tribe of Florida v. Florida,* 517 U.S. 44 (1996); *Alden v. Maine,* 527 U.S. 706 (1999); *Kimel v. Florida Board of Regents,* 528 U.S. 62 (2000).

26. *California v. Superior Courts of California,* 482 U.S. 400 (1987).

27. David C. Nice, "State Participation in Interstate Compacts," *Publius* 17 (Spring 1987), p. 70. See also Council of State Governments, *Interstate Compacts and Agencies* (1995), for a list of compacts by subject and by state with brief descriptions.

28. *McCulloch v. Maryland,* 4 Wheaton 316 (1819).

29. Joseph F. Zimmerman, "Federal Preemption Under Reagan's New Federalism," *Publius* 21 (Winter 1991), pp. 7–28.

30. Oliver Wendell Holmes Jr., *Collected Legal Papers* (Harcourt, 1920), pp. 295–296.

31. *U.S. Term Limits, Inc. v. Thornton,* 514 U.S. 779 (1995).

32. *Garcia v. San Antonio Metro,* 469 U.S. 528 (1985).

33. See, for example, *United States v. Lopez,* 514 U.S. 549 (1995). Also see Richard A. Brisbin Jr., "The Reconstitution of American Federalism? The Rehnquist Court and Federal-State Relations, 1991–1997," *Publius* 18 (Winter 1998), pp. 189–217.

34. *U.S. Term Limits, Inc. v. Thornton,* 514 U.S. 779 (1995).

35. *Seminole Tribe of Florida v. Florida,* 517 U.S. 44 (1996).

36. *Alden v. Maine,* 527 U.S. 706 (1999); *Kimel v. Florida Board of Regents,* 528 U.S. 62 (2000); *Vermont Agency of Natural Resources v. United States ex rel. Stevens,* 529 U.S. 765 (2000).

37. George Will, "A Revival of Federalism?" *Newsweek,* May 29, 2000, p. 78.

38. See *Jones v. United States,* 530 U.S. 1222 (2000).

39. *United States v. Morrison,* 529 U.S. 598 (2000).

40. John E. Chubb, "The Political Economy of Federalism," *American Political Science Review* 79 (December 1985), p. 1005.

41. Paul E. Peterson, *The Price of Federalism* (Brookings Institution, 1995), p. 127.

42. Donald F. Kettl, *The Regulation of American Federalism* (Johns Hopkins University Press, 1987), pp. 154–155.

43. See Paul J. Posner, *The Politics of Unfunded Mandates: Whither Federalism?* (Georgetown University Press, 1998).

44. Advisory Commission on Intergovernmental Relations, *Restoring Confidence and Competence* (Advisory Commission on Intergovernmental Relations, 1981), p. 30.

45. Cynthia Cates Colella, "The Creation, Care and Feeding of the Leviathan: Who and What Makes Government Grow," *Intergovernmental Perspective* (Fall 1979), p. 9.

46. Aaron Wildavsky, "Bare Bones: Putting Flesh on the Skeleton of American Federalism," in *The Future of Federalism in the 1980s* (Advisory Commission on Intergovernmental Relations, 1981), p. 79.

47. Peterson, *Price of Federalism,* p. 182.

48. John Kincaid, "Devolution in the United States: Rhetoric and Reality," in Nicolaidis and Howse, *The Federal Vision,* p. 144.

49. Eliza Newlin Carney, "Power Grab," *National Journal,* April 11, 1998, p. 798.

50. Luther Gulick, "Reorganization of the States," *Civil Engineering* (August 1933), pp. 420–421.

51. David E. Osborne, *Laboratories of Democracy* (Harvard Business School Press, 1988), p. 363.

52. Dye, *American Federalism,* p. 199.

53. Edward Felsenthal, "Firms Ask Congress to Pass Uniform Rules," *Wall Street Journal,* May 10, 1993, p. B4.

54. John J. DiIulio Jr. and Donald F. Kettl, *Fine Print: The Contract with America, Devolution, and the Administrative Realities of American Federalism* (Brookings Institution, 1995), p. 60.

55. Kincaid, "Devolution in the United States," p. 148.

Chapter 4

1. Robert D. Putnam, "Bowling Alone: America's Declining Social Capital," *Journal of Democracy* 6 (January 1995), pp. 65–78. See also Robert D. Putnam, *Bowling Alone: The Collapse and Revival of American Community* (Simon & Schuster, 2000), and Robert D. Putnam, "Bowling Together," *American Prospect* 13 (February 11, 2002), pp. 20–22.
2. See Pippa Norris, "Does Television Erode Social Capital? A Reply to Putnam," *P.S.: Political Science and Politics* 29 (September 1996), pp. 474–479. See also Everett Carl Ladd, *The Ladd Report* (Free Press, 1999), and Michael Schudson, *The Good Citizen: A History of American Civic Life* (Harvard University Press, 1998).
3. Putnam, "Bowling Together."
4. Clinton Rossiter, *Conservatism in America* (Vintage, 1962), p. 72.
5. Bernard Bailyn, *The Ideological Origins of the American Revolution* (Belknap Press, 1967); Gordon S. Wood, *The Creation of the American Republic, 1776–1787* (University of North Carolina Press, 1969).
6. See Ronald Dworkin, *Taking Rights Seriously* (Harvard University Press, 1977).
7. *Marbury* v. *Madison,* 1 Cranch 137 (1803).
8. "A Nation Challenged: Excerpts from President's Speech: 'We Will Prevail' in War on Terrorism," *New York Times,* November 9, 2001, p. B1.
9. www.commoncause.org/laundromat/stat/top50.htm.
10. Floyd Norris and Joseph Kahn, "Enron's Many Strands: The Overview; Rule Makers Take On Loopholes That Enron Used in Hiding Debt," *New York Times,* February 14, 2002, p. A1.
11. See Michael B. Katz, *The "Underclass" Debate* (Princeton University Press, 1993); Theodore Dalrymple, *Life at the Bottom: The Worldview That Makes The Underclass* (Dee, 2001); and Charles A. Murray, *The Underclass Revisited* (AEI Press, 1999).
12. When adjusted using the consumer price index (CPI), the percentage of households earning over $75,000 a year has risen from 10.1 percent in 1970 to 22.6 percent in 1999. U.S. Bureau of the Census, *Statistical Abstracts of the United States, 2001* (Government Printing Office, 2001), tab. 661.
13. Bailyn, *Ideological Origins.*
14. Robert A. Dahl, "Liberal Democracy in the United States," in William Livingston, ed., *A Prospect of Liberal Democracy* (University of Texas Press, 1979), p. 64.
15. Ibid., pp. 59–60.
16. Franklin D. Roosevelt, State of the Union Address, January 11, 1944, in *The Public Papers of the President of the United States, 1944* (Government Printing Office, 1962), pp. 371–394.
17. Harry S Truman, State of the Union Address, 1949, in *The Public Papers of the President of the United States, 1949* (Government Printing Office, 1964), pp. 1–7.
18. E. J. Dionne Jr., *They Only Look Dead: Why Progressives Will Dominate the Next Political Era* (Simon & Schuster, 1996), p. 13.
19. William Safire, "'To Fight Freedom's Fight,'" *New York Times,* January 31, 2002, p. A25.
20. Quoted in David Brooks, "Need a Map? The Right," *Washington Post,* October 31, 1999, p. B1.
21. David B. Magleby, *The Outside Campaign* (Rowman & Littlefield, 2001).
22. Warren B. Rudman, *Combat: Twelve Years in the U.S. Senate* (Random House, 1996), p. 270.
23. David B. Magleby, "Issue Advocacy in the 2000 Presidential Primaries," in David B. Magleby, ed., *Getting Inside the Outside Campaign* (Center for the Study of Elections and Democracy, Brigham Young University, 2000), p. 13. Also at www.byu.edu/outsidemoney.
24. Kathleen Day, *S&L Hell: The People and the Politics Behind the $1 Trillion Savings and Loan Scandal* (Norton, 1993).
25. Sylvia Nasar, "Even Among the Well-Off, the Rich Get Richer," *New York Times,* March 5, 1992, p. A1.
26. Irving Howe, *Socialism and America* (Harcourt, 1985); Michael Harrington, *Socialism: Past and Future* (Arcade, 1989).
27. Daniel Yergin and Joseph Stainslaw, *The Commanding Heights: The Battle Between Government and the Marketplace That Is Remaking the Modern World* (Simon & Schuster, 1998).
28. www.gp.org/fullplatform.htm.
29. Brian Faler, "A Polling Sight: Record Turnout," *The Washington Post,* November 5, 2004, p. A7.
30. Center for Political Studies, University of Michigan, *American National Election Study, 1990: Post-Election Survey,* April 1991.
31. Michael Kranish, "Discord Replaced by Desire to Win," *Boston Globe,* July 31, 2000, p. A10.
32. Earl Black and Merle Black, *The Rise of Southern Republicans* (Belknap Press, 2002).
33. Herbert McClosky and Alida Brill, *Dimensions of Tolerance: What Americans Believe About Civil Liberties* (Russel Sage Foundation, 1983).
34. Nat Hentoff, "Liberal Trimmers of the First Amendment," *Washington Post,* January 17, 1998, p. A25.
35. Dinesh D'Sousa, *Illiberal Education: The Politics of Race and Sex on Campus* (Free Press, 1991), p. 313.

Chapter 5

1. Franklin Delano Roosevelt, quoted in William Safire, *Lend Me Your Ears: Great Speeches in History* (Norton, 1997), p. 646.
2. Martin Gross, "Homeland Security—Flying High," *Washington Times,* February 1, 2002, p. A18.
3. "Islam Is Peace, Says President," press release, September 17, 2001, at www.whitehouse.gov/news/releases/2001/09/print/20010917-11.html.
4. Albert Einstein, quoted in Laurence J. Peter, *Peter's Quotations* (Morrow, 1977), p. 358.
5. Alexis de Tocqueville, *Democracy in America,* ed. J. P. Mayer, trans. George Lawrence (Doubleday, 1969), p. 278. Originally published 1835 (*Volume 1*) and 1840 (*Volume 2*).
6. Central Intelligence Agency, Directorate of Intelligence, *Handbook of International Statistics* (Government Printing Office 1999), tab. 41, pp. 52–53.
7. de Tocqueville, *Democracy in America,* trans. Henry Reeve, eBook at www.netlibrary.com.
8. U.S. Bureau of the Census, *Statistical Abstract of the United States, 1999* (Government Printing Office, 1999), p. 300.
9. V. O. Key Jr., *Politics, Parties, and Pressure Groups,* 5th ed. (Crowell, 1964), p. 232.
10. Earl Black and Merle Black, *The Vital South: How Presidents Are Elected* (Harvard University Press, 1992), p. 4.
11. Joseph A. Pika and Richard A. Watson, *The Presidential Contest,* 5th ed. (CQ Press, 1996), pp. 80–81.
12. U.S. Bureau of the Census, at www.census.gov/population/cen2000/tab01.pdf.
13. Robert S. Erikson, Gerald C. Wright, and John P. McIver, *Statehouse Democracy: Public Opinion and Policy in the American States* (Cambridge University Press, 1993).
14. U.S. Bureau of the Census, *Statistical Abstract of the United States, 2001* (Government Printing Office, 2001), p. 21.
15. Holly Idelson, "Count Adds Seats in Eight States," *Congressional Quarterly Weekly Report* 48 (December 29, 1999), p. 4240.
16. *Statistical Abstract, 2001,* p. 30.
17. Ibid., p. 46.
18. U.S. Bureau of the Census, at www.census.gov/population/socdemo/race/black/tabs99/tab16.txt.
19. Kevin M. Pollard, "America's Racial and Ethnic Minorities," *Population Bulletin,* September 1999. See also ibid.
20. *Statistical Abstract, 2001,* pp. 38–39.
21. U.S. Bureau of the Census, *The American Indian and Alaska Native Population, 2000* (Government Printing Office, 2002) p. 1.
22. Ibid., p. 13.
23. Ibid.
24. Robert D. Ballard, "Introduction: Lure of the New South," in *In Search of the New South: The Black Urban Experience in the 1970s and 1980s,* ed. Robert D. Ballard (University of Alabama Press, 1989), p. 5; *Statistical Abstract, 2001,* p. 24.
25. *Statistical Abstract, 2001,* p. 437.
26. Ibid., p. 442.

27. U.S. Bureau of the Census, *Poverty in the United States, 2000* (Government Printing Office, 2001); also at www.census.gov/hhes/www/poverty00.html.

28. *Statistical Abstract, 2001,* p. 433.

29. U.S. Bureau of the Census, at www.census.gov/hhes/www/wealth.

30. U.S. Bureau of the Census, *Household Wealth and Asset Ownership, 1991* (Government Printing Office, 1991), tab. H. See also ibid.

31. U.S. Bureau of the Census at www.bls.census.gov/cps/pub/hsgec_1095.htm.

32. *Statistical Abstract, 2001,* pp. 164, 169.

33. U.S. Bureau of the Census, 2000 summary file no. 1, at www.census.gov.

34. Mark R. Levy and Michael S. Kramer, *The Ethnic Factor: How America's Minorities Decide Elections* (Simon & Schuster, 1973). See also Mark Stern, "Democratic Presidency and Voting Rights," in *Blacks in Southern Politics,* ed. Lawrence W. Mooreland, Robert P. Steed, and Todd A. Baker (Praeger, 1987), pp. 50–51.

35. Harold W. Stanley and Richard G. Niemi, *Vital Statistics on American Politics, 2000–2001* (CQ Press, 2001), p. 122.

36. *Statistical Abstract, 2001,* p. 27.

37. See Frank R. Parker, *Black Votes Count: Political Empowerment in Mississippi After 1965* (University of North Carolina Press, 1990).

38. "Number of Black Elected Officials in the United States, by State and Office, January 1999," Joint Center for Political and Economic Studies, at www.jointcenter.org/databank/graphs/beo_99.pdf.

39. Ibid.

40. Rodolfo O. de la Garza, Louis De Sipio, F. Chris Garcia, John Garcia, and Angelo Falcon, *Latino Voices: Mexican, Puerto Rican, and Cuban Perspectives on American Politics* (Westview Press, 1992), p. 14. See also, Richard E. Cohen, "Hispanic Hopes Fade," *National Journal,* February 2, 2002.

41. Todd S. Purdum, "Shift in the Mix Alters the Face of California," *New York Times,* July 4, 2000, p. A1.

42. *Statistical Abstract, 2001,* p. 43.

43. Rodney Hero, F. Chris Garcia, John Garcia, and Harry Pachon, "Latino Participation, Partisanship, and Office Holding," *P.S.: Political Science and Politics* 33 (September 2000), p. 529. See also de la Garza et al., *Latino Voices,* p. 14.

44. *Statistical Abstract, 2001,* pp. 17, 27.

45. U.S. Bureau of the Census, *Profile of the Foreign-Born Population in the United States, 2000* (Government Printing Office, 2001), at www.census.gov/prod/2002pubs/p23-206.pdf.

46. *Statistical Abstract, 2001,* p. 139.

47. Ibid., p. 10.

48. U.S. Bureau of the Census, *Profile of the Foreign-Born Population.*

49. James West Davidson, William E. Gienapp, Christine Leigh Heyrman, Mark H. Lytle, and Michael B. Stoff, *Nation of Nations* (McGraw-Hill, 1990), pp. 833–834.

50. G. Thomas Edwards, *Sowing Good Seeds: The Northwest Suffrage Campaigns of Susan B. Anthony* (Oregon Historical Society Press, 1990), p. 136.

51. Paul Kleppner, *Continuity and Change in Electoral Politics, 1893–1928* (Greenwood Press, 1987), p. 172.

52. Margaret C. Trevor, "Political Socialization, Party Identification, and the Gender Gap," *Public Opinion Quarterly* 63 (Spring 1999), p. 62.

53. *Statistical Abstract, 2001,* p. 251; Sue Tolleson-Rinehard and Jyl J. Josephson, eds., *Gender and American Politics* (Sharpe, 2000), pp. 77–78.

54. U.S. Bureau of the Census, "Voting and Registration in the Election of November 2000," at www.census.gov/prod/2002pubs/p20-542.pdf.

55. Tolleson-Rinehard and Josephson, *Gender and American Politics,* pp. 232–233.

56. Diane L. Fowlkes, "Feminist Theory: Reconstructing Research and Teaching About American Politics and Government," *News for Teachers of Political Science* (Winter 1987), pp. 6–9. See also Sally Helgesen, *Everyday Revolutionaries: Working Women and the Transformation of American Life* (Doubleday, 1998); Karen Lehrman, *The Lipstick Proviso: Women, Sex, and Power in the Real World* (Anchor/Doubleday, 1997); Tanya Melich, *The Republican War Against Women: An Insider's Report from Behind the Lines* (Bantam Books, 1998); and Virginia Valian, *Why So Slow? The Advancement of Women* (MIT Press, 1998).

57. Barbara C. Burrell, *A Woman's Place Is in the House: Campaigning for Congress in the Feminist Era* (University of Michigan Press, 1994).

58. CNN, at www.cnn.com/ELECTION/2004/results/index.html.

59. Arlie Russell Hochschild, "There's No Place like Work," *New York Times,* April 20, 1997, p. 51.

60. Alexis Simendinger, "Why Issues Matter," *National Journal,* April 1, 2000, based on data from a Pew Center Poll conducted March 15–19, 2000.

61. *Statistical Abstract, 2001,* p. 440.

62. U.S. Senate Committee on Health, Education, Labor, and Pensions. *The Study of Government on Gender Wage Descrimination: Hearing Before the Committee on Health, Education, Labor, and Pensions.* 106th Cong., 2d sess., June 8, 2000.

63. Anna Quindlen, "Some Struggles Never Seem to End," *New York Times,* November 14, 2001, p. H24.

64. Elsa Brenner, "The Invisible Population," *New York Times,* November 14, 1999. See also www.census.gov/population/www/documentation/twps0034.html.

65. Robert T. Michael et al., *Sex in America: A Definitive Survey* (Little, Brown, 1994).

66. "A half-dozen Republicans ousted Democrats from their state Senate seats in November, due almost entirely to outrage over the passage of legislation legalizing civil unions for gay and lesbian couples." Elizabeth Mehren, "The Little State That Could, and Has," *Los Angeles Times,* May 24, 2002, p. A21.

67. Adam Clymer, "Senate Expands Hate Crimes Law to Include Gays," *New York Times,* June 21, 2000, p. A1.

68. *Boy Scouts of America v. Dale,* 120 S. Ct. 2446 (2000).

69. *Statistical Abstract, 1999,* p. 111.

70. *Statistical Abstract, 2001,* p. 59.

71. Ibid., p. 62.

72. *General Social Survey (GSS) 1972–2000 Cumulative Codebook,* at www.icpsr.umich.edu/GSS/index.html.

73. See Leni Yahil, *The Holocaust: The Fate of European Jewry* (Oxford University Press, 1990).

74. Stephen C. LeSuer, *The 1838 Mormon War in Missouri* (University of Missouri Press, 1987), pp. 151–153.

75. John Conway, "An Adapted Organic Tradition," *Daedalus* 117 (Fall 1988), p. 382. For an extended comparison of the impact of religion on politics in the United States and Canada, see Seymour Martin Lipset, *Continental Divide: The Values and Institutions of the United States and Canada* (Routledge, 1990), pp. 74–89.

76. www.september11news.com/PresidentBushSpeech.htm.

77. Robert N. Bellah, *Beyond Belief: Essays on Religion in a Post-Traditional World* (University of California Press, 1991).

78. Roper Center for Public Opinion Research, March 3, 2002, at roperweb.ropercenter.uconn.edu/cgibin/hsrun.exe/roperweb.

79. William H. Flanigan and Nancy H. Zingale, *Political Behavior of the American Electorate,* 10th ed. (CQ Press, 2000), p. 131.

80. *Statistical Abstract, 2001,* p. 55.

81. CNN, at www.cnn.com/ELECTION/2000/results.

82. *2000 American National Election Study* (Center for Political Studies, 2000).

83. Ibid.

84. Lyman A. Kellstedt and John C. Green, "Is There a Culture War? Religion and the 1996 Election," paper presented at the annual meeting of the American Political Science Association, Washington, D.C., 1997, at www.wheaton.edu/polsci\kellstedt.

85. CNN, at www.cnn.com/ELECTION/2000/results.

86. Organization for Economic Cooperation and Development (OECD), *National Accounts,* vol. 1, *Main Aggregates, 1960–89* (OECD, 1991), p. 145.

87. Raymond E. Wolfinger, Fred I. Greenstein, and Martin Shapiro, *Dynamics of American Politics,* 2d ed. (Prentice Hall, 1980), p. 19.

88. Thomas Jefferson, "Autobiography," in *The Life and Selected Writings of Thomas Jefferson,* ed. Adrienne Koch and William Peden (Modern Library, 1944), p. 38.

89. U.S. Department of Education, *Digest of Education Statistics, 2001* (Government Printing Office, 2001), p. 357.

90. Harold W. Stanley and Richard G. Niemi, *Vital Statistics on American Politics, 1999–2000* (CQ Press, 2000), p. 115.

91. Stanley Fischer, "Symposium on the Slowdown in Productivity Growth," *Journal of Economic Perspectives* 2 (Fall 1988), pp. 3–7.

92. www.kc.frb.org/PUBLICAT/SYMPOS/1998/S98katz.pdf.

93. U.S. Bureau of the Census, at www.census.gov/hhes/poverty/threshld/thresh01.html.

94. U.S. Bureau of the Census, at www.census.gov/hhes/poverty/poverty00/table5.html.

95. *Statistical Abstract, 2001,* pp. 442–443.

96. Ibid., p. 442.

97. W. Michael Cox and Richard Alm, "Why Decry the Wealth Gap?" *New York Times,* January 24, 2000, p. A24.

98. Mark Hertsgaard, "Unequal Parts," *New York Times,* January 7, 2002, p. C4.

99. *Statistical Abstract, 2001,* p. 417. "Real" means that inflation has already been taken into account.

100. Daniel Bell, *The Coming of Post-Industrial Society: A Venture in Social Forecasting* (Basic Books, 1973), p. xviii.
101. *Statistical Abstract, 2001,* p. 384
102. Ibid., p. 417.
103. Ibid., p. 384.
104. Mattei Dogan and Dominique Pelassy, *How to Compare Nations: Strategies in Comparative Politics,* 2d ed. (Chatham House, 1990), p. 47.
105. *Index to International Public Opinion, 1991–92* (Greenwood Press, 1992), p. 462.
106. Seymour Martin Lipset, *Continental Divide: The Values and Institutions of the United States and Canada* (Routledge, 1990), p. 170.
107. U.S. Bureau of Labor Statistics, at www.bls.gov/csx/1999/Aggregate/age.pdf.
108. *Statistical Abstract, 2001,* p. 443.
109. Ibid., p. 251.

110. CNN, at www.cnn.com/election/2000/results/index.epolls.html.
111. Seymour Martin Lipset, *Political Man* (Doubleday, 1963), pp. 283–286.
112. Thomas Jefferson to P. S. du Pont de Nemours, April 24, 1816, in *The Writings of Thomas Jefferson,* ed. Paul L. Ford (Putnam, 1899), vol. 10, p. 25.
113. *Statistical Abstract, 2001,* p. 137.
114. Ibid., p. 141.
115. Ibid., p. 169.
116. Herbert McClosky and John Zaller, *The American Ethos: Public Attitudes Toward Capitalism and Democracy* (Harvard University Press, 1984), p. 261.
117. John Gunther, *Inside U.S.A.* (Harper, 1947), p. 911.
118. Carl N. Degler, *Out of Our Past: The Forces That Shaped Modern America,* 3d ed. (Harper & Row, 1984), p. 322.

Chapter 6

1. Mike Lux, personal communication, December 14, 2000.
2. Ibid.
3. See David B. Magleby, ed., *The Other Campaign: Soft Money and Issue Advocacy in the 2000 Congressional Elections* (Rowman & Littlefield, 2003). See also David B. Magleby, ed., *Outside Money: Soft Money and Issue Advocacy in the 1998 Congressional Elections* (Rowman & Littlefield, 2000).
4. U.S. Bureau of Labor Statistics, at www.bls.gov/cps/cpsaat40.pdf.
5. Michael Podhorzer, Department of Political Research, AFL-CIO, personal communication, June 14, 2002.
6. Herbert B. Asher et al., *American Labor Unions in the Electoral Arena* (Rowman & Littlefield, 2001).
7. James MacGregor Burns and Stewart Burns, *A People's Charter: The Pursuit of Rights in America* (Knopf, 1991).
8. William R. Donohue, *The Politics of the American Civil Liberties Union* (Transaction Books, 1985).
9. David B. Magleby, ed., *The Other Campaign: Soft Money and Issue Advocacy in the 2000 Congressional Elections* (Rowman & Littlefield, 2002). See also David B. Magleby, ed., *Outside Money: Soft Money and Issue Advocacy in 1998 Congressional Elections* (Rowman & Littlefield, 2000), and Clyde Wilcox, *Onward Christian Soldiers: The Religious Right in American Politics* (Westview Press, 2000).
10. National Education Association, at www.nea.org/aboutnea.
11. Robert Salisbury, "Interest Representation: The Dominance of Institutions," *American Political Science Review* 78 (March 1984), p. 66.
12. V. O. Key Jr., *Public Opinion and American Democracy* (Knopf, 1961), pp. 504–507.
13. R. Kenneth Godwin, *One Billion Dollars of Influence: The Direct Marketing of Politics* (Chatham House, 1988).
14. Lucius J. Barker, "Third Parties in Litigation: A Systemic View of the Judicial Function," *Journal of Politics* 29 (February 1967), pp. 41–69; Jethro K. Lieberman, *Litigious Society,* rev. ed. (Basic Books, 1983).
15. Gregory A. Calderia and John R. Wright, "Organized Interests and Agenda Setting in the U.S. Supreme Court," *American Political Science Review* 82 (December 1988), pp. 1109–1127. See also Gregory A. Calderia and John R. Wright, "*Amici Curiae* Before the Supreme Court: Who Participates, When, and How Much?" *Journal of Politics* 52 (August 1990), pp. 782–806.
16. Karen O'Connor, *Women's Organizations' Use of the Courts* (Lexington Books, 1980).
17. Steven P. Brown, *Trumping Religion: The New Christian Right, Religious Liberty, and the Courts* (University of Alabama Press, October 2002), Ph. D. diss.
18. Lee Epstein and C. K. Rowland, "Debunking the Myth of Interest Group Invincibility in the Courts," *American Political Science Review* 85 (March 1991), pp. 205–217.
19. Kelly D. Patterson, "Campaign Consultants and Direct Democracy: Politics of Citizen Control," in *Campaign Warriors: The Role of Political Consultants in Elections,* eds. James E. Thurber and Candice J. Nelson (Brookings Institution, 2000).
20. For a discussion of the 1998 New Mexico race, see Lonna Rae Atkeson and Anthony C. Coveny, "The 1998 New Mexico Third Congressional District Race," in Magleby, *Outside Money,* pp. 135–152.
21. Ethan Bronner, *Battle for Justice: How the Bork Nomination Shook America* (Norton, 1989), pp. 50–55.

22. Hugh Heclo, "Issue Networks and the Executive Establishment," in *The New American Political System,* ed. Anthony King (American Enterprise Institute, 1978).
23. David Mayhew, *Congress: The Electoral Connection* (Yale University Press, 1974), p. 45.
24. John R. Wright, "Contributions, Lobbying, and Committee Voting in the U.S. House of Representatives," *American Political Science Review* 84 (June 1990), pp. 417–438.
25. For evidence of the impact of PAC expenditures on legislative committee behavior and legislative involvement generally, see Richard L. Hall and Frank W. Wayman, "Buying Time: Moneyed Interests and the Mobilization of Bias in Congressional Committees," *American Political Science Review* 84 (September 1990), pp. 797–820.
26. Edwin M. Epstein, "Business and Labor Under the Federal Election Campaign Act of 1971," in *Parties, Interest Groups, and Campaign Finance Laws,* ed. Michael J. Malbin (American Enterprise Institute for Public Policy Research, 1980), p. 112. See also Gary Jacobson, *Money in Congressional Elections* (Yale University Press, 1980).
27. Open Secrets, at www.opensecrets.org/pacs/index.asp.
28. Kelly Huff, Ron Harris, and Ian Stirton, "FEC Issues Semi-Annual PAC Count," at www.fec.gov/press/20020124pacno.html and www.fec.gov/press/paccnt_grph.html.
29. Federal Election Commission, at www.fec.gov/press/082101pac.html.
30. Federal Election Commission, at www.fec.gov/press/051501congfinact/051501congfinact.html.
31. Brody Mullins and Charlie Mitchell, "Soft Money Unleashed," *National Journal,* February 7, 2001, pp. 500–501.
32. Amy Dockster, "Nice PAC You've Got Here—A Pity If Anything Should Happen to It: How Politicians Shake Down the Special Interests," *Washington Monthly,* January 27, 1987, p. 24.
33. Hall and Wayman, "Buying Time," pp. 797–820. A different study of the House Ways and Means Committee found campaign contributions to be part of the representatives' policy decisions, but even more important was the number of lobbying contacts; see Wright, "Contributions, Lobbying, and Committee Voting."
34. Ronald Reagan, "Remarks to Administration Officials on Domestic Policy," December 13, 1988, *Weekly Compilation of Presidential Documents,* vol. 24 (December 1988), pp. 1615–1620.
35. Sylvia Tesh, "In Support of Single-Interest Politics," *Political Science Quarterly* 99 (Spring 1984), pp. 27–44.
36. California Commission on Campaign Financing, *The New Gold Rush: Financing California's Legislative Campaigns* (Center for Responsive Government, 1985), pp. 177–197. For a study of state lobby regulation, see Cynthia Opheim, "Explaining the Differences in State Lobby Regulation," *Western Political Quarterly* 44 (June 1991), pp. 405–421.
37. Adam Clymer, "Congress Sends Lobbying Overhaul to Clinton," *New York Times,* December 16, 1995, p. 36.
38. Legislative Resource Center's Lobbying Section, telephone interview, August 16, 2002.
39. U.S. Senate, at www.senate.gov/legislative/vote1042/vote_00168.html.
40. Common Cause, at www.commoncause.org/publications/jan02/img/appendix1_sec_study.pdf and www.commoncause.org/shaysmeehan/ney_enron_facts.pdf.

41. *Buckley* v. *Valeo*, 424 U.S. 1 (1976).

42. David B. Magleby and Eric A. Smith, "Party Soft Money in the 2000 Congressional Elections," in Magleby, *The Other Campaign,* p. 39.

43. Lorraine Woellert, "Oh, What a Sweet Soft-Money Scheme," *BusinessWeek,* May 22, 2000, p. 85.

44. Greg Hitt, "Democrats Move Ahead in Soft-Money Race," *Wall Street Journal,* August 17, 2000, p. A24.

45. Open Secrets, at www.opensecrets.org/industries/indus.asp?Ind+H04.

46. Marianne Holt, "Stealth PAC's Revealed: Interest Group Profiles." Press release, Center for Public Integrity, February 5, 2001.

47. David B. Magleby, ed., *Election Advocacy: Soft Money and Issue Advocacy in the 2000 Congressional Elections* (Center for the Study of Elections and Democracy, 2001), at www.byu.edu/outsidemoney.

48. David B. Magleby and Candice J. Nelson, *The Money Chase: Congressional Campaign Finance Reform* (Brookings Institution, 1990), pp. 72–97.

49. Factors that predict the formation of PACs include company size and the degree of regulation for corporations. See Craig Humphries, "Corporations, PACs, and the Strategic Link Between Contributions and Lobbying Activities," *Western Political Quarterly* 44 (June 1991), pp. 353–372.

50. Federal Election Commission, at ftp.fec.gov/fed.

Chapter 7

1. John E. Mueller, "Choosing Among 133 Candidates," *Public Opinion Quarterly* 34 (Fall 1970), pp. 395–402.

2. E. E. Schattschneider, *Party Government* (Holt, Rinehart and Winston, 1942), p. 1.

3. See Scott Mainwaring, "Party Systems in the Third Wave," *Journal of Democracy* (July 1998), pp. 67–81.

4. Joseph A. Schlesinger, *Political Parties and the Winning of Office* (University of Michigan Press, 1994).

5. James A. Thurber and Candice J. Nelson, eds., *Campaign Warriors: The Role of Political Consultants in Elections* (Brookings Institution, 2000).

6. Lizette Alvarez, "Senate to Divide Power and Money Equally in Panels," *New York Times,* January 6, 2001, p. A1.

7. Nick Anderson and Jonathan Peterson, "China Trade Vote: House OK's China Trade Bill," *Los Angeles Times,* May 25, 2000, p. A1.

8. Elizabeth A. Palmer, "Bill to Extend Residency Program Passes House After Six-Month Wait," *Congressional Quarterly,* March 16, 2002, p. 706.

9. See three books edited by David B. Magleby: *Outside Money: Soft Money and Issue Advocacy in the 1998 Congressional Elections* (Rowman & Littlefield, 2000); *The Other Campaign: Soft Money and Issue Advocacy in the 2000 Congressional Elections* (Rowman & Littlefield, 2002); and *Financing the 2000 Election* (Brookings Institution, 2002).

10. David W. Brady and Craig Volden, *Revolving Gridlock: Politics and Policy from Carter to Clinton* (Westview Press, 1998); James A. Thurber, ed., *Divided Democracy: Cooperation and Conflict Between the President and Congress* (CQ Press, 1991); James A. Thurber, ed., *Rivals for Power: Presidential-Congressional Relations* (CQ Press, 1996); Charles O. Jones, *Separate but Equal Branches: Congress and the Presidency* (Chatham House, 1995), chaps. 5 and 6; Jon R. Bond and Richard Fleisher, *The President in the Legislative Arena* (University of Chicago Press, 1990).

11. *California Democratic Party et al.* v. *Jones,* 120 S.Ct. 2402 (2000).

12. Bruce E. Cain and Elisabeth R. Gerber, eds., *Voting at the Political Fault Line: California's Experiment with the Blanket Primary* (University of California Press, 2002), pp. 341–342.

13. Arthur Sanders and David Redlawsk, "Money and the Iowa Caucuses," in *Getting Inside the Outside Campaign,* ed. David Magleby (Center for the Study of Elections and Democracy, 2000), pp. 20–29.

14. *The Book of the States, 2000–2001* (Council of State Governments, 2000), pp. 164–165.

15. CNN, at www.cnn.com/ELECTION/2000/results/, May 17, 2002.

16. William H. Riker, "The Two-Party System and Duverger's Law: An Essay on the History of Political Science," *American Political Science Review* 76 (December 1982), pp. 753–766. For a classic analysis, see Schattschneider, *Party Government.*

17. See Paul S. Herrnson and John C. Green, eds., *Multiparty Politics in America,* 2d ed. (Rowman & Littlefield, 2002), and J. David Gillespie, *Politics at the Periphery: Third Parties in Two-Party America* (University of South Carolina Press, 1993).

18. L. Sandy Maisel and John F. Bibby, *Two Parties—or More? The American Party System* (Westview Press, 1998).

19. Ted G. Jelen, ed., *Ross for Boss* (State University of New York Press, 2001), p. 88.

20. Steven J. Rosenstone, Roy L. Behr, and Edward H. Lazarus, *Third Parties in America: Citizen Response to Major Party Failure,* 2d ed. (Princeton University Press, 1996). See also Xandra Kayden and Eddie Mahe Jr., *The Party Goes On: The Persistence of the Two-Party System in the United States* (Basic Books, 1985), pp. 143–144.

21. On the impact of third parties, see Howard R. Penniman, "Presidential Third Parties and the Modern American Two-Party System," in *The Party Symbol,* ed. William J. Crotty (Freeman, 1980), pp. 101–117. See also Frank Smallwood, *The Other Candidates: Third Parties in Presidential Elections* (University Press of New England, 1983).

22. Barry C. Burden, "Did Ralph Nader Elect George W. Bush? An Analysis of Minor Parties in the 2000 Presidential Election," paper presented at the annual meeting of the American Political Science Association, San Francisco, August 30–September 2, 2001.

23. Benjamin Franklin, George Washington, and Thomas Jefferson, quoted in Richard Hofstadter, *The Idea of a Party System* (University of California Press, 1969), pp. 2, 123.

24. For concise histories of the two parties, see two studies by Robert A. Rutland, *The Democrats: From Jefferson to Clinton* (University of Missouri Press, 1996) and *The Republicans: From Lincoln to Bush* (University of Missouri Press, 1996).

25. See V. O. Key Jr., "A Theory of Critical Elections," *Journal of Politics* 17 (February 1955), pp. 3–18; Walter Dean Burnham, *Critical Elections and the Mainsprings of American Politics* (Norton, 1970), pp. 1–10; and E. E. Schattschneider, *The Semisovereign People: A Realist's View of Democracy in America* (Holt, Rinehart and Winston, 1975), pp. 78–80.

26. William E. Gienapp, *The Origins of the Republican Party, 1852–1856* (Oxford University Press, 1987).

27. David W. Brady, "Elections, Congress, and Public Policy Changes, 1886–1960," in *Realignment in American Politics: Toward a Theory,* eds. Bruce A. Campbell and Richard Trilling (Texas University Press, 1980), p. 188.

28. L. Sandy Maisel, *Parties and Elections in America: The Electoral Process* (Rowman & Littlefield, 2002), pp. 48–49.

29. Gerald Pomper, "Classification of Presidential Elections," *Journal of Politics* 29 (August 1967), p. 538.

30. CNN, at www.cnn.com/ELECTION/2000/results/index.epolls.htm.

31. V. O. Key Jr., *Political Parties and Pressure Groups,* 5th ed. (International Publishing, 1964). See also Paul Allen Beck and Marjorie Randon Hershey, *Party Politics in America,* 9th ed. (Longman, 1998).

32. Federal Election Commission, "Party Fundraising Escalates," November 3, 2000, at fecweb1.fec.gov/press/pty00text.htm.

33. Beck, *Party Politics in America,* 8th ed. (Longman, 1997), chap. 2.

34. Virginia Sapiro, "It's the Context, Situation, and Question, Stupid: The Gender Basis of Public Opinion," in *Understanding Public Opinion,* 2d ed., eds. Barbara Norrander and Clyde Wilcox (CQ Press, 2001), p. 41.

35. Jeff Zeleny, "Bush Picks Onetime Peer to Lead GOP; Racicot's Mandate: Win Votes in '02," *Chicago Tribune,* December 6, 2001, p. N14.

36. See L. Sandy Maisel, *From Obscurity to Oblivion: Running in the Congressional Primary,* rev. ed. (University of Tennessee Press, 1986).

37. The early Republican efforts and advantages over the Democrats are well documented in Thomas B. Edsall, *The New Politics of Inequality* (Norton, 1984), and Gary C. Jacobson, "The Republican Advantage in Campaign Finances," in *New Direction in American Politics,* eds. John E. Chubb and Paul E. Peterson (Brookings Institution, 1985), p. 6.

38. Steven R. Weisman, "Republican Feuds Yield a New Party Dialectic," *New York Times,* November 30, 1998, p. A22.

39. John F. Bibby, *Politics, Parties, and Elections in America,* 4th ed. (Nelson-Hall, 1999). For further data on these roles, see Cornelius P. Cotter, James L. Gibson, John F. Bibby, and Robert J. Huckshorn, *Party Organizations in American Politics* (Praeger, 1984).

40. See James L. Gibson, Cornelius P. Cotter, John F. Bibby, and Robert J. Huckshorn, "Assessing Party Organizational Strength," *American Journal of Political Science* 27 (May 1983), pp. 193–222. See also Cotter et al., *Party Organizations in American Politics.*

41. Paul S. Herrnson, *Party Campaigning in the 1980s: Have the National Parties Made a Comeback as Key Players in Congressional Elections?* (Harvard University Press, 1988), p. 122.

42. Jonathan S. Krasno and Daniel E. Seltz, *Buying Time: Television Advertising in the 1998 Congressional Elections,* report of a grant funded by the Pew Charitable Trusts (1998).

43. On the influence of local parties, see Kayden and Mahe, *Party Goes On.* See also John C. Green and Daniel M. Shea, eds., *The State of the Parties: The Changing Role of Contemporary Parties,* 3d ed. (Rowman & Littlefield, 1999), which presents recent case studies of parties at the local level.

44. Jill Newell, White House staff, personal communication, July 2, 2002. A list of many of these positions appears in *Policy and Supporting Positions* (Government Printing Office, November 9, 1988). For a general discussion of presidential appointments, see G. Calvin Mackenzie, "Partisan Presidential Leadership: The President's Appointees," in Maisel, *Parties Respond,* pp. 316–337.

45. *Marbury* v. *Madison,* 1 Cranch 137 (1803).

46. See Angus Campbell, Philip E. Converse, Warren E. Miller, and Donald E. Stokes, *The American Voter* (Wiley, 1960); Norman A. Nie, Sidney Verba, and John R. Petrocik, *The Changing American Voter,* enlarged ed. (Harvard University Press, 1979); and Warren E. Miller and J. Merrill Shanks, *The New American Voter* (Harvard University Press, 1996).

47. "At the Races: A Weekly Review of Campaign 2000," *National Journal* 39 (September 2000), p. 2991.

48. Campbell et al., *American Voter,* pp. 121–128.

49. Bruce E. Keith et al., *The Myth of the Independent Voter* (University of California Press, 1992).

50. See Byron E. Shafer, *The End of Realignment: Interpreting American Electoral Eras* (University of Wisconsin Press, 1991).

51. Michael F. Meffert, Helmut Norpoth, and Anirudh V. S. Ruhil, "Realignment and Macropartisanship," *American Political Science Review* 95 (December 2001), pp. 953–962.

52. Hedrick Smith, *The Power Game: How Washington Works* (Random House, 1988), p. 671.

53. Nine percent of all voters were Pure Independents in 1956 and 1960; Keith et al., *The Myth of the Independent Voter,* p. 51. In 1992, the figure was also 9 percent; *1992 American National Election Study* (Center for Political Studies, University of Michigan, 1992).

54. Earl Black and Merle Black, *The Rise of Southern Republicans* (Harvard University Press, 2002).

55. Ibid.

56. For the "optimistic view," see Ralph M. Goldman, *Search for Consensus: The Story of the Democratic Party* (Temple University Press, 1979), pp. 366–373; Kayden and Mahe, *Party Goes On*; Larry J. Sabato, *The Party's Just Begun: Shaping Political Parties in America's Future* (Scott, Foresman, 1988); Joseph A. Schlesinger, "The New American Political Party," *American Political Science Review* 79 (December 1985), pp. 1152–1169; and David E. Price, *Bringing Back the Parties* (CQ Press, 1984).

57. "Party Unity Background," *Congressional Quarterly Weekly Report* 60 (January 12, 2002), p. 142.

58. Barbara Sinclair, "Evolution or Revolution?" in Maisel, *Parties Respond,* pp. 263–285.

59. Herrnson, *Party Campaigning in the 1980s,* pp. 80–81.

60. See Magleby, *Outside Money and The Other Campaign.*

61. *Congressional Record,* March 19, 2001, pp. 524–534.

62. Common Cause, at www.commoncause.org/laundromat/stat/topdonors_all.htm.

Chapter 8

1. David B. Magleby, ed., *Election Advocacy: Soft Money and Issue Advocacy in the 2000 Congressional Elections* (Brigham Young University, Center for the Study of Elections and Democracy, 2001), monograph presented at the National Press Club, Washington, D.C., February 5, 2000, available at www.byu.edu/outsidemoney/2000general.

2. Gallup Organization, at www.gallup.com.

3. CNN, at www.cnn.com/ELECTION/2004/results/index.html.

4. Daniel Henninger, "American Opinion Knows the Face of Terror," *Wall Street Journal,* April 26, 2002, p. A10.

5. Robert Coles, *The Moral Life of Children* (Atlantic Monthly Press, 1986); Robert Coles, *The Political Life of Children* (Atlantic Monthly Press, 1986). See also Stephen M. Caliendo, *Teachers Matter: The Trouble with Leaving Political Education to the Coaches* (Greenwood, 2000).

6. Coles, *Political Life of Children,* pp. 59–60.

7. Pamela Johnston Conover, "The Influence of Group Identifications on Political Perception and Evaluation," *Journal of Politics* 46 (August 1984), pp. 760–785; Henry E. Brady and Paul M. Sniderman, "Attitude Attribution: A Group Basis for Political Reasoning," *American Political Science Review* 79 (December 1985), pp. 1061–1078.

8. Shawn W. Rosenberg, "Sociology, Psychology, and the Study of Political Behavior: The Case of the Research on Political Socialization," *Journal of Politics* 47 (May 1985), pp. 715–731.

9. Caliendo, *Teachers Matter,* pp. 16–17.

10. James Garbarino, *Raising Children in a Socially Toxic Environment* (Jossey-Bass, 1995).

11. Russell J. Dalton, "Reassessing Parental Socialization: Indicator Unreliability Versus Generational Transfer," *American Political Science Review* 74 (June 1980), pp. 421–431.

12. Suzanne Koprince Sebert, M. Kent Jennings, and Richard G. Niemi, "The Political Texture of Peer Groups," in *The Political Character of Adolescence,* M. Kent Jennings and Richard G. Niemi (Princeton University Press, 1974), p. 246. See also Richard G. Niemi and M. Kent Jennings, "Issues and Inheritance in the Formation of Party Identification," *American Journal of Political Science* 35 (November 1991), pp. 970–988.

13. National Association of Secretaries of State, *New Millennium Project, Part I: American Youth Attitudes on Policies, Citizenship, Government and Voting* (Washington, D.C.: National Association of Secretaries of State, 1999).

14. Margaret Stimmann Branson, "Making the Case for Civic Education: Educating Young People for Responsible Citizenship," paper presented at the Conference for Professional Development for Program Trainers, Manhattan Beach, Calif., February 25, 2001.

15. Kenneth Feldman and Theodore M. Newcomb, *The Impact of College on Students,* vol. 2 (Jossey-Bass, 1969), pp. 16–24, 49–56. See also David O. Sears and Nicholas A. Valentino, "Politics Matters: Political Events as Catalysts for Preadult Socialization," *American Political Science Review* 91 (March 1997), pp. 45–65.

16. Robert D. Putnam, "Bowling Together," *American Prospect* 13 (February 11, 2002), p. 20–22.

17. Quoted in Hadley Cantril, *Gauging Public Opinion* (Princeton University Press, 1944).

18. Everett C. Ladd and John Benson, "The Growth of News Polls in American Politics," in *Media Polls in American Politics,* eds. Thomas Mann and Gary Orren (Brookings Institution, 1992), pp. 19–31.

19. Benjamin I. Page and Robert Y. Shapiro, *The Rational Public: Fifty Years of Trends in Americans' Policy Preferences* (University of Chicago Press, 1992), p. 237.

20. George J. Church, "What in the World Are We Doing?" *Time,* October 18, 1993, p. 42.

21. "Poll Analyses: Which Freedoms Will Americans Trade for Security," *Gallup News Service,* June 11, 2002.

22. David R. Mayhew, *Congress: The Electoral Connection* (Yale University Press, 1974); Richard F. Fenno Jr., *Home Style: House Members in Their Districts* (Little, Brown, 1978).

23. Robert S. Erikson and Kent L. Tedin, *American Public Opinion: Its Origins, Content and Impact,* 5th ed. (Allyn & Bacon, 1995), p. 279.

24. David W. Moore, "Poll Analyses: Republicans, Democrats Tied in Congressional Races" *Gallup News Service,* April 2, 2002.

25. The 2000 National Election Study, Center for Political Studies, University of Michigan. The NES Guide to Public Opinion an Electoral Behavior at www.umich.edu/~nesguide/nesguide.htm.

26. Erikson and Tedin, *American Public Opinion,* p. 304.

27. Neil S. Newhouse and Christine L. Matthews, "NAFTA Revisited: Most Americans Just Weren't Deeply Engaged," *Public Perspective* 5 (January–February 1994), pp. 31–32.

28. National Opinion Research Center, *General Social Survey, 1996* (University of Chicago, 1996).

29. The 2000 National Election Study, Center for Political Studies, University of Michigan. The NES Guide to Public Opinion and Electoral Behavior at www.umich.edu/~nesguide/nesguide.htm; Ian Stirton, Federal Election Commission Clearinghouse on Election Administration, personal communication, March 5, 2001.

30. Frank R. Parker, *Black Votes Count: Political Empowerment in Mississippi After 1965* (University of North Carolina Press, 1990), p. 3.

31. Bernard Grofman and Lisa Handley, "The Impact of the Voting Rights Act on Black Representation in Southern State Legislatures," *Legislative Studies Quarterly* 16 (February 1991), pp. 111–128.

32. International Institute for Democracy and Electoral Assistance, "Voter Turnout from 1945 to Date: A Global Report on Political Participation," at www.idea.int/voter_turnout/index.html.

33. Raymond E. Wolfinger and Steven J. Rosenstone, "The Effect of Registration Laws on Voter Turnout," *American Political Science Review* 72 (March 1978), p. 24.

34. Raymond E. Wolfinger and Steven J. Rosenstone, *Who Votes?* (Yale University Press, 1980), pp. 78, 88.

35. Federal Election Commission, "Executive Summary," at www.fec.gov/votregis/nvrasum.htm.

36. See Raymond E. Wolfinger and Ben Highton, "Estimating the Effects of the National Voter Registration Act of 1993," *Political Behavior* (June 1998), pp. 79–104; Raymond E. Wolfinger and Jonathan Hoffman, "Registering and Voting with Motor Voter," *PS: Political Science and Politics* (March 2001), pp. 85–92.

37. "Voter Turnout Drops in 1998 Primaries," *New York Times,* June 30, 1998, p. A18.

38. For a discussion of the differences in the turnout between presidential and midterm elections, see James E. Campbell, "The Presidential Surge and Its Midterm Decline in Congressional Elections, 1868–1988," *Journal of Politics* 53 (May 1991), pp. 477–487.

39. David E. Rosenbaum, "Democrats Keep Solid Hold on Congress," *New York Times,* November 9, 1988, p. A24; Louis V. Gerstner, "Next Time, Let Us Boldly Vote as No Democracy Has Before," *USA Today,* November 16, 1998, p. A15.

40. U.S. Bureau of the Census, *Statistical Abstract of the United States, 2001,* p. 253.

41. Wolfinger and Rosenstone, *Who Votes?* p. 102.

42. Howard W. Stanley and Richard G. Niemi, *Vital Statistics on Politics, 1999–2000* (CQ Press, 2000), pp. 120–121; CNN, at www.cnn.com/ELECTION/2000/results/index.my.html.

43. See Angus Campbell, Philip E. Converse, Warren E. Miller, and Donald E. Stokes, *The American Voter* (Wiley, 1960). This volume is a foundation of modern voting analysis despite much new evidence and reinterpretation. See also Norman H. Nie, Sidney Verba, and John R. Petrocik, *The Changing American Voter* (Harvard University Press, 1976), and Ruy A. Teixeira, *Why Americans Don't Vote: Turnout Decline in the United States, 1960–1984* (Greenwood, 1987).

44. David E. Rosenbaum, "Democrats Keep Solid Hold in Congress," *New York Times,* November 9, 1988, p. A24.

45. Austin Ranney, "Nonvoting Is Not a Social Disease," *Public Opinion,* October–November 1983, pp. 16–19.

46. Thomas Byrne Edsall, *The New Politics of Inequality* (Norton, 1984), p. 181.

47. Frances Fox Piven and Richard A. Cloward, "Prospects for Voter Registration Reform: A Report on the Experiences of the Human SERVE Campaign," *PS: Political Science and Politics* 18 (Summer 1985), p. 589.

48. Ibid., p. 589.

49. Wolfinger and Rosenstone, *Who Votes?* p. 109.

50. E. E. Schattschneider, *The Semisovereign People* (Dryden Press, 1975), p. 96.

51. Stephen Earl Bennett and David Resnick, "The Implications of Nonvoting for Democracy in the United States," *American Journal of Political Science* 84 (August 1990), pp. 771–802.

52. Bruce E. Keith, David B. Magleby, Candice J. Nelson, Elizabeth Orr, Mark C. Westlye, and Raymond E. Wolfinger, *The Myth of the Independent Voter* (University of California Press, 1992), pp. 60–75; 2001 American National Election Study, Center for Political Studies, University of Michigan, Ann Arbor.

53. Martin P. Wattenberg, *The Rise of Candidate Centered Politics: Presidential Elections of the 1980s* (Harvard University Press, 1991), p. 1.

54. Barry Goldwater, quoted in Theodore H. White, *The Making of the President, 1964* (Athenaeum, 1965), p. 217.

55. William H. Flanigan and Nancy H. Zingale, *Political Behavior of the American Electorate,* 8th ed. (CQ Press, 1994), p. 173.

56. Kevin Sack, "The 2000 Campaign: The Democrats; Gore Surrogates Bluntly Question Bush's Competence," *New York Times,* October 20, 2000, p. A27.

57. See Alton Mitchell, "The 2000 Campaign: The Credibility Issue; A Sustained G.O.P. Push to Mock Gore's Image," *New York Times,* October 15, 2000, pp. 1, 28; Melinda Henneberger, "The 2000 Campaign: The Gun Lobby; Rallying Voters and Relishing a Leading Role," *New York Times,* November 3, 2000, p. A25.

58. CNN, at www.cnn.com/ELECTION/2000/results/index.epolls.html.

59. J. Merrill Shanks and Warren E. Miller, "Policy Direction and Performance Evaluation: Complementary Explanations of the Reagan Elections," *British Journal of Political Science* 20 (1990), pp. 143–235; Warren E. Miller and J. Merrill Shanks, "Policy Direction and Performance Evaluation: Comparing George Bush's Victory with Those of Ronald Reagan in 1980 and 1984," paper presented at the annual meeting of the American Political Science Association, Atlanta, August 31–September 2, 1989.

60. Amihai Glazer, "The Strategy of Candidate Ambiguity," *American Political Science Review* 84 (March 1990), pp. 237–241.

61. Robert S. Erikson and David W. Romero, "Candidate Equilibrium and the Behavioral Model of the Vote," *American Political Science Review* 84 (December 1990), p. 1122.

62. Morris P. Fiorina, *Retrospective Voting in American National Elections* (Yale University Press, 1981).

63. CNN, at www.cnn.com/ELECTION/2000/results/index.epolls.html.

64. Gerald H. Kramer, "Short-Term Fluctuations in U.S. Voting Behavior, 1896–1964," *American Political Science Review* 65 (March 1971), pp. 131–143. See also Edward R. Tufte, "Determinants of the Outcomes of Midterm Congressional Elections," *American Political Science Review* 69 (September 1975), pp. 812–826, and Andrew E. Busch, *Horses in Midstream: U.S. Midterm Elections and Their Consequences* (University of Pittsburgh Press, 1999).

65. John R. Hibbing and John R. Alford, "The Educational Impact of Economic Conditions: Who Is Held Responsible?" *American Journal of Political Science* 25 (August 1981), pp. 423–439; Morris P. Fiorina, "Who Is Held Responsible? Further Evidence on the Hibbing-Alford Thesis," *American Journal of Political Science* (February 1983), pp. 158–164.

66. Robert M. Stein, "Economic Voting for Governor and U.S. Senator: The Electoral Consequences of Federalism," *Journal of Politics* 52 (February 1990), pp. 29–53.

Chapter 9

1. *1994 Census of Governments* (U.S. Government Printing Office, 1995), vol. 1, no. 2, p. 1.

2. See U.S. Term Limits, at www.termlimits.org.

3. In the 1992 and 1994 National Election Studies, approximately 78 percent of Americans favored term limits; Center for Political Studies, University of Michigan.

4. *U.S. Term Limits Inc.* v. *Thornton,* 514 U.S. 799 (1995).

5. For an insightful examination of electoral rules, see Bernard Grofman and Arend Lijphart, eds., *Electoral Laws and Their Political Consequences* (Agathon Press, 1986).

6. Arend Lijphart, "The Political Consequences of Electoral Laws, 1945–85," *American Political Science Review* 84 (June 1990), pp. 481–495. See also David M. Farrell, *Electoral Systems: A Comparitive Introduction* (Macmillan, 2001).

7. As noted, one of Gore's electors abstained, reducing his vote from 267 to 266; CNN, at www.cnn.com/2001/ALLPOLITICS/stories/01/06/electoral.vote/index.html.

8. Paul D. Schumaker and Burdett A. Loomis, *Choosing a President: The Electoral College and Beyond* (Seven Bridges Press, 2002), p. 60. See also George Rabinowitz and Stuart Elaine MacDonald, "The Power of the States in U.S. Presidential Elec-

tions," *American Political Science Review* 80 (March 1986), pp. 65–87, and Dany M. Adkison and Christopher Elliott, "The Electoral College: A Misunderstood Institution," *PS: Political Science and Politics* 30 (March 1997), pp. 77–80.

9. See, for example, David R. Mayhew, *Congress: The Electoral Connection* (Yale University Press, 1974); Richard F. Fenno Jr., *Home Style: House Members in Their Districts* (Little, Brown, 1978); and James E. Campbell, "The Return of Incumbents: The Nature of Incumbency Advantage," *Western Political Quarterly* 36 (September 1983), pp. 434–444.

10. Gary King and Andrew Gelman, "Systemic Consequences of Incumbency Advantage in U.S. House Elections," *American Journal of Political Science* 35 (February 1991), pp. 110–137.

11. Alan I. Abramowitz, "Economic Conditions, Presidential Popularity, and Voting Behavior in Midterm Congressional Elections," *Journal of Politics* 47 (February 1985), pp. 31–43. See also Gary C. Jacobson, *The Politics of Congressional Elections,* 3d ed. (HarperCollins, 1992), p. 159.

12. See Edward R. Tufte, *Political Control of the Economy* (Princeton University Press, 1978); see also his "Determinants of the Outcomes of Midterm Congressional Elections," *American Political Science Review* 69 (September 1975), pp. 812–826. For a more recent discussion of the same subject, see Jacobson, *Politics of Congressional Elections,* pp. 123–178.

13. Alan I. Abramowitz and Jeffrey A. Segal, "Determinants of the Outcomes of U.S. Senate Elections," *Journal of Politics* 48 (1986), pp. 433–439.

14. This includes the postelection switch of Alabama Senator Richard Shelby to the Republican party.

15. Linda L. Fowler and Robert D. McClure, *Political Ambition: Who Decides to Run for Congress* (Yale University Press, 1989); Paul S. Herrnson, *Congressional Elections: Campaigning at Home and in Washington,* 3d ed. (CQ Press, 2000), p. 45.

16. Kathleen Hall Jamieson, *Everything You Think You Know About Politics . . . and Why You're Wrong* (New Replica Books, 2000), p. 38.

17. For a discussion of different explanations of the impact of incumbency, see Keith Krehbiel and John R. Wright, "The Incumbency Effect in Congressional Elections: A Test of Two Explanations," *American Journal of Political Science* 27 (February 1983), p. 140.

18. Roll Call, "Roll Call Casualty List," *Roll Call Politics,* November 5, 1998, p. 15; "Senate, House, Gubernatorial Results," *Congressional Quarterly Weekly,* November 11, 2000, pp. 2694–2703.

19. "Financial Activity of Senate and House General Election Campaigns," Federal Election Commission at ftp.fec.gov/fec.

20. D. Cover, "One Good Term Deserves Another: The Advantages of Incumbency in Congressional Elections," *American Journal of Political Science* 21 (August 1977), pp. 523–542; Morris P. Fiorina, *Congress: Keystone of the Washington Establishment* (Yale University Press, 1978); Mayhew, *Congress,* pp. 52–53.

21. Mayhew, *Congress,* p. 61; Richard F. Fenno Jr., *Congressmen in Committees* (Little, Brown, 1973); Steven S. Smith and Christopher J. Deering, *Committees in Congress,* 3d ed. (CQ Press, 1997).

22. See National Journal, at nationaljournal.com.

23. Candice J. Nelson, "Spending in the 2000 Elections," in David B. Magleby, *Financing the 2000 Election* (Brookings Institution, 2002), pp. 28–30.

24. Jonathan S. Krasno, *Challengers, Competition, and Reelection: Comparing Senate and House Elections* (Yale University Press, 1994).

25. Alan I. Abramowitz, "Explaining Senate Election Outcomes," *American Political Science Review* 82 (June 1988), pp. 385–403.

26. David B. Magleby, "More Bang for the Buck: Campaign Spending in Small State U.S. Senate Elections," paper presented at the annual meeting of the Western Political Science Association, Salt Lake City, March 30–April 1, 1989.

27. The Green Papers, "2000 Primary and Caucus Results," at www.thegreenpapers.com/PCC/Tabul.html.

28. The descriptions of these types of primaries are drawn from James W. Davis, *Presidential Primaries,* rev. ed. (Greenwood Press, 1984), chap. 3. See pp. 56–63 for specifics on each state (and Puerto Rico). This material is used with the permission of the publisher.

29. Paul T. David and James W. Caesar, *Proportional Representation in Presidential Nominating Politics* (University Press of Virginia, 1980).

30. See Rhodes Cook, "GOP's Rules Favor Dole, If He Doesn't Stumble," *Congressional Quarterly Weekly,* January 27, 1996, pp. 228–231. See also the Republican National Committee, at www. rnc.org.

31. www.nass.org/issues.html#primaryplan.

32. *The Book of the States, 2000–2001* (Council of State Governments, 2000), pp. 164–165.

33. David Redlawsk and Arthur Sanders, "Groups and Grassroots in the Iowa Caucuses," in *Outside Money in the 2000 Presidential Primaries and Congressional Elections,* ed. David B. Magleby, in *PS Online* (June 2001), at www.apsanet.org/PS/june01/redlawsk.cfm.

34. David B. Magleby, *Getting Inside the Outside Campaign: Issue Advocacy in the 2000 Presidential Primaries* (Center for the Study of Elections and Democracy, Brigham Young University, 2000). See also Magleby, ed., *Outside Money,* at www.apsanet.org/PS/june01, and Richard Moron, "A Look at . . . Political Momentum," *Washington Post,* February 6, 2000, p. B3.

35. The viewership of conventions has declined as the amount of time devoted to conventions dropped. In 1988, Democrats averaged 27.1 million viewers and Republicans 24.5 million. By 1996, viewership for the Democrats was 18 million viewers on average and for the Republicans, 16.6 million. See John Carmody, "The TV Column," *Washington Post,* September 2, 1996, p. D4. Viewership figures improved somewhat in 2000: Democrats averaged 20.6 million viewers and Republicans 19.2 million. See Don Aucoin, "Democrats Hold TV Ratings Edge," *Boston Globe,* August 19, 2000, p. F3.

36. Stephen J. Wayne, *The Road to the White House, 2000: The Politics of Presidential Elections* (St. Martin's Press, 2000), chap. 5.

37. Jeff Fishel, *Presidents and Promises* (CQ Press, 1984).

38. See White House, at www.whitehouse.gov/infocus/education.

39. CNN, "Burden of Proof," August 9, 2000.

40. Election Reform.org, at www.ballotaccess.org.

41. Sidney Kraus, *The Great Debates: Kennedy vs. Nixon, 1960* (Indiana University Press, 1962). See also Myles Martel, *Political Campaign Debates* (Longman, 1983).

42. "Televised Debate History, 1960–1996," at www.museum.tv/debateweb/html/history/1976/video.htm.

43. CNN, at www.cnn.com.

44. CNN, at www.cnn.com.

45. Commission on Presidential Debates at www.debates.org/pages/history.html.

46. Robert S. Erikson, "Economic Conditions and the Presidential Vote," *American Political Science Review* 83 (June 1989), pp. 567–575. Class-based voting has also become more important. See Robert S. Erikson, Thomas O. Lancaster, and David W. Romers, "Group Components of the Presidential Vote, 1952–1984," *Journal of Politics* 51 (May 1989), pp. 337–346.

47. David B. Magleby and Candice J. Nelson, *The Money Chase: Congressional Campaign Finance Reform* (Brookings Institution, 1990), pp. 13–14.

48. *Buckley* v. *Valeo,* 424 U.S. 1 (1976).

49. See Herbert E. Alexander and Monica Bauer, *Financing the 1988 Election* (Westview Press, 1991), and Frank J. Sorauf, *Money in American Elections* (Scott, Foresman, 1988).

50. Including federal funding, Federal Election Commission reports show that George W. Bush raised just over $193 million. "2000 Presidential Race: Total Raised and Spent," Center for Responsive Politics, at www.opensecrets.org/2000elect/index/AllCands.htm.

51. Federal Election Commission, Public Disclosure Office, personal communication, January 9, 2001.

52. Beth Donovan, "Parties Turned Soft Money Law into Hard and Fast Spending," *Congressional Quarterly Weekly,* May 15, 1993, pp. 1196–1197; David E. Rosenbaum, "In Political Money Game, the Year of Big Loopholes," *New York Times,* December 26, 1996, p. A1; "Party Fundraising Escalates" at www.fec.gov/press/01120/partyfunds.htm.

53. See Joseph A. Pika, "Campaign Spending and Activity in the 2000 Delaware U.S. Senate Race," in *Election Advocacy: Soft Money and Issue Advocacy in the 2000 Congressional Elections,* ed. David B. Magleby (Center for the Study of Elections and Democracy, Brigham Young University, 2001), pp. 51–61.

54. David B. Magleby, "Dictum Without Data: The Myth of Issue Advocacy and Party Building," at www.byu.edu/outsidemoney/dictum.

55. See Pika, "Campaign Spending and Activity."

56. Ibid.

57. David B. Magleby, ed., *The Other Campaign: Soft Money and Issue Advocacy in the 2000 Congressional Elections* (Rowman & Littlefield, 2002), p. 213.

58. Craig B. Holman and Luke P. McLoughlin, *Buying Time, 2000: Television Advertising in the 2000 Federal Elections* (Brennan Center for Justice, New York University School of Law, 2001), p. 33.

59. See Magleby, "Dictum Without Data."

60. Morton M. Kondracke, "McCain to Lead New Reform Fight for Free TV Time," *Roll Call,* May 30, 2002, at www.rollcall.com/pages/columns/kondracke/00/2002/kond0530.html.

61. Rick Hampson, "Former Banker Was Big Spender," *USA Today,* November 9, 2000, p. A9.

61. Rick Hampson, "Former Banker Was Big Spender," *USA Today,* November 9, 2000, p. A9.
62. Federal Election Commission, "Disclosure Data Base: PAS200.ZIP," at ftp.fec.gov/fec. See also David B. Magleby and Jason Richard Beal, "Independent Expenditures and Internal Communications," in *The Other Campaign,* ed. Magleby, p. 83.
63. Federal Election Commission, "Congressional Financial Activity Soars for 2000," press release, January 9, 2001.
64. Federal Election Commission, at ftp.fec.gov/fec.
65. See Robert Hunter, ed., *Electing the President: A Program for Reform, Final Report of the Commission on National Election* (Center for Strategic and International Studies, 1986); James L. Sundquist, *Constitutional Reform* (Brookings Institution, 1986); and Edward N. Kearny, "Presidential Nominations and Representative Democracy: Proposals for Change," *Presidential Studies Quarterly* 14 (Summer 1984), pp. 348–356.
66. Barbara Norrander and Greg W. Smith, "Type of Contest, Candidate Strategy, and Turnout in Presidential Primaries," *American Politics Quarterly* 13 (January 1985), p. 28.
67. John G. Geer, "Voting in Presidential Primaries," paper presented at the annual meeting of the American Political Science Association, Washington, D.C., September 1984. See also Albert R. Hunt, "The Media and Presidential Campaigns," in *Elections American Style,* ed. A. James Reichley (Brookings Institution, 1987), pp. 52–74.
68. Ben White, "After Drama Left the Primaries, Voter Turnout Fell Dramatically," *Washington Post,* September 1, 2000, p. A5.
69. George S. McGovern, "Considerations on Our Political Processes," *Presidential Studies Quarterly* 14 (Summer 1984), pp. 341–347.
70. Mark Sandalow, "Gore, Bush Sweep Six Southern Primaries—Nominations Cinched," *San Francisco Chronicle,* March 15, 2000, p. A1.
71. The President's Commission for a National Agenda for the Eighties, *A National Agenda for the Eighties* (U.S. Government Printing Office, 1980), p. 97, proposed holding four presidential primaries, scheduled about one month apart.
72. Nelson W. Polsby, *Consequences of Party Reform* (Oxford University Press, 1983), p. 118.
73. Thomas E. Cronin and Robert Loevy, "The Case for a National Primary Convention Plan," *Public Opinion,* December 1982–January 1983, pp. 50–53.
74. Neal R. Peirce and Lawrence Longley, *The People's President: The Electoral College in American History and the Direct-Vote Alternative,* 2d ed. (Yale University Press, 1981), describe and advocate the direct-vote alternative. Nelson W. Polsby and Aaron B. Wildavsky, *Presidential Elections: Contemporary Strategies of American Politics,* 10th ed. (Chatham House, 2000), favor the present system.

Chapter 10

1. Howard Kurtz, "Errors Plagued Election Night Polling Service: VNS Report Also Faults Networks in Florida Blunder," *Washington Post,* December 22, 2000, p. A1.
2. Marvin Kalb, "Financial Pressure Doomed Networks on Election Night," *Deseret News,* December 3, 2000, p. AA7.
3. CNN, at www.cnn.com/2000/ALLPOLITICS/stories/11/16/tauzin.networks/index.htm.
4. Pew Research Center for the People and the Press, "Media Seen as Fair, but Tilting to Gore," press release, October 15, 2000.
5. Pew Research Center for the People and the Press, "Web News Takes Off," press release, June 8, 1998, p. 1; and Pew Research Center for the People and the Press, Survey Reports, "Public's News Habits Little Changed by September 11," June 9, 2002. See http://people-press.org/reports.
6. James Fallows, *Breaking the News: How the Media Undermine American Democracy* (Pantheon Books, 1996), p. 3.
7. Paul Starobin, "Heeding the Call," *National Journal,* November 30, 1996, pp. 2584–2589.
8. William Rivers, *The Other Government* (Universe Books, 1982); Douglas Cater, *The Fourth Branch of Government* (Houghton Mifflin, 1959); Dom Bonafede, "The Washington Press: An Interpreter or a Participant in Policy Making?" *National Journal,* April 24, 1982, pp. 716–721; Michael Ledeen, "Learning to Say 'No' to the Press," *Public Interest 73* (Fall 1983), p. 113.
9. Leslie G. Moeller, "The Big Four: Mass Media Actualities and Expectations," in *Beyond Media: New Approaches to Mass Communication,* ed. Richard W. Budd and Brent D. Ruben (Transaction Books, 1988), p. 15.
10. Andrew Kohut, "Web Users Are on the Rise; but Public Affairs Interest Isn't," *Columbia Journalism Review,* January–February 2000, p. 68. One service that e-mails customized news and reminders to subscribers is infobeat.com.
11. U.S. Bureau of the Census, *Statistical Abstract of the United States, 2001* (Government Printing Office, 2001), tabs. 1125 and 1126.
12. *Media Use and Evaluation* (Gallup Organization, 2000).
13. Jim Rutenberg, "Media: Audience for Cable News Grows," *New York Times,* March 25, 2002, p. C8.
14. Marc Fisher, "TV Stations Offer a Clear Picture of Indifference," *Washington Post,* September, 26, 2000, p. B1.
15. Alliance for Better Campaigns, *Political Standard* 4 (March 2001), p. 6.
16. David B. Magleby, "Direct Legislation in the American States," in *Referendums Around the World: The Growing Use of Direct Democracy,* ed. David Butler and Austin Ranney (AEI Press, 1994), pp. 218–257.
17. See Ray Hiebert, Donald Ungarait, and Thomas Bohn, *Mass Media VI* (Longman, 1991), chap. 11.
18. *Statistical Abstract of the United States, 2001,* tab. 932.
19. Darrel West, *The Rise and Fall of the Media Establishment* (Bedford/St. Martin's, 2001).
20. Audit Bureau of Circulations, at abcas1.accessabc.com/ecirc.
21. Inktomi, "Web Surpasses One Billion Documents," at www.inktomi.com/new/press/billion.html, January 18, 2000.
22. Kohut,"Web Users Are on the Rise," p. 68.
23. Jeremy Derfner, "So, Was It a Net Election?" *Slate,* January 26, 2001, http://slate.msn.com/?id=97767; J. Scott Orr, "Web Becomes New Source of Untapped Campaign Cash," *Times-Picayune,* April 5, 2000, p. A10.
24. See Robert A. Rutland, *Newsmongers: Journalism in the Life of the Nation, 1690–1972* (Dial Press, 1973).
25. Quoted in Frank Luther Mott, *American Journalism,* 3d ed. (Macmillan, 1962), p. 412.
26. During the 1930s, more than 1,000 speeches were made by members of Congress on one network alone. See Edward W. Chester, *Radio, Television, and American Politics* (Sheed & Ward, 1969), p. 62.
27. Frances Perkins, quoted in James MacGregor Burns, *Roosevelt: The Lion and the Fox* (Harcourt, 1956), p. 205.
28. Gannett Corp., at www.gannett.com/map/gan/007.htm.
29. "California, Southland Focus; Tribune Gets Antitrust Approval in *Times* Deal," *Los Angeles Times,* April 7, 2000, p. C2.
30. Seth Schiesel, "FCC Rules on Ownership Under Review," *New York Times,* April 3, 2002, p. C1
31. Stephanie Storm, "Mergers for Year Approach Record," *New York Times,* October 31, 1996, p. A1.
32. Geraldine Fabrikant, "The Media Business," *New York Times,* October 11, 1996, p. D2.
33. Shanto Iyengar and Donald R. Kinder, *News That Matters* (University of Chicago Press, 1987).
34. Steven J. Simmons, *The Fairness Doctrine and the Media* (University of California Press, 1978).
35. "Political Fairness on TV," *Christian Science Monitor,* October 17, 2000, p. 10.
36. Harvey G. Zeidenstein, "News Media Perception of White House News Management," *Presidential Studies Quarterly* 24 (Summer 1984), pp. 391–398.
37. Elihu Katz and Paul Lazarsfeld, *Personal Influence: The Part Played by People in the Flow of Mass Communications* (Free Press, 1955).
38. See Doris A. Graber, "Say It with Pictures: The Impact of Audiovisual News on Public Opinion Formation," paper presented at the annual meeting of the Midwest Political Science Association, Chicago, April 1987, and Benjamin I. Page, Robert Y. Shapiro, and Glenn R. Dempsey, "What Moves Public Opinion?" *American Political Science Review* 76 (March 1987), pp. 23–43.
39. See, for example, Jack Dennis, "Preadult Learning of Political Independence: Media and Family Communications Effects," *Communication Research* 13 (July 1987), pp. 401–433, and Olive Stevens, *Children Talking Politics* (Robertson, 1982).
40. See Angus Campbell, Philip E. Converse, Warren E. Miller, and Donald E. Stokes, *The American Voter* (Wiley, 1960).
41. Paul Lazarsfeld, Bernard Berelson, and Hazel Gaudet, *The People's Choice: How the Voter Makes Up His Mind in a Presidential Campaign,* 3d ed. (Columbia University Press, 1968); Bernard Berelson, Paul Lazarsfeld, and William McPhee, *Voting: A Study of Opinion Formation in a Presidential Campaign* (University of Chicago Press, 1954).

42. Pew Research Center for the People and the Press, "Scandal Reporting Faulted for Bias and Inaccuracy: Popular Policies and Unpopular Press Lift Clinton Ratings," press release, February 6, 1998, p. 6.

43. Gallup Organization, at www.gallup.com/poll-archives/980926.htm.

44. Stuart Oskamp, ed., *Television as a Social Issue* (Sage, 1988); James W. Carey, ed., *Media, Myths, and Narratives: Television and the Press* (Sage, 1988).

45. Doris A. Graber, *Processing the News: How People Tame the Information Tide*, 2d ed. (Longman, 1988), pp. 107–113.

46. Times Mirror Center for the People and the Press, "Times Mirror News Interest Index," press releases, January 16 and February 28, 1992.

47. John K. Robinson and Mark R. Levy, eds., *The Main Source: Learning from Television News* (Sage, 1986).

48. Graber, *Processing the News*, p. 115.

49. Rush Limbaugh, *See, I Told You So* (Pocket Books, 1993), p. 326.

50. See Nelson Polsby, *Consequences of Party Reform* (Oxford University Press, 1983), pp. 142–146. See also Stanley Rothman and S. Robert Lichter, "Media and Business Elites: Two Classes in Conflict!" *Public Interest* 69 (Fall 1982), pp. 119–125.

51. Michael Parenti, *Inventing Reality: The Politics of the Mass Media* (St. Martin's Press, 1986), p. 35.

52. Rick Lyman, "Multimedia Deal: The History; 2 Commanding Publishers, 2 Powerful Empires," *New York Times*, March 14, 2000, p. C16.

53. David Broder, "Beware of the 'Insider' Syndrome: Why Newsmakers and News Reporters Shouldn't Get Too Cozy," *Washington Post*, December 4, 1988, p. A21; see also Broder, "Thin-Skinned Journalists," *Washington Post*, January 11, 1989, p. A21.

54. Robert Lichter, "Consistently Liberal—but Does It Matter?" *Forbes Media Critic* 4 (Fall 1996), pp. 26–39. These data are essentially the same as data reported a decade earlier. See David Shaw, "The Times Poll: Public and Press—Two Viewpoints," *Los Angeles Times*, August 11, 1985, pt. 1, p. 1.

55. Daniel P. Moynihan, "The Presidency and the Press," *Commentary* 51 (March 1971), p. 43.

56. S. Robert Lichter, Stanley Rothman, and Linda S. Lichter, *The Media Elite* (Adler & Adler, 1986).

57. Larry J. Sabato, *Feeding Frenzy: How Attack Journalism Has Transformed American Politics* (Free Press, 1991).

58. See Thomas Patterson, *Out of Order* (Knopf, 1993); Paul Weaver, *News and the Culture of Lying* (Free Press, 1993); and Anthony Munro, "Yet Another Conspiracy Theory," *Columbia Journalism Review* 33 (November 1994), p. 71.

59. Shanto Iyengar, Mark D. Peters, and Donald R. Kinder, "Experimental Demonstrations of the 'Not-So-Minimal' Consequences of Television News Programs," *American Political Science Review* 76 (December 1982), pp. 848–858.

60. Ibid.; Maxwell E. McCombs and Donald L. Shaw, "The Agenda-Setting Function of the Mass Media," *Public Opinion Quarterly* 36 (1972), pp. 176–187; Maxwell E. McCombs and Sheldon Gilbert, "News Influence on Our Pictures of the World," in *Perspectives on Media Effects*, eds. Jennings Bryant and Dolf Gillman (Erlbaum, 1986), pp. 1–15; Iyengar and Kinder, *News That Matters*.

61. Quoted in Michael J. Robinson and Margaret A. Sheehan, *Over the Wire and on TV: CBS and UPI in Campaign '80* (Russell Sage Foundation, 1983) p. xiii.

62. ABC News, at abcnews.go.com/sections/us/DailyNews/WTC_MAIN010914.html.

63. David B. Magleby, *Direct Legislation: Voting on Ballot Propositions in the United States* (Johns Hopkins University Press, 1984).

64. Peter Marks, "Costly Prescriptions: One Issue That Fits All," *New York Times*, October 1, 2000, p. A22.

65. Paul T. David, Ralph M. Goldman, and Richard C. Bain, *The Politics of the National Party Conventions* (Brookings Institution, 1960), pp. 300–301.

66. Richard Davis, *The Press and American Politics: The New Mediator*, 2d ed. (Prentice Hall, 1996), p. 279.

67. Frank I. Lutz, *Candidates, Consultants, and Campaigns* (Blackwell, 1988), chap. 7.

68. Larry J. Sabato, *The Rise of Political Consultants* (Basic Books, 1981).

69. See ibid.; James David Barber, *The Pulse of Politics: Electing Presidents in the Media Age* (Norton, 1980); and Fred Barnes, "The Myth of Political Consultants," *New Republic*, June 16, 1986, p. 16.

70. Quoted in Sabato, *Rise of Political Consultants*, p. 144.

71. Thomas E. Patterson, *The Mass Media Election: How Americans Choose Their President* (Praeger, 1980), chap. 12.

72. John H. Aldrich, *Before the Convention* (University of Chicago Press, 1980), p. 65. See also Patterson, *Mass Media Election*.

73. John Foley et al., *Nominating a President: The Process and the Press* (Praeger, 1980), p. 39. For the press's treatment of incumbents, see James Glen Stovall, "Incumbency and News Coverage of the 1980 Presidential Election Campaign," *Western Political Quarterly* 37 (December 1984), p. 621.

74. Priscilla Southwell, "Voter Turnout in the 1986 Congressional Elections: The Media as Demobilizer?" *American Politics Quarterly* 19 (January 1991), pp. 96–108.

75. William Glaberson, "A New Press Role: Solving Problems," *New York Times*, October 3, 1994, p. D6.

76. Patterson, *Mass Media Election*, pp. 115–117.

77. Raymond Wolfinger and Peter Linguiti, "Tuning In and Tuning Out," *Public Opinion* 4 (February–March 1981), pp. 56–60.

78. Lewis Wolfson, *The Untapped Power of the Press* (Praeger, 1985), p. 79.

79. Stephen Hess, *The Government-Press Connection* (Brookings Institution, 1984), p. 106.

80. Lloyd Cutler, "Foreign Policy on Deadline," *Foreign Policy* 56 (Fall 1984), p. 114.

81. Michael B. Grossman and Martha Joynt Kumar, *Portraying the President* (Johns Hopkins University Press, 1981), pp. 255–263; Fredric T. Smoller, *The Six o'Clock Presidency: A Theory of Presidential Press Relations in the Age of Television* (Praeger, 1990), pp. 31–49.

82. Susan Heilmann Miller, "News Coverage of Congress: The Search for the Ultimate Spokesperson," *Journalism Quarterly* 54 (Autumn 1977), pp. 459–465.

83. See Stephen Hess, *Live from Capitol Hill: Studies of Congress and the Media* (Brookings Institution, 1991), pp. 102–110.

84. Richard Davis, "Whither the Congress and the Supreme Court? The Television News Portrayal of American National Government," *Television Quarterly* 22 (1987), pp. 55–63.

85. For a discussion of the Supreme Court and public opinion, see Thomas R. Marshall, *Public Opinion and the Supreme Court* (Unwin Hyman, 1989), and Gregory Caldiera, "Neither the Purse nor the Sword: Dynamics of Public Confidence in the Supreme Court," *American Political Science Review* 80 (December 1986), pp. 1209–1228.

86. For a discussion of the relationship between the Supreme Court and the press, see Richard Davis, "Lifting the Shroud: News Media Portrayal of the U.S. Supreme Court," *Communications and the Law* 9 (October 1987), pp. 43–58; and Elliot E. Slotnick, "Media Coverage of Supreme Court Decision Making: Problems and Prospects," *Judicature*, October–November 1991, pp. 128–142.

87. Todd S. Purdam, "TV Political News in California Is Shrinking, Study Confirms," *New York Times*, January 13, 1999, p. A11.

88. Times Mirror Center, "Campaign '92," *Times Mirror*, January 16, 1992.

89. Quoted in Herbert Schmertz, "The Making of the Presidency," *Presidential Studies Quarterly* 16 (Winter 1986), p. 25.

Chapter 11

1. From a poll by Opinion Dynamics, Inc., for Fox News Channel, cited in *National Journal*, September 20, 1998, p. 1856.

2. Charles Warren, *The Making of the Constitution* (Little, Brown, 1928), p. 195.

3. Congressional Quarterly, *Origins and Development of Congress* (CQ Press, 1982), pp. 53–54.

4. Richard F. Fenno Jr., *Home Style: House Members in Their Districts* (Little, Brown, 1978), p. 168.

5. Alison Mitchell, "Redistricting 2002 Produces No Great Shake-Ups," *New York Times*, March 13, 2002, p. 1.

6. *Davis* v. *Bandemer*, 478 U.S. 109 (1986).

7. *Republican Party of North Carolina* v. *Hunt*, 841 F. Supp. 722 (1994).

8. *Bush* v. *Vera*, 517 U.S. 952 (1996).

9. *Hunt* v. *Cromartie*, 532 U.S. 234 (2001).

10. Frances E. Lee and Bruce I. Oppenheimer, *Sizing Up the Senate: The Unequal Consequences of Equal Representation* (University of Chicago Press, 1999).

11. Daniel Patrick Moynihan, introduction to Monica Friar and Herman Leonard, *The Federal Budget and the States: Fiscal Year 1994* (Kennedy School of Government, 1994).

12. R. P. Fairfield, *The Federalist Papers*, (Doubleday, 1961) p. 160.

13. See Roger H. Davidson and Walter J. Oleszek, *Congress and Its Members*, 8th ed. (CQ Press, 2002).

14. Richard F. Fenno Jr., *The United States Senate: A Bicameral Perspective* (American Enterprise Institute, 1982), p. 1.

15. For discussion of the modern Speakership, see Barbara Sinclair, "House Majority Party Leadership in an Era of Legislative Constraint," in *The Postreform Congress*, ed. Roger H. Davidson (St. Martin's Press, 1992), pp. 91–111, and Ronald M. Peters Jr., ed., *The Speaker: Leadership in the U.S. House of Representatives* (CQ Press, 1995).

16. Newt Gingrich, quoted in Adam Clymer, "Firebrand Who Got Singed Says Being Speaker Suffices," *New York Times*, January 22, 1996, p. 1.

17. Newt Gingrich, *To Renew America* (HarperCollins, 1995) and *Lessons Learned the Hard Way* (HarperCollins, 1998).

18. Dennis Hastert, quoted in Greg Hitt, "Hastert Is Tapped as House Speaker to Fill Vacuum Created by Livingston," *Wall Street Journal*, December 21, 1998, p. A20.

19. Richard E. Cohen and David Baumann, "Speaking Up for Hastert," *National Journal*, November 13, 1999, pp. 3298–3303.

20. For insightful memoirs by three recently retired U.S. senators, see Bill Bradley, *Time Present, Time Past: A Memoir* (Knopf, 1996); Warren B. Rudman, *Combat: Twelve Years in the U.S. Senate* (Random House, 1996); and Alan K. Simpson, *Right in the Old Kazoo: A Lifetime of Scrapping with the Press* (Morrow, 1997). See also the reflections of Joseph I. Lieberman, *In Praise of Public Life* (Simon & Schuster, 2000), and Adam Clymer, *Edward M. Kennedy: A Biography* (Morrow, 1999).

21. For an insightful set of essays on Senate leadership, see Richard A. Baker and Roger H. Davidson, eds., *First Among Equals: Outstanding Senate Leaders of the Twentieth Century* (CQ Press, 1991).

22. Barbara Sinclair, "Unorthodox Lawmaking in the Individualist Senate," *Extensions: A Journal of the Carl Albert Congressional Research and Studies Center* Vol. 3, no. 2 (Fall 1997), p. 11. See also Sinclair, *Unorthodox Lawmaking: New Legislative Processes in the U.S. Congress*, 2d ed. (CQ Press, 2000), chap. 3.

23. Norman J. Ornstein, "Prima Donna Senate," *New York Times*, September 4, 1997, p. A17. See also Carroll J. Doherty, "Senate Caught in the Grip of Its Own 'Holds' System," *Congressional Quarterly Weekly*, August 15, 1998, pp. 2241–2243.

24. Nicol Rae and Colton Campbell, "The Changing Role of Political Parties in the U.S. Senate in the 104th and 105th Congresses," paper presented at the annual meeting of the American Political Science Association, Boston, September 3–6, 1998, p. 21.

25. Sarah A. Binder and Steven S. Smith, *Politics or Principles? Filibustering in the United States Senate* (Brookings Institution, 1997).

26. David Baumann, "The Collapse of the Senate," *National Journal*, June 3, 2000, p. 1759.

27. For a criticism of recent confirmation hearings and various reform proposals, see Stephen L. Carter, *The Confirmation Mess: Cleaning Up the Federal Appointments Process* (Basic Books, 1994). See also G. Calvin Mackenzie and Robert Shogan, eds., *Obstacle Course: The Report of the Twentieth Century Fund Task Force on the Presidential Appointment Process* (Twentieth Century Fund Press, 1996).

28. Woodrow Wilson, *Congressional Government* (Houghton Mifflin, 1885; reprint, Johns Hopkins University Press, 1981), p. 69.

29. Christopher J. Deering and Steven S. Smith, *Committees in Congress*, 3d ed. (CQ Press, 1997).

30. Joel D. Aberbach, *Keeping a Watchful Eye: The Politics of Congressional Oversight* (Brookings Institution, 1990), p. 33. Aberbach's data exclude hearings by Appropriations, Administration, and Rules but do include Budget and the revenue committees.

31. Karen Foerstel, "Chairman's Term Limits Already Shaking Up House," *Congressional Quarterly Weekly*, March 24, 2000, p. 628.

32. Aberbach, *Keeping a Watchful Eye*.

33. "Résumé of Congressional Activity, 105th Congress," *Congressional Record, Daily Digest*, January 19, 1999, p. D29.

34. Ronald Reagan, quoted in Lawrence Longley and Walter Oleszek, *Bicameral Politics* (Yale University Press, 1989), p. 1.

35. For an example of intense bargaining on a major defense appropriation bill, see Pat Towell, "Camouflage-Green Defense Bill Poised for President's Signature," *Congressional Quarterly Weekly*, July 22, 2000, pp. 1819–1822.

36. Davidson and Oleszek, *Congress and Its Members*, p. 307.

37. For a history of the early Congresses, see James Sterling Young, *The Washington Community, 1800–1828* (Columbia University Press, 1966).

38. Davidson and Oleszek, *Congress and Its Members*, p. 30.

39. Polsby, "The Institutionalization of the U.S. House of Representatives," *American Political Science Association* (March 1968), pp. 144–168.

40. Norman J. Ornstein, Thomas Mann, and Michael Malbin, *Vital Statistics on Congress, 1999–2000* (AEI Press, 2000), p. 170.

41. Pew Research Center for the People and the Press, *Washington Leaders Wary of Public Opinion* (Pew Research Center, 1998), p. 30.

42. Herbert Asher, "The Learning of Legislative Norms," *American Political Science Review* 67 (June 1973), pp. 499–513.

43. See the case studies in Richard F. Fenno Jr., *Senators on the Campaign Trail: The Politics of Representation* (University of Oklahoma Press, 1996), p. 331. See also Benjamin Bishin, "Constituency Influence in Congress: Does Subconstituency Matter?" *Legislative Studies Quarterly* (August 2000), pp. 389–415.

44. Statistics from congressional Web sites (www.senate.gov; www.house.gov). See also the Library of Congress Web site (thomas.loc.gov).

45. For a fascinating comparison of two Rhodes scholars, one a liberal from Maryland and the other a conservative from Indiana, and what has shaped their votes over several terms in the U.S. Senate, see Karl A. Lamb, *Reasonable Disagreement: Two U.S. Senators and the Choices They Make* (Garland, 1998).

46. Richard E. Cohen, "A Shallow Bipartisanship," *National Journal*, February 2, 2002, p. 321. Update by author.

47. See Richard Morrin, "Tuned Out, Turned Off: Millions of Americans Know Little About How Their Government Works," *Washington Post National Weekly Edition*, February 5, 1996, pp. 6–7.

48. A 1999 CBS survey reported in "Poll Readings," *National Journal*, October 9, 1999, p. 2917.

49. Bradley, *Time Present, Time Past*, chap. 4.

50. Jackie Clames, "House Divided: Why Congress Hews to the Party Line on Impeachment," *Wall Street Journal*, December 16, 1998, p. 1.

51. Ornstein et al., *Vital Statistics on Congress, 1999–2000*, pp. 103–106.

52. Lieberman, *In Praise of Public Life*, p. 109.

53. Constance Ewing Cook, *Lobbying for Higher Education* (Vanderbilt University Press, 1998). See also Ken Kolman, *Outside Lobbying* (Princeton University Press, 1998).

54. Jill Barshay, "Bush Starts a Strong Record of Success with the Hill," *Congressional Quarterly Weekly*, January 12, 2002, p. 110.

55. See Jeffrey S. Peake, "Presidential Agenda Setting in Foreign Policy," paper presented at the annual meeting of the American Political Science Association, Boston, September 3–6, 1998.

56. Tim Penny, quoted in Lloyd Grove, "How a Bright Penny Just 'Wore Down,'" *Washington Post National Weekly Edition*, August 30, 1993, p. 12.

57. Joseph P. Kennedy II, quoted in Clifford Krauss, "How Personal Tragedy Can Shape Public Policy," *New York Times*, May 16, 1993, p. A16.

58. Sinclair, *Unorthodox Lawmaking*, p. 58. For a defense of riders as a means to cut wasteful spending, see Slade Gorton and Larry E. Craig, "Congressional Riders Rein in Excesses," *Walla Walla Union-Bulletin*, July 31, 1998, p. 4.

59. See David W. Brady and Craig Volden, *Revolving Gridlock: Politics and Policy from Carter to Clinton* (Westview Press, 1998). For two case studies on the way bills get treated in Congress, see Janet M. Martin, *Lessons from the Hill: The Legislative Journey of an Education Program* (St. Martin's Press, 1993), and Steven Waldman, *The Bill—How Legislation Really Becomes Law: A Case Study of the National Service Bill* (Penguin, 1996).

60. James Madison, *The Federalist*, No. 57, in *The Federalist*, ed. Jacob E. Cooke (Meridian Books, 1961), p. 385.

61. See Charles Lewis and the Center for Public Integrity, *The Buying of the Congress: How Special Interests Have Stolen Your Right to Life, Liberty and the Pursuit of Happiness* (Avon, 1998).

62. For an excellent treatment of ethical problems faced by members of Congress and what has been and might be done about them, see Dennis F. Thompson, *Ethics in Congress* (Brookings Institution, 1995).

Chapter 12

1. Gallup Poll, at www.gallup.com.
2. Pew Research Center for the People and the Press, at www.people-press.org.
3. Charles O. Jones, *The Presidency in a Separated System* (Brookings Institution, 1994), p. 295. See also Jean Reith Schroedl, *Congress, the President, and Policymaking* (Sharpe, 1994).
4. Richard Pious, *The American Presidency* (Basic Books, 1978).
5. This history of presidential powers draws heavily on Sidney M. Milkis and Michael Nelson, *The American Presidency: Origins and Development, 1976–1998*, 3d ed. (CQ Press, 1999).
6. *United States* v. *Nixon*, 418 U.S. 683 (1974).
7. It is difficult for the average citizen to assess the health and character of presidential candidates, but voters still try to do so. For various efforts, see Fred Greenstein, *The Presidential Difference* (Free Press, 2000); David Gergen, *Eyewitness to Power: The Essence of Leadership, Nixon to Clinton* (Simon & Schuster, 2000); and Stanley A. Renshon, *The Psychological Assessment of Presidential Candidates* (New York University Press, 1996).
8. For a penetrating and realistic analysis of Abraham Lincoln, see David H. Donald, *Lincoln* (Simon & Schuster, 1995). On the paradoxes and the heightened expectations we place on presidents, see Thomas E. Cronin and Michael A. Genovese, *The Paradoxes of the American Presidency* (Oxford University Press, 1998).
9. See Joseph G. Dawson III, ed., *Commanders in Chief: Presidential Leadership in Modern Wars* (University Press of Kansas, 1993).
10. See Thomas J. Weko, *The Politicizing Presidency: The White House Personnel Office, 1948–1994* (University Press of Kansas, 1995).
11. See G. Calvin MacKenzie and Robert Shogan, eds., *Obstacle Course: The Report of the Twentieth Century Fund Task Force on the Presidential Appointment Process* (Twentieth Century Fund Press, 1996).
12. See James P. Pfiffner, *The Strategic Presidency: Hitting the Ground Running*, 2d ed. (University Press of Kansas, 1996).
13. See Paul C. Light, *The President's Agenda: Domestic Policy Choice from Kennedy Through Clinton* (Johns Hopkins University Press, 1999).
14. *United States* v. *Curtiss-Wright Export Corp.*, 299 U.S. 304 (1936).
15. For commentary by analysts who believe the *Curtiss-Wright* ruling was too sweeping, see Harold H. Koh, *The National Security Constitution* (Yale University Press, 1990); Louis Fisher, *Presidential War Power* (University Press of Kansas, 1995); and David Gray Adler and Larry N. George, eds., *The Constitution and the Conduct of American Foreign Policy: Essays on Law and History* (University Press of Kansas, 1996).
16. On the president's major involvement in the budget process, see Allen Schick, *The Federal Budget: Politics, Policy, Process* (Brookings Institution, 1995).
17. Richard E. Neustadt, *Presidential Power and the Modern Presidents* (Free Press, 1991).
18. Albert R. Hunt, "Clinton Ends His Tenure on High Note," *Wall Street Journal*, December 14, 2000, p. A9.
19. See Sidney M. Milkis, *The President and the Parties: The Transformation of the American Party System Since the New Deal* (Oxford University Press, 1993), and James W. Davis, *The President as Party Leader* (Praeger, 1992).
20. See Bradley H. Patterson Jr., *The White House Staff: Inside the West Wing and Beyond* (Brookings Institution, 2000).
21. John Podhoretz, "Little Shop of Horrors," *Washingtonian*, November 1993, p. 52.
22. For the views on presidents and the White House staff of a highly placed White House aide in several administrations, see Gergen, *Eyewitness to Power*.
23. See Irving Janis, *Groupthink* (Houghton Mifflin, 1982).
24. See Shelley Lynne Tomkins, *Inside OMB: Politics and Process in the President's Budget Office* (Sharpe, 1998).
25. See Cronin and Genovese, *Paradoxes of the American Presidency*, chap. 9.
26. Letter, from Kathryn Hughes, secretary of the cabinet in the Clinton White House, February 1997. See also Robert B. Reich, *Locked in the Cabinet* (Knopf, 1997).
27. Former Vice President Dan Quayle's views are of interest in *Standing Firm* (Harper, 1995). Three useful general treatments on the vice presidency are Jules Witcover, *Crapshoot: Rolling the Dice on the Vice Presidency* (Crown, 1992); Paul Light, *Vice Presidential Power* (Johns Hopkins University Press, 1984); and Joel Goldstein, *The Modern Vice Presidency* (Princeton University Press, 1982).
28. Mark Hertsgaard, *On Bended Knee: The Press and the Reagan Presidency* (Farrar, Straus & Giroux, 1988). See also John A. Maltese, *Spin Control: The White House Office of Communications and the Management of Presidential News* (University of North Carolina Press, 1992).
29. Political scientists are unsure of these relationships. See Jeffrey E. Cohen et al., "State-Level Presidential Approval and Senatorial Support," *Legislative Studies Quarterly* Vol. 15, no. 3 (November 2000), pp. 577–590; Lyn Ragsdale, "Studying the Presidency," in *The Presidency and the Political System*, 6th ed., ed. Michael Nelson (CQ Press, 2000), pp. 29–63; and Paul Gronke and Brian Newman, "FDR to Clinton: A 'State of the Discipline' Review of Presidential Approval," paper presented at the annual meeting of the American Political Science Association, Washington, D.C., August 31–September 3, 2000.
30. Harold J. Laski, *The American Presidency: An Interpretation* (Harper, 1940), p. 38.

Chapter 13

1. David S. Broder, "A Weak Hand," *Washington Post National Weekly Edition*, December 25, 2000, p. 4.
2. George C. Edwards, "Building Coalitions," *Presidential Studies Quarterly* Vol. 18, no. 1 (March 2000), pp. 60–61.
3. See the arguments in David Gray Adler and Michael A. Genovese, eds., *The Presidency and the Law: The Clinton Legacy* (University Press of Kansas, 2002), and Louis Fisher, *Congressional Abdication on War and Spending* (Texas A&M Press, 2000).
4. James A. Thurber, "An Introduction to Presidential-Congressional Rivalry," in *Rivals for Power: Presidential-Congressional Relations*, ed. James A. Thurber, (CQ Press, 1996), p. 6.
5. See, for example, former Republican Senator Warren G. Rudman's memoir, *Combat* (Random House, 1996), chaps. 2 and 3. See also former Democratic Congressman Timothy Penny and Major Garrett, *Common Cents* (Little, Brown, 1995).
6. Sarah A. Blinder, "Going Nowhere: A Gridlocked Congress?" *Brookings Review* (Winter 2000), p. 18.
7. John R. Hibbing and Elizabeth Theiss-Morse, *Congress as Public Enemy: Public Attitudes Toward American Political Institutions* (Cambridge University Press, 1995).
8. David W. Brady and Craig Volden, *Revolving Gridlock* (Westview Press, 1998), p. 176.
9. Letter from Abraham Lincoln to his Illinois law partner W. H. Herndon, February 15, 1848, in *Abraham Lincoln, Speeches and Writings, 1832–1858* (Library of America, 1989), p. 175.
10. Leonard C. Meeker, "The Legality of U.S. Participation in the Defense of Vietnam," *Department of State Bulletin*, March 28, 1966, pp. 448–455.
11. Louis Fisher, *Congressional Abdication on War and Spending* (Texas A&M Press, 2000), p. 184.
12. Ibid., p. 170. See also Louis Fisher and David Gray Adler, "The War Powers: Time to Say Goodbye," *Political Science Quarterly* (Spring 1998), pp. 1–20.
13. Lee Hamilton, "The Role of the Congress in U.S. Foreign Policy," speech delivered to the Center for Strategic and International Studies, Washington, D.C., November 19, 1998.
14. Orrin G. Hatch, "Senate Isn't Guilty of Racism in Confirming Judges," *Wall Street Journal*, September 5, 2000, p. A34.
15. See Henry J. Abraham, *Justices, Presidents, and Senators: A History of U.S. Supreme Court Appointments from Washington to Clinton*, 4th ed. (Rowman & Littlefield, 1999), and Sheldon Goldman, *Picking Federal Judges: Lower Court Selection from Roosevelt Through Reagan* (Yale University Press, 1997).
16. Paul C. Light, "Our Tottering Confirmation Process," *Public Interest* (Spring 2002), pp. 57–83.
17. Raoul Berger, *Executive Privilege: A Constitutional Myth* (Harvard University Press, 1974).

18. Mark J. Rozell, "The Law: Executive Privilege—Definition and Standards of Application," *Presidential Studies Quarterly* (December 1999), p. 924.
19. *United States v. Nixon,* 418 U.S. 683 (1974).
20. See Mark J. Rozell, "Something To Hide: Clinton's Misuse of Executive Privilege," *PS: Political Science and Politics* (September 1999), p. 551. See also Mark J. Rozell, *Executive Privilege: The Dilemma of Secrecy and Democratic Accountability,* 2d ed. (University Press of Kansas, 2000).
21. See Nancy Kassop, "A New (or Old?) Understanding of the Separation of Powers: The Expansion and Contraction of Presidential Power under Clinton," paper presented at the annual meeting of the American Political Science Association, Washington, D.C., August 31–September 3, 2000. See also Christopher J. Deering and Forrest Maltzman, "The Politics of Executive Orders: Legislative Restraints on Presidential Power," *Political Research Quarterly* (December 1999), pp. 767–783.
22. Terry M. Moe and William Howell, "Unilateral Action and Presidential Power: A Theory," *Presidential Studies Quarterly* (December 1999), p. 856.
23. Edwards, "Building Coalitions."
24. Ibid., pp. 49–58.
25. Ibid., p. 63.
26. See Charles Walcott and Karen Hult, *Governing the White House: From Hoover through LBJ* (University Press of Kansas, 1995), and Bradley H. Patterson Jr., *The White House Staff: Inside the West Wing* (Brookings Institution, 2000).
27. See Paul C. Light, *The President's Agenda: Domestic Policy Choice from Kennedy to Clinton,* 3d ed. (Johns Hopkins University Press, 1998), for a discussion of the agenda-setting process.
28. Neustadt, *Presidential Power,* p. 7.
29. Lyndon Johnson, *The Vantage Point: Perspectives on the Presidency, 1963–1969* (Holt, Rinehart and Winston, 1971), p. 461.
30. Walter Mondale, quoted in Light, *President's Agenda,* p. 13.
31. See David R. Mayhew, *Divided We Govern: Party Control, Lawmaking, and Investigations, 1946–1990* (Yale University Press, 1991).
32. See Paul C. Light, "The Focusing Skill and Presidential Influence in Congress," in Christopher J. Deering, *Congressional Politics* (Dorsey Press, 1989).
33. Harold W. Stanley and Richard G. Niemi, *Vital Statistics on American Politics* (CQ Press, 1995).

Chapter 14

1. Andrew Kohut, *Deconstructing Distrust: How Americans View Government* (Pew Research Center for the People and the Press, 1998), p. 124.
2. These statistics are from Paul C. Light and Judith Labiner, "A Vote of Renewed Confidence: How Americans View Presidential Appointees and Government in the Wake of the September 11 Terrorist Attacks," a report of the Presidential Appointee Initiative, Brookings Institution, October 2001; and G. Calvin MacKenzie and Judith Labiner, "Opportunity Lost: The Rise and Fall of Trust and Confidence in Government After September 11," a report of the Center for Public Service, Brookings Institution, May 2002.
3. An exception is a book of essays in praise of innovations by federal agencies, John D. Donahue, ed., *Making Washington Work: Tales of Innovation in the Federal Government* (Brookings Institution, 1999).
4. Dennis Palumbo and Steven Maynard-Moody, *Contemporary Public Administration* (Longman, 1991).
5. Donald Kettl, *Leadership at the Fed* (Yale University Press, 1986).
6. Tom Ridge, quoted in Maureen Shirhal, "Ridge Hints at Border Agency Consolidation," *Government Executive Daily Briefing,* February 26, 2002, at govexec.com/dailyfed/0202/022602td1.htm.
7. James Fesler and Donald Kettl, *The Politics of the Administrative Process* (Chatham House, 1991).
8. See Paul C. Light, *Thickening Government* (Brookings Institution, 1995).
9. See Terry M. Moe, "The Politics of Structural Choice: Toward a Theory of Public Bureaucracy," in *Organization Theory: From Chester Barnard to the Present and Beyond,* ed. Oliver E. Williamson (Oxford University Press, 1990), pp. 140–162.
10. Leonard White, *The Federalists* (Macmillan, 1956), p. 1.
11. For an analysis of the use and abuse of the civil service system in the early twentieth century, see Stephen Skowronek, *Building a New American State* (Cambridge University Press, 1982).
12. Data on U.S. budget projections and employment can be located at www.whitehouse.gov/omg and www.gpo.gov/usbudget and in *Statistical Abstract of the United States* (Government Printing Office, annually).
13. See James Eccles, *The Hatch Act and the American Bureaucracy* (Vantage Press, 1981).
14. See Jeanne Ponessa, "The Hatch Act Rewrite," *Congressional Quarterly Weekly,* November 13, 1993, pp. 3146–3147.
15. Paul C. Light, *The New Public Service* (Brookings Institution, 1999), p. 25.
16. Theodore J. Lowi Jr., *The End of Liberalism,* 2d ed. (Norton, 1979).
17. Kent Weaver, *Automatic Government: The Politics of Indexation* (Brookings Institution, 1988), p. 1.
18. James Q. Wilson, *Bureaucracy: What Government Agencies Do and Why They Do It* (Basic Books, 1989), p. 257.
19. See David E. Lewis, "The Presidential Advantage in the Design of Bureaucratic Agencies," paper presented at the annual meeting of the American Political Science Association, Boston, September 3–6, 1998.
20. Morris P. Fiorina, "Flagellating the Federal Bureaucracy," *Society* (March–April 1983), p. 73.
21. See Steven S. Smith, *The American Congress* (Houghton Mifflin, 1995); see also Joel D. Aberbach, *Keeping a Watchful Eye: The Politics of Congressional Oversight* (Brookings Institution, 1990).
22. See Matthew McCubbins and Thomas Schwartz, "Congressional Oversight Overlooked: Police Patrols Versus Fire Alarms," *American Journal of Political Science* 2 (February 1984), pp. 165–179.
23. See transcript of proceedings in Alvin Felzenberg, ed., *The Keys to a Successful Presidency* (Heritage Foundation, 2000), chaps. 3 and 4.

Chapter 15

1. Alexis de Tocqueville, *Democracy in America,* ed. Phillips Bradley (Knopf, 1944), vol. 1, pp. 278–280.
2. Harold J. Laski, *The American Democracy* (Viking, 1948), p. 110.
3. See Carol Guarnieri and Patrizia Pederzoli, *The Power of Judges: A Comparative Study of Courts and Democracy* (Oxford University Press, 2002); Alec Stone Sweet, *Governing with Judges: Constitutional Politics in Europe* (Oxford University Press, 2000); and C .N. Tate and T. Vallinder, eds., *The Global Expansion of Judicial Power* (New York University Press, 1995).
4. Jerome Frank, *Courts on Trial: Myth and Reality in American Justice* (Princeton University Press, 1949), pp. 80–103. See also Martin Shapiro, *Courts* (University of Chicago Press, 1981), and Robert P. Burns, *A Theory of the Trial* (Princeton University Press, 1999).
5. *United States v. Students Challenging Regulatory Agency Procedures (SCRAP),* 412 U.S. 669 (1973).
6. *Flast v. Cohen,* 392 U.S. 83 (1968); *Lujan v. Defenders of Wildlife,* 504 U.S. 555 (1992).
7. Philip J. Cooper, *Hard Judicial Choices: Federal District Court Judges and State and Local Officials* (Oxford University Press, 1988), p. 15.
8. *Bordenkircher v. Hayes,* 434 U.S. 357 (1978). See also James Eisenstein, *Counsel for the United States: U.S. Attorneys in the Political and Legal Systems* (Johns Hopkins University Press, 1978).
9. *Luther v. Borden,* 7 Howard 1 (1849).
10. *Bush v. Gore,* 531 U.S. 98 (2000).
11. John Roche, "Judicial Self-Restraint," *American Political Science Review* 49 (1955), 762, 768.
12. See Charles Lopeman, *The Activist Advocate: Policymaking in State Supreme Courts* (Praeger, 2000), and Harry Stumpf and John H. Culver, *The Politics of State Courts* (Longman, 1992).

13. Eleanore Bushnell, *Crimes, Follies, and Misfortunes: The Federal Impeachment Trials* (University of Illinois Press, 1992), and Mary L. Volcansek, *None Called for Justice: Judicial Impeachment* (University of Illinois Press, 1993).

14. *Third Branch* (Administrative Office of the U.S. Courts, March 2002). For more information on the caseloads and operation of the federal courts, go to www.uscourts.gov.

15. C. K. Rowland, "The Federal District Courts," in *The American Courts: A Critical Assessment,* eds. John B. Gates and Charles A. Johnson (CQ Press, 1991), pp. 61–80.

16. *Peretz* v. *United States,* 501 U.S. 923 (1991).

17. See Christopher P. Banks, *Judicial Politics in the D.C. Circuit* (Johns Hopkins University Press, 1999), and Donald R. Songer and Susan B. Haire, *Continuity and Change in the United States Courts of Appeals* (University of Michigan Press, 2000).

18. See *Anastasoff* v. *United States,* 223 F.3d 898 (2000), and Jerome I. Braun, "Eighth Circuit Decision Intensifies Debate over Publication and Citation of Appellate Opinions," *Judicature* 83 (September–October 2000).

19. Neil D. McFeeley, *Appointment of Judges: The Johnson Presidency* (University of Texas Press, 1987), p. 1.

20. Harold W. Chase, *Federal Judges: The Appointing Process* (University of Minnesota Press, 1972); Sheldon Goldman, *Picking Federal Judges: Lower Court Selection from Roosevelt Through Reagan* (Yale University Press, 1997).

21. See Brannon P. Denning, "The Judicial Confirmation Process and the Blue Slip," *Judicature* (March–April 2002), pp. 218–226.

22. Lisa M. Holmes and Roger E. Hartley, "Increasing Senate Scrutiny of Lower Federal Court Nominees," *Judicature* (May–June 1997), p. 275.

23. George Watson and John Stookey, "Supreme Court Confirmation Hearings: A View from the Senate," *Judicature* (December 1987–January 1988), p. 193. See also John Massaro, *Supremely Political: The Role of Ideology and Presidential Management in Unsuccessful Supreme Court Nominations* (State University of New York Press, 1990).

24. Barbara A. Perry and Henry J. Abraham, "A 'Representative' Supreme Court? The Thomas, Ginsburg, and Breyer Appointments," *Judicature* (January–February 1998), pp. 158–165.

25. Goldman, *Picking Federal Judges,* pp. 161, 327–336.

26. Sheldon Goldman, "Bush's Judicial Legacy: The Final Imprint," *Judicature* (April–May 1993), p. 291.

27. Eleanor Dean Acheson, quoted in David M. O'Brien, "Judicial Legacies: The Clinton Presidency and the Courts," in *The Clinton Legacy,* eds. Colin Campbell and Burt A. Rockman (Chatham House, 2000), p. 101.

28. Robert A. Carp and C. K. Rowland, *Politics and Judgment in Federal District Courts* (University Press of Kansas, 1996).

29. Sheldon Goldman, "Reagan's Judicial Legacy: Completing the Puzzle and Summing Up," *Judicature* (April–May 1989), pp. 318–330.

30. Robert A. Carp, Donald Songer, C. K. Rowland, Ronald Stidham, and Lisa Richey-Tracey, "The Voting Behavior of Judges Appointed by President Bush," *Judicature* (April–May 1993), pp. 298–302.

31. David G. Savage, *Turning Right: The Making of the Rehnquist Supreme Court* (Wiley, 1992).

32. Naftali Bendavid, "Diversity Marks Clinton Judiciary," *Recorder* (December 30, 1993), p. 11.

33. O'Brien, "Judicial Legacies," pp. 96–117.

34. Tom Curry, "Bush Uses Judges as Campaign Issue: GOP Senate Majority Would Solve Impasse over Judicial Nominees," MSNBC, March 29, 2002.

35. Jeremiah Smith, quoted in Paul E. Freund, *Understanding the Supreme Court* (Little, Brown, 1949), p. 3.

36. Felix Frankfurter, letter to Justice Hugo Black, December 15, 1939, quoted in David M. O'Brien, *Constitutional Law and Politics,* 5th ed. (Norton, 2002), p. 74.

37. See Benjamin N. Cardozo, *The Nature of the Judicial Process* (Yale University Press, 1921), a classic. See also Saul Brenner and Harold Spaeth, *Stare Indecisis* (Cambridge University Press, 1995).

38. William O. Douglas, quoted in David M. O'Brien, *Storm Center: The Supreme Court in American Politics,* 6th ed. (Norton, 2003), p. 184.

39. Ibid., p. 30 (figures as of the end of the 2001–2002 term).

40. William Howard Taft, letter to Horace Taft, November 14, 1929; quoted in Henry Pringle, *The Life and Times of William Howard Taft* (Farrar, 1939), vol. 2, p. 967.

41. See David N. Atkinson, *Leaving the Bench: Supreme Court Justices at the End* (University Press of Kansas, 1999).

42. David M. O'Brien, *Judicial Roulette: Report of the Twentieth Century Fund Task Force on Judicial Selection* (Priority Press Publications, 1988), pp. 10–11.

43. White Burkett Miller Center of Public Affairs, *Improving the Process of Appointing Federal Judges* (Miller Center, University of Virginia, 1996).

44. See Citizens for Independent Courts Task Force on Federal Judicial Selection, *Justice Held Hostage: Politics and Selecting Federal Judges* (Century Foundation, 2000).

45. Donald Santarelli, quoted in Jerry Landauer, "Shaping the Bench," *Wall Street Journal,* December 10, 1970, p. 1. See also J. W. Peltason, *Federal Courts in the Political Process* (Doubleday, 1955), p. 32.

46. Michael A. Kahn, "The Appointment of a Supreme Court Justice: A Political Process from Beginning to End," *Presidential Studies Quarterly* 25 (Winter 1995), pp. 26, 39.

47. Ex parte *McCardle,* 74 U.S. 506 (1869).

48. Barry Friedman, "Attacks on Judges: Why They Fail," *Judicature* (January–February 1998), p. 152.

49. Tony Mauro, "Yipes! Stripes!" *Recorder,* February 8, 1995, p. 8.

50. William H. Rehnquist, quoted in John R. Vile, "The Selection and Tenure of Chief Justices," *Judicature* (September–October 1994), p. 98.

51. David Danelski, "The Influence of the Chief Justice in the Decisional Process of the Supreme Court," in *The Federal Judicial System: Readings in Process and Behavior,* eds. Thomas P. Jahnige and Sheldon Goldman (Holt, Rinehart and Winston, 1968), p. 148.

52. Robert J. Steamer, *Chief Justice: Leadership and the Supreme Court* (University of South Carolina Press, 1986).

53. Sue Davis, "The Supreme Court: Rehnquist's or Reagan's," *Western Political Quarterly* 44 (March 1991), p. 98. See also Sue Davis, *Justice Rehnquist and the Constitution* (Princeton University Press, 1989).

54. Savage, *Turning Right.*

55. David M. O'Brien, "The Rehnquist Court's Shrinking Plenary Docket," *Judicature* (September–October 1997), p. 58.

56. O'Brien, *Storm Center,* p. 63.

57. See H. W. Perry Jr., *Deciding to Decide: Agenda Setting in the United States Supreme Court* (Harvard University Press, 1991).

58. Edward Lazarus, *Closed Chambers: The First Eyewitness Account of the Epic Struggles Inside the Supreme Court* (Times Books/Random House, 1998).

59. O'Brien, *Storm Center.*

60. Lincoln Caplan, *The Tenth Justice: The Solicitor General and the Rule of Law* (Knopf, 1987); Rebecca Mae Salokar, *The Solicitor General: The Politics of Law* (Temple University Press, 1992).

61. Charles Fried, *Order and Law: Arguing the Reagan Revolution—A Firsthand Account* (Simon & Schuster, 1991).

62. Jeffrey A. Segal and Robert M. Howard, "How Supreme Court Justices Respond to Litigant Requests to Overturn Precedent," *Judicature* (November–December 2001), pp. 148–157.

63. Gregory A. Caldeira and John R. Wright, "Organized Interest and Agenda Setting in the U.S. Supreme Court," *American Political Science Review* 82 (December 1988), p. 1110; Donald R. Songer and Reginald S. Sheehan, "Interest Groups' Success in the Courts: *Amicus* Participation in the Supreme Court," *Political Research Quarterly* 46 (June 1993), pp. 339–354.

64. *Webster* v. *Reproductive Health Services,* 492 U.S. 490 (1989); *Roe* v. *Wade,* 410 U.S. 113 (1973); Susan Behuniak-Long, "Friendly Fire: *Amici Curiae* and *Webster* v. *Reproductive Health Services,*" *Judicature* (February–March 1991), pp. 261–270.

65. *United States* v. *Lopez,* 514 U.S. 549 (1951).

66. Caldeira and Wright, "Organized Interest and Agenda Setting"; Songer and Sheehan, "Interest Groups' Success in the Courts," *American Political Science Review* 82 (December 1988), p. 1118.

67. Tony Mauro, "The Supreme Court as Quiz Show," *Recorder,* December 8, 1993, p. 10.

68. Joyce O'Connor, "Selections from Notes Kept on an Internship at the U.S. Supreme Court, Fall 1988," *Law, Courts, and Judicial Process* 6 (Spring 1989), p. 44.

69. Tony Mauro, "No Comfort for Counsel After Court Review," *Recorder,* November 10, 1997, p. 8.

70. Mauro, "Yipes! Stripes!" p. 8.

71. Joan Biskupie, "Supreme Court Film Offers Glimpse Behind Justices' Closed Doors," *Washington Post,* June 17, 1997, p. A15.

72. William H. Rehnquist, *The Supreme Court: How It Was, How It Is* (Morrow, 1987), pp. 289–290.

73. Forrest Maltzman, James F. Spriggs III, and Paul Wahlbeck, *Crafting Law on the Supreme Court: The Collegial Game* (Cambridge University Press, 2000).

74. Daniel M. Berman, *It Is So Ordered: The Supreme Court Rules on School Segregation* (Norton, 1986), p. 114; Walter F. Murphy, *Elements of Judicial Strategy* (University of Chicago Press, 1964), p. 66; O'Brien, *Storm Center,* pp. 262–272.

75. Charles Evans Hughes, quoted in Donald E. Lively, *Foreshadows of the Law: Supreme Court Dissents and Constitutional Development* (Praeger, 1992), p. xx.

76. *Brown v. Board of Education of Topeka,* 347 U.S. 483 (1954).

77. *United States v. Nixon,* 418 U.S. 683 (1974).

78. Gerald N. Rosenberg, *Hollow Hope: Can Courts Bring About Sound Change?* (University of Chicago Press, 1991).

79. J. W. Peltason, *Fifty-Eight Lonely Men: Southern Federal Judges and School Desegregation* (University of Illinois Press, 1971); Gary Orfield, Susan E. Eaton, and the Harvard Project on School Desegregation, *Dismantling Segregation* (New Press, 1996).

80. See Shawn Francis Peters, *Judging the Jehovah's Witnesses* (University of Kansas Press, 2002); Clyde Wilcox, *Onward, Christian Soldiers? The Religious Right in American Politics* (Westview Press, 1996); Mark Tushnet, *The NAACP's Legal Strategy Against Segregated Education, 1925–1950* (University of North Carolina Press, 1987); and Karen O'Connor, *Women's Organizations' Use of the Court* (Lexington Books, 1980).

81. Cooper, *Hard Judicial Choices,* pp. 347–350.

82. Arthur S. Miller, "In Defense of Judicial Activism," in *Supreme Court Activism and Restraint,* eds. Stephen C. Halpern and Charles M. Lamb (Heath, 1982), p. 177. See also Richard Neely, *How Courts Govern America* (Yale University Press, 1981).

83. *United States v. Carolene Products,* 304 U.S. 144 (1938). Variations on this basic position have been restated in dozens of books. Halpern and Lamb, *Supreme Court Activism and Restraint,* and Mark Tushnet, *Red, White, and Blue: A Critical Analysis of Constitutional Law* (Harvard University Press, 1988), provide analysis from all perspectives. For another analysis of this great debate, see Lief H. Carter, *Contemporary Constitutional Lawmaking* (Pergamon Press, 1985). See also Terri Jennings Peretti, *In Defense of a Political Court* (Princeton University Press, 1999), and Stephen Macedo, *The New Right v. the Constitution* (Cato, 1986). Leslie F. Goldstein, "Judicial Review and Democratic Theory: Guardian Democracy vs. Representative Democracy," *Western Political Quarterly* 40 (September 1987), pp. 391–412, contains a useful bibliography.

84. J. W. Peltason, "The Supreme Court: Transactional or Transformational Leadership," in *Essays in Honor of James MacGregor Burns,* eds. Michael R. Beschloss and Thomas E. Cronin (Prentice Hall, 1988), pp. 165–180; Mark Silverstein and Benjamin Ginsburg, "The Supreme Court and the New Politics of Judicial Power," *Political Science Quarterly* 102 (Fall 1987), pp. 371–388.

85. *Planned Parenthood v. Casey,* 505 U.S. 833 (1992).

86. Thomas R. Marshall, *Public Opinion and the Supreme Court* (Unwin Hyman, 1989), p. 193. See also William Mishler and Reginald S. Sheehan, "The Supreme Court as a Counter-Majoritarian Institution: The Impact of Public Opinion on Supreme Court Decisions," *American Political Science Review* 87 (January 1993), pp. 87–101, and Helmut Norpoth and Jeffrey A. Segal, "Popular Influence on Supreme Court Decisions," *American Political Science Review* 88 (September 1994), pp. 711–724.

87. See John B. Gates, *The Supreme Court and Partisan Realignment* (Westview Press, 1992).

88. Rosenberg, *Hollow Hope,* p. 343.

89. Rehnquist, *Supreme Court,* p. 98.

90. Gallup Organization, "Confidence in Institutions," June 8–10, 2001, at www.gallup.com; Herbert Kritzer, "The Impact of *Bush v. Gore* on Public Perceptions and Knowledge of the Supreme Court," *Judicature* (July–August 2001), pp. 32–38.

91. Edward White, "The Supreme Court of the United States," *American Bar Association Journal* 7 (1921), p. 341.

Chapter 16

1. Jeffrey Smith, *War and Press Freedom* (Oxford University Press, 1999); Richard W. Steel, *Free Speech and the Good War* (St. Martin's Press, 1999).

2. *Felker v. Turpin,* 518 U.S. 651 (1996); *Winthrow v. Williams,* 507 U.S. 680 (1993); *McCleskey v. Zant,* 499 U.S. 467 (1991); *Stone v. Powell,* 428 U.S. 465 (1976).

3. *United States v. Lovett,* 328 U.S. 303 (1946).

4. Neil H. Cogan, ed., *The Complete Bill of Rights: The Drafts, Debates, Sources, and Origins* (Oxford University Press, 1997); Robert A. Rutland, *The Birth of the Bill of Rights, 1776–1791* (University of North Carolina Press, 1955).

5. *Barron v. Baltimore,* 7 Peters 243 (1833).

6. *Gitlow v. New York,* 268 U.S. 652 (1925).

7. Richard C. Cortner, *The Supreme Court and the Second Bill of Rights: The Fourteenth Amendment and the Nationalization of Civil Liberties* (University of Wisconsin Press, 1981).

8. Dorothy Toth Beasley, "Federalism and the Protection of Individual Rights: The American State Constitutional Perspective," in *Federalism and Rights,* ed. Ellis Katz and G. Alan Tarr (Rowman & Littlefield, 1996); Charles Lopeman, *The Activist Advocate: Policymaking in State Supreme Courts* (Praeger, 1999).

9. *Witters v. Washington Department of Services for the Blind,* 474 U.S. 481 (1986); *Zobrest v. Catalina Foothills School District,* 509 U.S. 1 (1993).

10. *Everson v. Board of Education of Ewing Township,* 333 U.S. 203 (1947).

11. *Lemon v. Kurtzman,* 403 U.S. 602 (1971).

12. *Capital Square Review Board v. Pinette,* 515 U.S. 753 (1995).

13. *Lynch v. Donnelly,* 465 U.S. 669 (1984).

14. *Allegheny County v. Greater Pittsburgh ACLU,* 492 U.S. 573 (1989).

15. *Bowen v. Kendrick,* 487 U.S. 589 (1988); *Lee v. Weisman,* 505 U.S. 577 (1992); *Board of Education of Kiryas Joel Village School District v. Grumet,* 512 U.S. 687 (1994).

16. *Mitchell v. Helms,* 530 U.S. 793 (2000).

17. *Agostini v. Felton,* 521 U.S. 74 (1997).

18. *Lee v. Weisman,* 505 U.S. 577 (1992); *Santa Fe Independent School District v. Doe,* 530 U.S. 290 (2000).

19. *Engel v. Vitale,* 370 U.S. 421 (1962).

20. *Edwards v. Aguillard,* 482 U.S. 578 (1987).

21. *Marsh v. Chambers,* 463 U.S. 783 (1983).

22. *Witters v. Washington Department of Services for the Blind,* 474 U.S. 481 (1986).

23. *Mueller v. Allen,* 463 U.S. 388 (1983).

24. *Zobrest v. Catalina Foothills School District,* 515 U.S. 1 (1993); *Agostini v. Felton,* 521 U.S. 74 (1997); *Mitchell v. Helms,* 530 U.S. 793 (2000).

25. Mark Walker, "State Voucher Programs," *Education Week,* October 3, 2001, p. 33.

26. *Zelman v. Simmons-Harris,* 122 S.Ct. 2460 (2002).

27. *Employment Division of Human Resources of Oregon v. Smith,* 494 U.S. 872 (1990).

28. *City of Boerne v. Flores,* 521 U.S. 507 (1997).

29. *Rosenberger v. University of Virginia,* 515 U.S. 819 (1995).

30. *Board of Regents of the University of Wisconsin System v. Southworth,* 529 U.S. 217 (2000).

31. Oliver Wendell Holmes Jr., in *Abrams v. United States,* 250 U.S. 616 (1919).

32. John Stuart Mill, *Essay on Liberty,* in *The English Philosophers from Bacon to Mill,* ed. Arthur Burtt (Random House, 1939), p. 961.

33. Robert Jackson, in *West Virginia State Board of Education v. Barnette,* 319 U.S. 624 (1943).

34. *Brown v. Hartlage,* 456 U.S. 45 (1982), reversing a decision of the Kentucky Court of Appeals based on the bad tendency test.

35. Oliver Wendell Holmes Jr., in *Schenck v. United States,* 249 U.S. 47 (1919).

36. *Dennis v. United States,* 341 U.S. 494 (1951).

37. *New York Times v. Sullivan,* 376 U.S. 254 (1964).

38. *Yates v. United States,* 354 U.S. 298 (1957).

39. *Brandenburg v. Ohio,* 395 U.S. 444 (1969).

40. *New York Times v. Sullivan,* 376 U.S. 254 (1964).

41. *Hustler Magazine v. Falwell,* 485 U.S. 46 (1988).

42. *Masson v. New York Magazine, Inc.,* 501 U.S. 496 (1991).

43. *Gertz v. Robert Welch, Inc.,* 418 U.S. 323 (1974).

44. Potter Stewart, concurring in *Jacobellis v. Ohio,* 378 U.S. 184 (1964).

45. John Marshall Harlan, in *Cohen v. California,* 403 U.S. 15 (1971).

46. *Miller v. California,* 413 U.S. 15 (1973).

47. *Young v. American Mini Theatres, Inc.,* 427 U.S. 51 (1976); *Renton v. Playtime Theatres, Inc.,* 475 U.S. 41 (1986); *City of Los Angeles v. Alameda Books, Inc.,* 122 S.Ct. . . . . (2002).

48. *Barnes v. Glen Theatre, Inc.,* 501 U.S. 560 (1991); *City of Erie v. Pap's A.M.,* 529 U.S. 277 (2000).

49. *New York v. Ferber,* 458 U.S. 747 (1982); *Ashcroft v. Free Speech Coalition,* 122 S.Ct. 1389 (2002).

50. *General Media Communications v. Cohen,* 524 U.S. 951 (1998).

51. See Catharine A. MacKinnon, *Only Words* (Harvard University Press, 1993), and compare another feminist, Nadine Strossen, *Defending Pornography: Free Speech, Sex, and the Fight for Women's Rights* (Scribner, 1995).

52. *Butler v. Her Majesty the Queen,* 1 S.C.R. 452 (1992).

53. *Chaplinsky v. New Hampshire,* 315 U.S. 568 (1942).

54. *Cohen* v. *California*, 403 U.S. 115 (1971).

55. *R.A.V.* v. *St. Paul*, 505 U.S. 377 (1992). See also *Wisconsin* v. *Mitchell*, 508 U.S. 476 (1993); and *Apprendi* v. *New Jersey*, 530 U.S. 466 (2000).

56. *44 Liquormart, Inc.*, v. *Rhode Island*, 517 U.S. 484 (1996).

57. *New York Times Company* v. *United States*, 403 U.S. 670 (1970).

58. *Near* v. *Minnesota*, 283 U.S. 697 (1930); ibid.

59. *Hazelwood School District* v. *Kuhlmeier*, 484 U.S. 260 (1988).

60. *R.A.V.* v. *St. Paul*, 505 U.S. 377 (1992). See also *Wisconsin* v. *Mitchell*, 508 U.S. 476 (1993).

61. *Branzburg* v. *Hayes*, 408 U.S. 665 (1972).

62. *Richmond Newspapers, Inc.*, v. *Virginia*, 448 U.S. 555 (1980). See also David M. O'Brien, *The Public's Right to Know: The Supreme Court and the First Amendment* (Praeger, 1981).

63. Oliver Wendell Holmes Jr., dissenting in *Milwaukee Publishing Co.* v. *Burleson*, 255 U.S. 407 (1921).

64. *Lamont* v. *Postmaster General*, 381 U.S. 301 (1965).

65. *Rowan* v. *Post Office Department*, 397 U.S. 728 (1970).

66. *McIntyre* v. *Ohio Election Commission*, 514 U.S. 334 (1995).

67. *Southeastern Promotions, Ltd.*, v. *Conrad*, 420 U.S. 546 (1975).

68. *Federal Communications Commission* v. *Pacifica Foundation*, 438 U.S. 726 (1978).

69. *Turner Broadcasting System* v. *Federal Communications Commission*, 518 U.S. 180 (1997).

70. *United States* v. *Playboy Entertainment Group*, 529 U.S. 803 (2000); *Denver Area Educational Television* v. *Federal Communications Commission*, 518 U.S. 727 (1996).

71. See and compare *Federal Communications Commission* v. *Pacifica Foundation*, 438 U.S. 726 (1978), and *Sable Communications* v. *Federal Communications Commission*, 492 U.S. 115 (1989).

72. *Reno* v. *American Civil Liberties Union*, 117 S.Ct. 2329 (1997).

73. Freedom Forum Online at www.freedomforum.org/assembly/1998/9/2/march.asp.

74. Lee C. Bollinger, *Images of a Free Press* (University of Chicago Press, 1991).

75. *Walker* v. *Birmingham*, 388 U.S. 307 (1967).

76. *Madsen* v. *Women's Health Center*, 512 U.S. 753 (1994); *Schenck* v. *Pro-Choice Network*, 519 U.S. 357 (1997); *Hill* v. *Colorado*, 530 U.S. 703 (2000).

77. *West Virginia State Board of Education* v. *Barnette*, 319 U.S. 624 (1943).

Chapter 17

1. *Vance* v. *Terrazas*, 444 U.S. 252 (1980).

2. G. Pascal Zachary, "Dual Citizenship Is Double-Edged Sword," *Wall Street Journal*, March 25, 1998, pp. B1, B15, quoting T. Alexander Aleinikoff of the Carnegie Endowment for International Peace. See also Mark Fritz, "Dual Citizenships Create Dueling Family Allegiances," *Los Angeles Times*, April 6, 1998, p. A1, and William Branigin, "Pledging Allegiance to Two Flags," *Washington Post National Weekly Edition*, June 8, 1998, p. 14.

3. *Slaughter-House Cases*, 83 U.S. 36 (1873).

4. *Ex Parte Milligan*, 71 U.S. 2 (1866).

5. *Korematsu* v. *United States*, 323 U.S. 214 (1944).

6. *Ex Parte Quirin*, 317 U.S. 1 (1942).

7. *Reid* v. *Covert*, 354 U.S. 1 (1957).

8. Dan Eggan and Susan Schmidt, "Suspected al-Qaeda Operative Held as 'Enemy Combatant,'" *Washington Post*, June 11, 2002, p. A1.

9. See Laurence H. Tribe, "Citizens, Combatants, and the Constitution," *New York Times*, June 16, 2002, p. WK13.

10. *Plyler* v. *Doe*, 457 U.S. 202 (1982).

11. Karen De Young, "Bush Lowers Refugee Quota to 70,000," *Washington Post*, November 22, 2001, p. A45.

12. *Sale* v. *Haitian Centers Council, Inc.*, 509 U.S. 155 (1993).

13. Christopher Marquis, "Census Bureau Estimates 115,000 Middle Eastern Immigrants Are in the U.S. Illegally," *New York Times*, January 23, 2002, p. A10.

14. Francis X. Clines, "Harsh Civics Lesson for Immigrants," *New York Times*, November 11, 2001, p. B7.

15. *Chicago Home Building & Loan Association* v. *Blaisdell*, 290 U.S. 398 (1934).

16. *Chicago, Burlington & Quincy Railway Co.* v. *Chicago*, 166 U.S. 226 (1897).

17. *First English Evangelical* v. *Los Angeles County*, 482 U.S. 304 (1987). See Richard A. Epstein, *Taking: Private Property and the Power of Eminent Domain* (Harvard University Press, 1985).

18. *Lucas* v. *South Carolina Coastal Commission*, 505 U.S. 647 (1992).

19. *Tahoe-Sierra Council, Inc.*, v. *Tahoe Regional Planning Agency*, 122 S.Ct. 1465 (2002).

20. *United States* v. *564.54 Acres of Land*, 441 U.S. 506 (1979).

21. *Mathews* v. *Eldridge*, 424 U.S. 319 (1976), restated in *Connecticut* v. *Doeher*, 501 U.S. 1 (1991).

22. *Meyer* v. *Nebraska*, 262 U.S. 390 (1923).

23. *Lochner* v. *New York*, 198 U.S. 45 (1905).

24. *Griswold* v. *Connecticut*, 381 U.S. 479 (1965).

25. Philip B. Kurland, *Some Reflections on Privacy and the Constitution* (University of Chicago Center for Policy Study, 1976), p. 9. A classic and influential article about privacy is Samuel D. Warren and Louis D. Brandeis, "The Right to Privacy," *Harvard Law Review*, December 15, 1890, pp. 193–220.

26. *Roe* v. *Wade*, 410 U.S. 113 (1973).

27. *Planned Parenthood of Southeastern Pennsylvania* v. *Casey*, 505 U.S. 833 (1992).

28. *Stenberg* v. *Carhart*, 530 U.S. 914 (2000).

29. *Bowers* v. *Hardwick*, 478 U.S. 186 (1986).

30. *Baker* v. *Vermont*, 744 A.2d 864 (1999); *Powell* v. *Georgia*, 510 S.E.2d 18 (1998); *Kentucky* v. *Wasson*, 842 S.W.2d 487 (1992).

31. "Family Feeling," *Economist*, March 30, 2002, pp. 27–28.

32. *Boy Scouts of America* v. *Dale*, 530 U.S. 640 (2000).

33. Antonin Scalia, dissenting in *Romer* v. *Evans*, 517 U.S. 620 (1996).

34. But see *Washington* v. *Chrisman*, 455 U.S. 1 (1982).

35. *Katz* v. *United States*, 389 U.S. 347 (1967).

36. *County of Riverside* v. *McLaughlin*, 500 U.S. 44 (1991).

37. *California* v. *Hodari D.*, 499 U.S. 621 (1991).

38. *Bond* v. *United States*, 529 U.S. 334 (2000).

39. *Terry* v. *Ohio*, 392 U.S. 1 (1968).

40. *Minnesota* v. *Dickerson*, 508 U.S. 366 (1993).

41. *Almeida-Sanchez* v. *United States*, 413 U.S. 266 (1973); *United States* v. *Ortiz*, 422 U.S. 891 (1975).

42. *United States* v. *Ramsey*, 431 U.S. 606 (1977).

43. *Coolidge* v. *New Hampshire*, 403 U.S. 443 (1971); *Arizona* v. *Hicks*, 480 U.S. 321 (1987).

44. *United States* v. *Ross*, 456 U.S. 798 (1982).

45. *Pennsylvania* v. *Mimms*, 434 U.S. 110 (1977), reaffirmed in *Ohio* v. *Robinette*, 519 U.S. 33 (1997).

46. *Chandler* v. *Miller*, 520 U.S. 305 (1997).

47. Randall Kennedy, *Race, Crime, and the Law* (Pantheon Books, 1997), pp. 136–168; David Cole, *No Equal Justice: Race and Class in the American Criminal Justice System* (New Press, 1999).

48. George Lardner, "On the Left and Right, Concern over Anti-Terrorism," *Washington Post*, November 16, 2001, p. A40.

49. *Treasury Employees* v. *Von Raab*, 489 U.S. 656 (1989); *Skinner* v. *Railway Labor Executives' Association*, 489 U.S. 602 (1989); *Vernonia School District 47J* v. *Action*, 515 U.S. 646 (1995); *Chandler* v. *Miller*, 520 U.S. 305 (1997).

50. *Board of Education of Independent School District No. 2 of Pottawatomie City* v. *Earls*, 122 S.Ct. 2559 (2002).

51. *Mapp* v. *Ohio*, 367 U.S. 643 (1961).

52. Senate Committee on the Judiciary, *The Jury and the Search for Truth: The Case Against Excluding Relevant Evidence at Trial: Hearing Before the Committee*, 104th Cong., 1st sess., (U.S. Government Printing Office, 1997).

53. *United States* v. *Leon*, 468 U.S. 897 (1984); *Arizona* v. *Evans*, 514 U.S. 1 (1995).

54. *Miranda* v. *Arizona*, 384 U.S. 436 (1966).

55. *Dickerson* v. *United States*, 530 U.S. 428 (2000).

56. Justice Felix Frankfurter, dissenting in *United States* v. *Rabinowitz*, 339 U.S. 56 (1950).

57. *United States* v. *Enterprises, Inc.*, 498 U.S. 292 (1991).

58. *Williams* v. *Florida*, 399 U.S. 78 (1970); *Burch* v. *Louisiana*, 441 U.S. 130 (1979).

59. *J.E.B.* v. *Alabama ex rel T.B.*, 511 U.S. 127 (1994); *Batson* v. *Kentucky*, 476 U.S. 79 (1986); *Powers* v. *Ohio*, 499 U.S. 400 (1991); *Hernandez* v. *New York*, 500 U.S. 352 (1991); *Georgia* v. *McCollum*, 505 U.S. 42 (1990).

60. "The Three-Strikes Law," *Economist*, April 6, 2002, p. 30.

61. *Benton* v. *Maryland*, 395 U.S. 784 (1969). See also *Kansas* v. *Hendricks*, 521 U.S. 346 (1997).

62. *Graham* v. *Collins*, 506 U.S. 461 (1993).

63. Lori Montgomery, "Maryland Suspends Death Penalty," *Washington Post,* May 10, 2002, p. A1.
64. *Penry v. Lynaugh,* 492 U.S. 302 (1989).
65. *Atkins v. Virginia,* 122 S.Ct. 2242 (2002).
66. Jerome Frank, *Courts on Trial* (Princeton University Press, 1949), p. 122. See also Steven Brill, *Trial by Jury* (American Lawyer Books/Touchstone, 1989).
67. Harry Kalven Jr. and Hans Zeisel, *The American Jury* (University of Chicago Press, 1971), p. 57. See also Jeffrey Abramson, *We, the Jury: The Jury System and the Ideal of Democracy* (Basic Books, 1994).
68. George Edwards, *The Police on the Urban Frontier* (Institute of Human Relations Press, 1968), p. 28. See also Jerome G. Miller, *African-American Males and the Criminal Justice System* (Cambridge University Press, 1996).
69. Sandra Bass, "Blacks, Browns, and the Blues: Police and Minorities in California," *Public Affairs Report* 38 (November 1997), p. 10.
70. See David Cole, *No Equal Justice: Race and Class in the American Criminal Justice System* (New Press, 1999); and Randall Kennedy, *Race, Crime, and the Law* (Pantheon, 1997).
71. See "Understanding Community Policing" (Bureau of Justice Administration), at www.community_policy.org.
72. Robert H. Jackson, *The Supreme Court in the American System of Government* (Harvard University Press, 1955), pp. 81–82.

Chapter 18

1. Andrew Hacker, *Two Nations: Black and White, Separate, Hostile, Unequal* (Scribner, 1992).
2. *Slaughter-House Cases,* 83 U.S. 36 (1873); *Civil Rights Cases,* 109 U.S. 3 (1883).
3. *Plessy v. Ferguson,* 163 U.S. 537 (1896).
4. *Brown v. Board of Education of Topeka,* 347 U.S. 483 (1954); *Brown v. Board of Education of Topeka,* 349 U.S. 294 (1955).
5. *Gomillion v. Lightfoot,* 364 U.S. 339 (1960).
6. Michael R. Belknap, *Federal Law and Southern Order: Racial Violence and Constitutional Conflict in the Post-Brown South* (University of Georgia Press, 1987), pp. 128–204.
7. Taylor Branch, *Parting the Waters: America in the King Years, 1954–1963* (Simon & Schuster, 1988). See also Harris Wofford, *Of Kennedys and Kings: Making Sense of the Sixties* (Farrar, Straus & Giroux, 1980).
8. See Charles Whalen and Barbara Whalen, *The Longest Debate: A Legislative History of the 1964 Civil Rights Act* (Mentor, 1985), and Hugh Davis Graham, *The Civil Rights Era* (Oxford University Press, 1990).
9. Aldon D. Morris, *The Origins of the Civil Rights Movement: Black Communities Organizing for Change* (Free Press/Macmillan, 1985); James Farmer, *Lay Bare the Heart: An Autobiography of the Civil Rights Movement* (Arbor House, 1985).
10. National Advisory Commission on Civil Disorders, *The Kerner Report* (U.S. Government Printing Office, 1968), p. 1.
11. Ellen Carol Du Bois, *Feminism and Suffrage: The Emergence of an Independent Women's Movement in America, 1848–1869* (Cornell University Press, 1978); Joan Hoff-Wilson, "Women and the Constitution," *News for Teachers of Political Science* (Summer 1985), pp. 10–15.
12. Susan M. Hartmann, *From Margin to Mainstream: American Women and Politics Since 1960* (Temple University Press, 1989); Susan Gluck Mezey, *In Pursuit of Equality: Women, Public Policy, and the Federal Courts* (St. Martin's Press, 1992).
13. *United States v. Virginia,* 518 U.S. 515 (1996). See also Philippa Strum, *Women in the Barracks: The VMI Case and Equal Rights* (University Press of Kansas, 2002).
14. David M. O'Brien, "Ironies and Unanticipated Consequences of Legislation: Title VII of the 1964 Civil Rights Act and Sexual Harassment," in *Congress and the Politics of Emerging Rights,* eds. Colton C. Campbell and John F. Stack Jr. (Rowman & Littlefield, 2002), pp. 27–44.
15. *Meritor Savings Bank, FBD, v. Vinson,* 477 U.S. 57 (1986).
16. *Oncale v. Sundowner Offshore Services,* 523 U.S. 75 (1998); *Faragher v. City of Boca Raton,* 524 U.S. 775 (1998); *Burlington Industries v. Ellerth,* 524 U.S. 742 (1998).
17. Gregory Rodriguez, "The Nation: Where Minorities Rule," *New York Times,* February 10, 2002, p. WK6.
18. Celia W. Dugger, "U.S. Study Says Asian-Americans Face Widespread Discrimination," *New York Times,* February 29, 1992, p. 1, reporting on U.S. Civil Rights Commission, *Civil Rights Issues Facing Asian Americans in the 1990s* (U.S. Government Printing Office, 1992).
19. Won Moo Hurh, *Korean Immigrants in America* (Fairleigh Dickinson University Press, 1984).
20. Antonio J. A. Pido, *The Filipinos in America: Macro/Micro Dimensions of Immigration and Integration* (Center for Migration Studies of New York, 1986).
21. Harold L. Hodgkinson, *The Demographics of American Indians: One Percent of the People, Fifty Percent of the Diversity* (Institute for Educational Leadership/Center for Demographic Policy, 1990), pp. 1–5.
22. Charles F. Wilkinson, *American Indians, Times, and the Law* (Yale University Press, 1987); Vine Deloria Jr. and Clifford M. Lytle, *The Nations Within: The Past and Future of American Indian Sovereignty* (Pantheon Books, 1984).
23. *County of Yakima v. Yakima Indian Nation,* 502 U.S. 251 (1992).
24. Theodora Lurie, "Shattering the Myth of the Vanishing American," *Ford Foundation Letter* 22 (Winter 1991), p. 5.
25. Spencer Rich, "Native Americans: They Can Still Get Free Health Care If They're Indian Enough," *Washington Post National Weekly Edition,* July 14, 1986, p. 34, quoting the Office of Technology Assessment.
26. *Idaho Employment v. Smith,* 434 U.S. 1 (1974).
27. *San Antonio School District v. Rodriguez,* 411 U.S. 1 (1973).
28. *Frontiero v. Richardson,* 411 U.S. 677 (1973).
29. *Califano v. Webster,* 430 U.S. 313 (1977).
30. *Mississippi University for Women v. Hogan,* 458 U.S. 718 (1982); *United States v. Virginia,* 518 U.S. 515 (1996).
31. *San Antonio School District v. Rodriguez,* 411 U.S. 1 (1973).
32. Matthew Bosworth, *Courts as Catalysts: State Supreme Courts and Public School Finance Equity* (State University of New York Press, 2001).
33. Sandra Day O'Connor, in *Kimel v. Florida Board of Regents,* 528 U.S. 62 (2000).
34. Ibid.
35. *Washington v. Davis,* 426 U.S. 229 (1976). See also *Hunter v. Underwood,* 471 U.S. 522 (1985).
36. Sandra Day O'Connor, concurring in *Hernandez v. New York,* 500 U.S. 352 (1991).
37. *Personnel Administrator of Massachusetts v. Feeney,* 442 U.S. 256 (1979).
38. *Smith v. Allwright,* 321 U.S. 649 (1944).
39. *Gomillion v. Lightfoot,* 364 U.S. 339 (1960).
40. *Harper v. Virginia Board of Elections,* 383 U.S. 663 (1966).
41. *Report of the United States Commission on Civil Rights* (U.S. Government Printing Office, 1959), pp. 103–104.
42. Harold W. Stanley, *Voter Mobilization and the Politics of Race: The South and Universal Suffrage, 1952–1984* (Praeger, 1987).
43. Abigail M. Thernstrom, *Whose Votes Count? Affirmative Action and Minority Voting Rights* (Harvard University Press, 1987), p. 15.
44. Thernstrom, *Whose Votes Count?* For a contrary view, see Bernard Grofman, Lisa Handley, and Richard G. Niemi, *Minority Representation and the Quest for Voting Equality* (Cambridge University Press, 1992).
45. *Morse v. Republican Party of Virginia,* 517 U.S. 116 (1996).
46. *Shaw v. Reno,* 509 U.S. 630 (1993).
47. *Hunt v. Cromartie,* 121 U.S. 1452 (2001).
48. Orlando Patterson, *The Ordeal of Integration: Progress and Resentment in America's "Racial" Crisis* (Civitas/Counterpoint, 1997), p. 67.
49. *Plessy v. Ferguson,* 163 U.S. 537 (1896).
50. *Brown v. Board of Education of Topeka,* 347 U.S. 483 (1954). See also J. W. Peltason, *Fifty-Eight Lonely Men: Southern Federal Judges and School Desegregation* (University of Illinois Press, 1971), p. 248.
51. *Brown v. Board of Education of Topeka,* 349 U.S. 294 (1955).
52. William Celis III, "Study Finds Rising Concentration of Black and Hispanic Students," *New York Times,* December 14, 1993, p. A1.
53. *Freeman v. Pitts,* 503 U.S. 467 (1992); *Missouri v. Jenkins,* 515 U.S. 70 (1995).
54. See Gary Orfield, Susan E. Eaton, and the Harvard Project on School Desegregation, *Dismantling Desegregation: The Quiet Reversal of Brown v. Board of Education* (New Press, 1996).

55. Raymond Hernandez, "NAACP Suspends Yonkers Leader After Criticism of Usefulness of School Busing," *New York Times,* November 1, 1995, p. A13.
56. Quoted in Peter Applebome, "Opponents' Moves Refueling Debate on School Busing," *New York Times,* September 26, 1995, p. A1.
57. William O. Douglas, dissenting in *Moose Lodge No. 107* v. *Irvis,* 407 U.S. 163 (1972).
58. *New York State Club Association* v. *New York City,* 487 U.S. 1 (1988).
59. *Boy Scouts of America* v. *Dale,* 530 U.S. 640 (2000).
60. *Civil Rights Cases,* 109 U.S. 3 (1883).
61. *Heart of Atlanta Motel* v. *United States,* 379 U.S. 421 (1964).
62. Darryl Van Duch, "Plagued by Politics, EEOC Backlog Grows," *Recorder,* August 18, 1998, p. 1; David Rovella, "EEOC Chairman Casellas: 'We Are Being Selective,'" *National Law Journal,* November 20, 1995, p. 1.
63. Charles M. Lamb, "Housing Discrimination and Segregation," *Catholic University Law Review* (Spring 1981), p. 370.
64. *Shelley* v. *Kraemer,* 334 U.S. 1 (1948).
65. Daniel Mitchell, quoted in CQ Researcher, *Housing Discrimination* 5 (February 24, 1995), p. 174.
66. John Marshall Harlan, dissenting in *Plessy* v. *Ferguson,* 163 U.S. 537 (1896).
67. *University of California Regents* v. *Bakke,* 438 U.S. 265 (1978). See Howard Ball, *The Bakke Case* (University Press of Kansas, 2000).
68. Sandra Day O'Connor, in *Richmond* v. *Croson,* 488 U.S. 469 (1989).
69. See *Adarand Constructors, Inc.,* v. *Pena,* 515 U.S. 2000 (1995).
70. *Shaw* v. *Reno,* 509 U.S. 630 (1993); *Miller* v. *Johnson,* 515 U.S. 900 (1995).
71. *Hopwood* v. *Texas,* 518 U.S. 1016 (1996).
72. Edward Walsh, "Affirmative Action's Confusing Curriculum," *Washington Post,* September 4, 2001, p. A2.
73. Michael Fletcher, "Use of Race in Law School Entry Upheld," *Washington Post,* May 15, 2002, p. A1.
74. "Affirmative Action in California Passed," *Economist,* April 8, 2000, p. 29.
75. Carol M. Swain et al., "When Whites and Blacks Agree: Fairness in Educational Opportunities," Institute of Governmental Studies, University of California at Berkeley, Working Paper 98-11, 1998, p. 6. See also Lee Sigelman and Susan Welch, *Black Americans' Views of Racial Inequality: The Dream Deferred* (Cambridge University Press, 1994), and Peter Skerry, "The Affirmative Action Paradox," *Society* 35 (September–October 1998), p. 11.
76. James Farmer, quoted in Rochelle L. Stanfield, "Black Complaints Haven't Translated into Political Organization and Power," *National Journal,* June 14, 1980, p. 465.
77. National Academy of Science, *A Common Destiny: Blacks and American Society* (National Academy Press, 1989); Donald Kinder and Lynn M. Sanders, *Divided by Color: Racial Politics and Democratic Ideals* (University of Chicago Press, 1996).
78. Gregory Rodriguez, "Where the Minorities Rule," *New York Times,* February 10, 2002, p. WK6.
79. Gary Orfield, "Separate Societies: Have the Kerner Warnings Come True?" in *Quiet Riots: Race and Poverty in the United States—The Kerner Report Twenty Years Later,* eds. Fred R. Harris and Roger W. Wilkins (Pantheon, 1988), p. 103. See also Nicholas Lehmann, *The Promised Land* (Knopf, 1991), and Desmond King, *Separate and Unequal* (Oxford University Press, 1995).
80. Patterson, *Ordeal of Integration,* p. 54.
81. Gary Orfield and Carole Ashkinaze, *The Closing Door: Conservative Policy and Black Opportunity* (University of Chicago Press, 1991), p. 26.
82. William J. Wilson, *The Truly Disadvantaged: The Inner City, the Underclass, and Public Policy* (University of Chicago Press, 1987), esp. chap. 5; Kevin Phillips, *The Politics of Rich and Poor* (Random House, 1995).
83. Orfield and Ashkinaze, *Closing Door,* pp. 221–234; A. Leon Higginbotham Jr., *Shades of Freedom* (Oxford University Press, 1996).

Chapter 19

1. Louis Uchitelle, "Job Cuts Take Heavy Toll on Telecom Industry," *New York Times,* June 29, 2002, p. B1.
2. See "National Debt," at www.jeffords.senate.gov/debt.html.
3. For a discussion of the budgetary cycle, see Allen Schick, *The Federal Budget: Politics, Policy, Process,* rev. ed. (Brookings Institution, 2000).
4. Efforts at past tax reform are described in Jeffrey H. Birnbaum and Alan S. Murray, *Showdown at Gucci Gulch: Lawmakers, Lobbyists, and the Unlikely Triumph of Tax Reform* (Vintage, 1988). See also Timothy J. Conlan, Margaret T. Wrightson, and David R. Beam, *Taxing Choices: The Politics of Tax Reform* (CQ Press, 1990).
5. Quoted in Frederick Lewis Allen, *Since Yesterday* (Harper, 1940), p. 64.
6. W. H. Beveridge, *The Pillars of Security* (Macmillan, 1943), p. 51.
7. The debate over Keynes and his economic theories is still alive in the United States. See Donald E. Moggridge, *Maynard Keynes: An Economist's Biography* (Routledge, 1992).
8. Environmental Working Group, at www.ewg.org.
9. Gary Burtless, Robert J. Lawrence, Robert E. Litan, and Robert J. Shapiro, *Globaphobia: Confronting Fears About Open Trade* (Brookings Institution, 1998), p. 29. For more information about GATT and the World Trade Organization, go to www.wto.org.
10. Mary Jordan, "Mexican Workers Pay for Success," *Washington Post,* June 20, 2002, p. A1.
11. Burtless et al., *Globaphobia,* p. 126.
12. Robert W. Crandall et al., *An Agenda for Federal Regulatory Reform* (American Enterprise Institute/Brookings Institution, 1997), p. 1.
13. Harold W. Stanley and Richard G. Niemi, *Vital Statistics in American Politics, 1999* (CQ Press, 1999), p. 258.
14. Stephen Moore, ed., *Restoring the Dream: The Bold New Plan by House Republicans* (Times Books, 1995), p. 156.
15. *United States* v. *E. C. Knight Co.,* 156 U.S. 1 (1895).
16. On the origins of the Federal Trade Commission and the role of Louis D. Brandeis, see Thomas K. McCraw, *Prophets of Regulation* (Belknap Press, 1984), chap. 3.
17. Don L. Boroughs with Betsy Carpenter, "Cleaning Up the Environment," *U.S. News and World Report,* March 25, 1991, p. 46.
18. For a useful history of airline deregulation, see Steven A. Morrison and Clifford Winston, *The Evolution of the Airline Industry* (Brookings Institution, 1995).
19. On Southwest Airlines and its longtime chief executive Herb Kelliher, see Kevin Freiberg and Jackie Freiberg, *Nuts!* (Bard Press, 1996).
20. *Reno* v. *American Civil Liberties Union,* 521 U.S. 844 (1997).
21. See Robert W. Crandall and Harold Furchtgott-Roth, *Cable TV: Regulation or Competition?* (Brookings Institution, 1996); Richard Klinger, *The New Information Industry: Regulatory Challenges and the First Amendment* (Brookings Institution,1996); and Lawrence Lessig, *Code and Other Laws of Cyberspace* (Basic Books, 2000).

Chapter 20

1. "Gifts to Rescuers Divide Survivors," *New York Times,* December 2, 2001, p. A1.
2. Michael B. Katz, *In the Shadow of the Poorhouse: A Social History of Welfare in America* (Basic Books, 1986).
3. This history draws heavily on Theda Skocpol's wonderful work on the subject, starting with "America's First Social Security System: The Expansion of Benefits for Civil War Veterans," *Political Science Quarterly* 108 (Winter 1993), pp. 64–87.
4. Ibid., pp. 85–86.
5. Joel F. Handler, *The Poverty of Welfare Reform* (Yale University Press, 1995), p. 21.
6. Gertrude Schaffner Goldberg and Eleanor Kremen, eds., *The Feminization of Poverty: Only in America?* (Greenwood Press, 1990).
7. U.S. Bureau of the Census, "Historical Tables—People," tab. P-40, at www.census.gov/hhes/income/histinc/p40.html.
8. June O'Niel and Solomon Polachek, "Why the Gender Gap in Wages Narrowed in the 1980s," *Journal of Labor Economics* 11 (Spring 1993), pp. 225–229.
9. See, for example, Margaret Weir, "Political Parties and Social Policymaking," in *The Social Divide: Political Parties and the Future of Activist Government,* ed. Margaret Weir (Brookings Institution, 1998).

10. Self-employed workers must cover both amounts, and many state and local government workers are not required to participate.

11. Martha Derthick, "No More Easy Votes for Social Security," *Brookings Review* 10 (Fall 1992), pp. 50–53.

12. Peter Francese, "Social Security Solution," *American Demographics* 15 (February 1993), p. 2. See also Terry Savage, "Can Social Security Find Its Way Back to Stability?" *Chicago Sun Times,* December 8, 1998, p. 6.

13. For a pessimistic view of the viability of Social Security, see Neil Howe and Richard Jackson, "The Myth of the 2.2 Percent Solution," at www.cato.org/pubs/ssps11es.html. Robert D. Reischauer of the Brookings Institution testified before the House Committee on Ways and Means on November 19, 1998, that Social Security will start running deficits by 2021 and that by 2032, "reserves will be depleted."

14. See Theda Skocpol, *Protecting Soldiers and Mothers: The Political Origins of Social Policy in the United States* (Belknap Press, 1992), chap. 9, for a history of the act.

15. Lyndon Johnson, speech at the University of Michigan, May 1964, in *Congress and the Nation, 1965–1968: A Review of Government and Politics During the Johnson Years* (CQ Press, 1969), vol. 2, p. 650.

16. For a history of Medicare and other Great Society programs, see James L. Sundquist, *Politics and Policy: The Eisenhower, Kennedy, and Johnson Years* (Brookings Institution, 1968).

17. Robert Pear, "House Sends Senate an Overhaul of Welfare System" *New York Times,* December 22, 1995, p. A37.

18. William J. Clinton, State of the Union Address, January 23, 1996.

19. William J. Clinton, acceptance speech, Democratic National Convention, Chicago, July 6, 1992.

20. Robert Pear, "Judge Rules States Can't Cut Welfare," *New York Times,* October 14, 1997, p. A1.

21. Administration for Children and Families, at www.acf.dhhs.gov/news/stats/aug-sep.htm.

22. Centers for Medicare and Medicaid Services, "Health Accounts," at www.cms.hhs.gov/statistics/nhe.

23. John Greenwald, "Ouch!" *Time,* March 8, 1993, p. 53.

24. U.S. Bureau of the Census, *Statistical Abstracts of the United States, 1999* (U.S. Government Printing Office, 1999), p. 448.

25. Ibid., p. 93.

26. Laurene A. Graig, *Health of Nations: An International Perspective on U.S. Health Care Reform* (CQ Press, 1993), p. 20.

27. According to the Public Citizens Research Group, the optimal number of C-sections is 12 percent of total births. But in the most recent year for which we have data, 21 percent of births were by C-section, producing an estimated 330,000 unnecessary surgical deliveries. National Center for Health Statistics, at www.cdc.gov/nchs/datawh/statab/pubd/4611s39h.htm.

28. Michael D. Lemonick, "Doctors' Deadly Mistakes," *Time,* December 13, 1999, p. 74.

29. Jennifer Steinhauer, "At Beth Israel, Lapses in Care Mar Gains in Technology," *New York Times,* February 15, 2000, p. B1.

30. "Medicare Funds Going Up in Smoke," *Deseret News,* May 17, 1994, p. A1.

31. "Big Tobacco Fights Legal Battles," at www.washingtonpost.com/wp-srv/national/longterm/tobacco/overview.htm.

32. Centers for Disease Control and Prevention, at www.cdc.gov.

33. U.S. Bureau of the Census, at www.census.gov.

34. Medicare HMO, "Managed Care National Statistics," at www.medicarehmo.com/mcmnu.htm.

35. "Measuring the HMOs," *Los Angeles Times,* October 3, 1998, p. B7.

36. Mary Agnes Carey and Rebecca Adams, "Managed-Care Conferees Agree on Appeals Principles; Key Details Remian Unresolved," *Congressional Quarterly Weekly,* April 15, 2000, p. 903.

37. James A. Klein, "Should Employers Select Health-Insurance Options for Workers?" *Dallas Morning News,* August 2, 1998, p. J1.

38. Institute of Medicine, Committee on Employer-Based Health Benefits, *Employment and Health Benefits: A Connection at Risk,* eds. Marilyn J. Field and Harold T. Shapiro (National Academy Press, 1993), p. 5.

39. The amount permitted for a medical savings account is 75 percent of the maximum total deduction for medical expenses for an individual or couple; see Internal Revenue Service, at www.irs.ustreas.bov/prod/forms_pubs/pubs/p96901.htm.

40. U.S. Department of Education, Office of Educational Research and Improvement, National Center for Education Statistics, *Federal Support for Education, Fiscal Years 1980 to 1998* (National Center for Education Statistics, 1998), p. iii.

41. National Center for Education Statistics, at www.nces.gov.nces.ed.gov/pubs99/digest98/d98t319.html.

Chapter 21

1. See James Steinberg, "Counterterrorism: A New Organizing Principle for American National Security?" *Brookings Review,* vol. 20, no. 3 (Summer 2002), pp. 4–7.

2. Condoleezza Rice, "Promoting the National Interest," *Foreign Affairs,* January–February 2000, pp. 46–47.

3. James M. Scott and A. Lane Crothers, "Out of the Cold: The Post-Cold War Context of U.S. Foreign Policy," in James M. Scott, ed., *After the End: Making U.S. Foreign Policy in the Post-Cold War World* (Duke, 1998), p. 5.

4. William J. Broad, "27 Countries Support New Atom Accord," *New York Times National Edition,* May 3, 1992, sec. 1, p. 9.

5. For a critical analysis of the new policy, see Ivo H. Daalder and James M. Lindsay, "A New Agenda for Nuclear Weapons: On Nuclear Weapons, Destroy and Codify," *Brookings Institution Policy Brief No. 94,* February 2002.

6. "A Dangerous Treaty," editorial, *Wall Street Journal,* February 19, 1997, p. A16. But see Pat Towell, "Clinton Pressures GOP to Act on Chemical Arms Ban," *Congressional Quarterly Weekly,* March 11, 1997, pp. 545–550.

7. Michael Mandelbaum, "Lessons of the Next Nuclear War," *Foreign Affairs,* March–April 1995, pp. 22–37. See also Paul H. Nitze, "A Threat Mostly to Ourselves," *New York Times,* October 28, 1999, p. A25.

8. For a readable summary of this dispute, see Bill Keller, "The World According to Powell," *New York Times Magazine,* November 25, 2001, pp. 18–39.

9. Karen De Young and Walter Pincus, "Crises Strain Bush Policies; Friends, Foes Find Lack of Coherence in Foreign Affairs," *Washington Post,* April 21, 2002, p. A1.

10. Condoleezza Rice, quoted in Glenn Kessler, "Rice Lays Out Case for War in Iraq," *Washington Post,* August 16, 2002, p. A1.

11. Warren Christopher, *In the Stream of History: Shaping Foreign Policy for a New Era* (Stanford University Press, 1998), p. 533.

12. U.S. Department of Defense, at www.defenselink.mil; U.S. Department of State, at www.stage.gov.

13. The case for continued reliance on vital U.S. embassies abroad is well made in Mary Locke and Casimir A. Yost, eds., *Who Needs Embassies? How U.S. Missions Abroad Help Shape Our World* (Georgetown University School of Foreign Policy, 1997).

14. For a fascinating history of U.S. intelligence operations, see Christopher Andrew, *For the President's Eyes Only: Secret Intelligence and the American Presidency from Washington to Bush* (HarperCollins, 1995). See also Rhodri Jeffreys-Jones, *The CIA and American Democracy,* 2d ed. (Yale University Press, 1998).

15. Chuck McCutcheon, "Tenet Gives CIA Credibility on the Hill," *Congressional Quarterly Weekly,* January 22, 2000, pp. 139–142.

16. For President Bush's recollections and surprise, see George H. W. Bush and Brent Scowcroft, *A World Transformed* (Knopf, 1998), pp. 302–333.

17. See Loch K. Johnson, *Secret Agencies: U.S. Intelligence in a Hostile World* (Yale University Press, 1996).

18. Daniel Patrick Moynihan, *Secrecy: The American Experience* (Yale University Press, 1998), pp. 221, 227.

19. Johnson, *Secret Agencies,* p. 201.

20. See George C. Wilson, *This War Really Matters: Inside the Fight for Defense Dollars* (CQ Press, 2000).

21. Steven Kull, "What the Public Knows That Washington Doesn't," *Foreign Policy,* Winter 1995–1996, p. 115. See also Steven Kull and I. M. Destler, *Misreading the Public: The Myth of a New Isolationism* (Brookings Institution, 1999).

22. Pew Research Center for the People and the Press, *Public Opinion in a Year for the Books* (Pew Research Center, 2002), p. 1.

23. Thomas L. Friedman, "India, Pakistan, and G.E.," *New York Times,* August 11, 2002, sec. 4, p. 13.
24. For an examination of how Japanese companies try to influence foreign policy and trade officials in Washington, see Pat Choate, *Agents of Influence* (Knopf, 1990).
25. "G.O.P. Returns $100,000 Gift," *New York Times,* January 20, 2001, p. A8.
26. For a useful review of how Congress has occasionally challenged and even more often failed to challenge the White House when it comes to the war power, see Louis Fisher, *Presidential War Power* (University Press of Kansas, 1995).
27. Trent Lott, quoted in Miles A. Pomper, "Philosophical Conflicts Complicate Iraq Debate," *Congressional Quarterly Weekly,* August 3, 2002, p. 2098.
28. For an analysis that asserts U.S. foreign policy is almost entirely shaped by self-appointed elites, see Eric Alterman, *Who Speaks for America? Why Democracy Matters* (Cornell University Press, 1998). More generally, see Ole Holsti, *Public Opinion and American Foreign Policy* (University of Michigan Press, 1996).
29. Dennis C. Jett, "The U.N.'s Failures Are Everyone's Fault," *New York Times,* May 22, 2000, p. A23. See also Christopher S. Wren, "Era Waning: Holbrooke Takes Stock," *New York Times,* January 14, 2001, p. 8.
30. "U.S. Foreign Aid Spending Since World War II," *Public Perspective* 8 (August–September 1997), p. 11.
31. Gallup Poll, May 2000, www.gallup.com.
32. See Sebastian Mallaby, "Why So Stingy on Foreign Aid?" *Washington Post National Weekly Edition,* July 3, 2000, p. 27.
33. Ibid. But see Doug Bandlow, "The Case Against Foreign Aid," *Christian Science Monitor,* September 29, 1999, p. 9, and Eric Schmitt, "Helms Urges Foreign Aid Be Handled by Charities," *New York Times,* January 12, 2001, p. A4.
34. Richard N. Haass, "Sanctions Almost Never Work," *Wall Street Journal,* June 19, 1998, p. A14. See also Richard N. Haass and Meghan L. O'Sullivan, eds., *Honey and Vinegar: Incentives, Sanctions, and Foreign Policy* (Brookings Institution, 2000).
35. Richard Lugar, in Gerald F. Seib, "Capital Journal," *Wall Street Journal,* June 17, 1998, p. A18.
36. Gary Hufbauer, "Foreign Policy on the Cheap," *Washington Post National Weekly Edition,* July 20, 1998, p. 22.
37. Gary Hufbauer and Jeffrey J. Schott, "Economic Sanctions and Foreign Policy," *PS: Political Science and Politics* 18 (Fall 1985), p. 278.
38. See Ivo H. Daalder and Michael E. O'Hanlon, *Winning Ugly: NATO's War to Save Kosovo* (Brookings Institution, 2000), esp. chap. 6.
39. John Prados, *The President's Secret Wars: CIA and Pentagon Covert Operations Since World War II* (Morrow, 1986); Moynihan, *Secrecy.*
40. Norman A. Graebner, "The President as Commander in Chief: A Study in Power," in *Commander-in-Chief: Presidential Leadership in Modern Wars,* ed. Joseph G. Dawson III (University Press of Kansas, 1993), p. 31.
41. Colin L. Powell, quoted in Steven Mufson, "From Soldier to Diplomat," *Washington Post National Weekly Edition,* December 25, 2000, p. 6.
42. Keller, "The World According to Powell," p. 14.
43. Kull and Destler, *Misreading the Public.*
44. Dana Priest, "Peacekeeping Is Putting Women in the Trenches," *Washington Post National Weekly Edition,* January 26, 1998, p. 9; Mark Thompson, "Boys and Girls Apart," *Time,* January 5, 1998, p. 104.
45. Evan Thomas and Gregory L. Vistica, "Falling Out of the Sky," *Newsweek,* March 17, 1997, p. 26.
46. Office of Management and Budget, *Budget of the United States, Fiscal Year 2003* (U.S. Government Printing Office, 2002).
47. Ibid.
48. John Spratt and Hugh Brady, "National Security v. Social Security," *Brookings Review,* vol. 20, no. 3 (Summer 2002), p. 12.
49. See, for example, James Kitfield, "Ships Galore!" *National Journal,* February 10, 1996, pp. 298–302.
50. Kenneth R. Mayer, *The Political Economy of Defense Contracting* (Yale University Press, 1991), p. 223.
51. Paul Wolfowitz, quoted in Molly M. Peterson, "Crusader Becomes Target in Defense Transition Debate," *National Journal,* May 15, 2002, p. 27.
52. On the bureaucractic and congressional politics of these panels, see Robert Scott Dering, "The Politics of Military Base Closures, 1988–1995," paper presented at the annual meeting of the American Political Science Association, Boston, September 3–6, 1998.

Chapter 22

1. Michael Cooper, "Brother, Can You Spare a Billion?" *New York Times,* March 31, 2002, p. A26.
2. For a discussion of what factors improve economic performance and state policy effectiveness, see Paul Brace, *State Government and Economic Performance* (Johns Hopkins University Press, 1993), and Susan E. Clarke and Martin R. Saiz, "Economic Development and Infrastructure Policy," in *Politics in the American States,* eds. Virginia Gray, Russell Hanson, and Herbert Jacob, 7th ed. (CQ Press, 1999), pp. 540–543.
3. Readers interested in understanding the enormous variety of political cultures within our states would do well to read books in the fascinating University of Nebraska series called "Politics and Governments of the American States." About 18 of planned volumes on the 50 states have been published, including studies of Arkansas, Colorado, Illinois, Kentucky, Michigan, New Jersey, North Carolina, and West Virginia. We rely on several of these studies in our chapters on state politics.
4. Robert S. Lynd and Helen M. Lynd, *Middletown* (Harcourt, 1929). See also their analysis of Muncie ten years later in *Middletown in Transition* (Harcourt, 1937).
5. Floyd Hunter, *Community Power Structure* (University of North Carolina Press, 1953). For a reassessment and rebuttal of Hunter's findings, see M. Kent Jennings, *Community Influentials: The Elites of Atlanta* (Free Press, 1964).
6. Robert A. Dahl, *Who Governs? Democracy and Power in an American City* (Yale University Press, 1961).
7. See the interesting study of San Jose, California, by Phillip J. Troustine and Terry Christensen, *Movers and Shakers: The Study of Community Power* (St. Martin's Press, 1982). See also Clarence N. Stone, *Regime Politics: Governing Atlanta, 1946–1988* (University Press of Kansas, 1989).
8. See, for example, Peter Bachrach and Morton S. Baratz, *Power and Poverty: Theory and Practice* (Oxford University Press, 1970); Matthew A. Crenson, *The Unpolitics of Air Pollution: A Study of Non-Decision Making in Two Cities* (Johns Hopkins University Press, 1971); and John Gaventa, *Power and Powerlessness: Quiescence and Rebellion in an Appalachian Valley* (University of Illinois Press, 1980).
9. Bryan D. Jones and Lynn W. Bachelor, *The Sustaining Hand: Community Leadership and Corporate Power,* 2d ed. (University Press of Kansas, 1993), p. 254. See also Stone, *Regime Politics.*
10. U.S. Office of Management and Budget, *Budget of the United States, FY 2000* (U.S. Government Printing Office, 1999); *New York Times Almanac, 2000* (Penguin, 1999), p. 155.
11. Stone, *Regime Politics,* p. 232.
12. For a detailed analysis of how the W. R. Grace Company and Beatrice Foods Company had to rely on law firms to fight legal actions surrounding their operations in Woburn, Massachusetts, see Jonathan Harr, *A Civil Action* (Vintage Books, 1996). See also Alan Rosenthal, *The Third House: Lobbyists and Lobbying in the States,* 2d ed. (CQ Press, 2001).
13. See Clive S. Thomas and Ronald J. Hrebenar, "Interest Groups in the States," in *Politics in the American States,* ed. Gray et al., pp. 122–158, and *The Book of the States, 2000–2001* (Council of State Governments, 2000), p. 397.
14. For a general discussion of ethics reform and enforcement efforts, see *Spectrum: The Journal of State Government* (Winter 1993).
15. On various efforts to improve ethical practices and professionalism in the state legislatures and the limits of these efforts, see Alan Rosenthal, *Drawing the Line: Legislative Ethics in the States* (University of Nebraska Press, 1996).
16. Jimmy Carter, *Why Not the Best?* (Bantam Books, 1976), p. 101. See also the memoir by Tom Loftus, a former speaker of the Wisconsin State Assembly, *The Art of Legislative Politics* (CQ Press, 1994), chap. 3.
17. Diane D. Blair, *Arkansas Politics and Government* (University of Nebraska Press, 1988), p. 118.
18. William P. Browne and Kenneth VerBurg, *Michigan Politics and Government* (University of Nebraska Press, 1995), pp. 241–245.
19. Paul Peterson, *City Limits* (University of Chicago Press, 1981), p. 124. See also the useful discussion of the challenge of covering state legislative politics in Browne and VerBurg, *Michigan Politics and Government,* pp. 242–245.

20. Joseph F. Zimmerman, *The New England Town Meeting: Democracy in Action* (Praeger, 1999).
21. See for example, Daniel Kemmis, *The Good City and the Good Life* (Houghton Mifflin, 1995), and David L. Kirp, John P. Dwyer, and Larry A. Rosenthal, *Our Town: Race, Housing, and the Soul of Suburbia* (Rutgers University Press, 1997).
22. Eugene F. Rivers III, "High-Octane Faith," in *Community Works: The Revival of Civil Society in America,* ed. E. J. Dionne Jr. (Brookings Institution, 1998), p. 61.
23. For the efforts of a big-city mayor and his team of advisers, see Buzz Bissinger, *A Prayer for the City* (Random House, 1997). See also the example of Milwaukee's mayor, John O. Norquist, *Wealth of Cities* (Addison-Wesley, 1998).
24. See Timothy Egan, "They Give, but They Also Take: Voters Muddle States' Finances," *New York Times,* March 2, 2002, p. A1.

Chapter 23

1. Temporary New York State Commission on Constitutional Revision, Effective Government Now for the New Century (Nelson A. Rockefeller Institute of Government, 1995).
2. Mario M. Cuomo, "Real Reform: It's Time for a People's State Constitutional Convention," *Rockefeller Institute Bulletin* (1993), pp. 41–46.
3. Richard Perez-Pena, "Voters Reject Constitutional Convention: Last-Minute Campaign Appears to Sway Ballot," *New York Times,* November 5, 1997, p. B1.
4. Michigan Department of State, Bureau of Elections, at www.sos.state.mi.us/law; Arkansas Government Relations, at www.uark.edu/~govinfo/PAGES/History/del.html; gopher://gopher.sos.state.mi.us/00 and _elect/genres1994/d90E90000000.
5. Gerald Benjamin, "The Functions of State Constitutions in a Federal System," paper presented at the American Political Science Association Round Table, Washington, D.C., 1984.
6. John Adams, quoted in Judith S. Kaye, "Federalism's Other Tier," *Constitution* 3 (Winter 1991), p. 50.
7. *Providence Journal,* July 7, 2000, as reported at www.projo.com.
8. G. Alan Tarr, *Understanding State Constitutions* (Princeton University Press, 1998), p. 47.
9. Donald S. Lutz, "Toward a Theory of Constitutional Amendment," in *Responding to Imperfection: The Theory and Practice of Constitutional Amendment,* ed. Sanford Levinson (Princeton University Press, 1995), pp. 237–274.
10. *The Book of the States, 2002–2003* (Council of State Governments, 2002), p. 3; John Kincaid, "State Constitutions in the Federal System," *Annals of the American Academy of Political and Social Science* 496 (March 1988), p. 14.
11. *Book of the States, 2002–2003,* p. 14.
12. Jack W. Strain, *An Outline of Oklahoma Government,* ed. Leroy Crozier and Carl F. Reherman (Bureau of Local Government Services, Department of Political Science, Central State University, 1984), p. 21.
13. South Dakota Constitution, Article XI, Section 8.
14. Alabama Constitution, Amendment 383 (1901).
15. Christopher W. Hammons, "State Constitutional Reform: Is It Necessary?" *Albany Law Review* 64 (2001), pp. 1328–1334.
16. Christopher W. Hammons, "Was James Madison Wrong? Rethinking the American Preference for Short, Framework-Oriented Constitutions," *American Political Science Review* 93 (December 1999), p. 838. See also ibid.
17. Kaye, "Federalism's Other Tier," p. 54.
18. Miranda S. Spivack, "How States' Rights Can Rectify the Wrongs of the Supreme Court," *Los Angeles Times,* June 16, 1991, p. M2.
19. *Michigan v. Long,* 463 U.S. 1032 (1983); "Our Judicial Federalism," *Intergovernmental Perspective* 15 (Summer 1989), pp. 8–15; William M. Wiecek, "Some Protection of Personal Liberty: Remembering the Future," and Kermit L. Hall, "Mostly Anchor and Little Sail: The Evolution of American State Constitutions," in *Toward a Usable Past: Liberty Under State Constitutions,* eds. Paul Finkelman and Stephen E. Gottlieb (University of Georgia Press, 1991), pp. 371–417.
20. According to the *Book of the States, 2002–2003,* p. 11, in 1998–1999, of the 266 legislative proposed amendments in the 49 states that require submission to the voters for ratification, 210, or 78.8 percent, were adopted.
21. "Mississippi Begins Analyzing Its Racist Constitution of 1890," *New York Times,* December 12, 1985, p. B2. See also Janice C. May, "State Constitutions and Constitutional Revision: 1988–89 and the 1980s," in *The Book of the States, 1989* (Council of State Governments, 1990), p. 23, and Tip H. Allen Jr., "The Enduring Traditions of the State Constitutions," in Dale Krane and Stephen D. Shaffer, *Mississippi Government and Politics: Modernizers Versus Traditionalists* (University of Nebraska Press, 1992), pp. XX–XXV.
22. *Book of the States, 2002–2003,* p. 14.
23. Ibid.
24. Ibid.
25. David B. Magleby, "Direct Legislation in the American States," in *Referendums Around the World: The Growing Use of Direct Democracy,* eds. David Butler and Austin Ranney (American Enterprise Institute Press, 1994), p. 225.
26. California Commission on Campaign Financing, *Democracy by Initiative: A Summary of the Report and Recommendations of the California Commission on Campaign Financing* (Center for Responsive Government, 1992), p. 25.
27. Katherine M. Mauk, "Approaches to Altering State Constitutions," research report of the Public Law Research Institute at Hastings College of the Law, 1995, p. 5. See also www.uchastings.edu/piri/ spring95/statecon.html.
28. *Amador Valley Joint Union High School District* v. *State Board of Equalization,* 22 Cal. 3d 208 (1978), quoted in Eugene C. Lee, "The Revision of California's Constitution," *CPS Brief: A Publication of the California Policy Seminar* 3 (April 1991), p. 1.
29. Mauk, "Approaches to Altering State Constitutions," p. 5.
30. *Book of the States, 2002–2003,* p. 11. See also Magleby, "Direct Legislation," p. 251.
31. Tarr, *Understanding State Constitutions,* p. 158.
32. Ibid., pp. 160–61.
33. Gerald Benjamin and Thomas Gais, "Constitutional Conventionphobia," in *State Constitutions: Competing Perspectives,* eds. Burton C. Agata and Eric Lane (Hofstra Law and Policy Symposium, 1996), vol. 1, p. 69; Tarr, *Understanding State Constitutions,* p. 25.
34. Caleb Nelson, "Majorities, Minorities, and the Meaning of Liberty: A Reevaluation of Scholarly Explanations for the Rise of the Elective Judiciary in Antebellum America," Yale Law School (1991), p. 51, elaborating the thesis of Gordon Wood, *The Creation of the American Republic, 1776–1787* (University of North Carolina Press, 1969), pp. 306–325.
35. Elder Witt, "State Supreme Courts: Tilting the Balance Toward Change," *Governing,* August 1988, p. 33.
36. G. Alan Tarr, Keynote Address, conference on State Constitutional Reform, May 4, 2000, at www.camlaw.rugers.edu/statecon/keynote.html.
37. Lee, "Revision of California's Constitution," p. 7. See also Lutz, "Toward a Theory of Constitutional Amendment," pp. 355–370.
38. Re Jan Ruggiero, Director of Elections, Elections Division, Office of the Secretary of State, Providence, R.I., at www.state.ri.us.
39. Common Cause of Rhode Island, "Separation of Powers," at www.common causeri.org/news.
40. Cecil Morgan, "A New Constitution for Louisiana," *National Civic Review,* July 1974, pp. 343–356.
41. Tarr, *Understanding State Constitutions,* p. 143.
42. Bob Egelko, "Court Rejects New Vote on Constitutional Convention," March 27, 1998, at www.sfgate.com/cgi-bin/art.
43. Beryl E. Pettus and Randall W. Bland, *Texas Government Today* (Dorsey Press, 1979), pp. 34–36. See also Janice C. May, "Texas Constitutional Revision and Laments," *National Civic Review,* February 1977, pp. 64–69.
44. Andre Henderson, "Selling a Constitution: California Desperately Needs a New Charter, That Doesn't Mean It Will Get One," *Governance,* December 1995, pp. 30–31.
45. B. Drummond Ayres Jr., "Alabama Governor Set for Tough Race," *New York Times,* February 27, 2002, p. A16.
46. Albert E. McKinley, "Two New Southern Constitutions," *Political Science Quarterly,* 18 (September 1903), pp. 480–511.
47. *Montgomery Advertiser,* December 11, 2002, the Associated Press, "Constitutional Work May Come in 2003," at www.Montgomeryadvertiser.com.
48. Alabama Citizens for Constitutional Reform, "Convention Schedule," at www.constitutionalreform.org.
49. Ibid.
50. Phillip Rawls, "Constitution Plans Incite Lawsuit," *Mobile Register,* January 14, 2002.
51. Diane Roberts, "Alabamians Go by an Outdated Book," *New York Times,* February 25, 2002, p. A23.
52. Bill Barow, "James Blast Calls for New Constitution," *Mobile Register,* February 14, 2001.

Chapter 24

1. Steven Erlanger, "Milosevich Pledges Harsh Crackdown on Strike Leaders," *New York Times,* October 4, 2000, p. A1.
2. CNN, "Serb Strikers Foil Police to Occupy Mine," October 4, 2000, at www.cnn.com/2000/world/europe/10/04/yugo.protest.03/index.html.
3. Steven Erlanger, "Yugoslavs Claim Belgrade for a New Leader; Police Join Crowd," *New York Times,* October 6, 2000, p. A1.
4. John F. Bibby, *Politics, Parties, and Elections in America,* 5th ed. (Wadsworth, 2003).
5. Florida Department of State, at election.dos.state.fl.us.
6. According to Todd Taylor, executive director, Utah Democratic party, these requirements are intended to promote gender equity; personal communication, November 18, 1998.
7. See Cornelius P. Cotter, James L. Gibson, John F. Bibby, and Robert J. Huckshorn, *Party Organizations in America* (Praeger, 1984).
8. Ronald E. Weber, ed., *American State and Local Politics: Directions for the 21st Century* (Chatham House, 1999), p. 174.
9. U.S. Bureau of the Census, at www.census.gov/population/www/socdemo/voting/p20-542.html.
10. Steven A. Holmes, "Heads Up: The Melting Pot Politics of 2000 Are Truly Soupy," *New York Times,* February 13, 2000, sec. 4, p. 1.
11. California Secretary of State, at www.ss.ca.gov/elections/ror_021902.htm.
12. Mary Clare Jalonick, "Utah GOP Floats a Salt Lake Split-Up," *Congressional Quarterly Weekly,* May 5, 2001, p. 1032.
13. Federal Election Commission, at www.fec.gov/pages/2000turnout/reg&to00.htm.
14. For a discussion of coordinated campaigns, see Paul Herrnson, "National Party Organizations and the Postreform Congress," in *The Postreform Congress,* ed. Roger Davidson (St. Martin's Press, 1992), pp. 65–67.
15. See Cotter et al., *Party Organizations in America.*
16. Richard Perez-Pena, "A Federal Soft-Money Ban Could Benefit State Parties," *New York Times,* March 22, 2002, p. B6.
17. Richard A. Oppel Jr., "Election Panel Rebuffs Effort to Weaken 'Issue Ad' Limits," *New York Times,* June 20, 2002, p. A1.
18. See Bruce E. Keith et al., *The Myth of the Independent Voter* (University of California Press, 1992), p. 52.
19. Jodi Wilgoren, "Gov. Ventura Says He Won't Seek Reelection," *New York Times,* June 19, 2002, p. A14.
20. William H. Flanigan and Nancy H. Zingale, *Political Behavior of the American Electorate,* 8th ed. (CQ Press, 1994), p. 171.
21. Willis D. Hawley, *Nonpartisan Elections and the Case for Party Politics* (Wiley, 1973), pp. 81–82. See also Brian F. Schaffner, Matthew Streb, and Gerald Wright, "Teams Without Uniforms: The Nonpartisan Ballot in State and Local Elections," *Political Research Quarterly* 54 (March 2001), pp. 7–30.
22. David E. Rosenbaum, "As Redistricting Unfolds, Power Is Used to Get More of It," *New York Times,* August 13, 2001, p. A14.
23. Terrel L. Rhodes, *Republicans in the South: Voting for the State House, Voting for the White House* (Praeger, 2000), p. 88.
24. Harvey L. Schantz, "Sectionalism in Presidential Elections," in *American Presidential Elections: Process, Policy, and Political Change,* ed. Harvey L. Schantz (SUNY Press, 1996), pp. 106–107. See also CNN, at www.cnn.com.election/2000/results/index.epolls.html.
25. U.S. Bureau of the Census, *Statistical Abstract of the United States, 2001* (U.S. Government Printing Office, 2001), p. 26.
26. Raymond E. Wolfinger and Steven J. Rosenstone, *Who Votes?* (Yale University Press, 1980), p. 130.
27. David B. Magleby, "Participation in Mail Ballot Elections," *Western Political Quarterly* 40 (March 1987), pp. 79–91.
28. Absentee ballots for all states are available from myabsenteeballot.com, at absenteeballot.net.
29. Diane Morgan, Office of the Washington Secretary of State, personal communication, March 22, 1999.
30. Bruce E. Cain and Elisabeth R. Gerber, eds., *Voting at the Political Fault Line: California's Experiment with the Blanket Primary* (University of California Press, 2002), p. 341.
31. *California Democratic Party et al. v. Jones, Secretary of State of California, et al.,* 530 U.S. 567 (2000); Linda Greenhouse, "Split Decisions: The Court Rules, America Changes," *New York Times,* July 2, 2000, sec. 4, p. 1.
32. Malcolm E. Jewell and David M. Olson, *Political Parties and Elections in American States,* 3d ed. (Dorsey Press, 1988), p. 121; Flanigan and Zingale, *Political Behavior of the American Electorate,* p. 195.
33. James I. Lengle, *Representation and Presidential Primaries: The Democratic Party in the Postreform Era* (Greenwood Press, 1981). For more on primary elections, see Larry M. Bartels, *Presidential Primaries and the Dynamics of Public Choice* (Princeton University Press, 1988); Jeane J. Kirkpatrick, *The New Presidential Elite: Men and Women in National Politics* (Basic Books, 1976); and Barbara Norander, "Ideological Representativeness of Presidential Primary Voters," *Journal of Politics* 51 (November 1989), pp. 977–992.
34. Federal Election Commission, at www.fec.gov/pages/cflaw2000.htm.
35. Other "clean money" states are Vermont, Arizona, and Massachusetts. Edward Zuckerman, "Maine Campaign Reform: Were Voters 'Hoodwinked' by Outside Groups?" *Political Finance and Lobby Reporter,* December 24, 1996, pp. 1–4.
36. David B. Magleby, "Campaign Spending and Referendum Voting," paper presented at the annual meeting of the Western Political Science Association, Albuquerque, N.M., March 1994.
37. *Financing California's Statewide Ballot Measures: Receipts and Expenditures Through December 31, 1998* (California Secretary of State, 1998), p. 2.
38. David B. Magleby, *Direct Legislation: Voting on Ballot Propositions in the United States* (Johns Hopkins University Press, 1984), chaps. 7–9.

Chapter 25

1. Robert Jubilerer, quoted in David S. Broder, "Legislatures Under Siege," *State Legislatures,* July 1991, p. 21. See also David S. Broder, "States of Renewal," *Washington Post National Weekly Edition,* September 13, 1999, p. 4.
2. For a vivid account of legislator-lobbyist relations, see Jay Michael and Dan Walters, *The Third House: Lobbyists, Money and Power in Sacramento* (Berkeley Public Policy Press, 2002).
3. William M. Bulger, *While the Music Lasts: My Life in Politics* (Houghton Mifflin, 1996), pp. 316–318. See also former Wisconsin legislator Tom Loftus, *The Art of Legislative Politics* (CQ Press, 1994), and former Minnesota legislator John E. Brandl, *Money and Good Intentions Are Not Enough* (Brookings Institution, 1998).
4. See Peverill Squire, "Uncontested Seats in State Legislative Elections," *Legislative Studies Quarterly* 35 (February 2000), pp. 131–146.
5. Alan Rosenthal, "The Legislative Unraveling of Institutional Fabric," in *The State of the States,* 3d ed., ed. Carl E. Van Horn (CQ Press, 1996), p. 118.
6. For a useful look at Nebraska's unique legislature, see Jack Rodgers, Robert Sittig, and Susan Welch, "The Legislature," in *Nebraska Government and Politics,* ed. Robert D. Miewald (University of Nebraska Press, 1984), pp. 57–86.
7. Richard A. Clucas, "Exercising Control: The Power of State House Speakers," paper presented at the annual meeting of the Western Political Science Association, Los Angeles, March 1998. See also Malcolm E. Jewell and Marcia Lynn Whicker, *Legislative Leadership in the American States* (University of Michigan Press, 1997).
8. *The Book of the States, 2000–2001* (Council of State Governments, 2000), p. 46.
9. See James D. King, "Changes in Professionalism in U.S. State Legislatures," *Legislative Studies Quarterly* 15 (May 2000), pp. 327–343.
10. Alan Rosenthal, *Legislative Life: People, Process, and Performance in the States* (Harper & Row, 1981), pp. 112–113.
11. Gary F. Moncrief, Peverill Squire, and Malcolm E. Jewell, *Who Runs for the Legislature?* (Prentice Hall, 2000).
12. *Book of the States, 2000–2001,* p. 70.
13. See Sue Thomas, *How Women Legislate* (Oxford University Press, 1994). See also Lesley Dahlkemper, "Growing Accustomed to Her Face," *State Legislatures,* July–August 1996, pp. 37–45, and Kathleen Dolan and Lynne Ford, "Change and Continuity Among Women State Legislators," *Political Research Quarterly,* Vol. 50 (March 1997), pp. 137–151.
14. National Conference of State Legislatures.

15. *Book of the States, 2000,* pp. 83–84.
16. See Richard Perez-Pena, "Lawyers Abandon Legislatures for Greener Pastures," *New York Times,* February 21, 1999, p. 3, and Karen Hansen, "Legislator Pay: Baseball It Ain't," *State Legislatures,* July–August 1997, pp. 20–24.
17. Tom Birmingham, quoted in Hansen, "Legislator Pay," p. 20.
18. Frank Smallwood, *Free and Independent: The Initiation of a College Professor into State Politics* (Stephen Greene Press, 1976), p. 223.
19. For fascinating comparative data, see *Inside the Legislative Process: A Comprehensive Survey by the American Society of Legislative Clerks and Secretaries* (National Council of State Legislatures, 1998).
20. Keith E. Hamm and Gary F. Moncrief, "Legislative Politics in the States," in Virginia Gray et al., *Politics in the American States,* 7th ed. (CQ Press, 1999), p. 184.
21. Lobbying strategies are outlined in Michael and Walters, *The Third House.* Other lobbying realities are discussed in Loftus, *Art of Legislative Politics,* chap. 10, and Alan Rosenthal, *Drawing the Line: Legislative Ethics in the States* (University of Nebraska Press, 1996).
22. Thomas Frank, "Ex-Legislators Use Contacts," *Denver Post,* July 5, 1996, p. 16A. See also Loftus, *Art of Legislative Politics.*
23. Samuel K. Gove and James D. Nowlan, *Illinois Politics and Government* (University of Nebraska Press, 1996), p. 53.
24. Garry Boulard, "Lobbyists as Outlaws," *State Legislatures,* January 1996, p. 20. See also David Fireston, "Arkansas Lawmakers Indicted in Vast Corruption Case," *New York Times,* April 28, 1999, p. A14.
25. Smallwood, *Free and Independent,* p. 165. See also Rosenthal, *The Third House,* but also "State Legislators Mix Public and Private Business, Study Says," *New York Times,* May 21, 2000, p. 26.
26. Joel A. Thompson and Gary F. Moncrief, eds., *Campaign Finance in State Legislative Elections* (CQ Press, 1998).
27. Winnie Hu, "Lobbying Code Puts an End to Lawmakers' Gravy Train," *New York Times,* April 11, 2000, pp. A1, A27. See also Christopher Swope, "Winning Without Food and Cigars," *Governing,* November 2000, pp. 40–46.
28. Charles Mahtesian, "The Ethics Backlash," *Governing,* October 1999, pp. 39–41.
29. Brandl, *Money and Good Intentions,* p. 58.
30. Quoted in David Ray, "The Sources of Voting Cues in Three State Legislatures," *Journal of Politics,* Vol. 44 (November 1982), p. 1081. See also John J. Kennedy, *The Contemporary Pennsylvania Legislature* (University Press of America, 1999).
31. Karl T. Kurtz, "The Old Statehouse, She Ain't What She Used to Be," *State Legislatures,* January 1994, pp. 20–23. See also Alan Rosenthal, *The Decline of Representative Democracy* (CQ Press, 1998).
32. Rosenthal, "The Legislative Institution," pp. 136–137. See also Alan Ehrenhalt, "An Embattled Institution," *Governing,* January 1992, pp. 28–33, and Karen Hansen, "Our Beleaguered Institution," *State Legislatures,* January 1994, pp. 12–17.
33. Alan Rosenthal, "The Legislative Institution: In Transition and at Risk," in *The State of the States,* 2d ed., ed. Carl E. Van Horn (CQ Press, 1993), p. 144.
34. See, for example, Christopher Conte, "Laptop Legislatures," *Governing,* November 1999, p. 36.
35. Carrie Koch, "A Room for a View," *State Legislatures,* May 1997, pp. 32–34.
36. Bette H. Dillehay, "E-Government as Virginia's Vision," in *Spectrum: The Journal of State Government* (Winter 2002), pp. 24–25.
37. Rich Jones, "The State Legislatures," in *The Book of the States, 1992–1993* (Council of State Governments, 1992), p. 125.
38. Michael Janofsky, "Idaho Legislature Repeals Term Limit Law, Undoing Voter Approved Measure," *New York Times,* February 2, 2002, p. A11. See also

Wayne Hoffman, "The Battle over Term Limits," *State Legislatures,* May 2002, pp. 25–29.
39. Janofsky, "Idaho Legislature," p. A11.
40. See John M. Carey, Richard G. Niemi, and Lynda W. Powell, *Term Limits in the State Legislatures* (University of Michigan Press, 2000).
41. Jack Quinn et al., "Redrawing the Districts, Changing the Rules," *Washington Post National Weekly Edition,* April 1, 1991, p. 23.
42. Gordon E. Baker, *The Reapportionment Revolution* (Random House, 1966), p. 47.
43. *Baker v. Carr,* 369 U.S. 186 (1962).
44. *Wesberry v. Sanders,* 376 U.S. 1 (1964).
45. *Reynolds v. Sims,* 377 U.S. 533 (1964).
46. *Brown v. Thomson,* 103 S.Ct. 2690 (1983).
47. *Shaw v. Reno,* 509 U.S. 630 (1993); *Abrams v. Johnson,* 138 L.Ed. 2d 285 (1997). For a summary of state and federal judicial cases on drawing legislative district lines, see *Redistricting Case Summaries from the '90s* (National Conference of State Legislatures, 1998); see also Ronald E. Weber, "Emerging Trends in State Legislative Redistricting," *Spectrum: The Journal of State Government,* Vol. 75 (Winter 2002), pp. 13–15; additional updates can be found at the National Conference of State Legislature Web site, www.ncsl.org.
48. Samuel Issacharoff, "In Real Elections, There Ought to Be Competition," *New York Times,* February 16, 2002, p. A31.
49. Ibid.
50. See Spencer C. Olin, *California's Prodigal Sons: Hiram Johnson and the Progressives, 1911–1917* (University of California Press, 1968).
51. See Joseph F. Zimmerman, *The Recall: Tribunal of the People* (Praeger, 1997).
52. Editorial, *New York Times,* October 29, 1993, p. A16.
53. Jennie Drage, "A Smorgasbord of Ballot Measures," *State Legislatures,* December 2000, p. 16.
54. See, for example, Eugene C. Lee, "The Initiative Boom: An Excess of Democracy," in *Governing California,* eds. Gerald C. Lubenow and Bruce E. Cain (Institute of Governmental Studies, University of California, 1997), pp. 113–136. See also David S. Broder, *Democracy Derailed: Initiative Campaigns and the Power of Money* (Harcourt, 2000). But see Elisabeth Gerber et al., "Minorities and Direct Legislation: Evidence from California Ballot Proposition Elections," paper presented at the annual meeting of the American Political Science Association, Washington, D.C., September 1–3, 2000. See also Elisabeth Gerber, *The Populist Paradox* (Princeton University Press, 1999).
55. See Peter Schrag, *Paradise Lost: California's Experience, America's Future* (New Press, 1998). See also the decidedly negative appraisal offered by Richard Ellis, *Democratic Delusions: The Initiative Process in America* (University Press of Kansas, 2002).
56. David B. Magleby and Kelly D. Paterson, "Consultants and Direct Democracy," *PS: Political Science and Politics* 31 (June 1998), pp. 160–161. See also Broder, *Democracy Derailed.*
57. David B. Magleby, "Ballot Initiatives and Intergovernmental Relations," paper presented at the annual meeting of the Western Political Science Association, Los Angeles, March 1998, p. 2.
58. Ibid., p. 13.
59. Thomas E. Cronin, *Direct Democracy: The Politics of the Initiative, Referendum, and Recall* (Harvard University Press, 1989).
60. Michael G. Hagen and Edward L. Lascher Jr., "Public Opinion About Ballot Initiatives," paper presented at the annual meeting of the American Political Science Association, Boston, September 3–6, 1998.

Chapter 26

1. See Thad L. Beyle, "Enhancing Executive Leadership in the States," *State and Local Government Review* (Winter 1995), pp. 18–35, and Thad L. Beyle, "The Governors," in *Politics in the American States: A Comparative Analysis,* 7th ed., eds. Virginia Gray, Russell Hanson, and Herbert Jacob (CQ Press, 1999), pp. 191–231.
2. Lamar Alexander, *Steps Along the Way: A Governor's Scrapbook* (Nelson, 1986), p. 112. Similar views can be found in former Vermont Governor Madeleine M. Kunin's memoir, *Living a Political Life* (Vintage, 1995).
3. See Earl H. Fry, *The Expanding Role of State and Local Governments in U.S. Foreign Policy* (Council on Foreign Relations Press, 1998). See also, for example, Alan Johnson, "Taft Shows He's Up to the Job on Foreign Grounds," *Columbia Dispatch,* February 14, 2000.
4. *The Book of the States, 1998–1999* (Council of State Governments, 1998), p. xxiii.
5. Ibid., tab. 2.3, p. 18.

6. This story is adapted from Robert S. McElvaine, *Mario Cuomo: A Biography* (Scribner, 1988), pp. 337–338. See also the assessment of Governor Pete Wilson's turbulent first years as governor of California in Robert Reinhold, "The Curse of the Statehouse," *New York Times Magazine,* May 3, 1992, pp. 27–28, 54, 58–59.
7. Thad L. Beyle, "Governors," *The Book of the States, 2002* (Council of State Governments, 2002), p. 135.
8. James M. Perry, "Virginia's New Governor Joins a GOP Trend," *Wall Street Journal,* February 11, 1998, p. A24.
9. Richard F. Winters, "The Politics of Taxing and Spending," in *Politics in the American States,* ed. Gray et al., p. 329.
10. Fred Branfman and Nancy Stefanik, "Who Says Raising Taxes Is Political Suicide?" *Washington Post National Weekly Edition,* February 13, 1989, p. 24. See also the excellent case studies of governors in Michigan, Massachusetts, Pennsylvania,

Arizona, and elsewhere who pushed through economic development programs in the 1980s, in David Osborne, *Laboratories of Democracy: A New Breed of Governor Creates Models for National Growth* (Harvard Business School Press, 1988).

11. In some cases, a governor's style and strategy alienate legislators. See, for example, Charles Mahtesian's analysis of Minnesota's Jesse Ventura, "Can He Govern?" *Governing,* May 2000, pp. 36–42. In contrast, Governor Bruce Babbitt worked effectively even with a legislature controlled by the opposition party. See David R. Berman, *Arizona Politics and Government* (University of Nebraska Press, 1998), pp. 116–117.

12. For a lighthearted commentary by a member of Governor Pete Wilson's Electronic Commerce Advisory Council, see Stewart Alsop, "Helping the Governor Figure Out E-Commerce," *Fortune,* June 8, 1998, p. 269.

13. "N.H. Veto Saves Death Penalty," *New York Times,* May 20, 2000, p. A16; Alan Rosenthal, *The Decline of Representative Democracy* (CQ Press, 1998), p. 297.

14. Cited in a profile of New York in *Governing,* February 1999, p. 66.

15. Thad L. Beyle, "Being Governor," in *The State of the States,* 3d ed., ed. Carl E. Van Horn (CQ Press, 1996), p. 89. See also Beyle, "Governors."

16. But see Governor Tommy Thompson's defense of using frequent vetoes, *Power to the People: An American State at Work* (HarperCollins, 1996), and the view of one of his main critics in the Wisconsin legislature, Tom Loftus, *The Art of Legislative Politics* (CQ Press, 1994), chap. 5. On the varied effectiveness of the line item veto as a tool for fiscal responsibility, see Glenn Abney and Thomas P. Lauth, "The Item Veto and Fiscal Responsibility," *Journal of Politics,* Vol. 59 (August 1997), pp. 882–892. On how a governor's rash use of the line item veto can infuriate legislators, see Mahtesian, "Can He Govern?" p. 40.

17. Ronald Smothers, "Mississippi Governor Bans Same-Sex Marriages," *New York Times,* August 24, 1996, p. 6.

18. *Perpich et al.* v. *Department of Defense,* 110 L.Ed. 312 (1990).

19. For background on this controversy, see Jonathan Alter, "The Death Penalty on Trial," *Newsweek,* June 12, 2000, pp. 26–34.

20. "Governor Ryan's Brave Example," *New York Times,* July 3, 2000, p. A20. See also Judy Keen, "Death Penalty Issue Looms over Bush Campaign," *USA Today,* June 16, 2000, p. 17A.

21. The entire Ryan Commission report is available online at www.idoc.state.il.us/ccp/. See also Francis Clines, "Death Penalty Is Suspended in Maryland," *New York Times,* May 10, 2002, p. A16.

22. For a scholarly analysis of the role political parties play in nominating and assisting governors, see Sarah McCally, *The Governor as Party Leader: Campaigning and Governing* (University of Michigan Press, 1998).

23. See Don W. Driggs and Leonard E. Goodall, *Nevada Politics and Government* (University of Nebraska Press, 1996), chap. 7.

24. Beyle, "Governors," p. 230.

25. Sarah F. Liebschutz et al., *New York Politics and Government* (University of Nebraska Press, 1998), p. 93.

26. Thomas Hardy, "The 'Weak' Governor," in *Mississippi Government and Politics,* eds. Dale Krane and Stephen Shaffer (University of Nebraska Press, 1992), p. 152.

27. See, for example, how hard it is for a governor to control the economic fortunes of a state, especially during a recession, in Paul Brace, *State Government and Economic Performance* (Johns Hopkins University Press, 1993).

28. *State Legislatures,* June 2000, p. 7.

29. Kunin, *Living a Political Life,* p. 382.

30. Beyle, "The Governors," in *Politics in the American States,* ed. Gray et al., pp. 224–226.

31. Thomas H. Kean, quoted in Barbara Salmore and Stephen Salmore, *New Jersey Politics and Government* (University of Nebraska Press, 1998), p. 136.

32. Jesse Ventura, *I Ain't Got Time to Bleed* (Signet Press, 2000), pp. 296–297.

33. Beyle, "The Governors," in *Politics in the American States,* ed. Gray et al., pp. 224–226.

34. Richard C. Elling, *Public Management in the States* (Praeger, 1992).

35. Alan Ehrenhalt, "Reinventing Government in the Unlikeliest Place," *Governing,* August 1993, pp. 7–8.

36. Richard C. Elling, "Bureaucracy: Maligned Yet Essential," in *Politics in the American States: A Comparative Analysis,* 6th ed., eds. Virginia Gray and Herbert Jacob (CQ Press, 1996), p. 308.

37. Jonathan Walters, "Fad Mad," *Governing,* Vol. 9, September 1996, p. 49.

38. Beyle, "Being Governor," in *State of the States,* ed. Van Horn, p. 106.

39. See the discussion of Governor George W. Bush and his relationship with his lieutenant governor in Jonathan Walters, "The Taming of Texas," *Governing,* July 1998, p. 20. See also "The Future of the Texas Lieutenant Governor," *Comparative State Politics,* October 1995, pp. 21–24.

40. But see Charles N. Wheeler III, "Why Illinois Still Needs Lieutenant Governor's Position," *Illinois Issues,* September 1994, pp. 6–7.

41. On the recent fate of attorneys general who have aspired to become governors, see Charles Mahtesian, "Blocked Path to the Big Job," *Governing,* March 1996, p. 47.

42. Attorney General Bob Butterworth, at legal.firn.edu.

43. Office of the Attorney General, State of California, at caag.state.ca.us.

44. Professor Thad L. Beyle at the University of North Carolina at Chapel Hill tracks state polls on governors' job performances and finds that Democratic, Republican, and Independent governors alike all averaged about 60 percent public approval in the 1990s.

45. Alexander, *Steps Along the Way,* p. 141.

46. Thomas H. Kean, *The Politics of Inclusion* (Free Press, 1988), p. 248.

47. Scott Matheson with James Edwin Kee, *Out of Balance* (Peregrine Smith Books, 1986), p. 186. See also the reflections of another popular western governor in Cecil Andrus and Joel Connelly, *Cecil Andrus: Politics Western Style* (Sasquatch Books, 1998).

Chapter 27

1. See Mark S. Hurwitz and Drew Noble Lanier, "Women and Minorites on State and Federal Appellate Benches," *Judicature* 85 (September–October 2001), p. 84, and Chris W. Bonneau, "The Composition of State Supreme Courts," *Judicature* 85 (July–August 2001), p. 26.

2. See Michael Solimine and James Walker, *Respecting State Courts: The Inevitability of Judicial Federalism* (Greenwood Press, 2000), and Matthew Bosworth, *Courts as Catalysts: State Supreme Courts and Public School Finance Equity* (State University of New York Press, 2001).

3. Lynn Mather, "Policy Making in State Trial Courts," in *The American Courts: A Critical Assessment,* eds. John B. Gates and Charles A. Johnson (CQ Press, 1991), pp. 119–157.

4. Henry R. Glick, "Policy Making and State Supreme Courts," in ibid., pp. 87–88.

5. Patrick Schmidt and Paul Martin, "To the Internet and Beyond: State Supreme Courts on the World Wide Web," *Judicature* 84 (May–June 2001), pp. 314–325.

6. Robert F. Williams, "In the Supreme Court's Shadow: Legitimacy of State Rejection of Supreme Court Reasoning and Results," *South Carolina Law Review* 56 (Spring 1984), p. 353.

7. Harry P. Stumpf and John H. Culver, *The Politics of State Courts* (Longman, 1992), pp. 8–11.

8. Hans A. Linde, "Observations of a State Court Judge," in *Judges and Legislators: Toward Institutional Comity,* ed. Robert A. Katzmann (Brookings Institution, 1988), p. 118.

9. Peter J. Galie, "The Other Supreme Courts: Judicial Activism Among State Supreme Courts," *Syracuse Law Review* 33 (1982), pp. 731–793.

10. Philip L. Dubois, "State Trial Court Appointments: Does the Governor Make a Difference?" *Judicature* 68 (June–July 1985), pp. 20–21.

11. Charles H. Sheldon and Nicholas P. Lovrich Jr., "State Judicial Recruitment," in *American Courts,* eds. Gates and Johnson, pp. 172–173.

12. William Glaberson, "Fierce Campaigns Signal a New Era for State Courts," *New York Times,* June 5, 2000, p. A22.

13. Thurgood Marshall, in *Renne v. Geary,* 501 U.S. 312 (1991).

14. *Republican Party of Minnesota* v. *White,* 122 S.Ct. 2528 (2002).

15. William Glaberson, "Court Rulings Curb Efforts to Rein in Judicial Races," *New York Times,* October 7, 2000, p. A8.

16. Glaberson, "Fierce Campaigns," pp. 1, 22.

17. Roy A. Schotland, "Financing Judicial Elections," in *Financing the 2000 Elections,* ed. David B. Magleby (Brookings Institution, 2002), p. 103.

18. "Judges Say Political Influence Threatens Independence of Judiciary," *Press and Dakotan,* at www.pressandakotan.com/stories/101797/judges.html.

19. Schotland, "Financing Judicial Elections."

20. Toddy Woody, "Gambling with Justice," *Recorder,* October 6, 1997, p. 12.

21. *Wells v. Edwards,* 409 U.S. 1095 (1973).

22. *Chisom* v. *Roemer,* 501 U.S. 400 (1991); *Houston Lawyers' Association* v. *Texas Attorney General,* 501 U.S. 419 (1991). See also Tracy Thompson, "The New Front in the Battle for Civil Rights: Judgeships," *Washington Post National Weekly Edition,* December 18, 1989, p. 34.

23. J. W. Peltason, *The Missouri Plan for the Selection of Judges* (University of Missouri Studies, 1945). The plan was previously known as the Nonpartisan

Plan for the Selection of Judges or the Kales Plan until called the Missouri Plan by this monograph.

24. Beth M. Henschen, Robert Moog, and Steven Davis, "Judicial Nominating Commissioners: A National Profile," *Judicature* 73 (April–May 1990), pp. 328–334.

25. Philip L. Dubois, "The Politics of Innovation in State Courts: The Merit Plan of Judicial Selection," *Publius* 20 (Winter 1990), p. 40.

26. Warren K. Hall and Larry T. Aspin, "What Twenty Years of Judicial Retention Elections Have Told Us," *Judicature* 70 (April–May 1987), pp. 340–347; Susan B. Caron and Larry C. Berkson, *Judicial Retention Elections in the United States* (American Judicature Society, 1980).

27. Larry T. Aspin, "Trends in Judicial Retention Elections, 1964–1968," *Judicature* 83 (September–October 1999), p. 79; "Evaluating the Performance of Judges Standing for Retention," *Judicature* 79 (January–February 1996), pp. 190–195.

28. Dexter Filkins, "Republican Group Seeks to Unseat Three Justices," *New York Times*, December 20, 2000, p. A17.

29. Traciel Reid, "The Politicization of Retention Elections," *Judicature* 83 (September–October 1999), p. 68.

30. Thomas E. Cronin and Robert D. Loevy, *Colorado Politics and Government* (University of Nebraska Press, 1993), pp. 251–253.

31. "Evaluating the Performance of Judges"; "The Need for Judicial Performance Evaluations for Retention Elections," *Judicature* 75 (October–November 1991), p. 124.

32. Henry Weinstein, "Forum Airs Questions of Jurist Independence," *Los Angeles Times*, November 22, 1998, p. A18.

33. Anthony Champagne and Greta Thielemann, "Awareness of Trial Court Judges," *Judicature* 74 (February–March 1991), p. 276.

34. Jeffrey Shaman, Steven Lubet, and James Alfini, *Judicial Conduct and Ethics*, 3d ed. (Lexis, 2000), sec. 15.07.

35. Jolanta Juskiewicz Perlstein and Nathan Goldman, "Judicial Disciplinary Commissions: A New Approach to the Discipline and Removal of State Judges," in *The Analysis of Judicial Reform*, ed. Phil Dubois (Lexington Books, 1982), pp. 93–106.

36. Franklin M. Zweig et al., "Securing the Future for America's State Courts," *Judicature* 73 (April–May 1990), pp. 297–298.

37. Beverly Blair Cook, "Women Judges in the Opportunity Structure," in *Women, the Courts, and Equality,* eds. Laura L. Crites and Winfred L. Hepperle (Sage, 1987), pp. 143–171.

38. *Burch v. Louisiana,* 441 U.S. 130 (1979); *Ballew v. Georgia,* 435 U.S. 223 (1978). See Reid Hastie, Steven D. Penrod, and Nancy Pennington, *Inside the Jury* (Harvard University Press, 1983), for a study showing that nonunanimous verdicts are more likely to bring convictions than those requiring unanimity. Federal courts often use juries of fewer than 12 for civil cases. For federal criminal trials, the Supreme Court still requires both the common law jury of 12 and unanimous verdicts.

39. Robert H. Jackson, quoted in Jack M. Kress, "Progress and Prosecution," *Annals of the American Academy of Political and Social Science* (January 1976), p. 100.

40. William K. Muir, *Police: Streetcorner Politicians* (University of Chicago Press, 1977).

41. Charles E. Silberman, *Criminal Violence, Criminal Justice* (Random House, 1978), p. 303.

42. Jay Livingston, *Crime and Criminology* (Prentice Hall, 1992), p. 474.

43. Silberman, *Criminal Violence,* p. 218. See also David Cole, *No Equal Justice: Race and Class in the American Criminal Justice System* (New Press, 1999).

44. Thomas M. Uhlman and N. Darlene Walker, "A Plea Is No Bargain: The Impact of Case Disposition on Sentencing," *Social Science Quarterly* 60 (September 1979), pp. 218–234. See also Malcolm M. Feeley, *The Process Is the Punishment* (Russell Sage, 1979).

45. Thomas Church Jr., "Plea Bargains, Concessions and the Courts: Analysis of a Quasi-Experiment," *Law and Society Review* 14 (Spring 1976), p. 400. For a contrary view, see National Advisory Commission on Criminal Justice Standards and Goals, *Report of the Task Force* (U.S. Government Printing Office, 1979).

46. Church, "Plea Bargains," p. 400.

47. Jonathan D. Casper, *American Criminal Justice: The Defendant's Perspective* (Prentice Hall, 1972), pp. 52–53. Abraham S. Goldstein, *The Passive Judiciary: Prosecutorial Discretion and the Guilty Plea* (Louisiana State University Press, 1981), is critical of judges for not supervising plea bargains more actively.

48. *Santobello v. New York,* 404 U.S. 257 (1971).

49. Edward Barrett, "The Adversary Proceeding and the Judicial Process," lectures to the National College of State Trial Judges, quoted in Lynn M. Mather, "Some Determinants of the Method of Case Disposition: Decision-Making by Public Defenders in Los Angeles," *Law and Society Review* 12 (Winter 1974), pp. 187–188.

50. Henry N. Pontell, *A Capacity to Punish* (Indiana University Press, 1985).

51. Lee Sechrest, Susan O. White, and Elizabeth D. Brown, eds., *The Rehabilitation of Criminal Offenders: Problems and Prospects* (National Academy of Sciences, 1979), pp. 3–6.

52. John Hagan and Kristin Bumiler, "Making Sense of Sentencing: A Review and Critique of Sentencing Research," in *Research on Sentencing,* eds. Alfred Blumstein et al. (National Academy Press, 1983), vol. 2; Susan Welch, Michael Combs, and John Gruhl, "Do Black Judges Make a Difference?" *American Journal of Political Science* 32 (February 1988), pp. 126–135.

53. William B. Eldridge, "Shifting Views of the Sentencing Functions," *Annals of the American Academy of Political and Social Science* (July 1982), pp. 104–111.

54. Bureau of Justice Statistics, "The Nation's Prison Population Growth Rate Slows," press release, August 9, 2000.

55. Eric Schlosser, "The Prison-Industrial Complex," *Atlantic,* December 1998, p. 52.

56. *New York Times,* December 4, 1993, p. 21.

57. Barbara Fink, "Opening the Door on Community Corrections," *State Legislatures,* September 1984, pp. 24–31.

58. Gary Enos, "Despite New Technology, Home Confinement Faces Risks, Public Opposition," *City and State* May 21, 1990, p. 14.

59. Quoted in Associated Press, "ABA 'Public Jurist' Considers Reforms in Legal System," December 1993.

Chapter 28

1. Jack D. Fleer, *North Carolina Government and Politics* (University of Nebraska Press, 1994), p. 198.

2. See Jacques Steinberg, "42 Failing Schools in Philadelphia to Be Privatized," *New York Times,* April 18, 2002, p. A1.

3. An excellent overview of counties is Donald C. Menzel, ed., *The American County: Frontiers of Knowledge* (University of Alabama Press, 1996).

4. Ellen Perlman, "Polite Tenacity," *Governing,* November 2000, pp. 34, 214.

5. For a history of suburban development, see Rosalyn Baxandall and Elizabeth Ewen, *Picture Windows: How the Suburbs Happened* (Basic Books, 2000).

6. See Paul G. Lewis, *Shaping Suburbia: How Political Institutions Organize Urban Development* (University of Pittsburgh Press, 1996).

7. Joel Garreau, *Edge City* (Doubleday, 1991).

8. For the views of three mayors on the good city, see Stephen Goldsmith, *The Twenty-First Century City* (Regnery, 1997); Daniel Kemmis, *The Good City and the Good Life* (Houghton Mifflin, 1995); and John O. Norquist, *The Wealth of Cities: Revitalizing the Centers of American Life* (Addison-Wesley, 1998).

9. *Rogers v. Lodge,* 458 U.S. 613 (1982); *Thornburg v. Gingles,* 478 U.S. 30 (1986).

10. For the experience of one mayor in a council-manager city, see the memoir by Cambridge, Massachusetts, Mayor Barbara Ackermann, *"You the Mayor?" The Education of a City Politician* (Auburn House, 1989).

11. See James H. Svara and Associates, *Facilitative Leadership in Local Government: Lessons from Successful Mayors and Chairpersons in the Council-Manager Form* (Jossey-Bass, 1994).

12. See Earl H. Fry, *The Expanding Role of State and Local Governments in U.S. Foreign Affairs* (Council on Foreign Relations, 1998), esp. chap. 4.

13. It is fascinating to examine how mayors of different cities view their roles and responsibilities. Excellent books about important mayors are Roger Biles, *Richard J. Daley: Politics, Race, and the Governing of Chicago* (Northern Illinois University Press, 1995); Adam Cohen and Elizabeth Taylor, *American Pharaoh: Mayor Richard J. Daley: His Battle for Chicago and the Nation* (Little, Brown, 2000); and Robert A. Dahl, *Who Governs? Democracy and Power in an American City* (Yale University Press, 1961), a classic study of Mayor Richard Lee of New Haven. See also two reflective books by mayors in medium-sized or smaller cities: Kemmis, *Good City and the Good Life,* and Ackermann, *"You the Mayor?"*

14. David R. Judd and Todd Swanstrom, *City Politics: Private Power and Public Policy,* 2d ed. (Longman, 1998), p. 7.

15. See, for example, the analysis of other groups such as the African Americans in Atlanta in Clarence N. Stone, *Regime Politics: Governing Atlanta, 1946–1988* (University Press of Kansas, 1989). See also Bryan D. Jones and Lynn W. Bachelor, *The Sustaining Hand: Community Leadership and Corporate Power,* 2d ed. (University Press of Kansas, 1993).

16. For suggestions on how to form community groups and effective alliances seeking progress in cities, see Michael Briand, *Practical Politics: Five Principles for a Community That Works* (University of Illinois Press, 1999).

17. Judd and Swanstrom, *City Politics,* p. 7.

18. For greater detail, see U.S. Bureau of the Census, "Standards for Defining Metropolitan Areas," at www.census.gov.

19. The legal constraints on Baltimore, for example, are outlined in David Rusk, *Baltimore Unbound: A Strategy for Regional Renewal* (Abell Foundation/Johns Hopkins University Press, 1996).

20. D'Vera Cohn, "A New Millennium for America's Cities," *Washington Post National Weekly Edition,* October 30, 2000, p. 34.

21. David Rusk, former mayor of Albuquerque, makes this case well in *Baltimore Unbound* and in *Cities Without Suburbs,* 2d ed. (Woodrow Wilson Center Press/Johns Hopkins University Press, 1995).

22. See Myron Orfield, *Metropolitics: A Regional Agenda for Community and Stability* (Brookings Institution, 1997); and Manuel Pastor, ed., *Regions That Work: How Cities and Suburbs Can Grow Together* (University of Minnesota Press, 2000).

23. See the recommendation often prescribed by a major proponent of regionalism, Neal R. Peirce, in Charles Mahtesian, "The Civic Therapist," *Governing,* September 1995, pp. 24–27. See also Neal R. Peirce, "Visions of a New Urban Policy," *National Journal,* October 26, 1996, p. 2302.

24. "The End of Urban Man? Care to Bet?" *Economist,* December 31, 1999, pp. 25–26.

25. See the thoughtful recommendations in Robert J. Waste, *Independent Cities: Rethinking U.S. Urban Policy* (Oxford University Press, 1998).

Chapter 29

1. See the summary by U.S. Department of Education, January 7, 2002, in *The Book of the States, 2002* (Council of State Governments, 2002), p. 472.

2. *Book of the States, 2002,* p. 282.

3. John W. Wright, ed., *The New York Times Almanac, 2002* (Penguin, 2001), p. 368. See also Thomas D. Snyder, *Digest of Education Statistics, 2000* (National Center for Education Statistics, 2001).

4. Thomas R. Dye, *Politics in States and Communities,* 10th ed. (Prentice Hall, 2000), p. 472.

5. National Center for Educational Statistics, "Statistical Analysis Report, September 2001: Overview of Public Elementary and Secondary Schools and Districts, School Year 1999–2000," at nces.ed.gov/pubs2001/overview.

6. See Gary Orfield, Susan E. Eaton, and the Harvard Project on School Desegregation, *Dismantling Desegregation: The Quiet Reversal of Brown* v. *Board of Education* (New Press, 1996).

7. National Commission on Excellence in Education, *A Nation at Risk: The Imperative for Educational Reform—An Open Letter to the American People* (U.S. Government Printing Office, 1983). Ernest L. Boyer, *High School: A Report on Secondary Education in America* (Harper & Row, 1983), based on observations of high schools, contains a detailed series of recommendations. See also the National Science Board Commission on Precollege Education, *Mathematics, Science, and Technology: Educating Americans for the 21st Century* (U.S. Government Printing Office, 1983), and Carnegie Forum on Education and the Economy, *A Nation Prepared: Teachers for the 21st Century* (Carnegie Forum, 1986).

8. James B. Steman and Wayne C. Riddle, *Goals 2000: Educate America Act Implementation Status and Issues* (Congressional Research Service, 1996), pp. 2–4.

9. Rochelle L. Stanfield, "Learning Curve," *National Journal,* July 3, 1993, pp. 1688–1691.

10. C. Eugene Steuerle, Van Doorn Ooms, George Peterson, and Robert D. Reischauer, eds., *Vouchers and the Provision of Public Services* (Brookings Institution, 2000).

11. Terry M. Moe, "Private Vouchers," in *Private Vouchers,* ed. Terry M. Moe (Hoover Institution Press, 1996), p. 35.

12. Ibid., p. 22. See also John F. Witte, *The Market Approach to Education: An Analysis of America's First Voucher Program* (Princeton University Press, 1999).

13. William H. Rehnquist, quoted in Richard Rothstein, "Failed Schools? The Meaning Is Unclear," *New York Times,* July 3, 2002, p. A14.

14. Elizabeth Kolbert, "Unchartered Territory," *New Yorker,* October 9, 2000, p. 36. For the example of charter schools being initiated in Rhode Island, see Maureen Moakley and Elmer Cornwell, *Rhode Island Politics and Government* (University of Nebraska Press, 2001), pp. 189–190.

15. Mary Gifford, "Arizona's Charter Schools: A Survey of Parents," in *Arizona Issue Analysis* (Goldwater Institute, April 1996). See also Chester E. Finn, Bruno V. Manno, and Gregg Vanourek, *Charter Schools in Action: Renewing Public Education* (Princeton University Press, 2000).

16. Ed Lazere, "Welfare Balances After Three Years of TANF Block Grants," report, Center on Budget and Policy Priorities, January 12, 2000, p. 1.

17. R. Kent Weaver, *Ending Welfare As We Know It* (Brookings Institution, 2000).

18. See Tommy G. Thompson, *Power to the People: An American State at Work* (HarperCollins, 1996).

19. See Burt S. Barnow, Thomas Kaplan, and Robert Moffitt, eds., *Evaluating Comprehensive State Welfare Reforms* (Brookings Institution, 2000); Carol W. Weissert, ed., *Learning from Leaders: Welfare Reform Politics and Policy in Five Midwestern States* (Brookings Institution, 2000).

20. For more information, see Center on Budget and Policy Priorities, at www.cbpp.org.

21. Peter Edelman, "The True Purpose of Welfare Reform," *New York Times,* May 29, 2002, p. A21.

22. Howard Dean, quoted in Robert Pear, "Study by Governors Calls Bush Welfare Plan Unworkable," *New York Times,* April 4, 2002, p. A14.

23. Trinity D. Tomsie, "Managing Medicaid in Tough Times," *State Legislators,* June 2002, p. 13.

24. Ibid., pp. 14–15.

25. David S. Broder, "States in Fiscal Crises," *Washington Post National Weekly Edition,* May 27, 2002, p. 4.

26. "Small Fees Will Improve State's Medicaid Program," editorial, *Walla Walla Union-Bulletin,* May 31, 2002, p. B2.

27. U.S. Bureau of the Census, *Statistical Abstract of the United States, 1998* (U.S. Government Printing Office, 1998), pp. 222, 308.

28. Christopher Surope, "Counting Cops," *Governing,* December 2001, pp. 40–42.

29. Jodi Wilgoren, "New Terror Alert Brings No Change in States' Security," *New York Times,* May 25, 2002, p. A11.

30. Ibid.

31. Larry Morandi, "Growing Pains," *State Legislatures,* October–November 1998, pp. 24–28.

32. Neal Peirce, "Parisian Green: A Hint for Us," Washington Post Writers Group, at www.npeirce@citistates.com, June 2, 2002, p. 1.

33. See Robert B. Albritton, "Subsidies: Welfare and Transportation," in *Politics in the American States: A Comparative Analysis,* 7th ed., eds. Virginia Gray, Herbert Jacob, and Kenneth Vines (CQ Press, 1999), and E. J. Dionne Jr., ed., *Community Works: The Revival of Civil Society in America* (Brookings Institution, 2000).

34. For a discussion of the evolution of environmental policy in a particularly interesting place, see Charles O. Jones, *Clean Air: The Policies and Politics of Pollution Control* (University of Pittsburgh Press, 1973).

35. Jacqueline Vaughn Switzer and Gary Bryner, *Environmental Politics,* 2d ed. (St. Martin's Press, 1998), pp. 64–66.

36. Jeff Dale, "Realistic Redevelopment," *State Legislatures,* February 1999, pp. 28–31.

37. John Nagy, "States Giving Anti-Growth Measures High Priority," in *State and Local Government, 2000–2001,* ed. Thad L. Beyle (CQ Press, 2000), p. 195.

38. Bruce A. Williams, "Economic Regulation and Environmental Protection," in *Politics in the American States,* eds. Gray et al. (CQ Press, 1996), pp. 478–515.

39. Ibid.

40. Bruce A. Williams and Albert R. Matheny, *Democracy, Dialogue, and Social Regulation: The Contested Languages of Environmental Disputes* (Yale University Press, 1995), p. 148.

41. Troy Gagliano, "Renewing the Energy Debate," *State Legislatures,* April 2002, pp. 14–21.

42. Alan K. Ota, "Congress Clears Huge Transportation Bill, Restoring Cut-Off Funding to States," *Congressional Quarterly Weekly,* May 23, 1998, pp. 1385–1386.

43. *The Book of the States, 2000–2001* (Council of State Governments, 2000), p. 394.

44. Nancy M. Davis, "Politics and the Public Utilities Commissioner," *State Legislatures,* May 1985, p. 20. See also William T. Gormley Jr., "Policy, Politics, and Public Utility Regulation," *American Journal of Political Science* 27 (February 1983), pp. 86–105.

45. Amy Wallace, "San Onofre Mitigation Plan Wins Approval," *Los Angeles Times,* July 17, 1991, p. A3.

Chapter 30

1. Michael Janofsky, "West's Governors Back Clinton Plan for Fighting Fires," *New York Times,* September 9, 2000, p. A1; Edward Walsh, "U.S. to Resume 'Prescribed Fires,'" *Washington Post,* October 27, 2000, p. A33.
2. *The Book of the States, 2002* (Council of State Governments, 2002), p. 305.
3. Ibid., p. 350.
4. *Elrod* v. *Burns,* 427 U.S. 347 (1976).
5. American Federation of State, County, and Municipal Employees, at www.afscme.org.
6. American Postal Workers Union, at www.apwu.org.
7. Service Employees International Union, at www.seiu.org/index.html.
8. Bureau of Labor Statistics, "Employment Cost Index," October 27, 2000, at 146.142.24/cgi-bin/surveymost.
9. Ibid.
10. Werner Z. Hirsch, "Factors Important in Local Government's Privatization Decisions," *Urban Affairs Review,* 31 (November 1995), pp. 226–243.
11. Edwin Blackstone and Simon Hakim, "Private Ayes: A Tale of Four Cities: New York, Philadelphia, Indianapolis, and Phoenix," *American City and County* 112 (February 1997), pp. 4–8.
12. Stephen Goldsmith, *The Twenty-First Century City* (Regnery, 1997), p. 10.
13. See Reason Public Policy Institute, a pro privatization think tank, at www.privatization.org.
14. See Henry S. Wulf, "Trends in State Government Finances," in *Book of the States, 2002,* pp. 269–277.
15. John Shannon, "The Deregulation of the American Federal System, 1789–1989," in *The Changing Face of Fiscal Federalism,* ed. Thomas R. Swartz and John E. Peck (Sharpe, 1990), pp. 17–34.
16. Roy W. Bahl Jr., "Changing Federalism: Trends and Interstate Variations," in ibid., p. 59.
17. *Book of the States, 2002,* p. 290.
18. For a brief history of the property tax, see Dennis Hale, "The Evaluation of the Property Tax: A Study of the Relation Between Public Finance and Political Theory," *Journal of Politics* 47 (May 1985), pp. 382–404. See also C. Lowell Harris, ed., *The Property Tax and Local Finance* (Academy of Political Science, 1983).
19. *Critical Issues in State-Local Fiscal Policy: A Guide to Local Option Taxes* (National Conference of State Legislatures, 1997), p 10. See also *Statistical Abstract of the United States, 2001* (U.S. Government Printing Office, 2001), pp. 278 ff.
20. See Roy Bahl, David L. Sjoquist, and W. Loren Williams, "School Finance Reform and Impact on Property Taxes," *Proceeding of the Eighty-Third Annual National Tax Association Conference, 1990* (National Tax Association, Tax Institute of America, 1991), pp. 163–171.
21. *Serrano* v. *Priest,* 5 Cal.3d 487, 96 Cal. Rptr. 601 (1971).
22. *San Antonio Independent School District* v. *Rodriquez,* 411 U.S. 1 (1973).
23. David L. Kirp, "New Hope for Failing Schools: State Courts Are Remedying the Shame of Inadequate Education Funding," *Nation,* June 1, 1998, p. 20. See also *Board of Education, Levittown, Etc.* v. *Nyquist,* 439 N.E.2d 359 (1982); *Washakie County School District Number One* v. *Herschler,* 606 Pac.2d 310 (1980); *Edgewood Independent School District* v. *Kirby,* 34 Tex. Sup.Ct. J. 386 (1991).
24. J. Richard Aronson and John L. Hilley, *Financing State and Local Governments,* 4th ed. (Brookings Institution, 1986), p. 138. See also U.S. Advisory Commission on Intergovernmental Relations, *Property Tax Circuit-Breakers: Current Status and Policy Issues* (U.S. Government Printing Office, 1975), and Steven D. Gold, "Circuit Breakers and Other Relief Measures," in *Property Tax and Local Finance,* ed. Harris, pp. 119–132.
25. David B. Magleby, *Direct Legislation: Voting on Ballot Propositions in the United States* (Johns Hopkins University Press, 1984), pp. 61–76.
26. See "Is There a Parade?" *Nation,* October 14, 1978, pp. 363–364, and Tom Bethell, "The Changing Fashions of Liberalism," *Public Opinion* 2 (January–February 1979), pp. 41–46.
27. *Survey of Legislative Fiscal Officers* (National Conference of State Legislatures, 1996); Mandy Rafool, NCSL tax specialist, personal communication, September 15, 1998.
28. *Book of the States, 2002,* pp. 299–300.
29. *World Almanac and Book of Facts, 2002,* p. 630.
30. Ernst & Young, "Global Online Retailing: A Special Report," p. 7, at www.ey.com.
31. James Popkin and Katia Hetter, "America's Gambling Craze," *U.S. News and World Report,* March 14, 1994, p. 43.
32. John L. Mikesell, "Lotteries in State Revenue Systems: Gauging a Popular Revenue Source After 35 Years," *State and Local Government Review* 33 (Spring 2001), p. 86–100; Charles T. Clotfelter et al., *State Lotteries at the Turn of the Century* (National Gambling Impact Study Commission, 1999).
33. David Brunori, "An Essay on the Future of Urban Taxation," *State Tax Notes,* June 15, 1998, p. 1943.
34. Kathryn A. Foster, *The Political Economy of Special-Purpose Government* (Georgetown University Press, 1997); Robert L. Bland and Wes Clarke, "Budgeting for Capital Improvements," in *Handbook of Government Budgeting,* ed. Roy T. Meyers (Jossey-Bass, 1999), pp. 653–677.
35. John Shannon, "The Deregulation of Fiscal Federalism," in *Changing Face of Fiscal Federalism,* eds. Swartz and Pecks, p. 31.
36. For a thorough discussion of issues related to intergovernmental competition in attracting business and related tax issues, see Robert L. Bland, *A Revenue Guide for Local Government* (International City Managers Association, 1989), chap. 9.
37. Charles Mahtesian, "The Stadium Trap," *Governing,* May 1998, p. 22.
38. See Mark Rosentraub, *Major League Losers: The Real Cost of Sports and Who's Paying for It* (Basic Books, 1997).

Chapter 31

1. Thucydides, *History of the Peloponnesian War,* trans. Benjamin Jowett (Prometheus Books, 1998).
2. Edith Hamilton, *The Echo of Greece* (Norton, 1957), p. 47.
3. The White House, at www.whitehouse.gov/news/releases/2001/09/20010911-16.html.
4. For a book advocating more direct democracy, see Ted Becker and Christa Daryl Slaton, *The Future of Teledemocracy* (Praeger 2000); for a contrary view, see Richard J. Ellis, *Democratic Delusions: The Initiative Process in America* (University Press of Kansas, 2002).
5. For more on the relationship between electoral institutions and party systems, see Maurice Duverger, *Political Parties: Their Organization and Activity in the Modern State* (Wiley, 1954).
6. John F. Kennedy, *Profiles in Courage* (Pocket Books, 1956), p. 108.
7. These three books will give you insight into the life of a politician: Bill Bradley, *Time Present, Time Past: A Memoir* (Knopf 1996); Warren B. Rudman, *Combat: Twelve Years in the U.S. Senate* (Random House, 1996); Mark Hatfield, *Against the Grain: Reflections of a Rebel Republican* (White Cloud Press, 2001).
8. For a contrary view of Madison's presidency, see Gary Rosen, *American Compact: James Madison and the Problem of the Founding* (University Press of Kansas, 1999).
9. See Warren Bennis and Patricia Ward Biederman, *Organizing Genius: The Secrets of Creative Collaboration* (Addison-Wesley, 1997).
10. See Lawrence R. Jacobs and Robert Y. Shapiro, *Politicians Don't Ponder* (University of Chicago Press, 2000); Christopher Beem, *The Necessity of Politics* (University of Chicago Press, 1999); and John E. McDonough, *Experiencing Politics* (University of California Press, 2000).
11. See Kareem Abdul-Jabar and Alan Steinberg, *Black Profiles in Courage* (Morrow, 1996).
12. Reinhold Niebuhr, *The Children of Light and the Children of Darkness* (Scribner, 1944), p. xi.
13. See Bernard Crick, *In Defense of Politics,* rev. ed. (Pelican Books, 1983), and Stimson Bullitt, *To Be a Politician,* rev. ed. (Yale University Press, 1977).
14. See Benjamin R. Barber, *A Passion for Democracy* (Princeton University Press, 1998).
15. See Nat Hentoff, *Free Speech for Me—but Not for Thee: How the American Left and Right Relentlessly Censor Each Other* (Harper Perennial, 1993).
16. William J. Brennan, commencement address, Brandeis University, May 18, 1986.
17. Arthur M. Schlesinger Jr., *The Disuniting of America* (Norton, 1993), p. 134.
18. John W. Gardner, *Self-Renewal,* rev. ed. (Norton, 1981), p. xiv.

PHOTO CREDITS

Chapter 1: © AFP Photo/Shawn Thew/Corbis: **xvi** © Timothy A. Clary/AFP Photo/Corbis: **2** Spencer Platt/Getty Images, Inc.—Liaison: **3** Corbis Digital Stock: **5** © Hiroko Masuike/AFP Photo/Corbis: **9** The Granger Collection: **15** (*left*) Corbis: **15** (*right*) Getty Images Inc.—Liaison: **16** Currier & Ives, "Give Me Liberty or Give Me Death!", 1775. Lithograph, 1876. © The Granger Collection, New York: **22**

Chapter 2: Paul Conklin/PhotoEdit: **26** AP/Wide World Photos: **34** The Granger Collection: **35** The Granger Collection: **26** (*top*) AP/Wide World Photos: **36** (*middle*) Fabian Bachrach/Getty Images, Inc.—Taxi: **36** (*bottom*) AP/Wide World Photos: **38** AP/Wide World Photos: **39** Zigy Kaluzny: **43** (*top*) AP/Wide World Photos: **43** (*bottom*)

Chapter 3: Mike Wilkins, Preamble, 1987. Painted metal on vinyl and wood. 96 X 96". National Museum of American Art, Smithsonian Institution. Gift of Nissan Motor Corporation in U.S.A./Art Resource, NY: **62** Ian Barrett/Corbis: **62** Donald McLeod-Pool/AP/Wide World Photos: **63** Jim Wilson/New York Times Pictures: **70** AP/Wide World Photos: **74** Mark Richards/PhotoEdit: **78** Tom Carter/PhotoEdit: **81**

Chapter 4: Michael Newman/PhotoEdit: **84** Richard Shock/Getty Images, Inc.—Liaison: **89** (*left column, bottom*) Myrleen Ferguson/PhotoEdit: **89** (*right column, top*) Tom McCarthy/PhotoEdit: **89** (*right column, bottom*) Jean Catuffe/SIPA Press: **91** UPI/Corbis: **93** Alex Wong/Newsmaker/Getty Images, Inc.—Liaison: **94** AP/Wide World Photos: **97** Newsmaker/Getty Images, Inc.—Liaison: **98** Greg Gibson/AP/Wide World Photos: **99** SIPA Press: **100** Mitchell Cohen: **101** Courtesy of The Libertarian National Committee, Inc.: **102**

Chapter 5: Corbis: **108** Library of Congress: **112** Lou Krasky/AP/Wide World Photos: **113** Tony Gutierrez/AP/Wide World Photos: **118** (*top*) Eric Gay/AP/Wide World Photos: **118** (*middle*) Mark Lennihan/AP/Wide World Photos: **118** (*bottom*) Larry Downing/Reuters/Corbis: **119** (*top*) Pablo Martinez Monsivais/AP/Wide World Photos: **119** (*bottom*) Barry Talesnick/IPOL Inc./Globe Photos, Inc.: **121** Arthur Hochstein/TimePix: **122** Ted Streshinsky/Corbis: **123** (*left*) Lee Stone/Corbis/Sygma: **123** (*middle*) Laura Rauch/AP/Wide World Photos: **123** (*right*)

Chapter 6: John Chiasson/Getty Images, Inc.—Liaison: **132** National Association for the Advancement of Colored People (NAACP): **134** (*all four photos*) Susan Jones/SIPA Press: **140** Getty Images, Inc.—Liaison: **141** (*top*) Celano Lee/Getty Images, Inc.—Liaison: **141** (*bottom*) AP/Wide World Photos: **142** Cynthia Howe/Corbis/Sygma: **144** Corbis: **148** © Sam Mircovich/Reuters NewMedia Inc./Corbis: **150** Jim Bourg/Corbis: **151** Crandall/The Image Works: **152** Doug Mills/AP/Wide World Photos: **155**

Chapter 7: Lee Marriner/AP/Wide World Photos: **160** Reuters/Jim Bourg/Getty Images, Inc.—Hulton Archive Photos: **165** John Harrington/Black Star: **169** Ed Betz/AP/Wide World Photos: **171** Paul Conklin/PhotoEdit: **172** Harry Cabluck/AP/Wide World Photos: **173** J. Scott Applewhite/AP/Wide World Photos: **177** Getty Images, Inc.—Hulton Archive Photos: **183**

Chapter 8: Vincent Bucci/Getty Images, Inc.: **190** Bob Daemmrich/Stock Boston: **192** AP/Wide World Photos: **195** UPI/Corbis: **196** Bob Daemmrich/Stock Boston: **199** Jeff Widener/AP/Wide World Photos: **200** Julia Malakie/AP/Wide World Photos: **205** Getty Images, Inc.—Liaison: **206** Walter Michot/AP/Wide World Photos: **209**

Chapter 9 Brian Snyder/Reuters NewMedia/Corbis: **214** Getty Images, Inc.—Liaison: **219** Danny Johnston/AP/Wide World Photos: **222** AP/Wide World Photos: **224** Mike Fiala/SIPA Press: **228** AP Wide World Photos: **229** (*left*) Shaun Heasley/Reuters/Corbis-NY: **229** (*right*) Dennis Brack/Stockphoto.com: **230** AP/Wide World Photos: **236** Charles Rex Arbogast/AP/Wide World Photos: **238** AP/Wide World Photos: **243**

Chapter 10: Cynthia Johnson/Getty Images, Inc.—Liaison: **246** Shannon Stapleton/Corbis: **249** (*top*) Win McNamee/Corbis: **249** (*bottom*) - Geostock/Getty Images, Inc.—Liaison: **251** Corbis: **253** (*top*) UPI/Corbis: **253** (*bottom*) © Mitchell Gerber/Corbis: **254** Getty Images, Inc.—Hulton Archive Photos: **263** (*top*) AP/Wide World Photos: **263** (*bottom*)

Chapter 11: Getty Images, Inc.—Hulton Archive Photos: **270** Brendan McDermid/Reuters NewMedia/Corbis: **270** (*top*) Corbis: **270** (*middle and bottom*) Dennis Cook/AP/Wide World Photos: **271** AP/Wide World Photos: **272** Alex Wong/Getty Images, Inc.—Liaison: **277** Robert Trippett/SIPA Press: **278** Alex Wong/Getty Images, Inc.—Liaison: **279** Mark Humphrey/AP/Wide World Photos: **280** Dennis Brack/Black Star: **284** Paul Conklin/PhotoEdit: **289** Alex Wong/Getty Images, Inc.—Liaison: **290** Hyungwon Kang/Reuters NewMedia/Corbis: **291** Mark Wilson/Getty Images, Inc.—Taxi: **292** AP/Wide World Photos: **300**

Chapter 12: AP/Wide World Photos: **304** AP/Wide World Photos: **308** AP/Wide World Photos: **310** AP/Wide World Photos: **311** Mark Wilson/Getty Images, Inc.—Taxi: **313** Stephen Jaffe/AFP Photo/Corbis: **317** Getty Images, Inc.—Taxi: **319** AP/Wide World Photos: **322** Joyce Naltchayan/Corbis: **324** AP/Wide World Photos: **325** Bruce Chambers/Corbis/SABA press Photos, Inc.: **326**

Chapter 13: Martin H. Simon/Corbis/SABA Press Photos, Inc.: **332** The Nashua Telegraph/SIPA Press: **334** Wally McNamee/Corbis: **337** AP/Wide World Photos: **341** Joe Marquette/AP/Wide World Photos: **342** Luke Frazza/AFP Photo/Corbis: **346**

Chapter 14: © Roger Ressmeyer/Corbis: **352** U.S. Department of Education: **355** John Neubauer/PhotoEdit: **357** Tom Horan/Sygma/Corbis: **360** Ken Karp/Omni–Photo Communications, Inc.: **364** David Saville/FEMA News Photo/FEMA: **369** AP/Wide World Photos: **371** Gail Mooney/Thomas A. Kelly/© Kelly–Mooney Photography/Corbis: **373**

Chapter 15: Brad Markel/Getty Images, Inc.—Liaison: **376** Clary/UPI/Corbis: **385** (*first column: top*) Carol T. Powers/AP/Wide World Photos: **385** (*first column: bottom*) Reuters/Corbis: **385** (*second column: top*) Reuters/Gary Hershorn/Corbis: **385** (*second column: bottom left*) Reuters/Steve Jaffe/Corbis: **385** (*second column: bottom right*) Damian Dovarganes/AP/Wide World Photos: **388** Dan Loh/AP/Wide World Photos: **392** C. Johnson/Getty Images, Inc.—Liaison: **393** Reuters/Gary Hershorn/Corbis: **396**

Chapter 16: Rob Crandall/The Image Works: **404** Rogelio Solis/AP/Wide World Photos: **409** LM Otero/AP/Wide World Photos: **411** Charles Tasnadi/AP/Wide World Photos: **412** Tom Uhlman/AP/Wide World Photos: **415** The Report Newsmagazine: **416** Jean Catuffe/SIPA Press: **420** Corbis: **422** (*top*) Adam Nadel/AP/Wide World Photos: **422** (*bottom*) Getty Images, Inc.—Hulton Archive Photos: **423**

Chapter 17: Andrew Lichtenstein/Corbis/Sygma: **426** David McNew/Getty Images, Inc.,—Liaison: **429** Corbis: **430** Joe Marquette/AP/Wide World Photos: **435** Mitchell Crooks/Getty Images, Inc.,—Hulton Archive Photos: **436** Blair Seitz/Photo Researchers, Inc.: **437** Bob Daemmrich/Stock Boston: **438** James Wilson/Woodfin Camp & Associates: **439** Seth Perlman/AP/Wide World Photos: **442** Damian Dovarganes/AP/Wide World Photos: **443**

Chapter 18: Damian Dovarganes/AP/Wide World Photos: **448** L.P. Winfrey/Woodfin Camp & Associates: **452** (*top*) AP/Wide World Photos: **452** (*bottom*) AP/Wide World Photos: **453** Corbis: **454** AP/Wide World Photos: **456** Eric Haase/Contact Press Images, Inc.: **457** AP/Wide World Photos: **458** Cleve Bryant/Photo Edit: **461** UPI/Corbis: **464** AP/Wide World Photos: **465** Raynor/SIPA Press: **468** (*top*) AP/Wide World Photos: **468** (*bottom*) Jon Roemer/Jon Roemer Photography: **470** Curiale Dellaverson Hirschfeld Kelly & Kraemer LLP: **471**

Chapter 19: AP/Wide World Photos: **474** AP/Wide World Photos: **481** Bob Daemmrich/Stock Boston: **484** Mike Theiler/Reuters/Corbis: **486** Andrew Wong/Reuters NewMedia/Corbis: **488** AP/Wide World Photos: **490** AP/Wide World Photos: **495** AP/Wide World Photos: **496** Reuters/Toshiyuki Aizawa/Getty Images, Inc.—Hulton Archive Photos: **497**

Chapter 20: Steve Schneider/SIPA Press: **502** AP/Wide World Photos: **504** Official White House Photo/Corbis: **506** AP/Wide World Photos: **509** Paul Conklin/PhotoEdit: **510** Nick Ut/AP/Wide World Photos: **511** AP/Wide World Photos: **512** AP/Wide World Photos: **513** The White House Photo Office: **514** Ed Kashi/Corbis: **521** AP/Wide World Photos: **524** Chris Martinez/Getty Images, Inc.—Liaison: **525**

Chapter 21: Jason Szenes/Corbis/Sygma: **528** Consolidated News Pictures/Corbis/Sygma: **533** Tauseff Mustafa/AFP Photo/Corbis: **534** Yariv Katz/AFP Photo/Corbis: **537** Eric Draper/The White House/Getty/Getty Images, Inc.—Hulton Archive Photos: **539** UPI/Corbis : **540** (*Marshall*) Corbis: **540** (*Dulles*) UPI/Corbis: **540** (*Rusk*) UPI/P. Skingley/Corbis: **540** (*Kissinger*) UPI/Corbis: **540** (*Vance*) UPI/Don Rypka/Corbis: **541** (*Shultz*) Reuters/Mark Cardwell/Corbis: **541** (*Baker*) Reuters/Jeff Mitchell/Corbis: **541** (*Christopher*) Joe Marquette/AP/Wide World Photos: **541** (*Albright*) Oleg Popov/Reuters NewMedia/Corbis: **541** (*Powell*) Mark Wilson/Getty Images, Inc.—Hulton Archive Photos: **543** (*top*) Dennis Brack/Stockphoto.com: **543** (*bottom left*) Tech. Sgt. Cedric H. Rudisill/Department of Defense/Reuters: **543** (*bottom right*) Tia Deatrick/AFP Photo/Corbis: **546** Corbis/Sygma: **550** AP/Wide World Photos: **551** (*top*) UN–DPI, John Isaac/AP/Wide World Photos: **551** (*bottom*) Mikhail Metzel/AP/Wide World Photos: **553** AP/Wide World Photos: **555** T. Campion/Corbis/Sygma: **557** United Defense Corporate Headquarters: **559**

Chapter 22: Alden Pellett/AP/Wide World Photos: **564** AP/Wide World Photos: **565** Margaret Ross/Stock Boston: **567** Steven Rubin/The Image Works: **569** Courtesy of the Urban League of Greater Miami: **572** (*top*) Bob Daemmrich/Stock Boston: **572** (*bottom*) J. Wilson/Woodfin Camp & Associates: **573** Tony Freeman/PhotoEdit: **574**

Chapter 23: Dale Atkins/AP/Wide World Photos: **576** Andy Levin/Photo Researchers, Inc.: **583** The Senate of the State of Texas/Senate Media Services: **587**

Chapter 24: R. Jenkins/SIPA Press: **590** Yukad/SIPA Press: **592** Rich Pedroncelli/AP/Wide World Photos: **596** David Sams/Stock Boston: **598** Tony Freeman/PhotoEdit: **603** John Gress/AP/Wide World Photos: **605** Alan Reininger/Contact/Woodfin Camp & Associates: **606**

Chapter 25: Bob Daemmrich Photography, Inc.: **610** Bob Daemmrich/Stock Boston: **616** Larry Davis: **617** Rogelio Solis/AP/Wide World Photos: **619** Rogelio Solis/AP/Wide World Photos: **621**

Chapter 26: Jacqueline Roggenbrodt/AP/Wide World Photos: **634** Lauren McFalls/AP/Wide World Photos: **636** AP/Wide World Photos: **637** (*left*) Deidre Eitel/AP/Wide World Photos: **637** (*middle*) Orin Wagber/AP/Wide World Photos: **637** (*right*) Rich Pedroncelli/AP/Wide World Photos: **639** Salem Governor's Office: **643** Seth Perlman/AP/Wide World Photos: **644** Jeff Christensen/Reuters NewMedia/Corbis: **646**

Chapter 27: Michael Newman/PhotoEdit: **654** Richard Hutchings/Photo Researchers, Inc.: **656** Sam C. Pierson, Jr. Photo Researchers, Inc.: **660** (*top*) William Hubbell/Woodfin Camp & Associates: **660** (*bottom*) Tony Gutierrez/AP/Wide World Photos: **667** Scott T. Baxter/Getty Images, Inc.—Liaison: **668**

Chapter 28: Elaine Thompson/AP/Wide World Photos: **674** Mike Segar/Reuters NewMedia, Inc./Corbis: **677** Kevin Horan/Stock Boston: **680** Farrell Grehan/Photo Researchers, Inc.: **682** Suzanne Plunkett/AP/Wide World Photos: **686** Andy Levin/Photo Researchers, Inc.: **689** Kathy Willens/AP/Wide World Photos: **692** Alan Schein Photography/Corbis: **693**

Chapter 29: Douglas C. Pizac/AP/Wide World Photos: **696** Clark Campbell/SIPA Press: **699** Bob Daemmrich/Stock Boston: **702** Monika Graff/The Image Works: **703** Lynsey Addario/AP/Wide World Photos: **706** Alon Reininger/Contact/Woodfin Camp & Associates: **708** Larry Mulvehill/The Image Works: **709** Obremski/Getty Images, Inc.—Image Bank: **711** Bob Rowan, Progressive Image/Corbis: **713** AP/Wide World Photos: **715** AP/Wide World Photos: **717**

Chapter 30: Charlyn Zlotnik/Woodfin Camp & Associates: **720** AP/Wide World Photos: **725** AP/Wide World Photos: **728** Bob Daemmrich Photography, Inc.: **729** Rob Crandall/Stock Boston: **732** Bob Daemmrich/The Image Works: **733** Brian Yarvin/The Image Works: **735** AP/Wide World Photos: **736**

Chapter 31: Reza Estakhrian/Getty Images, Inc.—Stone: **738** Bob Daemmrich Photography, Inc.: **741** Stan Orkin/AP/Wide World Photos: **746** Cassy Cohen/PhotoEdit: **747**

INDEX